American Foreign Policy
in the Nuclear Age

*With this book the author pays
tribute to Vassar College on
the occasion of its Centennial.*

American Foreign Policy in the Nuclear Age

Principles, Problems, and Prospects

by
CECIL V. CRABB, JR.
Department of Political Science
Vassar College

ROW, PETERSON AND COMPANY
Evanston, Illinois   Elmsford, New York

Acknowledgments

This book is a product of my experiences in teaching American foreign policy and international relations at Vassar College and of numerous opportunities afforded within recent years to observe certain aspects of the foreign policy process firsthand in the nation's capital. Especially valuable was my association with the Department of State, Office of Congressional Relations, during the summer of 1951. Then and subsequently I have had many opportunities to discuss American foreign relations with governmental officials in both the executive and legislative branches.

My students at Vassar—always challenging and intellectually stimulating —have provided a continuing impetus to present material as provocatively as possible and to keep abreast of significant developments in the field. Usually without knowing it, they have served as critics for many of the ideas and approaches incorporated into this book, and in many cases their reactions have provided helpful guidelines for revisions.

The manuscript was largely written during a year's leave of absence from the college. I am grateful to the Faculty Committee on Research and the administration of Vassar College for providing me a research grant during this period.

Research was undertaken chiefly at the Joint University Library, on the campus of Vanderbilt University, Nashville, Tennessee. The Director of the Joint University Library, Dr. A. F. Kuhlman, co-operated generously in making the facilities of the library available to me. Miss Clara M. Brown, Head of the Reference Department, and Mrs. Elizabeth W. Swint, Head of the Circulation Department, along with other members of the library staff, were unstinting in assisting me in various phases of research. The members of the library staff at Vassar College also extended their capable assistance.

Typing assistance was provided by Mr. and Mrs. James Stoltz, Mrs. Diane Maiello, and Mrs. Ruth Ashman. Special thanks are due Mrs. Ashman, the able departmental secretary; in cases far too numerous to mention she brought her judgment and experience to bear in solving problems encountered in preparation of the manuscript. My wife, Harriet, provided at every stage assistance and encouragement that was nothing less than indispensable—so much so that she fully deserves the title of co-author.

I am also grateful to my colleagues at Vassar, along with my co-laborers at other institutions, with whom I have discussed many of the ideas presented in this book. Their incisive criticisms resulted in improvement both in style and content. A special debt is owed Dr. Nelson E. Taylor, Jr., of the Political Science Department at Vassar, for his willingness to criticize my ideas on the philosophy of American foreign policy.

Finally, I wish to acknowledge the immeasurable debt owed my parents, to whom this book is fondly dedicated.

While recognizing the generosity and co-operation of friends and colleagues, I alone bear responsibility for errors of fact or judgment that may have found their way into this study.

CECIL V. CRABB, Jr.
Vassar College

Table of Contents

Introduction

This is an age of Sputniks and rocket flights to the moon, of recurrent international crises, of gigantic defense budgets. American preoccupation with foreign policy issues in peacetime has reached a scale never before witnessed in our history. Plainly, no lengthy justification is needed for another study of the principles, problems, and prospects of the nation's relationships with the outside world. Americans are becoming progressively conscious of how "domestic" are the implications of problems and decisions in the foreign policy field. While it is true that the level of citizen interest in, and awareness of, global issues has reached a new high in the postwar era, it is also true that the level of citizen enlightenment and understanding of the complexity of these issues has not reached the heights demanded for American success in the diplomatic sphere.

In a democracy, it is axiomatic that public opinion provides the context within which policy makers must always act and that public thinking very largely sets limits to the kinds of actions officials can take in meeting the challenge of external events. This study is offered to induce Americans to think more intelligently and critically about the nature of their country's relationship with other nations, and about the American approach to significant issues in the international community.

This book was written with two groups specifically in mind: college students enrolled in courses on American foreign policy, and interested laymen who desire to deepen their overall understanding of the nation's foreign relations. For both groups, my basic objectives are the same. First, I want to present the minimum factual information requisite for a proper understanding and intelligent judgment of the formulation and conduct of American foreign policy. Second, I seek to suggest the ways in which an analytical approach to major problems in foreign policy can proceed. And third, I wish to impart both needed basic familiarity with the subject-matter and sufficient incentive to motivate the reader to pursue on his own many of the problems and implications discussed in these pages. The interested reader will be able to use the extended list of references at the end of each chapter and at the end of the book as a helpful guide for further study.

The teacher and student of American foreign policy will find all the traditional facets of the subject covered. What is different about this book is its approach, which is designed to encourage the reader to examine foreign policy issues in an analytical way. Speaking generally, descriptive and chronologically-organized material has been kept to a minimum. Such material has been used mainly for more meaningful discussion of the problems growing out of America's new role in world affairs and for better assessment of the meaning and implications of these problems.

In the early chapters (Chapters 1 through 5) attention is focused on such issues as the growing complexity of foreign affairs, the greater total involvement of an ever-widening circle of governmental agencies, the overriding necessity for systematic co-ordination of government-wide efforts in the foreign policy field, and the almost inextricable connection between foreign and domestic policy questions. Chapter 6 analyzes the increasingly more difficult, but also never more urgent, problem of fostering harmonious executive-legislative relations and of achieving a "bipartisan" approach to foreign relations. Chapter 7 discusses the always vital matter of the relationship of public opinion to the foreign policy process.

The second part of this book (Chapters 8 through 18), dealing with the *substance* of American foreign policy, endeavors to follow a common approach in discussing the major geographic areas and the important global issues with which the United States has been deeply concerned in recent years. Each problem is identified initially and its importance for American foreign policy shown. Then, a brief historical background is presented to trace the evolution of this problem down to the post-World War II era. Next, in analyzing the problem's contemporary manifestations, its major elements are distinguished and treated in detail. Finally, the effectiveness or ineffectiveness of American efforts to deal with these problems is evaluated and significant implications for the future are emphasized.

What this distinctive approach means in specific cases may be illustrated by referring to the treatment of America's relationships with Western Europe in Chapter 10. An analysis of postwar problems is preceded by a brief treatment of the factors governing American-European relations in the prewar period. Recent issues prominent in American-European relations are then discussed within a four-fold

framework: containment, economic recovery, and rearmament; European economic integration; NATO and other strategic-military questions; and European political unification. After analyzing these separate issues, the overall effectiveness of American postwar foreign policy toward Europe is evaluated. This general pattern of development is followed throughout chapters 8 to 17.

Other innovations and differences in emphasis in the approach and coverage of this study may be mentioned briefly. Chapter 2 on American national character and Chapter 18 on the philosophy of American foreign policy were included because of my deep conviction that prevailing public images, stereotypes, sacred cows, traditional thought and behavior patterns —in short, the mental baggage of the American society—have a vital bearing upon the formulation and conduct of foreign policy. Intangible as national character and philosophy are, and difficult as it is to speak with certainty about them, no factors are of more crucial significance in the long run in shaping the nation's response to challenges in the external environment.

Chapters 8 and 9 provide somewhat fuller coverage of the all-pervading cold war than is found in similar studies. Chapter 8 especially, dealing with the enduring historic goals of Russian foreign policy and with American-Russian relations down to the Second World War, provides material not often found in books designed principally for use in the field of political science. This chapter stems from my belief that historical perspective is indispensable for any intelligent comprehension of the origins of the cold war and of major developments in the recent period on the cold war front. Similarly, Chapter 9 includes material, particularly on American-Russian competition in the economic and strategic-military realms, which is presented sparingly, if at all, in existing publications.

Chapters 16 and 17 dealing with international organization and disarmament, respectively, also differ from more orthodox approaches. In discussing the UN, peripheral attention is devoted to describing its structure and its history since 1945. Much greater attention is paid to describing how developments and trends in the UN have posed problems for the United States, to analyzing America's role in the UN since 1945 and the factors shaping that role, and to presenting persistent issues in the American approach to international organization. Discussion of disarmament centers upon the issues which have blocked agreement on arms-limitation proposals throughout the postwar era and on the implications of these issues for American foreign policy.

Finally, I have departed from the concept of objectivity current in some quarters, which holds that a scientific approach to subject matter, especially controversial subject matter, precludes the making of judgments about the adequacy or wisdom of public policy. I do not find this narrow view of scientific objectivity tenable. While it is true that the facts may speak for themselves, what they are saying is not always apparent. Objectivity, therefore, does not consist in withholding judgments; that,

indeed, is tantamount to an acquiescence in the status quo, which, in itself, is a value judgment. Objectivity consists rather in seeing to it that judgments made are supported by the available evidence and in recognizing that in many instances judgments must be tentative, until more complete and more reliable data become available. Not only is the writer in social science permitted to make judgments within these limitations, he is obligated to do so if he is to follow in the highest tradition of the scientific method. The reader will find many such judgments in this book.

If the reader gains a better grasp of the factual material necessary for an understanding of American foreign policy, if he finds that his own thinking about the subject has been stimulated and challenged, and if—above all—he receives some incentive to delve more deeply into problems and issues discussed here, this book will have largely fulfilled its purpose.

CHAPTER 1

Foundations of American Foreign Policy

Reduced to its most fundamental ingredients, foreign policy consists of two elements: national objectives to be achieved and means for achieving them. The interaction between national goals and the resources for attaining them is the perennial subject of statecraft. In its ingredients the foreign policy of all nations, great and small, is the same.

To say that foreign policy consists essentially of ends and means, however, is a statement that misleads by its very simplicity. Its breadth does not reveal the obvious differences in national goals and the methods used by various countries for attaining them. No one can doubt, for instance, that the foreign policies of the United States and the Soviet Union today are at antipodes in many respects. Similarly, there are many divergencies between the policies of Israel and the Arab states, India and Pakistan, China and Japan, Germany and France.

A thorough examination is needed of the ends of foreign policy, the means used to reach them, and the interactions between ends and means, before a country's policies can become intelligible. Let us begin by looking at the goals of American foreign policy, drawing comparisons with those of other countries as such comparisons illuminate our problem.

1. THE NATURE OF FOREIGN POLICY GOALS

The Pre-eminence of National Security

If self-preservation is the first law of nature, it is also the first law of foreign policy. Safeguarding the security of the nation is the foremost obligation of the statesman, irrespective of the country he represents or the character of its government. As Nicholas J. Spykman has phrased it:

> Because territory is an inherent part of a state, self-preservation means defending its control over territory; and, because independence is of the essence of the state, self-preservation also means fighting for independent status. This explains why the basic objective of the foreign policy of all

states is the preservation of territorial integrity and political independence. (33, p. 17).

Admittedly, this pre-eminent goal is seldom stated as baldly as this by national leaders. For instance, Secretary of State Dean G. Acheson phrased it this way: "To build our strength so that the things we believe in can survive is the practical and vitally necessary expression in times of our moral dedication" (1, p. 800). And Secretary of State John Foster Dulles declared that "The broad goal of our foreign policy is to enable the people of the United States to enjoy, in peace, the blessings of liberty" (11, p. 327). Yet in whatever phraseology it may be couched, it is the same goal. Every country operates upon the principle that its highest duty is to preserve its identity as a nation.

Accustomed to thinking in terms of the foreign policy differences that divide the world, especially on the plane of ideological discords, the reader may be surprised and doubtful that the foreign policies of the United States and its diplomatic opponent, the Soviet Union, accord to national security the same dominant role. These doubts should vanish if the reader remembers that national security is not identified as the *only* goal of foreign policy. As we shall see, there are many others, and sometimes these may disguise the centrality of the security issue. Moreover the term "national security" is not defined here, and no very satisfying definition of it can be given that would apply alike to all countries. Few concepts are so fundamental, and yet so elusive, as this one. In common with many other ideas that must be dealt with in the study of foreign affairs, it is a relative concept. Its meaning for individual nations will be determined by numerous variables: history, geography, cultural traditions, strategy and tactics in war, the nature of the economic system, and public opinion, to list but a few of the major influences. Nations may be, and frequently in history have been, mistaken in their estimate of what constitutes security. Hitler, no doubt, believed that attacking Poland and France, and later Russia, would promote German security. His miscalculation had disastrous consequences for his nation.

Security is one of those elastic terms like justice or equality or democracy. Almost every nation is in favor of it in the abstract, both for itself and generally for other nations. But nations disagree violently over what it means in concrete circumstances. So great may be the different conceptions of it that security for one country can mean disaster for another. For the Kremlin security might, and possibly does, mean nothing less than a communized world, directed from Moscow. For the United States it may entail the eventual extinction of communism as a militant ideology and of Russia as a great power. For England in the 19th century, it meant the establishment of *Pax Britannica,* accompanied by efforts to make certain

that the European balance of power was never disturbed in a manner inimical to Britain. For the United States during the 19th century it meant the opportunity to manage its affairs in the Western Hemisphere without interference by other countries. These and many other examples suggest that attempts to achieve security have led to a strange paradox: security is the underlying foreign policy goal of every state, but concrete efforts to achieve it are productive of endless insecurity throughout the international community as a whole.

Still another attribute of the security concept requires emphasis. A nation's conception of security is never static. It changes over the years —imperceptibly perhaps, even monthly and daily. The explosion of the first Soviet atomic bomb in 1949, for instance, revolutionized official American thinking about national security. By 1957 another major change in American ideas about security was necessitated by the success of the Soviet Union in launching the first earth satellite by means of a long-range guided missile. Security then is closely linked with technological progress. New inventions like the aircraft carrier and giant stratospheric bombers loaded with nuclear weapons contributed to the security of great sea and air powers like the United States and Britain. After their adversaries had gotten these weapons too, and a giant submarine fleet and guided missiles besides, the balance of military power swung more favorably to the sprawling land-mass of the communist empire.

Pre-eminent as is the role played by security in foreign policy, it can be overstressed. Nations can and have manifested an almost pathological fixation with this goal, to the exclusion of other goals. The fate of Hitler's Third Reich, and the consequences of certain steps in Soviet foreign policy under Stalin and his successors, illustrate a kind of inverse law about national security: the more a narrowly-conceived concept of security comes to dominate foreign policy, usurping other national goals, the more *insecure* the nation may ultimately become, after other nations also begin to take steps to safeguard their own well-being from what they regard as the ominous threat of hostile neighbors.

There can be no such thing as absolute security for nations any more than for individuals within nations. A measure of insecurity is inherent in life itself and may well be one basic force that spurs human progress. The eminent historian and one-time State Department official, George Kennan, notes that in international affairs, "there is no security in a search for the absolute defense. Security lies in accepting the moderate risks in order that the immoderate ones may be avoided" (23, p. 271).

Suppose it were possible for us to specify those conditions that would best promote the security of the United States, that would eliminate every possible threat to our national existence. What would those conditions be? Several ideas might occur to us. We might think that if only the threat of international communism were removed, the United States would have security. But upon reflection, we would remember that threats to our national existence arose long before communism became a powerful international force. We would see that our security could by no means be automatically guaranteed by eliminating the existing enemy.

Perhaps we might specify the triumph of democracy throughout the world. Wilsonian idealists believed that this would promote— some thought it would guarantee—international peace and justice. Yet we know that democratic countries, our own among them, can and do fight wars, and not always defensive wars. We think of the Mexican and Spanish-American wars in our own history. We recall the numerous colonial wars of Britain and France. We remember within our own experience that Britain, France, and Israel invaded Egypt in 1956 in pursuit of foreign policy goals, and that France has carried out what amounts to a war of extermination of rebel groups in its colonial domain in North Africa. These examples should make us strongly suspicious of any view which holds that international peace will prevail after all countries have adopted democratic philosophies or forms of government.

Perhaps we might reluctantly propose a *Pax Americana*. If the entire world could be put under American hegemony, or if other countries could be persuaded to accept American "leadership" in world affairs, surely that would eliminate all threats to American security. Such a view would also most likely prove false. It is a commonplace of history that world empires generate their own internal tensions and ultimately disintegrate from within. The historian Arnold Toynbee has identified the "universal state" as one of the stages of a civilization in decay—a civilization which is rapidly losing its power to preserve its identity. Internal conflicts —we may, for convenience, call them civil wars or revolutions—can tear an empire to pieces. Conflicts are in fact generated by the very effort of a nation to extend its hegemony beyond a certain optimum point. No one knows exactly what this point is. It is reached when the nation can no longer effectively integrate and communicate with the territories under its jurisdiction.

The American people have always had a peculiar propensity for believing that perfect or near-perfect security could be achieved. Yet it is difficult, if not impossible, for us even to think of theoretical circumstances that are not productive of some insecurity for the nation. The concept of security reminds us of certain doctrines of the world's great religions, such as the obligation of Christian believers to strive for the sinless life. Statesmen know that perfect security is not possible, yet they must constantly strive to attain it by all the means at their command.

Lesser Goals of Foreign Policy

Security of course is not the only goal of foreign policy. While it is the most fundamental one, other goals may be more evident in the day-to-day conduct of international affairs. The relationship between a nation's contemporary foreign policy goals and security may not always be evident and direct.

Take the history of American postwar foreign relations. A major plank in both the Democratic and Republican party platforms has been the promotion of reciprocal trade. Technical assistance to underdeveloped countries has received support by both parties. So has economic aid, cultural interchange, the United Nations, disarmament, political independence for colonial peoples, and peaceful development of atomic energy. These goals have formed important elements in American foreign policy since 1945, and in some cases they have become permanent features of that policy. We can more profitably reserve further discussion of them for later chapters, but several general observations can be made about them here.

Obviously, almost all these goals are related in some degree to the promotion of national security. Choose any of the goals listed—from the reduction of world trade barriers to the peaceful use of nuclear power—and their connection with security is not difficult to establish. Efforts to reduce trade barriers, for example, are based on the belief that economic tensions are productive of international tensions and war. One of the reasons for technical assistance is the belief that it will help underdeveloped nations to promote their own security from Communist domination, and in doing so, aid the defense of the free world. A similar relationship could be established for the other goals. Almost never is a foreign policy goal totally divorced from security considerations.

For some policies the relationship to national security is much more direct than for others. This leads to the thought that a nation's foreign policy will emphasize security aspects in direct ratio to the degree the nation believes itself threatened by other countries. No lengthy documentation is needed to prove that the policies of the United States toward Soviet Russia in the postwar era have been more concerned with security objectives than have its policies toward Canada and the North Atlantic community generally. Russia poses a visible and ominous threat to the United States and its allies; Canada and Western Europe do not. The United States will naturally be less motivated by security considerations in dealing with its friends and with neutral countries than with its avowed diplomatic enemies.

Besides preserving its independence as a nation, what is the United States seeking to achieve in world affairs? What objectives does it believe important in its relations with other countries? Answers to these questions are likely to vary greatly, depending upon circumstances prevailing at home and abroad in any given period. Moreover, they are likely to differ according to the vantage point of the individual answering the questions. Several lists of the goals of American foreign policy, ranging from broad principles to enumeration of detailed ob-

jectives toward particular problems, are published periodically in the volumes of the Department of State *Bulletin* and are contained in the testimony of executive officials before congressional committees. Almost never are these lists identical. Their differences hinge upon such considerations as the specific problems facing the nation at any time, the viewpoint of the official compiling the list, and perhaps the purpose for which the list was drawn up. In an age of growing specialization, the broad area of foreign relations, no less than other areas of national life, has become progressively divided and sub-divided among an ever-larger circle of governmental agencies. Agencies specializing in narrow segments of foreign policy find it difficult to relate their work to the nation's overall objectives in world affairs. The result often is that the totality of the nation's foreign policy goals is merely the sum of the goals of particular agencies, some of which are more skilled than others in generating support among private groups and high-ranking governmental officials for their point of view.

Indeed, it would not be too much to say that below the level of preserving national security, the selection of lesser goals of foreign policy and the assignment of different priorities to these goals is usually a process that goes on subconsciously, continuously, and for the most part accidentally. Rather than attempting to list the lesser goals of American foreign policy, therefore, it would seem more profitable to think in terms of categories of goals, proceeding from those of highest to lowest order of priority. First on the list is national security and its corollaries: provision for adequate defense, together with any other steps—extension of military and economic assistance to other countries, propaganda warfare, maintenance of strong military alliances, collaboration with the allies, preservation of a strong economic base at home—that directly or indirectly enhance the nation's security. Next on the list would be secondary goals: those objectives pursuance of which is desirable as long as there is no significant impairment of national security. Throughout the postwar period, the following objectives could be included in this list: peace, nonintervention in the internal affairs of other countries, respect for international law and treaties, support for collective security, worldwide economic advancement and human welfare, respect for human rights, and reciprocal trade. Last, there exists a category of objectives that might be labelled variously "desires, hopes, inclinations, and aspirations." These enjoy very low priority—so low that they will be sacrificed altogether when they conflict with the attainment of higher goals. Recent diplomatic experience indicates that the following might properly be included in this category: friendship with all countries, including Russia and Red China; liberation of the Eastern European satellite countries, Tibet, and other nations involuntarily embraced within the communist empire; universal peace; propagation of the democratic ideology and support for politically free governmental institutions; disarmament, significant reductions in the American defense budget, and withdrawal of the nation's armed forces from overseas; unimpeded cultural exchange, freedom of information, and termination of propaganda warfare; imposition of an enforceable system of world law, at least over selected areas of international intercourse; inculcation of ethical principles in the conduct of world affairs. It seems debatable whether objectives in this category can meaningfully be called "foreign policies" of the United States at all. For example, liberation of the communist satellites is no doubt a widely-held national hope, a profound desire; but it is not a foreign policy goal to which the nation is prepared to commit its energies and resources, since active pursuit of it would unquestionably entail serious risks to national security.

Quite clearly then all the foreign policy goals of the United States or any other country are not of equal importance and urgency. Choices must continually be made among them. Many of the goals included in the three categories outlined above are mutually exclusive. The United States could not, for instance, simultaneously seek friendship with Russia and Red China and arouse their ire by ringing the communist zone with military bases; nor could it at one and the same time commit itself to further worldwide economic advancement and slash its economic assistance programs to other countries.

What factors will determine the order of priority a nation establishes among its lesser goals of foreign policy? Completely satisfactory answers to this question would require volumes devoted to individual countries. For the answers involve nothing less than the history and cultural heritage of a nation, its basic philosophic tenets, its experiences, its religious, social, and political institutions, its hopes and aspirations as a society. America's foreign policies, said Secretary of State Dean Acheson in 1950, "grow out of, and are expressive of, our entire national life. They reflect our total culture" (**1**, p. 799).

At root, the question goes back to what kind of conception a society holds of the universe and man's place within it. From this underlying unity—for every organized society has a certain basic consensus on this question, else it would not be a society—many corollary beliefs are derived, relating to man's destiny, his potentialities and limitations, his tendencies for good and for evil. All these play their part in determining the order in which a nation will rank its subordinate foreign policy goals. In Chapter 2 we shall examine the effect of American national character on historic American foreign policy goals. In like manner, many scholars have identified important elements in the Russian historical experience and in communist ideology which have had far-reaching implications for Soviet foreign policy. The same point could be made about the importance of Hinduism in shaping India's outlook toward its economic conditions and its view of the outside world, or the importance of emperor worship in convincing the Japanese before the Second World War that they had a special mandate from heaven to dominate weaker countries.

These examples suffice to show that the hierarchy of lesser foreign policy goals is an exceedingly complex matter—that it is a product of almost every important influence that goes to make a nation what it is. The examples also suggest that until there is some supranational authority to which national societies give at least a portion of their allegiance, they will order their goals as their own society determines, thereby making inevitable conflicts among the foreign policies of nations in the international arena.

2. THE MEANS OF FOREIGN POLICY

Earlier we suggested that there were two elements in the foreign policy of any nation: objectives, and means for reaching them. Let us now look at the second of these. By what means do nations try to reach their goals in foreign affairs? This inquiry leads us directly to one of the most important and complex subjects basic to interstate relations: national power. Foreign policy is essentially a matter of how each nation tries to influence the actions of other nations. And this is what the concept of power is all about. *Power is the ability of a nation to influence the actions of other countries in a manner favorable to itself.* Its most fundamental aim is the preservation of national security. Americans are not accustomed to discussing international questions in the language of "power politics." Indeed, they have tended to believe that power politics could be eliminated altogether. But Americans are very accustomed to discussing the *reality* of power. They devote considerable time and energy to learning "how to win friends and influence people," how to get a promotion, how to put across a sales contract, and how to pass or defeat legislation in which they are interested. These are all efforts to exercise power. On a limited scale, such efforts resemble in many ways power politics on the international level.

The Manifestations of Power

One significant difference between power as exercised by individuals within the state and by nations within the world community resides in the role of force and coercion. Normally within a state, especially within a democratic state, force plays a relatively insignificant role in interpersonal and intergroup relationships. The government monopolizes force, using it to prevent violations of its laws when all other methods of restraint have failed. But in international affairs, force and coercion are used frequently by all members of the world community. In its most extreme manifestation, the use of force takes the form of war. On its most primitive level, national power is the capacity to preserve the identity of the nation by military force, construing this term broadly to include propaganda, economic, and other modern methods of warfare. That is why the power of a nation is often judged solely—and when solely, then erroneously—by the quantity and quality of its armed forces. Every other goal of foreign policy—the ability of the United States, let us say to preserve advantageous trade relations with the outside world, or to contribute to the advancement of economically backward countries, or to propagate democratic ideology—presupposes the continued existence of the nation. This is the *sine qua non* of all national policy, foreign or domestic.

Though military strength is the most basic element in a nation's power, it is by no means the only element, nor is it always the most important one in the day-to-day conduct of international affairs. The free world alliance against the communist bloc, for example, is not held together because of the overwhelming military superiority of the United States over its members. The cement of this alliance is to be found much more in recognition of a common danger, geographical proximity, ideological affinity, and a sense of common purpose. Decisions emerging from the alliance are a result more of persuasion than of coercion by the dominant nations within it.

Manifestly, there are limits to the usefulness of military power. It cannot be used to compel other nations, such as Burma in the postwar period, to accept American economic and technical assistance, even for their own good. Respect for American military strength has not always forced other nations, such as India in the past decade, to accept the American position on issues dividing the communist and non-communist worlds. Nor can the mere existence of great military power prevent widespread acceptance of communist ideology. This became apparent in American relations with Syria during 1957. In other words, *force is not always relevant to certain kinds of foreign policy situations.* Remembering the definition—that power is influence—the improper use of force may in fact result in lessened, rather than in increased, influence over the actions of other countries.

There are many manifestations of power.

Some of the more important of these are: persuasion and friendship; propaganda; economic aid (leading sometimes to economic coercion); ideological penetration; moral suasion; and public opinion. There is no necessity to examine these manifestations of power here. That can better be done in future chapters, when we discuss American foreign policy toward specific international problems in the recent past. At this stage, it is more important that we understand some of the general characteristics of power.

The Relativity of Power

One of the most basic facts to be grasped about power is this: *power is always relative.* We observed earlier that national security is a dynamic, not a static, concept. This is largely because of the relativity of power. When we ask, "what is the power of the United States in world affairs?" we are trying to solve an equation containing an almost infinite number of variables. No matter how skillful they may be in making judgments about the power of nations, no two experts from the State Department, the Pentagon, or any other governmental agency would answer this question in exactly the same way, because no final and completely authoritative answer is ever possible. The variables in the problem derive from the four important respects in which power is relative.

Power is relative with respect to time. The power of the United States has undergone a profound transformation within the past fifty years. This change has resulted principally from two facts: proven ability to wage war successfully, and the decision to play a more active role in world affairs, which has demanded that the United States develop and use some of its tremendous potential power during time of peace. Furthermore, America's power today is far vaster than it was immediately after World War II, when its armed forces had been stripped to skeleton strength, and before it had begun to develop nuclear weapons in large quantities.

The fact that power is relative to time is highlighted by the distinction between *potential* power and power *in being.* If it is asked, "what is the power of the United States and the NATO community to defend Western Europe from a possible Communist attack?" a major consideration would be the amount of time available to the free world to bring its military forces to bear in defense. Throughout the postwar period the United States has possessed great power in being, more than at any time in its entire history. Yet the existing power of the United States is only a fraction of its potential power. And, as Winston Churchill has said time and again, it is probably the great power potential of the United States, more than any other single factor, which has deterred further Communist intrusions into the free world.

Power is relative to the problem toward which it is directed. When we try to evaluate national power, we must always think in terms of power to reach certain specified objectives, to achieve concrete goals. America's power to defend its shores from aggression may be entirely different from its capacity to deal with communist influences in France, to establish friendly relations with Egypt, to raise living standards in Iran, or to prevent excessive use of the veto by communist countries in the United Nations. Success in foreign affairs requires skill in using appropriate weapons and skill in dealing with varied problems.

The power of one country is relative to that of other countries. The ability of the United States to affect the course of world events will almost invariably require comparative judgments about power. Knowing that the United States at any given time possessed 5 or 25 or 50 hydrogen bombs would tell us little or nothing of significance about American power. Such weapons might have little relevance to the problem under consideration. But even if they did, we could still not settle the issue until we asked: What is the power of the United States *relative to the power of other countries* that are actively concerned with the problem at hand? The issue of relative power has come into clear focus in recent years because of the steady accretion in Soviet nuclear and missile technology. In the immediate postwar period, the United States had a monopoly on nuclear weapons. In this one category its power was therefore infinitely greater than the Soviet Union's. Gradually, the USSR began to acquire such weapons, along with effective methods of delivering them. The Kremlin's rate of production for such weapons became relatively much faster than the American rate. If we assume that, by the end of the 1950's, the free world coalition had a two-to-one lead over the communist bloc in nuclear striking power, its relative position *vis-à-vis* the communist bloc had deteriorated greatly—so much so in fact that "nuclear parity" had been reached between the two camps. Both sides were equal, or nearly so, in the capacity to achieve objectives that might be sought by reliance upon nuclear weapons.

The same principle of course holds for non-military types of power, although differentials of strength are much more difficult, if not virtually impossible, to measure. What is the relative power of the United States and India to persuade masses throughout Asia to support a given course of action in foreign affairs? What is the respective influence of countries like Britain and Egypt in determining Arab attitudes toward the free world coalition? How much power does the United States possess to gain widespread acceptance of many of its policies within the NATO alliance? In international affairs, there is power and countervailing power, American push and Soviet or Indian or Egyptian pull. To decide what the power of a nation is, it is necessary to identify all the forces that are operative in any given international issue.

Power is relative to the country by which it is applied. Suppose, for purposes of illustration, that we measure the relative power of two countries by looking *only* at their military forces. What kind of evaluation is possible? No matter what the statistics show, the effective military power of two countries is never exactly comparable. This is true, even if it could be shown—and in reality of course it could not—that the military strengths of two nations were exactly equal. Why is it not possible to think that "ten divisions are ten divisions," irrespective of the country to which they belong?

Ignoring for the moment the fact that the divisions of two countries will differ markedly in firepower, number of troops, leadership, and many other respects, we may note that ten Russian divisions would be more easily available to the Kremlin for crushing the Hungarian Revolt than would ten American divisions to Washington for dealing with anti-American demonstrations in Egypt or Argentina. Few limitations exist on the Kremlin's ability to use troops for such purposes. Governmental leaders within the United States, on the other hand, must operate within a constitutional framework of civilian control over the military establishment and within a historical tradition which emphasizes non-intervention in the internal affairs of other countries.

Merely possessing power, along with even greater potential power, is no guarantee that a nation will exert strong influence in world affairs. Totalitarian regimes are often free to use all the powers at their command for diplomatic ends. Democratic nations, however, usually limit, sometimes severely, the ends for which certains kinds of power may be utilized.

3. THE INGREDIENTS OF AMERICAN POWER

The major elements that combine to make up the power of a nation are: geography, economic and technological resources, population, military forces, ideology, and national character. We shall treat the last three of these elements in separate chapters.

Geographical Determinants of American Power

Because they are the most permanent elements in a nation's power, and because they underlie other kinds of power, geographical attributes have been held by leading scholars to be the most fundamental in determining a nation's role in world affairs. "Power," the noted geographer Nicholas J. Spykman once wrote, "is in the last instance the ability to wage successful war, and in geography lie the clues to the problems of military and political strategy." He concludes that geography "is the most fundamental factor in the foreign policy of states because it is the most permanent" (33, p. 41). Such statements cannot be accepted without qualification. Geographical factors may have the greatest degree of permanence. But even these do change with the passage of time. Canals have been dug to connect important waterways; deserts have been made arable; swamps have been drained and converted into usable land; airplanes have conquered the obstacle of distances and overcome impassable land barriers; expeditions by the United States and other countries within recent years have shown that even the polar regions of the world can be made habitable. Consequently, it would be a mistake to regard geographical factors as fixed and unyielding before the efforts of man.

Another warning about trying to prove too much from geography is in order at the outset. There is the danger of falling into a kind of geographical determinism, popularly called "geopolitics". During the 1920's and 1930's, German geopoliticians especially were responsible for propagating the view that geographical pressures determine foreign policy; that German expansionism, such as the *Drang Nach Osten* (drive to the east), was dictated by certain natural and immutable geographical urges that gave Germany and its partners a special mandate to conquer Europe and eventually the world. Geopolitics thus became the tool of aggressive dictators. As Isaiah Bowman has written, it gave "territorial expansion a pseudoscientific justification," and clothed imperialistic schemes in supposedly scholarly garments (4, pp. 655-56). Such geopolitical thinking has been thoroughly discredited by reputable scholars. The prevailing view is that man's actions are not determined irrevocably by a supposed geographic destiny.

Keeping these qualifications in mind, let us examine the salient geographical facts about American power, starting with climate. The United States is in the temperate zone. This is the zone in which great nations have invariably been situated. Scholars since antiquity have sought to establish a correlation between national greatness and climate (2, pp. 70-1). That no precise correlation is possible is now conceded. Nevertheless, it seems that climatic extremes militate against a nation's becoming a great power in world affairs. Most of the United States escapes both extreme tropical heat and Arctic cold. Another climatic factor conducive

to energetic life is moderate variation in temperature, rainfall, humidity, and wind velocities. The United States escapes the stultifying effect of uniform climatic conditions for long periods. These facts are of cardinal importance for American economic pursuits, especially agriculture, and undoubtedly have some significance in shaping the character and outlook of the American people (2, pp. 70-4.).

No one ingredient in the power of a nation is likely to be so basic as its geographical location. Location determines the pattern of relations between a nation and other countries. It is crucial in national defense. The presence or absence of "natural frontiers," as Poland has discovered throughout its history, can decide whether or not national security can be preserved. Location is crucial in trade and commerce. Britain and Japan—small islands off the coasts of Europe and Asia—became great nations because of their ability to use the oceans as highways of commerce. Even the cultural and ideological influence exerted by a nation may depend on its location. Greek and Roman thought infused the European world because of the proximity of these nations to the European hinterland and the consequent ease of communication.

Long imbued with the idea of Western hemispheric solidarity, Americans have difficulty appreciating the objective facts about their geographical relationship with the rest of the world. Having expanded over a continent which contains few natural land barriers, the people of the United States have traditionally thought in continental terms. More specifically, this means they have believed that land connects and water divides. They have overlooked the fact that land, too, can present barriers, and that oceans may cease to be obstacles to contact between nations. For example, England and Japan were effectively separated from the continental mainland only until the advent of air power. In the 20th century, there is little or no difference between sea and land barriers. Travel is often easier by sea or air than by land. Freight can be hauled much more cheaply by water than by land. Military forces can often be transported more conveniently by sea or air than by land. The upshot is, as Eugene Staley has observed, that "the myth of the continents" is an illusion that the American people must abandon if they are to visualize their proper geographic role in the world and are to formulate policies which reflect this role (**35**, pp. 481-94).

Widespread reliance within the United States upon the Mercator map projection is partly responsible for erroneous notions about geographic relationships. Every map distorts global relationships to some degree. The peculiarity of the Mercator projection is that it gives credence to the idea that the United States is geographically isolated except from Canada and Latin America. Vast ocean distances seem to divide the United States from Europe and Asia. The accessibility of polar routes, first by airplanes and now by submarine, does not emerge. The Western Hemisphere appears to be a geographically compact unit, with the other great land areas of the earth scattered along its fringes. These "ship thoughts," as George T. Renner has labelled them, are largely the basis for the way the American people have traditionally thought about foreign affairs throughout their history (**30**, p. 38).

The only realistic perspective from which the salient facts about America's relationships with the rest of the world become apparent is to visualize them in global dimensions. More than at any other stage in history, the globe, not the map, needs to be the constant source of reference for every student of foreign policy. Once Americans adopt the perspective of the globe —thereby comprehending relationships that are obscured by flat map projections—they will understand several basic facts about their country's geographical location. One is that America is not isolated, nor has it ever been isolated to the degree imagined in the nation's folklore. The United States is not safely protected by two expansive oceans and by Arctic wastelands to the north. Stereotyped conceptions of the Western Hemisphere as a closely-knit geographic unit, sharply cut off from other centers of world power or arenas of international conflict, abound in the American mythology about foreign affairs. Yet arbitrary divisions of the world into hemispheres by lines running north and south possess virtually no military or strategic validity; such divisions are carryovers from the era of global exploration and colonization.

An almost infinite number of hemispheres can be projected on the globe, including of course those dividing the world along an east-west axis, or those created by lines running at an acute angle to the equator. And, as S. W. Boggs has observed, if hemispheres were projected embracing the United States, they could be drawn in such a way that there would be "no human being anywhere on earth" who did not "live in some hemisphere that includes *all* of the United States." Every major area of culture in the world would be part of some "American hemisphere" (**3**, p. 908).

Global thinking would also help us gain a proper understanding of distances between the United States and other countries. How much farther is it from New York City to Europe than to Brazil or Argentina? How much greater are the distances between the United States and Japan or the Middle East, on the one hand, and most countries in South America, on the other hand? Such questions reflect the ingrained belief of many Americans that the Western Hemisphere is the immediate backyard of the United States. A not untypical expression of this misconception was Wisconsin Governor Philip LaFollette's warning to Americans during the Second World War to beware lest they fight "not in this hemisphere where we can be supreme, but . . . with expeditionary forces four thousand miles away in Europe and six thousand miles away in Asia" (**35**, p. 485).

Few Americans are psychologically prepared to believe that Europe is the closest neighbor of the United States, excluding Canada, Mexico, and the Caribbean countries. The American people tend to minimize distances within the hemisphere and to maximize distances between the hemisphere and other great land masses of the world. For example, few Americans today would look upon a trip from Washington, D. C. to San Francisco (about 2,300 miles) as a particularly lengthy journey, especially if it were made by transcontinental airplane. Yet this is approximately the distance by air from Chicago to the southern tip of Greenland, to the Arctic Circle, or the Beaufort Sea north of Alaska and east of Soviet Siberia; from San Francisco to the Bering Sea adjacent to Siberia; from Denver to the Beaufort Sea and Baffin Island in the northeastern Arctic Ocean; from Cleveland to the Arctic Circle and the north Atlantic west of Greenland; and from Boston to Iceland. In the Western Hemisphere, this is also about the distance from New York to the Panama Canal —a distance farther than the mileage by plane or ship from the "bulge" of Africa at Dakar to the closest point in South America.

A careful study of comparative distances will go far toward correcting many geographical misconceptions prevalent in the United States. The erroneous conceptions underlying Governor LaFollette's statement quoted earlier are revealed by the fact that from Madison, Wisconsin, it is farther to Brazil than to Benghazi in North Africa; about equidistant to Ankara, Turkey, and Buenos Aires, Argentina; closer to every major European capital than to Buenos Aires (and only one, Athens, is as far as Rio de Janeiro); closer to Gibraltar than to Bolivia, Argentina, Chile, Paraguay, and Uruguay (and it is closer by sea to Gibraltar from the nearest American port than from Miami to the nearest point in South America); closer to Manchuria than to Buenos Aires (35, pp. 485-86). New York City is 3,700 miles from Gibraltar, about 3,000 miles less than the distance to Buenos Aires and nearly 1,800 miles less than the distance to Rio de Janeiro. Washington, D.C. is closer to Berlin than to Rio de Janeiro; Chicago closer to many points in Russia than to many Latin American countries; Boston closer to Moscow than to half the countries in Latin America (30, p. 39).

These facts possess added significance in an age of supersonic, long-range aircraft and guided missiles capable of being launched from remote sites and of traversing the shortest distances to selected targets. Ocean expanses, Arctic wastelands, deserts, and the like, present no obstacles to airplanes and missiles. To appreciate the impact these technological advances have had upon America's relation with the outside world, let us imagine that an enemy wished to attack this country. Both the United States and the Soviet Union now possess intermediate-range (1,500-mile) guided missiles, and both countries have at least limited stocks of these missiles available for their armed forces. Utilizing intermediate-range missile sites in Eastern Germany, Soviet Russia could bring the whole of Western Europe, including Iceland and Spain and the coastal fringe areas of North Africa, within its range. Using bases in Bulgaria, an intermediate-range missile attack could be launched against practically any point in the Mediterranean Sea, including about half of Algiers, most of Libya, all of Egypt, and about one-third of Iran. An arc drawn with a 1,500-mile radius centered upon New York City would extend into waters north of Newfoundland, into the central Atlantic, southward through Haiti and the Dominican Republic. An enemy submarine firing a 1,500-mile missile, submerged 500 miles in the Atlantic east of New York City, could bring most of the United States east of the Mississippi River within its range. The same submarine submerged 500 miles off the coast of California would command a field of fire embraced by an arc extending from the northern tip of Idaho, east to Colorado, and southeast to the Arizona-New Mexico boundary. Similarly, a submarine submerged in the Gulf of Mexico 500 miles south of New Orleans could fire an intermediate-range missile at Philadelphia in the northeast, Detroit in the north, Omaha in the northwest, and Pueblo, Colorado, in the west.

Both the United States and Soviet Russia are rapidly forging ahead with the development of long-range, 5,000-mile, guided missiles. When these weapons become available in quantity for military use, they will nullify any remaining vestige of protection afforded the United States by its geographical location. The arc formed by a radius of 5,000 miles centered on Moscow includes Alaska, sweeps through northern Oregon, passes through the north central and midwestern portions of the United States and embraces most of the eastern and Atlantic seaboard area, excluding only the extreme southern portions of the country. This means that the industrial heartland of the United States would be within range of missiles launched from behind the Iron Curtain.

Translating these data into general strategic terms, we may say that today almost every point in the United States is within range of an enemy armed with submarine- or ship-launched intermediate-range missiles or of aircraft with roundtrip range of 3,000 to 4,000 miles. When missiles with a 5,000-mile range are available, then no point in the United States or the Western Hemisphere will be outside the field of fire of enemy missiles. These facts demonstrate forcefully that any thought of hemispheric isolation or non-involvement by the United States in global affairs is a dangerous fiction. Richard Hartshorne has labelled the concept of the Western Hemisphere a mere "cartographic device" devoid of any strategic-political content (14, p. 386). S. W. Boggs has gone so far as to term the traditional boundaries of the Western Hemisphere—Meridians 20° West and 160° East of Greenwich—as lines "wholly lacking in geographical significance" (3, p. 906).

If the concept of hemispheres must be retained in the study of international affairs, a much more meaningful term would be "Northern Hemisphere." History, as Nicholas Spykman has emphasized, has in the main been made north of the equator. Here is the great locus of world power. A globe would show that the United States, by the ineluctable facts of geography, is placed in an intimate and inescapable relationship with the sprawling land masses of the Northern Hemisphere. Relationships among nations situated on that land mass will provide the dominant themes of international politics for years, perhaps generations, to come (33, pp. 42-3). Even the economic-political future of newly-independent countries in Asia, Africa, and Latin America, is likely to be shaped by their contacts with more powerful, richer countries in the Northern Hemisphere.

America's presence in the "North Atlantic quarter-sphere" writes Hartshorne, "is the most important aspect of our location, now as in the past" (14, p. 388). This zone includes Europe, North America, the greater portion of the Soviet Union, and the connecting and intervening oceans. It contains about one-third of the world's population and approximately nine-tenths of its industrial complex. With the exception of Japan, it embraces all the great military powers known to modern history (14, pp. 388-93).

The three pivotal facts about America's geographic relationship with the outside world are: its location in the Northern Hemisphere; its Atlantic orientation; and its proximity to Europe and northern Asia over the Arctic polar route. America's relationship with Europe will in all likelihood prove crucial for foreign policy, now as in the past, inasmuch as five of the great powers of recent history have been situated in Europe; since America's cultural heritage is predominantly from this region; since its economic relationships are much more extensive with Europe than with Asia; and since the nation's major allies are located on the European continent (33, pp. 90-1). America's strategic-political orientation toward Europe stands out forcefully when we view the position of the United States on a globe as it appears from the vantage point of the North Pole, or if we look at a polar coordinate map projection. Then it becomes apparent that the great land masses of the world stretch out from the North Pole like a starfish, with the northern continents much closer together than the southern continents. "The relations between North America and the two sides of the European continent," in the opinion of Nicholas Spykman, "are the base lines of world politics while the relations between South America, Australia, and Africa are unimportant" (33, p. 178).

Geographical facts and concepts have a vital bearing upon every goal of American foreign policy. They have, for example, largely determined the nation's response to the communist challenge since World War II. The American concept of containment has rested upon the premise that enemy control over the great land mass of Europe and Asia—what the eminent geographer Sir Halford Mackinder called the "world island"—would give an adversary a well-nigh impregnable position from which to extend its influence to other nations and regions. From Eurasia, an aggressor could soon overrun the Near and Middle East, the fringe lands of the Far East, and Africa. If an enemy succeeded in consolidating its hold upon these areas, it would then be able to isolate the United States from its major allies by cutting sea communication-transportation routes at key points, by imposing an economic blockade, and perhaps by penetrating South America politically and militarily. The huge Eurasian land mass contains two-thirds of the land area of the earth, five-sixths of its population, and a large proportion of its natural resources. Its possession in enemy hands would place the United States in a militarily and economically vulnerable position such that it could not, in all likelihood, continue to maintain its independence (**18**, *passim;* **33**, pp. 320-453; **35**, pp. 487-88).

The United States has no real choice about playing an active role in global affairs. That decision has been foreordained by the facts of geography and the economic-strategic corollaries deriving from those facts. The only real alternatives relate to the kind of role it will play. Will its policies be based upon realities? Or will they be based upon stereotypes and misconceptions concerning the nation's relationships with other important countries? The first alternative is of course no guarantee to success in the diplomatic field, but it is clearly a *sine qua non* of successful policy. The second, on the other hand, could jeopardize the continued existence of the United States as a great and independent power.

Economic and Technological Determinants of American Power

Since World War I it has become apparent that a nation's power—especially its capacity to wage war—is largely determined by its economic base. Without the ability to equip military forces, and to keep them supplied with materials of war for long periods, a nation cannot protect its security or its vital interests. Creation of a firm economic foundation to support its foreign policy, therefore, demands that a nation possess or have unimpeded access to important industrial raw materials.

In overall terms, the United States has been the most richly endowed nation on earth in the broad range of strategic raw materials needed to sustain an industrial economy. America is the leading producer of steel, with a capacity to produce over one hundred million tons annually. Increasingly, however, the nation is becoming dependent upon outside sources of high-grade iron ore, as its own high-grade reserves have become depleted. In 1957 the total iron ore reserves of the nation were estimated at 75 billion tons, of which only 10 billion tons were classified as high-concentrate ores. In that year approximately one-fourth of the iron ore consumed by the American steel industry was imported, chiefly from fields in Labrador and Venezuela (**42**, pp. 598-99).

The situation in regard to other metals is even more discouraging from the standpoint of industrial self-sufficiency. Domestic supplies of many strategic metals are either totally exhausted or very near the point of exhaustion. Especially critical are shortages of copper, high grade bauxite ore from which aluminum is derived, lead, zinc, manganese, and tin. The following chart shows the extent to which the United States is dependent upon imported supplies of strategic metals:

AMERICAN IMPORTS OF STRATEGIC METALS 1956-1957

Commodity	Imports As Percent of Consumption
Iron	20
Manganese	86
Chromite	94
Cobalt	79
Nickel	87
Tungsten ore	74
Copper	28
Lead	41
Zinc	54
Aluminum	83
Tin	79
Antimony	40
Cadmium	62
Mercury	54
Platinum	87
Asbestos	94
Fluorspar	65
Gypsum	32
Mica	95

(Source: **42**, volume 1, pp. 18-19).

The most significant fact about these domestic shortages is that the disparity between domestic supply and demand is certain to become even greater with the passage of time. The Paley Commission, a group appointed to study America's growing reliance upon foreign trade, reported to President Eisenhower in 1952 that the United States and its free world allies could expect the following percentage increases in the consumption of strategic raw materials between 1950 and the period 1970-1980:

PROJECTED INCREASES IN
RAW MATERIALS CONSUMPTION
1950 to 1970-1980

Commodity	United States Percentage Increase	Other Free World Allies Percentage Increase
Tin	18	50
Zinc	39	61
Copper	43	54
Iron Ore	54	73
Rubber	89	203
Nickel	100	100
Petroleum	109	275
Tungsten	150	150
Fluorspar	187	260
Aluminum	291	415

(Source: 16, p. 272).

Growing demand is not the only factor likely to create critical shortages of strategic imports. Our allies have lost many of their former co-lonial sources of supply; many mineral-rich countries are cutting down on their exports of these commodities, wishing to conserve these raw materials for their own use; throughout the Western world there is a lingering fear among investors about investing in new sources of sup-plies abroad, because of uncertainties about the world market, fear of political instability in many countries, and general apprehension about the risks involved; and finally, world trade patterns cannot be restored to normal, cannot be divested of what are often dominant military-strategic motivations, so long as the cold war persists (24, pp. 165-66).

These facts have an obvious and far-reaching bearing upon national security. Writing during World War II, Nicholas Spykman observed that an Axis victory would deny the United States needed imports of aluminum, manganese, mer-cury, tin, chrome, mica, tungsten, and nickel. If the United States could continue to import many of these strategic commodities from South

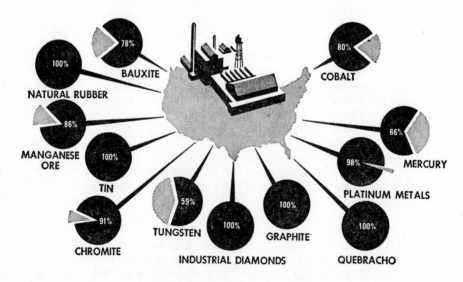

THE UNITED STATES MUST IMPORT
STRATEGIC MATERIALS FOR MAJOR INDUSTRIES

BAUXITE 78%
COBALT 80%
NATURAL RUBBER 100%
MANGANESE ORE 86%
MERCURY 66%
TIN 100%
PLATINUM METALS 98%
CHROMITE 91%
TUNGSTEN 59%
INDUSTRIAL DIAMONDS 100%
GRAPHITE 100%
QUEBRACHO 100%

*Natural graphite, strategic grade   DOMESTIC PRODUCTION   IMPORTS

Dept. of State, etc., *Mutual Security Program, 1959*, p. 8.

America, perhaps a reasonable degree of self-sufficiency could be maintained. But if it could not prevent an Axis penetration of South America—and, once Hitler overran Europe, this was a doubtful prospect—then the United States would be "surrounded by enemy territory and submitted to economic strangulation by the simple process of blockade through embargo" (33, p. 453). The situation would become even more critical today, since the nation now relies even more upon strategic imports than during World War II. Communist domination of the Eurasian land mass, providing a base from which to cut western hemispheric lines of trade and communication, could over the long run bring the American economy to a virtual standstill.

Turning to another important area of American technology, fuels and energy sources, we find a more promising picture. In 1957 total energy fuels consumed within the United States came from the following categories: anthracite coal, 1.5 per cent; bituminous coal, 30.9 per cent; petroleum, 36.3 per cent; natural gas, 27.7 per cent; and waterpower, 3.6 per cent (42, Volume 2, p. 4). Coal, petroleum derivatives, and natural gas thus are the mainstays of the nation's industrial and consumer fuel supplies. The United States is richly endowed with these primary fuels. In 1957, known reserves of coal were estimated at over 6 trillion tons, of which approximately half was regarded as accessible by existing extraction methods. At the present level of consumption, these reserves could supply the needs of the entire world for nearly 7 centuries. In 1900 coal supplied nearly 90 per cent of the total energy fuels consumed in the United States; a half-century later petroleum and natural gas had superseded coal as the principal source of consumer and industrial fuels. As the nation's petroleum reserves become depleted, however, coal may once more become the primary fuel. The process known as "coal hydrogenation" (the addition of hydrogen to coal), along with peacetime nuclear energy and, in the far-distant future, solar energy, may ultimately displace petroleum and natural gas as major sources of energy (5, p. 100). Possessing two and one-half times as large a coal reserve as the USSR, over three times as

much as the United Kingdom, and almost infinitely more than coal-deficit countries like India and many countries in Latin America, the United States will continue to rely heavily upon this vital resource to maintain its position as a great power.

Vast petroleum reserves have made possible the great industrial progress witnessed in America during the last century, and these reserves will also play a major role in future industrial expansion. In 1957 the nation derived more than one-third of its industrial and consumer fuels from petroleum, along with the overwhelming proportion of its lubricants. In that year the United States produced over 40 per cent of the world's total production of 6.4 billion barrels of oil. Geologists estimate the proved reserves of oil within the United States at 30 billion barrels. This figure does not count huge deposits of oil shales and oil sands which might someday become important sources of petroleum, provided technology can make extraction from these sources commercially feasible; nor does it include any estimate of new oil fields likely to be discovered in the future. In this same year, natural gas reserves were estimated at 246 trillion cubic feet. Impressive as these quantities seem, on the basis of an average production of 2.6 billion barrels of oil annually, the nation's known domestic petroleum supplies could be exhausted in a little more than a decade. Natural gas reserves, on the basis of present consumption levels, should last more than a century. Actually, projections of the nation's fuel and energy needs in the years ahead anticipate a doubling in these requirements every decade, for the next several decades ahead (21, p. 4). It is therefore reasonable to suppose that petroleum will also be depleted at a faster rate in the future than in the past. Three authorities from the California Institute of Technology predict that the United States, "which consumes liquid fuels at an extremely rapid rate, will undoubtedly pass through its peak domestic petroleum production at a considerably earlier date than will the world as a whole—perhaps as early as 1965-1970" (5, p. 100).

Today petroleum imports are vital for the maintenance of a strong industrial base at home. Imports in 1957 amounted to more than

1 billion barrels, net imports comprising 16 per cent of the total petroleum supply in that year.[*] Already, American industry is at work trying to discover alternative sources of oil—North Africa and parts of South America offer promise of containing large reserves—and to develop synthetic fuels that will compete commercially with petroleum products (28, p. 322). Countries in Western Europe are exerting intensive efforts to develop nuclear energy to reduce the free world's dependence upon outside sources of oil.

What is likely to be the impact of nuclear power and other technological changes, such as methods for harnessing solar energy, on the future energy needs of the United States? How will these developments affect dependence upon older sources of energy? Commercial use of nuclear power, solar energy, generation of power by the fusion process, and other recent innovations are still in their infancy, some of them barely beyond the experimental stage. Caution must therefore be exercised in making conclusions about their long-range impact upon either the technological-industrial processes within nations or upon the distribution of political-military power within the international community generally. Still, certain conclusions are warranted on the basis of available evidence. First, it seems clear that these newer forms of energy are not likely to replace traditional fuels in the United States for many years, possibly decades to come, principally because nuclear power is not yet competitive with existing sources of power, especially the generation of electricity from coal.[**] Second, other countries are likely to be motivated to accelerate the introduction of commercial nuclear energy by two considerations that are

much less applicable to the United States: desire to avoid deficits encountered in foreign trade from the importation of large stocks of fuel and desire to become economically self-sufficient, or as nearly so as possible. "Many nations will prefer an assured supply of nuclear power at relatively high but decreasing prices to less expensive but uncertain supplies of crude oil at prices which are destined to continue increasing" (5, p. 108). Other factors likely to retard the rapid growth of nuclear energy within the United States are: the location of long-established sources of energy adjacent to major industrial sites; the degree of economic risk involved in making a conversion to nuclear power; and the usual inertia to technological changes of far-reaching magnitude. Some observers anticipate that the United States will have greater difficulty overcoming these obstacles than will other countries, particularly those like the Soviet Union where such changes can be decreed by governmental fiat or like many underdeveloped areas where alternative sources of energy do not already exist in great abundance (19, pp. 182-86; 20, passim).

That nuclear energy generation within the United States will be a slow, evolutionary process is suggested by the following data: By 1957 there were 70 nuclear reactors in the country, 53 of which were owned by the United States Government. Of the 17 privately-owned reactors, only one was devoted to power generation, while the other 16 were devoted to research. By the end of 1957 the Atomic Energy Commission had granted 4 additional licenses for the construction of nuclear reactors and had granted one license for the operation of a power reactor (41, p. 542). A study prepared for the staff of the Joint Committee on

---

[*]Net imports is the quantity obtained by subtracting total American oil exports from total imports. The net import figures for 1957 do not convey fully the nation's dependence upon outside sources of oil, because in that year the United States increased its exports by approximately one-third above normal due to the interruption in oil exports from Middle Eastern countries occasioned by the crisis over the Suez Canal (42, Volume 2, p. 449).

[**]Citing data presented to the International Conference on the Peaceful Uses of Atomic Energy in Geneva in 1955, one study notes that "electricity can eventually be produced from nuclear energy at costs which are less than 1 cent (10 mills) per

kilowatt-hour. How much lower than 10 mills the cost can become, and how rapidly, are matters for conjecture." Optimistic estimates foresee a time when nuclear-generated power can be produced in the United States for 4 to 6 mills per kilowatt-hour. The study continues, however: ". . . nuclear electricity can probably compete with coal-generated electricity in other parts of the world long before it is competitive on a really broad base in the United States." Coal—America's greatest mineral resource—will remain the source of most electric power. Coal used for this purpose costs an average of $6 per ton in the United States, while in most European countries it costs from $13 to $20 per ton (5, pp. 106-07.)

Atomic Energy in August, 1958, calls attention to the slow pace that has characterized introduction of nuclear energy since explosion of the first atomic bomb in 1945. It observes that "experience has shown that probably several generations of intermediate and full-scale reactors of a given type will be required before the economic value of a given reactor concept can be determined. These technical and financial problems in turn have had a significant effect on the rate of progress in the civilian power reactor program" (**21**, p. 3). The stated goal of the peacetime nuclear energy program sponsored by the United States Government is to demonstrate by 1970 that nuclear-generated power can be made competitive with other sources of power. In the intervening years the Atomic Energy Commission is empowered by Congress to work closely with private industry to make this transition smoothly and economically (**21**, *passim*).

Just as important as America's position in respect to raw materials and fuels, is its capacity to produce and to convert its unequalled industrial strength to war and defense needs. The United States is believed to be approximately three-and-a-half times more productive than France, twice as productive as Britain, and eight times more productive than the Soviet Union (**24**, p. 118). The ability to convert America's economic system to war production was demonstrated during World War II when within four years the United States was producing goods and services for war at a new record rate. By 1944 the United States was outproducing the Axis powers by nearly 50 per cent and making nearly half of all the armaments turned out by all the belligerent nations combined. Postwar studies have shown that even this effort did not push the nation to its total industrial capacity. Considerable economic waste still existed and could, if necessary, have been partially eliminated (**9**, p. 5; **24**, p. 118).

Over the past one hundred years, the output of the American economy has increased twenty-five fold, an annual rate of increase of slightly more than 3 per cent. From 1950 to 1958 the Gross National Product—the total annual output of goods and services—increased from $350 billion to nearly $450 billion, an annual rate of increase of approximately 3¼ per cent. Conservative predictions for the annual growth of GNP use a rate of 2½ per cent through 1965; liberal predictions for the same period go as high as 5 per cent. Nevertheless the United States is unlikely to expand economically at a rate as great as that of its diplomatic antagonist, the Soviet Union. Under the seven-year plan instituted in 1959, the USSR expects to out-produce the United States in some fields by the mid-1960's; in the years thereafter, Russia's leaders claim that they will overtake and surpass the world capitalist giant in overall economic productivity. Though there are many grounds upon which to challenge communist predictions, it is undeniable that Russia's mounting economic strength will weigh heavily in determining the course of international affairs in the years ahead.

The productive strength of the American economy remains one of the cornerstones of the free world alliance. Unsuspected potential was realized during the Second World War, when —without resorting to manpower drafts for industry and without touching the bottom of the labor barrel—the United States supplied vast quantities of arms and commodities for the Allied war effort. As much as any other factor, the productive strength of the "arsenal of democracy" was crucial in tipping the scales in favor of the Allies. American productive enterprise was highly instrumental in sparking the recovery of Western Europe after the war and in launching many underdeveloped countries along the path of industrialization.

Considerable productive potential continues to exist. Between 2 and 3 per cent of all adult males do not have to work but could do so if national defense required it; the number of women in the labor force could be appreciably expanded; the average work-week could be lengthened perhaps up to the 60-hour week prevailing in most underdeveloped countries; productivity could be raised by the introduction of automation in many industries, better management techniques, and increased output per worker. Even without resorting to extraordinary measures deliberately designed to exact maximum production from American enterprise, one study foresees that production per man-hour in manufacturing will rise to an index of 236 by 1975, using the period 1947-1949 as an index of 100 (31, pp. 50-68 and Appendix, Table IV-A).

Population As A Determinant of National Power

Throughout history students of international affairs have been aware of the intimate connection between population and national power. This relationship is as complex as it is far-reaching in its implications. Military strength, economic productivity, scientific and technological know-how, national morale, the long-range goals of a society—all of these are functions of the size and character of the nation's population. Size of population is crucial in determining national power. Yet mere size alone cannot guarantee a nation great power status. If this were the case, global affairs would be controlled by heavily populated countries like India and China, which between them possess nearly 40 per cent of the total population of the world. Lacking another key ingredient in national power—adequate land and other resources requisite for a fairly high standard of living and a broad industrial base—the hundreds of millions of people living in these countries constitute more of a drain upon the power of the nation than an addition to it. The equation of national power contains many variables, and it is the relationship among these variables that largely determines whether nations will be weak or strong. Consequently, to decide whether a nation is "overpopulated," "underpopulated," or possesses an "optimum" population, consideration must be given to the capacity of the nation to support its people. Nevertheless, in recent history nations have been powerful only when they have possessed reasonably large populations. Perhaps the figure fifty million people could be taken as an approximate lower limit for nations that aspire to become great powers.

By the end of the 1950's, the United States had a population of more than 175 million—considerably larger than Britain, France or Germany, somewhat less than the Soviet Union, and much less than China or India. Throughout American history the rate of population growth has been phenomenal. The population quadrupled in the first half of the 19th century; trebled

during the last half; and has more than doubled since 1900. There has been an uneven growth during each decade, but the trend of the population curve has been steadily upward. The large population expansion during World War II and throughout the postwar era, when more than 43 million people were added to the society, surprised many demographers. Many had come to regard the United States as a country possessing a relatively stable population, compared with the rapid growth witnessed in regions like Africa, Asia, and Latin America. The census of 1950 revealed that they had underestimated the total population of the country by 5 per cent, which entailed an error of 41 per cent in predicting the growth of the population over the preceding decade. Consequently, in recent years demographers have become more cautious in predicting population trends. Now they normally make several predictions, utilizing different sets of assumptions concerning possible changes in the birth rate, death rate, median marriage age of the population, immigration, and related factors. That varying assumptions can yield significantly different results is attested by the following four predictions made by the Census Bureau for the growth of the American population in the period 1955-1980.

ESTIMATES OF TOTAL AMERICAN POPULATION 1975-1980

Series*	Total Population
I	272,557,000
II	259,981,000
III	245,409,000
IV	230,834,000

*Each series is projected upon the following assumptions: Series I, assumes a 10 per cent increase in fertility above present levels; Series II, projects 1955-57 fertility levels to 1975-80; Series III, assumes that 1955-57 fertility levels decline to levels prevailing in 1949-51 by 1965-70, remaining at that level to 1975-80; Series IV, assumes that fertility levels of 1955-57 decline to those prevailing in 1942-44 by 1965-70, then remain at that level to 1975-80.

(Source: 41).

Postulating a "medium" increase in the birth rate over the death rate, UN-sponsored projections forecast a total population for the United States of 217,000,000 people in 1975. Allowing for continued growth during the five-year interval to 1980, these figures are still below predictions made by the Bureau of the Census (**40**, p. 72).

Since 1950 the American population has been expanding at a rate of about 1.5 per cent annually, faster than the rate of 1.2 per cent annually prevailing over the preceding three decades, but only about half the growth rate recorded in the period 1700-1860 (**13**, pp. 20-1). In spite of unforeseen growth in recent years, the rate of population increase within the United States is considerably less than that prevailing in many other countries, notably those in Asia, Africa, and Latin America. Even on the basis of "high" assumptions regarding America's future population expansion, studies by UN agencies place the United States well down the list of countries that will experience a significant population expansion. Out of six categories, the United States is ranked next to last, along with Russia and other countries characterized by "moderate fertility, low mortality." When "low" assumptions are used, then the nation falls in the last category, along with its Western European allies, Russia and its European satellites, and other countries exhibiting "low fertility, low mortality." Irrespective of the assumptions relied upon, Africa, Asia, and Latin America head the list of countries destined to experience explosive population increases. According to high estimates, in the period 1975-2000, Africa's population is expected to double in size, Asia's and South America's will almost double (**40**, pp. 16-17, 70-71).

Judged by its capacity to support its growing population, the United States is acknowledged to be in a superior position among the nations on the globe. In 1950 the United States had 7.5 per cent of the world's people; yet it produced over 44 per cent of the world's total income in that year. Per capita income was nearly 600 per cent greater than the average of the world's per capita income in that year. Containing only slightly over 7 per cent of the total land area of the globe, in 1952 the United States produced the staggering total of 350 million tons of food-stuffs (**10**, pp. 36, 129). Scientists have estimated that American agri-

cultural production could be expanded as much as 50 per cent to feed the nation's expanding population (**6**, p. 119). Industrial productivity has far outstripped population gains. Thus, as measured by constant dollars (using the value in 1929 as a standard), the Gross National Product of the United States increased 335 per cent in the interval 1929-1957; in this same period the population grew by approximately one-third (**41**, pp. 5, 302). So phenomenal has been this rise in the American productive rate that the Twentieth Century Fund predicts: "if present rates continue, in another century we shall be able to produce as much in one 7-hour day as we now produce in a 40-hour week" (**6**, p. 2). Projecting a Gross National Product of approximately $500 billion for 1960, the Fund's study adds: "If we were forced into war emergency conditions similar to those of World War II, our total national output could approach $600 billion by 1960" (**6**, p. 3).

These data clearly indicate that the United States is not only able to support a large population at the present time without any diminution in the standard of living, but they also suggest further that even with population growth in future decades the nation can look forward to a gain in the per capita goods and services available to the American society. There will correspondingly be an absolute increase in the resources available to the nation's policy-makers to pursue national objectives at home and abroad and to protect America's vital interests in the world community.

Ever since 1798, when the English clergyman Thomas Malthus published his classic, *Essay on the Principle of Population*, students of politics have been conscious of the influence of population stimuli in determining national policies and global economic-political relationships. Modern scholarship has found many faults with Malthusian concepts, principally perhaps because they do not accord sufficient weight to man's ingenuity in overcoming adverse environmental factors and because Malthus tended to elevate observed population trends into inexorable "laws" purporting to govern the behavior of societies (**13**, pp. 108-24; **25**, *passim*). Yet one need not rely exclusively upon demographic determinism to anticipate the steady evolution of population issues as pivotal problems in world affairs, or to call attention to their new importance for American foreign policy. Kingsley Davis holds that the "most salient demographic change" in recent history is "the astonishing rise in the rate of growth of the world's total population." And within this broad trend another outstanding change has been that "the poorer countries are now contributing far more than their share to the inflated growth of the world's population." The crude birth rate in 1957 for countries like Mexico, Malaya, and the Union of South Africa, for example, is nearly twice that for the United States and almost three times that for several countries in Western Europe (**39**, p. 39). The disproportionate increase in the populations of these areas has many ramifications for global politics, but in Davis' view, "Above all, it means that the gap in wealth and power as between the rich and poor nations is becoming wider" (**8**, p. 294). Studies of per capita income reveal that the disparity between the "have" and "have-not" countries of the world is widening over the years. Thus in the late 1930's, the industrial nations of the West were ten times richer than underdeveloped countries in Asia, Africa, and Latin America; by the period 1952-54, they were eleven times richer. While there has been an increase in per capita *production* in many economically backward countries since 1929, in the same interval there has been a per capita decrease in *consumption* by populations within them. The calculations of a French demographer reveal that "In the aggregate, two-thirds of humanity consumes less than 5 per cent of the primary materials." (**8**, pp. 294-95).

Attempts to calculate the human absorptive capacity of the earth encounter innumerable obstacles, so many in fact as to render such calculations of questionable value (**25**, pp. 875-79). Nevertheless, it is crucial to know that reserves of many of the earth's resources are finite, and to observe that so far in history there has appeared no limit to the capacity of the human race to expand its numbers. Scientists will doubtless continue to ponder the theoretical capacity of the earth to sustain human life; the world's statesmen, however, will be much more vitally interested in such questions as: On what basis will the available resources of the globe be divided among the countries of

the world? What countries will make this determination? And by what criteria will it be made? Admittedly, such questions have always been present in some degree in international politics, and in some eras they have been uppermost. By the second half of the 20th century, however, they may well transcend other issues. In its bearing upon Soviet-American relations, for instance, such questions might ultimately prove pre-eminent. Possessing a common kinship in the richer industrial society of the West—a society that will be hardpressed to maintain its privileged position in a world of mushrooming population and of vocal demands for a greater share of the earth's resources by underdeveloped countries—both Russia and America may conceivably discover in that kinship a common bond that transcends prevailing national and ideological differences, just as they were driven to at least a minimum degree of unity to protect their vital interests during World War II.

Size alone is not the only important aspect of a nation's population. The character of the population is no less significant in determining the magnitude and nature of a country's power. For example, the ratio of younger people to middle-aged and elderly people within the society bears an intimate relationship to such elements in national power as the nature of the labor force and the size of the armed services. In recent years, the United States has experienced an aging process within its population. In 1850 the median age of the population was nineteen years; in 1950 it was thirty years, a 60 per cent increase in the median age. In 1860, 4 per cent of the population were over 65; in 1955, 8.5 per cent were in this group. In 1950 the average life expectancy had been pushed up to 66.3 years for males and 72.0 years for females. As life expectancy continues to climb, at perhaps slower rates, demographers expect that this aging process will go on. Projections of population estimates for 1980, on the basis of "high" assumptions concerning future growth, indicate that by that year approximately 9 per cent of the American people will be over 65 years of age. There has been an increase also in the proportion of children to the total population. In 1955 approximately 12 per cent of the population were under 5 years of age; the population projection for 1980 indicates that this proportion will rise to over 13 per cent.

These facts have manifold implications for American foreign policy and for closely related domestic issues. They mean that the "working population" between the ages of 21-65 years must support a larger percentage of dependents than formerly. In 1955 the employed labor force was 41 per cent of the total population; for 1975 Bureau of the Census estimates place this figure at 38 per cent of the total population (41, pp. 6-7, 204). Moreover, there will be a smaller percentage of the total population available for military service. A higher allocation of governmental expenditures will have to be directed toward providing services for the very young and the very old. And the aged as a group—to whom many political commentators ascribe a conservative, not to say reactionary, point of view about many national issues—will have a greater voice in shaping national decisions.

Another highly significant population trend has been the gravitation of masses of Americans to the cities and suburbs. As late as 1920 the American population was almost exactly divided between rural and urban elements. By the end of the 1950's, out of a total population of approximately 175 million, nearly two-thirds were classified as urban. Within this broad movement, a noteworthy trend has been the phenomenal growth in recent years of what the Bureau of the Census defines as "metropolitan areas": a county or group of contiguous counties which contains one city of 50,000 inhabitants or more. Census data reveal that in the decade 1940-1950 the population of metropolitan areas mushroomed, increasing by 22 per cent! By the close of the 1950's there were more than 170 metropolitan areas within the United States. The twenty-two largest ones—encompassing about 0.1 per cent of the land area of the country—contained nearly one-third of the people in the United States. Of the total population increase during the decade 1940-1950, more than 80 per cent took place in metropolitan areas (9, pp. 70-3; 41, p. 15). The gravitation of the American people to the cities and suburbs vitally affects the issue of national defense and foreign policy. In the age of nuclear weapons, supersonic aircraft, and missiles, the increasing

population concentration in such areas creates a progressively formidable defense problem. The American people have only dimly sensed the degree to which prevailing and projected population trends affect traditional concepts of national security and dictate military strategy for defense and offense. Discussion of these manifold ramifications at this point would carry us far afield.* Suffice it to say that the increasing vulnerability of the civilian population and of industrial sites to attack by enemy aircraft or guided missiles more and more calls into question the degree to which the United States can realistically rely upon a policy of "massive retaliation" against the communist empire in coping with Soviet Russia's expansive tendencies. At the present time, and for an indefinite period in the future, the United States is much more vulnerable to such attacks than its possible adversaries. Proposals designed to reduce the nation's vulnerability—an adequate civil defense program and dispersal of key industrial sites —have encountered widespread resistance and apathy among the population and have thus far had little impact (22, passim).

Other characteristics of the American population may be alluded to briefly. As the population gets older, an increase in chronic disease levels may be anticipated. Even today, population authorities refer to inadequate medical and dental care for the nation; to the prevalence of malnutrition among certain population groups; to poor housing and sanitation in the larger cities; to the inordinately high incidence of accidents, especially from automobiles—an incidence level so high as almost to qualify as a chronic epidemic in our highly industrialized-urbanized society; and to an alarming growth in mental illness over recent decades. Of great importance too is the existing and future need for added educational facilities required to accommodate the growing school-age population. Census figures for 1957, for example, show that only slightly more than one-third of the American male population had completed

---

*Discussion of the factors underlying American military and defense strategy vis-à-vis the Communist bloc is presented in Chapter 9, dealing with elements of the cold war, and in Chapter 10, dealing with the strategy of NATO.

high school and that less than 10 per cent had completed four years of college (**41,** p. 111). By the beginning of the 1960's, public opinion in the United States—severely jolted by the Soviet Sputniks and other evidences of rapid technological progress in the USSR—had come to see that the nation's destiny in world affairs could well be decided by the vigor, health, and educational level of its population. Perhaps in the long run these desiderata would determine the outcome of the cold war and the future role of the United States in global affairs.

REFERENCES

1. Acheson, Dean G. "The Shield of Faith," *Department of State Bulletin,* 23 (November 20, 1950), 799-801.

2. Barker, Sir Ernest. *National Character.* London: Methuen and Company, 1948.

3. Boggs, S. Whittemore. "Global Relations of the United States," *Department of State Bulletin,* 30 (June 14, 1954), 903-12. A cogent examination of America's geographic location in the world.

4. Bowman, Isaiah. "Geography vs. Geopolitics," *Geographical Review,* 32 (October, 1942), 646-58. This distinguished geographer effectively refutes German geopolitical theories.

5. Brown, Harrison, Bonner, James, and Weir, John. *The Next Hundred Years.* New York: The Viking Press, 1957. A broad projection for the next century of sociological, economic, demographic, and educational trends likely to influence the course of world events.

6. Carskadon, Thomas R., and Soule, George. *USA in New Dimensions.* New York: The Macmillan Company, 1957. A brief digest of findings by the Twentieth Century Fund concerning America's future economic needs and growth.

7. Cockcroft, John. "Peaceful Uses of Atomic Energy," *Science,* 129 (January 30, 1959), pp. 247-52. Reviews the results of the second Geneva Conference on the development of nuclear power.

8. Davis, Kingsley. "The Political Impact of New Population Trends," *Foreign Affairs,* 36 (January, 1958), pp. 293-302. A noted authority assesses significant implications of major population trends.

9. Dewhurst, J. Frederic, and Associates. *America's Needs and Resources.* New York: Twentieth Century Fund, 1955. A scholarly and comprehensive study of American human and economic capacities.

10. Doane, Robert R. *World Balance Sheet.* New York: Harper and Brothers, 1957. A comprehensive survey of world resources, providing a good background for evaluating America's power position.

11. Dulles, John Foster. "Our Foreign Policies in Asia," *Department of State Bulletin,* 32 (February 28, 1955), 327-31.

12. ———. "Principles in Foreign Policy," *Department of State Bulletin,* 32 (April 25, 1955), 671-75. Secretary Dulles here gives a forceful account of the principles guiding the United States.

13. Francis, Roy G., ed. *The Population Ahead.* Minneapolis: University of Minnesota Press, 1958. A compendium of the papers presented to the Second Symposium on Population Problems.

14. Hartshorne, Richard. "Where in the World Are We?" *Journal of Geography,* 52 (December, 1953), 382-93. Valuable for showing the geographical relationships of the United States.

15. Hatt, Paul K., ed. *World Population and Future Resources.* New York: American Book Company, 1952. Studies the impact of population problems on existing economic resources.

16. Hauser, Philip M., ed. *Population and World Politics.* Glencoe, Illinois: The Free Press, 1958. This symposium illuminates the manifold implications of population questions for world politics.

17. Hertzler, J. O. *The Crisis in World Population.* Lincoln, Nebraska: University of Nebraska Press, 1956. A sociological approach, with emphasis on the population problems of underdeveloped areas.

18. Hudson, G. F. "America and the World-Island," *Twentieth Century,* 158 (July, 1955), 35-44. Hudson relates Mackinder's ideas to the cold war.

19. Isard, Walter, and Whitney, Vincent. *Atomic Power.* New York: The Blakiston Company, 1952.

20. ———. "Atomic Power Politics," *Yale Review,* 38 (Spring, 1949), 399-409. These two studies examine the implications of nuclear power for the United States and other countries.

21. Joint Committee on Atomic Energy. *Proposed Expanded Civilian Nuclear Power Program.* Joint Committee Print. 85th Congress, 2nd Session. Washington, 1958. A brief summary of problems and prospects in the field of peacetime nuclear power in the United States.

22. Kaysen, Carl. "The Vulnerability of the United States to Enemy Attack," *World Politics,* 6 (January, 1954), 190-209. Especially valuable for showing the relation of population trends to national defense.

23. Kennan, George F. "Is War With Russia Inevitable?" *Department of State Bulletin,* 22 (February 20, 1950), 267-71.

24. Lincoln, George A. *Economics of National Security.* New York: Prentice-Hall, Inc., 1954. A thorough study of economic problems and their relation to national power.

25. McKelvey, V. E. "Resources, Population Growth and Level of Living," *Science,* 129 (April 3, 1959), pp. 875-81. A succinct evaluation of leading theories of population, with emphasis upon the relation of resources to standards of living.

26. Mackinder, Sir Halford. *Democratic Ideals and Reality.* New York: Henry Holt and Company, 1919.

27. ————. "The Round World and the Winning of the Peace," *Foreign Affairs,* 21 (July, 1943), 595-605. A classic statement by a world famous geographer of global geographic relationships. This article represents modifications of his earlier view in the light of World War II.

28. Miller, E. Willard. "Mineral Fuel Situation in the United States," *Journal of Geography,* 48 (November, 1949), 317-27.

29. Perkins, Dexter. "Geographical Influences in American History," *Geographical Journal,* 109 (January-March, 1947), 26-38. A distinguished historian examines the impact of geography on American development.

30. Renner, George T. "Air Age Geography," *Harpers,* 187 (June, 1943), 38-42. A perceptive presentation of basic geographical concepts for the United States.

31. Roos, Charles F. *Dynamics of Economic Growth: The American Economy, 1957-1975.* New York: The Econometric Institute, Inc., 1957. An enlightening projection of basic economic trends in the United States.

32. Schnitzer, Edward W. "German Geopolitics Revived," *Journal of Politics,* 17 (August, 1955), 407-23.

33. Spykman, Nicholas J. *America's Strategy in World Politics.* New York: Harcourt Brace and Company, 1942. This is probably the most penetrating study of geographic implications for American foreign policy.

34. ———— and Rollins, Abbie R. "Geographic Objectives and Foreign Policy," *American Political Science Review,* 33 (June, 1939), 391-410 and (August, 1939), 591-614. An analysis of the geographic origins and consequences of World War II.

35. Staley, Eugene. "The Myth of the Continents," *Foreign Affairs,* 19 (April, 1941), 481-94.

36. Stone, Adolph. "Geopolitics as Haushofer Taught It," *Journal of Geography,* 52 (April, 1953), 167-71.

37. Thompson, Warren S. *Plenty of People.* New York: The Ronald Press, 1948.

38. ————. *Population Problems.* New York: McGraw Hill Company, 1953. These two studies by a leading demographer provide valuable insight into demographic foundations of American policy.

39. United Nations. *Statistical Yearbook, 1958.* New York, 1958.

40. United Nations. Department of Economic and Social Affairs. *The Future Growth of World Population.* Population Studies, No. 28. New York, 1958.

41. United States Bureau of the Census. *Statistical Abstract of the United States: 1958.* (Seventy-ninth edition). Washington, D.C., 1958.

42. United States Department of the Interior. Bureau of Mines. *Minerals Yearbook, 1957.* 3 volumes. Washington, D.C., 1958.

43. United States Department of State. *Energy Resources of the World.* Washington: 1949.

44. "United States and Raw Materials," *World Today,* 7 (August, 1951), 338-46.

45. White, Theodore H. "The Challenge of Soviet Economic Growth," *The Reporter,* 8 (May 26, 1953), pp. 9-14.

CHAPTER 2

America Looks at the World

A Study in National Character

Objective factors—land, natural resources, economic capacities, population, and other elements—furnish the basis for a nation's power in world affairs. They cannot, however, determine what a nation will do with its power or how a nation visualizes its relations with the outside world. Nations may be strong enough to influence the course of world events in a manner favorable to themselves; whether in fact they will do so cannot be determined merely by studying statistics relating to military forces, capacity to produce steel, or national income. For three quarters of a century before the Second World War—omitting the interlude of World War I—the United States was a slumbering giant who did not know his own strength and was indifferent to the strength of other countries. It had some power in being and far greater potential power. But its citizens were captivated by the illusion that power was unimportant, that other countries did not care about America's power as America did not care about them, and that national security could be preserved irrespective of developments on the international scene. That illusion brought the nation almost to the brink of disaster.

The Role of National Character

What factors determine how the power of nations is utilized? In seeking the answers to

THE WAKING GIANT

Tom Little in *The Nashville Tennessean*, Dec. 1, 1957.

25

this question we must examine what has been called "national character." The question that Winston Churchill defiantly addressed to the Nazi Government early in the Second World War—"What kind of people do they think we are?"—is at once a necessary inquiry in any study of foreign policy and an inordinately complex one. As the historian Henry Steele Commager observed, it was because Hitler failed so completely to comprehend the importance of national character that the Nazi bid for world domination ended in catastrophe. His failure was

> fundamental and pervasive. . . . He failed to realize, as throughout history tyrants have failed to realize, that a people's character is, in the last analysis, the most important thing about them. . . . For material things cannot in themselves achieve something. They count only where there is a will to use them, and whether they count for weal or for woe depends upon the way that they are used. (10, p. xi).

When we ask: "What is the national character of the American people?" we shall focus upon the characteristics they exhibit as they look out upon the world. We want to establish the psychological perspective or frame of reference within which they approach foreign policy. We are searching for what an eminent English scholar, Sir Ernest Barker, called the "sum of acquired tendencies" and the "expectable action" of a nation. He elaborated this idea by saying:

> Each nation lives in a set of ideas (and of emotions associated with the ideas and even with the very words used to express the ideas), which is peculiar to itself. . . . Any man who has to act between nations . . . is bound to understand, to the best of his power, the peculiarities of each national fund of ideas. He must realize that there are as many atmospheres, and as many characters, as there are nations. . . . Nations are realities; and their characters—the set of their minds, and the atmosphere of their ideas—are as real as they are. (2, p. xi).

Put more simply, we are asking: Are there certain habits of mind that we can identify as the American approach to foreign relations? Many authorities agree that there are. Before we attempt to delineate them, however, certain reservations should be considered.

Pitfalls in the Study of National Character

In the first place, some authorities deny the existence of national character altogether. They believe that attempts to discuss it represent nothing more than impressionism and hasty generalization which scientific methodology cannot support (40). While their objections have some validity, most students agree that the subject is important, that it permits investigation, and that we can learn something about it, however tentative our conclusions must sometimes be.

Second, it is imperative that we avoid stereotyped thinking about our own national character and other nations' as well. All of us are familiar with stereotypes in this field. "The Germans are inherently militaristic and expansionist." The inference follows that peace with Germany is an illusion. "The French are decadent, immoral, and unreliable." Hence, they make very poor allies. "The Italians are opportunistic and cowardly." Hence, they are easily defeated in war and they too make poor allies. "The Latin Americans are ignorant and proud, politically immature, mercurial, and easily misled." Hence, they need guidance by the United States in solving their problems. Such sweeping characterizations are largely false and the inferences drawn from them are equally false. But there is a germ of truth in such stereotypes —enough to make them widely accepted. By choosing certain episodes in American diplomatic history one could also find enough evidence to make credulous people believe that the United States is imperialistic, money-loving, war-mongering, fickle, and xenophobic. These examples illustrate an important point in the study of national character: nations should be characterized by traits which are in accord with the overall pattern of the nation's history and ethos and which represent, as nearly as possible, typical behavior of the people described.

A third warning concerns the breadth of the field of study. Scholars in every branch of knowledge have something to contribute here. The physiologist and chemist tell us how our bodies perform; the geneticist enlightens us about the influences of heredity; the psychologist discusses the human personality in its complex ramifications; the social scientist informs us concerning the impact of political, social, economic, and cultural institutions upon man's behavior; and the historian supplies knowledge and interpretations of man's past. This list of course is not complete, for it must be re-emphasized that every discipline has something to offer. The study of national character resembles the creation of a mosaic. To complete the picture, pieces of different sizes, shapes and importance must be taken from diverse sources. Only then will a recognizable image emerge.

In the fourth place, it must be recognized that many of the traits of national character delineated in this chapter constitute subconscious premises growing out of historical experience, rather than explicit and clearly thought-out popular attitudes on matters of public policy. For this reason, inconsistencies persist among diverse traits of national character. To cite an example dealt with at length at a later stage: Americans in the past have exhibited a dogmatic attachment to "principle" in international affairs, while at the same time remaining devoted to expediency and trial-and-error methods in coping with many of their domestic problems. Yet such inconsistencies are seldom perceived by the average American, chiefly perhaps because he infrequently questions the basic values and beliefs that shape his attitudes toward problems at home and abroad.

A final warning concerns the danger of regarding national character as something fixed and unalterable. The character of neither individuals nor nations is cast in a permanent mold. Sir Ernest Barker wrote: ". . . There is no such thing as a given and ineluctable national character, which stamps and makes the members of a nation, and is their individual and collective destiny. Character is not a destiny to each nation. Each nation makes its character and its destiny" (2, p. 7). The proper analogy to illustrate national character is an organism — evolving, adapting to influences about it, learning from mistakes, ever-changing.

With these admonitions in mind, let us examine more closely the leading attributes of American national character.

1. AMERICAN ATTITUDES TOWARD POWER

No feature of the approach of the American people to foreign relations is more pronounced and has had more important consequences for their foreign policy than their attitude toward power conflicts, and specifically, toward war. Throughout most of their history, the American people have deprecated the role of power in international affairs. They have looked upon conflict as abnormal, transitory, and avoidable. Hostilities have existed among nations, not because their vital interests sometimes clashed, but because of "misunderstandings." These, it was believed, could be eliminated by a variety of means: agreements to denounce war "as an instrument of national policy," as in the Kellogg-Briand Pact of 1928; pledges to reduce armaments; solemn oaths to respect the territorial integrity of small countries; ratification of the charter of an international organization; resounding declarations of high principle such as the Fourteen Points or the Four Freedoms; faith in the "moral opinion of mankind" to deter aggressors; and belief that international student exchange programs and "good will missions" will reduce tensions, as the nations "get to know each other better."

Few writers have stressed the American misunderstanding of the fundamental role of power as frequently, and as pointedly, as Walter Lippmann. Our approach to foreign relations has ever been filled with "stereotyped prejudices and sacred cows and wishful conceptions," to the extent that we are often incapable of formulating workable policies. Our basic weakness is a failure to recognize, "to admit, to take as the premise of our thinking, the fact that rivalry and strife and conflict among states, communities, and factions are the normal condition of mankind" (28, p. 18).

Such habits of thought stem from a variety of influences in the nation's history. From America's own internal experience the people have taken the view that fundamental human conflicts did not exist, or if they did, that they *a reason for the American view*

THE American WAY OF LIFE

could be quickly resolved, because within its own borders remarkably few such conflicts have in fact persisted. Marxist ideology notwithstanding, the United States perhaps approximates more nearly than any other country the "classless society" (**25**, pp. 140-50). In America conflicts of all kinds—economic, religious, ethnic, racial—have produced relatively little enduring strife compared with the Old World and the newer nations of Asia and Africa. America has never experienced prolonged and irreconcilable divisions among its people. We have not pitted the Old Regime against the New, the proletariat against the owners of the means of production, religious dissenters against the orthodox, the inheritors of great wealth against the middle class. Somehow, America has learned to channel existing differences into non-violent avenues, to smooth them out, to make them seem secondary to the task of creating upon a continent the "American way of life." This has been done by providing unparalleled opportunities for material advancement; by steadily trying to offer equal opportunities for all in ever-widening spheres of national life; by de-emphasizing doctrinal and ideological differences in favor of immediate and attainable goals for human betterment; by listening to the demands of dissatisfied groups and, in time, meeting most of them; by insisting upon fair play in economic, social, and political life. Our experience has built in us the conviction that perseverance and will power can solve all problems.

Except for the Civil War, the United States has avoided these societal conflicts that have periodically torn older nations asunder and that, in many of them, have become endemic in their national life. Americans believe that conflict among peoples can be eliminated because they have to a remarkable degree proved it by their own experience.

Then too, the New World came to deprecate power because of the break it made, or thought it made, with the Old World after the Revolution. Throughout the 17th and 18th centuries settlers had come to America to escape the tribulations of the old order. Tyrannous monarchs and ministers of state, censors, religious persecutors, entrenched aristocracies, dynastic rivalries, diplomatic intrigues—these they were

leaving behind when they came to America. There they were carving out a "new society" where liberty, democracy, equality, freedom, and security for all would prevail. Power politics might be the keynote of the Old World; the dignity of the human spirit, progress, democracy—these came in the course of time to be the themes of the New World. Time and again after the Revolution, America's leaders asserted that Europe and America had separate interests. The United States had no stake in the quarrels of Europe. America wanted nothing so much as for Europe to mind its own business and, if Europe must continue to indulge in power struggles, to keep them away from the American shores.

Consequences for American Security

The consequences of America's attitude toward the role of power conflicts have been far-reaching and decisive. Such an attitude has heavily colored the nation's appraisal of the basis of its security. From superficial examinations of their own history, Americans have believed that their security could be explained by a variety of factors, none of which had anything to do with power. There was first the evident fact of geographical separation from Europe and Asia which, before the air age, did provide a substantial amount of military protection. Then there was the fact that the United States had repeatedly warned other countries to stay out of the Western Hemisphere—and, with few exceptions, the warning had been heeded. There was also the belief that if America chose to ignore the Old World, the Old World would respond by ignoring America. The illusion persisted that no vital interests connected the Old and New Worlds, that America could be secure no matter what transpired in Europe. From the time of the Monroe Doctrine in 1823 to the Second World War, the United States acted as though its security were a natural right; as though changes in the European balance of power could not affect it; and as though power played an inconsequential, if not altogether negligible, role in international relations. Walter Lippmann has written that for over a hundred years

The idealistic objections to preparedness, to strategic precautions, and to alliances came to dominate American thinking. . . . The objections flourished, and became a national ideology, owing to the historical accident that in that period Asia was dormant, Europe divided, and Britain's command of the sea unchallenged. As a result, we never had to meet our obligations in this hemisphere and in the Pacific, and we enjoyed a security which in fact we took almost no measures to sustain. (29, p. 49).

Throughout the greater part of its diplomatic experience, America has consistently failed to understand the difference between the *ability* of other countries to threaten American security and the *desire* of other countries to do so. Because they have threatened the United States infrequently, it has interpreted this to mean that other nations recognized and conceded that the Western Hemisphere and American overseas possessions belong within the American security zone. Because other nations have disturbed America remarkably little, America has believed they did not want to, that they were indifferent to America's role in world affairs.

Because the American mythology has traditionally de-emphasized power, the United States has lived off an unrecognized and unacknowledged inheritance: the British fleet ruled the seas, and the quarrels of Europe kept aggressors otherwise occupied. By the mid-20th century, the United States, like the Prodigal Son, had finally come to see that it could not go on living indefinitely off its inheritance and that it must at long last earn its own security.

A corollary of the American failure to accept the role of power has been the failure to understand that in the successful management of foreign affairs assets must equal or exceed liabilities. While it is true that power cannot be calculated with great precision, a rough kind of equilibrium must be maintained between a nation's foreign commitments and its ability to protect them. Bankruptcy, Walter Lippmann has argued, is the only word to describe American foreign policy at crucial intervals in history. American foreign policy was bankrupt for the same reason that we speak of a bankrupt business: obligations were assumed greater than the nation's resources, at least greater than the resources available to the nation's leaders at

any given time. The art of conducting foreign policy successfully, Lippmann has contended, "consists in bringing into balance, with a comfortable surplus of power in reserve, the nation's commitments and the nation's power" (29, p. 9).

In almost any period in American history since 1900, evidence of bankruptcy can be found. The American acquisition of the Philippines after the war with Spain was, in the words of the distinguished diplomatic historian, Samuel F. Bemis, "The Great Aberration." It was an aberration because annexation of these islands entailed responsibilities which the United States did not begin to appreciate. After some of the implications of extending America's boundaries thousands of miles into the Pacific—to the very doorstep of Japan—finally became apparent, the United States was still unwilling to take the necessary steps to protect its commitments there.

From the First World War to the Second World War this pattern of bankruptcy was repeated on an even broader and more ominous scale. At the very time when threats to its commitments were growing, especially in the Orient, America was reducing its military power. Not until 1941 did the American people begin to understand that America's refusal to use its power in behalf of its vital interests was in itself a policy. No nation, especially a powerful nation, can escape having an influence in world affairs. America's unwitting vote in this period was cast on the side of destroying the military security of the Atlantic Community, of turning over the military approaches of the Western Hemisphere to would-be conquerors, of giving Japan a free hand in the Pacific, in summary, of doing everything possible to insure bankruptcy in foreign affairs.

Wars Are Aberrations

Another corollary of America's failure to understand the role of power can be found in its attitude toward the causes and consequences of war. Clausewitz taught that war is but the continuation of policy by other means. Hence the cliché that America has never lost a war nor won a peace means that the American people have not had a clear grasp of the political issues leading to and growing out of war, and hence their policies for dealing with such issues have often been feeble and ineffective.

American history has been characterized by a recurrent failure on the part of public opinion to visualize the connection between foreign policy and national power, especially military aspects of national power. Viewing wars as essentially aberrations, instead of alternative methods of settling international disputes, the American people have evinced minimum historic awareness of the long-term political implications of military decisions. Following both world wars in which the United States has participated, the public failed to assess the implications of the changes wrought by war, either for their own country or for the international community as a whole. Instead, large segments of the population have tended to believe that the nation could return to the *status quo ante bellum,* apparently on the premise that the distribution of global power had not altered in any way that would impair their country's security.

This mentality is well illustrated by the revisionism that has characterized historical writing and literature following virtually every war in which the United States has been engaged. Recurrent themes in revisionist writings have been that responsibility for hostilities rested on both sides, and often more on the American side than on the enemy's; that the United States had no vital interests at stake and hence was under no necessity to fight; and that the American people had been deluded by a variety of influences—propaganda, munitions makers, Wall Street, political leaders—into believing that their security demanded recourse to arms (**41,** pp. 335-37). Revisionism, writes Dexter Perkins, has tried to convince the citizenry that "every war in which this country has been engaged was really quite unnecessary or immoral or both; and that it behooves us in the future to pursue policies very different from those pursued in the past." Behind such thinking, he continues, often lies "the assumption that the will to avoid war is sufficient to prevent war" (**36,** pp. 686, 695). Walter Lippmann has made this point even more forcefully. Writing in 1940, he explained the blindness of Americans

toward the Axis dictators by referring to "a falsification of American history." The American people had been "miseducated by a swarm of innocent but ignorant historians, by reckless demagogues, and by foreign interests, into believing that America entered the other war because of British propaganda, loans of the bankers, the machinations of President Wilson's advisers, and drummed-up patriotic ecstasy. The people have been told to believe that anyone who challenges this explanation of 1917 and insists that America was defending American vital interests is himself a victim or an agent of British propaganda" (**25,** p. 219).

America Reacts to Power

The unwillingness of many Americans to recognize the reality of power in world affairs, in the face of the persistence of conflicts on the world scene among competing powerful states, has resulted in several behavior patterns characteristic of the American approach to foreign relations. One of these patterns has been periodic retreat into an illusory isolationism. When it became clear after the First World War that power rivalries were as deeply embedded in international relationships as before, America's reaction was to retire from the field and "let Europe stew in its own juice." Similarly after World War II, with apparently little thought concerning the consequence of its actions, the United States brought its troops home from overseas and demobilized its armed forces. Reluctantly, it began to rebuild its military strength only after unmistakable evidence had convinced the nation that its continued security permitted no other course.

Paradoxically, widespread public misapprehension about the centrality of power in global relationships has also led to popular viewpoints and national policies that are diametrically opposed to isolationism. For example, Americans have shown an affinity for policies whose evident purpose was to make a frontal assault upon the problem of international conflicts in the hope of eliminating them altogether, much as medical science would concentrate its energies and skill to eliminate an epidemic. This pattern of behavior is illustrated by the eagerness many Americans display in embracing slogans and in participating in verbal crusades. Significant numbers of Americans expected that the First World War was "the war to end wars" and that victory would "make the world safe for democracy." Two decades later, the conviction prevailed widely that once the Axis was defeated the goal of "One World" would be achieved, perhaps by establishing the United Nations or by instituting the "Four Freedoms," one of which was freedom from fear. As co-operation among the wartime allies withered in the face of rising cold war tensions, basically the same mentality was displayed by the tendency of many Americans to think that reiteration of the determination to "stand firm" in the face of communist threats and intonation of militant phrases like "massive retaliation" would go far toward preserving national security.

Still another behavior characteristic that stems from misconceptions about the role of power in global affairs has been the tendency throughout much of American history to identify threats to national security with specific countries and to think that, once that threat was eliminated, international conduct would thenceforth be conducted within an atmosphere of harmony and good will. A logical corollary of this view is that a foreign policy aimed at the total elimination of the existing threat offers the greatest—some Americans might argue, the only—promise of ultimate security. This thinking has been widely exhibited by groups advocating an "interventionist" foreign policy in dealing with the communist bloc. Such groups have urged the nation to "strike at the root of the problem, once and for all" by "settling accounts" decisively with Moscow and Peiping. Specific policies supported by such groups have included "liberating" the Iron Curtain countries from the communist grip, expanding the Korean War to the Asiatic mainland, and countering the latest communist diplomatic maneuver with the threat of all out nuclear war. From time to time a small, but occasionally highly vocal, minority of Americans has advocated preventive war against the progressively stronger communist bloc.

Disillusionment must inevitably follow in the wake of utopian expectations. Expecting too much, the American people have ever been reluctant to settle for the attainable; and when they would not take the attainable, they frequently have preferred to absolve themselves of further responsibility for international peace and security. From apathy, to fervent involvement, to disenchantment, to apathy once more —this has been an all too familiar cycle in American foreign relations. The marked oscillation in moods in American foreign policy has engaged the attention of many writers (35, 114-28; 16). That there exists a regular frequency to such cycles may be doubted, although a number of writers have attempted to discover it. But the fact of violent swings in the American public temper toward foreign relations is a phenomenon no historian can deny. It is considered by informed commentators a serious obstacle to success in the foreign policy field.

People Are Good; Rulers Are Bad

America's failure to appreciate the role of power is also reflected in the contrast it draws between peoples and their rulers. Throughout its history the United States has had a profound suspicion of political authority (18, pp. 30-9). It has embraced Jefferson's dictum that "that government is best which governs least," and it has clung to this credo over the past half-century even while the powers of government on all levels were being expanded to unprecedented magnitudes.

In its foreign relations, the United States has periodically sought to explain the presence of conflict by distinguishing between the unfriendly acts of rulers and the supposedly peaceful inclinations of ordinary citizens (18, pp. 227-29). Admittedly, this distinction can be used advantageously as a diplomatic technique to encourage a rift between an unfriendly government and its people, in the hope that the leaders can thereby be induced to modify their existing policies. President Wilson undoubtedly was motivated by this hope when he repeatedly distinguished between the leaders and citizens of Imperial Germany. The Allies, he said, had no quarrel with the "German people" but only with their misguided rulers. During the Second World War, President Roosevelt took the same position toward the political hierarchies of Germany and Italy and, to a lesser degree, Japan. The people of these two countries, it was widely believed, had been seduced by their rulers into paths of military conquest. After World War II, much the same attitude could be discerned in America's relationships with Soviet Russia and Red China. Political orators proclaimed that the common people throughout the communist empire were essentially peace-loving and that they yearned for deliverance from their communist masters. Diverse motivations of course prompted these utterances: hope that public opinion behind the Iron Curtain would compel a softening of the totalitarian regimes prevailing, that it would induce a withdrawal of Russian power eastward, and that it would perhaps evoke a more receptive response to Western views on unresolved diplomatic issues than had been experienced through official diplomatic channels.

Distinctions between peoples and their leaders rest upon questionable assumptions. For one thing, they wrongly presuppose that rulers can govern without reference to the wishes of their subjects. For another thing, they fail to take account of the continuity between a nation's foreign policy goals and its historic goals and needs as a society. Third, citizens of other countries often actively share the goals of their leaders or, at a minimum, are relatively indifferent to foreign policy questions. Finally, even if the rulers of a country have advanced beyond the point of receiving explicit public approval for their policies, public opinion will oftentimes support such policies once the issue of patriotism is raised because of disputes with foreign nations. It is open to serious question, for example, whether many of the issues dividing Russia and the West today would melt away if Russia adopted democratic political institutions. Similarly, it is doubtful whether a liberalization of the communist regime in China would appreciably alter that country's determination to become the dominant power in the Orient. Optimistic hopes widely held by groups within the United States are but another evidence that America has consistently underestimated the role of national power in world affairs and has not sufficiently grasped the connection between it and foreign policy goals.

2. MORALISM: THE SHADOW

A second discernible trait in American national character is the emphasis placed upon moralism in relations with other countries. Moralism is not the same as morality, although both derive from a common etymological root. Morality has to do with the substance of behavior. It is conduct in accordance with a predetermined code of behavior, and throughout Christendom this refers to behavior sanctioned by the Christian faith. Moralism, as used here, is concerned with appearances, with the concepts and language employed in foreign relations, with the symbols used, and with the way that ends and means are visualized and expressed publicly. Moralism is not so much moral behavior but public recognition that such behavior is expected and is being carried out by one's own country. Thus it is possible for a nation devoted to moralism to be in fact moral, immoral, or amoral, however the case may be, in its actual conduct. Later in the chapter we shall have more to say about morality in American foreign relations. Now we are interested in the question: What forms has moralism taken in American foreign policy? What are its tangible evidences?

American Conceptions of "Manifest Destiny"

Americans have always drawn a significant contrast between their own territorial expansion and expansion by other countries. They have deprecated expansionism as a goal of foreign policy—even while in the midst of expanding. Denouncing the British Empire and applauding its dissolution; condemning Germany's territorial ambitions; castigating Soviet Russia's aggrandizements; and, as late as 1950, going to war to vindicate the principle that aggression cannot be condoned; these ideas have formed dominant themes in successive periods of American diplomatic history.

Toward their own experience of expansionism, Americans have taken a somewhat different view. Seemingly irresistible pressure—Americans called it "Manifest Destiny"—propelled American dominion westward to the Pacific and, after that, outward to the Caribbean and Pacific islands. Believing that this process had nothing in common with ordinary expansionism —soon forgetting that many great Indian tribes were almost exterminated in the process and the remainder confined to tiny or barren reservations—America looked upon westward expansion as a God-given right. As Ray A. Billington, a historian of westward expansion noted, when he wrote concerning the Mexican War:

Every patriot who clamored for Mexico's provinces would indignantly deny any desire to exploit a neighbor's territory. The righteous but ill-informed people of that day sincerely believed their democratic institutions were of such magnificent perfection that no boundaries could contain them. Surely a benevolent Creator did not intend such blessing for the few—expansion was a divinely ordered means of extending enlightenment to despot-ridden masses in near-by countries. This was not imperialism, but enforced salvation. So the average American reasoned in the 1840's when the spirit of manifest destiny was in the air. (Quoted in 25, p. 181).

Or as a Congressman from Massachusetts sardonically observed in the 1840's: Manifest Destiny was opening "a new chapter in the law of nations or rather, in the special laws of our own country, for I suppose the right of a manifest destiny to spread will not be admitted to exist in any other nation except the universal Yankee nation" (Quoted in 25, p. 183).

"No Compromise With Principle"

No nation in history has placed so much emphasis upon "principle" in dealing with other countries as the United States. "No compromise with principle!" is a perennial slogan of the American people. Before virtually every international conference in recent history, America's leaders have devoted an inordinate amount of time and energy to giving public assurances that principle would not be abandoned. During the 1950's, for example, a major obstacle to high-level diplomatic conferences among the great powers was widespread belief within the American population that such conferences in-

herently favored the enemy, that "sellout's" and "secret deals" would be well-nigh unavoidable. Indeed, it would not be too much to say that certain groups in American society had come dangerously close to equating the very process of diplomacy with "appeasement" and abandonment of principle. Undeviating opposition to appeasement by vocal groups within the United States placed many barriers in the path of a flexible and imaginative diplomacy.*

This emphasis, one might even say fixation, upon principle has its roots deep in the nation's past. The diplomatic historian, Dexter Perkins, has shown that it underlay America's failure to reach an accord with Great Britain after the Revolution and, against its own true diplomatic interests, America's affinity for the French cause during the Napoleonic period (35, pp. 68-0). The Monroe Doctrine in 1823 literally resounded with principles. In this period and in later ones, America identified itself with revolutionary causes abroad. In the mid-19th century, for example, American enthusiasm for European revolutionary causes threatened to precipitate several diplomatic incidents between the United States and European governments.

We have already alluded to the skillful manner in which many Americans justified expansionism upon moralistic grounds. Our attitude toward Spain late in the 19th century was shaped by the view that the Cuban rebellion accorded with our ideas of justice and morality.

---

*The widespread disrepute attached to the idea of appeasement in the West in recent years was surely both a symptom and a cause of the existence of international tensions. It was a symptom in that it symbolized the clash between antagonistic ideologies and the deep distrust displayed by one side toward the other. It was a cause, in that it perpetuated rigidities in conflicting national positions on major international issues and, in some instances, came close to rendering any "settlement" or accommodation on such issues impossible. Appeasement had come to be equated with the kind of sellout epitomized by the handing over of Czechoslovakia to Hitler in 1938 and by alleged "deals" made with Russia during the Second World War.

Synonyms for appeasement listed by Webster— to pacify, quiet, calm, sooth, allay—suggest that the idea is basic to human relationships and that there is nothing intrinsically immoral about the concept. Indeed, it is central to the attempt to resolve differences among nations by peaceful means.

At no time did our insistence upon principle emerge so clearly as during the First World War when it lay at the root of our quarrel with Germany and, by contrast, our long-suffering endurance of repeated British provocations. The allies were fighting for freedom and democracy; for freedom of the seas (even while they denied it to us); for self-determination and independence from monarchial and totalitarian rule; for the rights of small nations; and for international integrity. What did the Central Powers, especially Germany, stand for? They represented militarism and authoritarian rule within, expansionism and calloused opportunism without. They were breakers of treaties, violators of innocent nations, and, perhaps most heinous of all, insensitive to the ordinary standards of decency and morality expected of nations in the western community. American principles and German behavior, at least America's image of it, were at antipodes. It was this fact which more than any other finally drew the United States into the First World War.

Principle again pervaded the American attitude toward the dictators in the inter-war period. To many citizens, the most serious indictment of Japan's behavior during the 1930's was not so much that Japan was pillaging China and building up a formidable military threat to American security in the Pacific. It was rather that Japan was doing all of this in violation of its sacred word as embodied in the Washington naval treaties of the 1920's, the Kellogg-Briand Pact, and the Covenant of the League of Nations. Similarly, toward the European dictators the United States took the position that acts of aggression during the 1930's were reprehensible, not because they constituted in time an intolerable threat to the security of the Atlantic community, but because they stemmed from a theory that treaties were merely "scraps of paper," that defenseless nations had no rights, and that the pledged word of the nation could be violated with impunity. Not an awareness of American vital interests, but strong aversion to the actions of international gangsters imperceptibly but steadily drew the American people closer to the Allies (35, pp. 69-75).

Turning to the postwar period, moralism has pervaded American foreign policy toward a number of important international issues. Soviet Russia's exploitation of the eastern European satellites, for instance, was viewed as a calculating and willful violation of the agreements reached at Yalta and Potsdam concerning the treatment to be accorded conquered and liberated nations. So great was America's aversion to Soviet machinations in this area that the United States took a keener interest in events there—in an area where it had in fact very few vital interests—than in many other areas, such as southeast Asia or the Middle East or North Africa, where its own diplomatic interests were more direct and fundamental. Similarly, moral principle has been invoked repeatedly in America's attitude toward Red China, so much so that principle is perhaps the only explanation for America's attitude. The vast majority of Americans has felt that Red China cannot be permitted to "shoot its way into the United Nations" and that it must prove "by deeds and not words" that it is ready to become a peace-loving member of the family of nations before American recognition of the communist regime can even be contemplated.

Some Consequences of Moralism

America's affinity for moralism has had both positive and negative aspects. On the positive side it may be said that no other course accords with American experience and ideology. If Americans invoke principle more than most countries, it may be because the American people are more conscious than most of how often principle is lacking in international affairs. If they insist upon a "decent respect for the opinions of mankind," it is because of a deep conviction that mankind is tired of Machiavellianism, that it yearns for an international order in which justice, enforced by law, prevails. In common with all reformers, the American people concentrate upon the ultimate goal without gazing down at the pitfalls in the path of its attainment. If they are forever exhorting other nations and calling them to repentance, it is because they are so impressed with the need for charting new paths. Americans are asking other countries to pattern their conduct according to standards which, for the most part, Americans are willing to accept for themselves.

To foreigners, Americans must resemble nothing so much as the sombre Puritan: motivated by high ideals, austere, unshakable in his conviction that goodness will triumph in the end—but at the same time impatient with wrongdoing, sanctimonious, and at times insufferably self-righteous.

An uncritical attachment to principle also has its negative side. It can cause the nation to dispense with all colors on the political spectrum, leaving only black and white. When significant numbers of Americans evaluate prevailing global issues in terms of consummate righteousness versus consummate wickedness, habits of mind and practices are inculcated that seriously interfere with success in the foreign policy field. In dealing with problems in Asia, for example, a recurrent characteristic of American foreign policy has been its impatience and manifest lack of sympathy for "neutralism." The American approach has often rested upon the simple axiom: he who is not with me is against me. Injecting massive doses of principle into almost every important source of international controversy, the United States has exhibited very little understanding or enthusiasm for neutrals and fence-sitters. Countries like India, Burma, and Indonesia which did not "stand firm" with the West in opposing communism were, voluntarily or involuntarily, "helping communism." Despite its constant reiteration of principles like non-intervention in the affairs of other countries and self-determination, in many instances the United States has evidently been displeased with signs of too much "independence" on the part of its allies or other nations. Since many Americans have believed passionately that there could be no compromise with principle, they have expected other countries to support the United States on every major international question, at the risk of considering them in the camp of the enemy.

Informed commentators have stressed the tendency of the United States to postulate total extremes and mutually exclusive alternatives. For example, in wartime goals are delineated sharply: unconditional surrender or defeat; appeasement or victory; universal democracy or absolutism. International conflicts thus become, or are constantly in danger of becoming, Armageddons (28, pp. 19-20). Firmly convinced of the goodness of their cause, Americans often find it difficult to understand why it does not triumph and triumph speedily. "The illusion of American omnipotence," the perceptive British observer D. W. Brogan has written, resides in the belief that "any situation which distresses or endangers the United States can only exist because some Americans have been fools or knaves." Large numbers of Americans, he feels, have yet to learn that "the world cannot be altered overnight by a speech or a platform" (6, pp. 21, 28).

In practice, the American propensity to believe that there cannot be compromise with principle frequently resolves itself into the view that there can be no compromise at all. As a society, Americans have shown minimum preparedness to live with vexatious problems in the international community for extended periods of time. Their expectation is that problems will be "solved" and that tensions can be "eliminated." Frequently, they assume that threats to world peace and stability can be "removed," much as a housewife would summon an exterminator to deal with pests. So prominently does principle infuse their approach to such issues that the American people have often overlooked a lesson they have learned, or are still in the process of learning, in their own internal affairs. This is that very few problems in human relations are ever solved in a final sense. They are ameliorated, softened, mitigated, outlived, tempered, adjusted to—but seldom solved. This lesson emerges with striking force from any study of such diverse problems as divorce, delinquency, alcoholism, traffic accidents, crime, and a host of others. Nevertheless, sizable numbers of Americans confidently look forward to the elimination of the "communist problem" and, more generally, conflicts arising from clashing national interests. Their own experience could also teach them another pertinent lesson: few human problems yield before a dogged insistence upon principle, accompanied by short-lived and passionate crusades to eliminate the problem. More often, they yield instead to persistent and understanding efforts to deal with them and to an awareness that, if principle is present at all, it is likely to be present in some degree on both sides.

3. MORALITY: THE SUBSTANCE

The American people have been consciously more moralistic than others in their foreign affairs. Have they at the same time been more than ordinarily moral? What is their record in practicing the ideals they have professed and have tried to impose on others? In broad outline, the answer is that throughout their diplomatic history American citizens have placed a high value on moral behavior for themselves and for other countries as well.

The American Attitude Toward War

If we are to judge by the number of wars, both major and minor, in which the United States has engaged, the record does not indicate that the nation has been especially peaceloving. From the Revolution to the Korean War, there have been eight major wars and in between a host of small-scale ones. Reviewing this record, Dexter Perkins comments that "it does not seem to be a strikingly pacific one, at least not utterly out of line with the history of other nations." He adds also that we must keep in mind that territorial acquisitions—for which many other countries are forced to wage war—came to Americans primarily through purchase and negotiation (**35**, p. 84).

But the number of wars in which the United States has been engaged proves little or nothing about the extent of morality in its foreign policy. America has fought only one, the Mexican War, which could even remotely be construed as a war for territorial aggrandizement, and even then it compensated Mexico for the territory taken. America has traditionally been slow to anger. It has never gone to war over a "diplomatic incident." In its two greatest wars it has endured repeated provocations and has devoted months to seeking peaceful solutions before finally and reluctantly drawing the sword. This fact alone of course does not prove superior morality on the part of the American society; in part, the explanation derives from an overwhelming preoccupation with domestic pursuits and from a widespread inability to perceive the connection between events in Europe and national security. Nevertheless, the United States has probably been as un-warlike as any great power in history. In the vast majority of instances, only repeated provocations have forced the nation to enter military conflicts.

Moreover, the terms imposed upon vanquished nations have not, in the main, been severe. After both the First and Second World War, it was the United States that tried to mitigate the severity of the terms which the Allies wished to inflict upon the enemy. With rare exceptions, vindictiveness has not been a characteristic of the American mind. This may occasionally have been a passing phase, but it soon gave way to a sincere desire to help rehabilitate conquered nations, to aid them in re-entering the family of nations.

We have already alluded to America's reluctance to take foreign territories as a result of war. The United States has of course done so, but usually because, as in the Spanish-American War, there appeared no other alternative. Moreover, it has repeatedly refused to take reparations and indemnities. A classic case was the Boxer Rebellion (1900) when indemnities paid to the United States were set aside for the future education of Chinese students in America. Following all its wars in recent history, it has given generously through governmental and private agencies for the relief of suffering following in the wake of hostilities.

We conclude that America has never been a warlike country and that in victory it has been magnanimous.

Is America "Imperialistic?"

America's territorial expansion raises the question: Can the United States fairly be accused of being imperialistic? The answer depends in large part upon how imperialism is defined. If it signifies the acquisition of foreign territory, primarily for the exploitation and advantage of the mother country, only one judgment on American foreign policy is possible. It has been remarkably non-imperialistic.

As Dexter Perkins insists, a fundamental distinction must be maintained between expansionism and imperialism (35, pp. 30-1). The United States—beginning as a weak country along the fringes of the Atlantic Ocean and becoming within 150 years one of two super-powers—has expanded more than any country in recent history, with the possible exception of Russia under Czarist and communist rule. Most of America's territory was acquired by purchase or negotiation. That taken by conquest—by some interpretations Florida, the territory acquired after the Mexican War, the Philippines, and the Panama Canal region—was later compensated for by the United States. Admittedly, this account ignores the fact that most of the continental United States was in fact taken by conquest from its original inhabitants, the Indian tribes. And, parenthetically, it also ignores the fact that in dealing with the Indians the United States was guilty of violating practically every moral precept it has tried to follow toward other countries.

American domination over foreign territories, Perkins holds, has "always been rule with an uneasy conscience" (35, p. 32). Toward the vast continental landmass at home, one principle was consistently followed throughout American history: whenever the frontier lands were ready for statehood, they were admitted to the Union on an equal plane with the older states. Toward colonial societies a somewhat different, but closely related principle, has prevailed: they were to be tutored in the art of self-government and prepared for ultimate independence. Two overseas possessions—Alaska and Hawaii—were groomed for admittance into the Union, and were admitted in 1958 and 1959, respectively.

American administration of possessions and dependencies overseas has almost invariably led to marked improvement in their national life. Living standards were pushed up; modern sanitary practices were introduced; education was fostered and made available to ever-growing numbers; democratic political processes were encouraged among the inhabitants. After reviewing the broad stream of America's colonial record, Perkins concludes that "in the moderation which ought to go with strength, the United States has played and is playing a creditable role" (23, p. 45).

What America has done with its territories, however, may not be as significant as what it has not done. For, as Herbert Feis has emphasized, few countries in history have voluntarily foregone as many opportunities to acquire additional territory and to impose their will on weaker countries as the United States. Historically, the United States has refused to join with other strong countries in parceling out colonies and spheres of influence. Much of the tension developing between Japan and the United States during the 1930's, finally leading to Pearl Harbor, could be traced to America's refusal to join with Japan in staking out spheres of influence in the Orient; the Roosevelt Administration's refusal to acquiesce in unilateral Japanese expansionism further widened the gulf between the two countries. After World War II both Presidents Truman and Eisenhower steadfastly refused any *rapprochement* with the Soviet Union based upon a division of the world between the two power giants (14, *passim*).

The proper criticism to make of American foreign policy is not that it has been imperialistic, but that it has been slow to recognize that responsibility goes with power. Both in relations toward its own possessions and in its attitudes toward the colonial possessions of other countries, it has sometimes been quick to endorse the principle of self-determination for small countries, without realizing that for many weaker countries the choice lies between being protected by a benevolent great power or being taken over by aggressors. Experience in trying to carry out the doctrine of containment in the postwar period has called attention graphically to the stabilizing role in world affairs formerly exercised by institutions like the British Empire. Moreover, it has underscored the fact that freedom cannot be meaningful for any nation until that nation possesses the ability to safeguard its security.

America and Militarism

Another manifestation of the American national character is the attitude of its people toward the military establishment. We shall have more to say about this in Chapter 4. There we shall examine the constitutional and ideological restrictions which the American people have imposed upon their armed forces. Throughout their history, the American people have opposed a large standing army. They have preferred to raise troops by voluntary recruitment rather than by conscription. Today the United States is the only major power in the world that lacks a program of universal military training. A fundamental principle of the American constitutional pattern has always been civilian control over the military. So firmly have precedent and public opinion supported this doctrine that not even during time of war has there appeared significant danger of military domination of the government. President Truman's unceremonious dismissal of General Douglas MacArthur in 1951 caused a temporary public furor; but sober reflection convinced most citizens that Truman's action vindicated a principle that must be preserved. Even popular generals must be required to accept the strategy of the nation's elected political leaders on pain of instant dismissal.

The aversion of Americans to military service may also be seen in the rapidity with which the United States has demobilized conscripted forces at the end of major wars. After the Second World War it would be charitable to say that the army was demobilized; it would be more accurate to say that it disintegrated. America's historic bent for frenzied demobilization has had fateful consequences for national security and the security of the North Atlantic community to which the United States belongs. Following World War II, two years at least were required before public opinion accepted the fact that at a number of crucial points around the globe power vacuums had developed. The alternatives finally came to be seen as simple and painful: either the United States would rebuild its military machine to the level required for discharging its responsibilities as a great power, or else many of these strategic areas—Greece, Iran, Western Europe, North Africa, Japan, Korea—might well pass into the communist orbit.

Though America has been anti-militaristic, it has not been anti-military. The distinction here is fundamental. Americans have feared and distrusted the substance of military power, but they have applauded and glorified many of its trappings and incidentals. "I Love a Parade" describes America's attitude toward military pomp and ceremony. No other country in the world has so many "military academies" for the training of its youth—schools, it must be emphasized, which stress the building of disciplined minds, strong bodies, and courtly behavior, rather than trying to produce a military elite dedicated to bringing the nation glory through conquest. Few national holidays and athletic occasions are complete without an impressive parade, often including precision marching units from some military post or, if not that, then at least several civilian bands carefully trained in close-order drill.

America has found a substitute for militarism: it lies, in large part, in glorifying many of the superficial aspects of military life, while at the same time rejecting its substance (**5**, pp. 62-5; **18**, pp. 30-9).

"A Moral Equivalent for War"

The great American philosopher, William James, urged the nation to find a moral equivalent for war—some concept or activity that would elicit the same sense of dedication to a higher cause, the same spirit of sacrifice, the same passionate ardor that Americans had demonstrated during time of war. James' idea has lost none of its pertinency with the passage of time. In the post-World War II era Americans sometimes showed considerably more reluctance about supporting activities designed to assure peace and to attack the long-range causes of war than about making sacrifices once the nation entered into hostilities.

Nevertheless, from the time of the Jay Treaty with England in 1794, the United States has been in the forefront of nations seeking alternatives to force for settling international disputes. For example, it has time and again favored the arbitration of boundary and territorial disputes (**38**, pp. 143-54; 201-18; 347-52; 458-60). It has followed the same course toward controversies over neutral rights, such as occurred with Britain over the "Alabama claims" during 1866-72, and over violations of American neutral rights during the First and Second World War (38, pp. 315-19; 466-82; 634-45). It has sponsored and joined efforts to institutionalize arbitration, as when it accepted the Hague conventions of 1899 and 1907 and when it sponsored the Bryan arbitration treaties in the early 1900's (38, pp. 451-56).

In seeking a moral equivalent to war, it has taken the lead in establishing international organizations for dealing with threats to the peace. True, it refused to join the League of Nations. Nevertheless, it supported the League in a number of ways during the years that followed; and during the 1930's it cast its moral, though never its military, influence behind efforts of the League to deal with repeated aggressions by the Axis states. During the Second World War it very early took the initiative in planning for a new international security organization to preserve world peace. Since the war few countries have been more conscious of the necessity for strengthening the United Nations than the United States. Not that its record in the UN has been free from blame. America has ignored the UN in a number of important instances and to that extent has contributed to weakening its prestige. Still, it has worked diligently to establish the UN upon a firm foundation, and to endow it with enough power to deal effectively with international threats. In two major instances— the Korean War and the Middle Eastern conflict (1956-57)—the United States insisted that collective action to halt aggression take place through the United Nations. In the latter case, the influence of the United States was largely responsible for reaching a major milestone in the history of international organization: the creation of a UN police force endowed with sufficient power and moral authority to prevent further hostilities among the countries of the Middle East.

Since World War II America's ardent sponsorship of arbitration and the conference method for settling international disputes has also been tempered by the popular disillusionment growing out of postwar negotiations with the com-

munist bloc. The great emphasis accorded to "principle" in approaching cold war issues, along with the widespread popular equation of compromise with appeasement, has notably reduced America's traditional enthusiasm for conference diplomacy and arbitration techniques. Nevertheless, Americans have traditionally placed great faith in their ability to persuade other countries to settle differences rationally and without recourse to violence.

This, along with a number of other aspects of their national character discussed in this chapter, is at once one of their virtues as well as one of their weaknesses in foreign affairs. It is a virtue, because as long as diplomats are talking—even when their talk has degenerated into propaganda and irresponsible accusations—there is still hope that armies will not march. If war is to be avoided then a rational discussion of the issues that give rise to tensions would appear to be the only conceivable preventive.

But interminable talk, conferences, meetings "at the summit," and the like can also be detrimental. Optimistic by nature and dedicated to the view that the only barriers to human progress lie in the lack of human vision and resolute determination to overcome obstacles, Americans do not always appreciate the limitations inherent in diplomatic conferences. Productive negotiations require a will to peaceful solutions on the part of all participants. Fair and reasonable offers, as Chamberlain discovered in dealing with Hitler, and Roosevelt and Truman found out in dealing with Stalin, can furnish the basis for lasting accords only when the other side is also interested in discovering an equitable solution. When it is not, when instead it views concessions as but a prelude to further and greater concessions, then talk is not only unproductive; in some instances it can have the harmful effect of creating the appearance of achievement in the absence of reality, thereby encouraging the public to believe that prevailing international disputes have in fact been settled. This is not to suggest that endless diplomatic conferences between representatives of the West and the communist bloc, for example, are inevitably futile and should be discontinued. Barren as results have been in the recent period, diplomatic exchanges are obviously to be preferred to a military showdown. But public opinion should not expect too much from such conferences. When spectacular results are not forthcoming, the public should not dispair of reaching agreements in the future and should not condemn diplomatic techniques as a whole. Public disillusionment growing out of unreasonable expectations places an additional barrier in the path of sustained attempts to achieve a *modus vivendi* among nations with competing ideologies and rival national goals.

4. ISOLATIONISM IN WORD AND DEED

Isolationism has pervaded the American approach to foreign relations since the earliest days of the Republic. America's pattern of isolationist thought is well-illustrated by its foreign policies during the 1920's and '30's. What is not so widely recognized is that isolationism goes much deeper than merely the desire to avoid foreign entanglements. It is above all a habit of mind, a cluster of national attitudes, a feeling of spiritual separation from other countries, especially Europe, with roots penetrating deeply into the nation's heritage and experience.

Isolationism, as Albert K. Weinberg has aptly put it, is "not a theory of American foreign policy. Isolation is a theory about a theory of American foreign policy" (**43**, p. 539). It is more than a doctrine advanced to explain the objective facts of America's geographical relationship with the rest of the world. Instead, it is supposed to explain *what the American people believe to be the proper relationship between themselves and other countries.* Isolationist thinking permeates the American cultural experience, its philosophy, and what may be called more generally "the American way of life." It is basically a conviction that Americans are different from other people; that they do not look to foreigners for guidance but that foreigners should look to them; that their national destiny is to serve as a beacon to pilot all mankind into new paths of greatness—but that all this should be done primarily by precept and example.

The Roots of American Isolationism

The influences that have contributed to isolationist thinking are many and complex. Here we can do no more than allude to some of the more important ones (**4**; **18**, pp. 224-37; **29**,

passim; **36**, pp. 682-95; **31**). The desire for separation from the vicissitudes of Europe brought settlers to the New World. The wish to begin life anew, to leave behind the turmoil, the hopelessness, the bigotry of the Old World —these ambitions brought the religious dissenter, the peasant, the adventuresome aristocrat, the skilled artisan, the speculator, and the felon to American shores. From all walks of life they came, and with one objective: to find a new birth, as it were, in a far-off continent.

The Revolution cut the political ties with England, and as the years passed Americans came to believe more firmly than ever in their uniqueness. Washington and Jefferson both cautioned their countrymen that America and Europe had different interests and advised that America's best course was to concentrate on keeping these interests distinct. Very early in the nation's history isolationism became the underlying principle of foreign policy. One pretext after another, for example, was found to justify America's refusal to honor the French alliance during the Napoleonic wars. Against the wishes of many citizens, especially those in New England, the nation was finally drawn into a war against England in 1812. But within a little over a decade President Monroe in 1823 asserted that the United States had but one objective in its relations with the Old World: it wanted the European countries to mind their own business and, if they must persist in power struggles, to keep them out of the Western Hemisphere. Owing to an underlying identity of interests between the United States and Great Britain—an identity that did not become widely recognized until the post-World War II period—America, shielded by the British navy, experienced remarkably few challenges to the Monroe Doctrine during the course of almost a century.

America Looks Inward

From the Monroe Doctrine until the Second World War the American people were profoundly isolationist. We must regard participation in the First World War as an interlude. Its politico-strategic significance generally passed unnoticed within the United States. Historically, the energies, thoughts, and ambitions of the American people have been directed inward. Americans possessed a continent to populate and to incorporate within the boundaries of their country. They were feverishly creating out of their seemingly unlimited resources vast wealth and expanding opportunities for all. The ceaseless intrigues and struggles witnessed on the continent of Europe held no appeal compared with the challenge of creating the "American way of life." Passionately dedicated to the belief that human progress was limitless, the American people were tackling many of the formidable problems older civilizations had been unable to solve and, in most instances at least, they were solving them reasonably well: problems of unemployment, of unequal distribution of land, of racial and national minorities, of religious liberty, of illiteracy, of political oppression, of the pressure of population upon food supply, of the equitable distribution of wealth, and of hereditary rights. And if America's solutions to these and other problems left some groups unsatisfied, the solutions were at least good enough to force acknowledgment even from foreigners that the "new society" was becoming a reality across the Atlantic.

Isolationism derived then as much from the dominant concern of the American society with domestic affairs as it did from a deliberate rejection of foreign entanglements. The achievement of virtually every goal associated with the "American dream" demanded that internal interests receive primary attention. This fact prompted one of the nation's leading historians, Charles A. Beard, to prefer the term "continentalism," instead of isolationism, to characterize the nation's historic orientation in foreign policy. Elaborating Beard's idea, a contemporary American observer, Max Lerner, has written: "It was not so much a question of cutting America off from the world as it was

of rounding out and fully exploiting the part of the world that was America" (**27**, p. 888).*

America is the "New Society"

What then were the elements in this new society, this "American way of life?" We shall leave its dominant theme—belief in the perfectability of man and his institutions—for consideration later in the chapter. There was intense pride in the accomplishments of the American people. A perceptive English observer, D. W. Brogan, has written admiringly: "To have created a free government, over a continental area, without making a sacrifice of adequate efficiency or of liberty is the American achievement. It is a unique achievement in world history" (**5**, p. 101). A recent American writer credits the United States with two phenomenal accomplishments: it has succeeded in preserving, in an age of centralization and autocracy, the self-reliance of the individual and the autonomy of the local unit of government; and it has come closer than any nation in effecting a separation between the holders of economic and political power (**15**, p. 532).

Then too there was the theme of cultural separation that pervaded American literature

---

*Lerner's comprehensive study, *America As A Civilization,* affords many insights into the American mind. His discussion of isolationism is particularly illuminating. Lerner calls attention to the kinship existing between two seemingly antithetical schools of thought in foreign affairs, isolationism and interventionism. The isolationist wants to reduce the nation's foreign commitments and follow a go-it-alone philosophy in foreign relations. By contrast, the interventionist advocates greater reliance upon military power in dealing with threats to security and urges the nation to undertake diplomatic offensives to achieve goals like the liberation of the communist satellite countries or the overthrow of the communist regime in China. Despite the marked dissimilarities in their methods, Lerner contends, their underlying goal is basically the same: to create conditions throughout the world that will permit the United States once again to focus its energies on domestic affairs, with minimum involvement in foreign affairs. Both schools operate upon the assumption that the nation's destiny continues to be, as in the past, preoccupation with the American way of life (**27**, pp. 881-907, *passim*).

during the 19th century. Listen to James Russell Lowell in a "A Fable for Critics":

> Forget Europe wholly, your veins throb
>   with blood,
> To which the dull current in hers is but
>   mud; . . .
> O my friends, thank your god if you
>   have one, that he
> Twixt the Old World and you sets a
>   gulf of a sea; . . .
> To your own New-World instincts
>   contrive to be true, . . .
>   (25, p. 69)

This was a dominant strain of New World literature throughout the greater part of the 19th and 20th centuries. Not that American writers did not acknowledge their great dependence upon a common English and European literary heritage. But now they wanted a literature distinctly American, one that would express the nation's hopes and ideals in a way that European writers never could. This uniquely American flavor made Walt Whitman America's outstanding poet. "I Hear America Singing" may not have been his greatest poem, but it expressed better than most his abiding ambition: to chronicle in song the American way of life, to point to both its achievements and its unsolved problems, and to show the world that America was well on the way toward building a society based upon the principle of the brotherhood of man.

> Thou, too, sail on, O Ship of State!
> Sail on, O Union, strong and great!
> Humanity with all its fears,
> With all the hopes of future years,
> Is hanging breathless on thy fate!

These familiar lines from Longfellow[*] point to another consequence of the belief that America was the new society. America's example, it was thought, would be sufficient for other nations to take hope and, by tugging at their own bootstraps, as the American people had done, to raise themselves to new levels of human attainment. The United States, as Hans Kohn put it, has been the "universal nation" in two senses. First, American institutions, philosophies, and accomplishments have mirrored the hopes of mankind. Second, for over a century

---

[*]Henry Wadsworth Longfellow, "The Building of the Ship," (1849).

America's doors were open to receive the stranger and to provide him every opportunity for making the American dream come true (25, p. 139). This part of the American dream had been expressed by Jefferson in 1817, when he wrote that America's mission was

> to consecrate a sanctuary for those whom the misrule of Europe may compel to seek happiness in other climes. This refuge once known will produce reaction on the happiness even of those who remain there, by warning their taskmasters that when the evils of Egyptian oppression become heavier than those of the abandonment of country, another Canaan is open where their subjects will be received as brothers. . . . (Quoted in 25, p. 138).

Emerson was convinced that "Our whole history appears like a last effort of the Divine Providence in behalf of the human race . . ." (Quoted in 25, p. 140). And in 1839 John Louis O'Sullivan wrote an article entitled "The Great Nation of Futurity," the theme of which was that

> Our national birth was the beginning of a new history, the formation and progress of an untried political system, which separates us from the past and connects us with the future only; so far as regards the entire development of the rights of man, in moral, political and national life, we may confidently assume that our country is destined to be the great nation of futurity.

The writer concluded that America

> is destined to manifest to mankind the excellence of divine principles. . . . For this blessed mission to the nations of the world, which are shut out from the life-giving light of truth, has America been chosen. . . . (Quoted in 25, pp. 152-153).

By the 20th century, the belief that America was ordained by Providence to redeem the world by example had, like the early Christian expectation of the coming of the Kingdom, been modified in the light of realities. But as late as the post-World War II period such thinking persisted. Many Americans apparently saw no reason why underdeveloped countries all over the world could not repeat America's experience by evolving slowly from a "frontier" society to become in the course of time, and with American assistance, a mature industrial-urban nation. That many countries were not in the process of doing so was interpreted widely in the United States as a sign that they were indolent, ideologically misled, or willfully ignorant (**18**, pp. 223-24).

American isolationism then has positive as well as negative aspects. That Americans took little interest throughout most of their history in Europe's conflicts and in clashing imperialist interests in Asia and Africa was not solely because they did not wish to become embroiled in political controversies away from their own shores. In part at least their attitude was dictated by attachment to what they regarded as a far more fundamental and satisfying goal: demonstrating that the American society was the advance guard of a movement whose objective was nothing less than creation of the New Canaan.

Some Consequences of Isolationist Thought

The way in which isolationist thinking has shaped American foreign relations is a subject too vast to engage our attention here. It must be left for future chapters, when we examine American foreign policy toward major questions. But we can at least point to several specific corollaries of America's isolationist mentality.

A well-known maxim of American foreign relations, down to the post-World War II period, has been the desire to avoid "entangling alliances" in order to preserve freedom of action in world affairs. If America was to regenerate the world by example, it must remain free to save itself (**43**, pp. 539-41). Closely related to this idea is that of "non-intervention." America demanded that the Old World keep out of the New, and, in turn, was willing to forego intervention in the affairs of other countries. Moreover, America has until recently refused joint action with other countries. The Monroe Doctrine was proclaimed unilaterally, even though Britain had a desire to join in it. The United States refused to join the League of Nations. Toward the dictators in the 1930's it usually preferred to play a lone hand. Not until the postwar years has the United States been willing to engage in joint action for long periods of time.

Isolationism too has been manifested in America's reluctance to assume foreign territorial commitments. When they were assumed, every effort was made to reduce them as soon as possible. Territorial acquisitions in the wake of the Spanish-American War furnish a good example of this attitude (**43**, pp. 542-44). Even in the postwar period, this desire to shun foreign ties has been evident. Required to spend billions of dollars annually for defense and foreign aid, and to keep large military establishments in other countries, America has not yet become reconciled to foreign involvement as a permanent feature of its foreign policy. Every year Congress, invoking the pressure of public opinion, reduces the foreign aid budget below executive requests. A significant manifestation of residual isolationism occurred in 1957, when a minor diplomatic incident involving criminal jurisdiction over an American soldier, convinced many Americans that the United States should withdraw its troops from Japan rather than submit to supposed Japanese infringement upon American sovereignty.*

The great awakening which came in American national consciousness only after the Second World War was the realization that the United States was not isolated from the world and never had been. The United States might pretend that it was; it might delude itself into thinking that by will power alone the nation could avoid entanglement in the destiny of the world. But this mythology, the nation discovered through painful experience, courted national disaster. Other nations did not regard the United States as isolated. Other nations were very much interested in what America would do with its massive power. Other nations would not accept the view that America could remain aloof from political developments around the globe. After the Second World War the American people had at last come to see, if at times only dimly, that disengagement was possible only for a minor power, a decadent power, or a country that deliberately chose to imperil its own future security. What kind of involvement was it to be? What ought to be its objectives? What were the proper means

---

*In the "Girard case" Pvt. Girard, an American soldier, had killed a Japanese woman while, the army maintained, he was on military duty. Japan claimed the right to try him under the status-of-forces agreement with the United States; its right was upheld by the President and the Supreme Court.

to attain them? These were the questions that Americans in the mid-20th century were accepting as the overriding foreign policy questions of their age.

5. THE THEME OF PROGRESS AND HOPE

We have reserved the theme of progress and hope for consideration last, because it is most distinctively identified with the American national character. This theme pervades every aspect of the American way of life and has been a dominant note in American foreign relations.

Distinguished foreign visitors to America have agreed that America "was the land of perfectionism. The American knew that nothing was impossible, in his brave new world, and history confirmed his intuition. Progress was not, to him, a mere philosophical ideal but a commonplace of experience, and he could not understand why foreigners should see vulgar realities where he saw visions" (**10**, p. xix.). Lord Bryce found that in America "Men seem to live in the future rather than in the present. Not that they fail to work while it is called today, but that they see the country not merely as it *is* but as it *will be,* twenty, thirty, fifty, a hundred years hence, when the seedlings they have planted shall have grown to forest trees" (Quoted in **23**, p. 97). A more recent writer has stated that when he looked at America he saw "a people who, by everlastingly tugging at their own bootstraps, have raised themselves to a new peak of economic welfare" (Quoted in **23**, pp. 8-9). Contrasting the attitude of Americans toward world affairs in the postwar period with that exhibited by Europeans, Brogan writes: "Probably the only people in the world who now have the historical sense of inevitable victory are the Americans" (**6**, p. 22). And an American has written of his own country:

America pulses with life. It may, like a tree, have its rotten branches, its dead wood; but when those branches are cut away—as happens again and again—the tree goes on flourishing. This is something which cannot be said for any blueprint society, of the Left or Right, bureaucratic or theocratic. Contrary to what was taught by the Fascists 20 years ago, it is the democratic society that is dynamic and the doctrinaire society that is static. (**15**, p. 547).

The Well-Springs of Optimism

What explains this undeniable optimism, this belief in the limitless possibilities for the advancement of mankind? We have already touched many of the explanations, so that we shall treat them here only briefly. Let us answer the question by asking another: What *other* credo could possibly accord with America's philosophical and religious heritage, its material advancement, and the total pattern of history? Optimism and hope have ever pervaded American thought because in no other country in the world has there been so much ground for optimism and hope. If it was believed that the lot of mankind could be infinitely improved, that was because America had demonstrated it. When the Seabees chose their motto during the Second World War— "The difficult we do at once, the impossible takes a little longer"—they were expressing a great national creed.

The eminent American historian, Frederick Jackson Turner, showed that no influence was more important in instilling optimism than the frontier. As Ray A. Billington has phrased the Turner thesis: " . . . No one force did more to Americanize the nation's people and institutions than the repeated rebirth of civilization around the western edge of settlement during the three centuries required to occupy the continent" (Quoted in **25**, p. 21). An American orator in the 19th century, Edward Everett, commented that "the wheel of fortune is in constant revolution, and the poor, in one generation, furnish the rich of the next" (Quoted in **25**, p. 18). When Horace Greeley advised "Go West, young man!" he was in effect expressing the national conviction that a new start was always possible, that by will power alone an individual could leave his past behind and carve out a new future for himself and his posterity.

The closing of the frontier was a milestone in the nation's history, but not as important as sometimes supposed. After 1900 new frontiers beckoned: disease must be wiped out; corruption must be eradicated from American political life; industry must be compelled to operate within a context of the public interest; depressions must be prevented and protection afforded against unemployment; wealth must be distributed more equitably; religious, racial, ethnic and social barriers must be torn down; education must be made available to all; and new paths must be blazed in the one area which seemed most persistently to defy man's best efforts—the conduct of international affairs.

Underneath the conviction that mankind could and must improve itself lay firm philosophical and theological foundations. One was the religious heritage of Calvinism, with its emphasis upon predestination. An important part of this belief was that material blessings were an outward symbol of salvation. As the American dream unfolded it was easy for this belief to become corrupted into the view that material blessings *were* salvation. If faith could move mountains, then the moving of mountains, must surely be a sign of superior faith! Material progress and the view that America had been predestined by Divine Providence to lead in the spiritual regeneration of the world were the warp and woof of the New World's credo (37, pp. 93-105).

From Enlightenment philosophy America took a belief in the perfectability of man and his institutions. The Enlightenment philosophers had believed passionately in the inherent goodness of man as he was led by reason. Two political upheavals—the French and the American Revolutions—had tried to prove them right. Both tried to create the "new society." One failed and the other succeeded; but somehow Americans fixed their attention only on their own success. Scornful of religious dogmas emphasizing natural depravity and "the fall," fiercely devoted to the scientific study of nature, clinging doggedly to the conviction that "all men are created equal" and that they possess equal rights, Enlightenment philosophers and their intellectual descendants never doubted that good would conquer evil, if man would make the necessary effort.*

*That such habits of mind have diminished little throughout the course of American history is indi-

America, says the anthropologist Geoffrey Gorer, has always been a materialistic nation —not merely in the narrow sense of wishing to possess material goods and judging success by their acquisition, but in a much deeper sense. It has been materialistic because it has believed profoundly that personality, character, human qualities and actions can all be manipulated in the same way that man manipulates machines to create better products and achieve a higher standard of living. If matter is subordinate to the will, so is human character and personality (18, pp. 137-224). "The power of positive thinking" can remove all problems and eliminate all barriers to human progress. As D. W. Brogan has phrased it: "Many, very many Americans . . . find it inconceivable that an American policy, announced and carried out by the American government, acting with the support of the American people, does not immediately succeed" (6, pp. 25-6). Their history, he feels, does not prepare them to accept the fact that "great as is American power, it is not so great as to quell, by its mere existence, all opposition" (6, p. 23).

Some Consequences of the American Dream

Optimism and almost boundless confidence in man's ability—and possibly even more important, his desire—to improve his lot is reflected in a variety of attitudes and actions characteristic of the American people. We have

cated by a UN-sponsored study of public opinion in various countries, entitled *How Nations See Each Other*. Findings based upon surveys of public opinion within the United States are especially illumining. The "security index"—a device to measure overall satisfaction with a society's status—was very high for the United States. A high percentage of Americans (50 per cent) thought that human nature could be changed, although only half this number thought it was likely. Significantly, Americans scored higher than any other group polled in placing environment at the head of the list of factors determining national character, further suggesting the American people's belief in beneficial change. Slightly more Americans believed that world peace could be achieved than believed that it could not be achieved. All groups in the American society, even the most dissatisfied ones, characterized the United States still as the "land of opportunity." The adjectives which Americans relied upon heavily to characterize themselves were: peace-loving, generous, intelligent, progressive, hard working, and brave (9, pp. 52, 83-4).

already referred to the naïve belief that military force and "power politics" can and must be eliminated from the sphere of international relations. Until recent years it was difficult for many Americans to believe that other countries might plan and carry out aggression, exploit weaker countries, willfully violate treaties, and embark upon programs of aggrandizement. America has ever thought that good intentions could prevent war, especially if they were committed to paper and statesmen pledged the sacred honor of the nation to abide by them. The main thing, America has traditionally believed, is agreement on broad principles—justice, democracy, freedom, self-determination, peace—and trust that the good will of reasonable men will translate these into specific courses of action beneficial to all (35, p. 111). There is a close parallel, D. W. Brogan has observed, "between the optimism that led to the enactment of prohibition and the optimism which welcomed that international Volstead Act, the Kellogg Pact. In that optimism there was a strong element of the old-time religion, of belief in the old evangelical mass conversion. Hundreds and thousands had renounced the world, the flesh, and the devil . . . why should not the nations renounce mutual murder?" (5, pp. 62-3).

The optimism characteristic of the American society has had fortunate, as well as unfortunate, consequences for the pattern of international relations. Periodically, it has infused a new breath of hope into conduct among nations—sometimes when cynicism and disillusionment seemed on the verge of carrying the day. It has served as an antidote against the view that the international community is fated forever to witnesses violent clashes of rival national ambitions. In some periods, for instance at the time of the adoption of the League of Nations and in certain phases of disarmament negotiations after World War II, it was primarily American confidence that progress could ultimately be made that prevented the total collapse of quests for peace and security.

Yet America's buoyant optimism has also bred utopian expectations. Projecting their own domestic experiences upon the global scene, Americans have traditionally had bright visions and idealistic goals. When these had little immediate effect upon an unreceptive international environment characterized by power conflicts, large segments of the American society have often retreated into a crestfallen sulkiness. Throughout their history, Americans have been prone to believe that they had much to offer to the world: new ideas, political innovations, ambitious programs for the material and moral uplift of humanity and, above all, a new vision. When other countries were slow to respond, when they spurned America's pleadings and clung to old ways, America's instinctive reaction has been to turn inward once more and to get on with internal accomplishments, where the ingenuity and dynamism of the society could be put to dramatically successful results. The American people are inordinately sensitive. They solicit the friendship and approval of other societies but their pride is easily wounded when their proffered friendship is rebuffed and when other societies persist in following practices Americans deem outmoded. Eras of frustration and self-centeredness perhaps inevitably derive from an abiding conviction that, if only other nations would co-operate, America would lead the world community into a new era of human welfare.

Optimism is closely tied up with another American trait: affinity for expediency and pragmatism, and rejection of doctrinaire blueprints for remaking society. America's acknowledged material prosperity is an eloquent testimonial to ingenuity, improvisation, and experimentation. The quest for wealth at home has been accompanied by an easy tolerance of differing opinions, so long as these did not interfere with material progress (21, pp. 44-5). Few Americans have been struck by the contradiction between pragmatism at home and great emphasis upon "principle" often manifested in the nation's relationships with foreign countries. Lewis Galantière has written: "We are not doctrinaire, we have no dogmas to exalt; we are empiricists, and our defects are revealed when we are compelled to shift rapidly from the short to the long view. We leave ourselves free to act as seems rationally requisite or emotionally satisfying in any present situation" (15, p. 535).

Such habits of mind can and do place difficult barriers in the way of successful foreign policy, all the more so when the nation has emerged as the leader of a great coalition. Postwar experience has highlighted many of these limitations upon effective policy when sustained foreign commitments are demanded. Maintaining the long-run military effort required to implement the doctrine of containment, providing economic and technical assistance to other countries on a basis that will permit long-term planning, preserving continuous liaison with the allies, following consistent policies toward problems arising from international trade—evolving an effective foreign policy in these instances has been hampered from time to time by the pragmatic tendencies of the American people and has required them to commit themselves as never before to predictable and consistent courses of action.

REFERENCES

1. Adler, Selig. *The Isolationist Impulse: Its Twentieth Century Reaction.* New York: Abelard-Schuman, 1957.

2. Barker, Ernest. *National Character.* London: Methuen and Co., 1948. This volume, devoted primarily to Great Britain, is perhaps the best study of national character available.

3. Barzini, Luigi. *Americans Are Alone in the World.* New York: Random House, 1953. A discussion of American attitudes toward world affairs.

4. Beloff, Max. "The Foundations of American Policy," *The Spectator* (London), 194 (February 25 and March 4, 1955), 210-11, 247-49. A helpful analysis by a perceptive English observer.

5. Brogan, D. W. *The American Problem.* London: Hamish Hamilton, 1944.

6. ———. "The Illusion of American Omnipotence," *Harpers,* 205 (December, 1952), 21-8. The British scholar, D. W. Brogan, is a penetrating commentator on American attitudes and institutions.

7. Bruckberger, R. L. *Image of America.* New York: The Viking Press, 1959. A perceptive French priest analyzes American society.

8. Bryce, James. *The American Commonwealth.* New York: Macmillan and Company, 1891. 2 volumes. This classic remains indispensable to anyone who wants to understand significant propensities of the American society.

9. Buchanan, William and Cantril, Hadley. *How Nations See Each Other.* Urbana, Illinois: University of Illinois Press, 1953. An informative study of national character traits, as revealed in public opinion polls.

10. Commager, Henry S., ed. *America in Perspective.* New York: Random House, 1947. A useful compendium of writings by foreign visitors to the United States.

11. ———, ed. *The American Mind: An Interpretation of American Thought and Character Since the 1880's.* New Haven: Yale University Press, 1950. A collection of primary source materials and commentaries on the American mind.

12. Curti, Merle. *The Roots of American Loyalty.* New York: Columbia University Press, 1946. A valuable study of Americans' feelings of loyalty to their country, their institutions, and their ideology.

13. DeConde, Alexander, ed. *Isolation and Security: Ideas and Interests in Twentieth-Century American Foreign Policy.* Durham, N. C.: Duke University Press, 1957.

14. Feis, Herbert. "Is the United States Imperialist?" *Yale Review,* 41 (Autumn, 1951), 13-24. Feis convincingly refutes the charge that the United States has been imperialistic.

15. Galantière, Lewis. "America Today: A Freehand Sketch," *Foreign Affairs,* 28 (July, 1950), 525-48.

16. Ginsberg, Morris. "National Character," in *Reason and Unreason in Society.* Cambridge: Harvard University Press, 1948.

17. ———. "National Character and National Sentiment," in Hadfield, J. A., *Psychology and Modern Problems.* New York: Longmans, Green, 1936. National character is examined by a leading sociologist.

18. Gorer, Geoffrey. *The American People.* New York: W. W. Norton and Co., 1948. A provocative study by a cultural anthropologist, although the explanations offered appear sometimes oversimplified.

19. Halle, Louis J. *Civilization and Foreign Policy.* New York: Harper and Brothers, 1955.

20. ———. *Choice For Survival.* New York: Harper and Brothers, 1958. These two works by a former State Department official discuss many American characteristics in the realm of foreign policy.

21. Johnson, Gerald W. *Our English Heritage.* Philadelphia: J. B. Lippincott, 1949.

22. Kaplan, Lawrence S. "NATO and the Language of Isolationism," *South Atlantic Quarterly,* 57 (Spring, 1958), pp. 204-15. Analyzes contemporary manifestations of the isolationist impulse.

23. Klein, Ernest L. *Our Appointment With Destiny.* New York: Farrar, Straus and Young, 1952. Argues that the profit motive and pragmatism are the keys to America's greatness.

24. Klingberg, F. L. "The Historical Alternation of Moods in American Foreign Policy," *World Politics,* 4 (January, 1952), 239-73. A detailed examination of the moods in American foreign policy.

25. Kohn, Hans. *American Nationalism: An Interpretive Essay.* New York: The Macmillan Company, 1957. This is the most recent, and probably the best, study of American nationalism available. Kohn is perhaps the outstanding American scholar of nationalism.

26. Kust, Matthew J. "The Great Dilemma of American Foreign Policy," *Virginia Quarterly Review,* 34 (Spring, 1958), pp. 224-39. Deals with American attitudes toward colonialism.

27. Lerner, Max. *America As A Civilization.* New York: Simon and Schuster, 1957. This is one of the most comprehensive and incisive treatments of American civilization that has appeared in the recent period.

28. Lippmann, Walter. "The Rivalry of Nations," *Atlantic Monthly,* 181 (February, 1948), 17-20.

29. ———. *U. S. Foreign Policy: Shield of the Republic.* Boston: Little, Brown and Company, 1943. Among the numerous works of this distinguished observer, these examine most cogently American national character.

30. Mead, Margaret. *And Keep Your Powder Dry.* New York, Morrow, 1942. Written during World War II, this book examines the psychological strengths and weaknesses of the American people.

31. ———. "The Study of National Character," in Lerner, Daniel, *et al.,* eds. *The Political Sciences: Recent Developments in Scope and Methods.* Stanford: Stanford University Press, 1951.

32. Niebuhr, Reinhold. "The Cause and Cure of the American Psychosis," *American Scholar,* 25 (Winter, 1955-56), 11-20. An eminent theologian examines the American character, with particular respect to its unqualified optimism and utopianism.

33. Northrop, F. S. C. "Neutralism and United States Foreign Policy," *Annals of the American Academy of Political and Social Science,* 312 (July, 1957), pp. 42-68.

34. Pratt, Julius W. "Anticolonialism in U. S. Policy," *Orbis,* 1 (October, 1957), pp. 291-314.

35. Perkins, Dexter. *The American Approach to Foreign Policy.* Cambridge: Harvard University Press, 1952. One of America's leading diplomatic historians analyzes his country's approach toward a number of major international problems. Especially interesting is Chapter VII in which the "cycles" in our foreign relations are examined.

36. ———. "American Wars and Critical Historians," *Yale Review,* 40 (Summer, 1951), 682-95. Here Perkins evaluates the impact of revisionist historical writing upon the American mind.

37. Perry, Ralph Barton. *Characteristically American.* New York: Knopf, 1949. An eminent American philosopher examines the national character. This work is especially helpful for tracing America's philosophical and religious roots.

38. Pratt, Julius W. *A History of United States Foreign Policy.* New York: Prentice-Hall, 1955. This is a recent and scholarly one-volume history of American foreign relations.

39. Santayana, George. "Americanism," *Virginia Quarterly Review,* 31 (Winter, 1955), 1-26. One of America's most famous philosophers analyzes the American way of life. This is a helpful, though at times highly mystical, interpretation.

40. Shafer, Boyd C. *Nationalism: Myth and Reality.* New York: Harcourt, Brace, and Co., 1955. An up-to-date treatment, though focused more on other countries than America. Boyd doubts there is such a thing as national character, and he summons other writers to support his view.

41. Strout, Cushing. "The Twentieth Century Enlightenment," *American Political Science Review,* XLIX (June, 1955), 321-39. Valuable for showing the implications of revisionist history for American thought and for its criticisms of such history.

42. Warburg, James P. *The United States in a Changing World.* New York: G. P. Putnam's Sons, 1954. A readable survey of American diplomatic history, with insights into our national character.

43. Weinberg, Albert K. "The Historical Meaning of the American Doctrine of Isolation," *American Political Science Review,* 34 (April, 1940), 539-47.

44. Wickware, Francis S. "What We Think About Foreign Affairs," *Harpers,* 179 (September, 1939), 397-406. An analysis of public opinion polls on the eve of World War II.

CHAPTER 3

The President, the Department of State, and American Foreign Policy

Constitutional Appearance and Reality

In any discussion of American foreign relations, one must grasp at the outset the distinction between constitutional *appearance* and *reality*. Constitutional myth holds that the American government is divided into three co-equal branches and that each has certain clearly defined duties and prerogatives. Constitutional reality proclaims that—at least in foreign affairs, and very largely in domestic affairs also—this belief is at variance with American historical experience.

We may dispose of the Supreme Court's role in American foreign relations by saying that its function is mainly confined to prescribing the spheres of the other two branches and to keeping each within its proper orbit. Yet it is possible to exaggerate the importance of even this modest role. Time and again in American diplomatic history the Supreme Court has refused to mediate between the President and Congress, on the ground that disputes between them were "political" in nature and hence outside the jurisdiction of the Court. In foreign affairs its mediating role has been reluctant, limited, and tardy. The Court has chosen to leave twilight zones. One commentator writes that the Court "has fixed neither the outer

boundaries nor the inner divisions of the President's martial authority, and has failed completely to draw the line between his powers and those of Congress . . . " (30, p. 5). Typical of the cautious attitude of the Court was the verdict of Justice Swayne in 1870 that "The measures to be taken in carrying on war and to suppress insurrection are not defined. The decision of all questions rests wholly in the discretion of those to whom the substantial powers involved are confided by the Constitution."*

The Constitution divides the bulk of power in the foreign policy field between the executive and legislative departments. Yet, as we shall see more fully below, historical experience has greatly modified certain provisions of the Constitution and has added unforeseen tradi-

---

Stewart v. *Kahn,* 11 Wallace 493 (1871). Examples of questions the Supreme Court has held to be political, and hence subject to executive or legislative treatment alone, are: the determination of boundaries between countries; the determination of the country that possesses sovereignty over particular areas; whether a country ought to be classified as a belligerent under international law; whether a country has properly ratified a treaty; whether a person is properly accredited to the United States; whether the terms of a treaty are still in effect. For these and other examples, see 8, pp. 471-75.

49

tions and precedents to the American governmental system. The total impact of these changes is to magnify greatly the powers of the President and to reduce those of Congress over foreign relations. Admitting that today legislative influence in foreign affairs has increased significantly over the prewar period—reaching perhaps the highest plane in American history —the President is still the dominant influence in world affairs. Throughout history, writes a leading student of the Constitution, "the greatest single force in setting the course of American foreign policy has been Presidential initiative . . . " (6, p. 12, italics omitted). We now turn to a detailed investigation of the President's powers in foreign affairs.

These powers may be conveniently grouped into three categories: those specifically set forth in the Constitution; those which have evolved through usage and tradition; and—a special category of both—war or emergency powers giving the President authority to deal with national crises. Recognizing that these categories are often closely entwined, that no arbitrary and rigid compartmentalization is possible, let us look at each of them more fully.

1. THE PRESIDENT'S CONSTITUTIONAL POWERS

A. *The Treaty Making Process*

The Constitution provides that the President "shall have power, by and with the advice and consent of the Senate, to make treaties, provided two-thirds of the Senators present concur . . . " (Art. II, Sec. 2). Responsibility for treaties—formal and usually long range agreements in the international field—is thus divided between the President and Senate. The treaty process embodies two stages: negotiating agreements and ratifying them. The constitutional requirement for ratification is clearly set forth. Treaties become law only when two-thirds of the members of the Senate present approve them. However, controversy has always surrounded the provision that the President makes treaties with the "advice" of the Senate. Specifically what does this mean? How does the Senate give its advice? To what degree is this advice binding upon the President? Such questions have been productive of endless argument.* Various answers are possible. They may be grouped broadly into two schools of thought. The theory most frequently voiced by the Senate itself is that this clause compels the President to consult with the upper chamber from the *earliest stages* of negotiation, that it requires him to regard the Senate as an advisory council in reaching agreements with other countries. The second school—the view expressed by successive Presidents—is that "advice and consent" are in fact tantamount to the same thing. The President seeks the "advice" of the Senate when he requests its "consent" to a treaty already prepared and signed by executive officials.

Whatever the merits of the argument—the founding fathers probably held the first theory —there can be no doubt about which view has predominated. Throughout the entire process of treaty-making the President retains the initiative. Tradition and precedent have reduced the Senate's role largely to deciding whether treaties shall or shall not be ratified. The executive branch negotiates them, signs them in the name of the United States, presents them to the Senate for approval, and, after they are ratified, proclaims them as law. The Senate may refuse to ratify them, in which case the President has other means of achieving agreements with other nations. Moreover, the chief executive may refuse to accept amendments affixed by the Senate; he may withdraw the treaty from consideration by the Senate at any time; and he may even refuse to proclaim a treaty after it has been ratified, if he feels its terms no longer accord with the national interest.

So passive has the Senate's role become in the treaty-making process that even Senators themselves have cautioned that body against attempts to intrude into the President's direction of foreign affairs by construing the "advice and consent" clause broadly. Thus the highly respected Senator Arthur H. Vandenberg (Republican of Michigan) told his colleagues in 1948:

---

*For examples, consult: **10**, Chapter 1; **15**; **13**.

I think the Senate is entitled, at any time it pleases, to use the advice clause of the Constitution to tell the Executive what it thinks concerning foreign affairs. But I think it would be a tragic and unfortunate thing if the habit ever became general or too contagious because I respectfully submit, . . . only in those instances in which the Senate can be sure of a complete command of all the essential information prerequisite to an intelligent decision, should it take the terrific chance of muddying the international waters by some sort of premature and ill-advised expression of its advice to the Executive. (Quoted in **10**, p. 16).

Treaties are the traditional and most formal kind of international agreement, but they are by no means the only type. With increasing regularity, Presidents have come to rely upon "executive agreements" — understandings between heads of state—rather than upon more formal treaties to carry out foreign policy goals. George Washington negotiated such an agreement in 1792, providing for reciprocal mail delivery. Although other Presidents utilized executive agreements over the years that followed, Franklin D. Roosevelt raised them to a new pinnacle of importance as a technique of executive control over foreign relations. A well-known example is the "Destroyer Deal" made between FDR and Prime Minister Churchill in 1940, exchanging fifty obsolete destroyers for British bases in the Western Hemisphere. The following year FDR was granted authority by Congress to enter into agreements with the nation's allies for the provision of lend-lease assistance. During the war, allied conferences at Casablanca, Teheran, Yalta, and Potsdam resulted in a host of agreements concerning military strategy and postwar political settlements. None of these was submitted to the Senate for approval. Surveying the last half-century of diplomatic experience, one commentator has found that almost half of the international commitments made by the United States have been in the form of executive agreements. In more recent years they "have outnumbered treaties by perhaps ten to one" (**21**, p. 322).

Executive agreements are of two types: those reached by the President alone, and those that receive prior or subsequent legislative sanction. The former are exemplified by the Yalta and Potsdam agreements referred to above. Increasingly, however, Congress has participated in giving effect to executive agreements. Congress empowered FDR to enter into the lend-lease agreements alluded to earlier. The United Nations Participation Act of December 20, 1945, authorizes the President "to negotiate a special agreement or agreements with the Security Council which shall be subject to the approval of the Congress by appropriate Act or joint resolution" providing for the allocation of American military forces for the use of the Council in maintaining international peace (**8**, p. 445). Congress has also given the President authority to enter into agreements with other countries to reduce tariffs on a reciprocal basis.

Wherein do executive agreements differ from treaties? The Constitution designates treaties as the "supreme law of the land," whereas executive agreements are not so designated, unless they become the supreme law of the land by virtue of legislative sanction. The terms "treaties," "agreements," and "compacts" are used in the Constitution, but constitutional authorities do not feel that the courts have ever provided a clear differentiation among them.* And in Edward S. Corwin's view, "what difference there once may have been has been seriously blurred in practice within recent decades" (**8**, p. 433). Nevertheless, some differences are suggested by historical experience. Congress can change the terms of certain types of executive agreements, or repeal them by subsequent legislation, as exemplified by Congress' action in 1924 in superseding Theodore Roosevelt's 1904 "Gentleman's Agreement" with Japan on Japanese immigration to the United States. Asked in 1918 how long a particular executive agreement remained valid, Secretary of State Robert Lansing told the Senate Foreign Relations Committee that the agreement in question remained in force only so long as the President and his principal subordinates chose to abide by it (**8**, p. 436). This may be contrasted with treaty agreements, which customarily carry a stipulated time limit. Presumably, those executive agreements that have received congressional approval would be terminated if Congress withdrew its approval, although it

---

*For an extended treatment of the meaning of these terms, see the Supreme Court's opinion in *Holmes* v. *Jennison,* 14 Peters 540 (1840).

must be admitted that for certain categories of problems the President might continue to accept the existence of an understanding with foreign governments.

The Supreme Court has been most reluctant to intrude into the field of foreign relations. It expressed a typical view in *United States* v. *Pink* in 1942. This case involved FDR's agreement recognizing Soviet Russia. The court ruled that the President had recognized Russia following Russia's adherence to certain conditions and that the Court "would usurp the executive function if we held that that decision was not final and conclusive on the courts."* We must conclude that there are very few effective limitations upon the President's power to arrive at understandings with other heads of state by means of executive agreements and that such agreements constitute an important executive tool in the management of foreign relations.

Authority Over the Military Establishment

No clause in the Constitution has been more productive of disagreements between the President and Congress than Article II, Section 2, providing that "The President shall be Commander-in-Chief of the Army and Navy. . . ." As with the treaty power, Congress also possesses important prerogatives over the military establishment, such as the duty to provide for the army and navy, to regulate its size, to equip and support it, and to declare war. This fact places substantial limits upon the President's control of foreign relations, because success in foreign affairs is heavily dependent upon military strength.

Assuming then that Congress has provided for adequate military force, what agency of the government shall determine its use for foreign policy ends? By virtue of its powers in this field, and especially its power to declare war, can Congress instruct the President in the use of the military establishment in times of peace or war? Is the President limited in the use he can make of armed forces to the extent that he must not risk war without the consent of Congress?

The answer to all these questions is negative (**14**, *passim;* **30**, pp. 11-25; **6**, pp. 7-33). Once

the armed forces have come into being and their character (e.g., the proportion of ground, naval, and air forces to the whole) has been determined by Congress, the President alone utilizes them in behalf of national policy. It is difficult to unravel the exact intention of the founding fathers when they gave Congress the power to "declare war." In their era wars usually were "declared" formally, often weeks or months before hostilities actually began. Legislators could therefore safely debate the wisdom of going to war. Quite obviously this luxury is not afforded the nation today. In an age of nuclear weapons and German blitzkrieg tactics, the nation could be destroyed while its leaders deliberated. Speed in committing the armed forces for defense has thus come to be vital to national survival.

The facts of military life have largely rendered the right of Congress to declare war a dead letter, at least as far as this clause limits the power of the President to utilize the armed forces for foreign policy ends. The President, says Charles Fairman, is clearly "vested with power adequate to directing the defense of the United States" (**14**, p. 145). The controlling legal decision here, as with so many bearing upon the President's authority, goes back to Lincoln's action during the Civil War in blockading southern ports without a legislative sanction. In *The Prize Cases* the Supreme Court held that the President could not legally "initiate war," but he was "bound to accept the challenge without waiting for any special legislative authority."* This principle—that the chief executive may meet any threat arising to the security of the country—has stood for almost a century.

Stated differently, war has come to be regarded as a state of reality rather than a condition specified by legislative decree. The President must react to it, and react swiftly. A Senator observed over a century ago that "another country can commence a war against us without the cooperation of Congress" (**5**, p. 137). Richard Henry Dana, in arguing *The Prize Cases* before the Supreme Court, contended that war "is a state of things, and not an

---

*315 U. S. 203 (1942).

*2 Black 635 (1863).

act of legislative will."* President Eisenhower made essentially the same point when he said in 1954 that "hanging ought to be the fate of any President who failed to act instantly to protect the American people against a sudden attack in this atomic age" (7, p. 48).

In the postwar period, controversy over executive and legislative prerogatives relating to military affairs has taken place on three occasions: over President Truman's handling of the Korean War, over his proposal to send American ground forces to participate in NATO's defense efforts in Europe in 1951 and over President Eisenhower's request for Congressional support of the Eisenhower Doctrine in 1957. President Truman did not wait to receive legislative sanction before committing American troops to halt Communist aggression in Korea in 1950. Truman's action elicited scattered and futile protests on Capitol Hill, which were insignificant compared with the partisan storm generated by his dismissal of General Douglas MacArthur in 1951. In both instances Truman acted under his authority as commander in chief of the armed forces. In neither case was opposition to his actions effective.

Controversy also surrounded President Truman's plan in 1951 to station American troops on the European continent—the first time in history that American troops were to be stationed in friendly countries during peace for any significant length of time. Throughout the troops-to-Europe debate, the President and his advisers insisted that the White House did not "need" legislation authorizing this step, but that the administration would welcome it in the interest of demonstrating bipartisan unity. Ultimately, Congress voted to approve substantially the steps decided upon by executive policy-makers (10, pp. 87-96). Again in 1957 the issue of control over the military establishment arose when the Eisenhower Administration submitted a detailed program to Congress for dealing with recurrent crises in the turbulent Middle East. Secretary of State Dulles affirmed the traditional view when he declared that "under our constitutional system the President . . . is Commander in Chief of the Armed Forces . . . and, as such, has the right to

determine their disposition. That is a right which cannot be impaired by action of Congress." The Eisenhower Administration, however, sought the co-operation of the legislative branch to demonstrate the unity of American foreign policy in the face of ominous developments abroad.**

Maintenance of Diplomatic Relations With Other Governments

From Washington's administration onward, it has been a settled constitutional principle that as the Chief of State, the President alone maintains relations between the United States and foreign governments. The Constitution, said President Grant in 1877, "has indicated the President as the agency to represent the national sovereignty, and to receive all official communications" from other governments (5, p. 44).

Foreign diplomats are accredited to the President of the United States. Official communications from other governments are addressed to him or to his subordinate officials. Long-standing diplomatic protocol prohibits

---

**The quotation from Dulles was inserted into the *Congressional Record* on February 11, 1957 (Volume 103, p. 1870). In the course of Senate debate on the President's request, considerable background material on the scope of executive powers in foreign relations, particularly over the military establishment, was inserted into the *Record*. For a detailed recapitulation of precedents, see the remarks and insertions by Senator William Fulbright (Democrat of Arkansas) in Volume 103, pp. 1857-58.

The Eisenhower Doctrine evoked considerable controversy in Congress, especially among the Democratic opposition in the Senate. Its controversial aspects are discussed further in Chapter 6, where bipartisan techniques are analyzed. Meantime, we may note here that the President's request for legislative approval of standby authority to send troops to the Middle East if they were needed was sharply attacked by the President's critics. Senator Fulbright pointed out, for example, that President Eisenhower had asked for "a blank grant of power over funds and Armed Forces, to be used in a blank way, for a blank length of time, under blank conditions, with respect to blank nations, in a blank area. We are asked to sign this blank check in perpetuity or at the pleasure of the President—any President." Fulbright emphasized that under the Constitution, Congress was supposed to declare war *in individual cases* and that the request therefore represented "a blanket transfer to the Executive of the constitutional right vested in Congress to declare war" (*Congressional Record*, 103, 1957, p. 1856).

---

*2 Black 659-60 (1863).

foreign governments from having any official contact with other leaders or institutions within the American government or from appealing to public groups over the head of the President, upon pain of having diplomats violating this rule declared *persona non grata*, thereby requiring them to leave the country. On occasion, flagrant departure from this rule has led to strained diplomatic relations between the United States and foreign countries, as exemplified by tensions growing out of Imperial Germany's propaganda activities in the United States prior to the country's entry into World War I.

The severance of diplomatic relations often is the prelude to war between countries. When a nation has deliberately chosen to embark upon war or when it feels that war is unavoidable, it will recall its own diplomats and revoke the credentials of the diplomats of its enemies. The power to sever diplomatic relations belongs exclusively to the President, stemming from his position as the sole channel of communication with foreign governments.

Conversely, the principle that the President is the official spokesman for the United States in its dealings with foreign countries prohibits unauthorized *official* contacts between citizens of the United States and other governments. Citizens who violate this rule will almost certainly have their passport privileges revoked and may even be liable to criminal prosecution. In view of widespread foreign travel by congressmen and the general public, however, this rule is not likely to be enforced stringently unless such individuals embarrass executive policy-makers by working against established American policy.

Quite clearly the monopolistic position of the President in maintaining relations with other governments greatly enhances his already dominant position in the management of foreign relations. By such methods as cables and personal interviews, the chief executive and his subordinates are in constant communication with other countries. A steady stream of information about activities in the international community pours into the State Department, the Defense Department, the Commerce Department, and many other executive departments. Proposals affecting America's relations

with foreign countries, and their relations with this country, are channelled routinely through executive agencies. Such information, together with data gathered by the President's agents from other sources, gives the chief executive much of the knowledge requisite for sound decisions in the foreign policy field.

Intimately related to the problem of maintaining relations with other countries is the issue of recognition. Recognition of another government normally is followed by an exchange of diplomatic representatives with that government, entailing the two-fold process of sending American diplomatic officials abroad and receiving diplomatic officials accredited to the United States. Concerning the first of these acts, both the President and the Senate have certain prerogatives. The Constitution (Article II, Section 2) stipulates that high-level diplomatic appointments, along with all other major presidential appointments, must receive the confirmation of the Senate. Inasmuch as our principal interest here is examination of the President's powers, we shall reserve fuller treatment of the Senate's role for Chapter 5. At this point it is enough to point out that Presidents possess many ways of circumventing effective Senate control over their actions. They may rely upon "personal representatives" who may or may not already hold governmental positions. The chief spokesman for American foreign policy during the Wilson administration was Colonel Edward M. House, who performed many diplomatic functions at home and abroad, with minimum liaison with the State Department. Franklin D. Roosevelt leaned heavily upon Harry Hopkins, so much so that ultimately Hopkins was referred to in the press as "Roosevelt's personal foreign office." In the early months of World War II, Hopkins played a decisive role in cementing closer Anglo-American relations, a process made possible in part by his prolonged residence at Prime Minister Churchill's home (**31**, pp. 283, 285, 305, 328, 536). Then too Presidents may make "interim appointments" in the diplomatic field when the Senate is not in session. Even if the Senate ultimately refuses to confirm the individual so appointed, he may have already performed important duties, as was the case with Philip Jessup, President Truman's appointee as a member of the American delegation to the United Nations in 1951 (26, October 23, 1951).

Vigorous claims have been heard periodically throughout American history that the Senate's power to confirm appointments gives that body the right to determine the substance of American foreign policy by specifying the duties that appointees are to carry out. Yet after more than one hundred and fifty years, the Senate's power in this sphere is clearly peripheral. Determined and imaginative Presidents are seldom deterred from carrying out policies they believe the national interest demands, even when they encounter opposition in the Senate.

The second stage in recognition involves the reception of accredited diplomatic officials from other countries. Here the President has a completely free hand. The Constitution stipulates that the President "shall receive Ambassadors and other public ministers" (Article II, Section 3), leaving the chief executive free to exercise his discretion in the reception of foreign diplomats. He may receive them or refuse to receive them, as his conception of the national interest dictates. It is not unusual for foreign countries to inquire ahead of time whether certain individuals are acceptable, before sending them abroad. Moreover, having initially received a diplomat from abroad, the President may declare him *persona non grata*, whereupon he will be forced to leave the country. Although a wise President will always take account of opinion prevailing on Capitol Hill and throughout the country generally, he is under no constitutional obligation to heed congressional resolutions or other indications of public sentiment dealing with the question of recognition.*

---

*In spite of this fact, Congress has not been reluctant in recent years to express itself vigorously on matters like the recognition of Red China. Thus Section 105 of the Mutual Security Appropriations Act for fiscal year 1959 states: "The Congress hereby reiterates its opposition to the seating in the United Nations of the Communist China regime . . . the President is *requested* to inform the Congress insofar as is compatible with the requirements of national security, of the implications upon the foreign policy of the United States" if Red China is seated in the UN. See House Resolution 13192, 85th Congress, 2nd Session, August 23, 1958 (italics inserted).

Recognition involves much more than the mere formality of who shall represent the United States abroad and who shall be accredited to this country by other governments. Normally, the recognition of one country by another implies a willingness to conduct harmonious relations with that country. A government's refusal to recognize another government, on the other hand, usually signifies misunderstandings and tensions between them, as illustrated by America's refusal for many years to recognize the communist regime in Soviet Russia and its continuing unwillingness in the recent period to accord recognition to Red China.** Recognition then is an important tool of diplomacy available to the President. Its use in specific circumstances will be governed by the nation's objectives in foreign policy. Quite often, considerations of national security enter into the issue of recognition. During World War II, for instance, FDR and Secretary of State Hull succeeded in acquiring rights to Greenland—a vital base protecting the northeastern approaches to the continent—by refusing to recognize the existing Danish Government, which had capitulated to Hitler, and by dealing instead with the "Danish Government-in-Exile" which was amenable to the agreement (28, p. 642). After the war, relations with Soviet Russia were strained over a number of recognition questions. Both Truman and Eisenhower repeatedly refused to recognize Soviet incorporation of the Baltic States into the USSR; creation of the "East German People's Republic"; and Russian hegemony over formerly independent countries in eastern Europe. In the Far East, the overriding question involving recognition concerns Red China. Ever since the communist regime came into power in 1949, the United States has consistently refused to accord recognition to it or to approve its admission into the United Nations. As explained in Chapter 13, events have tended to call into question many of the assumptions underlying

---

**Non-recognition is not synonymous with a severance of diplomatic relations. Non-recognition usually implies coolness in the relations between two countries but does not usually lead to war. Conversely, nations—Russia and America are examples—may continue to recognize each other, although a considerable amount of tension prevails in relations between them.

America's policy. If and when recognition is eventually extended, the decision will be taken by the President and will be based upon his estimate of how such a step accords with the overall objectives of the United States in world affairs.

2. HISTORICAL–TRADITIONAL TECHNIQUES OF PRESIDENTIAL LEADERSHIP

Let us look next at certain important techniques of presidential leadership in the foreign policy field that are largely an outgrowth of history and tradition. Some of these techniques are not mentioned, except perhaps by indirection, in the Constitution. Yet many of them have become well-nigh permanent features of the American constitutional system.

The President's Control Over Information

Wise decisions in foreign policy, as in any field, require the collection and evaluation of information pertinent to the problems at hand. It follows therefore that executive leadership in foreign relations flows naturally from the ability of the executive branch to gather such information and, when national security demands it, to preserve its confidential character. Through the intelligence activities of the State Department, the Central Intelligence Agency, the military establishment, and other agencies, the President is in a unique position to know more about foreign policy problems than any other individual or group within the government.

Very early in American history Congress recognized the necessity to give the chief executive and his advisers wide discretionary powers to gather information and to keep it confidential. Alone among the executive departments, the Department of State has always been regarded by Congress as accountable to the President alone. Since 1947 this view has also governed legislative relations with the Central Intelligence Agency and the National Security Council. Other executive agencies may from time to time be *required* to furnish records and data for the guidance of Congress. In regard to the State Department and other agencies concerned with national security problems, however, Congress can only *request* the President to supply desired information

when such a step is "not incompatible with the public interest" (5, p. 177). The right—even the duty—of the chief executive to withhold confidential information bearing upon national security has been affirmed again and again throughout American history, not alone by the President but by the Supreme Court as well.* And much as individual congressmen from time to time complain about the "wall of secrecy" that surrounds the executive branch, Congress itself has done much to preserve the confidential character of information by approving legislation that provides severe penalties for the release of classified information dealing with such matters as the operations of the Department of Defense or information related to national defense, the activities of the Central Intelligence Agency, and unauthorized possession of any classified information (11, pp. 231-33). When the National Security Council, the highest interdepartmental committee in the government, was created in 1947, Congress deliberately ordered that it report solely to the President. Reporting to Congress, said one legislator, would be like "reporting to the entire world" (18, p. 149).

In recent years both Presidents Truman and Eisenhower have staunchly resisted efforts by congressional investigating committees to get confidential information from the executive departments. During the highly controversial Senate investigation of the army in 1954, instigated

---

*The case of *United States ex. rel. Touhy* v. *Ragen,* 95 L. Ed. 417 illustrates the Supreme Court's historic viewpoints on the matter of executive secrecy. This case also contains a lengthy annotation on court decisions dealing with this issue.

Reviewing prevailing legal opinion on this matter, one authoritative study concludes that unauthorized citizens have "no enforceable legal right to inspect any federal non-judicial records." Its overall finding is that "the opportunity of the people to know depends upon the favorable exercise of official grace or indulgence of 'discretion' " (11, p. 197).

by Senator Joseph McCarthy (Republican of Wisconsin), President Eisenhower instructed Secretary of Defense Charles E. Wilson to refuse McCarthy's demands for executive records. Wilson was directed to instruct his subordinates "not to testify to . . . conversations or communications or to produce any . . . documents or reproductions" (7, pp. 54-55). Toward the end of Eisenhower's second term, a number of the President's critics on Capitol Hill protested against withholding of information on Soviet missile and nuclear technology. Prominent figures in the Democratic-controlled Congress asserted that intelligent judgments could not be made about the President's military budget without a full disclosure of the enemy's strength. Executive officials, however, were visibly reluctant to reveal to the public, or in some cases even to legislative committees, available information on such matters, partially out of fear that sources of information relied upon by executive officials might be revealed and their usefulness thereby impaired. Under Eisenhower also, officials concerned with nuclear technology found themselves under increasing pressure to reveal information relating to radioactive "fallout"; scientific groups complained that the executive branch was suppressing information that national security demanded be made public so that the dangers from fallout could be widely understood.

In these and similar situations, neither elected officials in Congress nor the general public have independent sources of information that can rival those available to the President and his chief advisers. As foreign policy decisions more and more depend upon accurate knowledge about complex questions, the problem of the inadequacy of information available to the rank-and-file of citizens becomes magnified. Successful democracy presupposes citizen competence to judge public issues and to vote intelligently—capacities which will be severely limited by inability to secure, and perhaps understand, requisite information. Yet so long as the country is confronted by a ruthless and resourceful diplomatic opponent, there will exist a high premium upon preserving the confidential character of information that, were it disclosed, might impair national security. The problem facing the President is a delicate one.

The survival of democracy demands that as much information as possible be made public; the survival of the nation may require that vast quantities of such information be classified as secret. If the citizen and his representatives in Congress must accord the President considerable latitude in the disclosure of information, an equal obligation exists for the President and his advisers to make public as much information as national security permits, even when such information reveals incompetence among executive officials or widespread failures within the executive branch to deal with national policy questions successfully.

Congress of course has not always admitted the right of Presidents to withhold information. As a rule, however, legislators understand that the proper conduct of foreign affairs demands a wide area of secrecy, even from them; for most of them are aware that untimely "leaks" of information to the press can create embarrassing diplomatic incidents and, in extreme cases, can even prejudice national security. This realization in large measure underlies their acceptance of the fact that Congress can seldom command as comprehensive and accurate information about foreign affairs as the executive; it explains in no small part too why few congressmen are willing at critical junctures to pit their judgments of external events against the judgments of the President and his chief subordinates.

The President and Public Opinion

Although the role of the President as a molder of public opinion first came into clear prominence with Theodore Roosevelt, successive Presidents have sharpened public relations tools into powerful weapons for dealing with Congress, pressure groups, or dissident members of their own party. No President used this weapon with such telling effect as Franklin D. Roosevelt. He was the first to systematize the collection of data about public opinion, relying upon opinion polls, newspaper surveys, White House mail, and grassroots reports. And no President in American history has been so successful in generating grass-roots support for his programs with which to overcome legislative opposition. Binkley observes that FDR "had only to glance toward a microphone or suggest that he might go on the air again and a congressional delegation would surrender. They had no relish for the flood of mail and telegrams they knew would swamp them after another fireside talk to the nation" (1, p. 250). It was Roosevelt too who first encouraged reporters to *give him information* about how his policies were being received throughout the country. Today, Presidents regularly rely upon their press conferences to learn about currents in public opinion and to uncover problems within the government that require their attention (23, *passim*).

Presidents Truman and Eisenhower also cultivated public opinion, although not as successfully as Roosevelt. Truman utilized his numerous appointments—often as many as 95 a week—to familiarize him with public thinking. Eisenhower has leaned more heavily upon television appearances and "stag dinners," at which 15-20 guests are usually invited for an informal conference. Another significant development under Eisenhower has been the use of the Vice-President as a roving good-will ambassador who tries to interpret the President's program to the nation and to receive the public reaction to it. It has been estimated that by mid-1955, Vice-President Richard Nixon traveled over 52,000 miles in this capacity (7, p. 70).

When the President desires to address the nation, the facilities of every radio and television network are available to him. In the day-to-day conduct of government, his words and decisions are carried almost instantaneously by the wire services from the White House to every major capital of the world. No other governmental leader is provided with such extensive coverage, and none therefore has the opportunity, if he has both the desire and the ability to use it, to rally public opinion to his cause.

The President as Legislative Leader

According to the principle of separation of powers, the President should not have anything to do with legislation. It is doubtful that even the founding fathers believed in rigid adherence to this principle and it certainly has never been strictly observed in American govern-

mental practice. In many ways, the President is the foremost legislator in the government. Preparation of needed legislation, followed by efforts to secure its passage through Congress, is now recognized as one of the executive department's most time-consuming and compelling duties. Lawrence H. Chamberlain found that almost half of the major federal statutes enacted during the past seventy-five years emanated from the executive departments. About half the bills introduced into Congress annually originate in the executive branch (2, p. 73). So firmly ingrained has this practice become that Congressmen have been known to protest when the executive was derelict in preparing measures for their consideration. Thus Senator Homer Ferguson (Republican of Michigan) complained about President Truman: "If the President wants to tell the people he stands for a certain thing, he ought to come out with his proposal. He ought to come to the House and Senate with a message. And he ought to provide a bill that is exactly what he wants" (2, p. 74).

All of the great legislative enactments affecting American foreign relations in the postwar period—the British Loan of 1946, the Greek-Turkish Aid Program, the Marshall Plan, the China Aid Bill, the Point Four Program, the Mutual Security Program, reduction of tariffs, programs for developing peacetime nuclear energy—have had their origin in the executive branch. And after their initiation, executive officials have, at critical junctures, pressed for their adoption by Congress.* The scope of the present-day global commitments of the United States has drawn Congress more and more into the foreign policy process. But it has also drawn the executive more and more into the *legislative* process, requiring him, as in foreign affairs generally, to provide the direction and initiative needed for framing legislation bearing

---

*For example, see the impressive array of Cabinet officers who testified before the Senate Foreign Relations Committee on the Marshall Plan: Senate Foreign Relations Committee, *Hearings on European Recovery Program*, 80th Congress, 2nd Session, January 8-15, 1948, *passim*. Even greater urgency was attached by the executive to the North Atlantic Treaty. See Senate Foreign Relations Committee, *Hearings on North Atlantic Treaty*, 81st Congress, 1st Session, April 27-May 3, 1949, *passim*.

upon external affairs. In fact the success or failure of an incumbent administration is judged to a large extent by the degree to which it can claim a *legislative* record capable of dealing with existing foreign and internal problems.

The President As a Political Leader

Adequate discussion of the political role of the President would require a volume. The most we can do here is take for granted his preeminent political position and suggest some of the consequences of this position for foreign affairs. Historically, one of the President's most effective means for influencing the actions of legislators has been the patronage he has had to distribute to the party faithful, in the form of appointments to the federal service. No President in recent history has surpassed FDR in the skillful way he utilized this weapon (1, p. 246). Since the New Deal the importance of patronage has declined, because more jobs have been placed under civil service regulations.

In addition, the President plays an influential role in national elections. Every national candidate who is a member of the President's party desires to have his "endorsement" in a political campaign. The regularity with which candidates seek to "ride the President's coattails" is a well-known phenomenon in American political history, as illustrated by President Eisenhower's success in carrying a number of Republican candidates into office with him by his victories in 1952 and 1956.

Members of Congress do not follow a party line slavishly in their legislative actions. Still, they prefer when possible to work in close harmony with their party leaders, because such a course pays tangible political benefits. The party in power tries to establish a record which will generate wide voter appeal. Such a record can only be created if the party, led by the President, works in close harmony to produce it.

Power to Commit the Nation

Among those techniques available to the President to determine the course of foreign relations, none has probably become more sig-

nificant over the last half-century than the power to commit the nation publicly to certain specified policies. We have already pointed out that the President's pronouncements on national policy are flashed around the world and that he enjoys a uniquely powerful position in this respect. Virtually every major foreign policy undertaking today requires the approval of Congress at some stage, either legislative approval, as in such projects as the reciprocal trade program or revision of immigration quotas, or legislative appropriation of funds, or both combined as in programs of economic and military aid. The scope of congressional powers in foreign relations has therefore greatly expanded *on paper*. But because of the ability of the chief executive to commit the country, this expansion frequently is only nominal.

The postwar diplomatic experience of the United States is replete with examples. Take the Greek-Turkish Aid Program of 1947. After President Truman announced dramatically on March 12 that "it must be the policy of the United States to support free people who are resisting subjection by armed minorities or outside pressures . . . "[*] what choice did Congress have but to agree—and subsequently to vote the funds required to translate these words into effective policy for saving Greece from communist domination? The answer was provided by a *St. Louis Post Dispatch* editorial on the President's speech: "Congress may ponder and debate but the President's address has committed the nation to all-out diplomatic action just as a declaration of a shooting war must necessarily follow when the President asks for it" (26, March 13, 1947).

A similar result could be anticipated when President Eisenhower requested standby authority early in 1955 to protect Formosa and other Chinese off-shore islands from a threatened attack by Red China.[**] Once the request was made of Congress, no realistic alternative to its approval existed. Congress, as prominent Democrats were heard to complain,

---

[*]See President Truman's message to a joint session of Congress on March 12, 1947: *Congressional Record*, Volume 93, pp. 1980-81.

[**]Text in *Congressional Record* (daily edition), January 24, 1955, p. 497-99.

could not turn the President down without implying to the world that it was indifferent to the fate of Formosa and without conveying a strong impression abroad that it had repudiated executive leadership. To decline the request was to invite almost certain communist expansionism in the Orient (10, pp. 251-54).

Presidential pronouncements of this kind are like requests for all those who oppose sin and favor righteousness to stand up. Congress often is forced to cooperate lest it appear to favor communist expansionism or whatever threat to security the President has described. Nor is Congress prepared to deal with the grave international consequences that would flow from a repudiation of the President's leadership.

3. THE PRESIDENT'S EMERGENCY POWERS

Immediately after the Civil War, the Supreme Court declared that "the government, within the Constitution, has all the powers granted to it which are necessary to preserve its existence . . . "* This doctrine has been repeatedly affirmed, as in 1934 when the Court held that "the war power of the Federal Government . . . *is a power to wage war successfully. . . .*"** From the Civil War onward, national crises have called for the exercise of sweeping governmental powers, powers which many students have thought were unknown to the original Constitution. The point of principal concern to us is that exercise of these powers has entailed a vast expansion in executive authority to deal with national crises.

The emergency powers of the President derive primarily from two constitutional sources: his designation as commander in chief (Art. II, Sec. 2); and his obligation to "take care that the laws be faithfully executed" (Art. II, Sec. 3). Together these two clauses constitute the so-called "war powers" of the executive. Besides this constitutional source, Congress within the last half-century has added to the President's power to deal with national emergencies. Relying both upon his authority as commander in chief and legislative authority given him for coping with emergency conditions, Franklin D. Roosevelt created numerous new governmental agencies during World War II and made them responsible solely to himself, often by-passing established executive departments. In an executive order issued on February 19, 1942, Roosevelt directed his military commanders to bar

American citizens of Japanese ancestry from occupying designated areas on the West coast; this order was subsequently incorporated into an act of Congress (8, pp. 393-95). When President Truman, on December 16, 1950, proclaimed "the existence of a national emergency," according to the noted constitutional commentator Edward S. Corwin, he activated over sixty statutes or portions of statutes that become applicable during periods characterized as "a condition of emergency" or "in time of war or national emergency." In most cases, the President determines when such conditions prevail. His determination will greatly enlarge his powers, in part by removing limitations existing upon them during normal times (8, pp. 81-2).

Lincoln was the first President to claim broad executive powers for dealing with a national crisis. During the spring and summer of 1861, Lincoln took many steps which, up to that time, had been thought to lie largely or exclusively within the domain of Congress. He ordered a blockade of southern ports in the absence of a "declaration of war" and directed that ships violating the blockade be confiscated. He increased the size of the army and navy; called out the militia; closed the post office to treasonable correspondence; expended funds from the treasury without legislative authorization; and suspended the writ of habeas corpus. During the course of the Civil War, Lincoln also freed the slaves on his own authority and drew up plans for the "reconstruction" of the South that contemplated little, if any, active participation by Congress. Collectively, these actions asserted "for the President, for the first time in our history, an initiative of indefinite

---

*Ex parte Milligan, 4 Wallace 2 (1866).

**Home Building and Loan Association v. Blaisdell, 290 U. S. 398 (1934). Italics inserted.

scope in meeting the domestic aspects of a war emergency" (6, p. 19).

Lincoln's dynamic conception of presidential power to deal with national emergencies has become firmly incorporated into the nation's constitutional fabric. Speaking for the Supreme Court in the Neagle case,* Justice Miller in 1890 asked whether the President was limited "to the enforcement of acts of Congress or of treaties of the United States according to their *express terms. . . .* " He answered in the negative, holding that in the discharge of his constitutional obligation to take care that the laws be faithfully executed, the President also was required to include "the rights, duties and obligations growing out of the Constitution itself, our international relations, and all the protection implied by the nature of the government under the Constitution." Typical of President Wilson's expansion of executive authority during the First World War was his arming of American merchant shipping, in spite of the fact that Congress refused to pass a law giving him such authority (8, p. 493). The power of Presidents to take such steps was justified by Solicitor General John W. Davis in 1914 by his assertion that "in ways short of making laws or disobeying them, the Executive may be under a grave constitutional duty to act for the national protection in situations not covered by the acts of Congress, and in which, even, it may not be said that his action is the direct expression of any particular one of the independent powers which are granted to him specifically by the Constitution" (8, p. 496).

In the 1950's the scope of the President's emergency powers came to the fore sharply in the steel seizure case,** growing out of President Truman's seizure of a steel company to avert a strike in a vital defense industry. At first glance, the Supreme Court's opinion declaring Truman's seizure of the steel mills unconstitutional might seem a decisive setback for the concept of residual executive power for dealing with emergencies. Unquestionably, the Court's opinion was a landmark in attempting to set limits to that power. Nonetheless, the

Court's decision turned on the fact that Congress had already provided methods by which the President could deal with conditions like those prevailing in this case, but that the President did not avail himself of these methods before ordering seizure. The Court's opinion did not deny the existence of a vast reservoir of executive emergency power. On the contrary, according to one commentator the justices were in wide agreement that "the President does possess a residual of resultant power above, or in consequence of, his granted powers to deal with emergencies in the absence of restrictive legislation. . . . " The Court's opinion underscored the fact, however, that "any action of the President touching the internal economy of the country for which the justification of emergency is pleaded is always subject to revision and disallowance by the legislative power" (8, p. 499).

What then are the limitations upon the emergency powers of the President? One stems from the limitations imposed upon President Truman by the Supreme Court in the steel seizure case, in which the Supreme Court was reiterating long-standing precedent: when Congress has specified the means by which the President is to cope with emergencies, then the President is obligated to follow the procedure prescribed by law. Moreover, the President cannot take action that is plainly denied him by constitutional prohibitions, although admittedly Presidents in recent years have sometimes taken an extremely elastic view of constitutional provisions designed to keep governmental power within clearly defined boundaries.* In the long run, the dikes that will confine presidential power within its proper channels are to be found, as Clinton Rossiter suggests, in deeply-ingrained principles like the concept of separation of powers and federalism, the determination of Congress to resist usurpation of power by the President, the threat of impeachment, the operation of a healthy two-party system, and public opinion (29, pp. 31-53, *passim*). In the final analysis, these constitute the most effective barriers against presidential "dictatorship." Yet it must be confessed that these limitations are in almost every case *long-range*

---

*135 U. S. 1 (1890).

** *Youngstown Company* v. *Sawyer,* 343 U. S. 579 (1952).

*See, for example, the case of *Korematsu* v. *United States,* 323 U. S. 214 (1944).

checks upon the President, and that in the short run—especially when the security of the country may hang in the balance—very few restraints, beyond his own devotion to the American Constitution and prescribed courses of action under it, are likely to bind a forceful President. We must therefore conclude with Abbot Smith that

The President's activities in foreign affairs are such as almost to give him the power of war and peace; certainly the effective limitations on his power are political in nature and not constitutional; he would be ill-advised to move faster than the sentiment of the country will allow, but his constitutional disabilities alone will never actually prevent him from getting the nation practically into a state of war. (32, p. 229).

4. THE DEPARTMENT OF STATE: ITS FUNCTION AND ORGANIZATION

Our discussion thus far has centered upon the powers of the President in foreign relations. While the chief executive has the ultimate responsibility, the day-by-day conduct of foreign affairs is in the hands of executive officers under his control. The President must make high-level decisions; he must often resolve disagreements over foreign policy among his principal subordinates; and occasionally he will attend diplomatic conferences, where he will personally negotiate agreements with other heads of government. Yet the Department of State has overall responsibility for the routine management of external affairs. While a growing number of executive agencies has been drawn into the foreign policy process in the postwar period, it remains the function of the State Department to provide general guidance and coordination in all important foreign policy activities so that they are consonant with the declared objectives of the United States in world affairs, as defined by the President and Congress. We shall devote the remainder of this chapter to an examination of the State Department's role and to the problems that beset its effective operation.

The Challenge of New Obligations

The expanding global obligations incurred by the United States over the past quarter century have been mirrored in the phenomenal growth in the size and activities of the Department of State. In the infancy of the Republic, the State Department, headed by Secretary of State Thomas Jefferson, had five clerks in Washington, three ministers, and sixteen consular officials. And even in Jefferson's day there

existed some feeling in Congress that the State Department was overstaffed (17, p. 15)!

By the 1960's, the Department of State had over 35,000 employees, including almost 13,000 in the International Cooperation Administration. Of this total, nearly 3,500 were Foreign Service officers which formed the elite corps of diplomatic officials concerned chiefly with *political* aspects of foreign affairs. The State Department supervised nearly 300 overseas posts, located in 89 foreign countries, containing 78 embassies and 173 consulates. The Department's budget requests to Congress exceeded $250 million annually, compared with a budget of $5,950 in the first year of the department's existence. Somewhere between 1,500 and 2,000 cables and 35,000 pieces of mail a day flowed in and out of the State Department (26, April 19, 1959, Dispatch by Dana Adams Schmidt).

Several factors account for this phenomenal growth. As long as "isolationism" remained the keynote of America's relations with the outside world, State Department duties consisted largely of routine consular business, furnishing information on foreign trade and commerce, protecting American citizens abroad, and performing ceremonial functions. Since World War II the United States has been actively involved in global affairs as never before in its history. Its foreign policy activities have steadily grown in range and in cost. During the 1930's, foreign affairs took approximately 35-40 per cent of the federal budget; 95 per cent during World War II; and between 75-80 per cent as a rule in the postwar period. Similarly, the budget of the State Department alone rose from $15.4 million in 1930 to approximately $250 million by the end of the 1950's.[*]

But the increased *range* and *cost* of commitments undertaken by the United States in recent years is in many ways not as significant as their *character*. A fundamental trend since the 1930's has been the unprecedented expansion in economic, social, and cultural activities of the State Department and other governmental agencies. Judged by the number of employees in this broad area, economic, social, and cultural issues appear sometimes to overshadow political issues in the relationships among nations. Today there are more State Department employees in the former fields than in the latter. McCamy has calculated that out of the total number of governmental employees on the national level in the United States, only .0001 per cent are assigned to the country desk units of the State Department, which oversee political relations between the United States and other countries. He believes that traditional diplomatic problems may become neglected in favor of emphasis upon economic, social, and cultural issues (24, pp. 58, 65).

Informational and propaganda activities have also assumed a leading role in foreign relations in the recent period. World War II showed the importance of propaganda in making the nation's diplomacy effective. The cold war has injected propaganda issues into international relations on a scale seldom experienced in earlier years except during time of war. Consequently, the United States has had to expand its activities in this field.[**]

The Role of the State Department

Events in the international sphere during the past two decades and America's response to them have raised serious questions about the contemporary role of the Department of State in American foreign policy. Such questions seldom arose in the past, because the Department was recognized as having primary jurisdiction

over foreign relations. Today, however, it is encountering increasing "competition" from other governmental agencies, most notably from the military establishment, technical assistance and informational agencies, interdepartmental committees throughout the government, and, on a lesser scale, from virtually every executive department. In attempting to co-ordinate the manifold activities of a growing number of governmental agencies, the question arises: what specifically is the proper role of the State Department? This question was examined fully by the Hoover Commission. The Commission recommended that the following principles should guide the State Department's operations at home and abroad:

First, the department should concentrate on defining the objectives of American foreign policy, on formulating policies for achieving them, and on recommending the best means for carrying out these policies. Thus the State Department would become the designated organ of the government dealing with broad foreign policy *formulation*. Second, *operating* responsibility for programs involving foreign aid and psychological warfare should be entrusted to agencies other than the State Department. In line with this recommendation, the Marshall Plan was administered by the Economic Cooperation Administration; its successor, the Mutual Security Program, was handled by the Mutual Security Administration; technical assistance to backward countries was made the province of the International Cooperation Administration; and propaganda activities were carried on by the Voice of America and later put under the control of the United States Information Agency. Each of these agencies, however, looked to the State Department for overall policy direction and guidance, to assure continuity in all aspects of American foreign relations. Finally, the Hoover Commission recommended that the Department continue its traditional duties of representing the United States abroad, reporting to Washington from its overseas missions, and undertaking negotiations (24, p. 70).

Although the State Department today is not the only agency engaged in foreign affairs activities, it is the one which provides overall co-ordination and which takes primary, though

[*]For a fuller development of this point, see the chart in 24, p. 5.

[**]The organizational structure of the government dealing with propaganda and psychological warfare is discussed at length in Chapter 15.

ORGANIZATION OF THE DEPARTMENT OF STATE

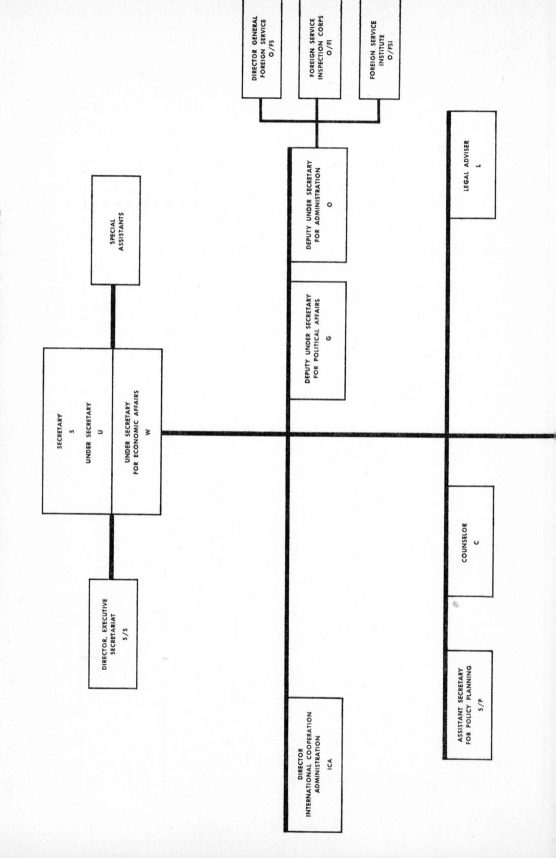

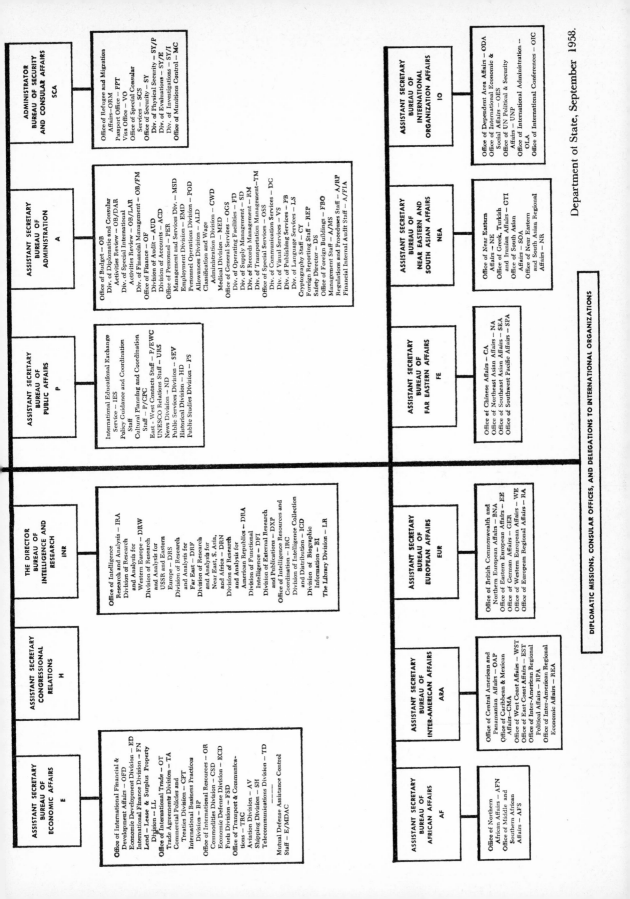

Department of State, September 1958.

ASSISTANT SECRETARY BUREAU OF ECONOMIC AFFAIRS — E

Office of International Financial & Development Affairs — OFD
Economic Development Division — ED
International Finance Division — FN
Land — Lease & Surplus Property Division — LL
Office of International Trade — OT
Trade Agreement Division — TA
Commercial Policies and Treaties Division — CPT
International Business Practices Division — BP
Office of International Resources — OR
Commodities Division — CSD
Economic Defense Division — ECD
Fuels Division — FSD
Office of Transport & Communications — TRC
Aviation Division — AV
Shipping Division — SH
Telecommunications Division — TD
Mutual Defense Assistance Control Staff — E/MDAC

ASSISTANT SECRETARY CONGRESSIONAL RELATIONS — H

THE DIRECTOR BUREAU OF INTELLIGENCE AND RESEARCH — INR

Office of Intelligence Research and Analysis — IRA
Division of Research and Analysis for Western Europe — DRW
Division of Research and Analysis for USSR and Eastern Europe — DRS
Division of Research and Analysis for Far East — DRF
Division of Research and Analysis for Near East, S. Asia, and Africa — DRN
Division of Research and Analysis for American Republics — DRA
Division of Functional Intelligence — DFI
Division of External Research and Publications — DXP
Office of Intelligence Resources and Coordination — IRC
Division of Intelligence Collection and Distribution — ICD
Division of Biographic Information — BI
The Library Division — LR

ASSISTANT SECRETARY BUREAU OF PUBLIC AFFAIRS — P

International Educational Exchange Service — IES
Policy Guidance and Coordination Staff
Cultural Planning and Coordination Staff — P/CPC
East - West Contacts Staff — P/EWC
UNESCO Relations Staff — URS
News Division — ND
Public Services Division — SEV
Historical Division — HD
Public Studies Division — PS

ASSISTANT SECRETARY BUREAU OF ADMINISTRATION — A

Office of Budget — OB
Div. of Diplomatic and Consular Activities Review — OB/DAR
Div. of Special International Activities Review — OB/LAR
Div. of Financial Management — OB/FM
Office of Finance — OF
Division of Audit — AUD
Division of Accounts — ACD
Office of Personnel — PER
Management and Services Div. — MSD
Employment Division — EMD
Personnel Operations Division — POD
Allowances Division — ALD
Classification and Wage Administration Division — CWD
Medical Division — MED
Office of General Services — OGS
Div. of Operating Facilities — FD
Div. of Supply Management — SD
Div. of Records Management — RM
Div. of Transportation Management — TM
Office of Special Services — OSS
Div. of Communication Services — DC
Div. of Visual Services — VS
Div. of Publishing Services — PB
Div. of Language Services — LS
Cryptography Staff — CY
Foreign Reporting Staff — REP
Safety Director — DS
Office of Foreign Buildings — FBO
Management Staff — A/MS
Regulations and Procedures Staff — A/RP
Financial Internal Audit Staff — A/FIA

ADMINISTRATOR BUREAU OF SECURITY AND CONSULAR AFFAIRS — SCA

Office of Refugee and Migration Affairs—ORM
Passport Office — PPT
Visa Office — VO
Office of Special Consular Services — SCS
Office of Security — SY
Div. of Physical Security — SY/P
Div. of Evaluations — SY/E
Div. of Investigations — SY/I
Office of Munitions Control — MC

ASSISTANT SECRETARY BUREAU OF AFRICAN AFFAIRS — AF

Office of Northern African Affairs — AFN
Office of Middle and Southern African Affairs — AFS

ASSISTANT SECRETARY BUREAU OF INTER-AMERICAN AFFAIRS — ARA

Office of Central American and Panamanian Affairs — OAP
Office of Caribbean & Mexican Affairs—CMA
Office of West Coast Affairs — WST
Office of East Coast Affairs — EST
Office of Inter-American Regional Political Affairs — RPA
Office of Inter-American Regional Economic Affairs — REA

ASSISTANT SECRETARY BUREAU OF EUROPEAN AFFAIRS — EUR

Office of British Commonwealth and Northern European Affairs — BNA
Office of Eastern European Affairs — EE
Office of German Affairs — GER
Office of Western European Affairs — WE
Office of European Regional Affairs — RA

ASSISTANT SECRETARY BUREAU OF FAR EASTERN AFFAIRS — FE

Office of Chinese Affairs — CA
Office of Northeast Asian Affairs — NA
Office of Southeast Asian Affairs — SEA
Office of Southwest Pacific Affairs — SPA

ASSISTANT SECRETARY BUREAU OF NEAR EASTERN AND SOUTH ASIAN AFFAIRS — NEA

Office of Near Eastern Affairs — NE
Office of Greek, Turkish and Iranian Affairs — GTI
Office of South Asian Affairs — SOA
Office of Near Eastern and South Asian Regional Affairs — NR

ASSISTANT SECRETARY BUREAU OF INTERNATIONAL ORGANIZATION AFFAIRS — IO

Office of Dependent Area Affairs — ODA
Office of International Economic & Social Affairs — OES
Office of UN Political & Security Affairs — UNP
Office of International Administration — OLA
Office of International Conferences — OIC

DIPLOMATIC MISSIONS, CONSULAR OFFICES, AND DELEGATIONS TO INTERNATIONAL ORGANIZATIONS

by no means exclusive, responsibility for formulating and evaluating American foreign policy.

Basic Organizational Structure

In common with other executive departments, the State Department within the past twenty-five years has experienced a great proliferation among its internal units. The Hoover Commission in 1948 found that the Department contained 94 separate units, with 25 officials reporting directly to the Secretary of State. After thorough study, a basic reorganization plan was proposed which, if it did not cut down drastically on the size of the Department, at least brought some semblance of order out of the administrative jungle previously prevailing (24, pp. 70-3).

In its simplest outline, the organizational structure of the State Department resembles a pyramid, with lines of authority moving downward from the Secretary of State, through his immediate subordinates, to the operating units at the bottom. But as the chart on pages 64-5 makes clear, the actual organizational pattern is considerably more complicated than this. The explanation lies in the Department's attempt to reconcile two contradictory administrative principles. One is the attempt to organize foreign affairs according to major geographical areas. Each area is subdivided into important regional groupings which, in turn, are divided into country desks for individual countries. Thus the Bureau of Far Eastern Affairs contains four regional offices: Chinese affairs, northeast Asian affairs, southeast Asian affairs, and southwest Pacific affairs. Diplomatic business relating to individual Asian countries will be handled by the appropriate regional office. The second principle is functional organization. Certain responsibilities of the Department of State are assigned to specialized agencies because these responsibilities cut across geographical boundaries and often concern many, sometimes all, the countries in which the United States has diplomatic interests. For example, the Bureau of Economic Affairs may be concerned with such widely prevalent issues as the impact of tariffs on international trade, promotion of economic development in backward countries, the relationship of economic problems to na-

tional defense, and the elimination of barriers to transportation and communication.

The Secretary of State is the chief foreign affairs adviser to the President, although since 1947 the National Security Council has become the highest interdepartmental committee concerned with national defense, a subject which often impinges upon foreign relations. The Secretary has Special Assistants to aid him. Two of them assume responsibility for co-ordinating State Department activities with the closely related fields of nuclear development and administration of the Mutual Security Program. The Mutual Security Program is under the jurisdiction of the Defense Department, since its main concern is enhancing the military strength of the non-communist world. The Secretary's chief subordinate is the Under Secretary of State, whose main duty it is to supervise the Department in the absence of the Secretary. In view of the frequent absences of the Secretary from Washington in recent years, the job has come to entail considerable responsibility. The Under Secretary is also Chairman of the Operations Coordinating Board of the National Security Council which checks that decisions arrived at by the Council and approved by the President are carried out throughout the government at large. Next in the State Department hierarchy is the Under Secretary for Economic Affairs. The existence of this office testifies eloquently to the growing importance of economic aspects of foreign policy and the ever-closer union between economic and political considerations in shaping the nation's relationships with the outside world.

Below these three officers are two Deputy Under Secretaries of State, one for political affairs and one for administration, plus the Director of the International Cooperation Administration. The Deputy Under Secretary for Administration supervises the internal administration and management of the State Department. The Director of the ICA administers American economic assistance to foreign countries. Co-ordination of ICA's activities with those of the State Department has sometimes been difficult and has occasioned requests on Capitol Hill that the Secretary of State ought to possess a greater voice in its operations. For broad policy guidance, the Director of ICA is therefore directly under the Secretary of State.

The position of Counselor was re-established in the State Department in 1937; it had existed in the 1907-1919 period. As a rule, the Counselor is an experienced and capable Foreign Service officer who advises the Secretary of State and the Under Secretary on important foreign policy questions and who undertakes special diplomatic assignments from time to time. The best-known counselor in the recent past has been George F. Kennan, a distinguished historian and recognized authority on the Soviet Union. More than any other official in the government, Mr. Kennan was responsible for providing a theoretical foundation for America's postwar policy of containment.

World War II and the years that followed called attention to the need for some kind of high-level diplomatic strategy board which, like the Joint Chiefs of Staff in the military establishment, could provide long-range estimates and calculations in foreign affairs. This need became pressing when the Greek crisis of 1947 showed that the United States could no longer "make policy on the cables" (**33**, p. 444). Consequently in 1947 the Policy Planning Staff was created. Staffed by experienced Foreign Service officers and headed by an Assistant Secretary of State, its role is to "formulate long-term plans for the achievement of the foreign policy objectives of the United States and to anticipate problems which the Department might encounter in the discharge of its mission" (**12**, p. 475). By 1951 PPS had been given the additional duty of co-ordinating the policies of the State Department and the National Security Council and of working in close conjunction with NSC's Planning Board to formulate and re-examine American foreign policy. Since its creation, PPS has had difficulty fulfilling its original conception as a top-level staff organ to advise the Secretary of State in somewhat the same manner as staff officers advise a military commander. Instead PPS has tended to be drawn into the day-to-day administration of foreign affairs, thereby impairing its usefulness as a nonoperating unit in the department whose chief function is to assess present and future developments and to present

estimates and judgments concerning the long-range direction of American foreign policy (**24**, p. 73).

The Legal Adviser is the chief law officer of the Department of State. He provides the Secretary of State and his subordinates with legal opinions on any subject of concern to the Department, from proposed or pending legislation affecting its interests to the interpretation of existing treaties.

The Functional Bureaus

On the next level are the functional bureaus, whose activities cut across regional and country lines. First, there is the Office of Intelligence Research, headed by a Special Assistant. It carries on intelligence activities on all matters of concern to the State Department. In this task, it works closely with the Central Intelligence Agency and other governmental intelligence units.

Next is the Office of Congressional Relations, headed by an Assistant Secretary. This office was created at the suggestion of the Hoover Commission in 1949. It has charge of all the Department's legislative programs, ranging from routine treaties and agreements with other countries to the Mutual Security Program and important treaties of mutual defense. Its services are available for answering inquiries by Congressmen—often sent to them by constituents; testifying before legislative committees or meeting informally with small groups of legislators who desire information about foreign affairs; arranging itineraries for legislative committees and subcommittees planning to travel abroad and furnishing State Department personnel to accompany such groups; and gauging congressional sentiment on outstanding foreign policy questions for the guidance of State Department officials (**10**, pp. 185-88).

The Office of Public Affairs, also headed by an Assistant Secretary, has a variety of duties which may conveniently be grouped under two broad headings: disseminating information about American foreign policy and the United States generally; and collecting and analyzing data on public opinion. Although this office does not actually administer the American overseas information program—that is done by the U. S. Information Agency—it co-ordinates all informational activities so that they are consistent with the basic principles of national policy. The Office of Public Affairs is also responsible for the Department's relations with the press and other communications media. Over the past several years, it has given out more than a thousand press releases annually. From time to time it arranges nationwide radio and television programs, as in the case of the Japanese Peace Conference in San Francisco in 1951, or when the Secretary of State wishes to address the nation It devotes considerable time to analyzing public reaction to American foreign policy, using newspaper editorials, public opinion polls, resolutions of interest groups, statements of prominent citizens, and departmental mail as indices of public opinion. Summaries of findings are prepared and circulated at frequent intervals for the guidance of policy-makers. The Office of Public Affairs also has charge of cultural exchange programs operated by the State Department. It may arrange for American cultural missions and "good will ambassadors" to visit other countries or for foreign groups to come to the United States. Another of its important continuing responsibilities is supervision of student exchange programs such as the Fulbright Act and the Smith-Mundt Act (1948). Finally, it is in charge of the historical division of the State Department, which publishes materials on various aspects of American foreign policy and makes diplomatic archives available to qualified scholars.

The Bureau of Security and Consular Affairs deals with such diverse matters as issuing passports and visas, handling refugee problems, and protecting the security of State Department property and personnel. The Bureau of Administration is concerned with the internal operation of the department, having charge of such matters as the budget, personnel and buildings.

The Geographic Bureaus

Relationships between the United States and other countries and with international organizations are dealt with by six regional bureaus: African affairs, Inter-American affairs, European affairs, Far Eastern affairs, Near East and South Asian affairs, and international organization affairs. These bureaus conduct the ordinary day-by-day diplomatic business of the United States with the countries or organizations under their jurisdiction. They channel communications between the State Department in Washington and its overseas diplomatic missions. While the bureaus are predominantly concerned with political issues, they also serve as the focal point for co-ordinating all aspects of America's foreign relations. Thus while the Indonesian desk in the Office of Southeast Asian Affairs, Bureau of Far Eastern Affairs, has no operating responsibility for American technical assistance programs in Indonesia—such programs are operated by ICA —it must see that technical assistance, along with cultural exchange programs, military policies, informational activities, and comparable aspects of the total pattern of America's relations with Indonesia, accord with the overall principles of American foreign policy. Effective co-ordination of activities by varied governmental agencies in foreign countries has sometimes been difficult. It is entrusted to the highest-ranking American diplomatic officials abroad.

The ambassador to France, the cultural attaché in Moscow, the consul in Venezuela, and other diplomatic officials regularly report to their country desks in Washington.* Moreover, information coming into other governmental agencies such as the Pentagon, the Treasury Department, the Atomic Energy Commission, or the Tariff Commission, is routed to the country desks of the State Department when liaison is required to assure continuity in policy. Positions on the country desks are filled by experts on the country in question—generally Foreign Service officers or other officials who have spent years residing in, and studying about, the country with which they are concerned. The Secretary of State, and ultimately the President, leans heavily upon the desk officers for advice in any problem involving American relations with specific foreign countries. More often than not, such advice is decisive. For the President or the Secretary of State "has no other choice except to gamble on his own hunches without benefit of analysis" (24, p. 61).

---

*The organization of overseas missions is clearly depicted by the chart in 20, p. 150.

The Bureau of International Organization affairs has an important role in supervising the relationships between the United States and international and regional organizations—chiefly, of course, the United Nations. The American Mission to the United Nations receives its instructions from this office and reports back to it regularly, so that the nation's foreign policy within the UN may be co-ordinated with policy toward other organizations, regions, and problems. This bureau also supervises the relationship between the United States and regional bodies such as NATO and the Organization of American States. In addition, the office handles necessary arrangements for international conferences in which the United States participates as a member or a sponsor. The number of such conferences has risen spectacularly—from approximately 75 per year in the 1930's to around 300 annually in the 1950's.

5. THE FOREIGN SERVICE

Its Role and Duties

Out of a total of over 12,000 personnel in the Department of State in 1958, nearly two-thirds were members of the Foreign Service. Down to the mid-1950's members of the Foreign Service were utilized predominantly to staff the overseas diplomatic missions of the United States. After a reorganization undertaken in 1954, however, the service was greatly enlarged by the admission of diplomatic personnel serving in Washington.

Several classifications exist in the Foreign Service. Overseas missions are headed by ambassadors or ministers—a chargé d'affaires, if they are absent. These top posts have customarily been awarded by the President to socially or politically prominent and wealthy individuals. Very few career diplomats can afford to take such assignments because of the comparatively low salaries these positions command and because of the great financial obligations they usually entail. In the larger countries, ambassadors and ministers must almost always spend several thousand dollars annually out of their own pockets to defray official entertainment expenses and other requirements. In recent years, however, a greater percentage than formerly of such appointments has been made from the ranks of career diplomatic officials.

Below ambassadors and ministers in rank are the members of the Foreign Service Officer Corps. Numbering over 3,400 individuals in 1958, this relatively small, well-educated, highly intelligent body of public servants constitutes the career diplomatic service upon which ambassadors and ministers in the field rely for the day-to-day administration of American foreign policy. Policy-makers in Washington lean heavily upon reports coming in from Foreign Service officers in the field in appraising significant developments in world affairs and their implications for the United States. In addition to reporting, Foreign Service officers perform consular functions, like processing visa and passport applications, providing services to American shipping, and handling problems related to the welfare of American citizens travelling abroad. Other duties include negotiation, representing the United States in other countries, and, on the average of three out of every nine years, serving in the State Department in Washington (35, pp. 15-30).

The Foreign Service Reserve Corps and the Foreign Service Staff corps are also part of the Foreign Service of the United States. The former constitutes a personnel reservoir, consisting mainly of specialists in selected fields, that can be tapped when the need arises. Reserve officers are appointed for a maximum term of five years. There were over 700 such officers in 1958. The Foreign Service Staff corps consists largely of typists and stenographers, clerical personnel, technicians, and custodial workers who assist the Foreign Service officers. Almost 10,000 foreign nationals were also employed in 1958 in routine capacities in American diplomatic posts overseas (36, pp. 5-6).

Organization and Reorganization

Throughout the greater part of the nation's history the selection of diplomatic personnel was haphazard. Very few guiding principles prevailed in the establishment of a professional corps of diplomats or in attempting to set up clearly-defined organizational precepts for its operation. For nearly a century and a half, political considerations more often than not entered into the making of appointments; almost always, low salaries compelled diplomats to subsidize their activities in foreign countries out of their own private funds (**36**, pp. 4-5).

The Foreign Service as it exists today owes its origin to the Rogers Act of 1924, when for the first time Congress spelled out requirements for entry into the service and set up a basic organizational structure. For the first time, the principle came to be widely endorsed that appointments to the Foreign Service ought to be on the basis of merit (**13**, pp. 206-7).

Since 1924 successful applicants for the career diplomatic service have been required to pass a battery of difficult written and oral examinations. These competitive examinations are open to any citizens between 20 and 31 years of age. The one-day written test is designed to test such skills as English expression general ability, overall educational background, and facility with foreign languages. The emphasis in the oral examination is upon personality traits, quickness of mind, poise, and general suitability for the Foreign Service. Impressive evidence of the difficulty of these examinations is afforded by the results among applicants in June, 1957: 2,616 men and women took the written examination; 556 passed. Of this number, 279 took the oral examination; 55 were notified of their acceptance into the Foreign Service; 16 were given a "deferred" status, mostly to permit the candidate to make up a deficiency in foreign languages. Once accepted, officers in the Foreign Service are evaluated by their superiors at periodic intervals. The principle of "up—or out" governs promotion policy in the service. Officers may reach the top grade— Class 1, for career ministers and career ambassadors. If they do not receive a promotion at periodic intervals, then they will be released from the service. In recent years, Foreign Service officers have reached such high positions as Under Secretary and Assistant Secretary of State (**36**, p. 7).

As would be expected, studies have revealed a very high educational level among the members of the Foreign Service officer corps. A high proportion are graduates of such schools as Harvard, Yale, Princeton, Georgetown, Stanford, and George Washington. McCamy and Corradini reported in 1954 that fourteen colleges and universities trained over half of the 1,306 Foreign Service officers whose backgrounds were investigated carefully (**25**, p. 1074). On the basis of their findings, it is possible to construct an image of the "typical" Foreign Service officer. He is male, between 31-50 years of age, and comes from the northeastern United States. He went to a private preparatory school and graduated from an Ivy League college or university with a B.A. degree or an M.A. degree. He had relatively little work experience before entering the Service, although he may have come from the field of education. Officers engaged in cultural-information activities at times have had experience in newspaper, radio, or television work (**25**, *passim*).

As long as the United States kept its foreign commitments to a minimum, few Americans were concerned about the adequacy of the Foreign Service. Only slight changes were made in the basic structure provided in the Rogers Act until the war called attention to increasingly serious problems of organization and morale. Many new agencies entered the foreign policy field during and just after the war. The relationship between them and the Foreign Service was often strained and on occasion threatened to interfere with effective administration of foreign affairs. Moreover, recruitment into the Service fell off during this period, with the result that Foreign Service duties had to be assigned to regular civil service employees —the Foreign Service Auxiliary—for the duration of the war emergency. In time Auxiliary officers came to outnumber regular Foreign Service officers in State Department activities at home and abroad. Serious morale problems for both groups resulted (**10**, pp. 207-09).

These considerations led to postwar efforts to reorganize the Service, efforts in which Foreign Service officers themselves assumed a prominent part. The State Department submitted its own detailed plan for reorganization to Congress, and Congress, with little opposition, passed the Foreign Service Act of 1946, substantially carrying out the Department's wishes.

Several thorough analyses of the Act have been made by other writers (13; 24, pp. 209-24). Here we need only make some general observations about its underlying purposes and scope. ⌜The Act did not contemplate sweeping changes in the Foreign Service. In the language of Congress, it attempted merely to "improve, strengthen, and expand" the existing corps. Salary scales for each officer grade were raised sharply, the number of grades was reduced, allowances, promotions, leaves, and retirement benefits were liberalized. The objective was to make the Service a more attractive career, and give it a better competitive position among other governmental agencies and with private industry. The principle of "promotion-up or selection-out" was introduced: after a specified period of time, officers would either have to be promoted to the next grade or released from the service. In addition, a Foreign Service Institute was established in Washington to train successful applicants for the Service and to provide periodic in-service training for officers already on the job (13, pp. 211-15). The Act of 1946 also set up a "career service" for clerical-secretarial employees. Primarily designed to grant them reasonably attractive salaries and job security rights, it also served to overcome their feeling of inferiority in being excluded from the Foreign Service.⌟

Throughout the years following these reforms new problems appeared. Many grew out of investigations by Congress into alleged communist influence in the national government. The State Department and Foreign Service were primary targets for such investigations, which caused grave problems of morale and administrative efficiency. George Kennan wrote in 1955 that the Eisenhower Administration had inherited a Foreign Service in "administrative ruin, packed with people who had never undergone the normal entrance requirements, hemmed in and suffocated by competing services, demoralized by anonymous security agents . . . a helpless object of disparagement and defamation at the hands of outside critics." He concluded that "it was no exaggeration to say that the experiment of professional diplomacy, as undertaken by the United States in 1925, had failed" (19, p. 98). Although many informed students regarded Kennan's judgment as ex-

treme, they nevertheless pointed to factors like declining recruitment rates and long delays encountered in processing applications to the Foreign Service as seriously impeding effective operation of the diplomatic corps (38, p. 7).

At length the Eisenhower Administration appointed a Public Committee on Personnel, headed by Dr. Henry M. Wriston of Brown University, to investigate problems prevailing in the Foreign Service and to make recommendations for its improvement. The Wriston Committee's recommendations were designed to repair some of the damage to morale sustained by the service within recent years by making it possible to attract and hold well-qualified individuals and by eliminating practices that had interfered with this goal. One key recommendation was integration of State Department personnel into the Foreign Service. Many State Department employees had heretofore been under civil service. This move, coupled with periodic rotation among officers serving in Washington and those serving overseas, was designed to improve morale and to broaden the experience of the nation's diplomats. To make the recruitment program more dynamic, entrance requirements into the Foreign Service were to be liberalized and prolonged delays in processing applications eliminated. Other recommendations entailed introduction of a program of scholarships for prospective Foreign Service officers who had passed the requisite examinations and introduction of a system of congressional appointments similar to that prevailing in the military officer schools.*

Another reorganization followed the Wriston Report. Over 1,440 State Department officials and 1,200 member of its "staff corps"—administrative specialists who had never taken the Foreign Service examination—were brought into the Service. Periodic rotation of officers be-

---

*For the principal recommendations of the Wriston Committee and the steps taken by Secretary of State Dulles to comply with them, see 9, 1954, pp. 58-61. To date, Congress has not instituted a scholarship system or a program of congressional appointments to the diplomatic corps. It has shown even greater reluctance to approve an idea advanced from time to time for further strengthening of the diplomatic service: establishment of a diplomatic "West Point" for prolonged training of future diplomats and for periodic in-service training of officers in Washington and in the field.

tween Washington and overseas posts became accepted practice. Foreign Service examinations were made somewhat less difficult, and recruitment was intensified. The Foreign Service Institute's program was expanded to provide more frequent in-service training for experienced officers. Throughout the years that followed, greater emphasis was placed upon acquisition of language skills by members of the diplomatic corps. On the whole, these changes were unquestionably beneficial. After 1954 morale in the Foreign Service improved, and a sharp upsurge took place in the number of applicants for entry into the diplomatic service.

Continuing Problems

In spite of these changes, several problems remain to hamper effective operation of the Foreign Service. For one thing, relationships between the overseas diplomatic missions and other American agencies abroad are not always smoothly co-ordinated, even though theoretically the former are the designated channels for providing central direction and guidance in overseas operations. At the State Department, Assistant Secretaries in charge of functional activities often have equal access to the Secretary of State with the Assistant Secretaries in charge of area bureaus (24, pp. 220-21). Consequently, lines of authority between political officers of the Department and those engaged in economic-social-cultural activities continue sometimes to be indistinct.

A second long-standing problem relates to the method by which ambassadors and ministers are chosen to represent the United States in foreign countries. No other country in the world appoints its top-flight diplomatic officials in such an illogical manner. Occasionally, ambassadors and ministers will be selected who have intimate knowledge of the country to which they are assigned, or who at least possess a general knowledge of foreign relations. But such appointments are more often than not accidental. Two criteria above all largely determine the selection of such officials: they must be wealthy and they must be members of—and the assumption is, contributors to—the party in power. A considerable outside income is indispensable, owing to the heavy financial demands made upon high-ranking diplomatic personnel, especially in the larger and more important capital cities. Career officers cannot as a rule therefore be considered for such posts, unless they possess sizable financial resources in addition to their salaries. That the appointee also be a faithful party man, and more often than not a big contributor, however, seems much less justifiable. Were it not for the training and experience of their subordinates many of these political appointees would have great difficulty discharging their duties competently.

The following case, admittedly an extreme one, illustrates the dangers latent in the prevailing system for appointing ambassadors and ministers. On July 2, 1957, the Senate Foreign Relations Committee met in executive session to consider the nomination of Mr. Maxwell H. Gluck, President Eisenhower's nominee for the post of Ambassador to Ceylon. Some significant highlights of this meeting are presented below.

Mr. Gluck: My qualifications generally are a varied business background. Ever since boyhood, I have had experience in industry, commerce, business, finance, and so forth.

I have never been in the diplomatic service before.

. . . . . .

Senator Fulbright: How much did you contribute to the Republican Party in the 1956 election?
Mr. Gluck: Well, I wouldn't know offhand, but I made a contribution.
Senator Fulbright: Well, how much?
Mr. Gluck: Let's see; I would say, all in all, twenty or thirty thousand dollars.

. . . . . .

Senator Fulbright: You don't think that is a pertinent reason for the appointment.
Mr. Gluck: I don't think it is the only reason.
Senator Fulbright: It is the principal reason, is it not?
Mr. Gluck: I don't think I want to admit that is the principal reason.

. . . . . .

Senator Fulbright: Why are you interested in Ceylon?
Mr. Gluck: I am not particularly interested only in Ceylon, but I am interested in a Government post where I can do some work and do some good at it.
Senator Fulbright: What makes you think you could do that in Ceylon?
Mr. Gluck: Unless I run into something that I am not aware of I think I ought to do a fairly good job in the job I have been nominated for.

Senator Fulbright: What are the problems in Ceylon you think you can deal with?

Mr. Gluck: One of the problems are the people there, not necessarily a problem, but the relationship of the United States with the people in Ceylon. I believe I can—I think I can establish, unless we—again, unless I run into something that I have not run into before—a good relationship and good feeling toward the United States.

. . . . . .

Senator Fulbright: Do you consider we are on friendly relations with India?

Mr. Gluck: Well, I think it is more—I think a lot depends on who is there, and what they do. I don't think we are on the friendliest relations with them, but I believe it can be strengthened a little more in one direction, or a little more in another direction, depending on what is done in that country.

. . . . . .

Senator Fulbright: Do you know who the Prime Minister in India is?

Mr. Gluck: Yes; but I can't pronounce his name.

Senator Fulbright: Do you know who the Prime Minister of Ceylon is?

Mr. Gluck: I have a list—

Senator Fulbright: Who is it?

Mr. Gluck: His name is a bit unfamiliar now. I cannot call it off, but I have obtained from Ambassador Crowe a list of all the important people there and I went over them with him.

I have a synopsis of all the people, both Americans, ambassadors, and officials from other countries, and I have from him also a sort of little biography or history of them, with what his opinion of them is; and so—

Senator Fulbright: That's all, Mr. Chairman.

Alone among the committee members, Senator Fulbright voted against this nomination, although even he confessed somewhat philosophically that "it is ridiculous to send [a] man with so little preparation to an area where these people are a sensitive and strange people, and I think it will do us no good. However, I am not going to raise cain. I know it is an old and evil custom that afflicts us."* In fairness to Mr. Gluck, it must be pointed out that his record in Ceylon was much more creditable than would have been expected on the basis of his seeming lack of qualifications for a diplomatic position or than has sometimes been the case with other individuals selected on a political basis.

_____

*These extracts are taken from: Senate Foreign Relations Committee, *Hearings on the Nomination of Maxwell H. Gluck,* 85th Congress, 1st Session, July 2, 1957, pp. 1-4.

A third recurring criticism heard of the Foreign Service is that its career officers constitute an intellectual elite which tends to regard its own judgments as infallible, or nearly so; that it seeks to create an officer caste system to dominate American foreign policy; and that it is often contemptuous of public opinion, Congressional sentiment, and the viewpoints of agencies outside the State Department. The stereotyped conception of the Foreign Service officer as the "striped-pants cookie pusher," is widespread and, what is more crucial, highly inimical to the development of a capable and dedicated body of diplomatic officials. This attitude may be but part of certain anti-intellectual currents that have swept American public opinion over the past decade.

Moreover, there remains the problem alluded to earlier: the comparative scarcity of Foreign Service officers who have expert knowledge of *political* developments in other countries and on the international scene as a whole. This phenomenon may result in part from the unparalleled emphasis of late upon economic-social-cultural aspects of foreign policy. Another contributing factor, as McCamy and Corradini found in their exhaustive study of Foreign Service personnel, is too frequent changes in diplomatic assignments. Assuming that five years' residence within a country is required to give an officer expert knowledge, it was found that over 80 per cent of the Foreign Service had stayed in one country less than six years; fewer than 13 per cent had stayed for 6 to 10 years; and just over 3 per cent had stayed over eleven years (**25**, pp. 1080-82).

Towering above all these problems, however, has been another which not only has affected the Foreign Service but all other governmental agencies as well. This is the incalculable damage done by irresponsible and sweeping accusations against loyal public servants over the past several years by such publicity-seeking individuals and groups as the late Senator Joseph McCarthy, the House Un-American Activities Committee, and certain members of the Senate Judiciary Committee. Quite clearly, legislative investigations of subversion and other problems are sometimes necessary and are legitimate activities of Congress, provided they take place within constitutional limits. But such investigations are supposed to bear some relationship to *legislation*. Instead, several well-publicized investigations in the postwar era have had little or no apparent connection with legislation. Quite openly they have sought to pry into the substance of American foreign policy, most notably toward the Far East, and into the day-to-day conduct of foreign relations by executive officials. Frequently, in seeking to "expose communist influences," they have tried to get, and to make public, information which could be, and sometimes clearly was, highly damaging to national security.

Even more disturbing than the investigations themselves, however, have been the fanciful and deluded assumptions often underlying them. Having postulated such misleading questions as "Who gave Eastern Europe to Stalin?" or "Who sold Nationalist China down the river?," legislators have sought to explain policy inadequacies—inadequacies, such as those apparent in our China policy, in which they often played a leading part—by reference to mysterious "subversive influences" in the State Department. It is disheartening to reflect upon the good that might have been accomplished if only half the time and energy spent in searching for subversive influences over the past decade had gone into objective, penetrating,

and prolonged study by Congressmen of the realities confronting the United States in foreign affairs!

Reckless and unfounded charges against leading Foreign Service officers and the diplomatic corps generally had, by 1950, brought the morale of the service to its nadir—to a point where capable officers were leaving the corps and qualified applicants were deterred from seeking admittance to it. Today the problem may have passed its zenith. In retrospect, we may date the improvement from Senator McCarthy's censure in 1954. Still, the injury done is not likely to be completely healed for many years. Writing in 1954 Walter Lippmann said of the Foreign Service personnel: "Their injuries are subtle. But they are deep. It will take a long time to repair them. A decade would be a conservative estimate" (**37**, December 27, 1954).

The scars left by this sorry episode in American history can serve as continual reminders of an ever-present problem in any democracy: widespread public suspicion and contempt for government servants at all levels may cripple the nation's efforts to carry out successful national policies and may, in the last analysis, adversely affect its very survival as a great and independent power.

REFERENCES

1. Binkley, Wilfred E. *President and Congress.* New York: Alfred A. Knopf, 1947. Valuable for historical background on executive-legislative relations.

2. ———. "The President and Congress," in *The Presidency in Transition* (a symposium). Gainesville, Fla.: University of Florida, 1949.

3. Borchard, Edwin M. "Treaties and Executive Agreements," *American Political Science Review*, 40 (August, 1946), 729-39. An informative comparison of treaties and executive agreements.

4. Buck, Philip W., and Travis, Martin B., Jr. *Control of Foreign Relations in Modern Nations.* New York: W. W. Norton and Company, 1957. Useful for background on foreign relations in other countries.

5. Corwin, Edward S. *The President's Control of Foreign Relations.* Princeton, N. J.: Princeton University Press, 1917. Though out of date,

this is still a classic work on the President's role in foreign relations.

6. ———. *Total War and the Constitution.* New York: Alfred A. Knopf, 1947. A penetrating study of the impact of war and emergencies on the Constitution.

7. ———, and Koenig, Louis W. *The President Today.* New York: New York University Press, 1956. A brief survey of the changing role of the presidency and executive techniques of leadership.

8. Corwin, Edward S., ed. *The Constitution of the United States of America*: *Analysis and Interpretation.* Legislative Reference Service, Library of Congress. Washington, D. C., 1953. This work, by one of the nation's foremost students of the Constitution, is an invaluable commentary on the Constitution, in the light of major court decisions, traditions, and understandings arising over the course of American history.

9. Council on Foreign Relations. *Documents on American Foreign Relations, 1938, et seq.* New York: Harper and Brothers, 1939. This series is a convenient compilation of documentary materials dealing with American foreign policy.

10. Crabb, Cecil V., Jr. *Bipartisan Foreign Policy: Myth or Reality?* Evanston: Row, Peterson and Company, 1957. Chapters I and VII discuss the President's role in foreign affairs.

11. Cross, Harold L. *The People's Right to Know.* Morningside Heights, N. Y.: Columbia University Press, 1953. A thorough treatment of the problem of access to information possessed by the government, together with an analysis of laws and departmental regulations dealing with confidential data.

12. "The Department of State, 1930-1955: Expanding Functions and Responsibilities," *Department of State Bulletin,* 32 (March 21 and March 28, 1955), 470-86 and 528-44. These two articles cover recent changes in the role and organization of the State Department.

13. Evans, Alona E. "The Re-Organization of the American Foreign Service," *International Affairs,* 24 (April, 1948), 206-17.

14. Fairman, Charles. "The President As Commander-in-Chief," in *The Presidency in Transition* (a symposium). Gainesville, Fla.: University of Florida, 1949.

15. Fleming, D. F. *The Treaty Veto of the American Senate.* New York: G. P. Putnam's Sons, 1930. Cites numerous examples of executive-Senate conflict over treaties.

16. Holt, W. Stull. *Treaties Defeated by the Senate.* Baltimore: The Johns Hopkins University Press, 1933. Provides helpful historical background on the Senate's role in treaty-making.

17. Hulen, Bertram D. *Inside the Department of State.* New York: Whittlesley House, 1939. A popular, but useful, treatment of the State Department. Especially interesting is Chapter XII, "One Day in the Department."

18. Huzar, Elias. "Reorganization for National Security," *Journal of Politics,* 12 (February, 1950), 128-52.

19. Kennan, George F. "The Future of our Professional Diplomacy," *Foreign Affairs,* 33 (July, 1955), 566-87. An analysis of the Foreign Service by one of its most distinguished officers.

20. Knappen, Marshall. *An Introduction to American Foreign Policy.* New York: Harper and Brothers, 1956.

21. Langer, William L. "The Mechanism of American Foreign Policy," *International Affairs,* 24 (July, 1948), 319-28.

22. Langer, William L., and Gleason, S. Everett. *The Undeclared War, 1940-1941.* New York: Harper and Brothers, 1953.

23. Leviero, Anthony. "The Press and the President," *New York Times Magazine,* August 21, 1949, pp. 10-11, 51-52. An experienced reporter analyzes the presidential press conference.

24. McCamy, James L. *The Administration of American Foreign Affairs.* New York: Alfred A. Knopf, 1950. Although somewhat dated, this is probably the best available one-volume treatment of the subject.

25. ——, and Corradini, Alessandro. "The People of the State Department and Foreign Service," *American Political Science Review,* 48 (December, 1954), 1067-82.

26. *New York Times.*

27. Plischke, Elmer. *Summit Diplomacy.* College Park, Maryland: Bureau of Governmental Research, University of Maryland, 1958. A recent evaluation of the President's role in negotiations.

28. Pratt, Julius W. *A History of United States Foreign Policy.* New York: Prentice-Hall, 1955. A scholarly, but highly readable, account of American foreign relations.

29. Rossiter, Clinton. *The American Presidency.* New York: New American Library, 1956. A readable and penetrating analysis of the presidency.

30. ——. *The Supreme Court and the Commander in Chief.* Ithaca: Cornell University Press, 1951. A capable treatment of legal and constitutional aspects of executive power.

31. Sherwood, Robert E. *Roosevelt and Hopkins,* Volume 1. New York: Bantam Books, 1948.

32. Smith, Abbot. "Mr. Madison's War," *Political Science Quarterly,* 57 (June, 1942), 229-46.

33. Stuart, Graham H. *The Department of State.* New York: The Macmillan Company, 1949. A history of the State Department, concentrating on its internal administrative changes and shifting responsibilities.

34. Sturm, Albert L. "Emergencies and the Presidency," *Journal of Politics,* 2 (February, 1949), 121-44. Analyzes the scope of presidential emergency powers.

35. United States, Department of State. *The Foreign Service of the United States.* (Department of State Publication No. 6608, "Department and Foreign Service Series," 74). Washington, 1958. A brief treatment of the Foreign Service.

36. ———. *The People Who Wage the Peace.* (Department of State Publication No. 6655, "Department and Foreign Service Series," 76). Washington, 1958.

37. *Washington Post - Times Herald.*

38. Wriston, Henry M. *Diplomacy in a Democracy.* New York: Harper and Brothers, 1956. Wriston's book is an analysis of the American diplomatic corps, based upon his findings as Chairman of the Public Committee on Personnel, appointed to investigate the corps.

CHAPTER 4

The Military Establishment
and Other Executive Agencies

1. THE MILITARY AND AMERICAN FOREIGN POLICY

Testifying before a congressional committee in 1945, former Secretary of State Cordell Hull observed that:

Soon after I came into the State Department, when I would be talking with the representatives of the thugs at the head of governments abroad . . . they would look at me in the face but I soon discovered that they were looking over my shoulder at our Navy and our Army and that our diplomatic strength . . . goes up or down with their estimate of what that amounts to. (**25**, p. 171).

And in 1951 General Omar N. Bradley, commander of army ground forces in Europe dur-

ing World War II and later Chairman of the Joint Chiefs of Staff, wrote in his memoirs:

The American army has . . . acquired a political maturity it sorely lacked at the outbreak of World War II. At times during that war we forgot that wars are fought for the resolution of political conflicts, and in the ground campaign for Europe we sometimes overlooked political considerations of vast importance. Today, after several years of cold war, we are intensely aware that a military effort cannot be separated from political objectives. (**2**, p. xi.)

These statements call attention to a trend of fundamental significance for American foreign policy in the postwar period. This is the new

PROGRESS!

S. J. Ray in *The Kansas City Star*, May, 1957.

role of the military establishment in the formulation and execution of foreign policy. Never
before in American history has there prevailed
such an awareness both within and outside the
government that national policy and military
power are closely interwoven. Governmental
officials and authorities on foreign relations
have devoted increasing attention to the interaction between policy objectives and the means
for attaining them. Thus Arthur W. Macmahon
conceives of national security in the form of a
triangle. At one corner is foreign policy. At
another is military policy. At the third corner
is economic policy. Together they encompass
the broad field of national security (**22**, pp.
5-6).

In this chapter we shall be concerned only
with the relationship between foreign and
military policy. Reduced to its essentials, this
relationship has been described by former Army
Chief of Staff, General Matthew B. Ridgway,
as follows:

> The statesman, the senior civilian authority,
> says to the soldier . . . : This is our national
> policy. This is what we wish to accomplish or
> would like to do. What military means are re-
> quired to support it?

The soldier studies this problem in detail.

> "Very well," he says to the statesman. "Here is
> what your policy will require in men and guns,
> in ships and planes." (**30**, p. 271).

This is a highly simplified version of how
civilian-military co-ordination is achieved in
practice.

An awareness that military leaders have a
part—and sometimes a decisive part—in foreign
policy has come only very recently in American
history. Military officers have occasionally assumed diplomatic roles, as when Commodore
Perry "opened up" Japan in 1854 or when
military commanders took over political responsibilities during the era of "gunboat diplomacy" in Latin America in the early 1900's.
Yet formal military participation in national
policy decisions was as a rule haphazard and
expediential before the Second World War.
After an intensive search of the evidence during the McKinley-Roosevelt-Taft period, for
instance, one writer has stated that "I have yet
to find a letter from a Secretary of State, asking

for a military cost accounting before some
diplomatic stroke." He found that before the
1930's, liaison among the Secretaries of State,
War, and Navy, was usually indirect, by letter
only (**25**, pp. 163-4).

The first proposal for a supra-departmental
agency to secure needed co-ordination was
made in 1919 by Acting Secretary of the Navy,
Franklin D. Roosevelt (**25**, pp. 167-8). The proposal was premature. Almost three decades
were required before the necessity for major
organizational changes toward this end came to
be widely admitted. Working co-ordination was
achieved during the Second World War by two
groups. For a time, they operated simultaneously, and their jurisdictions were not always
clearly delineated. One group was the Standing
Liaison Committee, consisting of the Under Secretary of State, the Chief of Naval Operations,
and the Army Chief of Staff. This was the "first
American agency for regular political-military
consultation on foreign policy" (**25**, p. 172).
The second group was the higher-ranking War
Council, consisting of the Secretaries of State,
War, Navy, and the Chiefs of Staff of the
armed forces. While this body did assure a
certain amount of consultation, on numerous
occasions President Roosevelt by-passed even
this body and worked directly through the
military commanders (**25**, pp. 173-4).

That civilian-military co-ordination was still
rudimentary and sometimes ineffectual was
clearly demonstrated by a number of vital and
far-reaching decisions made during the war.
Frequently, military considerations predominated in reaching such decisions. Military
insistence that Russia be brought into the
Pacific war, for example, had incalculable long-
range political implications, for it largely explains the concessions made by the West to
Stalin at the Yalta Conference in 1945.* The

---

*Throughout the war, the United States held
consistently to the position that Soviet participation in the conflict with Japan was necessary to
assure victory—a view that the Joint Chiefs of Staff
advanced as early as December 8, 1941 and that
was reiterated as late as the Potsdam Conference
in July, 1945. Interestingly enough, one of the foremost advocates of this view was General Douglas
MacArthur, who urged it upon his superiors in
the Pentagon on December 10, 1941. Until the
conference at Yalta, in February, 1945, American
strategists based their plans for conquering Japan

postwar boundaries of North and South Korea were fixed—as events revealed, permanently—because of a temporary military agreement between Russian and American military forces, establishing a line at the 38th parallel for purposes of receiving the Japanese surrender. Similarly, the zones of occupation in Germany, notably in Berlin, were determined with little or no thought of the ultimate political and economic, not to mention strategic, consequences of these boundaries (**8**, pp. 398-403; **10**, p. 409; **20**, pp. 321-2). So firmly ingrained was the idea that military considerations were uppermost during the war, that General Omar N. Bradley could write in reference to British and American views on Germany: "As soldiers we looked naïvely on this British inclination to complicate the war with political foresight and nonmilitary objectives" (**2**, p. 536). Soldiers of course have not been alone in ignoring Clausewitz's dictum that war is merely the continuation of policy by another means. During the period of occupation, the State Department showed considerable reluctance to relieve the army of the overall management of occupation affairs in Germany (**8**, pp. 441-2).

Except when militarism *per se* becomes the guiding principle of national policy, military

---

on the assumption that no atomic weapons would be available for this campaign, that somewhere between 500,000 and 1,000,000 men would be casualties in the invasion of Japan's home islands, and that it would require eighteen months after Germany's surrender (which did not take place until May, 1945) for Japan's defeat (**36**, pp. 133-57, *passim*).

Events showed of course that these estimates were inaccurate and that the Navy's contention—that Japan by early 1945 was in the process of being strangled economically—was substantially correct. Nevertheless, President Roosevelt relied upon the majority viewpoint among his military commanders and based his diplomacy at the Yalta Conference upon it (**35** and **40**).

action is always undertaken in behalf of *political* objectives.* Military decisions are therefore bound to have political connotations. Awareness of this fact is no doubt more widespread now than in any previous period of American history. Yet there still is perennial danger that it will be overlooked, especially in times of war. As recently as the Korean War, many congressmen and vocal groups of Americans apparently had difficulty seeing the connection between military actions and larger political considerations. General Douglas MacArthur's widely quoted remark that in war "there is no substitute for victory" reflects this difficulty, as does Senator William Jenner's (Republican of Indiana) question: "If our military are not permitted to develop a defense or to fight a war . . . but their strategy is diluted by political considerations of the State Department, what chance . . . do we have to defend this country . . . ?" (**38**, p. 5).

Senator Jenner's query raises a fundamental issue about the role of the military in American life. The threat of communist expansionism has forced the United States to devote somewhere between one-half and two-thirds of the total federal budget to national defense. Because of its sheer size and its obvious importance to the goal of security, the military establishment has come to possess an influence in national policy councils vastly exceeding its influence during any other period of American history, at least during time of peace. The problem of civilian-military relations is therefore a central one for foreign policy-makers.

---

*As the term is used here, "political objectives" refers to the larger goals of American foreign relations, as discussed in Chapter 1. Although such objectives obviously have a close connection with domestic politics, they are much broader than issues between the political parties within the United States.

2. THE NATIONAL DEFENSE ESTABLISHMENT

The Military Services Before World War II

Increasingly in the period before World War II, experience showed the futility of trying to preserve national security when civilian leaders ignored military factors. By the First World War, two problems of civilian-military co-ordina-

tion had already come to the forefront. First, internal reorganization of the military establishment was indicated in order to make it a more effective instrument of national policy. Second, new machinery was needed for co-ordinating military efforts with those of civilian agencies.

The First World War revealed the desirability of unification of the armed services. The emergence of air power as a major component of American military strength, and the dramatization of its effects by General Billy Mitchell during the 1920's and 1930's, provided new impetus to the unification movement. In the 1924-45 period over fifty bills were introduced into Congress calling for the merger of the armed services and the establishment of a joint military command. More than a dozen studies of the problem were carried out in this period by the executive branch (38, p. 11). Early in World War II the navy proposed a joint military command for all the service arms, with an army-navy staff whose head would be directly responsible to the President (3, p. 66). But the army, supported by the air force, opposed this move. Although studies of military unification continued throughout the war, little was done to make unification a reality. A consensus prevailed throughout all the agencies of government that so radical a change must await the end of hostilities. Before and during the war, when co-ordination was required among the military services it was usually reached by a process of "mutual agreement." The disaster at Pearl Harbor revealed forcefully how inadequate such agreements were for preserving national security. Yet until the postwar period high-ranking military officials clung to the idea that successful prosecution of six major wars in a century and a quarter demonstrated the feasibility of continued separation of the services (3, p. 65).

Within the military establishment disagreements arose over such issues as the proper roles of the army, navy, and air force in safeguarding national defense; over the best combination of the services to assure maximum co-ordination among them; over the establishment and operation of a joint command; and over the proper relationships to be set up between the nation's chief military commanders and their civilian superiors (38, pp. 68-9). Studies of these and equally complex problems continued during the war and into the immediate postwar era. In addition to the purely military aspects of modifications in the prevailing defense organization, there were urgent problems arising from rapid demobilization after the war and from conversion to a peacetime footing. Finally, on December 19, 1945, President Truman asked Congress to unify the armed services. His recommendations were patterned closely after a report prepared for the navy by Ferdinand Eberstadt. Extended legislative hearings and more detailed studies ensued, so that it was not until the spring of 1947 that Congress passed the National Security Act. This act, together with its later modifications,* provides the basis for the present defense establishment.

Reorganization of the Pentagon

The cardinal fact about defense reorganization in 1947 that substantially governed changes made in the years that followed was that the plan which finally emerged represented a compromise between two extreme positions, and as a compromise it satisfied no interested group completely. One extreme position favored no significant change whatever in American defense organization. There were fears about the emergence of anything resembling the German General Staff and apprehension lest the separate services lose their identities. Powerful vested interests like the Navy League, the Air Force Association, and the Associations of the United States Army opposed sweeping changes. These groups often had influential supporters on Capitol Hill. By the end of the 1950's, judging by the vocal opposition in Congress to some of President Eisenhower's recommendations, widespread fears existed that too great military centralization would usher in a "garrison state" and facilitate the emergence of a military dictator. Ranged against this group were advocates of radical change in the existing defense pattern. Advocates of sweeping reorganization pointed to innumerable instances in the nation's history—the most disastrous being Pearl Harbor—to support the view that America could no longer afford the luxury of three powerful services operating virtually autonomously. Crit-

---

*Writing in 1958, the *New York Times'* military analyst, Hanson Baldwin, observed that the National Security Act of 1947 had been *significantly* modified, either by law or executive action, thirteen times in the decade that followed; important, though not sweeping, alterations were made by Congress, at President Eisenhower's urging, in the summer of 1958 (27, March 2, 1958).

ics lamented that recurrent disputes over "service jurisdictions" and ineffectual efforts to secure "voluntary co-operation" among rival services had too long impaired national security.

The Act of 1947 tried to steer a middle course between these two positions, leaning perhaps more toward the former than toward the latter. It united the military branches, but not too closely. It placed the Department of Defense under the Secretary of Defense, but took pains to prevent his becoming a "military czar." It provided for a Joint Chiefs of Staff, but carefully circumscribed the group's powers and left its members as the *operating* commanders of their respective services. These compromises, and others, are explicable only if it is grasped that the plan of defense reorganization itself was above all a compromise and that, at least in some instances, it represented an attempt to synthesize viewpoints that were in the final analysis irreconcilable. With these general ideas in mind, let us examine specific changes introduced into the national defense establishment.

The apex of the organizational hierarchy in the Pentagon is the *Office of Secretary of Defense,* headed by a civilian *Secretary of Defense.* This officer represents the Defense Department in the Cabinet and in the National Security Council. Legally, the Secretary of Defense is the channel by which orders are transmitted from the President to the military services. Although the Secretary enjoys broad powers, such as preparation of the overall military budget, he is nevertheless restricted in his control over the direct operations of the separate military branches. Orders to the services which, by law, should be transmitted from the President to the Secretary of Defense, and thence to the services, have gone directly to the civilian secretaries at the head of each branch, thereby effectively by-passing the Office of Secretary of Defense. In 1949 Congress added to the authority of the Secretary of Defense, but with the clear stipulation that the military services were to be kept separate and that no "general staff" was to be imposed over them. Over succeeding years, a continuing problem in military coordination has been posed by the growth of the civilian bureaucracy in the Office of Secretary of Defense. In spite of changes in the Pentagon, the exact powers of the Secretary of Defense remain nebulous and ill-defined (27, March 2, 1958, Dispatch by Hanson Baldwin).

The second major innovation introduced by the defense reorganization of 1947 was establishment of the *Joint Chiefs of Staff.* This organ was to impart needed co-ordination in overall defense planning, while avoiding creation of a totally unified military command system. The Joint Chiefs comprise the military commanders from each of the three principal services plus the Commandant of the Marine Corps, when decisions affect its interests. A non-voting Chairman presides, with the chairmanship rotating among the services. The Joint Chiefs of Staff serves as the principal military adviser to the President, the National Security Council and the Secretary of Defense. Hanson Baldwin has summarized its duties by saying that:

> They are charged as a body with the preparation of strategic and logistic plans and the provision of "strategic direction" for the armed forces, with the establishment of unified commands, the formulation of policies for joint training and education of the armed forces, and the "review" of the services' manpower and equipment requirements. A grab-bag provision of the law also requires them to perform "such other duties" as are directed. (27, January 12, 1958, Dispatch by Hanson Baldwin).

Thus to avoid the extreme of overcentralization, the nation's highest military commanders are utilized in two rather contradictory capacities: *individually,* as operating heads of their respective branches, they are charged with carrying out assignments given to their service arms and with maintaining them as an effective fighting force; *collectively,* as the nation's highest military staff, they are responsible for formulating overall inter-service policies and programs designed to utilize *all* military branches in the way best calculated to promote national security. This kind of built-in ambiguity has well-nigh guaranteed that as an institution the Joint Chiefs would suffer from schizophrenic tendencies.*

---

*Problems arising from the operations of the Joint Chiefs are brought out clearly in General James Gavin's book, *War and Peace in the Space Age* (11). General Gavin emphasizes how the individual service chiefs are required simultaneously to think in terms of the interests of their own

The third category of changes brought about in 1947 and in subsequent years concerned the *military departments*. A major innovation in 1947 was elevation of the air force to a separate department, putting it on a plane of equality with the army and navy. Each of the services was now headed by a civilian secretary who, together with the senior military commander in each arm—who also served on the Joint Chiefs of Staff—administered the affairs of the department. Various provisions of the law of 1947 and later modifications tried to assure at least the semblance of co-ordination and liaison among the military departments in meeting common problems like procurement, manpower needs, and research and development. Experience with missile technology in later years, however, indicated that each military department retained a large measure of autonomy. Thus a decade later, a report by the House Committee on Government Operations found widespread waste and duplication in missile development. In common with a number of other reports over preceding years, it called for greater co-ordination and less competition among the service arms in weapons technology (4, Volume 14, p. 139).

In the years that followed passage of the National Security Act, Defense Department activities impinged increasingly on many politico-economic fields. After the Korean War, for example, the Defense Department was actively concerned with military aid programs to nations threatened by communist aggression, with strengthening the NATO alliance, and with

the rearmament of Germany and Japan. Political events literally anywhere in the world might affect the military security of the United States, thereby involving the Department of Defense. Consequently, in 1953 the position of Assistant Secretary of Defense for International Security Affairs was created. ISA—called by one writer "the State Department's Pentagon"—has three main areas of activity: American military assistance to other countries, politico-military-economic aspects of American defense policy, and relations between the Defense Department and the National Security Council (38, p. 45). In theory, ISA is the focal point for co-ordinating Defense Department relations with other governmental agencies whose activities touch the field of national security. That it has not completely resolved the problem of such co-ordination is indicated by the fact that the Joint Chiefs of Staff, for example, regularly maintain relations directly with the Department of State, giving high diplomatic officials policy "briefings" on the American military posture as it bears upon foreign affairs. The Joint Chiefs and the State Department also collaborated directly—by-passing ISA and even the Secretary of Defense—in working out instructions for American negotiators at the time of the Korean armistice talks (38, p. 56).

The National Security Council

In addition to reorganizing the military services, the National Security Act of 1947 also established a new high-level agency to facilitate co-ordination throughout the government for policies affecting national security. NSC has been called the "most important high-policy committee in the national government today . . ." (14, p. 136). It watches that "our foreign policies are consistent with our military capabilities and our domestic resources" (37, p. 536). In common with other executive agencies, however, NSC advises the President only; it has no independent powers to arrive at decisions and to declare governmental policies. That authority belongs to the President. It is only after he has approved Council decisions that they become binding upon other agencies as the official statement of American policy (37, p. 536; 38, pp. 32-3).

services and in the larger terms of the best conceivable co-ordinated plan for national security. More often than not, in such a contest, the interests of the individual services prevail. The system encourages "reciprocity" and "horse trading" among the service heads; not infrequently, decisions are made on a two-against-one basis. Gavin, whose views of course favor the Army side, believes this occurred in limiting Army missile development to weapons of no more than 250-mile range and in spending vast sums for "supercarriers." This condition in turn promotes, if it does not make wellnigh inevitable, attempts by the individual services to cultivate "sympathetic" viewpoints on Capitol Hill, largely breaking down the concept that the viewpoints of the Pentagon are co-ordinated through the Secretary of Defense. Whatever the motives of individual commanders, in Gavin's opinion *the system* perpetuates such phenomena (11, pp. 166-79, 257-65).

Under the Act of 1947 and its later modifications, the National Security Council is composed of the President as Chairman, the Vice-President, the Secretaries of State, Defense, and the Director of the Office of Defense Mobilization (ODM). From time to time the President may also invite other high-ranking executive officials to attend the Council's meetings, but these individuals have no vote. For instance, President Eisenhower has requested the attendance of the Chairman of the Joint Chiefs of Staff, the Director of the Central Intelligence Agency, and the Special Assistant to the President for Cold War Planning (14, p. 125).

Thus in the field of national security policy it was anticipated that functions would be separated as follows: Congress would determine overall goals and means for reaching them by fixing the size, composition, and appropriations for the military establishment. The President would allocate specific assignments to executive agencies, within the broad policies laid down by Congress. The Secretary of Defense would concern himself with unifying the efforts of the armed services in carrying out missions assigned to the Defense Department (16, p. 128).

Within NSC, three subordinate agencies play an important part in national security planning. Its Staff functions as a secretariat. It checks that papers presented for discussion are in proper form and language, that decisions are recorded accurately, and that the flow of ideas to and from NSC is expedited (38, pp. 32-2). We may visualize the roles of two other subordinate agencies—the Planning Board and the Operations Coordinating Board—by employing the metaphor used by Robert J. Cutler, a former Special Assistant to President Eisenhower for National Security Affairs. Cutler suggests that policy proposals must first flow "uphill" to the Council, and then back "downhill" to the agencies for action after a decision has been reached. The Planning Board controls the flow of proposals uphill. Composed of an official—usually an assistant secretary—from each agency represented on NSC, its function is to prepare proposals for Council consideration. Where do suggestions and ideas come from for consideration by the Council? Under

Eisenhower they have arisen from a wide variety of sources: from the necessity to reexamine policies carried over from the Truman Administration; from continuing review of policies already in existence; from progress reports submitted to NSC by its own staff and by other agencies; from external events which make changes in policy imperative; from proposals submitted by agencies active in the field of national security policy; and in some instances from the President himself (6, pp. 450-1).

After a decision has been reached, policy must then travel downhill to the agencies responsible for carrying it out. Investigations by the Hoover Commission in the early 1950's revealed that other executive agencies were not always complying fully with NSC's directives. Moreover, the Commission found that more frequent follow-up reports were needed to assure the continuance of sound policies. The Operations Coordinating Board was therefore established in 1953. OCB is composed of the Under Secretary of State as Chairman, the Deputy Secretary of Defense, the Director of the International Cooperation Administration, the Central Intelligence Agency, and the U. S. Information Service. Ad hoc representatives may be added to OCB from time to time, but they have no vote in its deliberations. It is significant that no provision was made for professional military representation on this board; there is no spokesman for the Joint Chiefs of Staff. Congress apparently believed that the military already had sufficient voice in the National Security Council; indeed on some issues NSC probably is topheavy with military representation (38, p. 34). OCB's principal function is "dovetailing the programs of the departments and agencies responsible for carrying out approved national policies." Like the National Security Council itself, OCB possesses no actual operating responsibilities. It is "a coördinator and an expediter and a follower-up and a progress reporter" (6, pp. 448-9).

The National Security Council has been utilized differently by Presidents Truman and Eisenhower. President Eisenhower has relied upon it for advice and guidance much more than his predecessor. Trained throughout his military career to utilize staff reports extensively, it was probably inevitable that Eisenhower would follow the same practice in civil affairs.[*] At the time of its establishment and in succeeding years, widespread apprehensions were voiced that the National Security Council might degenerate into an organ for promoting "compromise" within the government, rather than a body that would attack security problems forthrightly, thereby permitting an honest airing of often divergent opinions (20, p. 318). Defenders of the Eisenhower Administration, like Robert J. Cutler, contend that these fears have proved groundless. Evidently, Eisenhower has insisted upon full and frank debate within NSC; under his direction, in Cutler's opinion, that body has evolved into a "forum for vigorous discussion against a painstakingly prepared background and carefully studied papers." Conflicting opinions "which have developed at lower levels are not swept under the rug, but exposed" (6, p. 443). In spite of such assurances, by the beginning of the 1960's many observers had come to challenge's Cutler's assessment. As we shall see, such criticisms lay behind rising demands in Congress for a thorough evaluation of NSC's operations.

NSC in Action—A Case Study

The manner in which policy proposals affecting national security come to a focus in the National Security Council, and then go out from it to the operating departments and agencies of the government, can best be illustrated by a somewhat simplified case study.[**] Assume that the Department of State receives a report from one of the overseas diplomatic missions that a serious communist threat exists to the security of a given country. Copies of this report will also be sent to the Joint Chiefs of Staff and to ISA in the Defense Department. After considering the many implications of the threat,

[*]Cutler points out that under Eisenhower a fairly clear line of authority was established between NSC and the Cabinet. The former considers all questions directly related to security affairs; the latter all other questions upon which policy decisions must be made (6, p. 441).

[**]This case study is adapted from 38, pp. 58-61. For another interesting example involving American policy toward Trieste in 1949, consult 14, pp. 137-39.

the State Department then prepares a plan to counter it. The plan of course is first cleared within the Department, especially with the Policy Planning Staff. The Policy Planning Staff then transmits this plan to the National Security Council. Conceivably the plan might call for large-scale and prolonged American military, economic, and technical assistance to the country threatened. The Planning Board of NSC then sends the plan for further study as an NSC staff paper to the Defense Department and to all other government agencies affected.

Within the Defense Department, ISA will receive the staff paper and will circulate it throughout the Department for comments and recommendations. When these have been received, a Defense Department "position paper" will be drawn up on the proposal and this will be sent back to the Planning Board of NSC. The Defense Department's views will be sent to the Department of State and to other agencies for additional study.

Ultimately, after considerable study each departmental secretary will come to the Council meeting with his "position" clearly determined. The proposal in its original or modified form is placed on NSC's agenda, and when it comes up for discussion each member gives his opinion on it. Discussion ensues, and ultimately a "sense of the meeting" is taken. If the proposal is accepted, it is carefully put in final form and is submitted to the President for final approval. Only with his approval will it become national policy. If the proposal is rejected by a majority of the members, it may still come up again at a later date for further discussion. Or the problem may be studied more thoroughly to discover alternative courses of action for achieving the nation's objectives in foreign affairs. Conceivably, the President might still carry out any proposal that did not receive a majority vote in NSC, by executive order to the operating departments. The chances against this, however, are usually very great, since he would then be going against the views of his most trusted and best-informed advisers.

After the President approves the proposal, it is the responsibility of OCB to transmit the decision to the operating agencies. The members of OCB agree among themselves, presumably after consultation with their own departments, upon an allocation of functions among their respective agencies, so that the duties of, let us say, the State Department, the Defense Department, the U. S. Information Agency, and the International Cooperation Administration would be clearly defined toward any given problem. OCB's final operating plan will be distributed throughout the government. As time passes, it will be the responsibility of OCB to oversee the administration of the pro-gram adopted and to supply the Council with periodic progress reports on its operation.

.The entire process described above normally requires one to three weeks. In more urgent cases, such as the French defeat at Dienbienphu in Indochina in 1954, decisions may have to be made almost overnight. And occasionally, as in the Berlin Blockade of 1948, the President may even determine major national policies unilaterally.

3. CONTINUING PROBLEMS IN CIVIL-MILITARY RELATIONS

Establishment of the National Security Council and its subordinate agencies, together with changes made in national security organization since 1947, have done a great deal to supply needed co-ordination between political and military efforts. A number of significant problems, however, remain in this field.

Military Determination of Defense Requirements

The proper level of defense spending and the role of the military and civilian agencies in determining it remain unsettled. Since the Korean War especially, considerable controversy has raged within the government over two corollary problems: the *total* financial appropriation required to give the nation security in the nuclear age and the *proper allocation* of the total appropriation among the three military services. With respect to the first of these problems, the issue centers upon how this total shall be determined. One approach is for the Joint Chiefs of Staff, after thorough consultation with their respective military arms, to recommend to the Secretary of Defense, the National Security Council, and to the President, that a certain total sum is required for national defense. Theoretically, this would entail a purely *military* determination of what must be done to assure adequate defense. Upon receipt of their recommendations, the President and his advisers would prepare a federal budget that reflected the military estimates submitted.

Quite clearly, however, as Thomas K. Finletter, a former Secretary of the Air Force, has observed, no exclusively military determination of national defense requirements is ever possible. Any such determination of necessity makes certain assumptions about American foreign and domestic policies (9, pp. 261-2). Suppose that the President and the NSC have called for a military estimate from the Joint Chiefs in order to prepare the defense budget for fiscal year 1962. No estimate is possible without an evaluation by the Chiefs of the current foreign and domestic policies of the United States and without some kind of decision as to which of these policies should be retained, which modified, and which abandoned. How can military officials arrive at the required estimates without, for example, weighing such questions as the chances for a disarmament agreement between the non-communist and communist worlds; the danger of an outright communist attack or subversion in the NATO area, the Middle East, or other parts of the free world; an appraisal of the military strength of such small nations as Japan and Turkey compared to their security needs; and a determination of the extent to which the economic potential of the free world is sufficient to provide for prevailing security needs? Either the Chiefs must evaluate these and related issues or they must assume no significant change in the international situation and, accordingly, no change in existing American foreign policy commitments. Security and politico-economic questions are so closely enmeshed that it is well-nigh impossible to separate them. This means that the nation's military advisers cannot realistically make a purely *military* determination of defense requirements.

The second question to be decided in arriving at the total defense needs of the country is the proper allocation of funds among the military branches. It is commonplace knowledge that the military arms have a heavy prestige involvement in the amount of funds allocated to them; an evident spirit of competition prevails among them in dealing with appropriations. Against this background, it is not surprising that postwar experience has revealed a marked tendency on the part of the Joint Chiefs of Staff to decide upon mutually agreeable percentage distributions of available funds and to maintain these percentages with little significant variation from year to year. Not that national security is best served by such an approach, but it is the easiest way to preserve harmony and seeming unanimity within the military services. Since the "unification" of the armed forces in 1947, the nation's civilian superiors have expected military leaders to take unified positions. Sharp differences of opinion and "split papers" from the Joint Chiefs, says Finletter, "are not welcomed by their civilian superiors" (9, p. 249). The course of least resistance under these circumstances is for the Chiefs to execute a *de facto* "treaty" among themselves whereby defense funds are shared according to an agreed-upon formula. Unusual events, such as the obvious necessity for increased ground strength during the Korean War or congressional insistence upon increased air power, may modify this practice. But Finletter believes that in the absence of such pressures the military chieftains tend to gravitate to a position of allocating funds according to a fixed formula (9, p. 250).

Financial Considerations in Defense Policy

One method of arriving at a total budgetary figure for defense spending then is to request the Joint Chiefs to give a military estimate of the funds required. Though this method inevitably draws the Chiefs into the realm of foreign policy formulation, it will most likely be followed during times of war, when military considerations are uppermost in national planning. A second method, most prevalent in time of peace, is to reverse this process. Instead of the military advisers telling civilian policy-makers what ought to be spent for national defense, and then having the latter derive a budget from these estimates, an overall financial ceiling can be imposed upon the Department of Defense, just as on other departments. Then the Joint Chiefs will be ordered to do two things: 1) make a recommendation for the defense budget as a whole within this imposed ceiling; and 2) make an allocation for the three services within this total.

Under this system financial considerations become the key element in defense planning. The Chiefs are expected to stay within a budgetary limit; their military estimates therefore have to be drawn up within a framework imposed by their civilian superiors. In effect the President, after consultation with his economic advisers, says to the military: "This is what the nation can spend for defense activities. Draw up detailed plans making the most effective use possible of available funds."

Robert J. Donovan has described at length how this approach underlay the so-called "New Look" in national defense policy immediately after Eisenhower took office (7, pp. 51-64, 324-32). Because right-wing Republicans and Democrats and certain vocal segments of the general public pressed strongly for a reduction of taxes and the federal budget, the Eisenhower Administration came to rely increasingly upon air power alone for dealing with Soviet threats to the security of the free world. Air power thus became the mainstay for the doctrine of "massive retaliation" announced by Secretary of State Dulles on January 12, 1954, when he stated: "A potential aggressor must know that he cannot always prescribe battle conditions that suit him." Obviously referring to the recent Korean conflict, Dulles declared that the United States in the future would "depend upon a great capacity to retaliate, instantly, by means and at places of our choosing . . . " (7, p. 326).

In the months that followed, substantial cuts were made in American ground forces, and smaller reductions were made in naval forces. Air power, by contrast, was expanded. In spite of warnings by such individuals as Army Chief of Staff General Matthew B. Ridgway that the "New Look" seriously impaired the ability of the nation to deal with small "brush fire" type conflicts instigated by the Communists and with another possible Communist ground attack, as in South Korea, in the end financial considerations prevailed. "Again and again, during my tour as Chief of Staff," General Ridgway wrote later, "pressure was brought on me, in the name of economy, to keep the semblance, but not the reality, of a fighting force overseas" (30, p. 286). The defense budgets for 1955, 1956, and 1957 were based upon "directed verdicts" delivered to the military establishment. A financial ceiling was first decided upon by the President, after consultation with his economic advisers; then the Defense Department was ordered to prepare its budget within the prescribed financial limits. Finletter adds that the normal procedure in peacetime is that "high economic officials of the Government . . . step in and ask that a dollar limit be imposed on the Defense appropriations in advance of any final action by the Joint Chiefs of Staff or the National Security Council" (9, pp. 262-3). This practice, he believes, takes the determination of defense policy "largely out of the hands not only of the military experts but also out of the hands of the civilian head of the Department of Defense and . . . [gives] the economic experts in Government the right to make the most authoritative recommendations to the President on the subject" (9, p. 264).

Either method—permitting the Joint Chiefs to determine the defense *needs* first or permitting economic considerations to provide upper limits for defense spending—clearly has drawbacks. Under the first procedure the danger is that professional military men may have too great an influence on the broad field of security planning. Under the second procedure the danger is that they may have too little influence and that a desire for economy in the government may jeopardize national security. At the present time a satisfactory solution to the problem of achieving the desired balance remains to be found.

The Danger of Growing Military Influence

Other continuing problems have to do with the relationships between civil and military authorities under the American Constitution. The founding fathers were intensely suspicious

of military power.* They regarded it as one of the gravest threats to the survival of democratic government. Madison, for instance, believed that a standing army was "one of the greatest mischiefs that can possibly happen . . . " (17, p. 9). Accordingly, the founders placed many limits in the Constitution against military influence upon the government. The Constitution designates the highest civilian officer, the President, as the Commander in Chief of the military establishment. It provides that Congress shall raise and support the armed forces, make appropriations for their operation for periods no longer than two years,** and formulate rules and regulations for governing the conduct of the military branches. The Senate has the power to confirm the appointment of high-ranking military commanders. Two levels of military forces are envisioned under the Constitution: the national army, which the founders expected to be kept to a minimum level, and the state militia. The state militia is under the control of the States until it is called into the service of the United States. The founding fathers counted heavily on the local militias to provide safeguards against military usurpation. Important also was the provision in the Second Amendment assuring the citizenry the right to "bear arms." This was intended as an added obstacle to a possible military *coup*, although in practice the Second Amendment provision has virtually become a dead letter. Summarizing the various constitutional provisions, Elias Huzar has written that "Congress was to provide the sword which the President was to wield" (17, p. 21).

Throughout the greater part of American history, so long as the United States played a passive role in world affairs, no significant danger arose that the military would dominate the national government. Not once in the nation's history has there been any significant threat of a military *coup d'état*, even during

---

*Two valuable recent treatments of civilian-military relations within the United States are 15 and 19. Another helpful study, focusing more on constitutional questions, is 33.

**In practice, Congress makes military appropriations annually, although it does permit the defense establishment to "contract" for purchases and services extending over periods of more than one year.

time of war. Viewing the broad stream of American experience, Quincy Wright believes that the criticism to be made is not that there has been too much military influence in national councils but that, if anything, there has often tended to be too little (19, p. 126). This was undoubtedly true down to the Second World War.

Within recent years, however, disproportionate military influence on government policy has come to be recognized as a potential, if not sometimes an actual, danger. The great impact of the military on policy arises from the sheer size of national defense activities, as reflected in the federal budget; from the increasing complexity of modern technology as it bears upon military problems; from the fact that the overriding questions of the age almost always involve national security problems; and from the inability of civilian leaders to evaluate questions of military strategy and tactics competently. It is a widely accepted principle of public administration that the expert should "be on tap, and not on top." This is particularly urgent in the realm of civilian-military relations. Perhaps in no other field, with the possible exception of such scientific fields as nuclear energy, is it so difficult for public officials to form intelligent judgments (32, p. 283). Throughout the course of American history the nation's military leaders have, as a whole, been remarkably sensitive to constitutional limitations upon their role and have scrupulously stayed within their proper sphere. Granting this, how can non-military officials in the mid-20th century guard against the dangers often associated with the "military mind"?

What are some of the propensities of military leaders in their approach to national problems?* Traditionally, military leaders have been slow to abandon old ways and to see the potentialities in new inventions, though this attitude has been changing in the postwar period. They are as a rule supremely confident of the superiority of the military approach, characterized by such principles as unquestioning obedience, clearly delineated lines of authority, and extensive preliminary staff studies. As a matter

of course, military officials are prone to believe that the nation's defenses are inadequate, especially in peacetime. They often exhibit a super-patriotic and ultra-nationalistic attitude toward other countries. They are inclined to reduce diplomatic questions chiefly to questions of power and force and to gloss over political, economic, cultural and spiritual elements that enter into consideration of them. They are accustomed, particularly during wartime, to making decisions on the basis of immediate military expediency, neglecting to evaluate problems within the larger context of the nation's long-range diplomatic objectives (19, pp. 118-19; 34, p. 19).

Never before in American history has there existed such widespread realization that the military must play a part in national security planning. And never before has there existed a greater danger that, in playing this part, the military may predominate in formulating and executing national security policy. Burton M. Sapin and Richard P. Snyder, in their study of The Role of the Military in American Foreign Policy, suggest several possibilities for preserving the required civilian-military balance. First, vigorous and capable civilian leadership is needed, so that the military establishment does not gain the ascendancy by default. Second, there ought to be minimum use of military officials to "legitimate" policy: that is, to justify and defend civilian-made policy before congressional committees and public opinion generally. If professional military men are asked to defend policies, they often leave their field of competence and discuss non-military issues such as the proper level of federal spending and taxing or the economic resources of the country. While on such unfamiliar grounds, they frequently get caught in a crossfire of disagreement between Congress and the White House. When they give judgments on civilian questions, the military may become special pleaders. The impression may be created that their opinions have been formed by unalterable military considerations. In the long run, this practice could undermine the prestige of the military within the American government.

In the third place, the military officials must be constantly reminded of their important,

---

*For a more elaborate discussion of the characteristics of the military mind, see 1; 23; 26.

though *limited,* role in national policy-making, so that they have a heightened appreciation of their proper function under the Constitution. William T. R. Fox warns of the danger of "overco-ordination" within the government. Postwar awareness that civilian and military efforts must be successfully blended may encourage "kibitzing" on the part of the military leaders, on the theory that every important governmental question involves them to a degree, although they may have little competence in many corollary fields, such as financial policy, economic planning, and the day-by-day conduct of foreign affairs (10, p. 412). Fourth, Sapin and Snyder believe that military leaders must exercise greater discretion than they have sometimes shown in the past in making public statements, and especially statements taking issue with policies decided upon by their civilian superiors. The utterances of General Douglas MacArthur and General James Van Fleet attacking political decisions during the Korean War and of General Matthew B. Ridgway questioning the proper level of defense spending after the war are relevant examples (34, pp. 60-6).

Paul H. Appleby suggests another safeguard: unfaltering adherence to the principle of civilian superiority over the military, especially in time of war. He feels that the most important decision taken in this respect during World War II "was the decision to set up civilian war agencies." This principle may also be followed in two other important ways. First, civilian secretaries ought always to head the military departments. Second, an internal equilibrium should be preserved within the military establishment so that no one military branch becomes too powerful (19, pp. 72-3).

Concluding their study of the influence of the military within the American government, Sapin and Snyder urge that

. . . civilians must insist upon role clarification, self-restraint, and nonmilitary education on the part of the military. Even more important, civilians must decide precisely what meaningful civilian supremacy is . . . and must be prepared to check the expansion of the military functions beyond proper limits. If it is true that greater self-awareness and nonmilitary training are increasingly necessary for military leaders, it is equally true that civilians must be willing to exercise vigilance and to learn to evaluate military views. (34, pp. 76-7).

At a time when sound national policies demand a workable equilibrium between policy objectives and the means for reaching them, it is more crucial than ever that civilian and military leaders recognize their joint responsibilities and their mutual dedication to a common purpose. If military leaders need to be reminded constantly that their role is subordinate, it is also indispensable that civilian leaders, as General Ridgway has observed, must recognize the integrity of the military component. The civilian branch must permit the military to remain free from an arbitrary "party line" imposed from above, and to make impartial recommendations which reflect the military's best judgments on matters affecting the security of the United States (30, p. 270).

Unfinished Business in Defense Organization

In 1958, General James M. Gavin, former Army Chief of Research and Development, evaluated recent attempts to evolve an effective defense organization by saying:

Unity of purpose is fundamental to survival. However, purpose is one thing and accomplishment is another. . . . The divisive forces that bear upon decision-making in the Department of Defense are many: industrial interests, political pressures, professional competence or lack of it in committees, personal prejudices, and service interests. All work against unity of purpose. . . . Some of the most able and most intelligent Americans in public life have sought to bring order out of the decision-making maze of the Department of Defense, only to fail. It has been the organization that has defeated them. (11, pp. 257-58).

Echoing General Gavin's assessment, Robert A. Lovett, Secretary of Defense under Truman, wrote that the National Security Act of 1947 and its subsequent modifications possessed "the fault of all compromises . . . contradictions and straddles . . . " (27, January 5, 1958). And in 1957 the able *New York Times* reporter, James Reston, lampooned postwar attempts to achieve workable defense arrangements by saying that the Joint Chiefs of Staff were "The most expensive organization in America today, composed of three equally powerful officers who

HANDWRITING ON THE WALL!

W. J. McClanahan in *The Dallas Morning News*,
April, 1957.

preside over the military budget and govern a loose confederation of warring tribes." He characterized the role of the Chairman of the Joint Chiefs as one "who passes along the grievances and differences of 'the chiefs' to the Secretaries of the Army, Navy and Air Force, who in turn pass them to the Secretary of Defense, who sends them to the President, who returns them to the Pentagon for review" (27, November 10, 1957).

Such viewpoints call attention to the existence of considerable unfinished business in the Pentagon—a subject that received careful evaluation in two influential studies presented to the Eisenhower Administration in the late 1950's. One was the top-secret report submitted to the President by a study group headed by H. Rowan Gaither in 1957; the other was a report by the special studies project of the Rockefeller Brothers Fund early in 1958, which was very quickly released to the public

(31). Both of these studies re-enforced the viewpoints of critics of prevailing defense policy, whose admonitions became particularly intense after the launching of the first two Soviet earth satellites late in 1957. In the post-Sputnik period, public attention has centered, as never before in recent years, on the issue of national defense. The major conclusion of the Rockefeller Study—that "Unless present trends are reversed, the world balance of power will shift in favor of the Soviet bloc"—struck a responsive chord in many of the nation's leaders and interested public groups. Over the months that followed, executive, legislative, and private investigations into America's lagging missile and satellite programs attributed Russia's lead over the United States largely to costly inter-service rivalries and delays, on-again and off-again missile projects, bitter wrangles among high-ranking military spokesmen over "service jurisdictions" in developing and using missiles available for the armed forces, and an evident desire on the part of each service to reap maximum publicity value from technological developments. By 1958, these and other critical problems induced President Eisenhower to place further defense reorganization high on the list of urgently needed legislation and to make this subject the occasion for a special message to Congress.

The need for genuine unity in setting up and operating "unified commands" had become particularly pressing. Such commands were being utilized widely in the United States and abroad to carry out missions cutting across traditional service lines. The North American Air Defense Command, for example, used radar warning systems, ships and naval air power, and army aircraft and anti-aircraft installations, including short-range missiles, together with communications and supply components from all the services, to discharge its assigned mission. Considerable difficulty has been encountered at times in welding "unified commands" into smoothly functioning, fully coordinated teams. Designated commanders on occasion have found that they did not actually have authority over military contingents assigned from other branches of the service and that inter-service rivalries interfered with the command's effective operation. This situation was partially, though by no means wholly, corrected by a White House order in 1958 setting up a new "chain of command" extending from the President, to the Secretary of Defense, *directly to the commander of unified forces in the field.* This eliminates the separate civilian service secretaries, and the service representatives on the Joint Chiefs of Staff, as links in the new chain of command.

President Eisenhower's recommendations in 1958 also tried to remedy another acute problem in defense organization: the mushrooming of a top-heavy bureaucracy in the Pentagon, particularly in the Office of Secretary of Defense. The formidable bureaucratic labyrinth prevailing there was viewed as costly, as productive of prolonged delays in making vital decisions, and as clogging military channels of communication. Critics pointed to the contrast between the administrative structure currently existing and that which guided the nation to victory in World War II. With twelve million Americans in uniform in World War II, victory was achieved with a high-level bureaucracy consisting of a total of *eight* civilian officials in the War and Navy departments who held the rank of secretary, under secretary, or assistant secretary. In 1958, the United States had less than three million men under arms; at the Pentagon there were *thirty* civilians with the rank or equivalent rank of secretary, under secretary, or assistant secretary (27, March 2, 1958, Dispatch by Hanson W. Baldwin). And it was debatable by the end of the 1950's whether the nation was holding its own in military-security affairs in the face of a dynamic Soviet missile program.

This problem bears an intimate relationship to the nation's overall diplomatic position and, more specifically, to American military strength *vis-à-vis* the Soviet Union. Informed students of military affairs were apprehensive over the

GOOD LUCK!

Crockett in *The Washington Star*, December, 1957.

delay encountered in making decisions in the field of defense policy, a delay which they attributed partly to inertia inherent in the Defense Department's sprawling bureaucracy and partly to the extended periods of time required even under ideal conditions for making the transition from the drawing board to actual production of weapons. Thus nearly nine years were required from the time the Defense Department decided to approve production of the inter-continental Atlas missile until the weapon became operational. Six years elapsed between these same intervals for the Titan missile and nearly five years for the submarine-fired Polaris (27, August 2, 1959). The "lead-time" required for the United States to produce new weapons appeared to be expanding, in contrast to the time required by the USSR to produce comparable weapons. Thus on April 13, 1958, H. Rowan Gaither, a member of President Eisenhower's Science Advisory Committee and acknowledged authority on military technology, stated that "The relative strength of the United States in comparison with the Soviet Union and Red China is ebbing" (11, p. 13). This conclusion grew out of Mr. Gaither's assessment of two tendencies: the nation's enemies were gaining in military strength more rapidly than America and, at the very time when the United States was in danger of being outpaced by its enemies, it was assuming new commitments in foreign affairs— like SEATO, the "Eisenhower Doctrine" and bilateral commitments made to Asian countries —which further strained its already overtaxed military capacities.

When the lethargy encountered in making decisions in the Pentagon was added to the already extended period of time required to produce highly intricate weapons, distressingly long periods were needed to produce military hardware required to redress the military balance of power.* One student of military technology, Dr. Ellis A. Johnson, has observed: "During World War II our lead times were about 2½ years. Now the Russian lead time is five years. *Our lead time is ten years.*" And a study issued by the Stanford Research Institute concluded that "The central problem in the survival of the United States today *is the lead time race* with the Soviet Union for weapons superiority" (11, p. 240, italics inserted). Many military authorities predicted that the "missile lag" would not be appreciably overcome until 1963 or later, when the United States had perfected the solid-fuel Minuteman missile and the submarine-launched Polaris and, on the basis of experience gained, had discovered ways of producing missiles more rapidly. Even then there was no guarantee that Soviet technology would not preserve at least some of the gains which the Kremlin's intensified efforts to produce superior missiles had given it.

Basing his recommendations upon the findings of the Gaither and Rockefeller studies, President Eisenhower asked Congress in 1958 for significant modifications in the laws governing national defense. To increase the authority of the Secretary of Defense over the military services, the President requested that funds for the Defense Department be allocated to the Secretary of Defense, thereby giving that official broad discretionary power to grant funds to the individual service arms. This radical departure from existing practice found very little support on Capitol Hill. Legislators feared that this step would undermine Congress' constitutional prerogative to provide for and maintain the armed forces and that it would facilitate the emergence of a "defense czar" on the American scene. Even though the President modified many of his original recommendations

---

*For detailed accounts of how missile-satellite programs were delayed by a combination of inter-service rivalries, administrative delays, and other delays inherent in producing weapons of great complexity, consult 11, pp. 1-20, 135-57, 265-75.

While General Gavin makes no effort to disguise inter-service conflicts, especially those hindering programs desired by the Army, he properly cautions against a popular tendency to overemphasize the role of such conflicts in explaining deficiencies in

defense efforts. He points out that often powerful business groups have a deep vested interest in perpetuating such rivalries and in preventing the adoption of new weapons: "The amount of money that is spent on nation-wide advertising, by industry, for hardware that is obsolete is sizable, and the pressure that industry can place through lobbies in terms of employment, payrolls and effect upon constituents is impressive in Congress." He states that industries "will insist that . . . products be used long after they become obsolete." Consequently, in his opinion much seeming inter-service rivalry is in fact "fundamentally industrial rivalry" (11, pp. 255-57).

to take account of such criticisms, the House of Representatives was willing to accept very few of his proposals. Instead, it followed the leadership of influential legislators like Armed Services Committee Chairman Carl Vinson (Democrat of Georgia), by introducing changes which did little to alter the existing defense organization. The Senate, customarily more amenable to executive leadership in matters affecting the armed forces and functioning traditionally as a kind of court of review over House actions in this sphere, salvaged some of the President's proposals. The legislation that was finally enacted granted the Secretary of Defense somewhat greater authority over the separate military departments than he had previously possessed. It required, however, that any contemplated changes altering significantly the combat functions of the individual services be reported to Congress; an adverse vote in either the House or the Senate would prevent such changes. In addition, Congress by law preserved the right of any member of the Joint Chiefs of Staff or the civilian service secretaries to bring disputes over military organization or policy directly to Congress—a provision that President Eisenhower labelled "legalized insubordination." Now, as in earlier periods, Congress was clinging doggedly to its broad constitutional powers over military affairs, even if the exercise of such powers afforded a standing invitation for perpetuation of cliques and invited military and civilian officials to carry their grievances to Capitol Hill. In brief, Congress was no more prepared in 1958 than in 1947 to make radical changes in defense organization.

Events in the nuclear-missile age have made one fact abundantly clear: in many respects traditional organizational patterns and policies are about as useful in promoting national security as reliance upon the muzzle-loading cannon, sabre-wielding cavalry, or square-rigged schooners. Far-reaching changes in older forms and practices are essential. Said President

Eisenhower in 1958: "The first need is to assure ourselves that military organization facilitates rather than hinders the functioning of the military establishment. . . . Some of the important new weapons which technology has produced do not fit into any existing service patterns. They cut across all services, involve all services and transcend all services at every stage from development to operation" (**27**, April 13, 1958). Progressively, accelerating military technology and changes in strategy and tactics dictated by technological developments are bursting the seams of old defense garments. It is probable that the limit has been reached of putting new patches on these garments from time to time; additional attempts to "patch" may well impose intolerable strains.

Totally new concepts in warfare are emerging and in time these are bound to affect defense organization and policies. More and more, competent authorities are questioning the value of the traditional division of military forces into "ground, sea, and air" components. Missiles, for example, can be fired equally well from the air, the ground, the sea, and under the sea; they can be used for strategic bombing, tactical support on the battlefield, or defense. Similarly, the maintenance and protection of overseas bases calls for intimate co-operation among the three service arms. Organization of the military establishment along *functional* lines— e.g. logistics, communications, strategic attack forces, tactical forces, defense—appears to be the pattern of the future. If this pattern prevails, it will require a radical overhaul of national defense machinery.*

*A valuable background study of President Eisenhower's recommendations in 1958, and of Congress' treatment of them, relied upon heavily in this section is 4, volume 14, 1958, pp. 133-39. This account summarizes changes made in national defense organization since 1947 and contains opinions by influential legislators on the subject of defense organization. Students desiring to look more deeply into the subject will find this a useful guide to hearings, important speeches, and votes contained in reports of committee hearings and in the *Congressional Record.*

4. OTHER EXECUTIVE AGENCIES AND FOREIGN AFFAIRS

Our discussion thus far of the roles of the President, the State Department, and the

military establishment has revealed that co-ordination of the activities of governmental agencies is a central problem in formulating and executing an effective American foreign policy. The problem exists on three levels. First, the efforts of the President, the State Department, and the military services—the agencies most *directly* concerned with foreign policy—must be merged to assure sound policies at the top. Then other executive agencies must be included whose activities in foreign affairs may normally be tangential, but whose role may be highly important in selected phases of American foreign relations. Third, to unite all governmental efforts still further, executive activities must be co-ordinated with those of Congress. The remainder of this chapter is concerned with the second of these problems. The two chapters that follow will discuss the role of Congress and the problem of executive-legislative relations.

The unprecedented postwar growth in socio-economic-cultural aspects of foreign relations is reflected in the great increase in subordinate agencies within the State Department concerned with these phases of foreign policy. It is reflected also in the mushrooming in the number of other governmental agencies whose activities touch these fields. In 1950, there were nineteen executive agencies, including the President and State Department, involved directly with certain aspects of American foreign policy. If anything, this number has grown rather than diminished since the Korean War and since the inauguration of extensive foreign assistance programs following the war. Without attempting to discuss each of these agencies, let us endeavor to get some conception of their collective activities and to understand the methods by which at least minimal co-ordination within the executive branch may be achieved.*

The Cabinet

Before the establishment of the National Security Council in 1947 the Cabinet was the chief mechanism for providing high-level executive co-ordination of governmental policies. Since 1947, however, the role of the Cabinet in the foreign policy sphere has been heavily eclipsed by that of the National Security

Council. President Eisenhower particularly has tended to confine Cabinet discussions chiefly to considerations of domestic policy (6, p. 441).

While the Cabinet has been the principal advisory body to the President throughout the greater part of American history, its role has varied considerably under different Presidents. Forceful executives have often by-passed the Cabinet and even the State Department altogether. To achieve their foreign policy objectives, they have worked directly with diplomatic missions or agents abroad, with high-ranking military advisers, or through personal representatives. It must not be forgotten that the Cabinet, like the National Security Council, is an *advisory* body only. Final decisions must always be made by the President. How influential the Cabinet's views will be therefore depends upon a variety of factors: the competence of its members, the kinds and urgency of prevailing foreign policy problems, the willingness of its members to become well informed on complex issues, and the inclinations and viewpoints of the President himself. Under Eisenhower the Cabinet has profited immensely by sound organizational changes developed initially by the National Security Council, where the emphasis is upon full background preparation, members doing their "homework" before meetings, and relevant and frank discussion. In contrast to earlier periods when Cabinet discussions were often rambling and superficial, the Cabinet today operates in much the same way as NSC, thereby avoiding many of the pitfalls that have detracted from its usefulness in the past (6, pp. 446-47).

It is too early to predict that these innovations under Eisenhower have established a precedent binding upon future occupants of the White House. Eisenhower has elevated NSC, the Cabinet, and other staff agencies to a level of importance in both foreign and domestic affairs they seldom, if ever, achieved previously. FDR and Truman, on the other hand, tended to utilize the Cabinet for somewhat different purposes. Instead of regarding it as a body for making high-level collective judgments on paramount issues, they tended to view it as a mechanism for expressing divergent opinions within the government, for permitting the chief executive to gauge possible

---

*For more extended treatment of this problem, see 20, pp. 11-16.

public reaction to prevailing and anticipated policy, and for sensing the domestic political implications of current and future developments. One persistent barrier to more effective utilization of the Cabinet as a co-ordinating body is its notoriously poor record in preserving the confidential character of important information. Roosevelt and Truman apparently operated upon the assumption that information divulged in Cabinet meetings would sooner or later be "leaked" to the press or to Congress (22, pp. 41-4).

Economic Agencies and Foreign Affairs

In the economic field, there has been a tremendous proliferation of agencies whose activities impinge upon foreign affairs. This growth can be attributed chiefly to two factors: the vastly expanded activities of the national government in the economic realm generally since the New Deal, and the ever-growing attention devoted to economic aspects of international affairs since the Second World War. It is no exaggeration to say that today the operations of almost every executive agency have some major economic consequences. And the activities of a great many of these agencies bear directly upon foreign affairs.

The Treasury Department, for example, has obvious interests in this field. It must assure a sound national fiscal policy and must determine the level of governmental taxing and spending consonant with a healthy economic system. The Treasury Department, "has a strong influence on the proportion of the country's wealth to be devoted to national security, and this in turn tends to predetermine the ceilings under which foreign and military policies must operate" (38, p. 24). The department's well-known activities in suppressing traffic in illegal drugs and narcotics require it to work closely with the UN and other countries.

The Council of Economic Advisers serves as a staff organ to the President on overall economic policy and trends. In particular, it prepares his Economic Report, submitted to Congress early each year. CEA has no operating responsibilities. Moreover, its exact role within the government—notably its relation to other agencies engaged in economic activities—has never been precisely defined. Conflict between it and other agencies consequently has erupted at intervals in the postwar period. A good illustration is the 1949-50 period, when the Chairman of CEA, Edwin Nourse, indicated publicly his opposition to continued high taxes and expressed his belief that substantial reductions in spending by the national government —especially for defense purposes—were mandatory to assure a sound economy at home. In this instance Nourse was apparently also speaking for influential officials in the Treasury, Commerce, and Defense Departments. The President, supported by the Department of State, opposed any reduction in the defense effort or in America's overseas commitments. This impasse ultimately resulted in Nourse's resignation from the government (14, pp. 99-100).

Long-range planning for civilian and industrial mobilization was an outgrowth of World War II, when events, specifically the attack on Pearl Harbor, brought home forcefully how inadequate earlier hit-or-miss efforts had been in this area. Since then, there has been a bewildering succession of alphabetical agencies to deal with the problem.* The most recent one, the Office of Defense Mobilization, is an outgrowth of several earlier agencies. Its immediate predecessor was the National Security Resources Board, established by the National Security Act of 1947. ODM was created by executive order after President Truman declared a national emergency during the Korean war. In 1953 President Eisenhower merged NSRB and ODM to form a single organ with responsibilities for planning future manpower and industrial mobilization to assure maximum security. ODM prepares studies and estimates in such areas as civilian and military manpower, raw materials, industrial and agricultural production, economic stabilization, and telecommunications. It frequently works in concert with other federal agencies whose interests are similar. The Armed Forces Reserve Act of 1955, for example, grew out of collaboration between ODM and several other agencies which attempted to make the best possible use

---

*For an extended discussion of wartime and immediate postwar governmental efforts in this field, see 14, Chapters 3 and 7.

of civilian manpower to serve defense needs (38, p. 23).

The most influential agency concerned with economic affairs within the executive branch is the Bureau of the Budget, part of the Executive Office of the President. The Bureau of the Budget is the focal point of co-ordination for all budgetary matters within the executive branch and for drawing up a unified budget for presentation to Congress. It therefore has a key role in working with executive agencies to prepare their budgetary estimates. All budgetary requests by these agencies receive a thorough preliminary screening by Bureau officials before they are transmitted to Congress. Congress has come to rely heavily upon this screening to eliminate unnecessary governmental costs. Because the House and Senate Appropriations Committees generally heed the Bureau's advice on matters affecting national defense spending (16, p. 71), the Bureau often exercises a crucial voice in deciding the financial limits within which foreign, and related domestic, policies are formulated and carried out.

A number of independent regulatory commissions also have duties touching the sphere of foreign relations. The Tariff Commission is concerned with tariffs and reciprocal trade. Its recommendations to the President are often decisive in determining tariff rates; these rates have at times become sources of considerable international controversy. The Federal Aviation Agency controls air transportation within the United States and between it and foreign countries. The Maritime Commission supervises the American merchant marine fleet. Charged with overseeing all aspects of the development of nuclear power for military and civilian purposes, the Atomic Energy Commission has come to play a key role in the relations between the United States and other countries. The two largest deposits of uranium ore available to the free world are located in Canada and the Belgian Congo. AEC has also been actively concerned with such foreign policy issues as disarmament negotiations between the West and Russia, UN proposals for peacetime use and control of nuclear power, and analysis of radioactive "fallout" from the testing of nuclear weapons. In the contemporary period, after the

Soviet Union launched its first successful earth satellite in October, 1957, the Commission participated in Anglo-American efforts to increase the exchange of scientific information among the Allies in order to offset at least partially recent technological and scientific gains by the USSR (27, October 27, 1957).

The Commerce Department also has an important stake in foreign policy decisions. Established to promote business enterprise at home and abroad, it is concerned with any governmental policy that affects business conditions. This means that it is keenly interested in such questions as the level of defense spending, taxation, foreign aid, technical assistance to other countries, foreign investment, tariffs, the stability of foreign currencies, the merchant marine, and a host of other foreign and domestic problems. Similarly, the Department of Agriculture has come to have an important role in foreign relations. Its interests range all the way from trade agreements involving American agriculture to providing experts for technical assistance in the agricultural field to other countries, to disposing of American agricultural surpluses abroad.

Agencies Concerned with Foreign Assistance

Since the inauguration of the Greek-Turkish Aid Program in 1947 and the Marshall Plan in 1948, the provision of economic, military and technical assistance to other countries has been a consistent feature of American foreign policy. A great deal of organizational change within the national government has attended the administration of these programs. Providing liaison between the State Department and the agencies that have operating responsibilities for various aspects of foreign aid has been a recurrent problem.

Although foreign aid did not become a permanent feature of American foreign policy before 1947, a number of ad hoc and emergency programs existed before that date. Thus during the Second World War lend-lease was administered by the Lend-Lease Administration; other types of American assistance to the Allies were administered by the Foreign Economic Administration. At the end of the war these agencies went out of existence, and their functions were transferred helter-skelter to the State Department, the Commerce Department, the Agriculture Department, and the Reconstruction Finance Corporation (**38**, pp. 40-1).

With the inauguration of the Marshall Plan in 1948, Congress wanted to give operating responsibility for economic aid to Europe to a new agency, while leaving the State Department to determine the overall principles to be followed in administering such aid. Accordingly, the Economic Cooperation Administration was established. It was headed by an outstanding American businessman, Paul Hoffman, because Congress believed that sound business principles ought to govern the extension of aid to other countries, although legislators have recognized the necessity to gear this aid closely to the total pattern of American foreign policy (**39**, pp. 373-98).

After the Korean War—when economic and military assistance were combined under one program—ECA was superseded by the Mutual Security Agency, created in 1951. MSA existed until 1953, when it was replaced by the Foreign Operations Administration. FOA in turn was abolished in 1955, when an executive order divided its functions between the Department of Defense, for *military* assistance to foreign countries, and the International Cooperation Administration, for *economic-technical* assistance. ICA possesses a "semi-autonomous" role in the State Department. It administers economic and technical assistance within policy guidelines established by the State Department, and ultimately by the President (**38**, pp. 40-1). Since ICA has important operating responsibilities in foreign affairs, its Director is a member of the Operations Coordinating Board of the National Security Council.

Agencies Concerned with Informational Activities

We shall treat propaganda and ideological warfare as problems in American foreign policy in Chapter 14. At this point, however, we will refer briefly to the prevailing administrative pattern for conducting informational aspects of foreign relations. As with foreign assistance, this pattern has been rather complex over the past several years. During World War II, the Office of War Information was in charge of directing American propaganda at the Axis Powers. OWI was abolished at the end of the war, and many of its activities were transferred to the State Department. Then, under the necessity to counteract worldwide communist propaganda, the Voice of America was created within the State Department in 1948. From its inception, VOA has had a checkered existence. Congressional investigative committees often made it a prime target for ferreting out supposed communist influence within the government. Because of congressional antagonism, VOA's activities were heavily curtailed in the 1949-52 period and its prestige throughout the world seriously impaired.

In 1951 President Truman created the Psychological Strategy Board and made it directly responsible to the National Security Council. PSB was to determine the psychological objectives of American foreign policy and to co-ordinate and evaluate the work of psychological warfare agencies (**14**, p. 151). PSB was therefore like a general staff in the field of propaganda planning and execution. Yet ultimately widespread confusion developed over duplicating efforts in this field, prompting President Eisenhower on June 1, 1953 to ask Congress to approve a major re-organization. Congress accordingly abolished PSB and established the United States Information Agency and gave it responsibility for conducting all overseas information services (**14**, p. 152). Its Director supervises the administration of overseas information programs. He receives guidance in high-level policy from the Secretary of State. The Director is also a member of NSC's Operations Coordinating Board, although not of NSC itself.

Agencies Engaged in Intelligence Activities

A noteworthy innovation introduced by the National Security Act of 1947 was the establishment of the Central Intelligence Agency as a separate organ accountable to the National Security Council. CIA grew out of a widely prevailing conviction that American intelligence activities were inadequate for successful diplomacy in the cold war and out of an earlier awareness that more effective high-level co-ordination in the intelligence field was indispensable for sound policy determination. Pearl Harbor was still vividly remembered as the price that might be paid for inadequate and poorly co-ordinated intelligence operations within the government. CIA's duty is to "plan, develop, and co-ordinate all Federal foreign intelligence activity" (20, p. 289). It is the principal advisory body to NSC on intelligence matters. Although by law he is not a member of NSC, the Director of CIA is regularly invited by the President to attend its meetings.

Intelligence activities may be grouped broadly into two categories: the collection and evaluation of information required to formulate national policies, and covert operations involving such cloak-and-dagger functions as espionage, sabotage, arranging for refugees to escape from other countries, the breaking of foreign codes, and related activities. According to a former naval intelligence officer, the task of the intelligence expert in overall terms is to "winnow the extraneous data from the vital facts and to set these facts in proper perspective, thereby providing the factual basis for high-level policy decisions . . . " (13, p. 3). By this definition, virtually every agency within the government—from the State Department and Foreign Service, to the military branches, the F. B. I., the regular executive departments such as Treasury and Commerce, independent agencies like the Atomic Energy Commission, along with numerous congressional committees —routinely carry on intelligence operations, many of which impinge upon foreign affairs. Most information gathered by intelligence agencies, it must be emphasized, comes from "open sources": data gleaned from painstaking analyses of foreign newspapers, periodicals, technical-scientific journals, interviews, maps, statistical tables, scholarly studies, and the like. Probably less than 5 per cent of all information utilized by intelligence groups comes from reports submitted by secret agents (20, p. 282).

In addition to its information-gathering function, CIA also undertakes covert activities at home and abroad, such as espionage or any other steps demanded by national security. Understandably, information about CIA's covert operations is extremely difficult to come by, and often the most that can be done is to make an intelligent guess about its role in any given situation. It seems reasonable to believe, for example, that CIA was quite active in preventing a communist *coup* in Guatemala in 1954 and in speeding the evacuation of the remnants of Chiang Kai-shek's armies from northern Burma in 1952.[*] Citizens, including competent students of government, possess few methods for knowing what kind of job CIA is actually doing. It is one of the few governmental agencies that does not defend itself publicly from criticism or, more generally, provide documentary materials on its activities. Quite obviously, if it did endeavor to defend its record publicly, it would risk losing many valuable sources of information and might impair its own future effectiveness. Not even Congress is given information about its internal and external activities, since the annual appropriation for CIA is disguised within the budgets of several executive agencies.[**]

Inter-Departmental Committees and Agencies

While the National Security Council is the highest governmental agency concerned with unifying policies in the broad field of national security, there are a number of lower-level committees and agencies which also attempt co-ordination of selected aspects of American foreign policy. The Hoover Commission in 1948 found that, in addition to NSC, there were thirty-two inter-agency committees in the field of foreign affairs. About half of these had been created by agreement among executive departments and agencies in order to facilitate liaison among them. The remainder were created by departmental and presidential directives, informal agreements, and orders from the National Security Council (20, p. 145). Over half of these committees were concerned with economic affairs; two with the administration of the Foreign Service; five with national security and military affairs; three with social and cultural policy; and five with transportation

---

[*]Interesting, though sometimes highly speculative, treatments of CIA activities in the postwar period appear in 12 and 29. For more general accounts of intelligence operations, see 13 and 18.

[**]A select group of Congressmen each year is told the size and general nature of CIA's budget.

and communication. It is highly significant that "none existed specifically for the consideration of political foreign relations, which governed all other relations" (20, p. 146). These committees in 1948 were further subdivided into sixty-six standing subcommittees and sixty-four temporary working groups—for a total of one hundred and thirty subsidiary inter-agency committees involved in some phase of American foreign relations (20, p. 146)!

We can of course do little more in limited space than call attention to some of the more important inter-agency committees that have existed in recent years and to suggest the scope of their activities. In his study, *The Administration of American Foreign Affairs*, James L. McCamy refers to a number of such committees: the National Advisory Council on International Monetary and Financial Problems deals with American loans to other countries and participation in the International Bank and the International Monetary Fund. The executive Committee on Economic Foreign Policy considers selected phases of American foreign economic assistance. The Trade Agreements Committee works on draft trade agreements between the United States and other countries. The Committee on International Social Policy deals with problems in the fields of international labor relations, social welfare, health, and human rights. The Air Coordinating Committee concentrates on problems of domestic and international air transportation.*

Inter-Governmental Co-ordination—the Continuing Challenge

Throughout this chapter attention has been called to the importance of co-ordination in the work of numerous governmental agencies to assure successful American foreign policy. The sheer complexity of executive organization for the conduct of foreign affairs well-nigh defies comprehension. Moreover, because international developments are the overriding questions of the contemporary age, the always tenuous distinction between "international" and "domestic" policy questions has all but disappeared. Can anyone deny the significant domestic implica-

tions of the fact that well over half of the national budget is spent for defense? Conversely, can there be any realistic hope for a substantial reduction in taxes as long as the cold war keeps the international community in a state of continuing tension? Can the average citizen ignore the prospect that teen-agers must continue to enter the armed forces, that defense production levels affect economic stability, and that at any time the great industrial-urban centers of the nation may be subjected to lightening attack by long-range missiles carrying nuclear warheads? The informed student of American foreign policy has every reason to expect that domestic and foreign policy issues will become even more intermingled with the passage of time. Consequently, he can also expect the problem of assuring effective co-ordination among an expanding circle of agencies to become more, instead of less, difficult in the future.

By the opening of the 1960's, the nation's executive and legislative officials were clearly aware of the necessity for greater co-ordination and were undertaking studies to make it more effective. In the latter part of 1959, for example, a sub-committee of the Senate Committee on Government Operations had embarked upon an extensive examination of the operation of the National Security Council. The chief proponent of such a study, Senator Henry M. Jackson (Democrat of Washington) contended that NSC was not functioning properly. He criticized it specifically for its slowness in arriving at decisions and for its alleged tendency to arrive at compromise positions to avert open disharmony among powerful agencies, rather than agreeing upon clearcut and forceful statements of national policy. Press reports indicated that even President Eisenhower was dissatisfied with some features of NSC's operation and with other steps taken in the recent past to achieve co-ordinated policy. He indicated his support for a congressional investigation, provided it steered clear of domestic politics and conscientiously sought to propose needed improvements (27, August 2, 1959, Dispatch by Russell Baker). Detailed legislative proposals were not likely to be forthcoming from the committee, however, until the early 1960's.

---

*For a fuller discussion of the composition and functioning of inter-agency committees, see 20, pp. 146-50.

There is of course no tailor-made solution to the problem of providing the unity necessary in American foreign relations. Numerous expedients have been resorted to in recent years. According to Arthur W. Macmahon, these involve essentially four methods: 1) agencies to promote *formal*, continuous liaison among interested departments, as exemplified by the National Security Council; 2) *person-to-person contacts* among key officials concerned with selected problems; 3) *group meetings*, as typified by inter-agency conferences and committees; and 4) *informal liaison techniques,* as when State Department dispatches are routed to the Defense Department, the U. S. Information Agency, the CIA, and other agencies (**22**, p. 169). Experience has abundantly shown that no one of these techniques alone is adequate to impart the liaison required. On the other hand, a multiplicity of co-ordinating agencies might eventually mean the necessity for an agency to co-ordinate the co-ordination! Undoubtedly some progress has been made in the immediate past, especially since the National Security Act of 1947, to solve some aspects of this problem. That much more remains to be done, however, can hardly be doubted.

On top of the problem of unifying efforts *within* the executive branch, there must be added the problem of concerting executive-legislative relations in behalf of successful governmental policies. The next chapter is devoted to a discussion of the role of Congress in American foreign affairs, and the chapter following to a discussion of executive-legislative relations as they bear upon foreign relations.

REFERENCES

1. Baldwin, Hanson W. "The Military Move In," *Harpers*, 195 (December, 1947), 481-89.

2. Bradley, General Omar N. *A Soldier's Story*. New York: Henry Holt, 1951.

3. Cline, Ray S., and Matloff, Maurice. "Development of War Department Views on Unification," *Military Affairs*, 13 (Summer, 1949), 65-75. Traces emergence of the unification idea.

4. *Congressional Quarterly Almanac.*

5. Council on Foreign Relations. *The United States in World Affairs, 1931,* et seq. New York: Harper and Brothers, 1932.

6. Cutler, Robert. "The Development of the National Security Council," *Foreign Affairs*, 34 (April, 1956), 441-58. An illuminating evaluation of NSC.

7. Donovan, Robert J. *Eisenhower: The Inside Story*. New York: Harper and Brothers, 1956. A journalistic account, based on confidential sources.

8. Eisenhower, Dwight D. *Crusade in Europe*. Garden City, N. Y.: Doubleday and Company, 1948.

9. Finletter, Thomas K. *Power and Policy*. New York: Harcourt, Brace and Company, 1954. A penetrating criticism of recent developments in defense planning.

10. Fox, William T. R. "Civilians, Soldiers, and American Military Policy," *World Politics,* 7 (April, 1955), 402-18.

11. Gavin, James M. *War and Peace in the Space Age*. New York: Harper and Brothers, 1958. An illuminating treatment of defense organization and policies by an experienced military commander, especially valuable for suggesting emergent patterns in this sphere.

12. Harkness, Richard and Gladys. "The Mysterious Doings of CIA," *Saturday Evening Post,* 227 (October 30, November 6, and 13, 1954), pp. 19-24, 34-35, 30-32, respectively.

13. Hilsman, Roger. "Intelligence and Policy-Making in Foreign Affairs," *World Politics*, 5 (October, 1952), 1-45. A detailed treatment of intelligence problems.

14. Hobbs, Edward H. *Behind the President*. Washington, D.C.: Public Affairs Press, 1954. Discusses in detail roles and changes within executive agencies in the postwar period.

15. Huntington, Samuel P. *The Soldier and the State*. Cambridge: Harvard University Press, 1957. A perceptive analysis of civilian-military relations within the U. S.

16. Huzar, Elias. "Reorganization for National Security," *Journal of Politics*, 12 (February, 1950), 128-52. Analyzes the National Security Act of 1947 and later modifications.

17. ———. *The Purse and the Sword*. Ithaca: Cornell University Press, 1950. Examines congressional control over the military through appropriations.

18. Kent, Sherman. *Strategic Intelligence for American World Policy*. Princeton, N. J.: Princeton University Press, 1949.

19. Kerwin, Jerome G., ed. *Civil-Military Relationships in American Life*. Chicago: University of Chicago Press, 1948. A helpful symposium.

20. McCamy, James L. *The Administration of American Foreign Affairs*. New York: Alfred A. Knopf, 1950.

21. ———. "The Administration of Foreign Affairs in the United States," *World Politics*, 7 (January, 1955), 315-25.

22. MacMahon, Arthur W. *Administration and Foreign Affairs*. University, Ala.: University of Alabama Press, 1953. An incisive treatment of problems encountered in co-ordinating foreign policy activities.

23. Marquand, John P. "Inquiry Into the Military Mind," *New York Times Magazine*, March 30, 1952, p. 53 ff.

24. ———. "The U. S. Military Mind," *Fortune*, 45 (February, 1952), 91 ff.

25. May, Ernest R. "The Development of Political-Military Consultation in the United States," *Political Science Quarterly*, 70 (June, 1955), 161-81. Valuable study of co-ordinating civilian and military efforts.

26. Middleton, Drew. "The Enigma Called the 'Military Mind'," *New York Times Magazine*, April 18, 1948, p. 13 ff.

27. *New York Times*.

28. Puleston, Captain W. D. *The Influence of Sea Power in World War II*. New Haven: Yale University Press, 1947.

29. Ransom, Harry. *Central Intelligence and National Security*. Cambridge, Mass.: Harvard University Press, 1958.

30. Ridgway, General Matthew B. *Soldier: The Memoirs of Matthew B. Ridgway*. New York: Harper and Brothers, 1956.

31. Rockefeller Brothers Fund. *International Security—The Military Aspect*. New York: Doubleday and Company, 1958. Analyzes major problems in American defense policy.

32. Rogers, Lindsay. "Civilian Control of Military Policy," *Foreign Affairs*, 18 (January, 1940), 280-91.

33. Rossiter, Clinton. *The Supreme Court and the Commander in Chief*. Ithaca: Cornell University Press, 1951.

34. Sapin, Burton M., and Snyder, Richard C. *The Role of the Military in American Foreign Policy*. Garden City, N. Y.: Doubleday and Company, 1954.

35. Senate Armed Services and Foreign Relations Committees. *Hearings on the Military Situation in the Far East*. 82nd Congress. 1st Session, 1951. Pages 3328-3342 of these hearings contain a full statement by W. Averell Harriman of American military strategy in the Pacific during World War II. The relationship of military strategy to political decisions taken in this period is stressed.

36. Snell, John L., ed. *The Meaning of Yalta*. Baton Rouge, La.: Louisiana State University Press, 1956. A critical and dispassionate discussion of the Yalta Conference, bringing out clearly the relationship between military and political decisions.

37. Souers, Sidney W. "Policy Formulation for National Security," *American Political Science Review*, 43 (June, 1949), 534-43.

38. Stanley, Timothy W. *American Defense and National Security*. Washington, D. C.: Public Affairs Press, 1956. A scholarly analysis of national defense agencies.

39. Vandenberg, Arthur H. Jr., ed. *The Private Papers of Senator Vandenberg*. Boston: Houghton, Mifflin Company, 1952.

40. Zacharias, Ellis M. "Inside Story of Yalta," *United Nations World*, 3 (January, 1949), pp. 12-16. A discussion of the military miscalculations about Japan's strength in the Pacific that led to some of the agreements reached at the Yalta Conference.

CHAPTER 5

The Role of Congress in Foreign Relations

A striking phenomenon associated with the control of foreign relations in recent American history is the expanded role of Congress in virtually all phases of external affairs. As Representative Chester E. Merrow (Republican from New Hampshire) has declared, perhaps somewhat prematurely: "In practice the Congress has become a coequal partner with the Executive in giving substance to United States leadership" (**20**, p. 8).

The new role of Congress springs from a variety of factors. One of these is the greater involvement of the United States in world affairs since the Second World War. Another is the nature of contemporary foreign policy problems and programs accompanying America's new responsibilities. The underpinnings of American foreign policy today are vast and continuing programs of economic, military, and technical assistance; efforts to reduce world trade barriers; programs of cultural exchange and information dissemination; participation in the varied activities of the United Nations and regional associations such as the Organization of American States and NATO; and peacetime development of atomic power. New domestic policies too have been necessary to support national security. To maintain its position as leader of the free world coalition, the United States has had to preserve a strong and viable economic system at home. In the face of rapid technological progress by its diplomatic enemies, it has been compelled to give increasing attention to the development of new weapons and to scientific research generally. In short, the pressure of world events has compelled the United States to maintain a high degree of internal and external readiness to safeguard its security.

Expansion of congressional influence upon foreign relations has been an inevitable by-product, directly, by injecting Congress into the foreign policy process as never before, and, indirectly, by heightening its role in closely related domestic policies. In some foreign policies, such as assisting with the economic recovery of Western Europe or promoting trade throughout the free world, Congress has played a major role. In other policies, such as formulating a workable position toward the Nationalist Chinese government-in-exile or exchanging scientific information with America's allies, its part has been more tangential. But in the mid-20th century very few congressional activities are totally divorced from the area of foreign relations. Writing in 1953, one observer noted that "At least fifty public laws enacted in that session in the field of foreign relations were reported out of a committee other than Foreign Relations and Foreign Affairs" (**4**, p. 85).

Legislative Activities in Foreign Affairs
—A Case Study*

To illustrate the point, let us consider a case study of legislative activity in the foreign policy field by examining the work of the House Foreign Affairs Committee in 1957 and contrasting its activities with those of House committees in an earlier period. In the first session of the 85th Congress, the House Foreign Affairs Committee consisted of thirty-two members—seventeen Democrats and fifteen Republicans—with a staff of twelve employees. Internally, the committee was organized into eight standing subcommittees for the following important areas: Near East and Africa, International Organizations and Movements, Far East and the Pacific, National Security, Foreign Economic Policy, Europe, State Department Organization and Foreign Operations, and Inter-American Affairs. There were, in addition, two *ad hoc* subcommittees: one to study the creation of a commission for protecting American foreign investments and the prevention of claims against the United States; the other to study two bills seeking to curb foreign travel by "certain unaccompanied minors not possessing valid passports." Two conference committees were also established to reconcile conflicting House and Senate versions of a resolution on the Hungarian crisis of 1956 and differing House and Senate bills on the Mutual Security Program for 1958.

A detailed statistical breakdown of its activities for the year indicates that the Committee had 126 bills (including 61 duplicates) referred to it; that it considered 33 of these; that it reported 12 favorably to the House; that of these, the House passed 10 and these 10 were

---

*This case study is based upon material taken from 13, *passim.*

eventually enacted into law. It also considered 18 resolutions, out of which 7 were reported favorably to the House and eventually passed. The Committee held a total of 161 hearings, both public and executive, and accumulated 3,176 pages of testimony from 338 witnesses. Its reports on measures touching foreign affairs ran to 796 pages. The full committee met 79 times, and its subcommittees met 82 times, for a total of 161 meetings in all. The full committee devoted a total of 257 hours to its work—finally authorizing approximately $3.3 billion to be spent in the sphere of foreign relations.

These data take on added significance when compared with the committee's activities before the Second World War. Prior to the war, the House Foreign Affairs Committee was largely ornamental (29, pp. 13-26). It ranked far down on the list of desirable committee assignments in Congress, and it possessed little influence over American foreign policy. During 1933-34, for example, it held only thirty-seven full committee and nine subcommittee meetings. In that same period it recommended legislation requiring expenditures of approximately $200,000. By 1951, financial authorization voted by the committee had increased 70,000 per cent to roughly $14 billion (26, p. 67).

The statistical summary of activities of the House Foreign Affairs Committee for 1957 indicates both the cost and scope of congressional participation in foreign affairs. There remain, however, many other important aspects of legislative participation which must be examined, especially Congress' role in certain selected aspects of foreign relations. To do the latter, we shall first consider the constitutional powers of Congress in foreign affairs. Then we shall look at extra-constitutional methods for influencing foreign relations.

1. CONSTITUTIONAL POWERS OF CONGRESS OVER FOREIGN RELATIONS

Profoundly suspicious of executive power, and believing generally that too much power should not be conferred upon any one branch of the government, the founding fathers divided control over foreign relations. It is not surpris-

ing therefore that conflict between the two branches has characterized the management of foreign relations throughout the greater part of American history. With most important powers shared and—what may be more troublesome—

a twilight zone left between the executive and legislative branches, institutional conflicts are well-nigh inevitable under the American system of government. The Constitution provides a standing invitation for both branches to struggle for leadership, to jockey for position, to dominate the management of foreign affairs and governmental operations as a whole.

Senate Ratification of Treaties

Nowhere has conflict shown up more forcefully than in the treaty-making process. In Chapter 3 we discussed this process from the point of view of the President's powers to reach agreements with other countries. We shall not retrace the ground covered there, except to recall that the President has many methods of circumventing Senate control over his actions, the most important being the executive agreement.

What then is the real significance of the constitutional requirement that the President may make treaties with the advice and consent of the Senate? Before the Second World War, this provision was cited from time to time by the Senate in its efforts to influence the *substance* of American foreign policy. Periodically, the Senate has insisted on the right to determine whether negotiations ought to take place with other countries and on the conditions upon which they might take place (8, pp. 14-5). In the face of increasing executive control over treaty-making, dating from George Washington's determination to ignore the Senate until after agreements had already been reached with other countries, the Senate at intervals has tried to re-establish what it believed to be its rightful role (18, p. 127-31). That such efforts have done little to reverse the steady accretion of executive power to reach agreements unhindered by senatorial supervision is illustrated by events during the First World War era. Certain Republican Senators proposed sending eight of their number to France to acquaint themselves firsthand with Wilson's peace negotiations at Paris while these negotiations were still in progress. They believed this step amply justified under the advice and consent clause of the Constitution. It is significant that in the end they did not carry through with this inten-

tion. Wilson completed the negotiations leading to the Treaty of Versailles without any prior consultation with the Senate. He did take a nominal Republican with him to Paris, the former diplomat Henry White, but White in no sense spoke for Senate Republicans, nor did he have any power to reach agreements later binding upon them (21, pp. 397-404).

The later consequences of this episode drive home the point that although the Senate's role in treaty-making has declined, it was neither then, nor is it now, a mere formality. The Treaty of Versailles, for instance, was so emasculated with Senate modifications and amendments that Wilson would not accept it. When the Senate refused to yield, the resulting deadlock prevented American entry into the League of Nations. Until 1901, the Senate altered or amended eighty to ninety treaties placed before it. About one-third of these either failed of ratification or were later abandoned by the President as unsatisfactory. During the next quarter-century, fifty-eight proposed treaties were changed by the Senate; 40 per cent of them were abandoned or discarded by the President as no longer in the national interest (11, pp. 52-3).

These facts suggest that the contemporary importance of the advice and consent clause of the Constitution lies not primarily in giving the Senate a *veto* over agreements between the United States and other countries—the Senate can hardly prevent the President from reaching some kind of *de facto* agreement. Rather, the clause gives the Senate an opportunity to affect policy by attaching amendments and conditions and affords it an occasion to express its viewpoints. Because executive-legislative harmony has come to be indispensable to consistent and sustained efforts in foreign affairs, the chief executive is likely to take expressions of senatorial opinion seriously and, if possible, to formulate proposals that will be satisfactory to both branches.

To promote closer executive-legislative liaison, executive officials have sought the cooperation of the Senate Foreign Relations Committee in concluding most of the important treaties agreed to between the United States and other countries in recent years. Thus Senators Arthur H. Vandenberg (Republican of

Michigan) and Tom Connally (Democrat of Texas) played a prominent part immediately after the war in negotiating the minor Axis peace treaties. Considerable dissatisfaction was voiced with these treaties when they were put before the Senate, most notably about the treaty with Italy. But these Senators were able to convince their colleagues that the agreements were the best attainable under the circumstances. Similarly, the North Atlantic Treaty, signed on April 4, 1949, grew out of the "Vandenberg Resolution," expressing the sense of the Senate that a closer military association ought to be established among the nations of the North Atlantic community. Early drafts of the treaty were discussed continually with the Foreign Relations Committee, and the Committee was kept informed as negotiations proceeded with other countries (**28**, pp. 403-08). The most sustained effort to foster close collaboration between the executive branch and the Senate in treaty-making, however, occurred in 1951, when John Foster Dulles, then a special assistant to the Secretary of State, worked for a period of several months to generate unity throughout the government on a peace treaty with Japan. Dulles skillfully meshed executive views with those of the Senate to secure a treaty that was in every major particular acceptable to both branches (**10**, *passim*).

Postwar emphasis upon bipartisanship in foreign affairs and the evident need for more effective executive-legislative liaison when critical foreign policy issues are at stake have given the Senate, along with the House, a more dynamic role in the foreign policy process. Executive officials have consulted the Senate during the formation of important foreign policies more than at any other stage in American history. Even so, the Senate's role in treaty-making continues to be subordinate. It cannot initiate treaties, nor can it effectively prevent agreements the President believes to be in the national interest. It can reject treaties submitted to it or substantially modify them by amendments. It can express its opinions in a variety of ways. But in a showdown the President may still ignore the Senate, especially if he finds Senators obdurate and if agreements must be made speedily and decisively.

Senate Confirmation of Appointments

Along with its power to ratify treaties, the Senate also enjoys a unique prerogative in foreign affairs through its power to confirm executive appointments. In Chapter 3, we evaluated the President's ability to nullify this power too by utilizing personal representatives, executive officers, and by making interim appointments while the Senate is not in session. Nevertheless, as with the treaty power, the President will normally prefer to work with the Senate by having his appointments confirmed in the prescribed constitutional manner.

In the early period of American history the Senate was prone to use its powers of confirmation to pass upon the establishment of diplomatic missions abroad. This occurred for example in 1809 when the Senate refused to approve an exchange of ministers between the United States and Russia (**22**, pp. 281-83). The confirmation power has also been used to influence the treaty-making process, as when the Senate refused for some time to confirm negotiators who were to settle outstanding differences with Great Britain in Washington's Administration. Bitter and prolonged wrangling ensued between the President and Senate before the highly controversial Jay Treaty, signed in 1794, could even be negotiated. Under Cleveland, the upper chamber rejected a fisheries agreement with England because the President had sent negotiators who had not received Senate confirmation. The dispute over confirmation, however, may have been a pretext for defeating a treaty which many Senators, particularly those from New England, opposed anyway (**23**, pp. 290-91).

McKinley was the first President to utilize a personal diplomatic agent who had not been confirmed in his assignment by the Senate. Then and in the years that followed, the Senate has protested against this practice. One significant expression of disapproval was an amendment affixed to the Treaty of Versailles, providing that no diplomatic representatives could be sent to the League of Nations without prior senatorial confirmation. This was a clear rebuke to Wilson, who had ignored the Senate in negotiating the treaty. More generally, it was a firm enunciation of the Senate's right to pass on diplomatic appointments (23, pp. 292-93).

In the postwar period, along with other legislative prerogatives in the foreign policy field, the power of confirmation has received renewed emphasis. Two examples may be cited to illustrate the point. First, when the United States joined the United Nations, the Senate successfully insisted upon the right to confirm the appointments of high-ranking diplomatic personnel assigned both to existing and future UN agencies. Second, when Congress approved the Greek-Turkish aid bill in 1947, it added a proviso that the Senate must confirm the appointments of any high officials sent to oversee the administration of foreign aid in other countries. The following year, Congress also specified that the roving ambassador to supervise administration of the Marshall Plan should be confirmed by the Senate (23, pp. 294-98).

On a number of occasions conflict has prevailed over diplomatic appointments. A highly controversial episode was President Truman's appointment of Philip Jessup as a member of the U. S. delegation to the United Nations in 1951. This appointment was made in the face of well-nigh unanimous Senate opposition, based upon the belief that Jessup had been too closely identified with left-wing causes. Although the Senate refused to confirm Jessup's appointment, President Truman gave him an "interim appointment" after the Senate adjourned, so that he joined the United States delegation anyway. Then in 1957 many Democrats unsuccessfully opposed the appointment of Maxwell H. Gluck as Ambassador to Ceylon, on the ground that he was not qualified for the position.*

Senate influence upon foreign affairs through the power of confirmation, on the whole, affords very little direct opportunity to determine the substance of American foreign policy. Forceful Presidents are not likely to be deterred for long by Senate opposition. Wilson's use of Colonel House as his personal representative to carry out important missions and FDR's use of Harry Hopkins for similar purposes show that the confirmation hurdle can be circumvented.

*The Gluck appointment is discussed at greater length in Chapter 3.

Congressional Control Over Appropriations

"The great power which the legislative arm of the Government has," said Senator Robert M. LaFollette (Republican of Wisconsin) in 1943, "is the power over the purse strings" (15, p. 26). Mindful that the English Parliament had finally established its supremacy because of the monarchy's dependence upon it for funds, and recalling too that colonial legislatures had used this power effectively against colonial governors, the founding fathers counted heavily upon the power of the purse to assure congressional supervision over all phases of governmental activity. Important programs and policies almost invariably require funds for their implementation—all the more so in our age of recurrent international crises. One-half to two-thirds of the national budget approximately is now devoted to foreign policy and national defense.

Congress can use its power of the purse to affect foreign, and related domestic policies, in many different ways. It can of course simply refuse to appropriate funds for measures proposed by the executive branch. That is its prerogative. But such drastic action seldom occurs, chiefly because Congress is as aware as executive officials of the gravity of conditions prevailing in the international community. It has no desire to risk diplomatic defeat for the United States by ill-advised refusals to cooperate with the White House in formulating measures pertaining to national security. Moreover, the President may, and normally does, exert pressure upon Congress in a variety of ways to assure sympathetic consideration of his budgetary requests. These ways may involve personal appeals to Congress and to public opinion, close liaison with party leaders, testimony by his high-level advisers upon the necessity of proposed measures, and promises of support in forthcoming political campaigns.

A clear illustration of many of the points made about Congress' control over foreign relations through the power of the purse was afforded early in 1959. In the late 1950's, the Eisenhower Administration had instituted the Development Loan Fund which was making a constructive contribution to American foreign policy throughout Asia and Africa by advancing funds for capital improvements. By 1959 money had been utilized to finance roads, electric power facilities, port installations, cement and fertilizer plants and many other similar undertakings in the underdeveloped countries.

Early in January, 1959, President Eisenhower asked for a supplemental appropriation of $250 million to finance the Development Loan Fund, then nearing the end of its reserves. The powerful House Appropriations Committee, heavily staffed by conservative Republicans and Democrats, cut the President's request by $100 million. President Eisenhower branded this action as "irresponsible" and capable of inflicting the "gravest injury" on American foreign policy. Working with the recognized leaders of both political parties, the President was able to have the $100 million cut restored on the floor of the House. In other words, when committee action might endanger the nation's foreign policy, the House was willing to take the highly unprecedented step of overriding one of its most powerful committees and of following executive leadership (22, Dispatch by Rowland Evans, Jr., March 25, 1959).

Very seldom then does Congress refuse outright to approve expenditures requested by the executive branch for national defense and foreign policy. Rather the appropriations process affords opportunities for legislative inquiry into administrative policy. It allows committees and individual legislators to introduce amendments and sometimes to redraft executive proposals entirely. After funds have been voted, it permits continuing supervision by periodic investigation to see that expenditures are being made in accordance with law, that widespread waste and duplication do not exist, and that programs originally authorized are still in the public interest. Like legislative activity in other phases of the foreign policy field, the power of the purse chiefly affords Congress occasions to modify and amend policy proposals initiated by the executive branch. Virtually all of the great legislative enactments that have been foundations of postwar American foreign policy —the Greek-Turkish aid bill, the China aid program, the Marshall Plan, the Mutual Defense Assistance Program, programs of technical assistance to other countries—originated within the executive branch. In most cases, they were

modified partially or heavily by Congress, either initially by the foreign affairs committees or, in rare cases, other committees that might have jurisdiction, or later by the appropriations committees. The latter nearly always cut budgetary requests submitted by the White House, even when these had been approved in whole or in substantial part by the policy committees.

Postwar experience has called attention to a number of major problems arising from legislative control of appropriations for foreign policy. Legislation entailing expenditures in both domestic and foreign affairs must in effect go through Congress twice. A measure is considered first by a standing committee. If the committee approves it, it then goes to the full house, and if it is authorized there, then the Appropriations Committee of that chamber will consider it with a view to recommending funds for its implementation. Again assuming a favorable committee recommendation, the measure returns to the full house for passage as an appropriations bill. After the bill is approved by both houses, it is sent to the President for signature, after which it becomes law. Thus a measure relating to the Defense Department introduced in the Senate would go first to the Armed Services Committee for approval, then to the entire Senate, then to the Appropriations Committee, then back to the Senate once more, and ultimately to the other house, where the same basic process is repeated, and finally to the President for signature.

Now aside from the fact that this is a most cumbersome and time-consuming process, a number of other fundamental criticisms can be made of it, especially when foreign policy measures are involved. First, there is the inability of the appropriations committees, not to speak of Congress as a whole, to examine the executive budget *in its totality*. Not until the last stages of the appropriations process have been reached are the items of the budgets, like the pieces of a jig-saw puzzle, reassembled to form a meaningful picture. When the appropriations committee in each chamber receives the budget, it parcels out the separate items to its subcommittees—for agriculture, military affairs, foreign affairs, and other areas—for detailed study. These subcommittees maintain little effective liaison with the full committee and almost none with the standing committees of Congress which earlier authorized the program for which an appropriation is sought. Moreover, full appropriations committee review of subcommittee actions is hasty and highly incomplete. The consequence is that not even the parent committee has a clear conception of what actions its subcommittees have taken and the reasons for these actions. Not until all subcommittee reports have come in, usually just before the adjournment of Congress, is it possible to know what total appropriations Congress is making in any given year. Then when each chamber considers these reports it passes separate legislation for each major budgetary activity. Senator Harry F. Byrd (Democrat of Virginia), influential chairman of the Senate Finance Committee, complained in 1949 that "the budget picture is never seen again as a whole until after it has become the law of the land . . . There is no way of telling what total appropriations or expenditures are, and there is no way of comparing the effect of action on the bills with the revenue situation. . . . The bills are passed as separate and unrelated pieces" (15, pp. 396-7).

Another problem endemic in the organization of Congress is the difficulty of co-ordinating the efforts of the appropriations committees with those of the standing committees. With reference to national defense, one legislator defined their different roles by saying that it was the responsibility of the standing committee on armed services, for instance

> to recommend measures that will provide us with a defense establishment . . . adequate to the assurance of our national security. . . . It is the responsibility of the Appropriations Committee to recommend appropriations to effectuate such measures, and to see, as best it can, that the Nation will get value received in the expenditure of the funds made available. (15, p. 40).

The same distinction holds for the appropriations committees and all other standing committees. That the line between their jurisdictions is difficult to draw precisely, however, has been illustrated many times by events in the postwar period. The history of legislative action on the Marshall Plan in the 1947-48 period is a case in point. This undertaking had been preceded by what was most likely the most intensive joint executive-legislative stock-taking,

in American diplomatic history. Standing and select committees of Congress, executive agencies, and private study groups pooled their efforts to assure as thorough a study as time permitted of Europe's economic needs and of America's resources. Finally, in the spring of 1948, Congress authorized a long-range program of economic assistance to Europe that was to involve approximately twelve billion dollars in American funds (8, pp. 62-4).

Yet in the face of this impressive executive-legislative collaboration by a Republican Congress and a Democratic President, the House Appropriations Committee threatened to emasculate the Marshall Plan later in the summer by cutting the first year authorization by 25 per cent. Despite the unprecedented study that had gone on in previous months, the Committee had come to an incredible decision. In the words of its Chairman, John Taber (Republican of New York): "the architects of this worldwide relief program have no definite plan and no definite program . . . " (7, Volume 94, p. 7168). The committee's position prompted Senator Arthur H. Vandenberg, Chairman of the powerful Foreign Relations Committee, to denounce Taber's committee on the floor of the Senate—a highly irregular procedure—and to urge Congress vigorously to restore the reduction in funds. Not even Vandenberg's great prestige, however, was able to undo the damage completely, because in the end both houses had to agree to a cut in the earlier authorization (28, pp. 397-8).

This episode exemplifies a tendency that has become a major barrier to intelligent formulation of basic foreign policy programs: the inclination of individual legislators and committees of Congress to apply across-the-board percentage reductions in requested appropriations or, alternatively, to vote lump sum reductions in even figures, like fifty or one hundred or five hundred million dollars. Most infrequently is such an approach dictated by logic or concern for sound policy decisions. More often it stems from the inability of the average legislator to establish a priority among separate items in a complex budget, a prevailing feeling on Capitol Hill that economies must be effected somewhere, and a determination on the part of Congress to resist any intimation that it has become merely a rubber stamp in considering executive budget requests.*

Assignments to appropriations committees are highly prized by Congressmen. Like all committees of Congress, appropriations committees are fiercely independent. They resent any intrusion upon their prerogatives, and they sometimes show little inclination to be bound by the actions of other committees. Their hearings are almost always held in secret. Much of the testimony taken is "off the record," and hence not even available to other legislators. Their members know that very few legislators have the time or the expert knowledge to assimilate thousands of pages of the executive budget requests and "justifications" submitted along with the budget, to read hundreds of pages of testimony by expert witnesses, and to acquire detailed knowledge about a host of large and small executive expenditures. Committee recommendations are therefore usually accepted with little change by the entire house. Floor debate on their reports tends to be desultory and superficial. Almost never are amendments to their recommendations successfully made on the floor. *For all practical purposes the appropriations committees are Congress itself when dealing with expenditures.*

---

*Political motivations are also unquestionably present sometimes when Congress votes percentage or lump sum reductions, as indicated by the following incident related to the author by a high-ranking official in the Truman Administration. This officer was approached by a legislator who had consistently supported the administration's foreign policy programs. Now, however, the legislator said that he would be unable to support large foreign policy appropriations in the future, lamenting that "My political opponent is waging a very effective campaign against me by attacking my support of 'foreign give-away programs,' huge defense budgets, and high taxes. I must somehow convince my constituents that I am zealously looking after their economic welfare, else I am in danger of being defeated in the next election." The following strategy was accordingly agreed upon: the administration would deliberately ask Congress for 20 per cent more funds than it needed in certain categories of foreign aid; then the legislator could dramatically demand reductions in the "padded" executive budget by moving to pare it 20 per cent by "cutting the fat" from the budget. This strategy was carried out. The administration eventually got the funds it needed. The legislator demonstrated to his constituents that he was a trustworthy guardian of their pocketbooks, thereby aiding him in his successful campaign for reelection!

For reasons that will become apparent later in this chapter, the House committee is much more influential than its Senate counterpart. And the House committee's subcommittee on military appropriations, consisting of approximately five members, in effect largely determines legislative action on the national defense budget (**15**, pp. 53-6; **17**, pp. 386-7).

Congress and the National Defense Budget

The President, Elias Huzar has written, was designated commander in chief of the military forces, but he "was to command only those forces which Congress put at his disposal . . ." (**15**, p. 19). And General Omar Bradley stated before a congressional committee in 1949 that "Under our form of government, the military policy of the United States is shaped by the Congress not by the armed forces . . . because . . . Congress controls the appropriations which in the final analysis . . . control the military policy . . ." (Quoted in **15**, p. 132).

The founders counted heavily upon the power of the purse to guard against military usurpation and to assure that the armed forces would always be utilized in the public interest. Thus the Constitution gives Congress the power to raise and support the military forces of the nation and specifies that Congress may not make any military appropriation for longer than two years. In practice, Congress makes annual appropriations, thereby assuring itself an opportunity to review national defense policy at frequent intervals.* Congress, in Arthur W. Macmahon's phrase, exerts "continuing intervention" in governmental administration by means of its control over the purse strings. It does this initially by authorizing or withholding expenditures. Then it conducts hearings and investigations to see that expenditures are made according to law, that waste and unnecessary duplication is avoided, and that sound administrative practices are followed (**17**, pp. 164-5). All of these methods may be used, and have increasingly been used

---

*Some items in the military budget must be "carried over" from year to year to assure needed continuity. This is true, for example, of long-range defense contracts, research and development costs, and commercial leases.

in the postwar period, to control the military establishment.

Without legislative authorization of their activities, accompanied by appropriation of ample funds, military departments cannot operate. This fact has been borne in upon them with great force on a number of occasions when one or both houses have failed to complete action on the military budget before the new fiscal year began. In these instances, "interim appropriations" were required to tide the departments over until final action on the budget could be completed. Many items in the military budget tend to be recurrent and relatively fixed, such as military pay scales, and long-range research and development contracts. They are not subject to drastic alteration by Congress without interfering with a sustained defense effort. Still, opportunities exist every year for Congress to change the direction of national defense policy by amending budget requests to reflect the legislative will. These opportunities have been utilized repeatedly throughout the postwar period. Spurred by the recommendations of its Appropriations Committee, the House in 1949 was adamant in support of a fifty-five group Air Force—in 1948, it had approved a seventy group force—despite the fact that President Truman had recommended only forty-eight groups. Even though the Senate was inclined to support the President, in the end it too was forced to accede to insistent House demands for increased air power. Here was a forceful legislative attempt to determine an important phase of national security policy —a phase that had profound repercussions for foreign affairs—even over the opposition of the chief executive.

The final denouement of this issue brought into clear focus some aspects of executive and legislative prerogatives in this field. Although President Truman eventually signed the military appropriations bill for 1950 expanding the air force, he announced publicly that he did not intend to be bound by the action of Congress. Defense needs, he stated, had to be judged "in the light of total national policies and . . . in the light of our foreign policy and the economic and fiscal problems facing us domestically. . . . I am, therefore, directing the Secretary of Defense to place in reserve the

amount provided by the Congress . . . for increasing the structure of the Air Force" (Quoted in 2, p. 381). The President, in other words, could not be *compelled* to spend funds for national defense if, in his judgment, such an expenditure did not accord with the public interest. A similar controversy characterized debate over military appropriations during the Eisenhower Adminstration, when the Democratic majority in Congress sought to coerce Republican policy-makers into expanding American ground forces to meet localized communist incursions into the free world. Thus in 1958 the House and Senate added $1.25 billion to the Defense Department budget which the President had requested. Senator Chavez (Democrat of New Mexico), who led this move on the Senate floor, explained that the Appropriations Committee believed that the United States would not have adequate defense until the nation was prepared to fight several brush fire type wars at a time. He added: "I hope that all Members of this body who agree will do their utmost to convince those responsible in the executive branch that further cuts will imperil the foundation of our defenses." His colleague, Senator Humphrey (Democrat of Minnesota), admitted frankly that "the Congress cannot control expenditures" as long as the President imposed budgetary ceilings on his subordinates; he contended that even when Congress voted extra funds for defense, they would not be spent unless the Administration supported such a move (7, Volume 104, 15582-83, 15595).

Controversies of this kind call attention forcefully to a point made before: after more than a century and a half of experience under the Constitution, twilight zones exist regarding executive and legislative prerogatives in defense and foreign policy. The nature and scope of the powers possessed by each branch are still in the process of evolution.

In considering the defense budget, the appropriations committees of Congress have many opportunities to examine all phases of national security policy. A detailed study of the defense budget for 1950 showed that in the investigations and hearings accompanying legislative action on the budget, the House Appropriations Committee considered such subjects as aircraft procurement, loans to industry, the Berlin blockade, preventive medicine, naval shipyards, and "mortars, heavy infantry"—to cite but a small sampling of the thirty-five subjects discussed. Altogether, the hearings on the 500-page budget required two months, ran to almost four thousand printed pages of testimony, and included over four hundred statements by executive officials (2, p. 367). Recognizing that legislative scrutiny of a defense budget running into many billions of dollars is a staggering task, Congress grants its appropriations committees a privilege it gives other committees only under the most exceptional circumstances. This is the right to meet and conduct hearings even while Congress itself is in session.

Defense budget-making raises several other major questions about Congress' role in national defense. One of these, as we noted earlier, is the jurisdiction between the standing committees of Congress and the appropriations committees. Under the rules of Congress, appropriations bills are not supposed to contain substantive legislation; they are merely supposed to grant funds for purposes already authorized by Congress—authorized, that is to say, by the standing committees. In practice, however, this rule is seldom strictly obeyed, principally because it is a difficult one to enforce under any circumstances, and an almost impossible one to apply rigidly in the realm of national defense. How after all is it possible to decide separately whether there ought to be a seventy or fifty-five or forty-eight group air force—a question within the province of the armed services committees—and whether the country can *afford* an air force of a certain designated strength—a question within the province of the appropriations committees? Huzar wrote in 1950 that all the military appropriations measures "since 1933 have contained provisions bearing on military policy and administration . . . " (15, p. 45). A close scrutiny of appropriations bills after 1950 would undoubtedly reveal a similar pattern.

At times, appropriations committees invade the policy makers' preserves unduly. They may justify their intrusion into the field of national policy by citing the need to "correct the mistakes" of the standing committees and the necessity to "clarify" legislative intent. In re-

ality policy provisions may have been inserted into appropriations bills to forestall a presidential veto. The President cannot veto the policy without vetoing the appropriation. Frequently, policy provisions reflect the strong views on foreign and domestic policy questions that members of appropriations committees hold and wish to incorporate into law. This haphazard approach to defense policy is difficult to prevent because jurisdiction between committees usually can be delimited only by raising points of order in floor debate. But special rules on appropriations bills do not ordinarily permit raising points of order on the floor (17, p. 174).

If unified action among committees is not easy to maintain, it is also hard to co-ordinate activities *within* and *between* the two appropriations committees. We have already referred to the fact that the military subcommittees have considerable working autonomy. Members of the House Appropriations Committee, moreover, serve on no other congressional committee; members assigned to the military subcommittee are permitted to serve on no other subcommittee. This practice cannot be followed in the much smaller Senate, where legislators must serve on numerous committees and subcommittees. The result is that a division of labor has emerged between the House and Senate: the House committee—in practice, its military subcommittee—examines the defense budget in great detail and makes its recommendations; then the Senate committee acts as a financial supreme court, permitting the military services to "appeal" House cuts and to request restoration of needed funds. House and Senate conferees later reconcile higher Senate, and lower House expenditures, and merge them into a unified appropriations measure (15, pp. 29-39).

The average member of Congress has little influence in legislative action on the defense budget. The really effective force is the military subcommittee of the House Appropriations Committee and, to a much lesser extent, its counterpart in the Senate. How well are these subcommittees, consisting of approximately five Representatives and twenty Senators, prepared to do their job? Even for the House subcommittee, whose members devote full time to this one committee assignment, careful examination of the national defense budget is a well-nigh impossible task. Committee studies tend to be highly selective and often bog down into a discussion of petty details, frequently those relating to a member's constituency. Especially in time of war or cold war, committee members must lean heavily upon the judgments of military commanders. One legislator commented that during World War II, "The War Department, or . . . General Marshall . . . virtually dictated the budget" (**15**, p. 58). Legislators concede that they are not skilled military strategists and that they must often accept the word of military spokesmen that certain expenditures are necessary. A member of the House subcommittee told military officials in 1950 that " . . . we are not kidding ourselves. We know we cannot go into every dollar of expenditure. We can do our best, but we have to trust you gentlemen to wisely spend, under the policies which we approve, funds which we appropriate" (**15**, p. 62).

This dependence is reflected too in the tendency of the two appropriations committees to grant the military departments considerable discretion in spending, especially in time of national crises (**15**, p. 320). Flexibility is assured through a variety of bookkeeping devices such as transfer of funds from one budget item to another, carryovers from year to year, provision of funds under very broad titles, and emergency and contingent funds. A classic case was development of the atomic bomb during World War II. Over eight hundred million dollars was spent by the military before even the members of the Appropriations Committees knew that Project Manhattan was well under way (**15**, p. 336)! Normally the President and the Secretary of Defense have sizable contingent funds which they may use in whatever manner they think necessary to protect national security (**15**, pp. 337-41).

We have devoted considerable space in this chapter to the importance of Congress' control over the purse strings as a means of influencing foreign relations because this is a subject that has not yet received the attention its importance deserves. What then are we to conclude about this power? It is apparent that Congress today relies upon it perhaps more than upon any other technique to affect defense and foreign policy. Yet many significant obstacles remain in the path of intelligent and effective use of this power. Congress has come to see that great discretion must often be given to executive policy-makers if national security is to be preserved. While Congress has ultimate power of the purse, it understands today, perhaps more than at any time in American history, that the entire nation is dependent upon enlightened executive leadership.

The Congressional Power to "Declare War"

Another constitutional provision intended to give Congress substantial control over military and foreign policy is its right to "declare war." This power, as we noted in Chapter 3, has largely lost its original significance. No longer do nations give advance notice of their intention to go to war. Pearl Harbor and the Communist attack on South Korea in 1950 must be regarded as typical of the way aggressive nations today begin conquests.

The congressional power to declare war has seldom interfered with executive leadership in the foreign policy field. It "has never prevented war when the President wanted one" (**31**, p. 20). Historical evidence abounds to support this contention—from Polk's belligerent position toward Mexico in the 1840's, to Cleveland's militant stand during the Venezuelan boundary dispute with Britain in 1897, to FDR's "shoot on sight" order to the navy in dealing with Nazi U-boats before World War II, to Truman's intervention in the Korean War in 1950. Presidents have not hesitated to protect national security when they believed that it was threatened. When hostilities have actually occurred between the United States and other nations, the President has then usually recommended that Congress declare war. This declaration merely confirms the self-evident: that a state of war actually exists. Many times in American history military forces have been engaged in hostilities without such a declaration. The "undeclared" war with the French in Washington's Administration and Jefferson's war with the Barbary Pirates are examples from the early period. In the twentieth century, forces were sent to Latin America on many occasions; America carried on a *de facto* war with the Axis for several months before Pearl Harbor; and President Truman never asked for a declaration of war in the Korean conflict.

The right of Congress to declare war is less important as a legislative sanction than in two other particulars. One of these relates to public opinion. Nothing perhaps conveys so forcefully America's will to resist and to gain ultimate victory as the spectacle of both Houses of Congress approving, almost always by nearly unanimous votes, a presidential request for a declaration of war. This gesture both unites the home front and serves notice to other countries that all agencies of the government are wholeheartedly behind the war effort. Second, a congressional declaration of war has important legal consequences. Numerous legislative grants of authority to the President take effect during periods of war and national emergency. These give the chief executive vast powers he does not ordinarily possess in peacetime. A corollary issue is the question: when is the nation once more at peace? When do emergency and wartime measures cease having legal force? The power to "declare peace," is not explicitly granted in the Constitution. The founding fathers evidently expected that peace would be made by treaty, thereby giving both the Senate and the President a part in bringing hostilities formally to an end. Actually, several methods have been utilized for ending hostilities: treaties, legislation, and presidential proclamation. The commander in chief alone arranges for a cease-fire or armistice. Whatever the method used to end war formally, it is clear that the national government's powers to wage war extend to dealing with problems growing out of the war. Many measures valid during war are also valid during its aftermath, after the fighting has actually stopped. The war power, said Justice Douglas in 1947, "is plainly adequate to deal with problems of law enforcement which arise during the period of hostilities but do not cease with them."[*]

Fleming v. Mohawk Wrecking and Lumber Company, 331 U. S. 111 (1947). For fuller citation of legal authorities, see 27, pp. 78-86.

General Legislative Authority in Foreign Affairs

Along with its control over appropriations, Congress has general legislative authority over foreign policy measures. Most notably since the Second World War, American foreign policy has been based upon important legislative enactments: the Greek-Turkish aid program, the European Recovery Program, the Mutual Security Program, the Atomic Energy Act, immigration and trade laws, technical assistance programs, propaganda activities, and many others.

Congress determines the legal framework within which executive officials operate. This power may range from establishing an agency such as the National Security Council, specifying its powers and personnel, and maintaining supervision over its operations through the investigative power, to giving the President wide discretion in the realm of tariff reduction. Theoretically, most governmental activities at home and abroad must have some legislative sanction.

Yet, as Robert Dahl has written, "Perhaps the single most important fact about Congress and its role in foreign policy . . . is that it rarely provides the initiative. . . . in foreign policy the President proposes, the Congress disposes —and in a very large number of highly important decisions . . . the Congress does not even have the opportunity to dispose" (9, p. 58). Chapter 3 called attention to a number of techniques by which a forceful President may virtually compel congressional action. As a rule, Congress can pass upon executive proposals by accepting them, modifying them, or rejecting them; but it does not usually formulate them without considerable assistance from the executive branch. It realizes that intimate executive-legislative collaboration is required in the foreign policy field, because Congress possesses neither the requisite information nor the expert judgment nor the time to arrive at sound decisions unilaterally. The average legislator simply cannot assimilate fully all data relevant to decisions in this field, even when these data are available to him.

An illustrative episode occurred in 1948, when Congress was considering the Marshall

Plan. The Staff Director of the Republican Policy Committee* showed GOP Senators a stack of material eighteen inches high, consisting of documentary material already assembled on the Marshall Plan, exclusive of appropriations committee reports since these were not yet ready. Asked by a Senator how long it would take to assimilate this material, the Director replied that it would require him two months of reading, providing he had no other duties. The Senator then estimated that it would take the average member of Congress from four to five months to go through the material (9, pp. 129-30). The Marshall Plan of course was but one among many important measures considered by Congress in 1948. Subsequent years did not make this problem any less acute. As an illustration, the hearings conducted by the House Appropriations Committee on the Department of Defense appropriation for fiscal year 1960 totaled more than 4,000 printed pages! This voluminous record did not include separate hearings held on the provision of American military assistance to foreign countries. Added to the difficulty of assimilating such a tremendous volume of information is the often chaotic organization of material within the printed record of hearings and the tendency of committees to have statistics, charts, and other data scattered helter-skelter throughout several volumes of testimony. Moreover, the indexes to such hearings often are so sketchy as to make it nearly impossible to pinpoint information on selected subjects.

While Congress is traditionally more reluctant to take the initiative in proposing policy measures in foreign relations than in domestic affairs, it has by no means relinquished its power to do so. For instance, the House Foreign Affairs Committee in 1948 initiated a bill to provide military assistance to Western Europe, but the bill was abandoned when it failed to receive White House support. A year later, however, the Mutual Defense Assistance Program substantially embodied the committee's recommendations (6, pp. 80-1). In 1948 Congram substantially embodied the committee's four hundred million dollar assistance program

for Nationalist China. Then again in 1950 it granted a loan to Spain against the wishes of the White House (22, pp. 161-2).

Opportunities to affect the substance of policy exist too in the ability of Congress to add amendments and to make modifications in executive proposals. Amendments made to the Mutual Security Act in 1956 are an example.* Section 2 of this act, entitled "Statement of Policy," declared American policy to be expansion in "its own airpower, . . . guided missiles, or other advanced weapons, so as to be prepared at all times to resist any attack by Communist power" and "to make available to free nations and peoples upon request assistance of such nature and in such amounts as the United States deems advisable. . . ." The statement continued to the effect that nations assisted in their recovery by American aid ought in the future to "share with the United States to a greater extent the financial burden of providing aid to those countries which are still in need of assistance of the type provided under this Act."** Another principle inserted into the act was that foreign aid "shall be administered so as to assist other peoples in their efforts to achieve self-government or independence upon circumstances which will enable them to assume an equal station among the free nations of the world and to fulfill their responsibilities for self-government or independence." A later section of the act in effect required termination of American aid to Yugoslavia if that country should again develop close ties with the Kremlin, unless the President certified that providing aid to Yugoslavia advanced the national interest of the United States. Another section of the act granted the President $5,000,000 to finance various programs and activities designed to keep alive "the will for freedom, and . . . to encourage the hopes and aspirations of peoples who have been enslaved by communism." Still another

---

*This is a party, as distinct from a legislative, committee in the Senate.

*For the text of these amendments, see House Resolution 11356, 84th Congress, 2nd Session, June 29, 1956.

**Broad policy statements of this kind, it should be emphasized, have no binding force as law. They are merely advisory to executive officials, although such officials normally try to assess congressional thinking carefully and to formulate proposals that will be supported on Capitol Hill.

section of the act specified that officials who were engaged in administering programs fostering the peaceful uses of nuclear energy "shall give full and continuous publicity through the press, radio, and all other available media, so as to inform the people of the participating countries regarding the assistance, including its purpose, source, and character, furnished by the United States. . . ." And the last section of the act provided:

> It is the sense of Congress that in the preparation of the Mutual Security program, the President should take more fully into account the desirability of affirmatively promoting the economic development of underdeveloped countries, both as a means of effectively counteracting the increased political and economic emphasis of Soviet foreign policy and as a means of promoting fundamental American foreign policy objectives of political and economic self-determination and independence.

Other recent examples of forceful legislative initiative in the foreign policy field are congressionally-imposed requirements that American contributions to the United Nations be terminated if Communist China is allowed to be represented there; detailed conditions under which American economic and military assistance to foreign countries must be terminated (ten such conditions are listed in the Mutual Security Act of 1954); demands that Spain be invited to join NATO; and insistence that the countries of Western Europe make more impressive progress toward political and economic unification.

Congressional influence may also be expressed negatively, as when the legislature refuses to grant executive requests or substantially reduces their cost or scope. Thus in 1940 Congress tried to sever diplomatic relations with Russia, by attaching a rider to the annual State Department budget, to strike out the salary for the American Ambassador to Moscow. This rider carried initially, but was lost on a teller vote in the House by the narrow margin of 105-108 (**24**, p. 157). In the summer of 1951, the House—reflecting widespread legislative and public dissatisfaction with President Truman's Far Eastern policies—tried to compel the resignation of Secretary of State Acheson by eliminating his salary from the State Department budget. This move also eventually failed. Congress however was highly successful in forcing modifications in American overseas information programs by curtailing heavily the operations of the Voice of America in the early 1950's. In 1951 it cut President Truman's emergency request for VOA operations by 90 per cent; then it reduced VOA's regular budget for the next fiscal year by 25 per cent. Other manifestations of this power have been congressionally imposed "ceilings" on the total funds the United States can contribute to the budgets of the United Nations and other international bodies to which the United States belongs (**24**, pp. 161-2).

Although it concedes wide latitude to the executive to manage foreign relations, Congress nevertheless has come to expect prolonged executive-legislative consultation before important policies are announced and before international commitments are assumed that require implementing funds. Congress, said a subcommittee of the House Foreign Affairs Committee in 1948, can

> . . . no longer be confronted with agreements involving commitments requiring Congressional appropriations without prior consultation. Repeated attempts by the Executive to force Congressional action by this technique may result in embarrassing the Executive rather than the Congress. (**16**, p. 327).

The problem then, in the face of recurrent external crises requiring forceful American leadership, is that of co-ordinating executive and legislative efforts.

2. EXTRA–CONSTITUTIONAL AND INFORMAL TECHNIQUES

Legislative Investigations and Foreign Affairs

Few activities of Congress in the modern period have attracted so much attention and notoriety as its many well-publicized investigations into everything from subversive influences upon the State Department, to crime in interstate commerce, to the operations of the Voice of America. Within prescribed constitutional limits, investigation is a proper and necessary adjunct of law-making. Investigation, James A. Perkins wrote in 1940, is "the most important congressional instrument for scrutinizing the work of the executive and the administration, as well as the instrument par excellence for publicizing congressional opinion to secure public support" (25, p. 285).

Congressional investigations had comparatively little influence upon foreign policy before the Second World War. The only significant exception was the Nye Committee investigation during the 1930's into the influence of the munitions makers on American foreign policy before and during World War I. Its findings were highly instrumental in creating an isolationist climate of opinion within the United States on the ground that America had been drawn into the war by the intrigues of profit-hungry industrialists (25, p. 285).

During and after World War II legislative investigations probed virtually every phase of American foreign policy. Conducted by several important committees of Congress, whose members differed widely in knowledge about foreign policy and in attachment to traditional democratic principles of fair procedure, the results of these investigations were decidedly mixed. Some committees, such as the House Un-American Activities Committee and the Senate Judiciary Committee, unquestionably injured the prestige of the United States at home and abroad and jeopardized the stability of its foreign relations. Other investigations, such as those carried out by the Truman Committee during World War II and by the Foreign Relations–Armed Services Committees jointly over Far Eastern policy in 1951, resulted in needed clarifications of national policy and in improved administration.

One of the most fundamental clashes in American history between executive and legislative prerogatives over national defense policy occurred when the Committee on the Conduct of the War tried to compel President Lincoln to follow congressional advice during the Civil War. The Committee on the Conduct of the War

was encouraged . . . by the public impatience at the slowness with which military operations against the Confederacy were proceeding. . . .

They consistently urged a more vigorous prosecution of the war and less lenience toward the institution of slavery. . . . So far did the committee depart from its legitimate purpose that it became a veritable thorn in the flesh of the President. The members took over partial control of military operations. Their investigating missions to the front undermined army discipline and discouraged the more capable commanders. . . . Interrogating generals as if they were schoolboys and advising the President like military experts, they sought to intimidate Lincoln by threatening to arouse Congress against him. (3, p. 115).

This description might almost be made to fit certain postwar investigations of American foreign policy in the Far East, of the problem of East-West trade, and of the operations of the Voice of America.

Legislative investigations, however, have made important positive contributions to American foreign and closely related domestic policies. A model constructive investigation was that carried on by the Truman Committee during World War II.[*] Binkley believes that the Truman Committee represented the "highest development of the congressional investigating committee," and that Senator Truman perhaps contributed more than any other civilian except the President to the winning of the war (3, pp. 268-9). The Committee grew out of Senator Truman's conviction that Congress ought to carry on investigations while waste could still be eliminated from the war effort and unsound practices could be corrected, instead of waiting until after the war when it could do no more than try to assess the blame for failures. After World War I there had been over a hundred congressional investigations, most of them "motivated by partisan desires to fix blame on the opposition;" they had "raked over the coals for more than fifteen years after the war" (2, p. 296).

Executive officials, including the President, were at first apprehensive about the Truman Committee's activities, fearing a new version of the notorious Committee on the Conduct of the War. Their fears proved quite unjusti-

---

[*]This committee, known as the Special Senate Committee Investigating the National Defense Program, was established in March, 1941, and was named for its Chairman, Senator Harry S. Truman (Democrat of Missouri).

fied. Assisted by a skilled staff, the Committee went about its business with a minimum of fanfare. It scrupulously avoided spectacular publicity stunts, intimidation of witnesses, and ill-conceived attempts to intrude into executive management of the war effort. Patiently and quietly, it gathered evidence about deficiencies in the defense effort with a view to correcting them. Working in close coordination with executive agencies affected, its investigations covered such diverse subjects as the location of military camps, military procurement policies, unemployment, taxation, and housing. The Committee—in marked contrast with postwar procedure—made it a practice to show its reports to executive officials before they were made public. As a result of the committee's findings President Roosevelt, in January, 1942, ordered a major reorganization in the national defense structure. The War Production Board was created with wide powers to prevent abuses and waste like those brought to light by the committee (2, pp. 295-317). Eventually the Truman Committee became a kind of "umpire" of the war effort, working closely with executive agencies to straighten out conflicting jurisdictions and tightening up administration in behalf of a sound national defense policy. Its activities won praise from congressmen and executive officials alike. Thus Senator Scott Lucas (Democrat of Illinois) said that the Committee had done its work "in a systematic and careful way without any blare of trumpets. . . . Three distinct bills are now pending before various committees . . . all proposing legislation to cover conditions disclosed by this particular investigation. That is the primary reason back of practically every investigation" (2, p. 320).

Senator Lucas' dictum appears to have been forgotten by many investigating committees in the postwar period. The relationship between their activities and legislation was often nebulous, if not indeed non-existent. This was true especially of committees whose assigned jurisdictions were fields other than foreign affairs, such as the House Un-American Activities Committee, the Senate Judiciary Committee, or the Senate Committee on Government Operations. These and other committees roamed afield looking for officials responsible for the loss of Nationalist China and Eastern Europe to communism, for subversive intellectuals who supposedly possessed such a hold over public opinion and news media that un-American policies were foisted off on innocent policymakers, and for administrative officials who had led the nation astray at critical junctures throughout its recent diplomatic history. To say that these investigations had largely negative results would be charitable. Often the results were highly damaging to American foreign relations. They prejudiced relations between the United States and its allies, demoralized the diplomatic corps, raised doubts abroad about the constancy of American commitments, and undermined presidential leadership in the foreign policy process.

Probably the most fundamental long-range consequence stemming from these freewheeling investigations was to inculcate an utterly false—one might say potentially disastrous—illusion in the public mind. This was a new devil theory of diplomacy which held that if American Far Eastern policy left much to be desired in the postwar period, the only conceivable explanation must be that American diplomatic interests had been betrayed by subversive influences in high places. This mythology was undoubtedly as inimical to American success in the foreign policy field as many activities undertaken by the Kremlin. It was part of the "illusion of American omnipotence" based on the premise that the United States could at will alter world affairs to its liking. When experience proved otherwise, then betrayal—not ignorance, not lack of sound judgments, not failure to understand the significance of international events correctly—was advanced as the only possible explanation. Consequently, many legislative committees have spent their time throughout the postwar period chasing after a will-o'-the-wisp that constantly eludes them. If they have trouble identifying the "subversive elements" that sabotaged American policy toward Nationalist China it is because these elements were such obvious, but unspectacular, ones as widespread national ignorance about developments in the Orient, public apathy, unwillingness to pay the price of a more effective policy, and preoccupation with domestic affairs—failures, reflected as much in Congress as anywhere else.

Nevertheless, with all their apparent faults—many of which can be and ought to be corrected—congressional investigations can make a useful contribution to American foreign policy. A most valuable investigation in the postwar era was the joint Senate Foreign Relations—Armed Services Committee investigation into President Truman's dismissal of General Douglas MacArthur in 1951. MacArthur was a distinguished national hero. During the Korean War, he seemed to many citizens to stand unflinchingly against many unwholesome tendencies: appeasement of the Communists, kow-towing to the allies, and undue surrender of sovereignty to the United Nations. His dismissal precipitated what William S. White has called "the gravest and most emotional Constitutional crisis that the United States has known since the Great Depression" (**30**, p. 242). Seldom in American history has the principle of civilian control over the military been in such great jeopardy as when President Truman, after repeated provocations, finally ordered MacArthur home from Korea.

Under the strong leadership of Senator Richard Russell (Democrat of Georgia), the joint committee conducted a prolonged investigation into MacArthur's dismissal and in the process probed into recent American policies in the Far East. As the facts came to light, the congressional and national furor subsided. Not even Republicans cared to challenge the President's *right* to dismiss the General. Throughout its investigation, the committee sought unity among its members. Its final "Message to the American People," says White "dissolved a national emotionalism the exact like of which had not heretofore been seen. . . ." The committee "protected not only the American tradition of the pre-eminent civil authority; [it] halted what was then an almost runaway movement toward rejection of the United Nations" (**30**, p. 250).

The verdict then on investigative committees and foreign affairs is that as often as not they have been instruments for legislative mischief. If they followed the lead of several distinguished committees within American history they could be instruments for good and make a beneficial contribution to public policy and administration.

Congressional Resolutions

Congressional resolutions expressing the opinion of Congress on questions of public policy are not law, and have no binding force on the executive. Nevertheless, they can be important techniques by which Congress influences American foreign relations.

Numerous resolutions have been important in American postwar diplomatic experience. We have already mentioned the Vandenberg Resolution which initiated negotiations leading to the North Atlantic Treaty in 1949. This resolution constituted clear evidence to the executive that the Senate desired a closer military association between the United States and Western Europe. American relations with Red China were heavily conditioned by two legislative resolutions in 1951. Foreshadowing a similar resolution later by the United Nations, both Houses branded Red China an aggressor for intervening in the Korean War late in 1950. Then the Senate went further and expressed its conviction that Red China should not be admitted to the United Nations. These resolutions probably expressed the overwhelming viewpoint of the American people. Neither Presidents Truman nor Eisenhower have been prepared to abandon the positions taken by Congress (**19**, p. 50).

Other resolutions in the postwar period have requested the President to use his efforts to bring about the economic and political unification of Europe; to bring Spain into the NATO defense system; to investigate—with a view to curtailing—trade between America's allies and the communist bloc; to take the lead in condemning Soviet suppression of the Hungarian revolt of 1956; to sponsor various proposals for strengthening the United Nations; and to authorize the President to use force if necessary in achieving foreign policy objectives in the Far East and the Middle East (**8**, p. 252; **11**, p. 57; **19**, pp. 50-5).

Neither the legislative nor executive branch operates in a vacuum. Each is highly sensitive to public opinion and to the opinions expressed by officials in the other branch. Whenever possible, they prefer to adopt policies that can command wide public support. Congressional resolutions therefore are important barometers of opinion for the executive. They may reflect deep public concern about contemporary policy issues; they may call attention forcefully to widespread dissatisfaction with existing policies; and they may strengthen the President's hand in dealing with other countries by conveying the impression abroad of unanimity within the American government.

Speeches and Activities of Individual Legislators

Closely related to formal legislative resolutions as a means for affecting foreign policy are the speeches and activities of individual members of Congress. The lack of strict party discipline in the legislature, along with the tradition of legislative freedom of speech, most notably in the Senate, gives members almost unlimited freedom to comment publicly on outstanding public issues. They may do this by delivering formal speeches or impromptu remarks; by introducing bills and amendments to bills; by inserting material into the Congressional Record; by holding press conferences; by making speeches outside Congress, especially over radio and television channels; by "leaking" information to the press; by travelling abroad; and in many other ways. Expressions of congressional opinion are studied carefully by other governments, because they know that legislators often reflect public opinion within their local constituencies and that individual members sometimes exert a powerful influence upon the course of foreign relations (14, p. 235).

A few historical examples will suffice to show the importance of Congressional sentiment. During the Oregon boundary controversy in 1844 it prompted President Polk to insist upon the belligerent motto "Fifty-Four Forty or fight!" in dealing with Britain. After a considerable "war scare" the United States retreated from this adamant and untenable position. Congressional viewpoints were important too in shaping the course of American colonial policy after the acquisition of the Philippines in 1898. So strong and vocal were anti-imperialist forces in that period that from then on the United States followed the principle that colonial possessions were to be prepared for ultimate independence (14, pp. 245-6).

An important corollary of the Monroe Doctrine was enunciated in 1912 by Senator Henry Cabot Lodge (Republican of Massachusetts). The Lodge Corollary, aimed at Japan, stated that naval bases could not be established in the Western Hemisphere by a non-American power. Senate debate and ultimate rejection of the Treaty of Versailles as submitted by Wilson colored the American approach to international organization for the next two decades. Then in the 1920's Japanese-American relations were heavily damaged by the Senate's position on Japanese immigration. Reacting vigorously to what it thought to be a Japanese affront to national prestige, the Senate prohibited all Japanese immigration to the United States. This move became a "sore point in relations with Japan, to the discomforture of the Department of State" (14, p. 246).

Since World War II individual legislators time and again have exerted a significant positive or negative influence on the course of foreign relations. Thus until his death Senator Pat McCarran (Democrat from Nevada) was almost unilaterally responsible for shaping Congress' conservative attitude on questions of immigration and refugee relief. He and President Truman were at constant odds over the admittance of displaced persons from Europe. McCarran was a determined foe of any proposals seeking to liberalize immigration quotas (2, pp. 256-7). Until 1952 Senators Tom Connally and Arthur H. Vandenberg alternated as chairmen of the Senate Foreign Relations Committee when their party controlled Congress. Both were individuals of strong opinions about American foreign policy, and their voices carried considerable weight in the deliberations of their party. Both also maintained firm control over committee proceedings so that ill-considered and hasty legislation or measures the chairman did not support in the foreign policy field were usually killed. On one occasion, for example, Senator Connally admitted frankly what he intended to do with a measure introduced by Senator William Knowland (Republican of California), a staunch and persistent critic of the Democratic Party's record in the Far East. Pressed by Knowland for committee action on a proposal relating to policy in the Pacific, Connally stated: "I assure the Senator from California that this matter will have in the Foreign Relations Committee exactly the consideration that it so richly deserves . . . "—whereupon Connally looked up at the press gallery and drew his finger dramatically across his throat (**30**, p. 190)!

Throughout the postwar period the statements and activities of such legislators as Senators McCarran and Joseph McCarthy (Republican of Wisconsin) were constant threats to the stability of American foreign relations. From his position on the Government Operations Committee, McCarthy particularly fancied himself a self-appointed guardian of the State Department, possessing a mandate to pass upon current and pending foreign policy measures to assure their conformity with his own private conception of the national interest. McCarthy-instigated investigations pried into American Far Eastern policy, allegedly subversive influences upon the State Department and United Nations, the operations of the Voice of America, and the loyalty and competence of high-level executive officials. Operating upon the simple theory that people believe that where there is smoke there is fire, McCarthy was adept at planting smoke-pots, fanning them in full view of the television cameras, and then rushing in as a one-man fire department to locate and extinguish the blaze before the nation was consumed. Few individuals in modern American history were privy to so many high-level "conspiracies" to subvert the nation, conspiracies perpetrated by anonymous "subversive groups" whose identity and exact influence always remained shrouded in mystery. That the impact of these groups upon governmental policy could never quite be established proved only that their nefarious and subterranean operations were better-concealed than even the ingenious McCarthy had imagined! At times, McCarthy's activities posed a serious threat to the continuity of American foreign policy that had been established through the bipartisan labors of public-spirited, informed, and less publicity-conscious officials in the executive and legislative branches.

Having acceded to the chairmanship by virtue of length of service on the committee, chairmen of the more important committees have ample opportunities to exert individual influence upon foreign affairs. This is true because, in William S. White's expressive phraseology:

> A senate committee is an imperious force; its chairman, unless he be a weak and irresolute man, is emperor. It makes in its field in ninety-nine cases out of a hundred the real decisions of the Institution itself. What bills it approves are approved by the Senate; what bills it rejects are rejected, with rare exceptions. . . . To override, say, the Committee on Foreign Relations or the Committee on Finance involves a parliamentary convulsion scarcely less severe, as the Senate sees it, than that accompanying the overturn, say, of a British government. And in fact the one crisis . . . will hardly occur so frequently as will the other. (**30**, p. 181).

Under the rules of each chamber the chairman is in a position virtually to dictate what measures will be considered by his committee and hence by Congress as a whole. Only he can call the committee into session, and many chairmen have been dilatory about doing this to delay consideration of measures they did not support. Senator Pat McCarran, for instance, was able to delay legislative consideration of a displaced person act recommended by President Truman in 1948-1949, through prolonged and deliberate absence on an "inspection trip" to Europe. The committee could do little during his absence.

The McCarran case also illustrates another prerogative of committee chairmen: they often have a decisive voice in choosing the committee staff. Senator McCarran chose Richard Arens to be chief of staff for the immigration subcommittee of the Judiciary Committee. Arens "ruled with a firm hand one of the busiest subcommittees on Capitol Hill." Like McCarran, Arens opposed Truman's displaced persons bill. This fact became apparent from the way he undertook exhaustive studies purporting to show its disadvantageous features; from the manner in which he badgered executive department witnesses at hearings; and from the part he played in aiding legislators in preparing speeches against the bill (**2**, pp. 243-67 *passim*). Committee staffs often have a significant effect upon the voting behavior of legislators. The staff "can influence not merely by communicating and therefore interpreting events, but by suggesting, interpreting, and emphasizing the alternative policies available to meet the challenge of events. The congressional expert is a relatively new influence in Congress, but his long-run significance may prove to be exceptional" (9, p. 60).

A word from a powerful committee chairman often establishes the tone of legislative debate and determines the outcome of measures before Congress. When one of the patriarchs of the Senate, Harry F. Byrd (Democrat of Virginia), Chairman of the powerful Finance Committee, informed the Secretary of State what could and could not be done in the field of tariff legislation, the Secretary could take this as a definitive expression of legislative intent (30, p. 191). Similarly, when Senator Vandenberg informed the Truman Administration in 1949 that its Mutual Defense Assistance Program would have to be rewritten before he would support it, the program was rewritten because Vandenberg's support was a fundamental prerequisite to its passage (27, p. 504). Former Secretary of State Dean Acheson has noted that committee chairmen are as a rule individuals who are "more likely to influence than to be influenced by the views of others, including a President of their own party." From his own experiences under the Truman Administration Acheson concluded that bills might be retrieved from committees "often haggard and transformed by their imprisonment—by a presidential *habeas corpus;* if the demand is made often enough and vigorously enough" (1, pp. 25-6).

Congressional Travel

During the first six months of 1957, study missions from the House Foreign Affairs Committee visited the following countries:

Austria	Guatemala	Norway
Belgium	Luxembourg	Poland
France	Mexico	Spain
Germany	Netherlands	United Kingdom
Greece	Nicaragua	Yugoslavia

In this period, members of the committee also attended the NATO Parliamentary Conference, the autumn meeting of the 12th session of the United Nations General Assembly, and the inauguration of the President of Nicaragua (13, p. 6).

Congressional travel is a comparatively recent phenomenon. The first year in which legislators travelled abroad to inspect the operations of an overseas diplomatic mission was in 1936. Since that time individual legislators and study missions have travelled extensively. For example, a total of two hundred legislators went abroad in 1947-1948 to study conditions in Europe that necessitated the Marshall Plan. Today it is a rare congressman who cannot find one reason or another to go abroad every year or two on an investigation tour—whether it be studying the administration of technical assistance in India, conditions in American military posts in the NATO area, conflict along the Israeli-Egyptian border, or communist activities in Latin America.

Information gained by legislative travel now gives Congress a competence in foreign affairs it did not possess in a earlier period, when it had to depend almost entirely upon the judgments of executive officials. In certain cases investigations abroad can have highly significant consequences for foreign policy. Thus the Herter Committee which devoted weeks to collecting data abroad about Europe's economic condition in the 1947-1948 period was highly influential in generating legislative support for the Marshall Plan. Subsequently, numerous foreign trips by members of the foreign affairs, armed services, and appropriations committees, helped to maintain congressional support for the Mutual Security Program (5, p. 123). Studies growing out of these travels led to modifications in MSP that included efforts to bring Spain into the program, legislative insistence that recipient nations exert greater efforts to meet their own economic and military needs, attempts by the United States to eliminate barriers to American foreign investment, and establishment of a counterpart fund for the promotion of private enterprise within the recipient nations (5, pp. 123-4).

That foreign travel gives legislators additional opportunities to develop expert knowledge and insight in the realm of foreign affairs can hardly be doubted. The State Department, in fact, has on occasion even suggested to committees that some of their members go abroad to inspect overseas operations, such as administration of the Mutual Security Program. In such cases, and even when the initiative comes from the committee, the State Department works closely with legislative groups to plan itineraries, furnish liaison officers and guides, arrange interviews, and make whatever other arrangements are necessary for a profitable trip.

Within the past decade, the cost of these trips has been borne by "counterpart funds" contributed by countries receiving American economic and military assistance.* In a literal sense, however, these trips may actually cost little or nothing in the long run, since they often result in considerable savings to the taxpayer by uncovering waste and by pointing to the need for more efficient administration.

Congress and Foreign Policy—the Continuing Problem

The numerous and varied opportunities available to legislators to influence American foreign relations sometimes create serious obstacles in the formulation and execution of clear and sustained foreign policies. The public views and

---

*This fund of foreign currencies is supposed to be utilized for the administration of the Mutual Security Program. Even after legislative travel expenses have been met, the fund is seldom exhausted.

activities of 100 Senators and 435 Representatives can on occasion create a veritable cacophony in the foreign policy field. Other countries, unaccustomed to the vagaries of a government whose constitutional cornerstone is the doctrine of separation of powers, often have difficulty disentangling what they see and hear in the executive branch and in Congress and arriving at a true expression of American foreign policy. They fail to consider that speeches made by legislators may be calculated to assure and edify local constituents and to aid in re-election.

Within the United States, the governmental orchestra suffers from a superfluity of soloists. Players chronically tend to ignore the conductor—occasionally domestic and foreign observers may even wonder if all are playing the same music. In such cases the United States is at a grave disadvantage in the management of its foreign relations. Techniques have evolved throughout American history, and most notably in the postwar period, designed to assure a reasonable degree of harmonious orchestration. We shall examine these techniques in Chapter 6.

REFERENCES

1. Acheson, Dean G. A *Citizen Looks at Congress.* New York: Harper and Brothers, 1957. A challenging study of Congress' role by a former Secretary of State.

2. Bailey, Stephen K., and Samuel, Howard D. *Congress at Work.* New York: Henry Holt, 1952. Illuminating case studies of legislative activities.

3. Binkley, Wilfred E. *President and Congress.* New York: Alfred A. Knopf, 1947.

4. Cardozo, Michael H. "Committees Touching Foreign Relations Indirectly," *Annals of the American Academy of Political and Social Science,* 289 (September, 1953), 84-91. Treats comprehensively the foreign policy role of various legislative committees.

5. Carnahan, A. S. J. "Congressional Travel Abroad and Reports," *Ibid,* pp. 120-26.

6. Chiperfield, Robert B. "The Committee on Foreign Affairs," *Ibid,* pp. 73-83. A member of the committee analyzes its role.

7. *Congressional Record.*

8. Crabb, Cecil V., Jr. *Bipartisan Foreign Policy: Myth or Reality.* Evanston: Row, Peterson and Company, 1957.

9. Dahl, Robert A. *Congress and Foreign Policy.* New York: Harcourt, Brace and Company, 1950. Calls attention forcefully to a number of obstacles to further legislative participation in foreign affairs.

10. Dulles, John Foster. *A Peace Treaty in the Making.* San Francisco: Japanese Peace Conference, September 4-8, 1951. Gives details concerning drafting of Japanese treaty.

11. Gillette, Guy M. "The Senate in Foreign Relations," *Annals of the American Academy of Political and Social Science,* 289 (September, 1953), 49-57.

12. Holt, W. Stull. *Treaties Defeated by the Senate.* Baltimore: The Johns Hopkins Press, 1933. Indispensable for historical perspective on treaty making.

13. House Foreign Affairs Committee. *Survey of Activities of the Committee on Foreign Affairs.* 85th Congress, 1st Session, January 3 —August 30, 1957. The annual reports in this series, and similar reports by the Senate committee, are invaluable for material on Congress' participation in foreign affairs.

14. Hulen, Bertram D. *Inside the Department of State*. New York: Whittlesley House, 1939. Pages 233-46 provide an interesting analysis of the legislative role before World War II.

15. Huzar, Elias. *The Purse and the Sword*. Ithaca, N. Y.: Cornell University Press, 1950. This book is a definitive study of legislative control over the military through the power of the purse. Legislative attempts to control military policy by this power are discussed on pp. 62-296; efforts to control military administration on pp. 320-356.

16. Langer, William L. "The Mechanism of American Foreign Policy," *International Affairs*, 24 (July, 1948), 319-28.

17. MacMahon, Arthur W. "Congressional Oversight of Administration: The Power of the Purse," *Political Science Quarterly*, 58 (June and September, 1943), pp. 161-90; 380-414. An informative treatment of all aspects of legislative control through the power of the purse.

18. Mansfield, Mike. "The Meaning of the Term 'Advice and Consent,'" *Annals of the American Academy of Political and Social Science*, 289 (September, 1953), pp. 127-33.

19. Marcy, Carl, and Wilcox, Francis O. "Congress and the United Nations," *Foreign Policy Reports*, 27 (May 15, 1951), 50-60. Treats legislative activity bearing upon the United Nations, especially upon Charter revision.

20. Merrow, Chester E. "United States Leadership in a Divided World," *Annals of the American Academy of Political and Social Science*, 289 (September, 1953), 1-10.

21. Nevins, Allan. *Henry White*. New York: Harper and Brothers, 1930.

22. New York *Herald Tribune*.

23. Nigro, Felix A. "Senate Confirmation and Foreign Policy," *Journal of Politics*, 14 (May, 1952), 281-99. Provides useful background on Senate efforts to influence foreign policy through its confirmation power.

24. Nobleman, Eli E. "Financial Aspects of Congressional Participation in Foreign Relations," *Annals of the American Academy of Political and Social Science*, 289 (September, 1953), 145-64. Cites many examples of legislative efforts to control foreign relations through expenditures.

25. Perkins, James A. "Congressional Investigations of Matters of International Import," *American Political Science Review*, 34 (April, 1940), 284-94. Treats prewar legislative investigations in the foreign policy field.

26. Richards, James P. "The House of Representatives in Foreign Affairs," *Annals of the American Academy of Political and Social Science*, 289 (September, 1953), 66-72. A onetime chairman of the Foreign Affairs Committee examines the House's role.

27. Rossiter, Clinton. *The Supreme Court and the Commander in Chief*. Ithaca, N. Y.: Cornell University Press, 1951.

28. Vandenberg, Arthur H., Jr., ed. *The Private Papers of Senator Vandenberg*. Boston: Houghton Mifflin Company, 1952. An indispensable primary source about one of the most influential Senators in American foreign relations.

29. Westphal, Albert C. F. *The House Committee on Foreign Affairs*. New York: Columbia University Press, 1942. Provides useful historical insight into Congress' role.

30. White, William S. *Citadel: The Story of the U. S. Senate*. New York: Harper and Brothers, 1957. This study by an outstanding journalist is a provocative, though sometimes highly impressionistic, account.

31. Wright, Quincy. "International Law in Relation to Constitutional Law," *American Journal of International Law*, 17 (April, 1923), pp. 234-44.

CHAPTER 6

Executive-Legislative Relations and Bipartisanship

The astute Frenchman, Alexis de Tocqueville, once observed that a democracy

is unable to regulate the details of an important undertaking [in foreign affairs], to persevere in a design, and to work out its execution in the presence of serious obstacles. It cannot combine its measures with secrecy, and it will not await their consequences with patience. (**22**, p. 321).

That de Tocqueville's perceptiveness has stood the test of experience is plainly indicated by American diplomatic history. The eminent historian and former State Department official, George F. Kennan, has likened the American democracy to "one of those prehistoric monsters with a body as long as this room and a brain the size of a pin. . . ." He lies in the mud inert for long periods, but when aroused "he lays about him with such blind determination that he not only destroys his adversary but largely wrecks his native habitat." Like the monster, the American approach to foreign relations has often oscillated between "an undiscriminating indifference" and "a holy wrath equally undiscriminating" (**20**, pp. 66-7).

These comments—separated by over a century of American diplomatic history and by innumerable instances of public turmoil at home over important international issues—point to a problem that has increasingly engaged the attention of scholars and commentators. Some* have even wondered whether the American democracy is congenitally incapable of carrying out sustained and effective foreign policies in the midst of recurrent international crises, within a domestic environment of chronic citizen apathy and lack of understanding of complex external problems. The gravity of international problems in the nuclear age, coupled with the well-nigh infinite possibilities prevailing within the United States for disrupting the continuity and stability of foreign policy, create unprecedented difficulties for American policy-makers. Communist policy-makers are unhampered by such potentially divisive factors as a constitutional doctrine of separation of powers, an outspoken opposition party, active and resourceful pressure groups, or vocal public opinion. They therefore possess an enormous advantage over the United States and other democratic governments with respect to ability to formulate long-range diplomatic objectives and to carry them out with a minimum of opposition and disruption within the government and throughout the nation as a whole.

*The views of George Kennan on this subject are set forth in **20**. In addition to the opinions expressed in his syndicated column, Walter Lippmann has analyzed problems of policy-making in a democracy in **24**.

Events since World War II have given un-rivaled urgency to the problem of government-wide co-ordination of efforts in the diplomatic field and of finding means to reduce to a minimum the public turbulence that has char-acterized American foreign relations at intervals in the past. Yet if the necessity for greater unity has become apparent, so has the difficulty of securing it. Opportunities for internal con-tention over foreign policy and for intra-governmental conflict have multiplied with the growing complexity of international problems and with the greater American involvement in world affairs. The close entanglement of internal and external policy measures has compounded the problem, with the result that no clear de-lineation between them is possible in the modern period.

American diplomatic experience abounds with instances when dissension at home interfered seriously with diplomatic efforts abroad. Internal disunity over foreign policy questions not only can, but frequently has, dissipated the na-tion's energies in bitter domestic controversies and has placed many obstacles in the way of solving vexatious diplomatic problems. As long as the nation embraced an isolationist credo, and as long as political developments in Europe and Asia did not as a rule involve the United States directly, periodic disunity could be tol-erated. Only sporadic and usually ineffectual efforts were made prior to the Second World War to promote a unified approach to foreign relations. The contemporary emphasis upon cultivating unity at home when important foreign policy problems impend is accordingly a comparatively recent phenomenon, dating only from the Second World War.

Disunity in American Diplomatic History

As a generalization, it may be said that im-portant foreign policy questions in American history have always engendered various de-grees of dissension within the national govern-ment and throughout the country at large. The only significant exceptions are the major wars in which the nation was engaged—and even then internal disagreement ultimately pre-vailed over the causes of the war, the degree to which American vital interests were directly involved, postwar political and economic settle-ments, and related questions. Internal dissen-sion over foreign policy questions can be traced from the earliest days of the Republic over such major issues as the Jay Treaty, the Louisi-ana Purchase, and the War of 1812, on through the course of the 19th century over the Texas controversy and Mexican War, the many ramifications of the slavery issue, and Manifest Destiny, down to the mid-20th century.* As an example of disunity in the modern period, the student of American foreign relations has but to examine closely the fierce partisan and intra-governmental wrangle that characterized the Roosevelt Administration's efforts to deal with the rising Axis threat during the 1930's, and especially its efforts to secure repeal of American neutrality legislation (23, pp. 136-47, 280-91).

Of all the examples of disunity that might be cited one stands out—both because it precipitated an unusually intense domestic con-troversy over a diplomatic issue and because its ultimate consequences were of singular im-portance for the modern period. This was President Wilson's bitter fight with Senate Re-publicans over United States membership in the League of Nations. Wilson's opponents, led by Senator Henry Cabot Lodge of Massachu-setts, protested vigorously against his failure to consult the Senate in the early stages of plan-ning for the League of Nations and to include one or more of their number among his official negotiating party in Europe. Wilson had at-tempted a rudimentary kind of bipartisan col-laboration when he took the former diplomat and nominal Republican, Henry White, with him to Paris to provide liaison with the Republican opposition at home. Republicans, however, had little confidence in White, and he proved completely incapable of providing the expected liaison. Meanwhile, Republicans left no doubt about their intentions regarding the Treaty of Versailles; they would emasculate the League of Nations proposal with crippling amendments and reservations which would be completely unacceptable to Wilson (17, p. 700; 19, pp. 264-5; 25, pp. 397-404).

---

*The examples cited here are dealt with at length in 28, pp. 77-80, 86-104, 125-40, 201-19, 220-36, 237-62, 367-94.

For his part, Wilson indicated little awareness of the strength of his Republican foes, and of the isolationist bloc in the Senate. Nor did he demonstrate any inclination to try to reach agreements with it. He adamantly refused to accept even minor modifications of the treaty, and the Senate was equally unyielding. This dead-lock—resulting in America's refusal to join the League of Nations—colored the American approach to international relations for two decades thereafter. While it does not constitute a particularly praiseworthy chapter in American diplomatic experience, it at least taught valuable lessons for future policy-makers. This episode, for example, was the chief impetus in shaping the determination of President Roosevelt and Secretary of State Cordell Hull to avoid a partisan battle during and after the Second World War and to work for integrated governmental support for the new international organization growing out of the war. Wilson's experience in dealing with the Senate was also instructive in suggesting fruitful avenues for promoting greater unity in the future.

Sources of Conflict in Foreign Relations

The League of Nations controversy points to three potential sources of conflict over foreign policy issues: *institutional discord* between the President and Congress, or the Senate alone; *partisan controversy* over diplomatic questions;

and *personal animosity* between key individuals involved in the foreign policy process. Two additional sources of disunity have become especially pronounced since World War II: *controversy and poorly integrated efforts within Congress and within the executive branch*. In the postwar period, these last two sources of disunity have sometimes proved more troublesome than the more traditional sources.

Internal disunity over foreign affairs as a rule has its origins in a number of tributaries which often converge and re-enforce each other to form a floodcrest of controversy and factionalism. Institutional or personal discord may generate partisan disputes, and vice-versa. Disharmony within the executive branch may produce confusion and diffuse efforts within Congress. A number of techniques, most of them evolved during the postwar period, have been used for the prevention of internal instability when major foreign policy decisions confront the nation. Collectively, these techniques for generating unity comprise what has come to be called a bipartisan approach to foreign relations.*

---

*Occasionally other terms like "non-partisan" or "un-partisan" are used to designate the approach desired. Bipartisanship is employed throughout this chapter, however, because it conveys more forcefully the idea of *collaboration* in formulating important foreign policy measures. Such collaboration has come to be regarded as the principal prerequisite of a bipartisan approach.

1. BIPARTISAN TECHNIQUES AND PROCEDURES

Before analyzing the specific practices associated with bipartisan collaboration, a word of caution is in order. The concept of bipartisanship has been, and remains, an exceedingly fluid and elusive one. Admittedly, widespread agreement within the government has existed since World War II that unity is imperative when important diplomatic problems arise. Members of both political parties—from isolationist-inclined Republicans to the most internationalist Democrats—have usually been agreed on supporting the principle of unity. Yet throughout the postwar period substantial controversy has surrounded the question of the precise techniques and procedures best calcu-

lated to bring about unity. Some practices have received almost universal approval. Others have met with various degrees of opposition. Certain practices have been consistently advocated by the party in power or the executive branch, while others have been endorsed by the opposition party or Congress. New bipartisan techniques have appeared during the past decade, and old procedures are continually being modified in the light of experience. Even so, disagreement occasionally breaks out over the exact meaning and scope of the bipartisan concept. Its meaning has not been and, for reasons that will become apparent presently, perhaps cannot be defined with exactitude.

Prior Consultations on Foreign Policy Measures

Among the practices associated with bipartisan foreign policy, none is more fundamental than the requirement of prior consultation in the initial stages of policy formulation. Senator Arthur H. Vandenberg (Republican of Michigan), the foremost advocate of bipartisan co-operation in the postwar period, once defined the goal as a "meeting of the minds" toward problems prevailing in the international field (35, p. 550). Legislative action on important foreign policy measures since the Second World War has almost invariably been preceded by a greater or lesser amount of prior consultation between officials in the executive and legislative branches. A notable example was the United Nations Charter. State Department officials worked closely with the Senate Foreign Relations Committee over a period of almost three years to assure Senate acceptance of the nascent United Nations (35, pp. 90-171). Similarly, the Marshall Plan was finally approved by Congress in 1948 after what was probably the most intensive collaborative stocktaking in American diplomatic history. Legislative committees, executive officials, and private study groups all joined to investigate Europe's critical economic problems and America's ability to assist in European reconstruction.* Significant bipartisan consultation also preceded the China Aid bill of 1948, the North Atlantic Treaty, the Mutual Defense Assistance Program, and later programs of American economic, technical, and military aid to foreign countries (10, pp. 74-116). President Eisenhower's requests in 1955 and 1957 for legislative authority to use troops if necessary for preserving the security of Formosa and the Middle East from threatened Communist attack were eventually granted by Congress, but only after legislative and executive officials had discussed conditions existing in these areas and had agreed that Communist threats against them were imminent (10, pp. 251-4).

Although prior consultation is widely regarded as the *sine qua non* of bipartisan co-operation, no clear consensus exists concerning the nature of these consultations. Much depends on such diverse influences as the external problem under consideration, the amount of time available for decision, the personalities of the individuals involved in the decision, and the extent to which unity is believed to be a paramount goal. Quite clearly, consultations cannot be tailor-made in advance to fit all conceivable kinds of international situations. Considerable improvisation is therefore inevitable. Yet certain basic patterns of consultation have emerged. Liaison is provided on the highest level by the President, the Secretary of State, and their principal advisers, when basic policy measures are under consideration in the government. When new legislation is required, or when the State Department budget is being considered by Congress, the Secretary of State usually appears personally before the appropriate legislative committees. In some instances, the President himself may meet with legislative leaders at a White House conference to explain proposed undertakings and to review existing policies. President Truman, for example, held such a conference just before he ordered American troops to intervene in Korea (9, June 27, 1950, p. 9365). President Eisenhower did likewise before the Geneva Conference in 1955, in order to assure as wide an area of agreement as possible over the issues outstanding between the communist and non-communist worlds and over the fundamentals of American policy.

At a lower level, consultation is provided almost daily by the Office of Congressional Relations in the State Department and those officials on the White House staff and in other executive agencies charged with cultivating harmonious relations with Congress. Liaison on this level may range from legislative requests to the executive branch for information, to briefings for legislators conducted by the State Department, to informal get-togethers attended by legislative and executive officials, to formal appearances by subordinate executive officials before legislative committees.

The establishment of a subcommittee system in the Foreign Affairs and Foreign Relations committees, to correspond with the major geographical and functional divisions of the State Department, has facilitated exchange of infor-

---

*Preliminary studies of the Marshall Plan are described in 32.

mation between the legislative and executive branches. A former chairman of the House committee believes that:

> One of the most helpful signs in collaboration between the executive and legislative branches has been a greater use of the subcommittees. Today the Assistant Secretaries [of State] invariably seek out Members of the appropriate subcommittee and arrange a meeting to impart the latest developments in their particular fields of responsibility. This approach has provided a tremendous sense of participation even though Congressmen may be listeners. It builds up a mutual confidence on the part of both branches. (30, p. 71).

A corresponding change took place in the executive branch, as a result of the findings of the Hoover Commission, when the State Department established the Office of Congressional Relations, whose function it was to promote more intimate collaboration with Congress on foreign policy measures.

Yet in spite of considerable progress in establishing liaison procedures capable of assuring widespread consultation about certain kinds of foreign policy problems, there remains room for much improvement. For instance, many Congressmen were dissatisfied with the way the White House presented the Eisenhower Doctrine for legislative approval, early in 1957. A series of increasingly more ominous developments in the Middle East, resulting in a marked deterioration in Western influence throughout the region, led to a presidential request that Congress grant him standby authority to use American troops to safeguard the security of any Middle Eastern country threatened by international communism. Democrats objected not alone to the *substance* of the Eisenhower program but also *to the way in which it was proposed*. The Eisenhower Doctrine was labelled a "bipartisan" measure by the Administration. Yet, according to Senator William Fulbright (Democrat of Arkansas, and influential member of the Foreign Relations Committee), bipartisanship in actuality had consisted of "leaks to the press, speeches to specially summoned Saturday joint sessions (of legislative committees), and dramatic secret meetings of the Committee on Foreign Relations after dark one evening before the Congress was even organized, in an atmosphere of suspense and urgency. . . ." In Fulbright's opinion, "All of

this was designed to manage the Congress, to coerce it into signing this blank check."[*] Fulbright's opinions were echoed by a number of other Democrats. Senator Hubert Humphrey (Democrat of Minnesota), for example, condemned the Eisenhower Doctrine as a "diplomatic barbiturate, a diplomatic opiate, which calms one's nerves and puts him into a kind of slumberland, when, in fact, the illness still persists. . . ." He criticized the way in which the doctrine was presented to Congress, because in his opinion the Administration had not consulted the *recognized leaders*—"namely, the majority leader and minority leader and the heads of committees." Instead, it had engaged in a kind of high-pressure publicity campaign to convince Congress that the Eisenhower Doctrine ought to be adopted as a bipartisan measure. In dealing with the opposition party, the doctrine "was handled with a kind of Hollywood public relations treatment" (8, Volume 103 (1957), pp. 1877-78).

Legislators as Negotiators and Observers

A bipartisan practice that is rich with historical tradition is the use of legislators and members of the opposition party as negotiators and observers at international conferences. This custom dates back to the War of 1812, when two legislators participated in negotiating the peace treaty (17, pp. 596-7). McKinley followed the same practice at the end of the Spanish-American War; the treaty of peace with Spain might have been rejected by the Senate except for this fact (17, p. 598). Henry White's inability to provide liaison between President Wilson and Senate Republicans to assure acceptance of the Treaty of Versailles constituted a lesson which executive officials in later years were careful to observe: bipartisan support for policy is not likely to emerge unless care is taken to work through the *acknowledged leaders* of the opposition party.

The individual most closely identified with bipartisanship in the modern period was Senator Arthur H. Vandenberg. Vandenberg once

---

[*] 8, Volume 103 (1957), p. 1856. Other references to the nature of bipartisan procedures appear in Fulbright's speech on the Middle East, pp. 1855-69.

wrote of "wearing three hats" (**35**, p. 318). He was, first of all, the chairman of the Foreign Relations Committee in the 80th Congress (1947-48); then he was the acknowledged Republican spokesman on foreign policy questions; finally, he served as president of the Senate and consequently came in close touch with that body's opinions and activities. Because of his great prestige and influence with reference to foreign policy issues, Vandenberg could provide invaluable assistance to the Truman Administration in the immediate postwar period, especially in negotiating with the Soviet Union. His presence at the right hand of Secretary of State James Byrnes, during negotiations over the minor Axis peace treaties for instance, provided a forceful demonstration of American unity. On one significant occasion in 1946, when the Truman Administration's diplomatic efforts were severely challenged by the speeches of Secretary of Commerce Henry A. Wallace, Vandenberg's firm statement that the "authority of American foreign policy is dependent upon the degree of American unity behind it . . . " and that "most Republicans have been glad to join Democrats, thus presenting a united American front to the world," served blunt notice to the Soviet Union that the Administration's increasingly firm policies had solid bipartisan support (**26**, September 15, 1946). A more recent illustration of this technique occurred in 1951, when the Truman Administration asked a former Republican Senator from New York and foreign affairs adviser to Governor Thomas E. Dewey, John Foster Dulles, to generate wide bipartisan support throughout the government in behalf of the peace treaty with Japan (**13**). Commenting on the use of legislators as negotiators in an earlier period, D. F. Fleming has written that:

> When powerful Senate leaders act as negotiators of a treaty they acquire a paternal interest in the document and are likely to defend it vigorously. . . . Other Senators, too, are likely to look upon the treaty as made by capable, friendly hands and therefore to be attacked with much more restraint. (**15**, p. 169).

"Politics Stops at the Water's Edge"

"I ask Congress for unity in these crucial days," said President Truman on January 8, 1951. "I do not ask for unanimity. I do not ask for an end to debate. . . . Let us debate the issues, but let every man among us weigh his words and deeds. There is a sharp difference between harmful criticism and constructive criticism" (**8**, Vol. 97, p. 101). A theme recurrent in arguments supporting bipartisanship in foreign affairs is that considerable self-restraint must be exercised by those engaged in dealing with external problems. Participants are admonished not to "play politics" with the diplomatic interests of the country. They are urged to place the welfare of the nation ahead of partisan advantage. The ideal, said Senator Vandenberg in 1947, is "an unpartisan American foreign policy—not Republican, not Democratic, but American—which substantially unites our people at the water's edge in behalf of peace" (**26**, November 4, 1947).

As with other aspects of a bipartisan approach, it is not always easy to translate such generalities into specific practices and rules of behavior designed to achieve the goal of unity. Nevertheless, several corollary ideas follow from the precept that "politics stops at the water's edge." First, as suggested by President Truman's speech, when criticism of existing policy is necessary—and advocates of bipartisanship have repeatedly stated there must be no mora-

Uncle Sam: "A Clear Windshield Would Help"

Marcus in *The New York Times*, March 3, 1957.

torium on criticism—it should be constructive and not destructive. Obviously, this requirement, too, suffers from extreme vagueness. As an example, consider Senator Herbert Lehman's (Democrat from New York) criticism of the Eisenhower Administration's diplomacy:

> We must regard with deep misgivings the administration's strong inclination to formulate a slogan in place of a policy, its disposition to coin phrases rather than to develop programs, its habit of putting salesmanship ahead of statesmanship. (9, April 14, 1954, p. A2832).

Whether this can be designated "constructive" or "destructive" criticism is a question that will be decided largely by whether a Democrat or a Republican is asked to evaluate it.

A large area of independent judgment must always exist in deciding what kind of criticism is permissible. Still, as the former Democratic presidential candidate Adlai Stevenson has phrased it:

> . . . in politics, criticism divorced from honest and constructive purpose ceases to be a proper instrument of democracy. Criticism, as an instrument not of inquiry and reform, but of power, quickly degenerates into the techniques of deceit and smear. . . . If criticism is distorted into calumny, mud-slinging, and doubletalk . . . it is not simply this or that party or this or that political figure that must suffer. It is the Republic itself. (34, p. 33).

This may be accepted as a reasonably good description of the kind of criticism bipartisanship contemplates.

Second, the idea that politics stops at the water's edge presupposes that those individuals who join in bipartisan endeavors will do so *in good faith* and with a genuine desire to achieve great national purposes. As the Truman Administration discovered in dealing with Far Eastern problems, bipartisan procedures can avail little unless there is a sincere effort on the part of those using them to arrive at constructive policy decisions. Neither side should give the appearance of wanting unity in the government, when in fact it does not want unity at all, but is merely utilizing opportunities to collaborate with the opposite party for purely partisan ends. The Truman Administration, for example, was strongly suspicious that Senator Robert A. Taft (Republican of Ohio) and other influential Republicans in Congress did not really want bipartisanship. For his part, Sena-

tor Taft more than once expressed deep-seated reservations about bipartisan collaboration. Little constructive purpose therefore could be served by liaison techniques under these circumstances.

Third, bipartisanship contemplates that neither political party will seek to exploit foreign policy issues for partisan gains, particularly during political campaigns. Though this is the prevailing theory, it has not been followed to any significant degree by either party in the postwar period. Until 1953, Republicans repeatedly berated Democratic policy-makers for diplomatic failures in the Far East and tried to show that high-level decisions were, at worst, influenced by subversives and, at best, decided by individuals closely identified with left-wing causes. These themes were notably prominent in Republican campaigning during the elections of 1950 and 1952. Democrats of course have not neglected foreign policy issues in recent elections. They have accused Republicans of latent isolationism reflected in periodic GOP opposition to reciprocal trade, foreign aid, cultural exchange, and co-operation with the United Nations. They repeatedly criticized the swaggering braggadocio of Secretary of State Dulles, and they directed especially bitter criticism at the Eisenhower Administration's record in the Middle East.

Almost as a matter of ritual, candidates and politicoes are expected to endorse the *principle* of bipartisanship; having done that, they are apparently free to attack the opposite party's diplomatic record with impunity! Thus, in the presidential campaign of 1956, Democratic presidential nominee Adlai Stevenson confessed that any discussion of foreign policy ought to be "above politics." Then he proceeded to declare that the Eisenhower Administration had brought the nation to "bankruptcy" in its Middle Eastern diplomacy and added: "I doubt if ever before in our diplomatic history has any policy been such an abysmal, such a complete and such a catastrophic failure" (18, November 2, 1956).

While, ideally, bipartisanship contemplates self-restraint and a sense of mutual sacrifice among major participants in the foreign policy process and among candidates for public office, it has proved extremely difficult to translate this principle into rules for guiding the day-today conduct of policy-makers and rank-and-file party members. The evident disparity between widespread support for bipartisanship in theory and intense partisan controversy over foreign policy issues in practice must be explained by something more than the inability of politicians to follow their own preachments. This disparity is rooted in the political system itself and in the nature of democratic government.

Fortunately, sometimes there is value in merely the *appearance* of bipartisanship. It may convey the impression abroad of underlying public support for basic policy measures. It may make certain policies publicly acceptable. For instance, Secretary of State Dulles attempted to generate firm legislative support for the Eisenhower Administration's foreign policies. Many of these policies were carried over from the Truman Administration and had precipitated heated disunity within the government. But because they were viewed as bipartisan measures they could easily be supported as Republican policies under the Eisenhower Administration (**16**, p. 33).

Before examining certain troublesome problems accompanying a bipartisan approach, it is appropriate to ask how effectively has the bipartisan approach operated throughout the postwar period? In very general terms, the answer must be that greater unity has prevailed over foreign relations since World War II than might have been expected on the basis of earlier diplomatic experience. Both branches of the government and both major political parties stand united today behind certain broad policy goals and programs, chiefly those calculated to contain militant communism. The nation's friends and its diplomatic enemies have been able to count with reasonable assurance on the constancy of American leadership and on the fulfillment of its overseas commitments.

Yet if impressive unity has prevailed, so has substantial disunity. Not even Wilson's bitter wrangle with Senate Republicans equalled the level of partisan strife and public controversy witnessed toward selected aspects of postwar American foreign relations. Illustrative episodes include intense disputes over the Roosevelt and Truman Administrations' Far Eastern policies and vituperative criticisms directed at such executive officials as Secretaries of State Dean G. Acheson and, to a lesser extent, John Foster Dulles. The House of Representatives even tried in 1951 to compel Acheson's retirement by an unsuccessful move to eliminate his salary from the executive budget. Since World War II, no national election has failed to include widespread public controversy over aspects of America's relations with the outside world. In presidential years particularly, such as 1952, Republicans have discovered issues in this field that promised to be powerful vote-getting devices; both then and in 1956 such issues were of unquestioned importance in ending their twenty-year tenure as the opposition party. Allegations made during these campaigns were that the Democratic Party was the party of treason; that it had sold out Eastern Europe and Nationalist China to communism; that it had been content with a military stalemate, which many Americans equated with a defeat, in the Korean War; and that it had harbored subversive elements within the government.

Why has the unprecedented emphasis on bipartisan co-operation often failed to prevent schism over certain important American foreign policies, even though an underlying consensus has prevailed over many fundamentals of policy? What are the limitations inherent in, or frequently encountered in, a bipartisan approach?

2. BARRIERS TO UNITY

Constitutional Obstacles

Formidable barriers to bipartisan collaboration on foreign affairs are inherent in the American constitutional system. Thanks to the concept of separation of powers, the control of foreign relations was deliberately divided by the founders between the President and Congress, particularly the Senate. Whatever may have been the original intention of the founding fathers, American diplomatic experience has clearly elevated the

President into a position of leadership in foreign affairs. The role of Congress is important, and has become increasingly so in the modern period, but it is nevertheless a *subordinate* role. Congress may modify proposals made by executive officials; and, for short periods at least, it can block at least certain steps contemplated by the White House. But the initiative in foreign affairs rests with the President and his chief advisers. Efforts to achieve bipartisan co-operation, therefore, must always be carried on within a historic and constitutional framework of executive supremacy in foreign relations.

This fact has profound significance for bipartisanship. It means, first, that the President must always remain at the helm of the ship of state. Under the Constitution, it is his responsibility to preserve national security, and he cannot abdicate this responsibility merely because greater unity within the government might be ideally desirable. Obviously, attempts to create unity may contribute to the broad goal of national security. At times, however, as when President Truman decided upon American assistance to Greece in 1947 and intervened with troops in Korea in 1950, a chief executive must take steps demanded by the diplomatic interests of the country, regardless of whether such steps have received widespread initial bipartisan support. However useful bipartisan collaboration may be, there are times when it will have to be sacrificed to the paramount constitutional obligation of the President to manage foreign relations in the manner best calculated to assure national security.

Second, under the American Constitution Congress bears little or no direct responsibility for certain kinds of activities in the sphere of foreign relations. This is true, for instance, of the recognition of other governments, which is purely an executive function. It is difficult to see how completely satisfactory bipartisan procedures can be worked out within the existing constitutional framework to cover such problems. For if, on the one hand, the President permits Congress to share in making policies in these instances, then he is permitting the legislature to make decisions for which he alone is constitutionally responsible. If he excludes such questions from the area of bipartisan co-

operation, then he invites the charge that he has arbitrarily limited the bipartisan process, that he really does not want unity on the issue in question, and that he has freed the opposition party to criticize policy openly. No example from postwar experience better illustrates the complexities of this kind of problem for the bipartisan approach than the Truman Administration's diplomacy toward Nationalist China (**10**, pp. 93-116).

In the third place, a constitutional no-man's-land exists in regard to the control of domestic aspects of foreign relations, notably the use of troops in behalf of diplomatic objectives. After a century and a half of constitutional history, the exact boundaries between legislative and executive prerogatives remain shadowy. This well-nigh invites the two branches to struggle for supremacy, to maximize their own power, and to resist expansion in the powers of the other branch. Such considerations were undoubtedly behind the so-called Great Debate on American defense policy late in 1950 and early in 1951. Although the ostensible issues involved the commitment of American ground troops to Europe, this debate must be at least partially explained as a recurrence of a constitutional struggle that has erupted many times in American history over the exact scope of legislative and executive prerogatives in the military and defense field. Genuine bipartisan co-operation is predicated upon some kind of understanding as to the jurisdictions of the President and Congress, in order that a profitable division of labor in foreign affairs may result.

To summarize: under the American Constitution relations between the President and Congress are almost always in a state of actual or potential turbulence. This condition is not accidental. To avoid the extremes of dictatorship and of mass rule, the founding fathers deliberately sought to make unified governmental policy difficult and to place many obstacles in the way of co-ordinating activities among the branches. The founders, in other words, deliberately sought to prevent too much unity within the American government. In their view, divided responsibilities—bringing, as they must, inevitable disunity, perhaps even deadlock—would go far to preserve the Republic from domination by any one branch. While the founders obviously could not foresee the later historical consequences of disunity within the government, especially in the realm of foreign relations, it is difficult even today to overcome the constitutional doctrine of separation of powers altogether. As long as each branch continues to possess independent powers in foreign affairs, a certain amount of conflict and contention between them will likely prove inescapable.

Disunity Within the Executive Branch

The postwar emphasis upon bipartisanship would seem to suggest that internal divisions over foreign relations have their origins in hostile executive-legislative relations or partisan controversies. Yet it has become progressively apparent that considerable disunity may originate within the executive branch alone. A prerequisite for bipartisan agreements is agreement among executive officials themselves over basic policies and programs. In the absence of such agreement, bipartisan procedures can accomplish little. As Senator Vandenberg pointed out when Truman's Secretary of Commerce, Henry A. Wallace, publicly disagreed with the government's foreign policies, there can only be one Secretary of State at a time (26, September 15, 1946). Republicans wanted to collaborate with Democratic policy-makers, Vandenberg stated, but they had great difficulty doing so when doubt existed at home and abroad over the individuals who spoke for the administration and over what the fundamentals of policy were at any given time.

This problem became especially acute, almost endemic, with the Eisenhower Administration —so much so that the *New York Times* correspondent Cabell Phillips was led to observe in 1954 that a kind of "tripartisanship" was needed: the Administration had first to unify the speeches and activities of those within its official family before it could solicit the cooperation of the Democratic opposition (26, October 21, 1954).

Several examples may be cited briefly. The GOP Majority Leader in the Senate during 1953-54 was Senator William F. Knowland of California. Earlier, Knowland had been one of the chief critics of the Truman Administration's Far Eastern policies; after 1953 he appeared to be only slightly more satisfied with his own party's diplomatic efforts in that region. It was public knowledge that Knowland wanted the Eisenhower Administration to follow much more militant anti-communist policies in the Orient. In the field of defense policy, conflict also prevailed within the Administration. One group of Cabinet officers, led by Secretary of the Treasury George Humphrey, publicly expressed its belief that defense spending was too high. The President and his Secretary of Defense, Charles E. Wilson, maintained that it could be no lower without jeopardy to national security. Subordinate Defense Department officials, joined by the military chiefs, argued that the overall total was too low or that expenditures ought to be re-allocated more equitably among the armed services. Under these circumstances, Congress and the citizenry at large sometimes had considerable difficulty obtaining a clear picture of the level of defense spending the executive branch believed the national interest demanded. Conflict within the Administration was also evident over relations with Red China and disarmament negotiations with the Soviet Union. The President indicated in mid-1957 that some modification of the prevailing policy of non-recognition of Red China was possibly forthcoming, only to have Secretary of State Dulles follow the President's assertion with a speech of his own, in which he vigorously indicted Red China's recent actions and reaffirmed the Administration's determination to withhold recognition. Similarly, a veritable babel of voices was heard within the executive branch during 1957 over the question of disarmament. The Defense Department, the State Department, the Atomic Energy Commission, and the President's special assistant in charge of disarmament negotiations all took contradictory positions on the prospects for reaching agreement with the USSR and on the consequences of agreement for American security. In the midst of this confusion, it was not always clear just where President Eisenhower himself stood on the disarmament problem. Commenting on Eisenhower's remarks at a presidential press conference in this period, Walter Lippmann observed that the "President has acted the part, not of a statesman who has a policy but of a puzzled man who is thinking out loud" (26, July 2, 1957).

These illustrations highlight the fact that disunity within the government over foreign affairs is not exclusively a product of executive-legislative conflict or of partisan controversies. In view of the great complexity of foreign policy issues and the vast expansion in the size of the executive branch in recent years, it has become increasingly difficult to unify even executive efforts so that initially a reasonably clear understanding of American diplomatic intentions is possible and, after that, so that bipartisan collaboration may take place on the basis of carefully worked out executive proposals.

Disunity Within Congress

After reviewing the mechanism for controlling foreign relations within the United States W. Y. Elliott has concluded that:

> The Congress of the United States still remains without any very clear method of integrating the control of foreign policy in either house and certainly lacks any machinery for coordination in both houses, except in so far as party leadership may afford it. (14, p. 349).

For reasons to be discussed elsewhere in this chapter, party leadership seldom can be counted on to provide effective co-ordination of policy in Congress. The result is that collaboration between the President and Congress is sometimes considerably easier to bring about than integration of legislative activities alone.

It cannot be too strongly emphasized that congressional organization and procedure are not conducive to unified efforts in the foreign policy field. In spite of the Legislative Reorganization Act of 1946, congressional committees have tended to proliferate. By 1956 there were altogether a total of 231 standing and joint committees and subcommittees in both chambers. When this fact is coupled with growing interdependence of domestic and foreign programs, and with the traditional independence of legislative committees, the opportunities for disjointed and self-defeating efforts within Congress are almost without limit. As we noted in Chapter 5, some of the more serious sources of disunity within Congress are:

conflicting jurisdictions among standing policy committees; disagreements between policy committees and the appropriations committees; the extremely fragmentary treatment that Congress accords to the national defense budget; and the virtually inseparable relationship between internal and external policy measures.

The difficulties created by an unco-ordinated congressional approach to foreign policy were borne in with particular force upon the Eisenhower Administration shortly after it took office in 1953. At a meeting of the Cabinet on January 30, Attorney-General Herbert Brownell revealed that no less than ten separate legislative investigations of the State Department and American foreign policy were currently in progress (12, p. 85). Initially, President Eisenhower resolved to co-operate with these investigations, some of which quite plainly had publicity as their chief objective. But in time even Eisenhower was forced to refuse legislative demands for confidential data, on the firm constitutional grounds that such requests constituted attempts by the legislature to intrude into the confidential deliberations of the President and his chief advisers.

Another continuing source of disunity has existed in the role of the House Rules Committee, generally conceded to be the most influential committee on Capitol Hill. The Rules Committee is not a policy committee; theoretically it does not formulate legislation. Its assigned task is merely to regulate the flow of business in the House with a view to promoting legislative efficiency. In reality, the House Rules Committee has frequently exercised a veto over legislation in the foreign policy field. When it could not completely bottle up legislation it opposed, it could usually manage to delay legislative action and interpose all kinds of parliamentary barriers. In one case—when President Truman asked Congress for authority to send surplus American wheat to India in 1951 —the Rules Committee delayed congressional approval for several weeks, with the result that Soviet Russia supplied wheat to India before the United States. Dilatory tactics by the Rules Committee created the impression abroad that the United States was niggardly and that Congress was more interested in assuring repayment than in relieving famine conditions on the

Indian subcontinent. Even though Congress eventually approved Truman's request, the United States lost much of the goodwill and propaganda value that might have accrued if Congress had responded rapidly and enthusiastically. It was the membership of the strategic Rules Committee—legislators who had little experience or training in foreign affairs and who could probably not assess the consequences of their action—who frustrated what might have been a significant achievement in the foreign policy field (7, pp. 233-37).

A second factor that militates heavily against unified efforts within Congress is the weakness of party organization and the substantial freedom legislators possess to follow their own independent judgments on questions of national policy. Party lines within Congress* are seldom rigid and national political leaders have few weapons at their disposal for coercing errant party members into following a predetermined party line. National party platforms are not drafted by the party membership in Congress at all, but by delegates elected on the state and local level. It is not unknown for the presidential candidate himself to repudiate at least parts of the platform altogether; and legislative candidates on the state and local level are even less inclined to be bound by platform declarations. In political campaigns, especially for the House, candidates for Congress are primarily concerned with issues specifically affecting their states or districts. They do not hesitate to challenge positions taken by their national party leaders or even to oppose certain aspects of their own party's record in office.

The President and his chief political advisers have consequently come to depend far more on persuasion and conciliation to win support for their program among members of their own party than upon stern disciplinary measures. There are very few consistently effective disciplinary measures that can be taken against party defectors. Presidential interference in local elections is strongly resented and can often backfire to the detriment of the Presi-

dent's own prestige. Candidates for national office, of course, usually want the endorsement of the White House in forthcoming campaigns. But the President and the national party organization also need the support of state and local party leaders. The result is that the President usually endorses the candidacy of even those members of his party who openly opposed him on important domestic and foreign issues. Presidents from both parties customarily follow the principle that the election of *any* candidate from their own party is preferable to the election of a member of the opposition.

Given the extremely decentralized party organization within the United States, and the near impossibility of enforcing acceptance of a party line upon members, a major obstacle to bipartisan agreements in foreign relations lies in the difficulty of translating bipartisan understandings into agreements that are *binding upon Congress as a whole*. There is no guarantee that proposals carefully worked out between the two foreign affairs committees and the State Department will be accepted by other committees, such as the Rules or the Appropriations committees, or by rank-and-file party members. The two individuals who have been conspicuously successful in bringing about bipartisan collaboration in the postwar era— Senators Vandenberg and Walter F. George (Democrat of Georgia)—were singularly effective in surmounting this obstacle. Both men served as chairman of the Foreign Relations Committee, and both were also highly influential in the deliberations of their party organizations. Both were consequently in a position to reach agreements with reasonable assurance that they would be accepted by their colleagues in Congress. William S. White explained Senator George's role under the Eisenhower Administration in the following terms:

> He spoke, and speaks, on world affairs for the entire Democratic party in the Senate as few men can have done in history. In effect, he pledged, and indeed committed, the whole power of the Democratic party in this field to the President. And while he was at it he flung about the President the capacious cloak of the immense, incontestably conservative prestige of the Southern Democrats.
> . . . Thus, when Mr. George began to make it plain that he saw no reason whatever why the Administration should not negotiate with the

---

*Among the many studies of party organization within the United States, the following provide comprehensive coverage and interpretative insight: 4; 21; 31.

Communists, or move a bit away from the China Nationalists, it was impossible even for the most implacable Senate Republican right-wingers to cry out "soft on communism." (38, p. 34).

There is thus no particular mystery about why the Truman Administration had difficulty locating a successor to Vandenberg or why the Eisenhower Administration experienced the same difficulty finding a legislator who could replace Senator George. Their key roles in the bipartisan process were the result of a unique combination of talents and prerogatives: chairmanship of the Foreign Relations Committee, far greater than average influence in their party's deliberations, and great respect among the rank-and-file legislators. This combination appears infrequently, due to the organization of the party system and of Congress. And this fact poses a formidable roadblock in the path of arriving at enduring bipartisan understandings.

No treatment of the sources of disunity within Congress would be complete without reference to the influence of constituency pressures upon the activities of legislators. Among all the factors that may shape legislative behavior and viewpoints on both domestic and foreign issues, none is more fundamental at times than grass-roots opinion in state or local constituencies. Such pressures have been reflected most noticeably in the overall voting records of legislators from states containing large foreign-born populations, such as New York, Illinois, or Wisconsin. People in these states are more than ordinarily concerned with American relations with those countries from which local minority groups have come. Legislators from these states were especially vocal during the postwar period in demanding lenient Allied treatment of Italy, in questioning the Nuremberg war crimes trials, and in urging vigorous American protests against Soviet machinations in Eastern Europe (27, pp. 22-3).

William S. White has observed that in the Senate there is a "great pluralism of winds and cross-winds. There is in the Senate no possibility of finding and fixing a single economic interest, for this is a deliberately and unchangeably disparate place where unity in such an area of life is not only unacceptable but is consciously fought" (37, pp. 136-7). When foreign policy issues like the tariff arise that tend to break up an already loose party alignment into sectional and local interest groups, then the difficulty of achieving enduring bipartisan agreements is greatly compounded. Grass-roots constituency pressures are often much more decisive in influencing legislative behavior in regard to these questions than appeals to party loyalty or to the principle of bipartisanship.

Confusion Over Bipartisan Procedures

Some of the procedures for bringing about unity have come to be widely accepted as normally integral features of bipartisan collaboration. In regard to others, however, there has existed, and continues to exist, a substantial amount of controversy. Consider first the requirement that prior consultation ought to precede major decisions in the foreign policy field.

What exactly should be the nature of these consultations? Who ought to be included within them? To what extent should consultations permit the legislative branch to make significant modifications in proposals submitted by executive officials? To what degree does prior consultation bind the members of the opposition party to support resultant decisions, either initially or in the weeks and months that follow? Should consultations take place solely on foreign policy issues, or should they be extended to cover closely related domestic issues as well? These questions have repeatedly fomented misunderstandings throughout the postwar years, and to date no answers satisfactory to both branches of the government and both political parties have emerged.

As to the nature of consultations, Republicans complained on a number of occasions under Truman, and Democrats complained under Eisenhower, that many so-called "consultations" were in actuality only briefing sessions at which executive officials informed legislators of steps they intended to take to deal with critical external problems. As early as 1946, the GOP presidential aspirant, Harold Stassen, told the Truman Administration that "Republicans would like to be co-pilots in the foreign policy take-offs as well as in the crash landings . . . ," a view reaffirmed several times also by Senator

Vandenberg (26, April 15, 1955). There are, however, substantial limitations to this co-pilot conception of bipartisanship. External crises sometimes make decisive executive action mandatory. In these circumstances, Congress may be presented with a *fait accompli* it can either approve or disapprove, when it has any power to affect the decision at all. On other occasions, Congress may actually bear no responsibility for contemplated actions. Following a co-pilot conception of bipartisanship in these instances might result in substantial modifications of historic constitutional principles governing the scope of executive and legislative prerogatives in foreign affairs. Then again, the President, who must make the ultimate decision, may become convinced that certain steps are required in the diplomatic field, even though many legislators oppose these steps. Much as he might ideally desire unity, the President has a greater constitutional obligation to conduct foreign relations in the manner best calculated to protect national security.

The question of the individuals to be included in bipartisan consultations is also extremely complex and controversial. Obviously, officials from the State Department and the White House staff, along with representatives of other departments concerned with specific decisions, should participate. The two foreign affairs committees or their appropriate subcommittees in Congress should be consulted. What other groups should be drawn in? We have already noted that a significant trend in the postwar period is the extent to which the activities of many other congressional committees bear directly or indirectly on external affairs. A given foreign policy decision might conceivably be within the province of the armed services committees, the interstate and foreign commerce committee, the agriculture committees, to list but a few—and it will almost certainly be considered sooner or later by the appropriations committees. Furthermore, to assure bridging the gulf between the legislative committees and the party organization, the *political leadership* in Congress should also perhaps be included.

It is apparent that a law of diminishing returns governs the degree to which consultations can profitably be extended to include all groups within the government that might be directly or indirectly concerned with specific diplomatic decisions. Very often such decisions must be made quickly. Frequently too, constructive consultations require that confidential information be made available. The chances are great that such information will eventually become public if it is given to several committees and to individual party leaders. Moreover, there is the distinct probability that ever-broadening consultations will make the foreign policy process within the United States diffuse, discursive, and inordinately time-consuming.

Just what obligations are assumed by participants in the bipartisan process? Once they have agreed to join in bipartisan endeavors, how much are the participants obligated to support the policies that emerge? If the President seeks bipartisan support, is he required to accept changes proposed by Congress? After bipartisan consultations have begun, is either side free to withdraw from them because it disagrees with decisions taken? Postwar experience affords no very clear guidance on these questions. Their relevance and importance, however, can be gauged from the difficulties encountered by Secretary of State Dulles in trying to reach agreement with legislators over American foreign policy in Asia. After being bewildered on several occasions by Dulles' seemingly contradictory statements concerning American diplomatic intentions in the Far East, commentators in Washington concluded that these statements had their roots in the Administration's efforts to conciliate influential legislative critics. Paul Nitze, formerly chairman of the Policy Planning Staff in the State Department, distinguished between what he called Dulles' "declaratory policy" and his "operational policy." The former —often belligerently anti-communist and ultra-moralistic—was designed to win the support of such critics as Senator Knowland. His "operational policy," however, was covertly aimed at reducing American commitments to Chiang Kai-shek and avoiding open conflict with communism in Asia. As a price for winning and holding the support of influential legislators, the Administration was required, at least publicly, to take a "hard line" toward Asian problems. A realistic appraisal of events in Asia, however, led it to rely more upon its own independent judgment and, privately at least, to repudiate some of the positions taken in public speeches. Such behavior clearly risked making American foreign policy more obscure than ever to legislators not included in bipartisan consultations, to the allies, and to the citizenry at large (**16**, p. 32).

An additional difficulty in devising satisfactory bipartisan consultations relates to the range of subject-matter that ought to be included in them. If a prevailing conception of bipartisanship is that "politics stops at the water's edge," a necessary question is: in questions involving national security in the mid-20th century, just where does the water's edge begin? $E=MC^2$ is the basic scientific formula of the nuclear age. Its ramifications for national security touch such seemingly disparate questions as whether the level of governmental taxation is too high; whether the domestic economy is on a sound basis; and whether levels of education and scientific research are adequate to maintain long-range security. Should these and other closely related "domestic" questions be included in the scope of bipartisan consultations? If so, there would appear to be few important questions of governmental policy which could safely be omitted.

The lack of a clear dividing line between foreign and domestic questions leaves two basic alternatives for advocates of bipartisanship: either executive and legislative officials can conceive of foreign policy issues narrowly and confine consultations to these issues alone; or they can recognize the almost inextricable ties between internal and external questions and extend liaison techniques to include the broad range of important problems affecting national security. The former course well-nigh guarantees that disunity will appear within the government on closely related domestic questions and will almost certainly spread eventually to the realm of foreign relations. The latter course risks making a bipartisan approach cumbersome and time-consuming, if indeed it does not almost foreordain governmental paralysis and indecision in the face of recurrent and ominous external threats. To date, in the vast majority of cases, both Democratic and Republican administrations have preferred the former course. For instance, after initially suggesting that bipartisan co-operation should include relevant

domestic questions, the Eisenhower Administration dropped this proposal because of opposition from Republicans and Democrats alike (Dispatches by William S. White in **26**, November 24, 1954 and January 9, 1955).

Still another problem associated with bipartisan consultation centers on the question: who is entitled to speak for the opposition party and to reach agreements in its name? Factionalism, always present to some degree in American politics, afflicts the opposition party especially, because it lacks both a designated party leader and a clearcut program. One reason that bipartisan collaboration over the Treaty of Versailles foundered was because there was no individual who enjoyed the confidence of both President Wilson and Senate Republicans. Similarly, under the Truman Administration, influential members of the GOP complained that the two Republican advisers to the State Department, John Foster Dulles and John Sherman Cooper, prominent Republican from Kentucky, had no power, could not speak for them, and could not bind Congress to approve understandings arrived at with Democratic policy-makers.

The identical problem arose again in 1957 when President Eisenhower requested the former Democratic presidential candidate, Adlai Stevenson, to serve in his administration as a Democratic consultant on foreign affairs, with reference especially to defense policies. Stevenson accepted this assignment, even though a substantial question existed even in his own mind concerning just whom he actually represented. Stevenson had sometimes been called the "titular head" of the Democratic Party. But exactly what did this title signify? He held no official or political position, nor could it be said with any assurance that he was the opposition party's designated spokesman on foreign policy issues, a role much more likely to be performed in fact by legislators like Senators Mike Mansfield of Montana or William Fulbright of Arkansas (**5**). Moreover, at the very time Stevenson was presumably trying to promote closer bipartisan unity, another organization of the Democratic Party, in which former President Truman, Eleanor Roosevelt, Dean G. Acheson —and even sometimes Adlai Stevenson himself —played a prominent part, was severely criticizing the Republican record in the field of missile development and scientific research generally. Stevenson therefore served with the Administration for a few weeks only. After declining to attend a NATO Conference in December, Stevenson resigned his post because this assignment would have put him in a position which was, in his words, "without authority and necessarily identified with decisions I might not always agree with and could not publicly oppose" (26, December 8, 1957). Stevenson's not altogether satisfactory experience as an *ex officio* consultant on foreign policy had been foreshadowed by that of Wendell Wilkie during the Roosevelt Administration. Asked by the Administration to help convince Republicans to support preparedness measures in Congress, Wilkie refused to do so. He stated on August 9, 1940: "I do not think it appropriate for me to enter into advance commitments and understandings. If the National Administration . . . publicly takes any given position with reference to our foreign policy, I may on appropriate occasion comment thereon" (Quoted in 23, p. 754.)

Individuals who assume leading roles in providing bipartisan liaison must, so to speak, have one foot in each camp. The incumbent administration must thoroughly trust and respect them as straightforward and capable of giving their independent judgment about major foreign policy issues. An individual who is *persona non grata* to the party in power, such as Senator Taft was with the Truman Administration, can provide very little useful bipartisan liaison. Similarly, individuals so selected must always enjoy the confidence of their own party and be trusted by it not to become so closely identified with the administration in power that they ignore their own party's historic and current viewpoints on important international questions. A peculiar combination of talents and qualifications is demanded, so much so that remarkably few individuals in the postwar period have been conspicuously successful in bringing about enduring bipartisan accords.*

Finally, even if satisfactory consultations can be arranged, their cumulative burden may become extremely onerous and time-consuming for executive officials involved. The number of bipartisan consultations has grown impressively throughout the postwar period, as efforts to achieve unity within the government have been put on a more systematic and sustained basis. As an example, during the session of Congress from February 10 to July 28, 1953, Secretary of State Dulles and his principal advisers met with the full Senate Foreign Relations Committee or one of its subcommittees a total of twenty-five times. Subjects discussed ranged from American diplomatic activities in the Far East, to the Palestinian refugees, to the European Coal and Steel Community, to issues pending before the United Nations.** These consultations were with one legislative committee alone; a listing of consultations with the House Foreign Affairs Committee would show a roughly similar pattern. Nor does this list include White House conferences, at which the President himself reviewed foreign policy problems with legislators. From 1953 to 1957, Secretary of State Dulles met on two hundred and fourteen different occasions with legislative groups. Former Secretary of State Acheson has stated that during his service in the government it was not unusual for him to devote half of his working day in certain periods to bipartisan consultations! On the average about one-sixth of his time was devoted to this function (1, p. 65).

If anything, this problem has become more critical over the course of the years, both because the total *number* of high-ranking executive officials involved has increased and because the *time* devoted to such liaison activities has mounted. Significantly, the Secretary of Defense has more and more been drawn into such consultation. A tabulation of time spent by the Secretary of Defense during the year

---

*Out of his experiences as Secretary of State, Dean Acheson has given a detailed analysis of the personal qualities that are important for individuals prominent in the bipartisan process. See 1,

pp. 72-5. The subject is also discussed further in 10, pp. 217-20.

**An extensive list of bipartisan consultations, describing the groups included, the subjects discussed, and the dates held was inserted into the *Congressional Record*, Volume 101, pp. 2408-11, by Senator Knowland of California. This list shows all such consultations held under the Eisenhower Administration, to early 1956.

1958 to secure bipartisan support revealed that he testified before various committees of Congress, as follows:

HOUSE

Committee	Hours
Appropriations	15½
Armed Services	28½
Foreign Affairs	2½
Ways and Means	1½
TOTAL	48

SENATE

Committee	Hours
Appropriations	10
Armed Services	15
Foreign Relations	2
Preparedness	12
TOTAL	39

(*Source:* **26**, *February 15, 1959, Dispatch by Cabell Phillips.*)

It is open to serious question whether the total burden of consultations represents the most effective utilization of the time and talents of high-ranking executive officials, granting that some consultation is both desirable and unavoidable. Former Secretary of State Acheson is inclined to doubt it. He cites his own frequent, lengthy, and in many respects fruitless appearances before the Senate Armed Services-Foreign Relations Committees at the time of the investigation into General Douglas MacArthur's dismissal in 1951. This joint hearing entailed an extended, wide-ranging inquiry into recent decades of American Far Eastern policy. With some legislators participating in the investigation, partisan motivations abounded, as members of the Democratic and Republican parties sought to justify earlier positions of their parties. In Acheson's words, "Not more than an hour" of his interrogation "related to the relief of General MacArthur." On the basis of this and other experiences with bipartisan consultations, Acheson has concluded sardonically that "The understanding of relevance continues to elude the gentlemen of Capitol Hill" (**1**, pp. 65, 80-2). When major policy issues are at stake, important legislative committees are seldom content to question officials less exalted than the Secretary of State himself, or his highest assistants. And it is exceedingly difficult for executive officials to limit either the number or the scope of their appearances on Capitol Hill without inviting the charge that they are withholding information from Congress or that they do not really want bipartisan collaboration on particular issues. More and more legislative committees are being drawn directly and indirectly into external affairs. Acknowledging that many congressional hearings can have beneficial results, comparable to the joint investigation in 1951 that quieted the public furor over MacArthur's dismissal, such hearings can become enormously time-consuming for high-ranking executive officials—perhaps reaching the point of interfering with needed high-level executive planning in the international field.

Political Repercussions of Bipartisanship

In January, 1953, when the Senate Foreign Relations Committee was considering the confirmation of John Foster Dulles as Secretary of State, he was presented with certain of his own contradictory statements about, on the one hand, the compelling need for bipartisan co-operation and, on the other hand, his sharp criticisms of Democratic policy-makers throughout preceding months. His reply points to some of the political obstacles in the path of enduring bipartisan agreements:

. . . under our Constitutional system we have a general election every four years . . . one side presents his case, and the other side presents the other case, as two lawyers do when they go into court. At that stage the two parties are not judges and they are not judicial. In my opinion they should not be . . . but when that time is past, then I believe we should try to work together on a bipartisan basis. . . . (**16**, p. 29).

Dulles' statement calls attention to two contrary and powerful forces that tend to pull any discussion of foreign policy questions in opposite directions: the widely admitted need for maximum unity when important international issues are at stake and the equally compelling necessity for full and periodic debate on paramount questions of public policy.

Of all the pitfalls in the path of bipartisan collaboration, those inherent in American politics are in all likelihood the most persistent and formidable. Take first the long-standing principle that the party in power is held responsible by public opinion for the way it manages governmental affairs. Under a bipartisan approach, the principle that politics stops at the water's edge has been widely interpreted to mean that both political parties share equally successes and failures in the foreign policy field. Yet postwar experience points to two traditions of political behavior that virtually nullify this principle. These are, first, that the party in power takes credit publicly for significant achievements in internal and external affairs; second, that the opposition party dissociates itself from policy failures at home and abroad. Republicans, for instance, have consistently maintained, despite considerable evidence to the contrary, that the Truman Administration's unsuccessful Far Eastern policies were never part of the area of bipartisan agreement (35, p. 532). Likewise under Eisenhower, Democrats have repeatedly disavowed many Republican policies toward the Middle East which, on the most charitable interpretation possible, have not proved conspicuously successful (10, pp. 148-9). But in their attempt to end the long Democratic monopoly of the White House, Republicans particularly have found foreign policy issues to be remarkably effective in creating public sentiment favorable to their cause.

Recognizing that foreign policy questions are often exploited by self-seeking politicians, it is still true that gains and losses in external affairs cannot be shared equally between the two major parties. If the incumbent party has governed well, it is natural—in a democracy perhaps inevitable—that it should seek to be returned to office on the strength of its record. Conversely, an opposition party cannot voluntarily forego opportunities to inject international policies—especially unsuccessful policies—into the political arena without inviting the charge that it lacks alternative proposals of its own and that it can do no better than acquiesce in ineffectual efforts at home and abroad.

Then there is the fundamental political question: under a bipartisan approach, how is needed criticism of policy to emerge, and what is the role of the opposition party in providing it? Advocates of bipartisanship have maintained almost as a matter of ritual that there should be no moratorium on criticism, but only that criticism should be "constructive." Yet when unity becomes a dominant goal, the opposition party is always in danger of being compromised. Either it continues to attack policies that, in its judgment, need criticizing—thereby risking the charge that it is indifferent to the need for unity on the home front during periods of international tension; or it withholds criticism for the sake of unity or the *appearance* of unity—and risks perhaps the even more damaging charge that it is no longer an effective opposition and that it is equally responsible for feeble efforts in the diplomatic sphere. This dilemma is well illustrated by President Eisenhower's request early in 1957 for legislative authority to use troops if necessary in the Middle East. Democrats who, in this period, controlled Congress had deep-seated reservations about the President's proposal and about his past and contemporary policies in the Middle East. Yet, in the words of the *Christian Science Monitor* reporter, Richard L. Strout

. . . the Democratic group looks at the resolution as a vote of confidence which the administration requests under patriotic compulsions that cannot be resisted although lack of confidence in Mr. Dulles has visibly been growing. . . . In short, some of the Democrats feel they have been tricked. Faced with the alternatives of being branded as aiding communism against their own country, they are delaying action until they have made their own hostility to Mr. Dulles evident. Meanwhile, Mr. Dulles uses stronger and stronger terms in depicting the danger of the Middle East crisis. (6, January 25, 1957).

It cannot perhaps be too often emphasized that a cardinal distinction between totalitarian and democratic governments lies in the degree to which each believes the creation of unity to be a pre-eminent goal of policy-makers. Democracies operate upon the basis of consent, which inevitably implies a certain amount of dissent and dissension over important public issues. Totalitarian governments eliminate dissent openly and forcibly, but democracies may accomplish the same purpose, consciously or unconsciously, by more indirect and subtle means. Adlai Stevenson has observed that

. . . in many minds "criticism" has today become an ugly word. It has become almost *lèse-majesté*. It conjures up pictures of insidious radicals hacking away at the very foundations of the American way of life. It suggests nonconformity and nonconformity suggests disloyalty and disloyalty suggests treason, and before we know where we are, this process has all but identified the critic with the saboteur and turned political criticism into an un-American activity instead of democracy's greatest safeguard. (34, p. 32).

Under a bipartisan approach to foreign relations, there is not only the problem of *whether* criticism will emerge, but also the problem of *when* it emerges. Surely one purpose of enlightened criticism is to bring about needed changes in policy while there is yet time to prevent major policy failures. *Ex post facto* criticism whose purpose is merely to find out the individuals responsible for diplomatic ineptitude often serves little constructive purpose. This kind of criticism has been common in American diplomatic history. The many attempts by Republicans to investigate the Truman Administration's diplomacy toward Nationalist China are examples. Despite their claims to the contrary, Republicans participated in formulating a number of key foreign policy decisions toward China in the 1947-48 period (10, pp. 105-14). Penetrating criticism from the opposition party at that stage might possibly have averted what proved to be one of the most serious diplomatic defeats in the entire course of American history. Criticism eventually came—but by that time the only thing left to investigate was why Nationalist China had collapsed before the communist threat and why American diplomatic efforts had proved so ineffective.

One final point requires emphasis. "History," to quote Republican members of the House Foreign Affairs Committee, "is strewn with wreckage of countries that were united but on the wrong course." The paramount goal shared by both branches of the government and by both political parties is effective diplomacy. Unquestionably, bipartisan procedures sometimes contribute to reaching that goal. But sometimes too, other techniques and practices —firm executive leadership, clear public delineation of the issues by party spokesmen, replacement of inefficient incumbent officials by more capable ones—can advance the nation's diplomatic interests better than an uncritical attachment to the bipartisan principle. In the last analysis, one condition above all others is likely to prove the most durable incentive for unified efforts in foreign affairs: a conviction that the incumbent administration is aware of crucial problems in the international community and that it is working conscientiously to formulate the most intelligent and realistic policies possible for dealing with these problems.

REFERENCES

1. Acheson, Dean G. *A Citizen Looks at Congress.* New York: Harper and Brothers, 1957. A readable and incisive treatment of legislative problems, with emphasis on the congressional role in foreign affairs.

2. Bailey, Stephen K., and Samuel, Howard D. *Congress At Work.* New York: Henry Holt, 1952.

3. Bailey, Thomas A. *Woodrow Wilson and the Great Betrayal.* New York: The Macmillan Company, 1945. A scholarly treatment of the League of Nations controversy.

4. Brogan, D. W. *Politics in America.* New York: Harper and Brothers, 1954. This book by a noted English scholar is a valuable comparative study of the American political system.

5. Cater, Douglass. "Who Will Speak For the Democrats?" *The Reporter,* 15 (November 29, 1956), 22-3.

6. *Christian Science Monitor.*

7. *Congressional Quarterly Almanac,* Volume 7 (1951).

8. *Congressional Record.*

9. *Congressional Record* (daily edition).

10. Crabb, Cecil V., Jr. *Bipartisan Foreign Policy: Myth or Reality.* Evanston: Row, Peterson, and Company, 1957. Evaluates problems of bipartisanship and examines the pros and cons of such a policy for the American politico-governmental system.

11. Dahl, Robert A. *Congress and Foreign Policy.* New York: Harcourt, Brace and Company, 1950.

12. Donovan, Robert J. *Eisenhower: The Inside Story.* New York: Harper and Brothers, 1956. A journalistic account, based however on cabinet records.

13. Dulles, John Foster. *A Peace Treaty in The Making.* San Francisco: Japanese Peace Conference, September 4-8, 1951.

14. Elliott, W. Y. "The Control of Foreign Policy in the United States," *Political Quarterly,* 20 (October-December, 1949), 337-51.

15. Fleming, D. F. *The Treaty Veto of the American Senate.* New York: G. P. Putnam's Sons, 1930. Provides valuable insight in the Senate's historic role in treaty-making.

16. Harsch, Joseph C. "John Foster Dulles: A Very Complicated Man," *Harpers,* 213 (September, 1956), 27-34.

17. Haynes, George H. *The Senate of the United States.* Volume 2. Boston: Houghton Mifflin Company, 1938.

18. *Herald Tribune* (New York).

19. Holt, W. Stull. *Treaties Defeated By The Senate.* Baltimore: The Johns Hopkins Press, 1933. A valuable work on the Senate's role in treaty-making.

20. Kennan, George F. *American Diplomacy, 1900-1950.* Chicago: University of Chicago Press, 1951.

21. Key, V. O. *Politics, Parties, and Pressure Groups.* New York: Thomas Y. Crowell, 1947.

22. Langer, William L. "The Mechanism of American Foreign Policy," *International Affairs,* 24 (July, 1948), 319-328.

23. ——— and Gleason, S. Everett, *The Challenge to Isolation.* New York: Harper and Brothers, 1952. A scholarly and dispassionate treatment of American diplomacy in the 1937-40 period.

24. Lippmann, Walter. *The Public Philosophy.* Boston: Little, Brown and Company, 1955. Analyzes problems confronting the American democracy in foreign relations.

25. Nevins, Allan. *Henry White.* New York: Harper and Brothers, 1930.

26. *New York Times.*

27. "Power of Minorities in '46 Vote: Parties' Contest for Their Favor," *United States News,* 21 (October 18, 1946), 22-23.

28. Pratt, Julius W. *A History of United States Foreign Policy.* New York: Prentice-Hall, 1955.

29. Ratchford, B. U. "The South's Stake in International Trade—Past, Present, and Prospective," *Southern Economic Journal,* 14 (April, 1948), 361-75. An illuminating analysis of the South's changing position on the tariff.

30. Richards, James P. "The House of Representatives in Foreign Affairs," *Annals of the American Academy of Political and Social Science,* 289 (September, 1953), 66-72.

31. Schattschneider, E. E. *Party Government.* New York: Rinehart and Company, 1942. The author is a leading advocate of more disciplined parties, and a party re-alignment, within the United States.

32. Senate Foreign Relations Committee—House Foreign Affairs Committee, *The European Recovery Program,* Senate Document No. 111, 80th Congress, 1st Session, 1947. Contains a detailed analysis of preliminary studies leading up to the Marshall Plan.

33. Smith, Howard R., and Hart, John "The American Tariff Map," *Geographical Review,* 45 (July, 1955), 327-346. Discusses changing sectional alignments on tariff and trade legislation over the past half-century.

34. Stevenson, Adlai E. "Party of the Second Part," *Harpers,* 212 (February, 1956), pp. 31-34.

35. Vandenberg, Arthur H., Jr., ed. *The Private Papers of Senator Vandenberg.* Boston: Houghton Mifflin Company, 1952. A primary source for any study of bipartisanship in the postwar period.

36. *Washington Post - Times Herald.*

37. White, William S. *Citadel: The Story of the U. S. Senate.* New York: Harper and Brothers, 1957. An experienced journalist analyzes procedures and problems in the Senate.

38. ———. "Two Parties and One Foreign Policy," *New York Times Magazine,* August 7, 1955, pp. 12, 32-34.

39. ———. "Senator George—Monumental, Determined," *New York Times Magazine,* March 13, 1955, pp. 12, 42-47. An informative treatment of Senator George's contributions to the bipartisan process.

CHAPTER 7

Public Opinion and Decision Making

1. THE ANATOMY OF PUBLIC OPINION

In democratic societies it is axiomatic that governmental policies are heavily conditioned by public opinion. Authoritarian governments, to be sure, cannot totally disregard public sentiment. But they are not nearly as strongly compelled as democracies to take it into account in the day-to-day conduct of public affairs or to feel that it has fixed the outer limits beyond which officials dare not go for fear that their actions will later be repudiated by the citizenry.

At every stage in the foreign policy process —from the consideration of measures to be recommended to Congress, to the exchange of notes between governments, to speeches by representatives to the United Nations—public opinion must always be considered by policy-makers within the United States. Sometimes this opinion is clear and determinative, as illustrated by the almost unanimous public clamor demanding speedy demobilization after World War II. At other times, for instance toward the postwar problems of communist intrigue in Indochina or American policy toward Egypt, public opinion in recent years has been nebulous and difficult to measure. Even if policy-makers desired to take it into account, they often had great difficulty in deciding what the national consciousness demanded.

"Public Opinion"—A Many-Faceted Concept

Although the term public opinion did not come into wide currency until late in the 18th century (3, p. 669), philosophers and political sages have long been aware of the concept's pertinence to the study of government. Montesquieu referred to the *esprit général*, Rousseau to the *volonté général*, and German philosophers of the romantic school to the *Volksgeist*. Today popular usage has robbed the term public opinion of many of the incisive and specific qualities associated with it in earlier periods, so that prevailing definitions often cannot include all its nuances and subtleties of meaning. Wilhelm Bauer defines public opinion as a "deeply pervasive organic force" which "articulates and formulates not only the deliberative judgments of the national elements within the community but the evanescent common will . . . " (3, pp. 669-70). In less philosophical language, Cottrell and Eberhart hold that public opinion refers to the opinion of "the 'informed' public, the most vocal members of an elected official's constituency, the public represented by organizations, the kind of people with whom the speaker has some contact or whose opinions he esteems . . . " (12, pp. 9-10). These and other definitions that

145

might be cited* make it apparent that public opinion is an extremely variegated concept that admits of no brief yet complete definitions. How it is defined will depend heavily upon the facets of public opinion that are being investigated or upon the aspects of its influence that are being stressed.

Students of public opinion are in fairly general agreement that several elements are central to the concept. First, the term implies a greater or lesser degree of *public agreement* on important socio-economic-political questions. Second, the term presupposes a certain amount of *public discussion and awareness of contemporary issues*. Some issues provoke immediate and heated public debate and may lead to considerable group action for or against specified policies. In such cases public opinion may be thought of as a dynamic force. In other cases, public consciousness of issues may be hazy or even non-existent. Or, public opinion may be latent: when events arouse the population to a realization of the importance of public questions, then the citizenry may take an active part in debate over them. Third, most authorities believe that public opinion implies a *rational process*, that it involves "arriving at" decisions over a period of time, after the influences that go to formulate prevailing viewpoints have had a chance to become operative. Other writers have stressed, by contrast, that public opinion can be—and often is—an *irrational process*, and that sometimes irrational elements—personal and group antagonisms, prejudices, emotional reactions, snap judgments, and the like—predominate in shaping popular attitudes.

We shall better understand the complexities of public opinion after we have examined two questions about its basic nature and importance. What is the character of the *public* to which the term alludes? And what is meant by the *opinion* which the public supposedly reflects?

The "Public" and Its Components

Often the term public opinion carries the connotation of *the people as a unified entity*,

as suggested by the familiar constitutional phrase, "We, the people of the United States. . . . " It is possible to cite instances from American history to support the idea that occasionally the great body of the citizenry speaks with a clear and compelling voice in demanding or opposing certain governmental policies. This was the case during the 1930's, when the American people were profoundly isolationist and wanted nothing so much as to be left alone to manage their own internal affairs.

Instances when the population as a whole embraces one conception of the national interest are exceptional. More often than not, in regard to any specific issue confronting the nation, there are in reality *many publics and many opinions*. At any stage in American diplomatic experience a veritable cacophony of voices is likely to be heard by governmental officials advocating diverse and sometimes totally contradictory courses of action. The individual who seeks to assess the currents of popular sentiment will be struck by their dissimilarity, by the different levels of enlightenment reflected in the positions of various groups, and by the intensity of feeling with which conflicting viewpoints are championed. The shrill cries of xenophobic agitators, the machine-like efficiency with which certain pressure groups pass "resolutions" on controversial questions, the consistent left- or right-wing positions of segments of the American press, the quiet behind-the-scenes efforts of skilled lobbyists, the temporary flurries of public excitement over a reported diplomatic crisis —all these form part of that complex, elusive pattern called public opinion.

Once we recognize the inescapable fact that on most important national issues no clear majority sentiment binds the whole population together, the question arises: what group expresses "public opinion"? The loudest one? The most influential one? The wealthiest and most resourceful one? Those that can claim the largest memberships? Interest group lobbies who purport to speak in behalf of public opinion? When pollsters find that 51 per cent of the population expresses itself for or against a given proposal, have they at last uncovered what "public opinion" demands?

---

*For additional definitions, see 5, pp. 5-7 and 56, pp. 330-32.

These questions should make it apparent that the term public opinion as yet has no clearly defined and altogether satisfactory content. If the "public" means a majority of the adult population that has devoted serious thought to contemporary issues and has arrived at clearly thought-out verdicts about them, then in many cases no such thing as a reasonably uniform public opinion exists. Moreover, the proposition that governmental officials ought to formulate policies acceptable to public opinion rests on the debatable assumption that popular sentiment is rooted in a more durable basis than transitory moods or emotionalism.

Public Prejudices, Attitudes, and Opinions

Turning next to the question "What constitutes an opinion?," equally difficult problems arise. If by an opinion we mean *a reasonably enlightened and rational judgment* on any given issue, presupposing some background knowledge of the issue, it is evident that in practice "opinions" are rare. The great body of American citizens is poorly informed about many aspects of domestic and international problems, especially about international ones. Poll after poll has shown that a significant percentage of the population confesses openly that it has "no opinion" on major contemporary problems; and intensive studies of public opinion have indicated that even among those who express viewpoints, the level of understanding is discouragingly primitive.

On any given question in foreign affairs, somewhere between one-third and one-fourth of the American people probably have no opinion at all, in the sense of a point of view arrived at by thoughtful study of the issue in question. On the other hand, there are many relatively small groups who are interested and well-informed in foreign affairs—groups like the Council on Foreign Relations, the Foreign Policy Association and the members of its local branches, the American Association for the United Nations, the Arden House Study Group, and many less publicized professional and journalistic societies.

From time to time official and unofficial *ad hoc* committees are appointed to study and report on selected aspects of American foreign policy. One of the most influential of these in recent years was the Gaither Committee, appointed by President Eisenhower to investigate American defense problems in the light of spectacular Soviet gains in the missile field. The committee's findings, submitted late in 1957, pointed to many serious deficiencies in American defense planning and to the growing disparity between American and Soviet missile strength. Press reports indicated that the opinions expressed by the Gaither Committee were an important consideration in shaping President Eisenhower's budget recommendations in 1958, notably in the field of military-defense spending.*

There are thus great *qualitative* differences in public opinion. All opinions are not of equal merit, nor are all entitled to equal respect by policy-makers. Indeed, one may question whether certain kinds of viewpoints expressed by the public should be called "opinions" at all. Perhaps "attitudes" or "sentiments" or "prejudices" would be more accurate designations for viewpoints that are often largely intuitive, based upon hunch or emotionalism, and reflect no very clear appreciation of the complexities and subtleties surrounding major national issues (**56**, p. 332). Dexter Perkins has made the point as follows:

> We speak of "public opinion." The phrase suggests what the eighteenth century faith with regard to democratic government prescribed, that the average man makes up his mind by a purely rational process, by a study of the facts as they are laid before him. But is it not an illusion to assume that . . . is actually what takes place? The *facts*, if ascertainable at all . . . are often extremely complicated and are, for that matter, even when known, likely to be weighed subjectively. In the case of large groups of people, it might be better to speak of "public sentiment" rather than of "public opinion." For precise and detailed knowledge is not in the possession of the average citizen. His mood and prejudices are as important as his considered judgments. Indeed, they may influence policy more deeply. (**38**, p. 173).

---

*As a top secret document, the Gaither Committee report (named for its Chairman, H. Rowan Gaither, Jr.) was not released to the public. Much of its content, however, was "leaked" to the press, perhaps deliberately to arouse public sentiment to a greater sense of urgency about defense spending. For a summary of the report's findings, see *U. S. News and World Report*, Volume 44 (January 3, 1958), p. 57.

The Public Opinion Process

The formation and impact of public opinion have been described as a process divisible into four stages. The first stage is the reception of primary impressions, colored by prejudices, passions, rudimentary understanding, and sketchy information. Next, these impressions may be re-enforced, modified, or abandoned altogether and replaced by other ideas, as new information becomes available and as preliminary judgments are changed in the light of experience. Then, third, after public opinion has crystallized sufficiently, it will be expressed through a variety of techniques: elections and the political process, lobbying, the press and other media, communications to governmental officials, citizens' meetings and demonstrations, to list but a few well-known methods. Finally, majority sentiment will be embodied into laws, mores, customs and the major premises underlying the society in question (5, pp. 124-25).

To conceive of public opinion as a process requires that we view it as a phenomenon in constant flux and modification. Public opinion both determines events and—what may be just as basic for the governmental process—is in turn shaped by events. McCamy has observed that "The public interested in any subject is in constant change" (29, p. 309). The number of interested groups is changing; their internal composition is changing; their viewpoints toward contemporary issues are changing; their influence upon the government and upon opinion-molding forces is changing. Governmental officials who want to find out what public opinion demands and will support in terms of policy, therefore, are compelled to keep intimately in touch with it, to observe the close interaction between opinion and events, and to test such opinion at frequent intervals and from many vantage points.

We turn now to a consideration of the interaction between public opinion and public policy. In order to give as much concreteness as possible to our discussion, let us examine this interaction by means of a case study: the Roosevelt Administration's vital efforts to safeguard American security in the face of increasingly ominous threats from abroad during the neutrality era of the 1930's.

2. PUBLIC OPINION AND PUBLIC POLICY:
ACTION AND REACTION

The Neutrality Era—Case Study in Public Myopia

The drama of New Deal diplomacy toward the European and Asian dictators before World War II contained two underlying and contradictory themes: isolationism gripped the American people and compelled the Roosevelt Administration to follow policies of non-involvement in world affairs, while events in Europe and Asia at the same time tended to draw the United States more and more into the vortex of global crises. If isolationism drugged the American population into a kind of apathetic stupor, the actions of Germany, Italy, and Japan ultimately made new departures in foreign policy mandatory. Caught between the millstones of isolationism at home and the progressively greater danger from abroad, the Roosevelt Administration was required to formulate and carry out policies capable of pre-serving at least the barest essentials of national safety without precipitating a violent isolationist reaction among the citizenry.

Roosevelt had taken office in 1933 under circumstances that well-nigh guaranteed the existence of profound isolationist attitudes throughout the country. First, there was the overriding national preoccupation with domestic problems growing out of the Great Depression. Economic dislocations accompanying the depression had priority among governmental problems throughout Roosevelt's first term. Foreign policy issues were secondary (7, p. 263). Then, there was the historic heritage of isolationism, re-enforced by international events during the 1920's and early '30's. Except for the interlude of the First World War, the United States had consistently maintained a policy of non-involvement in European affairs and only limited involvement in Asian affairs.

And by the 1930's the majority of the American people had come to regard the First World War as an unfortunate and unnecessary departure from traditional American policy. Popular disillusionment with the war and its aftermath was widespread. Wilsonian idealism had crumbled rapidly before the forces of despair and disillusionment, as the Treaty of Versailles failed to create a noticeably better world, as the League of Nations proved incapable of defending weak nations and preventing violations of solemn international agreements, and as former friends and foes alike appeared unconcerned about repaying war debts and foreign loans owed to the United States. From the utopian expectation that the world was going to be transformed by the "Great Crusade" of 1914-1918, the American people had turned to the equally myopic view that their own lives could be divorced from events in distant parts of the world and that other powerful nations would respect America's profound yearning to be left alone.

These attitudes were powerfully re-enforced after 1934 by the investigation carried out by the Nye Committee of Congress into the reasons for American participation in World War I. After calling hundreds of witnesses and taking thousands of pages of testimony, the Nye Committee purported to have discovered these reasons in the sinister machinations of armaments-manufacturers and profit-hungry industrialists. This view, incidentally, accorded with Marxist interpretations of the causes of war and perhaps inadvertently gave credence to the viewpoints of Marxist-affiliated groups at home and abroad. Ready to believe that American participation in World War I had been a tragic mistake, the American public as a whole accepted these findings enthusiastically.

The Committee's revelations spawned a great outpouring of "revisionist" writing, both factual and fictional, which buttressed the prevailing mythology that the American people had been duped by a combination of Allied propaganda, credulous political leaders, and Wall Street into entering a conflict that was none of its business. Poll surveys on the question of American participation in the First World War indicate both the intensity of public feeling on the

subject and the way that public feeling came to be modified in time by the impact of crises abroad. Thus, in January, 1937, 70 per cent of those polled felt that American entry into World War I had been a mistake; by February, 1939, only 48 per cent still expressed this view; by October, 1939, the number had climbed to 59 per cent; then it fell again to 40 per cent in January, 1941, and to 21 per cent by December, 1941. That almost half the population could, by early 1941, see no connection between the security of the United States and the security of England and France is an eloquent testimonial to the extent of isolationist thinking.[*] As Secretary of State Hull pointed out later, it was tragic that the country "was thrown into deepest isolationism at the very moment when our influence was so vitally needed to help ward off the approaching threats of war abroad" (**20**, I, p. 399).

Except for brief flurries of popular resentment against the latest reported outrages of Hitler and Mussolini during the 1930's, American public opinion "remained virtually unaffected by international developments from the fall of 1935 until after the Munich crisis in September, 1938" (**22**, p. 48). The polls consistently showed an overwhelming majority, running often as high as 95 per cent, opposed to American military intervention in Europe on the side of Britain and France (**22**, p. 58). At the time of the Ethiopian crisis in 1935 only 29 per cent of the public was willing to join in League sanctions against Italy; and until 1938, a substantial majority of Americans favored selling American arms impartially to both sides (**22**, pp. 52-3). Public opinion was staunchly opposed also to any suggestion, such as that contained in FDR's "quarantine speech" of October 5, 1937, that the United States sever diplomatic relations with any country committing aggression (**39**, pp. 624-25).

After the Munich Conference in the fall of 1938, when it became abundantly clear that wholesale concessions would not satisfy Hitler's apparently insatiable demands for territory, American public opinion began to turn imperceptibly but steadily toward the cause of the Allies. Isolationism was still firmly en-

[*]For this and other poll surveys on World War I, see **8**, pp. 201-02.

trenched on Capitol Hill, so much so that FDR and Secretary Hull had no success during the first half of 1939 in having Congress repeal or modify existing neutrality legislation in order to permit the shipment of arms to countries threatened by the Axis powers (**39**, pp. 631-32). Public sentiment, however, was clearly moving ahead of congressional opinion. A Gallup poll taken in February, 1939, showed 69 per cent of the American people willing to take steps short of war to aid England and France. After Hitler invaded Poland in September, interventionist sentiment within the United States reached a new plane: 21 per cent of the people favored outright American intervention on the side of the Allies, and 46 per cent approved such a course if it appeared that the Allies would be defeated (**22**, p. 59).

Was this a transient mood between phases of ingrained isolationism, or had the American public at last awakened to the Axis danger? No clear answer is possible. Throughout the months that followed, the polls showed a higher percentage than formerly in favor of aid to the Allies, but the percentage of Americans supporting this course declined as the months passed. That the public temper was changing was also indicated by Congress' willingness, at long last, to repeal the arms embargo, permitting the United States to sell arms to the Allies on a cash and carry basis and authorizing the President to designate "combat zones" which American citizens would then be prohibited from entering (**39**, p. 636). During the "phony war" in Europe from September, 1939, to April, 1940, interventionist sentiment within the United States began to wane. Roosevelt's speeches advocating preparedness and aid to England and France met with widespread public disapproval. Prominent isolationists toured the country to warn against any American involvement in European and Asian crises and to discount public apprehensions that Axis victories might eventually endanger American security.

Isolationism receded somewhat after Hitler's attack against the Low Countries and France in the spring of 1940. With the collapse of France and the British military evacuation at Dunkirk, a revolution occurred in American thinking about the European conflict. Suddenly

the citizenry believed the nation to be in mortal peril! A great crescendo of public feeling demanding preparedness and large-scale aid to the Allies swept the country. One newsman wrote that "the millions are crying havoc with almost a single voice" (**25**, p. 505). Sensing, if not fully comprehending, the historic relationship between American security and British seapower, the American people forged ahead of the Roosevelt Administration in calling for an end to neutrality. The near-hysteria that erupted within the United States after the defeat of France prompted Roosevelt to resort to a "fireside chat" to calm the popular agitation (**25**, p. 479).

Although there were ups and downs in popular sentiment throughout successive months, by the end of 1940 isolationism was rapidly losing its hold upon the minds of most Americans. Powerful congressional isolationists continued to oppose measures recommended by the administration. But from late 1940 onward, Roosevelt won victory after victory against his opponents at home.* To illustrate, in October, 1940, Roosevelt asked Congress to provide for "total defense." Congress responded by granting nearly eighteen billion dollars—almost as much money as the United States had expended during World War I. Similarly, in this period, Congress voted conscription, a measure that the Administration had been most reluctant to propose earlier for fear that it would arouse formidable isolationist opposition (**25**, pp. 680-1). Before the end of the year the United States and Britain had consummated the destroyer deal, whereby fifty over-age American destroyers were exchanged for British hemispheric bases. Roosevelt labeled this step "the most important action in the reinforcement of our national defense . . . since the Louisiana Purchase" (**1**, p. 770). Constitutional lawyers could, and did, question the legality of this exchange without an act of Congress. Yet the polls showed that the public substantially approved this move, which wellnigh eliminated any lingering doubts about

---

*One indication of this change are the public opinion polls on the subject of conscription. In September, 1939, 39 per cent of the public supported it; by May, 1940, 50 per cent were in favor of it; and by October, 1940, 76 per cent believed it necessary (**8**, p. 458).

whether the United States was genuinely neutral (8, p. 1160). Isolationism flared up again early in 1941, when Congress debated and eventually passed the historic Lend-Lease bill. Again, the polls showed that popular sentiment was solidly with Roosevelt in providing "aid short of war" to England and France (22, p. 54). Henceforth, as relations deteriorated with Germany over American neutral rights, and as Japan prepared for its treacherous attack at Pearl Harbor, the United States was drawn relentlessly into the storm center of international crises.

Public Opinion and the Outer Limits of Policy

The most striking fact that emerges from the case study of Roosevelt's New Deal diplomacy is the degree to which public opinion within the United States established the boundaries within which the Administration was required to operate in its foreign relations. Until the Munich crisis of 1938, the Administration could do little more than accept this isolationist frame of mind as an unalterable national conviction that set rigid limits upon the foreign policies of the American government. After the Nye Committee's investigation especially the Administration, according to Secretary of State Cordell Hull, took the position that "There was no hope of success and nothing to be gained in combating the isolationist wave at that moment. To have done so would only have brought a calamitous defeat and precipitated a still more disastrous conflict on the whole basic question of isolation itself" (20, p. 400). As late as 1937, when Roosevelt delivered his forceful "Quarantine Speech"* against Axis aggressions, Hull characterized public thinking by saying: "The reaction against the quarantine idea was quick and violent. As I saw it, this had the effect of setting back for at least six months our constant educational campaign in-

tended to create and strengthen public opinion toward international cooperation" (20, p. 575).

During periods of isolationist ascendancy, Roosevelt and his advisers could do no more than hope international events would prod the American consciousness into at least a rudimentary understanding of the bases for national security. To have done more would almost certainly have risked sacrificing the limited gains already made in undermining isolationism and would have encouraged the rise of demagogues who were ready to capitalize upon existing isolationist yearnings. In few periods of American history has public opinion shaped American diplomacy as markedly as in the Roosevelt Administration from 1933 to roughly mid-1938.

Should policy-makers follow public sentiment or should they seek to mold it to support policies the national interest demands? We have already answered this question partially by saying that during certain intervals of the neutrality period policy-makers could follow no other course than to accept the overwhelming national sentiment in favor of isolationism. Yet Roosevelt's foreign policy activities during the 1930's suggest that the relationship between public opinion and policy-makers is reciprocal. Policy-makers are influenced by public opinion and, in turn, seek to create a favorable environment of national sentiment in behalf of needed policies. This leads us to consider the strength of public opinion in the short-run and in the long-run. As Roosevelt and Hull found out, for instance, during the period of the Nye Committee investigations, public sentiment over short periods of time may be well-nigh irresistible. Over the long run, policy-makers can try to educate the public to domestic and international realities and to raise the level of citizen enlightenment on complex government problems. Cordell Hull wrote in his *Memoirs*:

One of the basic principles I set myself for the conduct of foreign affairs was to stimulate an informed American public opinion on international events. . . . I intended to be as liberal as possible in making the workings of our foreign affairs visible to the people. I wanted them to see what was going on so that they could realize the nature of the new forces rising abroad and the vital stake their nation had in the peace of the world. (20, p. 218).

---

*The "Quarantine Speech" was prompted by renewed Japanese aggressions in China. The key idea was that the "epidemic of world lawlessness is spreading." To meet this epidemic, Roosevelt urged that the international community "quarantine" aggressor nations. For further commentary on the international implications of the speech, see 40, pp. 624-5.

As the relationship between American security and international events became gradually more apparent to the American people, the Administration grew bolder in forging ahead of popular thinking. Writing of the late 1930's Hull stated: "In our policies toward Europe, as in our policy toward Japan we sought to keep reasonably ahead of public opinion, even while seeking to educate public opinion to the importance of our position in the world and to the fatal fallacy of isolating ourselves" (20, p. 575).

Maintaining an equilibrium between opinion and policy required then, as always, a delicate touch, an acute sense of timing, and an ability to assess the currents of public sentiment with a high level of accuracy. Masterful as Roosevelt was in discerning what the popular temper demanded at any time, nevertheless there were periods when even Roosevelt failed to maintain this hair-line balance. In early New Deal days, for example, he tended to overemphasize the nation's indifference to international affairs and to underemphasize his own ability to provide leadership in awakening the country to the significance of events abroad. Moreover, in the early New Deal particularly, Roosevelt failed sometimes to differentiate between temporary flurries in public opinion and long-range fundamental tendencies (7, pp. 262-3). In the months immediately preceding the outbreak of war in Europe, and in the weeks that followed, public thinking appeared to be considerably ahead of the President in demanding preparedness and aid to the Allies (25, p. 505). Still, Roosevelt excelled in his ability to fathom popular thinking and to formulate policies acceptable to it. He perhaps appreciated the mutual influence of policymakers and public opinion as well as any man who ever occupied the White House.

Moods and Cycles in Public Opinion

Popular sentiment is subject to changing moods and sometimes the changes are sudden and vehement. Thus in the 1930's, many Americans moved all the way from a deeply entrenched isolationism to the furious "interventionism" evident at the time of the collapse of France. Between these extremes, the number of Americans favoring "aid short of war" for England and France varied considerably, depending largely upon international developments and their apparent relationship for American security.

Public opinion polls taken on the subject of American-Japanese relations during the 1930's are a good illustration of the cyclical nature of public opinion. The question was asked repeatedly: Should the United States risk war with Japan rather than let Japan continue its aggressions in Asia? When the question was asked in July, 1940, when events had reached a critical turn in Europe after France's collapse, only 12 per cent of the people polled favored firm American resistance to Japanese aggression. By March, 1941, this number had risen to 60 per cent, only to fall back to 52 per cent by July. By August, 1941, the number had reached a new high of 70 per cent (56, p. 352). Public responses to the question of whether the Allies or the Axis Powers would win the European war showed this same cyclical propensity. In the summer of 1939, immediately before the German attack on Poland, approximately 75 per cent of the American people thought England and France would win a European war. As Hitler's legions marched through Poland and attacked the Low Countries and France, deep pessimism was evident in the American attitude. By July, 1940, only 33 per cent of the Americans felt the Allies would win. Then the percentage began to rise rather spectacularly, to reach 65 per cent by November, 1940. Throughout the following months, it went down again, falling to 53 per cent by the spring of 1941, only to return to 70 per cent by the late fall (56, p. 352).

In the postwar period American opinion about the Korean War, within less than a year, showed the following changes on the question: Did the United States make a mistake in intervening in the Korean War?

Poll Date	Yes	No	No Opinion
August, 1950	20%	65%	15%
January, 1951	49%	38%	13%
March, 1951	50%	39%	11%

(40, p. 387)

On the question of providing American *military* assistance to foreign countries, a significant variation in public opinion during the period 1948-1956 was also evident. Favorable replies ranged from a low of 43 per cent to a high of 75 per cent in January, 1951, just after communist Chinese intervention in the Korean War, when it appeared that the United Nations forces might be driven from the peninsula. From that date until June, 1956, the percentage favoring military over economic assistance declined steadily (36, pp. 13, 15).

Allowing for a margin of error in polling techniques, these are wide variations in opinion on the same subject over relatively short periods of time. The reasons for such swings in popular thinking are even now not altogether clear. Some writers explain them on the basis of recurring "cycles" in American thinking about foreign affairs and have tried to plot the frequencies of these cycles (23, *passim*; 38, pp. 114-28). Considerable doubt remains, however, about whether such cycles appear automatically or whether their frequencies can be predicted accurately. A number of short-term causes may well explain sharp fluctuations in the public temper. These include the effect of new international events on public opinion and the degree to which citizens believe their nation's security to be intimately affected by such events. Not only is the citizenry likely to differ from time to time in the degree to which it is *informed* about global affairs, but it will also differ in the extent to which it feels *personal involvement* in them. Still another factor causing sudden changes may be the degree of confidence that the general public has in the nation's leaders. As the Axis threat became more ominous during the late 1930's, and as the American people in time began to sense the danger to their own security inherent in this threat, they exhibited confidence in the Roosevelt Administration's efforts to manage the country's foreign relations—so much so that many commentators ascribed Roosevelt's third term victory in 1940 substantially to this factor.

Whatever its causes, the mercurial nature of public opinion within the United States presents a formidable barrier to effective diplomacy in the nuclear age. Rarely in the nation's history has there been such a compelling necessity

for clear vision and steadiness of purpose for years, perhaps decades, to come. Confronted by an utterly unscrupulous, resourceful, and dedicated diplomatic enemy that is convinced of its own inevitable victory, the United States faces an unprecedented challenge in foreign affairs. And one of the factors that will decide the outcome of that challenge is the attitude of the American people. Even today, more than a decade after the announcement of the policy of containment, it remains to be seen whether the American people are psychologically able to continue a policy of no peace—no war for another ten or twenty-five, or fifty years, or perhaps even indefinitely. Will the American people revert to their characteristic behavior in earlier critical periods of history and oscillate between isolationism on the one hand and furious interventionism—this time perhaps with nuclear weapons—on the other hand? Will they continue to believe that the alternatives in international affairs are either to solve all problems totally or to pretend that they do not exist? No clear answers can yet be given, but on this question may well hang the issue of war or peace in our time.

Public Apathy and Ignorance About World Affairs

The isolationist era of the 1930's also calls attention to another characteristic of public opinion within the United States that presents a continuing problem for American foreign relations. James M. Burns has evaluated the influence of public opinion on New Deal diplomacy:

> Outside Washington were the millions of voters who held the destinies of foreign policy makers in their hands. And here was the most unstable foundation of all on which to build a consistent program of foreign relations. Great numbers of these voters were colossally ignorant of affairs beyond the three-mile limit. . . . the American people, lacking stable attitudes built on long experience in foreign policy making, swung fitfully from one foreign policy mood to another, from isolation to neutralism to participation in world politics. (7, p. 248).

"Dark areas of ignorance" characterize the approach of the American people to foreign affairs. After analyzing numerous public opinion polls and intensive studies of public opinion in local communities, one reporter concluded that in general

30% of the electorate is *totally unaware* of any given international event;

45% is aware of the event but cannot in any sense be considered "informed" about it;

25% shows a reasonably high level of enlightenment about foreign policy issues. (**33**, p. 51).

These findings are borne out by other studies and by an examination of the poll results when questions were asked about important global problems in the postwar period. Thus in 1946 only 25 per cent of the people had any clear conception of the purpose of the two billion dollar American loan to Britain. A little over one-third knew what the Greek-Turkish Aid Program of 1947 was all about. Later in the year, only 14 per cent could give even an elementary explanation of the purposes and nature of the Marshall Plan (**29**, p. 313). Similarly, a poll conducted in Cincinnati in this period showed that 30 per cent of the people interviewed had no conception whatever of the purposes for which the United Nations existed! Another 27 per cent had an inkling of its purposes, but were classified as "poorly informed" on the subject. Some 42 per cent could be called "better informed." But only 1 per cent of the total number could answer correctly six simple questions about the functions of the United Nations (**29**, p. 315).

More recent studies have tended to confirm the existence of widespread ignorance about foreign affairs and—what is much more disturbing—apparent public complacency about its own lack of knowledge. Successive polls taken in December, 1948, March, 1950, and February, 1951, showed that the percentage of people who were "unfamiliar" with the question of what country was winning the cold war was 46, 42, and 45 per cent, respectively (**40**, p. 399). The National Opinion Research Center quizzed a cross-section of the population on its interest in world affairs in March 1955. The results were:

Subject	Great Interest	Some Interest	No Interest
United Nations	21%	59%	19%
Formosa situation	37%	41%	20%
Hydrogen bomb tests	47%	41%	11%
U. S. relations with Central and South America	23%	42%	32%

(Note: Totals do not equal 100% because some respondents gave no opinion. Source: 35, *p. 6*.)

What factors explain the ignorance of the public about contemporary global issues and its manifest lack of interest in them? Some writers emphasize the inability of the public at large to inform itself, stressing the lack of information available to masses of the people about complex international questions. Such commentators are prone to believe that citizen enlightenment will be raised as additional and more "objective" information is put at the disposal of the public.* Yet, McCamy has pointed out that the American people "have available to them much more information about foreign affairs than they ever absorb. . . . If the information beats upon their eyes and ears, it is not taken in and retained" (**29**, p. 316). Citizen apathy and ignorance do not have their roots predominantly in the inability of the average citizen to inform himself, but rather in his unwillingness to do so. Most Americans could build up a more intelligent foundation for their opinions about world affairs readily enough by subscribing to one of the better

---

*This theme is especially pronounced in the writings of sociologists who deal with public opinion. Thus Bogardus argues that the public requires more "unbiased" information upon which to base its judgments. He advocates the issuance of "factual reports" so that the public can make up its mind on the basis of the latest research in the social science field. If a "social science digest" were made available in mass quantities, he contends, then "millions will read and be influenced." Overlooking the objection that writings in social science can ever be completely "impartial" (or the objection that they even ought to be so), American diplomatic experience affords little ground for believing that the average citizen would take the trouble to read and reflect upon such reports, even if they were easily available to him. See 5, pp. 59, 144.

metropolitan dailies like the *New York Times* or the *Washington Post-Times Herald,* by writing their Congressmen from time to time for copies of important legislative hearings, by obtaining informative publications available from the State Department, and by purchasing and studying an occasional serious book or periodical devoted to global issues. Overriding

preoccupation with routine day-to-day affairs, intellectual laziness, a willingness to substitute prejudice for opinion and to take his viewpoints second and third-hand, frustration growing out of his inability to comprehend intricate international problems and relationships quickly—these largely explain the ordinary citizen's disinterest in foreign relations.

3. MINORITIES, INTEREST–GROUPS, AND SECTIONALISM

American society is distinguished by the number of group associations that abound and the decisive part these groups often play in the political life of the nation. That America is a "nation of joiners" is a commonplace fact of unequalled significance for any understanding of American politics. Every American belongs to a number of groups: the family, the neighborhood, religious organizations, business associations and service clubs, labor unions, trade associations, political parties, and fraternal organizations. Besides these, he may be a member of a racial or national minority; his section of the country has distinctive viewpoints on at least some questions of public policy.

The central fact about the American, however, is not so much that he is a joiner, but that he belongs to a number of groups at once and that these create within him what the sociologists call "cross-pressures" in molding his opinions on contemporary issues. Kimball Young has defined a cross-pressure "as the operation of two or more determinants of opinion on the same individual or group" (**56,** p. 340).*

Because of cross-pressures most citizens lack consistency in their approach to foreign policy issues. At any given time their viewpoints are likely to be dictated by a combination of diverse influences. Judgments are made pragmatically and opinions changed at frequent intervals, as the number and intensity of these influences tend to change. The result is that very few actions of the government can be attributed to a single manifestation of public opinion such as economic interest-group pres-

sure or sectionalism. Decisions usually involve some kind of synthesis of competing pressures, so much so that it is difficult as a rule to isolate the exact influence any one pressure may have upon a particular policy.

With the realization then that multi-group membership is a distinctive feature of American life, let us examine its effect on public opinion within the United States. Specifically, let us look at the effects of interest-group activity, racial and minority group membership, and sectionalism.

Economic and Other Interest-Groups

The distinguishing feature of American life, writes the sociologist Bradford Smith, is the "enormous proliferation of special-interest associations . . . " (**46,** p. 253). Political scientists have long regarded such groups as providing a needed corrective to the non-ideological two-party system within the United States. If special economic, regional, racial, religious, professional and other interests are unable to get the two major parties to take strong and unambiguous positions on policy issues, they are able to express and agitate for their peculiar viewpoints through the thousands of pressure groups active within the nation. The role of interest-groups in the American politico-governmental system is a vast and fascinating subject. Here, we shall look briefly at some of the principal interest-groups active in foreign affairs and identify certain problems that have special pertinence for the study of foreign relations.

It would be well-nigh impossible to enumerate or perhaps even to count the total number of pressure groups within the United States.

---

*The influence of cross-pressures shows up with particular force in a study of voting behavior in 1944 by Lazarsfeld and Gaudet (**26**).

We may, however, get some idea of their multiplicity and variety by looking at the number that testify before legislative committees on specific measures. Take the Trade Agreements Extension Act of 1953. Between forty and fifty private interest-groups testified before the House Ways and Means Committee. A random sampling of these groups includes:

Nationwide Committee of Industry, Agriculture, and Labor on Import-Export Policy
National Foreign Trade Council
Atlantic Fisherman's Union
National Creamery Association
Synthetic Organic Chemical Manufacturers Association of the U. S.
Tuna Research Foundation
The Hat Institute
National Association of Hot House Vegetable Growers
Bicycle Institute of America
American Flint Glass Workers Union (AFL)
The Cordage Institute
Mushroom Growers Cooperative Association
Vitrified China Association
Pin, Clip and Fastener Institute
Wine Institute   (10, p. 211).

This list, as is apparent, does not include some of the best-known pressure groups within the nation. There are first the "big three" clusters—agriculture, labor, and business. Within the agricultural community, three major pressures groups exist, along with a host of regional and commodity organizations. The American Farm Bureau Federation, established during the First World War with the help of the government, has the largest membership and is usually regarded as the most influential agricultural pressure group. Its strength is located chiefly in the middle Corn Belt and the central Cotton Belt. In general the Farm Bureau's viewpoints are middle-of-the-road on internal and external issues. The National Grange is the next largest and the most conservative. Its membership includes many prosperous farmers, mainly dairy farmers, and the principal center of its strength is the northeast. The Grange has tended to take right-of-center positions on such issues as agricultural price supports and tariffs. On the matter of trade, for example, it has long advocated a moderately "protectionist" position. The National Farmers Union—the left-wing among agricultural pressure groups—is the smallest of the national farmers organizations. Drawing its strength from many of the mid-western communities that gave rise to the Populist Party and Bryanism, the Union consistently champions the cause of the "underprivileged" at home and abroad. As a rule, its foreign policy position is strongly "internationalist," with firm support for an increase in American foreign aid spending for other countries (45, pp. 627-30).

The merger of the two great American labor unions in 1955 has given labor the advantage of being able to speak for sixteen million members—eleven million from the older and more conservative American Federation of Labor and five million from the younger CIO. Recent events, however, indicate that organized labor is far from being completely unified. Powerful groups within the AFL-CIO, like the auto workers, the steel workers, the teamsters, the machinists, and carpenters compete for leadership and for influence in policy-making. The AFL-CIO has more than once since its merger been threatened with insurgency. Even today, nearly two million labor union members belong to "independent unions" that are not affiliated with the AFL-CIO (37, p. 1231).

In the business community, two major, and literally hundreds of smaller, interest-groups can be discerned. The two most influential on the national level are the United States Chamber of Commerce and the National Association of Manufacturers. The former is chiefly an organization for businessmen, with a large proportion of small businesses represented. The NAM, on the other hand, "speaks for industry;" its members are more than sixteen thousand large and small business corporations and it regards itself as the voice of industry in Washington (44, p. 113). Besides these two large and well known business groups, there are a host of trade associations and organizations established on a product, or regional, basis like the National Cheese Institute, Independent Petroleum Association of America, National Council of American Importers, Committee for a National Trade Policy, National Small Business Men's Association, Retail Druggists' Association, and many others. In most instances, these smaller groups are concerned primarily with safeguarding the economic interests of their own members rather than taking clear positions on broad national policy questions. For instance, they are not likely to agitate strongly on the question of American propaganda activities throughout the world. Issues like tariff reductions, taxation, deficit financing, and government controls, however are apt to elicit vocal and strong responses from such groups.

In addition to economic interest groups, there are a host of others that represent the viewpoints of veterans, religious denominations, reformers, study groups, racial and national minorities, and educational and professional associations. One of the most influential of these in the field of internal security legislation and veterans' benefits is the American Legion. With over three million members and 15,000 local posts, the Legion is in a strong position to generate grass-roots pressure upon legislators and executive officials. The Legion has been especially concerned with the patriotism of governmental officials, teachers, and others in positions of public leadership. Its preoccupation with "Americanism" has been as constant as it has been undiscriminating. The Legion has come close to relegating to itself a monopolistic position in defining Americanism and in differentiating the true patriot from the subversive. "To question the motive or ideals of the Legion's combined thinking is to question the fundamental principles of America," a Legion publication wrote in the recent past (48, p. 131). Another veterans pressure group, the Veterans of Foreign Wars, with over two million members, approaches national and international problems somewhat more liberally than the Legion.

Among the more influential religious organizations are the Roman Catholic Church, the National Council of Churches of Christ in America, various Jewish organizations like the American Jewish Committee, and other groups such as the Friends Committee on National Legislation. Professional and reform groups often prominent in the field of foreign relations are the United World Federalists, the American Association for the United Nations, the Foreign Policy Association, the Council on Foreign Relations, the League of Women Voters, the

American Association of University Women, the National Bar Association, the National Congress of Parents and Teachers, the National Education Association, and the General Federation of Women's Clubs.

This brief delineation of some of the more important interest-groups active in foreign affairs illustrates the extent of pressure group activity. It is of cardinal importance in understanding their significant role to remember that *economic, religious, professional and other groups are subject to the same cross-pressures that beset the individual citizen and that affect other manifestations of public sentiment.* For instance, one writer refers to the "big economic, regional, and commodity group cleavages" that are characteristic of American agriculture. These "make a united front very difficult to attain, except occasionally on a single issue" (13, p. 379). We have already mentioned that the American labor union movement has deep internal stresses within it, so much so that the merger of 1955 appears sometimes in danger of disintegrating. Business is not excepted from this rule. Within the business community it is not at all unusual for small and specialized business organizations to oppose the positions taken by the larger national bodies like the Chamber of Commerce and the NAM. The result is that agriculture, labor, business, and other segments of the American society are seldom unified in their approach to public issues. Even comparatively small groups that take positions on limited problems, like the United World Federalists, are frequently torn by internal differences of opinion.* To illustrate, let us look at the alignment of pressure groups on an important issue in 1956 involving the interests of agriculture, business, and labor: American affiliation with the General Agreement on Tariffs and Trade usually known as GATT. GATT's purpose is to foster international trade and eliminate world trade barriers. President Eisenhower had requested Congress to approve American membership in GATT in 1955 and again in 1956. Congress did not approve it at that time because of fear that

---

*For an illuminating treatment of the internal operation and formulation of policies by a small pressure group, see 18.

GATT might interfere with American tariffs.* Among the more important groups *opposing* American membership in GATT were:

American Farm Bureau Federation
National Cheese Institute
American Tariff League
Southern States Industrial Council
Wine Institute
U. S. Potters Association (labor)

Among the groups that *favored* American membership in GATT were:

U. S. Chamber of Commerce
National Grange
Committee for Economic Development
National Council of American Importers
General Federation of Women's Clubs
AFL - CIO
Chrysler Corporation
Committee for a National Trade Policy

In view of the divergent opinions expressed by the multitude of interest-groups within the United States, how are governmental officials to discern the public interest on any given national issue, especially one that arouses great controversy? Controversial questions like the tariff are likely to agitate interest-groups and generate strong sectional and regional viewpoints. Other questions like immigration will elicit vocal opinions from racial and national minorities within the United States. When such questions arise it is apparent that there is in fact no such thing as *a public opinion.*

Countless opinions, of varying degrees of intensity and enlightenment, are directed at Washington. One thing is certain: the *national* interest, however difficult it may be to formulate explicitly in specific situations, is something different from the sum total of competing group interests. Policy-makers cannot, and should not, seek to arrive at a conception of what the public demands merely by accepting the most clamorous or momentarily influential pressure groups as representative of public opinion. Pressure groups, like administrative experts, should be on tap, but not on top; their demands should be considered but not followed blindly. Clearly, they are and must be recognized as being only one segment of that im-

portant but elusive entity known as public opinion. Governmental officials can arrive at an intelligent assessment of what the public demands and upon its proper role in the formulation of public policy only as they balance competing interest-group attitudes, realizing all the while that in doing so they may be dealing with a very small minority of the citizenry. Ultimately, officials must balance all sources of opinion against the needs of the country—and in some cases they may conclude that the national interest will be best served by policies that are not currently advocated by large masses of citizens but for which public support could be secured if the President and his followers in the government believe a given step to be mandatory.

Racial and National Minorities

Throughout the greater part of its history, the United States has opened its shores to mass waves of immigrants from the Old World. President Tyler's message to Congress in 1841 sounded the keynote of the nation's policy toward the immigrant:

We hold out to the people of other countries an invitation to come and settle among us as members of our rapidly growing family; and for the blessings which we offer them, we require them to look upon our country as their country, and unite with us in the great task of preserving our institutions and thereby perpetuating our liberties. (**50**, p. 47).

From early in the nineteenth century until 1930 at least 60 per cent of the total immigration of the world came to the United States (**50**, p. 23). By 1947 almost forty million people had come (**50**, p. 73). Census estimates by 1950 indicated that there were approximately thirty-four million persons of foreign white stock and fifteen million Negroes in the United States (**55**, p. 323). Out of a total population of close to 180,000,000, between one-third and one-fourth belonged to some racial or national minority.

Yet size alone cannot account entirely for the decisive influence minority groups have often exercised in politico-governmental affairs. Since the same cross-pressures operate upon these groups as upon all citizens, and since the

---

*The controversy is fully treated in **11**, pp. **485-7.**

different racial and national minorities seldom see eye-to-eye on public issues, factors other than size usually account for their decisive role. One such factor is the pattern of their distribution throughout the population as a whole. While a few racial and national minorities, for example the Germans, the Scotch-Irish, and the Negroes, tend to be concentrated in the rural areas, most minority groups have gravitated toward the cities, especially cities along the eastern seaboard and in the middle western hinterland. This is notably true of the immigrants from Ireland, Italy, and Eastern Europe. The foreign population of New York City offers an interesting example. New York City contains approximately 1,800,000 people classified by the Census as belonging to a racial or national minority. The homelands of the thirteen largest groups were as follows: Asia, 32,000; Austria, 124,000; Canada, 61,000; England and Wales, 54,000; Germany, 186,000; Hungary, 52,000; Ireland, 142,000; Italy, 344,000; Poland, 180,-000; Rumania, 30,000; Scotland, 26,000; USSR, 315,000; Yugoslavia, 38,000. In addition, New York City has about 40 per cent (2,000,000) of the total Jewish population of the country (55, pp. 326, 328).

Minority groups often hold the political balance of power within the states. In pivotal states like New York, Ohio, and Illinois, this tends to give them an extremely influential voice in national politics. Since the 18th century, Tammany Hall in New York City has based its strength upon foreign-born and national minority elements. Until World War II its traditional source of strength was the Irish-American population. Since World War II its strength has depended more on the Italian, Puerto Rican, and Negro minorities.

Then too racial and national minorities have often had an important voice in shaping national policies because of the intensity with which their views are held and expressed. The general American public often is quite apathetic toward questions that can be counted on to provoke automatic and heated discussion among America's racial and national minorities. One of these is civil rights legislation. Another is the question of immigration. Minority groups as a whole tend to favor expanded immigration—especially if it affects their country of origin. American re-lations with the immigrants' old homeland may stir strong sympathies. Thus there was vocal minority group expression on American policy toward peace treaties with Germany, Austria, and the lesser Axis satellite countries; the controversy between Italy and Yugoslavia over Trieste; relations between Israel and the Arab world; Communist persecutions of the Roman Catholic Church in Eastern Europe; and relations with England over a host of issues, from colonial and Commonwealth problems to garrisoning American military forces on British soil.

The nation's racial and national minorities are likely to develop an even more active concern with some aspects of foreign affairs in the years ahead because of the increasing national and global interest in "minority problems" and the growing realization that these issues are no longer of exclusively national concern. Increasingly, they have come to the attention of the United Nations as root causes of global tensions. With the passage of time, minority groups all over the world have come to feel a certain kinship and have joined in efforts to solve their mutual problems. Carey McWilliams has written concerning America's minorities:

> Our 364,000 Indians are but part of some 30,000,000 Indians in the western hemisphere, and our 13,000,000 Negroes are but part of some 37,000,000 Negroes in the new world. It has become perfectly apparent, therefore, that the manner in which racial minorities are treated in America is no longer, if it ever was, a matter of parochial concern. A race riot in Detroit instantly provokes discussion in the far east; the mistreatment of Mexicans in Los Angeles immediately echoes throughout the hemisphere (32, p. 216).

Time and again in the postwar period executive officials have stressed the effect that America's treatment of its own minority groups has on dealing with nations in the Afro-Asian bloc. Former colonial countries like India are inordinately sensitive to racial questions and give considerable prominence in their news media to racial and minority group conflicts within the United States. Racial conflicts in Little Rock or Chicago are likely to influence the course of American foreign relations much more decisively than idealistic resolutions on the race question by such groups as the National Council of Churches or the AFL-CIO.

When we consider the evidence of influence that racial and minority groups have wielded in selected periods of American foreign policy, the importance of their role is impressive.* Jewish citizens and groups, for instance, were responsible for repeated protests by the State Department against Czarist persecution of Russian Jews early in the 20th century. The persecutions ultimately led to the termination of a Russian-American commercial agreement in 1911 (1, p. 560-n). Considerable influence can also be ascribed to the Jewish population in determining America's progressively militant position toward Hitler during the 1930's. The classic example, however, of a foreign policy shaped heavily by minority group pressure was the American position on the Palestinian issue during and immediately after World War II, climaxed by vigorous American advocacy of the partition of Palestine into separate Jewish and Arab states. Zionist pressure upon the White House was acknowledged by pro-Zionist President Truman as perhaps the strongest he encountered on any foreign policy issue during his tenure in the White House (49, II, pp. 156-62).

Several foreign-born groups, such as the Italian-Americans, have exercised a determinative influence on the course of American diplomatic history. During the 1930's Italian-Americans gradually swung toward admiration and sometimes vocal and economic support for Mussolini's fascist program at home and in foreign affairs. Their feelings helped to prevent a strong American stand against Italy's aggressive policies. As Mussolini's exploits brought new glory to the old homeland, many Italian-Americans felt, in the words of Max Ascoli, one of their number, that "there was a new dignity

---

*It is of course difficult to prove that any specific policy was "dictated" by minority group pressures. Other pressures (economic, political, religious, ideological) are almost always present in some degree. For a vigorous dissent from the view that American Jews have had an important influence on American foreign policy, see 19. Honor doubts that the American State Department was ever so concerned about Hitler's treatment of the Jews as is sometimes thought or that American foreign policy during the 1930's was substantially shaped by American Jewry.

in being an Italian" (30, p. 36). Mussolini's propaganda apparatus sought to exploit the "inferiority" felt by many Italian-Americans and to create in their minds as favorable an image as possible of the "old country." That this propaganda was not without some success is attested by the fact that during the Ethiopian War of 1935, many Italian-American women contributed their wedding rings to be converted into money for the Italian cause (30, p. 37).

During and after the Second World War, the United States took the lead among the great powers in championing lenient surrender and occupation terms for Italy. In time, Washington supported Italy's cause against Yugoslavia in the long-standing dispute over Trieste. To some extent, these policies were undoubtedly due to the sizable Italian-American minority within the American society and to its politically strategic role in the large cities, particularly in the east (31, p. 404).

Another nationality that has often played a crucial role in shaping American foreign policy is the German-American minority. From 1820 to 1948, some six million Germans emigrated to this country. By 1950, 85 per cent of this group lived in the north. German-Americans tended to be concentrated in New York, Illinois, and the mid-western states of Ohio, Iowa, Missouri, and the Dakotas (50, pp. 103-04). The astute political analyst, Samuel Lubell, has drawn attention to the influence of the German-American population in molding American isolationist attitudes during the interwar period, especially in the mid-West. After studying the voting records of legislators from the mid-Western isolationist belt, Lubell concluded that "by far the strongest common characteristic of the isolationist-voting counties is the residence there of ethnic groups with a pro-German or anti-British bias" (27, p. 132). Lubell may oversimplify a complex phenomenon when he ascribes the strong isolationist tendencies of the rural mid-West to two factors: existence of a large pro-German and almost always anti-British bloc of voters; and exploitation of these sentiments by shrewd politicians (27, p. 133). Thus, says Lubell, during the election of 1940, Roosevelt's popular vote fell approximately 7 per cent; but in twenty counties—nineteen having large German-American populations—his vote fell 35 per cent below the 1936 level. And in 83 out of 101 counties where his vote fell from 20-24 per cent below that of 1936, German was either the first or second largest nationality within the county (27, p. 132).

Lubell discovered what he labels the "most isolationist of all Americans" among the Russian-German farmers of the mid-West. The ancestors of this group, of which the largest concentration is in North Dakota, were originally Germans who settled in Russia during the period of Catherine the Great, late in the 18th century. They came to America in the late 19th and early 20th centuries. Preferring cultural isolationism, this group tends to live in closely-knit communities governed by customs brought over from the Old World. Education for the children is not encouraged, so that the group as a whole has a very low educational level. Yet Lubell warns that "The explanation is hardly the simple one, that isolationism stems from lack of education. Rather it would seem that resistance to education is a symptom of cultural isolation in which ethnic prejudices, once established, do not change" (27, p. 148).

On the basis of research into voting records and interviews, Lubell found deepseated opposition among the German-American population to war. One reason why this group consistently votes Republican is that it blames the Democratic Party for participation in the First and Second World Wars and the Korean War. The Korean War seemed to vindicate the position which many German-Americans took during World War II: that if Hitler were not left free to "deal with" communist Russia, then some day the United States itself would have to cope with the communist menace (27, pp. 150-52). "What really binds the former isolationists," writes Lubell, "is not a common view on foreign policy for the future, but a shared remembrance of opposition to American intervention in the last war. The strength of the Republican appeal to the former isolationist voters is essentially one of political revenge" (27, p. 152).

The Sons of Eire and American Foreign Policy

Among the minority groups who have had a significant influence upon American foreign relations, none has a record equal to that of the Irish-American population. From 1820-1947, some 4.6 million Irish immigrants entered the United States. Settling originally in the cities along the Atlantic seacoast, the Irish gradually pushed inland to inhabit the midwestern cities as well. Thus by 1950, Chicago had an even larger Irish-American population than Boston, a traditional center of Irish concentration. Over 90 per cent of the Irish-American population are city-dwellers (50, p. 110).

The influence of Irish citizens upon American domestic politics—and especially upon the organization and policies of the Democratic Party—is well-known and requires little elaboration here. Even in the contemporary period, Democratic political organizations in Boston, New York, and Chicago continue to rest heavily upon control of the Irish vote. Politics in these and other heavily Irish communities, moreover, has usually been characterized by great intensity of feeling, rampant emotionalism, deeply ingrained prejudices, raucousness, and not infrequent addiction to violence. A student of the Irish-American minority within the United States has observed: "The Irish developed many of the shoulder-hitting methods of American politics characteristic of the 19th century. There were many Irish

> Who think that freedom must consist
> In proving points, with sticks and fists."
> (53, p. 105).

That many of the distinctive traits and viewpoints associated with the Irish element would find expression in the realm of foreign relations was well-nigh guaranteed by the importance of the "Irish vote" in pivotal states and by the freedom which the Irish enjoyed—a freedom frequently denied them in their homeland—to rail against English bondage. After Irish immigration to the United States had reached substantial proportions, the influence of the Irish-American population upon American diplomatic history could be clearly discerned. Along with other foreign-born groups that came to America to escape persecution at home, the

Irish consistently advocated American support for revolutionary and anti-colonial movements abroad. Thus during the revolutionary ferment in Europe in 1848 and the years that followed, America's Irish citizens applauded the popular uprisings against autocracy in Europe; urged American intervention in the Crimean War (1853-56) on the side of Russia in the hope that Britain would thereby be defeated; and periodically sponsored rallies, in association with other foreign-born groups, to urge a more forceful American policy in behalf of political liberalism (53, p. 85).

Fierce and unshakable Anglophobia has characterized the Irish-American approach to foreign relations. Americans of Irish extraction have usually proceeded on the supposition that "the strongest and best hater of England is the best American" (53, p. 109). One episode which dramatically shows the lengths to which the Sons of Eire were prepared to carry their hatred of England was the Fenian-inspired invasion of Canada in the late 1860's and early 1870's. Feeding upon a long-smoldering antagonism toward England, numerous Irish "secret societies," including the Fenians, spent their time plotting against Great Britain. Irish resentment finally crystallized in an ill-fated expedition into Canada. This episode temporarily soured Canadian-American and Anglo-American relations. The historian Thomas A. Bailey believes that the invasion did much to destroy any lingering sentiment that existed in Canada favoring eventual union with the United States (1, pp. 408-09).

"Among all the immigrant groups in the United States," Wittke observes, "none has built up a folklore of fond remembrance for their native land comparable to that of the Irish. . . . " The "wrongs of Ireland" have welded successive generations of Irish-Americans into a vociferous anti-British phalanx (53, p. 161). The historic American affinity for "twisting the lion's tail" and railing against British colonialism can be ascribed in large measure to the influence of Irish groups. Anglophobia reached a peak, with fateful consequences for American foreign policy, at the close of World War I. For a variety of reasons, many of the provisions of the Treaty of Versailles aroused heated opposition among the foreign-born within the American popula-

tion. German-Americans were strongly opposed to the terms imposed upon their native land, and they blamed Wilson for the Allies' failure to live up to the principles enunciated in the Fourteen Points. Italian-Americans were disgruntled because of Wilson's unwillingness to honor secret agreements made with Italy and for that country's relatively limited territorial gains as a result of the peace settlement. Poles, Czechs, Jews, Chinese, and Japanese within the United States also voiced real or fancied grievances—leading a Boston newspaper to assert that the United States is a "country of quiet majorities and vociferous minorities" (2, p. 24).

No group in the United States, however, opposed the treaty with such fervor as the Irish. Before the United States entered the war, the Irish had been openly pro-German—not because they favored Germany but because of their violent opposition to England and because, almost as a matter of principle, they sided with England's enemies (2, p. 24). This endemic Anglophobia carried over into the war period and the period of the peace settlements. Unfortunately for the advocates of the League of Nations, debate over the Treaty of Versailles within the United States coincided with one of the most turbulent eras in the stormy history of Irish politics. The Irish independence movement had erupted into a new fight with England. Civil wars, riots, murders, hunger strikes, execution of Irish patriots, and wholesale arrests were taking place in Ireland while Americans were considering the Treaty of Versailles. Then in 1919 when the Irish leader and self-proclaimed "President" of the Irish Republic, Eamon de Valera, visited the United States, Irish citizens worked themselves up into a frenzy of hatred against England and against President Wilson, who was closely identified with British policies (2, p. 26).

These circumstances, along with certain highly controversial provisions of the Treaty of Versailles, generated solid Irish opposition to the League of Nations. The Irish were incensed because Wilson had failed to champion the cause of Irish independence at the Paris Peace Conference; because they feared that Article X of the League Covenant might be used by England to intervene in Irish domestic affairs; and because the hated British Empire received six votes in the League Assembly, while the United States received only one vote (**2**, p. 27; **53**, pp. 288-91). On top of all this, the Irish attacked the League as a British-inspired plot to gain control over the affairs of other nations and ultimately to extend the British Empire throughout the world! That most of these charges were without substance did little to detract from the strength of Irish opposition and shows only the lengths to which groups within the population sometimes go in substituting prejudice and emotional fervor for a rational analysis of public issues. Illogical as Irish opposition might be, it was a potent force. President Wilson's bitter fight with his arch foe Senator Henry Cabot Lodge, Republican of Massachusetts, may be at least partially explained by the strength of the Irish vote in Lodge's state. It is noteworthy that Lodge's colleague from Massachusetts, Senator David I. Walsh, himself of Irish extraction, was one of the few Democratic Senators who actively opposed Wilson on the League issue. Neither Senator could ignore the viewpoints of a significant minority of his constituents, irrespective of his party's position on the question (**2**, p. 25).

In subsequent years, the Irish also opposed America's entry into the World Court for substantially the same reasons advanced against the League in 1919-1920 (**14**, p. 119). Then throughout the 1920's and 1930's, as Germany, Italy, and Japan sought to extend their empires and as the activities of the dictators came to challenge the security of England and France more acutely, Irish-American sentiment reflected the anti-British animus characteristic of earlier periods. Irish groups repeatedly criticized Roosevelt for his policies of "aid short of war." After the defeat of France and in the midst of the Battle of Britain in 1940-41, relations became exceedingly tense between England and Ireland over the latter's neutrality. England feared that Ireland might be invaded by German forces; Ireland on the other hand appeared to fear British domination as much as German. During this controversy, Secretary of State Cordell Hull informed England that "the large Irish-American population in the United States would take serious offense if the British attempted to base troops in Ireland for defense

against Germany." The British Foreign Office in time replied that such was not England's intention. Differences between England and Ireland on this question were eventually worked out satisfactorily (**20**, p. 718).

With political conditions within Ireland, and relations between Ireland and England, relatively quiescent during and after the war no incidents like the Fenian episode or the debate over the League of Nations agitated the Irish-American population unduly. Age-old hostilities toward England, moreover, are bound to attenuate with the passage of time, as second, third, and fourth-generation Irish-Americans lose their attachment to the old country and as memories of "perfidious Albion's" treatment of the old country fade into the background. Polls taken during World War II, for example, showed comparatively insignificant differences between the viewpoints expressed by Irish-Americans on important questions of foreign policy and those expressed by cross-sections of the entire population. Asked as early as December, 1940, whether Ireland should abandon neutrality, 63 per cent of the people interviewed said yes; 40 per cent of the Irish-Americans interviewed said yes. Asked substantially the same question again in March, 1942, 71 per cent of the public felt that Ireland ought to abandon neutrality, while 56 per cent of the Irish-American population polled agreed with this view (**8**, pp. 377-78). This reply reflected patriotic compulsions as well as a decline in traditional Irish Anglophobia. That Anglophobia had not entirely disappeared, however, was indicated when the distinguished wartime British Prime Minister, Winston Churchill, visited the United States in 1946. Anti-British demonstrations sponsored by Irish groups were held in several American cities (**53**, p. 163). Strong animosities against England will likely come to the surface from time to time in the future, and political spokesmen for predominantly Irish communities can be expected, as a matter of political necessity, to give voice occasionally to the deeply ingrained sentiments of their Irish constituents.

Sectional Viewpoints on Foreign Affairs

Sectional viewpoints toward both domestic and foreign policy questions also constitute important specialized manifestations of public opinion within the United States. What constitutes a section? The sociologist, John Gillin, states that geographical divisions within the country that might be called sections or regions "subscribe to the general list of values of the national culture, but with certain additions, emendations, or special emphases more or less peculiar to themselves" (16, p. 111). He distinguishes sectionalism from regionalism by saying that "whereas 'sectionalism' implies conflict, regionalism implies an 'orchestration of diversity' within a total national cultural unity" (16, p. 110).

Another problem of definition that poses some difficulty in discussing sectionalism springs from the lack of uniformity in deciding the exact boundaries of geographic sections within the United States. After a thorough study of the sectional basis of congressional voting behavior, Grassmuck has concluded that "Sectional attitudes are not static but dynamic. They change in area and intensity as issues change and as time passes" (17, p. 14). Sectional lines within the United States are determined chiefly by the purposes for which such a delineation is made or by the data that one wishes to study on a sectional basis. Thus Grassmuck notes that "The Bureau of the Census has seen fit to make a sectional breakdown, which is ignored in turn by other organs of the government." There seems to be no uniform classification which can be used for all purposes (17, p. 35).

Yet we shall not depart unduly from prevailing usage if we think in terms of six major sections within the United States: the Northeast, the Middle Atlantic, the Southeast, the Southwest, the Northwest, and the Far West.* Within each section, there are important subsections, and sometimes these exhibit marked variations in attitudes on selected national issues. Gillin identifies four such subsections in the Southeast: the coastal fringe area, the low

country, the Piedmont, and the mountains (16, p. 111). Moreover, state-by-state breakdowns in public opinion polls show significant deviations from sectional attitudes among the states that are included within the area studies (8, pp. 460-1).

Sectional differences and discords have strongly influenced the course of American history. Until the last quarter-century sectional discords often embraced foreign policy issues. In the nineteenth century, for example, the slavery controversy generated intense sectional animosities. The agrarian South and commercial New England were sharply at odds over the annexation of Texas and over tariff questions. After the Civil War, agricultural communities generally opposed an expansionist foreign policy, while the commercial and financial East favored the extension of American influence across the seas, at least to the extent necessary to protect business interests.

In the modern period, sectional differences have tended to recede or in many cases to become outweighed by other differences within the population. During the neutrality era, for instance, " . . . at no time did surveys find a situation where one section of the country showed a majority favoring the principle of aid to Britain, while another section showed a majority opposed. *All* areas were in favor. . . . The differences were of degree—substantial majorities as compared to overwhelming majorities" (28, p. 36).

After studying public attitudes toward the United Nations and international co-operation generally in the postwar period, Frederick W. Williams still found some important variations based upon geographic differences. He concluded that the East, principally New England, continued to be rather strongly "internationalist" in its viewpoint, although many citizens did not appear to support concrete policies that would make greater international co-operation a reality. He also found a higher than average support for a policy of internationalism in the South and Southeast. Contrary to expectations, the Middle Atlantic states manifested considerably greater isolationist sentiment than might have been generally supposed; and again in contrast to what might have been anticipated, this sentiment was especially

---

*These are the sections proposed by Gillin (16, p. 111). In his study of sectional variations on congressional voting behavior toward foreign policy issues, Grassmuck followed a seven-fold classification: New England and the North Atlantic States, the Great Lakes States, the Border States, the Great Plains, the South, the Rocky Mountain States, and the Pacific Coast (17, p. 37).

marked in the *higher* socio-economic brackets. The most striking feature of public opinion within the Rocky Mountain states was the degree of diversity *within* the area, ranging from deep-seated attachment to isolationism to equally strong internationalism. As a whole, he found the level of internationalist thinking lower than might have been predicted. The Middle West, the traditional homeland of entrenched isolationism, continued to show a relatively low awareness of international realities and of America's responsibilities in world affairs. The Pacific Coast also showed comparatively little interest in American relations with Europe, lending credence to the view that the Far West region has never been closely identified with the Old World. Surprisingly strong isolationist attitudes existed, in spite of the fact that the Pacific Coast region showed the highest per capita educational level of any section studied. Williams concludes that while evidence of isolationist thinking remains even in the nuclear age, the nation as a whole has arrived at a new understanding of America's role in world affairs and is prepared to support policies necessary to discharge that role (**52**, *passim*).*

Grassmuck's study of congressional voting behavior on important foreign policy issues during the 1920's and 1930's points to other sectional attitudes. Sectional variations showed

---

*The term "isolationist" has unquestionably become a label of opprobrium since World War II. Thus when pollsters asked citizens in 1944 how they classified themselves, only 13 per cent were willing to call themselves isolationists; 64 per cent looked upon themselves as "internationalists"; while 23 per cent had "no opinion" (**8**, p. 367).

Such findings however, cannot be interpreted to mean that isolationism has disappeared from American thought. On the basis of a mail survey sent out to all daily newspapers in the country and to 10,000 citizens in all walks of life, Quentin Reynolds in 1952 received these replies to the following significant questions:

Are people impatient enough with the mounting difficulties of our foreign relations to want to withdraw? (a) from Europe: yes—43%; no—57%; (b) from Asia: yes—44%; no—56%.

Would one or two more acts of aggression make them mad enough to go to war (e.g. because of a Soviet attack against Iran or Yugoslavia)? Yes—17%; No—83%.

What do people within the United States think of the United Nations? Favorable—39%; Unfavorable—61%.

Are the American people going isolationist? Yes—67%; No—33%. (**42**, pp. 13-17).

up with particular force toward certain specific problems in foreign relations. Thus he found that legislators from the Northeast and, to a more limited extent, from the South could be counted on with great regularity to vote for military expenditures, especially naval appropriations. Evidently citizens in that section had a greater than average awareness of the dependence of national security upon armed strength and upon America's historical reliance upon seapower to preserve its independence and freedom of action (**17**, p. 40). Legislators from the Great Plains, on the other hand, consistently voted against naval expenditures because "Geographically, all parts of the section lie more than five hundred miles from salt water so that both invasion and shipbuilding were a long way off during the interwar period" (**17**, p. 48-9). Legislators from the Pacific Coast, however, joined the Northeast and South in supporting efforts to enlarge the Navy because "a firm desire for adequate naval protection is indeed a characteristic of the legislative attitude of Congressmen from coastal states" (**17**, p. 52). Grassmuck's study also confirms the important part often played by racial and national minorities in certain regions. To cite but one example, legislators from states like Rhode Island and Massachusetts, where there are large numbers of foreign-born citizens, tended to oppose the Washington Naval Armaments Treaty of 1922, for the classic reason that German- and Irish-American citizens "gave no indication of welcoming any alliance signed by Great Britain" (**17**, p. 67).

In the interwar period the Northeast led the way in favoring a reduction in the "war debts" and in foreign loans owed to the United States by other countries and, in the more recent period, in supporting measures that would contribute to greater economic stability and prosperity in Europe. This viewpoint may perhaps reflect the region's closer proximity to Europe. Or it may derive from awareness that "this northeastern part of the nation stood to benefit commercially from trade with Europe to a far greater extent than could other sections, save perhaps the South . . . " (**17**, pp. 107-08). Even in the postwar period a strong attachment to isolationism and a desire for minimum American involvement in world affairs characterizes prevailing viewpoints in the middle west. On the basis of 73 roll call votes in the House and 88 in the Senate on foreign policy measures, Smuckler found that the traditional heartland of isolationism continues to be a bloc of states including the Dakotas, Idaho, Kansas, Nebraska, Wisconsin, and Minnesota. On the basis of House votes alone, he concludes that the most "internationalist" section is the South, plus the states of Missouri, Oklahoma, Texas, New Mexico, Arizona, Utah, Wyoming, Nevada, and California (**47**, p. 391). Yet Smuckler cautions against trying to prove too much on the basis of legislative voting behavior. Isolationist sentiment also shows up from time to time in other areas, and many influences besides sectionalism are often decisive in shaping regional viewpoints on world affairs (**47**, pp. 400-01).

For many years, the South has enjoyed the reputation of being perhaps the most "internationalist" or, perhaps more accurately, "interventionist" of all sections within the United States. One distinguishing feature of Southern attitudes on world affairs has been the willingness of the South to support military preparedness measures. Throughout recent history Southern legislators have voted consistently for defense measures (**17**, pp. 41-2, 55; **28**, p. 37). Several Southern states pride themselves upon the number of "volunteers" they have contributed to the armed services during the nation's wars. Moreover, throughout the greater part of American history, a pronounced pro-British attitude has characterized Southern viewpoints. This may derive from a variety of factors: 90 per cent of the white population of the South looks upon itself as Anglo-Saxon in national origin; Britain has always been a good customer of Southern cotton exports; and during the Civil War, sympathy for the Confederacy was high in England (**21**, p. 312; **28**, p. 37). For reasons of geographical propinquity and economic self-interest, the South has always favored harmonious relations with Latin America and has encouraged programs to stimulate greater trade between North and South America (**21**, p. 316). Historically, the South has been committed to a policy of low tariffs, because of the necessity to import finished goods and to sell agricultural products in foreign markets. The low tariff position of the South is gradually giving way to pleas for protection by the many business concerns, especially in the textile fields, that have come into the area since World War II (**41**, pp. 361-9). The eminent historian of the South, C. Vann Woodward, has observed that, out of long and painful experiences in dealing with minority problems and being a minority within the nation, the South has certain valuable lessons to offer in the approach of the American people to foreign relations. More than any other section, the South has come to question the value of moral-idealistic crusades as fruitful methods for solving human problems. The South has experienced such a crusade, and is in a position to testify that moral fervor solves few problems. Above all the regions within the nation, the South can testify to the importance of perseverance, steadiness, and long perspectives in dealing with complex problems in human affairs (**54**, *passim*).

Yet as with any other single influence that determines popular thinking or legislative voting behavior, we must beware giving too much emphasis to sectionalism. Two broad qualifications must always be kept in mind, and these would apply with equal validity to other determinants of public attitudes. The first is that sectional viewpoints are likely to be much more pronounced on some issues than on others. The industrial East can be expected to favor expanded commercial agreements with other nations, but it may exhibit no strong opinion at all on the subject of political relations with Southeast Asia. Similarly, the South feels strongly about military preparedness measures, but it may manifest no more than average interest in providing Point Four assistance to Greece and Turkey.

The second qualification is that sectional differences are almost always heavily overlaid with other influences which may often be more significant than geographical boundaries or distinctive cultural outlooks. We have already referred to the close coincidence between sectional attitudes and the distribution of racial and national minorities throughout the country. In addition, political affiliation is often closely linked with sectional viewpoints. For example, the South gave Roosevelt overwhelming support for military preparedness measures during the 1930's. Grassmuck is inclined to ascribe this phenomenon much more to the South's traditional and solid alignment with the Democratic Party than to supposedly peculiar viewpoints inherent in Southern culture (17, 145). William G. Carelton offers much the same explanation of Middle Western isolationism, holding that the key element in shaping that region's distinctive viewpoints on world affairs has been its historic association with the Republican Party (9, pp. 378-85). Another factor that is often more important than sectional attitudes, and frequently gives a regional viewpoint its peculiar cast, is the presence of a large rural population. Numerous commentators have pointed to what appears to be an inherent provincialism in the thinking of rural people about international affairs. Friedrich goes so far as to maintain that this is a characteristic of rural folk wherever they are found (15, p. 50). Among the causes of this outlook are their attachment to the soil, their limited mobility, their usually lower than average educational and economic levels, and their limited contact with the foreign-born and with foreign countries (15, pp. 50-1). Whatever the reasons, there appears to be a definite correlation between isolationist attitudes and a rural population concentration (17, p. 101; 47, pp. 398-9).

Public Opinion in Perspective

Preceding chapters have called attention to the care with which policy-makers in both the legislative and executive branches seek to inform themselves about popular attitudes and to take them into account in formulating and carrying out governmental policies. Legislators are keenly sensitive to public opinion. An experienced Washington observer, Cabell Phillips, has stated that "In the final analysis it is the sentiment back home that determines how members will vote on most issues" (33, p. 87). Phillips believes that "The deliberations of Congress are followed by the greatest concentration of news and radio reporters anywhere in the world." But in his efforts to send out newsletters to his constituents, to appear on radio and television programs, and to get his name into the *Congressional Record* at frequent intervals, the "Congressman probably is not

aiming so much at influencing the voters' thinking on major issues of the day as at obtaining public approval of his own votes and speeches" (33, p. 83). That legislators pay close attention to public opinion can hardly be doubted. In fact, they pay entirely too much attention to it sometimes, in that they are not as inclined as they should be to discount transitory flurries of public excitement and do not devote enough attention to generating public support for needed policies. Phillips has concluded that "Congressmen put too much emphasis on their role as mirrors of public opinion, not enough on their role as moulders of public opinion" (33, p. 87).

In Chapter 3 we devoted considerable space to discussing the methods available to the President and the State Department for keeping abreast of public sentiment. In addition to systematic studies of public opinion as reflected in polls, editorial and press comment, the viewpoints of interest-groups, and interviews with individual citizens and visiting delegations, the President and his subordinates also rely heavily upon numerous informal means for testing national attitudes. Roosevelt and Truman regularly sent their advisers—who often travelled incognito—around the country to "take the pulse of the public" on outstanding contemporary issues. President Truman was apparently strongly influenced to run for office again in 1948 by his conviction, shared by very few of his advisers and by few political commentators throughout the country, that public opinion supported him and that there existed widespread dissatisfaction with the work of the Republican-controlled 80th Congress (33, pp. 70-1).

An elaborate organization exists in agencies like the State Department to apprise officials of public thinking. Short summaries of public attitudes, as revealed by the polls, newspaper opinion, and the like, are circulated daily throughout the State Department, and more comprehensive summaries are prepared and distributed at greater intervals. Moreover, the State Department keeps diplomatic posts in the field abreast of public sentiment at home. To what extent are such findings actually utilized by executive officials who formulate and carry out policy? There is a substantial question about the degree to which policy makers are influenced by such information. McCamy writes:

> In practice the officials who are primarily responsible for formulating foreign policy pay little attention to these particular factors of public opinion that might be relevant. . . . They may or may not read the written reports on public opinion, but they seldom consult the specialists in public opinion during the process of developing a policy. (29, p. 331).

And W. Phillips Davison adds that the geographic desk officers of the State Department often have little or no contact with officers who are investigating public opinion. An analysis of all documents circulating through the State Department showed that 95 per cent of those having to do with substantive policy were not even shown to the public opinion specialists. "In practice a policy maker may be more influenced by reading his customary newspaper in the evening and thinking through the arguments advanced by columnists and commentators than by scanning his office mimeographed reports on public opinion" (33, p. 130).

Two fundamental considerations perhaps foreordain that policy-makers should sometimes pay little or no attention to public attitudes in formulating policies. The first, as we have emphasized throughout this chapter, is that, except in rare instances, there is in reality no such thing as public opinion in the singular. Although used widely, the term is actually a convenient, but highly oversimplified, shorthand invoked to describe an extremely complex phenomenon. The term embraces many "publics" and significant quantitative and qualitative differences in the "opinions" expressed by them. Therefore, governmental officials are likely to find the task of evaluating the numerous and often contradictory currents of public sentiment a difficult and time-consuming pursuit. No two officials would likely arrive at identical judgments on what the public demands in respect to any given policy question. Indicative of the way public officials differ in their reliance upon methods for discovering public attitudes is the disparity between legislative and executive officials on the way they assess various means for testing public opinion. When asked to rank their preferences for al-

ternative methods of discovering public opinion, legislators and administrators differed as follows:

Method of Discovering Public Opinion	Administrators	Legislators
Public opinion polls	1	5
Visits to the public	2	2
Newspapers	3	3
Personal mail to officials	4	1
Visits from the public	5	4

(Source: 24, p. 334)

Since each of these methods has limitations as an accurate index of public opinion, undue reliance upon any one of them inescapably distorts the results obtained. For instance, it is axiomatic that personal mail to officials—the first preference on the list of legislators—is sometimes notoriously unreliable as a guide to popular thinking. Skillful lobbyists can and do generate grass roots "mail campaigns" to influence Congress. Moreover, legislators have found that citizens who oppose a measure are more likely to be heard from than those who favor it. The mere act of writing to an official usually indicates that the writer feels more strongly about the issue than the silent majority. Similarly, there are many well-known drawbacks to public opinion polls, the first choice of executive officials. Pollsters concede that their findings must always allow for a certain margin of error; and on some issues, this may be a fairly wide margin. A longstanding limitation, which pollsters have had only limited success in overcoming, is the difficulty of measuring qualitative differences in opinion and degrees of intensity with which views are held. Alternative methods of wording questions about public issues—especially if value-suggesting phrases like "Do you agree with President Eisenhower that . . . ?" are introduced—can produce widely varying results. Other methods for appraising public sentiment encounter comparable difficulties. No single method is completely reliable; nor is there any guarantee that all prevailing methods used collectively will yield a clear and unambiguous result, since the limitations inherent in each separate method are bound to show up in the final result. Such shortcomings of course do not argue in favor of abandoning any or all of these methods. But they re-emphasize the intricacy of public opinion evaluation.

Basically the role of public opinion in a democracy hinges on the question: to what extent ought public officials to be guided by popular thinking and to what extent should they attempt to create public support for policies they believe the national interest demands? Government "by the people" surely does not mean that officials must be guided by every passing whim of the public and must equate mere prejudice and emotionalism with reasoned judgment on national policy matters. Our study of Roosevelt's diplomacy during the 1930's indicates that there must always be a continuing interplay between public opinion and public policy. Few informed citizens or students of government would advocate that officials follow public sentiment blindly, irrespective of international and domestic events. In an age of total war, when decisions in the international field could easily determine the future destiny of the human race for generations to come, the statesman has as much obligation to lead and educate public opinion as to follow it. His record in office—and ultimately his place in history—is likely to be determined by the extent to which he can maintain a successful equilibrium between policies the citizenry will support and policies the public interest requires. Meanwhile, he must make an unceasing effort to raise the level of public enlightenment and to encourage more active and more intelligent citizen participation in the politico-governmental process.

REFERENCES

1. Bailey, Thomas A. *A Diplomatic History of the American People*. New York: Appleton-Century-Crofts, 1950.

2. ——. *Woodrow Wilson and the Great Betrayal*. New York: The Macmillan Company, 1945.

3. Bauer, Wilhelm. "Public Opinion," *Encyclopedia of the Social Sciences*. New York: The Macmillan Company, 1934, 12, pp. 669-73.

4. Bernays, Edward U. "Attitude Polls—Servants or Masters?" *Public Opinion Quarterly*, 9 (Fall, 1945), 264-68b. Discusses arguments for and against public opinion polls for measuring popular viewpoints.

5. Bogardus, Emory S. *The Making of Public Opinion*. New York: The Association Press, 1951.

6. Burdette, Franklin L. "Influence of Noncongressional Pressures on Foreign Policy," *Annals of the American Academy of Political and Social Science*, 289 (September, 1953), 92-9.

7. Burns, James M. *Roosevelt: The Lion and the Fox*. New York: Harcourt, Brace and Company, 1956. A readable interpretation of the Roosevelt era.

8. Cantril, Hadley. *Public Opinion, 1935-1946*. Princeton: Princeton University Press, 1951. A voluminous compendium of polls on various subjects.

9. Carelton, William G. "Isolationism and the Middle West," *Mississippi Valley Historical Review*, 33 (December, 1946), 377-90. Carelton argues that the extent of Middle Western isolationism has been greatly exaggerated.

10. *Congressional Quarterly*. Volume 9, 1953.

11. ——. Volume 12, 1956.

12. Cottrell, Leonard S., Jr., and Eberhart, Sylvia. *American Opinion on World Affairs*. Princeton: Princeton University Press, 1948.

13. Engelbert, Ernest A. "Political Strategy of Agriculture," *Journal of Farm Economics*, 36 (August, 1954), 375-87. Brings out clearly the many internal stresses that beset the agricultural community.

14. Fleming, D. F. *The United States and the World Court*. Garden City, N. Y.: Doubleday, Doran and Company, 1945. A significant study of the interaction between public opinion and American policy toward the World Court.

15. Friedrich, Carl J. "The Agricultural Basis of Emotional Nationalism," *Public Opinion Quarterly*, 1 (April, 1937), 50-61. Shows clear correlation between isolationist viewpoints and rural populations.

16. Gillin, John. "National and Regional Cultural Values in the United States," *Social Forces*, 34 (December, 1955), 107-13. Emphasizes regional viewpoints toward important socio-economic-political issues.

17. Grassmuck, George L. *Sectional Biases in Congress on Foreign Policy*. Baltimore: The Johns Hopkins University Press, 1951. An important study of sectional viewpoints as reflected in legislative voting behavior during the interwar period.

18. Hennessy, Bernard. "Case Study of Intra-Pressure Group Conflicts: The United World Federalists," *Journal of Politics,* 16 (February, 1954), 76-95. The writer brings out forcefully how cross-pressures occur within important pressure groups.

19. Honor, Leo L. "American Intercession in Behalf of the Jews," *Journal of Modern History,* 22 (March, 1950), 48-51. Analyzes the impact of American Jewry on foreign policy and evaluates certain literature on the subject.

20. Hull, Cordell. *The Memoirs of Cordell Hull.* New York: The Macmillan Company, 1948, volume I.

21. Irish, Marian D. "Foreign Policy and the South," *Journal of Politics,* 10 (May, 1948), 306-36. Discusses Southern attitudes toward world affairs and relates them to the influence of southerners on the government, especially Congress.

22. Jacob, Philip E. "Influences of World Events on U. S. 'Neutrality' Opinion," *Public Opinion Quarterly,* 4 (March, 1940), 48-66. An illuminating treatment of American public opinion and its impact on policy during the 1930's.

23. Klingberg, F. L. "The Historical Alternation of Moods in American Foreign Policy," *World Politics,* 4 (January, 1952), 239-73. Perhaps the most ambitious attempt yet made to establish certain recurrent "cycles" in American opinion toward world affairs.

24. Kriesberg, Martin. "What Congressmen and Administrators Think of the Polls," *Public Opinion Quarterly,* 9 (Fall, 1945), 333-37.

25. Langer, William L., and Gleason, S. Everett. *The Challenge to Isolationism.* New York: Harper and Brothers, 1952. This is one of the best studies of American foreign policy during the New Deal.

26. Lazarsfeld, P. F., and Gaudet, H. *The People's Choice.* New York: Duell, Sloan and Pearce, 1944.

27. Lubell, Samuel. *The Future of American Politics.* New York: Harper and Brothers, 1952. Lubell cites many instances of the influence of racial, nationality, and sectional viewpoints on American public policy, although he may well exaggerate the degree to which racial-nationality opinions are determinative.

28. Lydgate, William A. *What America Thinks.* New York: Thomas Y. Crowell, 1944.

29. McCamy, James L. *The Administration of American Foreign Affairs.* New York: Alfred A. Knopf, 1950.

30. MacIver, R. M., ed. *Group Relations and Group Antagonisms.* New York: Harper and Brothers, 1944. The chapter by Max Ascoli brings out clearly the influence of Italian-Americans on American foreign policy.

31. McNeill, William H. *America, Britain and Russia, 1941-1946.* London: Oxford University Press, Royal Institute of International Affairs, 1953. This authoritative study ascribes considerable influence to racial and national minorities on postwar U. S. policy. See pp. 21, 31-n, and 404.

32. McWilliams, Carey. "The Problem of Minorities," in Bliven, Bruce, and Mezerick, A. G., eds. *What the Informed Citizen Needs to Know.* New York: Duell, Sloan and Pearce, 1945.

33. Markel, Lester, ed. *Public Opinion and Foreign Policy.* New York: Harper and Brothers, 1949. A valuable symposium on various aspects of public opinion and foreign relations.

34. National Opinion Research Center, University of Chicago, "Occasional Reports," Series FA - No. 1.

35. ———. "Occasional Reports," Series FA - No. 3.

36. ———. "Occasional Reports," Series FA - No. 4.

37. Paschell, William. "Structure and Membership of the Labor Movement," *Monthly Labor Review,* 78 (November, 1955), 1231-39.

38. Perkins, Dexter. *The American Approach to Foreign Relations.* Cambridge, Mass.: Harvard University Press, 1952.

39. Pratt, Julius W. *A History of United States Foreign Policy.* New York: Prentice-Hall, 1955.

40. "The Quarter's Polls," *Public Opinion Quarterly,* 15 (Spring, 1951).

41. Ratchford, B. U. "The South's Stake in International Trade—Past, Present, and Prospective," *Southern Economic Journal,* 14 (April, 1948), 361-75. Focuses on changing southern viewpoints toward world affairs, especially trade questions.

42. Reynolds, Quentin. "The USA and the World," *United Nations World,* 6 (July, 1952), 13-17. An illuminating treatment of several important aspects of American opinion on international relations.

43. Rose, Arnold and Caroline. *America Divided.* New York: Alfred A. Knopf, 1949. Treats a number of instances of minority group influence on foreign relations. See pp. 9-11, 39, and 47-8.

44. Sayre, Morris. "The Stake of Industry," *Annals of the American Academy of Political and Social Science,* 259 (September, 1948), 113-21. A former president of the NAM outlines his organization's viewpoints on major issues.

45. Schultz, Theodore W. "Which Way Will Farmers Turn?" *Foreign Affairs*, 23 (July, 1945), 627-34. Examines the attitudes of agricultural groups on postwar problems.

46. Smith, Bradford. *A Dangerous Freedom*. Philadelphia: J. B. Lippincott Company, 1954. The freedom alluded to is "freedom of association"—and the writer brings out many implications of extensive group membership for American society.

47. Smuckler, Ralph H. "The Region of Isolationism," *American Political Science Review*, 47 (June, 1953), 386-401. A thorough study of forces contributing to American isolationist thinking, especially of sectionalist viewpoints.

48. Stavisky, Sam. "Where Does the Veteran Stand Today?" *Annals of the American Academy of Political and Social Science*, 259 (September, 1948), 128-35.

49. Truman, Harry S. *Memoirs by Harry S. Truman*. Garden City, N. Y.: Doubleday, and Company, 1955.

50. United States Senate, Committee on the Judiciary. *The Immigration and Naturalization System of the United States*, 81st Congress, 2nd Session. Washington: Government Printing Office, 1950. This is an extremely valuable reference work on immigration into the United States and the nature of the foreign-born population within the country.

51. Vaughan, Wayland F. *Social Psychology*. New York: Odyssey Press, 1948.

52. Williams, Frederick W. "Regional Attitudes on International Cooperation," *Public Opinion Quarterly*, 9 (Spring, 1945), 38-51. A helpful, if somewhat dated, breakdown on regional viewpoints about international questions.

53. Wittke, Carl. *The Irish in America*. Baton Rouge: Louisiana State University Press, 1956. An indispensable source for further study on the influence of this important minority group on American foreign relations.

54. Woodward, C. Vann. "The Irony of Southern History," *Journal of Southern History*, 19 (February, 1953), 3-19. A noted authority on the South relates southern viewpoints to the broad stream of American opinion on foreign policy issues.

55. *World Almanac and Book of Facts for 1957*. New York: New York World-Telegram, 1957.

56. Young, Kimball. *Social Psychology*. New York: Appleton-Century-Crofts, 1956.

CHAPTER 8

The Cold War in Historical Perspective

Thus far, we have studied the formulation of American foreign policy and evaluated the major influences and institutions that have an important role in it. We now begin a consideration of the substance of American foreign policy in the contemporary era.

In this and subsequent chapters we shall follow a similar approach: first, a brief historical background dealing with the past relations between the United States and other countries or with America's attempt to cope with important international questions is established; then, utilizing this background as a perspective within which to view contemporary problems, the basic issues that have given rise to such problems are analyzed. This chapter and the next examine relations between the United States and Soviet Russia. The sequence of

topics covered is indicative of the approach to be followed in the remainder of our study: enduring elements in Russian foreign policy; Russian-American relations to World War II; ideological conflict in the postwar period; strategic-territorial conflict in the postwar period; and economic-military conflict in the postwar period. This approach provides a more helpful frame of reference within which to evaluate current American foreign policy than would a chronological recital of major developments in Soviet-American relations since 1917.

Let us then look initially at certain influences in Russian foreign policy which must be properly understood in order to comprehend the issues that divide Russia and the United States in the contemporary era.

1. ENDURING GOALS OF RUSSIAN FOREIGN POLICY

The Centrality of Historical Insights

Engraved upon the National Archives Building in Washington are the words: "What Is Past Is Prologue." It is a central thesis of this first chapter dealing with substantive problems in American foreign relations that Americans seldom pay enough attention to the lessons of history in their attempt to understand the issues stemming from the dominant interna-

tional problem of their age—the cold war. It may appear unnecessary to remind a society as history-minded as the American that the past has much to teach the student of present-day world affairs. Yet Americans seem often more inclined to venerate the past than to learn from it. Applying this idea specifically to Russian-American relations, what we are suggesting is this: history shows a remarkable continuity in Russian foreign policy, whether that foreign policy is practiced by the Czars or the Communists. Continuity can be discerned in both the *goals* of Russian foreign policy and in the *methods* utilized for achieving them.

Two examples must suffice at this stage. Is world domination generally believed to be a cardinal diplomatic ambition of the USSR? "A strange superstition prevails among the Russians, that they are destined to conquer the world . . . ," said a State Department dispatch in the mid-nineteenth century (1, p. 62). And is the Kremlin thought by the West to be utterly unprincipled in its dealings with other countries, so much so that its promises are looked upon as worthless? A Russian historian once described Czarist diplomacy as follows:

> The diplomatic methods of the Muscovite boyars often threw the foreign envoys into desperation, particularly those who wanted to carry on their business forthrightly and conscientiously. . . . in order not to fall into their nets it was not enough to make certain that they were lying; it was also necessary to decide what the purpose of the lie was; and what was one to do then? If someone caught them lying, they did not blush and they answered all reproaches with a laugh. (2, p. 163).

At the time of the Russo-Japanese War in 1905, Theodore Roosevelt declared that "Russia is so corrupt, so treacherous and shifty . . . that I am utterly unable to say whether or not it will make peace, or break off negotiations at any moment" (1, p. 198). Western diplomats in the modern period would likely find these descriptions remarkably apropos in characterizing the difficulty of maintaining harmonious relations with the USSR.

These examples are cited at the beginning of our study of Russian-American relations to stress the importance of setting contemporary cold war problems within the requisite historical context. Americans are prone to think of the cold war as a conflict between Soviet communism and Western democracy. Ideological elements are unquestionably present. Yet such an oversimplified approach gives rise to many dangers and misapprehensions. Americans are likely to fall into the error of thinking that the Bolshevik Revolution of 1917 ushered in a *totally* new era in the relations between Russia and the outside world and in international politics generally. This of course is the view-

point assiduously cultivated by the Kremlin itself. Students of foreign policy, however, must not jump to the conclusion that Russian diplomacy before 1917 is unrelated to present-day Soviet diplomatic behavior. They must be skeptical of the viewpoint—a cardinal article of faith in the communist creed—that Marxist-Leninist-Stalinist ideological compulsions furnish the most useful keys to understanding Russia's activities in the international community since 1917. They must not try to arrive at a guide to Soviet diplomatic conduct merely by piecing together utterances and writings by high-ranking communist spokesmen. Nathan Leites' work, *A Study of Bolshevism*, is a valuable compendium of such utterances on a variety of themes. Yet, perhaps inadvertently, it conveys the impression that such influences as history, geography, strategic and economic factors—not to mention the pattern established by the day-by-day Soviet reaction to international events—are comparatively unimportant in explaining the Kremlin's diplomacy. The underlying assumption seems to be that of all the factors that shape Soviet foreign policy, ideology is far and away the most significant. As we shall see later in this chapter and in the chapter to follow, this is at best a questionable assumption (17, *passim*). What is basic for understanding Soviet diplomatic goals and methods at any stage is not so much what Lenin or Stalin or lesser communist luminaries *said* Soviet Russia was doing or going to do in world affairs, but rather what Russia has in fact *done* both in the Czarist and in the communist periods. Creation of "People's Democracies" by the bayonets of the Red Army in Eastern Europe does not differ from old-style Czarist imperialism in the same area merely because Stalin baptized his hegemony with quotations from Marx and Lenin. The Czars could invoke a variety of slogans too, such as "legitimacy" and Pan-Slavism, to justify what was in essence *Machtpolitik*. Communism as an ideology resembles other ideologies in that it both shapes events and is in turn shaped by events. As a dynamic, ever-growing faith, it is both a *cause of action* and a *justification for action* by the Soviet state.

Age-old Russian foreign policy goals and methods, blended and overlaid with communist ideological compulsions, provide the key to the foreign policies of the Kremlin. More and more since 1917 Soviet Russia has given evidence of diplomatic atavism, a characteristic which is not, of course, peculiar with Russia. One of the most fascinating aspects of Soviet diplomacy is the degree to which Stalin and his successors have ingeniously fused the historic diplomatic ambitions of Old Russia with the communist faith. As much as any other single factor, it is this union that confronts the free world co... ...tion led by the United States with a formi... ...and continuing challenge. Because A... generally give insufficient attention to... ...torical elements of Russian foreign... shall devote considerable space h... ...ing them.

Expansionism—The Keynote of Historic Russian Policy

A newspaper reporter during the Crimean War in the mid-1850's wrote of Russia:

The Russian frontier has advanced: towards Berlin, Dresden and Vienna . . . towards Constantinople . . . towards Stockholm . . . towards Teheran. . . . The total acquisitions of Russia during the last 60 years are equal in extent and importance to the whole Empire she had in Europe before that time.

And in another dispatch the same reporter declared that:

And as sure as conquest follows conquest, and annexation follows annexation, so sure would the conquest of Turkey by Russia be only the prelude for the annexation of Hungary, Prussia, Galicia, and for the ultimate realization of the Slavonic Empire. . . . The arrest of the Russian scheme of annexation is a matter of the highest moment.

So wrote a German correspondent—Karl Marx—who was to have no little influence on the future course of Russian history. The word that best characterizes Russian foreign policy throughout history and furnishes the most evident and important link between Russia's past and present policies in the international community is the word *expansionism*. Beginning as an insignificant twelfth-century city in the valley of the Dnieper, by the post-World War II period Moscow was the center of an empire that embraced one-fourth of the human race

and thirteen ...cluding countries li... ...are ideologica... 22-3).

The... alm... in...

...ssia ...; and ...ed and ...gainst the ...Russia, such ...malayas, the ...e river systems

...essive Czars pushed ...ussia, and in doing so ...d troublesome interna... ...er the Great finally won ...window on the West" when ...h of the Baltic region from ...erine the Great participated in Po... ...e partitions, in 1772, 1793, and 1795, ... pushed Russian frontiers steadily southward to encroach upon the Turkish Empire. Her successors continued the march southward and eastward by maintaining pressure against the frontiers of Turkey, Persia, Afghanistan, and India—thereby generating one of the most persistent diplomatic problems of the nineteenth century. At Tilsit in 1807, Alexander I and Napoleon attempted to divide most of Europe between them. And after Napoleon's defeat Alexander annexed Poland, Finland, and Bessarabia, and engaged in intrigues in virtually every country in Europe. Nicholas I and Alexander II sponsored explorations and colonization movements eastward into Central Asia and Siberia, bringing Russia ultimately into conflict with Japanese and, to a lesser extent, British and American diplomatic ambitions in the Orient.

It is instructive to recall Czarist territorial ambitions at the beginning of the First World War. Had Imperial Russia been victorious, it expected to push its territory westward to incorporate what was the Poland of 1919-39; annex East Prussia and all of the area west of the Vistula; annex Eastern Galicia; overthrow the defunct Turkish Government and realize Russia's ancient ambition to control the Straits;

and annex Turkish territories bordering Trans-caucasia (7, p. 11).

Czarist expansionism derived from several impulses. First of all, Russia pushed inexorably across the Eurasian plain in much the same way as Americans trekked across their con-tinent. Prince Michael Gorchakov wrote of his country's history that Russia, in common with all countries, was "forced to take the road of expansion dictated by necessity rather than by ambitions, a road on which the chief difficulty is to know where to stop" (10, II, p. 982). The tendency to expand into territorial vacuums is neither a peculiarly Soviet, nor even Czarist, trait.

Second, the expansionist tendencies of the Czarist state sprang in part from politico-strategic necessities. The vast, frontierless Eur-asian plain facilitated Russian internal expan-sionism, but it also greatly aided foreign incursions into the interior of Russia. Histor-ically, the response of the Czarist state was to provide for defense-in-depth by creating an extensive buffer zone around its vulnerable geographic heartland. Safeguarding the mili-tary approaches to the interior has been a cardinal principle of Russian diplomacy since the time of Peter the Great, as it would have to be a diplomatic principle of any great power faced with a comparable threat.

Third, expansionism by the 19th century came to have an economic rationale. Russia, along with the other great powers, wanted a stake in foreign markets, both to increase the treasury and Russian prestige. The search for colonies led primarily to Manchuria, where Russian imperialism clashed with the territorial and economic ambitions of Japan, England, and the United States. As in American and British imperialism, economic concessions necessitated protection by Russian diplomats and soldiers. From 1904 to 1905 the Manchurian venture drew Russia into the most humiliating war in its history when it was humbled by the small island kingdom of Japan.

Fourth, a recurrent motif in Russian ex-pansionism was the "historic mission" of Russia to deliver lesser people from their cultural and spiritual backwardness and to usher in the earthly millennium. Since we shall examine Russian messianistic thought in a later portion

of the chapter, we shall merely observe here that the messianic aspirations of certain secular and religious thinkers within Russia coincided perfectly at points with the diplomatic ambi-tions of the Czarist state. The foreign policies of Alexander I (1801-1825) illustrate the point. Alexander exhibited a calculating Machiavel-lianism, combined with a fervent and mystic idealism. He was capable of both the Treaty of Tilsit (1807), whereby he and Napoleon divided Europe between them; and of the high-minded, if totally impractical Holy Alli-ance (1815), whereby Christian principles were to be made the basis of international conduct. Europeans, writes a contemporary British historian, must have wondered whether Alexander was not "just a cunning hypocrite, cultivating liberal sympathies and evangelical piety as a cloak to hide vast plans of aggres-sive ambitions. . . . " He was apt to "identify his own interest, or whims, with the good of humanity." Professing that all men ought to be free—at the very time he was annexing Poland, Finland, and Bessarabia—Alexander, "desired all men to be free on condition they did what he wanted them to do" (20, pp. 33-4).

The Search for Warm Water Ports

Closely related to expansionism is Russia's age-old search for warm water ports. Land-locked around most of its borders, Russia has always needed accessible and usable outlets to the sea. The ports of Murmansk, Archangel, and Leningrad are ice-bound a considerable portion of the year. To the south, Russian traffic on the Black Sea has always been at the mercy of Turkey which controls the Darda-nelles, or Turkey's protectors, such as Great Britain and, to a lesser degree, France during the 18th and 19th century. Since 1947 the United States has filled the vacuum created by the decline of British power in the Straits area and throughout the Near and Middle East as a whole.

South and eastward, Russian diplomacy has sought to force a breakthrough to the sea by intermittent pressure upon Persia, Afghanistan, and India. In addition to furnishing rich prizes to incorporate into the Russian empire, acqui-sition of passageways through these countries would give Russia access to the trade-routes of the world. The modern American policy of containment had its origins along the Persian-Russian border and in the bleak hills of the Northwest Frontier in India during the 19th century. A dominant objective of British diplomacy during the age of *Pax Britannica* was to prevent Russian penetration of the Middle East. Throughout British colonial history Russia was continually probing soft spots in the British defense perimeter and endeavoring to enlist other people, such as the Afghan tribesmen along the Indian frontiers, to further Russia's diplomatic ambitions.

Still further eastward, Russia advanced over Siberia and Central Asia toward the shores of the Pacific. The Czars at last acquired outlets to the sea when they obtained or leased ports in Siberia and Manchuria late in the 19th century. With the completion of the Trans-Siberian Railroad by 1900, these ports became useful, even though they were ice-bound a goodly part of the year, were extremely vulnerable to foreign attack, as the Russo-Japanese War proved, and even though they were some 6,000 miles from European Russia. Russia's search for eastern seaports, coupled with the necessity to assure their accessibility over the railroads of north China, inevitably drew it into the maelstrom of great power imperialistic rivalry in the Far East (**10**, II, pp. 1262, 1270-71).

Are Soviet policy-makers today still seeking outlets to the sea? The question hardly requires an answer. Soviet incorporation of the Baltic States, hegemony over Albania, intermittent pressure on Turkey to give the USSR a larger voice in safeguarding the Turkish Straits and determining policy toward them; Communist intrigue in the northern provinces of Iran in 1946, support for the Greek rebels in 1946-47, more recent economic blandishments to Afghanistan, India, and Burma, Communist machinations in Syria, Egypt and other Middle Eastern countries—all of these indicate that there has been little diminution in the traditional Russian urge to the sea.

The "Iron Curtain Complex"

When Winston Churchill stated in 1946 that an Iron Curtain had descended over Europe, he was coining a phrase that applied equally well to earlier stages in the history of Russia's relations with Europe. An "Iron Curtain complex" has been characteristic of the Russian attitude toward the outside world for centuries. When a *cordon sanitaire* or formidable geographical barriers did not effectively seal Russia off from contact with its neighbors, then a spiritual Iron Curtain has done so during most periods of Russian history. Estrangement and hostility took many forms: rigorous government censorship of ideas and communications from abroad; limited contacts between Russian citizens and foreigners; official coolness, amounting often to outright discrimination, toward foreign diplomats in Russia; belief in the inherent superiority of Russian customs and institutions; and unwillingness to cultivate sincere and lasting ties of friendship with other countries. With some significant exceptions, almost every period of Russian history has exhibited a deep-seated xenophobia.*

In pre-Soviet history many factors engendered suspicion and hostility toward the outside world. In some periods, like the late 19th and early 20th century, Russia was militarily much weaker than other countries suspected. The Russo-Japanese War and the First World War showed this. Furthermore, Russia was economically backward. The contrast between its rate of industrialization and standard of living and that of its advanced western neighbors was a source of constant embarrassment and insecurity. Moreover, under both the Czars and the Communists, Russia has feared the impact of western political ideals upon a population restive under despotism. Then, too, neither the Czarist nor communist regime has relished having the whole apparatus of state oppression—the ubiquitous secret police, the massive bureaucracy, the Siberian prison

---

*While xenophobia has been characteristic of the Russian *government*, there existed a considerable interchange of cultural and political ideas between Russian citizens and the outside world under the Czars. Barghoorn in fact maintains that the Russian population as a whole has traditionally been highly receptive to ideas from abroad and that even under the Communists, Soviet citizens have shown keen interest in the viewpoints of foreigners (**2**, pp. 162-64). For an illuminating treatment of the impact of American political ideas upon the Czarist state in the 18th and 19th century, see **16**, pp. 31-139.

camps, the policies of censorship and suppression of designated minorities—exposed to the gaze and ridicule of the world. Lurid accounts of these aspects of Russian life have always fostered tension between Russia and other countries. To avoid unfavorable reports in foreign countries, Russia has preferred to close the door to foreigners entirely or to permit them to see only a few selected show places.

Intense suspicion and fear of the outside world has been engendered also by Russia's historical experiences both under the Czars and under the Bolsheviks. The motif of cataclysm, perennial danger from abroad, and impending doom is a recurrent theme in Russian literature and political writing. In large measure it is a product of Russian geography and of history dictated by geographical conditions. The eminent British scholar Sir Bernard Pares has written: "The Great Russian people were hammered out of peaceful, silent pacific elements by constant and cruel blows from enemies on all sides, which implanted into the least intelligent of Russians an instinct of national defense . . . " (**19**, p. 114). And Mazour adds that "The motivating background of Russia's foreign policy is predominantly the need for security. . . . " He continues:

> The Napoleonic Wars culminating with the occupation of Moscow, the Crimean War ending with the disaster at Sevastopol, the Russo-Turkish War . . . , World War I ending with Allied intervention, and above all World War II with its appalling devastation—these are experiences which no nation can forgive or forget.

Whether justified or not, he feels that inevitably Russia will seek "a *cordon sanitaire* in reverse, with its bayonets turned westward. . . . it is the ABC of national strategy" (**19**, p. 116).

Fostered by countless invasions throughout history, the Russian legacy of suspicion and fear of the outside world is exemplified in the attitude of the reactionary Pobedonostsev, adviser to Alexander III (1881-94). Pobedonostsev was convinced that "it is impossible to rely upon any of our so-called 'friends' and 'allies,' that all of them are ready to hurl themselves upon us at that very minute when our weakness or errors become apparent" (**27**, p. 132).

The "Third Rome" Idea and Russian Messianism

The communist hope of redeeming mankind through the "world revolution" and achieving utopia is a variant of a theme that pervades historic Russian theological and philosophical thought. In a penetrating study of Russian national character, Nicolas Berdyaev states that "Messianic consciousness is more characteristic of the Russians than of any other people except the Jews. It runs all through Russian history right down to its communist period" (**4**, pp. 8-9). Its earliest origins are to be found in the conception of Moscow as the "Third Rome." After the fall of Rome in the 5th century and the collapse of the Byzantine Empire in the 15th, the center of Orthodox Christianity shifted to Moscow. To Russian theologians this signified a profound and God-ordained change in the direction of history. Thus the monk Philotheus informed Basil III, Grand Duke of Moscow:

> The first Rome collapsed owing to its heresies, the second Rome fell victim to the Turks, but a new third Rome has sprung up in the north, illuminating the whole universe like the sun. . . . The first and second Rome have fallen, but the third will stand till the end of history, for it is the last Rome. Moscow has no successor; a fourth Rome is inconceivable. (**19**, pp. 51-2).

"The Mission of Russia," comments Berdyaev, "was to be the vehicle of the true Christianity . . . There enters into the messianic consciousness the alluring temptation of imperialism" (**4**, p. 8-9).

Strongly reinforcing the theological designation of Moscow as the Third Rome were the viewpoints of the Slavophils, and their 19th century successors, the Pan-Slavists. Compounded of Russian nationalism, mystic ties of race, German idealism, and Hegelian philosophy, Slavophilism predicted the inevitable decay of Europe and the redemption of mankind by the Slavs. "Western Europe is on the high road to ruin," Prince Odoevsky wrote. Advancing the theme of *ex Oriente lux* that permeates Russian philosophic and religious thought, he believed that:

> We Russians, on the contrary, are young and fresh and have taken no part in the crimes of Europe. We have a great mission to fulfill. Our

name is already inscribed on the tablets of victory: the victories of science, art and faith await us on the ruins of tottering Europe. (**19**, p. 31).

And the Russian mystic Peter Chaadaev believed that "we have a vocation to solve a great many of the problems of the social order . . . to give an answer to questions of great importance with which mankind is concerned" (**4**, p. 37). Describing man's quest for spirituality and holiness, the immortal Dostoevsky stated in 1880: "I speak only of the brotherhood of man, not of triumphs of the sword. . . . For I am convinced that the heart of Russia, more than any other nation, is dedicated to this universal union of all mankind . . ." (**19**, p. 19).

The Pan-Slav movement late in the 19th century also contained messianic elements. According to its leading spokesmen, Russian cultural-historical affinity with the Slavs gave the Russian state a special responsibility as protector and defender of their interests. The Pan-Slavs, writes Florinsky, "were in general agreement that it was the historic mission of Russia to liberate the Slavs from a foreign and religious and political yoke . . ." (**10**, II, p. 987).

Other influences evident in certain periods of Russian thought also supported messianism and assigned to Moscow a dominant role in achieving the salvation of mankind. One of these was nihilism. Another was anarchism. Berdyaev summarizes the viewpoint of the most famous Russian anarchist, Michael Bakunin, as follows:

What is needed is to set fire to a world-wide blaze; it is necessary to destroy the old world; upon the ashes of the old world, on its ruins, there will spring up a new and better world of its own accord. . . . Collectivism or communism will not be an affair of organization; it will spring out of the freedom which will arrive after the destruction of the old world. (**4**, p. 148).

Also important is the attention given in Russian Orthodox theological thought to the coming of the Kingdom of God. In contrast to Roman Catholic and Protestant thought, Russian Orthodox theology has always emphasized the early apocalyptic message of the Church. The coming of the Kingdom of God will mean the "transfiguration of the world, not only the transfiguration of the individual man." Salvation is conceived of as total and corporate for society (**4**, p. 195).

Russian messianism, concludes Berdyaev, is perfectly compatible with the mission of Marxism-Leninism-Stalinism to redeem mankind and recreate society anew upon the ruins of the old order. "Russian communism is a distortion of the Russian messianic idea; it proclaims light from the East which is destined to enlighten the bourgeois darkness of the West" (**4**, pp. 249-50). Analyzing the messianic elements in contemporary Soviet policy, Barghoorn observes that the Kremlin "holds out to mankind the vision and prophecy of the earthly paradise, the harmonious society without coercion and inequality. This is the utopian aspect of Soviet Russia's message to the world . . ." (**23**, p. 531).* The point is well exemplified by an article in *Izvestia* on February 22, 1948, which discusses Russia's contribution to humanity in the Second World War:

The Soviet Army . . . stretched out a brotherly, helping hand to the peoples of Europe languishing in Fascist Slavery. The European peoples have to thank the Soviet Army for their liberation. . . . The Soviet Army saved European civilization from the Fascist barbarians, honorably and worthily performed its historic liberating mission. . . . As always, the Soviet Army stands on guard to protect the peaceful labor and tranquility of the peoples. Always, it stands on guard for peace throughout the world. (**8**, p. 512).

*The continuity of Russian messianic thought between the Czarist and communist periods is provocatively discussed in a series of Arden House papers included in **23** pp. 473-550.

2. RUSSIAN–AMERICAN RELATIONS BEFORE WORLD WAR II

The Nineteenth Century Pattern

Relations between Russia and the United States in the late 18th and throughout most of the 19th centuries were governed by influences that were to shape many of their relationships in the more recent period. At first, Russia and America had relatively few direct contacts and hence few common problems. Geographically separated, their interests touched directly in only one part of the globe—the Far East—and even this occurred only toward the end of the 19th century, when the United States emerged as a Pacific power.

A second characteristic of their relations was official coolness, interspersed with periods of ideological hostility and suspicion. The leading democracy in the world and the Czarist autocracy had few ideas and institutions in common. To successive Czars, the American democracy was a fertile seed-bed for spawning revolutionary ferment; its very existence encouraged rebellion against established authority within Russia and throughout Europe as a whole. The policy of welcoming political exiles added to prevailing ideological tensions. To the United States, Czarist Russia was the quintessence of despotism and political backwardness—in short, the antithesis of every American Revolutionary ideal. Informed Americans were aware that it was Alexander I, in concert with the arch-reactionary of the age, Prince Metternich of Austria, who was invoking the principle of "legitimacy" to exterminate all vestiges of political liberalism in post-Napoleonic Europe. And, it was a common American misapprehension that President Monroe's blunt warning to the European powers in the famous Monroe Doctrine of 1823 had kept the Holy Alliance from extending its noxious activities to the American continent.

Given the incompatibility of American and Russian political ideals and institutions, it is understandable why relations between the two countries did not begin auspiciously. The first American Minister to Russia, Francis Dana, was kept cooling his heels in Moscow for almost two years; and even then he left Russia in frustration without being able to gain audience with Catherine the Great (1, pp. 6-7). Alexander I finally extended Russian recognition to America in 1809, long after other countries had done so. It was not until 1824 that treaty relations were established between the two governments (11, p. 388).

During the years that followed, ideological hostility colored relations between Russia and the United States on many occasions. Americans were vocally anti-Russian during the

Polish Revolt of 1830, which the Czar suppressed with characteristic ruthlessness (1, pp. 39-44). Again in 1863 American public opinion was strongly anti-Russian during the Czar's intervention in Poland, even though the American Civil War marked the high-tide of Russian-American friendship (5, passim).

As the 19th century waned, ideological estrangement between Russia and America intensified. Czarist oppressions, both within Russia and in surrounding countries, drove ever larger groups of refugees to American shores. The program of "Russification" inaugurated by Alexander III (1881-1894), resulting in oppressive measures against minorities within Russia and harsh pogroms against the Jews, aroused heated opposition within the United States, especially on the part of the foreign-born population. On top of this, in the same period there were a number of sensational exposés about Russia by American citizens who had travelled in that country. Especially significant in arousing anti-Czarist sentiment within the United States were the revelations of George Kennan,* whose graphic descriptions of life in the prison camps of Siberia stirred the American consciousness about Russia as perhaps no other influence had done in the Czarist period (16, pp. 293-320).

The American people entertained high hopes for the Russian Revolution of 1905. But its perversion by reactionary forces within Russia, coupled with continued persecution of the Jews and other minorities, finally led to a breach in Russian-American relations in 1911, when the United States abrogated the commercial treaty of 1832. Commercial relations between the two countries were not re-established until the period of the New Deal (1, p. 49).

While geographical separation and ideological estrangement were important factors in relations between Russia and the United States before World War II, there was a third and much more basic factor. Until the emergence of both countries as super-powers in the contemporary period, the controlling principle in their relations, as DeWitt Poole has phrased it, was that in critical times each nation was "for

---

*The George Kennan alluded to here was a distant relative of the contemporary historian and expert on the Soviet Union, George F. Kennan.

the other a potential friend in the rear of potential enemies" (18, p. 141). Until around 1900, for both Russia and the United States the potential enemy was in almost every case Great Britain. After 1900 it came more and more to be Japan; and during the period of the 1930's and World War II it was the Axis Powers. During the era of *Pax Britannica* when it was a dominant goal of British foreign policy to check Russian expansionism, Russian policy sought to undermine British power. For it was Great Britain alone or as the leader of the European coalition that frustrated such Russian objectives as penetration of the Dardanelles and the Middle East. In the same period the United States was also intensely suspicious of British diplomacy. It suspected Downing Street of seeking to exploit American domestic controversies, such as the Civil War, to advance Britain's imperial ambitions.

Until the Anglo-American *rapprochement* at the end of the century, mutual hostility and suspicion of Great Britain often bound Russia and America into concerted diplomatic activity. Russian and American Anglophobia explain every example that might be cited of Russian-American friendship during this period—Alexander's recognition of America in 1809, withdrawal of Czarist claims to the American Northwest in the early 1820's, American sympathy for Russia during the Crimean War (1854-56), the visit of the Russian fleet to America in 1863, the sale of Russian Alaska to the United States in 1867, the naval mission sent by the United States to Russia in 1866 to congratulate Alexander II upon escape from attempted assassination. Let us look at only one of these instances as illustrative of the point.

The period of the American Civil War witnessed the zenith of Russian-American friendship before the Second World War. In marked contrast with the other European Powers, Czarist Russia openly proclaimed its sympathy for the Union. The appearance of the Russian fleet in New York harbor in 1863 seemed to Americans to signify both that Russia was prepared to give tangible aid to the North and that it was serving blunt notice on other countries to keep out of American affairs. Historical research, however, has convincingly shown that this view was entirely erroneous. The Czar's pro-Union policies were dictated chiefly by fear that the European powers, led by Great Britain, were planning to intervene against Russian suppression of the Polish Revolt of 1863. To keep the Royal Navy from sweeping the small Russian fleet from the seas, the Russian fleet used New York harbor as a haven. If war broke out, this haven might become a base for attacking British commerce. More generally, the Czar wanted to preserve the United States as a strong power in the rear of Britain because this obviously fitted in with the Russian aim of undermining British influence in world affairs (1, pp. 81-94).

Essentially the same considerations shaped Russian-American relationships nearly a half-century later at the end of the Russo-Japanese War (1904-05). In this instance, however, the common interests between the United States and Russia derived from their mutual desire to check Japanese expansionism in the Orient. Throughout the war American public opinion was solidly pro-Japanese. Opened for contact with the Western world by Commodore Perry in 1853, Japan was regarded as America's protégé. Moreover, the island kingdom was the under-dog, fighting against one of the most corrupt and oppressive despotisms known to history. Besides, it was widely and erroneously believed that Japan was America's ally in the Far East and was prepared to accept the principle of the Open Door in China in good faith. While public sentiment within the United States favored the Japanese cause throughout the war and during the peace negotiations that followed (25, *passim*), Theodore Roosevelt's pro-Japanese position changed somewhat as a result of the spectacular Japanese victories over the Czar's forces. In time Roosevelt appointed himself "honest broker" and sought to mediate between Russia and Japan in arriving at a peace settlement. The negotiations resulting in the Treaty of Portsmouth (1905) constitute a fascinating study in international affairs. They illustrate graphically many important characteristics of Czarist and Japanese diplomacy and show that strategic-political realities often motivate ideologically unfriendly nations like Russia and America to pursue common diplomatic goals. Thanks largely to

Roosevelt's mediation, the peace terms were much more favorable to Russia than might have been expected on the basis of its ignominious defeat by Japan.

Roosevelt's mediation sprang from a desire to create a balance of power in the Orient to thwart what he had come to suspect were the ultimate imperialistic ambitions of Japan. While he had as little regard as ever for the Czarist autocracy, a stable balance of power required that he seek to preserve Russia as a reasonably strong power in Asia (**25**, p. 449). As in the earlier period when both Russia and America were motivated by Anglophobia, and thirty-five years later when the two countries were united against the Axis powers, relations between them were founded on the familiar and often indispensable diplomatic principle of cultivating the enemy of one's enemies. Of cordiality and genuine friendship between the two nations—not to mention ideological compatibility—there was virtually none. Even so, their diplomatic policies could sometimes be concerted on the basis of compatible national interests.

From 1905 to 1917

Powerful currents were at work after the dawn of the 20th century to destroy the fundamental identity of diplomatic interests that had provided the foundation for Russian-American relations in the past. One of these was the diplomatic revolution implicit in the long overdue *rapprochement* between Great Britain and the United States. The Hay-Pauncefote Treaties (1900-01)* and, in the same period, British support for the American policy of the Open Door in China, signified the end of diplomatic hostilities between the two countries. Instead of co-operating with Russia to check Britain's imperial ambitions, as time passed American officials were prepared to join with countries like Britain and Japan to block Czarist diplomatic aspirations in the Far East. The second force operating to alter the earlier pattern of Russian-American relations

*These treaties cleared the way for American construction of the Panama Canal, superseding the older Clayton-Bulwer Treaty (1850) which had given Britain preferential rights in potential canal routes in Central America.

was the emergence of the United States as a great power and, more significantly, as a Pacific power. Following the victory over Spain the United States acquired the Philippines as a strategic base in the Far East. This development, along with expanding American economic penetration of China under the mantle of the Open Door, foreordained eventual conflict between American and Russian policy goals in Asia.

Symptomatic of America's new diplomatic strategy in the Far East was the entente between the United States and Japan with respect to Asian affairs, beginning with the Root-Takahira agreement (1908). This understanding, which historians today are inclined to regard as an American diplomatic blunder, demarcated spheres of influence between the United States and Japan in the Orient. In effect, Japan received a free hand to challenge Russia for control over Manchuria. In return, Japan pledged a hands-off policy toward American territorial possessions in the Pacific. For approximately thirty years, the United States followed the policy of largely ignoring—and, by its failure to act, encouraging—Japanese expansionism in Asia. And coincidentally, it was not until the early 1930's, when communist Russia and the United States were confronted with powerful Japanese threats to their interests in Asia, that Moscow and Washington endeavored to heal the breach that had divided them since the Communist Revolution of 1917.

America and the Russian Revolution

When the Czarist autocracy disintegrated because of disastrous Russian defeats during World War I and long-smoldering revolutionary ferment on the home front, what was the policy of the United States toward this epoch-making development? Initially, the United States welcomed the revolutionary movement within Russia in the hope that at long last a moderate political order would emerge (**26**, pp. 91-2). From February to October, 1917, however, the United States did nothing tangible to sustain the Kerensky Government or to help it overcome its radical opponents. Beset by increasingly grave internal problems, and by the collapse of the Russian western front against Germany, the Kerensky Government was doomed. It was overthrown in October by the Bolsheviks led by Lenin. With the dissolution of the Constituent Assembly—the designated constitutional convention—early in 1918, all hope for the emergence of a moderate political order shaped along western parliamentary lines disappeared. From the beginning, American policy toward the Bolshevik regime was compounded of an extreme dislike for communism, a belief that the communist government would not last, and a profound disillusionment that Russia was willing to desert its allies and to make a separate peace with Germany (**6**, pp. 3-4; **26**, p. 109).

Russia's withdrawal from the war in 1918[*] imperilled vast stores of war matériel furnished to the Czarist government by the Allies. If these supplies fell into the hands of the Central Powers, the strength of the enemy's war machine would be greatly enhanced. Safeguarding these supplies was therefore the ostensible reason for Allied intervention in Russia during 1918-1920. At the same time, the Allies made no secret of their profound hostility toward the new communist order. Their later action in giving significant aid to the anti-Bolshevik White forces during the Russian civil war, testified to the fact that Allied intervention had political as well as purely military motivations. With the tangible and moral support of the Allies, White armies attacked the communists from all directions. Before they were finally driven back by the Red Army in the latter stages of the civil war they had reduced the borders of communist-controlled Russia to

---

[*]By the treaty of Brest-Litovsk Russia in 1918 ceded to Germany over 1.3 million miles of territory occupied by 62 million people. This was 25 per cent of Russia's area and 44 per cent of its population. It included 35 per cent of Russia's agricultural land, 89 per cent of its coal mines, 73 per cent of its iron ore, and 54 per cent of its industry (**7**, p. 12).

Communist rulers were only partially successful in getting this Carthaginian peace modified after Germany's defeat. Russia was not invited to the Paris Peace Conference. Invoking the principle of "self-determination," the peace makers created a number of independent states (e.g., the Baltic States and Poland) out of former Russian territory. Russia, in other words, had substantial grounds for feeling that it had been among the defeated powers.

roughly those of medieval Muscovy (**1**, p. 241).

Compared with the part played by England and France in the Allied interventions, America's role was never particularly significant. Officially, the United States was committed to non-intervention in Russian internal affairs. American military units did land at Archangel and in Siberia. In Siberia their mission was, as much as anything, to prevent wholesale Japanese annexations of Russian territory. To that extent, as Roosevelt and Hull pointed out to Moscow during the 1930's, American intervention may have helped the communist regime in this period more than it weakened it.

Nevertheless, besieged on all sides by hostile forces and with its very existence at stake, the new Soviet State "was in no mood to draw careful distinctions between the motives of its respective invaders" (**6**, p. 9). The Allies as a whole did not conceal their avowed hostility toward bolshevism and their sincere hope that it would be overthrown in favor of a more moderate political order. Consequently, Allied intervention seemed at the very inception of the communist regime to bear out Marxist-Leninist pronouncements about the ever-present "capitalist encirclement," as well as to confirm the fears of earlier Czarist officials that powerful countries would exploit every opportunity available to crush and dismember Russia.

Foreign intervention in Russia could be and was utilized by the Bolsheviks to justify an utterly ruthless policy at home. It furnished a powerful appeal—defense of the Russian Motherland against foreign invaders—to rally the Russian masses, millions of whom were initially hostile to communism, behind the Red Army's attempt to drive out the hated foreigners. The legacy of the civil war in determining future relations between Russia and the outside world can hardly be exaggerated. Allied antagonism to communism "led to intervention, which enabled the Bolsheviks to use nationalism as their rallying cry. The consolidation of Bolshevik power, an event considerably abetted by intervention, only deepened the enmity of American policy makers and heightened their determination to outlast the Soviet state" (**26**, p. 107).

Thus the Soviet Union was conceived in revolution at home and in conflict with the outside world. Having experienced the reality of being "an island of communism in a capitalist sea," communist leaders could be counted on to believe firmly that the outside world was unalterably hostile to Soviet Russia and that the policies of non-communist countries must be viewed with extreme suspicion.

From the Revolution to the New Deal

For nearly fifteen years after the Bolshevik Revolution, the policy of the United States toward Soviet Russia underwent little significant change. After it became apparent that the Soviet regime was not going to be overthrown, American policy under Wilson and successive Republican Presidents was shaped by three fundamental considerations: extreme ideological hostility between American democracy and Soviet communism; disagreements between the two countries over communist repudiation of Czarist war debts and confiscation of foreign-owned property; and communist intrigue in the internal affairs of other countries through the instrumentalities of the Third International and local communist parties directed from Moscow. As late as 1933 an official State Department memorandum cited these three reasons in support of continuing American refusal to recognize the Soviet government (9, pp. 6-9).

By the early 1930's certain influences growing out of internal affairs within the two countries and out of the international community were reshaping relations between them. One of these was the desire of both countries to expand their foreign trade. By the late 1920's Russia had embarked upon the ambitious First Five Year Plan, by which she hoped to substantially raise agricultural and, to a lesser extent, industrial output. Imports from America would greatly assist in this goal. Meantime, within the United States vocal groups throughout the country were calling for an extension of American markets to Russia and were bringing pressure to bear upon Congress and the White House to achieve that end (26, pp. 236-7).

On the international scene the imperialistic designs of Japan, Germany, and Italy signaled the end of traditional American-Japanese friendship and drove both the United States and Russia to take steps to promote their own security. Once again a common enemy was forcing the two nations to collaborate. The first step was the resumption of diplomatic relations. They were renewed between the two nations, after the Kremlin pledged non-interference in the internal affairs of the United States through communist groups directed from Moscow, and agreed to make a satisfactory settlement on repudiated Czarist debts and confiscated foreign property.*

Throughout the "appeasement era" preceding 1939, both Russia and the United States from time to time called for collective efforts by the League of Nations to halt Axis aggression and violations of solemn treaty commitments. At Geneva, Soviet Foreign Minister Litvinov was especially active in trying to arouse a reluctant League to deal with Hitler and Mussolini while there was yet time; and across the Atlantic, Roosevelt and Hull added their voices, though not their armies, in support of the hoped-for coalition against the dictators. Alone among the great powers, Russia and America counselled a united front against the Axis, though such appeals were almost never made jointly.

Were Soviet Foreign Minister Litvinov's impassioned appeals for collective action to preserve European security nothing more than communist propaganda? Were his pledges of Russian assistance—unilaterally if necessary—to countries threatened with incorporation into the Axis empire nothing more than empty promises? No definitive answer can be given. Whatever Russia's response might have been had its offers been accepted, it seems unarguable that the Kremlin in this period was less myopic to the long-range global implications of the Rome-Berlin-Tokyo Axis than other foreign offices of the world. The other great powers were insensitive to Litvinov's pleas. Believing, in the words of Winston Churchill, that the rulers of Russia were a "band of cosmopolitan

---

*Neither of these conditions was fulfilled to the satisfaction of the State Department. Tension characterized relations between the two countries from 1933 to World War II over such questions as the activities of the Comintern and the harassment of State Department officials in Moscow (9, pp. 132-4; 224-5; 446-51). Moreover, the debt question dragged on for years before it was settled, with the State Department convinced that Russia had never intended to settle the issue fairly.

conspirators gathered from the underground world," and thinking that the Red Army, seriously weakened by the Great Purges of the mid-1930's, was no military asset, England and France were unwilling to put Litvinov to the test.

Instead, in their diplomatic moves against the Axis, and in their deliberations with Hitler and Mussolini, they ignored Moscow altogether. And in the crowning act of appeasement—the Munich Conference of 1938 at which Russia was not present—they exhibited no reluctance about handing over the strategic gateway to western Russia to Hitler. To the Kremlin, the "peace with honor" achieved at Munich must have had all the earmarks of an understanding between the West and Berlin giving Hitler a free hand for his announced *Drang Nach Osten* (drive to the east), provided he did not jeopardize the security of the West. The sacrifice of Czechoslovakia at Munich could not fail to revive Russian memories of countless invasions through the southeastern gate of Central Europe and convince rulers already steeped in Marxist-Leninist-Stalinist visions of "capitalist encirclement" of the undying enmity the capitalist world bore the USSR.

Then came the reckoning of August 31, 1939—the black day of the Nazi-Soviet Pact.* Never did Stalin appear so treacherous and so unprincipled as the day he and Hitler, after the fashion of Alexander I and Napoleon at Tilsit in 1807, agreed to divide the major part of Europe between them. At Munich the appeasers had sowed the wind. Now—confronted with an ever more belligerent Axis and a neutralized Russia—they were reaping the whirlwind. Stalin was prepared, as he was prepared many times before and after, to lay aside communist ideological preachments for the sake of Russian strategic territorial gains and tradi-

tional diplomatic ambitions. Nothing could have been more at variance with Marxist-Leninist-Stalinist dogma than the spectacle of the great Socialist Motherland allied with that personification of capitalist degeneracy and avarice, Nazi Germany. Yet no other action fitted in so well with diplomatic necessity and with the enduring goals of Russian foreign policy. Reflect upon what Stalin got as a result of this pact: a breathing spell in which to prepare the Red Army for a possible showdown with Hitler; a large part of central and eastern Poland; most of the Baltic area, paving the way for reincorporation of Finland; a base from which to put increasing pressure on Turkey and to force a way through the Straits; and a broad security zone to protect Russia's ever-vulnerable western frontier—all the while advancing the communist aim of world revolution directed from Moscow. The Nazi-Soviet Pact was a disaster for the West and a master stroke of Soviet diplomacy. It revealed what the world had to confront when it faced traditional Russian foreign policy goals overlaid with communist ideology.

The Uses of History

Soviet foreign policy today is by no means *exclusively* a continuation of ancient Czarist policies, just as it is by no means purely an extension of the ideas of Marx, Lenin, and Stalin to the international plane. It is, however, a *blending* of these two elements along with certain others, including a heavy mixture of opportunism. To appraise present-day Soviet policy intelligently, it is important to understand communist ideology, as well as to become well-grounded in the diplomatic aspirations of Imperial Russia. For it is, after all, not just the threat of communism, but the threat of *Russian* communism, that engenders feelings of deep insecurity in the West and requires the United States as the leader of the free world coalition to devote three-fourths of its governmental budget to defense. Walter Lippmann has made essentially the same point:

> . . . the behavior of nations over a long period of time is the most reliable, though not the only index of their national interest. For though their interests are not eternal, they are

---

*The most thorough compilation of documents bearing upon the Nazi-Soviet Pact is the State Department Publication, *Nazi-Soviet Relations*, 1939-1941, edited by Raymond J. Sontag and James S. Beddie, Washington, D. C., 1948. This documentary approach has the disadvantage, however, of treating the pact outside the context of European diplomacy, thereby conveying the impression that the pact bore no relation to the dynamics of international events during the 1930's. For an excellent background study of this period, see **3**, pp. 49-167; 211-277.

remarkably persistent. We can most nearly judge what a nation will probably want by seeing what over a fairly long period of time it has wanted; we can most nearly predict what it will do by knowing what it has usually done. . . . Even when they adapt themselves to a new situation, their new behavior is likely to be a modification rather than a transformation of their old behavior. (18, p. 138).

The skeptic, especially the skeptic who looks for the most meaningful clues to Soviet diplomatic behavior in the Marxist-Leninist-Stalinist line, may reply: yes, but communist ideology is bound to have different goals than Czarist rule. To this it may be countered that the different symbols and language employed by the Soviet state do not *per se* mean (1) that the policies differ substantially from older Czarist policy or (2) that they differ from policies characteristic of other strongly entrenched and powerful totalitarian regimes known to history. We do not want to carry this point too far; any informed student of Russian diplomacy can cite important innovations wrought by the communists. Yet it cannot be emphasized enough how important it is to set the distinctive elements of communist thought and action into a perspective of Russian history. The fundamental identity of interests between declared historic Russian policies and more recent communist policies must continually be kept in mind.

As far as Russian-American relations before the Second World War are concerned, several insights are afforded by reflecting upon the historical record. First, until both countries emerged as super-powers in world politics as a result of the defeat of the Axis and the decline of British and French influence, relations between them were essentially episodic. America had no real foreign policy toward Russia until events compelled it in 1947 to formulate one. In the Czarist and early Soviet periods the foreign policy of the United States toward Russia was determined chiefly by American policies toward other great powers and important international issues. When Russia and America found themselves on the same side of an issue, this was more by accident than design. After the events that had forged a temporary bond were modified, the chances were great that the bond would sooner or later dissolve.

Since the pattern of Russian-American relations before World War II was established more by the actions and policies of other countries than by any direct and clearly thought out principles underlying relations between them, major changes in the international community were bound to affect Russian-American relations. One of the most basic of such changes that has fundamentally altered Russian-American relations has been the decline of Great Britain as a first-rank power. Many of the international obligations assumed by the United States in the present-day era have been taken over from Britain with little significant change. Even today many Americans do not appreciate fully the extent to which there has developed since 1900 a fundamental identity of interests between British and American security, and the extent to which this entente has driven a wedge between the United States and Russia. All around the globe Britain and America have been drawing closer together in their diplomatic activities, including attempts to contain Russian expansionism. When British power was insufficient to accomplish common objectives, it was supplemented by American power—until there came a time, by the end of World War II, when America was the principal source of Western strength. As the United States had been in an earlier period, its allies now were junior partners in resisting threats to the territorial and political *status quo* of the western world.

This is the real meaning of "America's rise to world power"—a process begun with the Spanish-American War and consummated by the Second World War. During the same period Russia too was becoming more powerful. The industrial revolution finally reached Russia under the Communists; and so spectacular was Soviet technological achievement that by the end of the 1950's the USSR appeared to be surpassing the United States in certain fields of technological-scientific progress.

From 1918 onward the Concert of Europe gradually disintegrated. One by one nations that had stood as buffers between Russia and America disappeared as first-rank powers. In the post-World War II period, the two super-powers for the first time in their history confronted each other directly. Inevitably, their policies toward a host of issues—not the least of which was the basis of their own security—came into conflict. No longer could their relations be episodic; now these relations would likely determine the future political destiny of the world. No longer could Russia and the United States shape their policies in terms of mutual hostility to a common enemy, for there was no common enemy. This direct confrontation between the United States and Soviet Russia around the globe was the dominant factor underlying the cold war. And the cold war was the overriding international problem of the mid-20th century.

By the end of the Second World War, the United States had to make a simple, painful choice: it could either fill the vacuum left by the waning of British, French, German, and Japanese power; or it could reconcile itself to the fact that at long last Russia would be in a position to fulfill its traditional foreign policy objectives, and, in the process, to acquire a strategic-territorial position that would make it well-nigh invincible against any coalition that might be raised to resist Russian diplomatic ambitions. In reality of course this was no choice at all. Failure to respond to the challenge posed by Soviet diplomacy in the postwar period could only end ultimately in the destruction of American security and, after that, almost certain Soviet mastery of the world.

This then—the direct confrontation of American and Soviet power—is the pre-eminent international question of our age, as it is likely to be for decades or even generations to come. What are the major issues that derive from this confrontation? How do the two sides compare in strengths and vulnerabilities? What basis is there for a possible settlement of outstanding issues of the cold war? These are the questions to which we shall direct our thoughts in the next chapter.

Is There Somewhere Else To Go?
Herblock's Here and Now, Simon & Schuster, 1955.

REFERENCES

1. Bailey, Thomas A. *America Faces Russia.* Ithaca, N. Y.: Cornell University Press, 1950. A history of American-Russian relations, focusing on the role of American public opinion.

2. Barghoorn, Frederick C. *Soviet Russian Nationalism.* New York: Oxford University Press, 1956. A well-known authority treats many enlightening aspects of Russian nationalism under the Communists.

3. Beloff, Max. *The Foreign Policy of Soviet Russia, 1929-1941.* New York: Oxford University Press, 1949. This is one of the most scholarly and objective treatments of Soviet foreign policy.

4. Berdyaev, Nicolas. *The Russian Idea.* New York: The Macmillan Company, 1948. A highly original, controversial, study of Russian national character.

5. Blinn, Harold E. "Seward and the Polish Rebellion of 1863," *American Historical Review,* 45 (July, 1940), pp. 828-33. Discusses a little-known chapter in American diplomatic history.

6. Browder, Robert P. *The Origins of Soviet-American Diplomacy.* Princeton: Princeton University Press, 1953. Traces out the influences that led the United States to recognize the USSR.

7. Carman, E. Day. *Soviet Imperialism*. Washington, D. C.: Public Affairs Press, 1950. A thoroughly documented account of Soviet expansionism since 1917.

8. Department of State. *Communist Perspective*. Division of Research for USSR and Eastern Europe, Office of Intelligence Research, 1955. This is probably the best single compendium available for communist doctrinal statements (in Russian and English).

9. ———. *Foreign Relations of the United States, The Soviet Union: 1933-1939*. Washington: 1952. Documentary material (published periodically by the State Department) on U.S.-Russian relations during the period covered.

10. Florinsky, Michael T. *Russia: A History and An Interpretation*. New York: The Macmillan Company, 1953. Contains a wealth of historical detail, a minimum of interpretation.

11. Graham, Malbone W. "Russian-American Relations, 1917-1933: An Interpretation," *American Political Science Review*, 28 (June, 1934), pp. 387-409. Argues that the United States has always been ideologically alienated from Russia, even under the Czars.

12. Haines, C. Grove, ed. *The Threat of Soviet Imperialism*. Baltimore: The Johns Hopkins University Press, 1954. A symposium, with papers by several leading authorities on the USSR.

13. Historicus. "Stalin on Revolution," *Foreign Affairs*, 37 (January, 1949), pp. 175-214. A cogent analysis of communist theory, holding that the USSR has never abandoned "world revolution" as its ultimate goal.

14. Huszar, George B., and Associates. *Soviet Power and Policy*. New York: Thomas Y. Crowell, 1955. A helpful symposium on various aspects of Soviet internal and external policy.

15. Kohn, Hans, ed. *The Mind of Modern Russia*. New Brunswick, N. J.: Rutgers University Press, 1955. A collection of excerpts (with commentary) from the writings of Russian thinkers.

16. Laserson, Max M. *The American Impact on Russia*. New York: The Macmillan Company, 1950. A distinctive historical work, concentrating on ideological and cultural interchange between the United States and Russia.

17. Leites, Nathan. *A Study of Bolshevism*. Glencoe, Illinois: The Free Press, 1953. An illuminating treatment of communist thought, with however minimum attention to its historical context or to its modifications in the light of events.

18. Lippmann, Walter. *U. S. Foreign Policy: Shield of the Republic*. Boston: Little, Brown and Company, 1943. Contains a provocative treatment of prewar American-Russian relations.

19. Mazour, Anatole G. *Russia: Past and Present*. New York: D. Van Nostrand Company, 1951. A textbook on Russian history, with many helpful insights and interpretations.

20. Middleton, K. W. B. *Britain and Russia*. London: Hutchinson and Company (no date). Discusses the relation of historic Russian foreign policy to the Soviet regime.

21. Mosse, W. E. "Russia and the Levant, 1856-1862," *Journal of Modern History*, 26 (March, 1954), pp. 39-48. Relates Russian policy in the Near East to the urge to the sea.

22. "Russian Opinion on the Cession of Alaska," *American Historical Review*, 48 (April, 1943), pp. 521-31. Relates sale of Alaska to broad Russian foreign policy aims.

23. Simmons, Ernest J., ed. *Continuity and Change in Russian and Soviet Thought*. Cambridge: Harvard University Press, 1955. This symposium contains a number of thought-provoking essays on aspects of Russian foreign policy.

24. Tompkins, Stuart R. *The Russian Mind*. Norman, Okla.: University of Oklahoma Press, 1953. Provides insight on Russian character and patterns of thought.

25. Thorson, Winston B. "American Public Opinion and the Portsmouth Peace Conference," *American Historical Review*, 53 (April, 1948), pp. 439-64. Treats an important episode in Russian-American relations.

26. Williams, William A. *American-Russian Relations: 1781-1947*. New York: Rinehart and Company, 1952. Although some of the writer's conclusions may be questioned, this work is valuable in relating the cold war to the broad context of relations between the United States and Russia.

27. Wren, Melvin C. "Pobedonostsev and Russian Influence in the Balkans, 1881-1888," *Journal of Modern History*, 19 (June, 1947), pp. 130-141. Illustrates many points of continuity between Czarist and Communist actions.

28. Wright, Edmond. "Russia and America," *The Political Quarterly*, 25 (July, 1954), pp. 217-28.

CHAPTER 9

Elements of the Cold War

The cold war infuses almost every problem in contemporary American foreign policy. It affects such diverse issues as American relations with Western Europe and Southeast Asia; tariff questions, reciprocal trade, and foreign aid; American participation in the United Nations and other international efforts directed at reducing world tensions. Because the cold war is all-pervasive, we begin our study of concrete problems in American foreign relations with that subject.

Our purpose here is to establish a frame of reference within which to evaluate more limited issues such as Soviet-American conflict in the Middle East or disarmament disputes. While the cold war may be aggravated by such specific disagreements, it has its origins in much more fundamental factors. Analysis of these fundamental factors will be our task in this chapter.

For convenience, we have divided them into three *fronts* of the cold war: ideological, strategic-geopolitical, and economic-military.

1. THE IDEOLOGICAL FRONT

Save perhaps for a profession that communist and Western democratic ideologies seek to achieve the best interests of humanity and strive to bring about a more just political-economic-social order, the two philosophies are antithetical on almost every concrete issue that confronts society. Their disagreement over most goals and, more crucially, over the means for reaching them, is so deep and all-pervasive that common agreement on seeking the welfare of society affords practically no real affinity between the two ideologies. Their differences necessarily color relations between communist and non-communist nations in international affairs. Our interest here centers on the limited topic of the relationship between communism as an ideology and Russian behavior in the sphere of foreign relations.* We shall explore

---

*The literature on communist ideology is voluminous. Among the helpful critical commentaries are: 16; 20; 23; 25; 30; 33; 45; 55; 13; 39; 22; 54; and 28.

In any discussion of communist ideology it must be kept in mind that the term communism itself is subject to differing interpretations. There are many varieties of communism: the type practiced by the early Christian community and by the "Brook Farm" experiment in early American history; the type advocated by such groups as the Mensheviks in Russian history from the early 1900's to 1917, which sought an evolutionary development into a communistic society and which was antithetical in many points to the communism espoused by Lenin; and the Marxism advocated by many groups in recent history, who disagree sharply with the Kremlin's brand of communism

that question first by examining the main tenets of communist thought and then relating this credo to the diplomatic behavior of the Soviet Union.

In Chapter 14 we shall discuss the ideological conflict between Russia and the West largely from the point of view of the propaganda struggle that has been a conspicuous feature of international relations in the postwar era, looking especially at the efforts of the two camps to influence the "neutralist" countries of the world.

Communist Ideology—An Overview

Communism is a materialistic creed. This means not so much that it is concerned with material advancement—which of course it is —as that it rejects supra-natural phenomena and confines what is known and can be known about human nature and behavior solely to historical experience. This fact at once places it outside the Greco-Roman-Christian tradition. Rejecting such Christian ideas as that man is a creation of the Almighty, that he is constantly tainted with sin, and that consequently no perfect social order can be established on earth, communism claims to "be able, through science and social action, to create an ideal order in which the needs and desires of mankind will be fully satisfied . . . " (23, p. 264).

Through the insights afforded by the processes of "dialetical materialism,"* communism purports to have found the key to social or-

ganization in the "mode of production." At any stage in history, whether in the feudal, capitalist, socialist, or communist era, the prevailing mode of production determines the nature of a society's laws, institutions, ethical and moral codes, class relationships, political systems—in short, every aspect of the societal order. But there is one feature common to all societies, until the communist utopia has been reached. This is the class conflict. In every precommunist society a struggle takes place between the owners of the means of production —under capitalism, the bourgeoisie—and the workers—the proletariat. The latter are denied their rightful share of the fruits of industry by the entrenched bourgeoisie. Until the prevailing system of production is overturned by revolution, this situation continues. Nothing short of a revolution can usher in a new socialist** order, since the entrenched owners will never relinquish control voluntarily. Ostensible improvements in the standard of living of the working class, through such techniques as higher wages and better working conditions, extensions of governmental regulation over economic enterprise, or democratic

---

and who are, in fact, violently opposed to the Soviet Union's policies.

When the term communism is used in this and later chapters, it is meant to describe a body of belief professed by the rulers of Soviet Russia. This ideology can more accurately be described as Marxism-Leninism-Stalinism or perhaps as Bolshevism, since at many crucial points its theories derive much more from Russian leaders and experience than from the writings of Karl Marx or other communist philosophers.

*Marxist thought took from Hegel the idea of the "dialetic"—that is, arriving at truth by the synthesis of opposites. One stage of human history (the thesis) gives rise to tendencies (the antithesis) that ultimately bring in a new stage (synthesis), which is formed by a combination of the old and new. Thus in Marxist thought feudalism engendered anti-feudal forces. The synthesis of these two stages ushered in the new stage, capitalism.

**Russia today neither is, nor calls itself, a communist state. The Soviet Union is still in the preparatory stage of socialism which, according to communist dogma, must precede the communist utopian era. Under socialism the "dictatorship of the proletariat" must be retained to protect the new workers' society from internal and external enemies. When this dictatorship will be abolished and when the state will "wither away," as classic Marxist thought predicts, remains uncertain. The Kremlin has never announced a time-table for this transition, although it has made it contingent upon realization of certain favorable circumstances at home and abroad. During the 1930's, Stalin made the withering away of the state dependent upon the disappearance of the capitalist encirclement, thereby linking the perpetuation of the dictatorship in Russia to progress made toward communism in the non-communist world. In effect, the onus for maintenance of a ruthless dictatorship inside Russia was now shifted upon the capitalist countries; if the Russian people became restive, the blame for authoritarian government could be shifted to the "Wall Street imperialists"! Then in 1952 he specified three other preconditions for entrance into the communist utopia: significant increases in industrial production, particularly productive tools; improvement in agricultural production, accompanied by control of "the whole product of social production in the interests of society"; and extension of educational facilities so that citizens could become "active agents of social development . . . " (47, p. 46).

political reforms, merely constitute efforts on the part of the bourgeoisie to consolidate its power by beguiling the proletariat into thinking that its lot is improving.

After the revolution, the "dictatorship of the proletariat" will destroy every institution of the old order and will prepare the way for the coming communist millenium. Led by the "vanguard of the proletariat," the Communist Party, revolutionary forces will radically alter governmental forms, social relationships, law, economic institutions, moral-ethical codes and, when the world revolution has been consummated, the international order, making all spheres of life responsive to the needs and wishes of the working class.

Inevitable Conflict and "World Revolution"

The attitude displayed by communist Russia toward its relations with non-communist countries is described in a famous passage from Lenin's writings in 1919:

> . . . We are living not merely in a state but in a system of states and the existence of the Soviet Republic side by side with imperialist states for a long time is unthinkable. One or the other must triumph in the end. And before that end supervenes, a series of frightful collisions between the Soviet Republic and the bourgeois states will be inevitable. (9, pp. 383-84).

The following year Lenin wrote that " . . . As long as capitalism and socialism exist, we cannot live in peace; in the end, one or the other will triumph—a funeral dirge will be sung over the Soviet Republic or over world capitalism" (9, p. 384).

A cardinal article of the communist faith then is inevitable and continuing conflict between communist and non-communist countries. So long as communist societies exist, or those that are passing through the transitional stage of socialism* into communism, tensions inherent in the class struggle will be projected into the international community, expressing themselves in the unalterable hostility exhibited by capitalist countries toward the bastion of world communism, the Soviet Union. The Russian expositors of Marx contend that capitalist nations, dominated as they are by a bourgeoisie that will never relinquish power voluntarily, must follow policies aimed at subverting communist regimes. Ultimately, as capitalist systems begin to disintegrate, as a result of the class struggle at home and colonial turmoil abroad, the leaders of world capitalism may even be driven in their desperation to undertake a final Armageddon against the communist world.

Hostility of the non-communist world toward the USSR is sometimes referred to in Marxist thought as the "doctrine of capitalist encirclement." Thus Stalin declared in 1930 that "capitalist encirclement means that around the USSR there are hostile class forces, ready to support our class enemies within the USSR morally, materially, by means of financial blockade and, when the opportunity offers, by means of military intervention" (9, p. 15). This view was reiterated by the Soviet Navy journal *Red Fleet* in 1946 when it warned that "so long as the capitalist world exists, the possibility of a new war and of bandit attacks on the USSR are not excluded" (9, p. 18).

---

*The reader is reminded that the term "socialism" in this context has a different meaning than it possesses in ordinary usage in the West. Not infrequently, the terms communism and socialism are used interchangeably by citizens in noncommunist countries. Russia, as we have noted, designates itself a "socialist republic." Nevertheless, the Kremlin's invectives against socialist orders outside of the Iron Curtain countries are scarcely less severe than those reserved for capitalist countries. Socialist systems like those prevailing in Britain or India are guilty of the sin of "petty-bourgeois reformism," which has been condemned repeatedly since 1917. This deviation, said Stalin in 1928, "represents a tendency . . . on the part of a section of Communists to depart from the revolutionary line of Marxism in the direction of Social-Democracy." What would be the result of this heresy? Stalin answered that it would mean the "consolidation and strengthening of capitalism, for Social-Democracy is the main bulwark of capitalism among the working class. Hence, the triumph of the Right deviation in the Communist Parties in capitalist countries favors the conditions necessary for the preservation of capitalism" (47, p. 52). Sometimes such socialism is branded merely "opportunism." The Kremlin has reserved some of its sharpest vituperation for socialists, writes Hunt, because "these parties are rivals with the Communists for the leadership of the masses" and because socialists stop short "of the absolute goal of revolution" (22, pp. xiii-xiv). In short, conflict must exist between followers of the Soviet Union and other countries that profess to be socialistic but which do not acknowledge Moscow's leadership.

The USSR—Bastion of World Communism

In the previous chapter we remarked upon the threat posed by the merger of traditional Russian foreign policy goals with the imperatives of Communist ideology. At this point, let us examine this identity more closely.

Time and again since 1915 communist leaders have called upon all who accepted the Marxist-Leninist-Stalinist faith to work unceasingly for the support of the diplomatic ambitions of the Soviet Union in world affairs. Following the diplomatic line laid down by the Kremlin is tantamount to advancing the interests of world communism. True believers in communism, said Stalin in 1925, will "support Soviet power and foil the interventionist machinations of the imperialists against the Soviet Union . . . mainstay of the revolutionary movement in all countries" (9, p. 177). And a Communist journal stated in 1948 that

> . . . the only determining criterion of revolutionary proletarian internationalism is: are you for or against the USSR, the motherland of the world proletariat? . . . A real internationalist is one who brings his sympathy and recognition up to the point of practical and maximal help to the USSR in support and defense . . . by every means and in every possible form. . . . The defense of the USSR . . . is the holy duty of every honest man everywhere. . . . " (9, p. 273).

Equation of Russia's interests as a state with the professed ideological goals of the world communist movement is a *tour de force* which, vastly enhances the power position of the USSR. First, it enlists communist groups everywhere as agents of the Kremlin and requires them to take any steps—treason and espionage not excepted—to carry out the interests of world communism. Second, it arrogates to the Kremlin alone the right to interpret what steps are necessary to reach the goals of communism, thereby automatically giving the Soviet Union a preferential position over such countries as Yugoslavia or Red China. Third, it baptizes the goals of Russian foreign policy—expansionism and imperialism, hostility toward the West, the search for warm water ports, and the rest —with idealistic garments that make such goals appealing to Communists, fellow travellers, and neutralists all over the world. Fourth, it eliminates any contradiction that might arise

in the future between the ideological precepts of communism and the diplomatic ambitions of the Soviet Union by declaring that these are identical to begin with and that the Kremlin is the sole expositor and interpreter of both. In short, this assertion entails nothing less than the preposterous claim that the purposes of the Soviet Union are the purposes of humanity at large and requires all believers in human welfare to serve the Soviet Union. That this claim is fantastic on its merits does not prevent it from being widely accepted, nor does it lessen the degree to which the Soviet Union, by virtue of the claim, sometimes enjoys an enormous diplomatic advantage over the United States and the free world generally.

The "Internal Contradictions" of Capitalism

In Stalin's authoritative work, *Problems of Leninism* (1924), three "internal contradictions" of capitalism are set forth. These have great significance in explaining the diplomacy of capitalist countries and, in turn, shaping the diplomatic response of the Soviet bloc:

> The first contradiction is . . . between labor and capital. . . . Imperialism brings the working class to revolution.
> The second contradiction is . . . among the various financial groups and imperialist powers in their struggle for sources of raw materials, for foreign territory. . . . This frenzied struggle . . . includes as an inevitable element imperialist wars. . . .
> The third contradiction is . . . between the handful of ruling, civilized nations and the hundreds of millions of the colonial and dependent peoples of the world. . . . This undermines the position of capitalism by converting the colonies and dependent countries from reserves of imperialism into reserves of the proletarian revolution. (9, p. 253).

Stripped of its verbiage, Stalin predicted three major sources of tension and conflict within the capitalist world that will ultimately so weaken it that it can no longer resist the onward march of communism: class struggle between the workers and the owners of the means of production; conflict between imperialist countries over markets and sources of raw material; and conflict between imperialist countries and their colonies and dependencies.

The implications of these allegedly inescapable developments for the foreign policy of the communist bloc are clear and fundamental. In general, it is incumbent upon communist countries and groups to encourage these conflicts within the capitalist camp, to accelerate them in every possible way. Communist strategy is therefore perennially aimed at fomenting divisions among the capitalist nations, at sowing seeds of discord among them, at trying to weaken and disrupt any alliances that may develop among them, and at hastening the downfall of the colonial systems upon which their economies are presumably dependent. *Pravda* sounded the keynote of the Kremlin's strategy in 1947:

> . . . Marxism-Leninism urges all the oppressed people to fight for their liberation, links the national liberation movement of oppressed people in the colonies and dependent countries with the revolutionary struggle of the proletariat. (**9**, p. 61).

And in 1946 the official journal *Bolshevik* declared that initiative in Soviet diplomacy was an important factor

> . . . because the Soviet Union has continuously experienced hostile international actions. . . . The conditions of capitalist encirclement require the application of extensive counter plans which would not only foil the enemy but would systematically improve the international position of the Soviet state and strengthen the economic and cultural contacts between the USSR and foreign countries. (**9**, p. 24).

Communist Tactics*

One well-known characteristic of communist philosophy is its emphasis upon expediency in advancing the professed ideological goals.

Communist "morality," said an official Soviet publication in 1941, is "that which facilitates the destruction of the old world, and which strengthens the new, communist regime." Invoking an unidentified quotation from Lenin, the article continues that " 'At the foundation of Communist morality lies the struggle for the strengthening and perfecting of Communism' " (**9**, p. 238).

Any policy, any move or maneuver that advances the aims of world communism is *ipso facto* moral; and conversely, immorality is the failure, by commission or omission, to work in behalf of the communist cause. Accordingly, the methods by which communism is to be achieved are exceedingly flexible. Whatever opportunism demands is acceptable. Said Stalin in 1923: "The strategy of the Party is not something permanent, fixed once and for all. It changes to meet historical shifts . . . " (**9**, p. 442). Or as Lenin had phrased it earlier in 1920: " . . . the strictest loyalty to the ideas of Communism must be combined with the ability to make all the necessary practical compromises, to 'tack' to make agreements, zigzags, retreats and so on" (**9**, p. 443).

The extreme flexibility of Communist methods has significant implications for Russia's relations with the outside world. It means that there is no predetermined time-table for ushering in the world revolution. As George Kennan has put it: the Kremlin "is under no ideological compulsion to accomplish its purposes in a hurry" (**27**, p. 82). Realization of the ultimate goals of world communism is made contingent

---

*Some recent writers on communist thought have differentiated rather sharply between strategy and tactics (the former being the long-range plan of action, the latter the short-run techniques utilized for carrying out that plan). It is by no means certain, however, that communist spokesmen themselves make such a clear delineation. It is true that Stalin declared "Strategy deals with the main forces of the revolution" and that it "remains essentially unchanged throughout a given stage. . . . " Yet he also said that "The strategy of the Party is not something permanent, fixed once and for all. It changes to meet historical turns and shifts. These changes are expressed in the fact that for each separate historical turn there is worked out a separate strategic plan appropriate to it and operating for the whole period. . . . For every historical turn there is a

strategic plan which corresponds to its needs and is adapted to its tasks" (**33**, p. 47).

This problem highlights the underlying ambiguity of Marxist thought and the impact of exigencies at home and abroad upon the viewpoints advocated by the Kremlin in any period. Whether or not the Kremlin does differentiate between strategy and tactics may be of interest chiefly as a matter of philosophic speculation. For our purposes, a more significant point may be the keynote that has recurred frequently in communist ideology. As expressed by Lenin in 1900, the theme urged loyal communists to utilize "all methods of political struggle, as long as they correspond to the forces at the disposal of the Party and facilitate the achievement of the greatest results possible under the given conditions!" For additional quotations on this subject, see **9**, pp. 440-55.

upon the development of favorable circumstances in the external environment. Time and again after 1917 Lenin and Stalin cautioned the party faithful against rashness and precipitate action that could only bring injury to the communist cause. They warned, in effect, that "enemies aim at the annihilation of the Party. . . . An all-out attack may come at any time. . . . Until final victory, the very survival of the Party is always uncertain; when the enemy is already severely wounded, he lashes out with unprecedented reckless ferocity" (**27**, p. 416). If the final victory of communism depends upon propitious developments in the non-communist world, then the "inevitable victory" of communism may be postponed indefinitely.

While the tactics of Communists are kept flexible so as to make the best possible use of circumstances, one principle has been elevated into the *sine qua non* of ultimate victory. This is preservation of the USSR as a great power. "By preserving the Soviet power," said Stalin in 1918, in justifying the Treaty of Brest-Litovsk, "we render to the proletariat of all countries . . . the best, the most effective support." And again in 1925 he declared to the party faithful their duty to "support Soviet power . . . since the Soviet Union is the mainstay of the revolutionary movement in all countries . . . " (**9**, pp. 345-46).

Expediency then is the keynote of the tactics of world communism. Certain broad principles for guiding strategy and tactics are laid down: fomenting class conflicts within non-communist countries, creating and exploiting differences between them, and utilizing colonial strife to hasten the downfall of the so-called imperialist powers. Above all, the Soviet Union must be preserved as a great power to serve as the hub from which communist influence may radiate out to the entire world.

Ideological Conflicts and International Tensions

What conclusions can we draw about the effects of ideological conflicts on Russian-American relationships in the contemporary era?

In the first place, the evident antithesis between Western and communist political ideals affects the very language employed in diplomacy. A good illustration is the long-standing controversy between Russia and the United States over interpretation of the Yalta and Potsdam agreements pertaining to Soviet occupation of former Axis territory in Eastern Europe. When the West and Russia talked in terms of establishing "democratic governments" and holding "free elections" in the Axis satellite territories overrun by the Red Army, they were talking a different language. The West obviously thought this agreement demanded free elections by secret ballot, as practiced in America, Britain, or France. It soon discovered that "free elections" according to the Kremlin's interpretation meant elections preceded by the elimination of all "fascist elements" and disfranchisement of "enemies of the people"—or in effect disfranchisement of all groups that could not be faithfully counted on to follow the line dictated by Moscow. The point here is not whether Moscow really intended to abide by the letter and spirit of the Yalta and Potsdam agreements; the point is that these agreements were couched in language bound to foment misunderstanding and ill-will in later interpretations. So fundamental is the divergence between Western political ideology and Marxism-Leninism-Stalinism that ordinary terms which formerly had a widely accepted meaning in diplomatic parlance no longer possess a clearly defined content. Ideological conflict means, in other words, that the two most powerful nations on earth sometimes *cannot even communicate* with assurance that their positions are being completely understood by the other side.

In the second place, injection of ideological conflict into international affairs on a scale seldom experienced in recent history has intensified existing sources of disagreement and made problems, which were already inordinately difficult, well-nigh insoluble. Select any problem that has engaged the attention of foreign policy-makers throughout recent history—maintaining the balance of power, establishing a system of collective security and international law, seeking disarmament agreements, trying to achieve solutions of colonial conflicts. All of these and more have served as focal points for intense ideological discord. It is difficult enough under optimum conditions to make a system of collective security operate, without having the United Nations perverted into a propaganda forum which resounds with Soviet vituperations against "capitalist warmongers" and "Wall Street imperialists" *ad nauseum,* and in which the West in turn and largely in self-defense excoriates Moscow's record in internal and external affairs. Over the course of time, in such bodies as the United Nations, both sides have given evidence of being more interested in proving the soundness of their ideological positions than in negotiating settlements of existing cold war tensions.

Even when ideological factors are not deliberately and consciously injected into international relations, the mere existence of rival ideological systems that are espoused by powerful nations and coalitions can infuse the pith and marrow of political relationships. To the degree that any nation's view of the outside world is colored by rigid adherence to a particular philosophic system, it will be difficult for that nation to plan its policies objectively. For example, by the time events in the outside world have been viewed through successive lenses of the communist telescope and have finally come to a focus at the eyepiece in the Kremlin, the images may have become so distorted that communist leaders may actually be dealing with conditions that exist only in the minds of communists. Even if the rulers were led, out of sheer self-interest, to seek resolutions of major disagreements in world affairs, they could be prevented from achieving this goal by distortions introduced through adherence to ideology expected from the vast Soviet bureaucracy.

Third, many students of communist philosophy believe that the ideological conflict foredooms any genuine or lasting settlement between the United States and the USSR or between the communist bloc and the free world. Pointing to doctrinal assertions by Lenin and Stalin, they argue that conflict between the two worlds is inescapable as long as "world revolution" remains the Kremlin's announced goal. According to this view, communist advocacy of "peaceful co-existence" is merely a siren song calculated to lull the West into complacency, to paralyze its defense efforts, and in the end to yield the world by default to communism. The only realistic course for the United States, therefore, is to accept communist pronouncements about the coming world revolution at face value and to prepare for continuing conflict, perhaps ultimately a third world war.

The overall role of ideology as an animating force in Soviet foreign policy will be analyzed later in this chapter. It is sufficient here to observe that a policy based on fear of world revolution, while entitled to serious consideration and possessing a measure of validity, is subject to many fundamental reservations. Profound ideological disagreements are not new to history. They have existed between Christians and Infidels; between Catholics and Protestants; between Jacobins and defenders of Monarchy; and between supporters of, and rebels against, established political authority. Moreover, it may be asked: since the West customarily operates upon the assumption that the Kremlin's pronunciamentos must be received with a healthy measure of skepticism, why should this principle not also apply to ominous ideological predictions? The most meaningful test of the validity of such predictions, as with all aspects of communist ideology, is the test of experience: assessing the degree to which they have actually entered into internal and external policy calculations since 1917. This evidence is evaluated in the next section.

Fourth, Marxist-Leninist-Stalinist philosophy gives the Kremlin a powerful advantage over its diplomatic opponents: belief in the inevitable victory of its ideological cause. Besides inculcating in communist groups a fanaticism and earnestness seldom seen outside religious groups in non-communist countries, conviction that communism is the "wave of the future," that it is being swept forward by the irresistible tides of history, serves as a powerful tonic to sustain the Kremlin and its supporters during lean years. It gives them a vision that, regardless of day-to-day adversities, remains undimmed; and it evokes loyalties to a cause worthy of their best and untiring efforts. In some degree this advantage partially accounts for the fact that the United States—in spite of its economic advancement, idealism, and remarkable lack of imperialistic motives—sometimes experiences great difficulties in countering communist propaganda and diplomatic maneuvers.

Ideology and Soviet Foreign Policy

. . . There will develop two centers on a world scale: the socialist center drawing together to itself the countries gravitating toward socialism, and the capitalist center drawing together to itself the countries gravitating toward capitalism. The struggle between these two camps will determine the fate of capitalism and socialism throughout the world. (33, p. 100).

Statements such as this, made by Stalin in 1927, focus attention upon a crucial question for the present age. The answer to it is likely to determine the course of international affairs for generations to come. To what extent generally can the communist credo as declared and interpreted by the Kremlin be taken as a reliable guide to the foreign policy of the Soviet Union? More specifically, does the communist world's professed belief in the inevitability of "world revolution" foreclose any possibility of averting a new global holocaust? The search for answers bristles with difficulties. At the outset, two simplistic answers must be rejected as inadequate. The first is that because world revolution has been an announced goal of the communist faith that this foreordains an eventual military showdown between communist and non-communist countries. History is not necessarily moving inexorably toward a Götterdämmerung climax merely because communist oracles have decreed it, any more than capitalist or neo-capitalist countries in the West are doomed to economic collapse because Marx prophesied this result. A second error is to dismiss communist prophesy of world revolution as "mere propaganda" on the grounds that every pronouncement emanating from the Kremlin must be received with skepticism, if not downright disbelief. Bewilderment with the perpetual zigzags of Soviet foreign policy, and even more with the dialectical technique of arriving at truth by a "synthesis" of opposites, must not lead us to discount completely the role of ideology and, in at least some cases, its importance as an actual goal.

To gain the needed perspective, we must keep certain basic considerations in mind. Since 1917 circumstances inside and outside Russia have compelled frequent modifications in ideology and Soviet diplomatic behavior. Though no elaborate search of communist writings and a point-by-point comparison of them with the domestic and foreign policies of the USSR since 1917 has as yet been undertaken by students of international relations, it would be exceedingly unrealistic to accept the Marxist-Leninist-Stalinist credo as a literal and infallible guide to the past, present, or future policies of the Soviet Union. The rulers of Russia since 1917 have professed themselves to be communists; and there is no reason to question the sincerity of their attachment to communist doctrine, as they define it. Yet these same rulers have repeatedly cautioned their followers against the sins of "dogmatism" and "Talmudism," which an authoritative communist source has identified as "the uncritical acceptance of dogma without considering the conditions of its application. . . . " Russia's communist rulers have urged the party faithful to support "creative Marxism," as a "progressive science which does not stand still but moves forward with life itself and moves life forward." Shortly before his death, in 1953, Stalin admonished the party not to regard formulae from Marx, Lenin, and their successors as principles which "will serve for every period and country, for every possible contingency" (22, pp. 67-9). Ironically, citizens of non-communist countries are sometimes more inclined than communists themselves to regard Bolshevik goals as fixed and unalterable! It would be most unrealistic to believe that communist leaders spend their time searching through available literature for the "correct line" on existing problems and then proceed to carry out policies that will automatically satisfy doctrinal requirements.

The role of communist ideology in Soviet foreign policy is far more subtle and complex than this. Moreover, ideology may shape Soviet policies subconsciously as often as it shapes them consciously. In common with any society, the Soviet Union must achieve some kind of a crude balance between what it ideally would like to do and what it is able to do. Its ideological professions undoubtedly influence —and what may be more crucial, they are influenced by—events inside and outside Russia. No less an authority than Karl Marx himself believed that ideologies derived from the "mode of production" that shaped the total culture in given historical eras. Marx's theory is little more than a truism: that ideas spring at least in part from the broad cultural context existing in any society. If the theory has any validity, then it applies to the Soviet Union no less than to other countries. This fact cautions against acceptance of the viewpoint—assiduously propagated by the Kremlin—that communist thought forms an unbroken philosophic chain from Marx to Khrushchev and his successors and that this ideology provides the key to history, rather than the reverse. The history of Soviet Russia itself of course contradicts such an interpretation. According to communist doctrine and predictions the long-awaited communist revolution never should have succeeded first in Czarist Russia, an agricultural, economically backward country, in which the "proletarian consciousness" was practically non-existent. Lenin's genius lay substantially in his ability to adapt Marxist precepts to what was, and in many ways remains, an inhospitable environment. In the process, Lenin so "adapted" Marxism to the Russian milieu as to make it unrecognizable to many violently anti-Bolshevik Marxists. Stalin, like Lenin, made sweeping reinterpretations of Marxist-Leninist thought to cope with events in the late 1920's and early 1930's.

There are a number of fundamental reasons why communist dogma can seldom be taken as a reliable guide to the understanding of Soviet foreign policies. First, it is difficult for the layman, and only slightly less difficult for governmental officials and students, to differentiate between communist ideological pronouncements *as propaganda* and the same pronouncements *as authentic explanations of Soviet behavior at home and abroad*. Take the doctrine of "capitalist encirclement." Does the Kremlin really believe that the communist bloc is surrounded by hostile nations bent upon annihilating communist countries at the first opportunity? Few Westerners are capable of answering this question with finality. But informed students of Soviet history do know this: the doctrine of "capitalist encirclement" has proved a tremendously useful propaganda weapon for enabling the communist regime to deal with both its internal and external enemies. For example, this doctrine enables the Kremlin to shift the onus for the existence of all the oppressive organs of the police state onto the capitalist world. When inquisitive minds inside and outside Russia ask how long the "dictatorship of the proletariat" will continue and when the state will "wither away," then the bogey of "capitalist encirclement" becomes the ritualistic explanation of why the state must be maintained, ever-strong and ever-vigilant against enemies at home and abroad. Paraphrasing Voltaire, if "capitalist encirclement" did not exist it would be necessary for the Kremlin to invent it—or risk widespread defection from the communist cause inside and outside Russia following any relaxation of the prevailing despotism.

In the second place, the communist creed is highly ambiguous. There are great gaps in the ideological heritage concerning such questions as the role of the Communist Party under socialism and communism, the circumstances under which the transition will be made from socialism to communism, and the exact nature of the society and international order that will prevail in the communist utopia. As a result, Bolshevik rulers enjoy abundant flexibility in adapting their ideology to fit existing conditions.

Third, communist ideology is highly inconsistent, containing innumerable contradictory statements. Nathan Leites finds it significant that the Party "has never allowed a detached analysis, or even an attempt at codification, of its ideology . . . " (27, p. 17). Undoubtedly it would be detrimental to the Soviet state to attempt a "codification" of communist dogma, if by that is meant a tightly knit, logically consistent philosophy constructed on the basis of a careful search of the literature. Such a development would deprive the communist hierarchy of one of its greatest assets—the extreme flexibility of its ideology, permitting frequent and rapid adaptations to prevailing realities. There are few instances in Soviet history when the Kremlin was bothered for long by discrepancies between communist doctrine and internal and external conditions. Whatever policies were demanded, sooner or later quotations from Marx, Lenin, Stalin or lesser luminaries were available to rationalize Soviet conduct. And when the discrepancy between avowed doctrine and reality could no longer be ignored, then the Kremlin was not above rewriting history to eliminate such contradictions. Far from being a drawback doctrinal inconsistencies in communist philosophy endow the rulers of Russia with an inexhaustible supply of varied ideological garments with which to clothe their necessary policies.

Fourth, many writers have called attention to the fact that Bolshevism is an ever-growing, dynamic faith. As early as 1920 Stalin cautioned against relying on "quotations and maxims" instead of "practical experience" as a guide to correct behavior. Again in 1950 he sternly warned certain party members against the erroneous view that Marxism was a

> collection of dogmas, which "never" change, despite changes in the conditions of the development of society. They think that if they learn these conclusions and formulae by heart and begin to cite them without rhyme or reason, they will be able to solve all problems. . . . But this can be the conviction only of people who see the letter of Marxism, but not its essence. . . . (27, p. 245).

These warnings should caution students of international affairs against regarding communism as an unalterable body of doctrine which the Kremlin pursues relentlessly and which forms the dominant impulse in Soviet diplomatic behavior. They suggest instead that ideology provides a frame of reference that shapes the communist world's outlook upon world affairs, but that it is a frame of reference which undergoes constant change in the light of experience.

Fifth, so far as understanding Soviet diplomatic behavior is concerned, more significant than philosophic incompatibility between communist and non-communist countries may be the fact that communism *as espoused and practiced by the rulers of the Russian state* foments international tensions. It is primarily *Russian* communism that threatens the West. Other countries would not be unduly alarmed about their security if Portugal or Honduras

was the main stronghold of the international communist movement. The proper guide to the diplomatic behavior of the Soviet Union is not so much what communist theoreticians have proclaimed they intended to do, but what Soviet policy-makers have in fact done since 1917. Judging from their actions, how have the rulers of Russia appraised the importance of their own ideology? Explicitly or tacitly, what value have they assigned to doctrinal purity and adherence to declared ideological goals? When Soviet Russia has faced, as every nation must periodically, a choice between dogged attachment to ideology and deviation from ideology to cope with conditions that militate against achievement of ideological objectives, how has it resolved this dilemma? In the process of passing the ideology through the test of experience, what has been the effect upon the ideology itself?

These are pivotal questions in any intelligent appraisal of Soviet foreign policy. Generally speaking, adapting the goals of communist ideology to conditions prevailing within and outside Soviet Russia has led to many significant modifications in that ideology. Communist theoreticians may explain these modifications as temporary "tactical shifts" or "reinterpretations" of classical thought under new circumstances, but more disinterested observers identify them as organic changes in communist thought, insofar as that thought can be said to possess a core of basic doctrines. The point is well illustrated by many episodes in Soviet history, particularly those in which the communist regime was faced with a difficult choice between the ends and means of policy. Consciously or unconsciously, the regime frequently has resolved the problem by so modifying its ideology that in effect the means of policy became the *de facto* ends, and the declared ends became primarily important as means.

This phenomenon is strikingly apparent in the impact of the demands of the Russian state and its ruling regime upon classic communist thought. Although Karl Marx's views toward specific nationalist movements in 19th century Europe were ambivalent, classical Marxist philosophy adhered to a reasonably clear interpretation of nationalism and the forces that sustain it. Marxists believed that the national state had been forged out of a feudal society by the bourgeoisie. To the degree that it served to overcome feudal particularism, the rise of the nation state had been beneficial. But in time loyalty to the nation had become perverted into a rallying cry whereby the bourgeoisie enlisted the support of the masses to solidify its control over the workers and distracted them from pursuit of their true interests. Since loyalty to the nation eventually became an anti-proletarian force, it was destined to be superseded by "proletarian internationalism" (**22**, pp. 10-16; 90-91). Occasionally this early conception of nationalism found its way into later Soviet ideological pronouncements, as typified by Stalin's statement that "a nation is an historical category belonging to a definite epoch, the epoch of rising capitalism" (**22**, p. 11). The natural inference, therefore, was that the nation state must disappear as the dominant political entity. The affinity existing among the laboring masses of the world would ultimately erode mass loyalty to the nation and unite the working classes in a supra-national proletarian brotherhood.

When this idea was passed through the furnace of revolutionary experience in Russia and then cooled by immersion in the realities facing Russia after 1917, it lost its validity and had to be modified. Forced to conclude a humiliating treaty with Germany that greatly reduced the size of Russian territory, and soon besieged on all sides by anti-communist "White" forces that initially had strong support among the peasantry and other classes in Russia, Lenin's new regime was in mortal danger of being overthrown before the world revolution could be consummated. Outside of Russia, events did not augur well for Bolshevik predictions that the establishment of a communist order in Russia would trigger a chain reaction of revolutions throughout Europe. Having counted heavily upon the occurrence of revolution in Germany, the Kremlin watched impotently as the abortive uprisings of 1919, 1921, and 1923 were stamped out by the German Government. Similarly, Béla Kun's revolutionary effort in Hungary was abortive. Nor did the British general strike of 1926, which climaxed several years of industrial conflict, usher in a communist system in Britain.

Meanwhile, during the early and mid-1920's, the communist regime in Russia found itself beset with a host of internal and external problems, not the least of which was the contest for power after Lenin's death in 1924. The chief contenders in this struggle were Joseph Stalin and Leon Trotsky. The outcome is well known: Trotsky was ultimately displaced in the communist hierarchy, exiled from Russia in 1927, and assassinated in Mexico by Stalinist agents in 1940. Developments in Russia during this period were, of course, amply rationalized by invocation of ideas and phrases from the sacred texts of communist thought. But what concerns us more directly here is the reverse process: the impact of the events upon communist ideology. The triumph of the supreme opportunist, Joseph Stalin, over the doctrinal purist, the unswerving advocate of "world revolution," Leon Trotsky, eliminated any remaining doubt about the extent to which ideological demands would be subordinated to the requirements of the Russian state, as interpreted by the clique governing Russia. Trotsky went to his grave convinced that Stalin had "perverted" the Revolution by foresaking its messianic mission to arouse the proletariat in other countries no matter what the consequences for Russia itself might be.

Stalin replaced the idea of world revolution with his concept of "socialism in one country." This ingenious innovation fused communist ideology to Russian national interests, making them one and the same. In the process it abandoned the earlier idea that the "typical state for the capitalist period is the national State" (**22**, p. 93). "Socialism in one country" meant in effect that the long-prevailing view—that communism in Russia could not survive unless it became part of a successful worldwide revolution—had been shelved in favor of a theory that accorded more realistically with circumstances at home and abroad. This was that communism was not thriving anywhere *except* in Russia. Therefore, unless the gains made in Russia could be preserved no further progress in spreading communism could be anticipated; preserving the security of the USSR by supporting the policies of its communist hierarchy became the dominant obligation of loyal adherents of the communist faith. This innovation clearly ranks as one of Stalin's strokes of brilliance. By equating the interests of international communism with the needs of the Soviet state he largely avoided a dilemma that had hampered his predecessors and has often posed obstacles for non-communist countries like the United States: the antagonism between ideological requirements and requirements of *Realpolitik*. Exactly how did Stalin resolve this problem? He did so by declaring that in any conflict between *Realpolitik* and ideological principles, the latter would be subordinated to the former—not of course by expressly repudiating outmoded or unattainable ideological goals, but by resorting to "reinterpretations" of them that not infrequently amounted to their repudiation and their replacement by new principles that would more adequately explain why the Kremlin embarked upon specific policies and programs.

Meanwhile, what happened to the earlier revolutionary fervor advocating "world revolution" and stressing that the welfare of the international proletariat was indivisible? Detailed studies have found no prediction of "world revolution" in communist sources after 1934 (**30**, p. 386; **19**, *passim*). The concept disappeared in favor of emphasizing the identification between communist objectives and support for the Soviet Union. Ideological pronouncements as well as the operational policies of the Soviet state made it plain that one interest was paramount: pursuing policies that served the purposes of the ruling hierarchy and eliminated threats to its existence both inside and outside Russia. The zigzags in Soviet foreign policy, accompanied by feverish revisions in the ideological line, could be explained almost predominantly on this basis. Reviewing the record of Soviet diplomacy, Barrington Moore, Jr. has concluded that:

> The evidence seems to indicate that Marxist doctrine has not made the Soviet Union join any coalition or abandon any alliance that it would not have joined, or abandoned, on grounds of simple national self-interest. . . . Russian expansion can be explained very largely without reference to Marxist ideological factors. For the most part, each step in Soviet expansion can be considered a logical move to counter a specific actual or potential enemy. (**30**, pp. 391-92).

Paradoxically, writes Louis J. Halle, it is communist doctrine that "has tended to become the 'opium of the people.' " He contends that "world revolution" is perhaps "still 'on the books' as much as ever," but that "the men in the Kremlin . . . find themselves extended to the utmost in dealing with the immediate, practical politics of power. And in the politics of power the prime element is survival of the fittest through competition" (**17**, pp. 137-40).

Any ideology tends to become modified by the experiences encountered in putting it into practice. Just as the early Christian community ultimately abandoned its conception of the imminence of Christ's return to earth and, in doing so, modified many doctrines and beliefs deriving from that expectation, so too has the indefinite postponement of the world revolution in favor of the proximate goals of the Soviet state had far-reaching repercussions for Russia's relations with the outside world. What began in the early Bolshevik period as essentially a *means* for realizing the eschatological goals professed by the communist creed —consolidating the regime in Russia and protecting it from hostile forces at home and abroad—*ultimately became the operating ends of the Kremlin's policies*. Whether it was in instituting successive purges against Stalin's opponents or shifting diplomatic alignments so as to serve Russia's national interests, retention of power became the dominant motif in the behavior of the Soviet hierarchy. The Soviet Union's occupation of eastern Europe and its ruthless suppression of successive revolts in the satellite zone after World War II had no more necessary connection with "world revolution" than did Julius Caesar's conquest of Gaul or Hitler's of Poland. But it had a great deal to do with maximizing the power position of the Soviet state and achieving goals which, however much they may be given a contemporary justification by Marxist jargon, differed in few material respects from those of Peter the Great or Alexander the First.

On the basis of Soviet experience since 1917, Louis J. Halle has aptly commented that the "contradiction of ends and means pervades the Communist movement and is basic to it." He continues:

We may take it as a practical fact . . . that where ends and means contradict each other the latter will prevail. In other words, the ends will be determined by the means rather than by the intentions of those who avow them. . . . For ends are only what we think about, while means are what we do. . . . Means, therefore, are determinative as ends are not. The man who marches northward from New York City may intend to reach Washington, but the direction he actually takes will determine his destination. (**17**, p. 125).

And Barrington Moore, Jr. asserts that "under the impact of political responsibility, goals and tactics, means and ends, have become jumbled up with one another and have often tended to change places. The familiar thesis that the Soviets have pursued a single aim through flexible tactics will not withstand the test of comparison with the historical record" (**30**, p. 393).

In his *Inquiry Into Soviet Mentality*, Gerhart Niemeyer deals incisively with the relation of ideology to Soviet behavior. He finds that it is precisely in the realm of the more altruistic and eschatological aspects of communist thought that "revisions" have most frequently taken place. In spite of Marxist and early Leninist expectations to the contrary, the repressive features of the regime have steadily increased. "In other words, the Soviet rulers wield dictatorial power but do not wield it for the sake of a practically realizable goal. What else then is this dictatorial power but an end unto itself?" Since, "the Soviet system does not set up an authority or a principle which its rulers are required to respect and obey," and since "the ruling elite holds the key to everything, including the only authentic version of the dialectic of history," then "must we not say . . . that Soviet power . . . is its own end, and is hence might without service?" (**33**, pp. 14-15). The same study locates the wellspring of Soviet behavior in "a rationalization purely incidental to a wholly irrational clash of wills" (**33**, p. 18). Irrespective of its ideological professions, the real goal of the Kremlin is "the end of imposing upon the vast majority of mankind the ideas and the will of a small minority that has discovered new ways of manipulating human beings into subservience to totalitarian power" (**33**, p. 38).

Defectors from behind the Iron Curtain and from the ranks of communism almost invariably concur in this assessment. Thus the former high-ranking Yugoslav communist, Milovan Djilas, has spoken of the "strengthening of the new class and the sovereignty not only of a single ideology, but the sovereignty of thought of a single man or group of individuals" as the force animating the Kremlin's policies. The result has been an "intellectual decline and impoverishment of the ideology itself. . . . The ideology's progress, its elements of truth, have declined in proportion to the increase of physical power of its disciples" (**10**, p. 129). Lamenting that at first communist ideology in Russia "was guided by the most beautiful, primordial human ideas of equality and brotherhood," Djilas ultimately discovered that "only later did it conceal behind these ideas the establishment of its domination by whatever means." As time passed, experience revealed that "Power is an end in itself and the essence of contemporary Communism" (**10**, pp. 129, 163, 169).

Returning to the question posed at the beginning of this section—What is the role of goals like "world revolution" and other announced objectives of Soviet foreign policy? —our answer must be (1) that communist ideology makes certain contributions in realizing goals of Russian statecraft and is unquestionably important in establishing the international environment within which contacts between communist and non-communist countries take place; (2) that there is very little evidence for believing that ideological goals are uppermost in the Kremlin's scale of priorities so far as operating policies are concerned; (3) that maximizing the power of the Soviet elite and entrenching its dominant position have displaced ideological objectives as the *de facto* goals of the communist hierarchy in the Kremlin. The longer the communist regime exists the more it exhibits all the earmarks of totalitarian and imperialistic countries throughout world history. Ruthless internal oppression imposed by ambitious men and cliques, repudiation of every principle of ethics and morality held sacred in the West, unprincipled exploitation of conquered territory for the benefit of the USSR, contempt for solemn international agreements, unceasing pressure upon the non-communist world to expand Russian territory and hegemony, utter contempt for the truth and ordinary standards of decency—this is the bill of particulars that must be filed against Soviet communism. Recent uprisings within the Soviet satellite empire, as well as continuing defections from the communist cause, bear witness to the fact that the professed long-term goals of communism are more and more losing their power to make such barbarous policies tolerable, even to groups who have long been schooled in political adversity.

What is of enormous significance for the West is the fact that the Kremlin is clearly reluctant to jeopardize Russian security by ill-advised, perhaps suicidal, diplomatic or military crusades undertaken for ideological reasons; that it is extremely sensitive to considerations of *Realpolitik*, especially to comparisons of Soviet and American power; that the communist elite keeps uppermost the necessity to perpetuate its despotic rule and privileged position and can be counted on with reasonable assurance to avoid policies that would bring its position into jeopardy. In brief, Russia's rulers, in common with the rulers of many great powerful states known to history, will place first their own security and well-being, in the hope that in the course of time all these other things will be added unto them.

2. THE STRATEGIC–GEOPOLITICAL FRONT

Centrality of the Strategic Problem

While the United States dislikes communism and other totalitarian ideologies wherever found, ideological conflict alone cannot explain why the threat of war continually hangs over the globe. Fear of world revolution causes no great perturbation in Washington, London, and Paris. What does cause grave concern is the fear of Soviet expansionism and the consequent imposition of a totalitarian political order directed from Moscow upon non-communist nations. Communism has confronted the West at least as far back as the publication of the *Communist Manifesto* in 1848. The novel element in international affairs is not therefore that Russia is communist, or even that there may be more support for communism in other countries now than formerly; it is rather that Russia has acquired a new geopolitical base from which to spread communism by force of arms and by infiltration of other countries. So formidable is its new geopolitical position that this alone would constitute a serious threat to free world security even if the communist Revolution of 1917 had never taken place. It is a safe prediction that the cold war would exist, even if it might be diminished somewhat, *irrespective of the internal character of the Russian government*, provided the strategic-geopolitical base of Russian power remained substantially what it is today.

The origins of the cold war late in World War II and in the immediate postwar period can be traced to the strategic-geopolitical conflict. When the military tide turned in the east after the Battle of Stalingrad (1943), the Red Army began to drive the Germans out of Russia, across the Eurasian plain to the north and toward Czechoslovakia in the south, and finally to the very gates of Berlin. In the process Russia overran and occupied the belt of small countries separating Germany from the USSR. Rounding out occupation of these countries with the Czechoslovak coup in 1948, Russia has remained in direct or indirect control of this territory to the present day.*

Why did Soviet annexation and control over the Eastern European satellite belt precipitate the cold war? There are many reasons. In the first place, Russia's action constituted eloquent testimony to Western policy-makers of Soviet duplicity and of the Kremlin's apparently insatiable appetite for territory. Secondly, the communization of Eastern Europe was at vari-

---

*The Soviet European satellite empire includes the following countries that were annexed and incorporated into the USSR: Latvia, Lithuania, and Estonia, together with parts of Poland, eastern Germany, Rumania, Czechoslovakia, and Finland. Nominally independent Soviet satellites include: Albania, Poland, Rumania, Bulgaria, Hungary, and Czechoslovakia. Finland preserves its autonomy, but it must be regarded as a part of the Soviet military security system.

ance with many wartime pledges, such as those given at Yalta, and in opposition to almost every principle of the United Nations Charter. Furthermore, by annexing these territories Russia was engaging in undisguised imperialism, after the fashion of Japan in Manchuria or Germany in Austria before the Second World War.

The Postwar Geopolitical Revolution

Yet beyond these reasons there was another which by itself would have necessarily fore-ordained the cold war. This was that World War II ushered in a geopolitical revolution which profoundly altered the world balance of power. John C. Campbell has described the significance of Russia's strategic gains by saying that the USSR has converted the satellite zone into a great military bastion and

> a deployment area of great strategic importance, by building up the satellite armies to over one million men . . . to the point where Soviet and satellite forces together cast their shadow over all of Europe and stand as a threat to the security of the free nations beyond their borders. Nothing brings home to free Europeans the reality of the Soviet threat more than to see the Russians encamped on the Elbe and the Danube, and to hear the ancient European capitals of Prague and Budapest speaking with the voice of Moscow. (16, p. 209).

Russian occupation of Eastern Europe, contemporaneous with the decline of Germany, Japan, and Italy as great powers, constituted in the words of one observer, the "fulfillment of the Western geopoliticians' bad dreams." As the largest land mass on the globe, Russia "is able, independently of the West, to organize and exploit," this satellite zone and "to choose the time for final decision" (18, p. 77). Soviet Russia has come dangerously close to holding the fate of the world in its hand if geopoliticians like Sir Halford Mackinder are right, that the nation which dominates the Eurasian land mass possesses a well-nigh impregnable position from which to control the political destiny of the world.° Acknowledging that

many of Mackinder's ideas must be modified in the light of present-day technological developments—such as strategic air power and missile systems for delivering destruction—it is nevertheless true that control over the Eurasian land mass by one country confronts the world with a strategic problem of unparalleled magnitude.

The communization of Eastern Europe realized six traditional goals of Czarist-communist foreign policy: it brought the Red Army to the very doorstep of Western Europe; it vastly expanded the territory directly under control of the Kremlin; it established a *cordon sanitaire* in reverse between Russia and its potential enemies from the West; it gave Russia an outlet to the sea in the Baltic region; it materially strengthened the ability of the USSR to penetrate the Mediterranean—Near East area; and it furthered the communist goal of world revolution. These six developments have in turn given rise to many sources of tension between the United States and Russia and their allies, tensions that have pervaded almost every other issue in international affairs since World War II.

Soviet occupation and control over the Eurasian heartland is the dominant geopolitical fact of the mid-20th century. Obviously, it shapes Soviet military, economic, political, and diplomatic strategy toward the non-communist world, and it largely determines the response that the free world must in turn make in countering the communist threat.

American Policy and the Strategic Imbalance in Europe

The ability of the Red Army to overrun Western Europe in the event of a new war prompted the United States initially to formulate the Marshall Plan for rehabilitating West-

---

°Mackinder's ideas were developed during World War I and reiterated, in modified form, during World War II. His most famous dictum was: "Who rules East Europe commands the Heartland; Who rules the Heartland commands the World Island; Who rules the World Island commands the World." East Europe was the area between the Volga and the Elbe Rivers. The Heartland, never precisely defined, was the great Eurasian hinterland, roughly coterminous with the USSR. The World Island was the land mass of the European-Asian-African continents. Thus Mackinder, in opposition to advocates of sea power like Captain Alfred Mahan, believed that ultimate victory belonged to a firmly entrenched, militarily impregnable land mass.

For commentary on Mackinder's views see 24, pp. 567-86; 18, *passim;* and 36, *passim.*

ern Europe's war-devastated economies and, after that, to create the NATO defense system as the sheet anchor of the free world's military efforts. Even now the spectre of Russian military supremacy hangs like the sword of Damocles over the heads of Western policy-makers. For in the event of war it is extremely doubtful in the nuclear-missile age whether Europe could be defended against the Red Army. The military collapse of Western Europe would present the United States with the pain-ful alternatives of raining atomic destruction upon its friends to "liberate" them from the communist yoke or of reconciling itself per-manently to the incorporation of Western Europe into the communist empire. The latter eventuality would almost certainly tip the economic-military scales sooner or later in favor of the Soviet Union.

Soviet evacuation of that part of Europe overrun by the Red Army toward the end of the Second World War has remained a fixed

STRATEGIC FACTS BEHIND THE AIRPOWER—MISSILE DEBATE

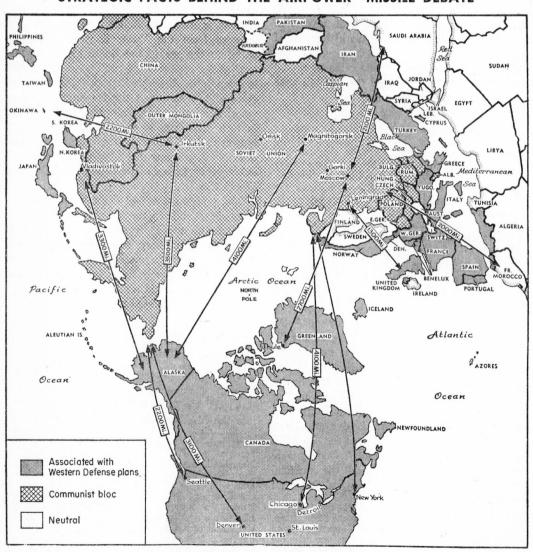

The New York Times, May 13, 1956.

goal of American foreign policy ever since 1945. Few diplomatic objectives in the postwar era have met with so little success. At the same time, the problem of Soviet domination of Eastern Europe is one of the root causes of conflict between the communist and non-communist worlds.

Settlement of issues growing out of Soviet military occupation of Eastern Europe was a major item on the agenda of the Yalta Conference (February, 1945). At Yalta the United States and Britain thought they had secured Soviet agreement to proposals guaranteeing the establishment of freely-elected, democratic political regimes in Eastern Europe, even while the West conceded that such regimes must remain "friendly" to Russia. Stalin, for example, had agreed to a four-part memorandum on Allied policy toward occupied countries in Eastern Europe, the key phrase of which was that the Big Three *jointly* would assist these countries to "form interim governmental authorities broadly representative of all democratic elements in the population and pledged to the earliest possible establishment through free elections of governments responsive to the will of the people." Former Secretary of State Byrnes records that "Agreement was quickly reached among the Big Three" on this proposal and that Stalin said " 'On the whole, I approve of the declaration' " (3, p. 33).

Agreements reached at the Yalta Conference thus bound the USSR (1) to establish democratic political orders in the liberated and occupied countries of Eastern Europe and (2) to carry out such steps in concert with the other major Allied powers.* Since 1945

the United States and its Western allies have protested in vain against the Kremlin's domination over the nations of Eastern Europe. Specific points at issue have been the failure of the USSR to agree upon a peace treaty for Germany that permitted the re-unification of the German nation under a freely-chosen democratic political system; the imposition of Kremlin-controlled communist puppet governments upon the people of Eastern Europe; the economic exploitation of these countries for the benefit of the USSR; and ruthless oppression carried out against individuals and groups that opposed Russia's mailed-fist rule.

There has been no significant change in the position of either Soviet or American policy toward Eastern Europe since 1945. Time and again the United States has demanded Soviet evacuation of this zone as a precondition for any lasting settlement of cold war tensions. Thus in a letter to Premier Bulganin on February 15, 1958, President Eisenhower placed the question of Soviet hegemony over Eastern Europe high on the list of subjects that must be discussed at any new summit conference. Eisenhower stated bluntly that "our people are . . . opposed to regimes which hold people against their will and which deny the principle on which our nation was founded, that governments derive their just powers from the consent of the governed and can never rightly deprive the governed of their inalienable right to life, liberty, and the pursuit of happiness." To Russia's contention that its control over Eastern Europe was not properly a matter for Western concern, Eisenhower replied: "Does the Soviet Union claim such a proprietary interest in these lands and people that to discuss them is solely a matter of Soviet domestic concern? If not, and if these lands and people can be

---

*For reasons that are not altogether clear, the American people have tended to equate the Yalta Conference with the Munich Conference of 1938 by referring to wholesale American "appeasement" of Stalin and to officials of the Roosevelt Administration who allegedly "handed Eastern Europe" to the USSR. Such judgments can derive from only two possible sources: gross ignorance of the context of events within which the conference took place and the agreement ultimately reached or unbridled partisanship.

As regards the Eastern European features of the agreement, the "concessions" made at Yalta were chiefly *Soviet* concessions—in the sense that the West had nothing to "concede" in this area. At the time of Yalta the area was rapidly falling under Soviet military domination. Therefore, Britain and the United States had essentially two

choices: they could leave the USSR in unilateral control of the area, or they could seek an agreement specifying *joint* control and the establishment of freely-elected governments. The latter course was followed. Of course, the USSR did not abide by the agreement reached. In the years ahead, this fact also posed two choices: either the Western governments could protest violations of the Yalta agreement (which they did unceasingly) or they could resort to military force to *compel* Soviet adherence to it, a course which would undoubtedly have triggered World War Three. For further commentary on the Yalta agreement and its later implications, see: 12; 40; 43.

discussed by Soviet leaders as an international problem, why cannot we both discuss them" (48, pp. 106-07)?

In preparation for a proposed great power conference early in 1958 both Russia and the West had formulated "package deals" for relieving global tensions. Crucial to both was the issue of Eastern Europe. The issue, as summarized by the *New York Times,* was: "The United States wants to discuss self-determination for the East European satellites. Russia has said, in effect, that the East European governments are none of the United States' business" (32, February 9, 1958). For well over a decade the impasse has remained. What are the chances that it may eventually be broken?

Prospects for a Strategic Realignment

Memories of invasion from the west—by Napoleon, by Germany and the Allies during World War I, by Hitler during World War II —are too deeply woven into the fabric of Russian national consciousness to be removed by mere promises from the West that Russia has no reason to fear for the security of its borders or by assurances that its security is safeguarded by the United Nations. For basically the same arguments were heard before the Second World War, when Russian security was presumably guaranteed by the French system of alliances in Eastern Europe and by the League of Nations. Both of these supports ultimately collapsed, permitting Hitler's war machine to penetrate to the gates of Moscow and, in the process, to inflict millions of casualties and billions of dollars worth of property damage on the USSR.

However much the West may believe Soviet fears to be irrational, it cannot be denied that they are *real* and that they enter heavily into Soviet diplomatic calculations. It seems clear that *de facto* Russian control over the military destiny of Eastern Europe is a fixed and unalterable principle of Soviet foreign policy, however unpalatable that may be to the West and to the American people. From Russia's viewpoint, it is no more arguable than whether the Western Hemisphere ought to be included within the American security zone. This at

least was the judgment of a number of leading experts on the USSR who were polled in 1957 by the staff of the Senate Foreign Relations Committee. The majority foresaw "little likelihood that the Soviet leaders would be willing to withdraw their troops from Eastern Europe, although some thought they might consider such a move under certain circumstances" (37, p. 11). In replying to the poll, Frederick Barghoorn observed that "as realistic students of international relations, we must understand that a great power does not welcome the establishment of what it considers to be outposts of enemy power in its own security zone" (37, p. 26).

The prospects for an *unconditional* withdrawal of Soviet power from Eastern Europe —as demanded by the United States since 1945—are therefore exceedingly remote. The only possibility would seem to be some kind of a negotiated, *quid pro quo* agreement between Russia and the West—chiefly the United States —that would make such a withdrawal contingent upon equivalent Western concessions. Public interest in this kind of settlement was revived late in 1957 and early 1958 by the speeches and writings of a number of prominent Americans and by an exchange of letters between the United States and Russia concerning the feasibility of a new great power conference. George F. Kennan, expert on Soviet affairs, in a series of lectures delivered in England, sharply criticized the rigidity of American policy toward Eastern Europe and declared that no progress could be made in settling this problem without reasonable concessions by the United States. To date, Kennan declared, American policy has called upon Moscow "to abandon . . . the military and political bastion in Central Europe which it won by military effort from 1941 to 1945, and to do this without a compensatory withdrawal of American armed power from the heart of the Continent." For the Kremlin to accept this demand, said Kennan, would inevitably "create the general impression of a defeat for Soviet policy in Eastern and Central Europe generally." Accordingly, Kennan believed that any reduction of Moscow's power within the satellites would have to be geared to agreement on the German question and to some reduction

PULLBACK IN EUROPE: WHAT RUSSIA WANTS

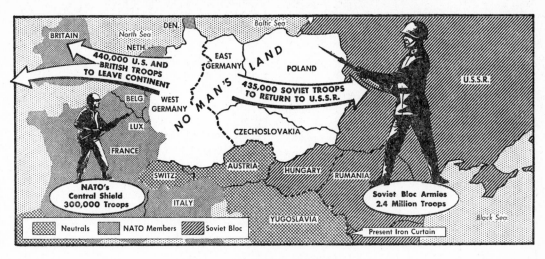

Newsweek—Magill, Feb., 10, 1958, p. 59.

of American armed forces in Europe (**32**, December 8, 1957 and January 19, 1958). Kennan's analysis was sharply contested by spokesmen for the Eisenhower Administration and by former Secretary of State Dean G. Acheson, one of the architects of American policy toward Russia. To Acheson's mind any diminution in American power in Europe was unthinkable, since it would leave the NATO countries defenseless against possible communist attack; moreover, he questioned whether the Kremlin would ever contemplate evacuating the satellites, since this would almost certainly result in the overthrow of Moscow's hand-picked political regimes there (**32**, January 19, 1958).

For the United States the problem of Soviet domination of Eastern Europe remains as baffling as it is crucial. Despite widespread sloganizing by certain high-ranking officials of the Eisenhower Administration about "liberating Eastern Europe" and "rolling back" the Iron Curtain (**11**, pp. 46-50), the simple truth is that the future of Eastern Europe lies in Soviet, not American, hands. Impressive as American power is in many fields, there is no way short of an all-out war to bring it to bear upon the problem of Russia's mastery over the Eastern satellite zone. This—rather than any

supposed "sell-out" by the Roosevelt Administration at Yalta—is the central fact that underlies the strategic revolution of the contemporary era. John C. Campbell has made the point as follows:

> Soviet successes . . . have been our failures, or rather our losses, in terms of the world balance. These are losses that were perhaps inevitable, given the postwar situation with which the United States found itself. We may regret instances of our lack of foresight, of misplaced hope and confidence, or of less than realistic negotiation. But the United States is not the arbiter of the world, least of all in areas which the Red Army overran in our common war against Hitler. (**16**, p. 217).

If any significant change in the strategic imbalance occasioned by Soviet occupation of Eastern Europe is possible, it is likely to be a product of two factors which must occur well-nigh simultaneously: progress in resolving other cold war issues, and widespread acceptance by the American people of the idea that in successful negotiations concessions cannot be expected from the other side alone. As long as public opinion within the United States believes widely that negotiation with the USSR, in which there will almost certainly have to be some American concessions, is *ipso facto* "appeasement," little progress can be expected.

3. THE ECONOMIC–MILITARY FRONT

How do the economic-military postures of the two sides in the cold war compare? What are the relative strengths and weaknesses?

Economic Postures and Potentialities

Measured in terms of sheer territorial size alone, the communist bloc has a substantial advantage over the non-communist world. The bloc includes one-fourth of the land area of the globe and occupies a strategic position giving it many geopolitical advantages. Counting Red China, the communist bloc contains about eight hundred and fifty million people, while the free world, counting the neutralist nations, totals just over one billion people.

When we consider economic and industrial capacities, a striking fact is the extent to which the Soviet Union has gained on the West economically since 1917. In recent years the USSR has increased its economic production at a more rapid rate than the United States or Western Europe (52 and 53), a phenomenon that is not surprising given the low rate of industrial production in Russia in 1917 and the great emphasis accorded to economic expansion by Stalin and his successors in the Kremlin. Ever since inauguration of the first Soviet Five Year Plan in 1928, it has been a fixed goal of Soviet policy-makers to outstrip the United States economically. This goal was interrupted by World War II. During the course of the war Nazi Germany overran and destroyed some 31,000 Soviet mines and factories, knocking out nearly one-third of Russia's industrial facilities. By 1953, however, the staggering job of rebuilding war-devastated industries had been completed, and the Kremlin gave every indication of returning to its old goal of surpassing American industrial levels (24, p. 88). After the great power conference at Geneva in 1955, communist propaganda organs vocally stressed the theme of "competitive coexistence." Economic advancement and competition with the West were dramatically elevated into major objectives of the communist bloc. Demonstrating his system's superiority in this sphere, said Premier Khrushchev in 1959, would "attract millions of new adherents to socialism" and, by 1970,

would alter the world balance of power decisively in favor of the communist world (32, February 1, 1959, dispatch by Harry Schwartz). Inauguration of a new seven-year plan in that same year—in which the Soviet Union planned to equal or surpass the United States in such productive categories as steel, oil, electricity, and even selective categories of consumer goods—testified to the importance attached to economic progress, and to economic aspects of the cold war, by the communist hierarchy.

The Soviet Union is second only to the United States in possessing the raw materials requisite to a strong industrial economy, and in some ways the bloc is even more self-sufficient in strategic raw materials than America (7, pp. 41-2). The USSR possesses well-nigh inexhaustible supplies of coal—2 trillion tons, out of a world reserve of seven trillion tons. It has adequate supplies of oil.* It has made prodigious efforts to expand generation of electric power and is continuing to build hydro-electric plants at a rapid pace. It has abundant supplies of iron ore, although the quality of both coal and iron available may decrease with the passage of time (24, p. 144). It is also well endowed with many lesser metals vital for making high quality steel and precision parts, possessing a number—manganese, asbestos, chromium, platinum—which the United States lacks. In respect to the newest strategic metal, uranium, Russia has available at least limited supplies from Czechoslovakia (7, pp. 37-40, 124).

---

*Accurate information about the extent of raw materials within the USSR, and especially one as vital as oil, is difficult to obtain. The oil situation within Russia has been subject to considerable speculation in the West, partly because much of the country remains unprospected (not only for oil but other raw materials as well). Soviet statistics are always suspect. Western geographers, for example, are inclined to take with considerable skepticism the Soviet claim that Russia has two-thirds of the oil reserves of the world within its borders. This claim is based upon huge reserves reportedly discovered east of the Volga (a kind of "second Baku") and along the base of the Caucasus. Although new discoveries have undoubtedly been made, Russia was heavily dependent upon imports of oil from the Allies during World War II (7, p. 45; 24, p. 36).

WORLD ECONOMIC RESOURCES

Percentage Distribution

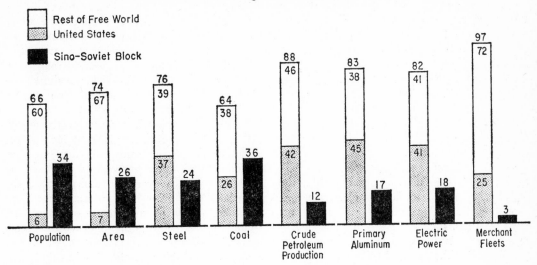

Adapted from Dept. of State, etc., *Mutual Security Program, 1959*, p. 21.

The Soviet Seven-Year Plan

Analysis of the Soviet seven-year plan, announced early in 1959, affords a convenient frame of reference within which to study problems and prospects in Soviet economic development and to assess the USSR's position *vis-à-vis* the United States. This plan must be viewed against the much-heralded Soviet aim to defeat the West on the plane of economic rather than military competition, a viewpoint reflected in increasing reliance by the Kremlin upon foreign assistance programs and trade agreements to woo countries in the Afro-Asian bloc. Addressing the Twenty-first Communist Party Congress early in 1959, Premier Khrushchev stressed the economic vitality and dynamism of the communist world as the key element in the conflict with the free world. Khrushchev asserted that the "world socialist system as a whole has caught up with the capitalist world system" in per capita industrial production; after 1965, the USSR would surpass the United States in the production of some commodities; five years later Khrushchev believed that Russia would surpass the United

States in per capita industrial output.* Faster economic growth rates for the Soviet Union —a rate of 8.6 per cent per year was postulated in the seven-year plan—was the "objective law of socialism" that would give the communist world economic supremacy in the near future. Khrushchev estimated the American economic growth rate in the immediate future at 2 per cent per year. American economists placed it at from 4 to 5 per cent annually, though some economists believed this rate to be optimistic in view of the fact that from 1950 to 1958 the American economy expanded at an average of only 3¼ per cent annually. Soviet projections foresaw a Gross National Product for Russia of over $300 billion annually by 1965. Conservative American forecasts called for the GNP of the United States to reach more than $500 billion by that date;

*Data relating to the Soviet seven-year plan are taken from material presented in 32, November 16, 1958 and February 1, 1959, Dispatch by Harry Schwartz; and 6, January 19, 1959, Dispatch by Paul Wohl, January 28, 1959, Dispatch by Paul Wohl, and February 5, 1959, Dispatch by Richard L. Strout.

liberal estimates, using a 5 per cent growth rate, figured on more than $600 billion by 1965. If 1957 productive levels for the United States were maintained, then the growth in the Soviet economy would bring the USSR abreast of the United States by 1980. If the United States continued its present rate of economic expansion, then the Soviet Union could not catch the United States economically until the year 2000 or later (32, November 17, 1957).

By 1965 the Kremlin expected to be producing from 86 to 91 million tons of steel annually; Soviet oil production called for nearly a 100 per cent increase over 1958 figures, to 230-240 million tons annually; the Kremlin hoped too to double electric power generation, producing 500-520 billion kilowatt hours by 1965. Increases were also planned to meet the growing demand for consumer goods in the USSR, although the Kremlin was making no attempt to rival American production in this sphere. For example, meat production was to be more than doubled; butter production was to go up more than 50 per cent; shoes and hosiery were also to be increased substantially; a moderate increase was to be made in automobiles and trucks.

The Soviet seven-year plan calls for an overall increase of 70 per cent in agricultural production by 1965—a most ambitious goal in the light of recent Russian experience in meeting agricultural problems. Even though the Soviet grain harvest in 1958 was the largest since the communist regime came into power in Russia, Russian agricultural production had increased only 10 per cent since 1913. Despite considerable attention to agricultural problems, the Kremlin had not been able to prevent Russia from falling behind average yields in Western Europe and the United States. In terms of comparative yields, Soviet Russia's position was inferior to its position before the First World War. Similarly, statistics released by Soviet sources covering the production of livestock indicated that Russia's position did not differ materially from its position in 1916. Figures made available by Soviet officials late in 1958 and early in 1959 showed rather conclusively that Western economists had *underestimated* the degree to which "official"

figures were substantially greater than actual production in many spheres of Soviet agriculture. Informed Western analysts were therefore inclined to look at agricultural projections in the USSR with considerable skepticism. During the early 1950's, for instance, Soviet production of industrial goods, electric power, and agricultural commodities lagged considerably behind the Kremlin's proposed schedules, so much so that the Sixth Five-Year Plan had to be abandoned prematurely.

At the same time, Western economists agreed that economic growth would continue in the Soviet Union at a faster rate than in the United States, and acknowledged the fact of significant growth over the course of preceding years. This by no means meant that they conceded Khrushchev's claim "to overtake" the United States; nor were they inclined to accept his projections as readily attainable goals. Always, the *diplomatic motivations* behind the Kremlin's claims for the past and future had to be recognized. If other countries *believed* Russia was winning the economic competition with the free world, this fact could have profound implications for the global balance of power.

Behind reported lags in Soviet production are certain hard economic realities, a great many of which are likely to prove unyielding even in the face of the Kremlin's most intensive efforts. First, there is the sharp imbalance between heavy industry and consumer goods industry. Not even a totalitarian state can go on indefinitely ignoring the demands of its population for substantial increases in the standard of living, if for no other reason than that declining civilian morale under forced industrialization will eventually bring about an industrial contraction. Then too there is the fact that while the communist bloc is remarkably self-sufficient in raw materials, it is by no means completely so. There are major gaps in the supply of needed raw materials: lead, nickel, tungsten, titanium, antimony, sulfur, mercury, tin, and, perhaps most serious of all, natural rubber. In the event of war Russian imports of rubber from Southeast Asia would be cut off or sharply reduced. If the experience of World War II is a reliable guide, there is ground for thinking that internal oil supplies are far from adequate to support a war economy. Even if new fields could be acquired by Soviet penetration of Turkey or Iran, these could easily be rendered useless by Russia's enemies.

Several basic factors are likely to limit future Soviet economic growth and may even bring about a decline in present productive rates. The *rate* of growth since 1917 cannot be taken too literally as a basis for predicting Soviet future economic output, since before 1917 Russia was predominantly an agricultural country possessing very little industry. At the start of the communist period Soviet technology was far behind technology in the West. A hundred-fold increase in the production of a given commodity may not mean much if there was negligible production of it from the start.

Moreover, the pace of forced industrialization within Russia has generated many new problems for the communist elite. An acute one in recent years has been a growing labor shortage in the USSR. By the end of the 1950's, Western studies found that the Soviet labor force was growing at the rate of 300,000 workers annually, contrasted with a gain of about 2,000,000 annually prior to World War II. An authoritative source found this critical manpower shortage to be "a serious, inherent weakness greatly impairing [Russia's] position —a weakness from which she could not quickly recover." As in Czarist days, part of the reason for Soviet secretiveness might well lie in the attempt to conceal this weakness from the outside world (5, July 6, 1959). The huge, seemingly inexhaustible, labor reserve traditionally provided by the peasantry appears to have dwindled rapidly, until today there are far fewer agricultural workers than conditions demand. In the future, shortages of capital too may be expected to cripple Soviet economic expansion, and output per unit of capital invested will most likely decline (35, pp. 74-6). Still another weak link in the Soviet economic system is transportation. Russia possesses some 60,000 miles of railroads—the United States has four times as much—supplemented by an extensive network of internal river and lake transportation. A modern highway system, however, is practically non-existent. Besides hindering the peacetime development of So-viet industry, Russia's primitive transportation system would undoubtedly be a considerable liability in time of war. The difference between the American and Soviet transportation networks might well spell the difference between defeat and victory for the USSR in a prolonged global war (51).

Yet compared with the Achilles' heel of the Soviet economic system — agriculture — these problems are perhaps of secondary importance. Agricultural crises were endemic under the Czars, leading frequently to widespread famines within Russia. Forced collectivization under the Communists, beginning in the late 1920's, resulted in the destruction of millions of heads of livestock; brought about a sharp decline in agricultural output from which the USSR has not yet recovered; and, perhaps most damaging of all, incurred the intense hostility of millions of Russian peasants. The Second World War witnessed indescribable devastation in the agricultural heart of Russia. When the Germans did not destroy everything in their path, then Russian partisans followed their traditional "scorched earth" policy in dealing with foreign invaders. Within more recent years recurrent droughts, brought on by adverse weather conditions and intensive farming techniques, have added their toll.

More permanent than man-made obstacles is the geographical fact that nature has not been kind to the USSR. Most of Russia lies in the same latitude as Canada, and much of the land is like that found around Hudson Bay. Out of a total area of some eight and a half million square miles, only one million square miles can be utilized profitably. Food can be grown on about 6 per cent of the land, or about 500,000 square miles, about the same as that available to the United States. Yet the USSR supports some two hundred million people—two hundred and fifty million by 1970. While the soil and growing conditions within Russia make agriculture always precarious, the United States, by contrast, has been faced within recent years with the problem of mounting agricultural surpluses that would undoubtedly add heavily to the strength of the free world in any conflict with communist coalitions.

What is the future of Soviet agriculture? In spite of prodigious efforts by the Kremlin, the future is not promising. Cressey, for example, believes that current Soviet agricultural production may "be near the limit under the techniques now available" (7, p. 26). Poor soil throughout much of Russia; millions of square miles of arid land; sparse rainfall—8-10 inches a year, compared with an average of around 20 inches in the United States; short growing seasons; limitations on the diversity of the crops grown; a historically rebellious peasantry—all of these add up to a continuing problem of great magnitude.

We must conclude then that while Russia under the Communists has made spectacular progress in many fields of economic endeavor, there are several chinks in the Soviet economic armour. In any military showdown with the West these vulnerabilities could be expected to weaken the Soviet military effort seriously over a prolonged period of time. The prospect remains, therefore, that barring some unforeseen scientific-technological developments that could alter the picture substantially, the economic strength of the free world coalition will stay ahead of the Soviet-led communist coalition for an indefinite period.

The Military Balance Sheet

The military historian, Samuel L. A. Marshall warns us that:

> War, and the risks of war, are never a matter of counting the chips on both sides of the table, and then coming forth with a plus or minus answer. The wisest man . . . could not forecast the true capability of the United States for a war with limits yet undefined, fought with weapons the effects of which remain unmeasured, engaging peoples whose moral strength in the face of unfathomed danger is unknown and unknowable. (16, p. 200).

Recognizing that comparisons of military capabilities can never be too precise, that much depends upon the exact circumstances under which forces are utilized, and that rapid changes in military technology sometimes quickly alter existing power configurations, let us examine more closely dominant factors in the East-West arms equation. First, there is the clear inferiority of the United States and

its allies in military manpower. By the late 1950's, the communist camp had more than eight and a half million men under arms. In time of war, Russia and its satellites could muster well over 500 divisions—creating a Red military Juggernaut that would dwarf NATO ground forces.* Western defense planners concede communist superiority on land, especially in armor and artillery. By the beginning of the 1960's the disparity between ground forces possessed by both sides was more favorable than ever to the communist bloc, owing to deep cuts that had been made for several years preceding in American defense spending for ground troops and weapons.

An approximate parity existed between the free world coalition and the communist bloc in numbers of military aircraft. Estimates give both sides somewhere around 50,000 airplanes. The Soviet bloc's air fleet appears to be heavily concentrated in fighter planes. The bloc was far behind the free world coalition in heavy bombers and even further behind in long-range military transports, with shortages in this sphere seriously crippling the range of bomber fleets under the Kremlin's control. The free world possessed a considerably greater number of long- and intermediate-range bombers than the USSR (32, July 28, 1957). Control of a ring of strategic bases around the borders of the communist world also greatly strengthened the offensive and defensive power of the free world.

In seapower, the American-led coalition enjoyed a marked superiority over the Kremlin and its satellites in major ship categories, with

---

*NATO's proposed ground strength for a number of years had been aimed at 30 divisions. By 1960, however, NATO could actually muster only 16-17 divisions. Success in realizing the goal of 30 divisions presupposed: (1) an eventual contribution of 12 divisions from Western Germany, (2) return of certain French military forces that were committed in North Africa, and (3) maintenance of British troop commitments at current levels. There appeared very little indication either that West Germany would make her long-delayed scheduled contribution to NATO or that France could materially reduce its military commitment in North Africa.

Data relating to Western and communist military strengths and weaknesses are based in large part on 41, p. 32 and 32, January 5, 1958, January 25, 1959, and April 5, 1959, dispatches by Hanson W. Baldwin.

a single exception: submarines. Informed military observers in the West placed the number of Soviet submarines at 450-500 by the end of the 1950's, including some capable of firing guided missiles. Although no Soviet nuclear-powered submarine had as yet made an appearance, there seemed little doubt that the USSR either had, or was on the verge of having, developed long-range nuclear-propelled submarines. Although Russia controlled a formidable submarine fleet the Western allies had closed the gap in recent years. All told, the allies had nearly 400 submarines. Over 30 of these were nuclear-powered, either completed or near completion. Moreover, in other categories of naval vessels, the advantage plainly lay with the allies. The NATO community had well over 100 aircraft carriers; so far as was known, Russia and its satellites had none, except for "baby carriers" that were incapable of long-range maneuvers. Basically the same imbalance prevailed for battleships, cruisers, and destroyers, with the free world enjoying an overwhelming superiority in surface shipping.

Nevertheless, by virtue of an intensive shipbuilding campaign undertaken since World War II, the Soviet Union was rapidly becoming the second most powerful naval country on the globe. Acquisition of the Baltic ports, coupled with incorporation of the fleets and ship construction facilities of Poland, East Germany, and the Baltic States, had greatly enhanced the USSR's naval posture since World War II. Stalin and his predecessors carried on an energetic ship-construction program in the Baltic region. Soviet submarine strength particularly constitutes a far graver danger to Western security than that posed by Nazi U-boats in the early years of World War II. Hitler launched the war against the West with only 75 U-boats in active service—and came perilously close to denying the Atlantic sea lanes to the allies. American military leaders have repeatedly called attention to the grave consequences inherent in Russia's gains in naval power. Thus Admiral Robert B. Carney believes that "The continuing increase in Soviet maritime strength will surely give rein to further Soviet ambitions. . . . " A major strategic objective of the Kremlin will be "to gain

and maintain control of the seas and deny their control to any enemy" (4, p. 10).

Yet for an indefinite period to come, despite greater attention in Western defense spending to air and missile power than to naval power, the free world will likely possess sufficient naval strength to keep control over the major sea approaches to the vast Soviet continental empire. The Soviet submarine fleet may be supreme in closed waters like the Baltic Sea and the Black Sea; during time of war, however, it would be in danger of being "bottled up" by blockades that deny the communist fleet egress to the world's great ocean expanses. Powerful naval units like the United States Mediterranean-based Sixth Fleet could serve as floating bases from which to launch devastating air strikes against the industrial heart of Russia in the event of war. A fleet of over 30 atomic-powered submarines, possessing almost indefinite cruising range, could hurl missiles onto almost any site located behind the Iron Curtain. Conversion of many standard submarines into missile-launchers, firing the 1,500-mile range Polaris missile, was also expected to add materially to the free world's naval strength.

The linchpin of Western defense throughout the greater part of the postwar period was, and for several years to come will likely remain, possession of a large stockpile of nuclear weapons and of the means for delivering them to selected targets. This combination of a varied stockpile of nuclear weapons and an effective delivery system was the *sine qua non* of a military policy of "deterrence" aimed initially at preventing aggression and, if aggression occurred, at instituting "massive retaliation" against an enemy. Even after impressive strides had been taken toward perfection of long- and intermediate-range missiles and in providing adequate supplies of such weapons to the free world's military forces, the Strategic Air Command remained the mainstay of Western defense. No point on the globe was inaccessible to SAC's nearly 2,000 bombers, many of which could be refueled while in flight. Estimates made in 1956 placed the nuclear weapons stockpile available to each side at over 5,000 for the West and around 1,000 for the USSR (35, p. 38-n). There was no doubt that quantitatively the free world was ahead of the communist bloc in nuclear weapons. Yet it was equally true that, allowing for variations in the potency of such weapons, the communist bloc was rapidly acquiring a sufficient stockpile to wreak widespread devastation if war should occur. The five to one advantage suggested by statistical comparisons of available nuclear bombs distorted the fact that both sides were fully capable of raining nuclear havoc on their enemies and that the West might actually have more bombs than it had suitable targets upon which to use them!

Soviet success in firing two earth satellites late in 1957 was the opening phase in spirited competition between Russia and the United States in missile technology. Almost every week one side or the other demonstrated some new device for pushing the frontiers of space ahead. Most of these developments of course had military application. Kaleidoscopic changes in missile technology threatened to make obsolete any balance sheet of military strengths and weaknesses and to outdate many features of military power that had made nations strong in the past. In the resulting "missile race," both sides gave full publicity to their latest achievements; and in some instances, for example, in Soviet pressures on Berlin in 1959, it seemed apparent that diplomatic moves were closely geared to temporary victories in rocketry and other phases of military technology. Whatever the precise impact of various categories of missiles on the military balance of power, it was clear that Soviet successes called attention graphically to Russia's scientific prowess and to its ability, at least in some capacities, to rival the West in productive skills.

As for competing missile claims, very few Westerners, especially those outside of governmental agencies, were in a position to make an accurate assessment. The available data on the status of the free world's missile stockpile and its proposed productive schedules were incomplete; and even less information was available to laymen about the missile strength of communist countries. Nevertheless, by the opening of the 1960's, there seemed fairly widespread agreement upon certain facts. The Soviet Union was unquestionably ahead of the West in the development of long-range guided missiles. Qualitatively, Russia's missiles had more powerful thrust than those demonstrated in the West; and judging from Russia's firing of missiles into space, they possessed very accurate guidance mechanisms. Quantitatively, Russia held a productive lead over the West, as measured by ability to make large numbers of missiles available to troops in the field. Perhaps most crucial of all, Russia appeared to have a significant advantage over its opponents in reducing the "lead time"—the time required to bring missiles from the drawing board to the firing site—in the production of missiles and satellites. The 1960-64 period was looked upon by many military analysts as a critical one for the United States, when Russia's quantitative lead over the United States in missiles was variously estimated as ranging from 3 to 1, to as high as 10 to 1. In this period too the USSR would doubtlessly convert a portion of its large submarine fleet to missile-firing vessels, thereby bringing every large city in the United States and most of the nation's industrial complex within Soviet missile range! These were the central elements in the "missile gap" that precipitated a heated controversy between executive and legislative policy-makers over the state of American defenses in 1959 and would undoubtedly occupy a major role in defense planning in the years thereafter.

Officials of the Eisenhower Administration, however, denied that the United States was losing the missile race or that its military position was inferior to the Soviet position. General Nathan Twining, Chairman of the Joint Chiefs of Staff, testified early in 1959: "I think we're all right. . . . I would much rather have the defense posture of the United States than that which the Soviet has today" (32, February 8, 1959). Over against Soviet missile advances, American officials set a number of other important facts. One was the continued striking power of SAC, as well as the West's powerful naval superiority. Another was the rapid strides which the West itself was making in missile technology, highlighted by perfection of the Thor missile, to be followed by introduction of the Titan missile. In turn, these liquid-fuel missiles were scheduled to be superseded by the solid-fuel Minuteman, planned for testing by 1961. The Minuteman would open a new phase in missile strategy, since it would be ready for almost instantaneous launching from "hard" sites built underground in remote areas, thereby greatly reducing the vulnerability of domestic and overseas bases. By 1963 also it was expected that the American fleet would be extensively armed with missiles capable of being fired from submerged submarines. While these developments would do much to restore the military balance in favor of the West, in the interim it appeared that the USSR was ahead in most aspects of missile technology and that its headstart might require years to overcome.[*] The Eisenhower Administration's assessment of American military strength *vis-à-vis* the Soviet Union was not without its vigorous critics. The Senate Democratic majority leader, Lyndon Johnson of Texas, accused the administration of falling behind Russia in space exploration. Senator Stuart Symington, a consistent critic of the administration's alleged "complacency," charged that, on the basis of testimony from civilian and military officials, by the early 1960's, Russia "could wipe out our entire manned and unmanned force" (**32**, February 8, 1959).

Admittedly, the critics had the better of the argument in this respect: what the *actual* balance of forces was on each side might not be so important in shaping diplomatic moves as what was *generally believed to be* the balance of forces. If the West were *thought* to be behind Russia, and if Russia or neutralist countries acted on this assessment, the consequences could be highly inimical for the security of the free world and for achievement of its diplomatic goals.

In summary, calculation of strengths and weaknesses on both sides revealed overwhelming communist superiority in military manpower and ground troops, probable superiority in fighter and short-range aircraft, submarines, and in certain phases of missile technology. The West had supremacy on the sea, in

bombers and transport aircraft, nuclear weapons, and perhaps in short-range guided missiles. The picture possessed all the earmarks of a military stand-off, with each side enjoying an advantage in some weapons and an inferiority in others. We shall have more to say presently about the consequences for the United States of what has been labelled the "balance of terror."

Variables in the Military Equation

Many imponderables complicate accurate calculations of comparative national power. What weight ought to be attached to such intangible, but absolutely fundamental, considerations as civilian and military morale on both sides? Are the Soviet satellite armies reliable, or for that matter is the Russian population itself prepared to support the communist hierarchy in the event of war with the West? While it would be foolish to count confidently upon widespread defection within the satellites and within Russia itself if war comes, it is nevertheless profitable to recall that this did occur when the German *Wehrmacht* entered Russia during World War II. Large numbers of Soviet citizens, especially ethnic minorities, defected, only to be repulsed by the brutal policies carried out against them by their Nazi conquerors.

The West of course is not free from morale problems, some of which could become critical in the event of a military showdown. How reliable are the NATO allies in the face of conflict between the United States and Russia, with the certain knowledge that Europe would be a major battleground and that America might be forced to rely upon widespread atomic devastation to "liberate" its allies from enemy control? Would alliances like CENTO and SEATO disintegrate when they were put to the test? Would many of the nation's far-flung bases be usable in areas where neutralist sentiment is strong? Might the United States be forced by world opinion to hold back its nuclear air power in meeting localized Communist thrusts into the free world? Such questions inevitably enter into the West's response to Communist military power.

---

[*]Data on Soviet and American missile strength are taken from **32**, January 18 and 25, February 8, and April 5, 1959, dispatches by Hanson W. Baldwin; from **6**, February 3, 4, and 5, 1959, dispatches by Robert R. Brunn; and **31**, February 14, 1959, dispatch by the military analyst S. L. A. Marshall.

216

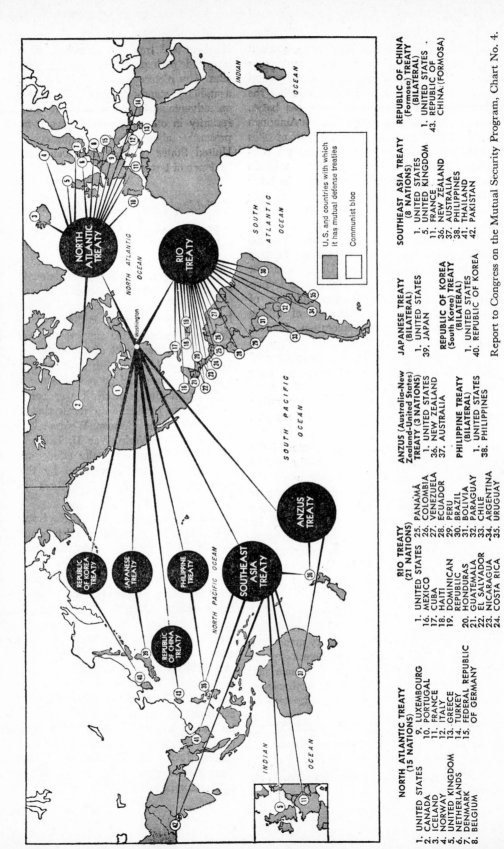

UNITED STATES COLLECTIVE DEFENSE ARRANGEMENTS

NORTH ATLANTIC TREATY (15 NATIONS)
1. UNITED STATES
2. CANADA
3. ICELAND
4. NORWAY
5. UNITED KINGDOM
6. NETHERLANDS
7. DENMARK
8. BELGIUM
9. LUXEMBOURG
10. PORTUGAL
11. FRANCE
12. ITALY
13. GREECE
14. TURKEY
15. FEDERAL REPUBLIC OF GERMANY

RIO TREATY (21 NATIONS)
1. UNITED STATES
16. MEXICO
17. CUBA
18. HAITI
19. DOMINICAN REPUBLIC
20. HONDURAS
21. GUATEMALA
22. EL SALVADOR
23. NICARAGUA
24. COSTA RICA
25. PANAMA
26. COLOMBIA
27. VENEZUELA
28. ECUADOR
29. PERU
30. BRAZIL
31. BOLIVIA
32. PARAGUAY
33. CHILE
34. ARGENTINA
35. URUGUAY

ANZUS (Australia-New Zealand-United States) TREATY (3 NATIONS)
1. UNITED STATES
36. NEW ZEALAND
37. AUSTRALIA

PHILIPPINE TREATY (BILATERAL)
1. UNITED STATES
38. PHILIPPINES

JAPANESE TREATY (BILATERAL)
1. UNITED STATES
39. JAPAN

REPUBLIC OF KOREA (South Korea) TREATY (BILATERAL)
1. UNITED STATES
40. REPUBLIC OF KOREA

SOUTHEAST ASIA TREATY (8 NATIONS)
1. UNITED STATES
5. UNITED KINGDOM
11. FRANCE
36. NEW ZEALAND
37. AUSTRALIA
38. PHILIPPINES
41. THAILAND
42. PAKISTAN

REPUBLIC OF CHINA (Formosa) TREATY (BILATERAL)
1. UNITED STATES
43. REPUBLIC OF CHINA (FORMOSA)

Report to Congress on the Mutual Security Program, Chart No. 4.

U. S. and countries with which it has mutual defense treaties

Communist bloc

It is an axiom of international politics that the effectiveness of a nation's or coalition's power will be heavily determined by the kind of situation toward which it is directed and by the circumstances prevailing at the time of its application. Quite obviously the Kremlin possesses an enormous initial advantage in case of a global nuclear war because of its ability to launch a surprise attack against its enemies. This advantage might well prove crucial at least in the early stages of a global conflict. Save perhaps by perfecting its defenses and warning systems, there appears no way for the West to overcome this advantage without departing from every precept of its ideology and its traditional foreign policy principles. One avenue that may offer hope lies in agreement on techniques for preventing surprise attacks. Yet as Field Marshall Viscount Montgomery has said, after the initial blow, "the advantage will go to that side which has the greater defensive strength, which can protect itself against attack, and can survive to strike back" (**29**, p. 105). All things considered, the free world coalition, relying upon the great productive capacities of the United States and Western Europe, could be expected to recover from the initial shock and to recapture its economic and military strength more rapidly than the communist bloc.

The Nuclear Balance of Terror

The steady accretion of Soviet atomic and hydrogen weapons, accompanied by demonstrated progress in producing missile delivery systems, has brought about a global balance of terror. Nuclear parity, by which is meant the ability of each side to devastate the other, will in all probability mean that future military conflicts will be decided by conventional weapons. If nuclear weapons from the arsenal of both sides cancel each other out, how then do the military positions of both camps compare? If the free world is denied use of its most powerful striking force—the American Strategic Air Command, together with missiles carrying nuclear warheads—this fact places it at a decisive military disadvantage in certain kinds of conflicts.

General Matthew B. Ridgway, former Army Chief of Staff, has summarized the military obligations of the United States, as head of the free world coalition, as follows:* to meet force with force; to "be prepared to meet and defeat limited aggression in small perimeter wars, whether or not nuclear weapons are used;" and to be able to defeat the USSR and its satellites "if general war should occur. . . . " General Ridgway informed the Defense Department in 1955 that "In my view, the present United States military forces are inadequate in strength and improperly proportioned to meet the above commitments . . . " (**14**, p. 144). This inadequacy arose chiefly out of one condition: lack of a strong mobile force, properly trained and equipped to meet Communist ground thrusts around the perimeter of the free world (**14**, pp. 144-45).

As long as its military power was concentrated chiefly in the Strategic Air Command and supplementary missile units, and secondarily in seapower, the dilemma confronting the free world coalition led by the United States would be: in the light of the alignment of military forces on both sides of the Iron Curtain, it (1) could seek to meet localized Communist aggression where it occurred on the basis of almost certain military inferiority; or it (2) could bring its overwhelming strategic air and missile power into play to meet Communist threats, thereby precipitating the third world war. Diplomatically, these two alternatives reduced themselves to settling for a negotiated peace, perhaps a *status quo ante bellum* as in Korea, or a disadvantageous settlement as in Indochina. Or by relying upon nuclear devastation, the United States could seek the complete elimination of the Soviet Union as a great power in world politics. Both of these alternatives have serious drawbacks. Nuclear war jeopardizes the future of civilization itself. Negotiated settlements on the basis

*The problem of relative communist and non-communist military power in an age of nuclear parity is cogently and succinctly discussed in General Ridgway's memorandum to the Defense Department of June 27, 1955, reprinted in full in **14**, pp. 141-48.

This problem has also come to engage the attention of academic and non-academic commentators. For two provocative and comprehensive treatments, see **26** and **35**.

of Western military inferiority risk having the defenses of the free world eroded and nibbled away by repeated localized Communist incursions. The clear inferiority of the West in conventional armaments therefore has almost compelled the United States to choose between two equally disastrous courses: localized appeasement and surrender or a worldwide nuclear holocaust.

To remedy this imbalance between the military might of the free world and the communist empire in localized conflicts, two basic steps at least are necessary. First, public opinion in the West generally, and in the United States specifically, will have to understand the fatal consequences of relying exclusively upon strategic airpower and nuclear weapons for dealing with international conflicts.

The public must reject the view that "in war there is no substitute for victory" because a desire for *total* victory and unconditional surrender of the enemy tends to expand even minor wars into global conflagrations. Second, the imbalance cannot be corrected without significant changes in the composition of the military forces of the West. Unless it is prepared to accept repeated Communist victories in localized engagements, the West, chiefly the United States, must expand its capacity to repulse such threats with conventional weapons. This of course means principally ground forces, supported by tactical air power. Without a reorientation in the Western defense effort to bring such forces into existence, the communist world will inevitably enjoy a formidable advantage in limited wars.

REFERENCES

1. Barghoorn, Frederick C. *Soviet Russian Nationalism.* New York: Oxford University Press, 1956. A leading student evaluates the interaction between communist ideology and Russian nationalism, emphasizing how each reinforces the other.

2. Brodie, Bernard. "The Anatomy of Deterrence," *World Politics,* 11 (January, 1959), pp. 173-92. A critical evaluation of the American strategy of deterrence, emphasizing the degree to which the United States might be more reluctant to initiate total war than would the USSR.

3. Byrnes, James F. *Speaking Frankly.* New York: Harper and Brothers, 1947. A first-hand account of Soviet-American relations in the immediate postwar era.

4. Carney, Admiral Robert B. "Principles of Sea Power," *Military Review,* 35 (February, 1956), pp. 3-17. Discusses increases in Soviet seapower and their consequences for the free world.

5. *Chicago Daily News.*

6. *Christian Science Monitor.*

7. Cressey, George B. *How Strong is Russia?* Syracuse: Syracuse University Press, 1954. Analyzes underlying geographic factors in the Soviet power position.

8. Department of State. *American Foreign Policy, 1950-55.* (Publication No. 6446, "General Foreign Policy Series," 117). Washington, 1957. An invaluable collection of documentary materials on American foreign policy.

9. ———. *Communist Perspective.* Division of Research for USSR and Eastern Europe, Office of Intelligence Research, 1955.

10. Djilas, Milovan. *The New Class: An Analysis of the Communist System.* New York: Frederick A. Praeger, 1957. A trenchant indictment of communism by a former high-ranking Yugoslav Communist.

11. Donovan, Robert J. *Eisenhower: The Inside Story.* New York: Harper and Brothers, 1956.

12. Fenno, Richard F. *The Yalta Conference.* Boston: D. C. Heath and Company, 1955. A collection of interpretive essays on the Yalta Conference.

13. Fisher, Marguerite J. *Communist Doctrine and the Free World.* Syracuse, N. Y.: Syracuse University Press, 1952.

14. Furniss, Edgar S. *American Military Policy.* New York: Rinehart and Company, 1957. Contains primary and secondary source materials on American defense policy.

15. Glabisz, General Kazimierz. "The Human Balance Sheet," *Military Review,* 35 (January, 1956), pp. 16-25. A comparative study of resources available to the communist and noncommunist worlds.

16. Haines, C. Grove, ed. *The Threat of Soviet Imperialism,* Baltimore: The Johns Hopkins Press, 1954.

17. Halle, Louis J. *Civilization and Foreign Policy.* New York: Harper and Brothers, 1955. This study by a former State Department official contains many helpful insights into contemporary American foreign relations.

18. Hammer, T. "The Geopolitical Basis of Modern War," *Military Review*, 35 (October, 1956), pp. 75-82. Analyzes the relation of geopolitical factors to the cold war.

19. Historicus. "Stalin on Revolution," *Foreign Affairs*, 28 (January, 1949), pp. 175-214.

20. Hook, Sydney. *Marx and the Marxists*. Princeton: D. Van Nostrand Company, 1955.

21. Hoopes, Townsend. "Overseas Bases in American Strategy," *Foreign Affairs*, 37 (October, 1958), pp. 69-83. Evaluates the importance of foreign bases in making the American doctrine of deterrence effective.

22. Hunt, R. N. Carew. *A Guide to Communist Jargon*. New York: The Macmillan Company, 1957. A valuable guide, in brief compass, to leading concepts in communist ideology, highlighting the evolution of these concepts to explain realities confronting the USSR.

23. ———. *The Theory and Practice of Communism*. London: Geoffrey Bles, 1957. A short but good critical evaluation of communism.

24. Huszar, George B., and Associates. *Soviet Power and Policy*. New York: Thomas Y. Crowell, 1955.

25. Kelsen, Hans. *The Political Theory of Bolshevism*. Berkeley: University of California Press, 1948. Another helpful commentary on communist ideology.

26. Kissinger, Henry A. *Nuclear Weapons and Foreign Policy*. New York: Harper and Brothers, 1957.

27. Leites, Nathan. *A Study of Bolshevism*. Glencoe, Illinois: The Free Press, 1953.

28. LeRossignoi, James E. *From Marx to Stalin*. New York: Thomas Y. Crowell, 1940. Analyzes the evolution of communist thought, bringing out significant changes in ideology under successive Russian leaders.

29. Montgomery, Field Marshall Viscount Bernard. "A Look at World War III," *Military Review*, 35 (June, 1955), pp. 99-109. A distinguished Western military leader analyzes the military position of the free world.

30. Moore, Barrington, Jr. *Soviet Politics—the Dilemma of Power*. Cambridge: Harvard University Press, 1950. An illuminating study, focusing on how internal and external pressures have affected the character of the Soviet regime.

31. New York *Herald Tribune*.

32. *New York Times*.

33. Niemeyer, Gerhart. *An Inquiry Into Soviet Mentality*. New York: Frederick A. Praeger, 1956. An illuminating analysis of the role of ideology in Soviet Russia. Attempts to lay down guidelines for predicting Soviet behavior.

34. Osgood, Robert E. *Limited War: The Challenge to American Strategy*. Chicago: University of Chicago Press, 1957. Assesses the extent to which the United States is prepared to fight limited wars.

35. Roberts, Henry L. *Russia and America*. New York: Harper and Brothers, 1956. This work analyzes outstanding issues in the cold war and weighs alternative policies for the United States.

36. Robinett, General Paul M. "Survey of the Land Routes into the Soviet Union," *Military Review*, 35 (August, 1955), pp. 6-12. Emphasizes important geographical factors that will influence any future war between the communist and non-communist nations.

37. Senate Foreign Relations Committee. *Control and Reduction of Armaments*, Staff Study No. 8, 85th Congress, 1st Session, 1957. Washington: 1957. Contains much valuable data on Soviet policies toward Eastern Europe historically and in recent years.

38. Shepley, James. "How Dulles Averted War," *Life Magazine*, January 16, 1956, pp. 70-80.

39. Simmons, Ernest J., ed. *Continuity and Change in Russian and Soviet Thought*. Cambridge, Mass.: Harvard University Press, 1955.

40. Snell, John L. *The Meaning of Yalta*. Baton Rouge: Louisiana State University Press, 1956. Probably the best account so far of the meaning and significance of the Yalta Conference.

41. Sokol, Anthony E. "Naval Aspects of European Integration," *Military Review*, 35 (June, 1955), pp. 26-36.

42. "Soviet Strength in the Baltic Area," *Military Review*, 36 (February, 1957), pp. 95-101. Calls attention forcefully to the implications of Soviet naval might.

43. Stettinius, Edward R. *Roosevelt and the Russians—The Yalta Conference*. Garden City, N. Y.: Doubleday and Company, 1949. A first-hand account of the Yalta Conference by a former Secretary of State.

44. Strausz-Hupé, Robert. "Nuclear Blackmail and Limited War," *Yale Review*, 48 (Winter, 1959), pp. 174-81. A highly critical analysis of the possibility of America's acceptance of the concept of limited war.

45. Tomasic, Dinko. *The Impact of Russian Culture on Soviet Communism*. Glencoe, Illinois: The Free Press, 1953. Discusses the interaction between Russian culture and communist ideology.

46. Toynbee, Arnold J. *Civilization on Trial*. New York: Oxford University Press, 1948. In chapter 9, a distinguished historian deals with forces that animate Russian policies, stressing the continuity with pre-Soviet history.

47. United States Information Agency. *Soviet World Outlook.* Washington, D. C.: 1954. This is a revised volume of a work published under the same title in 1950, bringing together quotations from leading communist thinkers on a variety of themes.

48. *United States News and World Report,* 44 (February 28, 1958), pp. 105-07. Contains the text of President Eisenhower's letter to Premier Bulganin on a proposed great power conference.

49. Vandenberg, Arthur H., Jr., ed. *The Private Papers of Senator Vandenberg.* Boston: Houghton Mifflin Company, 1952.

50. Vassiliev, M. F. "The Soviet Force Cuts," *Military Review,* 36 (February, 1957), pp. 101-03.

51. Wein, Otto. "Transportation as a Strategic and Economic Problem of the Soviet Union," *Military Review,* 36 (April, 1956), pp. 75-89. Concludes that transportation problems would greatly weaken the USSR in the event of war.

52. White, Theodore H. "The Challenge of Soviet Economic Growth," *The Reporter,* 8 (May 26, 1953), pp. 9-14. A provocative, though sometimes uncritical, assessment of the economic future of the Soviet Union.

53. Wiles, Peter. "The Soviet Economy Outpaces the West," *Foreign Affairs,* 31 (July, 1953), pp. 566-80. Clearly outlines the challenge of Soviet economic expansion on the basis of past performance.

54. Wolfe, Bertram D. *Khrushchev and Stalin's Ghost.* New York: Frederick A. Praeger, 1957. Deals with events in Russia after the death of Stalin.

55. X. [George F. Kennan] "The Sources of Soviet Conduct," *Foreign Affairs,* 25 (July, 1947), pp. 566-83.

CHAPTER 10

Western Europe

The New World and the Old

Here we begin a series of chapters devoted to concrete problems in recent American foreign policy. In each case our emphasis will be upon aspects of American relations that have proved to be major continuing problems since the United States assumed the leadership of the free world coalition after the Second World War. Our approach will therefore be topical-analytical instead of narrative-chronological. Sufficient background will be presented to enable the reader to put present-day issues into the necessary historical perspective; more than that we cannot do without departing materially from our purpose of focusing on principles, problems, and prospects of American foreign policy in the nuclear age.

A Century of the Monroe Doctrine

No better illustration can be found of the revolution in American foreign policy brought about by the Second World War than the relationships that evolved between the United States and Western Europe in the postwar era. With the signing of the North Atlantic Treaty in 1949, the United States intertwined its own security inextricably with that of its Western European allies—thereby finally reversing the principles that had governed American relationships with Europe for nearly a century and a quarter.

From the earliest days of the Republic, the United States has conceived of itself as a new and unique nation whose appointed mission required it to stand aloof from the quarrels and vicissitudes of the Old World. Geography separated the two worlds by thousands of miles of ocean; the American Revolution signified a spiritual-ideological breach. For well over a century thereafter, Americans were primarily concerned with domestic problems and challenges, especially expansion across the Continent. George Washington had sounded the keynote of the American outlook in his Farewell Address in 1796, when he declared that "Europe has a set of primary interests, which to us have none or a very remote relation." This view was also supported by Thomas Jefferson, who stated in 1813 that "The European nations constitute a separate division of the globe; their localities make them a part of a distinct system; they have a set of interests of their own in which it is our business never to engage ourselves." America, on the other hand, "has a hemisphere to itself. It must have its separate system of interests; which must not be subordinated to those of Europe . . . " (**27,** p. 168).

Thus when President Monroe delivered his classic message to Congress in 1823 he was adding very little to the position already taken by the United States in regard to European affairs since Independence. The key thought expressed by the Monroe Doctrine with respect to Europe,* was that "In the wars of European powers in matters relating to themselves we have never taken any part, nor does it comport with our policy so to do. It is only when our rights are invaded or seriously menaced that we resent injuries or make preparation for our defense." Warning the Holy Alliance to stay out of American affairs, Monroe stated "that we should consider any attempt on their part to extend their system to any portion of this hemisphere as dangerous to our peace and safety. With the existing colonies or dependencies of any European power we have not interfered and shall not interfere" (**27,** p. 169).

At the time neither the United States nor Europe was conscious that Monroe was enunciating a principle of American foreign policy that would apply for over a hundred years thereafter. The influences that prompted Monroe's speech were two-fold: threatened intervention by the Holy Alliance to return the newly-independent states of Latin America to Spain and machinations of Czarist Russia in the Northwest, climaxed by the Imperial ukase of 1821 which virtually proclaimed the Pacific Northwest a Russian sphere of influence (**27,** pp. 169-73). The Monroe Doctrine had been America's response to these two threats. Over the course of time it became the most famous principle of American foreign policy.

However, the self-abnegation pledge that the United States would not interfere in European affairs was not nearly so sweeping as is sometimes supposed. Monroe pledged only non-

---

*The Monroe Doctrine had two aspects one governing America's relations with Europe, the other governing Europe's relations with the Western Hemisphere. While the first aspect remained relatively unchanged for over a century, except of course for the First World War, the other was subject to numerous amendments and modifications in the years that followed 1823. The Western Hemispheric applications of the Monroe Doctrine are discussed in Chapter 12.

interference in "the wars of the European powers in matters relating to themselves. . . . " Thus the Monroe Doctrine from its inception applied only (1) to Europe's *wars* and (2) those wars that were *exclusively of European concern.*

Although President Monroe was not conscious of laying down a precept that would bind American foreign policy-makers through successive decades, the Monroe Doctrine's stipulations relating to America's relationships with Europe in fact became the guiding principles of American foreign policy until the Truman Doctrine was proclaimed in 1947. There were of course a number of exceptions to noninterference in Europe, notably America's participation in the First and Second World Wars. But even these examples can be deemed compatible with the Monroe Doctrine since in both cases American vital interests were very much involved in these European conflicts. German submarines forced the United States into World War I. The Japanese attack on Pearl Harbor, followed by the German declaration of war against the United States, compelled our entry into World War II. It is significant that all through World War II the United States believed that the greatest threat to its own security emanated *from Europe;* hence American policy-makers consistently gave a higher priority to the European theater of war than they did to the Pacific theater.

For nearly a hundred years after 1823, American involvement in the politics of Europe was episodic and transitory. Woodrow Wilson's ill-fated attempt to reorient American foreign policy around the principle of "collective security" is too well known to require elaboration here. Senate rejection of the League of Nations graphically reaffirmed American isolationist attitudes toward Europe. America did not officially participate in the League's activities, although it sent unofficial "observers" to attend League deliberations, and co-operated on a limited scale with a number of the League's social and humanitarian activities (**27,** pp. 527-28). Prolonged vacillation by the Senate in considering American membership in the World Court constituted further evidence of isolationist tendencies, with the World Court proposal being finally rejected by the Senate in 1935. (**12**, *passim;* **27**, p. 533). Then during the 1930's isolationism made the population insensitive to the most elementary facts concerning the nation's security and the security of the North Atlantic region with which America's destiny was increasingly linked. "Aid short of war" was the most that the American people would support—and sometimes there was very little public support even for this—prior to the Japanese attack of Pearl Harbor in 1941.

Prerequisites of an Isolationist Policy

For almost a hundred years isolationism accorded both with the desires of the American people and with existing geographic-diplomatic realities, although by the turn of the century many of these realities were beginning to change. At first, few Americans were aware of these changes—if indeed they are altogether aware of some of them today—preferring as late as the 1930's to cling to old ways long after conditions had passed that had made traditional habits of thought and policies possible. Isolationism was finally abandoned as the policy of the United States, not willfully, but as an inescapable reaction to the facts of international life in the postwar nuclear age, and more specifically a reaction to the inescapable challenge posed by the Soviet threat. Yet, even in the postwar period numerous Americans fail to understand why isolationism has been possible historically and why it is an untenable policy today.

Three conditions made possible America's historic withdrawal from the political affairs of the old world. These conditions have either disappeared altogether today or else they have so changed as to make an isolationist course by the United States nothing short of suicidal. What were these conditions?

(1) *America was geographically isolated from the world.* This fact, as much as any other, explains America's ability for over a hundred years to stay out of great power conflicts in Europe and to a lesser degree in Asia. America could follow isolationism as a policy because the United States was separated from the storm centers of diplomatic controversy by formidable geographical barriers. Thousands of miles of ocean cut America off from Europe

and Asia; the polar ice-cap and northern Canadian wastelands posed an impenetrable obstacle to the north; no threat could come from the weak, unstable governments that existed in Latin America. In the modern period, annihilation of distance by the fast ocean liner, the submarine, radio and telephone, and finally the jet airplane and supersonic missile has eliminated the geographical fact of isolation from the outside world. Within minutes destruction could be rained on American cities by a potential aggressor; and, conversely, American retaliatory power could be launched speedily against an enemy. Isolationism will not suffice as a policy, therefore, because isolation is no longer a reality.

(2) *Europe's diplomatic troubles were America's well-being.* The United States was also fortunate that suspicion and rivalry among the great powers of Europe prevented them from uniting behind an anti-American policy. As a rule, the United States had only one thing to fear from the Old World: a new grand coalition that might arise to despoil the young nation and to jeopardize its continued independence. Occasionally this danger appeared imminent, as illustrated by the Holy Alliance's threatened intervention in Latin America in the early 1820's. In the main, however, European countries could never subordinate their differences sufficiently to collaborate against the United States. Repeated diplomatic conflicts on the Continent during the 19th century—occasioned by Russia's several attempts to penetrate the Near East, France's efforts to re-establish its former position of greatness, countless nationalistic rebellions against entrenched autocracies, Bismarck's determination to make Germany a great power —kept the great powers in an almost constant state of diplomatic ferment and intensified existing hostilities. Europe's infrequent incursions into Western hemispheric affairs—such as French intervention in Mexico during the Civil War—produced controversies among the European states themselves, out of fear that one country would increase its power over the others. Meantime, on the Continent age-old jealousies and antagonisms made European countries reluctant to embark upon expansionist policies in the Western Hemisphere, so long as

the fear existed that the first danger to their security lay in Europe.

Continuance of this state of affairs in turn depended on several factors: the existence of a number of European states, roughly equal in power; determination by these states to fight wars for limited ends, in contrast to the doctrine of "total wars," followed by the principle of "unconditional surrender," that has been one factor making a balance of power inoperative in more recent years; recognition by the states of Europe that preservation of the balance of power system was in the best interests of all concerned. These conditions do not obtain in the contemporary age. They were destroyed by a combination of the First World War, the imperialistic ambitions of Hitler and Mussolini, the Second World War, the wartime and post-World War II policies of the USSR, independence movements in former colonial areas, the injection of ideological considerations into world politics on a far greater scale than in the 19th century—all contributing to the decline of Britain, Germany, and Italy as great powers on the European scene and militating against re-institution of a balance of power system comparable to that prevailing earlier.

(3) *American security was protected by the Pax Britannica and the subsequent Anglo-American entente.* The 19th century was the age of *Pax Britannica*—unquestionably one of the most stable and benign eras known to the history of international relations. Britain ruled the seas. Utilizing strategic bases in its scattered colonies, it intervened repeatedly to put down threats to international peace and order, whether they came from the diplomatic intrigues of Russia in the Near East, or Germany in Persia, or the Holy Alliance in Latin America. For more than a century after independence, the American people were suspicious of Great Britain, believing firmly that Downing Street harbored territorial ambitions on the American continent and, in more general terms, that it sought to frustrate American diplomatic goals. This frame of mind persisted until around 1900.

Actually, in spite of this prevailing antagonism toward Britain, a fundamental identity of interests lay beneath the surface of Anglo-American relations throughout most of the 19th century. Historians are agreed that British acceptance of the principles of the Monroe Doctrine—at least those parts relating to European activities in the Western Hemisphere—largely explains whatever success the doctrine achieved for several decades after 1823 in realizing American diplomatic objectives. Britain was perhaps even more concerned than America about the possibility of other great powers' establishing a strong position in Latin America, thereby enhancing their capacity to jeopardize British sea communications and trade routes. Britain could accept the idea, therefore, that this hemisphere was a special preserve of the United States—a country that possessed no navy worth mentioning and that harbored no expansive tendencies that would be at British expense.

Until about 1900 Americans rarely perceived the relationship between their own security and British power. After that date, however, both countries began openly to acknowledge their mutual interests. Britain feared the growing naval might and imperialist ambitions of Germany and Japan. The age-old imperialistic objectives of Czarist Russia threatened more than ever to infringe upon British colonial and trade interests in the Far East. America, although beginning to expand its navy, had few imperialistic designs that clashed with those of Great Britain. As maritime and trading countries, both nations shared a desire to preserve freedom of the seas and unimpeded access to world markets. Ideological affinity provided another link in the chain of Anglo-American co-operation. British support of the Open Door policy in China at the turn of the century and negotiation of the Hay-Pauncefote Treaty in 1901, preparing the way for American construction of the Panama Canal, signified the new official harmony that now characterized Anglo-American relations.

Nevertheless, it could not be said that American citizens as a whole understood the crucial role of this entente in preserving their security. Periodically, vocal citizens groups "twisted the lion's tail" and railed against the alleged evils of the British Empire. Anglophobia abated during World War I, but in the era of "normalcy" and isolation that followed the war, a majority of Americans appeared to be ignorant of the part played by Anglo-American co-operation in defending the vital interests of the United States. The "inarticulate major premise" of American foreign policy after 1900 has been the assumption that Great Britain and the United States are friends and that in an overwhelming majority of cases their diplomatic objectives are complementary, rather than antagonistic. Britain's dramatic decline as a great power after World War II, a process that actually began with World War I, drove home to Americans as never before how vital for international peace and stability had been Britain's former role as protector of the balance of power in Western Europe and chief

defender against Russian expansion across the frontiers of Europe, the Middle East, and Asia. Moreover, as America discovered painfully in the turbulent postwar period, in its colonial affairs Britain had contributed to international stability through its policies of preparing dependent peoples for orderly and enlightened self-government.

For nearly a century the United States enjoyed the benefits of *Pax Britannica*. In the postwar years the roles became reversed. Now it was Great Britain that was protected by a *Pax Americana* whose aims differed in few material respects from Britain's efforts to enforce the peace during the 19th century.

1. CONTAINMENT, RECOVERY, AND REARMAMENT

The Origins of Containment

By 1947 the Monroe Doctrine had been superseded by the Truman Doctrine's principle of containment as the guiding rule of America's relationship to Europe. Reduced to its essentials, the new policy anticipated firm and sustained American resistance to Soviet expansionist tendencies. Containment received its most persuasive justification at the hands of George F. Kennan, a high-ranking State Department official and recognized authority on Soviet Russia. In a widely-circulated article on "The Sources of Soviet Conduct" (37), Kennan enunciated the containment idea as America's response to the challenge of Soviet expansionism and hostility toward non-communist countries. The immediate postwar period had witnessed Soviet hegemony over Eastern Europe, communist intrigue in such countries as Iran, Turkey, Greece, Indochina, and China, as well as Soviet intransigence on such questions as disarmament and control of nuclear weapons. By 1947 it had become apparent on all sides that the wartime policy of great power collaboration had collapsed.

It was Kennan's belief, sharply challenged by other leading students of international politics (19), that successful implementation of the containment idea would not only prevent further Soviet incursions into the non-communist world but would also in time bring about a "mellowing" in the Kremlin's attitudes and

policies toward the outside world, possibly aiding the emergence of a less despotic, less xenophobic political order within the USSR.

Containment received its first application in the Greek-Turkish Aid Program of 1947 After that, came the Marshall Plan, the North Atlantic Pact, the Mutual Defense Assistance Program, and the Mutual Security Program. Hand-in-hand with these developments went efforts by the United States to encourage greater economic, military, and political integration on the Continent of Europe. All of these were manifestations of the containment idea, because the major impetus in each case was the threat to the security of the North Atlantic community posed by the expansionist policies and impressive military power of the communist bloc. Whatever specific forms America's relations with Western Europe in the postwar period might take, one goal remained uppermost: to make the North Atlantic area as impregnable as possible against threats to its security emanating from behind the Iron Curtain, irrespective of whether they came from a threatened Soviet military attack or communist intrigue in the political affairs of Western Europe.

European officials in the main shared Washington's assessment of the communist threat; but to their minds there were perhaps even more compelling reasons for co-operating with the United States to rebuild Europe's devastated economies, strengthen its defenses, and initiate movements aimed at transcending deeply-entrenched nationalistic tendencies on the Continent. One was to impart a feeling of greater security among Europe's citizens. Another was to lessen dependence upon the United States, a dependence which, in Europe's weakened position, was both inevitable and widely resented. Still another was ultimately to recreate Western Europe as a powerful independent force in world affairs. Throughout the postwar era the viewpoint has gained adherence among leaders on the Continent that the countries of Europe must forsake ancient nationalistic bickerings and pool their energies and resources if Western Europe is ever again to play the decisive role in international politics witnessed in earlier eras of modern history.

In examining these developments, our study will focus on four dominant problems in postwar American foreign policy toward Europe. These are: European economic recovery and rearmament; economic unification movements; defense and military collaboration within the North Atlantic region; and movements directed at the political unification of Europe.

The Greek-Turkish Aid Program

In an historic foreign policy address on March 12, 1947, President Truman declared that "it must be the policy of the United States to support free people who are resisting subjection by armed minorities or outside pressures" (6, pp. 1980-81). Truman's address was prompted by the crisis in Greece, where Communist-led rebels were seeking to overthrow the legitimate government. For almost two years British troops had supported the Greek government's effort to restore stability. But Britain was near bankruptcy. Some liquidation of British overseas commitments therefore became imperative, leaving the United States the alternative of either assuming many of these commitments or accepting further Communist intrusions into the free world. The situation in Greece took on added urgency because at long last Russia appeared on the verge of achieving its age-old desire to break through into the Mediterranean area.

President Truman consequently asked Congress for an appropriation of $400 million to resist communist expansionism in Greece and to bolster the defenses of near-by Turkey, which had also experienced intermittent Soviet pressures during and since World War II. After prolonged study Congress granted this request in May, thereby establishing the pattern of economic-military aid to countries struggling against Communist aggression. Such aid was to become a permanent feature of American foreign policy in the contemporary period. Along with Yugoslavia's later defection from the Soviet bloc, American economic and military aid proved to be of crucial importance in preserving the political independence of Greece and assuring its continued adherence to the free world alliance.

The European Recovery Program

Even before Congress had approved the Greek-Turkish Aid bill, the Truman Administration had begun studies of Western Europe's progressively critical economic plight. Wartime and early postwar relief programs like the United Nations Relief and Rehabilitation Administration (UNRRA) had done little or nothing to eliminate the causes of economic instability in Europe. By mid-1947 widespread economic distress, bringing in its wake political turbulence, impended in Europe. In a major foreign policy speech on June 5, 1947, Secretary of State George C. Marshall took note of Europe's crisis and suggested that America would be prepared to extend long-range economic assistance, provided Europe took the lead in presenting a carefully worked out plan for utilizing American assistance to promote lasting regional recovery. Europe was quick to respond. Even Soviet Russia and its satellites expressed an interest in participating in the Marshall Plan. By midsummer, however, communist propaganda organs had begun to denounce the Marshall Plan as an instrument of American imperialism. Neither Russia nor its satellites participated in the discussions that finally resulted in the presentation of a concrete program to the State Department. Lacking access to the Kremlin's archives, no Westerner can be certain of the reason behind Moscow's

AMERICAN ECONOMIC ASSISTANCE TO EUROPE

In Millions of U.S. Dollars

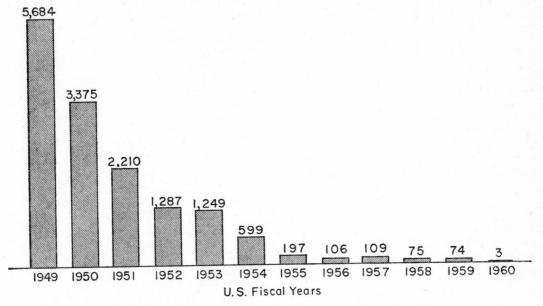

U. S. Fiscal Years

Adapted from Dept. of State, etc., *Mutual Security Program, 1959,* p. 67

refusal to participate in the Marshall Plan. No bars originally existed against Russia's association with the plan, although as time passed the program came more and more to be presented to Congress and the American public as an anti-communist measure. Several hypotheses may be suggested. Russia was apparently unwilling to accept any "conditions" for the use of American aid, particularly any that would involve extensive American "supervision" of its administration. Moreover, in the light of an increasingly anti-Soviet attitude within the United States and especially in Congress, Russia may have actually feared an expansion in American influence in the sensitive Eastern European satellite zone. Several countries in this area had expressed keen interest in participating in the Marshall Plan. Czechoslovakia, for instance, appeared highly enthusiastic about the prospect of American assistance. If extensive American aid to Eastern European countries led to significant progress in rehabilitating these countries, American prestige would be greatly enhanced to the detriment of Soviet influence. Ideological considerations

may also have colored Russia's decision. The Kremlin may have thought that long-awaited revolutionary forces could work more successfully in economically debilitated countries.

Whatever the reasons for the Kremlin's obduracy, it is apparent that Soviet refusal to join in the plan was a major blunder in Russia's postwar foreign policy. Perhaps more than any other factor, the Marshall Plan was responsible for the decline of communist influence in Western Europe after 1948. Initially there had appeared considerable opposition within the United States to so costly a measure. This opposition was largely overcome by presenting the plan to Congress as part of the "containment" strategy, a maneuver that would hardly have been possible had Soviet Russia been a participating country. Soviet participation, therefore, probably would have killed the Marshall Plan outright, or, at a minimum, sharply reduced its scope.

In accordance with American demands, the nations of Western Europe formed a regional association ultimately called the Organization for European Economic Cooperation (OEEC) to make exhaustive studies of the region's long-term needs and to draw up plans for using American assistance in the most effective way.* By mid-August OEEC had submitted a proposal calling for nearly $30 billion in American funds, an estimate that was eventually scaled down to $17 billion over a four-year period. By the end of the program, $12.5 billion had actually been appropriated by Congress for European recovery (4, p. 175).

The Marshall Plan officially came to an end in 1951. At the time of its expiration, there was no question but that it had largely achieved its basic purpose of rehabilitating the economic systems of the OEEC countries. By 1951 European production had either reached or exceeded prewar levels. Figuring 1947 as 100, the index of industrial output for major Western European countries and for the OEEC area as a whole showed the following prewar and postwar levels:

	1938	1947	May, 1951
Western Germany	295	100	334
France	105	100	148
United Kingdom	91	100	135
Western Europe	115	100	162

Progress was also impressive in the revival of European trade. By 1950 international trade had expanded by 11 per cent over prewar levels, with intra-European trade rising 25 per cent over the previous year (33, 1951, p. 219). This progress made it possible for the nations of Western Europe to contribute to their own defense on an expanded basis. In 1949 these countries were spending 5 per cent

*OEEC remained in existence after the Marshall Plan expired in 1951. In 1960 its members were Austria, Belgium, Denmark, France, the German Federal Republic, Greece, Iceland, Ireland, Italy, Luxembourg, Netherlands, Norway, Portugal, Sweden, Switzerland, Turkey, and the United Kingdom. The United States and Canada maintain an "informal association" with OEEC.

OEEC was Europe's organ for administering Marshall Plan funds. America's was the European Cooperation Administration (ECA), a semiautonomous body headed initially by Paul Hoffman, a prominent American businessman. Congress wanted the actual administration of European foreign assistance taken out of the State Department; yet it left ECA under State Department guidance for basic policy directives (34, pp. 388-92).

RUINING AN OLD NESTING PLACE

Justus in *The Minneapolis Star*, August, 1957.

of their Gross National Product, or $4.5 billion, on defense; by 1951-52 this had risen to 8 per cent of their GNP, or $9 billion (33, 1951, p. 353).

Deeply-rooted and vexatious economic and financial problems, however, remained by the end of 1951 and in the years thereafter. Many of these became especially troublesome as the emphasis in American foreign aid shifted from economic to military assistance and as the United States exerted greater diplomatic pressure upon its European allies to rearm.

The Shift to Military Aid

The change to military aid, for reasons to be discussed later, began in 1950 with the Mutual Defense Assistance Program. In 1952 economic, military, and technical assistance for underdeveloped countries were combined into a single program, known as the Mutual Security Program. In the years that followed, military-defense foreign aid was administered by the Defense Department. Economic and technical assistance was administered by the International Cooperation Administration (ICA), a semi-autonomous organ under the policy control of the State Department. MDAP and MSP, in conjunction with influence exerted by the United States through NATO, formal diplomatic channels and public opinion, resulted in a vast increase in Western Europe's defense efforts. By 1957 Europe was spending $13 billion on its own defense (17, Part V, p. 856). "Defense support,"* along with a significant improvement in the economic posture of Europe, had, according to a high-ranking State Department official, given the United States and its European allies a "7-to-2 lead over the Soviet Union and its satellites in industrial output" (17, Part V, p. 854).

Rearmament, however, had also generated formidable economic and financial problems for the European allies. Initially, officials of the European Cooperation Administration (ECA), had resisted efforts by American military spokesmen to divert Europe's productive facilities for military ends. OEEC countries themselves were reluctant to follow the ambitious rearmament pace proposed by military strategists within the United States, because of fears that this pace would destroy gains in economic recovery made thus far and would give rise to adverse economic tendencies within Europe. That these apprehensions were realistic was proved by events after 1950-51, when the burden of rearmament did indeed become onerous, generating both acute financial stresses within the OEEC countries and recurrent discord between the United States and its European allies. Consequently, in the 1952-53 period, there was a marked slowing down in the rate of the rearmament program. NATO had to adopt a "stretch out" schedule that postponed the creation of military units and bases the United States considered indispensable to the free world's defense. Beset with internal inflation, a growing disparity between imports and exports, and a public opin-

ion that was resisting further diversion of government revenues to military outlays, the countries of Europe demanded some relaxation in the proposed rearmament schedule (33, 1952, pp. 404-17; 33, 1953, pp. 153, 172).

American Assistance in Perspective

In 1958, a decade after inauguration of the Marshall Plan, the Mutual Security Program contemplated an expenditure of $4.4 billion, of which $2.4 billion was devoted to military assistance. Of this total, Europe was to receive $338,500,000, or a small fraction of the $13 billion being spent on defense by the European countries themselves. That American foreign assistance had achieved its most fundamental objective—creating within the North Atlantic community an economically healthy and well-equipped military complex—could hardly be questioned. Europe's recovery permitted the United States to divert the major share of its foreign assistance from Europe to the Middle East and Far East. In 1950, Europe had received some 79 per cent of American foreign assistance; by 1957, it was receiving only 10 per cent (17, Part V, p. 775).

How long would American aid to Europe have to continue? Asked this question in 1957 by the Senate Foreign Relations Committee, Secretary of State Dulles was unable to give a specific answer. The abiding objective, he stated was to "keep alive in these countries the hope and belief that they can lift up their economies without accepting the Communist alternative for doing so." Eventually, Europe and the other recipients of American assistance ought to be able to do this for themselves, but until that time came, assistance by the United States would have to continue (29, p. 404).

By the close of the 1950's, many groups within the United States were advocating a reduction in American foreign assistance, citing as arguments the mounting burden of taxation by all levels of government, the staggering national debt, and the persistence of unemployment in some regions of the country occasioned, it was charged, in part by competition from foreign goods. The White House found itself under intense pressure from Congress to cut the foreign aid provisions of the President's

---

*In 1957 Secretary of State Dulles told the Senate Foreign Relations Committee that "defense support" involved three elements: aid in terms of military equipment and supplies, or "end items"; support for the economic systems of non-communist countries to enable them to carry the burden of re-armament; and economic development programs to strengthen the military base of the free world alliance (29, p. 397).

budget. Spokesmen for the executive branch steadfastly maintained, however, that if the nation was to preserve its role of leadership in world affairs, foreign assistance now going mainly to the underdeveloped countries must be increased. It was still true, as it had been since World War II, that the chief beneficiaries of the billions of dollars loaned or granted to other countries were the American people. The recipient countries of course derived many benefits from such aid. But from the Greek-Turkish aid program onward, these programs had been formulated predominantly as part of America's response to the challenge of militant communism; their success was therefore America's own success in preserving its security and the security of its allies in the face of threats

posed by a resourceful diplomatic opponent. The observation of Assistant Secretary of State for European Affairs, C. Burke Elbrick, to the House Foreign Affairs Committee in 1957 has lost none of its validity in the intervening years:

> . . . if the mutual security program in Europe should be drastically reduced, it would mean that European defense efforts would be much smaller and far less productive . . . The only way we could compensate for this reduction would be to increase our own national defense expenditures by an amount several times greater than the amount of this program . . . the abandonment of our military assistance programs would not be an act of economy but an act of reckless extravagance. (17, Part V, 855).

2. EUROPEAN ECONOMIC INTEGRATION

The American Objective

As early as 1942, John Foster Dulles expressed the thoughts of many leading Americans when he stated that:

> Continental Europe has been the world's greatest fire hazard. This has long been recognized, but it has seemed impractical to do anything about it. Now the whole structure is consumed in flames. We condemn those who started and spread the fire. But this does not mean that, when the time comes to rebuild, we should reproduce a demonstrated firetrap. (8, I, p. 1442).

When the Senate was considering interim aid to Europe in 1947, Dulles told the Senate Foreign Relations Committee that the "basic idea should be, not the rebuilding of the prewar Europe, but the building of a new Europe, which, more unified, will be a better Europe" (8, I, p. 1442).

Consistently throughout the postwar period, the United States has encouraged the movements looking toward European unity or European integration. Congress in particular has been keenly interested in the progress of European integration and has not hesitated to express its viewpoints in legislation providing American assistance to Western Europe. Thus the Mutual Security Act of 1954 contained the following expression of Congressional sentiment:

> The Congress welcomes the recent progress in European cooperation and re-affirms the belief in the necessity of further efforts toward political federation, military integration, and economic unification as a means of building strength, establishing security, and preserving peace in the North Atlantic area. . . . the Congress believes it essential that this Act should be so administered as to support concrete measures to promote greater political federation, military integration, and economic unification in Europe. (30 p. 5).

Throughout the life of the Marshall Plan and in the foreign aid programs that superseded it, vocal minorities within Congress attempted repeatedly to make American assistance to Europe conditional upon greater progress in achieving economic unification on the Continent. In most instances such moves were defeated since coercion of our allies was usually opposed by the White House. But in 1950 Congress required the ECA Administrator to withhold $600 million in authorized funds, pending European agreement on the establishment of the European Payments Union (4, pp. 161-63).

Throughout the postwar period, America's support for the *idea* of European economic integration has remained more consistent than its conception of the precise forms such integration was expected to take and of the relationships that were to prevail among economic

MAKING WAY FOR A NEW SUPERMARKET

Burges Green in *The Providence Journal*, July, 1957.

unification movements on the Continent.* America's tendency has been to support *all* economic unification movements indiscriminately. Europe's response, deriving from the efforts of many of her own leaders to encourage

*The term European unification or integration possesses no very clearly defined content. The more specific term *economic* unification is also imprecise. According to Robert Marjolin, it contemplates "free circulation of goods, persons, and capital between the European countries," a "single tariff" for Europe, a "single currency with a single bank of issue, and a common budget. In a word, it would mean practically the creation of a single state." The term "European integration" is "any process which brings about a greater degree of unity" (13, p. 28).

A detailed study by the Brookings Institution of American assistance to Europe holds that the United States never possessed a clear conception of what it meant by European unification or integration, "except for references to the benefits derived by the United States from the possession of a single large domestic market, which could be interpreted as implying that Europe should copy the American model" (4, p. 162).

unification throughout history and, in the more recent period, from insistent American demands, have produced supra-national economic institutions which are a curious amalgam of high idealism, opportunism, and sweeping compromises. The consequence is that today a crazy-quilt pattern of supra-national organizations has been imposed upon the national economies of Europe. Each of these organizations in itself has a complex structure. Collectively, they are interlocked and mutually dependent. Adding to the complexity of the problem are the relationships prevailing between institutions in the economic field and those established to promote co-operation among European countries in the military and political spheres. Comprehensive treatment of individual organizations, and of relationships among them, must be left for other writers (4, pp. 270-315, 471-505; 13, *passim*; 20, pp. 409-534; 31, *passim*).

Forms of Economic Integration

One long-standing obstacle to greater economic co-operation among the nations of Europe until the postwar period was the existence of numerous national trade barriers and excessive customs duties. A customs union embracing Belgium, the Netherlands, and Luxembourg was established in 1944, but it accomplished little in the years immediately following its establishment. Several studies of customs barriers within Europe took place in 1947-48. At that time obstacles in the path of a European-wide customs union appeared insuperable. The most that could then realistically be expected was a sub-regional approach. Consequently, the Benelux countries revived their customs union. The Benelux nations looked forward ultimately to a complete economic merger, but this ambitious scheme has been repeatedly postponed. A second European customs union modeled somewhat after Benelux was established between France and Italy in 1949 (4, p. 274-5). Many of the goals implicit in the customs union were incorporated in the European Common Market, which began operations in 1959.

A second approach to European economic integration was through co-operative planning by OEEC, the organ that had been established by Western Europe at the time of the Marshall Plan. The Marshall Plan had been predicated upon the assumption that the European countries would draw up plans for utilizing American aid for the best interests of the region as a whole, thereby assuring a high degree of economic unity. The objective of the Marshall Plan, according to one authoritative study, was "the recovery of Western Europe in the form of an integrated unit, which, it was hoped, would be capable of maintaining itself economically, politically, and militarily" (33, 1951, p. 215). This was an ambitious undertaking bound to have far-reaching consequences for the nations concerned.

As the years passed, compromise after compromise had to be made to reflect existing realities within Europe, America, and the rest of the world. Lacking a supra-governmental political authority with power to compel national acceptance of economic directives,

OEEC became, in the words of Florinsky, "actually a forum of . . . national states pursuing divergent and, at times, irreconcilable policies" (13, p. 48). OEEC very early lost an important weapon with which to bring about further European economic integration: the power to allocate Marshall Plan funds to its members. Its control over the national economic systems of Europe was further weakened by the shift from economic to military assistance, which increased the influence of military bodies like NATO (20, p. 435). More and more, OEEC has had to depend upon persuasion and voluntary compliance. Consequently, it has experienced a great deal of non-compliance with its directives. Several times it has had to reduce its goals sharply or risk its own disintegration in the face of deeply entrenched nationalist attitudes. Yet in spite of its limitations, OEEC successfully tackled the problem of intra-European trade. By 1955 restrictions on 90 per cent of the private trade within Europe had been reduced. Owing in large measure to OEEC efforts in eliminating trade barriers, intra-European trade was 70 per cent higher than before the war (33, 1955, p. 79).

Still another noteworthy development in the movement toward regional economic integration was the European Payments Union (EPU), an outgrowth of a proposal drawn up by the members of OEEC in 1949. Its purpose was to facilitate intra-European trade by affording a mechanism whereby trade transactions could be settled by balancing a member's credits against its debits, in a manner similar to a bank clearing house. This mechanism accomplished many, though by no means all, of the goals that would have been realized by adoption of a common currency throughout OEEC.

EPU's most fundamental contribution lay in preparing the way for adoption of the more far-reaching European Common Market. EPU did much to remove trade barriers and to alleviate problems associated with currency convertibility on the Continent—so much so that by the end of the 1950's, European currencies as a whole were in a firmer position *vis-à-vis* the dollar than at any period in recent history. By that time, Britain and nine other European nations had made their currencies convertible. These steps, reported the *New York Times* early in 1959, were symptomatic of Europe's phenomenal economic recovery; Europe's currencies "stand 'eye to eye' with the dollar—to the point, indeed, where there has been some concern about the dollar's stability" (**24**, January 4, 1959). Building upon foundations laid by EPU and related organs, later movements like the Common Market heralded a significant advance down the path of further regional economic co-operation.

Progress toward European economic integration has also been achieved by the "sector approach," of which the European Coal and Steel Community (ECSC) is the best example. This approach anticipates "the establishment of a single market for a limited number of commodities within a restricted geographical area . . . " (**13**, p. 57). The impetus for ECSC originally came from French Foreign Minister Schuman in the 1949-50 period, when the United States was pressing for the end of the Allied occupation of Germany, to be followed by German rearmament and German participation in NATO. France had long opposed this move; but if it could not be prevented, then at least some of the dangers inherent in an industrially powerful, rearmed Germany could be eliminated by having the great Ruhr industrial complex under the control of a supra-governmental authority. The Schuman Plan, of which ECSC was an outgrowth, contemplated a "complete 'fusion' of national interests in one important sector. . . . an international organization controlling all the heavy industries of Western Europe . . . " (**4**, p. 301). Sweeping as this proposal was, its ultimate objective was even broader. It was widely believed by advocates of European integration that the successful operation of ECSC would lead to numerous other "sector" plans—a "Green Pool" was anticipated for agriculture—which would in turn lead to political integration, climaxed by establishment of a "United States of Europe" (**20**, pp. 471-93; **35**, pp. 248-58). Progress toward reaching the latter objective had not, by the beginning of the 1960's, been impressive, though another important sector plan had been established. The new regional organization— called *Euratom*—was charged with responsibil-

ity for developing peacetime nuclear energy on the Continent.

ECSC came into existence in 1952, when a fifty-year treaty among France, Belgium, the Netherlands, Luxembourg, Italy, and the Federal Republic of Germany was ratified. In establishing ECSC the signatory countries desired to follow the principle of "checks and balances" familiar to students of the American Constitution. This led them to set up an exceedingly complex administrative structure to carry out the plan, described here only in briefest outline. There are five organs. The executive organ is the High Authority, consisting of nine members from the participating states. These representatives are expected to discharge their duties independently of the wishes of the governments they represent; they are specifically prohibited from receiving "instructions" from their home governments. A Council of Ministers co-ordinates the activities of the High Authority with those of the participating governments. The Consultative Assembly and the Common Assembly formulate basic directives and proposals; and a Court of Justice is empowered to entertain appeals from the rulings of the High Authority.*

Officially, ECSC possesses sweeping powers. For example, it has authority to abolish import and export duties within its area, to eliminate restrictions on the movement of coal, to abolish discriminatory practices among producers, buyers, and consumers of its products, and to eliminate state subsidies. It is supposed to have authority to eliminate these and other practices interfering with the stated goal of promoting economic expansion, full employment, and an improvement in living standards within its area. While ECSC has made noteworthy progress in evolving common policies for its members in coal and steel production, it has encountered increasing obstacles inherent in the "sector" approach to regional problems. Decisions affecting the production of coal and steel could not be made *in vacuo*. Despite the sweeping powers possessed by the High Authority, many

---

*The administrative structure of ECSC is described at length in: **20**, pp. 471-93; **28**, *passim*; and **31**, pp. 235-68. These sources also contain interesting material on problems experienced by ECSC and case studies illustrating its manifold activities.

issues lay outside its jurisdiction. Prevailing national differences over social security systems, taxation, transportation, trade, finance, credit—all of these and more enter into the positions taken by member-countries toward questions dealt with by ECSC. The sharp delineation of certain questions as being within its province, while others were left to the national governments themselves, means that inescapably there is a limit to how effective its policies can be in evolving regional answers to basic economic problems on the Continent (21, pp. 142-43).

From the beginning numerous compromises have had to be made to reflect the strength of entrenched nationalistic forces within its area. Moreover, the experience of ECSC has raised a number of fundamental questions about the efficacy of the "sector" approach to Europe's problems. Writing in 1958, Ernst B. Haas concluded that "After five years of activity, ECSC clearly had not brought with it a general enthusiasm for supranational institutions and federal powers in limited spheres." At the same time it had given "an undoubted impetus to further integration" (15, p. 110).

Obviously, no final judgments on ECSC's effectiveness can yet be given. At the time of its inception, ECSC was frankly acknowledged to be an experimental measure. That it continues to function today—and that in the course of its activities it has been able to gain compliance with its directives on the basis of consent, rather than legal force—is evidence of at least some success to date. Only time will reveal how successfully the operations of limited organs like ECSC can be dovetailed with more all-inclusive schemes, as exemplified in the Common Market. Finally, the durability of ECSC must still be tested against what would surely generate the strongest forces tending to tear it apart: a major recession within Europe, triggering powerful nationalistic demands at the expense of mutual co-operation to advance regional goals.

The European Common Market

The European Economic Community, usually called the Common Market, can be viewed as the culmination of the movement towards European economic union in the immediate postwar period. The Common Market is far more comprehensive than Benelux and other customs unions. It laid the groundwork for what may ultimately develop into a substantial merger of the economic systems of the participating countries.

The Common Market came into existence on January 1, 1958, as the result of a 378-page treaty signed by France, the Federal Republic of Germany, Italy, and the Benelux countries (Belgium, the Netherlands, and Luxembourg) on March 25, 1957. The Common Market did not actually begin operations until January 1, 1959. Its purpose is to abolish within its jurisdiction all internal tariffs and barriers to trade and to create a new "trading area." Its ultimate status in international economic affairs is likely to be comparable to that of the "dollar area" and the "sterling area." By an evolutionary process, the members of the Common Market will so reduce existing tariffs and trade restrictions that trade among them will become completely free; concurrently, the Common Market will apply a uniform tariff toward non-members, which will be the arithmetical average of the six national tariffs prevailing on January 1, 1957. The uniform external tariff, however, will not be applied until four years after the Common Market began operations.

Advocates of the Common Market idea consider it the opening phase in Europe's "second industrial revolution." With the appearance of the Common Market, a great new industrial-commercial complex emerged to challenge the dominant positions of the "dollar area," the "sterling area," and the communist bloc in international economic affairs. In 1955, the members of the Common Market had accounted for approximately one-fifth of the world's trade, one-seventh of its coal production, one-fifth of its steel production, one-eighth of its electric power generation, and one-seventh of its automobile production (24, March 31, 1957). The six nations joining the Common Market have a population of more than 160 million people, creating a mass market rivalling that of the United States. And if, as appeared likely, other European countries associated themselves with this movement, an even larger market would emerge. For instance, concurrently with negotiations leading to the Common Market, Great Britain and smaller European countries (Sweden, Denmark, Norway, Austria, and Switzerland) sought acceptance of a plan calling for a much broader *Free Trade Area*. These countries were unsuccessful in preventing establishment of the Common Market, but by the beginning of the 1960's it appeared probable that they would ultimately become associated in some way with the Common Market. The total population of the mass market then would exceed 240 million people. These developments certainly indicated that, at least in the realm of economic affairs, Western Europe was rapidly on the way to achieving the position of a powerful "third force" on the world scene.

The eminent American business leader and former ECA Administrator, Paul Hoffman, has identified seven significant features of the European Common Market. First, as we have noted, within 12 to 15 years, the members will completely eliminate tariff and quota restrictions upon trade among themselves; other barriers, like discriminatory freight rates, will be sharply reduced. Second, restrictions on the unimpeded movement of labor and capital among the member-states will either be eliminated outright or reduced. Within the Common Market area, both labor and capital will be free to migrate without regard to national boundaries. Third, the Common Market will encourage co-operation among its members so that agricultural problems and price support programs will ultimately be dealt with as a whole throughout the Common Market area. Fourth, the Common Market recognizes the importance of European economic development, especially for underdeveloped areas like southern Italy, by providing for the creation of a European Investment Bank, with an initial capital fund of one billion dollars. Fifth, various provisions of the Common Market agreement are designed to ease the transition from national to regional trade policies. Twelve to fifteen years will be required before all the goals laid down in the Common Market accord have been reached; the European Investment Bank will make loans designed to prevent temporary economic disruptions; and such problems as unemployment and uprooting of workers will

be attacked on a regional basis. Sixth, a new tariff unit will confront the outside world, but a certain amount of flexibility is permitted to each country in waiving established tariffs, provided the interests of the Common Market area as a whole are not adversely affected. Seventh, new machinery, paralleling that established by the European Coal and Steel Community, was set up to operate and supervise the Common Market. Two executive agencies—a Council and a Commission—were created. The six-member Council, staffed by high-level representatives from each country, has primary responsibility for applying treaty provisions to the market's operations. For the first four to six years, the Council must function by unanimous vote, a customary feature of supra-national bodies established in Europe; thereafter it may take decisions by various kinds of majority votes. The day-to-day supervisory body is the Commission, whose personnel are chosen on the basis of expertise. In addition to these bodies, there is a legislative Parliamentary Assembly and a Court. The Court decides controversial issues relating to application of the treaty provisions governing the Common Market (16, pp. 3-5).

Summarizing the implications of the Common Market, Hoffman states that:

> . . . the Common Market goes far beyond a traditional customs union. It will lead to a new economic community with common rules of competition, a common labor force, a central investment fund, and joint institutions of considerable authority. It stops short, however, of a full economic union wherein members merge their budgets, centralize their banks, and adopt a common currency. Each nation retains control of its economic, fiscal, and credit policies. (16, p. 5).

Nevertheless, the Common Market clearly lays the groundwork for further transcendence above purely national economic policies. Jan Hasbrouck, economic analyst for the New York *Herald Tribune*, has predicted that over the years membership in the Common Market will force "a large measure of harmonization in wages, social conditions, taxes, fiscal policies and other factors in the costs of production." In addition, he believes that the advent of the Common Market will almost certainly generate additional pressures in behalf of a common currency.*

As with any politico-economic movement, inauguration of the Common Market perhaps raises as many new issues for the future as it resolves for the present. Many of these issues, during the 1960's and beyond, are likely to prove of lasting significance for American foreign policy. Consider initially the matter of Western unity and harmonious relations. The Common Market idea was opposed by Britain and many smaller countries of Europe which tend to follow London's lead in international economic affairs.

By the beginning of the 1960s, conflict continued to prevail in the North Atlantic community between members of the Common Market and the "Outer Seven" (or Free Trade Area), led by Great Britain. Concern over this conflict in Washington—together with adverse balances in America's own international trade position at the end of the 1950s and a mounting belief that the European Allies ought to shoulder greater responsibility for providing economic assistance to underdeveloped countries—prompted the United States to initiate new negotiations on these issues. Early in 1960 the United States called for a revitalization of OEEC. It hoped that this organization could successfully bridge the differences in viewpoints between members of the Common Market and the Free Trade Area and that, in addition, it could serve as a mechanism for providing greater co-ordination in foreign aid programs carried out by the North Atlantic Allies. Some observers interpreted this proposed strengthening of OEEC as an important effort to create the same degree of unity among the Allies in *economic* affairs as NATO provided in *military* affairs. Though tensions growing out of economic issues weakened the solidarity of the free world coalition, prolonged negotiations would undoubtedly be necessary before these differences could either be eliminated entirely or significantly reduced. Particularly troublesome was the dilemma involved in Britain's

desire to maintain close economic ties with the Commonwealth—which itself operates upon the basis of preferential tariff rates for its members —and its companion desire to associate itself more intimately with European unification movements. Until some means could be found to resolve this dilemma, a major barrier would exist to closer regional harmony on economic issues.

It could be safely predicted, furthermore, that the durability of the Common Market would in large measure be determined by tendencies within Europe itself as time passed. One of these was France's future under de Gaulle's leadership. From the first day he took office, de Gaulle made it clear that a primary objective was to secure a more influential role for France within the Atlantic Community and in world affairs generally. There seems little doubt that France championed the Common Market with this objective in mind, in the hope that, in Britain's absence, France might have a preponderant voice in its affairs, and that France would entrench itself in a stronger position from which to deal with an economically resurgent Germany. Whatever French motives, for France there is bound to be an interaction between the future of the Common Market and France's chronic internal economic problems, such as inflation, antiquated tax laws and outmoded productive methods. This same interaction will also be felt by other European countries.

Europe's supra-national economic organs in the postwar period, by and large, were launched in an era of almost uninterrupted rising demand for goods and services on the Continent. To this extent, they have been inaugurated under highly favorable conditions. As with the Coal and Steel Community, the durability of the Common Market has yet to be tested in the face of a major recession in Europe, which could be expected to trigger a resurgence of nationalist pressures and to engender rising pleas for "protection" on the part of domestic industries and employee groups.

The advent of the Common Market presents a challenge to the foreign economic policies of the United States, as regards both *official* policies and those of *private* business groups. Collectively, nations in the Common Market

---

*An illuminating series by Mr. Hasbrouck analyzing the nature and implications of the Common Market appears in 23 for February 2, 3, 4, 5, and 6, 1959. Our treatment of the Common Market, especially of implications for the future, draws heavily from this series.

form the world's largest trading unit, a unit which will be even larger if and when other European nations join this union. This fact will compel the United States to re-appraise its tariff and trade policies, especially "protectionist" features discriminating against European imports. Additionally, it will furnish a powerful leverage for forcing Washington to reconsider America's relations with the General Agreement on Tariffs and Trade (GATT). To date, protectionist forces within Congress have succeeded in preventing wholehearted American participation in GATT. In the light of the Common Market, however, European countries will be in a position as never before to take retaliatory action against any trade discrimination by the United States.

Yet the Common Market also presents great opportunities to the United States. Elimination of intra-European trade barriers greatly enhances trade and investment opportunities for American firms. These firms could establish themselves *within* the Common Market area and thereby avoid discrimination against their products from *outside* it. By the end of the 1950's American corporations were hastening to invest and to expand their operations within the Common Market area—a move that was welcomed by "the six" as expanding employment opportunities, introducing new productive techniques, raising levels of purchasing power, maximizing the supply of consumer and producer goods, and generally contributing to the overall objectives entertained by the members of the Common Market. Economic analysts predicted a period of tremendous economic growth for Europe, which would reflect itself in rising demands for goods and services of all kinds. The Common Market itself facilitated expanded American investment by adhering to reasonable tax policies and by permitting the repatriation of profits for outside business enterprises. Increased American investment in Europe could be expected to have a favorable impact upon world trade as a whole and upon the problem of supplying capital to underdeveloped areas. Producers using Europe as a base would often be able to circumvent problems occasioned by the "dollar shortage" and to utilize trade channels not ordinarily open to firms in the United States.

With inauguration of the Common Market, for the first time since World War II Europe was on the verge of possessing sufficient strength in its own right, at least in the economic realm, to make its long-held dream of becoming a "third force" in contemporary world affairs a reality. For the United States this development was at once a consummation of many of its own postwar policies toward Europe and the beginning of a new era in American-European relations. While the exact contours of these relations throughout the years ahead could not be predicted with assurance, this much was certain: as reflected both in the emergence of the Common Market and simultaneous developments in NATO, Europe was increasingly demanding—and was now in a position to receive—recognition as an equal with the United States in dealing with fundamental global issues.

Economic Integration in the Balance

Since 1948 the United States has tried to promote economic integration on the Continent. How far has this goal been attained? A number of supra-national bodies exist in Europe and these have made undoubted progress toward solving certain regional problems, even though in almost every instance their progress has fallen considerably short of their professed aims. At least some, such as ECSC, show signs of evolving into genuine supra-national organs, with power to enforce compliance by the member-states.

Yet some troublesome issues remain. American policy-makers have regarded economic and political unification as a panacea for many of Europe's age-old difficulties. Congress particularly has insisted on economic unification in Western Europe without having a very clear conception of what forms such unification was to take, or thinking through the relationships to be established among new and existing economic institutions in Europe, or devoting any sustained thought to the consequences of such integration either for Europe or the international community as a whole, or studying the major implications of unification movements in such separate, if interrelated, fields as military and political activities.

If economic unification were accomplished overnight, what would be Western Europe's relationship to that part of the Continent still under Soviet domination? To the Soviet bloc as a whole? To the "dollar area," and specifically the United States? To the British Commonwealth? To the underdeveloped countries? As an Italian authority, Ugo La Malfa, suggests, in the last analysis economic problems cannot be sharply disentangled from political problems. "A distinction between the two may be made at the risk of falling into abstraction, but even then it must be admitted that economic and political factors are always intermingled, that any differentiation between the two is arbitrary . . . " (14, p. 64). How much money Britain is willing to devote to armaments, France's decision to devalue the *franc*, Italian efforts to cope with pressing population and agricultural problems, Switzerland's de-

cision on cutting imports from the United States—these are basically political decisions to be made by *national* governments unilaterally or perhaps in concert with other regional groupings and associations existing outside the European continent. Many issues connected with European unification, and many of the solutions advanced to deal with these issues, have ramifications that might not appear to have much relevance to events on the European continent. Systematically exploring the implications of European unification for these areas, and evolving viable relationships between supra-national organs in Europe on the one hand and national governments and regional associations elsewhere on the other hand, will pose a continuing challenge to Western policy-makers for years and perhaps decades in the future.

3. NATO: SOVIET CHALLENGE AND WESTERN RESPONSE

Origins of NATO

A significant landmark in American postwar foreign policy toward Europe was the creation of the NATO defense community.[*] Just as

[*]The Text of the North Atlantic Treaty is reproduced in 8, I, pp. 812-15. Original signatories of the Treaty were the United States, Canada, the United Kingdom, Belgium, Luxembourg, Norway, Iceland, the Netherlands, Denmark, France, Italy, and Portugal. Countries that later joined NATO were: Greece and Turkey (1952) and the Federal Republic of Germany (1955).

A provocative study by the Council on Foreign Relations has called attention to the distinction which must be preserved between the geographical concept of *Western Europe* and *the North Atlantic area or community*. The latter—including as it does Western Europe, North America, and various territories encompassed by a belt from the Arctic Circle to Turkey and French North Africa—is a far more comprehensive concept. In turn, the territory embraced within the NATO agreement was linked with other territories in the Middle East and Asia by such treaties as the Baghdad Pact and the Southeast Asia Treaty Organization.

Embedded within the confusion which often arises through indiscriminate use of these terms is a problem that has plagued American foreign policy throughout the postwar period; it is one toward which a satisfactory answer has not yet appeared. The problem is: at the same time the United States was encouraging economic and political unification within *Western Europe,* joint defense planning encompassed the entire North

economic assistance to Greece and Turkey in 1947 had led to the much more comprehensive and prolonged European Recovery Program, so too was sustained economic assistance to Europe followed by efforts to bolster the military strength of the free world. Initially, these efforts took the form of a military alliance among the nations of Western Europe, which became the nucleus of the North Atlantic treaty. Within a short time this was supplemented by substantial American military assistance to NATO and to other regional defense organizations.

Several developments in the 1947-49 period spurred efforts within both the United States and Europe to establish a unified defense

Atlantic area. Yet in view of the fact that intimate economic-political collaboration is vital to full co-operation in the sphere of defense, many authorities have raised the question of whether even *military* policies could be successfully co-ordinated for essentially different geographical units. To achieve adequate defense, will the scope of economic-political co-ordination also have to be extended to the entire North Atlantic area? Otherwise, will nationalist tendencies rob area-wide defense planning of much of its effectiveness? Thus far, such questions have not figured prominently in America's relationships with its western allies (21, pp. 1-6, 64-9).

system for the North Atlantic area. European communist parties had agitated militantly against the Marshall Plan. During the late 1940's communist groups in such countries as France and Italy appeared to be gaining in strength. Moscow's propaganda organs meanwhile were carrying on a virulent anti-American campaign. In China, the Nationalist Government was collapsing before the communist rebel forces. Then in the spring of 1948 had come the Soviet-engineered *coup* in Czechoslovakia, an event that hastened favorable Congressional action on the Marshall Plan. There followed the Berlin Blockade of 1948-49. Here an avowed objective of Soviet foreign policy was to drive the West—and above all, the United States—out of Germany. Had the Kremlin succeeded in this goal, Western Europe would have been left in a highly precarious military-economic position.

Increasingly, Europe's leaders were aware of the need for closer military co-operation among members of the North Atlantic area. With the active encouragement of the United States, five of them on March 17, 1948, signed the Brussels Treaty.* This pact, formed a "collective defense arrangement within the framework of the United Nations Charter . . . " (8, I, p. 819). Concurrently, the Senate Foreign Relations Committee, working in close conjunction with the State Department, was attempting to draft a legislative resolution paving the way for American association with a European security system. This resolution, known as the Vandenberg Resolution in honor of its instigator, Senator Arthur H. Vandenberg, was approved by the Senate on June 11, 1948, by a vote of 64-6. It called for "Association of the United States, by constitutional process, with such regional and other collective arrangements as are based on continuous and effective self-help and mutual aid, and as affect its national security" (8, I, pp. 819-20). The Senate, in other words, was overwhelmingly in favor of a closer military union between the United States and Western Europe. Europe

*The text of the treaty is reprinted in 8, I, pp. 968-71. Original signatories were Belgium, France, Luxembourg, the Netherlands, and the United Kingdom. Italy and the Federal Republic of Germany joined the Brussels defense system in 1954.

had created the embryo of such a union under the Brussels Pact; it remained for the United States to join in this effort and for the pact to be extended to other countries. This was done under the North Atlantic Treaty, which the United States ratified on July 21, 1949.

The American Military Commitment Under NATO

By making explicit what had been implicit in the Greek-Turkish Aid Program, the Marshall Plan, and in the firm resistance to Soviet pressure during the Berlin blockade earlier, the North Atlantic Treaty signified that the United States had accepted the principle that its own security was inextricably linked with that of its North Atlantic neighbors. The North Atlantic Treaty is a short document, containing only fourteen articles. The key article, expressive of the philosophy behind this military union, was Article 5 by which "The parties agree that an armed attack against one or more of them in Europe or North America shall be considered an attack against them all. . . . " In the event of an attack, each signatory will exercise the "right of individual or collective self-defense" and will "individually and in concert with the other Parties" take "such actions as it deems necessary, including the use of armed force, to restore and maintain international peace and security" (8, I, p. 813).

In assessing the nature of the commitment assumed by the United States under NATO, it is profitable to think in terms of the *de jure* and the *de facto* obligation. Widespread fears existed in Congress in this period that American membership in NATO might jeopardize the constitutional right of Congress to declare war. Numerous legislators were apprehensive lest "automatic war" follow an attack against one of the NATO signatories. Therefore, the Vandenberg Resolution had carefully conditioned American participation in NATO upon observance of the "constitutional process" of the United States, which prescribes that only Congress can declare war (7, pp. 74-80; 34, pp. 399-421). Legally then the obligation assumed by the United States was limited to regarding an attack against one NATO country as an attack against all. Exactly how the United States or any other signatory would react to such an attack was left unspecified. Article 5 of the treaty, said Secretary of State Acheson in 1949, "does not mean that the United States would automatically be at war if one of the other signatory nations were the victim of an armed attack" (8, I, p. 822).

The *de facto* commitment assumed by the United States under NATO, however, is another matter. The nature of warfare in the modern period has tended to render the right of Congress to declare war virtually a dead letter. Secretary Acheson suggested as much when he told the Senate Foreign Relations Committee in 1949: "If we should be confronted again with an all out armed attack such as has twice occurred in this century and caused world wars, I do not believe that any other action than the use of armed force could be effective" (8, I, p. 822). And in recommending ratification of the treaty to the Senate, the Committee itself observed that as far as the United States was concerned Article 5 reflects a "realization brought about by its experience in two world wars that an armed attack in the North Atlantic area is in effect an attack on itself." Widespread realization of this fact, said the Committee, "should have a powerful deterring effect on any would-be aggressor by making clear to him in advance that his attack would be met by the combined resistance of all the nations in the North Atlantic Pact" (8, I, p. 835).

As the years passed the question of automatic war came to be largely academic. Virtually every precept of American defense strategy presupposed intimate collaboration between European and American military forces and rested upon the doctrine of instant and massive retaliation against an aggressor. The development of guided missiles carrying nuclear warheads gave the Soviet bloc the ability to devastate NATO bases within a matter of minutes. More than ever this fact put a premium upon the ability of the free world to retaliate speedily in the event of war. By late 1957 even Secretary of State John Foster Dulles admitted publicly that in case of a Soviet-instigated attack on Western Europe, the NATO commander (SACEUR—Supreme Allied Commander Europe) would "almost certainly fight back" without waiting for a declaration of war. The NATO forces, of which American forces were an integral part, would return the fire of any aggressor (22, November 21, 1957).

In summary then NATO entailed a profound change in American foreign policy by making clear the determination of the United States to fight beyond its own shores to protect the security of the Atlantic system. And it signified a *de facto*, if not *de jure*, alteration in the American constitutional system by notifying potential aggressors that the United States would retaliate instantly, without waiting for a declaration of war, if an attack occurred against its friends in the North Atlantic sphere.

Strategic Implications of NATO

American participation in NATO constituted a milestone in the history of American foreign policy by proclaiming to the world that the American security zone was recognized by Washington as extending in a belt from Norway to Turkey in Europe. Yet the nation's membership in NATO had even wider strategic connotations than this.

The accession of Greece and Turkey to membership in 1952, coupled with the establishment of regional defense systems in other parts of the world subsequently, both strengthened NATO by the addition of more armed forces and by forging links joining these regional defense organizations. Now the NATO alliance extended into the eastern Mediterranean-Near East area, a tinder box of conflict between Russia and Western countries throughout history. Greek and Turkish accession therefore gave the free world bastions for the protection of the military approaches to the Mediterranean, the Black Sea, the oil fields of the Middle East, the Suez Canal, and North Africa. Equally important, Turkey furnished a strategic bridge to the east by virtue of the fact that the Turks were at the same time members of NATO and of CENTO (Central Treaty Organization), the latter being a security system of anti-communist countries of the Middle East. By the close of the 1950's CENTO—the former Baghdad Pact—had been seriously weakened by the defection of Iraq. But Turkey, Iran, and Pakistan, the other members, remained pro-Western. Pakistan's membership simultaneously in CENTO and the Southeast Asia Treaty Organization (SEATO) extended the defense nexus further eastward. And, because the United States is in addition a member of several other military alliances in the Pacific, such as those based on the Korean Treaty, the Japanese Treaty, the Republic of China Treaty, the Philippine Treaty, and the Anzus Treaty, the defense chain, with its western anchor in NATO, reaches as far east as Korea and the Philippines. Finally, American membership in the Rio Treaty binding the nations of the Western Hemisphere brings the chain full circle.*

Thus as a member—far and away the most powerful member—of a defense cordon that extends from Britain and Iceland in the west to Japan and Australia in the east, the United States has translated the postwar doctrine of containment into a series of interlocking, mutually dependent, regional defense systems designed to safeguard the security of the non-communist world. The United States has gone far toward ringing its chief diplomatic enemy with a complex of defense alliances that prevents the Kremlin from using outright military attack to consolidate its position by incorporating many non-communist countries into its empire. To that extent, the defense structure, of which NATO is the cornerstone, materially enhances the military posture, and contributes to the morale, of the free world coalition.

At the same time, it is also true that the strategic implications of the free world's defense system raise troublesome problems. While the alliance system deters Soviet military aggression, it also makes it exceedingly difficult to localize conflicts between the communist and non-communist worlds. In this sense, the situation today is distressingly reminiscent of the pre-World War I era, when an initially insignifi-

cant conflict between the Triple Alliance and the Triple Entente and their satellites dragged the great powers into war. Communist intrigue in Syria in 1957-58, for instance, created considerable alarm in the West about the military security of Turkey. If Turkey's security were found to be threatened by communist machinations in the Middle East, then presumably the military guarantees contained in the North Atlantic Treaty and CENTO would become operative.

Admittedly, this risk was as well understood in the Kremlin as it was in the West, and this fact alone may contribute to deterring communist aggression. But regardless of the intentions of Washington or Moscow or other capitals, the possibility existed that an "incident" in a country like Turkey or Pakistan or Korea might trigger a chain reaction that might ultimately result in all-out military conflict among the great powers. The point being made here is that NATO and the regional defense pacts modelled after it have largely made the issue of global war or peace dependent upon the actions and intentions, of small, often defenseless, and sometimes irresponsible, nations along the perimeter of the Soviet empire. The United States could easily be pulled into a worldwide military conflagration by a momentary flareup of Arab nationalism that threatened a NATO country, or by an essentially nationalistic movement, abetted by communist elements, in Southeast Asia. To that extent, American membership in NATO and its companion organizations has substantially reduced the freedom of action of American foreign-policy-makers and has often made the policy of the United States merely a reaction to the policy of its allies.

Administrative Machinery and Principles

NATO presents a complex organizational pattern which has undergone several major administrative changes since 1949. From the beginning, NATO's constitutional framework was left flexible so that its structure could be modified in the light of experience. Consequently, its growth has been highly pragmatic. The highest policy-making body, the Council, is composed of the foreign ministers of the

---

*The defense treaties to which the United States is a party are reproduced in 18. See also the map on page 216, above. The nature of the obligations assumed under these treaties varies somewhat. Thus the commitment under SEATO is much less definite and forthright than under NATO. See specifically the Report of the Senate Foreign Relations Committee on SEATO, January 25, 1955 (8, I, pp. 929-45).

member-countries. The Council is empowered to create whatever subsidiary organs are necessary to advance NATO's purposes. It has established a Defense Committee, consisting of the defense ministers of each country, and a Military Committee, consisting of the military chiefs of staff of each member-state. The Military Committee serves as the highest-ranking military body. Its executive agency is known as the Standing Group and is composed of a military commander from the United States, Britain, and France. The Standing Group meets in Washington and carries out the policy decisions of NATO on a day-by-day basis. Other administrative organs of NATO deal with problems of finance, economics, and supply, as well as with a host of other issues that have a significant bearing upon the military security of the North Atlantic area. One fundamental trend since 1949 has been the degree to which NATO has closely collaborated with the supranational economic bodies of Western Europe and has broadened its scope so as to include studies of related problems like inflation, industrial production, and mobilization.

An important stage in the evolution of NATO's administrative-command structure occurred after the outbreak of the Korean War, when the non-communist world became more conscious than ever of its military vulnerability. Within NATO this led to an attempt to "integrate" what up to that time had been essentially national armies into a joint command system. SHAPE (Supreme Headquarters Allied Powers in Europe) was established to defend continental Europe and was given control over the ground and tactical air forces required for this purpose. Subsequently, the military command system was expanded by adding SACLANT (Supreme Allied Command Atlantic), with headquarters in Norfolk, Virginia. Headed by an American naval commander, SACLANT's mission was to safeguard the sea and air routes in the Atlantic area and to maintain trans-Atlantic communications. An American-Canadian Regional Planning Group was also given the mission of defending the North American continent against air attack.

One continuing problem encountered by NATO, a problem indigenous to any military alliance system, has been that of co-ordinating civilian and military efforts in behalf of the common goal. The complexity of this problem led to a significant organizational modification in 1951, whereby the North Atlantic Council was divided into two organs: a ministerial council meeting three times annually and a permanent representatives council meeting at much more frequent intervals. It was hoped that this would provide more effective day-to-day liaison among the participating governments, in the solution of the broad range of collateral economic and political issues affecting NATO (13, pp. 86-90).

Since its inception, NATO has sought the "integration" of the military forces available from its members. Although considerable progress toward reaching this goal has been achieved, NATO is still dependent upon military components supplied by member-governments; the raising of these forces, and their allocation to NATO, remains basically a *national* decision. In trying to fashion a collective defense force from national military components, NATO has emphasized three principles. First, NATO has sought *adequate* force contributions to enable it to discharge its military missions. Second, it has endeavored to secure *balanced* commitments, by which is meant that it has sought to maintain the correct proportion of ground, sea, and air forces and the proper allocation of specialized units within each of these categories. Third, it has stressed the principle of *equality*—the idea of "fair sharing" —among its members. Adherence to this principle has meant that NATO sought to take account of the peculiar problems and capabilities of each member, while at the same time trying to make each member contribute its just share to the common defense effort. On the whole, NATO has been highly successful in having outstanding issues thrashed out on a basis of consent. Important decisions within NATO must be taken by unanimous vote. Thus far most problems have eventually been solved by unanimous agreement among the participating governments (13, pp. 91-92; 21, pp. 76-89).

Accomplishments and Continuing Problems

What kind of verdict can be rendered as regards NATO's accomplishments and its future prospects? The answer to this question must necessarily depend upon what has been, and still is, expected of the organization. If it is conceived of within the narrow compass of its original purpose—to provide a military shield between the North Atlantic area and the Soviet bloc—its accomplishments to date have been impressive. Judged within a somewhat larger frame of reference, however, the verdict must be more qualified.

Summing up NATO's accomplishment in June, 1957, the Assistant Secretary of State for European Affairs, Burke Elbrick, told the House Foreign Affairs Committee that:

NATO today is a proven and successful alliance. The Communist western advance has been halted and not 1 inch of territory has been lost since the alliance was founded. Behind the security of the NATO shield the Western European peoples have regained their economic health and are taking new initiative toward economic integration. In most of the NATO countries the NATO alliance is the core and foundation of international security policy. . . . the essential unity, strength, and usefulness of the Alliance remains and will remain. (17, Part V, pp. 860-61).

Measured by the emergence of military forces under NATO's control, there was ample justification for this verdict. By 1956 NATO had 5.9 million troops, counting reserves; 150 usable airfields, including those being constructed; 2,300 combat naval vessels of all kinds; 12,000 conventional and nearly 11,000 jet aircraft—all of which constituted an impressive contribution toward fulfilling the mission of NATO as a "shield" to protect the West in the event of war, until the "sword" of strategic air and missile power could retaliate against aggression.

Equally impressive has been the degree to which America's European allies have contributed to their own defense effort. Very few Americans are aware that from NATO's inception, the European countries themselves paid most of the cost of raising and supporting the armed forces required for continental defense. In 1953, for instance, the United States contributed 20 per cent of this cost and Europe contributed 80 per cent. By 1957, the European countries had assumed 90 per cent of the burden of providing for their own defense,

thereby permitting a diversion of American foreign assistance from Europe to other areas. Thus in 1950, 79 per cent of American foreign assistance went to Europe; by 1957 this had shifted to 25 per cent for Europe, 27 per cent for the Middle East, and 46 per cent for the Far East.*

Judged by another standard—ability to prevent an attack upon Europe and to defend Europe if an attack should come—NATO's progress has also been highly encouraging. General Lauris Norstad, SACEUR in 1958, believed that NATO possessed sufficient power to deter Soviet aggression in Europe and to retaliate instantly if the communist bloc should attack. He was convinced that the thirty ground divisions contemplated for NATO, including twelve expected from Germany, would protect Europe long enough to permit NATO's strategic air and missile power to strike against the industrial heart of any aggressor. Moreover, NATO's forces were believed to be adequate for dealing with any localized communist military thrust across the Iron Curtain (17, Part IV, pp. 539-50; 24, January 5, 1958).

Impressive as these accomplishments are, a number of major problems remain. Increasingly, some of the NATO countries, such as Britain, France, and Germany, are finding the burden of rearmament difficult to maintain in the face of pressing internal economic demands that require substantial governmental outlays. These difficulties will obviously become more or less acute depending on the economic progress made by European countries. For as Warne has observed:

Defense is likely to remain one of the most important items of national expenditure for an appreciable period and would bear directly upon the whole range of government policy. National authorities could not be expected to give what amounts to a first call on national resources to a supra-national body in a sphere which would be likely to have wide repercussions in other fields. (36, p. 82).

Thus NATO's long-range future is likely to be heavily determined by the ability of such bodies as OEEC, ECSC, and the newly-

---

*Data on the military accomplishments of NATO to date are taken from the testimony, charts, and reports included in 17, Parts IV and V, and 24, March 3, 1957.

conceived pool for the utilization of peacetime nuclear energy, Euratom (1, *passim*), to deal successfully with fundamental economic problems on the Continent.

The issue of Germany also continues to hamper NATO's maximum development. When the Federal Republic of Germany was created in 1955, it was expected that Germany, within 3 or 4 years, would furnish NATO with twelve divisions, with accompanying sea and air power. But by 1960 Germany was still far from having made the anticipated military contribution. Delay was due to acute budgetary problems, sharp internal political controversies, and a militant Soviet threat to the entire Western position in Berlin. Two overriding problems continued to pervade Germany's approach to virtually every issue affecting its future: the fact that the country remained divided into free and communist-dominated Germany by boundaries wholly lacking in ethnic or historical significance; and the chance that the retirement of Germany's octogenarian postwar leader, Chancellor Konrad Adenauer, might bring a fundamental reorientation in Germany's foreign policy on such issues as participation in NATO and negotiations with the communist bloc on the vital question of German unification. During the latter years of his tenure, Adenauer had faced rising criticism from his political opponents who were demanding a more independent role for Germany in global political affairs.

America's relations with the NATO allies posed several problems which could be expected to endure for some time to come. Foremost among these was the growing spirit of independence manifested by countries like Britain and France, and, more generally, a mounting sense throughout the NATO community that the allies ought to possess a more decisive voice in shaping the free world's diplomatic and military policies. General de Gaulle's accession in France strengthened that country's determination to be accepted once more as a great power. Concrete evidences of this insistence were France's rapid progress in developing its own nuclear weapons stockpile and its lead in forging ahead with the European Common Market. Great Britain, still chafing under the humiliation of diplomatic defeat during the Suez Crisis of 1956, was also increasingly disposed to exert its own diplomatic initiative. Two developments exemplified this tendency. One was Britain's careful insistence late in 1957 that it retain substantial control over American missile bases established on British soil. The other, coming in 1959, was Prime Minister Harold Macmillan's visit to Russia. In bilateral conversations with Soviet Premier Khrushchev, Macmillan took the initiative in trying to evolve negotiable proposals with the USSR for resolving cold war antagonisms, such as the new and inflammatory Soviet threat against Berlin.

It could confidently be predicted that Washington would more and more be forced to take account of suggestions and criticisms coming from across the Atlantic from its progressively stronger, more prosperous, allies who were demanding a more influential role in managing NATO's affairs. Many of these suggestions were directed at making the policies of the United States more imaginative, pliable, and adaptable to what were often rapidly changing circumstances—and above all, at subjecting many long-standing American policies toward the communist bloc to constant scrutiny.

One of the most-criticized aspects of American policy was a sweeping Congressionally-imposed limit upon the exchange of American nuclear information and technology with the allies. Ever since the explosion of the first atomic bomb in 1945, executive officials had been largely prevented by law from making the fruits of America's expanding nuclear technology available to the NATO partners. This situation engendered misunderstandings within the NATO community both because of the symbolic significance—it seemed to imply that the allies were untrustworthy—and because it necessitated needless duplication of effort in the West in weapons development and in pushing ahead with projects that might ultimately have peacetime application. Until this issue was resolved, a lingering source of animosity within the NATO community would remain.

Vexatious political issues have also tended to create internal stresses within the North Atlantic community. France's fears of a rearmed and economically powerful Germany have

EUROPE AND THE INTERMEDIATE RANGE MISSILE

The New York Times, Dec. 22, 1957.

abated little, despite the apparent success of the European Coal and Steel Community and the Common Market in linking Germany's economic destiny with that of its European neighbors. By the opening of the 1960's much remained to be done before there existed a supra-national *political* authority within Europe capable of preventing a possible resurgence of militant German nationalism.

Under de Gaulle's leadership, the Fifth Republic of France finally moved closer in 1959 to end the protracted war in North Africa by offering the rebels a choice of three alternatives: complete independence, "integration" as a department of France, or "autonomy" within the French Union. French "colons" resident in Algeria stoutly resisted any new policy that did not contemplate total suppression of the rebel movement. By early 1960, the colons challenged the authority of the French Government itself, an uprising which de Gaulle finally defeated. His victory, however, by no means ended opposition to his policies among French elites in Algeria. Meanwhile, the Algerian rebels—deeply suspicious of Paris' good faith and its ability to control French elements in the country—showed no inclination to lay down their arms or even to enter into serious negotiations. De Gaulle's offer, therefore, led to no immediate diminution in the Algerian conflict, nor did it make possible any significant reduction in French military commitments there. As long as the Algerian crisis endured, France could not make its scheduled contribution to NATO. Although the United States had warmly endorsed de Gaulle's new approach, relations between the two countries remained somewhat strained. Frenchmen felt that the United States did not fully understand France's position, and they resented the fact that the United States often was unwilling to back French viewpoints in organizations like the United Nations.

By 1960, at least one long-standing issue dividing the NATO allies appeared to be in the process of resolution. This was the fate of the island of Cyprus where Greek and Turkish inhabitants, backed by their countries of origin, had fought bitterly over the governmental powers which Britain was about to surrender. Britain, Greece, and Turkey had at last agreed upon a plan that seemed acceptable to all parties to the dispute.

The inescapable fact about NATO is that in spite of its elaborate organizational structure and its expanded activities in many non-military fields, it is essentially a military alliance. As such, it is subject to the limitations and disabilities commonly associated with military alliances throughout history. Chief among these is the fact that its aims and goals are largely negative. NATO was conceived as the sheet anchor of Western defense against the threat of Soviet expansionism. Anti-communism was and remains its primary objective. Granted that many of NATO's activities since 1949 have

taken place in fields which have a remote relationship to defense, most of these activities are part of a larger objective of strengthening NATO as a bastion of Western military security.

Under these circumstances NATO's fortune can be expected to vary in almost direct proportion to the threat confronting it. A high degree of unity against an outside threat may perhaps force transcendence above national differences so long as the threat endures. In periods when no imminent threat exists, differences among the members come to the surface and generate internal controversy. An evident aim of Soviet "peace offensives" of course is to foster and exploit such differences for the Kremlin's purposes.

Differing estimates of the imminence and severity of a given threat to members of NATO can be expected to give rise to conflicting goals and methods for reaching these goals. It is the judgment of Warne that:

> If N.A.T.O. is allowed a period of peace, in which to develop, it will evidently be something more than a military alliance subject to the whim of an enemy. History would, nevertheless, seem to suggest that if N.A.T.O. wishes to be sure of out-living the external threat . . . it would be wise, if it can rise to the occasion, to develop common institutions involving a surrender of sovereignty . . . (36, p. 85).

One possibility is that NATO might evolve into the unified military arm of a politically united North Atlantic Community. Admittedly, this possibility at the present time seems remote. In any case, NATO's long-range future will likely be heavily contingent upon the extent to which unity takes place among its members in related economic and political spheres.

4. POLITICAL UNIFICATION: EDC AND WEU

Precursors of European Union

A committee of the Hague Congress on European unity in 1948 submitted a report summarizing the case for European political unification as follows:

> Judged from any standpoint—political, economic or cultural—it is only by uniting herself that Europe can overcome her immediate difficulties and go forward to fulfill her mission for the future. . . . It is impossible to keep problems of economic collaboration and defense separate from those of general political policy. Economic and

defense plans having been made, political power is required to implement them. . . . If the policy of mutual aid . . . is to bear any substantial fruit, it must be accompanied step by step with a parallel policy of closer political union. Sooner or later this must involve the renunciation or, to be more accurate, the joint exercise of certain sovereign powers. (25, pp. 6-7).

The dream of a politically unified Europe is as old as history. The list of famous personages advocating this ideal—Dante, Pope Leo X, Erasmus, Grotius, Thomas More, William Penn, Cruce, Sully, the Abbé de Saint-Pierre, Fichte, Kant, Mazzini, Briand, and Churchill—testifies both to the importance and the durability of the vision.* Yet until the Second World War the ideal of European political unification was a dream espoused chiefly by intellectuals. Even today, it has not caught the imagination of the masses, either within Europe or the United States. Not even Winston Churchill's dramatic offer of an organic union between Britain and France at the time of the French military collapse during World War II gained wide popular appeal (14, pp. 40-1).

Progress toward European political integration is an almost perfect example of the Toynbeean idea of challenge and response. The Soviet threat sufficed, where other inducements throughout history have failed, to fuse the countries of Western Europe into at least the rudiments of a political commonwealth. Soviet hegemony over the heartland of Eurasia, accompanied by the decline of England, France, and Germany as great powers, left Western Europe basically two alternatives: either it could strive for greater co-operation among its members to solve common regional problems, or it could continue to remain impotent in the face of a continuing military threat from the

east. The United States could and did temporarily assume the burden of promoting economic recovery and military stability in Europe; but eventually the problem of Europe's own resources and efforts in this connection had to be faced squarely.

Consequently, throughout the postwar period a number of groups within Europe have undertaken to sponsor political unification movements. Often several such movements were going on simultaneously. Some groups sought to impose a supra-national political authority from the top that would embrace the regional economic and military bodies already in existence. Other groups advocated a policy of gradualism and evolution, preferring to let the seeds of European political unification sprout from the soil already prepared by such organizations as NATO, OEEC, and ECSC. Meantime, these organizations were finding that their activities in the economic and military realms required them more and more to work for greater political co-operation among their members. In a literal sense, therefore, it is incorrect to speak of the *movement* in favor of European political integration, except insofar as this is acknowledged as the ultimate goal of *several* groups and organizations that have been active in postwar Europe. The student will find ample literature from which to trace out the progress made to date by these separate and often unco-ordinated efforts. (14, pp. 161-231; 25, *passim;* 8, I, pp. 968-1242). Our interest centers on those aspects of the European unity movement that most directly affected America's relations with Europe.

The Council of Europe

American influence, according to one European scholar, "has been applied continually and with increasing momentum in favor of a unification of Europe" since World War II. Moreover, "the American attitude toward unification has been a decisive factor in whatever initiative has been taken by European statesmen in this direction" (14, p. 48). Pressure from the State Department was almost in direct ratio to the intensity of the international crisis prevailing at any given time, reaching its apex in the 1948-50 period, when the Berlin block-

---

*Space is not available here to undertake a discussion of the historical antecedents of the European unification movement in the modern period. More extended discussion can be found in 14, pp. 11-37, 80-97; 13, pp. 1-27; 26, *passim.*

The terms European political integration or unification are often used in a variety of senses. In practice, three concrete proposals singly or in combination are usually implied by these terms: a European *federation,* with a central government and strong local governments; an *organic union* involving a strong central authority over the Continent; and a *functional union* that applies to a limited sector, such as the European Coal and Steel Community (13, p. 19).

ade and the Korean War focused America's attention as never before in the postwar era on national defense.

In March, 1948, the French National Assembly called for the creation of a European constituent assembly to lay the basis for a European federation. Accordingly, on May 5, 1949, the Council of Europe came into being as a result of agreement among ten nations.[*] It contained two major organs: a Committee of Ministers, empowered to make recommendations to the member states, and a deliberative body known as the Consultative Assembly, whose function was to make recommendations to the Council of Ministers. Neither from its inception nor in the years thereafter was the Council of Europe regarded as anything more than a consultative body permitting the nations of Western Europe to discuss their common problems. Despite an impressive superstructure, creating the appearance of an effective supra-national authority, the Council of Europe remains "an intergovernmental arrangement . . . in which the ruling organ is an assembly of representatives of national governments each of which has preserved its sovereignty entire." The Council of Ministers makes recommendations to the member governments, which the latter are free to accept or reject; the Consultative Assembly is "of little substantive importance. Only in a moral sense, that is, in the sense that it is a forum in which public opinion may be molded, is the Assembly other than a quite powerless body" (38, p. 46).[**]

Even so, the Council of Europe made a valuable contribution by working in close conjunction with such bodies as the United Nations, OEEC, NATO, and other organs concerned with selected aspects of European regional problems. Furthermore, it provided a forum for discussing Europe's problems on a high political level; it focused public attention on such issues as inflation and the threat of aggression; and it initiated studies of important socio-economic questions, such as human rights and social security (9, p. 7). Although the United States did not join the Council, American officials encouraged its operation and expressed the hope that ultimately it would evolve into a more effective instrument of political unity.

The Rise and Fall of EDC

The 1948-50 period witnessed a growing awareness of the military vulnerability of the non-communist world, accompanied by a switch in emphasis from American economic aid to military-defense assistance to Europe. In the same period leading figures within Europe advocated closer political integration among the nations of the continent.

These developments demanded a reorientation in the policy of the United States and its allies toward Germany. While not abandoning its often reiterated objective of eventually bringing about complete German reunification, the United States began to take the initiative in terminating the Allied occupation of Western Germany as a preliminary step toward making the military-economic resources of Germany available to the NATO defense complex. This goal was dictated by the two-fold realization that Germany's participation would not only greatly strengthen NATO, but that, by contrast, the possible incorporation of Germany into the Soviet bloc would place the West in what might ultimately prove a hopelessly inferior military position.

Yet restoration of sovereignty to Germany, followed by German participation in NATO, raised a number of vexatious issues. Foremost

---

[*]Original members were France, the United Kingdom, Belgium, the Netherlands, Luxembourg, Denmark, Norway, Sweden, Italy, and Ireland. Greece and Turkey joined in 1949. Iceland was admitted in 1950. The Federal Republic of Germany entered in 1951, with the Saar having an "associate membership." For detailed treatment of the governmental machinery and procedures established by the Council of Europe, see 9, pp. 2-7.

[**]A short-lived movement aimed at creating a new supra-national political authority in Europe was the European Political Community (EPC), which was closely tied to the European Defense Community, discussed below. Theoretically, EPC was to be the political organ erected to supervise the common army established by the European Defense Community; it was, in effect, a second attempt to arrive at a political confederation, in the light of the success already achieved in setting up the European Coal and Steel Community. After

---

the failure of the French Assembly to ratify the EDC treaty in 1954, however, EPC was also abandoned. Its nature and evolution is traced in 38, pp. 81-126.

among these was the danger that a re-armed Germany might some day embark upon a foreign policy of *revanche*. Because of geographical proximity and historic quarrels with Germany in the past, France was understandably more concerned about this danger than any other country. To many Frenchmen a re-armed, sovereign Germany was more threatening than a Soviet attack, which public opinion in Europe widely believed to be a remote danger (**25**, p. 163).

Efforts to reconcile American insistence upon German participation in NATO with French apprehensions about future German military hegemony over Europe led to a proposal known as the European Defense Community (EDC). An agreement to establish EDC was signed on May 27, 1952, by the Republic of Germany, Belgium, France, Italy, Luxembourg, and the Netherlands (**8**, I, pp. 1107-1150). Its immediate aim was to bring Germany back into the community of nations, while establishing a larger political framework that contained adequate safeguards against a revival of German militarism. EDC, moreover, had important long-run implications, for it was widely regarded in Europe as the forerunner of a genuine European political union.

EDC contemplated the most ambitious plan for the political integration of Europe witnessed to that time. Its purpose was establishment of a "European Defense Community, supranational in character, consisting of common institutions, common armed forces and a common budget." In time EDC was expected to deal with such thorny problems as common European citizenship and the merger of Europe's national economic systems into an integrated whole (**13**, pp. 96-103, 129-36).

From its inception, EDC was enthusiastically supported by the United States Government. On April 15, 1954, President Eisenhower pledged the "closest possible integration between the European Defense Community forces on the one hand, and United States and other North Atlantic Treaty forces on the other. . . . " In a candid statement to Europe that the United States regarded EDC as of the utmost importance, Eisenhower promised *indefinite* American association with NATO "when there is established . . . the solid core

of unity which the European Defense Community will provide" (**8**, I, pp. 1199-1200).

Yet as the months passed, opposition to EDC within certain European countries increased significantly. Paradoxically, it became most intense in France, the very country that had taken the lead in bringing initial agreement on EDC as the best method for dealing with issues arising out of German re-armament. As opposition to EDC grew in France, so too did American pressure upon the French Government to ratify the agreement. Through formal diplomatic and informal channels, the Eisenhower Administration made it clear that future American military-economic assistance to Europe might very well hinge upon establishment of EDC (**10**, *passim*). Finally, late in 1953, in one of the bluntest warnings ever issued by the United States to its cold war allies, Secretary of State Dulles served notice that French rejection of EDC would result in an "agonizing re-appraisal" of American foreign policy toward Europe. The implication was unmistakable that, if EDC were rejected, the United States would sharply reduce its military and foreign aid commitments to the Continent (**24**, December 15, 1953).

At the conclusion of an historic foreign policy debate on August 30, the French National Assembly rejected EDC. A number of influences were responsible for this decision, which found extreme right-wing and left-wing groups within the Assembly agreed, for fundamentally different reasons, that acceptance of the EDC was not in the national interest.* French unwillingness to join EDC temporarily imperilled the close association that had existed between the United States and its European allies since 1947. A revival of American isolationist attitudes, both inside and outside the government, seemed likely.

---

*One authority gives the following explanation of the French defeat of EDC: with the death of Stalin, France's fear of a Russian attack against Europe abated; the current emphasis upon nuclear weapons convinced the French that land armies in Europe were relatively unimportant; France was unwilling to surrender its forces, heavily committed in North Africa, to a joint European command; Britain continued to refuse to make a concrete military commitment to EDC; and—above all—France feared Germany more than Russia (**3**, pp. 129-30).

Origins of the Western European Union

Secretary of State Dulles termed French rejection of EDC a "saddening event." In language seldom employed among diplomatic allies, Dulles noted that "It is a tragedy that in one country nationalism, abetted by communism, has asserted itself so as to endanger the whole of Europe" (8, I, pp. 1471-73). That defeat of EDC was regarded with the gravest concern by the Eisenhower Administration was indicated on October 3, 1954, when Secretary Dulles told a nine-power conference in Europe categorically that American economic-military assistance in the past had been made available upon the expectation that Europe would move toward the goal of unity. The United States had counted heavily upon European ratification of EDC to assure that the United States "was not putting our troops in the midst of what has historically been the world's worst fire hazard." The participation of the United States in NATO had been a move of unprecedented significance in American foreign policy. With a forthrightness that left little to the imagination of Europe's leaders, Dulles continued:

> Now, a committal of that character is not lightly made, and I say in all frankness that as the situation stands today it would not be possible for the President . . . to renew that committal. There has been a great wave of disillusionment which has swept over the United States, and it is particularly manifest in the Congress—a great wave of disillusionment over what has happened, and a feeling that, after all, the situation in Europe is pretty hopeless and the United States had better not make any long-term committals to be part of it. . . . I cannot say at this moment that a renewal of that committal is possible. I can say, and must repeat that, as things stand today, it is not possible. (8, I, p. 1486).

At the same time, Dulles believed that a substitute for EDC could be found. If the European nations could evolve an acceptable alternative, the United States would align itself with the new proposal (8, I, pp. 1486-87). Among steps that could and should still be taken were restoration of sovereignty to Western Germany and participation of Germany in the NATO defense effort, after guarantees had been evolved to prevent a resurgence of German military hegemony over Europe.

The Anatomy of WEU

On October 23, 1954, the occupation of Germany was officially terminated, and concurrently the signatories of the Brussels Treaty of 1948 invited Italy and Germany to join their defense pact (8, I, p. 972). Protocols added to the Treaty of Brussels were designed to mollify France's fears of a re-armed Germany. These protocols specified limitations upon German re-armament by prohibiting the new Federal Republic from manufacturing atomic, biological or chemical weapons, long-range missiles and bombing planes, and large ships. Furthermore, the protocols prohibited any signatory from maintaining armed forces, except those used for internal police functions, without the consent of SACEUR. A separate body—the Agency for the Control of Armaments—was established to oversee the arms-limitations features of the agreement (8, I, pp. 978-84).

Failing acceptance of EDC the nations of Western Europe had drafted an acceptable, if much more limited, substitute. This new agreement, called Western European Union, was made possible in large part by an historic decision of the British Government. Foreign Secretary Anthony Eden informed the nine-power conference on September 29 that for the first time in its history Britain was prepared to station troops *permanently* on the Continent of Europe. While the total military contribution envisioned was not large—four divisions, with supporting tactical air power—this decision marked a fundamental reorientation in British thinking about its own security and that of Europe as a whole. Britain had finally abandoned even the pretense of "splendid isolation" and had cast its lot firmly with Western Europe. This move further allayed French fears of a re-armed Germany and considerably strengthened the hand of those European leaders who continued after the defeat of EDC to believe that greater European political unity was possible.

While the Western European Union* was an alternative proposal for EDC, it was far

---

*Signatories of the WEU agreement were: Belgium, France, the Federal Republic of Germany, Italy, Luxembourg, Netherlands, and the United Kingdom (8, I, p. 967).

from being a replica of it. WEU was predominantly a military agreement among the European countries, much on the order of the Organization of American States among the nations of the Western Hemisphere. In contrast to the plan contemplated under EDC, troop contributions to NATO from WEU countries were to be regarded as national forces, instead of being merged into a unified European army. The new Council of Western Europe was given authority to "consult with regard to any situation which may constitute a threat to peace, in whatever area this threat should arise, or a danger to economic stability" (8, I, p. 974). On matters of great importance, voting within the Council is by unanimous vote; on matters of lesser importance agreement can be reached by simple or two-thirds majority. As we have noted, a new organ, the Agency for the Control of Armaments, was established to supervise compliance with the arms-limitations clauses of the WEU agreement. Yet, the Agency's jurisdiction was from the outset circumscribed by so many exceptions and reservations that it could in no sense be viewed as a supra-governmental authority with powers to regulate all aspects of arms production within Western Europe.

The WEU agreement of 1954 declares a major goal to be "promoting the unity and . . . encouraging the progressive integration of Europe" (8, I, p. 973). In spite of such lofty professions, and in spite of an elaborate superstructure for making decisions on a co-operative basis, WEU's successes have been small. It possesses no armed forces or strategy of its own, having surrendered responsibility for these to NATO. Its effectiveness in promoting common policies among its members toward matters like arms standardization and establishing an arms production pool has been minimal. As time passed, its primary, almost its sole, activity was the carrying out of the arms-control provisions of the WEU agreement, directed particularly at preventing a resurgence of German militarism. Even these activities, however, do not embrace the whole of the NATO community, since Norway, Denmark, Iceland, Portugal, Greece, and Turkey do not belong to WEU and are not therefore subject to its arms-control limitations.

WEU's limited usefulness therefore highlights a problem for NATO and, more broadly, for other movements in the Atlantic community whose aim has been unification on various fronts. From the most comprehensive of these regional groupings—NATO—to more limited associations like OEEC, ECSC, the Common Market, and WEU, an intricate network of groups and sub-groups has appeared in Europe—so many in fact that an increasingly serious problem has been co-ordinating the policies of nations often belonging to different groupings within the North Atlantic area. In some cases at least, differing viewpoints *within* the North Atlantic region have become institutionalized by being given a more or less complex supra-national governmental structure. This phenomenon could conceivably make it more difficult than ever to achieve maximum collaboration among the national governments in respect to economic and political questions (21, pp. 121-124).

The United States looked upon WEU as substantially fulfilling American demands for greater political integration. In a message to the nations that joined WEU, President Eisenhower re-affirmed America's friendship with Europe and its intimate and continuing involvement in European security. Relations between the United States and Europe in the future, he emphasized, would be based on certain fixed principles, among which were: membership in and support for NATO; continued participation of American armed forces in the defense of Europe; encouragement of movements that might lead to even more effective European integration on all fronts; and acceptance of the principle that a military attack against Europe would be construed as an attack against the United States (8, I, pp. 989-91).

What are the prospects that WEU or other movements may evolve into genuinely effective instruments of European political integration? In answering this question, several considerations must be kept in mind. The first is that the progress made to date in achieving European unification has come about largely as a result of American pressure—and more specifically, of Congressional pressure. After the defeat of EDC, for example, there appears little doubt that the more circumscribed WEU was formulated predominantly out of fear that in its absence the United States would substantially reduce its commitments to Europe. True, European statesmen and intellectuals have engaged in interminable discussions throughout the postwar period, and have sponsored a variety of organizational plans that, given widespread public and governmental support within Europe, might evolve into a parliament of Europe. At the same time, however, there has always existed considerable reluctance within Europe to take the final step. In 1957 the former Italian Minister of Foreign Trade observed that "Europeans have sought to unite through various methods. But today, almost ten years later, although the national structures have been repaired, the fortress of national sovereignty has remained untouched, with few sporadic exceptions" (14, p. 67). The case *against* entrenched European nationalism is widely conceded on the Continent; but the case *for* a new supra-governmental authority is by no means as widely admitted. Many Europeans acknowledge the inability of the political *status quo* to solve their myriad problems. Emotionally and psychologically, however, they appear to remain firmly wedded to the old political forms. Similarly, they concede that American leadership is indispensable but resent it because it emphasizes the loss of their former military-diplomatic greatness (14, p. 169).

Whether the idea of European unity is a hot-house plant that will wither in a time of adversity, or whether its roots have at last sufficiently penetrated the hard crust of European nationalism so as to prosper in the years ahead is a question to which no definitive answer can be given. The germ of such a far-reaching change as the political unification of Western Europe can be implanted—perhaps more correctly re-invigorated—by an outside power like the United States. Yet over the course of time it will require more than American diplomatic pressure or the threat of Soviet expansionism to nourish the tender plant of unity through numerous vicissitudes until it has attained sufficient strength to survive in its native soil. Together, America and Europe have planted the seeds. Many have fallen on stony ground; a few show signs of prospering. Their future will provide a continuing challenge in American-European relations for years, if not decades, to come.

5. AMERICA AND EUROPE: CONTINUING ISSUES

In reviewing the record of American postwar foreign policy toward Western Europe—a record that has witnessed the merging of America's destiny in world affairs with that of its European allies—several significant facts and issues stand out. First, very few great powers can point to any episode in their history comparable to America's relations with the countries in the North Atlantic region since World War II. As one of the two super-powers, for a time possessing a monopoly of nuclear weapons, the United States could have imposed politico-military hegemony over its neighbors, especially after the nations of Western Europe became dependent upon Washington for economic, and later military, assistance. Few nations have had so rare an opportunity to create "satellites" as had the United States. And very few nations would have exercised such self-restraint in the face of such an opportunity. While denunciations against "American imperialism" have been heard from time to time in postwar Europe—and these denunciations have by no means emanated exclusively from communist circles—on the whole the United States has refrained to a remarkable degree from trying to dictate to its allies, much less to impose American political control over them. The overriding fact therefore that emerges from any study of relations between the United States and its Western European allies in the postwar era is that the allies have attained an impressive level of economic and military health and that they continue to preserve their political independence, both from the Soviet Union and from their powerful neighbor to the west. Thanks largely to American assistance, Western Europe continues to exist as a major force in world affairs; the future today is far more promising than might have been predicted in the mid-1940's.

Cynics, and those who can think in no other terms than *Realpolitik* when evaluating a nation's foreign policy, might interpret Europes' phenomenal recovery as a by-product of American policies of self-interest, above all its policy of militant anti-communism. The United States, they would contend, did not assist Europe chiefly because of idealistic support for European recovery *per se*, but because that goal coincided with the diplomatic objectives of the United States. That there is considerable validity to this contention cannot be denied. Even so, the high degree of co-operation that has prevailed between Europe and America since the Second World War points to a basic fact about the diplomatic conduct of nations. Admitting that America's policies have been based first and foremost on national interest, no better example could be cited to show that *statesmanship consists of bringing into balance considerations of national interest and ethical-humanitarian requirements.* While it is apparent that national interest and idealism sometimes *do* conflict in the diplomatic field, there is no compelling reason why they *must* do so. The story told in this chapter indicates that it is often possible to devise policies that achieve both immediate diplomatic ends and contribute to the general welfare of all the populations concerned. In that sense, America's pursuit of its national interest in Western Europe stands in glaring contrast to Soviet pursuit of its national interest in the Eastern European satellites. No Hungarian revolt, brutally suppressed, mars the record of American diplomacy. Friendship between America and Europe, in spite of temporary setbacks like the Suez crisis of 1956, is the foundation-stone of the free world alliance.

Admitting the success experienced by the United States in raising its European allies to a new level of economic, political, and military health, it is still true that American diplomacy toward Europe has raised a number of persistent troublesome issues. Take the American insistence upon European unification. Europeans have pointed to a sharp dichotomy between American pronouncements and American ac-

tions. Almost without letup, Europeans have heard the refrain "European integration" from Washington, particularly from Congress. Nonetheless, especially in the 1950-51 period, the United States has threatened to reduce its overseas troop commitments sharply. This threat has appeared and disappeared spasmodically, depending largely upon the extent to which the American people approved or disapproved of the policies of their allies, believed that government spending within the United States ought to be reduced, faced widespread unemployment or felt rebellious against unwanted global obligations necessitated by the cold war. In addition, the United States has not exercised any noteworthy leadership in broadening the jurisdiction of the United Nations, especially if it would entail a surrender of "American sovereignty." Similarly, the United States has shown marked reluctance to associate itself with many of the regional organizations that have appeared in Europe and to extend the jurisdiction of these organizations throughout the entire North Atlantic zone.

Regarding commercial policy and foreign aid, the United States has manifested considerably less idealism than it has urged upon Europe. Thus in 1958 President Eisenhower proposed to Congress that the reciprocal trade agreements program be extended for five years. The opposition to this request within Congress, however, was more formidable than it had been in years. Headlines like "Reversal of Foreign-Trade Policy is Goal of High-Tariff Bloc" (**24**, February 23, 1958) were not calculated to imbue Europeans with a high sense of America's ability to transcend narrow nationalist considerations or serve as a beacon lighting the path to supra-national co-operation. America's insistence that Europe forget petty nationalist bickerings and think in terms of the "common good" of nations on the Continent was not strengthened by the nation's own lapses into provincialism, as exemplified by protectionist amendments and conditions added on to foreign assistance programs, designed to give more business to the American Merchant Marine fleet, prevent nationalization of industries by the allies, or proscribe trade with the Soviet bloc (**4**, pp. 161-77, 561-69). Many Europeans also found it paradoxical that many

Americans, especially vocal members of Congress, threatened European countries with a resurgence of American isolationism if they did not make more rapid progress toward supranational co-operation. Critics argued that the most beneficial contribution the United States could make to supra-national causes in Europe was to associate itself more intimately with them!

In its insistence upon unification, the United States has tended indiscriminately to support each and every movement that had unification as its professed aim. How one movement related to another, now and in the future; what the overall pattern of these movements collectively might be; how developments in Europe affected, and were affected by, regional developments in other parts of the world—these questions have received minimum attention from the American advocates of European unification. Inevitably then, the result has been a formidable network of more and less effective supra-national organizations within Europe, most of which possess massive bureaucracies having intricate ties with each other and with the bureaucracies of the pre-existing national systems. The complex array of *de facto* and *de jure* relationships prevailing is surely one reason why the public in both Europe and the United States often finds the whole question incomprehensible.

The problem alluded to by a French political leader in the early 1950's has, if anything, become more acute in the years that followed. He observed that a *single* Europe had been the goal of those advocating unification on the Continent; but after the European Coal and Steel Community and the European Defense Community had been proposed the advocates of unification "had already made two Europes. . . . Were they going on along this particular road to construct a third Europe, and a fourth? A transport Europe . . . and then an agricultural Europe? . . . It would no longer be Europe; it would be anarchy" (38, p. 97). With the subsequent creation of the European Common Market and Euratom, the inquiry had lost none of its pertinency.

To some individuals, the diffuse pattern of supra-national authorities that had grown in Europe indicated unquestioned progress toward the announced goal of unification. To others, it signified something far more limited and less promising: Europe's often expediential response to intense outside pressures, resulting in considerable activity creating the *appearance* of unification but in very little actual success in piercing the armor of European nationalism, especially on the all-important political level. And because advocates of unification on both sides of the Atlantic have often been content to settle for appearance instead of substance, the goal of true European unity—assuming this to be a desirable goal—may have in fact become a more remote possibility.

Towering above all these difficulties is another which, though seldom discussed openly between leaders of America and Europe, explains in large measure why many postwar unification efforts have met with only limited success. Consciously or unconsciously, American insistence upon Western European unity has rested upon an assumption that is unacceptable to great masses of people in the North Atlantic region. This is that the postwar division of Europe into communist and anti-communist spheres is unalterable. This assumption emerges clearly from the fact that in the countless discussions and negotiations over European unification, insignificant attention has been devoted to the relationship of *Eastern* Europe to the unification movement.

Historically, the term Europe has been used to embrace the territory extending from Britain to Russia and from Scandinavia to Greece. Yet, when the United States insists upon "European unity," it is talking about *Western* European unity alone. In effect, the United States is asking the peoples of the West to abandon their historic ties with their Eastern neighbors and to set up a regional government for that part of Europe which—largely by historical accident—is presently west of the Iron Curtain. Aside from the fact that such a step, if successfully carried out, would likely aggravate cold war tensions, this would usher in a new historical era in the relations prevailing among the peoples of Europe, without the concurrence of a substantial part of the population on the Continent. This problem of course has been highlighted by the dilemma that has confronted Western Germany on the issue of unification. No German statesman could possibly admit that he had abandoned the ultimate "unification of Germany" as a cardinal goal of his country's foreign policy.

The problem is only slightly less acute for all the nations of Western Europe, especially in the economic realm. When American Congressmen insist upon "European integration," what they are calling for in essence is the establishment of a truncated political community, cut off from its neighbors, and its complementary economic nexus to the east—a community that would lack any real historical significance and from which the United States would undoubtedly continue to remain politically aloof.

Understandably, many Europeans are unenthusiastic about such a step, in spite of America's rather uncritical advocacy of it. Many geographers today question whether *Europe as a continent* can any longer be regarded as a distinctive and separate region. However that may be, clearly the continent must maintain very close ties in all fields with its Asian-Near Eastern–African hinterland. To presuppose therefore that Western Europe can be, and ought to be, cut off from the rest of Europe is to formulate a policy that conflicts with basic geographic realities. The compelling argument in favor of Western European integration is primarily a military-diplomatic argument occasioned by the Soviet challenge to the West. Western Europe can be regarded as a political region only because the remainder of Europe is in Soviet hands.

The division of Europe *as a whole* is thus the root problem. Its solution would appear to lie less in an approach that contemplates the permanent bifurcation of Europe by borders that lack genuine historical justification, than in an attempt to remove basic causes of international tension and, more specifically, an effort to heal the division of the continent occasioned by World War II.

REFERENCES

1. Armand, Louis. "Atomic Energy and the Future of Europe," *Foreign Affairs,* 34 (July, 1956), pp. 655-65. Discusses the impact of peacetime nuclear power for Western Europe.

2. Bailey, Thomas A. *Woodrow Wilson and the Great Betrayal.* New York: The Macmillan Company, 1945. Traces out the League of Nations controversy in the United States.

3. Bell, Coral, ed. *Survey of International Affairs, 1954,* New York: Oxford University Press, 1957.

4. Brown, William A., and Opie, Redvers. *American Foreign Assistance.* Washington: The Brookings Institution, 1953. Evaluates the American foreign aid program, with special emphasis upon American-European relations.

5. Calvocoressi, Peter. *Survey of International Affairs, 1953.* New York: Oxford University Press, 1956. This volume is part of the Royal Institute of International Affairs' annual series; it is especially valuable for the viewpoints of European countries on major issues.

6. *Congressional Record.* Volume 93.

7. Crabb, Cecil V., Jr. *Bipartisan Foreign Policy: Myth or Reality?* Evanston: Row, Peterson and Company, 1957. America's postwar relations with Europe are discussed in Chapters 3 and 4.

8. Department of State. *American Foreign Policy,* 1950-55 (two volumes). (Publication No. 6446, "General Foreign Policy Series" 117). Washington: 1957. This is an invaluable collection of documentary material on recent American foreign policy.

9. ———. "The Council of Europe," Office of Public Affairs, Publication No. 26, Spring, 1952. A brief though informative description of the Council of Europe and its implications.

10. ———. "A Report to the Nation on European Unity," address by Secretary of State Dulles on February 13, 1953. (Publication No. 4938). Washington, 1953. Secretary Dulles' speech typifies the official American viewpoint toward European unification.

11. ———. *The United States and Germany, 1945-1955.* (Publication No. 5827, "European and British Commonwealth Series" 47). Washington, 1955. Provides informative material on America's changing attitude toward Germany.

12. Fleming, D. F. *The United States and the World Court.* Garden City, N. Y.: Doubleday, Doran and Company, 1945. Discusses the controversy over American membership in the World Court.

13. Florinsky, Michael T. *Integrated Europe?* New York: The Macmillan Company, 1955. Evaluates European integration movements on a number of fronts and discusses the long-range implications of these movements.

14. Haines, C. Grove, ed. *European Integration,* Baltimore: The Johns Hopkins Press, 1957. A valuable symposium, bringing out divergent ideas about European integration.

15. Hass, Ernst B. *The Uniting of Europe.* Stanford, California: Stanford University Press, 1958. A critical evaluation of problems and prospects for European unification.

16. Hoffman, Paul G. *The New European Market.* New York: American Committee on United Europe, 1958. In this little booklet, the author assesses the implications of the Common Market for the United States.

17. House Foreign Affairs Committee. *Hearings on the Mutual Security Act of 1957,* 85th Congress, 1st Session, June 10-28, 1957.

18. ———. *Treaty Provisions Relating to the Use of United States Forces for Mutual Defense,* 84th Congress, 2nd Session, 1956. This publication contains the texts of all mutual defense treaties to which the United States is a party, together with maps illustrating the treaty relationships.

19. Lippmann, Walter. *The Cold War.* New York: Harper and Brothers, 1957. Lippmann challenges the doctrine of containment as set forth by George Kennan. While he makes many telling criticisms, he offers no feasible alternative to containment.

20. MacMahon, Arthur W., ed. *Federalism: Mature and Emergent.* Garden City, N. Y.: Doubleday and Company, 1955. Contains provocative material on European federalist movements in the postwar period.

21. Moore, Ben T. *NATO and the Future of Europe.* New York: Harper and Brothers, 1958. This study analyzes problems that have arisen since NATO's inception. It focuses on NATO's relation to other unification movements in Europe.

22. *Nashville Tennessean.*

23. New York *Herald Tribune.*

24. *New York Times.*

25. Northrop, F. C. S. *European Union and United States Foreign Policy.* New York: The Macmillan Company, 1954. An interesting, though at times highly mystical, treatment from the viewpoint of sociological jurisprudence.

26. Padover, Saul K., and Leonard, L. Larry. "Europe's Quest for Unity," Foreign Policy Association *Headline Series,* No. 97, January-February, 1953. A brief treatment of prewar and postwar unification movements.

27. Pratt, Julius W. *A History of United States Foreign Policy.* New York: Prentice-Hall, 1955.

28. Reynolds, P. A. "The European Coal and Steel Community," *Political Quarterly,* 23 (July-September, 1952), pp. 282-92.

29. Senate Foreign Relations Committee. *Hearings on the Foreign Aid Program,* March 20-April 15, 1957, 85th Congress, 1st Session, 1957.

30. ———. *Legislation on Foreign Relations,* 85th Congress, 1st Session, 1957.

31. Sennholz, Hans F. *How Can Europe Survive?* New York: D. Van Nostrand Company, 1955. European unification is examined from a viewpoint strongly favorable to *laissez faire* economic theory.

32. Shepley, James. "How Dulles Averted War," *Life Magazine,* 40 (January 16, 1956), pp. 70-82. This semi-official article sets forth Secretary Dulles' "brink-of-war" diplomacy.

33. *United States in World Affairs, 1947,* et seq. New York: Harper and Brothers, 1948. This annual series published for the Council on Foreign Relations provides an invaluable secondary source on current problems in American foreign policy.

34. Vandenberg, Arthur H., Jr., ed. *The Private Papers of Senator Vandenberg.* Boston: Houghton Mifflin Company, 1952. Congressional viewpoints on various phases of American-European relations are covered on pp. 337-421; 474-519.

35. Wandyez, Piotr S. "Regionalism and European Integration," *World Affairs Quarterly,* 28 (October, 1957), pp. 229-59.

36. Warne, J. D. *N. A. T. O. and Its Prospects.* New York: Frederick A. Praeger, 1954. A British observer evaluates NATO.

37. X. [George F. Kennan] "The Sources of Soviet Conduct," *Foreign Affairs,* 25 (July, 1947), pp. 556-83. In this article Kennan justifies the containment doctrine and outlines what he believes will be its ultimate consequences for the USSR; Kennan's viewpoints undoubtedly expressed the thinking of the Truman and later the Eisenhower Administration regarding America's proper response to the Soviet challenge.

38. Zurcher, Arnold. *The Struggle to Unite Europe, 1940-1958.* New York: New York University Press, 1958. A perceptive analysis of progress in achieving European unification, highlighting many problems and issues which appear to have gone largely unnoticed in the United States.

CHAPTER 11

The Middle East and Africa

Storm Centers of Diplomatic Conflict

Among the far-reaching changes in the international community brought about by the Second World War few surpass in importance the emergence of the Middle East as a maelstrom of great power conflict. And for the future, few problems will have higher priority for American policy-makers than evolving successful policies toward the continent of Africa.

In recent years, the Middle East has exhibited many of the characteristics associated with the Balkans of the pre-World War I era.* Turmoil and ferment, engendering manifold controversies and antagonisms among great and small powers, appear endemic to the region. While the United States at an early stage in its history developed a fairly well-understood body of principles that governed American diplomatic behavior toward

Europe and Asia, it had no foreign policy at all for the Middle East before the Second World War (25, pp. 422-23). This fact furnishes one key to American diplomatic efforts in the Middle East in the postwar period. Foreign policy officials in the United States have been required to formulate and carry out policies and programs toward an area with which they have had little or no historical experience and for which lessons from their domestic history afforded minimum guidance—and to do this at a time when turbulence within the area necessitated quick and difficult judgments. Time and again the urgency of crises has only been matched by their importance both within the immediate context of the Middle East and within the larger context of the international community.

How the United States has responded to the challenge of events in the Middle East in recent years is our central inquiry in this chapter. The issues that have confronted American policy-makers can be grouped into three categories, and we have subdivided the chapter accordingly: the Arab-Israeli conflict; Middle Eastern defense; and Arab nationalism.

*Contemporary usage varies considerably concerning the territory embraced by what was formerly called the "Near East" and now is generally known as the "Middle East." As used here, "Middle East" includes an arc of territories extending from Pakistan to Morocco, northward to Turkey, and southward to the Arabian peninsula and the Sudan. Geographically, Morocco, Algeria, Tunisia, Egypt, and the Sudan are in Africa, but in most respects their foreign policy orientation is toward the Middle East.

257

1. THE ARAB–ISRAELI CONFLICT

The United States had no foreign policy toward the Middle East prior to World War II because it thought it had no vital interests in this far-away and backward region. Great Britain, and to a lesser extent France, considered the Middle East their sphere of interest. Until the 1930's therefore, American activities in the region were limited chiefly to those carried on by educators, missionaries, and philanthropic groups. These groups won the friendship of the Arab populations that lasted until it was dissipated by the partition of Palestine in the 1947-48 period. During the 1930's, American oil companies began to acquire a stake in Middle East fields. By the postwar period American oil concessions surpassed those of any other country.

During the Second World War the United States became conscious as never before of the strategic-military role of the Middle East. One of the most decisive battles of the war was fought in the deserts of North Africa. Ports and airfields in the Middle East safeguarded Allied supply lines. Iran provided an indispensable base from which to send war matériel into Russia. Middle East oil was essential to the Allied war machine.

Nevertheless, during World War II, the United States was content to play a subordinate role in Middle Eastern diplomatic and political affairs. In the main it preferred, as in Europe, to defer the settlement of political issues until after the Axis defeat (20, II, p. 1533). Still, it was not beyond giving gratuitous advice to Britain and France concerning their colonial interests in the Middle East (20, II, pp. 1540-47). Advice on Palestine was particularly plentiful. Deeply concerned about the plight of European Jewry, high officials of the Roosevelt Administration, including the President himself, felt that Great Britain was being unnecessarily cautious in refusing to allow wholesale Jewish immigration to Palestine. Through official and unofficial channels, this viewpoint was communicated to the British Foreign Office (20, II, pp. 1528-36).

Immediately after the war the Middle East became a focal point of international discord. During 1946, for example, the nascent United Nations was compelled to deal with Soviet intrigues in the northern provinces of Iran, with complaints brought by Syria and Lebanon against French colonialism, and with the Soviet-instigated indictment against alleged British interference in Greek affairs. Concurrently, there was Soviet pressure against Turkey to revise the Montreux Convention of 1936, governing the passage of ships through the Dardanelles. Russia's European satellites were aiding the rebels in the Greek civil war. American influence in the postwar period helped in preserving the independence of Middle Eastern countries both from the threat of Soviet hegemony and from a resurgence of British and French colonialism, a fact that did much to win the friendship of the Arab countries (19, pp. 279-92).

Prelude to Partition

Whatever good-will existed toward the United States in earlier periods was soon dissipated by the inflamed passions aroused by the Palestinian issue, climaxed by the partition of that country into separate Jewish and Arab states in 1947. Partition was the culmination of a long and progressively bitter dispute among Arab countries of the Middle East, Great Britain as the League of Nations mandate power in Palestine, and Zionist groups.*

Great Britain had long taken an ambiguous position on the Palestinian issue, making contradictory promises to both sides (21, II, pp. 13-17, 25-27, 28-31, 103-06). By the 1930's, however, British policy came to have a distinctly pro-Arab cast. Meanwhile, the center of Zionist agitation had shifted to the United States. During and immediately after World War II intensive Zionist pressure was directed upon Congress, the White House, the State

---

*While Zionism has roots in the Hebrew religious faith, it is predominantly a *political* movement. Its objective has been the creation of a "national home" for the Jews in Palestine. Many Jews are Zionists, others are not; some are in fact vigorously anti-Zionist. Similarly, many non-Jewish groups and individuals support the Zionist cause. The writer has heard spokesmen for the Arab countries make the distinction between being anti-Semitic and being anti-Zionist.

Department and many other governmental agencies. American foreign policy began to reflect a deep concern for the Zionist cause, as witnessed by growing American diplomatic pressure upon Great Britain to relax restrictions against Jewish immigration into Palestine.

At the time, Great Britain was liquidating many overseas commitments, both because of its own internal economic problems and because many of these commitments had become untenable in the face of powerful nationalist movements. Confronted with recurrent armed clashes between British troops and Zionist terrorist organizations in Palestine, and despairing of ever finding a solution to the problem acceptable to Jews and Arabs alike, Britain decided to turn the problem over to the United Nations. From April to November, 1947, the General Assembly debated the Palestine question. Then it voted to partition the country into a Jewish and an Arab state. Events were soon to reveal this as an epochal decision haunting the international community for years, perhaps even generations, to come.

America and the Partition of Palestine

For the United States, the first and perhaps the most far-reaching consequence of partition of Palestine was that from 1947 onward, the Arab countries blamed Washington as the moving force behind the partition plan (34, passim). At one stroke the reservoir of Arab goodwill that had accumulated toward the United States was emptied; in its place there accumulated a reservoir of hatred, of suspicion and animosity, that did not lessen appreciably until the Suez Crisis of 1956. The United States supplanted Britain and France as the target of anti-Western animus in many Arab countries. In Arab eyes the United States personified the new "Western imperialism" that sought to establish an alien outpost in a predominantly Arab world. This conception was nourished by the fact that after the creation of the State of Israel, many private Jewish groups and their supporters in the United States sent millions of dollars of aid to Israel—a fact that was crucial in enabling that country to survive economically.

That American diplomats were exceptionally active in behalf of partition is undeniable. The United States voted for partition and used its influence widely to muster support for the partition plan among other countries, especially those in Latin America (26, passim; 17). Yet France and the Soviet Union also voted for partition. As time passed, the Kremlin's support for the Zionist cause was forgotten or deliberately overlooked in the Arab world. Until roughly 1955, the Kremlin did not intervene directly in Middle Eastern affairs. Ultimately, however, the Communist Party line acquired a pronounced anti-Zionist cast. By the late 1950's Moscow had become the self-styled champion of "Arab rights" and the defender of the anti-colonial cause against alleged Western imperialism in the Middle East. The Soviet Union sold arms to Egypt, though the latter's announced purpose was sooner or later to use them in a "second round" against Israel. The Kremlin's espousal of the cause of Arab nationalism relieved the onus of having originally voted for the creation of the State of Israel.

One striking and painful fact stands out about American advocacy of the partition of Palestine prior to 1947: the almost total insensitivity of American foreign policy-makers to the consequences of this act in terms of American-Arab relations and, more broadly, of Western-Middle Eastern relations. Time and again the Roosevelt and Truman administrations were warned by their own diplomatic officials in the field and by other countries, like Great Britain, that acceptance of Zionist demands would precipitate a crisis in the Middle East. The State Department and the military establishment apparently understood the force of Arab opposition far better than the White House, Congress, and American public opinion as a whole. Former Secretary of State Cordell Hull wrote: "In general the President [Roosevelt] talked both ways to Zionists and Arabs, besieged as he was by each camp." Leading American Zionists "believed that the President had made pledges to them. The State Department made no pledges" (20, II, p. 1536).

Former President Truman has admitted his deep suspicion of State Department officials regarding the Palestine question. Shortly after he took office, Truman told a leading American

Zionist that he would "do everything possible" to carry out Zionist demands. Moreover, Truman was "skeptical . . . about some of the views and attitudes assumed by the 'striped-pants boys' in the State Department." He felt them to be insensitive to the sufferings and privations experienced by European Jews (42, I, p. 69).

What induced the United States to champion the partition of Palestine? The heavy Zionist pressure brought upon all branches of the government during and after the Second World War constituted one of the most powerful lobbies ever organized in Washington (31, October 7, 1946). Even President Truman, who strongly sympathized with Zionist demands, was ultimately forced to close the doors of the White House to spokesmen for the Zionist cause (42, II, pp. 156-62). Two other influences were also important: the domestic political connotations of the Palestinian issue and American sympathy for the plight of thousands of Jewish refugees in Europe who had been cruelly persecuted by the Nazis. In pivotal states like New York, candidates from both parties outbid each other in attempts to win the Jewish vote by favoring the Zionist cause (31, October 5 and 7, 1946). Both Presidents Roosevelt and Truman believed that opening Palestine to homeless Jewish refugees would greatly alleviate the plight of European Jews (20, I, pp. 1531-32; 42, II, pp. 137-42).

Conflict after 1947

A depressing sequence of events followed the partition of Palestine. There were repeated clashes within the country between British troops and Jewish terrorist groups; thousands of Jewish immigrants entered the country illegally; and in the surrounding countries Arab leaders began making preparations to resist the partition of Palestine by force after the British evacuation. These developments induced the United States to re-examine its earlier policy favoring partition. In the spring of 1948, the American delegation to the United Nations proposed that the UN establish a "trusteeship" over Palestine. This proposal stemmed from belated American recognition of three salient facts: that Arab opposition to partition

was formidable and that Arab leaders were totally irreconciled to the creation of a Jewish state; that Britain, as the only nation in a position to exercise a stabilizing influence, was unsympathetic to the partition plan and would take no part in effectuating it; and that the United States itself was unprepared to assume any responsibility for preserving peace and stability after the expiration of the British mandate (43, 1947-48, p. 338). The American trusteeship proposal was doomed from the start. Except perhaps for the United States, it satisfied nobody. Zionists rejected it outright as a major retreat from the partition plan voted earlier. Arab nations by this time were disposed to accept nothing less than the continuation of Palestine as an Arab state.

When the British mandate expired on May 14, 1948, the State of Israel was proclaimed by the Jewish National Council in Tel Aviv and was immediately recognized by the United States. At once, Arab armies—bent on exterminating what they viewed as an illegal state imposed upon them by the West—crossed the borders of Palestine. The conflict that was to inflame the Middle East, and was to infuse virtually every other existing and future problem prevailing in that area, had begun.

"We Want To Make Our Position Perfectly Clear —"
The Herblock Book, Beacon Press, 1950.

Israel was spectacularly successful in driving back the decrepit Arab invasion forces. In the process Israel enlarged the territories under its control considerably beyond the boundaries laid down in the original partition proposal. Prolonged efforts by the UN to effect a truce finally bore fruit late in 1949, with an armistice established largely on the basis of the territorial *status quo*. Enlargement of Israel's borders beyond the original partition plan thus became, and remains, another source of tension in this already inflamed area.

The armistice of 1949 did little to end the conflict between the two sides. Chafing under the disgrace of a humiliating military defeat, Arab leaders periodically worked the masses into frenzies of anti-Israeli and anti-Western excitement. That their animosity toward Israel was genuine, and based upon a number of valid grievances, could hardly be doubted. Sometimes Israeli-phobia served as a convenient substitute for overdue internal reforms within many Arab countries and provided a justification for mounting expenditures on armaments. It also helped to perpetuate the hold excercised by ruling elites over poverty-ridden, ignorant masses. Much as communist leaders have relied upon the bogey of "capitalist encirclement" to rationalize authoritarian practices in Russia, so Arab leaders have talked incessantly of the coming "second round" against Israel. In preparation for this, many of them in time accepted Communist arms and Soviet military "advisers" for their armed forces.

While the Arab-Israeli dispute has waxed and waned in intensity since 1949, guerrilla warfare, commando raids and counter-raids, economic boycott and blockade, heated and incessant propaganda attacks, and non-collaboration in such fields as economic planning and cultural exchange have characterized relations between Israel and the Arab world. Bitter animosities engendered by this dispute have contributed greatly to the difficulties faced by Western policy-makers in coping with a host of other problems in the Middle East.

Obstacles to an Arab-Israeli Peace Settlement

What are the obstacles to a peace settlement between the Arab states and Israel? In the years following partition, the minimum demands of both sides have appeared as irreconcilable as ever. For Israel, the minimum demand is Arab acceptance of Israel's right to exist in peace and to carry on normal international intercourse unmolested by its neighbors. For many of the Arab states—Egypt is perhaps the leading example—the goal is nothing less than the total elimination of Israel as a sovereign state and return to the *status quo ante* partition, which is to say Arab control over Palestine. The presence of a UN police force between the two belligerent sides after the Suez crisis of 1956 prevented many earlier forms of overt conflict; progress toward removal of its underlying causes, however, appears as remote today as ever.

Numerous collateral issues affect, and are affected by, the Arab-Israeli conflict. At this point we shall mention only two of them: the plight of the refugees and the problem of regional economic planning. Beginning with the Arab invasion of Israel in 1948 and continuing thereafter, scores of Palestinian Arabs left the country. By the late 1950's, the number of Palestinian refugees totalled approximately one million persons, counting children born after 1948. Living conditions in the refugee camps were indescribably squalid. Uprooted from their homes and devoid of hope for the future, the refugees have naturally played an active part in keeping anti-Israeli sentiment alive. Many of them joined the "fedayeen", Egyptian commandos, who periodically raided Israel from the Gaza strip.

Both sides have disclaimed responsibility for the care and ultimate resettlement of the refugees. Consequently, the United Nations and the United States (unilaterally and through the UN) have largely taken on the burden of refugee relief. Israel refuses responsibility for the refugees on the ground that they left Israel voluntarily, with the expectation that sooner or later they could return in the wake of victorious Arab armies. For their part, the already overpopulated Arab countries do not desire to augment their hungry masses by nearly a million new citizens. The Arab states therefore demand that Israel restore the citizenship and the property formerly owned by the Arab refugees. To date the impasse on this crucial issue has proved insoluble (8; 13; 38).

After the Eisenhower Administration took office in 1953, American policy makers sought to bring agreement between Israel and its Arab neighbors, chiefly Syria and Lebanon, by encouraging them to collaborate on a Jordan Valley plan, a kind of Middle Eastern TVA. Benefits would include increased water supplies for irrigation and added electric power for old and new industries. Joint participation in the Jordan Valley plan might also integrate the economic interests of Israel and the surrounding Arab states more closely, thereby reducing political tensions between them. Then too this plan was expected to alleviate the refugee problem by creating new jobs (33, passim).

Technical difficulties abounded, not the least of which was how to apportion the water for irrigation made available under the plan. But overshadowing these technical difficulties was the root cause of disagreement: Arab unwillingness to accept Israel as a sovereign state, a step no Arab leader either could or would contemplate. This fact, in conjunction with the rising tide of militant Arab nationalism, doomed the Jordan Valley proposal to languish as an unfulfilled dream. Indicative of the Arab attitude in this period was the response that greeted an offer by Secretary Dulles in 1955 to provide American financial assistance for resettling the Arab refugees and to guarantee the borders of Israel that might be agreed on by both sides. An official of the Jordanian Government commented that "Dulles' very generous offer contained one fundamental flaw. He assumes the continued existence of Israel. We don't" (43, 1955, p. 177).

American Policy and the Arab-Israeli Conflict

Having been in the forefront of those countries that favored partition and steered the plan through the United Nations, since 1947 the United States has followed policies toward the Arab-Israeli conflict that have been hesitant and peripheral. Occasionally, as in the Tripartite Declaration of 1950 signed by the United States, Britain, and France (9, II, pp. 2237-38),

Washington has warned both sides against a renewal of hostilities and has offered to guarantee whatever borders might be established by negotiations between them. Sometimes too State Department officials have bluntly called upon Israel and the Arab world to face existing realities in the Middle East. In a remarkably plain-spoken address on April 9, 1954, Assistant Secretary of State Henry A. Byroade demanded that Israel look upon itself as "a Middle Eastern State" and plan its "future in that context rather than as a headquarters . . . of worldwide groupings of people of a religious faith. . . . " Byroade advised Israel to "drop the attitude of a conqueror." He was equally frank with the Arab countries, telling them that they should "accept this State of Israel as an accomplished fact. I say further that you are deliberately attempting to maintain a state of affairs delicately suspended between peace and war, while at present desiring neither" (12, passim).

Pronouncements aplenty have emanated from Washington on the Arab-Israeli controversy. Little fault can be found with an official policy that recognized some justification for the viewpoints expressed by both sides and that sought to maintain a position of objectivity in approaching this controversy. Commendable as might have been the logic of this position, and no matter how much it accorded with the traditional American policy of nonintervention in the affairs of other nations, countries inside and outside the Middle East often judged this policy not by its inherent logic or its conformity with historic American diplomatic principles, but by its practical effects in the Middle East storm center. When the policy was viewed in juxtaposition with the American position toward a host of other Middle Eastern issues—promotion of the Baghdad Pact security system, seeming endorsement of Arab nationalistic movements that tended to undermine British and French power in the area, provision of arms and economic assistance to the Arab countries—the impression frequently emerged that America's declared policy of "neutrality" in the Arab-Israeli dispute amounted in reality to a curious indifference toward the future fate of Israel and toward the repercussions of unbridled Arab nationalism and xenophobia.

The truth is that since 1947 American foreign policy toward the Arab-Israeli controversy has been bankrupt. As a major instigator of the partition of Palestine and as a leading member of the United Nations, the United States incurred obligations that it was not subsequently willing to carry out. Time revealed that the division of Palestine was fraught with many kinds of risks and consequences that should have been weighed before the United States championed the cause of partition. As the risks became more apparent and more formidable, America began to question the wisdom of coercing reluctant Arab states into accepting the existence of Israel. Continued friendship with the Arabs came to be viewed in Washington as the *sine qua non* for preserving Western influence throughout the Middle East and, more specifically, for maintaining access to Middle Eastern oil and countering the growing influence of the Communist bloc.

In trying to cope with the whirlwinds of Arab recrimination released by the partition of Palestine, American officials found themselves in a quandary from which there did not appear to be a satisfactory escape. The United States was seeking a middle-of-the-road course between two positions that could not, in the last analysis, be compromised: Israel's determination to exist as an independent state and the Arab states' equally fierce determination to exterminate Israel. Since partition, this question has been the pivotal issue in Arab-Israeli relations; all other issues like the refugee question or development of the Jordan Valley are secondary to it. Similarly, answers to the question of whether Israel is to be regarded as a permanent entity, or whether it is destined to be swallowed up in an Arab sea, will inevitably shape attitudes on collateral issues like Middle Eastern defense, economic development schemes, colonialism, and relations between Western and communist powers in the Middle East. As time passed, the Arab-Israeli dispute has become more and more intertwined with other critical issues in the Middle East, so much so that its disentanglement from these disputes is all but impossible. Preserving Western influence in the face of anti-Western currents in the Arab world, promoting political stability in the area, and maintaining a strong defense position more and more intrude into, and sometimes almost usurp, the Arab-Israeli question.

A belated American, or possibly UN, guarantee of the existence of Israel would trigger new waves of anti-Westernism in Arab countries. By the beginning of the 1960's, only one painful course offered promise of exorcising the Arab-Israeli canker from the body politic of the Middle East: an unequivocal Western guarantee—issued under the auspices of the United Nations if possible, but unilaterally by the United States if necessary—that the state of Israel will be protected against military attack by the Arab world. A companion guarantee would assure the Arab countries that Israel would not be permitted to expand its borders at the expense of its Arab neighbors.

By 1959, Arab fears of Israeli expansion were heightened by the arrival in Israel of waves of new immigrants from behind the Iron Curtain. Created as the "homeland" for world Jewry, Israel has permitted unrestricted immigration, although becoming more and more hard pressed to accommodate its growing population. Israel clings to the concept of unlimited immigration as a central article in the Zionist creed. This policy seems to confirm Arab fears that Zionism ultimately contemplates taking over a good part of the Middle East. And, given the fact that much of Palestine is arid wasteland, one must question whether Israel can go on adding to its population indefinitely *without* expanding into adjacent Arab territories. A Western guarantee of Arab security therefore ought to go a long way toward allaying Arab fears and, over the long run, might compel Tel Aviv to reassess its policy of unlimited immigration.*

Whatever the merits of the Arab-Israeli controversy, it must not be settled by recourse to arms. The minimum basis for accommodation must be the right of countries on both sides to exist in peace. Border guarantees would not necessarily "settle" the bitter Arab-Israeli dis-

*The arrival of immigrants from behind the Iron Curtain was viewed by some commentators as a deliberate attempt by the USSR to inflame the Arab-Israeli dispute.

pute in the sense that they would usher in an era of amicable relations between the two sides. They would, however, remove this dis-

pute as a source of *military* conflict that threatens to plunge the Middle East and possibly the entire world into a new war at any time.

2. STRATEGIC–MILITARY PROBLEMS IN THE MIDDLE EAST

The strategic significance of the Middle East makes it one of the central arenas of world politics. This strategic importance arises chiefly from three factors. First, the Middle East is a bridge connecting three continents. Land, sea, and air routes crisscross the area, linking Europe, Asia, and Africa. Second, the Middle East possesses a vast aggregation of human and natural resources. Here we shall deal with natural resources only. The goals and problems of nearly a half-billion Arabs, and America's involvement in them, are discussed later in this chapter. The outstanding natural resource of the Middle East is of course oil. Attempts by the great powers to acquire and retain control over the huge oil reserves of the region have been productive of continuing rivalries on the international scene in recent history. The Middle East contains two-thirds of the proved oil reserves of the world and nearly three-fourths of the oil presently available to the free world. Some 60 per cent of the oil concessions in the Arab world are held by the United States; another thirty per cent are held by Britain; and most of the remainder are held by French and Dutch companies. American concessions on the Arabian peninsula are particularly rich. Oil fields in the tiny Arabian kingdom of Kuwait, for example, produce over one million barrels of oil daily! Elsewhere, American companies hold substantial concessions in the oil fields of Iran, Iraq, and the small Persian Gulf island of Qatar. It appears certain that vast new fields have yet to be discovered in this area. French North Africa holds promise of containing vast resources in the arid wastes of the Sahara (31, January 12, 1958).

With the passage of time, the United States will become increasingly dependent upon the importation of oil supplies from the Middle East and elsewhere, just as America's major European allies have long been dependent upon

the Middle East, since very little oil is found in Europe. This dependence, driven home painfully during the Suez crisis of 1956, goes far toward explaining why European countries consider the oil flow from the Middle East the life blood of Europe's industries.

A third respect in which the Middle East is of immeasurable strategic importance to the United States is the area's role in the defense of the West against Communist expansion. The Free World's defense perimeter extends from Pakistan, through Turkey, to the air and missile bases located in Libya and Morocco. This defense cordon—from which intrusions into the free world may be resisted and from which strikes could be launched against an aggressor—safeguards the southern flank of NATO and protects the sea and air approaches across the south Atlantic to the Western Hemisphere. For the United States, the Middle East is an outer moat, defending the walls of NATO and, behind them, the inner fortress of the Western Hemisphere itself. Control of the Middle East by an enemy would gravely imperil the defense posture of the West. It would immediately cut off the flow of oil to industrial countries in the NATO alliance and would place one of the most strategically located areas on the globe in unfriendly hands. Now, even more than when Hitler tried to overrun the Middle East in World War II, such an eventuality would in the end be little short of disastrous for the maintenance of Western security.

The Middle East Defense Movement

These considerations, along with heightened appreciation of the Soviet challenge that followed the Greek-Turkish Aid Program in 1947, induced the United States to strengthen the defense posture of the free world. The North Atlantic Treaty and the NATO defense system, begun in 1949, were extended further eastward

THE OIL RESOURCES OF THE MIDDLE EAST

These Big Seven of the Middle East oil group together supply one quarter of the free world's petroleum needs. Of the Big Seven's output, 60 per cent goes to oil-hungry Western Europe, the rest to Asia and Africa, the Middle East for home consumption, the U.S., and other Western Hemisphere nations.

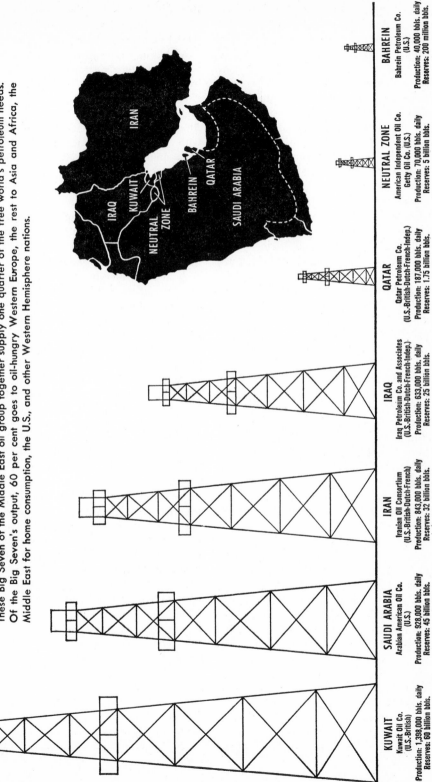

KUWAIT
Kuwait Oil Co.
(U.S.-British)
Production: 1,398,000 bbls. daily
Reserves: 60 billion bbls.

SAUDI ARABIA
Arabian American Oil Co.
(U.S.)
Production: 928,000 bbls. daily
Reserves: 45 billion bbls.

IRAN
Iranian Oil Consortium
(U.S.-British-Dutch-French)
Production: 843,000 bbls. daily
Reserves: 32 billion bbls.

IRAQ
Iraq Petroleum Co. and Associates
(U.S.-British-Dutch-French-Indep.)
Production: 633,000 bbls. daily
Reserves: 25 billion bbls.

QATAR
Qatar Petroleum Co.
(U.S.-British-Dutch-French-Indep.)
Production: 187,000 bbls. daily
Reserves: 1.75 billion bbls.

NEUTRAL ZONE
American Independent Oil Co.
Getty Oil Co. (U.S.)
Production: 70,000 bbls. daily
Reserves: 5 billion bbls.

BAHREIN
Bahrein Petroleum Co.
(U.S.)
Production: 40,000 bbls. daily
Reserves: 200 million bbls.

Adapted from *Newsweek*—Don Mackay, July 28, 1958. Production figures: April, 1958.

when Greece and Turkey joined in 1951. Increasingly, the American view came to be that an important gap existed in the containment fence to the east of Turkey. Small, weak, and sometimes politically unstable countries lay along the borders of Soviet Asia. For generations, Russia had sought to penetrate Persia, Afghanistan, and India, both to incorporate them into the Russian empire and to gain access to the southern seas. Immediately after World War II the USSR brought pressure against Iran (formerly Persia) in an evident attempt to extend Soviet control over Iranian oil fields and to gain an outlet on the Persian Gulf. In the years that followed, there was no reason for Western diplomats to believe that Russian officials had abandoned their ancient goals in the Middle East, no matter how much the Kremlin might temporarily give greater attention to areas like Europe or the Far East.

The United States therefore tried to establish a regional defense system, similar to NATO, embracing all the countries of the Middle East. Preliminary studies and negotiations soon revealed that this was impossible, owing largely to the anti-Western attitudes of Egypt and Syria (36, *passim*). Accordingly, a less ambitious scheme was devised to embrace the "northern tier" countries of the Middle East, using existing Greek and Turkish membership in NATO and the Anglo-Iraqui Treaty as nuclei. The Baghdad Pact of 1955 thus created a northern tier defense chain that bound Britain, Iraq, Iran, and Pakistan into an alliance system patterned after the NATO model (21, II, pp. 390-91).

The United States did not join the Baghdad Pact system (sometimes called the Middle East Treaty Organization or METO and renamed CENTO in 1959). Although not formally a member, the United States has been closely linked with CENTO by virtue of association with Turkey in NATO and with Pakistan in the Southeast Asia Treaty Organization or SEATO. Moreover, after 1955 the United States became associated informally with a number of CENTO's committees (15, pp. 419-20). Finally, policy declarations such as the Eisenhower Doctrine, analyzed below, committed the United States Government to regard an attack against a member of the Baghdad Pact with the utmost gravity. This eliminated any lingering doubt among potential aggressors about America's deep interest in Middle Eastern security.

What factors restrained the United States from joining the very pact it had originated? Ascending anti-Western sentiments in many Middle East countries aroused fears among American officials that America's association with the Baghdad Pact would trigger further Arab animosity and revive resentment against "Western imperialism." American and British sponsorship of the pact appeared to such capitals as Cairo to presage a resurgence of Western influence throughout the Middle East and to imply preferential Western treatment for the "northern tier" countries as opposed to those of the south (2, *passim*).

A second factor explaining the American government's reluctance to associate itself with the pact stemmed from relations with Israel. American officials were in a painful dilemma. Either the United States could propose Israeli membership in the Baghdad Pact with the almost certain result that the pact would then be unacceptable to Arab countries; or Israel could be excluded in the hope of winning Arab approval of the pact. Washington chose the latter course—a course that was viewed with considerable apprehension in Tel Aviv. Forthwith, American arms-aid began to flow to the member countries. Israel realized that these armaments could just as easily be used to invade Israel as to defend the recipient countries from outside threats. Moreover, the guarantees contained in the Baghdad Pact did not guarantee Israel against Arab aggression. Israel was not a party to the treaty, nor were some of its avowed and increasingly powerful enemies like Egypt. These considerations generated fears in Tel Aviv, echoed by Israel's supporters within the United States, about the long-range implications of American defense activities in the Middle East and about America's actual "neutrality" in the Arab-Israeli conflict.

The "Eisenhower Doctrine"

The next stage in America's efforts to bolster Middle Eastern defenses occurred as a response to growing communist influence in the area.

Egypt and Syria were receiving large stockpiles of arms from behind the Iron Curtain. During the Suez crisis of 1956-57, when British-French-Israeli troops attacked Egypt, there arose the possibility that "Soviet volunteers" might enter the Middle East ostensibly to rescue Egypt from British-French-Israeli domination. These threats prompted the Eisenhower Administration to ask Congress to approve what came to be designated the "Eisenhower Doctrine," making more explicit Washington's concern with Middle Eastern security. Congress gave the President substantially the authority he requested. A Joint Resolution passed on March 9, 1957, declared that "preservation of the independence and integrity of the nations of the Middle East" was vital to the American national interest. The key phrase in the resolution granted the President authority "to use armed forces to assist any such nation or group of such nations requesting assistance against armed aggression from any country controlled by international communism" (15, p. 45).

The Eisenhower Doctrine was in no sense a blanket guarantee of peace in the Middle East; initially it was directed solely at the danger of communist penetration. Even then, the guarantee was operative only under certain conditions: a request had to be made by one of the Middle Eastern countries before American forces could be used; the threat had to be identified as "armed aggression" as distinct, for example, from a purely internal *coup d'état;* and finally the threat must emanate from a country "controlled by international communism."

As the months passed, however, the Eisenhower Doctrine was broadened in scope, particularly by giving an elastic definition to the concept of "armed aggression." Events revealed that if the concept were interpreted in the usual sense of an outright armed attack by one state against another, then the Eisenhower Doctrine would have little practical application to power changes in the Middle East. Accordingly, Washington began to invoke the doctrine to deal with cases of "indirect aggression," citing a UN General Assembly resolution of 1949 calling on all states "to refrain from any threats or acts, direct or indirect, aimed at

impairing the freedom, independence, or integrity of any state" (7, 1957, p. 237). On July 1, 1958, Secretary of State Dulles stated that "we do not think that the words 'armed attack' preclude treating as such an armed revolution which is fomented from abroad, aided and assisted from abroad" (7, 1958, p. 300). And two weeks later President Eisenhower justified use of the doctrine when there was a threat to take over "a nation by means of indirect aggression; that is, under cover of a fomented civil strife the purpose of which is to put into domestic control those whose real loyalty is to the aggressor" (7, 1958, pp. 308-09).

The immediate occasion for this expanded interpretation of the Eisenhower Doctrine was the threat of internal subversion in pro-Western Lebanon. A rebellion against the regime of President Chamoun was being morally and materially aided by pro-communist Syria and Egypt, joined as the United Arab Republic. A revolution in nearby Iraq had also greatly enhanced communist influence in that country and had given anti-Western elements a new base of operations from which to threaten Lebanon. King Hussein in neighboring Jordan was able to maintain his authority only with the help of British troops. As the crisis mounted in Lebanon, local authorities requested the United States to render assistance. Accordingly, on July 15, 1958, President Eisenhower ordered American marines to enter Lebanon to preserve order in that internally-divided country. American intervention was of vital importance in enabling President Chamoun to maintain his authority throughout the country. For the time being, Lebanon was successfully held in the Western camp. Inside and outside the Middle East, however, widespread criticism was directed at the United States for utilizing troops to intervene in Lebanon's political affairs. Two questions would likely determine the future efficacy of the Eisenhower Doctrine in similar situations. In view of the shifting political tides characteristic of many Middle Eastern countries, what are the legitimate criteria for deciding that governments—particularly those undergoing violent domestic factionalism—have "requested" and should receive American assistance? And would the time gained by application of the Eisenhower Doctrine be used wisely by Western countries to grapple with bedrock sources of instability in the Middle East?

Middle Eastern Defense in the Balance

In weighing the effectiveness of efforts by the United States and its allies to strengthen the defensibility of the Middle East, one central fact dominates the asset side of the ledger. This is that by the end of the 1950's the four Middle Eastern members (and former members) of the Baghdad Pact—Pakistan, Iraq, Iran, and Turkey—retained their independence, despite a number of Communist-instigated threats against them since the pact was established. Turkey continued to serve as a vital connecting link between western and eastern segments of the free world's defense perimeter and to maintain its vigilant guardianship over the Straits waterway, against Soviet efforts to gain control over this access route to the Mediterranean Sea. No less crucial was the fact that the oil fields of Iran remained under the control of Western powers.

Entries on the asset side of the diplomatic ledger, however, were greatly exceeded by those on the liability side—so much so that by the beginning of the 1960's Middle Eastern defense continued to rank as one of the persistent issues facing officials in Washington, London, and Paris. By that time, the Baghdad Pact was rapidly disintegrating. Its foundations were being eroded by powerful nationalist and anti-Western currents throughout the Middle East. Even countries along the "northern tier" were affected. Iraq, Iran, and Pakistan were politically unstable. Political turbulence grew out of the same causes that fostered nationalist and xenophobic tendencies throughout the Afro-Asian bloc: grinding poverty; great social and economic inequalities; the impact of Western culture and technology upon ancient mores and cultural practices; anti-Israeli sentiment; lingering resentment against Western colonialism, fanned by new outbreaks of anti-colonialism in Africa; the diplomatic activities and ambitions of newly-independent countries like Egypt; and the blandishments and pressures emanating from the Kremlin and its followers within the Middle East. The con-

fluence of these forces threatened to engulf the Middle East in political turbulence and to sweep away remaining vestiges of Western influence. In the one area—erecting barriers against the threat of internal subversion and infiltration by communist and pro-communist groups—in which the Middle East was peculiarly vulnerable, such measures as the Baghdad Pact and the Eisenhower Doctrine furnished minimum assistance in advancing Western goals. Indeed, in some respects the very existence of the pact and the doctrine aggravated political strife within a number of Middle Eastern countries because adherence to these instruments was a hotly disputed domestic issue. A brief glance at recent events in an important Baghdad Pact country, Iraq, will illustrate these points.

Iraq, for many years regarded as a firm ally of the West, in the summer of 1958 experienced a political revolution that ushered extreme nationalist elements into power. As the months passed, strong right and left wing political factions began to fight for control of the country. Premier Kassim was forced to walk a tightrope between these equally matched factions. Although perhaps not communist-dominated, the left-wing in Iraqui politics contained an active and exceedingly vocal communist element; this wing favored more intimate relations with the USSR and a corresponding decrease in Iraq's dependence upon the West. The Soviet Union meanwhile had begun to strengthen its appeal by stepping up its propaganda activities to Arab groups and by promising to assist with the economic development of Iraq and other Arab countries. Shipments of Soviet arms began to arrive in Iraq. Throughout late 1958 and early 1959, press reports told also of intensive Communist attempts to infiltrate Iraqui governmental positions.

Rightist forces in Iraqui politics, on the other hand, strongly favored the alignment of their country with the Pan-Arab movement led by the United Arab Republic; if these elements carried the day in Iraq, ultimately the country might join the U. A. R. To become an influential force, the U. A. R. needed control over some of the Middle East's oil reserves. Iraq possessed the oil which both Syria and Egypt lacked.

Finally, early in 1959, Premier Kassim threw in his lot with the left wing, ousting rightist members from his regime. This move further weakened Iraq's ties with the West and opened the door for greater Soviet influence. Then on March 24, 1959, Iraq formally withdrew from the Baghdad Pact, thereby ratifying its *de facto* withdrawal over the course of preceding months. Left with only two Middle Eastern members—Turkey and Iran, neither of which was ethnically an Arab country—the Baghdad Pact had lost much of its original value as a guarantor of peace and security in this region. A compensating factor, however, was that the Eisenhower Doctrine—particularly as it was applied to the crisis in Lebanon—injected American power more decisively into the Middle East. Meanwhile, it could be confidently expected that instability would continue to characterize the Iraqui scene. Internally, right-wing groups still commanded a wide popular following; externally, tensions were growing between Iraq and Egypt, with Cairo becoming increasingly disenchanted with the Kremlin's intrigues in Arab affairs (31, February 15 and 22, March 25 and 26, 1959).

Western-sponsored defense measures also served to accelerate and solidify Arab unification movements. So antagonistic was the reaction of countries like Egypt, Syria, and Jordan to the Baghdad Pact that some of them turned to the Soviet Union for aid in countering Western defense schemes; shared antagonism to such schemes acted as a catalyst to speed up collaboration among some Arab nations. Egypt began to receive Communist arms and stepped up the tenor of its anti-Western propaganda, directing it more virulently than ever against "American imperialism." Soviet economic and technical experts arrived in larger numbers in the Middle East. Syria proved especially receptive to communist blandishments; arms and economic assistance flowed into the country, accompanied by the inevitable Soviet "technical advisers." By mid-1957 an openly pro-communist regime had taken control in Syria. Apart from affording a foothold for realization of age-old Soviet ambitions in the Middle East, this development threatened Turkey, America's most reliable ally in the Middle East. Turkey was in danger of being sandwiched between the military might of the USSR to the north and its new crypto-satellite, Syria. Considering the eclipse of British power in Suez and the subsequent Egyptian nationalization of the canal in 1956, communist control over Syria also entailed a major threat to the flow of Middle East oil, upon which the economic systems of Western Europe depended. Oil pipelines, connecting fields in Iraq and the Persian Gulf area with the Mediterranean, crossed Syria. Suez, the other major route for oil to the West, was under Egyptian control. To assure an alternative route, the Western powers have considered building a new pipeline from Iran into southern Turkey; but this proposal has met with strong opposition by Arab countries—particularly Iraq, Syria, and Egypt—that have objected to having the flow of Middle Eastern oil supplies dependent upon the co-operation of militantly pro-Western Turkey (31, September 22, 1957).

The conclusion seems unavoidable that American-instigated attempts to buttress the defenses of the Middle East by the Baghdad Pact and the Eisenhower Doctrine have produced decidedly mixed results. By the beginning of the 1960's, the vulnerability of the Middle East to communist penetration and influence—if not necessarily to overt military attack—was considerably greater than it had been in 1955. Widespread political unrest and intra-regional tensions continued to present a hospitable environment for the flourishing of extremist political movements and for the machinations of the Kremlin. It could not be fairly inferred that the deterioration witnessed after 1955 had been *caused* by the Baghdad Pact and the Eisenhower Doctrine. But it could be said that these measures were largely irrelevant to the elimination of underlying sources of instability in the Middle East. The Western powers had concentrated on military pacts and guarantees and had neglected to deal with fundamental sources of discord. Western efforts to buttress Middle Eastern defense were more vulnerable for what they *failed* to do than for what they did. None of these efforts supplied the ingredients that had been lacking in Western-Middle Eastern relations throughout most of the postwar period: projects and policies that somehow blended the interests of newly-independent Arab countries with those of Western countries, to form a broad, mutually agreed-upon approach to problems prevailing in the area. Success in finding this indispensable key in turn depended upon the ability of the West to understand the psychology of Arab nationalism and evolve policies and methods compatible with Arab nationalist demands. It is to a detailed examination of the nature and implications of Arab nationalism that we turn in the next section.

3. THE WEST AND ARAB NATIONALISM

The Sources and Nature of Nationalist Ferment

Since the end of World War II Arab nationalism has become a mighty stream fed by numerous tributaries. It has threatened to sweep away Western influence throughout the Middle East and to inundate that area in wave after wave of fanaticism and xenophobia, spawning numerous intra-regional tensions and inviting great power antagonisms.

Nationalism has infused virtually every issue troubling the Middle East in the contemporary era. The complaints in 1946 of Syria and Lebanon to the United Nations against French colonialism were anchored in nationalism. Part of the Arab states' opposition to the creation of Israel lay in their historical resentment of Western dictation. Nationalism was a key factor in the Iranian oil dispute which began in 1951 and was not settled until 1953, when Iran successfully nationalized the holdings of the Anglo-Iranian oil company (11, 892-95).

Not since the time of the Crusades have the Arab states been politically united. Their internal weaknesses have greatly facilitated the imposition of colonial domination over them. Pan-Arabism is a natural reaction against former colonial subjection and, in the minds of many Arab leaders, the necessary preliminary to restoration of the greatness that once belonged to Islam. Pan-Arabism is sustained by many forces, of which three have been of lasting historical significance: a common language—Arabic; a common religion—Islam; and common racial ties—Semitic. Since the First World War, other forces have fostered Arab unity. Most of the Arab states received their independence after the First World War from either Britain or France, their colonial masters. Economic backwardness and widespread poverty have given the Arab masses a sense of unity and feeling of separateness from the more advanced Western countries. To a greater or lesser degree all the Arab states resent involvement in the cold war and desire to retain their independence of action from both the communist bloc and the Western alliance. Finally, since 1947, there has been a powerful new bond of Arab unity: intense hostility to Israel.

Middle Eastern nationalism differs from other nationalist movements with which the student of history is familiar, such as those in 19th century Europe or in India under the leadership of Ghandi and Nehru. In Europe nationalism meant predominantly "self-determination," a goal that grew out of the philosophy of the French Revolution. But the Middle East "received nationalism in isolation, without liberalism, democracy, and the humanitarian aims . . . " (23, p. 7). That is why nationalism in the Middle East has so often "taken . . . the form of chauvinism, of emotional aggression, and of opposition to everything foreign rather than of genuine patriotism." In its overall manifestations, Middle Eastern nationalism

is distinguished by the over-estimation of one's own nation and the denigration of others, the lack of the spirit of self-criticism and responsibility, an ambivalent appraisal of the destiny of one's nation based on a feeling of inferiority, and a general tendency to attribute anything wrong with one's nation to the evil-doing of others. . . . (23, p. 8).

Arab nationalism has thus been deeply xenophobic and far less inclined than comparable movements in the Far East to acknowledge the benefits that have accrued from years of British or French colonial administration.

An even more basic feature of Arab nationalism has been its lack of constructive social, economic, and political programs to be carried out after the termination of Western colonial rule. Anti-Westernism has become an end in itself, a rallying cry permitting Arab elites to substitute their own despotic control for colonial power. Two British commentators have pointed out that:

> The Arab intelligentsia was even more hostile to the West than was, say, the Indian intelligentsia. . . . The explanation was that the Arab countries, just because the West had controlled their governments and not their peoples, never experienced the Western influence in its constructive, cultural, liberating aspect—less even than did the Chinese . . . because the Chinese accepted missionary influence and the Arabs on the whole did not. . . . the West never had the power to transform Arab society, to offer a new civilization, or to reorganize the educational and legal systems, as Britain did in India. (46, p. 19).

Arab nationalism has thus often tended to be negative, fanatical, and heavily opportunistic. Arab leaders have achieved freedom from alien domination; but nationalism has not produced many tangible fruits in terms of the economic, social, and political uplift of the inhabitants of the Arab countries. In recent years, nationalism has brought about the overthrow of the monarchy in Egypt and the accession of President Nasser's vocally anti-Western regime. It has produced a pro-communist order in Syria and an extreme leftist order in Iraq. In countries like Lebanon and Jordan, nationalist ferment imparts continuing instability to existing governments.

To a greater or lesser degree in every Arab country, revolutionary movements advocate radical solutions for age-old, chronic problems like poverty, illiteracy, disease, concentration of productive wealth and privilege in the hands of a few, and despotic political rule. To them "democracy" means freedom from mass exploitation by both foreign and indigenous elites. It means government programs to promote material advancement and human welfare. While there is agreement on basic goals, internal skirmishes continue over such issues as what groups will govern in newly-independent Arab countries, what groups will reap the benefits from oil royalties, and over the obligation of ruling cliques to advance the common

good. William Yale, a partisan for the Arab cause, has written:

> The Near East is going through changes so basic that they are profoundly revolutionary. These economic, social, and ideological changes are being brought about with increasing rapidity. . . . The ruling classes in the Arab countries, the landowners and tribal sheiks, are fearful lest these changes do away with their privileged position. . . . The religious leaders fear the weakening and undermining of Islam. . . . The well-to-do middle class fears the advent of socialism. . . . those with a stake in the maintenance of the old order dread internal revolution. (48, p. 431).

As a generality, Yale continues, "Most of the Near and Middle East is still in a transitional stage of development from a medieval to a modern society" (48, p. 432).

The manifold implications of the Arab nationalist ferment thus present officials in Washington and other Western capitals with many difficult choices. For example, shall the United States and its allies associate themselves with existing regimes like those in Iran and Jordan, knowing full well that in all probability nationalist tides will eventually sweep away monarchial institutions in these countries? Or should Western policies seek to encourage the emergence of more popular-based political orders, even at the risk of undermining established authority in these countries? Should economic assistance be provided by the West to friendly countries in the Middle East, irrespective of the socio-economic-political hierarchy prevailing within some of them and the degree of benefit for Arab populations as a whole? These are exceedingly difficult, but typical, questions with no clear-cut answers.

Mounting Tensions Over Suez

Many examples of Arab nationalism could be examined. We shall confine our attention to one only: Egyptian nationalism, climaxed by the Suez Canal crisis of 1956-57. Egyptian nationalism is selected both because of its own importance and because of its over-all ramifications for Western-Middle Eastern relations.

The roots of Egyptian nationalism go back at least as far as the mid-19th century. Nationalist ferment was kept alive by Egyptian intellectuals and by the unifying influence of Islam.

Britain occupied Egypt in 1881, and from that time on—as the British extended their influence within Egypt and throughout the Sudan and adjacent areas—many groups in Egypt sought to throw off British domination. For a long time, Britain successfully resisted Egyptian nationalist demands. By the 1930's, however, London began to make concessions. In 1936, Britain agreed to reduce its prerogatives in the Canal Zone sharply and to surrender them altogether by 1956, by which time it was hoped that Egypt would be strong enough to protect the canal alone.

In Egypt as elsewhere, World War II accelerated nationalist demands. Throughout the 1940's and early 1950's, Egypt demanded Britain's unconditional withdrawal from the Canal Zone. America's desire for establishment of a Middle Eastern defense system derived in part from the hope that such a system would safeguard the Suez Canal after the impending British evacuation. Egypt refused to discuss the problem of regional security until after British withdrawal from Suez. London, on the other hand, would not comply with Egypt's demand until some arrangement for the security of British interests in the Canal Zone had been made. The resulting impasse was not resolved until 1954, when both countries finally negotiated a new agreement that in effect met Egyptian demands. While leaving the canal in Egyptian hands, the agreement gave Britain the right to reoccupy the Canal Zone in time of war. Both countries reaffirmed their support for the Convention of 1888 which had proclaimed the canal an international waterway open to the traffic of all nations (**21**, II, pp. 383-84).*

Meantime, profound political changes were occurring within Egypt. King Farouk was over-

*At the time of this agreement, Egypt was already blockading Israeli shipping from the Suez Canal. Egypt has maintained that its pre-existing blockade was, at least tacitly, accepted under this agreement. Israel and the Western powers, however, have repeatedly demanded that Egypt lift the blockade, citing a resolution passed by the UN Security Council on September 1, 1951, calling on Egypt to "desist from the present practice of interfering with the passage through the Suez Canal of goods destined for Israel." To date, Egypt has successfully resisted Western demands to comply with this resolution (**9**, II, pp. 2251-54).

thrown by a military junta in July, 1952. In his place the Egyptian officer corps temporarily installed a figurehead, General Mohammed Naguib. Then in November, 1954, Naguib—who had manifested pro-Western sympathies—was overthrown by Colonel Abdel Nasser, who typified the young, fiercely nationalistic officer class. Nasser resembled many of the nationalist leaders who have risen to political prominence throughout the Middle East in recent years; his program symbolized the aspirations of nationalist groups in many surrounding states. First, the foundation of his power was the army, which contained many of the best minds and most ambitious leaders in the society. Schooled in discipline, conscious of the nation's economic and military inferiority, and yet proud of their country, this class could be counted on to support leaders who promised rapid progress in solving the nation's problems. Second, such groups defined "democracy" in different terms than the meaning commonly attributed to it in the West. Primary attention was to be devoted to achieving "social" and "economic" democracy. A long transition period would be required before the society was ready for "political" democracy as practiced in the West. Meantime, the established government must exercise firm direction and control over the country to eliminate public attachment to old ways and to pave the way for a new social-economic-political order. Third, Nasser's regime was similar to other newly-independent governments in the Middle East in that it exhibited a strong affinity for democratic forms and symbols for its official policies. The national legislative body, one observer noted, exists

to discuss and approve government measures. The various prerogatives with which it is endowed, according to the new Constitution, are hardly more than *pro forma* methods of sanctioning the Presidential will. (**32**, p. 36).

This description applied also to constitutional guarantees, popular elections, and other democratic trappings. These were more often than not instruments for maintaining Nasser and his coterie in power rather than mechanisms for protecting the rights of citizens or of expressing the popular will. Finally, Nasser's policies at home and abroad left no doubt concerning the dominating impulse in Egyptian foreign policy: advancing the national interests as Nasser defined them. Nasser's professed "neutralism" and his evident determination to pursue Egyptian goals—if necessary by playing off one great power against another—mirrored the viewpoints of nationalist leaders throughout the Afro-Asian bloc.

Nasser's writings reflect a belief in himself as a "hero in search of a role" (**29**, *passim*). Not only has he looked upon his mission as deliverance of Egypt from foreign bondage, but in time he placed himself at the head of the Pan-Arab movement and made Cairo the center of what he hoped would become an Arab federation. Nasser came to personify the anti-Western sentiment current throughout much of the Middle East. He fanned the flames of Arab hatred against Israel, against the Baghdad Pact, and against French colonial rule in North Africa. More covertly, Nasser aided anti-colonial movements, especially the rebellion in French North Africa (**49**, 1957, pp. 84-7). Then, in the summer of 1955, came Nasser's most serious flirtation with communism to date —the Egyptian-Czech arms agreement. For the first time Russia appeared to be getting a foothold in the Middle East. Israel, which had apprehensively watched American arms flow to the Baghdad Pact countries, now saw Communist arms flowing to Egypt. From there they would doubtlessly go to other Arab groups. Israel was gravely worried over this build-up in Arab armed strength. Urgent Israeli requests for American arms to maintain Israel's military strength proportionate to Arab military growth evoked only State Department assurances that the matter was under study. Secretary Dulles indicated his clear opposition to an "arms race" in the Middle East (**11**, 1955, p. 18). But, regardless of America's position, Egypt, encouraged by Soviet Russia, had already initiated an arms build-up which steadily weakened Israel's military posture in the Middle East.

After the Czech arms deal, Egyptian trade with Iron Curtain countries was expanded. In a move which was particularly galling to the United States Nasser extended Egyptian recognition to Red China. He also discussed technical assistance to Egypt by the USSR. These moves

DRILLING FOR OIL

Yoes in *The San Diego Union*, January, 1956.

by Cairo were taken in an atmosphere of mounting anti-Westernism and of increasing bellicosity toward Israel.

Side-by-side with Nasser's gravitation toward the communist camp had gone American-Egyptian negotiations over the construction of the Aswan High Dam on the upper reaches of the Nile. This project was designed to provide flood control, irrigation facilities, and electric power for Egypt and the other riparian states such as the Sudan and Ethiopia. One of the most ambitious engineering projects ever planned, the Aswan High Dam was to cost $1.5 billion or more and to require 10-15 years for completion. Nasser appeared determined to proceed with the project. Numerous and exhaustive studies of the dam's feasibility had uncovered several serious problems (**6**, *passim*). Nevertheless, the United States and, with its encouragement, the World Bank finally agreed to assist Egypt with a substantial loan for building the dam. In addition, Egypt would have to borrow heavily to complete the financial arrangements. American officials hoped that America's help would at least partially offset mounting communist influence over Nasser and

PLANS FOR THE ASWAN HIGH DAM

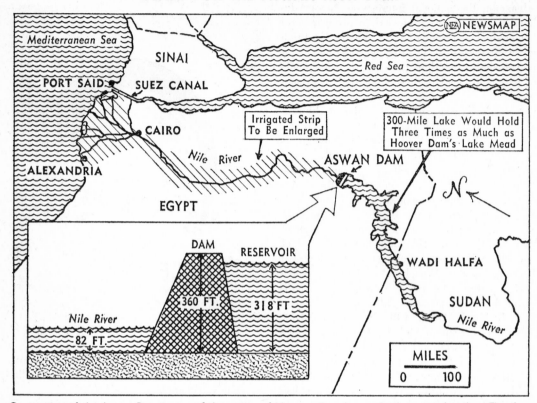

Construction of the Aswan Dam is one of the most ambitious engineering projects ever undertaken. The dam, which has been a central goal in President Nasser's program, will add two million acres of arable land to feed Egypt's rapidly expanding population. Retraction of an Anglo-American offer to finance the project triggered Nasser's nationalization of the Suez Canal in 1956 and the ensuing Anglo-French-Israeli invasion of Egypt. After extended negotiations, the Soviet Union in 1958 offered economic assistance to Egypt to erect the dam. Nonetheless, the total cost — between five and six hundred million dollars — will impose a severe drain upon Egypt's economy, thereby discounting heavily the net economic benefits accruing from the dam in the immediate future.

NEA Service, Inc., Oct. 24, 1958.

would restore in some degree waning Western influence in the Middle East.

But Nasser's policy of spurning the Western powers and cultivating the communist bloc eventually led to second thoughts in the United States about help for building the Aswan Dam. On July 19, 1956, Secretary of State Dulles retracted America's offer to assist in financing the project. He cited numerous technical and financial difficulties that purportedly created doubts about the dam's feasibility. Later, Dulles admitted candidly that the American offer had been withdrawn because of Egypt's anti-Western, pro-Soviet policies. To

his mind, the issue was: "do nations which play both sides get better treatment than nations which are stalwart and work with us?" (15, pp. 375-76).* Nasser's retort was to nationalize

---

*Speculation about Secretary Dulles' motives for withdrawing American assistance for the Aswan Dam construction continued for several months thereafter, especially among his Democratic critics in Congress. Leading Democrats alleged that Dulles had withdrawn this offer for the avowed purpose of precipitating a "showdown" with Nasser, after the latter's anti-Western activities had become galling to American officials. Thus, when the Senate considered the Eisenhower Doctrine early in 1957, Senator William Fulbright (Democrat of Arkansas) requested complete information from

the Suez Canal. This move not only ignited a new Middle Eastern crisis but, with Russia threatening to send "volunteers" to Egypt, it threatened an international conflagration.

The Suez Crisis of 1956

After Nasser nationalized the Suez Canal Company on July 26, 1956, Britain and France were ready to intervene with troops at once to assure that this vital waterway remained open to their commerce, especially to the oil tankers upon whose cargoes the economies of Western Europe were so dependent. The State Department, however, urged caution. Secretary Dulles took the lead in trying to resolve the dispute by negotiations intended to devise a plan that would be acceptable to the users of the canal as well as to Egypt.

As the weeks passed, Nasser refused to retreat from unilateral Egyptian control over the canal. He would not accept limitations upon his freedom of action demanded by Britain and France and other users of the canal. Complex talks and negotiations were going on, but there was little genuine progress in reconciling the demands of both sides. The Suez issue entered a new phase when it was presented to the Security Council of the United Nations in

the State Department on Aswan Dam negotiations. On the Senate floor he confessed that he had received "an adequate record" of these proceedings, but that "it was necessary to do some reading between the lines" and that he found "several . . . gaps in the information" furnished him.

After a careful study of the record made available, Fulbright concluded that the *official* reasons given (e.g., that other riparian states had not agreed to co-operate in building the dam, that it would cost Egypt too much, that Congress opposed the plan, etc.) were not valid reasons. He was strongly inclined to accept the view that the American move represented a calculated step by Secretary Dulles to have a showdown with Nasser. Fulbright noted, for instance, that aid to Egypt was cancelled against the advice of the American ambassador there and against the recommendations of the International Bank for Reconstruction and Development, which was to advance part of the funds. Fulbright attributed the following events directly to this move: Nasser's seizure of the Suez Canal; new opportunities for Soviet mischief in the Middle East; aggravation of the Arab-Israeli dispute; strengthening of the idea that the United States wanted satellites; diversion of the world's attention from the current Hungarian crisis. Fulbright's provocative analysis of Middle East problems should be read in full, in the *Congressional Record*, 103 (1957), pp. 14701-10.

October. It was during UN debate over the canal issue that Israeli forces, on October 29, 1956, invaded the Sinai Peninsula. Within hours they had cut through the thin line of Egyptian defenders opposing the Israeli advance toward the canal and had captured or destroyed vast quantities of Communist arms accumulated by Nasser in his desert supply depots. In the process they wiped out the hornets' nest of "fedayeen" commando bases in Gaza from which recurrent Egyptian attacks had been launched into Israel.

While the UN was still considering this outbreak of hostilities, Britain and France delivered an ultimatum to both Israel and Egypt requiring them to withdraw their troops from the canal area. When the ultimatum was not heeded, Britain and France, on November 5, parachuted troops onto Egyptian soil—allegedly for the purpose of "protecting" the Suez Canal. Primarily, however, the Anglo-French invasion of Egypt was precipitated by a growing disillusionment with Nasser and the hope that invasion would result in his overthrow. Instead, if anything invasion solidified Nasser's position and rallied masses throughout the Afro-Asian world to his cause.

In dealing with this new threat to the peace, which coincided with the Soviet suppression of the Hungarian Revolt, the United States took the initiative within the United Nations in arranging a cease-fire. The American position was that no matter what provocations had induced Israeli-British-French attacks against Egypt, diplomatic issues must not be settled by resort to military force (15, pp. 151-57). In a rare display of *mea culpa*, Secretary Dulles confessed that neither the United States nor the United Nations had displayed sufficient initiative in the past in dealing with sources of tension and instability in the Middle East (15, pp. 152-53). Nevertheless, he felt that the indispensable preliminary to any resumption of negotiations over these issues was the withdrawal of foreign troops from Egyptian soil.

Confronted with the moral censure of the world—and with the almost certain alienation of the Arab-Asian bloc within the United Nations —Britain and France reluctantly agreed to a cease-fire and to an evacuation of their troops.

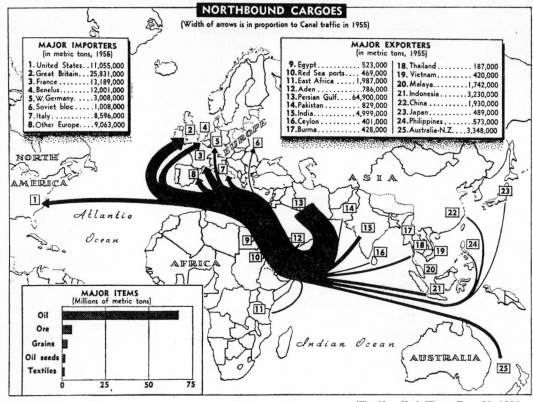

NORTHBOUND CARGOES
(Width of arrows is in proportion to Canal traffic in 1955)

MAJOR IMPORTERS
(in metric tons, 1955)

1. United States.. 11,055,000
2. Great Britain.. 25,831,000
3. France........ 13,189,000
4. Benelux....... 12,001,000
5. W. Germany.... 3,008,000
6. Soviet bloc.... 1,008,000
7. Italy.......... 8,596,000
8. Other Europe... 9,063,000

MAJOR EXPORTERS
(in metric tons, 1955)

9. Egypt.......... 523,000
10. Red Sea ports.... 469,000
11. East Africa..... 1,987,000
12. Aden.......... 786,000
13. Persian Gulf... 64,900,000
14. Pakistan....... 829,000
15. India.......... 4,999,000
16. Ceylon........ 401,000
17. Burma......... 428,000
18. Thailand........ 187,000
19. Vietnam........ 420,000
20. Malaya........ 1,742,000
21. Indonesia...... 3,230,000
22. China......... 1,930,000
23. Japan......... 489,000
24. Philippines..... 573,000
25. Australia-N.Z... 3,348,000

MAJOR ITEMS
(Millions of metric tons)

Oil / Ore / Grains / Oil seeds / Textiles

The New York Times, Dec. 23, 1956.

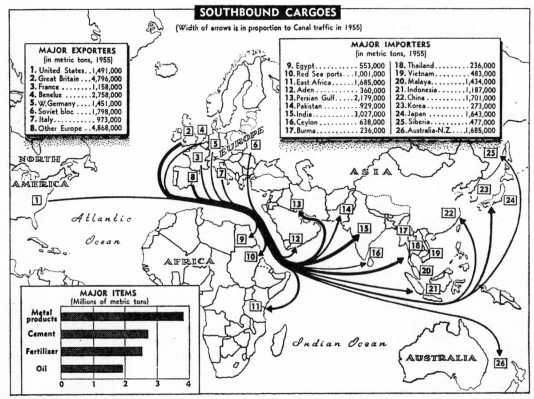

SOUTHBOUND CARGOES
(Width of arrows is in proportion to Canal traffic in 1955)

MAJOR EXPORTERS
(in metric tons, 1955)

1. United States.. 1,491,000
2. Great Britain.. 4,796,000
3. France........ 1,158,000
4. Benelux....... 2,758,000
5. W. Germany.... 1,451,000
6. Soviet bloc.... 1,798,000
7. Italy.......... 973,000
8. Other Europe... 4,868,000

MAJOR IMPORTERS
(in metric tons, 1955)

9. Egypt.......... 553,000
10. Red Sea ports.... 1,001,000
11. East Africa..... 1,685,000
12. Aden.......... 360,000
13. Persian Gulf... 2,179,000
14. Pakistan....... 929,000
15. India.......... 3,027,000
16. Ceylon........ 638,000
17. Burma......... 236,000
18. Thailand........ 236,000
19. Vietnam........ 483,000
20. Malaya........ 1,434,000
21. Indonesia...... 1,187,000
22. China......... 1,701,000
23. Korea......... 273,000
24. Japan......... 1,643,000
25. Siberia........ 477,000
26. Australia-N.Z... 1,685,000

MAJOR ITEMS
(Millions of metric tons)

Metal products / Cement / Fertilizer / Oil

Israel was much less ready to do so. By the spring of 1957 Tel Aviv finally agreed to ⟨...⟩ Gaza strip and to allow station-⟨...⟩ force throughout a neutral ⟨...⟩ Israel and its Arab neighbors.

⟨...⟩ Crisis

⟨...⟩is of 1956-57 had profound ⟨...⟩ng-range consequences, for ⟨...⟩ Eastern relations and, more ⟨...⟩American foreign policy toward ⟨...⟩ most obvious immediate con-⟨...⟩losure of the Suez Canal until ⟨...⟩red of the wreckage caused by ⟨...⟩uch more lasting and serious ⟨...⟩ed Afro-Asian apprehensions ⟨...⟩ imperialism." The Suez crisis ⟨...⟩isagreements within the British ⟨...⟩; temporarily imperilled the ⟨...⟩ce; further reduced the prestige ⟨...⟩ France in the Middle East; ser-⟨...⟩ed the Baghdad Pact; solidified ⟨...⟩sm and made Nasser a symbol of ⟨...⟩e to Western domination; created new Arab fears about the territorial ambitions of Israel; diverted world attention from the Kremlin's ruthless suppression of the Hungarian revolt; and facilitated Soviet penetration of the Middle East (46, pp. 15-16, 89-100). As the weeks went by it became apparent that Egypt's humiliating defeat had actually strengthened Nasser's hand inside and outside Egypt and that British and French prestige throughout the Arab world had reached their nadir. The Suez crisis had turned out to be highly damaging to Western influence throughout the Middle East. The humiliating circumstances under which Britain and France withdrew from Egypt, wrote one British observer, were an "open revelation of weakness" that would tend "to increase international instability. It is an invitation to others to 'have a go' at challenging Western influence . . . " (49, 1957, p. 100).

The Anglo-French invasion of Egypt was clearly a move of desperation, signifying that the Western powers had all but lost control of events in the Middle East. As one bastion after another of Western power crumbled in the area, the Anglo-French invasion seemed to admit the failure of Western statesmanship to cope with Nasser's brand of Arab nationalism. Since Western diplomacy had failed, Western powers out of blind and furious frustration would seek to exterminate Nasserism by one spectacular military blow. The Anglo-French invasion, much more than the Israeli one, was therefore the admission of diplomatic bankruptcy. This was widely perceived and bemoaned within the United States.

Less widely understood was the fact that the Suez crisis also called attention to major inadequacies in American foreign policy toward the Middle East since 1947. When the conflagration came, the United States labored creditably enough in its role as fireman; it had not, however, shown any significant foresight in the matter of fire prevention. Indeed, some of its earlier policies appeared to reflect a calloused indifference to the prospect that several inflammable issues were almost certainly sooner or later going to erupt into a diplomatic holocaust. That Washington should have been surprised when it came was eloquent testimony to the fact that American policy-makers had gravely misinterpreted developments in the Middle East and that their own policies had largely ceased to have any immediate impact upon shaping events in that region.

Arab Nationalism After Suez

Following the cease-fire in the Middle East, a UN police force patrolled the borders between Israel and the surrounding Arab countries. Israel was still denied access to the Suez Canal but had control of the Gulf of Elath to the south with its port at Aqaba, which Israel continued to hold after evacuating Egyptian territory. Otherwise, conditions that had engendered the Suez crisis showed little sign of improving. Nasser retained control of the Suez Canal; other countries used the canal on his terms. Arab antagonism toward Israel continued unabated, with Radio Cairo and other Arab voices in time beginning to speak of the coming "third round" against Israel. New waves of anti-Western sentiment swept the Arab world, in spite of the fact that the United States temporarily won the good-will of many countries in the area by demanding Anglo-French-Israeli evacuation of Egyptian soil. Soviet influence grew, with Egypt and Syria accepting communist arms and technical advisers.* Despite intimations by the United States during the Suez affair that more attention would be given to resolving tensions within the Middle East (7, 1957, pp. 261-72), little was done in succeeding weeks and months to bring many of these issues any nearer to solution.

Nasser used his enhanced position throughout the Arab world to the fullest to foment animosities against the West and other countries of the Middle East and to enlist support for his idea of a federation of Arab States under Egyptian sponsorship. Early in 1958, the political union of Egypt and Syria was announced. This move extended their collaboration initiated under the Damascus Pact, Egypt's countermove to the Baghdad Pact (31, February 2, 1958). Although Cairo invited other Arab states to join the United Arab Republic, only the tiny Arabian kingdom of Yemen seemed seriously interested. The other center of gravity of Pan-Arabism was Iraq. Deeply suspicious of Nasser's ambitions—and apprehensive over the fact that the New Egyptian-Syrian union was now in a position to block the flow of oil through Middle East pipelines—Iraq countered Nasser's move by agreeing to a union with Jordan. This union was called the "Arab Federation." Close family ties linked the Hashemite dynasties of Jordan and Saudi Arabia. At the time of its inception therefore the Arab federation was expected to maintain intimate ties with Saudi Arabia (31, February 6, 1958).

Tensions within the Arab community were further aggravated by the Iraqui revolution of 1958. At first, pro-Nasser forces had a major voice in the new regime. But as the months

---

*Nasser resisted the temptation during the Suez crisis to accept an offer of Soviet "volunteers" to help Egypt deal with the Anglo-French-Israeli invasion. The Soviet offer elicited a prompt American warning against Soviet military intervention in Middle Eastern affairs. Even Nasser, who has shown little awareness in some instances of the dangers of relying upon the Soviet Union, must have foreseen the ultimate consequences of permitting Soviet troops to enter Egyptian territory.

Additional testimony of Nasser's acumen—and of the strongly opportunistic bent of his foreign policy—is the fact that he has outlawed the Communist Party within Egypt.

passed, Premier Kassim threw in his lot with left-wing elements who had been alienated by Nasser's vigorous leadership in the Arab world and by his recent opposition to Communists within Egypt and other Arab countries. However much Arab nationalist leaders might consort with communism as a means of coercing the West, it was clear that there were fundamental points of conflict between Pan-Arabism as conceived by Nasser and co-operation with the Soviet Union as advocated by left-wing extremists in many Arab countries. Rivalries between Iraq and Egypt pointed to a continuing source of tension in the Middle East: clashes over who should lead the Pan-Arab movement and over what its relation should be with the cold-war antagonists.

Political differences dividing Arab countries have contributed in some measure to Israel's security. Hence Israel has viewed with dismay all serious progress towards political unification among Arab countries. Only time will reveal the future success of the Arab unification movement. But that the swirling currents of Arab nationalism will produce new tensions and crises in the Middle East can be predicted with assurance.

The Soviet Union and Arab Nationalism

Russia is no newcomer to the Middle East. Geography has made the USSR much more of a Middle East power than it has the United States and many of its allies. The most surprising aspect of Russia's emergence as an active diplomatic force in that area—and this was surely one of the most fundamental developments in international politics in the second half of the twentieth century—is not that it finally occurred but that it was deferred for so long. It was not until the mid-1950's that the Kremlin began to devote as much attention to penetrating the Middle East as it did to Western Europe or the Far East.

Historically Russia has sought to expand into the Middle East both for purposes of acquiring additional territory and gaining access to the sea. Since the discovery of vast oil deposits in this region, a new inducement has been to extend Soviet control over the oil-rich countries of the Arab world (27 and 28). The Middle

East has also possessed special significance for advancing communist ideological objectives, since it seemed an easy target for undermining capitalism by fomenting anti-colonial unrest. One of the first acts of the communist regime after it came into power in Russia was issuance of a proclamation signed by Lenin and Stalin and addressed to the "Labouring Moslems of Russia and the East." This urged the Moslem masses to undertake a holy war against their colonial oppressors (49, 1955, p. 153). Subsequent communist propaganda efforts have continually echoed variations on this theme.

Yet on the whole since 1917 Soviet diplomats have been chiefly occupied with other regions, so much so that the Middle East appeared to be a zone of peripheral importance to them. The USSR sought to push southward by the agreement with Germany in the Nazi-Soviet Pact of 1939. Then during the Second World War ineffectual efforts were made to break through the Dardanelles by pressure upon Turkey. Immediately after the war Soviet intrigue was evident in the northern provinces of Iran, but for reasons that are perhaps not fully known in the West, when these efforts met with resistance they were apparently abandoned. Soviet policy-makers diverted their efforts in the years that followed to more promising fields, leaving Western diplomats virtually a free hand throughout the Arab world (23, pp. 260-61).

By 1955, however, conditions within the Middle East clearly favored a renewal of Soviet diplomatic activity there, a fact that could be ascribed in large part to two developments: increasing estrangement between the West and certain Arab countries and the Geneva Conference of the great powers, at which a tacit agreement seems to have been reached that the cold war would be pursued primarily by non-military methods. The first development presented the Soviet Union with the opportunity to exploit Arab grievances against the West, engendered by such developments as the partition of Palestine, American insistence upon establishing a Middle East defense organization, and prevailing anti-colonial strife. The second development gave the Kremlin the opportunity to pursue its goals in the Arab

world with much less risk of triggering a third world war.

The most tangible manifestation of the new influence of Soviet Russia in the Middle East was the export of Communist arms to Arab countries and the emergence of an openly pro-Soviet government in Syria. "Good will" missions to Arab countries by communist officials increased markedly. There was a sharp intensification of Soviet propaganda efforts throughout the Arab region, a growing number of "cultural delegations" going in and out of Moscow, an expansion in the number of Soviet "technical advisers" visiting nations in the Middle East, new Soviet offers of loans and trade agreements with Arab countries, and a new peak of communist activity within nations in the area. The communist cause received new momentum as a result of the intense anti-Western sentiment growing out of the Suez crisis of 1956, when the USSR offered "volunteers" to Cairo and even invoked the threat of a missile attack if the invasion of Suez were not ended.

Wherever the Kremlin's fortunes were prospering in the Middle East it was because of the ingenuity of communist groups in exploit-

"Allah Be Praised — This Must Be The Technician . . . !"

Frank Interlandi in *The Des Moines Register,*
October, 1957.

ing mass discontent with poverty, economic oppression, colonialism, and foreign interference in Arab affairs. One weapon in the Communist diplomatic arsenal proved uniquely effective in this environment: the ability of the Soviet Union to identify its own diplomatic interests with those of Arab nationalists. Communist groups demonstrated great skill in playing upon three Arab phobias in particular —opposition to Israel, to Western political intervention, and to the influence of foreign corporations. For many groups in the Arab world, the USSR became a patron saint in "the Arab struggle against imperialism" and a vigilant custodian of "Arab rights" in international politics. By a remarkable exhibition of diplomatic legerdemain, Moscow succeeded in erasing several unpalatable facts from the minds of its Arab sympathizers: that the Kremlin had initially supported the partition of Palestine and had voted to create the State of Israel; that historically Russia had from time to time intervened in Arab affairs and had attempted to expand its borders southward; that communist rulers were currently exercising as brutal and exploitative a "colonial" domination over Eastern Europe as the world had ever seen; and that Russia's verbal solicitude for the downtrodden was largely belied by its record in dealing with minorities—including approximately 30 million Moslems—within its own boundaries (22, passim).

Basic to this diplomatic *tour de force* was what many Western observers identified as a fundamental reorientation in communist ideology regarding nationalist movements. What was the "correct line" of the Marxist-Leninist-Stalinist faith toward nationalist forces? Ambivalence had characterized the Soviet approach to this problem since the earliest days of the communist revolution, coming sharply to the fore in the Kremlin's attempt to define its relations with regimes like that of Kemal Ataturk in Turkey during the twenties (24, pp. 325-26). Insofar as nationalism served to embarrass the enemies of the communist state it should of course be supported. But the new nationalist leaders—designated the "national bourgeoisie"—had frequently turned out to be anti-communist and fiercely determined to preserve their country's independence, from Mos-

cow as much as from London, Paris, or Berlin. Until the mid-1950s, writes Walter Z. Laqueur, the Kremlin therefore "enjoined collaboration with the entire national movement in the Arab world . . . " (24, p. 327). But in the mid-1950s, communist spokesmen openly conceded that they had underestimated the role of the "national bourgeoisie" throughout the Arab world. Now Arab nationalist leaders were visualized as the "gravediggers of capitalism;" their regimes were necessary half-way houses along the road to the communist utopia in the Middle East. In the revolutionary scheme of things, control was expected to pass from the colonial powers, to Arab nationalists, to the left-wing elements of the Arab nationalist movements, and finally, after an alliance between these elements and the proletariat, to the Communist Party (24, pp. 325-26). Armed with this new ideological rationalization, the Kremlin after 1955 began to support Arab nationalist movements indiscriminately. The sole test of their acceptability was "not the class character of the party, nor its social and economic programs, nor its general stand on domestic issues—but only its foreign political orientation, its attitude towards West and East" (23, p. 296).

Yet by the close of the 1950s cracks had begun to appear in the wall of Communist-Arab solidarity. However much Arab leaders might opportunistically solicit Communist help as leverage against the West, many of them had come to realize that the Kremlin's interest in their cause was not purely altruistic. We have already alluded to the split in Iraqi politics between proponents of co-operation with the Pan-Arab movement and left-wing partisans of a loose federation of Arab countries in opposition to the United Arab Republic. Re-assessment of its links with communism was also going on in Egypt. After cutting most of Egypt's ties with the West, President Nasser was seeking to re-establish economic relations with the United States and European nations. Press reports attributed Nasser's about-face to concern in Cairo over Egypt's overly great dependence upon the communist bloc in economic and military affairs. Concurrently, open splits between Nasser and the Kremlin impended over the activities of communist groups throughout the Middle East. Governments friendly to

Egypt were beginning to question the compatibility of Soviet objectives with Arab objectives —so much so that at the Twenty-first Congress of the Soviet Communist Party early in 1959, Premier Khrushchev harshly criticized Arab nationalist leaders. In turn, Arab leaders began openly to denounce Soviet intervention in Middle Eastern affairs (31, January 4, 1959, dispatch by Dana A. Schmidt, and February 1, 1959, dispatch by Richard P. Hunt).

By the beginning of the 1960's, it appeared that communism, no less than the West, was on trial in the Middle East. The problem of the "national bourgeoisie" loomed as large as it had in earlier Soviet diplomacy. Arab leaders indicated their manifest reluctance to become merely a cog in the revolutionary machine, as was made clear by articles like the following from the Egyptian paper *Al Ahram* on January 4, 1959:

> In the past Communist organizations have stood by the nationalist forces in the bitter struggle against imperialism, pacts, imperialist collaborators, and feudalism. The struggle has ended or is about to end. What will be the attitude of the Communists in the future? Will they be deflected from the clear nationalist line in order to raise red flags in the Middle East? Or will they keep their mouths shut? (24, p. 331).

It is a commonplace of history that ententes can be held together most forcefully by common enemies and antagonisms. For a time, anti-Westernism served as a bridge between communist and Arab goals. And it would be utopian to suppose that this common denominator has entirely disappeared. But more and more communist policy-makers were facing the same challenge that confronted Western officials. As the years passed, the crucial question would likely become: could the collaboration between Arab nationalism and communism survive the transition from negative to positive goals, from opposition to advocacy of constructive programs acceptable to both sides? As Arab leaders tried to evolve concrete measures for grappling with problems in the Middle East, communism was only one means —and it could well be an expendable one— available for achieving their goals. For the Kremlin, by contrast, Arab nationalism was the means to achieve the communist bloc's diplomatic purposes. In the era of good feelings

that had characterized relations between Communist and Arab countries after 1955, the Kremlin had come dangerously close to overextending itself, to the point of arousing widespread Arab apprehensions about communist intentions. The result was that once more collaboration was being sought with the West by Arab leaders as a counterweight to Moscow's newly-gained influence.

In effect, the West was being given a "second chance" throughout the Arab domain. Whether Western governments proved capable of utilizing this new opportunity to restore relations with the Middle East upon a mutually profitable basis would constitute a persistent challenge to policy-makers in Washington and other capitals in the Atlantic community.

Profit and Loss in U. S. Middle Eastern Policy

Looking back upon American foreign policy toward the Middle East since World War II, what kind of over-all assessment can be made? On balance, the achievements were scarce. The area was probably more turbulent and unstable, Western influence was at a lower ebb, and prospects for at least some Soviet penetration of Middle Eastern affairs were much greater by the end of the 1950s than in the mid-1940s. The gains that might be cited— Israel still existed as an independent state, the major oil fields remained under Western control, no war convulsed the region, Soviet influence was less in some respects than might have been expected—were chiefly negative, in that the situation was not as inimical to Western interests as it might conceivably have become. Often in international affairs, when diplomats are dealing with adverse conditions and thorny problems, this kind of accomplishment represents a genuine gain!

Yet entries on the liability side of the ledger were conspicuous. With respect to the three problems that have been crucial in American relations with Middle Eastern countries—the Arab-Israeli conflict, regional defense, and Arab nationalism—in the main the United States and its Western allies were far from having established their policies upon solid foundations. Chronic flareups between Israel and the Arab states had been dealt with, and temporary solutions in many cases had been found. But little discernible progress had been made in resolving the bedrock question: was Israel to be regarded as a permanent member of the family of nations in the Middle East, and if so, what would be the principles governing its relations with the Arab world? Embedded within this fundamental question were a host of lesser ones involving such problems as establishing permanent boundaries for Israel, evolving a program for utilizing the waters of the Jordan River, and settling the incendiary Arab refugee problem. The West of course could not "solve" either the primary or secondary problems unilaterally. What it could be reasonably expected to do, however, was to supply sufficient initiative and inducements so as to maintain steady diplomatic pressure on the parties to these disputes in order that the search for solutions would continue. Instead, too often it has displayed notable diplomatic energy only when tensions have triggered a new diplomatic crisis. Success achieved in dealing with such crises in many cases was not followed by renewed vigor in preventing new ones from threatening the peace and security of the Middle East and possibly of the global community.

Varied results had also been achieved in coping with the issue of Middle Eastern defense. Here again, preoccupation with essentially secondary issues, such as the threat of an outright Soviet-instigated military attack against a Middle Eastern country, had diverted energies and resources from dealing with what was surely a far more basic and imminent threat: "indirect aggression," made possible by a number of mutually sustaining factors that favored communism and other forms of political extremism, often exploited by outside countries. The gravitation of certain countries like Syria, and in some periods Iraq and Egypt, toward the communist orbit was as much a symptom of instability in the Middle East as it was a cause of it. Almost indescribable

poverty, prolonged economic crises, illiteracy, fierce pride in having achieved independence and determination to have an active voice in world affairs, belief that progress could and must be made rapidly, historically-nourished resentments against outside intervention in their affairs—these were the root problems that often coalesced to incline Arab countries to seek assistance from the Soviet Union and to perpetuate various forms of political extremism. Accordingly, the West's success in promoting Middle Eastern defense would in no small measure be conditioned by its success in assisting Arab countries to resolve these contributory problems. More basic perhaps even than programs of Western military or economic assistance to the Middle East was creation of the requisite atmosphere of good faith and confidence, inducing Western and Arab countries to co-operate in the search for the most effective approaches to such issues.

In turn, creation of this atmosphere usually hinged upon relations between the West and Arab countries on the third issue considered earlier: Arab nationalism. So all-pervasive are the ramifications of Arab nationalism and so intermingled is this phenomenon with major problems extant in the Middle East in recent years, that it would not be amiss to regard it as the keystone of the arch of Western-Arab relations. And in dealing with Arab nationalist currents Western policy-makers have demonstrated singular inability to evolve policies and programs capable of achieving stated diplomatic goals. What factors account for this failure? Why, among all the problems that will color future Western relations with the Middle East, is this one likely to prove as crucial as any? What will be the central issues that must be recognized in any re-assessment of the free world's approach to this dynamic force? These questions can more intelligently be dealt with later in the chapter, after we have evaluated closely related developments on the African continent.

4. THE AWAKENING OF AFRICA

A Continent in Transition

By the second half of the 20th century Africa was awakening to play a prominent role in international politics after centuries of political and economic hibernation. It was no longer unusual to read news dispatches that riots had

DRUMS OF AFRICA

The Richmond Times-Dispatch, February, 1959.

erupted in the Belgian Congo, and had prompted the government of Belgium at long last to talk in terms of ultimate independence. By 1959 a colored majority in Nyasaland objected violently to being incorporated into the white-dominated Federation of Rhodesia—and future unrest seemed in the offing. Within the tiny and backward Republic of Congo, a part of the French Union, native groups fought each other for political dominance. The United Nations had found it necessary to debate the political future of trust territories such as the French and British Cameroons. Far to the north the Algerian war dragged on, in spite of President de Gaulle's new proposals to the rebels in 1959, holding out the prospect of ultimate independence from France as one possible alternative for Algeria. By the opening of the 1960's, this offer had produced little discernible change in the Algerian crisis (31, March 8, 1959).

Politically and economically, Africa was coming of age. It had finally begun to feel the impact of Western culture, political philosophy and technology. There was hardly a country on the African continent within which this impact was not unleashing powerful nationalist forces which, however poorly they might be articulated and despite their variation from country to country, had several points in common. African demands mirrored those voiced widely throughout the Middle East and Asia in the modern period—proof that Africa too was experiencing the "revolution in expectations" witnessed in other areas of the world. Foremost among them were insistence upon a greater measure of political freedom, leading to an end to colonial rule; progress in achieving higher living standards by such techniques as increased food production and attacks against prevalent diseases and—what often ranked first in African demands—an end to policies of racial-ethnic discrimination imposed in many countries by a handful of non-African groups upon a once-docile native majority.

Africa's progressively more crucial role in world affairs was likely to have far-reaching repercussions for the United States. Until the 1950's relations between the United States and Africa had been relatively inconsequential. Occasionally, as in America's role in creating the state of Liberia for the resettlement of emancipated slaves, the United States had some contact with African countries; but by and large, intimate contacts were non-existent. In discussing African questions as they relate to American foreign policy, therefore, we are discussing mainly emerging issues and future relationships. We are endeavoring to anticipate those questions which will come to the fore in Afro-American relationships over succeeding decades. Some of these issues already confront American officials with difficult policy choices; others are inherent in fundamental tendencies in Afro-American relations and in over-all developments in international affairs. Nevertheless, there is little room for certainty in the matter of Afro-American relations.

Profile of the "Dark Continent"

Encompassing an area four times that of the United States, the continent of Africa contains more than eleven million square miles, most of which is in the tropics. Africa is a region of infinite variety and contrasts. The northern portion of the continent is divided from east to west by the greatest desert on the globe, the Sahara; that portion lying athwart the Equator includes a dense, at some points an almost impenetrable, tropical rain forest. Elsewhere there is "small bush" country, isolated barren wastes, grasslands, and mountain ranges. Most of the interior of Africa is a great plateau. Africa has the shortest coast line, proportionate to its area, of any continent; with few exceptions, the coastline is unsuitable for the construction of harbors. Climate and geography have conspired to make transportation and communication ardous among African countries and between them and the outside world. Today, the only dependable method of transportation for much of Africa is the airplane.

In Africa's inhospitable environment, there dwell approximately 220,000,000 people, of whom about 5,000,000 are of European stock, with half of this latter total living in the Union of South Africa. Leading ethnic groups are the Arabs who inhabit much of North Africa; the Semitic-Hamitic peoples of Ethiopia, who do not regard themselves as colored; and Negroes or Bantu peoples who comprise the overwhelming majority of the native population. Over seven hundred languages and dialects are spoken throughout Africa. Major groups by religion show some sixty million Moslems, twenty-one million Christians, and the remainder pagan. Illiteracy has been estimated to run between 80 and 90 per cent of the *total* population; in twenty-five countries and dependencies, between 90 and 99 per cent of the population is illiterate (**1**, p. 230).

Africa is usually classified among the "underdeveloped" regions of the world. The classification is accurate in the sense that cultural-economic levels there are in general primitive, and that insufficient use has been made to date of the continent's resources.* Africa is the

source of many important minerals, a number of them vital for the defense program of the United States. Thus Africa produces virtually all the world's industrial diamonds. Expressed as a percentage of total world production, Africa supplies 94 per cent of the columbite, and 84 per cent of the cobalt, both vital ingredients in the making of high-grade steel products; 41 per cent of the beryllium, 33 per cent of the manganese, 29 per cent of the chrome, 21 per cent of the copper, 13 per cent of the tin, 50 per cent of the gold, and—perhaps most crucial of all for the free world's defense efforts—a substantial part of the uranium ore used in nuclear processes (**4**, pp. 51-2; **40**, p. 10). Besides Africa's proven reserves in these minerals, some authorities predict vast new discoveries, after the continent's resources are adequately surveyed. Chester Bowles has optimistically labelled Africa "the richest untapped source of mineral wealth still available to a world that is rapidly devouring its resources . . . " (**4**, p. 2). Among the richest potential resources of Africa are numerous sites for the generation of hydroelectric power.

Yet many qualifications must be borne in mind in evaluating optimistic assumptions that Africa lies as a great "underdeveloped" continent whose resources furnish the basis for an agricultural-industrial revolution. Measured by the value of mineral *output*, Africa ranks next to last among the continents. In fuels, Africa is especially poor, producing only 0.7 per cent of the world's total. Though Africa possesses vast forest reserves, totalling nearly 850 million hectares (one hectare equaling 2.471 acres), only 306 million hectares are classified as "productive," with the remainder classified as "inaccessible" in the light of present technology (**47**, p. 695). These are but some of the reasons why geographers like Derwent Whittlesey caution against roseate predictions about Africa's economic future. Certain illusions about Africa are widely current in the West. As an illustration, Africa's luxuriant tropical forests do *not* indicate the presence of fertile soil; to the contrary, most of this soil is highly infertile owing to severe leaching by incessant rains. Similarly,

---

*"Underdevelopment" is an ambiguous concept. If by underdevelopment is meant *a nation's capacity to raise its economic levels significantly,* then perhaps the United States is the most "underdeveloped" nation on the globe; and in this same sense, Soviet Russia also is high on the list. When a nation, or region, or continent is backward economically this does not automatically mean that it is underdeveloped. For it may not possess the resources, physical and otherwise, for improving its economic position substantially. Many so-called "underdeveloped" areas like the

---

Amazon Valley in South America or the mountains of northern India and Tibet may have little potential for further development.

the value of much of the "small bush" country of Africa is greatly impaired by heavy erosion and depletion of soil nutriments. Large portions of the grazing lands of Africa are unsuitable for the livestock industry because of the tsetse fly; usable ranges in many cases are already heavily overgrazed, consequently producing a poor quality of livestock. Again, as we have noted, Africa is rich in possible sites for hydro-electric facilities; but many of these sites are in the central, tropical region, far removed from possible markets for electric power and in some cases almost inaccessible for large-scale development. A physical map of Africa shows a network of rivers criss-crossing the continent, apparently offering many opportunities for the development of expanded internal communication and transportation. However, alternate floods and droughts, numerous rapids and waterfalls, and inaccessibility from the sea inhibit the usefulness of most of these rivers for communication-transportation (**40**, pp. 34-7).

Numerous other obstacles could be mentioned: the primitive skills of Africa's labor force, despite its impressive numbers; the fact that Africa's greatest mineral resources are owned by foreign corporations, with few benefits from these deposits being realized by the native populations; the low *percentage* (9.2 per cent by value) of Africa's mineral deposits compared with the world total. Africa lacks completely many of the major minerals required to support an industrial economy or even a more productive agricultural one. There are no chemical fertilizers, iron ore, coal, and, except for possible extensive deposits in the Sahara, no oil.*

For economically backward areas like Africa, whose major enterprise for centuries has been

---

*Forceful evidence of formidable problems confronting economic development in Africa can be obtained by reading selectively in the Twentieth Century Fund's authoritative study: **47**. This comprehensive work brings out graphically Africa's inferiority *vis-à-vis* other major regions in elements necessary for impressive economic growth. Thus statistics for the year 1948-50 show a per capita income for Africa as a whole of $50 annually. Again, Africa has just over 7 per cent of the world's population; yet it produces only 2.3 per cent of the world's income (**47**, pp. 391-93).

and will likely continue to be agriculture, land resources above all others are likely to prove decisive in shaping the economic destiny. For many African countries, the land is virtually the *only* economic resource; for all, it will remain high on the list of factors determining future growth. Yet here again, statistics do not paint an encouraging picture. Out of Africa's 7.3 billion acres of land, only 240 million—3.3 per cent of the whole—are suitable for agriculture (**47**, p. 316). Nowhere throughout that vast expanse of land do there exist large tracts of fertile soil, comparable to the Mississippi River Valley or the Nile Valley in earlier historical eras. For the entire continent, agricultural productivity ranges from low to moderate. Per capita agricultural yields tend to equal about half of the world average, approximately the yields also for Asia. In Africa, however, it is chiefly poor agricultural techniques, rather than lack of sufficient arable land as in Asia, that accounts for low productivity (**47**, pp. 315-20). Population increases have led to ever more intensive cultivation and grazing of lands, thereby reducing its fertility. For the bulk of Africa, the basic economic unit has been, and remains, the village or tribal economy producing food chiefly for its own consumption, with very little left for trade. The introduction of elementary scientific practices in agriculture aimed at preventing extensive soil erosion and depletion and at inculcating wise soil management techniques are steps urgently needed in many African countries to reverse the trend toward lowered per capita agricultural yields. Practically without exception, such steps are becoming matters of highest priority in every African country. With Africa's population presently increasing by 1.5 per cent annually, and greater increases expected in the short-run if economic levels are raised, many African countries will be hard pressed to maintain agricultural yields at their present levels.

At the risk of some oversimplification, it would not be too far amiss to regard land as the dominant problem in Africa, politically, as well as economically. The economic connotations of the land problem have major political and socio-cultural overtones, and vice versa. Land has often become the focal point of the political and racial antagonisms witnessed in Africa in the recent period. This is most graphically exemplified perhaps in the Mau Mau uprising that triggered prolonged and bitter conflict between European and native elements in British-controlled Kenya from 1952-55. In Kenya, as in many other African countries, despite ancient tribal traditions that land could not be permanently alienated, most of the fertile soil had passed under the control of non-native groups, which in Kenya comprised three per cent of the population. The native population, whose numbers were increasing rapidly, found itself more and more confined to government-created "reservations," carved out of less desirable lands. The pressure of the native population upon food supplies, combined with a growing sense of frustration and ill-will manifested toward Kenya's European elite, precipitated a long and bloody civil war which set back the long-range development of Kenya significantly and left a legacy of racial antagonism that may require decades to erase.

American Diplomatic Interests in Africa

Until the Second World War, relations between the United States and Africa, in the main, had been confined to the activities of Christian missionaries throughout the Dark Continent. From the "opening" of Africa by European powers early in the 19th century to the First World War, the whole of the continent rapidly fell under the colonial control of powerful European countries like Great Britain, France, Belgium, Portugal, Germany, and Italy. Such contacts as the United States had with Africa, therefore, had to be channeled through metropolitan governments in Europe.

The Second World War graphically altered the importance of Africa for the United States. America's concern with events in the African-Middle Eastern theater, and especially its participation with British forces in defeating the German *Wehrmacht* in the crucial North African campaign, testified to the realization in Washington that the nation's security was directly bound up with events in this theater. Enemy control over it would have outflanked the European allies, put Germany astride vital trade and communication routes, given Hitler strategic bases from which to control much of the south Atlantic, and ultimately jeopardized the defense of South and Central America. The possible implications of such developments for the security of the United States were manifold and serious.

In the years immediately following World War II, African questions tended to be overshadowed by major international problems in areas like Western Europe and Asia. Only in the late 1950's were there signs that American policy-makers envisioned a new era in Afro-American relations. Indicative of this was an expansion in State Department machinery for handling African problems; the assignment of more senior Foreign Service officers to the continent; greater requests by persons entering the Foreign Service for African assignment; expansion and improvement in the State Department's techniques for reporting on African affairs and for providing necessary training for diplomatic officials; and attempts to create a separate Bureau of African Affairs within the State Department. Also indicative of this new American interest was an expansion of American propaganda activities in Africa. The varied activities of the United States Information Agency were being stepped up throughout the Continent; and the number of psychological war specialists dealing with African questions was being increased. African affairs were also receiving considerably greater attention than before from collateral agencies like the Department of Defense, the Department of Labor, the Department of Commerce, and even the Department of Health, Education, and Welfare (1, pp. 193-203).

In the contemporary era and in the years ahead, four considerations guarantee that America's relations with Africa will be far more important than in the past: the continent's strategic importance for the free world; the threat of increased communist activity and Russian penetration throughout the Middle East and Africa; the inescapable responsibility of Western countries for joining with countries and dependencies in Africa in the attack upon formidable socio-economic problems; and the nationalist ferment that is the dominant fact

THE AFRICAN INDEPENDENCE MOVEMENT

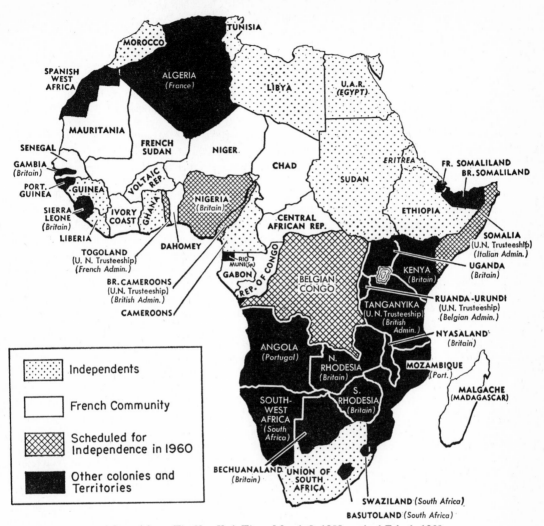

Adapted from *The New York Times*, March 8, 1959, revised Feb. 1, 1960.

of Africa's political life. Each of these factors merits detailed analysis.

America is likely to have more intimate and sustained relations with Africa in the years ahead than in the past because of the continent's magnified strategic importance. If anything, Africa's role in Western defense is more crucial now than during World War II. Its northern shoreline offers control over the Mediterranean and the southern European hinterland. Enemy occupation of territories adjacent to Gibraltar and Suez would make the Mediterranean a closed sea, diverting the free world's shipping to the more costly and slower routes around the tip of Africa. Enemy control over the eastern coast of the continent could imperil trade and communication lines between Europe and the Far East. In hostile hands, furthermore, Africa would afford bases from which the vital oil supplies of the Middle East could be denied oil-deficient countries in the West. The western "bulge" of Africa offers the most accessible base from which an enemy could undertake penetration of South and Central America and, simultaneously, dominate the vital sealanes of the south Atlantic.

The United States is now more vulnerable than ever to such threats, because the nation is becoming progressively more dependent upon the importation of strategic raw materials to maintain a strong defense position. Africa possesses singular importance in this connection, inasmuch as its uranium deposits comprise half of the proven reserves on the globe.

Other recent tendencies enhance Africa's significance for the United States. Throughout the postwar period, the policy of containment has necessitated establishment of numerous air bases and missile sites around the globe. Currently, major installations are located in Morocco and Libya. If "deterrence" fails to *prevent* aggression, they could be utilized to launch air strikes against an enemy. Conversely, enemy control over these bases would place enemy air and missile forces along the southern flank of the NATO alliance. With the range of missiles being pushed forward steadily, this would likely place at least portions of the United States itself within enemy missile range (**18**, pp. 55–63, *passim*).

Two current trends, somewhat contradictory in nature, could alter the strategic importance of Africa. The rapidly expanding range of modern missiles might, in the not too distant future, obviate the usefulness of the free world's military bases on African soil, since perfection of 5,000-mile range intercontinental missiles would bring targets anywhere in the world within range of allied bases. On the other hand, military spokesmen have called attention to the future importance of solid-fuel missiles which can be made ready for almost instantaneous launching from "hard" sites (i.e., concealed sites, built underground). Gradually the large, exposed American military installations established around the periphery of the USSR since 1947 may be superseded by small, carefully concealed launching sites for missiles, some of which might possibly be located in remote parts of Africa.

Intimately related to Africa's strategic significance is the problem of communism on the continent. Thus far, communism has not made impressive *numerical* gains throughout Africa. By and large its strength has been confined to pockets where there are large European and other non-native populations and where hostil-

ities between such populations and indigenous peoples have flared up. Communists have been active in the North African independence movement and in the Belgian Congo. Here and elsewhere, they have proved adept at fanning popular discontents against colonialism and racial discrimination to advance their cause. Although the Communist movement has comparatively few members in Africa—25,000 to 30,000 for the whole continent—numerical strength is not a sufficient key to the importance of the problem. Most especially when conditions favor the Marxist cause, Communists have demonstrated their ability to compensate for smallness of numbers by faithful dedication to their creed, superior training and organizational ability, and revolutionary zeal.

While the Kremlin appears to have accorded Africa low priority *vis-à-vis* the Middle East and Asia in the postwar period, the situation is rapidly changing. Since the Geneva Conference of 1955, the communist bloc's espousal of "peaceful co-existence" has led it to work more than ever through mass movements and to exploit prevailing popular discontents over colonial and racial questions. Africa provides a fertile ground for laborers in the Marxist vineyard, a realization that has apparently more and more colored the Kremlin's approach to African questions in recent years. Indicative of its newly-manifested solicitude for the welfare of African groups is the attention paid to them by the communist journal, *Moscow News*, late in 1956. Communist spokesmen took notice of "a great popular independence movement" springing up in Africa and praised the appearance of "political leaders of ability and energy" in African countries. Meantime, another communist organ cautioned against branding small countries in the UN as satellites of the United States "only because their official representatives sometimes are compelled to vote contrary to their own conviction under the pressure of American diplomacy" (**1**, p. 79). These and other signs presaged a fundamental reorientation in the Kremlin's approach to Africa (**18**, pp. 262–80; **40**, pp. 296–97).

A third respect in which America's relations with Africa are likely to become far more crucial in the future than in the past is the expanding role of the United States, working often in intimate collaboration with its European allies and native African governments, in attacking ancient and formidable socio-economic problems throughout the Dark Continent. So important is this aspect of Afro-American relations that extended treatment of emerging patterns and problems seems justified at this point.

Economic Aid and African Progress

In 1957, a decade after the United States inaugurated its postwar program of foreign assistance with the Greek-Turkish aid program, a special study group of the Senate Foreign Relations Committee called Africa "the world's most underdeveloped continent." It noted that until the late 1950's Africa had enjoyed rather low priority in American foreign assistance programs. Exclusive of Egypt it had received totals that ranged from eight to ten million dollars annually. These sums were supplemented of course by other grants and loans made available by European countries for their dependent territories, by the United Nations, and by other regional aid programs.* In the opinion of the study group, "the United States should be prepared to increase substantially its technical assistance programs" throughout Africa; such programs should be carried out "within the limits of each country's absorptive capacity, provided appropriate arrangements can be worked out with the government concerned." In regard to colonial and trust territories in Africa, the report continued that in the future, as in the past, the United States would have to work through the metropolitan governments in Europe, recognizing that "a developing Africa, in an atmosphere of tranquility, is very nearly as much in the interests of the United States as of the European powers who are somewhat more directly concerned" (35, pp. 8-9).

What concrete forms have American assistance programs to Africa assumed in recent

years? What problems in carrying out these programs have been encountered? Let us look briefly at some of the specific projects undertaken throughout Africa. After 1951 the United States made technical assistance available to Ethiopia for a number of objectives: increased food and other agricultural commodities production; improvement of agricultural processing and marketing techniques; expansion and modernization of the educational system; development of technical and sub-professional skills among the population; more effective utilization of water resources; and a number of steps designed to better governmental administration (35, pp. 470-71). By 1957 the United States had expended a total of nearly $12 million dollars on technical assistance programs in Ethiopia; in many of these projects Ethiopia's own expenditures exceeded those made by the United States. Concurrently with the implementation of these projects, Ethiopia received a $24 million credit from the Export-Import Bank (also an agency of the United States Government) for the purpose of expanding aviation facilities (35, p. 471).

Liberia, an African country with which the United States has had sporadic relations since 1847, has also received grants under the American technical assistance program. As is typical of many other African countries, the mass of the Liberian population is illiterate; its predominant economic enterprise is primitive agriculture. Because of its strategic importance in the African theater, Liberia received considerable aid from the Allies in World War II, much of which went into permanent improvements like harbor installations. In 1950, American technical assistance was extended for the first time to help in financing a five-year development program—later extended another four years—with total expenditures throughout the nine-year period reaching nearly $75 million. The Liberian Government was to make a minimum of 20 per cent of its current revenues available for its contribution to the plan. Projects have included development of roads, railroads, power facilities, water control, health and educational programs, agriculture, forestry, fisheries, and public administration. One major enterprise has been establishment of the Booker T. Washington Institute to promote technical

---

*The nature and range of economic assistance programs carried on by the United Nations, the British Commonwealth countries, regional bodies like the Organization of American States, and colonial powers, and the relationship of American programs to them, is analyzed in 35, pp. 270-96.

and vocational training. American assistance has also been supplemented by extensive loans from the Export-Import Bank and modest contributions under the United Nations expanded technical assistance program. Moreover, the Liberian government has encouraged the establishment and expansion of foreign corporations, like B. F. Goodrich Company, by imposing minimum currency restrictions and reasonable taxes. Added to these activities have been the contributions of philanthropic, educational, and missionary groups which, for example, operate half of the country's eight hundred schools (35, pp. 472-74).

A study of foreign assistance programs in Africa, prepared by the Library of Congress, notes that the cumulative impact of these programs in Liberia has been beneficial in many respects, as measured by indices of economic growth like the increase in Liberia's exports. Yet the study avers that "it is doubtful that benefits from the various aid programs have yet reached the great majority of Afro-Liberians." This reservation highlights a problem faced not alone for programs in Africa but in many other underdeveloped areas as well. Moreover, the report found a growing sentiment in Liberia that the country was becoming overly dependent upon the United States in economic affairs and that Uncle Sam was pursuing essentially "paternalistic" policies toward it (35, pp. 474-75).

Extension of economic aid to independent countries like Ethiopia and Liberia can be agreed upon by bilateral negotiations between the recipient countries and the United States. The interests of both parties can be freely considered. A different problem prevails when economic aid is given for colonial dependencies or trust territories. There is often little public awareness in the colonies or trust territories that the United States has extended assistance to them either in collaboration with metropolitan governments like Britain, France, and Belgium, or directly with the sanction of the colonial administration. A further difference from negotiations with independent governments is exemplified by experience in providing assistance to France's sub-Saharan dependencies. Writes the Library of Congress report cited above: "In the final analysis . . . development plans have represented the *French* interpretation of mutual interests, which is neither colonial exploitation nor purely altruistic regard for the welfare of the dependent populations" (35, p. 475, italics inserted). With the colonial powers often exercising the controlling voice over the kind of projects undertaken and, indeed, in deciding whether projects will be undertaken at all, America's relationships with dependencies are frequently remote. Nevertheless, the United States has made limited sums available to colonial areas in Africa. Funds channeled through France, for example, have been applied to a ten-year economic development plan inaugurated in 1947 for French West Africa, with major emphasis being placed upon non-income yielding projects like improvements in governmental administration, education, health and research. Similarly, in French Equatorial Africa, a ten-year development scheme launched in 1949 was directed at meeting acute economic problems in this tropical region, with high priority accorded to improving transportation and communication facilities (35, pp. 477-80).

Few colonial territories in the world are of more vital concern to the United States than the mineral-rich Belgian Congo, an area as large as America east of the Mississippi River. The Congo's mineral resources, most of which have not begun to be utilized, give it singular importance for the free world, not least because half of the known uranium deposits on the earth are located there. But despite its wealth of mineral ores, the Congo's leading economic pursuit remains agriculture. Although total funds provided under American assistance programs to the Congo have been small, in 1955 the Government of Belgium invited American co-operation in evolving a ten-year development program for the country, beginning with studies of its major economic problems and its resources for meeting them. Initial surveys called attention to the promising hydroelectric sites existing in the Congo and to the opportunities for developing heavy and light industry, utilizing the country's extensive mineral resources (35, pp. 480-82).

American participation in schemes like the ten-year Congo development plan brings into clear relief certain dilemmas and issues inherent in America's relationships with dependent territories in Africa. Belgium's own interest in fostering economic progress for the Congo was engendered in no small part by the hope that encouragement of a sense of "partnership" with native groups would erase ancient grievances arising from Belgium's earlier exploitation and would dampen nationalist demands for independence.* As time passed, however, Brussels was forced to make concessions to progressively more militant nationalist demands in the Congo. By 1960 Belgium had finally agreed to accept complete independence as the ultimate goal. Provision of American economic assistance within this context of pressures and cross-pressures highlighted problems confronting policy officials within the United States as they sought to formulate viable programs. Were colonial countries looking upon American assistance as one technique for *prolonging* their colonial regimes? Were anti-colonial groups regarding American aid as a method for *undermining* entrenched colonial systems? In the light of these conflicting forces, how did provision of assistance accord with Washington's own policies toward colonial disputes and toward corollary issues like relations with the cold war allies? Such questions arise inevitably out of the context of events in the Congo and countries with similar circumstances. Over the years, they would more and more demand clearly thought-out answers, answers that could only be forthcoming within a framework of consistent principles defining American policies toward still-dependent peoples.

Problems springing from American economic assistance to colonial areas in Africa are also brought into clear focus by experience in

Kenya. Kenya's already serious economic problems were greatly aggravated by the internecine Mau Mau uprising from 1952 until the end of 1955. Following successful British "pacification" of this uprising, fundamental economic problems were tackled. The initial plans, extending over three and one-half years, called for United States assistance from funds accruing from the sale of American agricultural surpluses to the United Kingdom. American contributions were to be matched by the government of Kenya. Raising agricultural productivity was the primary goal, with road-building, education, and health a close second. Although America's part in the development of Kenya has been relatively minor, the problems encountered have been typical of American participation in development schemes throughout Africa. Concerning Kenya, the Library of Congress' report concludes that:

> The outlook for Kenya is mixed. On the one hand, the European elements hold political supremacy and economic viability. On the other, the presence of vastly greater numbers of natives, many of whom will necessarily have to remain in depressed circumstances, at least in the present generation, creates an almost insuperable obstacle to the building up of a true nation, particularly in a continent where racial prejudice is so characteristic largely because of the once present threat of engulfment in the vast indigenous sea.

The report finds that "large numbers of the native groups are logical targets for the agents of communism" and, in what is if anything an underestimation of the difficulties involved, notes that successful programs in Kenya will call "for a very high degree of administrative wisdom coupled with moral as well as technical and economic aid from external sources" (**35**, pp. 496-97).

Our brief survey of American economic assistance to Africa permits certain general observations. First, it is apparent that the United States already has a part to play in the economic future of many African countries; it is a reasonable prediction that this role will assume even greater importance in the future. Second, along with assistance from the colonial countries and independent African governments, American aid has made a valuable contribution in promoting material progress on

---

*The African specialist, Rupert Emerson, has written that in colonial affairs the "magic word of the day is 'partnership,' but this term can embrace a multitude of divergent interpretations. The estimates of the partners as to their appropriate shares in the new community are sure to differ vastly and perhaps even catastrophically." He cites the example of Southern Rhodesia. Here, the European population, outnumbered by natives twelve to one, interprets "partnership to mean that *after some decades* the Africans would be granted equality, not on a man-to-man basis but as a community equal in status to the white community. For Africans, both partnership and democracy have a different meaning" (**1**, p. 7, italics inserted).

the continent. Third, economic assistance by the United States raises certain vexatious issues which, in some instances at least, are likely to become even more critical in the future. The Library of Congress report observes that:

> Improved standards of living in the dependent areas have not led so often to greater contentment and gratitude on the part of the recipients of economic and technical aid as to increased restlessness, awakening ethnic consciousness, and agitation for political concessions. (35, p. 502).

Referring to projects undertaken in British dependencies from 1945 to 1955, the report continues:

> There is a distinct possibility that the money spent . . . will have increased the mouths to be fed more than the money devoted to agriculture

and veterinary services in the same period has increased the production of food. . . . Already it is apparent that, when explosive increases of population occur as a result of the application of technical aid, as they have in parts of West Africa, it is not certain that the basic aim of development schemes will be realized to the extent originally anticipated. (35, p. 504).

Such conclusions point to the fact that programs evolved to date may in some cases have created as many new problems as they have resolved old ones. At any rate, they underscore the fact that the economic development of Africa is likely to prove a challenging, and sometimes frustrating, undertaking for an indefinite period. In addition, they suggest that economic change is likely to effect profound changes in political and socio-cultural affairs.

5. AMERICA AND AFRICA'S FUTURE

The pivot of America's future relations with countries on the African continent is likely to be the issue of nationalism. All signs point to an acceleration in the intensity of African nationalist demands and to the intimate concern of the United States with them. The change in the political status of the African countries since the First World War has been phenomenal. In 1914 two countries in the whole of Africa—Liberia and Ethiopia (or Abyssinia)—were independent; these two countries accounted for 5.5 per cent of the total population of approximately 170 million. By the late 1950s, about one-third of the Arab and Negro populations of Africa was living under independent governments. In 1957 the total number of independent countries stood at nine, embracing 86 million people, out of a total population of over 220 million. In the following year, the little country of French Guinea received its independence from the French Union. Moreover, the former Italian colony of Somalia, the former British colonies of Nigeria and the British Cameroons, and the former French colonies of Togoland and the French Cameroons were slated for independence in the early 1960's. Elsewhere in Africa—in Algiers, in the Belgian Congo, in Nyasaland—nationalist fires had consumed or were threatening to consume remaining vestiges of colonial, or

whatever the natives regarded as alien, control over African affairs.

Closely interwoven with the concept of political independence are demands for elimination of racial barriers imposed against colored populations in cultural, social, and economic affairs. Racial antagonisms have reached their peak in white-dominated countries like the Union of South Africa and the Rhodesian Federation. In the Rhodesian Federation, composed of Northern and Southern Rhodesia and Nyasaland, the last-named has a large colored majority. In common with Asian countries like India, many nations in Africa are extremely sensitive to international questions involving racial issues. In international organs like the UN Commission on Human Rights, these nations can be expected to champion the causes of minorities or racially-oppressed groups. Such viewpoints are part and parcel of African nationalist demands.

As nationalist movements successfully undermine existing colonial relationships, African countries will gain a greater voice than formerly in what has now become the dominant organ of the United Nations, the General Assembly. Relying upon their newly-acquired ability to influence the actions of the UN through the General Assembly—which, in contrast to the great-power dominated Security Council, operates upon the principle of "one nation, one vote"—African countries have already exhibited their determination to insist upon discussion of questions vital to *their* interests and have not been reticent about airing their grievances before the bar of public opinion. This tendency is likely to become magnified over the course of future years. By the end of the 1950s, the General Assembly had nine African members, compared with only three at the time of the UN's inception in 1945. Some commentators predict that by 1980 the number of African countries represented in the UN will rise to twenty-five, giving the African bloc somewhere between one-fourth and one-fifth of the Assembly's total membership (**31**, February 22, 1959, Dispatch by Thomas J. Hamilton)! Such an eventuality cannot fail to have a profound impact both upon the role of the UN in world affairs and upon official and unofficial American attitudes toward it.

The American Attitude Towards Colonialism

Discussion of America's past, present, and future response to African nationalism requires that attention be devoted to the historic policies of the United States toward freedom for dependent peoples. Specific manifestations of these policies, in the context of the Middle East and of Africa, have already been examined. It remains to relate these particular problems to the broad context of America's overall approach to such issues.

In dealing with nationalist ferment in the Middle East or in Africa or elsewhere, the broad objective of American foreign policy is plain enough: to evolve policies capable of blending its own interests, and those of its allies, with those of the indigenous populations to achieve the goal of human welfare. This task is as imperative as it is difficult. Varieties of nationalism, and collateral issues affected by nationalism, in regions like the Middle East and Africa, present American policy-makers with contradictions and anomalies on every hand. Progress made on certain fronts can easily cancel out progress made on other fronts. The objectives of parties affected by important issues—indeed the objectives sought by individual groups within particular countries or dependencies—can, and in some cases unquestionably will, prove well-nigh irreconcilable. In few spheres of diplomatic activity will the "illusion of American omnipotence"—the belief that all problems can be made to yield before determined American purposes and massive use of resources—be as much of a hindrance to progress as it will in Africa. Some concrete issues growing out of nationalist agitation may simply defy solutions acceptable to the West. In any case, for Western statesmen the premium will be upon acumen, foresight, sympathy, and diplomatic skill if even tolerable policies are to be evolved for coping with nationalist forces. Let us consider the leading elements that must be weighed in any reformulation of American foreign policy toward these problems.

First, there is the nation's historic attachment to the principle of self-determination and human freedom. Traditionally, the United States has sympathized with movements for political independence. President Wilson's advocacy of the principle of self-determination and President Franklin D. Roosevelt's endorsement of independence movements during World War II typified the national consciousness. Philip Bell summarizes America's historic attitudes by saying that the policy of the United States

has . . . been and continues to be one of condemnation of colonialism and in favor of independence for colonial peoples, with certain reservations added in small print—the grant of independence should not be too hurried and it should be given only to peoples who desire it and are capable of assuming responsibilities involved. (**3**, p. 86).

In some eras, the dominant motif of American policy—more often directed at the colonial empires of other countries than at its own colonial policies—has been unqualified endorsement of the principle of freedom for dependent peoples and insistence that such freedom be granted immediately. In other eras, the emphasis has been placed on the necessity for a prolonged "transition period" before dependent societies are ready for independence; and in a few cases American strategic interests have tended to overshadow even the ultimate goal of freedom for such societies.

The ebb and flow in American policies toward nationalist movements has been especially pronounced in the postwar period. Kaleidoscopic changes in political relationships throughout the world have meant that American policy-makers were even more hardpressed than usual to pursue consistent policies. As the United States assumed ever-growing obligations and was forced to take into consideration factors that had not entered significantly into earlier foreign policy decisions, its leaders found that evolving a satisfactory policy on colonialism constituted a formidable challenge. During and immediately after World War II, the United States tended indiscriminately to champion independence for countries like India, Burma, Ceylon, Indonesia, and Indochina; American diplomatic pressure was in no small way responsible for French evacuation from Syria and British evacuation from Lebanon, after these former dependencies had brought their cases to the United Nations in 1946. Even in the period of idealism rampant during and just after the war, however, two contradictory strains were evident in America's policies toward nationalism. Vocal as was its endorsement of the principle of independence for former colonies and dependencies, in crucial instances the American Government was not prepared to *do* anything to make this goal a reality. By and large, the United States refrained from using its dominant military position in the Pacific to prejudice reimposition of colonial regimes by Britain and France. Julius W. Pratt has written:

> In yielding the Southeast Asia command to the British, the United States in effect conceded that Burma, Malaya, Indochina, and the Netherlands Indies should, when reconquered from Japan, be returned to their former British, French, and Dutch masters. Then, it was hoped, would begin the process of guided governmental evolution on the Philippine pattern. (41, p. 132).

While the United States was often identified with anti-colonial forces in ensuing struggles by dependent peoples, key American military decisions taken during the war had guaranteed that such struggles would be bitter and prolonged. Washington's policies toward certain Japanese-held islands in the Pacific were also at odds with its viewpoints toward the dependencies of other countries. As a result of considerable pressure from the armed services, State Department and other civilian leaders decided to exclude these islands from the United Nations trusteeship system and to leave them under outright American control (41, p. 130).

Anti-Colonialism and the Cold War

As mounting cold war tensions increasingly colored colonial disputes, it became more taxing than ever to formulate a consistent policy toward such disputes that would carry out traditional American goals of ultimate freedom for dependent societies as well as new goals of mitigating global tensions, countering the intrigues of the communist bloc, and solidifying the position of the free world alliance. In some instances, like the British-Egyptian dispute over Suez or the French-Algerian dispute in North Africa, these objectives appeared to be mutually exclusive. Even in less extreme cases, retailoring American policy toward colonialism to fit widely varying circumstances often resulted in policies that appeared to be dictated chiefly by expediency and by a desire in Washington to temporize in the hope that prevailing disputes would somehow "work themselves out" satisfactorily. Official pronouncements echoed the nation's historic endorsement of freedom. Thus Ambassador Henry Cabot Lodge Jr. stated before the UN in 1953 that the "aspirations of peoples who are not now independent toward self-government always evoke sympathy and support from Americans." Speaking specifically of the North African conflict, Lodge hoped that France and its dependencies would "move continually closer together in achieving self-government . . . " (11, 1953, pp. 332-33). Verbal support for the Wilsonian principle of self-determination characterized American pronouncements on similar issues throughout the years that followed.

Yet other countries found a growing disparity between America's professed goals and its operating policies; and these countries were inclined to judge the nation's real sentiments more by the latter than by the former. A bewildering pattern has emerged from attempts to piece together the response of the

United States to specific colonial disputes. Alternately, the United States brought pressure to bear upon Britain, France, and other colonial powers to liquidate their empires and to grant a greater measure of freedom to societies still in a dependent status; counselled steadfastness on the part of its major allies in resisting nationalist demands; refused to take the side of colonial powers; issued sonorous statements endorsing the goals of nationalist groups; furnished its allies with economic and military means which enabled them to intensify their efforts to retain their possessions; and sporadically offered to serve as "honest broker" in mediating colonial conflicts. Chester Bowles, the able former Ambassador to India, has observed that at the very time American diplomats were delivering lofty pronouncements on the subject of independence for dependent peoples, the peoples of North Africa

are keenly aware that the French troops who pursue the Algerian nationalist guerillas through the hills are equipped with American small arms, artillery, tanks, planes, and helicopters given them under the NATO agreement. (4, p. 99).

Mr. Bowles quotes an unnamed governmental official as characterizing America's actual policy toward colonialism as one of "benevolent indifference" (4, p. 45). Whatever this may mean in theory, Bowles asserts, it "appears to others as indecision. Many leaders of the colonial powers regard us as blundering sentimentalists, while many African nationalists charge us with being timid hypocrites. Instead of making friends in each group, we are antagonizing both, without winning the respect of either" (4, p. 101). Nowhere perhaps was Bowles' assertion more clearly borne out than by American diplomacy in the Middle East. There, in the postwar period the United States has come dangerously close to alienating every country in the Middle East and every major power having vital interests in that region, with the exception of Turkey, which is often regarded more as a European than a Middle Eastern power. Other countries have not known whether the United States favored all Arab nationalist movements; whether it favored some and opposed others; whether it opposed most but favored a few; whether it favored a retention of British and French colon-

ial rule; or whether its policies toward colonial disputes were shaped predominantly by cold war considerations—or, in other words, whether the United States had an intelligible policy at all toward colonial controversies. Judging by what American diplomats have said and done in the postwar period, the United States has expressed all these attitudes in recent years, sometimes, by word and deed, several of them simultaneously. Other countries have not known, because the United States itself did not seem to know, the criteria by which America favored or opposed Arab nationalism in such areas as North Africa, Iran, or Egypt. Washington's attempts to serve as "honest broker" in Middle Eastern controversies often were cancelled out by open or covert support for one side or another, and sometimes for both!

Undeniably, bringing into satisfactory balance all of the diverse elements that had to enter into American calculations toward colonialism presented formidable difficulties. Consider the problem of the relations between the United States and its major allies. In the second half of the 20th century, the remaining "colonial powers" are European countries; in the Middle East and Africa they are three of America's principal allies: Britain, France, and Belgium. Britain and France are pillars supporting the NATO defense structure. Although colonial relationships have been rapidly dissolving everywhere since World War II, overseas dependencies continue to play a vital role in the economic destinies and—what may be no less crucial—in the *élan* requisite for the determination of certain European countries to make a maximum contribution for the free world's defense efforts. For example, 53 per cent of the free world's bauxite, 26 per cent of its chrome, 21 per cent of its copper, 50 per cent of its manganese, 40 per cent of its phosphate, 48 per cent of its tin, and 50 per cent of its rubber come from colonies and other dependent territories (3, p. 97). Britain and France each carries on trade valued at approximately $2 billion annually with its respective colonies. This amounts to one-seventh of Britain's total trade and one-third of France's total trade. Somewhere between one-eighth and one-fourth of all British overseas investments are in colonial territories. For selected commodities like oil and uranium, strong strategic compulsions argue in favor of continuing colonial relationships. In spite of assertions, heard since the time of critics of mercantilism like Adam Smith, that colonies were never "economical," that colonial countries often poured more resources into colonies than they took out, there remained the elusive but vital psychological factor. Countries like France and Belgium have spent hundreds of millions of dollars in colonial possessions since World War II in part because they were wedded to the idea that dissolution of their empires would impair their aspirations to exercise a more decisive voice in world affairs and would *permanently* relegate them to the ranks of second or third class powers. The United States could be indifferent to neither the economic-strategic nor the psychological reasons motivating its allies to perpetuate their colonial empires. Indeed, depending upon the intensity of prevailing cold war crises, American policy-makers have chosen support for, or at any rate lack of opposition to, European colonial regimes as the lesser evil, rather than risk almost certain disruption of the carefully-knit together Atlantic alliance system.

Anti-Colonialism and Rival National Interests

Along with traditional endorsement of freedom for dependent peoples and support for the cold war allies has gone another factor that must enter into any equation balancing conflicting interests on colonialism. The concept of "colonialism" is many-faceted; the term is often a misleading shorthand for superficially similar, but sometimes fundamentally different, phenomena. Stereotypes and clichés have so infused public thinking in the United States about colonialism that significant variations from country to country and region to region are almost totally glossed over. Stefan T. Possony has listed many prevailing popular conceptions—that every nation is entitled to immediate self-determination; that every society is capable of effective self-government; that every dependent people would benefit from independence; that expulsion of Western colonial powers would ensure permanent independence; that colonialism necessarily entails selfish exploitation; that the only alternative to continued dependence is absolute independence. Possony has shown the degree to which these ideas have captivated the public mind, irrespective of the circumstances actually prevailing in particular countries. As for the contention that every nation is entitled to immediate self-determination, he points out that many groups in the West believe that colonial peoples admire "the high-mindedness of the leading democracies" and that consequently

> youthful nations could be expected to side forever with the Western powers, and to behave with equal generosity to their own minority peoples. Enlightened self-denial expressed in anti-imperialist policies by the repentant imperial powers is ingenuously conceived as an infallible method of forging a solid alliance between the developed and the under-developed countries. The overwhelming body of recent evidence directly contrary to this naïve faith is summarily dismissed or glibly explained away. (41, pp. 18-19).

What would be the consequences of *immediate* independence for many colonial areas? What criteria exist for determining whether a body of people is "a nation," whose interests would be served by outright independence? Within countries containing diverse racial and ethnic groups, how far does the right of "self-determination" extend? If abolition of "foreign domination" is the stated goal, what steps must be taken to see that domination by one country is not superseded by domination by another? Assuming that some criteria are needed to test "political maturity" and "readiness" for independence, what standards should be applied and by whom? Fundamental questions of this kind inescapably plague attempts to evolve workable policies.

The central role of such questions is highlighted by events in the Middle East and Africa, where "anti-colonialism" may oftentimes be little more than a shibboleth, striking a responsive chord with native populations, but where problems attendant upon ending a colonial relationship receive minimum attention. In practice, what is objected to widely is merely *Western* colonialism, not the domination of one country by another, still less the exercise of substantial outside influence over smaller countries. As an illustration, vigorous advocacy of anti-colonialism has proved an effective weapon whereby President Nasser of Egypt has sought to undermine Western control, initially in Egypt and subsequently throughout the Arab world. Yet we have it on the authority of Nasser's own autobiography that Cairo watches the foreign policy orientation of neighboring African countries with keen interest, that in relationships with African countries Egypt conceives its own role in terms remarkably parallel to the mentality exhibited by advocates of European "colonialism" in an earlier age. Nasser has written:

> I say without exaggeration that we cannot . . . remain aloof from the terrible and sanguinary conflict going on there today between five million whites and 200 million Africans. We cannot do it for an important reason: we are in Africa. The peoples of Africa will continue to look to us, who guard their northern gate. . . . We will never in any circumstances be able to relinquish our responsibility to support, with all our might, the spread of enlightenment and civilization to the remotest depths of the jungle. (1, p. 71).

Spreading "enlightenment and civilization" was the rationale invoked also by self-appointed guardians of primitive cultures and advocates of the "white man's burden," like Benjamin Disraeli and Cecil Rhodes! The kind of "paternalism" implicit in such viewpoints does not become any less imperialistic because it is expressed by leaders of *non*-European countries; nor—on the basis of overall social and cultural affinity—could Cairo's claims be any more entitled to legitimacy than those of London or Paris. In brief, the American people and their policy-makers must be mindful of the fact that the cause of anti-colonialism *can be made to serve the national interests of other countries*, just as colonialism has traditionally served the interests of European powers. Consequently, colonial disputes frequently must be evaluated within the context of rival national interests. Realization of this fact will often rob such issues of the sharp moral-ethical overtones associated with them and will justify an American approach which also takes into account factors derived from national interest.

America's Choices

Still another fact that must animate the American response to colonial questions is this: the choice confronting policy-makers in the vast majority of cases lies among alternatives entailing greater or lesser evils. In many instances, no possibility exists for realizing what Western policy-makers might regard as "ideal" solutions. In dealing with the principal remaining center of colonial strife—Africa—the choices are likely to be continuation of colonialism, perhaps accompanied by efforts to mitigate its harsher features; political retrogression into a condition of chaos and anarchy among rival internal groups, in which process the indigenous masses are manipulated by contending cliques; and government by elites purporting to represent the interests of the native populations. None of these alternatives fits an American conception of what is ideally desirable. American officials may have to decide which alternative is *least disadvantageous* and to support it.

James S. Coleman has written that:

> Africa's diversity is nowhere more strikingly revealed than in the prevailing and emergent forms of government under which the African peoples live and are seeking to work out their destinies. All of the classical types of political systems are represented, ranging from a medieval monarchy, through black and white oligarchies and static colonial régimes, to new experimental democracies. . . . Policies welcomed and successful in one country may be rejected and totally inappropriate for another. Such political diversity obviously must be fully appreciated for any realistic assessment of the prospects for democracy and stability. (1, pp. 29-30).*

And another observer of African affairs, Vernon McKay, has cautioned that if "democracy" emerges at all in many African countries it is likely to be a type which varies markedly from Western models and which, in a literal sense, might not even be regarded as a democracy

---

*Coleman identifies the following types of government on the African scene: (1) in *independent* Africa he finds European oligarchies, African oligarchies, and emergent African states; (2) in *colonial* Africa he finds multiracial territories, Euro-African unions, and special status territories. Even less than in relations with Asia in recent years, American experience has ill-equipped the nation for dealing with novel governmental patterns extant throughout Africa (1, p. 30).

by traditional western standards. In many cases, a lengthy "transition period" will be required before democracy appears in formerly-dependent and newly-independent countries; after that, the "guided democracy" witnessed in contemporary Indonesia or the "presidential democracy" identified with Egypt under President Nasser or the "positive discipline" witnessed in the new nation of Ghana—where strong authoritarian control often underlies a democratic façade—are likely to be the guides for African political experience (1, pp. 84-5).

Finally, entering into any calculations of future American policies toward colonialism generally must be recognition of the fact that in many instances the influence of the United States on the future political development of dependent and newly-independent countries will probably be peripheral. With countries remaining in a dependent status, this point is obvious. For the most part, American influence will have to be exerted *indirectly*, through the metropolitan governments in Europe; and in the process, it is a virtual certainty that much of the initiative and energy applied by the United States will be filtered out before it reaches the grass roots in many colonial societies. In the last analysis, the colonial power itself will make the key decisions in the political realm. Pressure by the State Department on metropolitan governments may or may not achieve intended results. Even with independent countries in regions like Africa, however, relations with the United States are likely to be by and large tangential. Geographical remoteness, lack of experience in dealing with prevailing conditions, dissimilarity of backgrounds, and few points of direct contact—these and other limiting factors will militate against decisive American influence in shaping events.

Our lengthy analysis of the response of the United States to colonialism, focusing particularly on the Middle Eastern and African contexts, suggests several basic ideas that must enter into any attempt to evolve a more satisfactory approach to colonial issues.

(1) *The first task is elimination of deeply-embedded stereotypes and clichés that have characterized the nation's approach to colonial questions.* The challenge facing American pol-

icy-makers is vastly complicated by reliance upon emotionally-inspired nostrums and slogans in dealing with so complex a problem as colonialism. Postwar experience amply confirms that uncritical reiteration of idealistic *dicta* such as "self-determination" and "anti-colonialism" tends to becloud the question of American relations with specific colonial disputes and to divert officials from the difficult task of formulating workable proposals. Attachment to such slogans, in the absence of viable policies and programs, lends credence to the accusation that the United States is "hypocritical" in its approach to existing colonial controversies. The American public, no less than leaders of colonial and anti-colonial forces, requires assistance by its chosen leaders and by informed citizen groups in rethinking its customary, almost reflexive, response to such controversies.

(2) *The historic American goal of independence for peoples ready for such independence, and prepared to exercise its responsibilities, must be retained.* No other course accords with the mainstream of American diplomatic history, with the ideological propensities of the American people, or with the long-term national interests of the United States. Willingly or unwillingly, the American people themselves have engraved the desire for freedom on the consciousness of dependent peoples and have testified to the lengths societies are prepared to go to attain it. As much as any other factor, this consideration undergirds the American claim to leadership in global affairs and attracts other countries to its cause.

The goal of ultimate independence, however, must continue, as in the past, to be a qualified goal. Several corollaries derive from this fact. While the "conditions" requisite for independence may be generally specified, their application under dissimilar circumstances is likely to vary widely. Considerable flexibility will have to be exhibited in tailoring them to specific situations throughout the Afro-Asian bloc. Moreover, greater care and planning will have to enter into specification of these conditions. Obviously, the United States cannot realistically formulate and apply them unilaterally. This task can be accomplished better through deliberations of bodies like the UN

Trusteeship Council, the Committee on Non-Self-Governing Territories, and through intensive consultations with the allies and spokesmen for anti-colonial movements. The success of any reformulation of American policy toward colonialism is likely to be in direct ratio to success in achieving a wide consensus upon needed criteria and realization that agreement upon them will serve the best interests of all parties to colonial discords. Assuming some progress toward this goal, a collateral step will be more intensive "educational" campaigns to raise citizen enlightenment, within colonial countries, within societies living under a colonial relationship, and within the American society itself.

A necessary corollary of this maxim is also the idea that some societies are not yet "ready" for independence and will not likely be ready for an indefinite period in the future. For such societies, perhaps the most that America can promise throughout the years ahead is assistance in creating conditions that may someday lead to independence and assurances that the political relationship prevailing with such countries will be periodically reassessed.

(3) *By exercising foresight and applying preventive measures, the United States must seek to avoid having to choose between its allies and Afro-Asian societies.* The only "answer" to this doleful dilemma is for the United States to endeavor as far as possible to see that it does not arise. American diplomatic efforts ought to be directed at demonstrating that this dilemma is to the interest of no country involved in colonial disputes, not least its European allies. Their interests, no less than America's, are served to the extent that the United States is not pressed to choose between them and their dependencies. For it is doubtful in the long run whether their role in world affairs is enhanced even if the United States, perhaps out of cold war necessities, sides with them against their overseas possessions. Such a move may well mean a more complete break in the colonial relationship and a greater disruption to the metropolitan government's economy in the future than if reasonable concessions were made at periodic intervals.

Yet it would be utopian to imagine that all painful choices can be indefinitely avoided. No doubt situations will continue to arise in which Washington must cast its influence either for or against continuance of colonial systems. When hard choices of this kind must be made —when foresight and preventive measures have failed to prevent the dilemma from ever arising —the consequences will be plainly unpalatable. The injurious effects sometimes encountered in such a choice may, however, be mitigated somewhat by reflecting upon postwar experience and applying lessons learned. One observation that emerges with striking force is that a policy of attempting to please all parties to colonial disputes almost inevitably ends up pleasing nobody. There are times when a "middle of the road" position collides with traffic going in both directions and well-nigh guarantees that nations following such a course will be regarded by both sides more as a menace than a help. Furthermore, if temporary concessions, prompted by the gravity of world affairs, must be made to the point of view of the allies, then care should be taken to inculcate the view among dependent societies that these concessions are *temporary* and that the United States has not *abandoned* its traditional attachment to the principle of freedom. This would entail an obligation upon the United States to return to its support for the goal of independence as rapidly as circumstances permit.

(4) *Assistance should be provided by the United States to ease the transition for countries moving from a dependent to an independent status.* A clear necessity in American policy is moving further in the direction of providing needed assistance in resolving colonial disputes. In far too many instances, American assistance has consisted of gratuitous advice about matters concerning which it has had far too little first-hand experience. Basic to any successful American policy toward colonialism must be recognition—translated into programs designed to benefit colonial powers and their former dependencies alike—that independence for many countries is certain to give rise to numerous problems extending over a prolonged period. Demonstrating its sincere attachment to freedom will require that the

United States render whatever assistance its own resources permit in converting the abstract goal of freedom into a reality. Admitting many dissimilarities between conditions in Western Europe and the Afro-Asian bloc, the model of the Marshall Plan in dealing with the former can serve as the ideal for dealing with the latter. Even partial success in achieving this ideal would go far toward linking the national interest of the United States with the aspirations of hundreds of millions of people who are embarking upon a new, and unquestionably perilous, experiment in self-government.

REFERENCES

1. American Assembly. *The United States and Africa*. New York: Columbia University, 1958. These papers presented to an Arden House conference on Africa provide valuable insight into emergent African problems affecting American relations.

2. Atyeo, Henry C. "Arab Politics and Pacts," *Current History*, 30 (June, 1956), pp. 339-46. Discusses the impact of American-sponsored defense systems on the Arab world.

3. Bell, Philip W., "Colonialism As A Problem in American Foreign Policy," *World Politics*, 5 (October, 1952), pp. 86-109. Argues forcefully that America must rethink its position on colonialism and must acknowledge the benefits colonialism affords for native populations, the Western world, and generally in international relations.

4. Bowles, Chester. *Africa's Challenge to America*. Berkeley, California: University of California Press, 1956. Contains valuable insights into the influence of nationalism in parts of Africa and the Middle East for American foreign policy.

5. *Christian Science Monitor*.

6. Cooke, Morris L. *Nasser's High Aswan Dam*. Washington: Public Affairs Institute, 1956. Explores the implications of the Aswan High Dam project, with special reference to American-Egyptian relations.

7. Council on Foreign Relations. *Documents on American Foreign Relations, 1947*, et seq. New York: Harper and Brothers, 1948. The annual volumes in this series contain documentary material on American Middle Eastern policy.

8. Department of State. *Aid to the Palestine Refugees*. (Publication No. 4191, "Near and Middle Eastern Series," 4). Washington: 1951. Describes efforts by the United States and the United Nations to aid the Palestine refugees.

9. ———. *American Foreign Policy, 1950-55*. (Publication No. 6446, "General Foreign Policy Series," 117), Washington: 1957. Volume 2 of this helpful series contains extensive documentary material on the Middle East.

10. ———. *The Development of United States Policy in the Near East, 1945-51*. (Publication No. 4446, "Near and Middle Eastern Series," 5). Washington: 1952. Provides background on U.S. policy toward the Middle East in the immediate postwar era.

11. ———. *The Development of United States Policy in the Near East, South Asia, and Africa, 1951-52*, et seq. (Publication No. 4851, "Near and Middle Eastern Series," 9). Washington: 1953. The annual volumes in this series afford valuable treatments of contemporary American policy toward the Middle East.

12. ———. *The Middle East*. (Publication No. 5469, "Near and Middle Eastern Series," 16). Washington: 1954.

13. ———. *The Palestine Refugee Issue*. (Publication No. 3757, "Near and Middle Eastern Series," 3). Washington: 1950. Analyzes the issues in the refugee controversy.

14. ———. *United States Foreign Policy in the Middle East*. (Publication No. 4852, "Near and Middle Eastern Series," 10). Washington: 1953.

15. ———. *United States Policy in the Middle East*. (Publication No. 6505, "Near and Middle Eastern Series," 25). Washington: 1957.

16. Elwell-Sutton, L. P. "Nationalism and Neutralism in Iran," *Middle East Journal*, 12 (Winter, 1958), pp. 20-33. A brief, but illuminating, case study of nationalist and neutralist sentiment in the Middle East.

17. Glick, Edward B. "Latin America and the Establishment of Israel," *Middle Eastern Affairs*, 9 (January, 1958), 11-16.

18. Haines, C. Grove, ed. *Africa Today*. Baltimore: The Johns Hopkins Press, 1955. A symposium, presenting selected studies on Africa's varied problems.

19. Howard, Harry N. "The Arab-Asian States in the United Nations," *Middle East Journal*, 7 (Summer, 1953), 279-92. Contains helpful background treatment on America's relations with the Middle East prior to the partition of Palestine.

20. Hull, Cordell. *The Memoirs of Cordell Hull.* New York: The Macmillan Company, 1948.

21. Hurewitz, J. C. *Diplomacy in the Near and Middle East.* New York: D. Van Nostrand Company, 1956. An indispensable compilation of documents on great power relations in the Middle East. Volume 2 treats the post-World War I period.

22. Kulski, W. W. "Soviet Colonialism and Anti-Colonialism," *Russian Review*, 18 (April, 1959), pp. 113-26. Analyzes the reasons for the Kremlin's success in its anti-colonialist propaganda.

23. Laqueur, Walter Z. *Communism and Nationalism in the Middle East.* New York: Frederick A. Praeger, 1956. A perceptive treatment of the Arab nationalist movement, with emphasis upon the impact of communism on the Middle East.

24. ———. "The 'National Bourgeoisie': A Soviet Dilemma in the Middle East," *International Affairs*, 35 (July, 1959), pp. 324-31. A lucid analysis of challenges to Soviet diplomacy in reaching an accord with nationalist leaders in the Middle East.

25. Lenczowski, George. *The Middle East in World Affairs.* Ithaca, New York: Cornell University Press, 1952. Probably the best one-volume study of the Middle East available.

26. Leonard, L. Larry. "The United Nations and Palestine," *International Conciliation*, 454 (October, 1949), 607-786. An objective and comprehensive analysis of the Palestinian issue before the United Nations up to, and immediately following, partition.

27. London, Isaac. "Evolution of the USSR's Policy in the Middle East, 1950-1956," *Middle Eastern Affairs*, 7 (May, 1956), 169-79. A brief, but enlightening, treatment of the changing tactics in Soviet policy, leading to active Soviet intervention in Middle Eastern affairs.

28. Martin, H. G. "The Soviet Union and the Middle East," *Middle Eastern Affairs*, 7 (February, 1956), 49-56. An analysis of recent Soviet Middle Eastern policy.

29. Nasser, Gamal Abdel. "The Egyptian Revolution," *Foreign Affairs*, 33 (January, 1955), 199-212. The head of the Egyptian state explains his nation's role in world affairs.

30. New York *Herald Tribune*.

31. *New York Times*.

32. Peretz, Don. "Democracy and the Revolution in Egypt," *Middle East Journal*, 13 (Winter, 1959), pp. 26-40. Evaluates Egyptian "democracy" under Nasser, making significant comparisons with western models.

33. ———. "Development of the Jordan Valley Waters," *Middle East Journal*, 9 (Autumn, 1955), 397-412. Evaluates the Jordan Valley project as an outstanding issue in Middle Eastern affairs.

34. Polk, William R. *What the Arabs Think.* ("Headline Book," No. 96). New York: Foreign Policy Association, 1952. A good introductory study of Arab attitudes toward the United States, showing clearly Arab resentment over the creation of Israel.

35. Senate Foreign Relations Committee. *Technical Assistance.* 85th Congress, 1st Session, March 12, 1957. Contains studies of separate aspects of American foreign assistance; pp. 464-506 deal with development in Africa; the study of Soviet technical assistance, pp. 236-70, also contains material on the Middle East and Africa.

36. Spain, James W. "Middle East Defense: A New Approach," *Middle East Journal*, 8 (Summer, 1954), 251-67. The writer discusses the currents of conflict set in motion by American advocacy of a regional defense plan.

37. Stamp, L. Dudley. *Africa: A Study in Tropical Development.* New York: John Wiley and Sons, Inc., 1953. Focuses on the economic geography of Africa and its impact upon social, cultural, and political questions.

38. Stevens, Georgiana G. "Arab Refugees, 1948-52," *Middle East Journal*, 6 (Summer, 1952), 281-97. Weighs the pros and cons in the explosive refugee issue.

39. ———. "The Jordan River Valley," *International Conciliation*, 506 (January, 1956), 225-83.

40. Stillman, Calvin W., ed. *Africa in the Modern World.* Chicago: University of Chicago Press, 1955. A symposium covering selected aspects of Africa's present and future development.

41. Strausz-Hupé, Robert, and Hazard, Harry W., eds. *The Idea of Colonialism.* New York: Frederick A. Praeger, Inc., 1958. A symposium on various aspects of colonialism, with valuable chapters on American policies and attitudes.

42. Truman, Harry S. *Memoirs*. Garden City, N. Y. Doubleday and Company, 1955. Pages 156-62 of Volume 2 discuss Zionist pressures on the White House in behalf of partition and show President Truman's reactions to these pressures. Conflicting points of view within the government on this issue are brought out clearly in Chapters 10-12, Volume 2, *passim*.

43. *United States in World Affairs, 1945-47*, et seq. New York: Harper and Brothers, 1947. The annual volumes in this series by the Council on Foreign Relations are an enlightening secondary source on current American Middle Eastern policies.

44. Wheeler, G. E. "Russia and the Middle East," *International Affairs*, 35 (July, 1959), pp. 295-305. Traces Russian diplomatic goals in the Middle East, stressing continuity between Czarist and communist objectives.

45. Wilber, Donald N. "Prospects for Federation in the Northern Tier," *Middle East Journal*, 12 (Autumn, 1958), pp. 385-95. Calls attention to forces favoring and hindering regional co-operation in the Middle East.

46. Wint, Guy and Calvocoressi, Peter. *Middle East Crisis*. Middlesex, England: Penguin Books, Ltd., 1957. This little volume by two astute British observers provides a penetrating evaluation of the Suez crisis of 1956-57 and its contributory causes.

47. Woytinsky, W. S., and Woytinsky, E. S. *World Population and Production: Trends and Outlook*. New York: Twentieth Century Fund, 1953. This voluminous study affords a valuable source for understanding Africa's geographic and economic environment and for comparisons with other major regions.

48. Yale, William. *The Near East*. Ann Arbor: University of Michigan Press, 1958. A recent introductory survey of the history of the Middle East, written from a rather pronounced pro-Arab position.

49. *Yearbook of World Affairs, 1954*, et seq. London, England: Stevens and Sons, Ltd., 1954. The annual volumes in this series by the London Institute of World Affairs contain helpful essays on selected aspects of current international relations.

CHAPTER 12

The Western Hemisphere

Vicissitudes of the Good Neighbor Policy

Preoccupied in recent years with the all-pervading cold war, the people of the United States and their leaders sometimes neglect one of the most crucial areas in world politics: the Western Hemisphere. Though fairly well insulated from the eddies of great power antagonisms witnessed in Europe, the Middle East, and Asia, the Western Hemisphere is nevertheless of fundamental importance to policy-makers in Washington.

It would be difficult to justify the neglect of this hemisphere on rational grounds. With the passage of time all the American Republics and Canada are becoming more and more interdependent. Nearly half of the total foreign commerce of the United States is carried on with the Latin American states and Canada; trade by this country is divided almost equally between them (11, p. 25; 19, p. 20). As a market for our goods, Latin America in 1959 took approximately 20 per cent of the nation's exports. Within recent years Latin America has customarily received 50 per cent or more of its imports from the United States. Included in Latin America's exports to the United States were many strategic materials needed by defense industries in this country. Thus, as measured solely in statistics of trade, Canada and Latin America are about as important to

the United States as Western Europe and considerably more important than Asia or Africa (14, pp. 2-3; 19, p. 20).

Furthermore, Latin America is an area of outstanding potential, and a great deal of actual, economic growth. Spectacular economic expansion has occurred in the past quarter-century. Per capita income has grown by 2.25 per cent a year. From 1946 to 1952 it grew by 2.5 per cent annually. These gains become all the more impressive in light of the fact that population increases in that region are nearly the highest in the world; the population doubled from World War II to the late 1950's, and is expected to double again in the next quarter-century. If Latin American countries succeed in carrying forward programs of economic advancement—in which they will have to maintain the 2.5 per cent annual economic growth rate—then the Gross National Product throughout these countries will have to triple in the next twenty-five years (23, November 28, 1958, Dispatch by E. W. Kenworthy). Convinced that they have been "neglected" by Uncle Sam in recent years, citizens and leaders in Latin America believe that their future welfare will hinge upon generous assistance extended by the United States government and by the investment activities of private business concerns.

The overall strategic importance of Latin America to the United States has already been discussed at length in Chapter 1 and reviewed in Chapters 8 and 9. We shall not cover that ground again, except to stress once more that the security of the United States is dependent to a high degree upon keeping the military approaches to the Western Hemisphere in friendly hands and protecting the vital hemispheric lines of communications and trade from threats by the nation's avowed diplomatic enemies. For instance, of the imports needed by the United States for defense purposes, a goodly share comes from Latin America: 100 per cent of vanadium and quebracho (used

for tanning), 90 per cent of quartz crystals, 80 per cent of castor bean oil (used as aircraft lubricant), crude petroleum and fuel oil, and 40 per cent of the tungsten and zinc (**10**, p. 7).

The development of nuclear weapons and guided missiles has vastly enhanced the importance of Canada and the Arctic region for Washington's defense policy. The United States and Canada developed close defense ties during World War II. These have been greatly strengthened under the necessity to build effective defenses in the nuclear-missile age. "The Arctic," writes one geographer, "may become to the future what the Mediterranean was to the past—the axis of world power . . . This is the new strategic center of the world. It is the new Pivot Area, which has made the old Heartland

INDUSTRIAL RAW MATERIALS AVAILABLE IN LATIN AMERICA

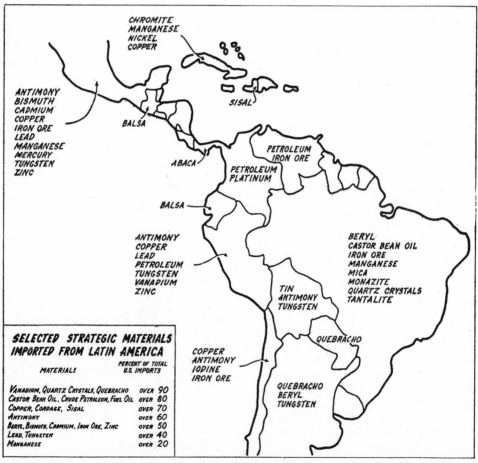

House Foreign Affairs Committee. *Hearings on the Mutual Security Act of 1958.* Part 12, p. 1501.

eccentric" (**39**, p. 40). A former chief of the United States Air Force, General Spaatz, has asserted that "Whoever controls the Arctic air lanes controls the world today" (**39**, p. 55). The new strategic significance of North America has been reflected in postwar agreements between the United States and Canada providing for joint construction and maintenance of a three-stage radar defense network extending into the Arctic and for general United States-Canadian co-operation in the field of defense planning. The St. Lawrence Seaway project also demands closer ties than ever before between the United States and Canada, especially in the sphere of expanding commercial co-operation. New vistas are thus opening up in the relations between the United States and its northern neighbor. Some authorities even foresee a gradual weakening of Canada's historic ties with the British Commonwealth and its ever closer association with the United States (**39**, p. 58).*

---

*Canada receives peripheral attention in this chapter. Extended treatments of relations between the United States and Canada historically and in recent years are: **2**, pp. 411-34; **15**, pp. 735-38; **38**, pp. 73-84; **40**, pp. 675-96; **20**; **21**; **24**; **3**.

This chapter will focus on the response of the United States to three problems: hemispheric security and solidarity; the communist movement in the Americas; and problems of foreign trade and aid.**

**In discussing relations between the United States and Latin America it is sometimes difficult to follow a satisfactory scheme of nomenclature without resorting to cumbersome phraseology. Our Latin American friends resent the fact that usage in the United States applies the term *American* to the United States alone. The people of Central and South America are fully as entitled to use this term as are the people of the United States.

Because it accords with popular usage, in other chapters of this book I have used the term "American foreign policy," to refer soley to the policy of the United States. To avoid confusion in this chapter, however, I have avoided such terms as "American foreign policy," which could conceivably mean the foreign policy of other countries in the Western hemisphere. Instead I have spoken of the foreign policy of the United States or the diplomacy of the State Department. Elsewhere in the book, the adjective *American* refers to the United States, on the theory that in those chapters there is minimum risk of confusion. The reader may wish to pursue the question of accurate nomenclature further in **1**, p. 32-n and **5**, pp. 79-81.

1. HEMISPHERIC SECURITY AND SOLIDARITY

The Monroe Doctrine

For over a century the Monroe Doctrine defined the diplomatic behavior of the United States toward the Western Hemisphere. Two developments in the third decade of the 19th century induced President Monroe to enunciate what came to be the most famous principle of our foreign policy. There were, first of all, Russian colonial activities in the West. Especially significant was the Czarist Imperial ukase of 1821. It virtually declared the Pacific waters around these Russian colonial outposts a closed sea, a pronouncement that seemed to the United States to presage renewed Russian colonizing efforts in North America. A second danger arose from the threatened intervention of the Holy Alliance in the affairs of the former Spanish colonies in Latin America. The United States feared that the Holy Alliance would invoke the principle of "legitimacy" in

an attempt to reimpose Spanish hegemony over newly-independent American possessions; or failing this, that another European country might supplant Spain as a colonial power in the Western Hemisphere.

The key portion of Monroe's message of December 2, 1823, was that:

The political system of the allied powers is essentially different . . . from that of America. . . . We owe it, therefore, to candor, and to the amicable relations existing between the United States and those powers, to declare that we should consider any attempt on their part to extend their system to any portion of this hemisphere as dangerous to our peace and safety. With the existing colonies or dependencies of any European power we have not interfered and shall not interfere. But with the governments who have declared their independence and maintained it . . . we could not view any interposition for the purpose of oppressing them, or controlling in any other manner their destiny, by any European power, in any other light than as the manifestation of an unfriendly disposition toward the United States. (16, p. 324).

Several points about Monroe's pronouncement require emphasis.* The first is that this was a *unilateral* declaration by the United States. The non-colonization principle, to be sure, was also supported by the British Foreign Office and, what was much more crucial for the continued independence of the Latin American states, enforced on several significant occasions by the Royal Navy. Yet other powerful nations were not inclined to regard the doctrine as a fixed canon of international law, much less as a precept to which they had freely given consent. As the history of the Monroe Doctrine made clear, its effectiveness depended predominantly upon one factor: the willingness and ability of the United States, backed in some instances by Great Britain, to enforce compliance with it. Second, as originally expressed, the non-colonization principle of the Monroe Doctrine prohibited *future* colonization by European countries. It did nothing to interfere with *existing* colonies; nor did it proscribe European diplomatic or economic influence throughout the New World. Later amplifications and corollaries of the Monroe Doctrine, which we shall treat below, broadened the scope of the non-colonization principle and introduced new prohibitions against European diplomatic activity in the Americas. But no such sweeping prohibitions were included in the original message.

Third, in the years following Monroe's proclamation the United States was unprepared on a number of occasions to back up the Monroe Doctrine with military and diplomatic force. This became evident almost immediately after 1823 when Latin American diplomats asked Washington for treaties of alliance that would commit the United States to support their continued freedom from Spanish colonial rule.

---

*Here our concern is with the Western hemispheric aspects of the Monroe Doctrine. The European aspects, by which the United States pledged itself not to interfere in wars on the continent of Europe, are discussed in Chapter 10.
The historic meaning and evolution of the Monroe Doctrine are ably treated in three studies by Dexter Perkins: 26, 27, and 28. A valuable compendium of documentary materials on the Monroe Doctrine is 16, pp. 301-425.

These requests met with an unenthusiastic reception on the part of the State Department. Moreover, when the nations of Latin America sought to cement closer hemispheric relations at the Panama Congress of 1826, the United States held aloof from the meeting. The viewpoint of the new President John Quincy Adams —"There is no community of interest or of principle between North and South America" —was in strange contrast with the community of interest which had seemingly been postulated by Monroe's message of 1823 (31, pp. 180-81).

From the time of its inception, and even after its scope had been broadened in the light of experience, the Monroe Doctrine remained essentially a unilateral response by the United States to conditions believed to threaten its security. In substance, wrote Robert Lansing in 1914, it reflected the view that "the United States considers an extension of political control by a European power over any territory in this hemisphere, not already occupied by it, to be a menace to the national safety of the United States." Compliance with the doctrine in the last analysis rested upon the "superior power of the United States to compel submission to its will . . ." (16, pp. 371-72). That the Monroe Doctrine had been proclaimed unilaterally by the United States meant, in the words of Secretary of State Charles Evans Hughes in 1923, that

the government of the United States reserves to itself its definition, interpretation, and application. . . . Great powers have signified their acquiescence in it. But the United States has not been disposed to enter into engagements which would have the effect of submitting to any other power or to any concert of powers the determination either of the occasions upon which the principles of the Monroe Doctrine shall be invoked or of the measures that shall be taken in giving it effect. (16, pp. 387-88).

Schooled as they are in the idea that Monroe's classic foreign policy principle was ideally suited to their country's historic desires and needs, it is difficult for North Americans to understand that the doctrine could arouse apprehension in their neighbors south of the border. Over the course of time, however, Latin American nations often viewed "Yankee imperialism" as a more imminent threat than reimposition of European colonial domination.

Occasionally, Latin American countries were inclined to regard the doctrine as nothing more than a thinly veiled scheme whereby the United States invoked hemispheric security as a pretext to exercise a *de facto* protectorate over weaker American states and, under the guise of protecting them from European intervention, practiced intervention itself in the affairs of nations to the south. In recent years, therefore, one recurring task of United States foreign policy-makers has been to try to convince the countries of Latin America that the Monroe Doctrine has not been directed against them but against powerful nations in Europe. Later portions of the chapter will illustrate how the United States has sought to translate the unilateral guarantees contained in the Monroe Doctrine into guarantees supported and enforced by all the countries belonging to the Inter-American system.

Corollaries of the Monroe Doctrine

Today when the student of American foreign policy studies the Monroe Doctrine, in reality he is studying an aggregate of diplomatic pronouncements and actions based upon President Monroe's message to Congress in 1823. Collectively, these have vastly expanded and modified the original meaning of the Monroe Doctrine in order to cover specific diplomatic situations that have arisen in the Western Hemisphere. Let us look briefly at some of the more important highlights in the evolution of this cardinal principle of American foreign policy.

The first important amplification of the Monroe Doctrine was the *Polk Corollary* in the period 1845-48. President Polk declared that the non-colonization principle of the Monroe Doctrine "will apply with greatly increased force, should any European power attempt to establish *any new colony* in North America . . . " (**16**, p. 330, italics inserted). A half-century later, in the midst of the Venezuelan boundary dispute with Great Britain (**16**, pp. 347-52), Secretary of State Richard Olney informed the British that the non-colonization principle of the Monroe Doctrine had been "universally conceded" and that it had been the "controlling factor" in the

"emancipation of South America" from Spanish rule. Olney, more gifted in the role of prosecuting attorney than historian or diplomat, went on to inform the British Foreign Office categorically that:

> Today the United States is practically sovereign on this continent, and its fiat is law upon the subjects to which it confines its interposition. Why? . . . It is because . . . its infinite resources combined with its isolated position render it master of the situation and practically invulnerable as against any or all other powers. (**16**, pp. 344-348).

The Olney letter translated the Monroe Doctrine into a pronouncement that in effect designated the Western Hemisphere as a Yankee sphere of influence, a claim which the nations of Europe and of Latin America were reluctant to accept.

Coincident with the age of "dollar diplomacy" toward Latin American and Asian affairs in the early 1900's was the *Roosevelt Corollary* to the Monroe Doctrine. Certain Latin American nations, chiefly in the Caribbean region, were notoriously lax in the management of their governmental and fiscal affairs. Outside intervention in their affairs for the purpose of collecting legitimate debts was consequently a perennial risk. President Theodore Roosevelt concluded that the United States could not prohibit foreign intervention to enforce payment of debts unless it were willing to assume responsibilities itself for preventing gross fiscal mismanagement by its southern neighbors. In 1901 Roosevelt stated that the Monroe Doctrine did not protect any Latin American country "against punishment if it misconducts itself. . . . " A year later he warned that it behooved each country in Latin America to "maintain order within its borders and to discharge its just obligations to foreigners." This line of reasoning ultimately led him to the conclusion in 1904 that any nation that "knows how to act with reasonable efficiency and decency" need not fear intervention. But:

> Chronic wrongdoing, or an impotence which results in a general loosening of the ties of civilized society, may in America, as elsewhere, ultimately require intervention by some civilized nation, and in the Western Hemisphere the adherence of the United States to the Monroe

Doctrine may force the United States, however reluctantly . . . to the exercise of an international police power. (16, pp. 360-64).

This then was the first Roosevelt's characteristically forthright response to the threat of intervention in Latin American affairs by European countries. Either the southern neighbors of the United States would keep their own affairs in order, thereby minimizing the risk of such intervention, or else the United States would be compelled under the Monroe Doctrine to undertake necessary house cleaning duties in such countries. This was no idle boast. On repeated occasions after 1904 the United States invoked the Roosevelt Corollary to justify intervention in Latin American affairs. This fact inevitably conveyed the impression to the other American republics that the Monroe Doctrine might protect them from the diplomatic ambitions of countries outside the Western Hemisphere, but that it could also be invoked to rationalize control over them by the United States, and to their minds this was often a distinction without a difference. Not until the administration of the second Roosevelt were all the military contingents of the United States finally withdrawn from Latin America.

The scope of the non-colonization principle contained in the Monroe Doctrine was also broadened by the *Lodge Corollary,* expressed in a Senate resolution of August 2, 1912. Prompted by threatened Japanese acquisition of parts of Lower California, this corollary held that the United States could not permit occupation of harbors within the Western Hemisphere "for naval or military purposes" by a foreign power, if such occupation would "threaten the communications or safety of the United States . . . " (16, p. 208).

The Good Neighbor Policy

The impact of Wilsonian idealism, along with the evident deterioration in relations between the United States and its hemispheric neighbors as a result of the Roosevelt Corollary from 1904 onward, demanded corrective measures on the part of the State Department. Recurrent outcries from the south against "Yankee imperialism" could no longer be ignored in Washington. A significant change in the foreign policy of the United States was therefore presaged by the "Clark Memorandum" of 1928, the gist of which was that the Roosevelt Corollary had been a perversion of the original intention of the Monroe Doctrine (16, pp. 401-07). Then with the election of Franklin D. Roosevelt came the "Good Neighbor" policy, enunciated in FDR's First Inaugural address and reiterated in a series of messages thereafter by Roosevelt and Secretary of State Cordell Hull. The first step in establishing good neighborly relations was to reassure the Latin American countries that the Monroe Doctrine was not a pretext to conceal Yankee imperialistic ambitions toward them. Secretary Hull stated in 1933 that the people of the United States believed that the so-called right of conquest "must be banished from this hemisphere and, most of all, they shun and reject that so-called right for themselves." In the same year FDR repeated Wilson's earlier pledge that the United States would never again seek additional territory by conquest. Paving the way for an effective inter-American system of defense and solidarity, Roosevelt observed that political turbulence and threats to hemispheric security were no longer of special concern to the United States alone, but that they were "the joint concern of a whole continent in which we are all neighbors" (16, pp. 165-66). As it related to the Monroe Doctrine, the new good neighbor policy came down to this: the traditional interest of the United States in Western hemispheric security must be translated into a policy shared by all the American countries. All must support it and all must act in concert to deal with conditions threatening the peace and stability of the hemisphere. This was in substance the purpose of the inter-American system.

The Pan-American Movement

No sooner had the countries of Latin America won their independence in the early 1800's than their leaders began to think in terms of a Pan-American movement to preserve their freedom, not alone from Europe but from their northern neighbor, the United States, as well. The great South American leader, Simon Bolivar, early took the lead in laying the basis for the Pan-American movement. The United States, largely for reasons of domestic politics and the desire to preserve an attitude of non-entanglement with other countries, did not participate in the first Panama Congress of 1826 (31, pp. 181-83). As was often characteristic of such conferences in the years that followed, the delegates were quick to pass resolutions proclaiming their mutual attachment to idealistic goals, such as political non-intervention and economic co-operation. But in this and later instances such resolutions frequently received little or no tangible support afterwards from the governments concerned. The first attempt to establish a Pan-American system therefore was a failure. For a half-century thereafter the dream of Pan-Americanism languished, despite the fact that considerable support for it existed in Latin America and within the United States.

Fifty years later the movement received new impetus under Secretary of State James G. Blaine, who proposed a meeting of all the American Republics in Washington in 1881 for the purpose of preventing war in the Western Hemisphere and of promoting closer economic collaboration among the nations of the region. A change in political administrations within the United States delayed these plans for eight years. But finally, in 1889, the conference was held. This conference was also devoid of tangible results, except for one: establishment of the Bureau of American Republics, later renamed the Pan-American Union, which in time evolved into one of the principal organs of the Inter-American System (31, p. 346).

The pace by which the Pan-American movement grew from little more than expressions of affinity among the American Republics, accompanied by occasional conferences at which actual gains were usually negligible, was leisurely between the late 1800's and the New Deal. Interventions carried out by the United States under the Roosevelt Corollary understandably made the other American republics highly suspicious of Uncle Sam's intentions. Uppermost in the minds of Latin American statesmen was the ubiquitous specter of Yankee domination; they consequently looked askance at frequent endorsements of the ideal of Pan-Americanism by the United States because

they feared domination of Latin American affairs by an international body controlled from Washington. Repudiation of the Roosevelt Corollary and the inauguration of the good neighbor policy were therefore necessary before significant progress could be expected toward establishing more intimate relations among countries in the Western Hemisphere.

Once the diplomatic atmosphere had cleared after 1932 Pan-American co-operation gradually became a reality. The threat of Axis aggression provided another stimulus, by binding the nations of the Western Hemisphere together against a common enemy and by emphasizing their economic interdependence. Beginning with the conference at Montevideo in 1933 the Inter-American System began to take shape. Here the United States accepted a resolution directed principally at itself, pledging all American Republics to a policy of non-intervention in the affairs of their neighbors. In return, the United States received widespread support by the Latin American governments for the New Deal principle of reciprocal trade, whereby national tariffs were lowered on the basis of mutual concessions (31, pp. 610-11). Three years later, at the Inter-American Conference in Buenos Aires, the American Republics accepted the principle of joint consultation among all the American countries in the event of a threat to the security of the hemisphere (16, p. 285). Additional conferences were held in 1938, 1939, 1940, and 1942. An important milestone was the conference at Mexico City in 1945, at which the Act of Chapultepec was adopted, formally declaring the determination of the American Republics to pursue a common policy in meeting any threat to their security from abroad (31, p. 765).

Building on these foundations, the Rio Conference of 1947 resulted in the Treaty of Reciprocal Assistance, signed on September 2. This regional defense agreement, like NATO and similar agreements, was drawn up under Article 51 of the United Nations Charter, providing for the right of individual and regional self-defense. Pending action by the Security Council of the UN, threats to the peace within the Americas were to be dealt with by the Inter-American system (31, pp. 767-68). Then at the Ninth Inter-American Conference at Bogotá in the spring of 1948 the formal machinery necessary to make these goals a reality—the Organization of American States (OAS)—was established. Finally the Pan-American movement had come to fruition. After nearly a century and a quarter the American Republics had moved from highly generalized and usually ineffectual declarations of mutual affinity to the creation of a regional defense system, containing permanent machinery for dealing with threats to the security and stability of the Western Hemisphere that might arise from such diverse sources as the activities of international communism, conflicts among individual American states, or widespread hemispheric economic dislocations.

OAS—Procedures and Principles

The Inter-American System rests upon three basic "charter documents" defining its scope and procedures. First, there is the Rio Treaty of mutual assistance safeguarding the defense of the Americas from an attack originating outside or inside the hemisphere; second, there is a document specifying the scope, organs, and duties of OAS; and third, there is a document setting forth procedures to be followed for bringing about the pacific settlement of disputes among members of the system (13, p. 157). Similarly, the Inter-American System has three principal organs: international conferences, the Pan-American Union, and specialized agencies. The high-level policy-making body is the international conference. General conferences are supposed to be held at 5-year intervals. Within shorter periods, lower-level conferences dealing with limited, sometimes highly technical, subjects are held. In the event of a threat to the security of the Americas, *Meetings of Consultation* are summoned immediately to deal with the threat. The foreign ministers of the member-states attend these meetings. The purpose of such meetings, in the words of a State Department document, is "to bring together on short notice the top spokesmen on foreign affairs of the executive branches of the 21 governments for rapid discussion and resolution of emergency issues" (13, pp. 158-59). We shall see below how the

Meeting of Consultation dealt with a specific complaint brought before the OAS in 1955.

The Pan-American Union is the permanent organ of the Inter-American System (13, p. 159). PAU maintains its headquarters in Washington. Its governing board consists of representatives chosen by each member-state. Frequently the state's highest diplomatic representative in the United States is selected. To assure that PAU would not become the diplomatic organ of one country alone, or would be too strongly influenced by one country, such as the United States, the chairman of PAU's governing board is not eligible for re-election. The Director General and his assistant, the highest administrative officials, serve for ten years, and they too are ineligible for re-election, nor can their successors be of the same nationality as the incumbents (13, pp. 159-60).

Established in 1910 primarily as an information-gathering and information-disseminating body, PAU's functions were largely confined to this task until after World War II. Much of its activity today is still devoted to the collection and spread of information of common interest to the American states in economic, social, technical, scientific, cultural, and legal fields. In addition, it has become the secretariat of OAS. It arranges for inter-American conferences, provides the required staff, and does the paper work that invariably accompanies such meetings. Moreover, many of the scientific and technical bodies associated with OAS operate under the supervision of the Pan-American Union. After the Rio Treaty of 1947, for the first time PAU acquired important *political* duties. Now it is empowered to act in response to a threat to the Inter-American System, until a Meeting of Consultation can be convened (13, p. 162-63).

The guarantees of hemispheric security contained in the Monroe Doctrine and its corollaries have been assumed by the Inter-American System. Certain precepts have emerged to guide OAS in dealing with threats to the peace. As far back as the end of the 19th century the states in the Western Hemisphere agreed to abstain from using force unilaterally in settling disputes among themselves. This principle was translated into a series of treaties during the 1920's and 1930's, providing that each state would rely upon the "good offices" of other countries, mediation, conciliation, and the like, in settling conflicts within the Inter-American System. Then during the Second World War the principle of "all for one, one for all" was incorporated into the Inter-American System. Any attack or threat against any part of the hemisphere would be regarded as an attack against all the American Republics. Under the Rio Treaty of 1947, therefore, OAS is empowered to deal with any threat to the hemisphere irrespective of whether the threat arises from within or outside the American system. Decisions taken by the Meetings of Consultation are binding on all members, regardless of whether they voted for the decision or not, provided the decision was taken by a two-thirds vote and with the further qualification that no state can be required to use armed forces without its own consent (13, pp. 165-168).

The five most salient features of the Inter-American System as it has evolved throughout a long, and sometimes discouragingly slow, historical process are: each member of the system is obligated to co-operate in resisting an actual or threatened attack against any American country; a two-thirds vote of a Meeting of Consultation is binding on all members; no distinction is made between a threat to the peace arising from outside or inside the hemisphere. The Pan-American Union now exercises political responsibilities, along with those in the cultural, social, economic and related fields; and finally, the Inter-American System is firmly integrated with the United Nations (13, p. 168).

OAS in Action—A Case Study

The machinery established under OAS to facilitate the peaceful settlement of disputes has been utilized on a number of occasions in recent years, with an impressively high level of success. Several specific disputes might be cited. We shall confine our attention to two examples.* Let us first look at the dispute between Costa Rica and Nicaragua, considered by the Organization of American States in 1955. Long-standing tension between these two countries, deriving largely from personal animosity between the two heads of states, erupted into armed hostilities in January. Upon the urgent appeal of Costa Rica, OAS was called into emergency session. It was asked to deal with an alleged threat to Costa Rica's security from rebels within the country who were supported and supplied with arms by groups in Nicaragua hostile to the Costa Rican government. The Meeting of Consultation promptly called upon both countries to desist from making any move that would aggravate prevailing tensions. A five-member investigating team from OAS immediately went to Central America, where it found substantial verification of Costa Rica's charges. By January 14, OAS had called upon the government of Nicaragua to halt border crossings by groups threatening the security of Costa Rica. Then two days later OAS called upon all member states to provide Costa Rica with military supplies designed to bolster its defenses. The United States promptly sent four military aircraft to the country, giving its government aerial supremacy over its borders.

On January 20 both Costa Rica and Nicaragua accepted an OAS-sponsored plan to create a "buffer zone" between the two countries. Troops from either nation were prohibited from entering this zone, while observation planes under the jurisdiction of OAS patrolled the skies over it. Within a few days, the threat to the security of Costa Rica had collapsed. By February, both governments had pledged that there would be no repetition of the incidents that had given rise to this conflict.

This case illustrates several significant characteristics of the Inter-American System. First, this controversy was handled *outside the United Nations.* Any threat to international peace is of course legally within the jurisdiction of the Security Council of the United Nations, but the successful operation of OAS

---

*The second example—the case of communism in Guatemala—will be considered in a later portion of the chapter. Other examples are discussed in the annual volumes of **37**, in **7**, I, pp. 1285-90, and **9**, *passim.*

The case study of OAS's response to the Costa Rican-Nicaraguan dispute is based upon material presented in **37**, 1955, pp. 221-22.

obviated the necessity for passing this case on to the Security Council. Second, very little actual coercion was required to resolve this issue. Planes and military hardware were furnished to Costa Rica, but in the main both countries complied voluntarily with OAS's directives. Third, this case calls attention to the profound change that has come about in relations between the United States and Latin America since the early 1930's. It is interesting to speculate upon what the reaction of the United States might have been if this controversy had arisen during the period of the Roosevelt Corollary or the Wilsonian era of heavy-handed American intervention in the affairs of our southern neighbors. In all probability the United States would have taken the initiative unilaterally in dealing with the dispute—and in doing so would have added to the prevailing antipathy within Latin America against Yankee interventionism. Now, however, although the United States had as strong an interest as ever in preserving peace in the hemisphere, the State Department remained very much in the background, deliberately seeking to avoid the accusation that OAS was merely a "tool" of Washington. The United States responded promptly to OAS's directives, and of course the State Department had exercised a voice, jointly with other OAS members, in shaping these directives. Thus the Costa Rican–Nicaraguan dispute was handled by all the American Republics *acting in concert*. Latin American participants had no reason to feel that the point of view of the United States had been imposed upon them.

Policies Toward Dictatorial Governments

At the fifth Inter-American Meeting of Consultation of the Organization of American States, held at Santiago, Chile, in August, 1959, the urgent problem on the agenda was one that has perennially troubled the waters of hemispheric relations in the modern period: what policies ought to be followed in dealing with dictatorial regimes throughout Latin America? By the opening of the 1960s, the problem appeared to be no closer to satisfactory resolution than before. It was particularly acute among nations adjoining the Caribbean, with

commentators speaking of the possible "balkanization" of that region into a number of antagonistic, unstable political systems, constantly in conflicts that threatened hemispheric peace and stability. Some nations, including countries like Argentina and Brazil, opposed summoning a Meeting of Consultation, out of fear that actions taken might result in an "interference" in their own domestic affairs and those of their sister republics. Other American states favored the meeting. It was clear that, at least in part, they hoped to advance their own diplomatic objectives by inducing OAS to take a strong stand against the policies of specific dictatorial regimes.

In dealing with this problem, the United States, now as in the past, was in a quandary. Firmly committed to the principle of "nonintervention" in the internal affairs of other countries, Washington was reluctant to take any step that might seem to violate this principle. Yet policy-makers in the United States were deeply troubled by conflicts between states like Cuba and the Dominican Republic and the activities of "rebel" groups against established political orders, when these groups were plainly supported and equipped by other countries. As expected, the Meeting of Consultation found no clearcut answer to this problem. Its response—setting up an "American Peace Commission" to observe, and perhaps mediate, recurrent tensions—testified to the durability and complexity of the issue in hemispheric relations (**23**, August 9 and 16, 1959, dispatches by Tad Szulc).

By the end of the 1950s, policy-makers in Washington conceded freely that the nation's position on the issue of dictatorships in the Americas remained ambiguous. In a report to the President on December 27, 1958, Milton S. Eisenhower stated that in his recent tour of Central American countries, "I pointed out with candor that from the beginning of our history until 1933, we had not been very consistent in our policies toward Latin America and that some of our actions in that period had clearly strengthened the hands of dictators. But I also pointed out that at Montevideo in 1933, we agreed to a vital change in policy. We agreed thereafter not to intervene in the internal affairs of our sister republics" (**23**, January 4,

1959). The "vital change" occurring after 1933 was perhaps more apparent to Washington than to other capitals in the hemisphere. At intervals thereafter, Washington was accused of too intimate relationships with dictatorial regimes—if in no other respect than that it did little or nothing to oppose them and that its usually "correct" policies toward them suggested indifference toward the kind of internal political orders prevailing in countries to the south. Admittedly, this issue has posed unpalatable choices for policy-makers in Washington. Intelligent insight into the problem can only be gained when the issue is viewed against the background of politico-diplomatic developments in Latin America and the principles governing the United States in its foreign relations.

Revolution is more often than not the means by which political changes are made within Latin American countries. Most of these countries exhibit and venerate the outward trappings of political democracy. As an illustration, the constitution of Argentina under the late dictator Juan Perón resounded with guarantees of civil liberties, restraints on autocratic governmental power, and other professed safeguards of freedom. In reality, elections and other practices which citizens of the United States regard as indispensable to democratic government are customarily resorted to in Latin America to ratify and maintain the authority of the latest revolutionary regime. Frank Tannenbaum noted that between 1930 and 1956 there were "over fifty violent, mainly military, upsets of government in Latin America, and many more abortive attempts that ended in failure" (41, 1956, p. 45). This pattern of course does not fit all Latin American states equally. Some, like Uruguay, are comparatively quiescent and democratically inclined; others, like Paraguay and Bolivia, appear to be addicted to perpetual revolutionary turmoil.

The problem of chronic revolutionary ferment in the Latin American states has confronted the United States ever since these countries began to throw off the colonial yoke in the early decades of the 1800s. The diplomatic response of the United States to the pattern of shifting political tides in these countries has been productive of endless controversy and misunderstanding within the Western Hemisphere. As an illustration, relations between the United States and Cuba became strained in the period 1958-59, when revolutionary forces led by Fidel Castro overthrew the military dictatorship of President Batista. Clinging to its customary policy toward Latin American dictators, Washington had maintained "correct"—its critics said overly friendly—relations with Batista's regime. Before Castro's revolution succeeded, his forces had been prevented from acquiring arms in the United States. His victory was followed by a wave of public trials and executions. These actions, conspicuously reported on millions of television sets in the United States and in lurid newspaper accounts, stirred deep antagonisms in public opinion. From public groups, influential newspapers, and Congress, the Eisenhower Administration was swamped by anti-Castro sentiments; for a time it appeared that this public crescendo might drive officials in Washington to intervene actively in Cuba's internal affairs. Castro's followers in Cuba and in the United States promptly complained that very few official or unofficial protests had been lodged against the long-standing and brutal excesses committed by Batista's henchmen. Castro's revolutionary regime ultimately began to exploit sentiment against it existing in the United States to solidify its hold upon Cuba. The result was that the United States government found itself for a time alienated from a country that was endeavoring to find its way toward a more democratic political order. Ironically, its dealings with Castro were considerably stormier than they had been with the unprincipled opportunist, Batista!

Many of the complexities and hard choices involved in the problem of relationships between the United States and dictatorial political systems in Latin America also came into sharp focus early in 1958 in regard to Venezuela. On January 23, a popular uprising ousted the dictatorship of General Marcos Pérez Jiménez. Until the time of Jiménez's overthrow, the United States had been careful to maintain "correct" relations with his government. At least publicly, the State Department refrained from any action that might seem to support the dictator's political opponents; and in some cases, as in Washington's awarding him a "Legion of Merit" and extending hospitality to his ruthless chief of police upon the latter's visit to the United States, it was apparent that Washington was "cultivating" harmonious relations with Venezuela.

After Jiménez's overthrow, resentment toward the United States mounted steadily—until it exploded into a bitter demonstration against Vice President Nixon, who visited the country in May. The United States was accused of having consorted with dictators and, by failure to act *against* Jiménez, of having helped maintain him in power. Letters were circulated purporting to show how diplomatic officials from the United States had sided with the dictator against his opponents. Meantime, actions taken in Washington seemed to lend credence to this view. As part of its attempt to curtail imports competing with domestic oil production, the United States began to impose "quotas" against the importation of Venezuelan oil—a move it had never taken when Jiménez was in power! On top of this, the United States, following precedents adhered to in many other such cases, granted political asylum to Jiménez and his notorious chief of police, a move that further inflamed popular antagonisms in Venezuela. As interpreted by many groups in Latin America, the actions of the United States had been dictated simply by a desire to safeguard access to Venezuelan oil.

Admittedly, the challenge confronting officials in Washington in dealing with conditions prevailing in Venezuela, and in comparable situations, is a formidable one. There appears to be no ideal solution to the problem. If Washington encouraged political movements aimed at unseating dictators like Jiménez, it would be accused of intervening in the internal affairs of weaker countries—a charge to which historically the United States has been peculiarly vulnerable in its dealings with Latin American governments. Yet when it maintained "correct" relations with dictatorial regimes, it courted the charge that it opposed only *communist* dictatorships and that it was indifferent to those in its own backyard, where political excesses often rivalled those behind the Iron Curtain (**23**, February 2 and May 18, 1958, dispatches by Tad Szulc).

Thus even in the second half of the 20th century, the problem of establishing and maintaining harmonious and constructive relations with Latin American governments plagues policy-makers in Washington. Several antagonistic, almost mutually-exclusive, principles of foreign policy and diplomatic interests must be reconciled. In some instances, the problem virtually defies satisfactory solution. Throughout the course of its diplomatic experience, the United States has sympathized with movements in other countries directed at expanding political freedom and widening popular participation in governmental affairs. At the same time, the principle of non-intervention in the internal affairs of other countries has demanded that the United States remain aloof from internal political struggles of other nations, even when they involved the issue of democracy versus dictatorship. It would not be amiss to say that the concept of non-intervention is the cornerstone of the edifice of hemispheric co-operation which the United States has tried to erect since it began advocating the policy of the Good Neighbor early in the 1930's.

Certain other strands in American foreign policy towards Latin America have tended to weaken the principle of non-intervention. Over against this principle, for example, has been the recognition policy of the United States which has been used to strengthen or weaken political movements in the hemisphere. Over the years, the United States began to evolve a set of principles to guide it in extending or withholding recognition. Before it would accord recognition to the newly-independent countries in Latin America in the early 1800's, the United States demanded: (1) that the government in power actually exercise effective control over the country in question; (2) that it have a reasonably good prospect for continued stability; and (3) that it be willing and able to carry out its commitments and obligations toward other nations (**31**, p. 174).

In the Wilsonian era a fourth criterion was added, when the United States was once again confronted with a revolutionary situation in Latin America, this time in Mexico. Wilson refused to recognize the Huerta regime because, in the President's words, it was a "government of butchers" which had come into power through violence and was, to Wilson's mind, antagonistic to the principles of democracy. Ultimately, Wilson intervened directly in Mexican internal affairs with the avowed purpose of overthrowing the Huerta government, on the dubious ground that in this way he would be advancing the welfare of the Mexican people (31, pp. 426-31). Wilson's viewpoint —that the United States should recognize only those governments whose character it approved —was incorporated into United States recognition policy, and on a number of occasions thereafter it became the dominant element in that policy.

Despite the idealism periodically expressed by the United States toward Latin America since 1932, Washington's unwillingness to recognize new governments in the American Republics unless they enjoy the State Department's approval has been productive of recurrent disagreements in inter-American relations. Pan-American conferences held during the 1930's, for instance, as a rule devoted considerable attention to the question of recognition. Other American countries sought to secure agreement on common principles of recognition policy that would prevail throughout the Inter-American System. Considerable support existed in Latin America for the Estrada Doctrine, named for a Mexican statesman, the gist of which was that recognition of new governments necessarily implied neither approval nor disapproval. The United States, however, consistently refused to endorse this doctrine. Each country within the Inter-American System continues to follow its own diplomatic precedents and inclinations in respect to recognition. And, although it amounts to intervention in the affairs of Latin American states, the United States continues on occasion to invoke Wilson's idea that a new government must be committed to democratic precepts and practices before cordial relations will be established and maintained with it (13, p. 173).

The non-intervention principle also faces a severe test when governments which have already been recognized embark upon policies held to be injurious to the diplomatic interests of the United States—perhaps by nationalizing foreign-owned corporations or becoming too

closely identified with international communism or engaging in virulent propaganda against the United States. An illustration is afforded by the history of relations between the United States and Argentina during and after World War II. Throughout most of the war Argentina was openly pro-Axis. Axis agents used the country as a base from which to carry out activities detrimental to the Allied war effort throughout the Western Hemisphere. Belatedly, and with visible reluctance, Argentina finally declared war on the side of the Allies; its contribution to the Allied victory, however, was minimal. Then after the war, the internal and external policies of the dictator Juan Perón alienated official and public opinion within the United States. Perón was skilled in exploiting Yankeephobia for his own political advantage. At periodic intervals waves of anti-United States feeling would sweep Argentina. In time it became apparent that Perón was using Uncle Sam as a scapegoat for Argentina's increasingly critical economic situation. Perón's fulminations against United States intervention did possess some validity, since State Department officials had intervened repeatedly in an effort to change the policies of the Argentine government. Despite United States intervention to discredit Perón and make him lose in the national elections of 1946, Perón won decisively, in part because he was adept at exploiting residual resentment against the United States to full advantage (25, passim). Not until Perón's overthrow in 1955 did relations between the United States and Argentina improve materially.

No matter how many provocations the United States might cite to justify its policies toward Argentina down to 1955, Washington's relations with Buenos Aires were not calculated to re-assure other American Republics that the prospect of Yankee intervention in their affairs had entirely disappeared. The problem remains as one of the most complex and delicate that has faced foreign policymakers throughout the diplomatic history of the United States: what course should be followed toward governments in Latin America and elsewhere whose internal and external policies are at variance with vital diplomatic objectives of the United States? In common with most foreign policy issues, the problem admits of no easy and clear-cut answer. Only the politically naïve would contend that the United States can view political developments throughout Latin America with indifference. Latin America is of critical importance to the United States; its politico-military orientation is therefore of the highest concern to officials in Washington. Yet it is equally clear that the era of the Roosevelt Corollary is over. No longer can the United States send troops into Latin American countries on one pretext or another to carry out its diplomatic purposes. This would be contrary to its membership obligations in the Organization of American States and the United Nations. Probably the most that can be done, therefore, is to follow certain precepts in dealing with revolutionary or unfriendly governments to the south.

One of these is to remember that *whether* the United States attempts to influence the course of events in the other American Republics is perhaps not so important as *how that influence is exercised.* Given the deeply ingrained and lingering sensitivity of the Latin American states to being dictated to by the United States, extreme tact, endless patience, and reliance upon persuasion and conciliation will likely accomplish far more than bluster and crude diplomatic pressure exerted upon the Latin American countries. John M. Cabot, former Assistant Secretary of State for Inter-American Affairs, has cautioned that:

> We cannot take the attitude that what is good for us is necessarily good for other nations under vastly different circumstances; that Uncle Sam knows best what is good for others, and will assume the responsibility for seeing that they get it; that it is wrong for Soviet Russia to impose Communism on foreign nations but permissible for us to impose democracy on them; that in the present state of international affairs we can afford to feud with every government whose internal policies don't altogether meet our approval. (6, p. 90).

Admittedly, it is a source of embarrassment for the United States to seem to be closely identified with Latin American dictators whose actions sometimes are little different from those of Hitler or Stalin. Some might raise the question: how can the United States simultaneously condemn Soviet oppression behind the Iron Curtain and in recent years condone or, at any rate, do very little to interfere with dictatorships in Cuba or Bolivia or Venezuela? The answer is as simple as it is fundamental. The United States government does not today, nor has it historically, opposed dictatorships in Russia or Germany or Japan or elsewhere merely because of the form of government existing, but because ultimately dictators in these countries endangered the security of the United States and of the international community as a whole. As a rule, no such threat has arisen from totalitarian orders in the Western Hemisphere.

The United States would obviously prefer to see democratic governments flourish in the Americas, as in other regions. What specific policies are calculated to serve this end? Vice President Nixon and Milton S. Eisenhower, brother of President Eisenhower, recommended to the President in the late 1950's that the United States enthusiastically greet democratic systems in the Americas but that it have merely "a formal handshake for dictators." This means more concretely, in Milton S. Eisenhower's words that

> . . . we refrain from granting special recognition to a Latin-American dictator, regardless of the temporary advantage that might seem to be promised by such an act. I most emphatically do *not* believe that we should withdraw our programs from Latin-American countries which are ruled by dictators. Non-recognition and non-cooperation would not help another nation achieve democracy. . . . By cooperating with them, even through dictators—by keeping open the lines of communication—one may hope that a growing understanding of the strength, glory, and basic morality of democracy will enable the people of a harshly ruled country to achieve and maintain democratic institutions of their own design. (23, January 4, 1959, italics inserted).

Quite clearly, there exists no panacea whereby policy-makers in Washington can avoid dilemmas and embarrassments inherent in this problem. For in the vast majority of cases, the overriding fact is that whether democracy or dictatorship exists in Latin American countries is a decision that, in the final analysis, must be made by the peoples of those countries. As Dexter Perkins has observed, "it is extremely doubtful whether the United States strengthens democracy in fact by active participation in the affairs of other states. Appeals from the outside by a government over the head of constituted authority in another country seem in general to have been unsuccessful in the past, and are likely to be unsuccessful in the future" (**29**, p. 165). This observation applies with special pertinence to an area that remains keenly sensitive to the real or imagined ambitions of the "North American Colossus;" to countries in which there are always groups willing and ready to fan the flames of xenophobia and to revive memories of State Department "big stick" diplomacy of an earlier era; and where, in at least some contexts, the alternative to authoritarian regimes might well be chaos.

Even though painful choices must sometimes be made in situations of this kind, some room for flexibility exists. For one thing, the United States can refrain from actions (such as awarding medals to dictators) which convey the idea that military juntas are *approved*, even if sometimes they must be *accepted*, by the State Department. Moreover, great care can be exercised to avoid even the *appearance* of undue support for dictators. Flexibility also exists in the administration of economic and military aid programs by the United States, even though there is the ubiquitous risk that Washington will be accused of "economic imperialism" in the administration of its aid programs.

Careful attention should be devoted especially to extension of military aid throughout Latin America. In the early 1950's, one of the leading journals published in democratic Uruguay, *Marcha*, asked how the United States could give military assistance to dictators—ostensibly for the purpose of "defending democracy"? Again, by this action the United States seemed to be suggesting that only *Communist-imposed* dictatorships were objectionable (**36**, 1954, p. 351).

Patiently, sympathetically, and with a minimum of fanfare, the United States can and must endeavor to assist in raising the level of political morality and enlightenment throughout Latin America, realizing all the while that political freedom and stability are not likely to endure unless there are firm socio-economic foundations and that, in most crucial respects, the future of Latin American countries will be determined by the populations of these countries. In many if not most instances, the influence of the United States is likely to be marginal. Any new flareups of xenophobia, triggered by genuine or fancied threats of intervention by the United States, will assuredly solidify latent anti-democratic tendencies and will postpone the emergence of orderly and effective governments, based upon respect for human freedoms.

2. PROBLEMS OF HEMISPHERIC TRADE AND AID

U. S. Assistance to Latin America

When Milton S. Eisenhower returned from a good-will tour of Latin America in 1953 he reported widespread misunderstanding of the United States in southern countries, "misunderstanding especially of our economic capacity and an underestimation of the degree of the sacrifices the people of the United States have made since 1941" (**14**, p. 7). Succeeding years witnessed no appreciable improvement in this aspect of American hemispheric relations. A reporter found the attitude prevailing at an Inter-American Economic Conference held in Washington late in 1958 to be "a sullen and growing revolt against economic conditions for which the United States, whether justly or

unjustly, was somehow held partly responsible." Expressing a complaint voiced widely throughout Latin America, one delegate stated: "The economic measures taken toward Latin America by the United States have always been very small ones, without the importance or magnitude required by the problems to be solved in Latin-American countries" (**23**, November 23, 1958, dispatch by E. W. Kenworthy).

Living in an area comparatively insulated from the cold war tensions that have heavily shaped the foreign policy of the United States toward other major regions, and yet sharing in the expectations commonly held by other underdeveloped areas, officials and citizens in

Latin America have been unable to comprehend why foreign assistance to their countries has been a small part of the foreign aid total extended by Washington since World War II and why Uncle Sam has often appeared far more generous toward its former enemies, such as Germany, Italy, and Japan, than toward its professed southern friends. In Latin American eyes the limited amount of foreign aid provided them since 1947 has seemed to imply that the United States has only a subordinate interest in helping these economically backward nations elevate their standards of living and levels of productivity (14, p. 7; 37, 1955, pp. 233-35).

Statistical data support Latin America's claim that the lion's share of foreign assistance by the United States has gone to Western Europe, the Middle East, and Asia. In postwar foreign aid provided by the United States through 1957, less than $2 billion, or a little over 3 per cent out of a total of $62 billion, went to Latin America. Out of the total flow of foreign capital into Latin American countries in the period 1950-1958, grants by the United States government totalled $2.3 billion, or 22.5 per cent of the total flow of $10.2 billion received by countries in this region. Latin American nations were keenly sensitive to the fact that this total from *all* sources was less than the United States government alone furnished Western Europe under the Marshall Plan and that grants from Washington to Latin American governments over this eight-year period were equal to about one-sixth of the total extended to promote European recovery (23, May 17, 1959, dispatch by Tad Szulc). As for military aid, Latin American countries contended that they had been virtually omitted altogether from Washington's largess, as indicated by the fact that these nations normally received 2 or 3 per cent of the total military assistance budget of the United States.

Latin America's place in the foreign assistance program of the United States can be brought into clearer focus by looking at the Mutual Security Act of 1959, authorizing expenditures for fiscal year 1960. The act entailed a total of $3.6 billion in foreign aid. Direct military support ($1.4 billion) and support for defense activities of other free nations

($ .751 billion) made a combined military aid program of $2.151 billion. Of this total, Latin America was granted $ .67 billion or 3.1 per cent of the funds earmarked for military assistance throughout the world. Although this percentage had remained fairly constant in recent years, considerable opposition had developed in Congress to providing military aid to Latin American countries, and the amount finally authorized was less than the Eisenhower Administration had recommended. Thus Congress cut out a proposal, endorsed by the Senate Foreign Relations Committee, that $31.5 million be given to the Organization of American States to encourage the creation of an international police force under OAS auspices. Furthermore, Congress believed that more stringent criteria ought to govern provision of military assistance to Latin America; it inserted a provision in the act specifying that "internal security requirements" within Latin American countries "shall not, unless the President determines otherwise, be the basis for military assistance to American Republics." The act stipulated further that "military equipment and materials may be furnished to the other American Republics only in furtherance of missions *directly relating to the common defense of the Western Hemisphere* which are found by the President to be important to the security of the United States."* Such provisions would almost certainly generate dissatisfactions south of the border. Intensely proud and desirous of building up their prestige in the community of nations, Latin American countries could not be expected to react sympathetically to any move in Washington that detracted from the strength of their already weak military forces. Tempers in these countries were not likely to be improved either by the fact that Latin America was omitted entirely from the list of countries

---

*The text of the Mutual Security Act of 1959, amending the same act for 1954, may be found in House Report No. 695, 86th Congress, 1st Session, 1959.

In addition to the provision of technical-economic assistance discussed above, Latin America shared in various multinational projects to which the United States contributed, such as technical assistance programs carried on by the UN and the atoms for peace program. For specific allocations under these categories in recent years, see 34, p. 2.

scheduled to receive $751 million in defense support funds.

The Mutual Security Act of 1959 provided $179.5 million for bilateral technical cooperation or economic assistance to foreign countries, out of which Latin America was slated to receive $43.7 million, 24.3 per cent of the total. In addition, the United States contributed $1.5 million to the technical assistance program carried on by the Organization of American States. Limited by law to a ceiling of no more than 70 per cent of the total budget of OAS-sponsored projects, the United States had contributed approximately that percentage in recent years (34, p. 21). Such projects involved activities like public health teaching programs, statistical training, construction of new housing, establishment of normal schools in rural areas, and encouragement of scientific practices in agriculture (35, pp. 31-32).

In the contemporary period, efforts by the United States have also been directed at dealing with emergency situations and other extraordinary conditions prevailing in particular countries, many of them in Latin America.

LATIN AMERICA RECEIVES MAINLY ECONOMIC AND TECHNICAL AID

U.S. Government Grants and Credits to American Republics in 1958 (In millions of U.S. dollars or equivalent)

Total: $594

Figures from *Survey of Current Business*, April, 1959, p. 19.

As in the past, assistance furnished in fiscal year 1960 emphasized "special assistance" programs for selected countries. As an illustration, Bolivia and Haiti had been hardpressed to maintain viable economic systems. With its top-heavy reliance upon tin—an industry that has traditionally felt chronic dislocations and was especially hard hit in the late 1950's—Bolivia required continued help from Washington. Haiti, severely damaged by "Hurricane Hazel" in 1954 and suffering from sharp fluctuations in the world coffee market, also required special assistance to maintain even minimum economic stability (33, Part 1, pp. 540-41).

Nations in the Caribbean, Central, and South America have also received financial assistance from other sources that are heavily supported by the United States government. Both the International Bank for Reconstruction and Development and the Export-Import Bank, the latter being an agency of the United States government, had advanced sizable loans to countries in this area. The newer Development Loan Fund, established specifically to make capital available to underdeveloped nations, by 1959 had provided over $63 million in loans to 14 Latin American nations. Yet, according to the Senate Foreign Relations Committee, DLF's resources were inadequate to the need existing,

LATIN AMERICA IS A MAJOR OUTLET FOR U.S. PRIVATE CAPITAL

U.S. Direct Private Investment in Latin America (In billions of U.S. dollars)

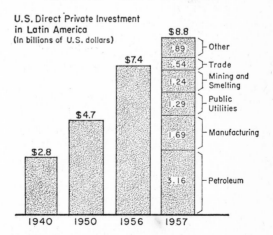

Figures from *Congressional Weekly Almanac*, June 19, 1959, p. 827; and Dept. of State, etc., *Mutual Security Program, 1959*, p. 111.

with requests for loans "increasing far beyond its capacity to provide assistance" (33, Part 1, p. 540).

Private investment by business concerns in the United States has also been an important aspect of the economic picture in countries to the south, providing more than half, $5.5 billion, of the total capital inflow of $10.2 billion in the period 1950-1958. By the late 1950's Latin America attracted some 30 per cent of all private, long-term overseas investments from private sources in the United States (14, pp. 2-3). In recent years, this capital was responsible for producing goods and services in these countries worth $5 billion annually and 30 per cent of the region's total exports. Some 20 per cent of the net output of all Latin American industries, over $1 billion in taxes collected by Latin American governments, and the employment of around 600,000 persons in these countries were made possible by private investment from the United States (37, 1955, p. 228).

Despite these facts, the other American Republics feel that the United States is neglecting their economic welfare. In answering these accusations, policy-makers in Washington have contended that Latin American countries have a major stake in the continued economic prosperity and military security of Europe and Asia, since considerable trade takes place between the Americas and the nations of Europe. Secretary of State Dulles also pointed out in 1955 that the American Republics should be thankful that they were spared the ravages of World War II and that in the contemporary period they have been relatively safe from the threat of Soviet domination (37, 1955, pp. 234-35).

In assessing future economic prospects in Latin America, officials within the United States have tended to stress the central role which has been and should be played by *private capital* in the economic development of countries in the Inter-American System. Thus by the end of the 1950's, approximately 80 per cent of all capital investment from the United States in Latin American countries came from *private* sources, with new capital from such sources entering Latin American countries at an average rate of $600 million

per year (23, January 4, 1959). Increasingly, however, it had become obvious that conditions in Latin America would have to be favorable for the continued provision of capital needed for economic expansion. United States citizens have been fearful that Latin American countries would nationalize foreign corporations, levy oppressive taxes, or otherwise discriminate against outside business concerns. John M. Cabot warned these countries in 1953 against the

> temptation to kill the goose that lays the golden eggs. They should realize that any arbitrary or unfair act may bring immediate advantages, and yet may prejudice the national interest for decades. Only years of good faith and fair dealing can restore shattered confidence, and, in the meantime, the nation must pay a heavy premium to counteract the apprehensions it has awakened among investors. (6, p. 70).

After a second good will tour of Latin American countries at the end of 1958, Dr. Milton S. Eisenhower stressed the importance of nongovernmental investments in Latin America's economic future but underscored the fact that "Private capital cannot be driven. It must be attracted." In view of the often unstable conditions prevailing in Latin America, and of the great demand for capital in "safer" environments like the United States itself or Western Europe, he was convinced that "Attracting private capital to Latin America . . . is not an easy matter." In his report to the President, he made a number of recommendations designed to improve the investment climate in Latin America and to extend assistance by the United States Government in accomplishing this goal (23, January 4, 1959).

The question of private capital versus governmental grants—in which the Latin American countries have shown a strong preference for the latter—has not yet been satisfactorily resolved. Policy-makers in Washington, sometimes vocally supported by American business interests, take the view that the economic advancement of Latin American countries is clearly a two-way street. Granting that the United States has been overly preoccupied with cold war considerations in allocating foreign assistance in Latin America and elsewhere, it is nonetheless true that conditions have not always favored greatly increased assistance, either through governmental grants or private business investments, to the American Republics. Some of them have entertained unrealistic conceptions about both the amount of aid that could legitimately be expected and utilized profitably and about the ability of the United States to correct long-standing economic dislocations prevailing within their economies and in their foreign trade (7, I, pp. 1338-40). Moreover, they have not always utilized private or public capital from the United States in a manner demonstrating concern for solid accomplishment or for enhancing the "investment climate" that would attract larger capital outlays in the future. Politico-economic conditions in Latin America often are precarious and therefore do not attract large-scale foreign investments. Greater realism, understanding, and co-operation on both sides are needed before either private or governmental sources in the United States will expand their investments throughout Latin America.

Inter-American Trade

Misunderstandings and tensions have also arisen within the Inter-American system over problems of foreign trade. In 1955 the value of United States-Latin American trade amounted to $7 billion, a total almost exactly balanced —though of course not necessarily for individual countries—between imports and exports. Trade is thus important both to the United States and to the nations of Latin America. The United States absorbs about 80 per cent of Latin America's copper exports, about 70 per cent of its lead and zinc exports, and about 70 per cent of its coffee exports. For its part, Latin America takes from 25-40 per cent of all food, textiles, machinery, vehicles, and chemicals exported by the United States (37, 1955, p. 229). Yet in one sense overseas trade is far more crucial for Latin American countries than for the United States. As a group, the Latin American countries are heavily dependent for their continued economic prosperity upon the export market; in some instances as much as 80 per cent of all commodities produced by these countries enters the export trade. And with most of them reliance upon a single exportable commodity is the rule. A sampling shows that Venezuela depends upon petroleum for 95 per cent of its exports; El Salvador depends upon coffee for 87 per cent of its

HEMISPHERIC TRADE PATTERNS

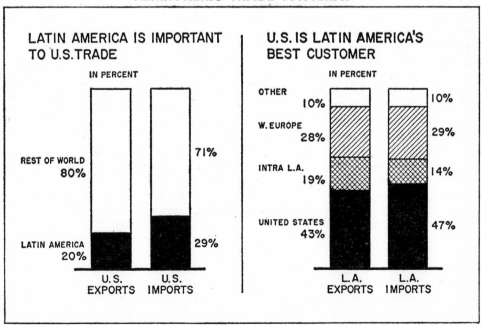

Dept. of State, etc., *Mutual Security Program, 1959*, p. 110

exports; Cuba depends upon sugar for 77 per cent of its exports; and Honduras depends upon bananas for 61 per cent of its exports. Thus Latin American countries are in a peculiarly vulnerable position when adverse conditions or trade restrictions interfere with their overseas commerce (11, p. 35).

Misunderstandings and tensions between the United States and its Latin American neighbors over economic issues are typified by recurrent disputes centering upon the production and sale of coffee. Throughout much of the postwar period, consumers in the United States complained that the price charged by Latin American coffee-growers was too high; many groups within the United States felt that producers were keeping the price artificially high to ensure large profits. Yet coffee producers explained the high prices charged by reference to a cardinal principle of capitalist economics: since coffee trees are slow to bear, the supply of coffee is relatively inelastic; therefore, when the demand goes up and the supply remains constant, the price increases. Remembering the lean years of the 1920's and 1930's when coffee glutted the market and when millions of pounds were dumped into the ocean, coffee producers were reluctant to increase their yields to meet what might prove a temporary expansion in demand. Their caution was dictated in part by the fact that once coffee trees begin to bear, they produce beans for forty years thereafter. Adding to the complexity of bringing the demand and supply for coffee into equilibrium was the fact that some fourteen American Republics produce coffee for the export trade. Consequently, it was well-nigh impossible to regulate production to meet world demand, in a manner that would assure the well-being of all countries concerned.

Nevertheless, in the postwar period most coffee-growing countries have expanded their production of this commodity to meet the new demand, so much so that by the late 1950's Latin American producers were beginning to face problems arising from an oversupply of coffee. Political leaders in these countries urgently requested United States assistance in resolving this problem. While officials in Washington encouraged studies of problems existing in the coffee-growing industry, and while they pledged co-operation in solving such problems on a long-term basis, they consistently refused to engage in any agreements that would keep the price of coffee artificially stable. For instance, at the end of 1958, Dr. Milton S. Eisenhower found that "Coffee is now being overproduced. Production is increasing at a faster rate than consumption." While he believed that the United States should make its services available to coffee-producing countries in efforts to prevent great price fluctuation and resultant economic distress in such countries, he reiterated the prevailing view in Washington that the United States could not join in schemes "the producing nations might develop to stabilize prices" (23, January 4, 1959).

By the end of the 1950's events suggested that sooner or later there might have to be some softening in the attitudes of policymakers in Washington. The distress produced by the fall in the price of coffee was paralleled by a calamitous decline in the price of copper, upon which the economic prosperity of Chile substantially depends. The price of copper had dropped from fifty-five to less than twenty-five cents a pound from the end of the Korean War to 1958. Venezuelan officials were apprehensive over the world market for oil; by the late 1950's, supplies of this commodity were also rising more rapidly than demand (23, September 14, 1958). These events took place within an overall economic context of a widening gap between the prices received for exports and the prices paid for imports, accompanied by a decline in the monetary reserves needed by many countries to finance their international transactions. Internally, a number of Latin American countries were suffering from mounting inflation and weakening currencies—developments which in turn led to political instability and ferment.

The United States proposed to assist Latin American governments in attacking these momentous problems by a variety of methods. As a result of prolonged study by an agency of the Organization of American States plans were announced in Washington early in 1959 for the creation of a long-desired inter-American development bank. Approximately half of the institution's capitalization of $850 million would come from the United States, with the remainder made up from contributions by other American republics. One important feature of this new institution would be its ability to make both "hard" and "soft" loans, the former being loans that meet prevailing banking standards for soundness and that require payment of interest in dollars, the latter being loans that might be considered less "sound" and that permit interest payments, perhaps at a reduced rate, in local currencies. The new bank would concentrate on the making of loans that would serve to expand economic productivity throughout the Americas (23, January 11, 1959, dispatch by E. W. Kenworthy). In addition to this development, the Central American governments had taken the initial step in launching a common market, possessing many of the earmarks of the European Common Market, discussed in Chapter 10. Defining the position of the United States toward this market, by relating this development to the overall context of the nation's foreign trade policies affecting both Latin America and other countries, would also pose a continuing problem for foreign policy officials in Washington. For ultimately the political future of Latin America, and hence the security of the United States, might well hinge upon the degree to which this and other attempts to cope with bedrock economic issues succeed in achieving their goal.

3. COMMUNISM IN LATIN AMERICA

The importance of Latin America as an arena of cold war hostilities may be gauged by recalling briefly the Nazi menace to the Western Hemisphere during World War II. Nazi agents were active in a number of Latin American states, particularly Argentina. There was perhaps never a time when the Axis powers were in danger of gaining control over Latin America—nor could the threat to the security of the United States existing in that quarter compare with the danger from Europe or Asia—but the United States was nonetheless compelled to divert over 100,000 troops for protection of that vital region (18, Part V, p. 925). Today, according to a high Defense Department spokesman, "In enemy hands the Latin American countries could provide bases for attack which would be dangerously close to the United States." The "bulge" of Brazil affords a tempting foothold for any enemy seeking to penetrate the Western Hemisphere across the South Atlantic, especially if the Middle East and northern and western portions of Africa were in hostile hands. Conversely, Brazil and its neighbors offer needed bases for air power and for radar defense units to safeguard the Americas and the South Atlantic sea lanes. Latin America also supplies the United States a number of strategic imports. One of the most important now is thorium from Brazil, used for thermonuclear technology. The states along the northern periphery of the South American continent and in Central America are in close proximity to the Panama Canal, while those along the continent's western fringe can protect vital sea and air approaches to the hemisphere. The armed forces available from these countries, while not large, add another increment to the military posture of the free world, as indicated by the fact that units from these countries played a valuable role in the UN's military operation in Korea (18, Part V, pp. 924-25).

Because of Latin-America's strategic-military importance to the United States, Washington has regarded the successful establishment of a communist bridgehead in the American Republics with the utmost gravity. Just how strong is the communist movement in Latin America? Measured solely by the size of national Communist parties, there is no cause for alarm within the United States. Membership varies from around 50,000 in Argentina and Brazil, to 30-40,000 in Chile and Cuba, to 500-1,000 in El Salvador, Guatemala, and Honduras, to negligible membership in Haiti and the Dominican Republic (18, Part V, p. 941). Yet a quantitative standard alone would be misleading as an indication of the threat posed by the intrigues of the communist movement in South America and the Caribbean. It is profitable to recall that communist groups in most countries, including Soviet Russia, are small minorities and that Marxist-Leninist-Stalinist theory supports this phenomenon. Communist infiltration of *other* political parties; utilization of popular social and economic reform movements to advance the Kremlin's diplomatic ambitions; gradual infiltration of governments through "united fronts;" skillful propaganda moves calculated to undermine the prestige and influence of the United States and to increase that of the Soviet Union; sabotage and espionage activities directed from Moscow—these are the dangers inherent in the presence of comparatively small, but dedicated and tightly disciplined, communist party and communist front organizations in the American republics.

Politico-economic conditions in Latin America often provide a fertile seedbed for the germination of communism. Poor, sometimes to the point of being poverty-stricken, dependent upon one-crop economies, saddled with antiquated social structures that favor privileged classes while depressing those at the bottom of the scale, handicapped by formidable geographical obstacles to economic betterment, and yet all the while believing in the desirability and possibility of material advancement, citizens in these countries can be expected to listen sympathetically to the siren song of the Kremlin that Marxism will fulfill their long-cherished dreams. As an example, a report by the International Cooperation Administration in 1957 characterized the favorable environment for the existence of communism in Boliva as one in which

> Widespread poverty, the political inexperience of the population, the existence of a large poorly paid working class, a civilian militia not wholly under Government control, and the low morale of the small national army and air force were factors which favored extremists. If the moderate forces had not been able to prevent economic deterioration, they would probably have lasted about as long as the Kerensky regime in Russia in 1917. (**17**, pp. 87-8).

Many of the general observations made about the communist movement in Latin America will come into sharper focus if we consider the crisis in Guatemala occasioned by the growth of communism in that country and the response of the United States to that challenge.

Crisis in Guatemala

The emergence of the communist movement in Guatemala cannot be divorced from the context of political events there within recent history. Revolutionary ferment had long marked the political scene in Guatemala, as elsewhere in Latin America, and non-communist groups had been unable to effectuate lasting socio-economic reforms. Like its counterparts in Asia, the Middle East, and other Latin American nations, the Guatemalan Communist Party was able to pose as the champion of nationalist aspirations while promising progress in solving bedrock economic problems. In the words of a British observer, "It is impossible to draw an exact boundary-line between nationalism and communism in Latin America today" (**36**, 1954, p. 368).

The year 1944 witnessed the beginning of a new revolutionary regime under Juan José Arévalo, who overthrew the government of the military dictator Jorge Ubico. The new government received substantial support from the lower middle classes and from the intellectuals, with many of the latter believing that a Marxist approach offered the best hope of progress for Guatemala. As is customary following revolutions in Latin America, a number of prominent and less prominent political exiles returned to Guatemala. Among these were influential individuals who espoused communism; some of these had received revolutionary training in Moscow. Until the early 1950's, however, Guatemalan Communists tended to operate clandestinely and to work through popular movements to advance their goals.

As time passed, Communists infiltrated the Guatemalan labor movement and other organizations commanding wide popular support. Through such groups Communists carried on intensive propaganda campaigns closely paralleling the diplomatic line of the Kremlin. The equivocal policies of President Arévalo, who encouraged "participation of Communists as individuals" in the government and labor movement while "discouraging the formation of an open organized Stalinist party," enabled communist groups to gain more and more control over Guatemalan affairs (8, p. 49). As the time for the national elections of 1951 drew near, the tempo of communist agitation and propaganda greatly increased. Election of the Communist-sponsored candidate, Colonel Jacobo Arbenz, as President was soon followed by the open establishment of the Guatemalan Communist Party (Partido Communista de Guatemala, PCG). At home Arbenz, supported by the PCG, embarked upon a long-overdue program of land reform. As the largest land-holder in the country, the United Fruit Com-pany—with headquarters in Boston—became the principal target of Arbenz's reform mea-sures. Guatemalan nationalism was also di-rected against the alleged power of the *Em-presa Eléctrica,* owned by investors within the United States, that generated four-fifth's of the country's electric power (**36**, 1954, pp. 376-78).

In external affairs, the Arbenz government was making little effort to conceal its growing hostility toward the United States. On a num-ber of occasions Guatemala gave the appear-ance of deliberately seeking to provoke the United States into some kind of ill-advised intervention in Central America. As an illustra-tion, Guatemala dramatically withdrew from the Organization of Central American States —a regional grouping that had long been ac-tively encouraged by officials in Washington —charging that OCAS had become merely a tool of State Department propaganda and an instrument whereby Uncle Sam dominated the affairs of weaker Central American coun-tries (**37**, 1953, pp. 334-35). As the months passed, policy-makers in the United States were convinced they detected the hand of Guatemalan Communists in fomenting political unrest in such countries as British Guiana and British Honduras. Guatemala provided a base for Communist-inspired intrigue throughout all the neighboring Central American states. In international affairs Guatemala's position co-incided with the Kremlin's with remarkable fre-quency, notably in respect to virulent propa-ganda attacks against alleged "Wall Street imperialism" and in denunciations of free world defense efforts generally (**37**, 1954, p. 372).

Quite naturally then, developments in Guate-mala were viewed with grave misgivings in Washington. On June 30, 1954, Secretary of State Dulles publicly called attention to the "evil purpose of the Kremlin to destroy the inter-American system. . . . " He noted that "For several years international communism has been probing . . . for nesting places in the Americas. It finally chose Guatemala . . . " (**8**, p. 30). Side-by-side with the consolidation of Communist power in Guatemala therefore went increasing diplomatic activity to deal with what the United States regarded as a menace to hemispheric solidarity and security. In an earlier period the United States would most probably have invoked the Monroe Doc-trine unilaterally. Now it sought to work through the Inter-American System. As early as April 7, 1951, the foreign ministers of the American republics, largely at the instigation of the United States, had issued the "Declara-tion of Washington," calling for "prompt action . . . against the aggressive activities of inter-national communism . . . " (**7**, I, p. 1292). But as it watched the steady accretion in the in-fluence of Guatemalan communism, the Eisen-hower Administration was persuaded that stronger measures were demanded. Hence Secretary of State Dulles personally attended an OAS meeting in Venezuela on March 28, 1954, where he was successful in getting the "Caracas Declaration" approved by an over-whelming vote. This sharply-worded resolution declared that

> the domination or control of the political insti-tutions of any American States by the interna-tional communist movement . . . would constitute a threat to the sovereignty and political inde-pendence of the American States, endangering the peace of America, and would call for a Meeting of Consultation to consider the adoption of appropriate action in accordance with existing treaties. (**7**, I, p. 1301).

The Caracas Declaration was widely hailed in the West, most especially in militantly anti-communist circles, as an outstanding diplomatic victory for the United States on the cold war front. Now the weight of the entire Inter-American System could be thrown against the "communist beachhead" in the Western Hemi-sphere. Discriminating observers, however, pointed to a number of signs indicating significant differences of opinion among the American Republics about the proper attitude toward Guatemalan communism. It was clear that Latin America was much less concerned about the threat of communism in Guatemala, and much more alarmed about State Department interference in hemispheric affairs, than the United States. An impassioned speech by the Guatemalan delegate to the Caracas Conference against "monopolistic interests" of the United States had received a resounding ovation from the meeting.

The Caracas Declaration had been approved by a vote of 17 to 1. Guatemala voted no and Mexico and Argentina abstained. During the conference, however, many Latin American delegates freely expressed their reservations about the declaration and, more generally, their misgivings about Washington's apparent fixation with the issue of communism. Many Latin American delegates were offended by the unseemly haste with which Secretary Dulles rushed back to Washington after he secured approval of the Caracas Declaration, a move which suggested that Washington's highest-level diplomatic officials cared strongly about nothing but stopping communism. A Costa Rican delegate felt that "global" issues were obscuring fundamental localized problems. A Bolivian delegate demanded "something more than a new way of fighting communism" from the conference, "something appropriate to improve . . . welfare and progress. . . . " A delegate from Uruguay confessed that he had voted for the declaration "without enthusiasm, without optimism, without joy and without feeling that we were contributing to the adoption of a constructive measure." In summary then the other American states were much less inclined to see the hand of the Kremlin in Guatemalan affairs, were far less concerned about the question of communism as a global issue, and were apprehensive lest the United States, in its conflict with the Kremlin, go too far in intervening in the internal affairs of Latin America (**36**, 1954, pp. 372-74; **37**, 1954, pp. 373-81).

Events moved toward a climax in the spring and summer of 1954, when Guatemalan Communists supported a strike in Honduras and when a shipload of arms from behind the Iron Curtain arrived in Guatemala. Denouncing Guatemala as already the "heaviest armed state" in Central America, the State Department moved immediately to increase the flow of armaments to other countries in that area (**7**, I, p. 1308). In the ensuing diplomatic tug-of-war Guatemala, supported by the communist bloc, sought to have the United Nations consider alleged United States intervention in Guatemala's affairs; Washington, on the other hand, was insistent that the United Nations did not have initial jurisdiction in the matter and demanded that it first be considered by the Organization of American States. Meanwhile, tension was growing in Central America. On June 18 an anti-communist force under Colonel Castillo Armas crossed into Guatemala from Honduras. Within a short time the pro-communist Arbenz government collapsed. "Each one of the American States has cause for profound gratitude," said Secretary of State Dulles. The "impressive solidarity" of the Inter-American System, he contined, "undoubtedly shook the Guatemalan Government." All Americans could rejoice that the citizens of that country "had the courage and the will to eliminate the traitorous tools of foreign despots" (**7**, I, p. 1315).

From one perspective—that of a dramatic victory of the free world against communism—the United States had scored an impressive diplomatic *coup* in the Guatemalan affair. Whatever else Armas was, and we shall examine this question more fully below, he was certainly anti-Communist. Temporarily at least, the "communist beachhead" in Guatemala had been eliminated.

But many Latin American countries, joined by some of the United States' western allies, were less given to unqualified rejoicing than were supporters of Secretary Dulles. If joy among the allies was noticeably restrained, there were several reasons why it should be. Skepticism, in the first place, was directed against State Department complicity in the counter-revolution that had ousted the Arbenz government. The extent of Washington's support for Armas will probably not be revealed for years to come; but the circumstances strongly pointed to widespread and decisive activity in Central American affairs by the super-secret Central Intelligence Agency (**23**, dispatch by James Reston, June 20, 1954; **37**, 1954, pp. 367-90; **30**, pp. 257-59). The British Labor Party leader, Clement Attlee, asked in the House of Commons how support by the United States for an *anti*-communist revolution in Guatemala differed materially from Red Chinese support for a communist revolution in Indochina (**37**, 1954, p. 383). Another commentator observed that for the United States, on the most charitable interpretation, to "tacitly condone" crossing of an international border by a revolutionist movement was disturbingly like the action of North Korea in crossing the 38th Parallel into South Korea (**30**, p. 257). Whatever the exact nature and scope of United States complicity in the Guatemalan anti-communist revolution, it was not such as to win friends within the Inter-American System and to dispel lingering apprehensions about *Yanqui* imperialism.

Then there was the matter of OAS's relations with the United Nations. Diplomatic officials within the United States had contended that the Guatemalan episode was not initially a matter for UN concern, implying that the UN was not entitled to consider issues involving the Americas until the OAS had first attempted a solution. This, to say the least, was a novel interpretation of the UN's jurisdiction, suggesting that American—as distinct from, let us say, Soviet or Middle Eastern—affairs enjoyed a privileged status outside the province of the international body designated to deal with *any* threat to international peace and security (**30**, pp. 258-59).

Finally, informed observers called attention to the fact that the defeat of communism in Guatemala might well prove a temporary victory. Much depended on Armas' willingness and capacity to deal with issues that had engendered political turbulence. Very early Armas showed that a platform of anti-communism was a double-edged sword that could be used to undercut the Kremlin's influence while providing a legitimate pretext for suspending constitutional guarantees and for ruling by extraordinary decree. In short, Armas gave every indication of following in the foot-steps of countless other Latin American *caudillos*. The evidence seemed incontrovertible, for example, that the Guatemalan elections of 1955 had been well "rigged" to produce the anticipated outcome: an overwhelming public endorsement of the new regime (**37**, 1955, pp. 204-05).

Guatemala's political future remained highly uncertain. Leaders friendly to the United States there or elsewhere could not govern indefinitely on a program of anti-communism. As one commentator has written, "The real issues antedate the anti-communist crusade; indeed, they antedate Communism" (**32**, p. 87). Another observer has pointed out that in Guatemala "the arguments are about land reform, imperialism, and so on, not Marxism versus capitalism or—at least not very frequently—Russia versus the United States" (**22**, p. 128). Communism appears to be merely one species of a perennial among the political flora that thrives in the soil of social, economic, and political turmoil. Western-style "democracy," however, is a tender plant. It has never been indigenous to Latin America; and only in recent years has any significant success been achieved in emplanting it in some Latin American countries. Even today, the most widely prevailing Latin American species of government—military juntas and *caudillos*—constantly threatens to choke out surviving democratic forms. If discernible progress is to be made in realizing democracy in the inhospitable environment found throughout Latin America, the most careful attention will have to be devoted to creating the conditions necessary for its survival and growth.

REFERENCES

1. Bemis, Samuel F. *The United States as a World Power.* New York: Henry Holt and Company, 1955. A textbook that provides a good introductory account of U.S.–Latin American relations.

2. Borchard, Edwin. "The St. Lawrence Waterway and Power Project," *American Journal of International Law,* 43 (July, 1949), pp. 411-34.

3. Brebner, John B. *North Atlantic Triangle.* Toronto: The Ryerson Press, 1945. Treats

Anglo-American-Canadian relations historically.

4. Bureau of the Census, *Quarterly Summary of Foreign Commerce of the United States, January-March, 1958.* Washington: Department of Commerce, July, 1959. This is the Commerce Department's official summary of foreign trade statistics.

5. Burnett, E. C. "The Name 'United States of America,'" *American Historical Review,* 31 (October, 1925), pp. 79-81.

6. Cabot, John M. *Toward Our Common American Destiny.* Medford, Mass.: The Metcalf Press, 1955. A series of speeches and essays by a former Assistant Secretary of State.

7. Department of State. *American Foreign Policy, 1950-1955.* (Publication no. 6446, "General Foreign Policy Series" 117), Washington: 1957. Provides invaluable documentary material on U. S.-Latin American relations for the period indicated.

8. ————. *Intervention of International Communism in Guatemala.* (Publication no. 5556, "Inter-American Series," 48). Washington: 1954. This document presents the "case" of the United States against Guatemalan communism; for a more balanced understanding of the issue, it should be utilized in conjunction with other treatments of the Guatemalan issue listed below.

9. ————. *Keeping Peace in the Caribbean Area.* (Publication no. 3918, "Inter-American Series," 41). Washington: 1950. Describes efforts by OAS to preserve the peace among Caribbean countries.

10. ———— *Military Assistance to Latin America.* (Publication no. 4917, "Inter-American Series," 44). Washington: 1953. Discusses nature and scope of U. S. military aid programs to Latin America.

11. ————. *Objectives of U. S. Foreign Policy in Latin America.* (Publication no. 6131, "Inter-American Series," 51). Washington: 1955. A series of addresses by Assistant Secretary of State Henry F. Holland on U. S.-Latin American relations.

12. ————. *Our Foreign Policy in Latin America.* (Publication no. 5285, "Inter-American Series," 46). Washington: 1953. An analysis of Latin American economic problems by Nelson A. Rockefeller.

13. ————. *Sovereignty and Interdependence in the New World.* (Publication No. 3054, "Inter-American Series," 35). Washington: 1948. Examines the evolution and operation of the Inter-American System.

14. ————. *United States-Latin American Relations.* (Publication no. 5290, "Inter-American Series,"

47). Washington: 1953. This document contains the report of Milton S. Eisenhower, after he made a "good-will tour" of Latin America.

15. Eisenhower, Dwight D. "The Canadian-American Partnership," *Department of State Bulletin,* 29 (November 30, 1953), pp. 735-38. President Eisenhower discusses the bases of Canadian-American relations.

16. Gantenbein, James W., ed. *The Evolution of Our Latin-American Policy.* New York: Columbia University Press, 1950. A helpful compendium of official sources on the historic policy of the U. S. toward Latin America.

17. House Foreign Affairs Committee. *Building a World of Free Peoples,* 85th Congress, 1st Session, March 1-April 9, 1957.

18. ————. *Hearings on the Mutual Security Act of 1957,* 85th Congress, 1st Session, June 17-20, 1957. This (along with earlier and later legislative hearings on the Mutual Security Program) contains illuminating data on U. S. foreign policy toward Latin America.

19. International Monetary Fund. *International Financial Statistics,* Volume 12 (September, 1959), p. 20. This publication affords a valuable source of information on United States relations with Latin America and other regions.

20. Keenleyside, Hugh L. *Canada and the United States.* New York: Alfred A. Knopf, 1952.

21. Kent, Tom. "The Changing Place of Canada," *Foreign Affairs,* 35 (July, 1957), pp. 581-92. Analyzes Canada's evolving role in world affairs.

22. Lewis, Flora. "The Peril Is Not Red," *Nation,* 178 (February 13, 1954), pp. 127-29. Examines the conditions within Guatemala that sustained the communist movement.

23. *New York Times.*

24. O'Hearn, Walter. "How We Stand With The Canadians," *The Reporter,* 18 (March 6, 1958), pp. 22-5. Focuses upon dominant issues in recent United States-Canadian relations.

25. Pattee, R. "The Argentine Question: The War Stage," *Review of Politics,* 8 (October, 1946), pp. 475-500. Analyzes U. S.-Argentine relations during the war years.

26. Perkins, Dexter. *The Monroe Doctrine, 1823-1826.* Cambridge: Harvard University Press, 1927.

27. ————. *The Monroe Doctrine, 1826-1867.* Baltimore: The Johns Hopkins University Press, 1933.

28. ————. *The Monroe Doctrine, 1867-1907.* Baltimore: The Johns Hopkins University Press, 1937. These are perhaps the most authoritative studies available on the Monroe Doctrine.

29. ———. *The United States and the Caribbean.* Cambridge: Harvard University Press, 1947. A survey of U. S.-Caribbean relations.

30. Pike, Frederick B. "Guatemala, the United States, and Communism in the Americas," *Review of Politics,* 17 (April, 1955), pp. 232-61. This is one of the best analyses available of the Guatemalan crisis.

31. Pratt, Julius W. *A History of United States Foreign Policy.* New York: Prentice-Hall, Inc., 1955. Contains a number of helpful chapters on U. S.-Latin American relations.

32. Rosen, Bernard. "Counter-Revolution: Guatemala's Tragedy," *Nation,* 179 (July 31, 1954), pp. 87-9. A highly critical treatment of U. S. policy toward Guatemala.

33. Senate Foreign Relations Committee. *Hearings on the Mutual Security Act of 1959,* April 23 to May 14, 1959. 86th Congress, 1st Session, 1959.

34. ———. *The Mutual Security Act of 1959.* Report No. 412, 86th Congress, 1st Session. Washington: 1959.

35. Special Committee to Study the Foreign Aid Program. *Foreign Aid Activities of Other Free Nations,* 85th Congress, 1st Session, Washington: 1957. The foreign aid programs of OAS are discussed on pp. 31-32.

36. *Survey of International Affairs, 1954,* et seq. New York: Oxford University Press, 1956. This scholarly series by the Royal Institute of International Affairs provides a different perspective on U. S. foreign policy than American sources.

37. *United States in World Affairs, 1952,* et seq. The Council on Foreign Relations' annual volume contains a comprehensive and balanced treatment of U. S. policy toward Latin America.

38. Wade, William W. "Canada's New Role in World Affairs," *Foreign Policy Reports,* 27 (June 15, 1951), pp. 73-84. Brings out clearly Canada's "emergence" as an important nation after World War II.

39. Weigert, Hans W., *et al.,* eds. *New Compass of the World.* New York: The Macmillan Company, 1953. Chapters 2 and 3 analyze the strategic importance of Canada today.

40. Willoughby, William R. "Canadian-American Defense Co-operation," *Journal of Politics,* 13 (November, 1951), pp. 675-96. Traces out Canadian-American collaboration in the field of defense policy.

41. *Yearbook of World Affairs, 1956,* et seq. London: Stevens and Sons, Ltd., 1957. The annual volumes in this series by the London Institute of World Affairs contain selected essays on Latin American problems.

CHAPTER 13

Asia

New Nations and Ancient Problems

In the turbulent postwar period no region has presented the United States with so many diplomatic challenges as has that far-flung arc of territories extending from Afghanistan to Japan and southward to Indonesia and the Philippines. As in the Middle East, the United States has been compelled to formulate viable policies toward countries and problems in this area when the swift unfolding of events often left very little time for working out intelligent decisions.

Guidelines from earlier diplomatic experience toward Asia unfortunately offered minimum help to American policy-makers in today's world. Some authorities doubt whether, prior to the Second World War, the United States ever possessed what can meaningfully be called a "foreign policy" toward Asia in the sense of a realistic conception of its diplomatic interests there, together with reasonably effective methods for advancing them. As late as 1955, Reischauer observed that "We have still to determine what are our basic interests in Asia—what are the dangers to be avoided and the hopes to be fulfilled in that part of the World. We have reached no agreement on what really is happening in Asia, how this may affect us, and what we should do about it" (**36**, p. 4). Broad segments of American public opinion and even influential political

and government leaders tend to seek guidance for contemporary policy in America's historic relations with Asia. Their attachment to images and conceptions derived from this experience goes far toward explaining many of the nation's policy inadequacies in that vital region during

"What's Our Firm, Unswerving Asia Policy Today"?
Herblock's Here and Now, Simon & Schuster, 1955.

recent years. Let us look briefly at the highlights of America's relations with Asia in the past.

Three episodes were of singular importance: Commodore Perry's opening of Japan to Western influence; proclamation of the Open Door policy toward China; and America's acquisition of the Philippines and other strategic bases in the Pacific. The visit of an American naval expedition under Commodore Perry to Japan in the mid-1850's climaxed a period of westward continental expansion at home. By 1848 the United States had acquired a 1,200-mile Pacific coastline, thereby whetting its interest in the affairs of Asia. Perry's visits in 1853-54 at last forced the hermit-like kingdom of Japan to open its doors to Western influence and, more specifically, to trade with the outside world (35, pp. 270-78). In the years following Perry's visit, Japan became America's protégé in the Orient. Long after contrary evidence had accumulated, the American people and their leaders continued to believe that the interests of the United States and Imperial Japan in the Orient were compatible. Only after Tokyo had dropped even the pretext of a pro-American, generally pro-Western policy, and embarked upon a course of outright military conquest in Manchuria early in the 1930's did Americans forsake their image of Japan as a benign, pacifically-inclined, crypto-Western country. Much the same image of Japan, however, re-appeared during the period of the American occupation following World War II. Tokyo's apparent willingness to accept sweeping occupation-imposed changes in social, economic and political affairs convinced many Americans that Japan's aggressive moves during the 1930's and 1940's did not really accord with the wishes of the Japanese people.

The second historic landmark in American policy toward Asia was proclamation of the Open Door policy toward China at the end of the 19th century. Preservation of the Open Door remained a professed goal of American foreign policy until World War II. Even after the victory of communism in China in the period 1949-50, part of America's resentment toward the communist government derived from the fact that Soviet Russia enjoyed a preferential position in Chinese affairs. Peiping had abandoned the Open Door policy. Just what was this policy? What were its implications for later American-Asian relations?

Strict accuracy should make us hesitate to call the Open Door a policy at all. In a brilliant diplomatic *coup*, on March 20, 1900, Secretary of State John Hay announced that he had been able to secure British, German, Japanese, and American concurrence to a pledge which, in the words of a British diplomat, assured that these countries would "maintain free and equal commercial relations for all time in the Orient" (13, p. 107). More concretely, Hay professed he had secured agreement to the general principle that future economic concessions granted to one of these governments by China must be granted on the same basis to the other governments. The gist of the three-fold pledge was that: each party agreed not to interfere with commercial spheres of influence currently maintained by other powers in China; Chinese tariffs would apply equally to the goods imported from these countries; and harbor dues, railroad charges, and the like, within any power's sphere of influence would be the same for other powers using these facilities (13, pp. 109-10).

Actually, Hay had not secured the agreement of the powers to these terms, but after his public announcement the countries involved hesitated to deny their acceptance of what appeared to be a fair, almost idealistic, agreement respecting diplomatic rivalry in China.

Historical scholarship has shown convincingly that the Open Door policy grew out of competing diplomatic ambitions in China, not the least of which were ambitions entertained by the United States. The policy was aimed specifically at Czarist Russia, whose advances in the Orient caused widespread alarm among other imperialistic countries, not so much out of abstract concern for the territorial integrity of China as out of fear that Russia's seemingly insatiable diplomatic appetite might eventually close China, Manchuria, and Korea to Western influence (13, p. 107). The United States was insisting upon equality of treatment chiefly because recent concessions wrested from China by other countries threatened to imperil America's position in the current economic rivalry and, most especially, to jeopardize American access to the lucrative Chinese trade. The Open Door was Washington's way of trying to safeguard its own political and economic interests in China at a time when an all-out diplomatic struggle for control of that country —in which America had neither the inclination nor the means to compete vigorously—would almost certainly result in the disappearance of American influence. Says Werner Levi of the Open Door: " . . . every nation sought its own advantage in the policy, not the least its official originator . . . " (26, p. 52).

In the light of these facts, it may seem strange that over the course of time the Open Door policy came to be widely regarded by the American people as the quintessence of a moral, unselfish foreign policy whose dominant purpose was preservation of Chinese territorial integrity against powerful imperialist forces. Several reasons explain what amounted to a kind of sanctification of the Open Door policy by the American people. Americans were unwilling to comprehend or admit that insistence upon the Open Door accorded with their own nation's diplomatic ambitions in China, the chief one of which was maintenance of unimpaired trade relations. This mentality was part of the larger and persistent belief that only other countries were capable of "imperialistic" motivations. Then too the Open Door policy seemed to foreshadow certain idealistic Wilsonian principles such as self-determination. In time the American people tended to ascribe to the Open Door policy a much wider and more humanitarian compass than its instigators had intended, converting it ultimately into a blanket guarantee of Chinese economic and political integrity.

Yet the Open Door policy did nothing whatever to interfere with *existing* foreign concessions in China; nor did it prevent future ones, so long as the countries enumerated above were treated *equally* by China. A four-way monopoly of Chinese trade was by no means prohibited under the Open Door policy —if indeed this was not what its framers ultimately anticipated. The Open Door policy said nothing about the *political* inviolability of China. The principle of equal concessions applied to commercial matters only, and it did not apply to all of them. For instance, future industrial or railroad concessions were excluded. Whatever influence the Open Door may have had in protecting Chinese sovereignty was therefore largely incidental. The objective was to assure equality of treatment for the United States in the midst of an impending imperialist struggle on the Chinese mainland (13, pp. 110-11). That China itself greeted the Open Door with something less than unrestrained enthusiasm was indicated by the fact that it did not formally adhere to the principle until it signed the Nine-Power Treaty in 1921 (26, p. 55).

More basic still in evaluating the implications of the Open Door policy in shaping the future American outlook toward Asia is the fact that neither at the time nor later was the United States prepared to take steps to enforce compliance with its provisions. Chester Bowles equates the Open Door policy with "so many of the statements of moral principle which we too frequently like to identify with foreign policy. It amounted to no more than a pious wish that the great powers should refrain from carving up China" (5, p. 380). As the years passed after 1900, American foreign policy in the Far East sometimes appeared deliberately designed to undermine the Open Door, perhaps not so much by commission as by omission. The United States was either unwilling or unable to halt progressive Japanese encroachments against the Open Door principle; and willfully or through ignorance, American policies sometimes actually facilitated Japanese expansionism at the expense of the Open Door (26, pp. 287-97).

Nevertheless, the Open Door policy was one of the most profound influences which shaped popular attitudes toward China and, more broadly, toward Asia as a whole. Its most lasting consequence was to inculcate the view that in China's relations with the outside world, the United States occupied a preferential position. This idea had a number of important corollaries: that China was a kind of "ward" of the United States and that it looked to Washington for guidance in its internal and external affairs; that China's leaders were highly amenable to American suggestions and leadership in all fields; that China was unshakably pro-American in its attitudes and could be counted on to remain America's firm ally in Asia; that China was moving slowly but perceptibly down the path of political democracy and economic stability; that China owed a great "debt of gratitude" to the United States for moral and material help extended to it after 1900 and that this debt would weigh heavily in shaping China's attitudes toward domestic and foreign issues.

Since World War II Americans have been psychologically unable to accept the fact—and this has been a key element in explaining the ineffectuality of their policies—that events inside and outside China have long since overtaken the Open Door policy. That policy was postulated upon the existence of a weak, internally divided China which was an easy prey to foreign influence. In general these conditions persisted until the end of World War II. Even during the war and in the immediate postwar period, however, Chiang Kai-shek had demonstrated time and again that *China's interests* were uppermost in his mind and that in critical areas of policy the United States and other foreign countries could be expected to exert minimal influence over Chinese affairs. This fact was made even plainer after communism's victory under Mao Tse-tung. The American people have been unable to adjust their thinking and their policies to the existence of a politically unified, ambitious, self-confident China. Deriving their images of China from the by-gone (and what history is likely to show as a most untypical) era of the Open Door policy, Americans have been left with a policy vacuum. They have demonstrated very little ability to fill that vacuum with constructive policies in recent years. Current American policies toward China are still groping for a new approach to replace the Open Door.

The third landmark in American Far Eastern policy before the Second World War was acquisition of the Philippines in 1899. This climaxed the acquisition of other Pacific islands such as Midway and Hawaii, obtained in 1867 and 1898, respectively. Its new strategic island bases for the first time made the United States a "Pacific power" in the military sense (**35,** pp. 387-92). This fact drew America deeper and deeper into the vortex of great power rivalry there, ordaining that sooner or later conflict would arise between the United States and the rising Imperial Japanese Empire, whose diplomatic ambitions led it eventually to challenge the United States and Great Britain for mastery over the western Pacific area.

With other territories in Asia—India, Burma, Southeast Asia, Indonesia—the United States had no significant and direct relations at all before World War II. Washington recognized British primacy in India and Burma, French in Indochina, and Dutch in Indonesia. At intervals the United States did not hesitate to offer gratuitous advice to European countries about the management of their colonial affairs. But it was not until former dependencies emerged as independent nations after World War II that the United States established formal and direct diplomatic relations with them.

The principal elements of American foreign policy toward the Far East in the prewar period afforded very poor preparation for the new role of responsible American leadership of the West's policies towards Asian affairs throughout the postwar period. Novel and complex problems, often totally alien to American experience and arising under conditions of unprecedented urgency, required a fundamental reorientation in American policies. Among these problems, three categories were fundamental. They provide the framework for our analysis of American-Asian relations at mid-century: the challenge of Asian nationalism, America's response to economic and trade issues throughout Asia, and the communist threat to the Far East.

1. THE CHALLENGE OF ASIAN NATIONALISM

Over one billion people in Asia have been involved in nationalist movements since World War II. Out of the fires of Asian nationalism nine newly-independent nations have been forged: Pakistan, India, Burma, Ceylon, Indonesia, North and South Vietnam, the Philippines, and Korea. In addition, profound social, economic, and political transformations have taken place as a result of the Communist victory in China and changes carried out in Japan by the American occupation authorities. No nation in the Orient has been entirely free from nationalist agitation; and even today, in the words of Edwin O. Reischauer, nationalism may still prove "the nuclear weapon of the situation in Asia" (36, p. 269).

Contemporary manifestations of nationalism differ from country to country and from region to region. They also vary markedly from the familiar standard of European nationalist movements in the nineteenth century. In a region as culturally diverse and as rich in historical tradition as Asia, inevitably nationalism will mean something different to a Burmese, a Malayan, an Indian, or an Indonesian. Even within the same country, different economic and social groups will interpret nationalism differently. Nevertheless, there is an affinity among the nationalist movements that have swept Asia in recent years. Two generalizations can be made. One is that these movements nearly always contain rational and irrational elements, emotional as well as logical goals. One writer describes Asian nationalism as a "huge emotional reservoir which can be tapped and used for good or ill depending on the kind of leadership which captures it" (19, p. 5). What nationalist groups throughout Asia are *against*—and of course the *bête noire* has been Western colonialism— often emerges more clearly than what they are *for* in pressing their demands.

Second, Asian nationalism is a fluid concept, more fluid perhaps today than during the Second World War and the years immediately following. In that period the principal articulate goal was abolition of outside colonial domination. Today, having achieved that goal on a broad scale, national aims are preserving newly-won freedoms, non-alignment in great power conflicts, and attention to urgent domestic problems facing societies throughout Asia. John Kerry King has written that these nations

are determined to maintain their independence. . . . to perfect their independence by minimizing outside cultural influences and their economic dependence on outside powers. . . . to achieve the form and substance of international status, prestige, and equality. . . . to formulate and pursue their own domestic and foreign policies in their own way. They aspire to rapid industrialization and economic development. . . . Above all they want to complete the transition from a dependent colonial society and economy to an independent national society and economy. (23, p. 48).

How are these broad goals expressed by individual countries? How do they create problems in terms of Western-Asian relations? How has the United States responded to the challenge of postwar Asian nationalism? To answer such questions as concretely as possible we have chosen to examine them within the context of two case studies. Our first case study will center on India, which exerts great influence throughout Asia, and where manifestations of nationalism are typical of much of the Orient. The second case study, dealing with relations between the United States and Red China, will illustrate still other characteristics of Asian nationalism and of America's response to it.

Indian Nationalism—Sources and Manifestations

Geographically situated so as to serve as a bridge between west and east Asia, and isolated from the sprawling continental hinterland by the formidable Himalayan range, India occupies a strategic position in Asia. Because India is at the crossroads of Asia, its leaders regard their country also as an ideological link between the East and West. In the words of an Indian spokesman, India is "the centre of gravity of the ideologies of the world" (28, p. 42). Its leadership throughout the Orient has been widely acknowledged by other Asian countries. The future course of political developments in that area is likely to be determined by the contest between India and Red China for the allegiance of the smaller nations in the Far East. When Prime Minister Nehru of India speaks on foreign policy issues, writes the former American Ambassador to India, Chester Bowles, "he expresses not only his own convictions but also the yearnings and the attitudes of the vast majority in free Asia and in Africa. . . . I am convinced that what Nehru says, most free Asians think" (5, p. 111).

One key to Indian foreign policy, and to the policies of countries like Burma and Indonesia whose outlook often parallels that of New Delhi, is the high priority assigned to the solution of age-old internal problems. What has been termed a "revolution of expectations" has occurred throughout most of the Far East (33, p. 187). At the very time many of these countries are breaking away from Western political control they are determined to follow the example of Western countries in industrializing and solving bedrock agricultural problems indigenous to most Asian states.

Asian leaders visualize a parallel between their experience and that of the American people after the Revolution. In both cases domestic problems were of primary, almost exclusive, concern. The American people had a continent to populate and to consolidate politically. The Indian people have new frontiers too; not literally of course, but symbolically, in the new horizons which beckon in the spheres of human welfare, material advancement, alleviation of widespread economic misery and social disorganization, elimination of disease, the fight against illiteracy and ignorance—in short, the creation of firm socio-economic-political foundations at home in order that newly-achieved freedoms may be maintained and that they may lead to tangible benefits for the peoples concerned. If Indians sometimes appear indifferent to global diplomatic issues, it is because they are "concerned less with their country's future as a Great Power than with its present as a very medium one" (46, p. 181). Nehru has stated that "Ultimately foreign policy is the outcome of economic policy" and that "until India has properly evolved her economic policy" her "foreign policy will be rather vague, rather inchoate and will be groping" (28, p. 26). Regardless of whether Nehru is correct or incorrect in attributing foreign policies to economic stimuli —and this is surely a debatable hypothesis— the really significant fact is that Indians *believe* that pressing internal economic problems shape their outlook on foreign affairs. This belief is highly symptomatic of their overwhelming preoccupation with domestic issues.

Other important keys to India's foreign policy can be discerned in the fact that the country has just recently emerged from a colonial relationship, that it is inhabited by what many Westerners regard as colored peoples, and that it is strategically situated at the cross-roads of Asia. No factor shaping India's outlook toward world affairs surpasses in importance the impact of its colonial experience. In this respect its history parallels that of many Afro-Asian nations. Reischauer has oberved that "If there are any attitudes common to all Asians, they are a fundamental resentment against Western domination in the recent past, a deep suspicion of Western motives in the present, and a very real fear of Western actions in the future. . . . there undoubtedly is an underlying anti-Western bias in the whole Asian response" (36, p. 75). And Nehru has declared that "Great countries like India, who have passed out of the colonial stage, do not conceive it possible that other countries should remain under the yoke of colonial rule" (28, pp. 46-7). Consequently, there are very few global issues which India and its like-minded partners in the Afro-Asian bloc do not relate to what they envision as the never-ceasing struggle against colonialism. For many years after World War II this issue was far more a "matter of principle" to such countries than the hypothetical danger of attacks from Soviet Russia or Red China. The intentions of former colonial countries in the West aroused far more apprehensions in the minds of peoples once dominated by the West than current oppressions carried on in the Soviet satellite zone. Events by the late 1950's, however, had altered this prevailing Asian view somewhat. The brutal Red Chinese incorporation of Tibet, followed by the dramatic escape of Tibet's rulers after an heroic trek across the Himalayas into India, and subsequent Chinese threats against India's northern provinces like Bhutan and Sikkim drove the point home to masses and rulers throughout Asia that Western "colonialism" was not the only kind that might threaten their security. Growing apprehensions about Red China did not result in any diminution in fears concerning the intentions of powerful Western countries. Asians have learned from their own experience that nations like Britain,

France, and The Netherlands are capable of professing lofty ideological principles and of disclaiming imperialistic ambitions, but that these pronouncements seldom resulted in any change in the colonial rule maintained over millions of dependent peoples. The mere fact that Western countries possess the *ability* to dominate smaller nations is often interpreted as proof that they are in fact constantly on the verge of doing so.

A strange ambivalence is often evident in Asian attitudes toward the communist world and the free world. Asians sometimes appear curiously indifferent to the facts that (1) Western countries have liquidated their empires in the postwar era on a scale unwitnessed before that time; (2) the United States—now perhaps the most powerful nation known to history—has the most non-imperialistic record of any great nation; and (3) the USSR has established and maintained one of the largest, most ruthlessly exploited, empires ever witnessed. That Asian spokesmen are perfectly sincere in their animosity toward colonialism wherever it is found must be admitted. Nevertheless, it is also true that anti-colonialism, like anti-Israeli sentiment throughout the Arab world, serves conveniently as a scapegoat on which comparatively slow progress in socio-economic fields can be blamed. The Western nations find themselves pictured in the incompatible roles of friends of the Asian states—reservoirs of large amounts of capital, that ought to be given generously to economically backward countries—and as opponents of Asian states—seeking reimposition of colonial rule upon helpless societies, through economic footholds from which political control can then be extended! These attitudes—natural in countries that recognize their dependence upon Western nations, but at the same time deeply resent that dependence—create psychological blocks that hamper satisfactory relations with Asia on a great variety of issues, ranging from the provision of economic assistance to military defense.

Side-by-side with anti-colonialism must be placed the preoccupation of India and Asian countries that share its attitudes with racial discrimination and conflict throughout the world. India is inordinately sensitive to racial

issues wherever they are found. Sometimes its own diplomatic interests are directly involved because of the problem of the "overseas Indians," approximately four million of whom live in foreign countries, chiefly South Africa, East Africa, Ceylon, Malaya, and Burma. The lot of the overseas Indian has often been painful, partially because they do not always assimilate easily and partially because, as in Burma, they have sometimes attained positions of economic eminence which naturally generate resentments against them. New Delhi has repeatedly denounced policies of racial discrimination in such countries as the Union of South Africa and Kenya. And even when its interests were not directly involved, as in the case of racial discrimination within the United States, India has watched with deep concern (28, pp. 55-59).

India's geographical location also is of great significance in explaining its outlook on world affairs. Its foreign policy reveals many characteristics of the earlier American policy of isolationism, largely because India is in fact isolated from the main currents of world political developments. Insulated from the Asian heartland by the virtually impenetrable Himalayan barriers and, what may be even more basic, protected throughout history by British diplomacy which proved highly successful in "neutralizing" such potential bases of invasion as Tibet and Afghanistan, India has come to look upon isolationism as a kind of natural right, as a patrimony bequeathed by years of British rule. Oftentimes New Delhi has shown no more astuteness than Washington exhibited before World War II in understanding the strategic realities underlying national security. India has yet to learn a lesson the United States appears to have learned after painful diplomatic experience: a policy of isolationism, resting upon conditions existing in one stage of history, may not be feasible when these conditions have changed.

In spite of their oft-expressed opposition to "militarism" and their deprecation of defense preparedness measures, Indians are becoming increasingly conscious of possible threats to the security of their own country. On the surface, New Delhi accepted Red Chinese hegemony over Tibet in 1950 with apparent equanimity, in order to demonstrate, according to one Indian spokesman, "a gesture of good will to New China" and to express India's "earnest desire" for cordiality between the two countries (**28**, p. 132). As the months passed, however, India evinced no little apprehension over the security of its northern borders. Red China's hegemony over Tibet and its ominous moves along India's Himalayan frontier prompted New Delhi to strengthen its military position in the states of Sikkim, Bhutan, and Nepal, with which India had concluded military security treaties earlier. India's obdurate position on the thorny Kashmir question derives at least in some measure from the reluctance to surrender control over a strategically located area on the northern border of the subcontinent (**1**, pp. 128-43). A new concern for national defense has also pervaded New Delhi's approach to the vital Northwest Frontier region, containing the only militarily usable passes from Central Asia through the Himalayan range into India.

In terms of intra-Asian relations, one issue to date has towered above all others: India's relations with Pakistan. Informed observers believe that New Delhi evaluates most questions in foreign affairs within the context of the smoldering Indian-Pakistani controversy stemming from the partition of India into separate Moslem and Hindu states in 1947. The centuries-old Hindu-Moslem "communal conflict" by no means came to an end in 1947. Suspicion and hostility have marked relations between the two countries ever since. They have colored the entire range of issues from trade questions, to disputes over care of refugees, to the extension of American economic and military aid to one or both countries, to alignment or non-alignment of both countries in great power diplomatic blocs. The focal point of these tensions has been the controversy over control of the Kashmir region which has been a source of discord between India and Pakistan ever since their creation as independent countries. The conflict has major implications for determining attitudes displayed by each country toward each other and toward a host of regional and global issues. Both New Delhi and Karachi, for example, have assessed American military assistance programs and sponsorship of alliances in Asia very largely in terms of how these developments affect the military balance of power in the Kashmir dispute (**31**, pp. 141-47; **8**, pp. 159-73, 241).

Finally, there remains the question of India's relations with the great powers and its cold war diplomacy. India's foreign policy since 1947 has been one of "neutralism." This term, like nationalism, is deceptive because the concept embraces numerous, sometimes contradictory, elements. Neutralism is merely a convenient label to designate a cluster of ideological propensities and expediential responses to critical global issues (**46**, p. 179).

Basic to the idea of neutralism is the principle of non-alignment in great power conflicts and diplomatic blocs. Nehru stated in 1946 that India would take part in international affairs

as a free nation with our own policy and not merely as a satellite of another nation. . . . We propose . . . to keep away from the power politics of groups, aligned against one another, which have led in the past to world wars and which may again lead to disasters on an ever greater scale. (**28**, p. 14).

India's leaders have emphasized that neutralism, in contrast to what is sometimes believed in the West, does not contemplate a merely negative or passive foreign policy. "Our foreign policy is not a negative or neutral policy," Nehru has explained, "but a positive policy naturally helping those forces that we consider right and disapproving of those that we consider wrong, but fundamentally keeping apart from other countries and other alignments of powers which normally lead to major conflicts" (**28**, p. 75).

Attachment to a foreign policy of neutralism, in the Indian conception, also means working assiduously in behalf of peace. Indians emphasize the positive aspect of this obligation, looking upon peace as something more than merely the absence of war and the reduction of international tensions. Working for peace consists of cultivating harmonious and fruitful contacts among nations in all their activities, to the end that an atmosphere of good will and security in world affairs may flourish. This goal has led India to cultivate friendly relations with both great power blocs, with Red China, with the neighboring states of west and Southeast Asia, and with its former ruler, Great Britain. It has likewise led India to denounce what it regards as periodic perversion of the United Nations into an instrument for perpetuating cold war antagonisms and a sounding board for rival propagandas. Similarly India has objected vigorously to the formation of hostile alliance systems and to the steady accretion in world armaments. In theory, if not always in practice, India rejects the premise that disputes in international relations can be resolved by recourse to arms and by reliance for security upon military pacts. Thus an editorial in the Indian periodical *United Asia* in 1954 challenged the argument that military strength was required to prevent war and safeguard the world from tyranny. It held that "war itself is a kind of tyranny" and that the "favourite device" of powerful and aggressive countries in the past was "resorting to war to end a tyranny;" wars, the editorial continued, have "created more tyrannies than they have destroyed" (29, p. 261). Mindful of the non-violent methods successfully utilized by Gandhi in achieving Indian independence, New Delhi believes that these same methods can produce constructive results in international affairs. This is the stated ideal, no matter how reluctant New Delhi remains to apply the same reasoning to its own relations with Pakistan in the explosive Kashmir dispute.

Summarizing the manifold ideas and influences that go to shape Indian foreign policy and policies of countries whose viewpoints often parallel those of India, we may say that these policies are compounded of elements derived from earlier colonial experience, geographic location, and urgent internal problems. In the words of Chester Bowles, millions of people in the Afro-Asian bloc "reveal the same preconceptions about Western materialism and Eastern spirituality, the same attitude toward the Cold War and the atomic bomb. They will condemn with equal vigor American racial discrimination wherever it comes to light. They will react with equal quickness to every evidence of foreign domination from any source" (5, p. 387). As in any other country or region, peoples in the Afro-Asian bloc have their stereotypes and their shibboleths. They also have pressing internal and external requirements. And because they are newly-independent countries, they are more than ordinarily inclined to believe for a long time to come that their own needs, as they define them, properly constitute the first claim upon their energies and their diplomatic efforts.

The United States and Red China

By the end of 1949 the United States had suffered one of the most far-reaching reverses in its entire diplomatic history, when the Nationalist Government of Chiang Kai-shek collapsed before the victorious forces of the Communists under Mao Tse-tung.[*] Basically, communism won in China because, in spite of massive quantities of American aid of all kinds, Chiang's government was unable to hold the allegiance of the masses, unwilling to eliminate corruption from its own ranks, and incapable of offering a constructive program to the people of China as an alternative for Mao's forward-looking, if ruthlessly autocratic, platform.[**]

---

[*]Relations between the United States and Nationalist China during and after World War II are treated in numerous works, many of which are highly subjective and emotional in character. The official position of the United States Government is set forth in the documentary account, **10**. Among the more scholarly and objective studies are: **26**, pp. 1-265; **16**, *passim*; **15**, *passim*; **13**, pp. 232-63; and **17**, pp. 200-10.

[**]Among the factors blamed by American public opinion for the communist victory, few have loomed as large as the Far Eastern consequences of the Yalta conference in February, 1945. In order to induce Soviet entry into the Far Eastern war, in the hope of reducing American casualties in the expected invasion of Japan, at Yalta Roosevelt made a number of concessions to Stalin. In the main, these were confirmations of long-standing Russian diplomatic ambitions in the Orient, such as assuring Soviet hegemony over Outer Mongolia, the return of southern Sakhalin Island to Russia from Japan, and recognition of Russia's pre-eminent interests in the railways and ports of Manchuria and North China. In return, Stalin pledged to recognize Chinese sovereignty over Manchuria and to support the Chinese Nationalist Government. FDR was to see that, in his words, this agreement was "unquestionably fulfilled" by Chiang Kai-shek (**26**, pp. 240-41).

The most charitable thing that can be said about these concessions is that they stemmed from a gross American military miscalculation about the strength of Japan and the resultant necessity to bring Russia into the Pacific war. The atomic

Ever since the Communist accession in China in 1949, the United States has steadfastly followed a policy of non-recognition of the Red regime. This policy has had three important phases: refusal to establish diplomatic relations with Peiping; unyielding opposition to Red China's admission to the United Nations and replacement of Nationalist by Red Chinese delegates there; and imposition of an embargo on Sino-American trade and leadership in imposing at least a partial embargo on trade between China and the free world. Tension between the two countries has been heightened by a number of developments since 1949. Red China's entry into the Korean War late in 1950 turned what looked like a certain United Nations victory over the entire peninsula into a stalemate truce settlement along the 38th parallel. American diplomatic initiative was in turn responsible for a United Nations resolution which branded Red China an "aggressor" in Korea (11, II, pp. 2602-09). More than ever, Americans became convinced that China could not be permitted to "shoot its way into the United Nations," a feeling which was re-enforced by repeated Chinese violations of the armistice negotiated in 1953. Especially galling to the United States has

---

bomb, however, had not yet been perfected; considerable doubt about its feasibility at this stage remained. American military advisers, especially from the Army, greatly underestimated the effect upon Japan so far of the American naval blockade and virtual mastery of the Pacific.

In retrospect it seems indefensible that these concessions should have been made without China's *prior* concurrence in them. Nevertheless, the Yalta concessions were probably of minimum significance in bringing about a communist victory in China. The initial reaction of both Chinese and American opinion to these agreements was not unfavorable. Chiang Kai-shek believed that he had gained a Soviet pledge not to assist the Chinese communist rebels—a pledge which Stalin kept throughout most of the ensuing civil war. Many Chinese spokesmen believed that this understanding therefore was preferable to leaving Russia a completely free hand in Chinese affairs. Moreover, Russia's subsequent looting of industrial equipment in Manchuria after Japan's defeat weakened the Communist effort far more than the Nationalist, since the Communists were concentrated in north China. Russia's looting has since greatly detracted from Red China's ability to industrialize.

In brief, both Soviet and American actions were of marginal significance in determining the outcome of the Chinese civil war (2, p. 107; 26, pp. 234-37; 24, pp. 89-138).

been Peiping's reluctance to release American prisoners of war still held in captivity.

Then as the Korean War drew to a close, Peiping began to express mounting belligerency toward the Nationalist-held islands of Formosa and the Pescadores, which Peiping regarded as belonging to the mainland. The United States was determined to prevent Communist domination over these islands, both because Washington felt a strong moral obligation to protect Chiang Kai-shek and his faithful men from the Communists and because high-ranking American military spokesmen considered Formosa vital to the preservation of American security. As Peiping's bellicosity grew, the Eisenhower Administration decided that a forthright declaration of American policy goals was necessary to avert the threat of open hostilities. In a message to Congress on January 24, 1955, President Eisenhower declared that Red Chinese military activities in the Formosa Straits posed a "serious danger to the security of our country and of the entire Pacific area and indeed to the peace of the world." He requested Congress to pass a resolution which would "reduce the possibility that the Chinese Communists, misjudging our firm purpose and national unity," might attempt to challenge the strength of the free world (11, II, p. 2485). Congress responded four days later by approving the "Formosa Resolution" authorizing the President to "employ the Armed Forces of the United States as he deems necessary for the specific purpose of security and protecting Formosa and the Pescadores against armed attack . . . " (11, II, p. 2487). In the same period Washington issued blunt warnings to Peiping that new outbreaks of Chinese aggression anywhere in Asia—the most likely point was Indochina—would encounter firm American resistance which would not necessarily be confined to the immediate territory in which aggression took place nor be limited solely to the use of conventional, non-nuclear, weapons (11, II, pp. 2370-71, 2373-76).

Greatly aggravating these specific sources of tension has been the overall atmosphere in which official and unofficial relationships between Washington and Peiping have been carried on since 1949. This atmosphere has been one of intense ill-will, recrimination, and

mutual suspicion. The United States has described Peiping's foreign policy as an attempt
to "destroy the way of life of the free countries
of the world and bring about the global
dominion of communism" and as reflecting
"fundamental hostility to the United States and
the free world as a whole. . . . " In a publicly
released State Department memorandum on
American foreign policy toward China, the
United States accused Peiping of seeking ultimate dominance throughout Asia. This memorandum asserted that the communist regime in
China was unrepresentative of the wishes of
the Chinese people. And it continued: "The
United States holds the view that communism's
rule in China is not permanent and that it one
day will pass. By withholding diplomatic recognition from Peiping it seeks to hasten that
passing" (30, August 10, 1958).

For its part, Red China gave no indication
of desiring more cordial relations with the
United States or other Western countries. Long
before Chiang's military collapse, the United
States had become a prime target of the
Chinese propaganda apparatus. After 1949 the
"Hate America" campaign became a permanent
fixture of Peiping's foreign policy. Waves of
vituperation against the United States alternated with rhapsodic tributes to the Soviet
Union. In Peiping's view the United States
was a "rotten imperialist nation" and the "headquarters of reactionary degeneracy" throughout
the world. Red China expressed contempt for
the United States as a "paper tiger," whose
alleged military might could not intimidate
Peiping. Virtually every failure or oppression
by the new communist order was rationalized
by reference to some fancied threat of American interventionism (26, pp. 284-307). From
the end of the Korean War onward, Red China
exerted intermittent pressure against Formosa
and other off-shore islands, even though the
United States warned that this might provoke
it into a war; yet in each case Communist
pressures would be relaxed just enough whenever necessary to prevent an overt military
conflict between the United States and China.
Communist agents from China were active in
most Asian countries, including those which
were members of SEATO. Then in 1959, a
new Chinese thrust was directed against the

mountainous country of Tibet; while Tibet's
rulers sought sanctuary in India, Peiping
tightened its grip upon a country that had
already entered Red China's sphere of influence. The attempt to convert Tibet into a
"people's democracy" aroused widespread condemnation throughout the free world, and it
resulted in considerably more than usual criticism of Red China by countries in the Afro-
Asian bloc. In brief, since the accession of
communism in China, the country's rulers have
given no indication of desiring friendly relations
with the United States nor of desiring to settle
outstanding differences between the two countries upon a mutually satisfactory basis.

Granting Red China's disinclination to arrive at a *rapprochement* with the United
States, the depressing sequence of events which
has characterized Sino-American relations since
World War II is instructive for the student of
American foreign relations. In the first place,
it illustrates certain habits of mind, stereotypes,
and mental blocks which have seriously interfered with the emergence of policies that serve
the United States' interests. The astute English
commentator, D. W. Brogan, has referred to
the "illusion of American omnipotence" (7,
passim). Nowhere is it better illustrated than
in the public slogans about how the United
States "lost China to communism" and how
certain State Department officials and prominent students of Chinese affairs "sold Chiang
Kai-shek down the river." Such thinking reflects at least three highly questionable assumptions: that the United States—either in
the postwar period or earlier—exercised significant influence over *political* developments
in China; that the United States could have
prevented a Communist victory after the war;
and that the primary causes of Nationalist
China's collapse in 1949 lay in the pro-
Communist activities of private and public
groups within the United States.

The "China was sold down the river" mentality is remarkably parallel to other instances
of American demonology in the past, such as
the Nye Committee's explanations during the
1930's of the origin of World War I. In Chapter
7 we analyzed the effect which this theory
had in shaping and re-enforcing American isolationist attitudes during the New Deal period.

Today, foreign propagandists, the machinations of Wall Street, and the nefarious intrigues of profit-hungry munitions makers have been replaced by Communists, fellow-travelers, left-wing foundations and study groups, and influential writers as scapegoats on which major inadequacies in the nation's foreign policy may be blamed. The public fails to see that these inadequacies more often than not had their source in illusions in the public mind as a result of ignorance about Sino-American relations throughout history and about international affairs generally. Few diplomatic issues throughout the nation's history have spawned so many investigations and so much official soul-searching, with such conspicuously barren results, as the collapse of Nationalist China. The nation's energies have been dissipated in searches for scapegoats and in wild-goose chases often motivated more by a desire for publicity than for enlightenment. The same time and energy could far more profitably have been expended in a searching, dispassionate investigation into the whole range of Asian problems confronting the United States, with particular emphasis upon those which are alien to American experience and those which have proved unyielding in the face of past diplomatic efforts. Such an investigation would have revealed that the forces which ushered in communism in China are widespread throughout Asia today. Merely understanding the problem confronting the United States is no guarantee of course that a solution to it can be found, or even that one exists. But if the United States expects to achieve any greater success in dealing with these forces it will have to demonstrate greater acumen than it displayed toward the Chinese civil war.

Whatever arguments may be made for or against non-recognition of Red China, the American people and Congress would probably have countenanced no other course for several years after 1949-50. Yet by the early 1960's it had become increasingly apparent that non-recognition—however psychologically satisfying it might be to masses of Americans —was a stagnant policy in terms of achieving the nation's basic diplomatic interests. Its wisdom could be challenged on a number of grounds. Non-intercourse with China offered

little prospect for improving Sino-American relations and of removing an outstanding cause of global tensions. Such a policy did little or nothing to lessen China's dependence upon Russia; to the contrary, it seemed to close the door upon any extensive contact between China and Western countries, thereby almost guaranteeing that China's rulers would have to turn to Moscow for support and advice in dealing with their critical internal problems. Furthermore, non-recognition did little to improve the climate of Afro-Asian opinion toward the United States. Always sensitive to signs of Western imperialism, some countries interpreted America's refusal to recognize China as evidence that the West demanded acceptance of its diplomatic line from newly-independent countries. China's exclusion from the family of nations also left an important question mark behind international disarmament negotiations. How could disarmament ever become a reality as long as one of the most heavily-armed nations of the world was excluded from negotiations? Even more basic, it is a truism that foreign policy must be based upon the world as it actually exists, that it cannot be effective in the long run so long as it is built upon illusions and utopian expectations. To continue a policy for more than a decade on the supposition that Chiang Kai-shek's regime on Formosa was the "legitimate" government of China, that it represented the "true interests" of the Chinese people, approached the ultimate in diplomatic pipe-dreams. A hypothetical analogy might be the willingness of European countries as late as 1875 to "recognize" Jefferson Davis as the "legitimate" President of the defunct Confederacy.

It could be safely predicted, therefore, that American officials would eventually be required to rethink the assumptions supporting a policy of non-recognition of Red China, just as it was not inconceivable that eventually Red China too would find it in its own interests to arrive at some kind of accommodation with the United States. To some degree, an improvement in the climate of Sino-American relations might hinge upon future relations between Red China and Russia. By the opening of the 1960's, it was clear that clouds were gathering on the horizon, sufficient perhaps to make the two giants of world communism conflict over their rival national interests and ambitions.

America's Response to Asian Nationalism

Recognizing the obstacles to effective American policies in Asia, it is still true that the United States has not succeeded as much as it might in evolving approaches linking Asian goals and American goals. Stereotypes, sacred cows, emotional loyalties to hopeless causes, a large measure of public apathy, failure to look at prevailing issues from the Asian viewpoint and to understand Asian nationalism—all of these have hindered the evolution of dynamic and imaginative American policies, capable of commanding widespread support among leaders and masses in the Orient. The central fact about nationalism in Asia is that it seeks to free Asian peoples from domination and influence by *the West*. In the Asian context, nationalism has first of all meant anti-colonialism, which means freedom from powerful Western countries. In this sense, Western attempts to co-operate with Asian countries begin with two strikes against them; any *rapprochement* with Asian countries must *start* by overcoming latent anti-Western sentiment; thereafter policies must be evolved that are mutually advantageous to both Asian and Western countries. Asian leaders may and do admit the *potential* danger of colonial domination by Soviet Russia or Red China; but they have experienced the *actual* domination of the West and this experience has left an indelible impression on their minds. History has therefore given the Communist side a marked advantage *vis-à-vis* the West in winning the loyalty and support of masses in Asia. Western officials, far more than Communist ones, are obliged to come forth with policies and programs that are capable of overcoming residual hostility and of demonstrating that Western aims and Asian aims are reconcilable. It is Peffer's harsh but substantially accurate conclusion that:

> Russia made use of the forces of the twentieth century in the nonwhite parts of the world. It did not create them. But this, too, must be said: the Western world played into Russia's hands. By its own obscurantism, its own blindness to what

was moving in Asia, its own inability to see that conditions had changed or, when it did see, its unwillingness to make the concessions that change imperatively called for, the West left Asia to go to Russia by default. (34, pp. 294-95).

Great respect for the United States existed throughout Asia during and immediately after the Second World War. Asians identified America, and especially its wartime President, Franklin D. Roosevelt, as their friend; they looked to Washington to assist them in attaining their freedom from European colonial domination; they believed that idealistic pronouncements, like the Atlantic Charter enunciating the "Four Freedoms," presaged a new dispensation for formerly dependent and economically backward peoples. American prestige in Asia grew after President Roosevelt endorsed freedom for India and Indochina, after the United States itself relinquished control over the Philippine Islands, and after it publicly supported the cause of Indonesian independence from the Netherlands (5, pp. 230-31, 380-81; 8, pp. 269-70; 23, pp. 108-09).

Gradually, however, disillusionment began to grip Asians regarding their relations with the United States. In time the United States often found itself lumped together with the "Western imperialist countries" so distrusted by countries in the Afro-Asian bloc. The United States was suspected of harboring a covert desire to dominate weaker states—if not directly, at least to the point of demanding conformity to its announced diplomatic line *vis-à-vis* the communist world. Factors which reshaped wartime and early prewar Asian attitudes toward the United States were realization that the "Four Freedoms" were not going to be speedily translated into generous, American-financed measures and programs for the material betterment of Asia; awareness that the power of the United Nations to fulfill Asian political and economic aspirations was limited; American equivocation regarding prolonged French rule in Indochina, coupled with later American economic and military assistance to France; pressure from Washington upon Japan to rearm, in spite of American occupation-imposed constitutional barriers prohibiting it; unwillingness of public opinion within the United States to accept the consequences of

Communist victory in China; inability of the United States to compel evacuation of remnants of Chiang Kai-shek's army from northern Burma; initial priority for Europe in American foreign assistance programs; attachment of conditions to foreign assistance grants, many of them unacceptable or humiliating to the sensitive pride of Asians; and an announced American defense policy of "massive retaliation," suggesting Washington's willingness to use nuclear weapons against aggression in the Orient, while letting countries in that area furnish required ground troops for defense (23, pp. 106-09; 8, pp. 270-73).

Asians were also offended by the tendency of the United States to evaluate every global issue very largely in terms of how it affected the West's diplomatic-military position in the cold war. Many Asians gained the impression that the United States had very little interest in their problems *per se*. Its only apparent concern seemed to be in rallying Far Eastern countries behind an American-led coalition against communism. Apart from clashing head-on with the widespread neutralist objective of non-alignment in diplomatic blocs, this policy implied that Asia was important to the West only in the degree to which Asians contributed enthusiastically, on terms specified by the West, to the containment activities of the free world (5, pp. 230-37, 381-94; 8, pp. 270-76; 14, pp. 101-07; 42, pp. 215-16).

Added to these sources of misunderstanding have been differing Asian and American viewpoints on the question of neutralism. The American people have exhibited no very astute understanding of the psychology of Asian neutralism and even less sympathy toward countries espousing a neutralist philosophy. They have tended to believe that Asian leaders like Nehru of India or U Nu of Burma were "soft" on communism, since their governments and other governments in the Afro-Asian bloc stubbornly refused to join the anti-communism coalition, sometimes opposed the United States outright on specific global issues such as seating Red China in the UN, and on occasion even sided with Soviet Russia as, for instance, in demanding a halt to nuclear weapons testing. Despite their own record of preserving an essentially neutralist position for over a hun-

dred years, Americans have believed that only ignorance or willful following of the communist line could explain the unwillingness of many Asian states to side with the United States on a matter of principle like Soviet aggrandizement in Eastern Europe or Red Chinese failure to respect the Korean armistice agreement.

Prevailing American skepticism over Asian neutralism has expressed itself from time to time in official statements and policies. Thus a study group report issued by the House Foreign Affairs Committee in 1954 recommended that "Such sums as we can grant for technical assistance must go to those who are standing on our side even at the expense of aid to those who are neutral" (23, p. 234). Apprehensions in Congress over the implications of neutralism also explained the long delay in 1951 in granting legislative authority to send surplus American wheat for relief of famine conditions in India. Wheat was finally sent, but not before Moscow dramatically announced that Russian wheat was on the way.

Arguments heard within the United States against the neutralist position have a certain superficial plausibility which gives them wide public appeal. In essence the case comes down to saying: any country which does not declare itself forthrightly against the communist menace is indirectly abetting it by failing to cooperate with the free world in countering Moscow's and Peiping's aggressive designs. Forced to assume the unwanted burden of free world leadership, it is altogether natural that the United States should want to present a united diplomatic front against the communist bloc and that it should desire less powerful non-communist countries to contribute their share to free world defense efforts.

Yet in the long run neutralism is likely to prove a more durable foundation upon which to build political stability in Asia than is insistence upon following the American diplomatic line. This is true for several reasons. One is that neutralism has evolved as *Asia's own answer* to critical diplomatic issues. As a tactical matter, therefore, genuine neutralism—by which is meant both the *willingness* of a country to pursue an independent course and its *ability* to do so—ought to receive every encouragement by the United States. It is not sufficiently appreciated within America that neutralist leaders like Nehru are as politically *conservative* and as *pro-Western* in their foreign policy orientation as Asian leaders are likely to be and still hold the allegiance of the masses. The United States ought to support, or, at any rate, ought not to disapprove neutralism, since the alternatives to neutralism in Asia are likely to be far worse. Given the residue of anti-Westernism inherited from the colonial period, the fact that neutralist leaders have supported the West as often as they have on important global issues is something of a miracle. To insist that they support the West's policies on every issue is almost certainly calculated to undermine the influence of responsible political leaders throughout the Orient and to prepare the way for extremists who will exploit every opportunity to discredit governments in power. If such groups can label these governments the "lackeys of Wall Street" and the "running dogs of American imperialism," as communist propaganda organs have labelled them, the West will be in danger of forfeiting all opportunity to influence events favorably in the Far East.

Neutralism ought to receive a more sympathetic hearing within the United States also because our own ideology makes it the only possible course to hold out to weaker countries. The United States does not want satellites. Domination over weaker countries and imposition of a diplomatic line upon them is one of the chief indictments in the West's bill of particulars against the Soviet Union. A dominant objective of American foreign policy from the time of the Greek-Turkish Aid Program in 1947 has been creation of strong, freedom-loving allies and friends in the international community. This inevitably implies that America wants associates who are in a position to formulate and exercise their best independent judgments concerning outstanding global issues. Sycophants make very unreliable allies in times of adversity. Moreover, the free world's collective efforts will be enriched immeasurably by viewpoints expressed by countries with varied problems and experiences. Encouraging Asian countries to exercise true freedom of choice is the only conceivable goal in the light of American history and ideology and the most fruitful one in terms of American diplomatic strategy in the nuclear age.

2. ECONOMIC AND TRADE PROBLEMS IN ASIA

Poverty is one great common denominator that promotes a feeling of kinship among nations in the Afro-Asian bloc. By Asian standards, the lowest paid economic groups within the United States would appear wealthy beyond belief. By the end of the 1950's, the United States had a per capita income of more than $2,500 annually; Western Europe's was $1,150. The annual per capita income in Burma was $56 and in India $68. India's per capita income was close to the median for Asian countries, which means that many countries have considerably lower standards of living than India. China's per capita income at the beginning of the 1950's, for example, was estimated at $27 annually (**31**, p. 351; and **30**, September 6, 1959, dispatch by E. W. Kenworthy).

Another common denominator is the determination of most Asian countries to raise their standards of living and to translate newly-won political rights into tangible material benefits for their economically primitive societies. This goal dictates determined attacks by Asian countries on economic problems whose roots trace far back into history. They have caught a new vision of a better life in the material realm, but are sorely taxed to solve these problems within the limits of their own resources. In virtually every case they need outside assistance, no matter how hesitant they are to take substantial outside help, either from governmental or private sources.

American Economic Assistance to Asia

The early 1950's witnessed a major shift in large-scale economic assistance by the United States from Western Europe to nations in Africa, the Middle East, and Asia. In the mid-

1950's new technical assistance projects were inaugurated by the United States in Cambodia, Indonesia, South Korea, Laos, the Philippines, Thailand, and South Vietnam. By 1957 the pattern of technical assistance had shifted heavily in favor of countries in the Afro-Asian bloc, while Europe and Latin America received a small fraction of the total allocated by the United States for such purposes (20, Part VI, p. 1027-28). A corresponding shift occurred in the extension of *military* assistance funds. With the defeat of the French forces in Indochina in mid-1954, the United States began to exhibit a new interest in defense problems throughout Asia. A later portion of the chapter will call attention to many implications of this shift for American foreign policy. Here it is sufficient to observe that the overwhelming proportion of American assistance to Asian countries continues to be devoted to projects closely related to strengthening their military security positions.* According to a high-ranking ICA official, "There has been no uniformity in the pattern of aid given, such as in general characterized aid to Europe under the Marshall plan. Programs developed as the Communist menace spread progressively

---

*Data relating to individual countries are taken chiefly from a study of technical assistance programs throughout the Far East, Southeast Asia, and the Middle East, included in 40, pp. 527-48 and from subsequent hearings before the House Foreign Affairs Committee and the Senate Foreign Relations Committee on the President's budget allocations for the Mutual Security Program. Extensive information on the scope and nature of U. S. aid to Asian countries, together with discussions of problems encountered in providing such aid, is contained in the testimony of executive officials before these committees.

By the beginning of the 1960's, the Mutual Security program distinguished the following categories of foreign aid: *special assistance,* rendered to deal with emergency or extraordinary situations in particular countries; *technical assistance,* designed to make American technical know-how available, with the recipient countries providing most of the needed equipment; outright *military assistance,* designed to strengthen the host country's armed forces; and *defense support,* provided to enable weak countries to carry the economic burden that an expanded military effort entails. By the opening of the 1960's, out of a total of $1.2 billion requested by the Eisenhower Administration for Asian countries, about 75 per cent was allocated for military assistance and defense support activities, with this percentage nearly equally divided between these two categories.

through the Far East, and interests of the United States became increasingly affected" (20, Part VI, p. 1102). Programs evolved largely to meet specific needs of Asian countries, often as these needs were revealed by national economic surveys and plans for long-range economic development, and by the proximity of particular countries to centers of cold war conflict. The nature of American assistance will become clearer if we examine such assistance briefly within selected Asian countries.

Since the restoration of sovereignty to Japan in 1951, the United States has given that country limited technical assistance. The Japanese Productivity Center, a group of Japanese businessmen, has used the bulk of this aid to send Japanese industrial teams to the United States and to bring American business consultants to Japan. The goal has been to attack Japan's age-old foreign trade imbalance by increasing exports, while decreasing costs at home so as to make Japanese goods competitive throughout Asia.

In the economic assistance granted to the Republic of China on Formosa, the emphasis has been upon expanding educational facilities and upon increasing agricultural and natural resources production. Inevitably, the uncertain political future of Nationalist China has precluded the most effective use of long-range American assistance. The little state of South Vietnam, which came into existence after the conclusion of the armistice in Indochina in 1954, has faced baffling economic problems since its existence. Keeping the truncated state alive and out of the communist orbit has naturally had highest priority with the State Department. Worthwhile long-range projects for American technical assistance scheduled by the late 1950's were the introduction of "fish farming" in the rice paddies to provide an invaluable dietary supplement, trachoma control, malaria control, and public health training.

Thailand was among the first Asian nations to receive American economic assistance. American aid made possible limited progress in the fields of public administration, education, transportation, and public health. Maladministration by Thai officials and profiteering by entrenched economic groups have detracted from the program's value for the country as a whole.

Beginning in 1952, the United States extended economic assistance to Pakistan. Major projects have been undertaken in such fields as agriculture and natural resource development, industry, and mining. Poor administrative practices by both American and Pakistani officials, however, have marred the record of American assistance in this important country. For instance, in 1953 the United States made available a large shipment of wheat to relieve famine conditions in Pakistan; this shipment arrived with reasonable promptness but was allowed to lie in warehouses until the new wheat crop had come in the following year!

In India the United States by the 1960's had provided substantial economic assistance; India desired no outside military assistance. A Senate Foreign Relations Committee Study concluded in 1957 that "There are few American-aid programs outside Europe which have been more successful" (40, p. 543). In contrast to many other Asian states, India had made a careful survey of its needs and had scheduled five-year plans designed to attack problems systematically. The first plan, which ended in 1956, emphasized increased agricultural production and was from 80-90 per cent successful in achieving its goal. The second plan gives highest priority to heavy industry and capital goods expansion. The long-range goal is to double the Indian national income within ten years (3, *passim*). Under the second plan however, as under the first, India will have a sizable foreign exchange deficit, from $800 million to $1 billion dollars. Closing this gap will undoubtedly require outside assistance. Paradoxically, writes Chester Bowles, Indians are scornful of "American materialism," yet "the same champions of Indian timelessness are in a hurry, a terrible hurry, to develop and to catch up. They are thirsting after the material progress of the West and are determined that in India and in Asia it will be shared more broadly among all men" (5, p. 97).

Spectacular accomplishments on a limited scale have been achieved by the use of American funds in India for rural redevelopment and village planning. For the first time in centuries, a minority at least of India's teeming rural millions have caught a new vision of economic betterment and are being induced to cast aside ancient practices that perpetuate misery and backwardness. While India's economic problems remain in some ways as acute as ever, at least a beginning has been made. What may be more fundamental, a new spirit of enterprise and optimism permeates all levels of government and society (5, pp. 322-47; 40, pp. 542-44).

The New Communist Economic Offensive

The mid-1950's witnessed a significant increase in the tempo and scope of Soviet economic and military aid to countries outside the communist orbit. After the great power conference at Geneva in 1955, preceded by the settlement of the Korean and Indochinese conflicts, both sides stepped up their inducements to the uncommitted world. Pursuing its theme of "peaceful co-existence," the Kremlin sought to broaden its sphere of influence by reliance upon persuasion, reasonableness, and renewed interest in the material progress of backward countries. Said Khrushchev in 1956: "Today the underdeveloped countries need not go begging for up-to-date equipment" (33, p. 197). The objective was to convince nations in the Afro-Asian bloc that the cooing of the Soviet dove of peace would be translated into generous and continuing economic assistance from the communist bloc (40, p. 401).*

The distinguishing feature of the new Soviet economic offensive has been reliance upon liberal trade agreements, characterized by favorable prices, low interest rates for long-term loans; willingness to supply commodities, especially heavy industrial goods and technical know-how, needed in Africa, the Middle East, and Asia; and willingness to accept payment in the exportable products of these countries, chiefly agricultural surpluses. That Soviet offers have been highly appealing to many uncommitted nations can hardly be doubted. The capitalist United States has found itself faced with a shrewd competitor on the economic front. Successfully meeting this competition has challenged, and will continue to challenge,

---

*Data on communist bloc aid to non-communist countries are taken from 40, pp. 239-67; 399-462. These staff studies for the Senate Foreign Relations Committee are thorough and illuminating.

SOVIET TECHNICAL ASSISTANCE TO CRITICAL COUNTRIES

In Millions of U.S. Dollars, to mid-1959

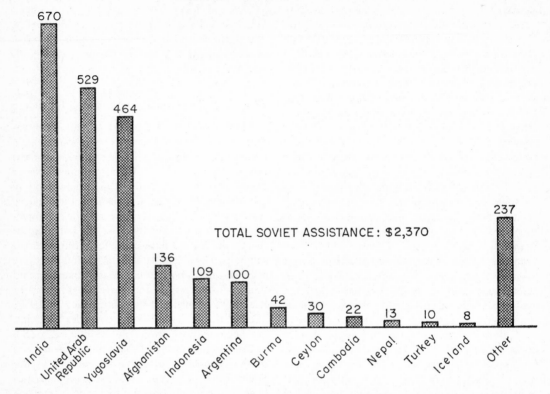

TOTAL SOVIET ASSISTANCE: $2,370

670 India
529 United Arab Republic
464 Yugoslavia
136 Afghanistan
109 Indonesia
100 Argentina
42 Burma
30 Ceylon
22 Cambodia
13 Nepal
10 Turkey
8 Iceland
237 Other

Figures from House Foreign Affairs Committee, *Hearings on the Mutual Security Act of 1958*. Part 7, p 908; and *Foreign Commerce Weekly*, 1959, *passim*.

the ingenuity of American policy-makers to the utmost. More concrete understanding of the nature of this challenge can be gained by looking at its manifestations in selected countries.

The strategically-located state of Afghanistan has been one target of Soviet economic penetration. All along, the Soviet Union had stressed the kinship that united the peoples of Afghanistan with the peoples living in neighboring Soviet Asian Republics. Then early in 1950 the USSR negotiated a new trade agreement with that country. This was followed in 1953 by a Soviet-Afghan loan agreement, by which Moscow extended assistance at low interest for the construction of wheat storage facilities. There followed still other trade agreements providing for Russian installation within Afghanistan of textile machinery, oil pumps, bakery equipment, and hospital equipment. By

1954 the Soviet Union had agreed to construct a 60-mile pipeline for oil, to build storage facilities, and to assist with oil surveys. Soviet help in paving the streets in the capital city, Kabul, provided eye-catching evidence of Russia's willingness to help and, as much as any other project, impressed Afghan opinion favorably. Other trade agreements followed, by which the Soviet Union agreed to provide consumer and industrial goods in exchange for Afghanistan's cotton and wool exports. The visit of Premier Bulganin and Communist Party chieftain Khrushchev late in 1955 resulted in a gift to Afghanistan of a 100-bed hospital and new buses for the city of Kabul. Then in 1956 a new Soviet credit of $100 million for 30 years at 2 per cent interest was made available, with repayment to be made in Afghanistan's exportable goods. By the spring of 1956, civil airline services had been established between Moscow and Kabul.

No country has been subject to as many Communist economic blandishments and offers of assistance as India. Stressing the theme that the USSR was not interested in an "armaments drive," the Kremlin has sought to convince India that its needs are of deep concern to communist countries. Trade relations between New Delhi and Moscow since Indian independence have not always been cordial, chiefly because India balked at Soviet prices and hesitated to admit large numbers of Soviet "technical advisers" into the country. But with the new communist "soft sell" after 1955 the Kremlin has spared no pains to make its terms palatable to New Delhi.

A new 5-year trade agreement was signed late in 1953. In it Russia's prices were considerably below earlier demands; the USSR promised to accept payments in Indian rupees; industrial goods sorely needed in India were to be supplied by Russia; and industrial installations were to be erected in India by Soviet technicians. Early in 1955 a Soviet-Indian agreement was reached providing for Russian construction of a one million ton steel mill, costing close to $100 million, at an interest rate of 2.5 per cent for twelve years. A follow-up agreement in 1956 provided for an Indian purchase of $105 million worth of Russian equipment for this plant. More limited forms of Soviet economic aid were studies of diamond mining in India, importation of Soviet tractors, and tours within Russia by Indian industrial and cultural groups.

The Bulganin-Khrushchev tour of Asia in 1956 brought further economic benefits to India. Significantly and typically, very little gratis assistance was furnished to India by Russia. A new agreement was reached, however, providing for expanded trade between the two countries. Items to be supplied by Russia met India's needs under its five-year plans: steel and heavy equipment for oil production and mining. Because of India's critical steel shortage and because of difficulty in buying steel at prices India could afford, the Soviet offer was "advanced at the precise moment when it could have a most favorable psychological effect" (**40**, p. 423). There was

no letup in the Soviet economic offensive in India after the Bulganin-Khrushchev visit. Later Soviet offers involved help to India in expanding electric power generation, aluminum production, establishment of air transportation between Moscow and New Delhi, additional equipment and technical advice for the oil industry, a gift of agricultural machinery, a new shipping agreement and agreements in several additional fields. By 1956, even Soviet European satellites—Poland, Rumania, and East Germany—had made offers to furnish industrial equipment required by New Delhi.

Offers from Russia, its satellites, and Red China have also been made to Indonesia to supply textile machinery, a ceramics plant, a rubber plant, a cement mill, and hydroelectric facilities. In Indonesia, as throughout Asia as a whole, the Kremlin has sought to capture the imagination and respect of peoples by lavish participation in trade fairs and industrial exhibitions, at which the theme is the "achievements" of Russia under communism and Russia's ability to collaborate with Asian states in the solution of their material problems. Such an approach has undoubtedly been effective. An American correspondent wrote concerning the Indonesian Trade Fair in 1954 that "The United States is taking a propaganda beating —by default—and the Russians are making propaganda hay . . . " (**40**, p. 433).

Two poignant examples of communist-free world economic competition are afforded by the cases of Burma and Ceylon. Divided internally in the recent period by communist and other factions, and deeply conscious of contiguous borders with Red China, Burma has been at pains to emphasize its neutrality in the cold war. In the 1953-54 period this course prompted Burma to terminate an American economic aid program. This step was also interpreted in the West as a protest by Burma against the inability or unwillingness of the United States to apply diplomatic pressure for ending intervention in Burma's northern provinces by remnants of Chinese Nationalist forces. Then early in 1954 a new Sino-Burmese trade agreement was announced, providing that China would take part of Burma's large rice surplus, along with beans, minerals, timber, and cotton; China in return would provide consumer goods and industrial raw materials. Soon the USSR announced its intention also of taking Burmese rice and of supplying industrial equipment.

Late in the same year Burma asked the United States to buy Burmese surplus rice for distribution to rice-deficient Asian countries. In exchange, Burma would buy industrial equipment and would employ American technicians to assist in economic expansion programs. The initial reaction of the United States to this proposal was hesitant, since the United States itself is one of the largest exporters of rice in the world market. At length, however, an agreement was reached for a comparatively small purchase, 10,000 tons of Burmese rice, in exchange for American technical services in Burma. Meantime, a Soviet-Burmese agreement on July 1, 1955, called for Burma to provide from 150,000 to 200,000 tons of rice and to receive metals, hardwood, rubber, and various kinds of industrial equipment from the USSR. Still other agreements followed, in which the USSR accepted additional rice and other Burmese exports for commodities needed in Burma.

Ceylon is another country in which the United States was in danger of being outmaneuvered by the communist bloc on the trade front. In 1952 Ceylon signed a 5-year trade agreement program with Red China calling for the shipment of rice to Ceylon and of rubber to Red China. This agreement—negotiated while the Korean War was still in progress—was strongly condemned in the West on the grounds that Ceylon had violated a resolution of the United Nations General Assembly of May 18, 1951, prohibiting trade in strategic goods with the communist bloc. Ceylon's reply was that the agreement had been reached only after the United States refused to buy Ceylonese rubber at favorable prices, had offered American rice at higher prices than Ceylon could pay, and had turned down a Ceylonese request for $50 million in American economic assistance. Communist China, on the other hand, bought Ceylonese rubber at 40 per cent above the world price. American-Ceylonese relations improved over the months that followed when a new economic aid agreement was worked out. This involved $5

million in aid for fiscal year 1956 and $6 million in aid for 1957. In addition to these sums, Ceylon also received over $16 million worth of aid in the period 1952-56 from Britain, Canada, and the Colombo Plan.*

Speaking generally, what kind of response ought the United States make in countering diplomatic maneuvers of this kind by the USSR? Undeniably, the Soviet Union possesses a marked advantage over the United States in its ability to subordinate economic and trade considerations to the achievement of political objectives. America neither can nor desires to approach economic issues on this basis. Still, in some cases it perhaps ought to take political and diplomatic interests more into account, even to the point of making "unprofitable" economic exchanges, when it is apparent that other countries, like Burma, are heavily dependent upon one or a few commodities for their economic, and very substantially their political, stability.

Persistent Issues in Aid to Asia

The United States, together with its allies and international bodies like the United Nations, has indicated its willingness to provide assistance to Asian nations that want outside

*This plan—officially called the "Colombo Plan for Cooperative Economic Development in South and Southeast Asia"—evolved out of a meeting of the foreign ministers of the British Commonwealth early in 1950. One authoritative study says that it is "not really a plan at all" but a "collection of plans, each of which is individually developed and implemented and none of which bears any necessary relationship to any other" (40, p. 211). Eventually seventeen countries joined this plan, including the United States which contributed to it directly and through the Export-Import Bank. The purpose of the plan was to deal with devastation and conditions of maladjustment growing out of World War II. Aid to Asian countries is made available on a bilateral basis between the donor and the recipient country (40, pp. 211-14).

In discussing the question of economic assistance in Asia, mention must also be made of the efforts carried on by various organs of the United Nations. Normally, the United States contributes from one-third to one-fourth of the budgets of such bodies as the Food and Agriculture Organization, the World Health Organization, the UN Educational, Scientific, and Cultural Organization, and the International Labor Organization. These bodies have done valuable work in such fields as disease control, improved sanitary practices, education, care of children, and medical training. For details, see 40, pp. 179-204; 41, pp. 18-28.

aid and demonstrate their capacity and willingness to utilize it beneficially. As in Western Europe, this aid has formed an important element in the free world's response to the threat of communist expansionism. In Asia it has helped in overcoming anti-Western sentiment and in furthering Western-Asian collaboration to combat widespread human misery. In certain countries in the Orient, American aid may well have been decisive in preventing, or at least mitigating, political crises which would almost certainly have increased the receptivity of these countries for communism or other species of authoritarian orders.

Our analysis thus far discloses a number of recurrent problems involving American economic assistance and trade with countries in the Far East. A dominant one is the sharp imbalance between the need for capital, as Asian countries define that need, and the ability of the United States, helped in some instances by other Western nations, to supply it. Very few countries in Asia believe that they are receiving as much Western assistance as they require. Even if aid were increased substantially, this would still be true, because their economic requirements are staggering. Nor are individual countries satisfied with any scale of priorities which allocates more American assistance to other countries than to them. Some countries receiving foreign aid tend to "compete" for American assistance and to feel that in some degree their national prestige hinges upon the extent to which they are successful in getting it. This is one reason why American officials have attempted, usually unsuccessfully, to keep confidential at least the amount of military and defense support aid earmarked for individual countries (**30**, May 31, 1959, dispatch by E. W. Kenworthy).

The apportionment of assistance between economic-technical and military-defense support categories also has occasioned considerable concern among officials of the American government. By 1960 a rift had developed between high-ranking executive officials and an influential group of legislators on this issue. The Eisenhower Administration's critics challenged the wisdom of continued large-scale military-defense support assistance to economically weak countries in Asia and elsewhere.

They doubted that such aid in most cases made any really constructive or enduring contribution to improving living standards in such countries or in raising industrial and agricultural productivity. Instead, they contended that nations accepting sizable military-defense support aid from the United States were inevitably required to divert a larger share of their own resources than formerly to non-productive ends, thus hindering their economic advancement. These critics argued that the surest road to security for such countries— particularly those that were comparatively remote from a Russian or Chinese military threat —was gradually to build firm foundations at home to support their own freely chosen political institutions. Greater emphasis by the United States upon this goal would more closely fulfill both America's purposes in shoring up free governments and the purposes of such governments in moving ahead economically and promoting human welfare.

This reasoning led the House Foreign Affairs Committee in 1959 to reduce the President's requests for military aspects of Mutual Security in Asian and Latin American countries. At the same time, the House increased allocations for economic assistance and, in a move strongly supported by influential Democratic members of the Senate Foreign Relations Committee, increased the lending authority of the Development Loan Fund, established to make loans to underdeveloped countries that were unable to get capital from existing sources. Concurrently, executive officials—who opposed expansion in *economic* assistance to underdeveloped countries only if it were done at the expense of *military* aid programs—proposed still other techniques for meeting the requirements of economically backward nations. One plan called for an International Development Authority, to be placed under the UN-sponsored International Bank for Reconstruction and Development (or World Bank). These proposals were made within an overall context of heightened awareness in Washington that (1) the level of economic assistance to underdeveloped nations must be increased, and (2) new departures and policy guidelines—emphasizing assistance through multinational bodies like the United Nations—were demanded.

Aid programs also are troubled by the always delicate matter of finding an equilibrium between America's insistence upon effective use of aid and the recipient country's sensitivity about infringements, real or fancied, upon its sovereignty. Both interests are of course legitimate. But whether they can always be reconciled in specific situations, and the specific forms attempted reconciliations take in individual cases, are problems that challenge to the utmost the ingenuity of policy-makers both in Washington and the Far East.

The United States desires, within the limits of its resources, to aid foreign countries to advance economically, both for humanitarian reasons and because this goal accords with America's overall cold war strategy. Unquestionably, the latter reason is often a stronger motivating impulse than the former. At the same time, the United States properly demands that foreign countries utilize American aid in a manner specified in bilateral aid agreements, the conditions of which are in turn laid down by Congress or, in some cases, left to the discretionary power of the President. Both logic and international law support the proposition that any country is theoretically free to make its resources available to other countries on terms acceptable to itself and to insist upon compliance with conditions agreed upon. Moreover, experiences like the fiasco of massive aid to the Nationalist Government of China right after World War II ought to have shattered any lingering illusion that indiscriminate American aid *per se* achieves the nation's diplomatic purposes. Even so vigorous an advocate of expanded economic assistance programs as Chester Bowles emphasizes the necessity for continuing supervision and careful planning of projects. While he labels American technical assistance programs "the most powerful constructive program against chaos and communism which the free world has devised," he believes nonetheless that "Our assistance is generally a waste of money in any country which is unwilling to put its own house in order" (5, pp. 324, 334).

Despite increasing departures from it within recent years (18, pp. 209-324), officially the United States remains as attached as ever to the historic doctrine of "non-intervention in the internal affairs of other countries." The nation's dedication to the principle is resoundingly affirmed on every appropriate occasion, especially if the United States is dealing with Anglo-French intervention in Egypt, Russian intervention in Hungary, or Chinese intervention in Tibet. The principle is at the core of the free world's efforts to keep non-communist countries out of the communist orbit. Furthermore, other nations, especially those that have experienced Western colonialism, are apt to judge America by the degree to which it adheres to its professed creed. The conflict between the non-intervention principle and America's natural desire to see its aid utilized beneficially, therefore, presents formidable difficulties for foreign policy officials. Insistence upon adequate safeguards to insure proper use of aid clearly risks violation of the non-intervention principle—to the point perhaps that some nations might follow the lead of Burma in refusing for a time to participate in foreign assistance programs. A take-it-or-leave-it attitude in Washington may be psychologically satisfying to many Americans, but it does not achieve the objectives sought in the foreign aid program, the chief of which is building the security of the non-communist world. On the other hand, provision of aid without any "strings" can be equally futile, if aid is siphoned into black markets and private bank accounts or dissipated on extravagances and projects of questionable merit.

Perhaps the middle course between Scylla and Charybdis—attaching as few strings as possible and insisting upon the minimum degree of American "supervision"—is the proper approach. In fact, this has tended to be the course followed by the United States in dealing with many countries in the Afro-Asian bloc. As the least of evils, it may be the only feasible alternative. Yet the shortcomings of this policy too must be recognized. In seeking to escape from both extremes, this approach can encounter still other obstacles. Officials and segments of public opinion within the United States can become convinced that so few conditions for accepting American aid exist that, for all practical purposes, no significant control is exercised by the American government at all. Officials and groups in recipient countries can become convinced that the "strings" existing are sufficient to constitute an intolerable threat to their sovereignty and to prove that in practice America has abandoned the non-intervention principle. In short, a policy of moderate conditions and supervision can possess the weaknesses of all compromises: by seeking to satisfy everyone, the policy may satisfy no one. The quest for the best of both worlds sometimes achieves merely the worst of both worlds.

The conclusion to be drawn may be merely the obvious truth that in foreign affairs, as in all other spheres of human experiences, there sometimes exists no attainable "ideal" solution to outstanding problems. The tension between the desirable and the possible pervades all levels of political behavior, affecting some

problems more than others. In problems of this kind, the "solution," if it can be called that, clearly is to be found in efforts both by the United States and countries receiving its assistance to avoid doctrinaire positions that make agreements impossible, to recognize a mutual interest in resolving deadlocks, and to accept the fact that neither side is likely to be totally satisfied with agreements reached. The American people and their officials will probably have to reconcile themselves to more waste and inefficiency in foreign aid programs for Afro-Asian countries than was the case, for example, with the Marshall Plan, viewing this as part of the price that must be paid for *any* reasonably successful aid program involving countries that are still deeply sensitive to the faintest intimation of Western control over them.

3. DEFENSE AND SECURITY IN THE PACIFIC

The strategic importance of Asia arises from a number of factors. India and Southeast Asia, along with Indonesia, lie athwart the main sea and air routes connecting Europe and the Middle East with the Far East. Japan, Formosa, Okinawa, the Philippines, and many lesser Pacific islands, form links in the defense chain safeguarding the military approaches to the Western Hemisphere and to two stalwart Western allies, Australia and New Zealand. Southeast Asia offers sources of food and raw materials needed both within and outside Asia. This region, for instance, supplies 90 per cent of the world's natural rubber and 55 per cent of its tin. Added to these considerations is the fact that the outcome of the ideological conflict that has divided the world since World War II could well be decided by the ultimate direction taken by several key nations in Asia.

Threats to the peace and security of the Far East can arise from a variety of sources. We have already discussed one of these: economic dislocations fostering political turbulence. Two additional threats exist: the danger of outright Soviet or Chinese, or possibly joint, aggression in Asia; and the danger of Communist infiltration and subversion of governments in this vital region. These threats merit detailed examination.

Diplomatic Ambitions of Russia and China

Throughout history both Russia and China have exhibited imperialistic ambitions toward Asia. Afghanistan, India, Tibet, and China, especially its mineral-rich northern province of Manchuria, were objectives of Russian diplomacy under the Czars, both because these territories would be valuable additions to Imperial Russia's domain and because they would advance the ancient Russian goal of finding outlets to the sea. Russian territorial designs in Afghanistan and along India's northern borders were in the main unsuccessful. Great Britain, working in close collaboration with the anti-Russian Chinese Imperial government, successfully "neutralized" these strategic approaches to southern Asia, thereby preventing Russian penetration into countries bordering the Indian Ocean. Greater success crowned Russian expansionist efforts in China itself. By the end of the 19th century, wholesale concessions in Central Asia, Manchuria, and the ports and railroads of north China had been wrung from the weak Chinese government. Even after the Communist victory in China in the recent period, Moscow has been reluctant to part with concessions and privileges exacted from feeble Chinese governments in the past, includ-

354

COMMUNIST CHINA PRESSES OUTWARD

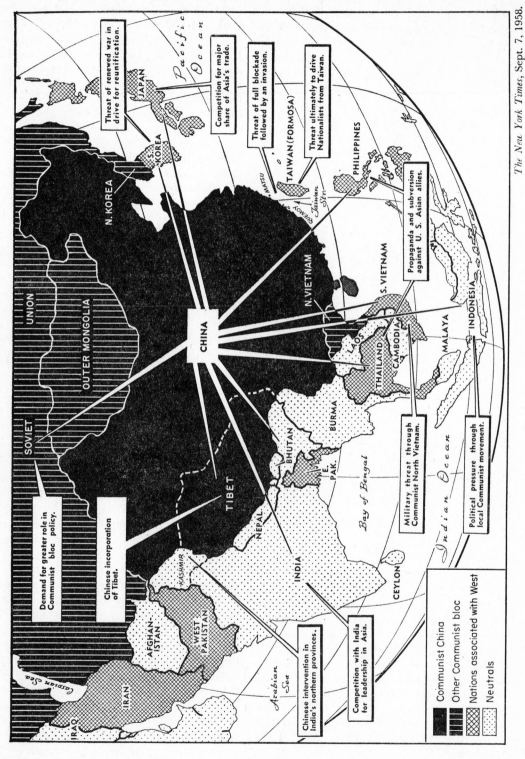

The New York Times, Sept. 7, 1958.

Threat of renewed war in drive for reunification.

Competition for major share of Asia's trade.

Threat of full blockade followed by an invasion.

Threat ultimately to drive Nationalists from Taiwan.

Propaganda and subversion against U. S. Asian allies.

Demand for greater role in Communist bloc policy.

Chinese incorporation of Tibet.

Military threat through Communist North Vietnam.

Political pressure through local Communist movement.

Chinese intervention in India's northern provinces.

Competition with India for leadership in Asia.

Pacific Ocean

Indian Ocean

Arabian Sea

Caspian Sea

Bay of Bengal

SOVIET UNION

OUTER MONGOLIA

JAPAN

S. KOREA

N. KOREA

CHINA

TAIWAN (FORMOSA)

MATSU

QUEMOY

Taiwan Str.

PHILIPPINES

N. VIETNAM

S. VIETNAM

LAOS

THAILAND

CAMBODIA

MALAYA

INDONESIA

BURMA

BHUTAN

NEPAL

E. PAK.

INDIA

TIBET

KASHMIR

AFGHAN-ISTAN

WEST PAKISTAN

IRAN

IRAQ

CEYLON

Communist China

Other Communist bloc

Nations associated with West

Neutrals

COMMUNIST CHINA: POWER GIANT OF ASIA

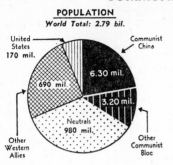
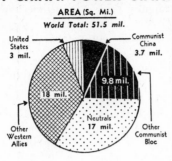
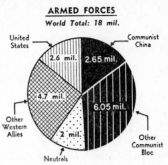

The New York Times, Sept. 7, 1958.

ing those gained by Russia at the Yalta Conference in 1945. In the light of the present-day Moscow-Peiping Axis, it is ironic to reflect upon the fact that Russian diplomatic ambitions in the Orient were largely responsible for American advocacy of the policy of the Open Door late in the 19th century.

Far less well understood in the West today, however, is the extent to which threats to the security of Asia have arisen, and continue to arise, from Chinese diplomatic ambitions. Americans, as was emphasized early in this chapter, have clung to an idealized image of China which has neither accorded with the mainstream of Chinese history nor facilitated the evolution of more realistic American policies toward that country. They have believed that China was a peace-loving, democratically-inclined country which over the course of history has been more sinned against than sinning. This conception is at variance with the Chinese diplomatic record. China's most consistent diplomatic ambition under the Communists and earlier regimes has been

the establishment of China as a recognized world power with a position of primacy in East Asia. This is not a uniquely Communist aim; it is one which has deep roots in traditional Chinese thinking. . . . Traditional Chinese attitudes have led many Chinese to believe that their country naturally deserves leadership in Asia and hegemony over surrounding areas. Chinese do not forget that if one views the last two millennia rather than the past century China had been the strongest country in Asia over long periods, and many Asian countries have at some time been tributary to China. (2, p. 147).

Werner Levi points out that in the contemporary period Red China presents itself as "the savior of all Asia, leading its peoples to a glorious future." Especially significant to an understanding of present-day Chinese policy is the fact that "the area of major interest, Southeast Asia, is also the area in which imperial China had or claimed a paramount position . . . " (26, p. 329). Creation and maintenance of a system of satellite countries—known in earlier diplomatic parlance as "client states" —has been a recurrent practice in Chinese policy throughout history. In earlier periods Chinese dominion extended over what are now the states of North and South Korea, North and South Vietnam, Laos, Cambodia, Thailand —formerly Siam—, Burma, Tibet, Nepal, and parts of Malaya and Indonesia. A recent report by an authoritative British study group holds that today "the Central People's Government will aim at the formation around China of a ring of satellites under Chinese influence, following in many respects the Chinese political way of life, insulating China's borders from undesirable contacts" (37, pp. 58-9).

The evidence since 1950 strongly supports this prediction. Peiping has scored considerable success in achieving its goal: North Korea is a *de facto* Chinese satellite; North Vietnam may not be a satellite, but Ho Chi Minh has established intimate ties with China; the political future of South Vietnam, even by the early 1960's, remained in considerable doubt, with the threat of a Chinese-engineered *coup* an everpresent possibility; the Kingdom of Laos has been shaken periodically by the Communist-led "Pathet Lao" forces, aided by China; Burma, while professing neutralism, has been careful to avoid antagonizing Peiping; Indonesia intermittently shows evidence of gravitating closer and closer to the communist orbit; the little country of Thailand is, on the surface, militantly anti-communist, but Bangkok is obviously becoming increasingly conscious of the necessity to reach some kind of *modus vivendi* with the Chinese colossus to the north (37, pp. 60-3; 43, 1955, p. 127).

Two factors within recent years have enhanced the ability of Peiping to influence the actions of surrounding states in Asia. One is the new posture of reasonableness and seeming friendship toward its neighbors which China was at pains to exhibit until the late 1950's, when its ruthless incorporation of Tibet and its machinations in India's northern provinces began to arouse formerly friendly nations against its ambitions. The desire of Red China to conciliate its neighbors emerged graphically at the Bandung Conference of Afro-Asian states in 1955, where Foreign Minister Chou En-lai's apparent willingness to maintain harmonious relations with smaller countries stood in marked contrast to Red China's earlier truculence and bellicosity in approaching a variety of issues in Asia (32, pp. 65-83; 43, 1955, pp. 106-07). Both Moscow and Peiping have found—especially in the light of the Soviet suppression of the Hungarian revolt in 1956—that policies of reasonableness and co-operation toward weaker states can sometimes accomplish more than policies of bluff and bluster. The second factor that enhances Red China's ability to exercise great influence throughout Asia is the presence in many of these countries of substantial "overseas Chinese" minorities. As far back as the 14th century, Chinese have emigrated to other countries, and after the 19th century this movement reached large proportions. Estimates today place the total number of overseas Chinese at from ten to thirteen million people, with the vast majority living in Southeast Asia and Indonesia. Chinese governments in the past have always looked upon these peoples as citizens of China, irrespective of where they lived or even whether they had acquired citizenship in other countries. Although Peiping has attempted to reassure surrounding Asian countries that their Chinese residents will not be disloyal, their mere presence—coupled with

the fact that they often occupy positions of economic power—constitutes a persistent source of tension between China and neighboring states (27, pp. 258-71; 37, pp. 75-90).

The Moscow-Peiping Axis

How does the professed ideological affinity between the two most powerful communist states on the globe, Russia and China, affect the problem of security in Asia? Certainly the prospect for preserving the independence of still-free Asian states grew dimmer with the forging of the Moscow-Peiping Axis after 1949. When the nearly six hundred million people of China are added to the more than two hundred million people in Russia, and to the people in the Soviet satellites, the free world faces somewhere around one billion people in the communist orbit. Territorially, the communist world stretches from the Pacific and the China Sea to the Adriatic, the gates of Berlin, and the Baltic Sea. Not since the time of Genghis Khan has such an empire appeared in history.

Outwardly, the Moscow-Peiping Axis has appeared monolithic and immune to the stresses and strains often characteristic of alliances between powerful countries—so much so that a State Department memorandum in mid-1958 stated that "the two partners in the Sino-Soviet alliance clearly realize their mutual dependence and attach great importance to bloc unity *vis-à-vis* the free world." The memorandum held there was "no evidence" for believing that "it would be possible to exert leverage on the Peiping regime which might ultimately be successful in weakening or even breaking the bond with Moscow" (30, August 10, 1958). Outwardly, both countries have tried to prevent misunderstandings from weakening the bonds between them. Russia has been more conciliatory in dealing with Red China than with any other country in the international community since 1917. In a number of instances the USSR has evidently compromised on potential sources of disagreement, even when Russian national interests might have dictated a firmer policy (26, pp. 310-18; 4, pp. 142-98).

Ideologically, the Moscow-Peiping Axis is held together by the postwar innovation in communist thought which concedes that there are "different paths to Socialism." Having confounded earlier communist oracles by experiencing a revolution based almost exclusively on the peasantry, China has since attempted to reconcile its experience with classic Marxist-Leninist-Stalinist dogma. The result has been the ingenious "different paths" theory which, in the words of an announcement from Peiping in 1951, means that "The classic type of revolution in the imperialist countries is the October revolution" in Russia. But the "classic type of revolution in the colonial and semicolonial countries is the Chinese revolution, the experience of which is invaluable for the peoples of these countries" (4, pp. 42-3).

Existence of the Sino-Russian *entente* raises formidable problems for Western defense efforts in the Pacific. By precept, example, and tactics designed to woo Asian states rather than by outright military aggression, the new communist axis is likely to make its influence felt for decades to come. Boorman believes that:

As Moscow and Peking look out on Communist Asia, they feel confident that, in a more or less prolonged period of relaxed tension, their growing political, economic and military strength will bring great gains, especially through their efforts to monopolize the emotions released by waves of anti-imperialism, national liberation, and modernization. . . . The expectation of Moscow and Peking is that, after a period of "peaceful competition," their axis will be stronger, and its opponents weaker, than they are now. (4, p. 227).

And yet there may have been some tendency within the United States, and throughout the West generally, since 1949-50 to accept far too uncritically Communist claims about the durability of the Moscow-Peiping Axis and to ignore a number of actual and potential sources of conflict between these two poles of the international communist movement. Let us analyze first the sphere of ideological kinship in which the two countries have professed the closest affinity and unity of purpose. Even here, officials in Moscow and Peiping have not altogether succeeded in hiding differences over the proper interpretation of the Marxist creed. The very existence of the communist order in China is a refutation of Marxist truth, as expounded by the Kremlin. Mao Tse-tung and his followers showed that a successful commu-

nist movement could be created and maintained primarily by the peasantry rather than an urban proletariat. As we have already observed, this required a significant modification of Marxist-Leninist-Stalinist thought, resulting in the "different paths to Socialism" theory. There have been many other disagreements over the meaning and application of Marxist principles between Russian and Chinese Communists since the 1920's. Not until the postwar period, after it became reasonably apparent that communist forces were winning the Chinese civil war, did Moscow evince any significant willingness to work in close and continuing harmony with indigenous communist leaders in China. Following Chiang Kai-shek's overthrow, the two great centers of global communism seemed to co-operate in complete harmony. Gradually, however, Western observers have begun to detect symptoms of major doctrinal disputes within the communist orbit.

An illustrative incident occurred late in 1958 when there were evident differences between Moscow and Peiping over the question of how and when communist countries like Russia and China were to make the transition from socialism into the ultimate utopia, communism. The Chinese Communist hierarchy thought it had discovered the answer: the promised land of communism would be reached by adoption of the "commune" system whereby hundreds of millions of people were enlisted in tightly regimented labor forces and put to work raising productive levels in agriculture and industry. Despite the fact that the communes were meeting opposition from China's vast, family-oriented peasantry, Peiping offered the commune system as the long-missing key that would open the door to the final communist stage, the stage of material plenty and the "classless society." As Harry Schwartz has written, this was in effect a claim "to ideological leadership of world communism, since it implied that Peiping had found a magic formula for doing in a few years what Moscow has not been able to do in more than four decades" (30, February 15, 1959). This bold assertion of initiative in doctrinal affairs did not go unchallenged in Moscow. At the meeting of the Twenty-first Soviet Party Congress early in 1959, a meeting from which Chinese party leaders were conspicuously absent, Premier Khrushchev and other party functionaries sharply criticized the ideological innovations emanating from Chinese quarters. Furthermore, in an interview with United States Senator Hubert Humphrey (Democrat from Minnesota) in the same period, Khrushchev stated flatly that the Chinese commune system, remarkably like Soviet efforts to "collectivize" the Russian peasantry, would fail. Moscow's open disapproval ultimately resulted in a not totally unexpected "correction" in the viewpoints of communist leaders in Peiping. It did not escape notice in the West that a new trade agreement giving China urgently needed industrial machinery was announced during this same period (**30**, February 15, 1959).

What country is the *ultimate* interpreter of communist thought, the infallible source of Marxist truth? This is the pivotal issue in this and other ideological differences. Before the communist victory in China, there was no doubt about the answer. Evidence is accumulating, however, that Peiping is no longer content with an inferior status. As a group, China's communist leaders are "senior" to those who have governed Russia since the death of Stalin. Russia's Premier Khrushchev achieved prominence only after 1953; and most of the followers of Stalin who survived his death and the purges instituted afterward have been removed from positions of power in the USSR. The communist movement in China gained victory under leaders like Mao Tse-tung, who have labored in the communist vineyard for over thirty years. Moreover—and this fact could hardly be exaggerated in understanding Sino-Soviet relations—the Chinese Communists came into power with minimum help from the USSR. Unlike the "people's democracies" that have been propped up by the bayonets of the Red Army in Eastern Europe, the Chinese communist government owes very little to Moscow. Instead, there may well exist a reservoir of ill-will and mistrust deriving from Russia's niggardly support during the period when the future of communism in China hung in the balance and from Russia's obvious lack of concern for the future of China when the Red Army looted Manchuria at the end of World War II.

These considerations well-nigh guarantee that Peiping will reserve considerable freedom of action in defining China's role in the communist family of nations. For example, Peiping made no secret of its support for movements in countries like Poland and Hungary, aimed at securing some relaxation of the Kremlin's iron grip upon these countries. It has not hesitated to cast its weight against the Soviet Union's virtual monopoly of power in weaker communist countries (**30**, June 30, 1957, dispatch by Harry Schwartz). Evident dissatisfaction and lack of enthusiasm in Peiping were visible both during the visit to the United States by Russia's First Deputy Premier Anastas I. Mikoyan early in 1959 and the visit of Premier Khrushchev in September. Mikoyan's visit did not stop Peiping's propaganda machine from grinding out scurrilous anti-American sentiment, calculated to imbue the masses with the proper incentive to support China's "big leap" forward in economic affairs. Constant reference to America's hostile intentions toward China apparently was one effective spur to greater efforts by the masses.

With both Mikoyan's and Khrushchev's visits, the Kremlin faced the same embarrassment growing out of the actions of its powerful Asian partner. At the very time the USSR was calling vocally for a "lessening" of world tensions and bearing down upon its theme of "peaceful co-existence," Peiping was maintaining a heated propaganda barrage against the United States and the free world generally. During Khrushchev's tour, obvious Chinese intervention in the affairs of Laos, aimed at subverting or overrunning that government, weakened Khrushchev's contention that the two camps could live in peace. In his contacts with the American people, Khrushchev seemed unusually sensitive to any references about the actions of Red China. Off and on during the late 1950's, Peiping appeared determined to make one point clear to the international community: Red China did not intend to stand idly by and watch the crucial questions in world politics negotiated at a "summit" meeting among heads-of-state of powerful Western countries and Russia. China might be a *communist* power; but it also was a great power whose rulers showed no inclination to have key decisions made "for them" by the Kremlin!

Paul Wohl has astutely commented that " . . . Soviet-Chinese relations have two sides —party relations and power relations." And it could well be the latter—which Wohl defines as dealing with "the respective dynamism of the two great Communist states"—that could prove crucial in shaping future relations between Moscow and Peiping (9, February 5, 1959, dispatch by Paul Wohl). For it is even more in this realm than in the ideological that fissures have appeared in the wall of communist solidarity. This fact should surprise no Westerner familiar with Asian history, least of all students familiar with the broad stream of American diplomatic history. It need only be recalled that it was largely to prevent further *Russian* expansionism and influence in China that the Open Door policy was formulated at the turn of the century. Throughout history, the Russian and Chinese empires have clashed over important territories like Manchuria, Outer and Inner Mongolia, Sinkiang, and Tibet. Both countries have been propelled by imperialist tendencies in the Orient, not infrequently at the expense of each other. Nathaniel Peffer makes the following judgment about the new Communist diplomacy toward China: " . . . the strategy for world revolution coincided point for point with the historic strategy of old Russia. It worked to the interest of world revolution to strike at Great Britain in Asia; but it had also worked to the interest of Tsarist expansion to strike at Great Britain in Asia." Imperialist-minded Russian Czars "might gleefully have burned Lenin at the stake, but they would also have applauded his foreign policy." Referring to more recent experience, Peffer asks: "Was Russia in Asia after World War II Marx on the march or Peter the Great and Nicholas II on the march?" (34, pp. 288-89). About Soviet Russia's demands upon China at the time of the Yalta Conference of 1945, Peffer comments:

. . . while China's sovereignty was restored and all special rights cancelled by other Powers, Russia—once more, titular patron of all downtrodden colonial peoples—got back all its classical imperialist tokens. In this respect in the Far East Russia has never acted out of its traditional character since the Bolshevik revolution. (34, p. 421).

Even today, it is probable that Peiping would be only slightly less reconciled to Soviet hegemony over countries like India or Burma than to American hegemony over them. Similarly, Moscow cannot be totally insensitive to the possible implications of Chinese expansionism into Tibet, to China's colonizing activities along the Sino-Soviet border, and to Peiping's self-assumed mandate to provide "leadership" in lifting Asian countries out of their backwardness. In several instances since 1949, power conflicts have penetrated the veil of Communist solidarity. Western observers spotted significant differences between Moscow and Peiping over the fate of Formosa and the off-shore Chinese islands. Red China has been uncompromising in its declared determination to "liberate" these islands from Nationalist rule and alleged "American domination." Moscow seems deeply impressed with the seriousness of this lingering Far Eastern crisis as a possible cause of a new global war; apparently, the Kremlin has tried to temper Chinese belligerency toward the Formosa issue. Russia's proposal early in 1959 for the creation of a "zone of peace" in the Pacific, however, elicited no enthusiasm in Chinese circles (30, February 15, 1959). Similarly, by the late 1950's Soviet officials were making no attempt to disguise their apprehensions over Chinese offers to provide economic assistance to countries like Mongolia, Albania, and Yemen; such offers were competing with Soviet activities in these areas. In the same period, too, informed Western observers detected signs of Soviet displeasure at Peiping's policy of resettling nearly 1.5 million Chinese in underpopulated provinces bordering the USSR; the Kremlin had experienced minimum success in luring large numbers of settlers to these areas (9, February 5, 1959).

Tensions have also cropped out in Sino-Soviet economic relationships. Two specific issues—the nature of Soviet economic assistance to China and the terms of trade between the two countries—have engendered controversies that could not be altogether concealed behind the façade of ideological kinship. As an illustration, a new nine-year trade agreement was announced early in 1959, in which the USSR agreed to send China $1.25 billion in industrial machinery and technical assistance, or a modest average of about $140 million per year. The Soviet Union generally provides economic assistance in the form of loans as opposed to outright grants, although the interest on such loans and the terms of repayment are often generous. Even Russia's chief ally was no exception to this practice; China would have to repay the principal and interest charges out of its future production. The nine-year trade agreement, while undoubtedly tailored to satisfy China's needs, could hardly be labelled generous; it provided only a fraction of the assistance necessary to raise the country's agricultural and industrial productivity appreciably. The agreement left the question open whether China could meet its needs completely by relying upon the USSR or whether with the passage of time China might decide that it is advantageous to cultivate more friendly contacts with Western countries.

Evidence available to Western observers about the actual course of Sino-Soviet relations may be likened to an iceberg: conflicts that are visible may be no more than suggestive of those beneath the surface of outward collaboration between China and Russia. Often it is possible only to speculate about such matters, on the basis of very few clues and reasonable hypotheses. Nevertheless, recent experience is certainly sufficient to caution against uncritical acceptance of Communist declarations of complete unity of purpose or suggestions that the Moscow-Peiping Axis is immune from the ordinary stresses and strains known to all alliances in history. For there remains one force not yet alluded to that, more than any other factor, will test the durability of that alliance: China's exploding population. By the opening of the 1960's, demographers estimated China's population at approximately 650 million persons—one-fourth of the human race! The population of China is expanding at a rate well above the world average, with 15 million people added annually. Studies by agencies of the United Nations estimate that China's population in 1975 will be nearly 900 million, and that by the end of the century China will possibly have

more than 1.5 billion people! As China's mushrooming population presses against the country's limited food supplies and productive capacities, despite economic expansion in the years ahead, there may well set in an almost irresistible temptation for millions of Chinese to push into adjacent territories. Russian territories, may offer the most promising sites available for untold millions of Chinese.

Since 1949 Russia has been the more diplomatically pliable partner of the Moscow-Peiping Axis, has been less addicted to recklessness and adventurism in dealing with the West, and has manifested more "maturity" in that it has repeatedly sought to prevent disputes with the West from igniting a new global war. Thus Soviet pressure on China was likely a key factor in securing agreement on an armistice ending the Korean War and in gaining a settlement of the Indochinese conflict in 1954. And by the late 1950's it was Moscow again, in the face of evident diplomatic foot-dragging in Peiping, that was taking the lead in proposing summit discussions with Western officials (**26**, pp. 52-8, 234-35; **4**, pp. 46-7, 101-103, 202-07; **2**, pp. 147-62; **30**, August 17, 1958).

The most significant fact about China today may be not so much that it has a communist government as that, after many years of internal weakness and vulnerability to outside control, China is a politically unified country. For the first time in decades, China's rulers possess both the power and the determination to pursue foreign policy objectives of their own. This is far from suggesting that by the opening of the 1960's the Moscow-Peiping Axis was on the verge of disintegration. It is merely to point out that, with the passage of time, China's steady accretion in power, coupled with the resurgence of many of its historic policies in Asia and its expanding population, may drive the country's rulers into a course of growing independence in world affairs. In brief, China's accession to the ranks of the great powers may ultimately prove as revolutionary for Sino-Soviet relations as it has proved for relations between China and the West. It is not inconceivable that China might decide someday that its own national interest was better served by improving rela-

"We Can Always Expand Into Russia"
© 1958, *New York Herald Tribune*, Inc.

cause? What will be the future overall context of communist bloc—free world relations, within which relations with Red China will have to be evaluated? These are variables in the equation of Sino-American relations. The only certainty would seem to be that American relationships with Red China will not long remain static, that they are bound to be shaped by important trends in the international community. The continuing problem facing foreign policy officials and citizens in the United States, therefore, will be weighing the impact of these forces carefully and re-assessing America's approach to the greatest power on the Asian scene in the light of them. For if one thing is plain on the basis of recent American experience in dealing with events in China, it is that policies that have lost touch with reality, that are based upon stereotyped thinking and emotional attachment to hopeless causes, are a sure road to diplomatic impotence. Persistence in the kind of thinking that has supported such policies might ultimately jeopardize the role of the United States as the leader of the free world coalition.

The Appeal of Communism in Asia

Closely allied to the danger of outright aggression by communist powers in Asia is the imminent threat of widespread communist infiltration and subversion of free governments in the Orient. In many of these countries the harvest is ripe and the communist laborers are many, dedicated, and exceedingly capable.

A number of intertwined and mutually dependent factors coalesce to make Asia peculiarly vulnerable to communist penetration. Uppermost, because it is probably the most basic condition favoring communism, is the continuing nationalist ferment in Asia, especially in its more extreme manifestations. Communists have had significant success in identifying their cause with the aspirations of hundreds of millions of Orientals. Countries like India, Indonesia, Burma, and Laos do not disguise their open admiration for at least certain features and achievements of the Soviet state since 1917. Political leaders in these countries find many parallels between problems confronting their own people and those faced throughout

tions with the West than by too intimate reliance upon a country whose policies dictate subordination of the interests of weaker states to those of the Kremlin. And it cannot be completely ruled out that as the years pass, both Russia and countries in the free world will find it to their mutual advantage to arrive at a *rapprochement* to safeguard their vital interests against this expansive Asian giant!

The exact implications for American foreign policy of the factors and possibilities discussed above—forces that may well take generations to become fully operative—cannot of course be determined with precision. Will Red China, like Soviet Russia, ultimately subordinate many of its professed doctrinal goals to the solution of pressing internal problems? As the communist regime matures, will it lose much of its truculence and hostility to powerful Western countries? Will China's rulers ultimately come to see that the results of a new global war would be disastrous for them, as well as for their enemies? Will the United States in time decide that communism is in China to stay and no amount of wishful thinking can restore the defeated Nationalist recent history by the Soviet society. Particularly impressive to their minds has been the USSR's ability to deal with age-old agrarian problems, to make spectacular progress toward industrialization, and to abolish racial and ethnic discriminations, at least officially. To a greater or lesser degree these goals are common to every country in Asia. Even more than Russia, however, Red China's record has been closely watched throughout Asia. China's problems—landlords versus peasantry, poor agricultural yields, the pressure of population on food supplies, the termination of foreign concessions within the country—are more common to Asia than are many of Russia's problems.

Referring to communism's appeals to Asians, Van Der Kroef observes that

> no other ideology, religious or political, has offered as understandable an explanation of their present predicament, or has stressed so heavily the need for loyalty and sacrifice to a program of action designed to solve their problems. (45, p. 297).

Communist groups in Asia have experienced considerable success in "running against" the bogey of Western colonialism, long after many Western colonial empires in Asia and elsewhere had been liquidated or were in the process of liquidation. The anti-colonialist issue has persisted because it is emotionally satisfying to certain groups and peoples in Asia and because it has its roots in widespread Asian disillusionment over the continued existence of deeply imbedded social cleavages, formidable economic difficulties, and conditions of political disequilibrium. Asian nationalist groups held high hopes for their countries after colonial domination had been terminated. Many of these hopes were undoubtedly utopian and have not been realized. According to Van Der Kroef, "The bright greeting of the Millennium did not await Southeast Asians on the day of liberation, as so many of them had confidently expected." He continues that "It is doubtful if the average Southeast Asian is economically any better off today than when he was in the colonial period . . . " (45, p. 297). The morning after, so to speak, has brought realization that bedrock problems remain to be solved and that most Asian societies

will be sorely challenged to solve them for an indefinite period in the future.

This condition is ready-made for successful and prolonged communist agitation throughout Asia. Communist spokesmen can assert that nationalist revolutions must be continued under their direction, that they must be "completed" by those uniquely fitted for such tasks. Pending creation of stable conditions in Asia, Communists exploit the omnipresent spectre of Western imperialism, a force supposedly ever-vigilant for new opportunities to reimpose colonial bondage on Asia. Communists contend that they alone possess the leadership qualities and insights necessary to achieve nationalist demands and, in the process, to preserve national security in the face of the ubiquitous imperialist threat (45, pp. 291-97; 23, pp. 74-105; 22, pp. 159-67).

Yet whatever its current appeal for Asians, Americans ought to be wary of overemphasizing international communism's role in *creating* disequilibria throughout the Far East. For it was Western countries that initially ignited the fuse of Asian nationalism and held out a new vision of material progress; and in this process the United States played a central role. In providing an impetus for nationalism in Asia, no force was more revolutionary than Wilsonian idealism. Referring to the reception accorded Wilson's Fourteen Point in politically-backward areas, Nathaniel Peffer has written that "It may not be an exaggeration to say that in modern times only the Communist Manifesto of Karl Marx was more subversive. Indeed, in the relations of empires and colonies Marx was probably less subversive than Wilson." Peffer is convinced that idealists like Wilson did more to bring about political ferment in Asia "than Nikolai Lenin and Josef Stalin. Certainly he prepared the ground for Lenin and Stalin" (34, pp. 272-73).

Nationalist demands in Asia then originated from Western sources. The Kremlin did not create widespread unrest in political, social, and economic affairs in Asia. Nor would conditions in many Asian countries necessarily be more favorable for the West if the Communist Revolution in 1917 had never occurred. Asia's problems have their roots in many of the same conditions that prepared the way for communism in Russia and later in China. Surely this is one key to the Kremlin's success on the Asian scene. One of these conditions is the wide gulf in most Asian countries separating a handful of well-educated, capable leaders from illiterate, poverty-ridden multitudes. This situation naturally facilitates the imposition and maintenance of a political oligarchy on Asian masses. Lenin's conception of the Communist Party as the "vanguard of the proletariat" has its counterpart in widespread Asian acceptance of a political elite and the necessity for prolonged "tutelage" before mass participation in politics and government can be achieved. Edwin O. Reischauer thinks that communism

> forms in some respects an almost perfect continuity of tradition with the supposedly benign autocracies of Asia's past. . . . There is no part of Asia in which democratic methods of organization and control do not represent a far greater and more difficult break with past political practices than does Communist dictatorship. (36, p. 165).

Communist shibboleths extolling the Soviet Union as the "fatherland of the international proletariat" and the "defender of peace and a champion of the freedom and independence of nations small and large" may evoke nothing more than feelings of aversion and incredulity in the West. In Asia, however, communist slogans and political nostrums often strike a favorable response among peoples who favor greater "democracy" in all fields but who possess neither experiences facilitating its growth nor appreciation of the conditions under which its existence has been made possible in democratic states of the West. Soviet and Red Chinese versions of democracy therefore are often cited in Asia as a more useful guide than Western versions.

American Military Assistance to Asia

In justifying American military assistance to free nations in Asia, Assistant Secretary of State Walter Robertson told the House Foreign Affairs Committee in 1957 that the necessity for such aid arose from six key factors: the strength of the Moscow-Peiping Axis; the continued threat to international peace that arose from Communist aggressiveness; the new threat posed by increased Communist foreign aid to countries like Burma, Indonesia, Cambodia, and Laos; the fact that two-thirds of more than 900 million Asians lived under Communist rule in China, North Korea, and North Vietnam;[*] the continued existence in Asia of strong nationalist currents, expressing themselves in demands for material betterment; and the fact that free nations in Asia were keeping over 1.5 million men under arms. Mr. Robertson declared that the United States had attempted to meet the "continuing buildup of military power throughout Communist-held areas of the Far East" by a three-pronged program of firm resistance to aggression in Korea or elsewhere, creation of a system of Far Eastern alliances, and provision of Mutual Security funds to enable Asian countries to strengthen their defense postures (20, VI, pp. 1092-93).

By far the greatest quantity of American foreign assistance to Asian countries has gone to nations which had actually experienced, or were in danger of experiencing, military conflicts with the communist bloc. Military aid and defense support continue in the early 1960's to comprise the major categories of American aid to such countries, with the bulk going to vulnerable nations like Cambodia, Laos, the Republic of China, South Korea, and South Vietnam. Despite strong pressure coming from the President's Democratic critics and private citizens groups demanding reduction in military and increases in economic aid, the administration has clung to its conviction that sizable military assistance to weaker countries is a prerequisite to their survival and to their enjoyment of future benefits deriving from economic expansion. In some countries, it feared that already too little was being spent to assure military security. No significant reduction in military aid would be possible until the threat that had given rise to such aid had materially lessened (39, Part 1, pp. 353-400, *passim*).

Few definitive conclusions concerning the effectiveness of American military assistance to Far Eastern countries are possible. What the future of many of these countries would have

---

[*]Mr. Robertson's total of 900 million Asians omits the populations of Burma, India, Pakistan, and Afghanistan.

been in the absence of such assistance is a matter of speculation. In certain countries— South Vietnam, Thailand, South Korea, and the Republic of China on Formosa—it is entirely probable that American assistance has been and remains of crucial importance in enabling these countries to preserve their independence and in laying the basis for security in the future. And in all Asian countries receiving American defense support aid, foundations are being laid which can reasonably be expected to contribute to more stable economic and political conditions. Yet by the early 1960's the growing strength of communism in countries like Indonesia and Laos argued against drawing too many optimistic conclusions about the relationship between American military assistance programs and peace and security in Asia.

Origins of a Pacific Defense System

Military aid was but part of the larger pattern of the total American response to defense problems in the Pacific area. Following the outbreak of the Korean War in 1950, the step-up in communist activities in Indochina, and the growth of neutralist sentiment in other parts of Asia, the United States began to lay the basis for a Pacific security system. Creating a more durable basis for free world defense efforts required negotiation of a treaty to end the war with Japan, followed by the termination of the American occupation. Studies toward that end were carried on during 1950-51. Sovereignty was finally restored to Japan by the San Francisco Conference during the fall of 1951. Concurrently, a new treaty of defense between the United States and Japan was drawn up giving the United States the right to "dispose . . . land, air and sea forces in and about Japan."*

The end of the occupation in Japan raised the issue of safeguarding Far Eastern countries

---

*Quotations from the texts of treaties between the United States and Asian countries here and in the remainder of the chapter are taken from 21, *passim.* This document provides a valuable comparative study of all defense treaties to which the United States is a party, pointing out significant differences in the obligations and other clauses assumed under them.

from a renewal of Japanese aggression, a matter causing apprehensions particularly in Australia and New Zealand. Accordingly, a security treaty among Australia, New Zealand, and the United States—popularly called ANZUS—entered into force on April 29, 1952. Under Article V each party recognized that "an armed attack in the Pacific Area on any of the Parties would be dangerous to its own peace and safety and declares that it would act to meet the common danger in accordance with its constitutional processes." Then on August 27, 1952, a United States-Philippine treaty of defense became operative. Article IV of this treaty duplicates Article V of the ANZUS treaty. On November 17, 1954, following the armistice in the Korean War, a mutual defense treaty between the United States and the Republic of South Korea entered into force. Article III of this treaty contained the same key stipulation as found in the ANZUS and Philippine treaties. Then on March 3, 1955, a new defense treaty was signed between the United States and the Republic of China on Formosa. Article V of this treaty was similar to the articles contained in the treaties cited above.

SEATO—Organization and Principles

During this period, sentiment was growing both within the United States and within allied countries in the Pacific in favor of a regional security system modelled after the earlier NATO pattern. Far Eastern security problems assumed new urgency after the French military collapse in Indochina in the summer of 1954, which raised the possibility that renewed communist agitation might erupt somewhere else in Asia. Consequently, after extended consultations, the South East Asia Collective Defense Treaty was signed at Manila on September 8, 1954, by the governments of the United States, United Kingdom, France, Australia, New Zealand, the Philippines, Pakistan, and Thailand. The South East Asia Treaty Organization (SEATO) began operating on February 19, 1955. To allay apprehensions among neutralist countries that SEATO threatened their freedom, there was attached a "Pacific Charter" which put the signatories on record as favoring the principle of self-determination and pledging to assist Asian states in maintaining it.

SEATO's organizational structure is basically a replica of NATO's. The highest policy-making body is the Council, composed of the foreign ministers of the signatory countries. A subordinate body known as the Council Representatives meets in continuing session at SEATO's headquarters in Bangkok, Thailand, where it carries out assignments given it by the Council, prepares recommendations for the Council's consideration, and supervises activities in such fields as economic mobilization and defense support, education, anti-subversion, and strengthening of the SEATO defense network. The Military Advisers carry on studies and planning in the defense field (37, pp. 118-24).

While SEATO bears a superficial resemblance to NATO, there are several fundamental points of contrast. The heart of SEATO is Article IV providing that in case aggression occurs each party will "act to meet the common danger in accordance with its constitutional processes." The same article declares that threats of internal subversion or other threats to the peace, shall oblige the signatories to "consult immediately in order to agree on the measures which should be taken for the common defense." The treaty area is defined as the general area of southeast Asia up to 21 degrees 30 minutes north latitude. A separate protocol to the treaty, however, designates the states of Cambodia, Laos, and South Vietnam as lying within the treaty area. In still another protocol the United States expressed its understanding that references in the treaty to aggression and armed attack apply only to *Communist-instigated* attacks. If aggression arises from any other quarters, the United States will consult with the SEATO powers concerning appropriate steps to be taken.

Several points require elaboration. First of all, the obligation assumed by the United States actually commits it to nothing more than to "act to meet the common danger in accordance with its constitutional processes" —action which the United States could, and undoubtedly would, take in the absence of SEATO. As a practical matter, American intervention in the Korean War, along with re-

peated unilateral warnings against a resumption of Communist aggression elsewhere in Asia, have left no doubt what the United States would do if there were a renewal of outright, undisguised Communist aggression. Repeatedly since the end of hostilities in Korea and Indochina, the State Department has warned both Russia and China that a new wave of Communist aggression would encounter the resistance of the free world which would not necessarily be confined (1) to the immediate area of aggression or (2) to use of so-called "conventional" weapons. The communist bloc, in other words, has been warned that new threats to the peace might encounter retaliation at points, and by methods, of the West's own choosing (11, II, pp. 2326-28, 2370-71, 2373-76, 2388-90).

As regards the threat of subversive activities carried out against non-communist governments, the SEATO agreement, in the words of one study, "bristles with difficulties" (37, p. 14). The treaty binds the parties to "consult immediately" to counter such threats. Yet no action can be taken to check subversion without the invitation and consent of the country threatened. And there are a number of countries, Thailand, Laos and Indonesia for instance, where this consent might be extremely difficult to obtain. Conceivably, the SEATO nations might be put in the position of being "requested" by an anti-communist faction to intervene in a country where Communists had come into power by legal and orderly means.

In dealing with subversion and peaceful penetration by communist elements, SEATO's usefulness as an instrument to preserve peace and security in Asia is hampered by the absence of a consensus among its members, and between them and non-member Asian states, on how "subversion" or "indirect aggression" are to be distinguished from legitimate nationalist movements or perhaps civil wars. Communists have demonstrated great skill in exploiting such movements for their own advantage. The United States, much more than some of its SEATO allies, is inclined to see the controlling hand of Moscow or Peiping in virtually every case of political turbulence within the Afro-Asian bloc. Neutralist nations, and to some extent the other members of

SEATO, are more inclined to believe that political instability in the Far East springs essentially from *bona fide* nationalist demands and pressing internal problems, even though communist elements undoubtedly aggravate already unsettled conditions. So long as basically different viewpoints on this question exist within the SEATO community, and within the larger Asian context, SEATO's ability to guarantee peace and security in the Orient is bound to be limited.

Progress in resolving this issue and increasing SEATO's value as a guarantor of security could be detected by the summer of 1958, when the United Nations General Assembly took cognizance of threats to the peace in the Middle East. For the UN's ability to deal constructively with such threats in the Middle East and elsewhere was likely to be determined by its ability to evolve a widely acceptable definition of "indirect aggression" and a set of procedures to be followed in coping with it. However, completion of this task would probably require the intensive efforts of statesmen for years, if not decades, to come.

SEATO—Problems and Prospects

SEATO's comparatively brief existence cautions us against making final judgments concerning its effectiveness. But the evidence is sufficient to permit tentative conclusions. In common with other military alliances, SEATO has been subjected to a number of internal stresses. Among these, none perhaps is more basic than divergence among its members concerning the defense philosophy that ought to guide its activities. After the Eisenhower Administration took office in 1952, the United States relied heavily upon the doctrine of "massive retaliation" in dealing with threats emanating from the communist bloc. The major premise underlying this doctrine is that the free world's security in the last analysis rests upon two foundations: the deterrent effect of strong air power, armed with nuclear weapons; and failing deterrence, the ability of the Western coalition to retaliate instantly and massively against aggressors. Many of the allies, however, question the doctrine of massive retaliation. They believe it is unduly rigid, allow-

ing very little flexibility in dealing with communist maneuvers in what are often highly varied circumstances in Asia and elsewhere. They think that it may be all but useless in dealing with communist penetrations and infiltrations which can be expected to take place in the kind of environment Asia provides. The allies, much more than the United States, are inclined to discount the possibility that another Korea-type aggression will be launched by Soviet Russia or Red China, both because the free world has demonstrated its determination to meet force with force and because other methods are likely to advance Communist ends with far greater success and with far less danger of triggering a nuclear war.

Many of the difficulties and limitations inherent in SEATO came into sharp focus at the meeting of the Council of Ministers in the spring of 1958. Over the preceding months, communist groups in Asia had utilized the theme of "peaceful co-existence" to undertake intensive propaganda campaigns in Asia directed at arousing popular support for economic and social reform programs, at counteracting the idea that Asian communist groups were puppets of Moscow, and at blaming the American-led anti-communist coalition for Asia's persistent problems. In this period Indonesia's government was heavily infiltrated by communist and ultra-nationalistic groups. Throughout the Indonesian archipelago a militantly anti-communist faction was challenging Jakarta's authority. As time passed, however, the Jakarta government successfully suppressed the anti-communist forces—a success which imperilled SEATO's sea and air communications by placing a pro-communist regime athwart these vital lifelines. Similarly, in the little Kingdom of Laos, communist elements had successfully created a political "patriotic front" which scored significant gains in the elections of 1958. Informed observers believed that Communists would most likely score even larger gains in 1960 (**24**, March 23 and May 18, 1958).

Less serious perhaps, but indicative of the threats confronting SEATO, were growing communist strength in Japan and on the vital American military base of Okinawa. Elsewhere in the SEATO area, Burma continued to receive substantial Soviet economic assistance; corrupt and inefficient government in the Philippines detracted from the strength of democracy there; and Thailand—militantly anti-communist throughout the post-war period—showed increasing evidence of gravitating toward the neutralist camp because of its evident apprehensions concerning the strength of Red China and North Vietnam (43, 1955, pp. 100-101, 127; 30, March 16, 1958). Meanwhile, the neutralist states of Asia continued to oppose SEATO on the ground that military alliances aggravated international tensions and increased the prospects of global war (38, pp. 11-12).

By the late 1950's, therefore, it was clear that SEATO had created almost as many problems in Western-Asian relations as it had solved. Perhaps the overriding continuing danger was that the American people would tend to place too much reliance for security upon an agreement whose scope and utility were severely limited from the outset, whose purposes were interpreted differently by the signatories, and whose value as a diplomatic instrument was open to serious question.

REFERENCES

1. Alexandrowicz, C. H. "India's Himalayan Dependencies," *Yearbook of World Affairs, 1956.* London: Stevens and Sons, Ltd., 1957, pp. 128-43. Analyzes India's defense problems along its northern and western borders.

2. American Assembly. *The United States and the Far East.* New York: Columbia University Press, 1956. Papers presented to an Arden House conference on Asian policy.

3. Bareau, Paul, *et al.* "India's Second Five-Year Plan," *International Affairs,* 33 (July, 1957), pp. 301-09. Discusses India's economic problems since independence.

4. Boorman, Howard L., *et al. Moscow-Peking Axis.* New York: Harper and Brothers, 1957. This illuminating study by the Council on Foreign Relations brings out clearly strengths and weaknesses in the Sino-Soviet alliance.

5. Bowles, Chester. *Ambassador's Report.* New York: Harper and Brothers, 1954. A valuable first-hand account of India's problems and outlook by a former American ambassador.

6. ———. "New India," *Foreign Affairs,* 31 (October, 1952), pp. 79-94.

7. Brogan, D. W. "The Illusion of American Omnipotence," *Harpers,* 205 (December, 1952), pp. 21-8. A searching analysis of certain American stereotypes about foreign affairs.

8. Brown, W. Norman. *The United States and India and Pakistan.* Cambridge, Mass.: Harvard University Press, 1953. Provides valuable historical insight on U. S. relations with these countries.

9. *Christian Science Monitor.*

10. Davis, Kingsley. "The Other Scare: Too Many People," *New York Times Magazine* March 15, 1959, pp. 13, 108-14. A succinct analysis of population projections and their implications for international affairs.

11. Department of State. *American Foreign Policy, 1950-1955.* (Publication no. 6446, "General Foreign Policy Series," no. 117). Washington: 1957. An invaluable source book for American relations with Asia.

12. ———. *United States Relations with China.* (Publication no. 3573, "Far Eastern Series," no. 30.) Washington: Office of Public Affairs, 1949. Traces out Sino-American relations since the period of the Open Door.

13. Dulles, Foster Rhea. *China and America.* Princeton: Princeton University Press, 1946. A helpful, but somewhat dated, secondary account.

14. Fairbank, John K. "The Problem of Revolutionary Asia," *Foreign Affairs,* 29 (October, 1950), pp. 101-13. A leading authority discusses barriers to an effective Asian policy.

15. ———. *The United States and China.* Cambridge, Mass.: Harvard University Press, 1958. An illuminating treatment of historic Sino-American relations.

16. Feis, Herbert. *The China Tangle.* Princeton: Princeton University Press, 1953. Perhaps the most dispassionate account available of U. S. relations with Nationalist China.

17. Fifield, R. H. "American Foreign Policy in the Far East, 1945-50," *World Affairs,* 5 (April, 1951), pp. 200-10. A brief but lucid interpretation.

18. Graber, D. A. *Crisis Diplomacy.* Washington, D. C.: Public Affairs Press, 1959. Analyzes the non-intervention principle in American foreign policy, emphasizing modifications in the principle in the light of experience.

19. Holland, William L., ed. *Asian Nationalism and the West.* New York: The Macmillan Company, 1953. The papers presented to the eleventh conference of the Institute of Pacific Relations bring out clearly the manifold aspects of Asian nationalism.

20. House Foreign Affairs Committee. *Hearings on the Mutual Security Act of 1957*, 85th Congress, 1st Session, May 22-June 28, 1957. This voluminous record provides a wealth of information on all aspects of the American foreign aid program.

21. ———. *Treaty Provisions Relating to the Use of United States Forces for Mutual Defense*, Committee Print, 84th Congress, 2nd Session, 1956. This document reproduces all the defense treaties to which the United States is a party, showing their similarities and differences.

22. Katona, Paul. "Soviet Propaganda to the Colonial World," *Yearbook of World Affairs, 1955*. London: Stevens and Sons, Ltd., 1955.

23. King, John Kerry. *Southeast Asia in Perspective*. New York: The Macmillan Company, 1956. An enlightening treatment of the area, bringing out clearly the obstacles to a more effective Western policy there.

24. Latourette, Kenneth S. *The American Record in the Far East, 1945-1951*. New York: The Macmillan Company, 1952. A succinct account by a leading authority on the Far East.

25. Levi, Werner. *Free India in Asia*. Minneapolis: University of Minnesota Press, 1952. Discusses the leading elements in India's foreign policy.

26. ———. *Modern China's Foreign Policy*. Minneapolis: University of Minnesota Press, 1953. Traces China's foreign policy from the period of the Open Door through the communist period.

27. Mallory, Walter H. "Chinese Minorities in Southeast Asia," *Foreign Affairs*, 34 (January, 1956), pp. 258-71. Analyzes the implications of the problem of the "overseas Chinese."

28. Murti, B. S. N. *Nehru's Foreign Policy*. New Delhi: Beacon Information and Publication Co., 1953. A semi-documentary account, written from a strong pro-Nehru position.

29. "Neutralism Becomes an Acceptable Creed," *United Asia*, 6 (December, 1954), pp. 261-2. This journal, published in Bombay, strongly reflects the neutralist position on world affairs.

30. *New York Times*.

31. Palmer, Norman D. "The United States and Pakistan," *Current History*, 34 (March, 1958), pp. 141-47. Focuses on the impact of U. S. economic and military aid for Indian-Pakistani relations.

32. Parkinson, F. "Bandung and the Underdeveloped Countries," *Yearbook of World Affairs, 1956*. London: Stevens and Sons, Ltd., 1956.

33. ———. "Soviet Aid to Underdeveloped Countries," *Yearbook of World Affairs, 1957*. London: Stevens and Sons, Ltd., 1957. Analyzes the impact and technique of the Soviet economic offensive in backward countries.

34. Peffer, Nathaniel. *The Far East*. Ann Arbor: The University of Michigan Press, 1958. A penetrating volume in the University of Michigan's history of the modern world. Especially outstanding is Peffer's history of events in China and of America's response to them.

35. Pratt, Julius W. *A History of United States Foreign Policy*. New York: Prentice-Hall, 1955.

36. Reischauer, Edwin O. *Wanted: An Asian Policy*. New York: Alfred A. Knopf, 1955. A perceptive treatment of recent U. S. policy toward Asia.

37. Royal Institute of International Affairs. *Collective Defense in South East Asia*. London: Oxford University Press, 1956. This report by a Chatham House study group evaluates defense organization and problems in the Far East, with special attention to SEATO.

38. Sawer, Geoffrey. "Problems of Australian Foreign Policy," *Politics and History*, 3 (November, 1957), pp. 1-17. Another analysis of SEATO, from the Australian point of view.

39. Senate Foreign Relations Committee. *Hearings on the Mutual Security Act of 1959*. 86th Congress, 1st Session. Washington: 1959.

40. ———. *Technical Assistance*, Report no. 139, 85th Congress, 1st Session, 1957. A compilation of detailed studies on various aspects of American technical assistance programs.

41. Special Committee to Study the Foreign Aid Program. *Foreign Aid Activities of Other Free Nations*, Committee Print, 85th Congress, 1st Session, 1957.

42. Spender, P. C. "Partnership with Asia," *Foreign Affairs*, 29 (January, 1951), pp. 205-18.

43. *United States in World Affairs, 1955*, et seq. New York: Harper and Brothers, 1957. This annual series by the Council on Foreign Relations provides a valuable background study of U. S. policies toward Asia.

44. Van Alstyne, Richard W. "Myth Versus Reality in the Far Eastern Policies of the United States," *International Affairs*, 32 (July, 1956), pp. 287-97. A diplomatic historian challenges many preconceptions that have guided America's Asian policies in the past.

45. Van Der Kroef, J. M. "The Appeals of Communism in Southeast Asia," *United Asia*, 7 (December, 1955), pp. 290-97.

46. Zinkin, Taya. "Indian Foreign Policy: An Interpretation of Attitudes," *World Politics*, (January, 1955), pp. 179-208. An experienced journalist evaluates the soundness of the Indian neutralist approach and finds many weaknesses in it.

CHAPTER 14

Psychological Warfare

Logomachy at Mid-Century

In the all-pervading conflict of the present age, the cold war between the free world alliance headed by the United States and the communist bloc headed by the Soviet Union, the front is everywhere. It is where armed forces from both sides watch each other across the sights of machine guns along the Korean armistice line; where delegates from both sides present their viewpoints, and in the process engage in heated propaganda exchanges in the United Nations; where highly trained secret agents from each side attempt to penetrate the security precautions of the other and transmit secret information about the opponent's capabilities and intentions; where technical assistance teams from each camp seek to carry out beneficial economic programs in countries like Iran and Burma; where propaganda experts on the Voice of America and Radio Moscow vie with each other to gain worldwide support for their ideological cause; and where each side continuously assesses the military posture of the enemy and tries to develop new weapons and new defenses.

Apart from these manifestations of the cold war conflict, however, there is another which embraces them all. No matter where the most active scene of the conflict may be at any given time, it is part of a larger battleground:

the continuing struggle for the allegiance of masses everywhere, the never-ending campaign to convince peoples the world over of the rightness of the ideological cause with which each side is identified. For in the last analysis, the battle on this front may very well decide the final outcome of the struggle that has engaged the major powers of the world since World War II. Victory in the battle of ideologies may shape the course of international relations for decades, perhaps generations, to come. Here the communist empire has scored some of its most impressive gains. Thus a public opinion poll in 1958 conducted in twelve capitals of the world asked the question: "Who is ahead in the cold war, Russia or the West?" Russia was rated ahead in ten capitals, sometimes by a four- and five-to-one majority; the West was rated ahead in only two capitals (2, p. 94).

Military commanders have long known that the morale of soldiers, and of civilians behind the lines, can be the decisive element in the outcome of battles. So it is with the paramilitary conflict which today is designated the cold war. The morale on both sides over extended periods, the predispositions of hundreds of millions of peoples in the uncommitted nations, the ability of both sides to keep their citizens psychologically prepared for the sacrifices required while at the same time attempting to promote defections within the enemy's camp—these may turn out to be the crucial determinants of the cold war conflict.

Americans have been slow to recognize the importance of psychological-ideological aspects of world affairs. By contrast, since long before the communist revolution of 1917, communism has accorded psychological warfare high priority in advancing internal and external policy goals. Specifically what is "psychological warfare?" What is its relation to other manifestations of national power like military force or economic coercion? How do the capabilities of both sides compare in the psychological warfare realm? What efforts have been made by the United States in the recent period to counter the Soviet ideological offensive, and how successful have these efforts proved? These are the fundamental questions to be investigated in this chapter. We shall explore them within a three-fold frame of reference: first, by a general inquiry into the nature and uses of psychological warfare, with emphasis upon propaganda as a major diplomatic weapon; second, by an analysis of the communist propaganda offensive against the West; and third, by a detailed description and evaluation of the postwar American "Campaign of Truth."

1. PSYCHOLOGICAL WARFARE: ITS NATURE AND USES

Psychological warfare is as old as history. When the Greeks failed to capture Troy by force of arms, they resorted to skillful deception —the Trojan Horse—to bring them victory. In early American history, one purpose of the *Declaration of Independence* was to gain widespread support in England and Europe for the colonial cause by identifying it with the political aspirations of Western society as a whole. One of the most famous books in American literature, *Uncle Tom's Cabin*, probably did more to arouse public support for the anti-slavery cause than the thousands of impassioned speeches made by all the Abolitionists combined. During the First World War, tons of propaganda in the form of press releases, leaflets, posters, booklets, pictures, and the like, emanated from the Allied side. These were acknowledged by German military leaders as having been singularly effective in undermining the military and civilian morale of the Central Powers and in turning neutral opinion against their cause. One of the most brilliant Allied propaganda victories in the period was won through the proclamation of President Wilson's "Fourteen Points," which were of inestimable value in shortening the war by weakening the will to resist among populations in the enemy camp (**13**, pp. 72-3, 84-5, 276).

Two of the most powerful nations in recent history, Nazi Germany and Soviet Russia, were created in large part by the successful application of psychological warfare techniques at home and abroad. We shall defer a consideration of the Soviet emphasis upon these techniques for a later portion of the chapter. Meanwhile, we may note that few individuals have surpassed Joseph Goebbels, the ingenious head of the Nazi propaganda machine, in recognizing the value of psychological warfare in statecraft and in developing methods for waging it successfully. Whether it was in working the German masses into ecstatic public demonstrations supporting Hitler, or in drumming up anti-Semitic sentiment throughout Germany, or in undermining the morale of Germany's weaker neighbors, or in sustaining the Nazi war effort long after the Third Reich's defeat had become inevitable, Goebbels had few peers in his expert use of psychological warfare.

Some Basic Concepts

No universally accepted definition of "psychological warfare" exists; and, indeed, it is difficult to formulate an altogether satisfactory definition of the concept. Its goal can be stated quite simply: to persuade other countries—especially the nation's diplomatic enemies —to accept one's own point of view as a basis for action. Nations utilize psychological warfare during periods of military hostilities to undermine the enemy's will to fight, thereby hastening his capitulation. In periods of peace or cold war, psychological warfare techniques are valuable diplomatic tools used (1) to avoid military hostilities altogether, if possible; (2) to assure victory for one's own country if war comes; and (3) to assure that diplomatic victories won with or without resort to arms will be achieved as inexpensively as possible. In its simplest terms then, psychological warfare is the effort to influence the actions of other countries at a minimum cost in national resources, the most important of which is human life. Such warfare is "psychological" in two senses. It is directed at the enemy's will and emotions. For its successful implementation, it requires the most careful study of the enemy's history, habits, thought patterns, culture, mythology, aspirations—in short, a study of everything about the enemy's national behavior.

A great variety of techniques can be invoked to wage psychological warfare. Propaganda can be carried on by radio, leaflets, sound trucks or speeches before bodies like the United Nations. The enemy may be intimidated by "saturation bombing" of civilian population centers, military demonstrations held for visiting diplomats, appropriately-timed naval "maneuvers" close to global troublespots, opportune announcements of important technological developments, like a successful rocket launching to the moon. There may be economic assistance programs or, conversely, economic blockades and boycotts; support for internal subversive movements within other countries; stratagems designed to keep other countries "benevolently" neutral during time of war or when war threatens. These are only a few of the better-known techniques utilized to wage psychological warfare. As is apparent, psychological warfare cannot be sharply differentiated from military and other forms of national power; it can be used separately or in conjunction with the latter.

What is the relationship between psychological warfare and ordinary diplomatic intercourse among nations? Is the United States engaging in psychological warfare, for example, when it exerts pressure to influence the outcome of crucial elections in France or Italy, by threatening to withhold, or sharply reduce, Marshall Plan aid if the Communists win the election? Is the appearance of a strong American naval force that is—by a convenient coincidence—engaging in maneuvers off the coast of Greece or Lebanon when political crises prevail in these countries a form of psychological warfare? If so, how do such cases differ in principle from routine diplomacy, in which every nation has as its basic goal protection of its own security and the countering of every threat that might arise to its self-preservation? There are plainly many borderline cases in international relations that defy completely satisfactory classification. Today, even the traditional line between war and peace is exceedingly difficult to draw precisely. Most ordinary diplomatic contacts among powerful countries contain at least rudimentary elements of psychological warfare; and in some periods relations among these countries can have many of the earmarks of relations customarily prevailing during time of war. So variegated are these relationships that it is even possible to have war on the ideological plane at the very time leaders are attempting to cultivate "better understanding" through devices like cultural exchange.

Recognizing that no hard and fast differentiation between ordinary diplomatic techniques and psychological warfare is possible, some differences, at least in degree, may be suggested. Psychological warfare is usually carried on against a nation's diplomatic enemies during periods of cold war or military hostilities. It will be used to defend the nation's vital interests, perhaps in the hope that military force will not have to be used in their defense. Normally, it is engaged in for a sustained period of time, perhaps for several years. A great variety of techniques—propaganda, economic inducements and pressures, covert diplomatic machinations, military force—will be utilized collectively to mount a continuing "offensive" and to counter psychological warfare activities of the other side.

In this chapter we shall concentrate upon propaganda as a major technique of psychological warfare, defining it as the effort of one group or nation to influence the actions of another group or nation *by primary reliance upon methods of systematic persuasion, including methods of verbal coercion and induce-*

ment. Propaganda is to be distinguished from other forms of psychological warfare by its utilization of the written and spoken word. Successful utilization of methods of persuasion depends in no small degree upon the effectiveness of other weapons in the arsenal of national power like economic strength and military force. Threats, unsupported by the requisite military power, are usually ineffectual; promises and inducements, without the willingness and capacity to make good on them, are equally worthless as diplomatic tools.

Several further points about propaganda require emphasis. A popular misconception is that propaganda is inherently false. This misconception explains in some measure why Americans have often been loath to support the propaganda activities of their government. Knowing that certain information is "propaganda" tells us nothing about the veracity or falsity of that information. The etymology of the word "propaganda" enables us to keep this point clearly in mind. Its root is the Latin verb *propagare,* meaning to propagate, to spread, to disseminate, to extend, to transmit. The term first came into historical currency after the establishment of the College of Propaganda by Pope Urban VIII (1623-44), to promote the missionary activities of the Roman Catholic Church. Throughout the greater part of history, propaganda possessed none of the insidious connotations later associated with it in the Nazi or communist periods. It meant merely the process of trying to gain converts to a particular cause, initially the Christian gospel as expounded by the Vatican. The process of propaganda then is the act of disseminating a belief; or propaganda may describe the belief so disseminated.

Confusion can enter into any discusssion of propaganda, however, when we inquire: what is good and bad propaganda? In a *tactical* sense, good propaganda is that which attains its intended result—gaining converts for the belief in question—and bad propaganda is that which fails to attain this result. In an *ethical* sense, according to the Judaeo-Christian tradition prevalent in the West, good propaganda is that which accords as nearly as possible with objective truth, and bad propaganda is that which relies heavily upon various forms of deception, falsehood, and chicanery. Whatever the ethical standards by which propaganda is judged, however, *any* propaganda, including of course American, is to be distinguished from an objective search for truth. Irrespective of whether it is the lobbyist trying to influence the legislator, the advertising agency trying to influence the consumer, or the Voice of America trying to influence public opinion in Indonesia, the object of all propaganda is to utilize *carefully selected* data to induce the hearer to accept a predetermined point of view. In that sense, because propagandists routinely emphasize facts and ideas which favor their cause, while ignoring or de-emphasizing those which weaken it, all propaganda ought to be examined critically by students of foreign policy. While propaganda need not be false, in evaluating it students can profitably recall the legal distinction between "the truth" and "the *whole* truth." Facts may be accurate, but they may be—and in propaganda almost always are—so arranged as to give a distorted conclusion.

The extent to which propaganda has emerged as a significant diplomatic weapon in the past half-century is well-known to students of history. Doubtless, many propaganda techniques arouse aversion in citizens who believe that ethical considerations ought to enter more heavily into the conduct of inernational affairs. Yet, from another perspective, propaganda must be looked upon as a possible alternative to military force. And the ideal conception of international relations in the Western religio-political tradition is one in which coercive methods have been eliminated altogether or greatly reduced. Bodies like the United Nations and the World Court exist to confine global disputes to the arena of persuasion and argumentation—which, according to the definition followed here, is the arena of propaganda. Wars and lesser forms of violence occur whenever peaceful techniques of international intercourse fail to safeguard the essential interests of nations in the world community.

The ultimate objective for the United States and its Western allies ought not to be the elimination of propaganda from the world scene, any more than it is eliminated from the domestic scene. Rather it should be the substitution of words for bullets, so that argument may accomplish in the future what machine guns, howitzers, and bombs have accomplished in earlier epochs. For no matter how weary Americans may become of tedious and seemingly barren propaganda exchanges in international affairs, it is far better that diplomats hurl words—even occasional insults—at each other than that their armies should hurl hand grenades and guided missiles. This is not to imply that beneficial improvements cannot and should not be made in the methods of present-day propaganda efforts by all countries; still less is it to sanction the practice of the communist bloc in waging a kind of "total war" against its enemies by all-out, scurrilous propaganda blasts. The tone of international relations could be vastly improved by universal agreement, accompanied by practicable means of enforcement, on the proper limits of propaganda exchanges between nations. The ultimate goal is creation of a framework of world law, so that propaganda activities in the world community, like these same activities within countries, would be subjected to enforceable rules of conduct. Yet after acknowledging the need for correction of evident abuses, it remains true that the more nations rely upon techniques of persuasion and conviction, the less likelihood there will be that instruments of destruction like hydrogen bombs and germ warfare will be summoned to enforce national demands.

The American people are prone to derogate "mere talk," to believe that "talk is cheap," and to demand "action instead of words." Historically, Americans have been doers, not philosophers; they have admired the man who "gets things done" more than the man who looks for the meaning in action or who seeks to change the thought patterns upon which past or future action takes place. Americans are therefore suspicious of diplomats who "do nothing but talk," often about highly technical, dull subjects frequently beyond the comprehension of a majority of citizens. This attitude inevitably places barriers in the way of those who urge greater national efforts in psychological warfare (**13**, pp. 345-46).*

---

*Paradoxically, no nation known to history has geared its economic life so closely to the efforts of the advertising industry, which deals in only one

The Interdependence of Diplomatic Weapons

In common with all aspects of national power, the effectiveness of propaganda as an instrument of foreign relations is heavily conditioned by the *totality* of the nation's response to the outside world. Nearly every action undertaken by a state in world affairs has propaganda connotations in terms of creating a favorable or unfavorable image of that country in the minds of foreigners. That image is an amalgam of a large number of diverse influences, most of which bear no relation to deliberate efforts by the country in question to create an attractive image of itself abroad. To illustrate, if the United States promises economic assistance to countries like Bolivia, Turkey, or South Vietnam, its ability to make propaganda capital out of this fact will be determined by the following major considerations: whether the United States has the resources to make good on its promise; whether public opinion and Congress will support the pledges given by executive officials; whether such aid is administered so as to advance the program's objectives; whether American aid is compatible with or, at a minimum, does not conflict with the emotional aspirations of the peoples concerned; and whether American aid is visualized by the recipients as meeting their needs more constructively than perhaps Soviet or Chinese aid.

Propagandists are much like individuals engaged in "retouching" photographs. In their effort to create as pleasing a likeness as possible, they are limited by the quality of the original picture. No amount of retouching can compensate completely for an unflattering

---

product: persuasion. Somehow, Americans see very little connection between the role of advertising in the economic field and what is essentially the same task in the diplomatic field.

The story is told that one day the great British Prime Minister Benjamin Disraeli was accosted in the halls of the House of Commons by an individual who had listened to hour after hour of dull debate on the floor. This individual was condemning the futility of "mere talk" and was highly resentful of the fact that his time had been taken up in lengthy discussions that involved "only matters of opinion." Disraeli finally bested his tormentor by saying: young man, opinion rules the world!

image conveyed by words and deeds which paint a totally adverse portrait of the nation abroad. Similarly, as the United States has discovered repeatedly in recent years, a favorable image of the country may survive, even after propaganda efforts have been feeble and uninspired. A strategically-timed announcement, such as President Eisenhower's "Open Skies" disarmament proposal at the Geneva Conference in 1955, can be worth more than a hundred routine Voice of America broadcasts in turning the propaganda tide in favor of one's own country. Conversely, all the millions of dollars invested in American libraries overseas cannot cancel out the ill-will which prevails toward the United States in many parts of the Arab world because of the partition of Palestine nor can it erase still-vivid memories of earlier American interventionism in Latin America.

These considerations suggest that propaganda *is not a policy itself but merely a reflection of a policy.* Nations do not engage in propaganda for its own sake. They do so to advance some pre-existing goal of statecraft. Thus success in the psychological warfare field will be determined to an important degree by prior success in clarifying the basic goals of policy toward major issues and areas. If American policy toward colonial peoples is vague and contradictory, American propaganda efforts will inevitably reflect this weakness and, for that reason, will be only moderately successful. Technicians in psychological warfare can perhaps tell the State Department how to put across a certain viewpoint most effectively in Saudi Arabia or Thailand; they cannot tell the State Department what viewpoints ought ultimately to be propagated as reflections of basic national policies.

Propaganda differs from other weapons in the arsenal of a nation's power, in that its effectiveness is far more difficult to measure precisely than is the case, let us say, with the application of military force. Whether victory, defeat, or perhaps stalemate has occurred on the battlefield is comparatively easy to assess. The attempt to evaluate the results of propaganda, however, is far more complicated and promises far less certainty of judgment. This fact has emerged with particular force whenever American propaganda officials have been called upon to present their "results" to skeptical Congressional committees. A former high-ranking State Department official, Edward Barrett, has aptly said:

> No one could prove last year's funds had been well spent by producing a cage filled with 7,000 Russians who had deserted Communism. The committee could see and touch new post offices; it could not see ten million Indians or Britons who had been made a little less suspicious of America than they were a year earlier. (1, p. 85).

How much could the East German, Polish, and Hungarian revolts against the Kremlin's rule be attributed to Western broadcasts and leaflet campaigns carried on intensively by unofficial anti-communist groups? To what degree are communist propaganda messages to India successfully countered by the Voice of America, American assistance in raising the level of village life, and American support for New Delhi's Second Five Year Plan?

Quite obviously, these questions cannot be answered definitively. One reason is that even individuals who are the targets of propaganda cannot determine its precise influence upon their actions. Propaganda is likely to be one among many stimuli shaping their conduct. It often acts as a catalyst in speeding up what is already a predisposition on the part of the hearer to behave in a certain way. For instance, it may hasten the surrender of already dispirited military forces or spur restive populations to set up guerrilla activities against an alien government. Successful propaganda is always cast in terms that are psychologically compatible with the pre-existing views of the hearer. During World War II impassioned Allied propaganda outbursts designed to prove Hitler's obvious lack of mental balance could be expected to elicit a negligible response on the part of the German soldiers. On the other hand, sober and reasonably accurate point-by-point refutations of Goebbel's roseate promises of an early Nazi victory proved a rewarding method for destroying German military and civilian morale (13, pp. 242-58, 416-33).

Similarly, individuals with experience on the psychological warfare front of the cold war have found that in America's approach to a country like India, a perfectly frank acknowledgment of the existence of racial problems within the United States, coupled with emphasis upon progress being made to deal with them, greatly strengthens the American indictment of Soviet oppression at home and abroad. Moreover, it enables the Americans to raise questions about religious and caste discriminations in India, and about its stormy relations with Pakistan, without alienating Indian opinion (3, pp. 296-321).

The aim of propaganda, it must be remembered, is *to persuade,* not preach or orate or ignite verbal pyrotechnics. That is why many of the Voice of America's messages have not been stridently and repetitiously "anticommunist" or "pro-American" enough to suit many ultra-nationalistic legislators and public groups. Demagogic outbursts over the Voice of America could be expected to win very few friends for the United States in the international community and would re-enforce the stereotype already prevailing in some countries that Americans are overbearing, intolerant of the opinions of others, and anti-communist to the exclusion of all else.

To summarize: the purpose of psychological warfare is to convince other countries to accept a certain point of view and to base their actions upon it, in the hope that violent forms of conflict and coercion may be avoided; if clashes cannot be altogether avoided, then propaganda can contribute to reducing their scope and duration and to assuring ultimate victory for one's own country. Valuable as psychological warfare may be as a tool of foreign relations, however, it is but one such tool available to nations in the international community. Its effectiveness will almost always be determined by the nature and use to which these other tools in the diplomatic arsenal have been, and are being, put. It is the *total* image of the nation in the eyes of the outside world which counts. This image generally is more a product of other influences than of deliberate efforts in the psychological warfare field.

2. THE COMMUNIST IDEOLOGICAL OFFENSIVE

Few Americans in the contemporary age need to be reminded of the central place ideological hostility among nations occupies on the current international scene. One day newspapers are filled with heated exchanges between communist and free world spokesmen over the question of disarmament. Another day the headlines may feature a tour by prominent Communists throughout the neutralist world, in which the uncommitted nations are wooed by various economic and propaganda blandishments. Still another day prominence may be given in the press to findings by a Congressional committee listing Soviet treaty violations since 1917, or first-hand accounts by communist defectors about life in Soviet slave labor camps, or disclosures of communist fifth-column activities within the United States and Canada. Hardly a day passes which does not witness some effort by one bloc or the other to make propaganda capital out of important developments in international affairs.

Communist Ideology and the Outside World

Chapter 9 discussed the nature of communist ideology and assessed its implications for Soviet foreign policy. Here our interest centers upon examining efforts made by Moscow and its supporters since World War II to wage an intensive psychological warfare offensive against the non-communist world. Since the United States is the strongest power in that world, this means predominantly an anti-American propaganda offensive.

Central to the Marxist-Leninist-Stalinist conception of world affairs is the idea, expressed by Stalin in 1950, that "History never does anything of moment without some particular necessity" (12, p. 67). Events in history are governed by the "laws of dialectical materialism," as expounded by Marx and his latter-day disciples. History is supposedly moving toward a mighty denouement which will witness the collapse of capitalism and the ultimate victory of communism. As long as capitalism and communism continue to exist, said Lenin in 1920, "We cannot live in peace; in the end, one or the other will triumph—a funeral dirge will be sung either over the Soviet Republic or over world capitalism" (**12**, p. 415).

Communist thought of course admits of no doubt concerning the system which will ultimately triumph. But meanwhile the "revolutionary struggle" must go on. Devoted Communists must simultaneously consolidate their own position while trying to weaken the position of the enemy. Three specific kinds of tensions within the enemy's camp must be encouraged and exploited: those between the proletariat and the bourgeoisie, between imperialist nations and their colonial possessions, and among the capitalist powers themselves (**12**, pp. 391-98). How long will this state of conflict last? There is no predetermined time-table; Communist theoreticians have tended to push the expected world revolution farther and farther into the future. Said Stalin in 1925:

> The epoch of world revolution . . . may occupy years or even decades. In the course of this period there will occur, nay, must occur ebbs and flows in the revolutionary tide . . . The revolution does not develop along a straight, continuous and upwardly aspiring line, but along a zigzag path . . . an ebb and flow in the tide. . . . (**12**, p. 478).

This analysis of the future course of world events therefore leads communist spokesmen to exercise caution, to avoid precipitous "adventurism" which, under prevailing circumstances, offers no hope of victory, to stress the necessity for patience and endurance in a struggle which may extend over decades or even generations to come. All the while, the foremost goal is to preserve the security of the USSR, the fountainhead of the world revolutionary movement, which, said Stalin, "stands like a huge rock surrounded by the ocean of bourgeois states" (**12**, p. 410). A prolonged "softening up" process is therefore required to make non-communist countries "ripe" for revolution. This has been a professed communist goal since 1917, although of course it has received more emphasis in some periods than in others. Psychological warfare as an instrument of Soviet diplomacy received a new impetus after the great power Geneva Conference

of 1955, where both sides acknowledged that a new nuclear war might well threaten the existence of civilization itself. After 1955 the new theme of communist foreign policy became "competitive co-existence," whereby the Kremlin challenged the free world to battle for the minds and loyalties of mankind (**23**, 1955, pp. 2-3).

The Soviet Propaganda Apparatus

A detailed discussion of the Soviet propaganda apparatus, and its manifold relationships to other organs of the Soviet state, would carry us beyond the compass of our study.* At the center of the Soviet propaganda effort stands the Communist Party of the Soviet Union (CPSU), the "vanguard of the proletariat." Lenin likened the Party to an army which, "inspired by a single will," leads "millions of people" to change their minds and actions "in accordance with the changing circumstances and demands" of the class struggle (**10**, p. 34). The Communist Party is the repository of Marxist truth. Its monolithic nature assures that this truth will filter down to, and be binding upon, all inferior organs of the communist state. The National Party Congress theoretically chooses—in reality, its actions are governed by—the ruling bodies of the party, such as the Central Committee, whose Presidium is the policy-determining body of the Party, and hence of the entire Soviet state. Lower-echelon party organs like the Cadre Department train communist leaders and oversee the execution of party directives throughout the Soviet government (**9**, pp. 34-7).

Specifically charged with propagating the communist faith around the world is the organ known as *Agitprop*, which is responsible directly to the Central Committee of the CPSU. After the "party line" toward any domestic or foreign issue has been determined, it is incum-

---

*The subject is fully discussed in two evaluations of Soviet propaganda activities in recent years. See **10**, pp. 28-43 and **9**, pp. 1-35. The charts showing the connection between propaganda and Communist Party organs, both within the Soviet state and for "Communist front" organizations, are especially illuminating. These studies also bring out clearly examples of communist propaganda tactics and themes toward particular countries in the recent period.

bent upon *Agitprop* to act as planner, director, and watchdog of all communist media engaging in propaganda dissemination. *Agitprop* directs the flow of information to important communist news media like *Pravda* and *Izvestia;* supervises the preparation of films; supplies information on the correct party line to foreign communist operatives by means of radio broadcasts, communist theoretical journals and publications, conferences among leading Communists, sponsorship of exhibits and cultural exchanges, and in many other ways. One highly important agency operating under *Agitprop's* direction is VOKS (the All-Union Society for Cultural Relations with Foreign Countries) which, though it feigns an autonomous status, is in reality a subordinate body within the total communist propaganda structure (**10**, pp. 38-40).

Supplementing the propaganda activities within the Soviet State are the attempts by communist groups to infiltrate non-communist bodies within the free world. Such infiltration has a number of objectives: to promote person-to-person contact with non-communists, to provide popular support for communist causes, to conceal communist operations behind a façade which makes them acceptable to ignorant peoples, and to recruit and train future party members. Among these Communist-infiltrated groups are such organizations as the World Peace Council, the World Federation of Trade Unions, the International Union of Students, and The World Federation of Teachers' Unions (**9**, p. 43).

Some Basic Characteristics of Soviet Propaganda

Steeped in the view that Marxist-Leninist-Stalinist canons can unlock all mysteries of human experience, Communists naturally place a high premium upon mastering the "techniques" of revolutionary agitation, in which propaganda has a high place. Technique of course includes a variety of skills in knowing when to attack and when to retreat, how to adapt revolutionary activity so as to make the most effective use possible of prevailing environmental factors, how to undermine morale in the enemy's camp, how to recognize vulnera-

bilities in both one's own position and the enemy's position, and how to utilize this knowledge successfully.

Perhaps the most basic element in communist technique, however—an element which makes the communist challenge to the free world one of inordinate difficulty—is recognition that in spreading the communist gospel, no measure, stratagem, or tactic is impermissible. Every move that offers any hope of success to the communist cause must be utilized to maximum advantage by the communist faithful. In one of the most unambiguous utterances in the catalogue of highly ambiguous communist pronouncements, Lenin declared forthrightly in 1921 that

> our morality is entirely subordinated to the interests of the class struggle. . . . We say: morality is that which serves to destroy the old exploiting society and to unite all the toilers around the proletariat . . . Communist morality is the morality which serves this struggle. . . . (**12**, p. 103).

Thus the free world faces an unscrupulous diplomatic opponent who is prepared to ignore the ordinary amenities of international conduct and morality, who, except as a matter of tactical importance, cares nothing for "a decent respect for the opinions of mankind," and who is ready to invoke every Machiavellian device which seems suitable for realizing its aggressive foreign policy ambitions.

One of Lenin's publications was entitled *Two Steps Forward, One Step Backward,* calling attention to the ebb tides and flood tides in the revolutionary struggle. Communist policymakers are expert in adapting their methodology to the exigencies of the hour; and indeed, in this process, they have had few equals throughout history. A striking characteristic of Bolshevik propaganda since 1917 has been the Kremlin's ability to shift from a "hard" to a "soft" propaganda line, in much the same way as an individual might alternately open and close the hot and cold taps of a faucet.

When external conditions favor launching a militant psychological offensive—usually when the Communist world is strong and its enemies weak—the men in the Kremlin open the spigot marked "hot." There pours forth a stream of propaganda abuse and belligerent ideological declarations aimed at non-communist countries. High on the list of propaganda themes during such periods are the "inevitable conflict" between communist and non-communist societies; the ultimate consummation of the "world revolution;" the inevitability of "frightful clashes" before communism emerges victorious; the perfidy and unalterable hostility displayed by capitalist countries toward the USSR and its followers; and the necessity for stepped up revolutionary agitation throughout the world. Interspersed among these themes is emphasis upon the "durability" of the communist system and its ability to survive even military conflict with its enemies.

Different conditions in the external environment—for example, when the Communist world and its enemies are nearly equal in strength or possibly when the former may be weaker than the latter—can prompt the communist hierarchy to turn on the "cold" propaganda spigot. Then there emanates from communist propaganda organs a soothing "soft" line, calculated to advance Moscow or Peiping's interests by reliance upon methods of persuasion, conciliation, compromise, and reasonableness. "Nods and becks and wreathéd smiles" become the order of the day for communist diplomats.

Outstanding themes of communist propaganda during such periods are the necessity for "peaceful co-existence" among powerful countries having different ideologies; the imperative need for a "relaxation of tensions" in the international community; permissibility of "different paths to socialism"; and the obligation resting upon "progressive forces" to take the lead in solving age-old material problems in human society. Such themes have been prominent in communist ideological pronouncements ever since the buildup in Western military strength after the formation of NATO in 1949, followed by extensive American economic and military aid programs to the free world allies, and by firm United Nations resistance to communist aggrandizement in Korea in 1950. Domestic troubles inside Russia after the death of Stalin in 1953; acute economic problems within the communist bloc; revolts in a number of Soviet satellites; widespread realization among humanity at large that guided

missiles and nuclear weapons imperil the future of the planet—all of these have induced the Kremlin to place more attention than formerly upon non-violent methods for achieving its diplomatic purposes.

The Communist Ideological Crusade in the Balance

In the utilization of psychological warfare techniques in international affairs the Kremlin enjoys several important advantages over the United States and its free world allies. One of these is the great backlog of experience possessed by communist groups in carrying on a war of nerves against their opponents. Bolshevism was conceived in conspiracy against the Czarist government; its leaders devoted years before 1917 to preparing the political soil of Russia for the advent of communism; they undermined the Kerensky government by propaganda and intrigue; and ever afterwards they have waged unceasing psychological warfare against internal and external foes. Advocates of Marxism-Leninism-Stalinism possess a cause which they espouse with all the fervor of religious fanatics and for which they are willing to suffer persecutions, not excluding martyrdom. Furthermore, the claim that the unfolding of history is on their side, that communism is the wave of the future, that their ultimate victory is inevitable, provides an invigorating tonic to sustain them during periods of adversity. And this claim often gives them an initial advantage in enlisting the loyalty of self-styled "progressive" groups throughout the world. Then too Communists have proved highly successful in finding and utilizing an ingredient which experts on psychological warfare deem to be indispensable for success: personalized "devils." "Capitalist warmongers," "Wall Street imperialists," and "fascist beasts," could be blamed for conditions deemed unfavorable for realizing many of mankind's aspirations. In addition, as we have already emphasized, communist propagandists do not hesitate to utilize distortion, outright falsehood, as well as truth, or any combination of these, to advance their objectives. Finally, there is the enormous advantage deriving from a monolithic political system that enables communist countries to make required adjustments in their diplomatic offensive with a minimum of hesitation or hardship. To a greater or lesser extent, all of these assets are possessed by Moscow and Peiping and are denied nations in the free world alliance.

Yet in spite of these advantages, it must not be supposed that communist propaganda efforts have met with unbroken success since the Kremlin launched its ideological offensive against the non-communist world in the immediate postwar period. There have been some spectacular communist propaganda fiascoes and any number of lesser failures. For instance in 1951, in reply to a serious disarmament proposal made by President Truman, Soviet Foreign Minister Andrei Vishinsky stated publicly: "I could hardly sleep all night after having read that Truman speech. I could not sleep because I kept laughing." Vishinsky's remarks made a very poor impression throughout Europe and the neutralist world, especially when the United States followed them up by an intensive propaganda campaign which depicted communist spokesmen laughing over the deadly serious question of disarmament in the nuclear age (1, pp. 135-37). A somewhat similar episode occurred in 1958, when communist diplomats brusquely rejected President Eisenhower's plan for a disarmament "Arctic inspection zone."

Far more crucial than momentary lapses in communist propaganda efforts in determining the success or failure of the Soviet psychological attack, however, is another consideration. Since propaganda is an integral part of the total pattern of a nation's responses to the outside world, what the Soviet Union and its satellites *do* in world affairs, testifies much more eloquently about the nature of the communist system *than what they say they do or are going to do.* Prodigious propaganda efforts are required to erase vivid impressions of the ruthless Soviet suppression of the Hungarian revolt in 1956, of widespread realization that the USSR holds millions of Eastern Europeans in economic vassalage, and of Russian and Chinese aggression in Korea. The theme of "peaceful co-existence" becomes a mockery when other countries know that the Kremlin demands absolute conformity with its announced policies and is prepared if necessary to enforce conformity at gun point. Admittedly, these facts about the communist system are more widely known in some countries than in others. Yet it is probably true that there has come about a heightened appreciation in most countries concerning the true nature of communism. Even in countries where anti-Western sentiment is high, like Egypt, Iran, and Burma, there is often a visible reluctance to accept communist claims at face value and to become overly dependent on Soviet economic and military assistance.

Much as the disciples of Marx scoff at the supposedly bourgeois ideas of objective truth and the existence of natural law principles of honesty, justice, and fairness in human relations, their rejection of these ideas does not prevent other countries from judging Moscow's or Peiping's pronouncements by the record of powerful communist nations in putting lofty communist *ipse dixits* into practice at home and abroad. Bridging the gulf between utopian visions and barbarous behavior is a challenge that taxes the ingenuity of communist propagandists to the utmost. The injunction that faith without works is dead is a precept which lies at the heart of a successful propaganda campaign and which nations cannot violate except at the risk of jeopardizing success in the diplomatic field.

3. THE AMERICAN "CAMPAIGN OF TRUTH"

The propaganda campaign inaugurated by the United States as a counter-measure to Soviet ideological warfare went into high gear in 1949, when impressive communist propaganda gains were being registered against the free world coalition. What are the principal instrumentalities and techniques by which the United States seeks to present its message to the world?

The Voices of America

The broadcasting service operated by the United States Information Service to give world-wide publicity to America's position is known as the Voice of America. However, it is not the only voice of the United States. In democratic countries there exists a multitude of "voices" which convey diverse messages to the outside world. This cacophony is a great obstacle in waging successful psychological warfare but at the same the greatest asset of a politically free society.

Among America's voices there is first of all the official voice of the American government, speaking through diplomatic pronouncements, speeches, notes, conferences, press releases, and in myriad other ways. Under the Constitution, this official voice is under the direction of the President and his immediate subordinate, the Secretary of State. But increasingly there has come to be an ever-widening circle of official and semi-official voices in American foreign policy. The Defense Department may call for greater reliance upon armed forces in meeting threats to national security. The Treasury Department may wish to reduce American economic commitments overseas for the sake of a balanced budget. The Atomic Energy Commission may demand the continued testing of nuclear weapons. All of these and many more may be heard from time to time within the executive branch alternately re-enforcing or competing with the official policy of the government as proclaimed by the President and the State Department.

Then there are five hundred and thirty-five individual voices in Congress, supplemented by the voices of many legislative committees and of hundreds of employees in the legislative branch. The voices of Congress may be heard in a variety of ways. They may be expressed by a bill authorizing generous foreign assistance programs or by amendments to such programs denying funds to individual countries which have incurred legislative displeasure. They may be embodied in a legislative resolution upholding the President in dealing with international crises or in a resolution attacking the nation's diplomatic allies. They may find expression in patient and thorough legislative collaboration with executive officials to solve major international problems or in irresponsible and precipitate public statements by individual legislators, which beget strains

within the free world alliance or create embarrassment for the State Department in dealing with neutralist countries. There may be painstaking and constructive investigations into important aspects of the nation's diplomatic history or heresy-hunting expeditions, conducted with an eye to the headlines, that cast doubt upon the loyalty and competence of the entire diplomatic corps. Intelligent discussions of existing global issues may be heard on the floor of the House and Senate or there may be free-wheeling oratorical outbursts calculated to enhance the political fortunes of legislators. These voices all compete with the Voice of America for the attention of the outside world. And sometimes they can cancel out within a few minutes what has been achieved over the course of months by experts in psychological warfare in creating a favorable image of the United States in foreign minds.

Finally, there is the voice of thousands of groups and millions of citizens embraced in that amorphous, but immensely important, force known as public opinion. There are the voices of competing interest groups, some calling for a higher tariff and some for a lower tariff; some calling for more idealism in the nation's foreign policy and some for more reliance upon military force; some favoring higher immigration quotas and some wishing to exclude foreigner's altogether from America's shores; some demanding greater progress toward world government and some ultrasuspicious of any seeming diminution of "American sovereignty"; some wishing to see greater collaboration among the free world allies and among nations generally and some demanding a go-it-alone policy for the United States; some believing that the only feasible course for the nation is to co-exist with the communist enemy and some believing that this is the surest road to national disaster.

Forming the arena in which these competing groups seek to be heard on governmental policy are millions of citizens who in the ordinary course of events have a limited interest in foreign policy issues and whose knowledge of such issues is confined to that gained from the newspapers, radio, or perhaps weekly news journals. On highly technical questions, such as the proper tariff rate to be charged on textile imports from Japan, or the precise agreement the United States might make with Egypt to finance the Aswan High Dam, or the extent to which the State Department ought to encourage the formation of a regional "agricultural pool" in Western Europe, the mass of the people expresses no opinion whatever. And on a great many other, more fundamental, questions it is at least debatable whether the general public has what can legitimately be called an "opinion." Nevertheless, the voice of public opinion is sometimes heard in a final and authoritative way. The principle *vox populi, vox Dei* is at least valid to the extent that in democratic societies few governments can ignore a strong public opinion on vital issues. Examples in recent years include public insistence upon frenzied demobilization after World War II, upon a policy of increasing "patience and firmness" in dealing with Russia in the immediate postwar period, upon continued non-recognition of Red China, upon careful safeguards and extensive preliminary moves before the United States negotiates with the USSR at a new summit conference, and upon the continued testing and development of nuclear weapons. Very seldom does there occur a nearly unanimous expression of the public will; but when it does occur then it may be said that the authoritative "voice of America" has been heard.

Finally, in common with Soviet Russia and all other nations engaging in propaganda activities, the most influential voice of the nation at any given time may well be its deeds and its actions in the international community. As a State Department official expressed the point in 1952: "Propaganda is 90 percent deeds and only 10 percent words." To illustrate this point, he cited the case of the free world's determination to remain in Berlin in the face of repeated Soviet efforts to compel American evacuation of occupied Germany. The most convincing propaganda that could be made to support the West's position was the fact that during the Berlin blockade American airships landed at the Tempelhof Airdrome in Berlin every three minutes to supply West Germans with the necessities of life denied them by the Soviet Union's blockade (**6**, II, pp. 3172-73). Similarly, American pronouncements on the is-

sue of international peace were enforced graphically when President Eisenhower in 1958 expressed the nation's willingness to create an arms-free neutral zone over the Arctic polar region, even though this offer would have made America's defense effort in the vital Canadian-Arctic area vastly more difficult.

At times propaganda efforts by the United States have been weakened as a result of the nation's behavior in internal and external affairs. As an illustration, whatever influence the nation has had throughout Asia in recent years has sometimes been seriously impaired by racial antagonisms within the United States. Countries within the Afro-Asian bloc are inclined to judge the sincerity of America's attachment to the principle of equality far more by how the American society actually treats national minorities than by idealistic pronouncements from the Secretary of State. Similarly, the extent of America's dedication to the cause of peace is apt to be evaluated by the Western European allies much more by Washington's efforts in seeking to formulate negotiable proposals with the Soviet Union than by lofty resolutions introduced by the American delegation to the United Nations. In the same manner, Latin American countries are likely to test the sincerity of America's belief in the principle of non-intervention in the affairs of other countries by how well that principle is carried out in Latin America.

Forerunners of Postwar Propaganda Efforts

The United States was a comparative latecomer in recognizing the centrality of psychological warfare as an instrument of foreign policy. During World War I, the Creel Committee carried on an intensive campaign of propaganda which made a significant contribution to the Allied war effort. But from 1919 until the late 1930's the United States carried on no noteworthy psychological warfare activities as a part of its foreign relations. Then in the late 1930's several agencies within the government, particularly the Division of Cultural Relations in the State Department, began to undertake propaganda operations directed toward Latin America, where the threat of

Axis penetration had become imminent (**6**, II, p. 3161).

A host of civilian and military agencies with responsibilities in the propaganda field emerged during the Second World War. Among the more important of these were the Office of Strategic Services, the Office of War Information, branches of Army and Navy intelligence, and the Coordinator of Inter-American Affairs who took the place of the Division of Cultural Relations mentioned above. All of these carried on psychological warfare activities designed to shorten the war and to assure ultimate victory by the Allies. In the process, many valuable insights into the nature of such warfare were obtained, and for the first time the United States began to acquire a backlog of experience and of personnel trained in the propaganda field.* These were to pay enormous dividends when cold war compulsions finally forced the United States to initiate its first peacetime campaign of systematic propaganda operations.

After the war many of the functions of these agencies were either eliminated altogether or transferred helter-skelter to the Department of State. Yet neither in the government nor in public opinion was there any noteworthy support for a continuation of psychological warfare efforts. Consequently, in spite of a number of State Department reorganizations designed to bring about greater success (**6**, II, p. 3162), American propaganda efforts languished because of lack of interest and lack of funds required to undertake a successful program.

Then on the eve of the Korean War President Truman committed the nation to undertake a "Campaign of Truth." Explosion of the first Soviet atomic bomb, continuing National Security Council studies of inadequacies in defense policy, followed by the Communist in-

vasion of South Korea on June 25 gave new urgency to this campaign. As set forth by the President, the goals were:

> . . . to present the truth to the millions of people who are uninformed or misinformed or unconvinced . . . to reach them in their daily lives, as they work and learn . . . to show them that freedom is the way to economic and social advancement, the way to political independence, the way to strength, happiness, and peace . . . [to] make ourselves known as we really are —not as Communist propaganda pictures us. (**6**, II, p. 3165).

On June 20, 1952, President Truman created a Psychological Strategy Board to carry on "more effective planning, coordination, and conduct . . . of psychological operations" (**6**, II, p. 3168). In January, 1952, he established within the Department of State the United States International Information Administration (IIA), where responsibility for overseas informational activities was lodged. When the Eisenhower Administration took office in 1953, these agencies were abolished (**6**, II, pp. 3169-72).

The United States Information Agency

On the recommendation of the Eisenhower Administration, the United States Information Agency (USIA), headed by a Director and Deputy Director appointed by the President, was established on August 1, 1953. The State Department was divested of operating responsibility for foreign information programs, although it continued to administer educational and cultural exchange programs.* USIA, by

---

*Space is not available to undertake an extensive treatment of the wartime and early postwar psychological warfare activities of governmental agencies. A number of excellent first-hand accounts and commentaries on the subject are available, including: 5; 1; 13; 14; 22; 24; 19.

The student of foreign policy will find it extremely difficult to assess the intricacy of psychological warfare, to understand the pitfalls that must be avoided and the precepts that must be followed for success, unless he at least samples some of the above accounts.

*A program of educational and cultural exchange-of-persons with other countries was inaugurated by the Fulbright Act of 1946 and was broadened under the Smith-Mundt Act of 1948; the former provides for an exchange of students and professors with other countries, while the latter encourages broader cultural exchange designed to promote better understanding among nations. Other exchange programs are operated under later legislative authority, such as the use of sums accumulated through the sale of surplus agricultural surpluses abroad (**6**, II, pp. 3198-99).

Appropriations for these programs have equalled between $20-30 million annually. One high-ranking diplomatic official has called such programs "among the most fruitful of our activities in the foreign field," citing his first-hand experiences in countries like India and Iran to prove their value (**21**, pp. 53, 580-81). For a provocative analysis of the limitations inherent in such programs as a means for promoting goodwill in international affairs, see **18**, *passim*.

statute, is semi-autonomous but looks to the State Department for guidance on basic foreign policy directives (6, II, p. 3185). A USIA publication in 1955 defined the agency's objectives as: explaining American policies and diplomatic objectives; countering anti-American propaganda disseminated by other countries; demonstrating the "harmony of U. S. policies with the legitimate aspirations of other peoples;" and presenting abroad "aspects of American life and culture which will promote understanding of U. S. policies and objectives" (6, II, p. 3188). By 1958 approximately $100 million annually was being spent on USIA's "Campaign of Truth," with moderate increases requested by the White House for the years ahead.

To carry out these duties, USIA relies upon a variety of techniques and approaches. It maintains over two hundred "overseas information posts" in eighty-two nations. These posts are under the supervision of a Public Affairs Officer working under the American Ambassador or highest-ranking diplomatic official resident in the country. Each PAO has a staff consisting of Americans and residents of the host country. Information activities are carried on by means of exhibits, films, libraries, bookmobiles, posters, radio, television, lectures, comic books, press releases, participation in trade fairs—in short every conceivable technique which promises to advance USIA's objectives within a particular country. Widely varying approaches for different nations and for different levels of society within nations are required. Where illiteracy is high, the emphasis might be upon simple films and comic books. Where educational levels are high, greater reliance can be placed upon booklets, news journals, libraries, and lectures.

Six days a week overseas USIA posts are provided with a lengthy news file which becomes the basis for their propaganda activities. USIA posts utilize this file to prepare press releases, news features, commentaries, newspaper and magazine articles, booklets, exhibits, and other projects which offer promise of success in creating a climate of opinion favorable to the United States abroad (8, pp. 45-117).

The Voice of America (VOA) handles USIA's radio broadcasting services to other countries. VOA operates seven days a week, twenty-four hours per day, broadcasting in approximately forty languages and sending out more than seventy-five programs daily over its facilities. A breakdown of its broadcasting schedule in 1957 showed the following geographical division:

VOA Target Area	Hours Broadcast Daily
Europe	19½
Near East — South Asia — Africa	16¼
Far East	9
Worldwide English broadcasts	4¾
Latin America	51½
	(8, pp. 501-02).

VOA maintains a fourteen-studio broadcasting station in Washington, with million-watt transmitters located in Germany, the Philippines, and Okinawa. A floating radio transmitter is located in the Mediterranean for broadcasting to the USSR and the Middle East. VOA broadcasts are repeated over different wave lengths and at frequent intervals in order to overcome, at least partially, intensive Soviet "jamming" efforts (6, II, pp. 3189-90).

More and more, USIA has successfully used films to convey America's message to foreign lands. Films have been produced in nearly forty languages; more than two hundred film libraries have been established overseas; over 6,000 16mm. film projectors have been put into service. To provide film service for economically backward areas USIA has more than three hundred mobile units capable of producing their own electric power (6, II, p. 3190). One film which has proved unusually effective is entitled "A Nation in Torment." It depicts Soviet suppression of the Hungarian revolt of 1956. In one instance, after this film had been shown to a group of "hard core" Communists in jail in Greece, twenty of this group immediately defected to the free world (8, p. 134). The former American Ambassador to India, Chester Bowles, has praised the success achieved by USIA in India by reliance upon simple, but carefully prepared films to disseminate the free world's message to illiterate and poverty-stricken masses (3, pp. 305-11).

Certain private organizations are currently supplementing the work of USIA in seeking friends for the United States abroad. Two groups particularly have taken the lead in radio broadcasting across the Iron Curtain. These are Radio Free Europe and Radio Liberation. Both of these organizations exist to expose the weaknesses of the communist regime in order to promote defection within communist-dominated countries. Radio Liberation puts particular stress on keeping alive the hope that ultimately deliverance will come to enslaved peoples behind the Iron Curtain (19, pp. 33-6). The Ford Foundation has carried on a continuing program designed to help political refugees become assimilated into the American society and the societies of other countries. The Rockefeller Foundation has underwritten a number of projects in the Middle East, the Far East, and Latin America, aimed at raising health and sanitary levels in these areas. Work undertaken by these and other foundations has paid profitable dividends in terms of promoting goodwill for the United States (19, pp. 219-20).

Past Patterns and Future Prospects

When Robert Burns penned

> O wad some Power the giftie gi'e us
> To see oursels as ithers see us
> It wad frae monie a blunder free us,
> An' foolish notion. . . .

his words accurately described the central problem of carrying on a successful propaganda campaign in foreign relations. Americans are inclined toward complacency and smugness about the impression their official and unofficial behavior makes on the outside world. Passionately convinced of the rightness of their cause, they either believe that reports of anti-American sentiment abroad are unfounded or perhaps Communist-inspired, or that it makes little difference how other countries view the United States.

Careful studies of the viewpoints held by foreigners about the United States reveal many unfavorable views which could be dispelled by more skillful propaganda (20, passim). A UN-sponsored study, for example, showed that while other societies often applied the words "practical" and "progressive" to the United States, words not applied to this country—which were often used to describe other nations—were "brave" and "self-controlled" and, perhaps most depressing of all, "peace loving" (4, p. 9). A study of French attitudes toward the United States revealed that the French are fearful of becoming "Americanized" and of "being victimized by the blunders of a nation which, for all its good intentions, seems . . . politically maladroit and lacking in experience." Many Frenchmen felt that American foreign policy "vacillates incoherently between extremes of isolation and aggressiveness" (7, p. 37). Certain English viewpoints toward the United States were even less flattering. Phrases like "a lot of simple plebeians," an "overgrown child," and "an impulsive nation, composed of decidedly immature people" were used to describe the American nation (7, pp. 38-39). A writer who analyzed German opinion toward the United States found widespread German support for the idea that Americans are "superficial, fickle, unprincipled, extremely naïve at best" (15, p. 55). A study of the impressions formed by Japanese students who had come to the United States was that the American people were "subject to changing whims" and that they were "overly materialistic, uncultured, impulsive, disorderly, shallow, superficial, too individualistic". These students believed that America "looks down on Japan and colored races" (17, p. 88). Running through these and other studies of foreign opinion of the United States are the themes that Americans are anti-intellectual, that they are becoming a nation of conformists, that they are intolerant of the opinions held by other societies, and that they believe heavily in the efficacy of military power to solve problems in the sphere of foreign policy.

Whether these images and stereotypes are true or false is not, for our purposes, the essential point. The point instead is that they exist and that they undoubtedly color relations between the United States and other countries in all spheres. Moreover, their continued existence calls attention to the abiding necessity for more intensified, and more successful, American efforts in the psychological warfare field than have been expended in the past.

A basic problem in this field is the question: how can results obtained be evaluated? Informed students of the subject agree that evaluation techniques are often crude and highly subjective. Frequently they permit little more than an informed guess concerning the results derived from different kinds of psychological warfare tactics. USIA relies upon a variety of tests to measure how well its activities are succeeding: reports of visitors and defectors from communism concerning American informational activities abroad; statements by foreign officials; use of USIA material by foreign news media; surveys of public opinion in free countries; reports by American diplomatic missions overseas; counteractions taken by communist countries such as "jamming" activities or public acknowledgment of VOA programs; actions taken and statements made as a result of USIA activities abroad; and audience mail (8, p. 159).

Testifying before a Congressional committee in 1957, the Director of USIA, Arthur Larson, stated that the only way to measure this agency's effectiveness accurately was to watch "what happens in the respective countries in connection with our foreign relations" (8, p. 153). Presumably, if other countries or groups take actions advocated by organs like the Voice of America, or if their behavior suggests that they have been influenced favorably by what they heard there, then the United States is doing a competent propaganda job. Yet this is a far from reliable criterion. Two parallel phenomena do not necessarily prove cause and effect, as indicated by the classic pitfall in logic: the rooster crows at dawn, the sun comes up, therefore, the rooster made the sun come up. The fact that a hundred defectors from communism cross the border into Western Germany, at a time when the Voice of America is depicting barbarities committed by the Soviet-controlled East German government, does not prove that VOA was responsible for these defections. Similarly, in the case cited earlier of Communists in Greece who defected to the West after seeing a film about the Soviet suppression of the Hungarian revolt, it might be natural to assume that the film

prompted the defections; in reality, these Communists might have been, and some of them undoubtedly were, considering defection sooner or later anyway. It is a commonplace of psychological warfare to design techniques to elicit behavior that the enemy may already be contemplating. The most that can be said sometimes, therefore, is that various propaganda devices accelerate such behavior or that they re-enforce predispositions that already existed. USIA officials are the first to admit that precise measurements of cause and effect in this field are fraught with difficulties.

Nevertheless, there is ground for thinking that American psychological warfare activities have met with limited success. The interrogation of defectors from behind the Iron Curtain reveals an encouragingly high listening rate to the Voice of America in communist-controlled areas. One defector stated: "There are only two moral sanctuaries for the oppressed people of our country—the Church and the American broadcasts" (19, p. 32). The wave lengths of VOA broadcasts are frequently found written in prominent places throughout the Soviet satellite zone (6, II, p. 3181). The USIA believes that in spite of Soviet jamming activities, VOA gets through to certain regions within Russia and the satellites, especially to rural and semi-urban areas. From time to time, communist publications acknowledge that listening to VOA is widespread enough throughout the communist empire to cause concern to Moscow and its puppet governments. The American broadcasts often succeed in disseminating news which Radio Moscow and other news media behind the Iron Curtain have suppressed. This was notably true in respect to revolts in the Soviet satellites during 1955-1956. Communist news outlets were forced to discuss these developments after Western sources had spread the news to people under the Kremlin's control (8, p. 163).

Throughout the free world, the evidence indicates that USIA gets its message across with reasonable success. In West Berlin, for instance, surveys have shown that 98 per cent of the people listen to the Voice of America (6, II, pp. 3179-80). Other studies have indicated that about one million Frenchmen listen to VOA daily; this number grows to two or three million on Sundays. Surveys have revealed that in countries like Germany, France, and Sweden, high percentages of youth and public opinion leaders listen to broadcasts by the United States and its allies (6, II, pp. 3181-82). Stories and articles appearing in the Arab press show that Voice of America broadcasts are monitored regularly for information later utilized by Arab news channels (8, p. 163). In countries like Pakistan, tabulations made of mail received by VOA outlets reveal a high listening rate and a relatively high proportion of letters that are favorable to the American point of view (8, p. 164). As always, of course, the evidence regarding the *actual influence* exerted by the Voice of America in these and other countries is highly inconclusive. Policy-makers in Washington are often required to fall back on hunch and supposition in evaluating the effectiveness of their programs.

Basic to the success of efforts in the propaganda field too is the degree to which these efforts are understood and supported by the American people. The climate of opinion at home has improved substantially over that prevailing in the late 1940's and the early 1950's. During that period the American population seemed to be gripped by a frenzied psychological compulsion on the subject of communism, leading them to believe that agencies of the government like the State Department and Voice of America were rife with communist agents and fellow-travellers. Wholesale, usually unsubstantiated accusations against loyal public servants, not excluding the Secretary of State himself, came dangerously close to cancelling out the progress achieved thus far in creating a favorable image of the United States in the minds of foreigners. United States prestige suffered severely when, as a result of harassment by vocal but poorly informed legislators, USIA officials actually burned books in American overseas libraries because they were deemed pro-communist, or at least not sufficiently anti-communist, in tone (23, 1953, pp. 48-9). Fortunately, the era of countrywide hysteria over the menace of communism appears to have abated. Many Americans now realize that national jitters over the communist danger is precisely the reaction sought by the men in the Kremlin, and that cool heads are better than panic or demagoguery in countering the communist threat. By the late 1950's the atmosphere was much more favorable than formerly for realistic and far-sighted American efforts in the psychological warfare field.

Yet despite substantial gains at home and abroad the truth is that in some respects the free world lags behind the communist bloc in utilizing psychological warfare to advance its diplomatic purposes. One writer quotes the remarks of a German defector from communism, who commented on the feebleness of the free world's propaganda efforts by saying that inside the Communist orbit "you have every opportunity you could possibly wish for," including "a political party afraid of its own shadow," an "economic system that doesn't work," an "atmosphere loaded with tension, suspicion, and instability," and "national conflicts that are explosive." He felt that any trained Communist could make a "revolutionary situation" out of these raw materials and added that "You've got a long way to go before you even catch Lenin" (19, p. 236).

It is surely one of the supreme ironies of all time that the nation which has a "revolutionary" heritage, an historical experience of creating a viable democratic political order of continental dimensions, and a diplomatic record as free of aggressive tendencies as any powerful country known to history, should frequently be bested on the psychological warfare front by an unprincipled, expansionist despotism. The German defector from communism was struck particularly by the free world's apparent lack of preparation, and its consequent paralysis of policy, for dealing with the anti-communist revolt that erupted in East Germany in June, 1953. Western officials possessed no policies capable of utilizing it for the free world's advantage (19, pp. 226-36). No significantly greater acumen was demonstrated by Western officials in dealing with the later revolts by Poles and Hungarians against Soviet domination. As we have noted, some propaganda advantage was reaped by the West by Voice of America broadcasts and films depicting Soviet oppressions; and these perhaps did have some impact upon "neutralist" countries in their assessment of communism. But from the viewpoint of peoples behind the Iron Curtain, a sharp bifurcation has been evident in American policies. Propaganda declarations carried on by official and semi-official organs have sharply diverged from official actions and policies. From time to time, it has appeared to other countries that the United States embraced the "liberation" of Eastern Europe and the "rollback" of the Iron Curtain as official diplomatic goals. Propaganda organs have declared that enslaved peoples had not been "forgotten" by the West; and such organs have at least intimated that the free world would "come to the help" of groups seeking to break the communist yoke. Yet when the crisis came, the United States and its allies did little more than condemn Soviet actions and provide for refugee relief. The net result of the revolt was probably a tighter authoritarian regime for captive nations than before.

Admittedly, there was little that the United States and is allies could do in such cases unless they were willing to fight Soviet Russia, most likely by all-out nuclear war. Under these circumstances, a more realistic propaganda campaign would have exercised greater caution in promising, or suggesting promises for, dependent peoples that the West would support rebellions against Russia's rule over them. How receptive are audiences behind the Iron Curtain *now* to the Voice of America and Radio Free Europe? Only speculative answers are possible, but it would be logical to believe that their receptivity has dropped sharply after they received graphic proof of the inability of the free world to follow up its propaganda messages with deeds. And it is perhaps not amiss to think that years will be required for the United States—assuming that it profits from the lessons of experience—to repair the damage done to its propaganda program by these episodes.

Apart from selected instances of Western maladroitness on the propaganda firing line, throughout the postwar period American foreign policy has suffered from what seems to be a congenital inability to inspire confidence in American leadership among the allies or neutralist countries and to convince other countries that the United States is not perhaps "equally" to blame for the existence of cold war tensions. Uninspired and feeble American

policies have of course played their part in perpetuating this state of mind. Undeniably also, the United States must shoulder some of the blame for the barrenness of negotiations over critical problems like disarmament or the ineffectualness of the United Nations in dealing with conflicts among the great powers. Still, communist-instigated "peace offensives" during the postwar era have too often successfully conveyed the impression widely throughout the world that it was only because of State Department rigidity that oustanding issues were not settled. In far too many cases— Premier Khrushchev's visit to the United States in September, 1959, is an instructive example —the United States has allowed Soviet Russia to pre-empt the goal of "peace" and to create the impression that the only obstacle to achieving it is America's lack of enthusiasm for the abstract goal. The American people and their officials of course know that this is not true. But they have registered no very conspicuous success in showing the fallacies in this claim to other countries.

Gradually, however, the United States is learning valuable lessons through experience in waging psychological warfare. A former information service official, Edward Barrett, has stressed the importance of the rule: "If you must say 'No', say 'No' affirmatively." It makes a far more favorable impression on global opinion to counter offers from the Soviet Union, that quite possibly were intended for propaganda purposes only, with counteroffers of constructive proposals by the United States, by requests for "clarifications" of the Soviet scheme and for "more specific information," than to reject them flatly out of hand as "mere propaganda" (1, p. 141). The United States also cultivates a more favorable image of itself abroad when it expresses its "willingness to negotiate" outstanding causes of global tension, and itself takes the initiative in proposing negotiations, even when it believes that little progress will be made in actually resolving international differences. In short, Barrett suggests that in assessing the reaction abroad to official American policy there is the ever-present necessity to "think back from the headlines." Far better when the "Campaign of Truth" was launched that the headlines should read "U. S. Undertakes 'Campaign of Truth'," than that they should read "Truman Launches Propaganda War against Russia" (1, pp. 72-3).

Should USIA's messages be truthful, even if they are sometimes uncomplimentary to the United States, or should they strive to create a favorable impression abroad regardless of the truth? Some people, especially some legislators investigating USIA's operation, believe that the latter alternative should be followed. For instance, when Saudi Arabia's King Saud visited the United States in 1957, the King received a decidedly cool reception by the people of New York City because of his admitted anti-Semitism. Much to the chagrin of some congressmen, USIA made no effort to disguise this fact in its broadcasting. There is a basic principle of strategy involved in cases of this kind. Said one USIA official in defending this action: "I think the most important thing in the world . . . is that our audience should acquire the conviction that we are telling them the straight story and not an invented, polished, glossed-over version" (8, p. 128).

In propaganda work, establishing and maintaining credibility is one prerequisite for success. Nine out of ten escapees from communist-controlled Hungary stated that they listened to the Voice of America and the British Broadcasting Company because they believed they were receiving a truthful presentation of world events (8, p. 163). How long would audiences of this kind last if they thought VOA propaganda was indistinguishable from that heard over Radio Moscow? The issue posed here penetrates to the roots of the free world's ideology. If the free world coalition routinely engages in duplicity and falsehood in its dealings with other countries, then what inducement is there for other countries to follow its lead instead of Moscow's or Peiping's?

Another continuing problem is the unsympathetic public attitude in the United States toward waging psychological warfare. When headlines like "U. S. Propaganda Post Called Thankless Job" appear in leading newspapers, little room for complacency exists. A reporter with experience in the propaganda field has written that "Perhaps the least sought-after and most inglorious of all [posts in the government] is the job of Director of the United States Information Agency." Heavily contributing to this condition is the fact that "The American people and press have never been fully reconciled to the need for a Government propaganda agency. And Congress, just as suspicious, has seldom been well-disposed toward a bureau that is almost friendless in the nation" (16, October 20, 1957).

Many of the deficiencies in the postwar American psychological warfare campaign came into clear focus with the launching of the Soviet Sputniks late in 1957 and early in 1958. The psychological impact of this scientific achievement in enhancing the prestige of the USSR the world over could hardly be exaggerated. The experienced news commentator, Arthur Krock, wrote that the Sputniks enabled the Soviet Union "to score over the United States the greatest psychological triumph in a contest of this sort between nations throughout history" (16, p. 12). Several months later, another reporter concluded that on the psychological warfare front, "the Soviet Union is scoring propaganda victory after victory," while the impact of the activities of USIA "on the public opinion of the world is marginal" (16, Dispatch by Dana Adams Schmidt, April 13, 1958).

What factors explain the West's, and specifically the United States', inadequacies in the arena of psychological warfare? One obvious explanation is the disparity between the magnitude of Soviet and American efforts in this field, as reflected in the funds each country devotes to this purpose. The USSR annually devotes as much money to jamming the Voice of America as is spent for all the activities carried on by USIA combined. In other words, Soviet "counter-propaganda measures" in the realm of radio transmission alone are about equal to everything the United States spends for its entire psychological warfare campaign. As regards positive measures in the propaganda field, it has been estimated that the USSR spends close to ten times as much to get its message across to the outside world as does the United States (23, 1954, pp. 43-4; 2, p. 94; 19, p. 81).

Also basic to the West's lack of success in the realm of psychological warfare is the fact that the American-led free world coalition has shown no conspicuous ingenuity in evolving slogans and symbols capable of firing the imagination of masses the world over, comparable to "the war to end wars" or the "Four Freedoms" in earlier eras. In far too many cases the West's *policies* have been singularly uninspired in dealing with problems which are of the utmost concern to hundreds of millions of people throughout the world. Writes Chester Bowles: "We have done very little since 1945 to capture the imagination of the Asian peoples, or even to reaffirm concretely our historic position as champion of expanding political and economic freedom for all men" (3, p. 381). Other critics have lamented the absence of a "dominant idea" which could form the nucleus of the West's propaganda counter-attack against militant communism (1, pp. 260-70; 19, pp. 222-25). The threadbare complaint that America's approach has often failed to rise above the level of anti-communism unfortunately remains as valid as ever.

It must be freely conceded that remedying this deficiency in the West's propaganda campaign is no simple matter. In dispensing their political snake-oil, the men in the Kremlin enjoy all the advantages possessed by charlatans throughout history. In a loud voice, their salesmen offer a cure-all for humanity's assorted ills; if prolonged doses do not bring noticeable improvement they can always tell the patient that doses must be continued a little longer before progress is observed; if unfortunate side-effects appear the patient is reassured that these will be as nothing compared with the state of bliss soon to be attained; meanwhile, the patient becomes so debilitated and so dependent upon political quacks that it is next to impossible for him to break away.

The United States and its allies, on the other hand, have no nostrums, no panaceas, to offer the world. The United States cannot claim that wholesale adoption of the "American way of life" will usher in the millennium for millions of backward peoples. Responsible officials and informed citizens in the West know that it will take more than acceptance of the secret ballot or the capitalistic system to satisfy the aspirations of peoples in Egypt, Afghanistan, and South Korea. The West can emphasize that man does not live by bread alone, that progress is most meaningful where mankind is free. It can insist that what counts most is the dignity of the human soul and socio-economic-political programs which recognize the centrality of ethical truths such as those contained in the Judaeo-Christian tradition. It can offer to make limited assistance available to countries which face their problems in ways acceptable to the West and desire outside help. It can summon other peoples to mutual dedication to freedom, to hard work and discipline, to sober analysis of needs and resources, to realistic expectations of their future prospects—all the while exposing the communist system for the cruel hoax it has revealed itself to be in practice since 1917. Above all, the West can see to it that its own behavior accords with its preachments to the international community. More than this the West cannot do without itself departing from its own fundamental ideological precepts.

That this approach sometimes fails to captivate masses of restless and impatient people, especially when they are also being wooed by the seductive slogans of the Kremlin, is understandable and inevitable. To some degree, this condition is inherent in the nature of the ideological conflict which grips the world. Still, it seems undeniable that the West can make a more persuasive effort than it has made in getting its message across successfully. The problem is complex; but it is also of paramount importance—so important that, in the words of Wallace Carroll's book, the continuing challenge facing the free world coalition may well be *Persuade or Perish*.

REFERENCES

1. Barrett, Edward W. *Truth is Our Weapon.* New York: Funk and Wagnalls Company, 1953. An experienced psychological warfare expert analyses American efforts on the propaganda front.

2. Benton, William. "Five Ways to Breach the Iron Curtain," *New York Times Magazine,* March 16, 1958, pp. 9, 94-5. A former Senator and State Department official recommends major changes in American propaganda efforts.

3. Bowles, Chester. *Ambassador's Report.* New York: Harper and Brothers, 1954. The necessity for more intensive American propaganda activities permeates Bowles study of U. S.-Indian relations.

4. Buchanan, William. "How Others See Us," *Annals of the American Academy of Political and Social Science,* 295 (September, 1954), pp. 1-11. Discusses foreign images of the United States as revealed in UN-sponsored studies.

5. Carroll, Wallace. *Persuade or Perish.* Boston: Houghton Mifflin Company, 1948. Describes U. S. propaganda activities during World War II.

6. Department of State. *American Foreign Policy, 1950-1955.* (Publication No. 6446, "General Foreign Policy Series," 117). Washington: 1957.

7. Freymond, Jacques. "America in European Eyes," *Annals of the American Academy of Political and Social Science,* 295 (September, 1954), pp. 33-41. Analyses European viewpoints and stereotypes about the United States.

8. House Appropriations Committee. *Hearings on Appropriations for the Departments of State, Justice, the Judiciary and Related Agencies, 1958,* 85th Congress, 1st Session, 1957. This document contains a wealth of information about contemporary and past operations of USIA and about problems encountered in its field.

9. Kirkpatrick, Evron M. *Target the World.* New York: The Macmillan Company, 1956.

10. ——. *Year of Crisis.* New York: The Macmillan Company, 1957. These two studies carefully analyze communist propaganda activities in the years 1955 and 1956 respectively. Data for individual countries are given.

11. Krock, Arthur. "Why We are Losing the Psychological War," *New York Times Magazine,* December 8, 1957, pp. 12, 91-5. Emphasizes the impact of the Soviet Sputniks in enhancing the Kremlin's prestige around the world.

12. Leites, Nathan. *A Study of Bolshevism.* Glencoe, Illinois: The Free Press, 1953. Contains numerous doctrinal statements from communist sources on propaganda warfare.

13. Lerner, Daniel, ed. *Propaganda in War and Crisis.* New York: George W. Stewart, 1951. Focuses primarily on propaganda experience during World War II.

14. Linebarger, Paul M. A. *Psychological Warfare.* Washington: Infantry Journal Press, 1948. An illuminating study of World War II propaganda activities.

15. Muhlen, Norbert. "America and American Occupation in German Eyes," *Annals of the American Academy of Political and Social Science,* 295 (September, 1954), pp. 52-61.

16. *New York Times.*

17. Passin, Herbert, and Bernett, John W. "The American-Educated Japanese, I," *Annals of the American Academy of Political and Social Science,* 295 (September, 1954), pp. 83-96. An informative study of Japanese opinion of America.

18. Riegel, O. W. "Residual Effects of Exchange-of-Persons," *Public Opinion Quarterly,* 17 (Fall, 1953), pp. 319-28. Challenges many myths and misconceptions as to the efficacy of exchange programs.

19. Scott, John. *Political Warfare.* New York: The John Day Company, 1955. One of the most astute and scholarly studies of American propaganda efforts.

20. Sellin, Thorsten, ed. "America Through Foreign Eyes," *Annals of the American Academy of Political and Social Science,* 295 (September, 1954), pp. 1-221. Careful reflection upon papers in this symposium will impart needed perspective on how the United States appears to other countries.

21. Senate Appropriations Committee. *Hearings on Appropriations for the Departments of State, Justice, the Judiciary and Related Agencies, 1958.* 85th Congress, 1st Session, 1957. Contains information on American propaganda activities at home and abroad.

22. Thomson, Charles A. H. *Overseas Information Service.* Washington: The Brookings Institution, 1948. A thorough evaluation of U. S. wartime informational activities.

23. *United States in World Affairs, 1953,* et seq. New York: Harper and Brothers, 1955. These volumes by the Council on Foreign Relations provide a valuable annual review of issues on the psychological warfare front.

24. Zacharias, Ellis M. *Secret Missions.* New York: G. P. Putnam and Sons, 1946. Describes one of the greatest Allied propaganda victories of World War II: the undermining of Japanese civilian morale, leading to Japan's early surrender.

CHAPTER 15

Foreign Economic Policy

The World's Creditor on Trial

As one of the supporting pillars of a nation's diplomacy, foreign economic policy is of utmost concern to students of international affairs. An example from recent American diplomatic experience will illustrate the centrality of the subject.

Dollars and Diplomacy

In the spring of 1958 Vice President Richard Nixon undertook a "good will tour" of Latin America. Throughout his tour Mr. Nixon encountered anything but good will toward the United States. Extreme anti-American sentiment time and again was manifested by masses in Latin America. Mobs in countries like Peru and Venezuela heaped indignities upon him and the country he represented and threatened his very life. Behind these incidents lay many contributing causes: resentment because the United States often appeared to sanction dictatorial regimes in countries to the south; prolonged efforts by communist-led groups to discredit the United States; festering grievances which have led to sporadic outbursts of Yankee-phobia in the past.

The cause relevant to our discussion here, however, was a deeply imbedded disillusionment with portions of the foreign economic policy adopted by the United States. Latin Americans had long been chafing under the conviction that the United States was "taking them for granted," that their region had consistently played second-fiddle to Europe and Asia in most phases of American foreign economic relations, and that Uncle Sam had been penurious and self-centered in his policies relating to foreign aid and trade questions. Latin Americans were also disturbed over the effects of the American recession of 1957-58, which were beginning to be felt widely throughout the Western Hemisphere. Most Latin American countries rely heavily upon single commodity exports and experienced foreign exchange deficits, as their exports to the United States declined. And because foreign trade was vital to their continued economic well-being, economic crises aggravated existing political turbulence. Anti-American groups found further reason for hostility toward the giant to the north in higher tariffs imposed by Washington on lead, zinc, copper, and oil imports; these commodities often formed an important part of the trade of Latin American countries (25, May 18 and May 25, 1958).

All these grievances and apprehensions coalesced in the hostile reception manifested toward Vice President Nixon. Nixon's tour re-

391

sulted in intensive soul-searching in high diplomatic circles in Washington over United
States-Latin American relations, particularly
economic aspects of those relations. The necessity for more vigorous leadership and a more
imaginative approach to these phases of American foreign policy was widely admitted by
officials of the Eisenhower Administration.
Thus C. Douglas Dillon, Under Secretary of
State for Economic Affairs, proposed a substantial increase in funds for the promotion of
economic growth in Latin America and other
backward areas. Concurrently, he favored participation by the United States in schemes to
stabilize world prices in key commodities and
to impart greater financial strength to such institutions as the International Monetary Fund
and World Bank in order that a decline in
world prices would not precipitate economic
crises in individual countries.

Yet Washington realized that more than
Latin America's problems and needs had been
highlighted by the Nixon tour. Problems there
mirrored those of underdeveloped areas as a
whole. As was emphasized by our discussion
of Africa and Asia, the formulation of effective
policies toward underdeveloped regions will
present a continuing challenge to American
officials for the indefinite future. In dealing
with these areas, economic issues are likely to
be of paramount importance. Nor will there be
any lessening in the importance of economic
questions in relations between the United
States and Western Europe or in the free world
coalition's relations with the communist bloc.

In this chapter our approach will focus upon
three broad categories of problems: American
tariff and trade policies, foreign assistance programs and their consequences, and miscellan-
eous other problems in American foreign economic relations. Analysis of these subjects will
be more meaningful, however, if we first discuss their historical setting.

Basic Economic Trends

Basic to an understanding of present-day
international issues is America's transition from
a debtor to a creditor—in the modern period,
the richest creditor—in the international community. From the first World War onward

there was an outflow of American capital to
other countries. Economic dislocations caused
by two world wars and by the Great Depression destroyed Great Britain's historic position
as the world's creditor. As was the case in
other aspects of international affairs, Britain's
former role was assumed by the United States.
With the precipitous decline in world trade
during the 1930's, much of the world's gold
supply flowed into the United States. Consequently, by the late 1950's the United States
held nearly $23 billion worth of gold, out of a
total world supply of nearly $39 billion (14,
p. 134). Having depleted their gold reserves—
and World War II took most of the reserves
which had been maintained through the Great
Depression—and having cashed in their foreign
investments to finance the war, the nations of
Western Europe emerged in the postwar period near the brink of bankruptcy. Yet they
were faced with the prodigious challenge of
reconstructing their economies and of attempting to restore normal patterns of economic intercourse upon which their future prosperity
depended. Had it not been for vast quantities
of American assistance to such countries, and
to more backward countries in Latin America
and Asia, many of these nations might not
have survived. The world-wide demand for
capital goods and raw materials in war-devastated countries, joined with the inability of
these countries to pay for required imports, led
to the so-called "dollar gap" which was a more
or less consistent feature of the pattern of international economics in the postwar period
(8, pp. 668-76).

A second trend of fundamental significance
in shaping America's response on questions of
international economics has been the increasing reliance the United States must place upon
imports of raw materials and commodities
needed both for civilian consumption and for
defense needs. A cessation of imports of such
consumer goods as coffee, pineapples, tea,
spices, cocoa, olives, tuna fish, sugar, and many
more would cause the American housewife dis-
comfiture and would also have adverse repercussions for certain segments of the American
economy. Far more crucial, however, is America's reliance upon foreign trade to maintain a
strong defense posture. Especially critical are

the domestic shortages of ferroalloys: metals needed to make high-grade steel products, such as airplanes, projectiles and bullets, armor-plating, vehicles, and ships. The following chart highlights America's dependence upon these imports.

Ferroalloys	Imports As Per Cent of Domestic Consumption (1954)
Manganese	98
Chromite	91
Cobalt	85
Nickel	95
Columbite and tantalite	99
Vanadium	60
Tungsten	65

(Source: 32, p. 36)

Manufacture of a particular type of jet airplane, according to a State Department publication, requires the following imported metals:

Material	Pounds Utilized	Per Cent Imported
Chromium	3,659	92
Nickel	2,117	97
Aluminum (bauxite)	46,831	76
Copper	436	88
Cobalt	2,309	35

(Source: 7, p. 11)

These are, or ought to be, sobering figures. They indicate the degree to which the United States is presently dependent upon the outside world for some of its most basic security needs. They constitute perhaps the most convincing refutation possible of an "isolationist"

UNITED STATES AND COMMUNIST BLOC AID TO CRITICAL COUNTRIES
In Millions of U.S. Dollars, mid-1955 to 1959

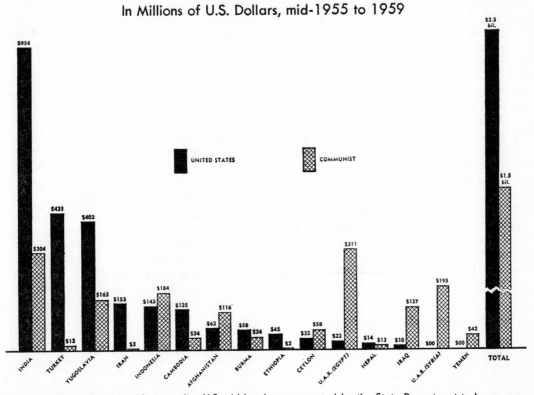

Communist bloc aid is primarily in credits. U.S. aid has been computed by the State Department to be as comparable as possible to the Communist program. U.S. figures include obligations by the International Cooperation Administration, the Development Loan Fund and Export-Import Bank, as well as Public Law 480 loans arising from U.S. surplus food sales overseas.

Adapted from *The New York Times*, March 29, 1959.

approach to foreign affairs. Projections for the future anticipate ever-increasing reliance upon imports in such categories as iron ore, crude oil, aluminum (bauxite ore), copper, lead, zinc, and virtually all the other ferroalloys, (8, p. 716).

Third, issues in the sphere of foreign economic policy assume unprecedented magnitude because of the communist economic offensive against the free world after the Geneva Conference of 1955. Communist Party boss Nikita Khrushchev admitted candidly to a visiting group of American legislators that "We value trade least for economic reasons and most for political reasons" (15, p. 732). This was no mere idle comment. From 1954 to 1957 the USSR doubled its trade with the underdeveloped countries of the world, raising it from $840 million in the beginning of the period to $1.7 billion at the end of the period. Over 150 trade agreements were negotiated by the USSR with nations in the free world (10, p. 36). Simultaneously there had come about a spectacular rise in the number of communist bloc "technicians" visiting countries still within the free world; the communist propaganda apparatus undertook an intensive campaign to discredit American assistance to other countries as "capitalist imperialism" whose purpose was to bring about the "enslavement" of weaker states; and communist countries stepped up their participation in trade fairs and exhibitions (e.g., by creating an impressive and expensive display at the Brussels World's Fair) at which the "achievements" of the communist people's democracies could be demonstrated to all mankind (33, pp. 1-3). The total impact of these moves was to put the free world coalition on the defensive in many critical areas throughout the world.

Domestic Policy and Foreign Policy

Finally, mention must be made of the extent to which economic developments within the United States affect, and are in turn affected by, international trade and finance. The aphorism that "When the United States catches a cold, Europe sneezes," has no greater validity than in the economic realm. In the postwar period fundamental economic trends within

the United States have had a far broader impact than upon Europe alone; their ramifications have extended throughout the civilized world. The total level of spending by the United States government, the proportion of the federal budget devoted to national defense, the national income generated in any given year, the number and composition of the civilian labor force, the level of domestic prices, the depletion of natural resources, the present and future well-being of domestic agriculture —all of these enter into calculations of national power, capabilities, and intentions. Capitals like Moscow, London, Paris, New Delhi, and Tokyo are keenly interested in the entire gamut of so-called "domestic" issues within the United States. Thus effective American consumer demand for textiles will in turn affect the level of Japanese industrial production, which will go far toward shaping the total pattern of Japanese foreign trade, which will be a significant element in determining Japan's relations with Southeast Asia and Red China, and so on. While the long-run consequences of economic phenomena within the United States may pass through a number of intermediate stages before they trigger major developments on the world scene, their ultimate effect upon the course of international affairs cannot be doubted. The growing interdependence between what were formerly "internal" and "external" policy matters is surely one of the most fundamental trends of interest to students of world affairs in the mid-20th century.

Furthermore, if it is of the utmost importance that the United States maintain a position of strength from which to lead the free world coalition, problems of international trade and finance become high priority issues. Few Americans realize how much their own security and the security of their diplomatic friends are tied up with the maintenance of a high level of American exports. Looked at purely from the point of view of domestic economic welfare, exports have played a progressively more important role in creating a position of economic strength and in supporting a high standard of living. Even "isolationists" would agree to the principle that full production and employment cannot be maintained within the United States without access to the world market though, as we shall see, they often do not see the companion necessity for a high level of imports. Brief attention to a few statistics will pinpoint the relationships discussed here.

For the year 1957 the total volume of exports by the United States approximated $19.4 billion, while imports equalled only $13.3 billion, leaving an export surplus of $6.1 billion in America's balance of international trade.* This gap was substantially closed by payments of the United States Government to other

---

*Students are cautioned about the necessity for precision in the use of certain basic terms and concepts of international economics. Thus the term "balance of payments" must be carefully differentiated from the term "balance of trade." The former is merely a record of the international transactions of a nation over a specified period of time, usually one year. "Credits" show up in this record as claims of one country, let us say the United States, against other countries. Credits show that other countries have bought certain exports or services from the United States. "Debits" show up as claims other countries have against the United States, the most common of which are imports and services purchased by Americans from these countries. Consequently, this record of international transactions must always "balance" in the sense that for everything the United States sends abroad it receives something of value in return —imports, "invisible" items like insurance protection or shipping services, or perhaps promises by other countries to pay in the future (loans).

There is therefore literally no such thing as a favorable or unfavorable balance of payments except in the sense that a country might like a different distribution of percentages on the credit and debit sides of the ledger. Thus the United States might have preferred that other countries send more imports to it in 1957 to close the export gap, rather than that the gap be narrowed by United States Government expenditures for military purposes.

The term "balance of trade," on the other hand, is much more restricted, referring only to the difference between the value of exported and imported *goods* in a given year. In Mercantilist thought of the 17th and 18th centuries, it was believed that the balance of trade was "favorable" when a nation exported more than it imported, receiving payment in gold—a view which, carried to its logical extreme by all nations, would have dried up international trade altogether. In the modern period, economists do not accept this concept. The ratio of exported goods to imported goods in itself has very little significance; and in some instances it may be positively advantageous for countries to import more than they export. In any event, the trade position of a country will be determined by the *totality* of its transactions, including such "invisible" transactions as shipping and freight charges, travel expenditures by its citizens, interest and dividends on foreign investments, government aid and settlements, and many more (**12**, pp. 71-81; **37**, pp. 61-80).

---

countries for the maintenance of American troops and military installations overseas. In addition, excluded from this calculation is military and economic-technical assistance to other countries. Had this gap between the cost of exports and imports not been closed by the payments described above, one of two alternative courses would have become inevitable: either the United States would have had to reduce its sales in foreign markets or else it would have had to increase its imports and use of foreign services (**14**, pp. 133-35; **13**, p. 28).

Stated differently, in contrast to what is widely supposed, the United States does not demonstrate altruism in "buying from other countries." Such purchases are an investment in its own continued prosperity, enabling other countries to purchase goods and services from business enterprises within the United States. The disparity prevailing in recent years between what the United States has sold abroad and what it has bought abroad could not be maintained without substantial governmental grants and loans from the United States, permitting other nations to accumulate dollars necessary for purchases from America; otherwise, such countries would inevitably be required to curtail their orders from the United States. Viewed strictly from the point of view of the economic welfare of the United States, therefore, the only alternative to continuing large-scale governmental grants and loans to other countries is maintenance of a high level of imports. Otherwise, an economic contraction within the United States would be inescapable.

As with all aggregate figures, export totals in any given year disguise the extent to which individual industries within the United States are dependent upon sales in foreign markets to maintain prosperity. The table at the top of page 396 shows a partial listing of important products entering the export market.

Corresponding percentages for agricultural goods run much higher. In the period 1956-57, 85 per cent of the rice, 54 per cent of the wheat, 26 per cent of the tobacco, and 61 per cent of the cotton produced in the United States entered foreign markets (**21**, p. 693). Testifying before the House Ways and Means Committee in 1958, Secretary of Commerce Sinclair Weeks observed that the livelihood of

Product	Exports As Per Cent of Total Production
Copper sulfate	45
Track-laying tractors	40
Civilian aircraft	33
Sulphur	29
Penicillin	29
Construction and mining equipment	26
Trucks and buses	19
Coal	14
Machine tools	11

(Data compiled from: **14**, p. 135; **21**, p. 693).

some 4.5 million workers in the United States —about 7 per cent of the total labor force— depended upon foreign trade (**2**, p. 112).

Under certain circumstances different, but no less deleterious, consequences for the domestic economy can follow when the nation buys more than it sells in the world markets. Throughout the greater part of the period since World War II, when other countries were economically debilitated and heavily dependent upon the United States, the opposite tendency—for exports to exceed imports— usually prevailed in American foreign trade. By the 1950's, however, economic recovery had been achieved in Western Europe, and some economic progress had been made in more underdeveloped countries. By the end of the decade many of these countries were selling comparatively more goods and services to America than they were buying from America. *Merchandise* exports from America in 1959 were estimated at $15 billion annually, while *merchandise* imports were estimated at $14 billion annually, as contrasted with *merchandise* exports of $19.4 billion against imports of $13.3 billion in 1957. Thus other countries had increased their sale of goods and commodities to America by more than $5 billion annually between these two years. Overall, payments *by* the United States in international economic transactions exceeded by $3.7 billion payments

THE PATTERN OF U.S. FOREIGN TRADE

In Billions of U.S. Dollars, 1958

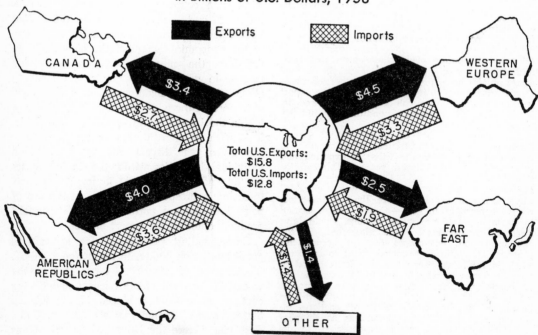

Adapted from *The New York Times*, Feb. 23, 1958; figures from
Statistical Abstract of the United States: 1959, pp. 894-5.

made *to* the United States by other nations. One result of this deficit was an outflow of gold from this country; another was a building up of dollar reserves by other nations—the latter tendency promoting greater "liquidity" in the foreign trade accounts of these nations.*

Many complex factors accounted for this change in America's trade position, most of them too intricate to be discussed here (**19**, *passim*). There were a number of possibly transitory, non-recurring causes and some much more long-range and fundamental ones. Foremost among the latter were: the enhanced economic position of other countries *vis-à-vis* the United States; repayment of obligations owed by other countries to the United States at a more rapid rate than had been anticipated; a decline in the flow of governmental and private capital from the United States, caused in part by more stringent credit requirements and higher interest rates at home; a decline in the foreign sales of certain classifications of American exports; and an increase in the purchase of foreign-made goods by Americans—highlighted by the sale of 27,000 foreign-produced automobiles in America in 1953 versus 432,000 in 1958!

---

*The concept of "liquidity" is explained at length, and its implications for American foreign policy assessed, in a later section of the chapter.

America's adverse trade position could, in the long run, exert a deflationary effect upon the domestic economy and could weaken the nation's overall role in international trade. The ultimate solution, in the words of one observer, lies in "the strengthening of our competitive position . . . both in foreign and in domestic markets." Specifically, this means maintaining and perhaps improving the comparative advantage that the United States possesses in designated areas of production, such as chemicals, synthetic rubber, aircraft, railroad and various categories of construction equipment, food processing equipment, and certain agricultural commodities. With underdeveloped countries, substantial improvement in America's trade position will depend in no small measure upon the ability of these nations—relying upon assistance from more economically advanced countries—to raise their consumption levels and hence to expand their foreign purchases (**19**, p. 24).

Recent trends in American economic relationships with the outside world have been sketched to call attention to the importance of economic aspects of foreign policy and to demonstrate the intimate association between foreign and domestic policy issues. With these considerations in mind, we turn now to an examination of specific problems in the economic relations between the United States and other countries.

1. AMERICAN TARIFF AND TRADE POLICIES

Few issues have engendered such controversy throughout American history as the tariff. Significantly, the second law passed by Congress under the Constitution was the Tariff of 1789, upon which the government was heavily dependent for revenue. Major stages in the development of United States tariff policy thereafter occurred in 1816, when the first tariff for the protection of American domestic industry from foreign competition was passed; in 1890, when President McKinley was given limited authority to adjust tariff rates after tariff concessions had been obtained from other countries; in 1916 when the United States Tariff Commission was created to study trade

questions and make recommendations to the President concerning rate adjustments; in 1930, when American tariff rates under the Smoot-Hawley Tariff reached their highest level in history—52.8 per cent of the value of dutiable imports. Thereafter, in large measure as a result of the Great Depression, of the barriers erected by the Smoot-Hawley Tariff, and of retaliatory steps taken by other countries against American imports, the foreign trade of the United States declined spectacularly, dropping from over $10 billion in 1930 to less than $3.5 billion in 1933. The early 1930's also witnessed a proliferation of trade restrictions throughout the international community. This was the period, for example, of the emergence of the "British Imperial preference system," whereby more favorable tariff rates were applied to nations within the British Empire and Commonwealth than to nations outside it (20, pp. 895-98).

The Reciprocal Trade Program

It was against this background of virtual stagnation of international trade, accompanied by the multiplication of barriers to its revival, that President Roosevelt and Secretary of State Cordell Hull proposed a reciprocal trade program. After vigorous leadership by the White House, Congress inaugurated the program in 1934 as an amendment to the Smoot-Hawley Tariff. The President was authorized for a three-year period to enter into trade agreements with other countries. He was permitted to reduce American tariff rates to a limit of 50 percent of prevailing rates, provided that other countries made equivalent concessions in their tariff rates on American goods.

The reciprocal trade program, technically known as the Trade Agreements Act of 1934, was renewed at intervals, and with some modifications, over the course of the years which followed. No significant change was made in its provisions in the renewals of 1937, 1940, and 1943. The apex in a philosophy of free trade was reached in the TAA renewal of 1945, when the President was given authority to cut tariff rates on a reciprocal basis up to 75 per cent of prevailing 1934 rates.

In 1947 the United States and twenty-two other nations negotiated the General Agreement on Tariffs and Trade (GATT); its purposes and provisions will be described below. In 1948, with Congress under the control of the Republican Party, the TAA was extended for an additional year. Certain "protectionist" features, to which we shall refer presently, were also introduced into the reciprocal trade program. In the same year fifty-three nations, including the United States, signed the Charter of the International Trade Organization (ITO) at Havana, Cuba. This agreement, like GATT, was designed to bring about a reduction in world trade barriers. ITO, however, has never received Senate ratification and prospects do not appear favorable for its ratification in the future.

The year 1949, with Democrats once again in control of Congress, witnessed a three-year extension of TAA. Again in 1951 TAA was renewed for two years, but with reinsertion of protectionist features which had been dropped in 1949. At this time too Congress prohibited American tariff concessions to countries carrying on trade in strategic goods with countries behind the Iron Curtain. Under the first Republican Administration in twenty years, in 1953 Congress extended the TAA for one year. At the same time it accepted President Eisenhower's recommendation for the appointment of an impartial commission, known as the Randall Commission[*], to study, and bring in recommendations in the field of American foreign economic policy.

Acting upon the Randall Commission's suggestions, in 1954 President Eisenhower requested a three-year extension of the TAA. Congress granted only a one-year extension. A year later, however, Congress accepted the White House's request for a three-year extension of the program. By the summer of 1958 Congress had agreed once again to give the President substantially the authority he asked for in tariff reduction. The President had requested an unprecedented five-year extension of the TAA, with authority to reduce tariffs by 5 per cent a year for this period. The state of international affairs—crises in the Middle East and recent Soviet advances in scientific research and development—vastly strengthened the President's hand in dealing with Congress on this issue. The necessity for preserving intimate ties with the allies and for demonstrating dynamic American leadership throughout the free world was never more urgent. Even so, the Administration was required to make concessions to "protectionist" sentiments in Congress by strengthening provisions designed to give relief to domestic producers who were threatened by foreign competition. With these concessions, the White House was able to secure wide support within both political parties for a four-year extension of its trade program

---

[*]A lengthy excerpt from the Randall Commission's report is included in 5, II, pp. 2898-2929.

(2, pp. 97-9, 128; 25, August 10, 1958). By the late 1950's, the United States had trade agreements with more than 40 countries (35, p. 45).

"Peril Points" and "Escape Clauses"

Trade agreements legislation contains two provisions designed to safeguard American producers from injury sustained from expanded imports into the United States. One is the "peril point" clause. Specifying that *new* reciprocal trade agreements should not lower tariffs below a level that would seriously harm domestic industries, the TAA requires the Tariff Commission to determine the "peril point" —the tariff rate below which reductions would jeopardize domestic producers—for imported commodities. The Commission informs the President of its findings and also makes them public. Supposedly, executive officials take these findings into account when they negotiate trade agreements with other countries.

Closely akin to the peril point idea is the "escape clause" provision in trade legislation, which may be invoked *after* trade agreements have been negotiated with foreign countries. In 1951 Congress directed that an "escape clause" be inserted into all new trade agreements and that it be incorporated into all existing ones as soon as possible. The basic idea of this provision is that if imports are found to threaten American producers substantially, then tariff rates for such imports will be raised to give relief to home industry. The Tariff Commission is required by law to carry on continuing studies of the impact of imports upon the economy. These studies may be initiated upon its own authority, or at the request of the President, Congress, and private groups. If the Commission finds that domestic industry is being seriously impaired, it reports its findings to the President and to Congress.

With both peril point and escape clause provisions, however, the President is free to accept or to reject the Commission's recommendations. In any case, he may not reduce tariff rates below the minimum levels prescribed by law. The publicity often given the Commission's studies by private business groups, lobbying and advertising carried on by businesses affected, and constituency pressures upon Congress and the executive branch frequently create forces well-nigh compelling the President to grant tariff relief fully or partially. In some cases the President may become convinced that such relief is well justified to protect segments of American industry from foreign competition. For example, from the inception of the "escape clause" provision in 1951 through mid-1958, the President made decisions under the clause affecting twenty-three commodities, granting tariff relief to American businesses on nine and refusing to grant relief on fourteen (2, p. 112). Complaints of alleged hardships to American industry are investigated and reinvestigated by the Tariff Commission. Thus during 1957, the Commission held its fourth inquiry into the effect of the importation of "spring clothespins," ultimately finding that imports were damaging domestic industry. Accordingly, the President doubled the tariff rate on this product. In the same year, a third investigation into the effects of bicycle imports was undertaken. In this case, the Commission unanimously found that no tariff relief was justified. Consequently,

VESTED INTERESTS!

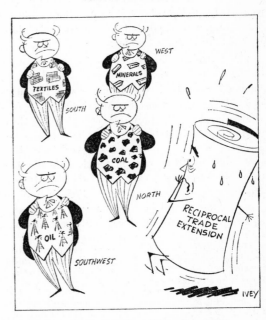

Jim Ivey in *St. Petersburg Times*, July, 1958.

the President took no action to raise tariffs on bicycles (**35**, pp. 9-10).*

While the aggregate number of instances in which the "escape clause" has been utilized to curtail imports has been relatively small, the mere existence of the clause in American tariff legislation doubtless has a deterrent effect upon the inclination of other countries to increase their imports to the United States sharply. As an illustration, the United States achieved a substantial reduction in Japanese imports without actually invoking escape clause provisions. By the 1950's Japanese textile producers were sending large quantities of goods to compete with an already depressed American textile industry. Japanese imports never ran more than 2 per cent annually of the total American consumption of textiles; but in selected categories —cheap blouses, corduroy, gingham, velveteen —competition with Japanese-produced goods was causing acute distress to American firms. Rather than risk almost certain and probably drastic action by the American government to restrict Japanese imports, Japan voluntarily imposed quotas upon its own manufacturers who exported to the American market. To forestall a recurrence of this problem, an American trade mission to Japan in 1956 strongly urged Japanese manufacturers to diversify in order to reduce the threat of retaliatory action against floods of Japanese goods into countries like the United States (**36**, pp. 200-01).

Yet Japan's voluntary reduction of exports to the United States by no means disposes of Japan's foreign trade problem; nor was this action ideal even from an American point of view. As much as any other nation in the world, Japan must trade or die. The Japanese are dependent upon the outside world for the vast bulk of their raw materials. To obtain them the Japanese must sell their finished products in foreign markets. For example, Japan is the second best customer of American agricultural exports, buying large quantities of

*For insight into the extreme complexity of problems arising under both "peril point" and "escape clause" provisions, and the numerous factors that must enter into decisions to raise tariff rates or maintain them at existing levels, the student is urged to read the case studies set forth in **35**, pp. 1-34 and in subsequent issues in the same series.

American-grown cotton annually. In 1957, Japan bought $1 billion worth of goods from the United States, leaving a trade deficit with America of over $600 million. In the month of February, 1958, 114 textile firms in Japan went bankrupt. Either Japan can dispose of a substantial part of its exports throughout the free world, with the United States taking its fair share, or else Japan will be forced for reasons of self-preservation to cultivate stronger trade ties with the communist bloc, and especially with its historic "natural markets" in Red China and North Korea. Japanese gravitation toward the communist bloc in the realm of trade would greatly increase its dependence upon the bloc in the political realm. In turn, this would significantly weaken the free world's defense posture throughout the Pacific region. Yet, as Under Secretary of State Christian A. Herter stated bluntly in 1958: "If the West closes the trade door in Japan's face, Japan must turn to the Communist bloc" (**15**, p. 734).

As with most questions in foreign policy, the issue of free trade versus "protection" admits of no simple solution. Policies embracing one viewpoint or the other—or policies that seek to bring about a "compromise" between the two positions—achieve some purposes while failing to achieve others. Choices must be made, however, and some kind of *de facto* scale of priorities among competing goals must be established. On balance, as we shall see at a later stage, the advocates of free trade have the stronger case; the most persuasive argument put forward by advocates of protectionism is perhaps the idea that certain industries are vital for defense—but even this argument does not necessarily prove that *tariffs* are required to sustain these industries. Pressed to its logical conclusion, the protectionist mentality would dry up international trade almost altogether. Even in its more moderate manifestations, it must be regarded as a concession to what is, in some quarters, a strongly entrenched isolationism, a tendency to equate private interests with the national interest, and lack of comprehension about the complex process of foreign trade—specifically, the relationship between buying and selling in world markets.

The Problem of East-West Trade

No better example of the central importance of commercial relations as an aspect of international relations can be found than the issue of East-West trade during the postwar period. Trade between nations now behind the Iron Curtain, including Communist China and North Korea, and those in the rest of the world was never impressive in the aggregate, totalling only 7.4 per cent of the world's trade in 1938. While the dollar volume of trade was higher in 1955, the percentage by that date was only 2.6 per cent of world trade (**17**, p. 1). As we shall see, however, in many respects the issue of East-West trade had assumed an importance far beyond the extent justified by these statistics, not least as a subject of contention between the United States and its chief allies in the cold war.

The Marshall Plan originally had contemplated re-establishment as nearly as possible of the traditional flow of trade between the western and eastern portions of Europe. The Kremlin's mail-fisted rule within its satellite zone, however, reduced the satellites to a position of economic vassalage and redirected their trade toward the USSR. Steadily deteriorating relations between the free world and the communist bloc from 1947 onward were reflected in the stiffening attitude of the United States toward trade with countries behind the Iron Curtain. Beginning in December, 1947, the American Government undertook to tighten trade restrictions toward the communist world to prevent the outflow of goods and commodities which would simultaneously weaken the free world and strengthen the communist empire. Even more severe congressionally-imposed restrictions on East-West trade were incorporated into legislation authorizing the Marshall Plan, which prohibited the ECA Administrator from delivering American foreign assistance to any country sending strategic goods behind the Iron Curtain.

After this, progressively more rigid limitations were placed by Congress on East-West trade, culminating in the "Battle Act," officially known as the Mutual Defense Assistance Control Act of October 26, 1951. This act sought to compel greater free world collaboration in behalf of trade restrictions against the communist bloc. Under its provisions embargo lists were prepared, with trade goods ranked in order of their strategic importance. A total embargo was imposed upon raw materials and finished goods having an obvious military application, while limited trade was permitted with the bloc in semi-strategic and non-strategic items. The Battle Act, which has no termination date, applies alike during periods of peace and war. It provides that American foreign assistance to other countries *must* be terminated to countries violating the embargo lists, although the President is authorized to make an "exception" when he feels the national interest so demands (**17**, pp. 1-13).*

Efforts to assure maximum free world collaboration in maintaining trade controls toward the communist bloc eventually led to the creation of formal machinery by which multi-national agreements could be reached. A Consultative Group, consisting of the United States, its Western European allies, Turkey, and Japan was formed to arrive at common policies. Within the CG, two subordinate bodies exist, one concentrating upon trade affecting the European satellite zone and the USSR, the other on trade questions affecting Red China, North Korea, and North Viet Nam. Both groups operate upon a basis of unanimity. Decisions reached, however, are subject to acceptance by each member state, so that in the last analysis the power of these groups is limited solely to making recommendations (**17**, pp. 17-18).

After the wars in Korea and in Indochina, Washington was being subjected to continuing pressure by the allies to relax existing trade controls against the communist world. Pressure mounted as the European allies were expanding their trade volumes, as American foreign economic assistance declined, as fears of a

---

*"Exceptions" have been the rule under this act. Although certain recipients of American foreign assistance have continued to send goods behind the Iron Curtain in violation of the act, in virtually every instance the United States has made an "exception" in these situations, chiefly because these goods were shipped under trade agreements antedating passage of the Battle Act and because the national interest would be more damaged by terminating aid than by continuing it under these circumstances. For details see **17**, pp. 45-6 and **16**, pp. 83-7.

third world war abated, and as the communist nations made attractive overtures for new trade agreements with the outside world. Following extensive study and negotiation, therefore, by the summer of 1954 the Consultative Group agreed to lift many restrictions on trade with the European communist bloc. Totally embargoed goods were reduced in number from 260 items to 170, the total quantity of many other goods which were permitted to move to the communist nations was expanded, and the "surveillance list" of goods for which total shipments were to be carefully watched by the free world was reduced from 100 items to 60 items. These changes, however, applied only to communist countries in Europe. Moreover, such outright military items as arms, ammunition, and nuclear raw materials were still embargoed (**17**, pp. 28-9). After CG agreement on these changes, the United States made corresponding modifications in the Battle Act to liberalize trade restrictions.

A moderate expansion in trade between East and West followed, although of course it was not altogether caused by, these modifications. For example, trade between America and Russia in 1956 reached the highest peak in any year since 1948, with the USSR sending almost $25 million in exports to the United States and the United States sending about $5 million in imports to Russia—in itself a bare trickle of trade and still considerably less than almost $90 million in Soviet exports to America and $30 million in imports from America in 1948. After 1956 trade declined somewhat again, tending to climb back to the 1956 level by the end of the decade. By quantitative standards, trade between the United States and the Soviet Union remained inconsequential, equaling about one-hundredth of the USSR's total trade of $2.25 billion with the free world as a whole. America's trade with the entire communist bloc throughout the postwar period has been insignificant and, despite large percentage increases in recent years, remains of incidental importance (**25**, August 16, 1959).

The same cannot be said, however, for trade between the communist bloc and America's chief allies. Old trade patterns have been broken; evolving trade patterns by the mid-1950's showed that the cycle whereby raw ma-

terials from the east were exchanged for finished goods from the west is giving way to a highly "diversified" kind of trade. More and more, Eastern Europe is sending finished steel and engineering goods abroad and is reducing its exports of raw materials, many of which are doubtless going to the USSR (**16**, pp. 2-3). During the 1950's trade increased significantly between the communist bloc and the European allies, notably the Federal Republic of Germany, the United Kingdom and France (**16**, p. 4).

Besides taking the initiative in imposing restrictions on trade between the free world and the communist zone of Europe, the United States has tried even harder to curtail trade with Red China and lesser communist countries in Asia. The Sino-Soviet *entente* after 1949 had radically altered China's historic trade pattern. By 1956 Red China carried on over three-fourths of all its trade with the communist bloc, whereas in the prewar period nearly all of its trade had been with countries now in the free world (**17**, p. 31). Besides a deliberate recasting, part of this change could be attributed to American leadership in imposing progressively severer controls upon free world trade with Red China. The United States imposed a blanket embargo upon its own trade after Chinese intervention in the Korean War; and American leadership was responsible for passage of a resolution by the UN General Assembly on May 18, 1951, declaring a sweeping embargo on all trade bound for Red China and North Korea (**17**, pp. 33-4).

Since that time, the United States has been hard pressed to maintain free world cohesiveness on the issue of trade with Red China. Embargo lists were far more sweeping than corresponding lists for communist Europe; revisions of the latter lists did not apply to China. By the late 1950's it was clear that the United States and its principal allies disagreed substantially on this question. After the armistices in Korea and Indochina, our allies, led by Great Britain, maintained that the "China differential" was illogical, since goods acquired from the West could readily be transshipped from other parts of the communist world to China. While the allies favored a continued embargo of *strategic* goods, they did not favor

By the end of the 1950's, the matter was under continuing investigation by the Tariff Commission, which had been directed to report to the House Committee on Ways and Means and the Senate Committee on Finance a plan that would: (1) establish logical and up-to-date tariff classifications; (2) eliminate existing anomalies and illogical classifications; and (3) simplify the determination and application of tariff classifications. On the basis of the Commission's studies, Congress was expected to make required changes in tariff legislation in the near future (35, pp. 40-1).

The General Agreement on Tariffs and Trade

In 1947 the United States and twenty-two other countries signed an agreement to promote world trade, known as the General Agreement on Tariffs and Trade (GATT). By 1958 thirty-seven countries belonged to GATT. GATT's purpose was to facilitate the expansion of multilateral trade by securing widespread agreement to its three guiding principles: (1) nondiscrimination by one member of GATT against the other members; (in other words, the "most favored nation" principle governs, whereby trade concessions made to one country in GATT will be made equally to all members); (2) agreements among all members for reciprocal tariff reductions; and (3) elimination of "import quotas" and other barriers to the exchange of goods and services among members (6, p. 7). Negotiations between the United States and other members of GATT have resulted in American tariff concessions on a larger dollar volume of imports to America than exports from America. On the other hand, several other countries reduced their tariff *rate* under GATT below the percentage rate reduction granted by the United States. The Senate has never formally ratified the executive agreement whereby the United States joined GATT. As we saw in Chapter 3, such agreements may nonetheless determine the official position of the United States Government in foreign affairs, even though Congressional acceptance of it would give a much firmer basis to American membership in GATT. In the absence of that

acceptance, GATT's future cannot help remaining obscured by a cloud of uncertainty.

Trade Policy—the Road Ahead

The judgment to be rendered upon American tariff and trade policy since the nation assumed leadership of the free world after the Second World War depends upon the prior assumptions within which one operates in deciding what kind of policy is in the national interest.

The economic conservative and "protectionist" will complain that today the President possesses sweeping authority to reduce tariffs—even to the point of injuring segments of domestic industry; the level of imports into the United States is at an all time high—approximately $13 billion annually—with the result that the "trade gap" is much narrower today than in the early postwar era; the average American tariff on dutiable goods has fallen from around 38 per cent in 1940 to under 15 per cent in 1955; and the tariff rate of the United States is considerably below rates levied by such countries as Italy, France, and the United Kingdom (25, December 16, 1956 and February 2, 1958). All of these considerations will be cited as evidence that the United States has already gone far in the direction of free trade and that no sweeping liberalization of tariff rates is required in the future. Indeed, protectionist groups argue that the dominant requirement today is to safeguard American industries threatened by ever-broadening streams of imports (2, pp. 109-23).

Advocates of a liberal trade philosophy, on the other hand, reject the premise that the postwar record in American tariff and trade policy furnishes an adequate guide to present and future conduct. They believe that protectionist features of the tariff law like the "peril point" and "escape clause" provisions cancel out much of the good which the reciprocal trade program was designed to accomplish. They believe the existing disparity between American exports and imports is unnatural and that it could only continue because the United States Government is closing this gap by direct payments to other governments. They point to the important role played by exports in maintaining a high level of economic enterprise within the United States and believe that in the future even greater exports will be demanded to pay for necessary imports. They cite the nation's growing reliance upon imports and are convinced that, far from harming the domestic economy, imports are vital to the maintenance of prosperity at home.

From most standpoints, it would appear that advocates of a more liberal trade policy have the stronger case. A maximum exchange of goods and services among nations accords with the fundamental economic concept of "comparative costs," which should encourage nations to specialize in producing those commodities they can make most cheaply, exchanging these for goods and services other nations can produce more cheaply. Exchange on this basis results in the most profitable transactions for all concerned. Even assuming that a nation could produce everything more cheaply than its neighbors—which of course it cannot—trade would still be beneficial because it would permit nations to concentrate upon those goods and services in which their productive advantages were most accentuated.

Nevertheless, it must be conceded that there do exist problems generated or rendered more acute by further tariff reductions. Declining production and unemployment in industries producing textiles, pottery, toys, watches, optical equipment, and bicycles have been caused or aggravated by expanding imports in the postwar period. The defense needs of the country demand that at least minimum protection be afforded domestic producers of such goods as optical equipment so that their products will be readily available to the United States in time of war. Assuming that the enemy were Soviet Russia, it would be realistic to expect the massive Soviet submarine fleet to be at least partially successful in severing normal trade arteries, thereby preventing the United States from acquiring defense products from other countries. Moreover, it would have to be assumed that some of the free world's industrial complex—particularly that located in Western Europe—would pass under enemy control, or that it might be obliterated by bombers and missiles.

The nation's defense requirements, however, do not necessarily argue in favor of significant increases in tariff levels, certainly not to the point of excluding certain categories of imports altogether. Governmental "stockpiling" of strategic goods and perhaps in some cases outright governmental subsidy to defense industries, comparable to that paid for years to sustain the American merchant marine fleet, could go a long way toward meeting defense requirements. In defense and non-defense industries alike, the deleterious consequences attending expanded imports can also be successfully dealt with by long-range collaborative planning by local, state, and national governments to ease the transition from high tariffs to low tariffs for communities hard-hit by imports. Such planning can inaugurate training programs for workers in depressed industries; in co-operation with private groups, help in the "relocation" of industries and the attraction of new industries to depressed areas; seek methods for reducing the cost of production for American firms; and encourage productive pursuits in which the United States has a comparative advantage over foreign competitors.[*]

As for the oft-repeated allegation that domestic producers cannot compete against foreign-made goods manufactured with "cheap labor", the answer is that the cost of labor *alone* proves nothing in evaluating the competitive position of American producers *vis-à-vis* foreign producers. The "unit cost of production," including of course wages and all other costs, is the only meaningful criterion. Measured by this criterion American producers more often than not have a powerful advantage over their foreign competitors. The American worker has the greatest variety and quantity of capital available to him of any worker in the world. As a spokesman for the Committee for a National Trade Policy told the House Ways and Means Committee in 1958: "... we have on the whole less to fear from cheap foreign labor than foreign countries have to fear from our machines and our tremendous

---

[*]Local-state-national programs of this kind have already proven their worth in such communities as Danbury, Connecticut, coal-mining areas in southern Illinois and Pennsylvania, and textile-producing communities in New England. For fuller details, see 1, pp. 14-15.

productivity in both production and distribution" (2, p. 126).

Then there is the further fact, omitted from the arguments advanced by protectionist groups, that for every decline in imports there must be a corresponding decline in exports. Normal trade cannot be a one-way street. Protectionists would impose high tariffs to shield certain segments of domestic industry from foreign competition, at the expense of firms whose prosperity depends upon the export trade. These latter firms have already demonstrated their ability to compete successfully in the world market. Efficient firms, that is to say, would be penalized at the expense of inefficient ones, or firms whose efficiency has not yet been demonstrated. In the process the consumer pays higher prices for domestic or comparable foreign-made goods. The elementary principle that a nation cannot continue to export without being willing to import lies at the heart of the foreign trade process. Unless they receive outright grants and loans from the United States, other countries cannot get dollars without selling their goods to the United States or perhaps to other countries which have acquired dollars by selling to America. Quite clearly, the American people do not desire that the gap between exports and imports be bridged indefinitely by such extraordinary devices as grants and loans to other countries. They anticipate a more "normal" trade pattern whereby exports of all kinds are in near balance with goods and services purchased from other countries.

Towering above these arguments in behalf of an enlightened trade policy, however, are those which relate questions of international trade and finance to America's broad diplomatic objectives. As the world's creditor, and simultaneously as one of the two super-powers in world politics, the United States constantly seeks to strengthen the economic-military position of itself and its allies. Foreign trade, while important for the United States, is indispensable for many of the allies. Without it their industrial plants would grind to a halt and their agricultural production would be seriously impaired. The resultant economic paralysis would in turn generate political unrest and turbulence, of which only the Kremlin would

be the beneficiary. Western European countries export nearly one-third of their Gross National Products, or nearly four times more than the ratio for the United States. The ratio for Europe is approximated by Latin America. Certain countries in the Middle East export as much as 60 per cent, or about nine times the American ratio, of their Gross National Products. The problem of maintaining a high level of exports is unusually critical for most of the one-crop economies found in Latin America, many of which send between one-third and one-half of their exportable goods to the United States. Any clogging of world trade channels adds to endemic political instability in these and many other economically backward regions and therefore has more than ordinarily serious consequences (21, p. 694).

Then there are what might be called the psychological effects of American trade policy

IS THIS WHAT HE WANTS?

Alexander in *The Philadelphia Bulletin*, May, 1958.

on the outside world. As the acknowledged leader of the free world coalition, the United States is expected to take the initiative in marking a path through the jungle of trade barriers and currency restrictions which grew up after the Great Depression and which reflect lingering nationalistic tendencies. It is expected to manifest some of the idealism successive American Presidents and Secretaries of State have urged upon other countries in overcoming provincialism and narrowly-conceived national interests. A strange dichotomy sometimes pervades American foreign policy. On the one hand, judged by the complex network of interlocking military alliances created by the United States as part of its cold war strategy, its national security policies are geared to the possession of strong allies and to intimate co-operation among free world nations. On the other hand, judged by certain features of its trade policies, the United States seems to cling to an isolationist philosophy, a kind of go-it-alone urge which assumes that in time of war allies will be unavailable. This thinking has dictated an approach emphasizing self-sufficiency for national defense industries which is difficult to reconcile with Washington's emphasis upon collaboration among free world countries in other spheres (39, pp. 77-80).

A test case involving America's approach to international trade issues arose in the period 1957-58, when the United States was called upon to formulate policies toward the emergent Common Market. The Common Market, as explained more fully in Chapter 10, had been established by France, West Germany, Italy, Belgium, the Netherlands, and Luxembourg in 1957; it began operations in 1959. Its members agreed to abide by the principles of GATT in their trade relations. This meant that

their terms of trade would be established upon a reciprocal basis with other countries. The Eisenhower Administration therefore urged Congress in 1958 to renew the Trade Agreements Act for an additional five years—Congress approved four years—thereby giving the President authority to reduce tariffs on a reciprocal basis for extended periods. Lacking such authority, the Chief Executive would be handicapped in trying to evolve long-term agreements on trade questions with other countries and regional institutions like the Common Market. Moreover, the countries would be in a far stronger position than formerly to impose retaliatory restrictions against American trade if "protectionist" features predominated in shaping American trade policy. Political and economic integration in Europe had been encouraged by the United States since World War II, as had the principle of eliminating existing barriers to world trade. Other countries therefore would be keenly interested to observe if the United States co-operated in trade relationships or reverted to economic isolationism (11, p. 601; 20, pp. 895-98; 22, passim). Realization of this fact by the executive branch was a major factor in motivating President Eisenhower to request a five-year extension of the Trade Agreements Act in 1958. Although Congress did not grant this request in full, agreeing only to a four-year extension, America's willingness to continue the Roosevelt-Hull tradition of reciprocal trade and to extend basic legislation for an unprecedentedly long period went far toward establishing mutually beneficial trade relations between the United States and the nascent European Common Market and to remove any temptation European countries might feel to consolidate behind "retaliatory" trade policies.

2. THE FUTURE OF FOREIGN AID

Earlier chapters dealing with Western Europe, the Middle East, Latin America, and Asia have scrutinized American postwar foreign assistance programs as they related to these areas. In this chapter our interest centers on *overall* aspects and implications of foreign aid. What have been the extent and nature of

American foreign aid programs since World War II? What significant trends in the provision of foreign assistance can be discerned? How does foreign aid affect the American domestic economy? What future developments are likely to prove of major importance for American foreign relations? These are some of the

U.S. EXPENDITURES FOR ECONOMIC AND MILITARY FOREIGN AID

In Billions of U.S. Dollars, World War II to 1959

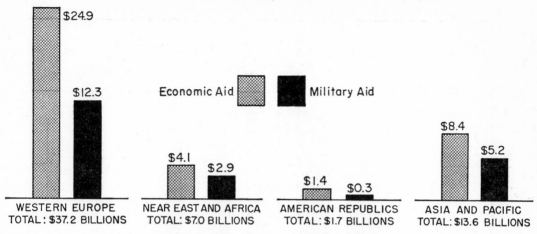

Adapted from NEA Service, Inc., Jan. 14, 1959.

dominant questions which must be discussed if our treatment of the foreign aid problem is to be complete.

Scope and Nature of U. S. Aid

Extensive foreign assistance is no new phenomenon in American history. In the post-World War I period the United States advanced nearly $10 billion in loans to some twenty countries. Most of these loans were never repaid. Negotiated agreements between America and its debtors, coupled with the Hoover debt moratorium during the Great Depression, turned most of these loans into outright grants.

Huge sums were advanced by the United States to its allies during the Second World War and to deal with severe crises in the immediate postwar period. The Greek-Turkish Aid Program and the Marshall Plan inaugurated continuing programs of economic and military assistance. From 1948 to 1958 the United States extended over $43 billion in aid to other countries, of which nearly $34 billion went for outright grants and $9.5 billion for loans. Approximately one-third of the aid extended in grants was spent for military services and supplies to America's allies and to other free world governments. The remainder paid for economic and technical assistance, admin-

istered unilaterally or through agencies of the United Nations and other international bodies (**31**, pp. 3-6; **25**, May 31, 1959, Dispatch by E. W. Kenworthy).

Certain important trends have characterized the American foreign assistance program. One of these has been the shift in the proportion of economic and military assistance. From the end of World War II to the Korean War, economic assistance tended to predominate, taking nearly all of the funds provided for foreign aid. From 1951 on expenditures for military assistance rose graphically, reaching a new peak in 1953. Thereafter the United States was expending more for military assistance to foreign countries than for economic-technical assistance. Thus in President Eisenhower's foreign aid proposal for fiscal year 1959, outright military assistance and "defense support" activities totalled $2.6 billion out of a foreign aid budget of $3.9 billion. The remainder of the foreign aid budget was devoted to the following categories: "special assistance" to meet emergency situations abroad, $212 million; Development Loan Fund, $625 million; future contingencies, $200 million; Point Four technical assistance programs, $142 million; UN Children's Fund, $106.6 million; UN technical assistance programs, $20 million; Organization of American States, $1.5 million (**38**, February

ANNUAL U.S. MILITARY ASSISTANCE PROGRAMS

In Billions of U.S. Dollars

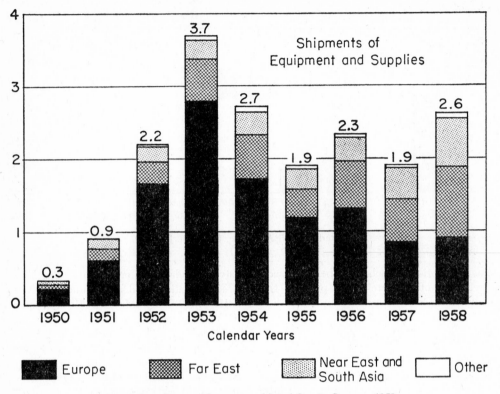

Adapted from Dept. of State, etc., *Mutual Security Program, 1959;*
1958 figures from *Survey of Current Business*, April, 1959, p. 19.

28, 1958, p. 91). No significant departures from these categories were evident in President Eisenhower's foreign aid budget for fiscal year 1960, when a total of $3.93 billion was requested, with nearly $2.5 billion scheduled for military assistance and defense support activities (25, March 22, 1959, Dispatch by Russell Baker). By the opening of the 1960's the foreign aid proportions of one-third for economic assistance and two-thirds for various types of military assistance seemed to have become fairly constant.

Equally significant has been the shift in the geographic direction of American foreign assistance. Taking the postwar era as a whole, Western Europe has been the beneficiary of close to $40 billion in aid from the United States, with nearly $25 billion going for economic assistance and the remainder for military assistance. The American Republics have received a total of only $1.5 billion; the Near East and Africa $5.5 billion; and Asia $13.1 billion. Yet upon the termination of the Marshall Plan and the end of the Korean War, Western Europe's share fell substantially, while that of the underdeveloped countries in the Middle East, Africa, and Asia rose appreciably. In President Eisenhower's budget recommendations for fiscal year 1959 Europe was to receive $1.2 billion in military assistance but a mere $39 million in economic assistance. Asia and the Pacific area, on the other hand, were scheduled to receive more economic assistance ($888 million) than military ($633 million). The proportion of assistance earmarked for the Middle East and Latin America also increased somewhat during this period (25, February 23, 1958).

MAJOR RECIPIENTS OF U.S. ECONOMIC AID

In Billions of U.S. Dollars, mid-1945 to 1958

WESTERN EUROPE
TOTAL: $24.9 BILLION

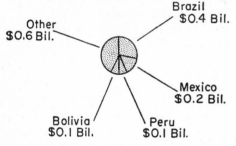

Other
$5.5 Bil.

United
Kingdom
$7.1 Bil.

Italy
$2.9 Bil.

W. Germany
$3.9 Bil.

France
$5.5 Bil.

NEAR EAST AND AFRICA
TOTAL: $4.1 BILLION

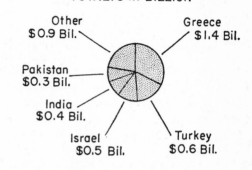

Other
$0.9 Bil.

Greece
$1.4 Bil.

Pakistan
$0.3 Bil.

India
$0.4 Bil.

Israel
$0.5 Bil.

Turkey
$0.6 Bil.

AMERICAN REPUBLICS
TOTAL: $1.4 BILLION

Brazil
$0.4 Bil.

Other
$0.6 Bil.

Mexico
$0.2 Bil.

Bolivia
$0.1 Bil.

Peru
$0.1 Bil.

ASIA AND PACIFIC
TOTAL: $8.4 BILLION

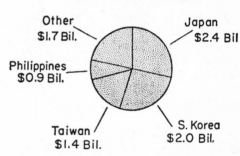

Other
$1.7 Bil.

Japan
$2.4 Bil

Philippines
$0.9 Bil.

Taiwan
$1.4 Bil.

S. Korea
$2.0 Bil.

For this period, a preponderance of aid went to Western Europe as part of the Marshall Plan to promote European economic recovery. Since the mid-1950's economic assistance to Europe has been curtailed. A larger proportion of aid has gone to the Near East, Africa, and Asia, for economic assistance to "underdeveloped" areas. Assistance to Latin America has always been a small percentage of the total — a fact that has occasioned much dissatisfaction throughout the sister American republics.

Adapted from NEA Service, Inc., Jan. 14, 1959.

Foreign Assistance in the American Context

The effects of American foreign assistance upon the recipient nations has been in the main highly beneficial. But what has been its impact upon the United States itself? This question receives very little attention on the part of commentators and writers interested in American foreign policy, yet its implications for future American foreign policy may be far-reaching.

Individuals and groups who attack foreign aid programs as "give-aways," who think that "charity begins at home" and that money expended for foreign aid ought to be used instead for tax cuts or possibly subsidies for depressed segments of American industry, overlook one fact about the foreign aid program which is of cardinal importance in evaluating its worth. This is that from the beginning the United States has provided assistance to other countries *predominantly to advance its own national interest and secondarily to benefit the countries receiving such aid.* Whether this impulse *ought* to be the basic philosophy of the foreign aid program is of course debatable. But that it has been the guiding philosophy especially since the Greek-Turkish aid program of 1947 is not open to serious challenge. The reconstruction of Europe, the elimination of malaria in countries like Iran, the building up of India's economy under the Second Five Year Plan, the stabilization of the tin industry in Bolivia and the nitrate industry in Chile—these things were done first and foremost because the security and diplomatic interests of the United States required that they be done. In this sense, the United States has been the chief beneficiary of the foreign assistance program.

Nevertheless, increasing public doubt about the benefits accruing to the United States from its foreign aid programs led the Senate Foreign Relations Committee to sponsor a series of studies on these programs in the 1956-57 period, in order that future requests for aid might be more intelligently evaluated.* After investigating the effect of foreign aid upon the American domestic economy, one study by the National Planning Association concluded that "the costs of the foreign aid programs seen in the perspective of the economy as a whole have been relatively small." In support of this conclusion it adduced the following data:

Since 1948, the average share of our gross national product which has gone for foreign aid has been 1.7 percent. In 1956, this share has dropped to around 1.1 percent. During this latter year, the United States per capita cost of foreign aid programs, after deducting repayments from foreign countries, has been $23.07. Foreign aid, in 1956, accounted for about 6.4 percent of total

*These studies, initiated by the Foreign Relations Committee but supervised by the Special Committee to Study the Foreign Aid Program (pursuant to resolutions of the 84th and 85th Congresses), provide the most comprehensive and objective studies available of the subject. Major studies were undertaken of ten overall problems: military assistance, the objectives of U. S. economic assistance, foreign assistance activities of the communist bloc, American private enterprise and foreign economic development, the use of private contractors in foreign aid, the role of foreign aid in the development of other countries, foreign aid and the American economy, agricultural surplus disposal and foreign aid, foreign aid activities of other free nations, personnel for foreign aid programs, and administrative aspects of foreign aid. In addition, ten "on-the-spot" investigations of foreign aid activities within selected countries and regions were carried out.

United States Government expenditures. The average for the period 1948-55 has been 9.4 percent of total United States Government expenditures. (32, p. 1).

The National Planning Association noted that about 1.5 per cent of America's total industrial, agricultural, and mining production had been sent to other nations through aid programs. During periods of inflation, foreign aid probably added to inflationary trends; but in periods of recession foreign aid provided stability to the economy. In the immediate postwar years American agricultural commodities were a more important aspect of the program than industrial goods; in more recent years, however, manufactured goods have risen in importance. Approximately 600,000 workers have been employed in manufacturing, processing, and distributing goods sent abroad through aid programs. A highly significant conclusion is that "Foreign aid, both in terms of goods and services, has helped to increase the flow of necessary commodities and raw materials to the United States. Some of these items are critical to our stockpiles and defense needs. Others tend to raise standards of living and cut costs of consumer goods." The Association concedes that foreign aid may have strengthened the position of foreign industries which compete with American industries. But it adds that "foreign aid has also brought about the development of industries and of stabilized economies abroad. Thereby, it has created an increasing demand for goods and services produced in the United States ..." (32, pp. 1-3). To the charge that foreign assistance has hurt American domestic industry by creating greater competition abroad, the Association answers that competition from abroad can arise in the absence of foreign aid; that foreign industries cannot obtain a long-range comparative advantage over American industries by relying upon foreign aid; that much of the technical know-how obtained by foreign industries is also available to domestic producers; and that competition would likely have developed, though more slowly, in the absence of foreign aid (32, p. 15).

Two branches of the American economy which have benefited appreciably from the American foreign aid program deserve special mention. One is the merchant marine fleet. By and large the American merchant marine has a poor competitive position in the world carrying trade, partly because it is older, and hence less efficient, than the fleets of many of its competitors. The Merchant Marine Act of 1936 provided a government subsidy to the fleet to assure that the nation would always have sufficient cargo vessels for its needs, especially in wartime. In the postwar period "cargo preference legislation" allocates to the American fleet 50 per cent of the carrying trade provided by American foreign assistance. Besides this, preference is also given it on inbound cargoes purchased by the United States Government, on the transportation of agricultural goods under federal disposal programs, and on transportation needed for "offshore procurement" by the United States of defense equipment and commodities bought in other countries (32, pp. 24-7).

American domestic agriculture has also benefited heavily from foreign aid programs, notably when the emphasis was upon providing relief and promoting economic recovery.

Thus during the three year period 1948-1950, over half of all agricultural exports from the United States were in the foreign aid category. Before the United States government embarked upon a systematic program for the disposal of domestic agricultural surpluses in 1954, according to the view of the National Planning Association, American domestic agriculture was saved from further depression by the foreign aid program. Without the program, agriculture would have been faced either with the necessity for a price decline for agricultural commodities or else expanded governmental purchasing to maintain a stable market (32, pp. 41-3).

Present Patterns and Future Prospects

Foreign aid appears to have become a permanent tool of American diplomacy, with somewhere between $3.5 billion and $5 billion being allocated for this purpose annually. The greater part of this total in recent years has been budgeted for military equipment and services, with smaller allocations for emergency

THE MUTUAL SECURITY PROGRAM

In Millions of U.S. Dollars, 1960

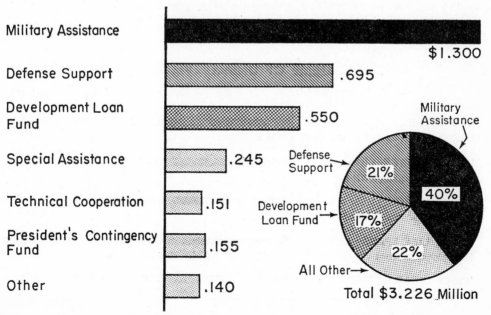

Figures from *Congressional Quarterly Weekly Reports*, Sept. 18, 1959, pp. 1282-4.

and technical assistance to underdeveloped countries. That there can be any sizable reduction in the *military* aspects of foreign assistance seems unlikely while international tension remains at a high peak. Indeed, in view of the increasing complexity and cost of modern warfare, the rapid obsolescence of weapons, the epochal developments in space flight, and the creeping inflation which has characterized price levels within the United States over the greater part of the postwar period, it is logical to predict that allocations for military aid will go up instead of down.

What can be expected in the realm of economic-technical assistance? In the first place, it seems unlikely that the United States will embark in the near future upon economic aid programs comparable to the Marshall Plan for Western Europe. Economic-technical aid is likely to remain a relatively small part of the overall foreign assistance pattern. Even so, some new and noteworthy developments can be expected in this field.

For some time, American officials have been aware of the inadequacy of the foreign assistance allocations available to backward countries which seek to expand their economic enterprise and to do it rapidly. Some of these countries would be considered "poor risks" by existing lending institutions, whether governmental or private. Throughout the underdeveloped countries the demand for capital far exceeds the available supply. The prospect that these countries can generate sufficient investment capital out of savings remains exceedingly remote. One estimate places the supply of investment capital available from all the underdeveloped countries combined at $17 billion annually, whereas $146 billion anually in investment capital is available from the Gross National Products of the industrial countries within the free world (25, June 29, 1958). Capital-deficient countries often do not possess adequate collateral to obtain loans from customary sources. Such countries therefore face a twofold problem: they urgently need new capital for economic expansion, but they cannot give satisfactory assurances that repayment will be made on terms acceptable (e.g., in dollars or other "hard currencies") to governmental and private lending institutions.

These considerations prompted the Eisenhower Administration during the late 1950's to take several steps designed to increase the supply of capital available to underdeveloped countries. The American contribution to the International Bank for Reconstruction and Development was raised, as was its contribution to the International Monetary Fund (3, July 23, 1959, p. 437). The United States also took the lead in providing greater flexibility in the lending power of IBRD, as well as its own Export-Import Bank. In addition, Washington sponsored the creation of two new lending in-

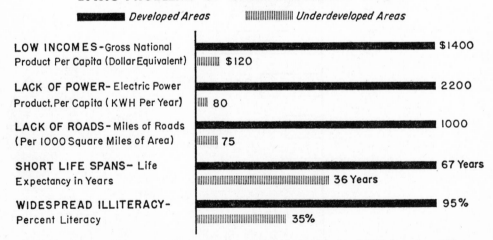

BASIC PROBLEMS OF UNDERDEVELOPED AREAS

■■■■■ *Developed Areas* |||||||||||||||| *Underdeveloped Areas*

LOW INCOMES-Gross National Product Per Capita (Dollar Equivalent) $1400 |||||||| $120

LACK OF POWER- Electric Power Product. Per Capita (KWH Per Year)   2200 ||||| 80

LACK OF ROADS- Miles of Roads (Per 1000 Square Miles of Area)   1000 |||||||| 75

SHORT LIFE SPANS- Life Expectancy in Years   67 Years |||||||||||||||||||||||||||||||| 36 Years

WIDESPREAD ILLITERACY- Percent Literacy   95% |||||||||||||||||||||||||| 35%

House Foreign Affairs Committee *Hearings on the Mutual Security Act of 1958*, Part 7, p. 900.

stitutions—the Development Loan Fund and the Inter-American Development Bank—established specifically to meet the needs of capital-deficient countries. The Development Loan Fund was approved by Congress in 1957 and began its operations the following year. It started with an original capitalization of $300 million. With applications for loans considerably exceeding funds at hand, the Eisenhower Administration requested an additional $625 million for fiscal year 1959. After some controversy within the government—with Democrats in Congress leading the fight to raise DLF's capital even further—Congress approved an American contribution of $700 million for fiscal year 1960 and *authorized* a contribution by the United States of $1.1 billion for fiscal year 1961.*

The Inter-American Development Bank was set up to make funds available throughout the Western Hemisphere. Its total assets were to be $850 million, with $400 million in paid-in capital stock. The United States was to subscribe $150 million, leaving $250 million to be subscribed by Latin American states. The remainder of the assets was to be in the form of "callable capital"—in effect, guarantees by the sponsoring governments of loans entered into by I-ADB—of which America's responsibility was to be $200 million. Plans called for I-ADB to raise its assets even further by 1962, provided the member governments agreed. I-ADB proposed to concentrate upon providing technical assistance and extending funds for long-range economic development projects that would raise productive levels in capital-deficient countries (**3**, May 15, 1959, p. 665).

Besides these steps, the Eisenhower Administration took the lead in planning still another innovation: a multi-national agency to be known as the International Development Association, which would be under the jurisdiction of the World Bank. Like its counterpart within the United States, the Development Loan Fund, IDA would also concentrate upon "soft loans"** for worthwhile projects for which capital was not readily available from existing institutions. The United States proposed that IDA begin with a capitalization of $1 billion, either in dollars or their equivalent in other "hard currencies," with the United States initially contributing $300 million and other countries contributing the remainder. By the close of the 1950's, the charter of IDA was in the process of being drafted, after which it would have to be ratified by the governments sponsoring the World Bank. IDA was not likely to be ready before 1961 to begin operations, assuming that sponsoring governments could agree quickly on its details (**9**, pp. 565-67; **34**, pp. 26-7; **24**, October 3, 1959).

These steps, however, were viewed by some American officials as still inadequate to supply the demand for capital urgently needed by underdeveloped countries. By 1959 the Eisenhower Administration found itself under fire from Democratic critics on Capitol Hill, who demanded a significant expansion in the economic, as opposed to the military, aspects of the foreign assistance program. Influential Democrats like Senator William Fulbright, Chairman of the Foreign Relations Committee, contended that extensive military assistance to small, poor countries seriously overburdened their fragile economies. In Fulbright's opinion the ultimate solution lay in broadening the economic base in such countries, thereby permitting them to sustain the required military establishment without risking financial ruin. In the face of firm opposition from the administration, many of whose spokesmen favored economic retrenchment and a balanced budget, such critics lacked the votes required to in-

---

*An *authorization* to spend must, of course, be followed by an actual *appropriation* of money. Congress could conceivably *appropriate* less than the $1.1 billion authorized for DLF in 1961.

"Soft loans" are not loans of doubtful validity; nor is the term a euphemism for outright grants. Soft loans are commitments "to repay and a reasonable expectation that the borrower will ultimately have the capacity to repay. . . . such loans, however, may be at a lower rate of interest and extend over a longer period of time than is now the general practice" (31**, p. 16). Or, as the President of the World Bank stated late in 1959 in reference to IDA: IDA would make "soft loans" but would not be a "soft lender"; it proposed to "operate in accordance with the same high standards as the bank" (**24**, October 3, 1959).

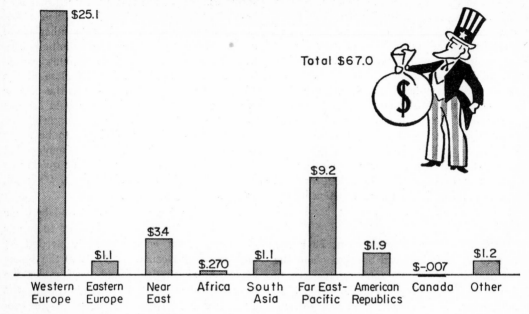

U.S. FOREIGN GRANTS AND CREDITS—BY REGIONS
In Billions of U.S. Dollars, mid-1945 to 1959

Total $67.0

Western Europe	Eastern Europe	Near East	Africa	South Asia	Far East-Pacific	American Republics	Canada	Other
$25.1	$1.1	$3.4	$.270	$1.1	$9.2	$1.9	$-.007	$1.2

The net figures used here are obtained by subtracting repayments and other credits extended by foreign countries to the United States from aid payments made by the United States.

Figures from *Statistical Abstract of the United States: 1959*, pp. 874-5.

crease the Eisenhower budget appreciably. It was also clear that expansion of foreign assistance found very little support in public opinion.

In its final report, the Special Committee to Study Foreign Aid Programs pointed to several ways in which these programs could be improved in the future. It felt that the objective of the programs might be more clearly set forth, that the rate of expenditure for certain programs, notably military aid, ought to be reduced when this could be done without damage to national security, that the Secretary of State ought to assume a stronger role in providing overall policy guidance in all phases of existing programs, that changes ought to be made in personnel policies and practices, and that a development fund ought to be estab-

lished to advance needed capital to backward countries (which, as we have seen, was done in 1957). The committee was in no doubt that foreign aid, on the whole, had served the national interest well and that continued aid for military, economic, and technical purposes would be required for some time to come. It reiterated the viewpoint that the objective of such programs was advancement of the diplomatic goals of the United States and asserted that these programs could not be terminated until conditions in the outside world rendered them no longer necessary (31, pp. 26-32). It would be a reasonable prediction that such conditions would not materialize for years, possibly even decades, to come.

3. OTHER ASPECTS OF AMERICAN FOREIGN ECONOMIC POLICY

American Private Overseas Investment

As the world's creditor, Uncle Sam has provided tremendous outlays of capital to other countries since World War I. Private and governmental institutions have both played a part in this process, with conditions in the post-

World War II period assigning the dominant role to the latter.

Much of the opposition voiced within the United States to a continuation of foreign aid, at least in its economic-technical aspects, stems from the conviction that assistance to backward countries can better and more cheaply be rendered by *private* capital. Expanded overseas investment by business concerns within the United States, it is widely contended, is a more natural and promising way of promoting economic growth than is the indefinite extension of governmental grants and credits. With the extension of private capital would go the provision of American technical skill and know-how vitally needed in economically primitive regions. In time productive levels would be raised in these regions and the international economic environment strengthened as a whole.

In absolute terms, private investment from the United States in foreign countries stands at the highest level in history. The following table shows overseas investment trends over almost two decades:

FOREIGN INVESTMENT OF THE UNITED STATES

(In Billions of Dollars)

	1939	1950	1957
Total United States Investment	$11.4	$32.8	$54.2
Private Investment	11.4	19.0	36.8
Governmental credits and claims		13.8	17.4

(Adapted from a table in **3**, June 19, 1959, p. 827)

As the table shows, *total* United States investments almost quintupled between 1939 and 1957; *private* investments tripled over this period. As a percentage of the national income, however, private investment by the United States was lower in the late 1950's than in the 1920's, averaging one per cent in the latter period and from one-third to one-half of one per cent in the postwar period (**30**, pp. 1-2). Moreover, the nature of this investment has changed sharply since the 1920's, with nearly four-fifths of the total in the 1950's being in the form of "direct investment"—outright ownership of plants and equipment—rather than "portfolio investment"—ownership of foreign securities (**30**, p. 3).

Highly significant also is the fact that a comparatively small percentage of the total private investment of the United States is located in the underdeveloped countries, exclusive of Latin America. The following table shows the distribution of this investment:

PERCENTAGE OF AMERICAN INVESTMENT BY AREA

(Through 1957)

Country-Area	Total Investment	Per Cent Distribution
Canada	$ 8.33 billion	33
Latin America	8.81	35
Western Europe	3.99	16
Middle East	1.28	5
Other Areas	2.27	9
International Agencies	0.57	2
	$25.25	100

(Adapted from **3**, June 19, 1959, p. 827).

Canada, Latin America, and Western Europe account for approximately 85 per cent of the total private investment of the United States. Stated differently, about half of American private investment is *outside* Canada and Western Europe, but of this proportion about three-fourths is in Latin America alone.

Still another trend of interest—symbolized by the fact that the preponderance of investment in the Middle East is in oil holdings—is the great increase in postwar investments in extractive industries abroad, rather than industries which manufacture and process finished goods. Mining, smelting, and petroleum have been the chief enterprises attracting private American capital. Several factors account for this trend: the growing demand for raw materials within the United States, realization that investments that "pay off" in raw materials and commodities can often bypass the "exchange controls" imposed by other countries against the outflow of profits, the attraction possessed by extractive industries in greater profits both *vis-à-vis* other kinds of overseas investments and *vis-à-vis* possible investment at home (**30**, pp. 3-7).

In the light of what has been labelled the "revolution in rising expectations" which has swept underdeveloped countries, estimates place the total amount of capital needed from outside sources as high as $10 billion annually (25, dispatch by Edwin L. Dale, June 29, 1958). It is apparent therefore that the private capital market within the United States has a major role to play in making needed funds available (23, *passim*). Many benefits can come from the provision of such capital. A Department of Commerce study in 1955 showed that American private investment in Latin America produced some $5 billion in goods and services annually, with $1.5 billion of this entering the export market. U. S. firms contributed about 5 per cent to the national income of Latin American countries; close to $1 billion in wages had been paid to over 600,000 employees, the vast majority of whom was native; more than $1 billion were paid by U. S. firms in the form of taxes, furnishing 15 per cent of government revenues in that area; and these firms paid out close to $2 billion for locally-produced goods and services (30, p. 14). By the close of the 1950's considerable sentiment had built up in Washington, especially in Congress, in favor of greater reliance upon private capital to meet the needs of underdeveloped countries. For example, a provision attached to the Mutual Security appropriation for fiscal year 1960 directed the State Department and other governmental agencies to strengthen the role of *private* capital in the economic development of other countries, presumably in the hope that the role played by *governmental* grants and loans could be correspondingly reduced (3, July 24, 1959, p. 1014). This viewpoint had been re-enforced by two studies in 1959 bearing upon the subject. One was the report of the Committee on World Trade Practices, appointed by President Eisenhower, which submitted its findings on March 2; the other was a special report undertaken for the State Department entitled "Expanding Private Investment for Free World Economic Growth," submitted on April 1. Both reports agreed that the United States ought to take greater initiative to improve the "investment climate" abroad, particularly in economically backward nations (3, June 19, 1959, p. 827).

One proposed method for achieving this goal was to revise provisions of the Internal Revenue code so as to eliminate excessive taxation of industries with foreign subsidiaries and to extend the existing 14 per cent tax reduction given firms with investments in the Western Hemisphere to firms investing outside the hemisphere. A subcommittee of the House Ways and Means Committee studied this matter during 1959 but took no action, owing in some measure to disunity within the executive branch on the proposal. Officials of the State and Commerce Departments favored such revisions. Those from the Treasury Department were opposed, believing that "inherently unattractive situations" for overseas investors "cannot be made attractive by artificial stimulants." A no less fundamental objection was the fact that the Treasury Department stood to lose several hundred million dollars annually in tax revenues by this change!

Other, and perhaps much more formidable, obstacles hamper the flow of private American capital to foreign countries. Sometimes such countries prefer, and often have a good chance of getting, *governmental* assistance from countries like the United States or multi-national organs like the World Bank. The worldwide dollar shortage, somewhat less acute by the end of the 1950's, has meant that profits earned by American capital cannot readily be converted into dollars, and that investments cannot always be liquidated without considerable loss. Some countries impose discriminatory tax-rates against foreign corporations. Fear of expropriation or nationalization of foreign firms and actual or potential internal political instability can create skepticism in the minds of possible investors, especially when attractive investment opportunities can be found under more favorable conditions (30, pp. 8-10).

To counteract at least some of these risks, in recent years the United States Government has underwritten a program of "investment guaranty." Upon payment of a premium, this program offers insurance protecting the investor against such threats as inconvertibility of capital and profits into dollars, expropriation, and war. Insurance under this program can be written for new investments only or for additions to existing holdings overseas. If the investor suffers damage to his holdings because of risks covered by the program, then the United States Government compensates him for damage sustained; title to his property in this case passes to the government, after which Washington negotiates directly with the foreign country involved to reclaim damages sustained to the investment (30, p. 56).

Thus far the investment guaranty program has been utilized only sparingly by entrepreneurs in the United States, and even then not always for the purpose for which the program was established. The risks covered by the program are limited. It does not, for example, protect American firms against what is sometimes called "creeping expropriation:" progressively discriminatory treatment by foreign governments which over the course of time amounts to expropriation. Furthermore, foreign countries—notably those that have experienced colonialism—are sometimes reluctant to have the United States Government acquire title to private business holdings out of fear that a new era of "dollar diplomacy" may be inaugurated or that, at a minimum, the United States may acquire too direct a stake in their economic systems. These considerations have convinced one competent study group that the program's usefulness is decidedly limited and that it cannot be expected to play any very impressive role in stimulating the flow of private American capital to underdeveloped nations (30, pp. 57-8). This viewpoint is confirmed by the fact that by late 1958 five-eighth's—$250 million out of $400 million of total guaranties—of the insurance written was granted to American firms doing business in Western Europe. Risks of course existed in that area too, but far fewer risks on the whole than existed in regions like Latin America, not to mention many countries in Africa and Asia. And nations in Europe had many more opportunities to generate their own capital, or attract it from the outside, than countries in the underdeveloped regions. Proposals made to broaden the coverage of the investment guaranty program have thus far met with considerable opposition in Congress (3, June 19, 1959, p. 827).

Promoting "Liquidity" in World Trade

In a manner roughly comparable to private business firms, nations must maintain a fund of "reserves" or operating capital to finance current international trade transactions. The sale of exports adds to the fund; the purchase of imports depletes it. When adverse economic or political conditions in the outside world compel reductions in a country's exports, while imports remain stable or perhaps even increase, then that country will be required to draw upon its reserves to pay for purchases abroad. The extent to which its reserves are adequate to pay for necessary imports determines a country's "liquidity" in international trade and commerce. If its imports and reserves both equaled X amount of currency units, then the country would be 100 per cent "liquid"; if its imports were valued at X currency units and its reserves at one-half X, then it would be only 50 per cent liquid.

The problem of maintaining adequate liquidity in the face of a rising volume of world trade, in an environment of rising prices and depleted reserves, had become a critical issue in international economic relations by the end of the 1950's. In 1937, total world imports and world reserves were nearly equal; by 1957, world imports were nearly twice as large in dollar volume as world reserves. Collectively, the importing nations of the world were only 50 per cent liquid in their international transactions. Some countries, however, were in a far more critical condition than others. Great Britain, for instance, had reserves of only $3 billion to cover imports of around $50 billion annually (25, June 15, 1958).

These facts took on added urgency after the United States experienced a recession in 1957-58. Fortunately, the recession did not unduly disrupt the economic stability of the nation's allies; but it did increase the pressure against their reserves, owing to a moderate decline in American imports. A mild decline in exports by trading countries would not markedly affect their liquidity. A substantial decline, however, could greatly aggravate an already serious problem. For if a country cannot maintain a high enough level of exports to pay for imports, it must then dip into its reserves; and if its reserves are rapidly diminishing, it has only one alternative other than receiving grants and credits from other countries: to stop making payments on its international obligations. Britain, France, and Chile have all experienced "exchange crises" of varying intensity in the recent past occasioned by the imbalance between reserves and obligations owed for necessary imports.

Two multi-national institutions—the European Payments Union, discussed at length in Chapter 10, and the International Monetary Fund —have played an active part in softening the effect of such crises. Both of these institutions, however, have been subjected to the pressures of sharply increased demands for their funds at a time of shrinkage in the value of their available funds caused by rising prices. As an emergency measure, a third institution, the United States-owned Export-Import Bank, has also made loans to countries enabling them to stabilize their financial positions. Yet when the Export-Import Bank uses its funds for this purpose it decreases its ability to make loans for long-range development projects overseas. All three of these institutions have been sorely pressed to meet the existing demand for their services.

The problem of achieving and maintaining liquidity in world trade is many-faceted. One approach—that probably in many cases offers little more than short-term relief—is strengthening institutions like those described above. In the long run, however, more fundamental approaches will be required. These include such steps as achieving reasonable stability in world prices, expanding trade so as to bring the imports and exports of given countries into closer equilibrium, raising consumption levels around the globe, and perhaps reducing the proportions of national budgets that must be devoted to armaments and other defense measures. Only as progress is made in these spheres is the problem of liquidity likely to recede as a major issue in international economic relationships.

Disposing of Farm Surpluses Abroad

Ever since World War II the United States has experienced steadily mounting agricultural surpluses at home. These have required a variety of programs by the national government to stabilize agricultural prices; meantime, however, the Commodity Credit Corporation which purchases these surpluses has found its stocks rapidly increasing. How could they be disposed of without impairing price structures at home and without disrupting normal patterns of world trade?

This problem increasingly engaged the attention of officials in both the legislative and executive branches and finally led Congress to establish the agricultural surplus disposal program. Besides concern over greater surpluses at home, Congress believed that the United States could not continue indefinitely to hold the surpluses off the world market when other nations were disposing of theirs, often under a "price umbrella" provided by American agricultural support programs. Congress sought some scheme whereby these stocks could be moved without damaging the trading positions of other countries, but with the hope that such stocks could be put to a profitable use, especially in agricultural-deficit countries (29, p. 12).

Accordingly, under legislation adopted in the 1953-57 period, agricultural surpluses could be disposed of abroad by four methods: sale for foreign currencies; grants for disaster and famine relief; donations to private welfare organizations for distribution overseas; and barter for goods and materials required to promote American defense efforts. During 1956-57 nearly half of all agricultural exports from the United States were moved under the disposal program, with higher percentages obtaining for commodities like wheat, dairy products, coarse grains, cotton, and rice. Measured in terms of the *value* of commodities involved, the most important method of disposal was the sale of surpluses for foreign currencies. The most geographically widespread *method* of surplus disposal, however, was donations to private welfare groups, with surpluses ultimately going to eighty-four countries and territories (29, pp. 2-4).

In the beginning phase of this program, and to a lesser extent throughout the years that followed, other countries expressed apprehension that the extensive disposal of surpluses by the United States would amount to a ruinous "dumping" of goods on the world market at bargain prices, thereby undermining the position of countries which depend upon agricultural exports for their continued prosperity. In the main, these fears have not been realized. Officials within the United States have given assurances that the disposal program will be conducted according to principles accepted by such groups as the Food and Agriculture Organization of the United Nations. The United States will compete fairly, both in terms of price and in terms of quality of goods, on the world market and it will assist other countries in every way to maintain their required level of exports (**28**, p. 1066). Private study groups within the United States and agencies of the United Nations alike agree that the American surplus disposal program has not disrupted world trade nor has it exerted undue pressure upon countries which normally export agricultural goods (**29**, pp. 21-22).

Meantime, the United States continues to build up sizable credits in foreign countries because of sales of its agricultural surpluses abroad. These balances, which cannot in most cases be converted into dollars, can be and are being used for a number of purposes. They have been utilized primarily for underwriting economic development projects, such as electric power plant construction in Japan and Israel, reforestation and watershed programs in Spain, highways in Chile, irrigation systems in Peru. Such balances have also been used to pay off United States obligations in these countries, such as leases of military installations in foreign lands and the acquisition of military supplies and equipment. Balances have been spent for building up demand for American exports and for a number of other purposes. Among these categories, however, the first

three mentioned account for using up over 90 per cent of foreign currency balances accumulated to date (**29**, pp. 9-10).

As the 1960's opened, the Eisenhower Administration endeavored to make even greater use than formerly of the nation's agricultural abundance to achieve diplomatic goals. In his budget message for fiscal year 1960, the President included a "food for peace" plan which was the culmination of studies undertaken over preceding months directed at attacking the twofold problem of mounting agricultural surpluses and the economic needs of other countries. The aim was to make these surplus stocks available to meet widespread human need by donating them to establish "food reserves" in needy countries. Congress, however, was unwilling to go far in this direction in 1959. The most it would do was permit up to $5 million received in foreign currencies through the *sale* of surplus commodities to be donated to the proposed food reserves. Conceivably, this could be the initial step towards achieving a program closely paralleling Eisenhower's recommendation. But with the sentiment in Washington, and most especially on Capitol Hill, running against further *grants* by the United States and in favor of more initiative by other countries to "help themselves," the President's "food for peace" plan did not appear to have a bright future. Agricultural abundance—a phenomenon many Americans may be inclined to view as more of a headache than a bonanza—is in reality one of the nation's greatest economic assets. It is a boon that very few nations in history have enjoyed, and none has experienced it in the degree witnessed in the United States. If imaginatively utilized, it could play a useful role in achieving ends shared by virtually every country in the family of nations.

REFERENCES

1. Committee for Economic Development. *United States Tariff Policy.* New York: 1954. An enlightening brief treatment by a non-partisan study group.
2. "Congress and the Reciprocal Trade Act," *Congressional Digest,* 37, April, 1958, pp. 97-127. An informative background study of

U. S. tariff and trade policies in the contemporary era.
3. *Congressional Quarterly Weekly Report.* This publication, together with the annual volumes, provides an invaluable analysis of congressional activities and a helpful guide to the *Congressional Record.*

4. Department of Commerce. *U. S. Income and Output*. Washington: 1958. This study, prepared by the Office of Business Economics, is a convenient source of data on American foreign trade.

5. Department of State. *American Foreign Policy, 1950-1955*. (Publication No. 6446, "General Foreign Policy Series," 117). Washington: 1957. Foreign economic policy is covered in Volume II, pp. 2886-3161 in this invaluable documentary collection.

6. ————. *General Agreement on Tariffs and Trade*. (Publication No. 6348, "Commercial Policy Series," 158), Washington: 1956. A description and analysis of GATT.

7. ————. *Together We Are Strong*. (Publication No. 6571, "Commercial Policy Series," 164), Washington: 1958. Highlights America's growing dependence upon foreign trade.

8. Dewhurst, J. Frederick, and Associates. *America's Needs and Resources*. New York: The Twentieth Century Fund, 1955. Projections for America's future dependence upon foreign trade are especially revealing. See pp. 711-16.

9. Dillon, Douglas. "Views of the Department of State on Proposal to Establish an International Development Association," *Department of State Bulletin*, 38, (April 7, 1958), pp. 565-68. Presents the case for the establishment of IDA.

10. Dulles, John Foster. "Vital Importance of Extension of Trade Agreements Act," *Department of State Bulletin*, 39, July 7, 1958, pp. 34-8. Secretary of State Dulles relates the TAA to the broad context of American diplomacy.

11. Eisenhower, Dwight D. "The Trade Agreements Program: Its Relation to National Well-Being and Security," *Department of State Bulletin*, 38, (April 14, 1958), pp. 591-601. President Eisenhower stresses the need for enlightened American relations with the emergent European Common Market.

12. Enke, Stephen, and Salera, Virgil. *International Economics*. New York: Prentice-Hall, 1947. This (along with the book by Lawrence Towle, listed below) are among the good basic texts available for students who need to learn (or perhaps review) basic concepts in international economics.

13. "Foreign Transactions," *Survey of Current Business*, 39 (July, 1959), pp. 27-28. This entire issue is designated the "National Income Number" and contains statistical summaries of national income and output.

14. Heilperin, Michael A. "U. S. Foreign Economic Policy," *Fortune*, 57, (June, 1958), pp. 133-35, 160-68. A highly competent secondary source on important aspects of the nation's international economic relations; its evident bias, however, is pro-free trade.

15. Herter, Christian A. "International Trade and Our National Security," *Department of State Bulletin*, 38, (May 5, 1958), pp. 731-34. Emphasizes the increasing demand for capital —and limited sources for securing it—among backward nations.

16. International Cooperation Administration. *East-West Trade Developments, 1956-1957*, Tenth Report to Congress, Washington: 1958.

17. ————. *The Strategic Trade Control System, 1948-1956*, Ninth Report to Congress, Washington: 1957. These two authoritative studies by ICA provide invaluable data on the subject of East-West trade. The latter study is especially valuable for showing trends and long-run implications of this issue.

18. Kerber, E. S. "Foreign Grants and Credits in 1958," *Survey of Current Business*, 39 (April, 1959), pp. 17-20.

19. Lederer, Walter. "Adverse Balance in Foreign Payments," *Survey of Current Business*, 39 (June, 1959), pp. 15-24.

20. Mann, Thomas C. "American Trade Policy and the Lessons of the 1930's," *Department of State Bulletin*, 38 (June 2, 1958), pp. 895-900. A high diplomatic official warns that American provincialism in trade may provoke retaliatory measures by other important trading countries.

21. ————. "The Trade Agreements Program and American Prosperity," *Department of State Bulletin*, 38, April 28, 1958, pp. 692-95. A strong plea—backed by impressive evidence— for a reduction in trade barriers.

22. Marjolin, Robert. "Prospects for the European Common Market," *Foreign Affairs*, 36, October, 1957, pp. 131-42. Examines problems to be faced by the Common Market, especially in its relations with the United States.

23. Millikin, W. F., and Rostow, W. W. "Foreign Aid: Next Phase," *Foreign Affairs*, 36, (April, 1958), pp. 418-37. The writers argue convincingly that underdeveloped countries must have more *private* assistance and that private and public institutions must collaborate in their assistance programs.

24. New York *Herald Tribune*.

25. *New York Times*.

26. "Payments Excess in International Business Continues High," *Survey of Current Business*, 39 (March, 1959), pp. 4-10.

27. Pizer, Samuel, and Cutler, Frederick. "Capital Flow to Foreign Countries Slackens," *Survey of Current Business*, 39 (August, 1959), pp. 25-29. Evaluates trends in the movement of private capital from the United States to other countries.

28. Roberts, Ralph S. "International Cooperation to Solve Food and Agricultural Problems," *Department of State Bulletin*, 38, (June 23, 1958), pp. 1066-74. Relates American agricultural programs disposal to global economic problems.

29. Special Committee to Study the Foreign Aid Program. *Agricultural Surplus Disposal and Foreign Aid*. 85th Congress, 1st Session, Washington: 1957.

30. ———. *American Private Enterprise, Foreign Economic Development, and the Aid Programs*. 85th Congress, 1st Session. Washington: 1957.

31. ———. *Foreign Aid* (Final Report). 85th Congress, 1st Session. Washington: 1957.

32. ———. *The Foreign Aid Programs and the United States Economy*. 85th Congress, 1st Session. Washington: 1957.

33. ———. *Foreign Assistance Activities of the Communist Bloc and Their Implications for the United States*. 85th Congress, 1st Session. Washington: 1957. The reports in this series, prepared at the request of the Senate Foreign Relations Committee, provide a comprehensive and objective analysis of the gamut of problems encountered in American foreign assistance programs.

34. "Strategy for Economic Cold War," *Business Week*, No. 1503, (June 21, 1958), pp. 26-7. A succinct treatment of economic aspects of the cold war.

35. Tariff Commission of the United States. *Forty-Second Annual Report*. Washington: 1959. This report, covering the fiscal year ending June 30, 1958, and other reports in this series provide useful information on foreign trade problems growing out of the reciprocal trade program.

36. ———. *Operation of Trade Agreements Program*, Ninth Report, July 1955 to June, 1956, Washington: 1957. The annual volumes in this series contain a wealth of data on tariff and trade questions.

37. Towle, Lawrence, W. *International Trade and Commercial Policy*. New York: Harper and Brothers, 1956. A good basic text in the field.

38. *United States News and World Report*, Vol. 44, February 28, 1958.

39. Vernon, Raymond. "Foreign Trade and National Defense," *Foreign Affairs*, 34, (October, 1955), pp. 77-89. Focuses on the relation of American tariff policies to defense.

CHAPTER 16

The Quest for World Peace and Security

Over two millennia separate the mutual defense leagues established by the ancient Greeks from the United Nations organization set up at the end of World War II. Yet statesmen dedicated to the goal of world peace and security in the modern period follow a path through the jungle of international anarchy which has been blazed by countless predecessors. Oftentimes the trail has grown dim; frequently it has veered off into the tangled thickets of wars and the quagmires of competing national interests. The ultimate destination has sometimes been obscured by clouds of suspicion, hate, ignorance.

But the vision has persisted and, in spite of obstacles and digressions in the unfolding of historical events, the quest has gone on. Gradually mankind has acquired renewed faith in its ability to reach the final goal, greater skill in the use of techniques and institutional devices to cultivate harmonious intercourse among nations, and heightened awareness that the abolition of war as an instrument of national policies may well be a prerequisite for survival of civilization on the planet. Every age has added its legacy to the reservoir of insights and tools available to contemporary statesmen. We must confine our attention to those most directly relevant to American foreign relations.*

---

*Limited space prevents me from dealing extensively with pre-United Nations efforts to achieve a workable international organization and respect for world law. Students are strongly urged, however, to familiarize themselves with these earlier movements by reading some of the worthwhile studies available. See especially the following (and the bibliographies contained in them): 1; 9; 7; 20, 21; 31; 34; 35; 36; 53.

1. INTERNATIONAL ORGANIZATION BEFORE WORLD WAR II

Nineteenth Century Antecedents

Conditions in the 19th century were peculiarly conducive to impressive strides toward reaching the goal of effective international organization and toward inculcating acceptance of world law. After 1815, techniques for "consultation" among powerful European countries emerged within the Concert of Europe. The Holy Alliance sought, admittedly with limited success, to inject Christian principles into the conduct of international affairs. Significant progress came about in socio-economic-administrative aspects of inter-state relations by agreements establishing such bodies as the Rhine River Commission (1868), the International Telegraphic Convention (1865), the Universal Postal Union (1874), and many others (34, pp. 67-90).

Meantime international law was being strengthened. Noteworthy developments included international agreements on the abolition of the slave trade; various conventions dealing with fisheries and marginal territorial waters; agreements aimed at mitigating the barbarities of naval and land warfare; and the Hague Conferences late in the 19th century which established machinery for arbitrating disputes among nations and for reducing armaments (34, pp. 105-20; 8, pp. 19-42).

By 1900 the United States had assumed an active role in these activities. It supported the Permanent Court of Arbitration at the Hague by submitting cases to it. An attempt was made by President Taft to broaden the area of disputes which the United States would submit to arbitration; but it encountered formidable resistance in the Senate, where so many exceptions were demanded that Taft finally abandoned the effort. President Wilson's idealistic and pacifistically-inclined Secretary of State, William Jennings Bryan, resumed the crusade. Eventually, thirty "cooling-off treaties" were negotiated between the United States and other countries, of which twenty-one were ratified by the Senate and proclaimed. These provided for arbitration of disputes by impartial bodies. The signatories were not required to accept recommendations made, but they pledged not to begin hostilities until after the arbitration commission had submitted its report (41, pp.454-60).

The League of Nations

The League of Nations was the culmination of an evolutionary movement often proceeding on many fronts at once, directed at gaining adherence to principles of international law and at securing formal and informal agreements for the peaceful settlement of disputes among nations. What looked like the total collapse of efforts to avert war in the period 1914-1918 was in reality but a temporary though crucial deviation from the charted course in the history of international organization. World War I witnessed physical destruction, blood letting, and social disorganization on a scale seldom equalled in human society to that time, It furnished a powerful stimulus

to an often complacent Victorian world for eliminating war and creating machinery for non-violent adjustment of disagreements in the world community. Out of the "war to end wars" and to "make the world safe for democrary" came intensive and widespread study of methods for setting up a viable international organization. From numerous sources, both official and private, suggestions and proposals were made which finally coalesced into the Covenant of the League of Nations, the first international organization in history providing a continuously functioning body to study and deal with issues affecting peace and security for all nations.

In many respects the structure and operating principles of the League of Nations foreshadowed that of its successor, the United Nations. Three major organs were created. The *Council*, a revised version of the Concert of Europe, consisted of Britain, France, Italy and Japan, plus four smaller nations elected by the Assembly. The *Assembly* embraced the total membership of the League, initially forty-two countries; it was roughly analogous to national legislatures. The *Secretariat* was the permanent administrative body, whose head, the Secretary General, was nominated by the Council and approved by the Assembly. The World Court was the League's legal tribunal. In addition, there grew up a host of lesser agencies in the economic-social field.

An imprecise boundary separated the functions of the two major policy-making agencies, the Council and the Assembly. The Covenant gave both certain independent functions; yet both were also empowered to deal with any question affecting world peace and security. Theoretically, the Council was expected to address itself to issues *directly* affecting peace and security, such as disarmament and the threat of war, while the Assembly was to consider more indirect contributory causes of international instability. The founders of the League, like the founders of the UN, envisioned that the smaller Council, where the great powers had a preponderant voice, would provide leadership and guidance to the larger Assembly in arriving at decisions on major causes of international tension (53, pp. 81-4). And in time the Council indeed came to speak for the League, as corroborated by the fact that it held 106 meetings throughout the League's existence, whereas the Assembly met only once a year from 1920 to 1940 (**34**, pp. 132-33).

Uppermost among the League's objectives was the maintenance of peace. The Covenant required members to submit disputes to judicial organs or to the League Council and to observe a ninety-day "cooling off" period before resorting to hostilities over a dispute. The League's fatal weakness showed up when it had to grapple with aggressions by ambitious dictators after Japan's invasion of Manchuria in 1931. The League possessed no independent power to *compel* acceptance of its decisions by recalcitrant members and non-members. Recommendations by the Council, reports by fact-finding commissions, impassioned appeals to protect the "sovereign rights" of weaker countries, aroused public opinion, moral suasion, conferences among the great powers—all of these were used to no avail by the League to dissuade aggressive countries. Dictators in Germany, Italy, and Japan, continued to defy the League with impunity because the great powers hesitated to use collective force to stop them. With each successful aggression the League was rendered more and more impotent.

In some fields, however, the League of Nations accomplished lasting good. Its subsidiary organs vigorously and often successfully attacked problems like wide-spread disease, narcotics traffic, government barriers to communications, sub-standard conditions of labor, and the slave trade. Many of the League's less publicized activities made an undeniably valuable contribution in eliminating underlying causes of war and human misery. Moreover, the League's contribution was of inestimable importance in another respect: experience gained in establishing and successfully operating the first permanent international organization in history provided a rich backlog of precedents and insights which was drawn upon in innumerable instances by the founders of the United Nations.

The United States did not join the League of Nations, in spite of the fact that one of its greatest Presidents had secured Allied acceptance of it at the Paris Peace Conference. The overwhelming election of Republican President Warren Harding in 1920 was widely—and probably incorrectly—interpreted as a resounding public rejection of the League. The Senate refused to ratify the Treaty of Versailles as submitted by President Wilson, and Wilson refused to accept modifications which would make it palatable to the Senate. The impasse was never resolved, dooming the United States to remain outside the League.

Nevertheless, as time went on the United States sent "unofficial observers" to Geneva. Working without fanfare, the observers cooperated with certain League activities, particularly in fields like suppression of narcotics rings and white slave traffic. They were able to communicate the American government's position on prevailing international issues to statesmen at Geneva. In 1934 the United States finally joined the International Labor Organization, which was loosely affiliated with the League, and in the same year it agreed to register its treaties at League headquarters (**41**, pp. 527-28). That isolationism still was the dominating impulse in American foreign affairs, however, was indicated in 1935, when not even the politically adroit President Roosevelt could prevail upon two-thirds of the Senate to approve American membership in the World Court.

The United States held officially aloof from the proceedings of the League of Nations dealing with global political developments after 1920. American initiative in sponsoring the Washington Naval Armaments Conference (1921) and the Kellogg-Briand Pact (1928) denouncing war as an instrument of national policy, however, was indicative of America's willingness to work for peace. In the critical decade of the 1930's, the United States as a rule applauded efforts by the League to deal with aggression in Europe and Asia; and occasionally Roosevelt and Secretary of State Hull took the initiative in trying to prod the League to even greater efforts. From time to time vigorous condemnations of German expansionism and of Japanese perfidy emanated from Washington. But American officials were always restricted by two prohibitions: they dared not commit the country to a policy which demanded action, and particularly military action, to halt aggression, nor could they risk the accusation that American policy was being "dictated" by the rejected and still unpopular League of Nations (41, pp. 580-81). These limitations, coupled with prolonged indecision in Washington regarding the long-run implications of Japan's expansionism in the Orient, meant that the United States was unprepared to render any tangible assistance to the League of Nations in a showdown and that its own unilateral response to repeated international crises was seldom an improvement over the growing paralysis displayed by the League of Nations. Considering the profound isolationist propensities of the American people, it was perhaps of no crucial significance that the United States failed to join the League of Nations. There is no evidence that, had the United States been a member, it was prepared to go beyond the feeble efforts exerted by England, France, and Russia in meeting the challenge of aggression head-on, with military force if necessary. Anything less could scarcely have averted the League's eventual demise.

The United Nations

Hitler's attack against Poland in the fall of 1939 ignited the Second World War. Soon every major power of the world was drawn into the vortex of that struggle. After the United States entered the war following the Japanese attack against Pearl Harbor on December 7, 1941, American officials moved rapidly to integrate Allied war efforts and, more importantly for our subject, to lay the basis for a durable peace in the postwar era. By 1942 the State Department had initiated intensive preliminary studies of problems that would be encountered in assuring international stability after the Axis defeat. Executive and legislative officials collaborated intimately to generate support within the government and throughout the country at large for an international organization to facilitate maintenance of world peace. Careful attention was paid to the experience of the League of Nations.

In a series of conferences dating from early 1942, step by step the contours of the nascent United Nations emerged, as agreements were secured among the Allies concerning its pur-

poses and guiding principles. At Moscow in the autumn of 1943, at Tehran in December, and finally at Dumbarton Oaks in the autumn of 1944 the "Big Five" (Great Britain, France, China, Soviet Russia, and the United States) negotiated agreements laying the foundations for the United Nations. The Dumbarton Oaks agreements indicated that the UN was to be much like its predecessor. The two major policy-making bodies were to be the Security Council and the General Assembly. The former, possessing primary responsibility for dealing with questions of international peace and security, was to reflect the preponderant influence of the Big Five in world affairs. These states were to be the "permanent" members, and seven smaller countries were to be rotating "non-permanent" members elected for two years by the General Assembly. The Assembly's function theoretically was confined to discussing all other matters within the jurisdiction of the UN and, more broadly, to promoting human welfare. The League's Permanent Court of International Justice, renamed the International Court of Justice, was retained as the judicial organ of the new international organization.

Finally, the Dumbarton Oaks proposals included a Secretariat, to be headed by a Secretary-General who, according to Article 97 of the UN Charter, is designated "chief administrative officer of the Organization." The Secretariat was to be the UN's continuing executive office, charged with facilitating the carrying out of policies and taking an active part in their formulation. As we shall see, one of the most profound changes in the UN after 1945 was the emergence of the Secretary-General as an active force in negotiations seeking to eliminate causes of international tension.

After Dumbarton Oaks there remained the crucial question of voting within the Security Council—a question involving the guiding philosophy upon which the United Nations was to be constructed and operated thereafter. The great powers had been primarily responsible for the impending Axis defeat. Moreover, they had taken the initiative in planning for the UN, virtually presenting the smaller powers with a *fait accompli*. Two extreme alternatives were possible: either the emergent UN, following in the footsteps of the Concert of Europe after the Congress of Vienna, might become merely a mechanism whereby the great powers imposed their will upon the international community. Or else the UN would accept the principle of "one state, one vote," carrying the concept of the equality of nations to the point of giving all states regardless of size and power an equal opportunity to shape decisions. The first course led back to the wastelands of a world dominated by the great powers in which global decisions were made by a handful of governments representing a small minority of the earth's population. The second path led to the swamp of futility, with the new international organization rapidly becoming impotent because decisions were made by a preponderance of weak states which possessed neither the power nor inclination to carry them out in the face of great power opposition. In short, a formula had to be found which in some way would blend the realities of the existing international power structure with the broad principles of equality, responsibility, and respect for the rights of weaker countries.

Such a formula was agreed upon at the Yalta Conference in February, 1945. Here it was decided that Security Council decisions involving *procedural* (i.e., presumably minor) questions could be made by a majority of any seven members of the Council. But on *substantive* matters (i.e., highly important questions affecting peace and security) decisions could only be reached by the *unanimous* vote of the great powers, plus the affirmative votes of two of the non-permanent members. Parties to a dispute before the Council, however, were prohibited from voting. Each permanent member in effect possessed a "veto" —a term not mentioned in the Charter. If the Security Council could not act in matters affecting peace and security with the concurrence of *all* the great powers, then it could not act at all.

The UN Charter was drawn up and signed at the fifty-nation San Francisco Conference held April 25 - June 26, 1945. The smaller states objected vigorously to the preponderant voice given to the Big Five in the Security Council. While the great powers remained adamant on retention of the veto, other concessions were made to accommodate the view-

points of smaller countries. As an example, the draft Charter was amended to make more forceful the UN's concern for "fundamental human rights," "social progress" and "better standards of life"—matters of the highest concern to newly-independent and dependent countries throughout Asia and Africa. A vastly strengthened Economic and Social Council, was elevated into a major organ of the UN.* A completely new body, the Trusteeship Council, was also added and given responsibilities for supervising governments of dependent people and of advancing their welfare.

The UN—Basic Assumptions and Underlying Concepts

For a proper understanding of the United Nations and of America's relationship to it, it is essential to grasp certain assumptions and underlying concepts upon which the UN was founded. Failure to understand these and their implications has often led to widespread confusion in American public attitudes toward the UN and has sometimes placed unnecessary obstacles in the path of the successful utilization of the UN as an instrument for world peace and security.

---

*The Charter provision permitting the Economic and Social Council to negotiate working relationships with specialized agencies active in the economic-social field proved especially important. In some cases, these agencies already existed; after 1945 their efforts were co-ordinated as closely as possible with the UN. In other cases, the UN created certain specialized agencies. Agencies already in the field, and later brought under the jurisdiction of the UN, include the Universal Postal Union (UPU), the International Labor Organization (ILO), the Food and Agriculture Organization (FAO), the International Monetary Fund, and the International Bank for Reconstruction and Development. Agencies which were in the formative stage or were created after 1945 include the International Civil Aviation Organization (ICAO), the UN Educational, Scientific and Cultural Organization (UNESCO), the World Health Organization (WHO), the International Refugee Organization (IRO), and the International Trade Organization (ITO).

A total of eleven "specialized agencies" of the UN exist. While they possess a certain degree of autonomy, they are also loosely under the jurisdiction of the General Assembly and the Economic and Social Council. For a fuller treatment of their precise relationship to the UN, see 23, pp. 73-8. An informative treatment of their activities and accomplishments is 3, *passim.*

First, the United Nations was designed to be, and it remains, *a league of sovereign states, not a world government.* This distinction has sometimes been blurred by both advocates and critics of international organization. The UN was established to facilitate harmonious relationships among *sovereign* countries to achieve ends specified in the UN Charter. While the Preamble to the Charter speaks of "the *peoples* of the United Nations," it goes on to observe that "our respective *Governments* . . . have agreed to the present Charter . . . " (italics inserted).

The UN possesses virtually none of the attributes associated with sovereign political entities: the power to tax, to pass laws, to impose its will directly upon citizens, and to punish *individuals* who violate its laws. Exceptions exist in one sphere only: enforcement of Charter provisions against violators of international peace and security. Article 2 of the Charter expressly prohibits the UN from intervening "in matters which are essentially within the domestic jurisdiction of any state," leaving it to the states concerned to decide what these matters are. A committee of the San Francisco Conference held that any nation would be free to withdraw from the UN "if its rights and obligations . . . were changed by Charter amendment in which it has not concurred and which it finds itself unable to accept" (**23**, p. 21). In countless ways the preliminary wartime studies of the UN, the debates at San Francisco, and the Charter itself leave no doubt that the founders were establishing an institution which accepted national sovereignty as supreme except in the case of threats to the peace. They sought to create an international environment in which sovereignty could be exercised more beneficially for the welfare of mankind (**23**, pp. 20-1; **8**, pp. 76-7).

In the second place, the United Nations was envisioned by its originators as predominantly an instrumentality *to preserve and maintain peace and security.* The implications of this fact for the later development of the UN, and for its subsequent influence upon world affairs, can hardly be exaggerated. For in many crucial respects the United Nations presupposed the existence or the early establishment of the peace it was expected to preserve; it was not designed to bring that peace into existence.

In at least three important respects, however, the peace which the UN was expected to preserve was not achieved after 1945 and has not been altogether achieved today. The most obvious instance was in relations among the great powers themselves. "Great power unanimity," the keystone of the arch of collective security, began to disintegrate after 1945 in the face of cold war antagonisms between two rival diplomatic blocs. Having postulated its existence and future effectiveness upon a continuation of wartime unity among the great powers, the UN possessed very few methods for creating an essential condition which its founders had taken for granted. The United Nations was set up to deal with *future* threats to the peace which met a twofold definition: (1) situations which the great powers *unanimously* recognized as endangering international tranquility; and (2) those with which the great powers were prepared to deal on a basis of *collective action.* Quite obviously, disputes among the great powers themselves do not meet this test—a fact which as much as any other explains why the UN's influence in settling cold war disputes since 1945 has often been peripheral.

Another sphere in which the UN presupposed an established peace was in restoring defeated Axis countries to the family of nations. The founders deliberately divorced the UN Charter from the peace treaties for all defeated Axis powers, in order to escape the stigma attached to the League of Nations because of its intimate identification with what proved in some countries a highly unpopular peace settlement. The UN has taken no role in negotiating Axis peace treaties since World War II. One of the issues which lies at the heart of continued cold war tensions—the territorial division of Germany—remains an issue toward which the UN has made, and can make, little positive contribution, so long as the great powers remain divided.

Still another sphere in which the peace the UN was supposed to safeguard did not materialize was in relations between colonial countries and their possessions. Here again the founders of the UN either did not anticipate postwar tensions over colonial questions, or else they counted on "great power unanimity" to resolve problems which might arise. In any event, the UN was given no formal jurisdiction over the vast majority of pre-existing colonial relationships. Charter provisions pertaining to dependent areas, in the words of one commentary, applied only to a limited number of "territories administered under League mandates or for which at a later time trusteeship agreements might be negotiated" (23, p. 408). While certain obligations were assumed by all members of the UN in administering their colonial affairs, no mechanism or procedures were set up whereby international control could be exerted to assure compliance with Charter obligations.

Immediately after the war, the UN did experience some success in dealing with colonial disputes, as in Indonesia, Syria, and Lebanon. But in many other critical instances, involving French colonialism in Indochina and North Africa, British colonialism in Kenya and Cyprus, and what can be correctly designated as Russian colonialism in Eastern Europe, the UN has been conspicuously unsuccessful in preserving the peace, largely because peace did not exist in many of these areas at the time of the UN's establishment and, throughout the years that followed, the UN possessed very few facilities for resolving these tensions. When colonial conflicts became intertwined with cold war issues, progressively involving the diplomatic ambitions and interests of the great powers, the difficulties facing the UN became well-nigh insurmountable.

Because the UN was forced to seek to realize conditions—the achievement of peace in vital sectors of international affairs—which its founders either had taken for granted or had deliberately excluded from the UN's jurisdiction, its influence has often been tangential. Concentration on these war-born problems inevitably meant that, in many significant respects, the UN would become a very different institution from the one its originators had anticipated.

2. THE UN AND THE POSTWAR WORLD

Since our task is confined to describing and assessing problems of international organization as they bear upon the foreign policy of the United States, we cannot undertake a comprehensive treatment of the evolution and major activities of the United Nations after 1945.* Nevertheless, some familiarity with the UN's development and its efforts to cope with leading international issues is indispensable for our purpose.

*Bibliography on the United Nations is copious. Aside from the *Official Records* of the UN's principal organs, described in the *United Nations Documents Index* issued monthly, a number of valuable summaries and commentaries exist. Official publications include the *Yearbook of the United Nations,* summarizing annual activities; the *United Nations Bulletin* issued bi-weekly; and the *Annual Report of the Secretary-General on the Work of the Organization.* These also cite relevant documentary materials for further reading in selected cases. Also valuable is the State Department's publication entitled *U. S. Participation in the United Nations,* issued annually, summarizing the UN's activities with emphasis upon America's role.

Helpful secondary studies include the summaries and articles appearing in the journal

Decline of the Security Council

Critics of the UN often overlook the solid record of accomplishment which it has amassed throughout the postwar period. Notable achievements have been the withdrawal of Soviet troops from Iran's northern provinces in 1946; termination of colonial rule over Syria and Lebanon in the same year; resolution of the conflict between Indonesia and the Netherlands in the period 1947-49; successful adjudication of a dispute between Great Britain and Albania in 1947; assistance in preserving the sovereignty of Greece in 1946-48; prevention of war between India and Pakistan over Kashmir after 1948; partial responsibility for ending

International Organization, which contains resumés of UN activities in its quarterly issues; publications in the Carnegie Foundation's series *International Conciliation,* which contains a number of illuminating studies on selected cases involving the UN; studies in the State Department's "International Organization and Conference Series;" and the summaries and essays in New York University's series, *Annual Review of United Nations Affairs.*

the Berlin blockade in 1949; resistance to armed Communist attack against South Korea from 1950 to 1953 and supervision of the Korean truce; conclusion and subsequent supervision of an armistice between Israel and the Arab states in 1950; termination of hostilities growing out of the Anglo-French and Israeli invasion of Egypt in 1956 and continuing enforcement of the armistice agreement by a United Nations Emergency Force stationed on the Israeli-Egyptian border; and intensive efforts late in 1958 to deal with crises in the Middle East involving Iraq, Lebanon, and Jordan.

While these achievements are an eloquent tribute to the contribution of the United Nations in its comparatively brief existence, it cannot be denied that in one vital area—mitigating tensions between the Soviet-led communist world and the American-led free world coalition—the UN's role has often been minimal. With rare exceptions, such as ending the Berlin blockade, the Security Council has been able to accomplish very little in adjusting disagreements between these two antagonistic power blocs. Time and again Soviet vetoes have prevented the Security Council from taking action in critical international disputes. In the face of a relentless bombardment of Russian *"nyet's,"* the Council's ability to discharge its duties under the Charter has inevitably declined and the overall prestige of the United Nations has been seriously impaired. Yet, as we shall see, the United States cannot wholly escape responsibility for the growing paralysis of the Security Council. The United States has never vetoed an important measure dealing with peace and security. More perhaps by omission than by commission, by subtle means rather than by deliberately obstructionist tactics, the United States has also played a part in weakening the Security Council's influence. The Council's decline is reflected in the decrease in the number of its meetings. In 1946 the Security Council held 88 meetings; in 1948, 168 meetings; in 1950, 73 meetings; in 1952, 42 meetings; and in 1954, 32 meetings (**16**, p. 14). Repeated deadlocks in the Council over inflammatory cold war issues at length resulted in a kind of constitutional revolution whereby

the Council's functions have more and more been assumed by the General Assembly.

What factors explain this profound change in the character of the United Nations? The obvious answer is to point to instance after instance in which the Security Council was immobilized by the Soviet veto—a total of eighty-five by mid-1958. Yet this is a superficial explanation which mistakes symptoms for causes. Excessive Soviet use of the veto is not in itself the *cause* of the Council's inability to deal with threats to the peace involving the great powers. Impotence stems from the fact that the world remains divided into powerful sovereign nations which are prepared to fight, if necessary, rather than to see their "vital interests" infringed, whether by nations acting jointly under UN auspices, or acting in coalition, or acting unilaterally. Under these conditions the veto furnishes the only possible way out for an international organization which must depend upon the voluntary consent and strength of its members for its enforcement powers. When UN action is contemplated against one of the strongest members as, for example, was widely advocated in the case of Soviet intervention in Hungary in 1956, then one of two possible alternatives exists: either the UN attempts to compel acceptance of its decrees by international malfactors at the risk of starting the third world war, or else it agrees that enforcement action under the circumstances is impracticable.

Abuse of the veto then can only be interpreted as symptomatic of the fact that peace does not exist among the great powers and that the UN was not designed to achieve it. Outright abolition of the veto in the Security Council would in no way alter the underlying international power structure which has contributed to the Council's ineffectualness in the face of recurrent cold war tensions. If the Council were permitted, by a simple majority vote, to take a decision, let us say, on Soviet intervention in the affairs of the Baltic states, the Council would sooner or later have to make the choice of fighting Russia to enforce the decision or of giving up the proposed action as unattainable. Little is to be gained, therefore, in blaming the veto for the Security Council's impotence. Assuming the continuance of the cold war, there is virtually no prospect that elimination of the veto would restore the Council to the position originally assigned to it by the founders.

Emergence of a Strengthened General Assembly

Contemporaneous with the eclipse of the Security Council has been transformation of the General Assembly into the UN's most influential organ. Our discussion has called attention to attempts in the Charter to distinguish rather sharply between the functions of the Council and the Assembly, assigning primary responsibility to the former for dealing with issues affecting peace and security. The Assembly, on the other hand, in the words of Article 10 of the Charter,

> may discuss any questions or any matters within the scope of the present Charter or relating to the powers and functions of any organs provided for in the present charter, and, except as provided in Article 12 [prohibiting the Assembly from making recommendations on issues pending before the Security Council], may make recommendations to the Members of the United Nations or to the Security Council or to both on any such questions or matters.

Save for questions directly pertaining to peace and security, therefore, the founders intended that the General Assembly should possess very broad powers and that it should deal with sundry "indirect" and long-range causes of international instability. However, the Assembly is limited to "making recommendations" on matters within its jurisdiction.

Founded upon the principle of the equality of all members, the General Assembly was to be a great international forum in which countries great and small would have an opportunity to discuss any subject within the purview of the Charter. Military behemoths and pygmies alike were given an equal voice and an equal vote. At San Francisco, the United States had joined with the small states in demanding broad powers and equality of voting in the Assembly. One of the crises at the Conference had come when Soviet Russia refused to accept such a conception, only to give way in time to avert a total impasse (27, pp. 11-18). A significant advance was made over the As-

sembly of the League of Nations, where unanimity was required for decisions, by the Charter provision that the Assembly could make decisions on an "important matter" by a two-thirds majority and on less important questions by a simple majority (Article 18). Apprehensive lest some of the smaller states lead the Assembly to discuss questions not properly within the competence of the United Nations, the American delegation at San Francisco took the initiative in inserting the Charter provision already cited (Article 2, Section 7) prohibiting *all* organs of the UN from intervening in matters which were "essentially within the domestic jurisdiction of any state" (27, pp. 18-20).

As cold war antagonisms increasingly paralyzed the Security Council, the General Assembly began to emerge as the authoritative voice of the United Nations. A critical period was 1947-48, when the General Assembly voted to "partition" the strife-torn land of Palestine into separate Jewish and Arab states and was called upon to deal with the violence which this act precipitated. After the Communist attempt to gain control over Greece in 1946-48, the United States took the initiative in converting the Assembly into the UN's primary organ for dealing with political tensions and possible causes of war.

An important evolutionary step was the American-sponsored "interim assembly" plan introduced in 1947, whereby an interim committee could deal with inflammable international issues between sessions of the Assembly (27, p. 37). This was merely the forerunner of a much more sweeping transformation of the Assembly's powers. That step was the American-initiated "Uniting for Peace" resolution, presented in the fall of 1950 and passed by the General Assembly on November 3. Carefully taking note of the Security Council's inability to discharge its primary obligations under the Charter, the resolution observed that this did not "relieve Member States of their obligations or the United Nations of its responsibility under the Charter to maintain international peace and security." The resolution therefore provided that when the Security Council was deadlocked or failed to act "where there appears to be a threat to the peace" then the General Assembly

> shall consider the matter immediately with a view to making appropriate recommendations to Members for collective measures, including in the case of a breach of the peace or act of aggression the use of armed force when necessary, to maintain or restore international peace and security.

If the Assembly were not in session when a threat to the peace occurred, it could meet in emergency special session within twenty-four hours; the request for an emergency meeting could be made by any seven members of the Security Council or by a majority of the Members of the United Nations. Other important provisions of the resolution were establishment of a Peace Observation Commission under the auspices of the Assembly; recommendations that all governments co-operate with the Commission; requests to each Member to survey the resources it could make available to support efforts of the Council or the Assembly for enforcing peace; and establishment of a Collective Measures Committee to study and report on methods for strengthening international peace and security (10, I, pp. 187-92).

The impact of these changes, in the words of Clark M. Eichelberger, was that the General Assembly became the "paramount organ" within the United Nations for adjusting international disputes. Eichelberger believes that the old balance between the Security Council and the Assembly "is not likely to be restored" (16, pp. 15, 19). Increasingly, it has fallen to the Assembly's lot to take over responsibility from the Security Council, as when the Assembly stationed a commission along the Greek border in 1947 to observe conditions there after the Council refused to act; when it gradually assumed the burden of successfully prosecuting the Korean War; and when it sought to enforce compliance with the Korean armistice agreement after 1953 (16, p. 16).

When the Assembly had to deal with successive crises in Egypt and Hungary in 1956, the "Uniting For Peace" resolution was put into effect for the first time. It was of no avail in attempting to terminate Soviet oppression of the Hungarian revolutionary movement. This proved once again that the Assembly, where there is no veto, was no more successful than the Security Council, in dealing with issues on which one of the world's two power giants refused to accept UN directives (47, pp. 46-71). The Assembly debates on the Suez dispute left no doubt that public opinion the world over was opposed to the Anglo-French and Israeli invasions of Egypt. As a result of negotiations which took place both inside and outside the UN, these countries agreed to withdraw their troops. For the first time in history a "United Nations Emergency Force," consisting of military contingents from ten member-states, was created. Its task was to patrol the always tense Israeli-Egyptian frontier and to prevent further hostilities from erupting between these countries (22, *passim*). Whatever other results the Suez crisis of 1956 may have had, one of them was to enhance the prestige of the United Nations and to revivify its sometimes waning fortunes. In turning to the General Assembly in this crisis, it was the United States as much as any other country which took the lead in giving the UN responsibility for restoring stability to the Middle East (50, 1956, pp. 358-60).

It was the turbulent Middle East which again in mid-1958 posed the most critical threat to world peace and security. The collapse of the pro-Western government of Iraq, accompanied by grave political unrest in Lebanon and Jordan, once more presented the UN with critical international tensions and the prospect of regional, perhaps even global, war. So delicate was the Middle Eastern situation that on August 13 President Eisenhower personally addressed the General Assembly, presenting a new American-sponsored plan for restoring stability to this crisis-ridden area. Significantly, it was to the General Assembly that the world looked for a resolution of the Middle Eastern conflict. Over succeeding months turmoil and great power tensions in the Middle East abated somewhat, owing largely to factors having little or nothing to do with the direct influence of the United Nations. The United Nations continued to station military forces along the borders of Israel, thereby preventing the tense situation between Israel and the Arab states from deteriorating sharply by new outbreaks of military hostilities. Otherwise, the

UN's role in coping with fundamental causes of instability in the Middle East was marginal. In the fall of 1959, the General Assembly listened to a new indictment of Egypt's blockade against Israeli shipping in the Suez Canal. As in the past, however, it appeared unable to do anything about this clear violation of its own resolutions and of the Suez agreement of 1888 governing Egypt's administration of this vital waterway.

The United States, which has been chiefly responsible for strengthening the General Assembly, has had to face a number of new problems growing out of the Assembly's expanded role. Taking full advantage of their numerical majority in the Assembly and of their new found opportunities to influence the course of world events, the small nations have utilized the Assembly as never before to air their grievances and demands. Nations in the Afro-Asian bloc particularly have come to rely upon the Assembly as an arena within which to wage their own brand of "cold war" against colonialism and economic backwardness, by gaining support among richer countries for expanded UN technical assistance programs, by hastening the process of independence for still-dependent peoples, and more generally by broadening the UN's concern for bedrock issues affecting human welfare and human rights (4, pp. 464-67). No longer does a straight division of voting along cold war lines, as was usually evident in the Security Council, prevail. Now four major blocs are discernible within the Assembly: a five-nation Soviet bloc, a thirteen-nation Arab-Asian bloc, a twenty-nation Latin American bloc, and a twenty-two nation NATO and non-Asian British Commonwealth bloc. With increasing frequence, on major international issues the larger Latin American bloc and the smaller Arab-Asian bloc hold the balance of power (4, p. 470; 2, pp. 3-31).

Thus the United Nations has become an agency in which the full panoply of global issues is debated and acted upon. While the United States can normally expect to muster a minimum of twenty or so votes among its NATO allies, it has found itself outvoted by the remainder of the eighty-one members of the UN and it has found that many of these nations often feel much more strongly about

other issues than about world communism. This is not to suggest that the Assembly consistently takes an anti-American line. Congressmen who have served as U. S. delegates to the Assembly have emphasized that respect for the United States is high in the Assembly and that American leadership is still highly effective in shaping decisions (29, pp. 2, 43-5). Nevertheless, as time goes on, as the strength of the Arab-Asian bloc increases, the West can be expected to face impatient demands of governments representing a majority of the human race, whose overriding concern appears to be human betterment in all walks of life. Mounting pressure has been exerted upon the "have" nations by the "have-not" nations, and this pressure can be expected to become even more intense in the future. Already the United States has been placed in an increasingly vulnerable position within the Assembly on issues involving colonialism, racial discrimination, and expanded UN assistance programs. One consequence of these developments has been to make American officials more inclined than formerly to support the principle of "weighted voting" within the Assembly, whereby the "capacities" of states would determine the number of votes they would have in making certain kinds of decisions (43, pp. 192-203).

The United States, in other words, has discovered that a strengthened General Assembly is a double-edged sword. If it could cut the shackles that bound the UN as long as the Security Council was veto-ridden, it could also slash away at the bonds of colonialism and racism, and it could occasionally prod reluctant countries in the West to take more vigorous action on issues of vital concern to a substantial number of the UN's members. And on these issues, the United States sometimes finds itself outvoted by the same impressive majorities it has tried to marshal against the communist bloc.

The UN's role in peace and security issues obviously has not measured up to the expectations of its founders. Yet, though the UN's progress in dealing with threats to the peace has not been spectacular, it has been steady; and though the UN has experienced no striking success in settling disputes among the great powers by utilizing charter procedures, it has

NATIONAL ALIGNMENTS AND VOTING IN THE UNITED NATIONS

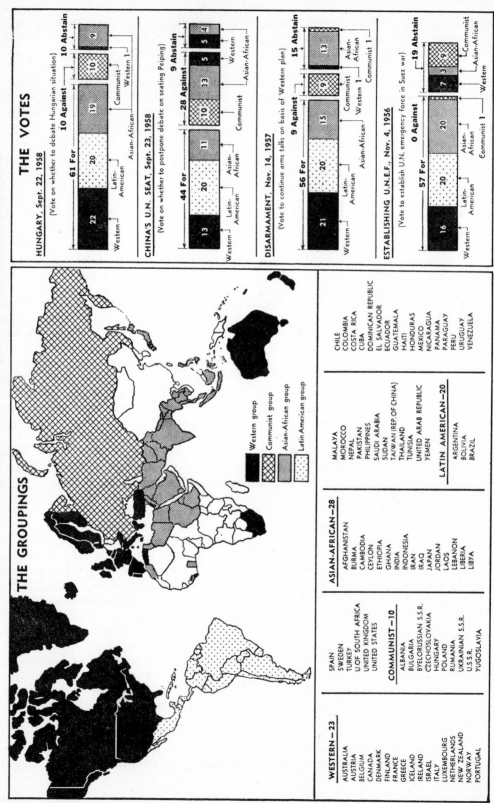

THE GROUPINGS

THE VOTES

HUNGARY, Sept. 22, 1958
(Vote on whether to debate Hungarian situation)

CHINA'S U.N. SEAT, Sept. 23, 1958
(Vote on whether to postpone debate on seating Peiping)

DISARMAMENT, Nov. 14, 1957
(Vote to continue arms talks on basis of Western plan)

ESTABLISHING U.N.E.F., Nov. 4, 1956
(Vote to establish U.N. emergency force in Suez war)

The New York Times, Sept. 28, 1958.

Western group
Communist group
Asian-African group
Latin American group

WESTERN — 23

AUSTRALIA
AUSTRIA
BELGIUM
CANADA
DENMARK
FINLAND
FRANCE
GREECE
ICELAND
IRELAND
ISRAEL
ITALY
LUXEMBOURG
NETHERLANDS
NEW ZEALAND
NORWAY
PORTUGAL
SPAIN
SWEDEN
U. OF SOUTH AFRICA
UNITED KINGDOM
UNITED STATES

COMMUNIST — 10

ALBANIA
BULGARIA
BYELORUSSIAN S.S.R.
CZECHOSLOVAKIA
HUNGARY
POLAND
RUMANIA
UKRAINIAN S.S.R.
U.S.S.R.
YUGOSLAVIA

ASIAN-AFRICAN — 28

AFGHANISTAN
BURMA
CAMBODIA
CEYLON
ETHIOPIA
GHANA
INDIA
INDONESIA
IRAN
IRAQ
JAPAN
JORDAN
LAOS
LEBANON
LIBERIA
LIBYA
MALAYA
MOROCCO
NEPAL
PAKISTAN
PHILIPPINES
SAUDI ARABIA
SUDAN
TAIWAN (REP. OF CHINA)
THAILAND
TUNISIA
UNITED ARAB REPUBLIC
YEMEN

LATIN AMERICAN — 20

ARGENTINA
BOLIVIA
BRAZIL
CHILE
COLOMBIA
COSTA RICA
CUBA
DOMINICAN REPUBLIC
EL SALVADOR
ECUADOR
GUATEMALA
HAITI
HONDURAS
MEXICO
NICARAGUA
PANAMA
PARAGUAY
PERU
URUGUAY
VENEZUELA

evolved other techniques for accomplishing these purposes. Chief among these are the dramatic application of the force of world opinion, initiative in spurring negotiations outside the UN, strong leadership by the Secretary-General in seeking resolution of thorny international issues and, perhaps above all, relentless pressure upon the great powers to continue the search for a mutually agreeable basis upon which to settle outstanding differences without resort to war. The Assembly may have "solved" very few issues between the communist and non-communist worlds. It has, however, softened great power conflicts and made them more tolerable to the international community.

Economic and Social Activities

Sometimes overshadowed by the activities of the United Nations in peace and security matters are the myriad activities carried on by the UN in economic-social affairs touching hundreds of millions of people. An earlier portion of the chapter called attention to the fact that, to conciliate the small states, provisions for a strengthened Economic and Social Council were added to the Charter at San Francisco. The Economic and Social Council consists of eighteen members elected by the General Assembly, each member serving for three years. As defined in Article 62, its province is sweeping, permitting it to "make or initiate studies and reports" relating to "international economic, social, cultural, educational, health, and related matters;" to "make recommendations . . . to the General Assembly, to the Members of the United Nations, and to the specialized agencies;" and to "make recommendations for the purpose of promoting respect for, and observance of, human rights and fundamental freedoms for all."

Under the Economic and Social Council are eight functional commissions and three regional bureaus. In addition, it has several "operating bodies" like the UN Children's Emergency Fund (UNICEF), the UN Relief and Works Agency for Palestine Refugees, and the UN Korean Reconstruction Agency. There are also eleven semi-autonomous "specialized agencies," which were enumerated earlier in this chapter.

Measured by the volume and quality of studies and publications turned out, the subsidiary organs of the Economic and Social Council have done a staggering and immensely valuable job. Frequent publications include a *World Economic Report, Review of International Commodity Problems, Statistical Yearbook, Demographic Yearbook, and Yearbook of International Trade,* to list merely a few titles from among the hundreds of comprehensive and limited studies released so far.

Besides study and publication, economic and social agencies of the UN have undertaken worthwhile projects on the national and local levels within selected countries. A description of these projects would carry us far afield, but some idea of their nature and scope can be gained by using the year 1955 as an illustration. The International Bank for Reconstruction and Development (IBRD) loaned $406.5 million to twenty member-countries and provided guidance in solving national economic problems. In the same year the three regional commissions of the Economic and Social Council carried forward their continuing studies of economic problems and trends in Europe, Asia, and Latin America. The UN Expanded Program of Technical Assistance received total pledges amounting to over $28 million, with the United States contributing nearly half. Typical projects undertaken by this program were training courses in accounting and bookkeeping in Libya, training programs and facilities for railroad operation within Pakistan, drives to eliminate rinderpest and poultry disease in Thailand, Burma, Afghanistan, and India, and provision of power-driven fishing boats to villages in India.

Relief and rehabilitation programs were conducted for Palestine refugees, with the UN spending nearly $30 million in 1955, and for Korea, with UN-sponsored projects going on in 3,800 sites and costing $123 million. The Narcotic Control Commission sought to tighten international supervision over traffic in narcotics, with growing emphasis upon diminishing traffic in marihuana. The Children's Fund (UNICEF) carried on 268 programs in 92 countries, with well over 90 per cent of its projects falling in the category of long-range "self-help" programs undertaken through joint collaboration between the UN and the country concerned. UNICEF concentrated particularly upon assistance to promote child welfare and child-care training, eradication of children's diseases, leprosy control in countries like Ethiopia and the Solomon Islands, and improvement of feeding and nutritional standards for children (13, 1955, pp. 110-57).

There has been an important shift in emphasis among most UN agencies, away from providing relief and emergency aid toward providing assistance and guidance to achieve economic growth, cultural progress, and health improvement in backward nations. Concurrently, increasing emphasis has been discernible upon long-range, as opposed to short-range, programs; these are often sponsored jointly by UN agencies and national governmental agencies, sometimes with private organizations playing a part. In recent years also, underdeveloped countries have received increasing quantities of UN assistance and advice. Within the UN itself, agencies have spent larger percentages of the budget on "grass roots" projects and less on programming and administrative costs. At the same time, however, American officials and some students of the United Nations contend that its activities in the economic-social realm are not always as fully co-ordinated as they might be, that efforts are sometimes diffuse, and that a limited number of the projects undertaken have been of doubtful value (11, *passim*).

Of most direct concern to the United States has been the growing demand within the underdeveloped countries for capital development funds, a demand which has been expressed within the UN as well as outside it. A UN Expanded Program of Technical Assistance, administered by the Economic and Social Council, was inaugurated in 1949, receiving at least some of its impetus from the American Point Four Program of technical assistance announced in the same year. EPTA's budget for the year 1958 was slightly over $30 million, with the United States contributing nearly half the total. Congress has stipulated, however, that America's contribution to EPTA must be reduced by stages, to reach no more than one-third the total budget by 1960 (29, pp. 24-68).

Most of the economically backward members of the United Nations regard EPTA's budget as inadequate to meet the worldwide demand for capital funds. For several years, these countries have urged creation of a Special UN Fund for Economic Development (SUNFED). As envisioned by these countries SUNFED would possess a greatly enlarged budget, made possible by greater contributions from the richer industrial countries of the world. The United States has opposed SUNFED for two reasons: Uncle Sam favors increasing utilization of *private* sources of capital for backward countries and, so long as cold war requirements necessitate a heavy defense burden, the United States is not prepared to increase its pledge to UN-sponsored assistance programs. American officials have stated publicly that their position on SUNFED might change if progress could be made in reducing the burden of armaments, so that defense costs could be utilized for programs of human betterment. Until that time, and in spite of growing sentiment within the UN for adoption of SUNFED, the United States has withheld its support (29, pp. 24-34). Meanwhile, the United States continues to advocate increased contributions to EPTA by all the members of the United Nations, a suggestion which has found very little support among the other UN members. Reporting on the Twelfth Session of the General Assembly in late 1957, the American delegates observed that "any consensus to the effect that the nations should all get together and boost their contributions [to EPTA] so as to avoid a curtailment of the program was notable by its absence" (29, p. 25).

Human Rights and Self-Determination

Also less well publicized than the UN's efforts to deal with situations endangering world peace are activities carried out in the realm of human rights. Since 1953, the United Nations has had before it for consideration two documents, a draft covenant on civil and political rights and another on economic, social and cultural rights. Discussion of these documents within the UN has sometimes been stormy, paralleling in many respects public consideration of them within the United States. To the

United States, a particularly controversial provision of the draft on economic rights has been Article 1, Section 3, providing that "The right of peoples to self-determination shall also include permanent sovereignty over their natural wealth and resources. In no case may a people be deprived of its own means of subsistence on the grounds of any rights that may be claimed by other States" (46, p. 267). Support for this idea, and for even stronger expressions of it after 1953, has naturally come chiefly from the underdeveloped countries, which have sought to apply the principle of "self-determination" broadly. By contrast, the United States and its European allies have feared that such a conception of self-determination might encourage nationalization or otherwise expropriate foreign corporate holdings in other countries. Among the deleterious consequences of such action, one would be to impair the investment climate in many of these countries and to reduce the prospect of attracting increased private overseas investment (13, 1955, pp. 166-68).

Despite strong official support from time to time for the human rights activities of the UN (10, I, pp. 228-31), the United States has taken a conservative position both on what the UN can and ought to try to accomplish in this field. Few activities of the United Nations have engendered so much apprehension within American public opinion concerning possible infringements upon national sovereignty and loss of constitutional guarantees than those carried on in the field of human rights. Deep public concern about this issue underlay much of the agitation in favor of the "Bricker Amendment" and other efforts to limit the treaty-making powers of the national government late in the Truman administration and early in the Eisenhower administration. Because of widespread citizen misgivings, and because American officials challenged the UN's authority to deal with essentially "domestic" questions, the United States has not ratified the two covenants on human rights alluded to above, the Convention on Genocide adopted by the Assembly in 1948, or the Convention on the Political Rights of Women adopted by the Assembly in 1952.

The American position on such issues was succinctly set forth in a letter of instructions from Secretary of State Dulles on April 3, 1953 (46, pp. 262-64). Here it was emphasized that while the United States supported efforts of the UN to promote respect for human rights, American experience indicated that "nationwide observance of fundamental human rights did not spring into being upon the enactment of statutes." Dulles felt that greater emphasis ought properly be put upon "developing throughout the world a human rights conscience which will bring nearer the goals stated in the Charter." The State Department therefore believed that "we should not at this time become a party to any multilateral treaty such as those contemplated in the draft Covenants on Human Rights, and that we should now work toward the objectives of the Declaration by other means."

UN human rights agreements and declarations are not binding upon the United States until they are ratified by prescribed constitutional processes. Thus Mrs. Franklin D. Roosevelt told the General Assembly in 1948, in reference to one such agreement: "It is not a treaty; it is not an international agreement. It is not and does not purport to be a statement of law or legal obligation. It is a declaration of basic principles . . . " (46, p. 252). It was the opinion of Attorney General Herbert Brownell in 1953 that "no amendment of the Constitution appears to be needed to prevent abridgement by treaty or executive agreement of the essential liberties guaranteed by the Bill of Rights or by the Constitution as a whole" (46, p. 337). Reflecting the views of the Eisenhower administration, Senate opponents of the Bricker Amendment asserted that "No treaty or covenant drafted in the United Nations, its agencies, or any other international organization can bind this Government to anything it does not wish to be bound. . . . " UN-sponsored agreements and conventions are binding upon the United States only when approved by the President and two-thirds of the Senate (46, p. 359).[*]

Caution by American officials, and divergent attitudes between industrialized and under-

---

[*]For a treatment of American policy toward the highly controversial UNESCO, see 54, passim.

developed countries, have also characterized UN consideration of political self-determination for still-dependent peoples. When they ratified the Charter, all members of the United Nations pledged themselves to support Article 73 setting forth principles to govern colonial relationships. According to these principles the interests of the inhabitants living in dependencies "are paramount," colonial responsibilities are a "sacred trust," the ultimate goal is to "develop self-government." Articles 75 through 91 set forth provisions regulating the international trusteeship system established under the UN for territories placed directly under international control. These territories are supervised by the Trusteeship Council.

As would be expected, the Afro-Asian pre-occupation with colonialist issues has found reflection both within Trusteeship Council discussions and in General Assembly discussions dealing with colonial issues not under the Council's jurisdiction. "The United Nations," said an Indonesian delegate, "is the best agency through which a burial of colonialism could be sought" (4, p. 467), a viewpoint widely accepted throughout the Afro-Asian countries. Within the Trusteeship Council, discussion has often centered on the pace with which independence ought to be granted to trust territories. In most cases the countries of the East have favored rapid independence, while those of the West have called attention to the necessity for adequate preparation and to internal and external dangers facing weak states all over the globe (25, pp. 9-21).

Anti-colonialist forces have tried repeatedly to force the United Nations to intervene in such disputes as that between France and its possessions in North Africa and to take cognizance of official policies perpetrating racial discrimination in the Union of South Africa. The UN has had virtually no influence upon the North African conflict, chiefly because none of the great powers except Soviet Russia has supported the anti-colonialist cause. Nor has it experienced any notable success in mitigating racial tensions in South Africa; the only discernible result has been the Union of South Africa's almost complete withdrawal from the United Nations. France and South Africa, however, have not been alone in challenging the competence of the UN to deal with colonial and racial issues. In General Assembly considerations in 1953 of South African racial discrimination, the American Representative to the UN, Henry Cabot Lodge, Jr., stated that while the United States would vote to place the matter on the agenda, the United States had doubts about the competence of the Assembly to deal with it. He continued: "The United States has observed with increasing concern the tendency of the General Assembly to place on its agenda subjects the international character of which is doubtful. In our view, this presents a problem of increasing concern for the organization." He felt that the jurisdiction of the UN over matters of this kind ought to be studied carefully in preparation for any review or amendment of the Charter in the years ahead (46, p. 283).

3. THE U. S. AND THE UN: SOME PERSISTENT ISSUES

In tracing out the movement toward world international organization and world law before World War II, and in treating the establishment and evolution of the United Nations, we have attempted to lay the groundwork for more intelligent understanding of America's relationship with the United Nations in the postwar period. We have already suggested some of the key elements in that relationship. In the remainder of the chapter, we shall explore that subject in greater detail. Important questions guiding our inquiry will be: To what extent

has America's membership in the UN posed problems for the foreign relations of the United States? What is the nature of these problems and what are their implications for the present and future? What are likely to be some of the more significant factors shaping public and official attitudes within the United States toward the United Nations throughout the years ahead? Our discussion will focus particularly upon those aspects of America's relationships with the UN which have tended to detract from the UN's usefulness and from enlightened

American leadership in the realm of international organization.

American Policy Formulation and the UN

The United States is represented at the United Nations by the U.S. Mission to the UN, which has two separate but intimately related functions: to provide representation at annual and special meetings of the General Assembly and to provide continuous representation to all other UN agencies (42, pp. 22-3). Heading the Mission is the United States Representative to the United Nations, appointed by the President and confirmed by the Senate. Since 1953 the Representative has been former Republican Senator from Massachusetts, Henry Cabot Lodge, Jr. Mr. Lodge has a large staff to assist him in representing the nation adequately before all UN organs.

Officials representing the United States at UN Headquarters in New York are "instructed" officials, which is to say that their function is to carry out American foreign policy as formulated in Washington under the ultimate supervision of the President. During the preliminary planning leading to the San Francisco conference in 1945, machinery had already been created within the State Department to provide guidance and continuity for American foreign policy in the field of international organization. After several organizational changes, some of which were prompted by the Hoover Commission's recommendations in 1949, a bureau now called the Office of International Organization Affairs, headed by an Assistant Secretary of State, was established. This office became the focal point for co-ordinating policy in Washington with policy in the United Nations (6, pp. 7-9). Theoretically, policy decisions affecting the UN flow from the Office of International Organization Affairs in the State Department to the U.S. Mission in New York. Sometimes broad principles of policy are passed on to the Mission, with the latter applying these to specific issues which arise within the United Nations. In other cases policymakers in Washington may issue detailed instructions to the UN Mission (30, pp. 22-28).

In practice, however, there is an interchange of ideas and recommendations between officials in Washington and New York in arriving at positions on important questions. An illustration is afforded by the formation of American policy during the Tenth Session of the General Assembly in 1955, where the communist bloc was successfully wooing uncommitted states by emphasis upon expanded economic assistance programs and trade. Officials in New York observed the impact of communist strategy and suggested to officials in Washington certain counter-strategy to meet the new communist threat. As publicly expressed by the Secretary of State on January 11, 1956, the United States sought to make "newly independent and newly articulate peoples feel that they can best satisfy their wants by becoming and remaining part of the community of free nations." Spurred by informative reports from the UN Mission, Secretary Dulles noted that "We are in a contest in the field of economic development of underdeveloped countries which is bitterly competitive. Defeat in this contest could be as disastrous as defeat in an armaments race. We could lose this economic contest unless the country *as a whole* wakes up to all its implications" (28, pp. 3-4, italics in original).

The existence of recognized machinery and procedures for co-ordinating diplomatic efforts in Washington and New York, however, has not always guaranteed effective liaison or fully concerted policies. Some informed commentators have called attention to the anomalous position occupied by the Office of International Organization Affairs within the State Department. This bureau is theoretically on a par with the geographical bureaus in formulating American foreign policy. Two factors, however, have detracted from its position. First, the Assistant Secretary of State for International Organization Affairs has been outranked by the U. S. Representative to the United Nations. Mr. Lodge, for instance, has held the rank of Ambassador; he has been a close political adviser to the President and a member of his Cabinet. Ambassador Lodge therefore has had almost equal access to the President with the Secretary of State and far greater access than almost all subordinate executive officials within the government. Thus the channels of communication between the State Department in Washington and the UN Mission in New York appear to be as much an outgrowth of the impact of key personalities on the foreign policy process as the result of precise legislative or executive determination.*

A second factor tending to interfere with smooth co-ordination of policy between Washington and New York since 1945 has to do with relationships between the Office of International Organization Affairs and other executive agencies. The prestige of IOA, and of the UN itself, was heavily damaged by disclosures and allegations made at the time of the "Hiss case" in the period of intense anticommunist agitation which gripped the country in the late 1940's and early 1950's. One result was that IOA experienced difficulty in becoming fully assimilated and "accepted" within the

---

*One commentator has written that shortly after his appointment, Ambassador Lodge let it be known that he did not intend to function on the basis of detailed "instructions" from IRO in the State Department (6, p. 10). *Time* magazine's account holds that Lodge frequently got his instructions changed and "usually wins his point" in differences with the State Department. It continues that "Sometimes the 'instructions' he gets from Washington are verbatim playbacks of what he wrote himself," in part because developments "happen too fast to rely upon specific instructions." (49, p. 13).

Insight into the part played by Mr. Lodge in his interesting role as a member of the Cabinet is afforded by Robert J. Donovan's account of Eisenhower's first term. In the vast majority of cases, Mr. Lodge's remarks in Cabinet meetings pertained to subjects like social security, highway construction, or taxes. Not once did he present a *critique* of problems within the UN, which may be perhaps explained entirely by the fact that the National Security Council is the highest governmental agency concerned with foreign policy and defense issues (15, pp. 14, 16, 27, 32, 61, 64-5, 86, 141, 157, 387, 394 ff).

An interesting sidelight provided by Donovan's book is the paucity of treatment accorded to the United Nations—a total of four pages. Index citations to this subject are about equal to those for headings like American Bar Association, Bricker Amendment, housing program, and patronage; they are. fewer than headings for budget, balanced, Gettysburg farm, McCarthy, Joseph R., and Yalta agreements. This may or may not be an indication of the importance ascribed to the UN in recent American foreign policy. In any event, it would certainly seem to confirm the fact that the United States is in no danger of losing its sovereignty to the UN because of the overriding fixation with that institution on the part of American policy-makers; and it would strongly suggest that instead the problem may be relying far too *little* upon the UN in certain aspects of American foreign relations.

State Department because of the taint derived from its close connection with an organization many people believed to be heavily Communist-infiltrated. The change in its earlier title, Office of United Nations Affairs, to IOA in part symbolized the Department's awareness that many activities of the UN had become controversial public issues and that within Congress "the United Nations" was not always a psychologically acceptable term.

The influence of IOA upon American policy in the UN was further weakened by the gradual replacement of "specialists" on the United Nations—who had entered the State Department by means of civil service appointments during and after the war—by field officers from the Foreign Service. A similar process has taken place within the U.S. Mission. Both IOA and the Mission have lost many of their highly trained experts on the United Nations. Their successors from the Foreign Service sometimes appear to have neither the knowledge nor the inclination requisite for forthright and dynamic American leadership on the plane of international organization (6, pp. 12-13).

Finally, maximum United States participation and leadership within the United Nations has inevitably been hampered by the growing complexity of foreign affairs, as reflected in the increasingly intimate connection between foreign and domestic policies. One result has been the continuing necessity to integrate the efforts of an ever-widening circle of executive and legislative agencies involved in major foreign policy decisions. Harmonizing and dovetailing the interests and demands of a large number of such agencies—and to do this sometimes under conditions of global crises —have clearly emerged as most difficult, and yet most urgent, continuing tasks facing officials dealing with foreign relations. New proposals, suggested modifications in existing policy, counter-moves to answer communist strategy or the latest moves of neutralist countries—all of these must be referred to the State Department and possibly to the National Security Council for study and consultation by an expanding number of departments, bureaus, and commissions within the national government. After a decision is eventually reached and passed on to the U.S. Mission in New York, which in turn presents it before the appropriate UN organ, the process may have to be repeated before major modifications can be made to accommodate the wishes of countries with which the United States desires to preserve friendly relations.

The necessity for almost endless co-ordination of policy within the government means that proposals sometimes become blunted and watered down, lose their dynamism and originality in their passage through the bureaucratic labyrinth. As often as not bargains are arrived at, and compromises are reached, producing a kind of lowest common denominator policy, acceptable to agencies because it proposes nothing startlingly new nor requires too many adjustments in prevailing policies. There comes about what Bloomfield has aptly described as a "cross-sterilization of ideas" (6, p. 15). The final resolution of conflicting viewpoints within the government on any important issue pending before the United Nations, like French colonialism in North Africa or cessation of nuclear weapons testing or expanded UN technical assistance efforts, not infrequently leaves the United States resting on dead center. By first trying to evolve a widely acceptable position *within* the government, and then in the next stage trying to reach a mutually agreeable solution with *other* governments, the result is sometimes a policy which does not *offend*—but yet at the same time does not *please*—groups at home and abroad concerned with the issue. The end product is often a "middle-of-the-road policy" which is perpetually in danger of colliding with traffic going in both directions.

The knowledge that greater reliance upon the United Nations will add still another dimension to the already extremely complicated process of co-ordinating foreign policy encourages a standpat philosophy among American officials both in Washington and New York. Within the United Nations, the strategy of the United States has sometimes been to "let sleeping dogs lie" on a number of vexatious issues. This propensity can be attributed at least partially to bureaucratic inertia, to an understandable reluctance on the part of responsible officials to raise questions which will precipitate

interminable consultations among governmental agencies, when the final result of countless meetings and mountains of paper work may be the quiet interment of new proposals and the reiteration of declared policy (6, pp. 3-4, 15).

Changes in the UN and American Policy

A number of implications for American policy inherent in the rise of a vastly strengthened General Assembly have already been suggested. Let us review these very briefly and add others that are basic to an intelligent appraisal of the transformations witnessed within the UN since 1945.

The Assembly's enhanced position means that nations associated with neither the free world coalition nor the communist bloc now possess greater influence in the deliberations and actions of the United Nations. A diplomatic third force has arisen in recent years, a force whose urgent problems and demands in the world community are often quite different from those of Washington, Moscow, London, or Paris. The newly-found strength of the neutralist position has also come to the fore in some aspects of the increased influence of the Secretary-General in international negotiations aimed at eliminating and mitigating sources of global tensions. In 1958 Secretary-General Dag Hammarskjold noted that "Over the years, the weight of the work of the Secretary-General has increasingly moved from what are conventionally regarded as political and administrative tasks to the diplomatic ones." More and more, Mr. Hammarskjold found himself devoting his time to mediating between the two great power blocs and to extending his "good offices" in resolving international controversies (26, p. 15).*

*An illuminating account of the rise of the Secretary-General as a force in global political affairs can be found in the memoirs of former Secretary-General Trygve Lie (33). Mr. Lie makes clear that all along he favored a *maximalist* conception of the Secretary-General's powers, i.e., that he ought to "influence the course of debates" and "emerge as a bold leader of international thought and action, as a genuinely international figure stimulating the Member States to rise above their nationalistic dispositions." This role found graphic expression in the "peace mission" undertaken by Mr. Lie in the spring of 1950,

What Mr. Hammarskjold's predecessor called the "United Nations view" (33, p. 421) has progressively been brought to bear upon international conflicts, especially those involving the communist world and the free world. Mr. Hammarskjold has experienced limited success in resolving such issues as continued Red Chinese imprisonment of American soldiers, in bringing about British-French-Israeli withdrawal from the Suez area in 1956 and in persuading the Soviet Union to participate more wholeheartedly in disarmament discussions. In a new outbreak of Middle Eastern crises in mid-1958 it was again the Secretary-General who took the initiative in finding solutions acceptable to the countries concerned. Roscoe Drummond reported in the New York *Herald Tribune* in the summer of 1958 that as the General Assembly deliberated the Secretary-General "will prove to be the most influential single force to turn this controversy-laden session into useful channels" (37, August 13, 1958).

Spurred by American efforts to find a detour around the veto-blocked Security Council, the members of the United Nations greatly strengthened the General Assembly. In time the Assembly, whose spokesman more and more has come to be the Secretary-General, has proven its ability to force concessions from sometimes obdurate great powers and to induce a more conciliatory approach from both sides in an attempt to eliminate threats to the peace.

Other ramifications of the Assembly's new role relate to the broad field of diplomatic method and procedure. Here we can only suggest some of the most direct connotations for American foreign policy. America's role in expanding the powers of the General Assembly is but one manifestation of a movement visible in American diplomatic history over the past half-century, aimed at "democratizing" the conduct of international affairs. This movement found its most outspoken champion in

when he made the rounds of the world's capitals in an attempt to find bases for lessening world tensions. In Washington, he told President Truman that "the trend of discussions" in the UN "seems to relate to means for *winning* the 'cold war' instead of *ending* it." In Moscow, he strongly urged Soviet leaders to take a more conciliatory attitude in dealing with still unsolved global problems (33, pp. 41, 283-293, 307).

Woodrow Wilson, whose insistence upon "open covenants, openly arrived at" was a key provision of his famous Fourteen Points. Wilson's influence was of singular importance not only in shaping the future direction of American foreign policy in many fields but also in mapping the course along which diplomatic practice throughout the world was to move in the years ahead. Owing at least partially to popular disillusionment following the first World War and to Wilson's crusade against "secret diplomacy," Americans have become highly suspicious of professional diplomats whose natural propensity, in the existing folklore, is to make nefarious deals giving away sovereign rights or perhaps selling out weaker countries. Lingering citizen misgivings about the Yalta and Potsdam Conferences of World War II have intensified public apprehensions about secret diplomacy in the modern period.

In recent years, informed students of international affairs have challenged the efficacy of "open diplomacy," as epitomized by discussions in the UN General Assembly. Particularly when deliberations are televised to millions of viewers and the galleries are open to the public, proceedings are apt to degenerate into propaganda contests, in which each side tries to outscore the other in verbal sparring. Officials from democratic countries are peculiarly tempted to pursue such tactics because of the ubiquitous influence of public opinion. Above all, officials think they must avoid the slightest intimation that they are "appeasing" the enemy or failing to "protect" the national honor. Some insight into what passes for diplomacy under these circumstances can be gauged from a *Time* magazine article in 1958. It attributed mounting public confidence in the United Nations to the fact that America's chief spokesman "answers every Russian thrust with a hard-hitting counterthrust." The public could be assured that "the U. S. is not being pushed around in the U. N. and is not likely to be." Frequently, after lively propaganda exchanges, Ambassador Lodge would be greeted by citizens who said "Good work, Mr. Lodge" or "Keep giving it back to them, Ambassador" (49, p. 11).

Propaganda duels in the UN may provide a scintillating hour of television, but can they properly be called diplomacy? Do they really fulfill the purposes for which the UN Charter was drawn up and signed? The answer is obvious when we recall that the chief purpose of diplomacy is to *settle* outstanding disagreement among nations, to find a basis upon which negotiations can be successfully carried through to a mutually satisfactory result. The essence of the diplomatic method is a willingness to make concessions in the expectation that the other side will also make concessions. This process becomes virtually hopeless in televised and public meetings. An experienced American diplomatic official has stated that "it is extremely difficult—often impossible—to retreat from a position taken in public" (**24**, p. 12). Positions taken in public quickly become encrusted with considerations of the nation's "honor and prestige;" for that reason they tend to become rigid and frozen. The customary process of reaching diplomatic agreements, in which almost invariably both sides state certain maximum demands and then retreat to their minimum demands, is replaced by dogged attachment to, and tiresome reiteration of, positions announced before the entire world. An eminent British scholar, Sir Harold Nicholson, has stated that genuine progress in resolving international disputes cannot be made before public assemblies in the United Nations but that it must be made "elsewhere, in accordance with those principles of courtesy, confidence, and discretion which must forever remain the only principles conducive to the peaceful settlement of disputes" (**39**, p. 58). Attempts to follow the concept of "open covenants, openly arrived at" more often than not end in open disagreements, openly arrived at; in most cases the best interests of the international community are served by following the principle of *open agreements, secretly arrived at*, whereby results are made public but deliberations leading to results are conducted in private, away from the corrosive influence of television cameras and a powerful, if often impatient and poorly informed, public opinion.

The UN in the Cold War Context

Soviet Russia, far more directly and dramatically than any other country, has frustrated the operation of the UN and thwarted collective action against machinations of the communist bloc. The latest Soviet veto in the Security Council or the most recent "walkout" by tight-lipped Soviet officials are featured in headlines around the world. Our concern here, however, is not with Soviet culpability on this point, nor with trying to draw up a balance sheet between Soviet and American derelictions in the United Nations. While acknowledging wholesale Soviet iniquities, we must move on to deal with inadequacies in America's own role in the United Nations. For in less spectacular, but perhaps no less fundamental ways, the United States has also weakened the United Nations. On a number of occasions it has failed to exhibit the statesmanship which both its own citizens and its friends in the international community might reasonably have expected from what is in most respects the most pacifically-inclined and overtly idealistic great power known to history. It is primarily in utilizing the United Nations as an adjunct of the State Department, to carry out America's cold war strategy against the communist bloc, that American policy toward the UN is most vulnerable.

This tendency has been manifested in several ways. First, mention can be made of the extent to which the United States has consistently by-passed the United Nations in the postwar period. Beginning with the Greek-Turkish Aid Program of 1947, marking the official inauguration of the American policy of containment, and going through the China Aid Program of 1948 and the European Recovery Program of the same year, the Mutual Defense Assistance Program and the Point Four Program in 1949, the United States embarked upon programs and policies which were of lasting importance in shaping the course of international economic and political developments. All of these programs were undertaken outside the United Nations; and some were inaugurated in the face of visible opposition on the part of important countries within the United Nations. Admittedly, there was considerable evidence to support the viewpoint of American officials that the UN was too weak and inexperienced—and, when programs related intimately to the cold war, too hindered by the veto—to carry out some of these undertakings successfully. Yet there was an evident predisposition on the part of the United States to conclude that the UN was incapable of administering many of these programs, without seriously testing the UN's ability or willingness to handle them. American policy-makers seemed largely unaware of what bypassing the UN would do to that body's prestige or that, in some cases, UN action might actually be more effective for some problems than unilateral administration.

Other examples of bypassing the United Nations when fundamental problems affecting peace and security were being dealt with include settlement of the Indochinese war in 1954, American policy relating to Formosa and the Pescadores, and the threat of communism in the Americas.

A case whose consequences ultimately proved far-reaching, involved simultaneous American neglect of the United Nations and impressive American statesmanship in elevating that body to the highest pinnacle ever reached by an international organization in meeting threats to the peace through the collective action of its members. This occurred during the course of the Korean War. The dualism characteristic of America's approach to the UN during that conflict is not untypical of America's approach toward a number of other issues relating to international organization in the postwar period. When the communist state of North Korea attacked South Korea, the United States moved rapidly to meet this aggression head-on, without waiting for the sanction of the United Nations. Then, in what may well have been a turning point in the history of international organization, on June 25, 1950, the day when U. S. troops had moved into Korea, President Truman requested the Security Council to find that the Communist invasion of South Korea constituted a "threat to the peace" and to invoke Charter provisions for dealing with such threats. Thanks to an earlier Soviet "walk-out," the Security Council was able to respond promptly and effectively. It called upon members to render all possible assistance to the United States. By the end of the war contributions had come from almost forty countries, with the United States of course carrying the principal burden of the military commitment demanded in Korea. For the first time in his-

tory, an international organization met gangsterism in the world community with adequate force, made possible by the collaborative efforts of its members. In retrospect, the Korean War might well have been a test case in the precarious existence of the United Nations, and it was largely owing to American leadership that it met that test forthrightly.

Then, having converted what began as unilateral American resistance to Communist expansionism into a collective UN effort, officials in Washington throughout the ensuing months appeared to relegate the UN more and more to the sidelines, while American military commanders in the field carried out vital decisions affecting politico-diplomatic questions. None had more profound consequences for the international community as a whole than General Douglas MacArthur's crossing of the 38th Parallel into North Korea, after which he pursued retreating Communist armies up to the Yalu River border of Red China. Not only was there no clear UN mandate for such action, but in all probability a majority of the members opposed it. Red China's subsequent entry into the war converted what had been a spectacularly successful UN operation to "repel aggression" into a protracted, bloody, and probably avoidable military conflict which eventually ended in stalemate and, in the process, intensified hostilities between the United States and Red China, inflaming global tensions for an indefinite period thereafter. Official American reluctance to consult with the United Nations, partly stemming from the public aversion to "interference" on the part of the UN's members, was also apparent in arranging for truce negotiations in the Korean conflict and in determining the composition of the UN truce negotiating team.

The United States, in other words, sought the moral sanction and broad support of the United Nations in meeting aggression head-on in Korea; at the same time, it did not want to relinquish any significant control to the UN in shaping military strategy, which often involved global and regional *political* issues of vital concern to other countries, or to permit extensive United Nations' participation in the resultant truce negotiations. In some cases, it appeared that the South Korean Government of

Syngman Rhee had considerably more voice in shaping American policy than did the United Nations (16, pp. 22-28; 48, pp. 186-88).

It must be conceded that numerous obstacles have existed for relying upon the United Nations in every major instance involving global conflicts since 1945. Admittedly, as one American diplomatic official has phrased it, the United States sometimes had no choice but to "work outside the United Nations in our continuing efforts to assure a just peace. . . . " In many other cases, however, Swift's judgment is substantially correct when he asserts that "unfortunately, we never really gave the United Nations a chance to do some jobs we have undertaken ourselves . . . " (48, pp. 184, 193).

America's neglect of the United Nations in matters affecting its cold war strategy is also apparent in other ways. By the late 1950's, when American officials considered holding high-level or lower-ranking diplomatic conferences with the communist bloc, the United Nations was seldom mentioned as a possible meeting place; and no evidence existed from official American statements on this subject that the UN was even being seriously considered as a place in which global tensions might be reduced. Then in the summer of 1958 President Eisenhower surprised the world, and in the process scored a dramatic propaganda *coup* for his country, by inviting Communist Party boss Khrushchev to a heads-of-state meeting at UN headquarters in New York. Khrushchev's final reaction was to decline the invitation. For once, this put the onus squarely on Russia for bypassing the UN and for "blocking the road to peace." In many earlier instances, it had been the United States which had too often taken the lead in arranging major diplomatic conferences, affecting political developments throughout the world, outside the United Nations. For the sake of gaining broader global support for its own policies, and for contributing to the prestige and strength of the United Nations, it could be hoped that President Eisenhower's action heralded a new era of American leadership in strengthening the UN. Greater American reliance upon the UN had also been witnessed earlier in the field of disarmament and peaceful utilization of nuclear energy. In 1953 President Eisenhower had pre-

sented his statesmanlike Atoms-For Peace proposal to the United Nations and had offered immediately to place the program under UN auspices. Then in 1958 the United States had also proposed its Arctic Inspection Plan for promoting disarmament. Both of these developments will be discussed at greater length in Chapter 17.

American foreign policy has also tended to convert the United Nations into a propaganda forum in which to indict Soviet Russia, while justifying America's own policies before the world. Sonorous pronouncements, typified by Secretary of State George C. Marshall's view that the UN "is the symbol of the aspirations of mankind," President Truman's view that the Charter is "an expression of the moral nature of man's aspirations" (12, pp. 14, 18), and Secretary Dulles' view that the Charter "represents man's most determined and promising efforts to save humanity . . . " (10, I, p. 323), have emanated from American officials at periodic intervals. Official assurances that the UN is the "cornerstone of American foreign policy" have, over the years, become part of the liturgy of American foreign relations.

Yet on occasion American officials have also been candid enough to admit some of the less exalted objectives which the United States pursues within the United Nations and which were not envisioned by the Charter. Thus Secretary of State Marshall in 1948 conceived it to be a "fundamental task" of the UN to "dispel the misconceptions of the Soviet leaders and to bring about a more realistic view of what is impossible in the relationships between the Soviet Union and the world at large" (12, p. 12). President Eisenhower in 1954 called the United Nations "the only real world forum where we have the opportunity for international presentation and rebuttal. . . . It is a place where the guilt can be squarely assigned to those who fail to take all necessary steps to keep the peace . . . " (50, 1954, pp. 431-32). A report to Congress on the Tenth Session of the General Assembly in 1955 asserted that "the fundamental, although not the sole, value of the United Nations to the United States is that it provides us with a forum where we can meet the Soviet threat to the free world and expose that threat for what it is before the whole world" (28, p. 11).

While it must be admitted that American officials can hardly do otherwise than "answer" Soviet propaganda outbursts against the United States, and that the United States is by no means unilaterally responsible for the extent to which propaganda exchanges often substitute for serious negotiations, it is also true that the United States has, at times, stooped too far to the level of its enemies. Policies and conduct based upon propaganda objectives are not calculated to *reduce* tensions and to advance the evolutionary process by which the UN becomes a more active influence in global affairs, in time perhaps acquiring some capacity to deal with disputes among the great powers. In pursuing its national objectives, the United States has sometimes resorted to tactics to which it and its allies have objected vigorously when applied to themselves and that are of doubtful constitutionality under the Charter. This has been notably true of issues that lie exclusively or predominantly within the domestic jurisdiction of states. The United States has pushed studies of "genocide" which were clearly aimed at exposing oppressive Soviet policies toward cultural and economic minorities within the USSR, many of whom have been virtually liquidated by the communist regime since 1917. To say the least, international law relating to genocide is cloudy. Many activities of the Soviet government, morally reprehensible as they may be, cannot legally be called "genocide" and condemned as such. An even clearer case has been American advocacy of UN-sponsored studies of Soviet "slave labor" and other iniquitous features of the communist system. In such activities Western officials have drawn hasty and inexact analogies with international law prohibitions against "slavery." The same officials have not protested far more flagrant cases of slavery in the Arab world. However much the free world is repulsed by barbarous treatment of citizens of other countries, it must be remembered that these matters are in the vast majority of cases excluded from the jurisdiction of the United Nations under Article 2, Section 7 of the Charter—a prohibition which the United States took the lead in inserting into the Charter.

One final aspect of America's often dominant concern for cold war considerations in its approach to the United Nations remains to be examined. The United States on many occasions has looked upon the UN as a place in which to register resounding "majorities" against the communist bloc in behalf of policies and programs sponsored by Washington. Perhaps out of a desire to convince critics at home that American participation in the UN does not jeopardize national sovereignty or give communist nations control over American foreign policy, official publications have made statements like the following: "The United States has never been defeated on any important political question in the United Nations. On the other hand the Soviet Union can usually count on only 5 out of 60 votes [before 1955] in the General Assembly" (14, no page numbers). A report submitted to Congress on the Twelfth Session of the Assembly in 1957 makes the statement that "On nearly all issues . . . where the Soviet Union vigorously attacked our position, the majority of the United Nations members supported the United States" (29, p. 43).

Such statements, while perhaps comforting to groups within the country which are apprehensive about the UN, inescapably raise the question: What would be the attitude of the United States toward the UN if the American position on most issues did *not* command overwhelming majorities? Does the thinking behind such statements imply that the United States ought to support the UN because, after all, the United States usually gets its way there? These questions are far from academic. With the growth in power of the eighty-two nation General Assembly, able as never before to subject the foreign policies of free world and communist countries alike to searching examination, such questions will become more and more pertinent to American policy-makers and may well require a new appraisal of certain objectives present in the American approach to the United Nations.

What are the sources of the striking success which the United States has experienced in mustering sizable UN majorities for its announced policies? Obviously, this phenomenon must be attributed partially to the fact that on a great variety of issues American policies command wide respect because they are believed to be sound and in accordance with the interests of a majority of the countries represented in the UN. On their merits they deserve support. There are, however, other explanations. One is that on a number of occasions the United States has foreclosed serious UN discussion of certain issues, such as admitting Red China, by announcing its position beforehand and by threatening, at least tacitly, to veto an adverse decision. This has had the effect of forestalling a possible American defeat. Moreover, the United States has deliberately refrained from bringing certain other issues, for instance, America's response to Communist intervention in Guatemala, before the United Nations, when it was apparent that widespread skepticism existed toward American conduct.

Accumulation of large majorities behind American-supported policies within the UN is therefore a complex process, involving many overt, and perhaps even a greater number of subtle, relationships. An illuminating commentary on this process was provided by the remarks of a Greek diplomatic official who said to an American official:

> I do not accuse you Americans of twisting arms very often. You do not usually have to do so. Here is what happens. Among those 82 members of the United Nations, many do not care at all about the Cyprus question. Some of them do not even know where it is. It does not make any difference to them. . . . But they do have some problem which is either before the United Nations or which might come before it that is of direct concern to their countries. They would all like to get the support of the United States on problems in which they have a particular interest.
> You can see people watching Mr. Cabot Lodge, and when Cabot Lodge holds up his hand to vote on a question, an average of at least 20 hands go up just because Cabot Lodge raised his hand. Those people want to be able to come around and say . . . "You see, we voted the way you did on this question and this question and this question. Now when our question comes up we hope very much you will remember that and vote with us." (45, Part I, p. 221).

The frankness of such a statement may surprise us; its description of how plain self-interest sometimes sways other countries to support the United States should not. A proper understanding of the dynamics of international organization demands that we recognize that America, no less than the Soviet Union or other countries, possesses and utilizes a variety of inducements for winning friends in foreign relations. This understanding should caution us against mistaking an impressive record of formal votes in the UN favoring American positions for evidence that American foreign policies in all their aspects are necessarily approved by these majorities. In their conception of the role the UN ought to occupy in their relations with other countries, furthermore, the American people could profitably keep in mind Secretary of State Marshall's admonition in 1947. He cautioned against "possible abuse of the Charter" when nations utilize the UN merely to "better a bargaining position, to obtain a larger forum for propaganda, or to create greater rather than less international friction" (12, p. 188).

The UN and Military Alliances

One of the consistent objectives of American postwar foreign policy which has raised troublesome issues respecting America's relations with the UN has been creation of an interlocking system of military alliances around the periphery of the communist world. The Rio Treaty, NATO, the Baghdad Pact, SEATO, and other mutual defense treaties which the United States has sponsored and to which it is a party were all technically negotiated under Article 51 of the Charter, providing for "the inherent right of individual or collective self-defense if an armed attack occurs against a Member of the United Nations. . . . " All of these pacts were intended as "defense treaties." Throughout the postwar period American officials have been at pains to emphasize that there was no conflict between these treaties and the Charter. To the contrary, in the American view their stated purpose was to strengthen the ability of the UN to deal with threats to the peace (10, I, pp. 796-873, 917-45).

Accepting American professions as true, it still is questionable how far these defense alliance systems, and the consequent increase in levels of armaments which has always accompanied them, is consonant with the *spirit* of the Charter and with the broad purposes for which the United Nations was founded. That the United States intended these alliances for "defensive" purposes may be fully granted. But ostensibly, so does every nation which enters into any military alliances. Regardless of the motives of the instigators, the creation and proliferation of competing, heavily-armed alliance systems is an important contributory cause of global tensions and wars. Alliances almost always provoke counter-alliances; a buildup in the "defense forces" of one system is followed by a counter-buildup in the forces of the other system, with the result that sooner or later nerves on both sides become taut, an atmosphere of mounting tension pervades the world community, and the chances of an "incident" igniting a war in which most great powers are involved are magnified. D. F. Fleming has described the "deadly spiral" which often grows out of competing alliance systems as follows:

> Great Power A is afraid of Great Power B and decides to arm for defense. This makes B uneasy, for fear that its superior position may be lost. B therefore increases its armaments, and thereby convinces A that B has aggressive intentions. Accordingly A adds to its arms, which is plain evidence to B that A is a potential aggressor. B passes another arms increase bill . . . A calls up more troops and that is clear notice to B that A is out to conquer the world. B is equally positive that A has unlimited ambitions and means to rule the earth.
>
> Are you confused by this time, quite uncertain about who started the arms race? At this stage nobody knows who started it. Both sides are wholly convinced that the other began the struggle. Each is absolutely sure that his own arms are strictly for *defense* and wholly certain that the arms of the other are intended for *offense.* (**19**, p. 353).

We might add that from the internal momentum generated by an arms race, it is but a step to the view that war has "become inevitable." On both sides, the tension mounts and the prevailing mentality comes to be epitomized by the familiar expression: we don't care who started it, but "we intend to finish it."*

---

*In his scholarly study of the origins of World War I, the distinguished historian Sidney B. Fay observed that "The greatest single underlying cause of the War was the system of secret alliances which developed after the Franco-Prussian War."

However much prevailing strategic requirements have dictated American reliance upon defense alliances and growing military stockpiles in the postwar period, this phenomenon has detraced from the influence of the United Nations in at least two significant ways. First, America's dependence upon these for its security has constituted a kind of vote of "no confidence" in the organization established to deal with threats to international peace. Second, the creation of alliances and mounting military forces have injected one more incendiary element into what has been a chronically inflamed global political situation since the Second World War.

Naturally, these considerations do not argue in favor of the immediate and total abandonment of America's military alliance system. In light of the evident weaknesses of the UN, some of them—particularly NATO and the Inter-American system—are the only attainable alternatives that will serve the national interest. Others, like SEATO, the Baghdad Pact, and some of the bilateral guarantees between the United States and other countries, are of far more questionable value. With them, their alleged advantages may well be outweighed by the mounting damage done to the prestige and influence of the United Nations by America's addiction to "pactitis" in recent years. America cannot indefinitely discount the impact upon the United Nations of continued multiplication of military alliances.

Charter Review and Revision

The UN Charter, like the American Constitution, has demonstrated a remarkable capacity to adapt to the exigencies and demands of the age. Important changes have come about in the UN through usages, precedents, informal under-

---

Designed as defensive moves, "the system also made it inevitable that if war did come, it would involve all the Great Powers of Europe." The second underlying cause of the war was held to be militarism, a central feature of which was ever-larger armies and larger military stockpiles. "Armaments were alleged to be for defense and in the interests of peace, according to the fallacious maxim *si vis pacem, para bellum*. They were intended to produce a sense of security. . . . What they really did was produce universal suspicion, and hatred between nations" (**17**, pp. 34-5, 38-40).

standings and agreements, contraction in some powers granted under the UN and corresponding expansion in other powers granted. The process of formal Charter amendment, as set forth in Article 108-109, has never been utilized to date.

According to the Charter, amendments shall normally be made when they have been adopted by two-thirds of the General Assembly and ratified by two-thirds of the member-states, including *all* of the permanent members of the Security Council. Article 109 provides, however, that a Charter review conference may be held at any time designated by two-thirds of the Assembly and by seven members of the Council. If such a conference had not been held prior to the tenth annual session of the Assembly (in 1956) then the proposal to call it was to be placed automatically on the agenda of the tenth session. There a simple majority vote in the Assembly, plus any seven affirmative votes in the Council, could summon a review conference for the purpose of exploring desirable changes in the Charter.

Characterizing prevailing world opinion on the question of Charter revision, one study in 1955 concluded that "few governments were in a hurry to get on with the conference, and few could say what, precisely, the conference would achieve when it met" (**50**, 1955, p. 270). Progress to date has been confined to intensive study of the matter by a committee of the General Assembly, appointed in 1955. The Twelfth Session of the Assembly in 1957 voted to keep this committee in being and directed it to bring in recommendations on the matter of Charter review not later than the Fourteenth Session in 1959 (**32**, p. 117). By the opening of the 1960's it was apparent that the Assembly's lethargy in considering Charter revision seriously was more calculated than accidental. It could be predicted with near certainty that many months would be required for the Assembly to "study" recommendations eventually made to it on Charter revision; that an even longer interval would likely be required for the Assembly to act favorably on such recommendations and set forth the schedule and agenda of a revision conference; and, in the unlikely event that a Charter revision conference were actually scheduled, that

its results—presupposing no significant change in the attitudes of the great powers—would be minimal.

The United States has favored holding a Charter review conference—drawing the distinction all the while between *reviewing* the Charter and actually *revising* the Charter. Charter review, in the American conception, is desirable for several reasons: it is required to discharge a tacit pledge made to the smaller countries at San Francisco that features of the UN to which they objected would at least be re-appraised in the light of experience; it would perhaps generate greater citizen interest in, and support for, the UN; and it might conceivably lead to desirable changes in the Charter (**18**, pp. 213-31).

Interest in the issue of Charter review and revision has stimulated considerable study within the Executive branch and within Congress. As early as 1948, in passing the "Vandenberg Resolution" (**51**, pp. 399-421), the Senate expressed itself as favoring restriction upon the use of the veto in the Security Council, particularly as it affected the admission of new members. In 1953 the Senate Foreign Relations Committee appointed a special subcommittee to study possible changes in the Charter. The subcommittee issued a number of valuable studies and reports (cited in **10**, II, p. 324), dealing with issues which might arise at a review conference. Having found no compelling reason why such a conference should not be held (**13**, 1955, p. 214), the subcommittee was content to leave the question of whether a conference ought to be held to officials in the Executive branch.

The prevailing disinterest among the members of the United Nations toward the holding of a Charter review conference undoubtedly derives in large measure from skepticism concerning what such a conference could accomplish. There is no very assuring prospect that the difficulties experienced by the UN in such areas as maintenance of world peace or disarmament could be overcome by a Charter review conference, any more than they have been overcome throughout the life of the UN since 1945. Some countries have feared that a conference might degenerate into another propaganda battle between communist and free world countries, or perhaps between colonial and anti-colonial countries. The same forces which had frustrated effective operation of the UN in the past might be expected to block sweeping changes in the Charter. Under Charter provisions, for example, Russia could still veto a proposal to restrict the veto in the Security Council.

The American attitude on Charter *revision* therefore has been mixed. American officials have opposed attempts to bring about sweeping changes in the UN, on the premise, as phrased by Secretary Dulles, that "The United Nations as it is, is better than no United Nations at all" (**10**, I, p. 329). Nevertheless, certain aspects of the Charter have been cited as offering perhaps some prospect for successful modification. One of these is elimination of the veto as applied to questions of membership in the UN. Another is the question of voting in the General Assembly. The United States has come to favor the principle of "weighted voting" in the Assembly so that, in the words of Secretary Dulles, "nations which are themselves unable to assume serious military or financial responsibilities cannot put those responsibilities on other nations . . . " (**10**, I, p. 327). Still another area in which the United States believes progress to be possible is in encouraging respect for, and strengthening, international law (**10**, I, pp. 327-8).

The United States does not support attempts to convert the United Nations into a "world government." Its unaltered conception of the United Nations as a league of sovereign states is indicated by its consistent position on the veto in the Security Council. From the time of the Dumbarton Oaks conference onward, Washington has demanded retention of the veto principle; and at the time of the San Francisco Conference the American delegation made it plain that a veto-less Charter would not be acceptable to the United States. American officials, however, have proposed that the great powers voluntarily refrain from using it whenever possible. Referring to America's desire for a more limited use of the veto, Secretary of State Dulles said that "Presumably, the United States would itself hesitate to move further than this in now surrendering its 'veto power'" (**10**, I, p. 327; **44**, pp. 1057-65).

In summary then, the United States favors calling a Charter review conference and has suggested certain benefits which might accompany such a conference, less by way of actually changing the UN than by way of generating widespread public support for international organization. Finding very little demand on the part of other countries for a Charter review conference, however, the United States has exercised minimum initiative in pressing the issue of Charter review and revision.

REFERENCES

1. American Association for the United Nations. *An Eleven Year Review of the League of Nations*. New York: League of Nations Association, 1931.

2. Ball, M. Margaret. "Bloc Voting in the General Assembly," *International Organization*, 5 (February, 1951), pp. 3-31. Explores the implications of greater influence by small countries in the UN.

3. Beckel, Graham. *Workshops for the World: The Specialized Agencies of the UN*. New York: Abelard-Schuman, 1954.

4. Bell, Coral. "The United Nations and the West," *International Affairs*, 29 (October, 1953), pp. 464-72. Emphasizes the newly-found strength of the Afro-Asian states and implications for countries like America and Britain.

5. Blelloch, David. "Bold New Programme: A Review of United Nations Technical Assistance," *International Affairs*, 33 (January, 1957), pp. 36-51. Analyzes UN technical assistance activities and assesses progress to date.

6. Bloomfield, Lincoln P. "American Policy Toward the UN—Some Bureaucratic Reflections," *International Organization*, 12 (Winter, 1958), pp. 1-17. A particularly illuminating treatment of the UN's role in American foreign policy and of factors shaping that role.

7. Carr, Edward H. *International Relations Between the Wars*. London: The Macmillan Company, 1947. Discusses the League of Nations against the background of rising world tension.

8. Claude, Inis L. *Swords Into Plowshares.* New York: Random House, 1956. A recent and provocative study of the United Nations.

9. Davis, Edgar E. *Pioneers of World Order.* New York: Columbia University Press, 1944. A valuable background study on international organization.

10. Department of State. *American Foreign Policy, 1950-1955.* (Publication No. 6446, "General Foreign Policy Series" 117). Washington: 1957. Pages 134-390 of Volume I contain documentary material on the UN.

11. ———. *Coordinating the Work of the United Nations.* (Publication No. 5999, "International Organization and Conference Series III," 109). Washington: 1955. Discusses trends and problems in social-economic activities of the UN.

12. ——. *Principal Statements Regarding the United Nations.* Office of Public Affairs, Division of Historical Policy Research, 1950. This mimeographed document is a collection of official statements about the UN.

13. ——. *U. S. Participation in the UN, 1955,* et seq. (Publication No. 6318, "International Organization and Conference Series III," 115). Washington: 1956. The annual installments in this series provide a valuable summary of American actions in, and policies toward, the UN.

14. ———. *You and the United Nations.* (Publication No. 5887, "International Organization and Conference Series III" 105). Washington: 1955.

15. Donovan, Robert J. *Eisenhower: The Inside Story.* New York: Harper and Brothers, 1956.

16. Eichelberger, Clark M. *UN: The First Ten Years.* New York: Harper and Brothers, 1955. A perceptive evaluation of the first decade of the UN.

17. Fay, Sidney B. *The Origins of the World War.* New York: The Macmillan Company, 1941. This is probably the most dispassionate and scholarly treatment of the causes of World War I; many of its conclusions still have relevance to the conduct of international affairs.

18. Finkelstein, Lawrence. "Reviewing the United Nations Charter," *International Organization,* 9 (April, 1955), pp. 213-31. Analyzes the question of Charter revision, with emphasis upon the American position.

19. Fleming, D. F. "Are We Headed Toward Another World War?" *Western Political Quarterly,* 5 (September, 1952), pp. 342-65. A trenchant critique of American foreign policy by an outstanding scholar.

20. ———. *The United States and the League of Nations, 1918-1920.* New York: G. P. Putnam's Sons, 1932.

21. ———. *The United States and World Organization.* New York: Doubleday, Doran and Company, 1945. In these two books the same author discusses the League of Nations and America's association with it.

22. Frye, William R. *A United Nations Peace Force.* New York: Oceana Publications, 1957. A capable journalist examines problems associated with the UN Emergency Force in the Middle East.

23. Goodrich, Leland M., and Hambro, Edward. *Charter of the United Nations.* Boston: World Peace Foundation, 1949. An invaluable reference work on the evolution and meaning of the UN Charter.

24. Gross, Ernest A. "Five Rules for Diplomatic Diplomats," *New York Times Magazine,* October 25, 1953, pp. 12, 42-4. An experienced negotiator examines current diplomatic practices.

25. Haas, Ernst B. "The Attempt to Terminate Colonialism," *International Organization,* 7 (February, 1953), pp. 1-21. Deals with the origin of the Trusteeship Council and with American viewpoints on colonialism.

26. Hammarskjold, Dag. "Why the United Nations?" *United Nations Review,* 5 (July, 1958), pp. 14-17. The Secretary-General assesses the UN's value and interprets his own role in international negotiations.

27. Haviland, H. Field, Jr. *The Political Role of the General Assembly.* New York: Carnegie Endowment for International Peace, 1951. One of a series of helpful studies on problems and trends in the UN.

28. House Foreign Affairs Committee. *Report on the Tenth Session of the General Assembly of the United Nations.* 84th Congress, 2nd Session. Washington: 1956.

29. ———. *Report on the Twelfth Session of the General Assembly of the United Nations.* 85th Congress, 2nd Session. Washington: 1958. Reports in this series, written by legislators who have served in official capacities in the UN, afford valuable summaries of UN activities and of American policies toward the UN.

30. Hyde, James N. "United States Participation in the United Nations," *International Organization,* 10 (February, 1956), pp. 22-34. Focuses on the formal machinery and processes of American decision-making in the UN.

31. Institute on World Organization. *World Organization: A Balance Sheet of the First Great Experiment.* Washington: American Council on Public Affairs, 1942. An assessment of the League of Nations.

32. "International Organization: General Assembly," *International Organization*, 12 (Winter, 1958), p. 117. This periodical provides up-to-date summaries on the activities of all UN organs.

33. Lie, Trygve. *In the Cause of Peace*. New York: The Macmillan Company, 1954. A former Secretary-General gives a first-hand account of the operation of the UN.

34. Mangone, Gerard J. *A Short History of International Organization*. New York: McGraw-Hill Book Company, 1954.

35. Miller, D. H. *The Drafting of the Covenant*. New York: G. P. Putnam's Sons, 1928. A standard reference work on the origins of the League of Nations.

36. Murray, Gilbert. *From the League to the U. N.* New York: Harper and Brothers, 1951. A valuable background study of continuity between the League and the UN.

37. New York *Herald Tribune*.

38. *New York Times*.

39. Nicholson, Harold. "An Open Look at Secret Diplomacy," *New York Times Magazine*, September 13, 1953, pp. 17, 47-8.

40. ———. "The Faults of American Diplomacy," *Harpers*, 210 (January, 1955), 52-8. A distinguished British observer examines current diplomatic methods.

41. Pratt, Julius W. *A History of United States Foreign Policy*. New York: Prentice-Hall, 1955.

42. Richardson, Channing B. "The United States Mission to the United Nations," *International Organization*, 7 (February, 1953), pp. 22-34. Another helpful study of how American policy is formulated and carried out in the UN.

43. Russett, Alan. "Large and Small States in International Organization," *International Affairs*, 31 (April, 1955), pp. 192-203. Deals with the implications of expanded small nation influence in the UN.

44. Senate Foreign Relations Committee. *A Decade of American Foreign Policy*. 81st Congress, 1st Session. Washington: 1950. Contains documents relating to America's early postwar role in the UN.

45. ———. *Hearings on Review of Foreign Policy, 1958*. 85th Congress, 2nd Session, Washington: 1958. Part of a comprehensive review of U. S. policy undertaken by the Committee.

46. ———. *Review of the United Nations Charter, A Collection of Documents*. 83rd Congress, 2nd Session. Washington: 1954.

47. "The Situation in Hungary," *United Nations Review*, 3 (December, 1956), pp. 46-71. A thorough account of the UN and the Hungarian revolt.

48. Swift, Richard N. "United States Leadership in the United Nations," *Western Political Quarterly*, 11 (June, 1958), pp. 183-94. A critical appraisal of America's role in the UN.

49. "United Nations: The Organized Thrust," *Time*, 72 (August 11, 1958), pp. 11-14. A highly journalistic account of American activity in the UN, focusing on Ambassador Lodge.

50. *United States in World Affairs, 1945-1947*, et seq. New York: Harper and Brothers, 1947. This series by the Council on Foreign Relations provides a readable summary of America's year-by-year activities in the UN.

51. Vandenberg, Arthur H., Jr., ed. *The Private Papers of Senator Vandenberg*. Boston: Houghton, Mifflin Company, 1952. A revealing compilation from the papers of one of the nation's most influential legislators in the foreign policy field.

52. Walters, F. P. *A History of the League of Nations*. London: Oxford University Press, 1952. A scholarly and recent account of the League's activities.

53. Watkins, James T., and Robinson, J. William. *General International Organization*. New York: D. Van Nostrand Company, Inc., 1956. A collection of relevant documents.

54. Wilcox, Francis O. *UNESCO and American Foreign Policy*. Department of State, 1956. Written by the Assistant Secretary of State for International Organization Affairs, this booklet should lay to rest fears expressed by American citizens about UNESCO.

CHAPTER 17

Disarmament

Turning Swords into Plowshares

When the League of Nations was founded no one anywhere doubted that the race in armaments had been largely responsible for the first World War. Therefore, "disarmament" was the largest single item in the peace movement of that time, and there was universal agreement that the first and greatest test of the League of Nations would be its ability to carry out a "reduction and limitation of armaments," which was the more cautious expression for the popular term, disarmament. (**24**, p. 10).

That the disarmament question had lost none of its urgency in the intervening years was indicated by the view of American legislators who attended the Twelfth Session of the UN General Assembly in 1957. In their judgment, "The political issue regarded as most important by most members of the twelfth session . . . was disarmament. . . . It was said . . . that the peoples of the world were so insistent that progress be made . . . that the delegates could not return home without a record of positive accomplishment" (**10**, p. 14). And when Soviet Premier Khrushchev visited the United States in the fall of 1959, the *New York Times* summarized issues dividing the communist and

non-communist worlds by saying: "Both sides recognized that the critical question was an issue on which East and West have negotiated fruitlessly for fourteen years—disarmament" (**15**, September 20, 1959).

With the constantly increasing destructive power of modern weapons and the growing stockpiles of arms in the hands of rival nations, disarmament had clearly emerged as one of the paramount issues in world politics. "The Powers' inability to agree on the regulation of armaments, and particularly on the control of atomic energy," has been called "the greatest single obstacle to the full implementation of that system of security . . . so carefully and hopefully planned in 1945," when the United Nations was established (**12**, p. 10). If collective endeavors to assure peace through international organization is one side of the coin of the quest for world peace, disarmament is surely the opposite side of the same coin. No problem possesses more of a life-or-death quality, bristles with more formidable difficulties, and has proved so unyielding before the earnest efforts of statesmen throughout history

1. DISARMAMENT IN HISTORICAL PERSPECTIVE

Some Basic Concepts

Several factors explain the unyielding nature of the disarmament problem. First, the very

term disarmament is, literally speaking, a misnomer. No nation has ever advocated *total* abolition of military force from the world scene.

The ultimate goal was clearly expressed by the League of Nations' Covenant, which called for "the reduction of national armaments to the lowest point consistent with national safety and the enforcement by common action of international obligations." The juxtaposition of this provision—just preceding Article 10, providing for collective action against aggression—is a key to the intimate relationship described here (**26**, I, pp. 48-9). The many-faceted nature of the disarmament problem was illustrated even more sharply by a League of Nations Assembly resolution in 1922, which specified a four-step process by which the levels of armaments might be lowered: agreements by all countries to cut military force levels; a satisfactory guarantee of the security of each country; a plan for collective action against aggression; and adherence by all countries to a mutual defense treaty (**18**, pp. 76-7).

The League Covenant identified three cardinal ingredients in any successful approach to disarmament: agreement that arms-limitation would entail significant benefits for mankind; belief that effective alternatives to armaments must be found and made operable in the international community; and conviction that the vital interests of nations, most fundamentally their right of self-preservation, must be safeguarded. Disarmament thus is really not a *single* problem, but a *cluster* of intimately related problems. Progress in resolving any one will likely determine the extent to which progress can be made in resolving closely associated ones. The attack against the causes of war and global insecurity must therefore proceed on many fronts at once.

The often bewildering intricacy of disarmament negotiations springs from the fact that few issues in global affairs have such widespread and important ramifications for the entire spectrum of problems and relationships existing among nations as does the question of arms-limitation. This is why it has proved so difficult for statesmen to make the transition from almost universal support for the *principle* of disarmament to detailed plans carrying out that principle in different historical periods and under highly varied circumstances.

Do high levels of armaments actually *engender* conflicts in the international community? Or are they merely reflections of the fact that hostilities *already exist* among nations, expressed in an increasing reliance upon military force among powerful countries? Impressive evidence can be cited to support both viewpoints. Statesmen and competent observers of international affairs have generally accepted the view that high levels of armaments are at once both a *cause* and a *symptom* of global tensions. In the present stage of knowledge, there appears to be a well-nigh indissoluble cause-and-effect relationship between world tensions and growing stockpiles of armaments. Perhaps in time the advancing frontiers of knowledge will impart greater precision in diagnosing the exact role of armaments as a cause and as an effect. Meantime, statesmen must continue to deal with the armaments problem in all its complex ramifications.

Would the total abolition of armaments *per se* restore stability, and greatly enhance the chance for peace, in a strife-torn world? Several answers are suggested on the basis of experience. Armaments usually are not an end in themselves. Normally, nations seek power—a central ingredient of which is armaments—to achieve certain goals in international affairs such as security, a more favorable strategic position, colonies, greater territory, an enhanced economic position, revenge for past hurts and slights against national honor, and a variety of other objectives. Implicitly or explicitly, every nation establishes some kind of scale by which an order of priority among its goals is determined. Its attachment to military force, as with all other kinds of power, will be determined in large measure by (1) the extent to which it is determined to realize its diplomatic goals in the face of possible military opposition by other countries and (2) the precise nature of these goals and their amenability to being achieved by military, violent means.

The mere possession of impressive military force does not *per se* guarantee that a nation will be successful in achieving its goals of statecraft. The United States has become very conscious of the inherent limitations of military force, for example, in dealing with widespread anti-Western sentiment throughout the Afro-Asian bloc in recent years. America's great stockpile of nuclear weapons does not make

India or Iraq more favorably disposed toward the free world coalition, nor does it help solve problems of poverty in Africa. There exist many problems of this kind for which the question of armaments has minimum relevance. Consequently, it is reasonable to think that the reduction or even the total abolition of armaments would have no significant impact upon a number of enduring sources of tension and instability in global affairs.

Total or partial disarmament might usher in a breathing spell in which these issues could be attacked; and unquestionably, it might impart a different tone to international negotiations, perhaps cooling tempers among hostile countries and greatly reducing the chance that an "incident" could set off a world conflagration. A prolonged period of disarmament conceivably could permit human and national behavior to change sufficiently so that a new era might dawn in the conduct of relationships among nations. Invaluable by-products of disarmament might also be strengthening international organization and gaining useful experience in the use of techniques like global "inspection" to facilitate maintenance of peace. But sooner or later, the frustrating spiral is encountered: significant progress toward disarmament would foster progress in solving major political problems; but the solution of many of these problems is a prerequisite for commencing major disarmament. Disarmament alone evidently cannot afford a guarantee that war would be abolished or that feelings of insecurity might not trigger a new arms-race. If history affords a reliable guide, disarmament instead could, under some circumstances, furnish new impetus to reliance upon military force, if nations believed their vital interests were in jeopardy. This was the case with the United States in the immediate postwar era, when its military weakness compared with the USSR forced a new buildup in American armed strength, which most probably set off renewed activity in military technology in the communist world.

In addition to the belief that a reduction of armaments will contribute to strengthening the prospects for peace, and that it accords with broad ethical-humanitarian considerations, disarmament movements throughout history have often been motivated by still other goals. One

motivation has been the desire to divert huge expenditures for armaments to projects designed to promote human welfare. Today this has become one of the most persuasive arguments advanced in behalf of disarmament. The United States, for example, has repeatedly stated that it cannot support the proposed Special United Nations Fund for Economic Development (SUNFED), which has been vigorously espoused by nations in the Afro-Asian bloc, until the economic burden necessitated by high levels of armaments has been reduced (10, pp. 24-8).

Propaganda motivations are almost always present in proposals advocating disarmament. Indeed, throughout the postwar period, it has sometimes seemed that propaganda considerations were uppermost in positions assumed by the two power giants, Soviet Russia and the United States. President Eisenhower's "Open Skies" plan and his later offer to establish an "Arctic Inspection Zone" were in large measure designed to enhance the position of the United States on the propaganda front, where Soviet Russia had scored impressive victories in preceding months. Down to the late 1950's, the value of both proposals to the United States lay more in the realm of psychological warfare than as measures calculated to break the stalemate reached in disarmament negotiations. The Soviet approach, too, has been heavily colored by propaganda overtones. The Kremlin's insistence upon such steps as outright prohibition of nuclear weapons and destruction of existing stockpiles, its call for cessation of nuclear weapons testing, its unilateral reductions in Soviet armed force levels, and its assaults against the West for alleged "germ warfare" in Korea have all been undertaken at least partially to cultivate a favorable reaction among neutralist countries, to undermine the military strength of the free world, and as part of the familiar postwar Soviet-instigated "peace offensive."

Propaganda overtones abounded in Premier Khrushchev's dramatic appearance before the UN General Assembly in September, 1959, during his visit to the United States. Khrushchev's grandiose scheme for immediate and total disarmament; his skillful and lengthy association of this plan with the "needs" of the underdeveloped countries and the crushing "armaments burden;" his choice of the General Assembly for a platform, instead of the disarmament sessions that had been in progress for some time in Geneva; subsequent insistence by Soviet diplomats that the proposal be fully discussed in ensuing Assembly meetings—these moves were calculated to have the maximum propaganda effect in cultivating the image that Russia was in the forefront of nations seeking the goal of peace. This of course does not necessarily suggest that the Soviet proposal was "nothing but propaganda," that there were not some worthwhile suggestions in it. It is merely to underscore the fact that because of its pre-eminence as an issue confronting mankind and its sweeping ramifications for other thorny global issues like national economic progress, the disarmament question lends itself admirably to the reaping of maximum propaganda capital.*

Finally, in evaluating disarmament efforts undertaken in recent years, account must continually be taken of another motivation almost invariably present in such efforts. Practically without exception, nations formulate their positions on arms-limitation in terms of how progress toward that goal affects their power position generally and, more specifically, how agreements reached leave them *vis-à-vis* potential enemies. Thus President Coolidge lamented, concerning an Anglo-French disarmament understanding in 1928, that "foreign governments made agreements limiting that

_____
*The *New York Times* reporter at the United Nations, Thomas J. Hamilton, foresaw that the United States would be placed in a delicate position in dealing with debate ensuing over Khrushchev's proposals, in which *specific* propositions dealing with highly controversial aspects of the disarmament problem—like inspection and control—had been conspicuously absent. As debate progressed, the United States would find itself in this dilemma: "If they [American officials] cross-examine the Soviet delegation too closely on the question of control and other issues . . . they may be accused of intransigence and of driving away the millennium. But if they fail to bring these obscurities into public view, there is a danger that the Assembly will refer the proposal to the ten-nation group [of communist and non-communist countries currently studying disarmament problems] with at least partial endorsement. If this happens, the Soviet Union will obtain a propaganda triumph of enormous proportion. . . ." (**15,** September 27, 1959).

class of combat vessels in which we were superior, but refused limitation in the class in which they were superior" (**16,** p. 556). Countries routinely demand sweeping reductions in weapons in which their enemies are strong, while finding convincing reasons why there is no urgency about reducing weapons in their own arsenals, perhaps on the ground that such weapons are "defensive" or because the "right of self-defense" demands that they be retained.

In no case throughout recent history has any nation really approached the question of disarmament "on its merits." National policies were nearly always compounded of liberal amounts of idealism and of cooly calculated *Realpolitik;* and in a majority of cases, it was the latter which ultimately determined the position taken by the country's diplomats in trying to arrive at agreements with negotiators from other countries.

Let us now focus more sharply on three aspects of the arms-limitation problem: basic trends in disarmament negotiations throughout modern history; enduring issues encountered throughout the postwar period; and implications of the peaceful utilization of nuclear energy.

Canada, the United States, and the "Unguarded Frontier"

It is a curious fact that one of the most effective disarmament plans ever carried out in international affairs is also the oldest agreement in existence. This is the demilitarization of the Canadian-American border, provided by the Rush-Bagot agreement of 1817 and agreements growing out of that accord. The ideal of demilitarization stemmed from settlement of the War of 1812 and from suggestions made by John Jay and John Adams much earlier. Within England the realization was growing that if a race ensued for naval supremacy on the Great Lakes, the United States would most likely win eventually. For its part, the United States was glad to arrive at an understanding which prevented an arms-race along its northern frontier. The Rush-Bagot agreement therefore provided that warships on the lakes would be limited solely to those required for patrol duty and customs inspection, an agreement which has remained in effect ever since.

Starting with an initial accord governing only *naval* armaments, agreements were later formulated which, at least by tacit consent, covered land armaments and fortifications along the border as well. Significantly, broadening of the Rush-Bagot agreement was accompanied by the evolution of arbitration and other non-violent methods for settling disputes between the two nations (16, pp. 143-45).

The "unguarded frontier" between the United States and its northern neighbor has not always enjoyed as peaceful a history as is sometimes supposed. Periodically, strife between the two countries has threatened to abrogate the demilitarization accord. The United States, for example, was on the verge of terminating the agreement during the Civil War.

How much relevance has the history of the Canadian-American "unguarded frontier" for the broader problem of arms-limitation within the international community at large? A number of special features in Canadian-United States relations caution against uncritical attempts to hold this out as a "model" to be applied generally throughout the world. With rare exceptions, neither the United States nor Canada has regarded the other as a threat to its existence, has nurtured ancient grievances toward the other or coveted the other's territory. To the contrary, over the course of time each has come to feel a community of interest with the other and to appreciate the extent to which the security of both countries was indissolubly linked. By the late 1950's, there had come about a virtual merger in the two nations' strategic defense system established to protect the Northern Hemisphere from surprise attack.

The Hague Conference

If we view the Rush-Bagot agreement as a special case, then we must date systematic disarmament proposals among the great powers from the emergence of the Hague Tribunal in the late 19th century. In 1898 the government of Czar Nicholas II, alarmed by the rapid expansion in German military technology, especially by the spectacular buildup in artillery firepower, proposed an international conference to deal with the rising spiral of armaments. All of the arguments heard today—that ever more destructive armaments were increasing the likelihood and barbarity of war, that funds and energies could better be devoted to more beneficial purposes, that all mankind yearned for a better way to settle world conflict—were voiced by advocates of disarmament in this period. A British scholar has written: "To these arguments, which were as cogent at the time as they are today, the Powers reacted in a manner that set the pattern for the next 50 years. They did accept the principle; they did not allow the preparations for the conference to interfere with the execution of their existing [armaments] programmes." The Hague Conference sought a modest beginning: merely a moratorium on the *future* production of weapons, without proposing the abolition of existing military forces. Concurrently with this limited beginning, it was hoped that an alternative for force could be found in greater reliance upon arbitration procedures for settling differences among countries (12, pp. 28-29).

Yet, in microcosm, the Hague Conferences of 1899 and 1907 mirrored tendencies typical of disarmament negotiations throughout the years that followed. Not even the limited hope of freezing existing levels of armaments and of gradually substituting organized procedures for the peaceful settlement of disputes proved attainable. The most that could be accomplished was acceptance of rules designed to "humanize war," such as pledges not to use expanding ("dum-dum") bullets and asphyxiating gases (18, pp. 170-71). That such rules were valuable in later years is conceded. But in the judgment of Martin, the Hague Conferences nevertheless diverted attention from the primary problem of *avoiding* war to the distinctly secondary problem of "humanizing war" and "by so doing they . . . helped to delay political and social pressures for the setting up of a strong and comprehensive international organization for peace" (12, p. 30).

Disarmament Movements in the 1920's and 1930's

Sporadic and unsuccessful attempts were made to gain support for disarmament proposals from 1907 down to the First World War (**12**, pp. 30-1). The next stage of importance dates from President Wilson's proposals relating to the League of Nations and disarmament. Four ideas were emphasized: compulsory adjudication of international disputes; a scheme whereby the security of large and small states was to be guaranteed; a new institutional framework, the League of Nations, whereby these goals could be carried out; and, finally, immediate adoption of a disarmament plan upon termination of hostilities, to be applied first to Germany, Austria, and the other defeated countries. It would be an oversimplification to say that disarmament failed in this period because the League of Nations ultimately failed; to some degree it might have been the other way around. In any case, the whole "package deal" envisioned in Wilson's proposals eventually broke down for a number of reasons, most fundamentally perhaps because nations were unwilling to make a wholehearted commitment to its requirements. Even granting a sincere desire on the part of certain League members to achieve disarmament within a context of functioning collective security, the chances for success were dim on a number of thorny "technical" questions inherent in disarmament schemes. These had to do with such issues as establishing a system of inspection to determine violations, a method for carrying out sanctions and punishments against lawbreakers, an equitable formula for determining the military force levels necessary for maintenance of internal order and defense, and criteria for determining comparability of various categories of weapons (**12**, pp. 31-2). However, League of Nations disarmament efforts served to dispel the notion that the only major barriers to arms-limitation were technical ones. It became clear that the thorniest issues associated with disarmament were "political" questions. Ancient national rivalries like that between France and Germany must be set at rest before disarmament could be successful and there had to be workable machinery to facilitate application of non-violent methods of international intercourse (**12**, pp. 33-4).

As a non-member of the League of Nations, the United States was not a party to disarmament deliberations undertaken within that body. Yet it was highly desirous of reducing the level of world armaments. Consequently, the United States sponsored and participated in a number of developments during the interwar period which sought to eliminate the scourge of war. As an outgrowth of the Hague Conferences, the United States had taken a leading role in sponsoring arbitration treaties. Although the United States had refused to enter the League of Nations, these treaties indicated that it shared many of the goals expressed in the League Covenant. Furthermore, its initiative in sponsoring disarmament negotiations testified to its acceptance of many of the League's professed purposes.

Perhaps the most impressive beacon of disarmament in the troubled seas of arms competition was the Naval Armaments Conference of 1921. Significant results included the establishment of a ratio of 10:10:7 for Great Britain, the United States, and Japan, respectively, for capital ships; an agreement to scrap certain types of older ships and to declare a ten-year moratorium on the construction of new capital ships; limitations on the total tonnage and the armaments of certain kinds of existing capital ships; and a pledge by the United States, Great Britain, and Japan not to strengthen fortifications on their possessions in the Pacific. The agreement was to remain in force until the end of 1936, whereupon it could be terminated by two years notice from any of the signatories. Following its aggressive moves in Manchuria in the early 1930's, Japan gave notice in 1934 that it would no longer honor the treaty obligations after 1936. Evidence uncovered during and after World War II revealed that, long before its expiration date, Japan had covertly violated this agreement, especially its prohibition against the fortification of Pacific territories and the construction of new battleships.

While the Naval Conference was widely hailed as a significant step forward, especially within the United States, its results do not look so impressive in hindsight. True, it did make a beginning in limiting increasingly more powerful weapons of destruction on the sea. Even more important, it slowed the momentum of the naval arms race whereby great and lesser countries competed for mastery, or at least parity, on the seas. Yet it encouraged the view that greater strides had been made toward peace than was actually the case; it left great loop-holes in naval armaments whereby certain powers were able to continue their armaments buildup in such categories as submarines, small aircraft carriers and small cruisers. From the point of view of the American national interest, it re-enforced the already prevailing misconception that the nation's Pacific commitments were safe from possible Japanese imperialism, that a minimum national effort was required to protect and safeguard them. Finally—and some might regard this more as an asset than a liability—it ultimately revealed the utter futility of having disarmament agreements dependent upon voluntary compliance and mere promises of compliance. This weakness, which perhaps guaranteed the failure of the Washington agreements, at least pointed forcefully to an indispensable requirement for future agreements in the disarmament field.

The Washington naval agreements are also significant to students of international affairs because they reveal clearly the principle that nations always approach disarmament in terms of its relationship to their own security. One major impetus in predisposing the United States to favor the conference was recognition within the executive branch that Congress was not prepared to provide funds for the kind of naval force the country's defense commitments required. What better way, therefore, of achieving maximum defense under these circumstances than to seek a reduction in the forces of possible enemies, primarily Japan and secondarily Britain? This motivation showed particularly in regard to the Anglo-Japanese treaty of alliance in the Pacific, which Washington regarded as directed at least partially against the United States. This treaty was superseded by agreements reached at the conference, in which both Britain and the United States received Japanese pledges to respect Chinese sovereignty. As a result of arms-reduction pledges among these Pacific powers, Washing-

ton and London thought they had fairly well guaranteed that Tokyo would not be in a position to dominate the Pacific militarily. Events were to show, of course, that this calculation was erroneous (**16**, pp. 548-53).

Japan accepted the limitations upon its freedom of action in the Pacific for two reasons predominantly: it had no intention of honoring some of the agreements anyway over the ensuing years; and even its position of seeming inequality in the 10:10:7 naval formula probably left it militarily superior to its rivals in the Pacific. Britain and America's arithmetic advantage in capital ships was more than cancelled out by the difficulty of defending their far-flung Pacific possessions from a strongly-entrenched Japan and by strategic commitments in other waters (e.g., the Atlantic and the Mediterranean) which did not dissipate Japan's naval strength.

In a strategic sense, therefore, a strong case can be made for saying that Japan "won" the Washington Naval Armaments Conference. The lack of any enforcement machinery and the nature of the strategic problem in the Pacific —permitting it to focus its strength against rivals far removed from the scene—meant that it could go about its carefully laid plans for expansionism in the Orient without being seriously impeded by agreements reached at the Washington Conference.

A Decade of Failure

Two other attempts to reach disarmament agreements before World War II deserve brief mention. Owing to expanded construction of certain types of cruisers, destroyers, and submarines exempted from the Washington agreements, the United States had come to believe that the prohibitions laid down in 1921 ought to be broadened. This led to the calling of the Geneva Conference in 1927. As events turned out, the atmosphere could hardly have been more prejudicial to success. France and Italy refused to attend; jealousy and suspicion colored the approaches of the erstwhile Atlantic allies, Britain and America. Each country pursued the customary policy of trying to "regulate" armaments which were conspicuous in the other country's arsenal, while showing no particular propensity to reduce its own. The conference ended in total failure.

One development in this same period prevented failure of the Geneva Conference from triggering a renewed race for military supremacy (16, pp. 555-56). That was the signing of the Kellogg-Briand Pact (or Pact of Paris) on August 27, 1928. This agreement, ultimately signed by nearly all civilized countries in the world, solemnly condemned "recourse to war for the solution of international controversies" and pledged the signatories to "renounce it as an instrument of national policy in their relations with one another." Numerous powerful signatories accepted the pact only after attaching various "qualifications" and "understandings." The United States, for instance, declared that the pact did not impair the "right of self-defense," did not exclude the use of force to uphold the Monroe Doctrine, or entail any obligation to participate in sanctions against countries violating the pact. Furthermore, American officials rated the pact of marginal importance in attacking the root-causes of war and violence in world affairs. According to the diplomatic historian, Julius Pratt, it was perhaps indicative of prevailing attitudes in the Senate that, immediately after ratification of the pact, the Senate voted appropriations to construct fifteen new 10,000-ton cruisers to add to the nation's naval strength (16, pp. 538-39).

The last significant act in the drama of disarmament negotiations before World War II was the London Conference of 1930, at which the United States and Britain manifested as much of a spirit of conciliation as they had shown suspicion and hostility earlier. The old 10:10:7 ratio set by the Washington Conference for the United States, Britain, and Japan, respectively, was preserved and applied now to cruisers. Japan, however, gained a position of parity in submarines, a fact which strengthened its naval position in the Orient even more than formerly. Agreement was also reached that submarines should not be used against passenger shipping and should be used in accordance with rules already recognized in international law. An "escalator clause" permitted the great naval powers to exceed adopted quotas if countries not party to the

accord embarked upon a naval arms-race (16, pp. 556-57).

The London Conference marked the finale in progress toward disarmament in the inter-war period. Following Japanese invasion of Manchuria in 1931-32, the world drifted inexorably toward the abyss of war. Japan gave notice of withdrawal from treaty prohibitions upon naval construction, effective at the end of 1936. Thereafter, the level of armaments began to climb toward the peak reached in World War II. Not until the postwar period were sustained efforts made to initiate new disarmament negotiations.

Disarmament Efforts in the Early Postwar Period

In evaluating progress made throughout recent history in the vexatious disarmament issue, Inis Claude cautioned in 1956 that:

It is important to avoid confusing long hours of international debate, vast piles of printed documents, and elaborate charts of institutional structure with meaningful accomplishment. Aside from certain limited and ephemeral successes which were achieved outside the League structure in the interwar period, the movement for arms reduction and limitation has been as unproductive of results as it has been productive of words. The tremendous display of military fireworks from 1939 to 1945 was only the final and most tragic bit of evidence that the League's efforts had been an abject failure, and the equally complete sterility of the work thus far undertaken by the United Nations in this field is one of the most glaring facts of international life. (3, p. 303).

As the destructive power of modern weapons has risen by almost geometric proportions since World War II, the postwar period has been characterized by interminable and highly technical meetings of negotiators from powerful countries; by carefully drafted and exceedingly complex disarmament proposals and counter-proposals; by mounting pressure from public opinion around the world for renewing the search for a way out of the disarmament impasse; and, down to the early 1960's, by remarkably little genuine progress in resolving the issues which have blocked great power acceptance of an operable disarmament plan.

The postwar period began auspiciously enough with the total demilitarization of once-powerful Axis countries like Germany and Japan, followed by significant reductions in the military forces of the Allied governments. In the light of hindsight it is clear that the United States government, bowing to insistent public demands, reduced its armed strength to levels dangerously below those consistent with the nation's security and its expanding diplomatic commitments around the world. Alone among the great powers, only Soviet Russia continued to maintain a large military establishment, although there was some reduction from the peak reached during World War II.

But a new element had entered the picture. Toward the end of the war, the United States had perfected the atomic bomb, using it to administer the military *coup de grâce* to the Japanese Empire. The awesome power of what came to be called the "absolute weapon" for a time focused world opinion on the compelling urgency of controlling nuclear weapons. In the new era—the nuclear age—the problem of non-nuclear (or "conventional") weapons for a time seemed insignificant compared with the necessity of assuring that nuclear energy was utilized for human welfare.

As the only country which had actually produced atomic bombs, and the one which possessed a clear head-start in nuclear technology, the United States took the initiative in presenting a plan for international control of atomic energy. The American position was based upon an Anglo-Canadian-American declaration of November 15, 1945. This statement described the atomic bomb as a "means of destruction hitherto unknown, against which there can be no adequate military defense. . . . " It held that only the "prevention of war" offered genuine protection to civilization. It declared further that, in the judgment of the three countries which had collaborated to perfect the atomic bomb, dissemination of information about its manufacture "before it is possible to devise effective, reciprocal, and enforceable safeguards" might intensify feelings of insecurity throughout the world. The statement therefore proposed immediate establishment of a UN commission to prepare recommendations aimed at utilizing nuclear energy solely for peaceful purposes. Enunciating a principle which has been consistently advocated by the United States throughout the greater part of the postwar period, the statement held that "The work of the Commission should proceed by separate stages, the successful completion of each one of which will develop the necessary confidence of the world before the next stage is undertaken." As we shall see, the matter of "staging" has proved one of the most controversial issues associated with disarmament within recent years (**17**, pp. 1076-77).

Following this tripartite declaration, on June 14, 1946, elder statesman Bernard Baruch presented a proposal—later known as the "Baruch Plan"—to the newly-created Atomic Energy Commission of the UN. The plan provided for establishment of an International Atomic Development Authority with broad powers to own and control all nuclear energy facilities "potentially dangerous to world security." The agency would control, inspect, and license all nuclear activities, would foster beneficial uses of nuclear technology, and sponsor research and development basic to scientific progress. After these steps had been taken, there would be cessation of production of all nuclear weapons, disposal of all existing stockpiles of such weapons, and transmission to the Authority of complete information concerning nuclear technology. The proposal envisioned rigid enforcement of the provisions of any disarmament proposal adopted, with "immediate, swift, and sure punishments," on the order of the Nuremberg war crimes trials, to be meted out to violators. The Security Council would have no veto of the Authority's findings and operations (**17**, pp. 1079-87).

On June 19, Soviet Russia offered a counterproposal to the Baruch Plan. Cardinal features were: an immediate international agreement pledging nations "not to use atomic weapons in any circumstances whatsoever," and requiring them to terminate current production of nuclear weapons and to dispose of existing stockpiles of nuclear weapons within three months after the agreement was reached; a pledge that signatories would regard violation of the agreement as a crime against humanity; and a further pledge that within six months the signatories would "pass legislation providing severe penalties" for violations of the provisions of the agreement (**17**, pp. 1090-91).

These two proposals were of lasting significance in shaping the course of disarmament negotiations over the next several years. The proposals defined the positions of the two rival power blocs whose relations colored most global political issues. Each plan reflected certain underlying assumptions indicative of each side's approach to disarmament and closely related questions in international affairs. Although there were some modifications on the part of each side in the years ahead, the deadlock on disarmament which ensued over these two conflicting proposals remained essentially unchanged thereafter.

The cardinal ingredients in the American plan were establishment of foolproof international inspection and control over all phases of nuclear technology, cessation of nuclear weapons production, disposal of accumulated atomic weapons stockpiles, and surrender of full information concerning nuclear technology to the Authority—in that order. The fundamental elements in the Soviet plan were immediate and unconditional prohibition of the use and manufacture of atomic weapons, destruction of existing stockpiles, and establishment of a nationally-operated inspection and control system—in that order.

Behind each of these proposals were certain hard realities. The United States possessed the atomic bomb; the USSR did not. Therefore, America was unwilling to relinquish its advantage until international control over nuclear processes had been guaranteed. Lacking the atomic bomb, but possessing formidable ground- and air-forces, the USSR was following the ancient stratagem of seeking to deprive its opponent of its strongest weapon, thereby leaving the communist bloc an overwhelmingly advantageous position in non-nuclear weapons. Meantime, pending negotiation of an acceptable disarmament scheme, Russia would press on rapidly to expand its own scientific-technological knowledge in the field of nuclear energy.

The American-sponsored Baruch Plan was widely hailed as a generous and statesmanlike gesture designed to assure that nuclear energy would forever be used for the benefit of mankind. Few other great powers would have been prepared to relinquish control over the greatest destructive force ever developed, especially when they were beginning to have serious doubts about the intentions of their most powerful diplomatic rival. Generous as it may have been from an American point of view, however, the Baruch Plan was probably foredoomed to failure as a measure acceptable to the Soviet Union. Two features of the plan virtually guaranteed this result. One was insistence upon iron-clad inspection and control by the Authority as a prerequisite to any functioning disarmament agreement. The other was that the efficacy of the inspection-control system had to be clearly demonstrated *before* the United States was prepared to relinquish its atomic monopoly. Given the extreme sensitivity Russia has displayed throughout history about the security of its borders and the hostility it has demonstrated toward foreigners, coupled with more recent re-enforcement of these anxieties and propensities by communist ideological preachments, it is extremely doubtful whether Russia would have accepted any plan calling for hordes of foreign "inspectors" in Russia, who possessed sweeping powers to inquire into virtually every aspect of Soviet society and industry. Under the Baruch Plan, the powers envisioned for the nuclear Authority were vast and without any very clearly specified limits (**17**, pp. 1093-1102).

But it was perhaps the second requirement which posed the most enduring obstacle to agreement in 1946 and in the years thereafter. America's insistence that successive stages in the disarmament agreement be completed before its own monopoly of nuclear weapons would be relinquished amounted to saying to the USSR: If you are willing to demonstrate your "good faith" by satisfactory compliance with the Baruch Plan; if we are completely convinced that you are genuinely endeavoring to meet its requirements; if, in short, the USSR's conduct over the course of months or possibly years is acceptable to the United States—then, and *only then,* will the American government place itself on a plane of nuclear parity with other great powers. If, however, at any stage, Soviet behavior does not meet with American approval, then "the deal is off," and the United

States is left free to exploit the advantage which its prior stockpiling of nuclear weapons and its headstart in nuclear technology have given it. The Soviet Union, that is to say, was to be put on probation for an unspecified period, with the United States acting as probation officer to decide whether Soviet behavior met required standards. If it did not, if for any reason the step-by-step disarmament plan did not prove feasible, then the United States would be left in a clearly superior position in any ensuing arms race.

From the point of view of Soviet national interest, there was little incentive for the Kremlin to accept the Baruch Plan. The United States was asking its most powerful antagonist to do something which it would never itself have contemplated doing if the roles had been reversed: to trust America not to exploit the great advantage its atomic monopoly gave it in world affairs, pending ultimate conclusion of an international disarmament agreement. In later years it became a cardinal principle of American foreign policy that no disarmament agreement could rest upon "mere promises;" yet this was in effect what Washington was prepared to offer Moscow for an indefinite period in the future. When the stakes were nothing less than the global balance of military power, this was asking a good deal of *any* state and entirely too much of a state whose outlook on world affairs had been conditioned by centuries of suspicion and hostility toward the outside world and whose ideology permitted no room for doubt about the hostility of other countries toward the communist bloc.

As for the Soviet counter-plan, its weaknesses were even more glaring and just as fundamental as those of the Baruch Plan. The Kremlin wanted the United States to relinquish its monopoly in atomic weapons—virtually the *only* weapons available to the West as a counterpoise against the crushing might of the Red Army—in exchange for vague Soviet promises of future compliance with an international disarmament agreement and bland assurances that in good time an effective system of global inspection and control would be set up and function satisfactorily under purely *national* auspices. The Soviet proposal required an even greater act of faith than the American, especially in view of recent Soviet machinations in Eastern Europe, indicating to the West the Kremlin's patent unwillingness to be bound by solemn promises made earlier in the Yalta and Potsdam agreements. Whatever weaknesses might be singled out in the Baruch Plan, no impartial student of American diplomatic history would seriously contend that the United States was contemplating a surprise attack against Russia in some future period, or that it was plotting to impose its rule over debilitated countries in Europe and Asia. The same could not be said for the Kremlin's intentions toward weaker nations. Already, these were beginning to be widely suspected in the Western world; and having demobilized their armies, Western officials could never give up their only protection against the overwhelming superiority of the Red Army in exchange for paper promises of Soviet good behavior in the future.

2. PERSISTENT ISSUES IN DISARMAMENT NEGOTIATIONS

The positions taken by the two super-powers, and their allies and satellites, in the period of UN debate on the Baruch Plan were, in most particulars, identical with positions held throughout the disarmament negotiations in the years thereafter. Proposals, counter-proposals, and attempts to create syntheses between them, resulted in negotiations that were as prolonged and intricate as they were fruitless in attacking the problem of steady accretions in national armaments and the destructive power of

modern weapons. These negotiations took place within an environment of progressively worsening relations between the free world and the communist world. By 1947 the United States had openly proclaimed the doctrine of containment, requiring a significant buildup in American military forces. In the absence of a workable disarmament agreement, both sides pressed forward rapidly in the field of nuclear technology. Soviet Russia broke America's monopoly of the uranium bomb in 1949. The

United States, meanwhile, was developing the thermonuclear (hydrogen) bomb, which it perfected in 1952. Less than a year later the USSR had succeeded in making a "hydrogen device," thereby re-establishing approximate nuclear weapons parity with the United States. The Korean War had prompted a considerable increase in the level of "conventional" weapons* throughout the non-communist world. Furthermore, the war had shown that, contrary to what some governments believed in the immediate postwar era, conventional weapons were far from outmoded in the nuclear age; their degree of destructiveness was at an all-time high. Establishing some kind of international control over their production and use was only slightly less urgent than controlling nuclear weapons.

The ebb and flow of tensions between rival, heavily armed, power blocs both caused, and were in some measure caused by, the stalemate over disarmament questions within the United Nations. Now, as in earlier eras, nations always had to consider the global context within which decisions respecting disarmament were to be made. How would acceptance of a particular disarmament scheme alter the nation's power relative to the power of its diplomatic opponents? How would reductions in specified categories of weapons affect the capacity of the nation to carry out its diplomatic commitments? These and many other questions weighed heavily in the approaches of all countries involved in the disarmament discussions. As rapid progress was made in nuclear technology, and as powerful nations perfected new methods, particularly missiles, for delivering nuclear weapons, the urgency of discovering fruitful approaches to the problem of arms-limitation mounted.

Throughout months and years of prolonged and often sterile negotiations, certain key issues persisted. Insight into the intricacies of the disarmament question since World War II can more profitably be gained by focusing our attention on these questions instead of tracing out chronologically the pattern of disarmament negotiations since 1946.**

The Scope of Disarmament Proposals

A central issue in all disarmament negotiations is the question: Shall statesmen strive for *total and comprehensive* agreements, covering all major aspects of the armaments problem, or shall they seek separate agreements covering only *limited* aspects of the problem? The choice lies between trying to reduce the total level of armaments to the lowest point consistent with the maintenance of law and order and a step-by-step process which, it is hoped, will sooner or later achieve a substantial reduction in military forces.

The former procedure was epitomized by the remark of Soviet Foreign Minister Maxim Litvinov during the 1930's that "the way to disarm is to disarm." This same mentality was reflected more than two decades later in Soviet Premier Khrushchev's dramatic plea before the UN General Assembly late in 1959, when he presented a new Russian proposal calling for total disarmament within four years. Schemes advocating total disarmament have the merit of simplicity: they urge powerful countries, by a supreme act of self-abnegation, to scrap their military forces at one blow, thereby relieving mankind of the evils growing out of the exist-

---

*The term "conventional" weapons does not have a universally accepted definition. In Martin's words, it means "all armaments and armed forces except atomic, radioactive, lethal-chemical and biological weapons, and all future weapons having comparable destructive characteristics" (12, p. 81).

For that matter, the distinction between armaments and non-armaments is exceedingly difficult to draw. For example, does the steel-making potential of a country count as part of its "armaments"? Normally it does not; yet in any future armaments-race, the side that possesses the greatest industrial capacity can be expected to win that race in the end. Again, students must be reminded that designations and measurements of the elements in a nation's power are highly inexact.

**A variety of sources is available to students who wish to follow disarmament negotiations on a year-by-year basis. Annual developments are summarized in the official *United Nations Yearbook;* good secondary accounts are the annual volumes in the series, *Annual Review of United Nations Affairs,* published by New York University. Informative sources for American policy toward disarmament are the annual installments in the State Department's series, *U. S. Participation in the UN,* and a number of titles in its "International Organization and Conference Series." Documentary material is included in *A Decade of American Foreign Policy* (17) and *American Foreign Policy, 1950-1955* (4, II, pp. 2739-2887).

ence of large armaments stockpiles and military forces. A tacit assumption of such proposals is that disarmament schemes fail because of the weakness of human will, rather than inability to agree upon "technical problems" or other issues. Consequently, an arms-free era of international good will would be ushered in if only countries would "make up their minds" to take the ultimate step.

In view of the evident reluctance of powerful, often hostile, countries to take so radical a step in the absence of settlements of vital political issues, the greatest weakness of total disarmament schemes is the fact that their comprehensiveness is their undoing. Whatever theoretical merits such plans possess, experience in recent history affords very little evidence for believing that heavily armed nations are prepared to accept such schemes. As with many "all or nothing" proposals, insistence upon *complete* reform as often as not results in *no* reform.

A limited disarmament scheme, on the other hand, recognizes that some *actual* progress is better than mere theoretical agreement on the desirability of sweeping disarmament measures. Modest beginnings which are successful may pave the way for more far-reaching steps in the future. Said Secretary of State Dulles in 1955: " . . . it is the beginning, the initial breakthrough, that is often decisive" (4, II, p. 2847). That at least appears to have become the prevailing view among the great powers by the 1960's, based upon the two-fold realization that there is virtually no prospect for adoption of a comprehensive agreement embodying the major demands of both sides and that global opinion is becoming increasingly insistent that some sign of progress, no matter how limited, be demonstrated in breaking the disarmament dead-lock. Accordingly, by the 1960's, the most promising approach appears to be a "package deal" incorporating several elements: a trial period in which the testing of nuclear weapons would be suspended; designation of an experimental "inspection zone"—possibly adjacent to the North Pole, in Europe, or both—in which experience would be gained in trying to carry out a reduction of armaments within a comparatively small area; and establishment of a verification-control system charged with super-

vising compliance with the agreement. Summarizing the attitude which had emerged after more than a decade of futile postwar disarmament negotiations, British Foreign Minister, Selwyn Lloyd, stated that "the scope of a disarmament agreement must be confined to measures which can either be controlled in an acceptable manner or are of such a limited character that a certain looseness of control can be accepted" (1, p. 5). The steps enumerated above appear to meet these criteria. Above all, they offer more promise than any other measures advocated throughout the postwar period of at last penetrating the hard shell of the disarmament problem at some point and of halting what has become a run-away arms race among the military giants of the earth. While many details remain to be worked out, and may still frustrate application of the above steps, a consensus on the principle that a limited beginning ought to be made was widely interpreted as a stride forward.

Political Issues and Agreement on Disarmament

The necessity for a "relaxation of tensions" throughout the international community has been a motif in Communist propaganda within recent years. For example, a Soviet statement on disarmament made before the United Nations on May 10, 1955, expressed the view that:

> Until an atmosphere of trust has been created in relations between states, any agreement on the institution of international control [of national armaments] can only serve to lull the vigilance of the peoples. It will create a false sense of security, while in reality there will be a danger of the production of atomic and hydrogen weapons and hence the threat of surprise attack and the unleashing of an atomic war with all its appalling consequences. . . . (4, II, p. 2850).

Few individuals would quarrel with this diagnosis of conditions requisite to ushering in an era of genuine peace and security for mankind. No theme has been more prominent in Western, and especially American, foreign policy than that an atmosphere of trust is indispensable to any kind of permanent resolution of cold war issues. Yet agreement upon sonorous principles like those enunciated in the Soviet statement just cited can be, and often has been, followed by violent disagreement over the precise steps needed to create the atmosphere conducive to harmonious international relations.

As an illustration, we have but to remember that the Russians have consistently demanded a ban of all nuclear weapons, destruction of existing nuclear stockpiles, cessation of further testing of nuclear weapons, dismantling of foreign (i.e., predominantly American) military bases—steps which, according to communist spokesmen, would automatically pave the way for great power agreement on other aspects of disarmament and corollary political issues. References to the *prior* settlement of long-standing political issues which divide the world have, however, been conspicuously absent from Soviet disarmament proposals. The United States, joined by many of its cold war allies, has tended to take the position that some progress in settling political issues was a *sine qua non* to any permanent relaxation of tensions in the international community. Very little progress could be expected so long as such issues remained unresolved.

The American approach to disarmament is thus part of a pattern of the nation's diplomatic response to the communist challenge in the postwar era. A fundamental element in this response has been insistence upon "deeds and not words" on the part of the communist world. Said Secretary of State Acheson in 1950, in dealing with tensions between the United States and the USSR:

> No one who has lived through these postwar years can be sanguine about reaching agreements in which reliance can be placed and which will be observed by the Soviet leaders in good faith. We must not, in our yearning for peace, allow ourselves to be betrayed by vague generalities or beguiling proffers of peace which are unsubstantiated by good faith solidly demonstrated in daily behavior. . . . What is required is genuine evidence in conduct, not just in words, of an intention to solve the immediate problems and remove the tensions which divide us (4, II, p. 1935).

This view, substantially unchanged, has been voiced by spokesmen for the Eisenhower Administration. Early in 1953, Secretary of State Dulles spoke of three obstacles to reaching an accommodation with the USSR, listing as basic sources of tensions the fact that the USSR was a heavily-armed totalitarianism which had greatly extended its borders by force, that communist ideology was intensely hostile to non-communist states, and that Soviet leaders recognized no moral inhibitions upon their actions. He declared that "so long as these three conditions persist . . . we must not . . . assume that the danger is over and that we are living in a peaceful world which requires neither armaments nor our allies" (4, II, pp. 1962-63).

It is not possible to list those political questions which the United States demands be settled before substantial progress can be made on disarmament. In fact, American officials have said that there is no such list and that the United States is prepared to make at least a beginning toward disarmament without prior settlement of these issues (5, 1956, p. 26). Nevertheless, one issue high on the American list is the unification of Germany. One authoritative study reports that in May, 1957, President Eisenhower assured German Chancellor Konrad Adenauer (1) that the nation would make no disarmament agreement which might prejudice later German unification and (2) that any comprehensive disarmament proposal necessarily presupposed solution of the German question. This viewpoint was accepted by Britain and France later in the year (25, 1957, p. 130).

Present-day disagreements over the relationship between armaments and political issues are of course merely contemporary disputes over the ancient question: do national apprehensions growing out of political disagreements give rise to armaments, or do high levels of armaments generate global anxieties and rigidities in national policies, thereby making political problems far more difficult to resolve? If an either-or choice must be made, events in the postwar period would seem to confirm the former viewpoint, advocated by the West. For it is a matter of record that Western rearmament appeared as a *response* to a pattern of increasingly ominous Soviet threats against the security of the free world. Once rearmament had been undertaken, and had perhaps prompted a renewed military buildup on the other side, momentum inherent in this situation itself greatly intensified feelings of world wide insecurity.

Yet there is no compelling reason why alternatives must be mutually exclusive. Britain and France, joined by many countries in the neutralist bloc, have advocated a simultaneous, multi-front attack against *all* major causes of tension in world affairs. After 1952-53, when both great power blocs had acquired thermonuclear weapons, pressures arising from world public opinion and growing revulsion against the terrible destructive power of modern weapons forced the great powers to compromise. By the late 1950's agreement had been reached that at least in the *initial* phase of a disarmament scheme, concessions could be made to the demands expressed by both sides. Thus the United States declared its willingness to take limited steps in the disarmament field, deferring further progress until the next stage, after success had been achieved in resolving at least some existing political questions. Concessions were forthcoming too from the USSR, which retreated from such demands as that the United States liquidate its overseas bases and dismantle NATO before genuine progress could be expected either in the disarmament field or in removing corollary cold war issues.

However, any progress *beyond* this initial stage, at least in the prevailing Western view, would necessarily require success in breaking the deadlock over major political questions. Moreover, it must be remembered that agreements "in principle," as diplomats throughout history have discovered, by no means guarantee that the all-important *details* of a disarmament scheme will prove acceptable to all participants. Western officials want no more vaguely-worded, elastic pledges like those contained in the Yalta and Potsdam agreements reached at the close of World War II. Nor, on the basis of later experience in the truce arrived at in Korea and Indochina, do they want pledges which rely merely upon the good faith of the participating nations to assure compliance. Thus far, not even the details of a circumscribed first-step plan have been worked out on a mutually satisfactory basis, not to mention details of a comprehensive plan entailing a sequence of stages.

Our discussion above has introduced a crucial concept in the disarmament deadlock since 1946. This is the question of "staging" and its pivotal role in negotiations looking toward arms-limitation.

"Staging" as an Issue in Disarmament

A staff study written for the Senate Foreign Relations Committee holds that "At the present time, some of the issues of disarmament revolve less around what is to be done than when it is to be done" (**21**, p. 21). The matter of "staging" (sometimes called "phasing") has caused endless controversy among the great powers. The American position, as stated by Secretary of Defense Charles E. Wilson in 1956, is that:

> Any agreement for reductions under the terms of a comprehensive disarmament program must be carried out by stages. These stages must be clearly defined and should be progressive, beginning with areas of least sensitivity. Each of the succeeding stages should only be initiated after the preceding stage has been satisfactorily completed. (**19**, Part 4, p. 165).

The United States has envisioned three important stages, to be followed in this sequence: (1) establishment of an effective system of international inspection and control to verify and enforce any agreement reached; (2) reductions in the levels of "conventional" armaments, accompanied by progress in resolving major collateral political issues which divide the world and in strengthening the inspection-control system set up earlier; (3) finally, elimination of existing nuclear and conventional weapons stockpiles, accompanied by prohibitions against the use of designated categories of weapons and by measures to assure compliance by all countries.

Soviet proposals, on the other hand, have never dealt as explicitly with the matter of staging as Western proposals. For many years after 1946, the USSR favored a treaty which would embody sweeping disarmament provisions to be carried out simultaneously, or nearly so. After 1954, however, its proposals shifted in the direction of more limited disarmament schemes, including staging schemes. Gradually the contours of a three-stage plan began to emerge, though they were never as clearly delineated as in Western proposals. The USSR contemplated the following successive stages: (1) total prohibitions against the manufacture of nuclear weapons and the use of existing ones; (2) reductions in the stockpiles of both conventional and nuclear weapons, together with cuts in military manpower; and finally (3) establishment and operation of a system of international inspection and control (7, p. 337). The Soviet position has always been hazy on just when important political problems were to be solved; presumably, progress in this area would take place throughout all three stages.

Great controversy has not only surrounded the exact *order* of stages to be followed, but it has also prevailed over the circumstances under which transitions will be made from one stage to the next. The experienced French diplomat, Jules Moch, has distinguished three attitudes on this question. The USSR has favored *automatic* transition from one stage to the next; Britain and France have tended to favor *semiautomatic* transition; and the United States has favored *optional* (or non-automatic) transition. For the sake of simplicity, let us envision a first stage disarmament plan, with only one requirement: prohibitions against the manufacture of nuclear weapons. Let us suppose that a contemplated second stage involved two requirements: destruction of nuclear weapons stockpiles and reductions in the levels of conventional weapons and in military manpower. Under what circumstances would the transition be made from the first stage to the second?

Throughout most of the postwar period, the USSR has taken the position that satisfactory compliance with the requirements of each stage ought to be determined by each state for itself and that the entire process of moving through successive stages ought to take place automatically, within designated time intervals, until all major categories of armaments have been brought under international control. The United States, on the other hand, has insisted upon satisfactory compliance with the obligations laid down within each stage before the next stage was entered; and—even more basic as a source of disagreement with the USSR—it has demanded that satisfactory compliance be verified by an international control agency. Implicit in America's position has been the assumption that if any country failed to honor commitments assumed in the first stage, then no further progress toward disarmament would be undertaken until full compliance had been made. This was a cardinal element in the Baruch Plan, and it was reiterated in American disarmament proposals after 1946. In practice, of course, this meant that the United States refused to relinquish its superiority in nuclear weapons until it was satisfied that it could do so without prejudice to its own security and the security of the non-communist world.

Britain and France have sought to combine the Soviet and American positions into the idea of semi-automatic transition from stage to stage. That is, whenever an international control agency—applying criteria agreed to previously by the great powers—certified that compliance with first-stage obligations was complete, then acceptance of second-stage requirements would become obligatory (7, p. 11).

The American position on staging is a logical outgrowth of the free world's reliance upon "nuclear deterrence" as the key concept of its defense effort. Confronted by the overwhelming might of the Red Army, coupled with Soviet advances in nuclear and missile technology, Western officials are in full agreement that strength in nuclear weapons must be preserved until such a time as global conditions favor their reduction without prejudice to the security of nations outside the communist bloc. The concept of "deterrence" is the heart of the West's defense efforts. As expressed by Sir Winston Churchill in 1955:

> After a certain point has been passed, it may be said, the worse things get the better. The broad effect of the latest developments is to spread almost indefinitely and at least to a vast extent the area of mortal danger. This should certainly increase the deterrent upon Soviet Russia by putting her enormous spaces and scattered population on an equality, or near equality, of vulnerability with our small, densely populated island and with Western Europe.
> . . . The hydrogen bomb with its vast range of destruction and the even wider area of contamination would be effective also against nations whose population hitherto has been so widely

dispersed over large land areas as to make them feel that they were not in any danger at all. (**18**, p. 233).

Secretary of State Dulles asserted categorically that "As against the possibility of full-scale attack by the Soviet Union itself, there is only one effective defense, for us and for others. That is the capacity to counterattack. That is the ultimate deterrent" (**18**, p. 235). It therefore has been a fixed premise of the American approach to disarmament that deterrent power will not be relinquished until the threat which called it into existence has also been removed.

The Soviet approach of course has been colored by vastly different considerations. Repeatedly, the USSR has invoked the principle of non-interference in the internal affairs of countries to oppose any inspection by other nations or an international agency to evaluate Soviet compliance with various stages of an arms-limitation agreement. It has been unwilling especially to leave that judgment to its arch-rival, the United States, since Washington might conceivably decide that Soviet behavior at any stage was unacceptable, leaving America with its postwar superiority in nuclear stockpiling and technology. Two interpretations of the Soviet Union's attitude on staging are possible. Many leading authorities on the USSR, joined by many governmental officials and laymen, doubt that the Kremlin is sincerely interested in *any* binding disarmament scheme which involves international inspection and control (**22**, *passim*). If so, the Kremlin's reluctance to accept a requirement of full compliance with first-stage provisions is fully explicable. Even if Soviet good faith in approaching disarmament negotiations is conceded, the USSR may be taking out a kind of insurance to guarantee that breakdown of an arms-limitation agreement at some later point would not leave Russia in an inferior military position. It is conceivable of course that both of these motivations are present in some degree.

The crucial role played by the question of staging was brought into clear focus by Premier Khrushchev's disarmament plan late in 1959. Khrushchev's speech contained no reference to the difficulties encountered over the years in solving the problem of staging satisfactorily. At the same time, he did propose that his plan

be carried out gradually "by stages." The first stage contemplated a reduction in the armed forces of the Soviet Union, the United States, and Communist China to 1.7 million men each; Britain and France would be allowed 650,000 men each. The second stage would witness the total liquidation of all armed forces and the long-advocated Soviet goal of the elimination of all foreign military bases. Finally, an international control agency would be set up, after all categories of military weapons had been destroyed. In large measure, these proposals merely reiterated the Soviet position throughout the postwar era. The order of staging—with inspection and control left for the last phase—remained unchanged; and, unless amplifications by Soviet diplomats in later UN debates introduced something new, the USSR clung to its staunchly-held viewpoint that transition from stage to stage would be an automatic procedure, with compliance left to the determination of each state for itself (**15**, October 4, 1959, dispatch by Thomas J. Hamilton).

Khrushchev's plan did not throw light on two other great stumbling-blocks associated with the staging issue. Shall an international control agency be semi-autonomous or shall its operations be subject to the same veto that prevails in the Security Council? We shall discuss the implications of that question below. Secondly, shall a disarmament scheme be discontinued if there is non-compliance with requirements laid down for any stage? The West believes the answer to the latter question must be affirmative. The communist bloc has left the issue in suspension, refusing to make specific proposals as to what ought to be done in case of deliberate violations of any disarmament accord reached (**21**, p. 22). By the opening of the 1960's, the position of the USSR remained as obscure as it had been over preceding years.

Conventional Weapons and Disarmament

So preoccupied were the great powers with the new magnitude of destructive force attained in nuclear and thermonuclear weapons in the years following World War II that they gave only incidental attention to the problem of conventional armaments. In 1947 a Commission for Conventional Armaments had been established under the United Nations; meantime, its companion body, the UN Atomic Energy Commission, was considering the problem of nuclear weapons. Negotiations in each body were carried on without any significant liaison and co-ordination with the other agency. Deliberations in the Commission for Conventional Armaments lagged throughout successive months, indicating that the great powers were almost exclusively concerned with the threat of nuclear devastation (21, pp. 5-7).

As always, positions on disarmament, however, were responsive to important developments in the international environment. Three such developments were of particular significance: by acquiring the uranium bomb (1949) and the hydrogen bomb (1953), the Soviet Union finally achieved at least approximate parity with the West in nuclear weapons; over this same period, the Western countries themselves raised their levels of conventional weapons and military manpower, thereby narrowing the gulf between themselves and the communist bloc in ground forces; and despite a widely prevalent conception in the West that the atomic bomb was the "absolute weapon," the Korean and Indochinese wars—fought entirely with non-nuclear weapons—demonstrated that control over conventional armaments was indispensable to further progress toward world peace and security.

In 1950 President Eisenhower proposed that the two questions of controlling nuclear and conventional armaments be considered jointly. This change in the American position led in 1952 to amalgamation of the two separate disarmament bodies into a new agency, the UN Disarmament Commission, charged with considering the entire spectrum of problems associated with disarmament.

Before this move, the United States and the Soviet Union had taken widely divergent positions on the relationship between conventional and nuclear weapons. From the beginning of postwar disarmament talks, the USSR has linked the two categories of weapons closely together and demanded simultaneous cuts in both categories—a demand which led to the specific proposal in 1948 that the great powers cut their ground, sea, and air-forces by one-third and, at the same time, unconditionally ban nuclear weapons. The American position, on the other hand, was that controlling conventional armaments was secondary to controlling nuclear weapons; once the latter had been achieved, then the former problem could be dealt with constructively (21, pp. 6-7).

A joint Anglo-French-American proposal to the Disarmament Commission in 1951 marked a fundamental modification in the Western view. At least some of the elements in earlier Soviet proposals were accepted by calling for a census of all military forces and armaments and for imposition of a "ceiling" on armed force levels and future weapons production. Subsequent amplifications of this plan called for a ceiling of 1 to 1.5 million troops for the USSR, the USA, and China, from 700,000 to 800,000 troops for the United Kingdom and France, and for much smaller ceilings—roughly one per cent of the population—for lesser powers (4, II, pp. 2760-61). The initial Soviet response was cool. Until 1955 the Kremlin merely reiterated its familiar demand for an *immediate* one-third reduction in the force levels of all great powers. This demand came to have a greater than ordinary appeal for neutralist countries when, in the months that followed, the USSR announced that Russia and its Eastern European satellites were making unilateral cuts in their military manpower. The West, however, continued to reject a flat, across-the-board percentage cut in armaments, because such a cut would merely perpetuate the Communist bloc's preponderance in ground forces; nor would the West accept any approach based upon unilateral disarmament, when such a move was unaccompanied by international inspection and control (21, pp. 8-9).

Finally, in 1955, the Soviet Union expressed its willingness to accept the principle of armed force ceilings as specified in the Anglo-French-American proposals cited above. Premier Khrushchev before the UN in 1959 proposed 1.7 million men each for Russia, the United States, and Communist China, leaving Britain and France 650,000 men each. Presumably, the armed forces of lesser powers would be reduced in approximately the same ratio, or perhaps even more drastically, since the USSR had argued for several years that the lesser powers ought to have their armed forces cut substantially. Although the gap between communist and free world positions was considerably narrowed by this suggestion, the disarmament dead-lock continued because of disagreement over the pivotal question of inspection and control. The West believed that no progress could be made in reducing conventional armaments without a fool-proof system of inspection and control. Specifically, it insisted upon two preconditions: a military census to determine existing national force levels and, in the light of information obtained, assurance that the Soviet Union would not be left in a position of preponderance in ground forces (**21**, pp. 19-20).

Other issues also remained unresolved. Among these was the age-old question of whether it is more important to control weapons or manpower. In a letter to Premier Bulganin in 1956, President Eisenhower stated that "disarmament should be sought primarily, though not exclusively, in terms of limitations on armaments rather than on men. The former are more subject to supervision, regulation and control than the latter" (**5**, p. 7). Western officials have been plainly apprehensive lest certain so-called "police forces" in the communist countries, along with large groups of "reserves," be excluded from imposed ceilings. Therefore, to the West the control of available weapons appears to offer surer promise of holding down overall military force levels than does an attempt to impose manpower limitations. Finally, no agreement has been reached on the permissible distribution of armed forces *within* agreed-upon ceilings. Quite obviously, comparative national strengths and weaknesses in ground, sea, and air-power are a matter of great international concern. Under certain circumstances, ratios in these categories could be decisive in tilting the global balance of power.

Establishing An Inspection-Control System

Along with the question of staging, the issue of an effective inspection-control system has proved to be a rock against which disarmament negotiations within recent years have broken. Not only have the free world coalition and the communist bloc differed over the stage at which a system of inspection-control ought to be inaugurated; they have also differed widely over many other fundamental issues associated with such a system. In many respects, their positions today have changed little from positions assumed at the time of the Baruch Plan and the Soviet counter-proposal in 1946.

The powers which an international control agency ought to possess are controversial. Should it have sweeping powers, to investigate *all* national activities which might conceivably entail a violation of a disarmament scheme? Or should its powers be confined to clearly designated sites and to specified activities within national territories? The United States has favored sweeping powers for the control agency. Said Secretary of Defense Charles E. Wilson in 1956, "it would be illusory to condition the execution of an arms-limitation agreement solely upon the good faith of the contracting parties. This emphasizes the requirement that any arms-limitation agreement be safeguarded by an effective inspection and control system which does not depend upon good faith alone for effective operation" (**19**, Part 4, p. 163). The Soviet Union has assigned no such priority to the question of inspection and control, believing that (1) establishment of such a system should *follow* a ban upon the use and manufacture of nuclear and conventional weapons and (2) that the powers given to such a system ought to be carefully specified so as to prevent any infringement upon national sovereignty.

It would be no exaggeration to say that disagreement between the free world and the communist bloc over the issue of inspection and control has been the ultimate source of the deadlock in disarmament deliberations since World War II. As we have already noted, in most essential respects both sides adhere to positions outlined in the Baruch Plan and the Soviet counter-plan submitted in 1946. These positions in turn might be looked upon as involving disagreement over two basic questions: the *scope* of the powers to be possessed by an international control agency in verifying compliance with any disarmament accord reached, and the ability of this agency *to deal with violations which are uncovered.* American officials demand sweeping powers of inspection, together with sufficient power to deal with violations—which means that the agency's operations must not be subject to "veto" in the Security Council of the UN. The USSR favors limited and selected inspection; its few statements on the matter of control indicate that it would leave violations largely to be dealt with by the countries themselves.

Following the Geneva Conference of 1955, both sides appeared more conscious than ever of the compelling necessity for peaceful coexistence, and disarmament negotiations turned increasingly on various inspection-control plans. In a dramatic move, at the conference President Eisenhower had put forward his "Open Skies" plan calling for reciprocal and unimpeded aerial inspection by Russia and America. Shortly thereafter, the Soviet Union countered with a "ground inspection" plan which paralleled the President's proposal in many important respects. We shall look at each of these plans more fully below. Each stemmed from a revolution in the thinking of powerful countries about the key issue of inspection. The new conception, as stated in a Soviet proposal of May 10, 1955, was that "opportunities which cannot be covered by the international control system exist for evading such control and for organizing clandestine manufacture of atomic and hydrogen weapons" (19, Part 4, p. 164).

The great powers were now agreed, in other words, that the heart of the disarmament problem was prevention of surprise attack by countries which might have secreted stores of nuclear and conventional weapons. A consensus existed among the great powers that there was no known way of establishing a foolproof inspection-control system over *existing* stockpiles of weapons, although the future manufacture of them might be controlled. The overriding function of an inspection-control system therefore was to provide security against a surprise attack against a disarmed country. In the Western view, this was the *sine qua non* of such a system (5, 1956, pp. 20-1; 25, 1957, pp. 132-34; 2, pp. 52-4). These were the considerations which prompted Eisenhower's "Open Skies" proposal.

The United States believed that unrestricted aerial surveys carried out on a reciprocal basis, together with an exchange of military blue-

prints among the great powers, would go a long way toward relieving mounting global tensions. Russia's initial response to the "Open Skies" proposal was negative, on the ground that it contemplated no real disarmament and that it was a thinly disguised plot by Western countries to gain intelligence data about the communist world (9, 1955-56, pp. 19-20). In succeeding months, however, Russia countered with a program of "ground inspection," to be carried out within a carefully delimited area —a proposal which many countries came to regard as complementary, rather than antagonistic, to the American plan.

By the beginning of the 1960's there was little evidence that the long-standing impasse on inspection and control could be circumvented. Khrushchev late in 1959 talked in *general* terms about the importance of effective inspection and control, claiming that:

> We are in favor of strict control over the implementation of a disarmament agreement when it is reached. . . . We are in favor of general disarmament under control, but we are against control without disarmament. (15, September 20, 1959).

Moreover, Khrushchev stated that during the first stage disarmament would be carried out "under appropriate controls"; during the third stage, the Soviet plan contemplated setting up an international control agency. In an attempt to clarify the meaning of his plan later, Khrushchev told the press that "appropriate inspection and control" would take place throughout the entire process of disarmament and that "the controllers" would remain "in order to make sure that the agreement is fully observed" (15, October 4, 1959, dispatch by Thomas J. Hamilton).

Obviously, the latest Soviet plan left much to be desired in terms of spelling out concrete details for a workable inspection-control system. Western statesmen were no more inclined by 1960 than they were earlier to make substantial concessions in the hope that the USSR would later bring forth an acceptable and detailed system of international supervision. At the very least, they wanted to await such details before expressing any notable enthusiasm for this new Soviet gesture. The absence of specific details made Western observers think that the USSR had not abandoned its opposition to demands considered essential by the free world. The first was assurance that officials of an inspection-control agency would be able to travel freely in performance of their duties. Khrushchev's emphasis upon "appropriate" controls strongly implied that he still believed that the agency proposed by the West would be engaged in gathering "intelligence data" for Western countries. The second related to the actual *power* to be possessed by such an agency to deal with suspected or actual violations. Soviet officials gave no sign that Russia had retreated from its insistence that such powers be subject to the same veto that prevails in the UN Security Council. Thus the new Soviet proposal differed in no material respect from the Kremlin's position all through the postwar period.

Proposals for an Experimental "Test Zone"

The last half of the 1950's witnessed more rapid progress in gaining consent to a concrete arms-limitation plan than has been witnessed before throughout most of modern history. The great powers at last seemed in agreement that a limited disarmament plan ought to be undertaken and that experience gained in carrying it out ought to afford valuable lessons for the future. Accordingly, diplomats from both sides of the Iron Curtain began to express interest in some kind of a "pilot project" in which the practical difficulties encountered in implementing a disarmament scheme could be brought to light and evaluated. Global interest centered upon President Eisenhower's suggestion in the spring of 1958 that an "Arctic Inspection Zone" be created, to include all territories within the Arctic Circle, plus parts of Alaska and Soviet eastern Siberia. Within this zone, nations would report the location of all military bases and the disposition of their armed forces; international "inspection teams," containing at least one representative from the United States and the USSR, would be given unimpeded access to inspect military activities and to supervise whatever actual disarmament steps might be agreed to within the zone; equipment needed for inspection—reconnaissance aircraft, vehicles, electronic devices—would be furnished by the great powers. In May, 1958, an overwhelming majority of the nations in the Security Council approved this plan. Only Russia's eighty-third veto prevented its adoption (**15**, May 4, 1958).

The USSR has not, however, rejected the principle of a pilot study modelled after the Eisenhower proposal. In an exchange of letters with President Eisenhower in 1956, Soviet Premier Bulganin had called for establishment of a test zone in Europe, to be bounded by lines eight hundred kilometers east and west of the present border between the NATO countries and the Soviet satellites (**5**, 1956, pp. 21-22). After the United States had presented its plan for Arctic inspection, it expressed willingness to combine elements of its own plan with proposals for ground inspection made by the USSR. By the summer of 1958, America had submitted a three-part scheme calling for: a test inspection zone embracing the whole of the United States and the USSR; or its original Arctic inspection plan; and, in addition to one of these, a European zone embracing an arc of territories from Great Britain through all of Western Europe, including the USSR up to a line drawn from the North Pole southward to the Caspian Sea (**15**, August 4, 1958). Moreover, to meet the repeated Soviet objection that test inspection plans contemplated no actual *reduction* in armaments, the United States also accepted the principle that an inspection zone approach might be combined with a first-stage disarmament scheme, in which at least limited steps could be taken to cut military force levels (**21**, pp. 14-15). Establishment of an arms-free zone in Europe (with the boundaries of such a zone unspecified) was included in Khrushchev's disarmament proposals to the UN in September, 1959.

By the end of the 1950's the great powers appeared to be closer to a breakthrough in another aspect of the disarmament problem. This was the matter of nuclear weapons testing. With ever-growing intensity, world public opinion demanded a cessation of such testing, citing the dangers to mankind inherent in the "fallout" of radioactive particles over the globe. The Soviet Union made propaganda capital out of its insistent demands for a cessation of testing. All the great powers, however, pressed forward with tests. A total of forty-three test explosions took place in the year 1957 alone (**25**, 1957, p. 132).

Within the United States government the question of test suspension had precipitated a deep division between Defense Department and Atomic Energy Commission spokesmen on the one hand, who demanded continuance of testing until real progress toward disarmament had been achieved, and officials from the White House and State Department, joined by many scientists, who believed that continued testing was highly inimical to human life and who were deeply disturbed by communist propaganda gains on the testing issue (**15**, August 24, 1958). American defense officials had repeatedly denied that testing entailed any serious danger to life, and insisted that, for the nation's own security and that of the free world, the Western powers had to continue their weapons development and testing program, partially in the hope that a "clean" thermonuclear bomb (i.e., one which produced little or no radioactive fallout) could be perfected. In view of the fact that the United States had built its defense posture upon a wide variety of nuclear weapons, it was clear that a decision on test suspension posed some exceedingly unpleasant choices for officials engaged in foreign policy formulation.

In evaluating possible alternatives, the military analyst Hanson W. Baldwin summarized the arguments pro and con by saying that a suspension of tests could ease international tensions; possibly provide a first step toward disarmament; restore some initiative to the United States on the psychological warfare front, especially in Asia; and possibly limit the amount of radioactive material already in the atmosphere. From the American viewpoint, however, a test suspension would also impair the development program undertaken by the Atomic Energy Commission by breaking the program's momentum; interfere with the development of certain new "defensive" weapons already begun by the United States and prevent creation of "clean" nuclear weapons; "freeze" certain aspects of the current missile program, in which the USSR already had a clear lead in some categories; perhaps interrupt peacetime development of atomic power; and possibly "provide the form of arms-limitation

without the substance," thereby relaxing tensions to such a degree that NATO and other alliance systems would ultimately be impaired (**15**, August 24, 1958).

Global agitation in behalf of nuclear test suspension received new impetus when a UN-sponsored scientific study of the implications of radioactive fallout, released in the summer of 1958, sharply challenged the prevailing American view that testing carried out thus far and anticipated for the future entailed no noteworthy hazard for the human race. Admitting that there were great areas of scientific ignorance about the *precise* consequences of exposure to radiation, the study nevertheless reported that the *verifiable* consequences were injurious to life. It predicted that from 2,500 to 100,000 babies would be born with genetic defects attributable to nuclear testing already carried out; it also predicted that from 400 to 2,000 leukemia cases would develop from such testing. It emphasized that the damage from testing varies widely throughout the earth, depending upon wind currents, rainfall patterns, dietary habits, and numerous other factors. For example, the highly dangerous radioactive element, strontium-90, is assimilated into the human body (predominantly in bone tissue) in place of calcium. Societies which rely upon calcium-rich diets are therefore in much greater danger than those which do not. Rice is an even richer source of calcium than milk. This is one reason why nations like India, Japan, and others in the Afro-Asian bloc, are peculiarly sensitive about the dangers inherent in continued nuclear weapons testing. In general, the UN report re-affirmed what many countries were saying about the entirely too optimistic conclusions emanating from the American Atomic Energy Commission about the consequences of further testing (**14**, August 11, 1958; **15**, August 17, 1958). Voluntary and well-dramatized Soviet suspension of nuclear weapons testing from time to time provided still further impetus for world public opinion to demand curtailment of nuclear experiments.

In response to this demand, scientific groups representing countries advanced in nuclear technology, began to study the feasibility of international inspection and control over nuclear weapons testing. By August 1958, the scientists had concluded that test inspection and control was feasible. Diplomatic discussions then ensued on establishment of a worldwide monitoring system for detecting explosions. The great powers were in accord that an acceptable monitoring system was possible and that it could be operated with reasonable assurance of success. They differed on the details. (14, September 12, 1958). A system of inspection and control for nuclear weapons testing unlike other inspection systems proposed in prior years would be largely "self-enforcing". Its ability to detect violations depended upon delicate scientific instruments already possessed by advanced industrial nations. To a minimum degree, therefore, it would be forced to rely upon pledges of voluntary compliance with the demands of an inspection plan and expressions of good intentions by the great powers. On the problem of *control*, however—the steps to be taken in case violations actually occurred—there was little unanimity. Presumably, if widespread violations took place, the plan for regulation of nuclear weapons would simply be abandoned.

Representation in Disarmament Negotiations

Toward the end of the 1950's the quest for arms-reduction was further complicated by disagreements about the nations to be "represented" in negotiations, and the relative influence of great and small powers. Two developments in the late 1950's brought these problems sharply to the fore. Throughout the greater part of the postwar period, disarmament negotiations had been carried on in the Disarmament Commission of the United Nations. After 1957, however, the USSR "boycotted" this organ, ostensibly on the ground that the communist bloc did not enjoy "parity" with the West in the determination of the commission's membership. Partially for this reason, disarmament negotiations were then shifted away from the UN to Geneva, where confidential deliberations took place over ensuing months. Here, as we have already noted, the great powers made some progress toward establishing an experimental "arms-free test zone," to be supervised by an international inspectorate. Substantial agreement was also reached on a moratorium on nuclear weapons testing. By the end of 1959 the great powers had decided that implementation of these and other steps that might be agreed to would be under the control of a ten-nation body, consisting of themselves and other designated countries—but containing none of the "neutralist" nations. This understanding largely met the Soviet objection about lack of "parity," but it aroused considerable resentment among nations not aligned with either power bloc.

These nations—possessing a far greater voice in UN affairs than formerly because of the emergence of the General Assembly as the dominant organ—demanded expanded representation in disarmament negotiations and in carrying out any plan reached. The small nations were spearheading a movement aimed at having a thorough review by the Assembly of any disarmament scheme formulated "outside" the United Nations—even at the risk that extended UN debate might imperil understandings carefully worked out in the sessions at Geneva. In part, this demand grew out of a heightened awareness on the part of lesser powers that, even though they did not possess impressive military forces, the nature of modern warfare jeopardized their existence no less than the existence of military giants. Accordingly, they reasoned that they ought to have a more decisive voice than formerly in preventing war.

Would the problem of "representation" cast a pale over further progress among the great powers on disarmament issues? Would Washington, Moscow, London, and Paris be willing to accord countries like Ceylon and Ghana greater influence in disposing of armed forces on both sides of the Iron Curtain? Would intrusion by the small countries into the sphere of disarmament negotiations perhaps weaken the overall influence of the United Nations in dealing with the issue? The implications of these developments for the future could not be fully assessed. It was clear, however, that American policy-makers and their counterparts in other powerful countries would be compelled to evolve reasonably satisfactory answers if further progress toward disarmament was to be achieved.

Disarmament—Retrospect and Prospect

What have innumerable and frequently highly technical disarmament negotiations carried on since World War II actually accomplished? In view of the inordinate complexity of the disarmament problem, and the great variety of relationships which exist among constituent parts of that problem, it may be well to recapitulate very briefly progress made to date.

Thus far, in spite of Soviet Russia's return to the concept of total disarmament in 1959, the great powers have concentrated upon partial disarmament in preference to comprehensive disarmament. Partial disarmament has been chosen out of widespread realization that more sweeping proposals have little or no chance of being universally accepted. Moreover, it seems widely conceded that experience gained in putting partial disarmament schemes into operation will provide statesmen with valuable lessons and will perhaps increase confidence that greater progress can be made.

No clearcut agreement has emerged on the always-controversial question of the relation of armaments to collateral political issues. Each side has tended to abandon an either-or position: Russia has expressed its willingness to relate such issues intimately to disarmament and perhaps to let negotiations over them proceed *concurrently* with reductions in weapons and manpower; America has expressed its willingness to take at least *limited* steps toward disarmament before or while political issues are being negotiated. A fundamental divergence is still discernible, however, in the weight accorded solution of political issues by each side. The free world continues to demand significant progress before embarking upon extensive arms-limitation programs; the communist world is willing to make some concessions, but demands that substantial arms-reduction come first.

Compromises have been made on staging also, with the position of neither the United States nor the Soviet Union as inflexible as it was during the 1940's. America has agreed to the principle that limited disarmament can take place before an effective inspection system is established, or perhaps while such a system is in the process of establishment. Nevertheless, the United States has made it clear that it wants to see early evidence of Soviet good faith before it proceeds very far with arms-reduction. The Soviet Union has modified its earlier insistent demand that the West agree to elimination of nuclear stockpiles and conventional weapons, and that it liquidate foreign bases, before an inspection-control system comes into being. It has accepted the idea in principle that inspection can be carried on within a specified geographical area *concurrently* with an actual reduction in armaments and that the powers of an inspection-control agency can grow apace with the lowering of arms levels. Recent Soviet statements on the question of inspection are, on the whole, less belligerently negative than they were during the 1940's and early 1950's. Yet, formidable differences on the question of staging remain to be overcome. American insistence that transition from stage to stage be certified by an international agency unhampered by veto, and Soviet insistence that certification be by each country or by an agency under the Security Council's auspices, seem almost as irreconcilable as ever. The same can be said about the matter of control. No consensus has emerged concerning what measures ought to be taken, and by whom, against violators of an international arms-limitation agreement.

Both sides have apparently accepted the view that conventional armaments and nuclear armaments are intimately tied together and that genuine disarmament requires that they be so approached. There is near agreement on the desirability of "ceilings" for great and small powers, though there is as yet no agreement on composition of military forces within those ceilings.

Inspection and control, as we have already suggested, is perhaps the most firmly embedded obstacle to agreement on disarmament. Some progress has been made. Each side has moved closer to the position of the other side —but it is still a long way from American insistence upon genuinely effective inspection-control and Soviet insistence upon preserving the "sovereignty" of nations by curtailing the activities of an international inspectorate, perhaps to the point that its powers could become nil. The most heartening development on this issue is the apparent interest expressed by both sides in launching some kind of experimental plan whereby an inspectorate would gain experience in supervising an "arms-free zone" in an area like the Arctic or Europe. Implementation of such a plan could go far toward clarifying the actual problems an inspectorate would encounter with disarmament schemes on a larger scale.

The most noteworthy progress in curtailing the manufacture of weapons has come in the realm of nuclear weapons testing. No formal international agreement has been reached, but in response to world public opinion the great powers seem to have reached a *de facto* agreement to suspend tests for long periods and to regulate more carefully the conditions under which testing takes place. The prospects for a formal agreement in this matter are perhaps more favorable than for any other agreement relating to disarmament.

There are two other disarmament issues on which there is as yet no consensus and which have received little more than passing attention by diplomats seeking agreements on arms-reduction. One is the role of the second greatest land power on earth—Communist China—in any proposed disarmament scheme. Thus far, the United States has refused to consider the possibility of including Red China in deliberations on arms-reductions, a fact which is bound to raise a substantial question about the degree to which genuine disarmament can ever be achieved. As Senator Hubert Humphrey (Democrat of Minnesota) declared on February 28, 1958, "I think you can go on with the first step, but ultimately, this whole problem of China, this great land mass with approximately 700 million people must be brought within the scope of some kind of agreement that is going to protect the security of the United States. I cannot imagine anybody wanting our great Nation to be disarmed and have Red China an armed mass . . . " (20, Part 14, p. 1358). The other problem relates to the control of outer space for peaceful purposes. The United States has proposed that this question be included in disarmament discussions; but to date this request has received nothing more than perfunctory attention.

3. "ATOMS-FOR-PEACE"

With monotonous regularity, diplomats from the great powers plowed their way through highly technical disarmament proposals over the course of the postwar period, only to leave the disarmament impasse largely unresolved. The seeming futility of these negotiations contrasted with the growing determination of statesmen from countries with advanced levels of nuclear technology to make its benefits available to mankind. If scientific knowledge and technical skill could not be diverted from military to peacetime uses, then progress in the latter sphere perhaps could at least keep pace with the steady accretion in stockpiles of nuclear weapons.

Momentum for more rapid strides in making the benefits of nuclear advances available for human betterment instead of human destruction was supplied by the incessant demands of underdeveloped countries. More and more, it looked as though the nuclear "balance of terror" was leaving the West in a vulnerable position in terms of competing with the communist bloc on the economic-psychological warfare front.

These and other factors compelled the United States to re-examine its hitherto stringent policy against release of information about nuclear technology until a workable disarmament agreement could be negotiated. Legislation in the early postwar period had prohibited any significant exchange of nuclear information between the United States and other countries. This policy was more and more alienating the nation's friends in the international community. As the country which professed lofty ideals for international conduct, the United States was expected to find some way of making the benefits of the nuclear age available to the world community, even in the absence of agreement on disarmament, especially when nuclear power seemed—as events have revealed, in most instances erroneously—to be "the answer" to the economic needs of the underdeveloped countries.

The Atoms-For-Peace Proposal

Briefly, this was the background against which President Eisenhower on December 8, 1953, made what was widely interpreted as one of the most imaginative suggestions advanced by the United States in the postwar period. This was the "Atoms-For-Peace" plan, in which the President outlined steps which might be taken under the United Nations to extend the benefits of nuclear technology to all countries (4, II, pp. 2798-2805). Apart from the belief that the President's proposal would have wide appeal and utility for the underdeveloped regions, Eisenhower's speech scored at least a temporary victory for the United States on the propaganda front by undercutting what was up to that time a highly successful communist propaganda offensive depicting Uncle Sam as animated by "atomic imperialism" and determined to deprive other countries of the benefits of nuclear technology by clinging doggedly to a policy of "atomic secrecy." Within the UN, the initial response to the President's plan was instantaneous and, almost without exception, favorable (11, pp. 16-17).

Unfortunately, several months passed before the atoms-for-peace proposal began to take concrete form. Within the United States, the President faced formidable opposition from isolationist legislators and from those who feared to divulge nuclear information to other countries. Having recognized the President's statesmanlike act, underdeveloped nations waited impatiently for the details of his plan. In explanation, Washington replied that the President envisioned that atoms-for-peace would be a UN-sponsored undertaking in which *all* the great powers would share and that so far the Kremlin had given no indication of supporting the plan. Finally, late in 1954, the Administration announced that it would contribute to atoms-for-peace even if the USSR failed to participate; within a few days, the Kremlin announced that it, too, would contribute its resources to the plan (11, p. 16-18).

Thus far, however, atoms-for-peace amounted to nothing more than a *plan*. And it largely remained so until November 15, 1954, when the American Representative to the United Nations, Mr. Lodge, again electrified public opinion by announcing that the United States was prepared to make available one hundred kilograms of fissionable material—the equivalent of one atomic bomb—under the atoms-for-peace proposal. This move once more restored the propaganda advantage to the United States by revealing that Washington was prepared to *act*, as well as to propose, for the sake of launching peacetime atomic development.

The International Atomic Energy Agency

Ever since the President's speech in 1953, negotiations had been carried on to create an international agency to operate and supervise the atoms-for-peace proposal. Negotiations were prolonged and exceedingly technical, but finally a draft agreement was drawn up and signed at a conference held at UN Headquarters from September 20 to October 26, 1956. Signatories were the USSR, Great Britain, France, the United States, and eight lesser powers (23, p. 2). On June 18, 1957, after lengthy committee consideration and floor debate, the Senate by a vote of 67-19 ratified the treaty establishing the International Atomic Energy Agency. In response to prevalent fears that national security might someday be imperilled by American membership in IAEA, the Senate appended a reservation to the effect that if the treaty were ever amended in a manner unacceptable to the Senate, then the United States would be required to withdraw from the agency (25, 1957, pp. 81-2).

The highest governing body of the IAEA is the General Conference, consisting of one representative from each member-state. The Conference meets annually or more often if necessary. The Board of Governors carries on the day-by-day activities of the agency; its members are chosen by a complicated formula to assure majority control by countries in the forefront of nuclear development (23, pp. 4-5).

The treaty establishing IAEA specifies that the transmission of nuclear information to it by member-states is purely *voluntary;* information acquired by the agency, as a result of assistance to members, however, must be shared with all member-states. Members agree to notify the agency concerning the quantity and quality of fissionable materials they are prepared—in conformity with regulations laid down in their own domestic law—to make available under the atoms-for-peace agreement. After studying the treaty's provisions, the Senate Foreign Relations Committee concluded that "Contributions are on a completely voluntary basis. Members are free to supply or to withhold materials, or to make available such quantities as they deem advisable, and on such terms as are agreed with the Agency . . . " (23, p. 6).

The Committee's report continues that the heart of the treaty is Article XII, "which contemplates a system of safeguards and security to prevent materials and facilities furnished for a particular project by the Agency from being diverted to a military use, and to require observance of any health and safety standards prescribed by the Agency" (23, p. 7). Under the treaty, IAEA possesses the right to examine and approve equipment and reactors used under its auspices by member-states, to require strict accounting for all fissionable materials granted to members, to demand project reports, and to demand return to the agency of any excess fissionable materials produced or reserved by member-states. The agency may employ inspectors to verify compliance with its regulations and to report any suspected diversion of fissionable materials for military use. Reports of suspected non-compliance are made to the Board of Governors and to the General Conference; ultimately, the UN Security Council and General Assembly are notified. If a state fails to take corrective measures after a finding of non-compliance has been made, it is denied further participation in the atoms-for-peace plan and, in case of flagrant wrongdoing, it may be suspended from membership (23, pp. 7-8).

As is apparent, the atoms-for-peace program thus has lasting implications for the corollary field of disarmament. The agency's inspection-control powers are far from iron-clad; they probably are not sufficient to prevent a country from violating the agreement at least the *first* time. Thereafter, of course, that country would be denied any further participation in the benefits of the atoms-for-peace proposal. According to Secretary of State Dulles, conformity derives essentially from two forces: the reluct-

ance of countries to cut themselves off from any further benefits of the plan for the sake of a temporary and probably indecisive advantage in nuclear weapons; and the moral suasion which would be exercised against such a country by the rest of the world. While there is always the risk that a country can violate the agreement, there is, in the words of one American official, "no possible way to prevent peaceful atoms from being perverted to warlike purposes if someone wants war badly enough. . . . But if we are going to live in the atomic age, we have to take the risks that are normal to that age" (11, p. 19). The most significant thing about the inspection-control system set up under the atoms-for-peace agreement then is not that this system is foolproof; it obviously is not. Rather it is that in establishing the system at all, the great powers were willing to take a step based upon faith and, before abandoning the search for a mutually acceptable inspection-control system, to test whether one based very largely upon voluntary compliance and self-interest can be made to work. If experience reveals that the step was justified, then this fact will unquestionably have an enormous impact upon companion movements in the disarmament field.

Atoms-For-Peace and the Future

No definitive judgments about the atoms-for-peace plan are possible. At this stage, very little can be said except that establishment of the International Atomic Energy Agency represented a heartening step forward and that, in the months following, the prospects seemed bright that it was going to function in the way its sponsors had anticipated. The global demand for its services in no way diminished; there appeared to be no insuperable barriers to its operation.

Yet by the early 1960's it was also apparent that some of the luster had worn off the atoms-for-peace plan because of widespread realization that nuclear energy was not the panacea it had been widely believed to be, particularly by underdeveloped countries. Development of peacetime nuclear power was a case of "to him that hath shall be given. . . . " Immediate and widespread use of nuclear power demanded the prior existence of a reasonably high level of industrial technology and scientific knowledge. Nations which lacked these elements were not likely to possess either the resources or the know-how, and possibly not even the demand, which would rapidly usher in the "nuclear age" and make it an era of unparalleled material advancement. Nuclear energy, after all, was but the *final* stage of a long evolutionary process which began in the West with the Industrial Revolution. It was, so to speak, the climax of that movement. It was not likely, therefore, that nations could jump from primitive economic levels, often based upon depressed conditions of agriculture, into the atomic utopia. Advanced nuclear technology demanded rapid parallel progress in all phases of industrial development (15, September 7, 1958, dispatch by John W. Finney).

That the most rapid progress toward the application of peacetime nuclear energy was apt to occur in countries which were already highly advanced industrially was born out by subsequent events. On January 1, 1958, six nations—France, Western Germany, Italy, Belgium, the Netherlands, and Luxembourg—joined in establishing the European Atomic Energy Community, popularly called *Euratom*. Euratom was designed to promote the peaceful uses of nuclear power for its members. Unlike the American Atomic Energy Commission, it has no interest in the development of atomic weapons, leaving it to individual countries—the principal one in Europe being France—to develop their own nuclear military technology (13, pp. 1-2). In common with many other institutions witnessed in postwar Europe, Euratom is essentially a body for promoting voluntary collaboration by its members in the solution of common problems (13, p. 3). It is based upon mutual self-interest. Ben T. Moore has called it a "first attempt to enact community legislation on nuclear problems" (13, p. 4).

Euratom sponsors research and development among its members, facilitates the exchange of technology, develops a "common market" for fissionable products, sponsors studies and regulations to assure safety and good health, facilitates investment in the nuclear energy field,

and is the focal point of relations between its members and outside countries touching nuclear problems (13, *passim*). Among the more specific goals of Euratom is reducing Western Europe's dependence upon Middle Eastern oil supplies. Success in this direction could go far toward reorienting Europe's political relationships with the strife-torn Middle East (13, pp. 33-34).

There has been impressive progress in breaking down barriers of nationalism in the field of scientific exchange on problems of nuclear energy. At international scientific conferences on the subject held in 1955 and 1958 there was a remarkably free exchange of information about problems of harnessing the atom for mankind's welfare. The conference in 1958 predicted that nuclear electric power generation would become competitive with existing methods by the 1960's in Europe and the 1970's in areas of "higher cost" like the United States and the USSR. Widespread use of atomic power in more backward countries, in the view of most scientists, would require an even longer period. Atomic energy would first have to be produced more economically and in forms—such as small reactors—which were usable in such countries. In one area however—the use of radio-isotopes in fields like medicine, industry, and agriculture—the nuclear age had already provided immeasurable good to mankind. And on the horizon lay the possibility of "controlled" thermonuclear reactions for the production of usable energy. If such reactions could be controlled, then the oceans might provide the world with a virtually inexhaustible source of fuel (15, September 7, 1958, Dispatch by John W. Finney).

Science has proved that the atom can be made to yield vast riches for the human race. Plans have been put into execution for sharing nuclear technology among all nations. How far mankind will ultimately benefit from these steps will depend of course upon the degree to which progress is achieved in dispelling the ever-present spectre of war, waged with new weapons capable of returning 20th century man to the Stone Age.

REFERENCES

1. British Information Service. "Disarmament," Text of a Speech by Foreign Minister Selwyn Lloyd on July 23, 1957. New York, July 26, 1957.

2. Cavers, David F. "The Challenge of Planning Arms Controls," *Foreign Affairs,* 34 (October, 1955), pp. 50-67. Explores many implications of the disarmament problem.

3. Claude, Inis L., Jr. *Swords into Plowshares.* New York: Random House, 1956. A provocative treatment of disarmament and other issues related to international security.

4. Department of State. *American Foreign Policy, 1950-1955.* (Publication No. 6446, "General Foreign Policy Series," 117). Washington: 1957. Volume II contains documentary material on the American position toward disarmament.

5. ———. *U. S. Participation in the UN, 1956,* et seq. (Publication no. 6577, "International Organization and Conference Series, III," 124). Washington: 1957. This series provides up-to-date data on the course of disarmament proceedings.

6. "Disarmament: The Continuing Quest for Agreement," *United Nations Review,* 3 (May, 1957), pp. 6-11. Analyzes the disarmament stalemate in terms of continuing issues causing the deadlock.

7. "Disarmament: Proposals and Negotiations, 1946-1955," *World Today,* 11 (August, 1955), pp. 334-48. Summarizes a decade's negotiations on disarmament.

8. Dulles, John Foster. "Disarmament and Peace," *Department of State Bulletin,* 37 (August 12, 1957), pp. 267-74. Discusses major differences in American and Soviet disarmament proposals.

9. Eagleton, Clyde, and Swift, Richard N. *Annual Review of United Nations Affairs, 1955-56,* et seq. New York: Oceana Publications, 1957. This series is a valuable source for tracing out disarmament negotiations under the UN.

10. House Foreign Affairs Committee. *Report on the Twelfth Session of the General Assembly of the United Nations,* 85th Congress, 2nd Session. Washington: 1958. Relationships between disarmament and other major global problems like foreign aid are forcefully brought out in this report.

11. Lear, John. "Ike and the Peaceful Atom," *Reporter,* 14 (January 12, 1956), pp. 11-21. Traces out the evolution of the atoms-for-peace plan under Eisenhower.

12. Martin, Andrew. *Collective Security.* Paris: UNESCO, 1952. A review and analysis of collective security and disarmament efforts under the League and the UN.

13. Moore, Ben T. *EURATOM: The American Interest in the European Atomic Energy Community.* New York: The Twentieth Century Fund, 1958. Discusses significant trends in the peaceful use of atomic energy as they affect Western Europe.

14. New York *Herald Tribune.*

15. *New York Times.*

16. Pratt, Julius W. *A History of United States Foreign Policy.* New York: Prentice-Hall, 1955. A valuable source for an overall view of America's approach to disarmament problems throughout history.

17. Senate Foreign Relations Committee. *A Decade of American Foreign Policy, 1940-49,* 81st Congress, 1st Session. Washington: 1950. Provides documentary material on the disarmament problem for the period covered.

18. ———. *Disarmament and Security: A Collection of Documents, 1919-1955.* Committee Print, 84th Congress, 2nd Session. Washington: 1956. Documentary materials covering disarmament in both the League period and the UN period.

19. ———. *Hearings on the Control and Reduction of Armaments.* Part 4. 84th Congress, 2nd Session, March 15, 1956. Washington: 1956.

20. ———. *Hearings on the Control and Reduction of Armaments.* Part 14. 85th Congress, 2nd Session, February 28, 1958. Washington: 1958. Hearings on the disarmament problem, conducted periodically by the Committee, contain valuable information on various aspects of that problem.

21. ———. Staff Study No. 3. *Control and Reduction of Armaments: A Decade of Negotiations, 1946-1956.* 84th Congress, 2nd Session. Washington: 1956.

22. ———. Staff Study No. 8. *Control and Reduction of Armaments: Attitude of Soviet Leaders toward Disarmament.* 85th Congress, 1st Session. Washington: 1957. These two studies of major issues associated with disarmament are part of a continuing series undertaken by the committee. The entire series illuminates many facets of the thorny disarmament controversy.

23. ———. *Statute of the International Atomic Energy Agency.* 85th Congress, 1st Session. Washington: 1957. Traces out the atoms-for-peace plan, culminating in the IAEA.

24. Shotwell, James T., and Salvin, Marina. *Lessons on Security and Disarmament from the History of the League of Nations.* New York: King's Crown Press, 1949. Provides valuable background for understanding the contemporary disarmament problem.

25. *United States in World Affairs, 1945-1946,* et seq. New York: Harper and Brothers, 1947.

Affords up-to-date information on the course of disarmament negotiations, with emphasis upon America's role.

26. Walters, F. P. A *History of the League of Nations.* London: Oxford University Press, 1952. An authoritative study of the League's efforts in disarmament.

CHAPTER 18

The Guiding Principles of American Foreign Policy

After reflecting upon the course of international affairs since World War I, a penetrating observer of Western society, Walter Lippmann, concluded that " . . . There is a deep disorder in our society which comes not from the machinations of our enemies and from the adversities of the human condition but from within ourselves" (14, p. 5). He found symptoms of this "deep disorder" in the people's "incapacity to cope with reality, to govern their affairs, to defend their vital interests and, it might be, to insure their survival as free and democratic states . . . " (14, p. 6). In his judgment "there was nothing to show that the Western democratic governments were in control of their affairs and capable of making the necessary decisions. They were reacting to events and they were not governing them" (14, p. 4).

Among competent students of international affairs a conviction has been growing that conduct in the sphere of foreign relations is substantially determined by the philosophical frame of reference within which a society operates in evaluating developments on the world scene and out of which the nation's responses to these developments are derived. Judgments at any given time in history about how a country's foreign policy *is* being conducted and

what *is* being accomplished, necessarily presuppose a prior conception of how foreign policy *ought* to be conducted and what it ideally *ought* to accomplish. Otherwise, foreign policy degenerates into a series of irrational, episodic responses to problems in the outside world. If a society fails to evolve some conception of what is *normative* in its approach to external issues, or fails to adhere to this conception, then its policies toward specific issues and problems are bound to reflect this neglect.

The question of the fundamental guiding principles of American foreign policy has engaged the attention of a host of commentators in recent years. For it has been most especially in this realm—failure to evolve and adhere to a reasonably consistent "philosophy of foreign relations"—that some of the greatest deficiencies in American foreign policy in the modern period have been most glaringly revealed. Americans are unphilosophical and unspeculative by nature. They are far more interested in devising plans for *carrying out* some project in foreign affairs designed to meet a specific challenge than they are in asking themselves *why* the challenge ought to be met in the first place, *why* some policies would meet it better than others, and above all, what the cumulative impact of a series of pragmatic decisions taken over an extended period of time in foreign relations is likely to be in terms of establishing a *discernible pattern* in the nation's approach to the outside world. The nation's diplomatic fortunes might greatly benefit from widespread, sober consideration by the citizenry of the basic principles which *ought* to animate the nation's diplomacy. This is the subject to which we direct our attention in this final chapter.

1. THE POSTWAR RE–EXAMINATION OF AMERICAN POLICY

The Need for Re-examination

More than any previous age in American history, the period since World War II has witnessed a continuing and searching re-examination of the underlying tenets of the nation's foreign policy. This re-examination has been spear-headed by a group of self-styled "realists," whose viewpoints are represented most pointedly in the writings of Professor Hans J. Morgenthau of the University of Chi-

cago; Mr. George F. Kennan, former State Department official and recognized authority on the Soviet Union; and to a lesser extent by Mr. Walter Lippmann, one of the nation's leading journalists and commentators on American society; Mr. Hanson W. Baldwin, military analyst for the *New York Times;* and Professor Robert Strausz-Hupé of the University of Pennsylvania.

The "realist" approach has been sharply challenged by another school of writers who, for want of a better term, might be somewhat inaccurately characterized as "idealists." By and large, these writers have tended to reiterate traditional foreign policy principles, especially as they were expressed by President Woodrow Wilson, Secretary of State Cordell Hull, and President Franklin D. Roosevelt. Because these principles have been discussed extensively in earlier chapters of our study, in this chapter we shall concentrate primarily upon the "realist" challenge. Leading proponents of the "idealist" position have been Frank Tannenbaum, an authority on Latin America; former American Ambassador to India, Chester Bowles; the leading theologian Reinhold Niebuhr; Thomas I. Cook and Malcolm Moos of the Johns Hopkins University; and the well-known diplomatic historian, Dexter Perkins.[*]

While there are admitted differences among the "realists" concerning selected aspects of American foreign relations, most of them have placed strong emphasis on the frequent disparity between what the United States has *tried* to accomplish in foreign relations and what it has actually accomplished. They have found the gap between high hopes and disappointing

PERILS OF THE STANDARD BEARER

Haynie in the *Greensboro Daily News*, May 15, 1958.

[*]Fuller acquaintance with the viewpoints of each school may be gained by consulting the following: 1; 3; 4; 5; 7; 8; 11; 13; 14; 15; 16; 19; 20; 21; 22; 23; 24; 25; 27; 33; 34; 35.

results to be a recurrent, almost an ingrained, feature of America's relationships with the outside world. Closely associated with this problem is a second: the pendulum-like oscillations in American public opinion between energetic, passionate attempts to remake the world and periods of cynicism and disillusionment toward events in the external realm. "Realists" have endeavored both to explain this phenomenon and to emphasize its consequences for national security.

Third, the "realists" have been particularly conscious of the *relationship between ends and means in foreign affairs*. This has led them to emphasize and re-emphasize what is surely the key concept of politics—*power*. They have cited instance after instance in which America, whose citizens remain curiously indifferent to the centrality of power, had what Walter Lippmann describes as a "bankrupt" foreign policy. American statesmen lacked or were unwilling to use the power necessary to protect diplomatic commitments and safeguard American security. "Realists" have found in this imbalance between the goals of foreign policy and the means necessary to achieve them another problem which appears well-nigh inherent in the American approach to foreign relations.

Fourth, the "realists" have emphasized what may well be in some respects the parent-problem of all those alluded to above: sharp differences between the way Americans visualize events in the outside world and the actualities of international politics. It is widely conceded by well-informed students of American foreign policy that the wholesale existence of stereotypes, sacred cows, utopian images, vast areas of ignorance, and substantial apathy in the public mind seriously interfere with the formulation and execution of sound foreign policy decisions.

In brief, the re-examinists have summoned the nation to take a critical look at itself and its propensities in the realm of foreign relations. They have sought to lead the nation back to first principles, to help it develop a clear sense of purpose, to evolve guiding principles which will enable it to meet challenges in the external environment by something more than a pattern of expediential responses to outside pressures. In seeking to surmount what is

often a *de facto* approach based upon "one problem at a time," the re-examinists are rendering an invaluable service to national, and ultimately perhaps to international, security.

To lend as much concreteness as possible to our consideration of the viewpoints of the re-examinists, let us concentrate primarily on the writings of Professor Hans J. Morgenthau and secondarily on the writings of other leading figures in this movement.

"National Interest"—The Pole Star of Diplomacy

No task is more urgently needed to assure success in the foreign policy field, according to Professor Morgenthau, than to "relearn the great principles of statecraft which guided the path of the republic in the first decade and—in moralistic disguise—in the first century of its existence" (21, p. 833). Among these principles highest priority must be given to a realization that the United States has acted "on the international scene, as all nations must, in power-political terms; we have tended to conceive of our actions in non-political, moralistic terms" (21, p. 836). However much it may have been concealed by heavy encrustations of moralism and legalism, the underlying reality behind America's historic policies toward Europe, Asia, and Latin America down to World War I was maintenance of the balance of power. In the Western Hemisphere specifically, American policy, as epitomized by its most famous foreign policy principle, the Monroe Doctrine and its numerous corollaries, was aimed primarily at preserving "the unique position of the United States as a predominant power without rival" (21, p. 844). American policy toward Europe sought to prevent "the development of conditions . . . which would be conducive to a European nation's interference in the affairs of the Western Hemisphere or to a direct attack upon the United States" (21, p. 844). A threat to American security would arise "if a European nation had gained such predominance that it could afford to look across the sea for conquest without fear of being menaced at the center of its power, that is, in Europe itself" (21, p. 835). America's historic diplomatic goals toward Asia were never so explicitly delineated and understood; moreover, they were subjected to moralistic influences in a measure from which the European and hemispheric policies were largely free. Yet principles, like the Open Door policy, which have been present in America's historic relations with Asia at least suggested the nation's concern with the balance of power concept (21, pp. 834-35).

From about 1900 onward, however, this fundamental objective of policy—preserving the balance of power—came to be neglected by the United States. Instead, foreign policy, in Morgenthau's words, became "either improvisation in the face of an urgent problem . . . or —and especially in our century—the invocation of some abstract moral principle in the image of which the world was to be made over" (21, pp. 833-34). George Kennan has made essentially the same point: " . . . I see the most serious fault of our past policy formulation to lie in something that I might call the legalistic-moralistic approach to international problems. This approach runs like a red skein through our foreign policy of the last fifty years" (13, p. 93). Woodrow Wilson personified the new approach to foreign relations; it was epitomized by such World War I slogans as "the war to end wars" and "the war to make the world safe for democracy" and by resounding principles like "self-determination," "freedom of the seas," "collective security," and "non-interventionism." Concurrently, the legalistic-moralistic approach dictated renewed diplomatic activities in areas like arbitration, disarmament, pacts to outlaw war, and pious declarations like the "Stimson Doctrine" (1932) withholding American "recognition" of territorial changes brought about in the Orient by military force. Permeating these activities, George Kennan has stated, was a firm belief "that it should be possible to suppress the chaotic and dangerous aspirations of governments in the international field by the acceptance of some system of legal rules and restraints" (13, p. 94).

Wilson's cardinal error—and, in the judgment of the "realists" it was a cardinal one in terms of shaping the direction American policy was to take in the future—was his unwillingness to accept the centrality of power in international affairs, his naïve belief that power both could be, and would be, eliminated. On the level of operating policy, Wilson's fatal blunder was, in Morgenthau's words, that he did not seek "restoration of the European balance of power, traditional guarantor of American security." Instead, he substituted for "the concrete national interest of the United States the general postulate of a brave new world where the national interest of the United States, as that of all other nations, would disappear in a community of interests comprising mankind" (21, p. 849). This kind of thinking colored the American approach to foreign relations throughout subsequent decades and was in large measure responsible for the nearly disastrous neglect of national security during the 1930's.

As the United States was drawn into the vortex of World War II, basically the same error was committed that had been committed during and after World War I: the nation's diplomatic goals were expressed in resounding declarations of idealistic principles, typified by such documents as the Atlantic Charter proclaiming the "Four Freedoms"[*] and the UN Charter, which also expressed exalted goals toward which it was believed the international order was moving. The wartime demand for "unconditional surrender" was one of the most glaring examples of foreign policy being shaped in response to emotional-moralistic pressures, without any regard for the long-range politico-strategic interests of the nation. "The people wanted to be told," asserts Walter Lippmann, "that when this particular enemy had been forced to unconditional surrender, they would re-enter the golden age. This unique war would end all wars. This last war would make the world safe for democracy. This crusade would make the whole world a democracy" (14, p. 21). Hanson W. Baldwin has listed "unconditional surrender" among "the seven great mistakes of World War II" (1, passim). No action could have been more antithetical to the balance of power principle because, as events after the war confirmed, the total elimination of Germany and Japan and, to a lesser extent, Italy from the

---

[*]For the text of the Atlantic Charter and other wartime documents in the same vein, see 29, pp. 1-32. The four freedoms enunciated in the Charter were: freedom from want, freedom from fear, freedom of speech, and freedom of religion.

ranks of the great powers inevitably created a power vacuum in Europe and Asia. The existence of this vacuum was an open invitation to Soviet expansionism into these areas. And it was this expansionism primarily which triggered the cold war between the free world and the communist world.

For nearly half a century American foreign policy has been predominantly actuated by impulses arising out of Wilsonian idealism, whose basic goals were to usher in a new order of international society by abolishing power conflicts among hostile nation-states. It required more than a century after 1789 for legalism-moralism "to drown out the older notion that international politics is an unending struggle for power in which the interests of individual nations must necessarily be defined in terms of power" (**21**, p. 840). Once this transformation occurred, a basic confusion—founded upon the romantic premise that power conflicts could be eliminated from the international scene—entered into American foreign policy. What Strausz-Hupé calls "pernicious abstractions" took hold of the American mind (**34**, pp. 637-82, *passim*). A statesman who said he did not believe in power and the necessity for a balance of power, Morgenthau has written, was "like a scientist not believing in the law of gravity . . . " (**21**, p. 853). The alternative to power is not a "higher morality," as Wilsonians would have it, but it is "moral deterioration through either political failure or the fanaticism of political crusades . . . " (**21**, p. 854).

Acceptance of the concept of "national interest" as the pole star of foreign policy, Morgenthau contends, would lead to an admission that throughout most of American history (until the era of Wilsonian idealism) the nation's foreign policy was "hard headed and practical and at times ruthless." The American society's treatment of the Indians is cited as an example. If we are honest and realistic:

> We know that this is the way all nations act when their interests are at stake—so cruel, so faithless, so cunning. We know that the United States has refrained from seeking dominions beyond the seas not because it was more virtuous than other nations, but because it had the better part of a continent to colonize. (**19**, pp. 970-71),

To the oft-repeated charge that the concept of national interest is elusive and almost indefinable, the "realist" replies that it is comparable to other ideas, including such moralistic-legalistic concepts as "general welfare," "justice," and "freedom," whose precise content must be determined in the light of history and circumstances. In its most fundamental sense, national interest means self-preservation—the meaning which emerges most forcefully in time of war—and, even more specifically, the protection of the nation's territory (**19**, pp. 972-73). In peacetime, its exact connotations are admittedly more elusive; such forces as dominant personalities, public opinion, economic, sectional and minority interest groups, and the like, converge upon it and obscure its meaning (**19**, pp. 973-74). The realists' concept of national interest rests upon the assumption that there will be "continuous conflict and threat of war" among nations and that this must "be minimized through the continuous adjustment of conflicting interests by diplomatic action" (**19**, p. 978).

For the "realist" there is, and can be, no conflict between moral values on the one hand and national interest—what we might call "political morality"—on the other. Quite the contrary, Morgenthau asserts, "the antithesis between moral principles and the national interest is not only intellectually mistaken but also morally pernicious. A foreign policy derived from the national interest is in fact morally superior to a foreign policy inspired by universal moral principles" (**20**, pp. 38-9). "Realists" condemn the "moralizing approach to foreign policy" because "it is derived from a false antithesis between morality and power politics, thus arrogating to itself all moral values and placing the stigma of immorality upon the theory and practice of power politics" (**20**, p. 34).* As formulated by another advo-

___

*Policies based upon national interest, according to Morgenthau, are morally superior to those based upon supposedly universal moral principle because the latter derive from the former. Morgenthau finds a "profound and neglected truth" in observations of the 17th century British philosopher Thomas Hobbes that, in Morgenthau's words, "the state creates morality as well as law and that there is neither morality nor law outside the state. Universal moral principles, such as justice or equality, are capable of guiding political action only to the extent that they have been given concrete concate of the concept of "political morality," if power is defined as *"the capacity to effect results,"* then conflicts between different moral systems and values ("consciences-in-conflict") can "find no resolution save in compromise of power-claims" (32, pp. 693, 695; italics in original). George Kennan has made essentially the same point by saying that a great deficiency in the American approach to foreign relations has been "the carrying-over into the affairs of states of the concept of right and wrong, the assumption that state behavior is a fit subject for moral judgment" (13, p. 98).

Whether in domestic or foreign relations, according to the "realistic" conception, true morality consists of bringing rival national claims based on power into equilibrium, of achieving a "balance of power" which will hold these competing forces in check. Such a policy, in the words of T. V. Smith, makes possible the "progressive enlargement of compromise-areas" (32, p. 695). Or as Robert Strausz-Hupé has phrased it more concretely as a diplomatic goal, "The problem of U. S. foreign policy is the restoration of the balance of power in Europe and Asia" (33, p. 77). Such, in brief, are the significant elements in the "realistic" position concerning the guiding principles which ought to activate American foreign policy.

The Uses of "National Interest"

Advocates of a "realistic" approach to foreign policy problems have made a number of immensely valuable contributions to a more intelligent understanding of America's relations with the outside world and have identified

---

tent and have been related to political situations *by society*" (20, p. 34, italics inserted).

We shall evaluate the assumptions underlying "realism" later in the chapter. At this stage, however, it is worthwhile to point out that in deriving morality from the *nation state,* Morgenthau confuses two very basic ideas: the difference between the *nation state*—one of several possible political units—and *society itself.* It may be agreed, as Morgenthau contends, that morality is derived "by society;" this does not prove, however, that it is derived by society as it is organized along *national* lines. It could be, and before the dawn of the nation state was, derived from different political units. Morality, therefore, could continue to be derived "by society" and yet be identified with *supra-national* political organizations just as much as with national ones.

numerous weak spots in the armor of the nation's diplomacy. They have shown great skill in diagnosis, and, because correct diagnosis is usually the prerequisite to improvement in any sphere, have prepared the way for needed changes in the pattern of America's relationships with the outside world. Their contributions have been notably significant in the following specific ways.

First, the "realists" have directed their attack against one of the most conspicuous weaknesses of the American approach to foreign relations in the last half-century: the tendency to equate a resounding declaration of policy intentions with the actual realization of these intentions. As George Kennan wrote about the Open Door policy toward China:

> Neither the obvious lack of practical results, nor the disillusionment of [Secretary of State John] Hay and the other persons involved, nor our unwillingness to bolster the policy in any forceful way, nor our subsequent departure from it ourselves—none of these things succeeded in shaking in any way the established opinion of the American public that here, in this episode of the Open Door notes, a tremendous blow had been struck for the triumph of American principles in international society—an American blow for an American idea. (13, p. 41).

Basically the same observations might be made about Wilson's Fourteen Points, the Kellogg-Briand Pact outlawing war, official denunciations of aggressive dictators during the 1930's, the Atlantic Charter, the Charter of the United Nations, enunciation of the doctrine of containment in 1947, announcement of the Point Four program in 1949, proclamation of Dulles' doctrine of "massive retaliation" and veiled proposals suggesting the "liberation" of Eastern Europe under the Eisenhower Administration. In each instance, there was a greater or lesser tendency on the part of public opinion to believe that official proclamation of a stated goal was tantamount to achieving it.

Utopian expectations surrounding these steps have sooner or later bred a disillusionist reaction, conspicuous features of which were cynicism and indifference—translated in most cases into isolationism—toward events in the outside world. Within a comparatively brief time, Wilson's conception of a strife-free world had crumbled; the popular ecstasy which had supported the "war to end wars" gave way to a feeling of national disgust and bewilderment, translated into a willingness to "let Europe stew in its own juice." Similarly, after World War II, when the massive injection of American power into the conflict, coupled with enunciation and reiteration of idealistic goals like the "four freedoms" failed to assure a better life for countless millions in Asia or guarantee a stable international order, America demobilized and reduced its diplomatic commitments to a minimum. In this instance, the retreat into isolationism was short-lived. In response to progressively more ominous threats to national security, American diplomacy entered a new era which soon began to exhibit many of the earmarks of the First and Second World War periods. Out of their growing recognition of the menace posed by international communism and their stiffening determination to resist it, Americans came dangerously close to attributing all their vexatious problems in foreign affairs to the machinations of the Kremlin, just as they had attributed them to the Kaiser or Hitler or Tojo in earlier eras, and to believing that if only this root-source of their problems could somehow be "dealt with," then all their annoyances and challenges in the external realm would disappear.

The American society, as was emphasized in Chapter 2, is by nature optimistic, youthful, and supremely confident of its ability to solve human problems. Progress remains its watchword today as much as ever. Americans have almost limitless faith in their ability to bring forces in the internal and external environment into a socially beneficial equilibrium, much as a mechanic adjusts the engine of an automobile to achieve a smooth synchronization of all its parts. They have tended to believe—and this has been strikingly characteristic of their domestic "reform movements"—that righteous zeal is the universal solvent for society's problems; if problems are not dissolved by this solvent, then the answer is *more* righteous zeal, passionately applied! And, with all the evangelistic fervor characteristic of old-fashioned Gospel meetings, this is the way they have been inclined to attack thorny diplomatic problems. As a society which, on the whole, has experienced remarkably little difficulty in

evolving and maintaining a national consensus upon its guiding principles, America has projected its own experience onto the international scene. Its citizens have believed that once reasonable men were in general agreement about what ought to be done, and most especially after they had solemnly committed their agreement to paper, the process of advancing rapidly to a concrete solution was merely a matter of detail. Americans have exhibited very little psychological capacity to cope with a world in which other societies sometimes share neither America's *desire* for radical change nor its belief that such change is possible.

The "realist" position therefore provides a check against rampant utopianism in foreign affairs, against highly romanticized expectations regarding what America's active involvement in global issues can reasonably be expected to accomplish. Impressive as it is, American power is nonetheless *finite*. It cannot "make the world safe for democracy" or guarantee that vast multitudes throughout the world possess "freedom from want" as a kind of natural right. America's good intentions may know no bounds. Its *power* to effectuate these intentions however is often severely limited. In some instances it is virtually nil. Recognition of this fact, as the "realists" properly insist, will go far toward preventing the emergence of utopian hopes, followed by the disillusionment which inevitably sets in when these hopes are largely unfulfilled.

Closely related to this contribution is another for which students of foreign policy are indebted to the "realist" school of thought. This is the renewed focus on the all-important concept of power, as perhaps the key issue in politics, domestic and foreign. Political scientists are in wide agreement that power is the pivotal concept in the study of group relationships, both within states and among states. Power is ubiquitous and inescapable—save perhaps in the cemetery. It is therefore the omnipresent raw material of politics. In this sense, the term "power politics" is a tautology. Politics is by definition concerned with power—its nature, its control and regulation, its distribution and utilization by competing groups and states.

The "realists" are correct in insisting that an intelligent approach to international affairs can never overlook the centrality of power. In the two preceding chapters, on international organization and disarmament, it was emphasized how great nations have repeatedly approached questions in these fields on the basis of how their power positions are likely to be affected by contemplated decisions. Every nation admits the theoretical necessity for disarmament; practically, no nation is willing to take the steps required to achieve it, largely out of fear that its own power position will thereby be jeopardized.

Americans have not been reluctant to acknowledge the centrality of power considerations in the foreign policies of *other* nations. They have been much slower to recognize its importance in the foreign policy of their *own* country. They have been prone to conceive of power as an "Old World" concept which has no relevance for diplomatic conduct by the "New World." They have tended to believe that somehow they have transcended "power politics" and that their conduct is on a more altruistic-humanitarian plane than the conduct exhibited by other countries. The "realists" therefore offer a needed admonition against cant and hypocrisy by the United States in dealing with other nations. And their arguments caution that, in periods when Americans thought they were "rising above" power considerations, they were more often than not entering a diplomatic fantasyland, only to have power considerations ultimately thrust themselves upon the nation in a form which threatened its very existence.

In the third place, in their analysis of American foreign policy the "realists" have laid the foundations for the kind of diplomatic conduct which is indispensable to national security in the nuclear age: continuous, soberly-considered involvement in world affairs, as distinct from episodic involvement, characterized by alternating cycles of violent interventionism and sulky isolationism. The lesson which has been driven home painfully in the postwar period is that the vital interests of the nation require thoughtful assessment and protection at all times. The steady and rational application of moderate doses of American power can be ex-

pected to yield richer diplomatic dividends than dissipation of that power in ill-defined, emotionally-satisfying crusades.

Fourth, the "realists" have called attention to the connection between ends and means in foreign policy. Neglect of this relationship easily qualifies as one of the most serious deficiencies in American foreign policy since 1900. In critical instances, Americans have evinced minimum awareness that an approximate balance must be struck between the goals of foreign policy and the means available for reaching them. They have tended to err in one of two directions. As we have already observed, sometimes they have become preoccupied with goals to the almost total exclusion of the means required for their realization. At other times, America has confused what are essentially the *means* of foreign policy with *ends* of policy.

One example of the former tendency is acquisition of the Philippine Islands and other Pacific possessions before and after the Spanish-American War. These territorial acquisitions entailed new diplomatic commitments. Yet as time passed, Americans manifested no significant awareness that their own security was involved in Asian affairs as never before or that diplomatic astuteness demanded a corresponding re-allocation of national resources to protect these commitments (13, pp. 9-25; 2, pp. 463-79). These observations also apply to the Open Door policy, which, in Kennan's words, "was not a policy that in general had a future. . . . It was not a policy that we Americans cared enough about to support in any determined way or for the results of which, if implemented, we were prepared to accept any particular responsibility" (13, p. 40). An example from more recent experience is the policy of containment, the dominant goal of American foreign policy since 1947 toward the communist bloc. This policy—surely the most ambitious ever undertaken in peacetime throughout American history—has demanded, and will continue to demand, prodigious national efforts, vast sums of money, and unceasing diplomatic vigilance for its successful implementation. Yet it may be questioned whether the average American is even now fully cognizant of the price that must be paid in the years ahead to carry out a goal which enjoys overwhelming popular support.

Taking the means of policy for policy itself has been evident during and immediately after each major war in which the United States has been involved since 1900. The "realists" insist upon the validity of Clausewitz's famous dictum that war is but the continuation of policy by other means. War is not an end in itself; it solves no political problems. War is always undertaken in behalf of *political* goals and is resorted to when non-violent methods for protecting the diplomatic interests of nations have failed to accomplish this result. Victory in war can do nothing more than create the conditions within which diplomatic goals can be achieved. For this to occur, nations must possess a reasonably clear conception of their diplomatic goals and how they are to be realized by resort to war.

Neither in the First World War, nor in the Second, nor in the Korean War could it be said that the American people possessed a clear understanding of why the nation was at war, the political aims it hoped to accomplish by fighting, and the methods by which it hoped to accomplish them. For instance, much of the public agitation within the United States surrounding issues accompanying the Korean War stemmed from a deep-seated confusion in the public and even in the official mind over the precise "war aims" of the United States. Were they to unify Korea politically? To eliminate communism from the Korean peninsula and perhaps from the mainland of China itself? To "repel aggression" by driving the Communist forces north of the 38th parallel? Or were the nation's war aims some combination of these goals, or possibly some other goals? These questions were never answered explicitly so that no clear public consensus existed about them. The "realist" insists that, difficult as it may be, attempts to answer such questions are vital to diplomatic success. Diplomatic action undertaken in behalf of cloudy, ambivalent, and poorly thought-out goals can never be expected to produce satisfying results in the foreign policy field.

The most valuable contribution made by the "realists" to public thinking about global issues may well be their insistence that, in a world of power politics, differences among nations must be accommodated, harmonized, and compromised by the techniques of diplomacy. "Realists" warn against the belief that tensions among powerful states can be finally and forever "eliminated." No nation can expect to get its way on every issue dividing the world. Indiscriminate injection of "moral principle" into international disputes is likely to engender almost insoluble problems for the world community, because nations, especially *democratic* ones, find it well-nigh impossible "to compromise with principle." And where compromise is ruled out, the only method remaining for safeguarding diplomatic interests is war or perhaps cold war.

These admonitions are especially apt for the United States, which in the postwar period has come dangerously close to equating compromise with "appeasement." The very process of holding negotiations with the Russians, it is widely believed, is not only a waste of time but a sacrifice of vital principles. So militantly opposed are Americans to the main tenets of communist ideology that they are likely to reason that there exists no basis for accommodation with demands growing out of Russia's needs *as a state*. Yet if Russia, in common with all other countries, is actuated primarily by power considerations, this at least holds out the possibility that there does exist a common denominator upon which mutually satisfactory agreement might be achieved. This point possesses special pertinence in connection with the widely prevailing assumption that the Russians cannot be counted on to keep diplomatic agreements. George Kennan has replied by saying:

> They have their own interests, and I do not think that they practice deceit for the sake of practicing it. If you make an agreement with them which is in their interests, as they see it, and then see to it that it remains in their interest to observe, it will sometimes be observed. (**30**, Part II, p. 1008).

Mr. James P. Warburg makes essentially the same point when he declares:

> I submit that nations do not make agreements relying upon each other's good faith. They rely

upon each other's intelligent pursuit of self-interest. History shows that the international agreements most likely to be broken are precisely those which are negotiated by one side or the other from a "position of strength"—that is, under some degree of duress. On the other hand, the agreements most likely to be kept are those negotiated on a give-and-take basis from a position of mutually recognized equality.

The agreements which endure are those freely entered into because they serve the self-interest of both parties and thus become self-enforcing. That is the sort of agreement we must seek. (31, Part 4, p. 762).

Uncovering the basis for such agreements, and concluding settlements upon them, is surely among the most urgent diplomatic challenges in the mid-twentieth century.

2. TOWARD A PHILOSOPHY OF FOREIGN AFFAIRS

Valuable as they are in supplying correctives for widely acknowledged weaknesses in the American approach to foreign relations in the modern period, the arguments of the "realists" must be subjected to careful scrutiny before they are adopted *in toto* as the guiding principles of the nation's foreign policy. For these arguments possess far greater validity in the realm of specific diplomatic practice than they do in the realm of political philosophy. Their greatest poignancy derives from their description of *how nations actually behave* in the international community; their greatest weaknesses are manifested when they purport to explain either *how nations must or ought to behave*. At the level of value judgment and moral principle, realist arguments lose much of their appeal.

"National Interest" in the Mainstream of History

The starting point for a critical evaluation of the "realistic" philosophy of foreign relations is recognition that there is nothing intrinsically new or startling in the proposals made by writers like Hans J. Morgenthau, George F. Kennan, or Robert Strausz-Hupé. The "realism" advocated by such writers represents a philosophical atavism. Clear antecedents can be discerned in the writings of Niccolò Machiavelli (1469-1527), Francis Bacon (1561-1626), Thomas Hobbes (1588-1679), Johann Fichte (1762-1814), Georg W. Hegel (1770-1831), Heinrich von Treitschke (1834-1896), Friedrich W. Nietzsche (1844-1900), Karl Marx (1818-1883), Nikolai Lenin (1870-1924), and their twentieth century disciples. Obviously, it would be impossible in limited space to trace out the philosophical stream which has culminated in the "realistic" philosophy of today. So as to at least indicate something of the nature of this continuum, as well as to lay the basis for an evaluation of the "realistic" position, let us look briefly at the writings of one of the most famous and influential philosophers who ever lived: the Renaissance Florentine, Niccolò Machiavelli.* One reason for our selec-

---

*Students who wish to carry an evaluation of the "realistic" position further could do no better than to study this position in the light of classical political philosophy. Such a study would suggest numerous parallels and would indicate many of the difficulties besetting the realistic position in a much fuller way than is possible here.

My colleague, Professor Nelson E. Taylor, has warned against oversimplification in our treatment of Machiavelli. It ought to be emphasized that much of present-day "realism" is a reinterpretation of Machiavelli's thought in the light of writings by later philosophers, particularly Thomas Hobbes.

Cf. the following Hobbesian passages: " . . . I put for a general inclination of all mankind, a perpetual and restless desire of power after power, that ceaseth only in death. . . . kings, whose power is greatest, turn their endeavours to the assuring it at home by laws, or abroad by wars. . . . Competition of riches, honour, command, or other power, inclineth to contention, enmity, and war. . . . To this war of every man, against every man . . . nothing can be unjust. The notions of right and wrong, justice and injustice have there no place." And "so in states, and commonwealths [nations] not dependent on one another, every commonwealth . . . has an absolute liberty, to do what it shall judge . . . most conducing to their [sic.] benefit. But withal, they live in the condition of a perpetual war . . . " (26, pp. 63, 83, 140).

Cook and Moos associate the philosophical roots of present day "realism" with ideas current in Europe in the 19th century. Hegel "made the evolution of the state the growth of reason and the progressive achievement of God on earth. The state was the very embodiment of right." A Swiss philosopher, Johann Casper Bluntschli, equated the state with a living organism; humans were its cells! Heinrich von Treitschke emphasized the

THE GUIDING PRINCIPLES OF AMERICAN FOREIGN POLICY 495

tion of Machiavelli is that in Hutchison's words "the truth in Machiavelli is more apparent in 1950 than it was in 1850 or even 1900 to most Western readers (11, p. 86).

The problem engaging Machiavelli's attention within Italy was basically the same problem which has prevailed within the international community in modern history. This was how to create a system of law and order out of conditions of anarchy and political turmoil. With the decline of the two central authorities capable of maintaining order throughout Italy— the Holy Roman Empire and the Medieval Church—Machiavelli could foresee nothing but continued barbarism, bloodshed, and turbulence, as self-seeking groups pursued their own interests. And it was to this problem that Machiavelli addressed himself in his immortal classic, *The Prince*. His book was a plea for a powerful ruler to bring stability to the strife-torn Italian peninsula and a handbook telling him how it might be done.

Force, fraud, violence, duplicity, faithlessness, hypocrisy—none of these was excluded as methods to be employed by the prince. The prince ought to *appear* to act morally, but he could never afford the luxury of being animated predominantly by morality. Any methods were therefore legitimate for the prince so long as they achieved their intended result. From Machiavelli's pen the world received the most explicit formulation of the idea of *raison d'état*. Put in its simplest form, *raison d'état* meant that the actions of the state were exempt from the ordinary moral and ethical strictures applicable to the actions of individuals and groups *within* the state. In Ebenstein's words, Machiavelli "thus separates power from morality, ethics, religion, and metaphysics, and sets up the *state* as an *autonomous system of values*

necessity for the state to be strong, to dominate other states, to hold no scruples against imposition of its will by force. "National interest" was its watchword. "Other purposes were subordinate and instrumental, and the welfare of the nation's citizens was incidental. Politics was a matter of competition between nations. Their purpose was to maintain and increase their own power. . . . The relations of nation-states were a Hobbesian war of all against all . . ." (8, pp. 114-15).

Hutchison emphasizes the "secularization" of philosophy from the 18th century onward as a major tributary giving rise to present-day "realism" (11, pp. 92-6).

independent of any other source" (9, p. 280, italics in original).

In Machiavellian thought the actions of the states could not properly be categorized as "moral" or "immoral." The state's actions were *amoral* in that they could not be judged by the canons of a moral-ethical code. Morality was any action that enabled the prince to establish and perpetuate his power; his actions were morally condemnable to the degree that they failed to achieve this end.

Machiavelli is generally acknowledged as the first "scientific" philosopher known to history. The ideas expressed in *The Prince* and his other writing grew out of careful observation of human behavior. His reflections upon human conduct and his assessment of human nature—in which Machiavelli's cynicism and pessimism were only surpassed by his overriding desire to see political stability restored to his native land—stemmed from his own immersion in Italian life during the infamous age of Cesare and Lucrezia Borgia. Accordingly, his "scientific" characterization of the nature of mankind in general, on the basis of behavior he observed all around him, achieved a pinnacle in "realism." Writes Ebenstein: "If Machiavelli had painted, in medieval fashion, the devils who inhabit hell, his impact would have been much less intense on his contemporaries and on posterity. What Machiavelli did, however, was to portray something worse, real human beings . . ." (9, p. 280). And it was to provide insight for the ruler, who had to impose his authority over self-willed, power-seeking individuals, that Machiavelli wrote *The Prince*.

The Relevance of Philosophic Insight

The contemporary student of American foreign relations has but to make appropriate substitutions in the thought of writers like Machiavelli and many of his philosophical descendants to arrive at essentially the theory of political realism expounded today. If one substitutes the idea of "national interest" in its most elementary sense—self-preservation—for Machiavelli's goal of strong political authority in Italy, and projects Machiavelli's observations about power-motivated human behavior *within* states to the realm of *inter-state* relations, if one elevates the concept of *raison d'état* into the impulse which motivates nation-states in their relationships with each other, then Machiavelli's thought becomes practically indistinguishable from the philosophy of present-day "realists."

Accordingly, weaknesses inherent in Machiavelli's thought are also present in the thought of his contemporary imitators. Foremost among these perhaps is the assumption that value judgments about how human society *ought* to conduct itself can be derived from a study of empirical data showing how it has conducted itself throughout history. From observations of human conduct, present-day Machiavellians purport to have discovered scientific laws of statecraft, based upon the supposedly inherent nature of states. No one has attacked this view more cogently than Reinhold Niebuhr. According to one commentator, "Niebuhr's heaviest blow is his claim that the fatal sin to which realism is constantly tempted is to make that which is universal in human behavior normative as well" (**12**, pp. 172-73). Professor Morgenthau, for example, categorically asserts that all nations act "in power-political terms" (**21**, p. 836); that "politics is an unending struggle for power in which the interests of individual nations must necessarily be defined in terms of power" (**21**, p. 853); that a statesman who says he does not believe in the "balance of power" is comparable to "a scientist who says he does not believe in the law of gravity" (**21**, p. 853); and that "the national interest is . . . the last word in world politics" (**19**, p. 972).

Now such conclusions may be accepted as "scientific" insofar as evidence can be adduced for showing that they accurately describe the *actual* conduct of states. They are patently unscientific, however, in the very area in which they lay claim to the greatest scientific objectivity: as they purport to derive principles governing (1) what states *must* do and (2) what states *ought* to do, from empirical data. For it is in the area in which the highest scientific validity is asserted that conclusions are least amenable to scientific verifications. "Realists" maintain that states *ought* to do what they *must* do, because of their inherent domination by power impulses. Such a conception

completely ignores any explicit consideration of the *ends* for which states exist and the goals they may legitimately pursue in their relationship with each other. It postulates the survival of the states as an end in itself and makes that end the highest goal of statecraft. It neither raises nor answers the question of *why* the survival of the state itself is a desirable goal; much less does it discuss the value of this end in relation to other ends for which human society might strive. But in classical political thought, as typified especially by writers in the Judaeo-Christian tradition, it is precisely this question —how the state contributes to the ends of human society—which has been one of the most fundamental questions of political thought through the ages. Actually, under the guise of a "scientific" approach to the study of foreign policy, the operating assumption of the "realists"—the conception that pervades their entire philosophy—is that the power-seeking nation state in its 20th century manifestations represents the apex of political achievement and morality which man is capable of attaining. *Assuming* this to be true—and the assumption is a corner-stone of the philosophical structure erected by "realists"—any action taken by a nation to maintain and perpetuate its power is not only permissible, but becomes the quintessence of virtue and morality (**35**, pp. 161-65).*

---

*To be sure, Morgenthau and other "realists" acknowledge the theoretical possibility that other viable political units might evolve in history to take over at least some of the functions of the nation state, as suggested in the idea that "above the national societies there exists no international society so integrated as to be able to define for them the concrete meaning of justice or equality, as national societies do for their individual members." This being so, "In the absence of an integrated international society, the attainment of a modicum of order and realization of a minimum of moral values are predicated upon the existence of *national* communities capable of preserving order and realizing moral values within the limits of their power" (**20**, pp. 34, 38, italics inserted).

"Realists" therefore may acknowledge the possibility that political organizations above the nation state could emerge. But this admission has no significant place in their philosophy, as reflected in (1) their identification of true morality with pursuit of the *national* interest, (2) their deeply-entrenched pessimism about the likelihood of any international organization emerging to supersede the nation state or fundamentally modify its powers, and (3) the almost total absence in their

Now the shortcomings of such a philosophy are as apparent as they are far-reaching. The grave defect in such reasoning is that it involves a logical contradiction. If "realists" are correct that it is an unalterable quality of mankind's nature—a kind of political law of gravity —to elevate power to the top of the hierarchy among possible goals, then there is no intrinsic reason why present-day civilization—including one of its most characteristic institutions, the nation state itself—is to be preferred over past or future eras of history, with their characteristic institutions. "Realists" contend that institutions and policies are "good" or "bad" depending upon the degree to which they contribute to the acquisition and maintenance of power. The political unit that we call the nation state —the *raison d'être* of which is pursuit of power —thus possesses no superiority of its own; it is merely a convenient mechanism evolved by society in a certain historical era for channelling and directing the search for power. Conceivably, other mechanisms—including supranational authorities—can be, and in history have been, *more* convenient than the nation state for realizing power objectives. Acknowledging this to be true, we arrive at the paradox that the pursuit of power can lead statesmen to subordinate and limit the power of individual countries to that of mankind as a whole, as expressed in supra-national institutions resting upon a broad consensus in the international community. The continued pursuit of power thus can erode the principle of national interest, just as in earlier eras it eroded the concepts of "city state interests" or "feudal interests."

"Realists" cannot have it both ways. They cannot rationalize anything a nation might do to further its "national interest," by claiming that such steps are legitimate in the quest for power, and then contend on the other hand

philosophy of emphasis upon the means—not to speak of the need—for evolving supra-national institutions that would set limits to the power-seeking propensities of heavily armed nations. "Realists" are far more (one might even say exclusively) concerned with what foreign policy *is* than what it is capable of becoming, as reflected in Morgenthau's viewpoint that "Foreign policy, like all politics, is in its essence a struggle for power, waged by sovereign *nations* for *national* advantage" (**20**, p. 92, italics inserted).

that the pursuit of power *requires* a state to pursue national interest. They cannot apply purely expediential criteria to the conduct of *all* states and *all* political phenomena and then maintain that there is any inherent and paramount virtue in perpetuating only one particular species of political organization known to history—the nation state. Quite obviously there are times when limits upon the conduct of nation states are most conducive to achieving and maintaining power. According to a philosopher who epitomized *Realpolitik*, Thomas Hobbes, mankind left a state of nature—where life was "nasty, brutish, and short"—precisely because of his conviction that the untrammeled quest for power among unrestrained individuals endangered the security of society itself; self-preservation demanded that limits upon human conduct be imposed. It is not necessary to be Hobbesian to see the application of this idea to 20th century international relations. Unfettered addiction to power goals by heavily armed nation states can jeopardize the continued existence of the human race, thereby inevitably threatening the existence of individual nations that are a part of it. Attachment to a narrowly-conceived, egocentric "national interest," therefore, is one of the ways best calculated to endanger the ultimate security— the *continued* capacity to pursue power—of every nation, including those most animated by national interest. Conversely, a national interest that realizes the interdependence of nations, that concedes the common stake of all in mitigating power conflicts and eliminating certain kinds altogether, and that conceives policies reflecting this realization constitutes a far greater "realism" than is manifested by 20th century advocates of *Realpolitik*.

The philosophy of present-day "realism" manifests the same contradiction that stands at the heart of Marxist-Leninist-Stalinist thought. Marxist thought derisively rejects any "natural law" precepts or inviolable moral-ethical principles. Marxists claim—by arguments remarkably parallel both to those of Machiavelli and his latter-day imitators—that the strictures imposed upon human society by legal codes, norms, moral-ethical values, and the individual conscience, are nothing more than attempts by the bourgeoisie to rationalize its dominant power position, to perpetuate its control over the proletariat. But if it is inherent in the nature of the bourgeoisie to do these things —if strictures upon human conduct represent *merely* rationalizations of the power-seeking propensities of the dominant class in any historical era—then the bourgeoisie cannot logically be condemned for doing them. There is nothing ethically "wrong" with oppression of the proletariat, since Marxist philosophy tells us that there can exist no absolute concept of "right" and "wrong," that these concepts are themselves products of the "class struggle." Presumably, the bourgeoisie is free to eliminate the proletariat outright (superseding it someday perhaps with electronically-run machines), since this would only be condemnable if it *failed* to enhance the bourgeoisie's power position. The extent to which this action injured the proletariat would be irrelevant in determining its legitimacy.

As a matter of fact, we know that Marxists do *not* reason this way. They condemn the bourgeoisie precisely because its behavior injures the proletariat's welfare. Now the only possible ground for such inexcusable "value judgments" is the assumed existence of some kind of "proletarian ethic," which by Marxism's own dogma is "unscientific" because it postulates a standard of human conduct which has never existed, since the proletariat has not been in a position to dictate moral and ethical codes, laws, and other precepts of human conduct. The adherents of "scientific socialism" are thus the true utopians, in holding forth the image of a future society in which humans successfully abjure the ancient pattern of pursuing power, a pattern supposedly inherent in their nature. Ironically, it is this ultimate promise held out to mankind—that the human race in some communist Promised Land will behave as it has never behaved in the past— that imparts to Marxist thought much of its appeal as a global ideology.

A similar defect lies at the heart of Professor Morgenthau's elevation of the "national interest" into the guiding principle of statecraft and his equation of it with consummate political virtue. If states are inescapably propelled by power goals, if they "can't help" pursuing them above all other goals, then upon what basis

does *American* national interest, or that of any other country, become preferable to all other competing national interests? Except as it *fails* to enhance American power, why should American domination of weaker allies be condemned as a policy? Or why, with the same exception, should Soviet hegemony over Eastern Europe—or possibly even the world—be denounced? Upon what basis should other countries choose to side with America or Russia or other great powers, except upon a fine calculation of which is the most powerful? In short, what grounds exist for questioning the belief that the national interest of one country could perhaps best be achieved by totally subordinating the interests of all other countries to its control? When looked at in purely tactical terms, diplomatic experience amply confirms the fact that America has promoted its own national interest to the degree that it convinced other countries there *was* some relationship between America's well-being and theirs; and its diplomatic interests have been impaired on many occasions when other countries became convinced that exclusive pursuit of national interest by the United States resulted in policies that were inimical to *their* national interests.

Yet "realists" do not as a rule draw the extreme conclusion that unswerving pursuit of national interest by any one state can legitimately result in damage to the national interest of other states, perhaps to the point of calling into jeopardy their continued existence as nations. Instead, they cite the "balance of power" principle which will presumably hold competing national interests in some kind of an equilibrium. Professor Morgenthau equates the balance of power concept with the law of gravity. States pursue power, just as matter obeys the law of gravity. But this analogy is faulty in several particulars. First, if nations have no more choice in obeying political "laws" than matter has in obeying physical laws, then the debate over whether the United States *ought* to follow national interest or the balance of power principle is entirely academic: it *does* follow the principle inexorably. It cannot help doing so, any more than a weight can help falling to the ground when it is dropped. It would be entirely superfluous to admonish statesmen to obey a "law" which they cannot avoid obeying and which they obey all the time! And if this is true, then the question may legitimately be asked: why is it necessary for "realists" to call for a *return* to principles of statecraft that the nation has never left and by its nature is incapable of leaving? How did it happen that President Wilson, for example, led the nation into a diplomatic quagmire by refusing to pursue balance of power, when Wilson and all other leaders of nation states are presumably motivated by forces over which they have no control? And if they have no choice, then how can they be condemned for doing what they were irresistably driven to do?

An escape from this *reductio ad absurdum* is to admit that statesmen *do* have a choice about whether to elevate concepts like national interest and balance of power into dominant foreign policy goals. Once this admission is made then of course there is no real analogy with the law of gravity, for it is conceded that man is not merely physical matter that responds automatically to "laws" beyond his control. The inquiry that follows next is: *why* should statesmen choose national interest or balance of power over other possible goals? What are the criteria for selection? Assuming that choices in foreign affairs are made rationally (an assumption of course that is not always valid) there must exist, implicitly or explicitly, some standard for discriminating among competing goals. What are these standards and how are they derived? Discussion of this point necessarily involves us in a problem to which "realists" devote insufficient attention; and yet it is inextricably related to the question of why certain objectives in foreign affairs are to be preferred over others. This is the question of the *ends* for which political power is utilized and the relationship of means to the achievement of these ends. We shall have more to say about this question at a later stage. It must suffice to note here that "realists," no less than their philosophical adversaries, the "idealists," make certain assumptions about the ends to which political power is to be directed. More often than not, these assumptions are implicit in their thought, rather than explicitly elaborated. They are no less present, and no less crucial in shaping ultimate conclusions, because

"realists" assert that the student of international politics can approach this subject-matter on an "assumptionless" basis.

One final objection to the "realist" equation of diplomatic principles with laws in the physical realm may be noted briefly. Man realizes many of his fullest potentialities to the very degree that he discovers ways of freeing himself from limitations imposed by natural phenomena like the law of gravity. The air and space-age would not have become possible if the law of gravity had been accepted as the last word in natural science or in technology based upon science. At this point, Hutchison's remarks about man's nature seem apropos:

> We note . . . in morality and ethics a primary difference between man and the animals. The ends or aims of animal life appear to be given by nature. . . . Thus if my dog satisfies his needs for activity, food, sex, etc., he appears to have a good life. Man possesses a great many such needs. . . . But of any such aim or desire man may ask the question: *Ought* I to satisfy this need? Is it right or wrong? Such questions mark off and open up the field of morality. (11, p. 32, italics in original).

As regards foreign affairs, all that observations resting upon empirical data can tell statesmen is what nations *have* done in the past and how alternative courses of action can contribute to the realization of ends whose legitimacy must, in the last analysis, be tested by reference to something other than studies of how mankind has behaved in earlier eras. Machiavelli differed in this respect from many of his contemporary imitators: he possessed a compelling vision of a better life for his native Italy, a conception of what "might be" in his native-land, which he could not possibly have taken from the pattern of internecine strife he saw all around him. Power was *instrumental* for the realization of ends whose legitimacy Machiavelli took for granted.

But this conception is totally lacking in the supposedly "realistic" approach to the study of international affairs widely advocated today. There is no recognition that human society, imperfect as it is, retains the capacity to discriminate between the ideal and the actual, between what man is and does and what he is capable of being and becoming. Difficult as it may be sometimes for students of inter-state relations to see tangible evidences of it, mankind does possess at least a vision of a more desirable international order; and occasionally, if far too infrequently, man demonstrates an ability to transcend his own self-centeredness. Machiavellians are right when they emphasize and re-emphasize that moral considerations *are* often totally absent from political affairs and that, on the basis of an objective study of political behavior, there is often very little ground for optimism that this condition is likely to change spectacularly. To that extent, admonitions against efforts to remake the international order by evangelical crusades and pious exhortations in foreign affairs are well-founded and timely.

But Machiavellians betray a massive unrealism of their own when they postulate the pattern of inter-state relations in 19th and early 20th century Europe—in which the balance of power presumably operated with maximum efficacy—as normative. Under the *Pax Britannica*, the balance of power may have worked moderately well, so well in fact that moral-ethical ends may have been better served under a British-regulated balance of power than in most other historical eras (8, pp. 106-111). Yet a strong case can be made for saying that its inherent instability led to the First World War, which in turn gave rise to conditions which largely rendered the traditional balance of power inoperative in today's world. In the nuclear-missile age, characterized by bi-polarity of power on the world scene, conflicts engendered by hostile, increasingly powerful countries motivated by "national interest," imperil the future of civilization. To assert that mankind can do no better than continue to conduct its relationships upon the basis of national interest and balance of power, to declare that this is true because history teaches that it has been true, and to allege that this kind of conduct, far from being both morally reprehensible and potentially disastrous, represents the highest type of "morality," constitutes the ultimate in subjective judgments about what are essentially metaphysical questions relating to the nature and destiny of mankind on earth and in the universe.

One final point about the philosophical shortcomings of Machiavellian thought in both its earlier and more recent manifestations requires emphasis. This has to do with the interaction between the ends and means of policy. Machiavelli had little or nothing to say about the legitimacy of the ends for which the prince was to use his virtually unlimited power. He simply took it for granted that these ends—restoring law and order to Italy—were legitimate. To Machiavelli, many of the more traditional goals enunciated for the state in earlier philosophic thought, such as peace, justice, a well-ordered society, prosperity, and happiness, were predicated upon imposing a strong political authority upon an internally-divided Italy.

Events in Italy and in many other European countries over the course of time revealed that once sheer expediency and opportunism (*raison d'état*) become the accepted means, these things more often than not become the ends for which the state exists and is perpetuated. It is therefore no surprise that the age of "Absolute Monarchy" and the "Divine Right of Kings" followed the spread of Machiavellian thought within Europe, and that political philosophers in later periods, like Jean Bodin, John Locke, Hugo Grotius, Jean J. Rousseau, Edmund Burke, and Thomas Jefferson, were primarily concerned with defining the limits upon what had become almost limitless governmental authority and with redefining the ends for which that authority might legitimately be utilized. In the modern period, a philosophy of "realism" might be looked upon as merely a statement of the "Divine Right of Nations."

These philosophical principles have importance for America's relationship with the outside world. It is one thing to acknowledge that the United States, in common with all other countries, sometimes fails to live up to its professed ideals. There are episodes in American foreign policy which typify a diplomacy based exclusively upon *Realpolitik*. Examples might include America's treatment of the Indians, the Mexican War, the Spanish-American War, the acquisition of the Panama Canal, numerous chapters in the history of America's relations with Latin America, and retention of the Japanese-owned Pacific islands at the end of World War II. Yet it may be less important to acknowledge that such episodes have taken place than to admit that they were aberrations and that, in many cases, later efforts were made to bring America's professions and its conduct more into harmony. Inauguration of the "Good Neighbor" policy in the early 1930's is an example of what this recognition meant in terms of reorienting the nation's Latin American policy as a result of this admission. Indispensable to changes of this kind, however, is recognition that the nation's earlier diplomacy was not consonant with its highest conception of moral-ethical conduct.

The Relationship of Ends and Means in Diplomacy

The relationship between ends and means in foreign policies is inordinately complex and baffling. Perhaps the means utilized to achieve stated goals are never, and in a human society cannot be, as morally commendable and as perfectly consonant with the ends as might be desired. As "the art of the possible," politics often demands compromises with moral principles, unless political processes are to lose touch altogether with the affairs of fallible man. Yet this is not to say that *any* legitimate end justifies any means for its realization. As Crane Brinton has put it:

> . . . men's ethical ideas and ideals, even though they do not stand in a simple causal relationship to men's deeds, stand in *some* relation to men's deeds. . . . Machiavelli makes the mistake still made by some of our deliberately hard-boiled writers on politics and morals; he writes off men's profession of good just because they do not wholly live up to them. (6, p. 360).

Examination of the interaction between the ends and means of foreign policy is no merely academic, philosophically hair-splitting speculation. For it is precisely this problem upon which the outcome of the cold war today may very well hinge. For example, nations in the Afro-Asian bloc are much more apt to judge America's policies toward colonialism by what the United States *does* in dealing with colonial issues than by abstract pronouncements from the State Department about what it *believes* on the subject. The means actually utilized (or not utilized) to carry out the announced

end are likely to be pivotal in shaping certain aspects of the nation's relationships with the outside world. The attachment of the United States to the goal of peace is judged by the same criteria. Endless reiteration of the nation's dedication to the goal of peace are far less persuasive in creating favorable viewpoints about the United States than what the nation actually does to make peace a reality. And if, as has happened repeatedly in the postwar era, other countries think, by looking at the *means* of American policy, that the United States is half-hearted and lethargic in working toward the goal, then properly or improperly these countries will decide that America does not really believe in peace, despite its ceaseless affirmations that this is a cardinal goal of American statecraft.

The USSR has confronted the same dilemma growing out of the relationship between the ends and means of policy. By "realistic" criteria, no moral condemnation attaches to Russia's domination of Eastern Europe, save perhaps as its policies have failed to enhance Russia's power position. The ruthless suppression of the Hungarian revolt in 1956 is only condemnable to the degree it could be shown such conduct in the long-run weakened Soviet power. If this did not happen, then Russian policies are, by "realistic" canons, the quintessence of "political morality."

Now this reasoning may be perfectly consistent according to "realistic" terms of reference. We know from recent events, however, that it is unacceptable to an ever-growing circle of nations, who are becoming progressively disenchanted with the foreign policies of Russia and Communist China, as these policies are revealed in the deeds of the communist world. As a high-ranking American official wrote concerning Soviet suppression of the Hungarian revolt:

> The Soviet leaders have been pinned under the spotlight of the moral judgment of the world. The dilemma they face is for them a hard one. They must respond to this moral judgment in increasing degree or forfeit the influence they covet to exert in much of the world. (18, p. 378).

And another American official has written that, if for no other reason than in its own self-interest, the United States must do everything possible in global affairs to prevent other nations from conceiving the cold war "as a battle of the we's against the they's in which the only important consideration is that the we's win" (**28**, p. 685). It is the *means* of policy by which the legitimacy of the ends are judged, rather than verbal attachment to abstract ideological goals. This is the reason why other countries regard Russia or Communist China or, in some instances the United States, as a menace to their existence.

Leaving out any question of whether immoral means ought to be used to achieve legitimate ends, it is clear that on the much lower level of operating policy, power (applied overtly or covertly, as expediency dictates) cannot for long achieve the goal which "realists" postulate for states in the international community: national security. Reinhold Niebuhr has called attention to the paradox in the elevation of security to the pinnacle of diplomatic goals:

> . . . the more man establishes himself in power and glory, the greater is the fear of tumbling from his eminence. . . . The will-to-power is thus an expression of insecurity even when it has achieved ends which . . . would seem to guarantee complete security. . . . There is no level of greatness and power in which the lash of fear is not at least one strand in the whip of ambition. (**12**, p. 166).

There is, in other words, as the USSR is likely to discover sooner or later, a law of diminishing returns governing the extent to which even the limited goal of national security can be achieved by a policy dictated solely by *raison d'état*. The unending pursuit of power ultimately results in insecurity, not only for the international community, but for any nation-state that is a member of that community. This is the point well understood by Secretary of State William H. Seward, who once said that "If one state has a right to intervene in any other . . . then every state has the same right to intervene in the affairs of every other nation. . . . The principle of intervention, thus practically carried out, would seem to render all sovereignty and independence, and even all international peace and amity, uncertain and fallacious" (**35**, p. 61). And as Gauss has said of Machiavelli's thought: "hypocrisy works only because the majority of men are not hypocrites and are therefore not suspicious. When all princes practice deceit it soon fails to get results for any of them" (**10**, p. 23).

"National Interest" as a Guide to Statecraft

Having examined some of the more glaring weaknesses in the "realistic" philosophy, there is another level on which this philosophy must be subjected to careful scrutiny. This is the plane of *operating* policy. Just how useful are the concepts of "national interest" and "balance of power" in the formulation and conduct of American foreign policy? Admittedly, as we have already suggested earlier in the chapter, the concepts have value as antidotes, as correctives against tendencies that have interfered with successful foreign policy in the past. They caution specifically against two dangers. The first is confusion of the concrete "interests" of groups within the state with the interest of the state itself. Thus emphasis upon the "national interest" goes far toward assuring that policy will be something more than a mere summation of powerful group interests. The second danger is believing that groups within states and states themselves can transcend attachment to their "interests" altogether and can submerge them in a quest for something called loosely "the good of mankind" or "the welfare of all nations." Nations do have interests that can never be ignored by statesmen. Pretending that interests do not exist—and that they do not sometimes clash fundamentally— is the ultimate in unreality and is an almost certain road to diplomatic ineptitude.

Yet in recognizing that ideas like "national interest" are valuable because they caution against unfortunate tendencies, we must at the same time recognize many limitations in the concept of "national interest" that prevent it from becoming a useful guide to diplomatic conduct. Speaking generally, it is clear that the concept of "national interest" raises more questions than it answers. In specific situations adherence to the concept of national interest may tell us a good deal about what statesmen ought *not* to do; but it tells us little or nothing about what they *ought* to do. Indeed, it would be no exaggeration to say that *determination of the national interest in a never-*

ending series of problems confronting the nation is the continuing challenge facing foreign policy officials. "Realists" imply that all that is needed is for American officials to proclaim their attachment to the principle of "national interest" to assure diplomatic success. But every official in the government—from the State Department and other executive agencies to Congress—is convinced that his ideas about American foreign policy are identical with the national interest. The overriding problem therefore—and it is a problem to which "realists" give little or no attention—is how the national interest is to be determined and whose determination of it is to be binding upon the government. An experienced American diplomat has written concerning the selection of alternative lines of policy:

> I know of no case . . . in which the settlement of an issue of our national policy . . . would have been facilitated by injecting the question: Shall we or shall we not try to serve the national interest?
> The question . . . is not whether, but *how,* to serve the national interest. That involves the question of what is the national interest in a particular situation.
> . . . there are many national interests, not just one. The difficulties arise in the conflict of one interest with another; for example, in the clash of the interest in peace with the interest in preserving national institutions. . . . (16, pp. 665-66, italics inserted).

This diplomat emphasizes "the inconclusiveness of the national interest as a guide in any particular policy problem" and holds that it is "inadequate and misleading even as a broad concept upon which to found a policy" (16, p. 666).

Unless it is assumed (and "realist" thought strongly suggests this) that the "national interest" is fixed and readily-apparent, then the crucial questions in foreign policy formulation revolve around how, and by whom, and according to what criteria competing versions of the national interest are to be chosen. Take a concrete example like American security in the Western Hemisphere. It is possible to agree with the "realists" that the national interest demands prevention and elimination of any threat to American security in this area. Officials and citizens may agree upon this and disagree violently on whether economic assistance pro-grams, the Pan American system, intervention in the affairs of the American Republics, non-recognition of other governments, military aid, propaganda tactics and a host of other possible steps in fact accord with the national interest. That all participants agree broadly the United States ought to safeguard its national interest is a fact that has minimum relevance in coping with the hard realities and choices confronting officials and citizens concerned with evolving an intelligent foreign policy.

Concepts like national interest and balance of power must also be viewed skeptically as adequate guides to diplomacy on the ground that they cannot indefinitely assure the well-being of the American people. This follows from what we know about the nature of power, about the conditions under which the balance of power can be maintained, and about the concept of national interest. At the outset, it may be observed that any analogy between the pursuit of power by groups and individuals *within* a state and the same objective *by* states themselves are faulty in at least one important particular. Pluralism within a state—the balancing of one competing interest against another —can result in a tolerable kind of power equilibrium among self-seeking groups precisely because this power struggle takes place within the context of dominant governmental authority. The existence of law within the state, and the monopoly of force which the state possesses to assure compliance with it, makes this constant pushing and pulling among power-seeking individuals and groups within the state endurable, without calling into jeopardy the continued existence of the state itself. Quite obviously, this is profoundly different from the situation obtaining within international relations. There the unending struggle for power among hostile states *does* imperil the continued existence of the participants and, increasingly, the non-participants.

This is but another way of saying that in reality there is no "balance of power" within states between the governmental authority and lesser groups. The power of the government *vis-à-vis* other groups is supreme; the state itself brooks no rivals among lesser groups to its legal strictures. It is prepared to compel obedience by force if necessary. This is the only condition within which a struggle for power can go on endlessly among competing groups without jeopardizing the very basis of society itself.

Our knowledge of the nature of power also cautions us against acceptance of "national interest" and "balance of power" as the ultimate goals of foreign policy. Many of the most basic ingredients of national power—national character, civilian and military morale, the leadership potential of the nation, the nation's ability to "bounce back" from initial military reverses—are statistically immeasurable. Comparisons between the power differentials of two rival states must therefore be exceedingly crude. The only ultimate test is the very test from which "balance of power" is supposed to save us: a military showdown. Naturally, this is an undesirable, potentially a suicidal, way of measuring power differentials among nations. Other criteria, inexact as they are, must be applied on a day-by-day basis in foreign policy to measure the power potentials of nations.

Recognition that the measurement of national power is highly inaccurate is of vital significance in evaluating the feasibility of balance of power as a goal of foreign policy. For this means that if there ever exists an equilibrium of power among hostile nations, it is an equilibrium which is largely accidental and outside of direct control by statesmen. This is so because the elements of national power are (1) by and large immeasurable and (2) undergoing a constant state of change. Many of the elements which enter into the determination of American power—morale, scientific-technological know-how, prevailing political leadership, and diplomatic astuteness—often are not amenable to deliberate calculation and control, even by the United States, except over very long periods of time. And certainly it would be impossible for the United States to calculate and control these same elements within the USSR. This means that, in the light of such forces as education, expanding scientific knowledge, and industrial technology, the balance of power is becoming more and more inherently unstable as a mechanism for preserving world peace or for safeguarding American security.

These considerations largely explain why the term "balance of power" itself is used by "realists" and others in at least two contradictory senses. It may mean that America ought to strive for an *equilibrium* of power between itself and possible enemies like Soviet Russia or, more broadly, between nations in the free world and the communist bloc. Or, it may mean that America ought to seek a *preponderance* of power—the kind of "balance" Morgenthau suggests was sought by America under the Monroe Doctrine—for the free world against the communist world. Whatever may be the theoretical meaning of the term "balance of power," in the vast majority of cases it is the latter meaning which actually emerges as the operating goal of diplomacy. Preponderance may be the embraced and announced goal, as in the case of Nazi Germany; or it may simply occur because of the nature of national power itself which, being largely incalculable, is not amenable to being brought into an equilibrium in world affairs. Even the United States must eventually seek a preponderance of power because it can accurately gauge neither its own power, nor the power of its rivals. It must therefore allow a wide "margin of error" by overestimating its own defense requirements so as to "play safe" against the danger of being too weak in a military showdown. Even if, accidentally, it did achieve an absolute parity with the Soviet Union at any time, the United States could not be certain this parity would remain for any significant period. In spite of the best of intentions on both sides, it is almost a certainty that it would not be preserved, owing to the dynamic nature of power itself.

If American officials must "play safe" by overestimating their power needs in comparison with Russia, Soviet officials must do likewise. Even though ideally they too might desire an equilibrium of power with the United States, they dare not risk the eventuality that their country will be too weak to protect itself if war comes. They must consequently allow an additional increment as a kind of insurance, so as to tilt the scales in their favor if a conflict comes. It is out of this situation that run-away arms-races begin and that they are perpetuated, even though no nation may be deliberately attempting to "upset" the balance of power and to provoke war. Given the best of intentions all around, national policies derived from the balance of power principle can have no other result in the long run than to keep the world in a constant state of tension and apprehension, to generate forces like armaments-races, to foster the belief that "war is inevitable," to create an international atmosphere which makes the resolution of tensions virtually impossible, and, in the last analysis, to imperil the very goal—national security—which the statesman who starts out seeking balance of power is trying to achieve.

In their emphasis upon the balance of power in global affairs, the "realists" are correct to this extent: national security cannot be preserved if any nation gets a preponderance of power, so that it can dominate other nations and ultimately perhaps the world. Such a condition must be regarded as the *summum malum* of international affairs. Balance of power thus may be a necessary instrument of statecraft. It is not an end in itself. Nor, for that matter, in the light of history is it to be regarded as a means which is always and automatically capable of achieving the results intended by statesmen. Balance of power must be recognized for what it is: essentially an expedient which *may* facilitate national security but which certainly cannot in any long-range sense guarantee it. Balance of power may sometimes have to be depended upon because there is no feasible alternative to replace it. Genuine realism demands, however, that its progressive unreliability be recognized and that the ultimate goal of statecraft be the mitigation of conflicts arising out of the power-seeking propensities of nations by the evolution of a system of world law.

The American Approach to Foreign Relations

Our lengthy appraisal of contemporary "realist" thought has indicated the main elements of what must be the American approach to foreign relations. It remains merely to make explicit, and to summarize briefly, what has been implicit in preceding pages.

First, credit must be given to the "realists" for restoring an imbalance in the American approach to external affairs in recent years by cautioning against the dangers of sentimentality and starry-eyed utopianism, which seek forthwith to "grasp this sorry scheme of things entire" and "remould it nearer to the heart's desire" by grandiose plans which, however commendable their intentions, make no concessions to the frailties and the finiteness of man. Uncritical advocacy of such plans inevitably breeds disillusionment and side-tracks nations from a steady, realistic approach to the formidable problems of human existence in a world of sovereign states. Perhaps the most significant contribution of the "realists" is their insistence that noble ends must always be realized with *imperfect* means. The translation of these ends into policies and programs therefore can never completely satisfy the idealists. Failure to recognize this fact can lead idealistic movements into a blind-alley of despair and impotence when they eventually confront the realities of human behavior.

In the second place, however much the "realists" have rendered a service by focusing attention upon the facts of national behavior, the American approach to foreign relations must preserve inviolate the distinction between what nations *do* and what they *ought* to do. Such an approach must reject any pseudo-scientific conception of man's destiny as nothing more than a perpetual struggle for power, a struggle which is equated with incarnate virtue. This conception is antithetical to the mainstream of Western humanistic philosophy and the Judaeo-Christian tradition.

Instead, a proper philosophy of foreign relations must continue to preserve the duality which has been a conspicuous feature of Western thought for well over two millennia. It is the duality present in Augustine's *City of God* which stands in contrast with the city of man. It is the duality present in the "Two Powers" philosophy of the Middle Ages, which postulated one kind of behavior for the Church and another for the state. In more recent philosophy, this duality is suggested in the titles of two of Reinhold Niebuhr's books, *Moral Man in Immoral Society* and *The Children of Light and the Children of Darkness*. This duality refers to the tension, always present in human society, between what man is and does, on the one hand, and what he wants to do and is capable of becoming, on the other hand. It was most succinctly expressed in St. Paul's lament: "The Law is spiritual; we know that. But then I am a creature of the flesh, in the thraldom of sin. I cannot understand my own actions; I do not act as I desire to act; on the contrary, I do what I detest. . . . The wish is there, but not the power of doing what is right. I cannot be good as I desire to be, and I do wrong against my wishes" (Romans 7:15-20, Moffat's translation). In his book *Christianity and World Issues,* T. B. Maston has described what this tension between man as he is and man as he ought to be means for the church and, more broadly, for any movement aimed at human betterment:

> . . . that tension should not become so great that the church will lose all opportunity to minister to the world. If we think of that tension as a rubber band . . . the speed with which the world is lifted toward the Christian ideal will be determined by the tautness of the rubber band. On the other hand, if the tension becomes too great the rubber band may break. If such happens the church has isolated itself from the world . . . the individual Christian or group that ministers most effectively to the world must start where the world is and progressively lift the world toward the Christian ideal for the world. This means that the Christian ideal, for the world as for the individual, is fleeting. As we move toward it, it moves ahead of us. (17, p. 353).

Third, if what is must be the starting point for achieving what might be, a necessary corollary is that America can never relinquish the ultimate vision of greater perfectability of the political order. That vision cannot be abandoned because, as the "realists" properly insist, its attainment in any historical era can never be anything more than approximate. If "idealists" are always in danger of erring on the side of imparting to man a greater capacity for rapid self-improvement than man's history justifies, the "realists" commit what is a far more grievous error. In rejecting the view that there can be a heaven on earth because of man's inherent egoism—in theological terms, his sinfulness—"realists" go to the extreme of saying in effect that man's vices are his virtues, that man is forever predestined to act as though he were in hell and that this hell is in reality his heaven!

However freely it may be admitted that mankind strives for power, this propensity must be recognized for what it is: a trait which derives from man's own pride and his deliberate attachment to self-interest. It follows both that "all have sinned and come short of the glory of God" and that mankind comprises a community knit together both by the trait of self-centeredness and the capacity for transcendance over self. The Judaeo-Christian tradition avers that man is not God, but that he is "made in the image of God," that he is "a little lower than the angels." This means , in Hutchison's words, that man possesses "transcendent and creative freedom. . . . The divine image is man's capacity in imagination to stand clear of himself and his world. . . . Because he can stand clear of himself and see himself, man possesses (always within limits) the capacity for self-determination. He can determine his own ends, and remake his own self; and for better and/or worse he is continuously doing so" (11, p. 24).

Applying these ideas to the specific realm of foreign policy we must accept what Cook and Moos have called the "realism of idealism" (8, *passim*). American "national interest" cannot be conceived as something rigid and immutable —and certainly not something which, by the nature of things, stands in opposition to the national interests of all other states. There is no such thing as a "national interest" divorced from broad human goals such as progress toward the good life, in which the highest development of human personality is the universal goal. This is the true "national interest" of every state—perceived as never before in the nuclear age, when "one world" has become a fact because of unprecedented strides in scientific knowledge and technology. Moreover, the nuclear-missile age has driven home as never before that the quintessence of Utopianism is to imagine that any powerful nation can enjoy its security while remaining indifferent to the needs and aspirations of humanity at large, of which it is a part. Recognition of this fact, along with awareness that political action based upon it can never accomplish perfect results, is the beginning of political wisdom.

A satisfactory philosophy of American foreign policy must therefore reject that brand of contemporary "realism" which is a corruption of Renaissance humanistic thought, with engraftings from 19th century German romanticism and Marxism. It accepts Hutchison's view that in any human world "there will be egotism, and this egotism will express itself in the will to dominate. Power impulses and the consequent clash or conflict of such power impulses are pervasive and perennial human facts. Wherever they occur it will be necessary to balance them in some sort of tolerable order" (11, p. 155). But a true conception of the "national interest" of the United States does not stop there. It goes on to assert that the United States, in concert with every nation in the world community, must endeavor to create the conditions in international affairs that prevail in domestic affairs and that are the *sine qua non* of security for individuals within states: a system of world law, together with adequate powers of enforcement, that will permit competition among rival interests to go on *within carefully prescribed limits,* without calling into question the continued existence of organized society, perhaps even of the human race itself.

"Realists" are fully correct in asserting that this is a formidable challenge, that the path is filled with obstacles, and that progress will sometimes be dishearteningly slow. They are incorrect in asserting that the goal is totally unattainable and that mankind is chained to an increasingly devastating cycle of war and peace. A sincere dedication to the goals of self-preservation, national interest, security and other national objectives requires them to join with "idealists" in discovering ways to achieve the framework of world law and order that is the only ultimate guarantor of security for the United States or any other nation on the world scene.

REFERENCES

1. Baldwin, Hanson W. *Great Mistakes of the War.* New York: Harper and Brothers, 1950. Among these mistakes, the writer puts "unconditional surrender" high on the list.

2. Bemis, Samuel F. *A Diplomatic History of the United States.* New York: Henry Holt and Company, 1950. One of the most scholarly diplomatic histories available.

3. Bowles, Chester. *Africa's Challenge to America.* Berkeley: University of California Press, 1956.

4. ———. *Ambassador's Report.* New York: Harper and Brothers, 1954.

5. ———. *American Politics in a Revolutionary World.* Cambridge: Harvard University Press, 1956. The writings of the former Ambassador to India bring out strikingly how America's adherence to its own ideals will be a crucial factor in shaping the course of world affairs in the future.

6. Brinton, Crane. *Ideas and Men.* New York: Prentice-Hall, 1950. A provocative treatment of leading thinkers in political philosophy.

7. Brogan, D. W. "Illusion of American Omnipotence," *Harpers,* 205 (December, 1952), pp. 21-8. Sharply challenges many elements in American folklore about world affairs.

8. Cook, Thomas I., and Moos, Malcolm. *Power through Purpose: The Realism of Idealism as a Basis for Foreign Policy.* Baltimore: The Johns Hopkins Press, 1954. Perhaps the most cogent book available directly challenging the "realistic" approach to foreign policy.

9. Ebenstein, William. *Great Political Thinkers.* New York: Rinehart and Company, 1956. A good starting point for students who wish to relate political philosophy to foreign affairs.

10. Gauss, Christian, ed. *The Prince* by Machiavelli. New York: The New American Library of World Literature, Inc., 1952. A convenient source for Machiavelli's thought, with a valuable introduction by the editor.

11. Hutchison, John A. *The Two Cities.* Garden City, N. Y.: Doubleday and Company, 1957. A provocative discussion of the relationship between Christian ethics and politics.

12. Kegley, Charles W., and Bretall, Robert W., eds. *Reinhold Niebuhr: His Religious, Social, and Political Thought.* New York: The Macmillan Company, 1956. Several writers evaluate the relevance of Niebuhr's thought; chapters on his view of politics are especially relevant for understanding foreign policy.

13. Kennan, George. *American Diplomacy, 1900-1950.* New York: The New American Library, 1952. One of the leading re-examinists of American foreign policy states his views.

14. Lippmann, Walter. *The Public Philosophy.* Boston: Little, Brown and Company, 1955.

15. ———. *U. S. Foreign Policy: Shield of the Republic.* Boston: Little, Brown and Company, 1943. These two, among the many books by Walter Lippmann, will indicate his approach to foreign affairs, an approach which, as the former book makes clear, perhaps places Lippmann more in the "idealist" than the "realist" camp.

16. Marshall, Charles B. "The National Interest," in Robert A. Goldwin, *et al.,* eds. *Readings in American Foreign Policy.* New York: Oxford University Press, 1959.

17. Maston, T. B. *Christianity and World Issues.* New York: The Macmillan Company, 1957. Another helpful study of the relationship between ethics and politics.

18. Merchant, Livingston T. "The Moral Element in Foreign Policy," *Department of State Bulletin,* 37 (September 2, 1957), pp. 374-79.

19. Morgenthau, Hans J. "Another 'Great Debate': The National Interest of the United States," *American Political Science Review,* 46 (December, 1952), pp. 961-88.

20. ———. *In Defense of the National Interest.* New York: Alfred A. Knopf, 1951.

21. ———. "The Mainsprings of American Foreign Policy," *American Political Science Review,* 44 (December, 1950), pp. 833-54. In these sources, the writer who is perhaps the strongest advocate of political "realism" states his position.

22. Niebuhr, Reinhold. *The Children of Light and the Children of Darkness.* New York: C. Scribner's Sons, 1944.

23. ———. *Christian Realism and Political Problems.* New York: C. Scribner's Sons, 1953.

24. ———. *Christianity and Power Politics.* New York: C. Scribner's Sons, 1940.

25. ———. *The Irony of American History.* New York: C. Scribner's Sons, 1952. These selections from the writings of America's greatest living theologian will provide insight into the problem of a proper philosophy of foreign affairs.

26. Oakeshott, Michael, ed. *The Leviathan* by Thomas Hobbes. New York: The Macmillan Company, 1947.

27. Perkins, Dexter. *The American Approach to Foreign Policy.* Cambridge, Mass.: Harvard University Press, 1952. A scholarly analysis of the leading elements in America's approach to external problems.

28. Robertson, Walter S. "Report to the Founders on Foreign Affairs," *Department of State Bulletin,* 36 (April 29, 1957), pp. 682-87.

29. Senate Foreign Relations Committee. *A Decade of American Foreign Policy, 1941-49.* Document No. 123, 81st Congress, 1st Session. Washington: 1950.

30. ———. *Hearings on the Control and Reduction of Armaments.* Part 11, January 9-10, 1957, 85th Congress, 1st Session, 1957.

31. ———. *Hearings on Review of Foreign Policy, 1958.* Part 4, June 3-6, 1958, 85th Congress, 2nd Session, 1958.

32. Smith, T. V. "Power: Its Ubiquity and Legitimacy," *American Political Science Review,* 45 (September, 1951), pp. 693-702. A forceful statement of the omnipresence of power and of the power-is-morality position.

33. Strausz-Hupé, Robert. "U. S. Foreign Policy and the Balance of Power," *Review of Politics,* 10 (January, 1948), pp. 76-83. The writer is another advocate of a philosophy of "realism" in international relations.

34. ———, and Possony, Stefan T. *International Relations.* New York: McGraw-Hill Book Company, 1954.

35. Tannenbaum, Frank. *The American Tradition in Foreign Policy.* Norman, Okla.: University of Oklahoma Press, 1955. This is a highly critical and forceful attack upon the "realistic" approach to foreign relations.

36. Welles, Sumner. *Seven Decisions that Shaped History.* New York: Harper and Brothers, 1950. This analysis by a former Under-Secretary of State brings out clearly how rampant idealism during World War II interfered with sound foreign policy.

SUGGESTIONS FOR FURTHER READING

This bibliography is designed to supplement the list of references appearing at the end of each chapter. Normally, titles listed there have not been repeated. Instead, studies have been included here that relate various aspects of American foreign policy to the broad international environment that forms the context within which America must shape its response to the outside world. For convenience and ease in utilizing both the list of references at the end of chapters and this bibliography, references have been arranged here in the same order as the subject matter of the book. A list of bibliographies and general references precedes the topical reading lists.

Bibliographies

American Political Science Review. Baltimore, 1907. The quarterly issues of this journal contain comprehensive bibliographies on American foreign policy and closely related subjects.

Beers, H. P. *Bibliographies in American History.* New York: H. W. Wilson Company, 1942.

Bemis, Samuel F., and Griffin, Grace G. *Guide to the Diplomatic History of the United States, 1775-1921.* Washington, D. C.: Government Printing Office, 1935.

Council on Foreign Relations. *Foreign Affairs Bibliography, 1919-1932.* New York: Harper and Brothers, 1933.

———. *Foreign Affairs Bibliography, 1932-1942.* New York: Harper and Brothers, 1945.

———. *Foreign Affairs Bibliography, 1942-1952.* New York: Harper and Brothers, 1955.

Handlin, Oscar, *et al. Harvard Guide to American History.* Cambridge: Belknap Press, 1954.

Library of Congress. General Reference and Bibliography Division. *American History and Civilization: A List of Guides and Annotated or Selective Bibliographies.* Washington: 1951.

Rips, Rae E., ed. *United States Government Publications* (3rd ed. rev.), New York: H. W. Wilson Company, 1949.

United Nations. Headquarters Library. *Bibliographical Series.* Titles listed in this series include *Latin America, 1939-1949* (1952); *A Bibliography of the Charter of the United Nations* (1955); and *Industrialization in Underdeveloped Countries* (1956).

———. *Ten Years of United Nations Publications, 1945-1955.* Provides a convenient source for locating UN publications on a variety of subjects.

———. *United Nations Documents Index.* This publication is indispensable in using documentary sources relating to the UN.

United States Government. *U. S. Government Publications—Monthly Catalogue.* Washington, D. C. An invaluable guide to the use of materials published by all branches of the American government.

General References

Carnegie Endowment for International Peace. *Institutes of International Affairs.* New York: 1953. Describes organizations within the United States and abroad interested in international relations.

Council on Foreign Relations. *The United States in World Affairs.* New York: Harper and Brothers, 1931——. This annual volume provides a readable secondary treatment of the main trends in American foreign policy.

Department of State. The Department of State publishes a number of continuing series devoted to selected aspects of American foreign relations. The following would perhaps be of greatest interest to the student:

Commercial Policy
Conference
Department and Foreign Service
Documents and State Papers
European and British Commonwealth
Far Eastern
General Foreign Policy
Inter-American
International Organization

Near and Middle Eastern
United States and the United Nations
London Institute of World Affairs. *The Year Book of World Affairs*. London: Stevens and Sons, Ltd., 1946——. This series contains articles on selected aspects of international affairs.
Periodicals. The following are scholarly periodicals dealing directly or indirectly with American foreign policy:

American Political Science Review, 1907 ——.

Annals of the American Academy of Political and Social Science, 1890——.
Current History, 1941——.
Department of State Bulletin, 1939——.
Foreign Affairs, 1922——.
International Affairs, London, 1922——.
International Conciliation, 1907——.
International Journal, Toronto, 1946——.
International Organization, 1947——.
Journal of International Affairs, 1947——.
Journal of Politics, 1945——.
Middle East Journal, 1947——.
Middle Eastern Affairs, 1950——.
Pacific Affairs, 1928——.
Political Science Quarterly, 1886——.
United Nations Review, 1954——.
Virginia Quarterly Review, 1925——.
Western Political Quarterly, 1948——.
World Affairs, 1901——.
World Politics, 1948——.
Yale Review, 1911——.

Royal Institute of International Affairs. *Documents on International Affairs, 1928*, et seq. London: Oxford University Press.

Savord, Ruth, and Wasson, Donald. *American Agencies Interested in International Affairs*. New York: Council on Foreign Relations, 1955. Describes the activities of agencies and groups within the United States active in the sphere of foreign relations.

United Nations. *Yearbook of the United Nations*. New York: Columbia University Press. A valuable summary of proceedings in the UN, providing a guide for further exploration in documentary sources.

World Peace Foundation. *Documents on American Foreign Relations, 1939*, et seq. Boston: 1939——. A convenient documentary source.

Foundations of Foreign Policy—Chapter 1

Berkner, Lloyd V. "Science and Military Power," *Bulletin of the Atomic Scientists*, 9 (December, 1953), pp. 359-65.

Bidwell, Percy W. *Raw Materials: A Study of American Policy*. New York: Harper and Brothers, 1958.

Bush, Vannevar. *Modern Arms and Free Men*. New York: Simon and Schuster, 1947.

Carlson, Lucile. *Geography and World Politics*. New York: Prentice-Hall, 1958.

Colling, Edward M. "Clausewitz and Democracy's Modern Wars," *Military Affairs*, 19 (Spring, 1955), pp. 15-20.

Davis, Kingsley. "The Political Impact of New Population Trends," *Foreign Affairs*, 36 (January, 1958), pp. 293-301.

Esposito, Vincent J. "War As A Continuation of Politics," *Military Affairs*, 18 (Spring, 1954), pp. 19-26.

Finletter, Thomas K. *Power and Policy*. New York: Harcourt Brace and Company, 1954.

Hauser, Philip M., ed. *Population and World Politics*. Glencoe, Ill.: The Free Press, 1958.

Jones, S. B. "Economic Geography of Atomic Energy," *Economic Geography*, 27 (July, 1951), pp. 268-74.

Marshall C. B. "The Nature of Foreign Policy," *Department of State Bulletin*, 26 (March 17, 1952), pp. 415-20.

Possony, Stefan F. *Strategic Air Power*. Washington, D. C.: Infantry Journal Press, 1949.

Senate Interior and Insular Affairs Committee. *Critical Materials: Factors Affecting Self-Sufficiency Within Nations of the Western Hemisphere*. 84th Congress, 2nd Session, 1956.

Slessor, Sir John. "Air Power and World Strategy," *Foreign Affairs*, 33 (October, 1954), pp. 43-53.

Thomas C. S. "Strategic Considerations for Effective Defense of the Free World," *World Affairs Interpreter*, 25 (January, 1955), pp. 348-60.

Weigert, Hans W., *et al. New Compass of the World*. New York: The Macmillan Company, 1953.

National Character—Chapter 2

Adler, Selig. *The Isolationist Impulse: Its Twentieth Century Reaction*. New York: Abelard-Schuman, 1957.

Agar, Herbert. *The Price of Power*. Chicago: University of Chicago Press, 1957.

Aldridge, John W. *After the Lost Generation*. New York: McGraw-Hill Publishing Company, 1951. A critical study of writings on World Wars I and II.

Brogan, D. W. "Trends in American Policy," *International Affairs*, 25 (April, 1949), pp. 125-36.

Buehrig, Edward H. *Wilson's Foreign Policy in Perspective*. Bloomington, Ind.: University of Indiana Press, 1957.

Current, Richard N. "The Stimson Doctrine and the Hoover Doctrine," *American Historical Review*, 59 (April, 1954), pp. 513-42.

Department of State. *The United States and Non-Self-Governing Territories*. (Publication No. 2812.) Washington, D. C.: 1947.

Dulles, Foster R. *America's Rise to World Power, 1898-1954*. New York: Harper and Brothers, 1955.

Graham, Malbone W. *American Diplomacy in the International Community*. Baltimore: The Johns Hopkins University Press, 1948.

Morgenthau, Hans J. "Lessons of World War II's Mistakes," *Commentary*, 14 (October, 1952), pp. 326-33.

Pratt, Julius W. *America's Colonial Experiment*. New York: Prentice-Hall, 1950.

———. *Expansionists of 1812*. New York: The Macmillan Company, 1925.

———. *Expansionists of 1898*. Baltimore: The Johns Hopkins University Press, 1936.

Strausz-Hupé, Robert, and Hazard, Harry W. *The Idea of Colonialism*. New York: F. A. Praeger, 1958.

Weinberg, A. K. *Manifest Destiny*. Baltimore: The Johns Hopkins University Press, 1935.

The President and Department of State—Chapter 3

Acheson, Dean. "The Responsibility for Decision in Foreign Policy," *Yale Review*, 44 (September, 1954), pp. 1-12.

Anderson, Dillon. "The President and National Security," *Atlantic Monthly*, 197 (January, 1956), pp. 42-6.

Barron, Bryton. *Inside the State Department*. New York: Comet Press Books, 1956.

Brookings Institution. *The Administration of Foreign Affairs and Overseas Operations*. Washington: Government Printing Office, 1951.

Brownlow, Louis. *The President and the Presidency*. Chicago: Public Administration Service, 1949.

Cheever, Daniel S., and Haviland, H. Field, Jr. *American Foreign Policy and the Separation of Powers*. Cambridge: Harvard University Press, 1952.

Childs, James R. *American Foreign Service*. New York: Henry Holt, 1948.

Commission on Organization of the Executive Branch of the Government. *Foreign Affairs —A Report to the Congress*. Washington: 1949. This is the Hoover Commission's task force report on foreign policy machinery.

Corwin, Edward S. *The Constitution and World Organization*. Princeton: Princeton University Press, 1944.

Driggs, Don W. "The President As Chief Educator on Foreign Affairs," *Western Political Quarterly*, 11 (December, 1958), pp. 813-20.

George, Alexander L. "American Policy-Making and North Korean Aggression," *World Politics*, 7 (January, 1955), pp. 228-32.

Guerrant, Edward O. *Modern American Diplomacy*. Albuquerque, N. M.: University of New Mexico Press, 1954.

Hamilton, William C. "Some Problems of Decision-Making in Foreign Affairs," *Department of State Bulletin*, 37 (September 9, 1957), pp. 432-36.

Laski, Harold J. "The American President and Foreign Relations," *Journal of Politics*, 11 (February, 1949), pp. 171-205.

Milton, George F. *The Uses of Presidential Power, 1789-1943*. Boston: Little, Brown and Company, 1944.

Plischke, Elmer. *The Conduct of American Diplomacy*. Princeton: D. Van Nostrand, 1950.

Potter, P. B. "Power of the President of the U. S. to Utilize Its Armed Forces Abroad," *American Journal of International Law*, 48 (July, 1954), pp. 458-9.

Wriston, Henry M. *Diplomacy in A Democracy*. New York: Harper and Brothers, 1956.

———. "The Secretary of State Abroad," *Foreign Affairs*, 34 (July, 1956), pp. 523-41.

Military and Other Executive Departments—Chapter 4

Commission on Organization of the Executive Branch of the Government. *The National Security Organization*. Washington: 1949. This is the Hoover Commission's task force report on security organization.

Fox, William T. R. "Civil-Military Relations Research," *World Politics*, 6 (January, 1954), pp. 278-88.

Gulick, Luther. *Administrative Reflections from World War II*. University, Alabama: University of Alabama Press, 1948.

Haviland, H. Field. "Foreign Aid and the Foreign Policy Process," *American Political Science Review*, 52 (September, 1958), pp. 689-725.

Kent, Sherman. *Strategic Intelligence for American World Policy*. Princeton: Princeton University Press, 1949.

Library of Congress. Legislative Reference Service. *The Concept of Civil Supremacy Over the Military in the United States (1774-1950)*. Washington: 1951.

Masland, John W. *Soldiers and Scholars: Military Education and National Policy*. Princeton: Princeton University Press, 1957.

Millis, Walter. *Arms and the State*. New York: Twentieth Century Fund, 1958.

——, ed. *The Forrestal Diaries*. New York: The Viking Press, 1951.

Platt, Washington. *Strategic Intelligence Production: Basic Principles*. New York: F. A. Praeger, 1957.

Ransom, H. H. *Central Intelligence and National Security*. Cambridge: Harvard University Press, 1958.

Rockefeller Brothers Fund. *International Security, The Military Aspect*. Garden City, N.Y.: Doubleday and Company, Inc., 1958.

Senate Foreign Relations Committee. *The Executive Branch and Disarmament Policy*. 84th Congress, 2nd Session, 1956. This study examines the role of the President's special assistant for disarmament.

Smith, Louis. *American Democracy and Military Power*. Chicago: University of Chicago Press, 1951.

Social Science Research Council. *Civil-Military Relations: An Annotated Bibliography, 1940-1952*. New York: Columbia University Press, 1954.

Van Riper, P. P. "Survey of Materials for the Study of Military Management," *American Political Science Review*, 49 (September, 1955), pp. 828-50.

Warren, Unna. "CIA: Who Watches the Watchmen?" *Harpers*, 216 (April, 1958), pp. 46-54.

Congress—Chapter 5

Brabner-Smith, J. W. "Concluding the War—The Peace Settlement and Congressional Powers," *Virginia Law Review*, 34 (July, 1948), pp. 553-68.

Carroll, H. N. *The House of Representatives and Foreign Affairs*. Pittsburgh: University of Pittsburgh Press, 1958.

Colegrove, Kenneth W. *The American Senate and World Peace*. New York: The Vanguard Press, 1944.

Dillard, H. C. "Treaty-Making Controversy: Substance and Shadow," *Virginia Quarterly Review*, 30 (No. 2, 1954), pp. 178-91.

Dulles, John Foster. "The Making of Treaties and Executive Agreements," *Department of State Bulletin*, 28 (April 20, 1953), pp. 591-5.

Galloway, George B. "The Operation of the Legislative Reorganization Act of 1946," *American Political Science Review*, 45 (March, 1951), pp. 41-68.

Harley, J. E. "A Reexamination of the Treaty Power and the Constitution," *World Affairs Interpreter*, 23 (Autumn, 1952), pp. 275-92.

McConaughy, James L. "Congressmen and the Pentagon," *Fortune*, 57 (April, 1958), pp. 156-60.

Schubert, G. A. "Politics and the Constitution," *Journal of Politics*, 16 (May, 1954), pp. 257-98.

Sherwood, Foster H. "Foreign Relations and the Constitution," *Western Political Quarterly*, 1 (December, 1948), pp. 386-99.

Young, Roland. *The American Congress*. New York: Harper and Brothers, 1958.

Bipartisanship and Executive-Legislative Relations—Chapter 6

Acheson, Dean G. "Legislative-Executive Relations," *Yale Review*, 45 (June, 1956), pp. 481-95.

Cohen, B. C. *The Political Process and Foreign Policy: The Making of the Japanese Peace Settlement*. Princeton: Princeton University Press, 1957.

Crabb, Cecil V., Jr. "An End to Bipartisanship," *The Nation*, 188 (February 21, 1959), pp. 155-59, 167.

Freeman, J. L. *The Political Process: Executive Bureau—Legislative Committee Relations*. New York: Doubleday and Company, Inc., 1955.

Hillsman, Roger. "Congressional—Executive Relations and the Foreign Policy Process," *American Political Science Review*, 52 (September, 1958), pp. 725-45.

Westerfield, H. Bradford. *Foreign Policy and Party Politics: Pearl Harbor to Korea*. New Haven: Yale University Press, 1955.

Public Opinion—Chapter 7

Adamic, Louis. *A Nation of Nations*. New York: Harper and Brothers, 1945.

Adler, Selig. "The War-Guilt Question and American Disillusionment," *Journal of Modern History*, 23 (1951), pp. 1-28.

Baker, R. *The American Legion and Foreign Policy*. New York: Bookman Associates, 1954.

Beloff, Max. *Foreign Policy and the Democratic Process*. Baltimore: The Johns Hopkins University Press, 1955.

Bowers, David F., ed. *Foreign Influences in American Life*. Princeton: Princeton University Press, 1944.

Burdick, Eugene, ed. *American Voting Behavior*. Glencoe, Ill.: The Free Press, 1959.

Cole, Wayne S. *America First: The Battle Against Intervention, 1940-41*. Madison, Wis.: University of Wisconsin Press, 1953.

Elder, Robert E. "The Public Studies Division of the Department of State," *Western Political Quarterly*, 10 (December, 1957), pp. 783-92.

Graebner, Norman A. *The New Isolation: A Study of Politics and Foreign Policy Since 1950*. New York: Ronald Press, 1956.

Handlin, Oscar. *The Uprooted*. Boston: Little, Brown and Company, 1951.

Hansen, Marcus L. *The Immigrant in American History*. Cambridge: Harvard University Press, 1940.

International Political Science Association. *Interest Groups on Four Continents*. Pittsburgh: University of Pittsburgh Press, 1958.

Johnson, Walter. *The Battle Against Isolation*. Chicago: University of Chicago Press, 1944.

Kane, J. J. *Catholic-Protestant Conflicts in America*. Chicago: Regnery, 1955.

Karson, Marc. *American Labor Unions and Politics*. Carbondale, Ill.: Southern Illinois University Press, 1958.

Lederer, William J., and Burdick, Eugene. *The Ugly American*. New York: W. W. Norton Company, 1958.

Lippmann, Walter. *Public Opinion and Foreign Policy in the United States*. London: Allen and Unwin, 1952.

Nevins, Allen. *The United States in a Chaotic World, 1918-1933*. New Haven: Yale University Press, 1950.

Rauch, Basil. *Roosevelt: From Munich to Pearl Harbor*. New York: Creative Age Press, 1950.

Seldes, George. *The People Don't Know: The American Press and the Cold War*. New York: Gaer Associates, 1949.

Symposium. "The Press and World Affairs," *Journal of International Affairs*, 10 (No. 2, 1956).

Wiggins, James R. *Freedom or Secrecy?* New York: Oxford University Press, 1956.

The Cold War—Chapters 8 and 9

Beloff, Max. "No Peace, No War," *Foreign Affairs*, 27 (January, 1949), pp. 215-32.

Berliner, J. S. *Soviet Economic Aid*. New York: F. A. Praeger, 1958.

Brodie, Bernard. "The Anatomy of Deterrence," *World Politics*, 11 (January, 1959), pp. 173-92.

Campbell, John C. "Negotiation with the Soviets: Some Lessons of the War Period," *Foreign Affairs*, 34 (January, 1956), pp. 305-20.

Dean, James R. *The Strange Alliance*. New York: Viking Press, 1947.

Goldman, Eric F. *The Crucial Decade*. New York: Alfred A. Knopf, 1956.

Halle, Louis J. *Choice for Survival*. New York: Harper and Brothers, 1958.

Historicus. "Stalin on Revolution," *Foreign Affairs*, 27 (January, 1949), pp. 175-215.

Hoopes, Townsend. "Overseas Bases in American Strategy," *Foreign Affairs*, 37 (October, 1958), pp. 69-83.

Hunt, R. N. Carew. *A Guide to Communist Jargon*. New York: The Macmillan Company, 1957.

Ingram, Kenneth. *History of the Cold War*. New York: Philosophical Library, 1955.

Kennan, George F. *Soviet-American Relations, 1917-20*. Princeton: Princeton University Press, 1956.

Kertesz, Stephen D. "Reflections on Soviet and American Negotiating Behavior," *Review of Politics*, 19 (January, 1957), pp. 3-37.

Kohn, Hans. *The Mind of Modern Russia*. New Brunswick, N. J.: Rutgers University Press, 1955.

Library of Congress. Legislative Reference Service. *Trends in Russian Foreign Policy Since World War I*. Washington, 1947.

McNeill, William H. *America, Britain, and Russia: Their Co-operation and Conflict, 1941-1946*. New York: Oxford University Press, 1953.

Osgood, Robert E. *Limited War: The Challenge to American Strategy*. Chicago: University of Chicago Press, 1957.

Society of Friends. *The United States and the Soviet Union.* New Haven: Yale University Press, 1950.

Soloveytchik, George. *Russia in Perspective.* New York: W. W. Norton Company, 1947.

Strausz-Hupé, Robert. "Nuclear Blackmail and Limited War," *Yale Review,* 48 (Winter, 1959), pp. 174-81.

Tompkins, Pauline. *American-Russian Relations in the Far East.* New York: The Macmillan Company, 1949.

Ulam, Adam B. "Soviet Ideology and Soviet Foreign Policy," *World Politics,* 11 (January, 1959), pp. 153-73.

Warburg, James P. "Cold War Tragedy," *Western Political Quarterly,* 7 (September, 1954), pp. 325-45.

Wish, Harvey. "Getting Along with the Romonovs," *South Atlantic Quarterly,* 48 (1949), pp. 341-59.

Wohlstetter, Albert. "The Delicate Balance of Terror," *Foreign Affairs,* 37 (January, 1959), pp. 211-35.

Zyzniewski, Stanley J. "Soviet Foreign Economic Policy," *Political Science Quarterly,* 73 (June, 1958), pp. 206-34.

Western Europe—Chapter 10

Allen, H. C. *Great Britain and the United States.* London: The Macmillan Company, 1955.

Altstedter, Norman. "Problems of Coalition Diplomacy," *International Journal* 8 (Autumn, 1953), pp. 256-66.

Aron, Raymond, *et al. America and the Mind of Europe.* New York: Library Publishers, 1952.

Bolles, Blair. *The Big Change in Europe.* New York: W. W. Norton, 1958.

Brebner, John B. *The North Atlantic Triangle: The Interplay of Canada, the United States, and Great Britain.* New Haven: Yale University Press, 1947.

Brinton, Crane. *The United States and Great Britain.* Cambridge: Harvard University Press, 1948.

Council of Europe. *European Yearbook.* Strasbourg, France: 1955——. Relates important yearly developments in European integration.

Dean, Vera M. *Europe and the United States.* New York: Knopf, 1950.

Department of State. *Documents on German Foreign Policy, 1918-1945.* Washington: Government Printing Office, 1949.

Deutsch, Karl, *et al. Political Community and the North Atlantic Area.* Princeton: Princeton University Press, 1957.

Earle, Edward M. "A Half-Century of American Foreign Policy: Our Stake in Europe, 1898-1948," *Political Science Quarterly,* 64 (June, 1949), pp. 168-88.

East, W. Gordon. "The Mediterranean: Pivot of Peace and War," *Foreign Affairs,* 32 (October, 1953), pp. 48-67.

Epstein, L. D. *Britain: Uneasy Ally.* Chicago: University of Chicago Press, 1954.

Gould, Lincoln. "NATO and European Integration," *World Politics,* 10 (January, 1958), pp. 219-32.

Heckscher, August, and Aron, Raymond. *Diversity of Worlds.* New York: The Viking Press, 1957. Deals with American-French relations in the recent period.

Hughes, H. Stuart. *The United States and Italy.* Cambridge: Harvard University Press, 1953.

Kennan, George F. "Disengagement Revisited," *Foreign Affairs,* 37 (January, 1959), pp. 187-211.

McKay, Donald C. *The United States and France.* Cambridge: Harvard University Press, 1951.

Marjolin, Robert. *Europe and the U. S. in the World Economy.* Durham, N. C.: Duke University Press, 1953.

Patterson, Gardner. *NATO: A Critical Appraisal.* Princeton: Princeton University Press, 1957.

Roberts, Henry L. *Britain and the United States.* New York: Harper and Brothers, 1953.

Scott, Franklin D. *The United States and Scandinavia.* Cambridge: Harvard University Press, 1950.

Symposium. "The Western Alliance," *Journal of International Affairs,* 12 (No. 1, 1958).

Ward, Barbara. *Policy for the West.* New York: W. W. Norton and Company, 1951.

Wolfers, Arnold. "Europe and the NATO Shield," *International Organization,* 12 (Autumn, 1958), pp. 425-40.

Woodhouse, C. M. "Attitudes of the NATO Countries Toward the United States," *World Politics,* 10 (January, 1958), pp. 202-19.

The Middle East—Chapter 11

Bullard, Sir Reader, ed. *The Middle East: A Political and Economic Survey.* New York: Oxford University Press, 1958. This volume is a recent revision of a study issued earlier by the Royal Institute of International Affairs.

Campbell, John C. *Defense of the Middle East: Problems of American Policy.* New York: Harper and Brothers, 1958.

Cragg, Kenneth. "The Intellectual Impact of Communism Upon Contemporary Islam," *Middle East Journal,* 8 (Spring, 1954), pp. 127-38.

Ford, Allan W. *The Anglo-Iranian Oil Dispute of 1951-1952.* Berkeley, Calif.: University of California Press, 1954.

Hoskins, Harold. *The Middle East: Problem Area in World Politics.* New York: The Macmillan Company, 1954.

Hourani, Albert. "The Decline of the West in the Middle East," *International Affairs,* 29 (January, 1953), pp. 22-43 and (April, 1953), pp. 156-84.

Issawi, Charles. "The Bases of Arab Unity," *International Affairs,* 30 (January, 1955), pp. 36-48.

Reitzel, William A. *The Mediterranean: Its Role in American Foreign Policy.* New York: Harcourt Brace and Company, 1948.

Royal Institute of International Affairs. *Great Britain and Egypt, 1914-1951.* New York: Royal Institute of International Affairs, 1952.

Rustow, Dankwart A. "Defense of the Near East," *Foreign Affairs,* 34 (January, 1956), pp. 271-87.

Schonfield, Hugh J. *The Suez Canal in World Affairs.* New York: Philosophical Library, 1953.

Thomas, Lewis V. *The United States and Turkey and Iran.* Cambridge: Harvard University Press, 1951.

Latin America and Canada —Chapter 12

Alexander, R. J. *Communism in Latin America.* New Brunswick, N. J.: Rutgers University Press, 1957.

Bemis, Samuel F. *The Latin American Policy of the United States.* New York: Harcourt Brace and Company, 1943.

Burr, Robert N., ed. *Documents on Inter-American Cooperation.* Philadelphia: University of Pennsylvania Press, 1955.

Jensen, Amy E. *Guatemala: A Historical Survey.* New York: Exposition Press, 1955.

Keenleyside, Hugh L. *Canada and the United States.* New York: Alfred A. Knopf, 1952.

McGee, Gale W. "The Monroe Doctrine—A Stopgap Measure," *Mississippi Valley Historical Review,* 38 (September, 1952), pp. 233-50.

Miller, Edward G., Jr. "A Fresh Look At the Inter-American Community," *Foreign Affairs,* 33 (July, 1955), pp. 634-48.

Munro, Dana G. *The United States and the Caribbean Area.* Boston: World Peace Foundation, 1934.

Padilla, Ezequel. "The Meaning of Pan-Americanism," *Foreign Affairs,* 32 (January, 1954), pp. 270-82.

Palmer, Thomas W. *Search for a Latin American Policy.* Gainesville, Fla.: University of Florida Press, 1957.

Santos, Eduarto. "Latin American Realities," *Foreign Affairs,* 34 (January, 1956), pp. 245-58.

Sellin, Thorstein, ed. "A Crowding Hemisphere: Population Change in the Americas," *Annals of the American Academy of Political and Social Science,* 316 (March, 1958). This symposium explores a frequently neglected aspect of foreign policy.

Symposium. "Problems and Progress in Latin America," *Journal of International Affairs,* 9 (No. 1, 1955).

Tansill, Charles C. *Canadian-American Relations, 1875-1911.* Toronto: The Ryerson Press, 1943.

Thomas, David Y. *One Hundred Years of the Monroe Doctrine, 1823-1923.* New York: The Macmillan Company, 1923.

Whitaker, Arthur P. *The United States and Argentina.* Cambridge: Harvard University Press, 1954.

———. *The United States and South America: the Northern Republics.* Cambridge: Harvard University Press, 1948.

Asia and The Pacific—Chapter 13

Battistini, Lawrence H. *Japan and America.* New York: John Day Company, 1954.

———. *The United States and Asia.* New York: F. A. Praeger, 1956.

Berkes, Ross N., and Bedi, Mohinder S. *The Diplomacy of India: Indian Foreign Policy in the United Nations.* Stanford, Cal.: Stanford University Press, 1958.

Bisson, Thomas A. *American Foreign Policy in the Far East, 1931-1940.* New York: Institute of Pacific Relations, 1940.

———. *America's Far Eastern Policy.* New York: Institute of Pacific Relations, 1945.

Bozeman, Adda B. "India's Foreign Policy: Reflections Upon Its Sources," *World Politics,* 10 (January, 1958), pp. 256-74.

Bro, Marguerita H. *Indonesia: Land of Challenge*. New York: Harper and Brothers, 1954.

Clyde, Paul H. *United States Policy Toward China: Diplomatic and Public Documents, 1839-1939*. Durham, N. C.: Duke University Press, 1940.

Dulles, Foster R., and Ridinger, G. E., "Anti-Colonial Policies of FDR," *Political Science Quarterly*, 70 (March, 1955), pp. 1-18.

Fairbank, John K., *Chinese Thought and Institutions*. Chicago: University of Chicago Press, 1957.

————. *Documentary History of Chinese Communism*. Cambridge: Harvard University Press, 1952.

————. *The United States and China*. Cambridge: Harvard University Press, 1958. This recent revision of an earlier volume on this subject is one of the most provocative treatments of Sino-American relations in the modern period.

Gross, Ernest A. "Some Illusions of Our Asian Policy," *Far Eastern Survey*, 26 (December, 1957), pp. 177-83.

Grunder, Garel, and Livezey, William E. *The Philippines and the United States*. Norman, Okla.: University of Oklahoma Press, 1951.

Hinton, Harold C., *et al. Major Governments of Asia*. Ithaca, N. Y.: Cornell University Press, 1958.

Isaacs, Harold R. *Scratches on Our Minds: American Images of China and India*. New York: John Day Company, 1958.

Klein, Sidney. "Capitalism, Socialism, and the Economic Theories of Mao Tse-Tung," *Political Science Quarterly*, 73 (March, 1958), pp. 28-47.

Masani, M. R. "The Mind of Asia," *Foreign Affairs*, 33 (July, 1955), pp. 548-66.

North, Robert C. *Moscow and Chinese Communists*. Stanford, Cal.: Stanford University Press, 1953.

Palmer, Leslie H. "Indonesia and the West," *International Affairs*, 31 (April, 1955), pp. 182-92.

Purcell, Victor. *The Chinese in Southeast Asia*. New York: Oxford University Press, 1951.

Reischauer, Edwin O., *et al. Japan and America Today*. Stanford, Cal.: Stanford University Press, 1953.

Sellin, Thorstein, ed. "Asia and Future World Leadership," *Annals of the American Academy of Political and Social Science*, 318 (July, 1958). This symposium contains articles dealing with a number of aspects of America's relations with Asia.

Spear, Percival. *India, Pakistan, and the West*. London: Oxford University Press, 1952.

Strausz-Hupé, Robert, *et al. American-Asian Tensions*. New York: F. A. Praeger, 1956.

Symposium. "Communism in Asia," *Current History*, 27 (November, 1954).

Symposium. "Southeast Asia in Transition," *Journal of International Affairs*, 10 (no. 1, 1956).

Taylor, Edmond. *Richer By Asia*. Boston: Houghton Mifflin Company, 1947.

Wei, Henry. *China and Soviet Russia*. Princeton: D. Van Nostrand Company, 1956.

Wolf, Charles, Jr. "Soviet Economic Aid in Southeast Asia," *World Politics*, 10 (October, 1957), pp. 91-102.

Propaganda and Psychological Warfare—Chapter 14

Barghorn, Frederick C. *The Soviet Image of the United States*. New York: Harcourt Brace and Company, 1950.

Berding, Andrew H. "The Battlefield of Ideas," *Department of State Bulletin*, 38 (June 23, 1958), pp. 1043-48.

Cooper, Kent. *The Right to Know*. New York: Farrar, Straus and Cudahy, 1956.

Doob, Leonard W. *Public Opinion and Propaganda*. New York: Henry Holt, 1948.

Evans, Frank B., ed. *Worldwide Communist Propaganda Activities*. New York: The Macmillan Company, 1955.

Ferreus. "The Menace of Communist Psychological Warfare," *Orbis*, 1 (April, 1957), pp. 97-121.

Harter, Donald L. *Propaganda Handbook*. Philadelphia: 20th Century Publishing Company, 1953.

Katz, Daniel, *et al.*, eds. *Public Opinion and Propaganda: A Book of Readings*. New York: Dryden Press, 1954.

Lasswell, Harold D., *et al. Language of Politics*. New York: G. W. Stewart, 1949.

Lerner, Daniel, ed. *Propaganda in War and Crisis*. New York: G. W. Stewart, 1951.

Levine, Harold. *War Propaganda and the United States*. New Haven: Yale University Press, 1940.

Martin, Leslie J. *International Propaganda: Its Legal and Diplomatic Control*. Minneapolis: University of Minnesota Press, 1958.

Smith, Bruce L., and Chitra, M., *International Communication and Political Opinion: A Guide to the Literature.* Princeton: Princeton University Press, 1956.

Stephens, Oren. *Facts to a Candid World.* Stanford, Cal.: Stanford University Press, 1955.

Summers, Robert E., ed. *America's Weapons of Psychological Warfare.* New York: Wilson, 1951.

Foreign Trade and Aid—Chapter 15

Aubrey, Henry S. *United States Imports and World Trade.* New York: Oxford University Press, 1957.

Buchanan, Norman S., and Ellis, Howard S. *Approaches to Economic Development.* New York: Twentieth Century Fund, 1955.

Commission on Foreign Economic Policy. *Report to the President and Congress.* Washington: 1954. This is the Randall Commission's report, on which many of the Eisenhower Administration's trade policies were based.

Elliott, William Y. *The Political Economy of U. S. Foreign Policy.* New York: Henry Holt, 1955.

Johnston, Bruce F. "Farm Surpluses and Foreign Policy," *World Politics,* 10 (October, 1957), pp. 1-24.

Lubin, Isador, and Murden, Forrest D. *Our Stake in World Trade.* New York: Foreign Policy Association, 1954. Headline Book No. 106.

Rippy, J. Fred. "Foreign Aid and the Problem of Non-Intervention," *Inter-American Economic Affairs,* 11 (Winter, 1957), pp. 23-47.

Shannon, Lyle W., ed. *Underdeveloped Areas: A Book of Readings and Research.* New York: Harper and Brothers, 1957.

Symposium. "The Underdeveloped Areas," *Current History,* 33 (August, 1957).

Thorp, Willard L. *Trade, Aid, or What?* Baltimore: The Johns Hopkins University Press, 1954.

Wiggins, J. W., and Schoeck, Helmut, eds. *Foreign Aid Reexamined—A Critical Appraisal.* Washington, D. C.: Public Affairs Press, 1958.

Woytinsky, W. S., and E. S. *World Commerce and Governments: Trends and Outlook.* New York: Twentieth Century Fund, 1955.

International Organization —Chapter 16

Bloomfield, Lincoln P. "The U. N. and National Security," *Foreign Affairs,* 36 (July, 1958), pp. 597-610.

————. *Evolution or Revolution? The United Nations and the Problem of Peaceful Territorial Change.* Cambridge: Harvard University Press, 1957.

Goodrich, Leland M., and Simons, Anne P. *The United Nations and the Maintenance of International Peace and Security.* Washington, D. C.: Brookings Institution, 1955.

Green, James F. *The United Nations and Human Rights.* Washington, D. C.: Brookings Institution, 1956.

MacLaurin, John. *The United Nations and Power Politics.* New York: Harper and Brothers, 1951.

Moor, Carol C., and Chamberlain, Waldo. *How To Use United Nations Documents.* New York: New York University Press, 1952.

Murray, James N. *The United Nations Trusteeship System.* Urbana, Ill.: University of Illinois Press, 1957.

Riggs, Robert E. *Politics in the United Nations: A Study of United States Influence in the General Assembly.* Urbana, Ill.: University of Illinois Press, 1958.

Sady, Emil J. *The United Nations and Dependent Peoples.* Washington, D. C.: Brookings Institution, 1956.

Schwebel, Stephen M. *The Secretary-General of the United Nations: His Political Power and Practice.* Cambridge: Harvard University Press, 1952.

VanAlstyne, Richard W. *American Crisis Diplomacy: The Quest for Collective Security, 1918-1952.* Stanford, Calif.: Stanford University Press, 1952.

Disarmament and Nuclear Energy —Chapter 17

Angell, Sir Norman. *The Great Illusion.* New York: G. P. Putnam's Sons, 1913.

Biörklund, Elis. *International Atomic Policy During A Decade.* Princeton: D. Van Nostrand Company, 1956.

Bolté, Charles G. *The Price of Peace.* Boston: Beacon Press, 1956.

Bretscher, Willy. "The Case for Conventional Armaments," *Orbis,* 1 (January, 1958), pp. 435-47.

Conway, John S. "Disarmament Reconsidered," *International Journal,* 13 (Spring, 1958), pp. 100-09.

Dean, Gordon. "Atoms for Peace: An American View," *International Journal,* 9 (Autumn, 1954), pp. 253-61.

———. *Report on the Atom.* New York: Alfred A. Knopf, 1953.

Flanders, Ralph E. *Letter to a Generation.* Boston: Beacon Press, 1956.

Frye, William R. *Disarmament: Atoms Into Plowshares.* New York: Foreign Policy Association, 1955. Headline Books, No. 113.

"International Atomic Energy Agency," *United Nations Review,* 3 (January, 1957), pp. 37-41.

Joint Committee on Atomic Energy. *Peaceful Uses of Atomic Energy.* 84th Congress, 2nd Session, 1956.

Kissinger, Henry A. "Nuclear Testing and the Problem of Peace," *Foreign Affairs,* 37 (October, 1958), pp. 1-19.

Nitze, Paul. "Atoms, Strategy, and Policy," *Foreign Affairs,* 34 (January, 1956), pp. 187-99.

Senate Foreign Relations Committee. *Control and Reduction of Armaments.* 84th Congress, 2nd Session and 85th Congress, 1st Session, December 12, 1956–January 17, 1957, Parts 1–14, Washington, D. C.: 1956-1957. This voluminous study of disarmament contains a wealth of material on various aspects of the problem.

Vinson, John C. *The Parchment Peace: The United States Senate and the Washington Conference, 1921-22.* Athens, Ga.: University of Georgia Press, 1955.

Williams, B. H. *The United States and Disarmament.* New York: McGraw-Hill Book Company, 1931.

Guiding Principles of American Foreign Policy—Chapter 18

Acheson, Dean G. *Power and Diplomacy.* Cambridge: Harvard University Press, 1958.

Bowles, Chester. *The New Dimensions of Peace.* New York: Harper and Brothers, 1955.

Buehrig, Edward H. *Woodrow Wilson and the Balance of Power.* Bloomington, Ind.: Indiana University Press, 1955.

Fosdick, Dorothy. *Common Sense and World Affairs.* New York: Harcourt, Brace and Company, 1955.

Kennan, George F. *Realities of American Foreign Policy.* Princeton, N. J.: Princeton University Press, 1954.

Lefever, Ernest W. *Ethics and United States Foreign Policy.* New York: Meridian Books, 1957.

Merchant, Livingston T. "The Moral Element in Foreign Policy," *Department of State Bulletin,* 37 (September 2, 1957), pp. 374-79.

Morgenthau, Hans J. *Dilemmas of Politics.* Chicago: University of Chicago Press, 1958.

Osgood, Robert E. *Ideals and Self-Interest in America's Foreign Relations.* Chicago: University of Chicago Press, 1953.

Stevenson, Adlai E. *Call to Greatness.* New York: Harper and Brothers, 1954.

Symposium. "The Idea of National Interest," *American Perspective,* 4 (Fall, 1950), pp. 335-401.

Tucker, Robert W. "Force and Foreign Policy," *Yale Review,* 47 (March, 1958), pp. 374-92.

INDEX

519

522

France:
and Algeria, 245-6
colonial system of, 290, 295
and EDC, 249
and Egypt, 275-7
and European economic unity, 237
and German occupation, 249
Free Trade Area, 235 (*see also* European Common Market)
Frontier, role of in American history, 44-5
Fuels and energy, requirements by U. S., 15-7 (*see also* Nuclear energy; Raw materials)
Fulbright, Senator William:
and "Eisenhower Doctrine," 53-n, 129, 275-n
and foreign aid, 415
and Gluck appointment, 72-3
Fulbright Act, 68, 382-n

Gaither, H. Rowan, 92
Gaither Committee, 90, 147, 147-n
Galantière, Lewis, 46
Gavin, General James M., 81-n, 89, 92-n
General Agreement on Tariffs and Trade (GATT), 398, 405
interest-group views on, 157-8
views of U. S. toward, 237
General Assembly: *see* United Nations, General Assembly
Geneva Conference (1955), 474
"Genocide," UN activities on, 439, 448
Geography, influence on U. S. policy, 8-13
"Geopolitics," 9, 202-8
George, Walter F., as bipartisan leader, 136-7 (*see also* Bipartisanship)
German-Americans, and U. S. policy, 160-1
Germany, during World War I, 34
Germany, Federal Republic of:
and disarmament, 468
occupation, ending of, 248-9
rearmament of, 243-4, 250
Germany, Nazi, 9
division of, 79
propaganda by, 370
"unconditional surrender" of, 488-9
Gillin, John, 164
"Girard case," 43, 43-n
Gluck, Maxwell H., 72-3, 107
Goebbels, Joseph, 370
"Good Neighbor Policy:" *see* Inter-American System; Monroe Doctrine
Gorchakov, Prince Michael, 176
Gorer, Geoffrey, 45
Grassmuck, George, 164
Great Britain:
and Common Market, 237

decline of, 186-7 (*see also Pax Britannica*)
and Egypt, 275-7
Irish-American hate for, 162-3
and Monroe Doctrine, 306
and Palestine, 258-9
relations with U. S., 224-5
and Western European Union, 250
"Great Debate" on troops to Europe, 53, 133
Greece, 225-6
Greek-Turkish Aid Program:
appointments concerning, 107
formulation of, 225-6 (*see also* Truman Doctrine)
Greenland, U. S. occupation of, 55
Guatemala:
CIA's role in, 98
communism in, 324-7
political future of, 327
U. S. intervention in, 325-7

Hague Conference, 459
Hague Congress on European unification, 246-7
Halle, Louis J., 200
Hammarskjold, Dag, 443-4 (*see also* United Nations, Secretary-General)
Hartshorne, Richard, 12
Hasbrouck, Jan, 235-6
Hay, John, 332
Hay-Pauncefote Treaty, 182, 182-n
Hegel, Georg F., 190-n
Herter, Christian A., 400
Hobbes, Thomas, 494-n, 497
Hoffman, Paul, 97, 228-n, 235
Holy Alliance, 180, 222
Hoover Commission, 129
study of national security, 83
study of State Department, 63, 66
views on executive committees, 98
Hopkins, Harry, 54, 107
House, Colonel Robert, 107
House Appropriations Committee:
activities in 1949, 111-12
and Air Force expansion, 111
and defense budget, 112-13
and defense budget investigation in 1960, 115
and Development Loan Fund, 108
and European recovery, 109
House Foreign Affairs Committee
and bipartisanship; *see* Bipartisanship
case study of work, 104
and military aid to Asia, 351
and military aid to Europe, 115
role before World War II, 104
subcommittees of, 104, 128-29
travel by, 122
views on bipartisanship, 143
views on executive branch, 116
views on neutralism, 344

House Government Operations Committee, 82
House Rules Committee, 135
House Un-American Activities Committee, 117
House Ways and Means Committee, 156
Hughes, Charles E., 306
Hull, Cordell, 77, 151
"Human rights" controversy in UN, 438-9
Humphrey, Hubert, 111, 129, 134, 358, 479
Hungarian revolt:
U. S. policies toward, 386-7
and Voice of America, 383-4
Hutchinson, John A., 499, 507
Huzar, Elias, 87, 110

"Idealism," philosophy of in foreign affairs, 486 (*see also* "Realism")
Ideology:
barriers to spread of free world's, 388-9 (*see also* Democracy)
and international conflicts, 189-202, 369-89
in Soviet foreign policy, 185-6 (*see also* Communism; Propaganda)
"Illusion of American omnipotence," 35, 118
Immigration:
early U. S. policies toward, 42
Congress' attitude on, 120-1
to U. S., 158-9
"Imperialism," in U. S. policy, 36-8 (*see also* Colonialism)
Imports, "strategic minerals" by U. S., 13-4 (*see also* International trade; Raw materials)
India:
and communism, 336-7
domestic problems in, 336
five-year plans in, 347
goals of, 335-9
and Kashmir, 338
neutralism in, 336-9
opposition to alliances, 338
and Pakistan, 338
and Red China, 337-8, 356
Soviet assistance to, 349
U. S. assistance to, 347
and U. S. racial policies, 159
U. S. shipment of wheat to, 135
"Indirect aggression," 267 (*see also* "Eisenhower Doctrine;" Southeast Asia Treaty Organization)
Indonesia, communism in, 349, 366
Industry, in the U. S., 13-8
Information:
availability to public, 57, 154-5
"leaks" by Cabinet, 95
legislative sources of, 122
president's control over, 54, 56-7, 135

524

527

United States—*continued*
and Europe, Western, 42, 221-55, 408 (*see also* North Atlantic Treaty Organization; Europe, Western)
exports of, 394-7
foreign aid to Africa, 288-92
foreign aid to Asia, 345-7, 351-3, 363-4
foreign aid to Europe, 228-30 (*see also* European Recovery Program)
foreign aid to Latin America, 317-21
foreign aid, trends in, 408-16
foreign economic policies, 391-421 (*see also* Foreign aid; International trade; Investments)
goals in foreign policy, 1-6
"Good Neighbor Policy," 308 (*see also* Inter-American System; Monroe Doctrine)
and Guatemala, 324-7
imports of, 392-4, 406
income, per capita, 19-20
industrial potential, 17-8
and Inter-American System, 309-10
interventions in Latin America, 307-8
investment "guaranty" program, 418-9
investments, 319-21, 416-9
isolationism in, 40-4
and Israel, 260 (*see also* Arab-Israeli dispute)
and Japan, 181-2, 332, 400
and Latin America, 303-27 (*see also* Monroe Doctrine)
and League of Nations, 427-8
and "limited war," 217-8 (*see also* "Deterrence;" "Massive retaliation")
means of foreign policy, 6-8
and the Middle East, 257-300
military strength of, 212-6 (*see also* Military establishment)
"missile lag" in, 92
and Monroe Doctrine, 221-2, 305-8
morale in, 215-7
"moralism" in foreign policy, 32-6
national interest of, 487-94 (*see also* National interest; "Realism")
and NATO, 238-46
naval strength of, 212-3
and "neutralism," 344-5
as "new society," 41-3
oil holdings in Middle East, 264 (*see also* Oil)
"Open Door Policy," 332-4 (*see also* China, Republic of)
optimism in, 39-40, 45-7
Pacific interests of, 182 (*see also* Asia; Far East)
and Pakistan, 338

and Palestine, 259-60 (*see also* Arab-Israeli dispute)
and Pan-Americanism, 309 (*see also* Inter-American System; Latin America)
population in, 18-22
principles of foreign policy, 485-507
propaganda by, 382-4, 388-9 (*see also* Propaganda; U.S. Information Agency)
recognition policy of, 314-7
recognition by Russia, 180
re-examination of foreign policy, 485-94 (*see also* "Realism")
and Russia, Czarist, 179-87
and Russia, Soviet, 173-9, 180, 182-7, 189-218, 401-4, 445-9 (*see also* "Cold War;" Communism; Disarmament; Middle East; Propaganda; Union of Soviet Socialist Republics)
and SEATO, 364 (*see also* Southeast Asia Treaty Organization)
and "Suez crisis," 275-7
and SUNFED, 437-8
territorial possessions of, 36-7
trade patterns of (*chart*), 396
trade policies of, 253-4, 397-400, 407-8
trade with China, Communist, 402-4
trade with Latin America, 303, 317-23
trade with U. S. S. R., 403-4
and underdeveloped countries, 414-6 (*see also* Foreign aid; Underdeveloped countries)
and United Nations, 350-n, 425-52
as "universal nation," 42
and Venezuela, 313-4
wartime diplomatic goals of, 493
United States Information Agency:
activities in Africa, 286
duties of, 97, 382-3
effectiveness of, 385-7
unpopularity in U. S., 388
"Voice of America," 383-4 (*see also* Propaganda)
"Uniting for Peace" resolution, 433 (*see also* United Nations, General Assembly)

Valera, Eamon de, 162
Vandenberg, Arthur H., 50-2, n, 105-6, 109, 120, 122, 128-30, 136 (*see also* Bipartisanship)
"Vandenberg Resolution," 106, 119, 239, 451 (*see also* North Atlantic Treaty Organization)
Van Der Kroef, J. M., 362
Venezuela, 313-4

Versailles, Treaty of, 105-7, 126-7, 162-3
Veterans organizations, 157
Vice-President of the United States, 58
Vietnam, South, 346
Vinson, Carl, 93
"Voice of America," 97, 116, 383-6 (*see also* Propaganda; U. S. Information Agency)

Wallace, Henry A., 130
Walsh, David I., 163
War:
American attitudes toward, 36
Congress' power to declare, 113-4
political goals in, 493
President's powers in, 60 (*see also* President)
relation to foreign policy, 30
"undeclared wars," 113-4
Warburg, James P., 493-4
War Production Board, 118
Washington, George, 105, 221
Washington Naval Armaments Conference, 460-1
Weinberg, Albert K., 40
Western European Union (WEU), 250-2
Western hemisphere:
communism in, 323-7
conception of in U. S., 9-13
U. S. investments in, 417
U. S. relations with, 303-27
White, Henry, 105, 126
White House conferences, 139-40 (*see also* Bipartisanship)
White, William S., 119, 121, 136-7
Whitman, Walt, 42
Wilkie, Wendell, 140
Williams, Frederick W., 164
Wilson, Charles E., 134, 469, 473
Wilson, Woodrow, 61, 105, 126, 162-3, 314-5, 362, 370, 444, 460, 488
Wohl, Paul, 359
Women, political rights of, 439
Woodward, C. Vann, 166
World Bank, 351
World Court, 163, 222-3
World government, 452
"World revolution" in communist thought, 191-2 (*see also* Communism)
World War II, 51, 78-9, 117-8
Wright, Quincy, 88
"Wriston report" on Foreign Service, 71-2

Yale, William, 271
Yalta Conference, 78-9, 205, 339-n, 429
Youngstown Company v. Sawyer (1952), 61
Yugoslavia, 115, 226

Zionism, 160, 258-60 (*see also* Arab-Israeli dispute; Israel)

532